Liberty, Equality, Power

A HISTORY OF THE AMERICAN PEOPLE

COMPACT FIFTH EDITION

John M. Murrin
PRINCETON UNIVERSITY, EMERITUS

Paul E. Johnson
UNIVERSITY OF SOUTH CAROLINA, EMERITUS

James M. McPherson
PRINCETON UNIVERSITY, EMERITUS

Alice Fahs
UNIVERSITY OF CALIFORNIA, IRVINE

Gary Gerstle
VANDERBILT UNIVERSITY

Emily S. Rosenberg
UNIVERSITY OF CALIFORNIA, IRVINE

Norman L. Rosenberg
MACALESTER COLLEGE

THOMSON
WADSWORTH

Australia • Brazil • Canada • Mexico • Singapore • Spain
United Kingdom • United States

THOMSON

WADSWORTH

Liberty, Equality, Power: A History of the American People, Compact Fifth Edition

John M. Murrin, Paul E. Johnson, James M. McPherson, Alice Fahs, Gary Gerstle, Emily S. Rosenberg, and Norman L. Rosenberg

Publisher: Clark Baxter
Senior Acquisitions Editor: Ashley Dodge
Development Editor: Margaret McAndrew Beasley
Assistant Editor: Kristen Tatroe
Editorial Assistant: Ashley Spicer
Senior Marketing Manager: Janise Fry
Marketing Communications Manager: Tami Strang
Senior Content Project Manager: Joshua Allen
Senior Art Director: Cate Rickard Barr
Print/Media Buyer: Barbara Britton
Permissions Editor: Roberta Broyer
Production Service: Lachina Publishing Services

Photo Manager: Sheri Blaney
Photo Researcher: Sarah Evertson
Cover Designer: Cheryl Carrington
Cover Printer: Transcontinental—Louiseville
Compositor: International Typesetting and Composition
Printer: Transcontinental—Louiseville
Cover Art: William Sidney Mount (American, 1807–1868). *The Power of Music.* 1847. Oil on canvas, 43.4 × 53.5 cm. © The Cleveland Museum of Art, 2002. Leonard C. Hanna, Jr. Fund 1991.110

Thomson Higher Education
25 Thomson Place
Boston, MA 02210-1202
USA

For more information about our products, contact us at:
Thomson Learning Academic Resource Center
1-800-423-0563

For permission to use material from this text or product, submit a request online at
http://www.thomsonrights.com

Any additional questions about permissions can be submitted by email to **thomsonrights@thomson.com**

Library of Congress Control Number: 2007924446

Student Edition
ISBN-13: 978-0-495-411017
ISBN-10: 0-495-41101-9

Instructor Edition
ISBN-13: 978-0-495-502432
ISBN-10: 0-495-50243-X

About the Authors

JOHN M. MURRIN *Princeton University, Emeritus* John M. Murrin is a specialist in American colonial and revolutionary history and the early republic. He has edited one multivolume series and five books, including two co-edited collections, *Colonial America: Essays in Politics and Social Development,* Fifth Edition (2001), and *Saints and Revolutionaries: Essays in Early American History* (1984). His own essays on early American history range from ethnic tensions, the early history of trial by jury, the rise of the legal profession, and the political culture of the colonies and the new nation, to the rise of professional baseball and college football in the 19th century. Professor Murrin served as president of the Society for Historians of the Early American Republic in 1998–99.

PAUL E. JOHNSON *University of South Carolina, Distinguished Professor Emeritus* A specialist in early national social and cultural history, Paul E. Johnson is also the author of *The Early American Republic, 1789-1829* (2006); *Sam Patch, the Famous Jumper* (2003); *A Shopkeeper's Millennium: Society and Revivals in Rochester, New York, 1815-1837,* 25th Anniversary Edition (2004); co-author (with Sean Wilentz) of *The Kingdom of Matthias: Sex and Salvation in 19th-Century America* (1994); and editor of *African-American Christianity: Essays in History* (1994). He has been awarded the Merle Curti Prize of the Organization of American Historians (1980), the Richard P. McCormack Prize of the New Jersey Historical Association (1989), and fellowships from the National Endowment for the Humanities (1985–86), the John Simon Guggenheim Foundation (1995), and the Gilder Lehrman Institute (2001) and the National Endowment for the Humanities We the People Fellowship (2006–2007).

JAMES M. McPHERSON *Princeton University, Emeritus* James M. McPherson is a distinguished Civil War historian and was president of the American Historical Association in 2003. He won the 1989 Pulitzer Prize for his book *Battle Cry of Freedom: The Civil War Era.* His other publications include *Marching Toward Freedom: Blacks in the Civil War,* Second Edition (1991); *Ordeal by Fire: The Civil War and Reconstruction,* Third Edition (2001); *Abraham Lincoln and the Second American Revolution* (1991); *For Cause and Comrades: Why Men Fought in the Civil War* (1997), which won the Lincoln Prize in 1998; and *Crossroads of Freedom: Antietam* (2002).

ALICE FAHS *University of California, Irvine* Alice Fahs is a specialist in American cultural history of the 19th and 20th centuries. Her 2001 *The Imagined Civil War: Popular Literature of the North and South, 1861–1865* was a finalist in 2002 for the Lincoln Prize. Together with Joan Waugh she published the edited collection *The Memory of the Civil War in American Culture* in 2004; she has also edited Louisa May Alcott's *Hospital Sketches* (2004), an account of Alcott's nursing experiences during the Civil War first published in 1863. Fahs has published on the cultural history of the Civil War and gender in such journals as the *Journal of American History and Civil War History*. Her honors include an American Council of Learned Societies Fellowship and a Gilder Lehrman Fellowship, as well as fellowships from the American Antiquarian Society, the Newberry Library, and the Huntington Library. She is currently at work on a study of popular literary culture in the late 19th and early 20th centuries, focused on the emergence of mass-market newspapers during an age of imperialism.

GARY GERSTLE *Vanderbilt University* Gary Gerstle is a historian of the 20th-century United States. His books include *Working-Class Americanism: The Politics of Labor in a Textile City, 1914–1960* (1989), and *American Crucible: Race and Nation in the Twentieth Century* (2001), winner of the Saloutos Prize for the best work in immigration and ethnic history. He has also published three coedited works: *The Rise and Fall of the New Deal Order, 1930–1980* (1989); *E Pluribus Unum: Immigrants, Civic Culture, and Political Incorporation* (2001); and *Ruling America: Wealth and Power in a Democracy* (2005). His articles have appeared in the *American Historical Review, Journal of American History, American Quarterly*, and other journals. He has served on the board of editors of both the *Journal of American History* and the *American Historical Review*. His honors include a National Endowment for the Humanities Fellowship and a John Simon Guggenheim Memorial Fellowship.

EMILY S. ROSENBERG *University of California, Irvine* Emily S. Rosenberg specializes in U.S. foreign relations in the 20th century and is the author of *Spreading the American Dream: American Economic and Cultural Expansion, 1890–1945* (1982); *Financial Missionaries to the World: The Politics and Culture of Dollar Diplomacy* (1999), which won the Ferrell Book Award; and *A Date Which Will Live: Pearl Harbor in American Memory* (2004). Her other publications include (with Norman L. Rosenberg) *In Our Times: America Since 1945*, Seventh Edition (2003), and numerous articles dealing with foreign relations in the context of international finance, American culture, and gender ideology. She has served on the board of the Organization of American Historians, on the board of editors of the *Journal of American History*, and as president of the Society for Historians of American Foreign Relations.

NORMAN L. ROSENBERG *Macalester College* Norman L. Rosenberg specializes in legal history with a particular interest in legal culture and First Amendment issues. His books include *Protecting the "Best Men": An Interpretive History of the Law of Libel* (1990) and (with Emily S. Rosenberg) *In Our Times: America Since 1945*, Seventh Edition (2003). He has published articles in the *Rutgers Law Review, UCLA Law Review, Constitutional Commentary, Law & History Review*, and many other journals and law-related anthologies.

Contents in Brief

Contents in Detail

3 • England Discovers Its Colonies: Empire, Liberty, and Expansion • 90

4 • Provincial America and the Struggle for a Continent • 133

Features

Note: Maps with "CI" page numbers appear in Color Inserts.

Maps

History through Film

To the Student: Why Study History?

Why take a course in American history? This is a question that many college and university students ask. In many respects, students today are like the generations of Americans who have gone before them: optimistic and forward looking, far more eager to imagine where we as a nation might be going than to reflect on where we have been. If anything, this tendency has become more pronounced in recent years, as the Internet revolution has accelerated the pace and excitement of change and made even the recent past seem at best quaint, at worst uninteresting and irrelevant.

But it is precisely in these moments of change that a sense of the past can be indispensable in terms of guiding our actions in the present and future. We can find in other periods of American history moments, like our own, of dizzying technological change and economic growth, rapid alterations in the concentration of wealth and power, and basic changes in patterns of work, residence, and play. How did Americans at those times create, embrace, and resist these changes? In earlier periods of American history, the United States was home, as it is today, to a broad array of ethnic and racial groups. How did earlier generations of Americans respond to the cultural conflicts and misunderstandings that often arise from conditions of diversity?

How did immigrants of the early 1900s perceive their new land? How and when did they integrate themselves into American society? To study how ordinary Americans of the past struggled with these issues is to gain perspective on the opportunities and problems that we face today.

History also provides an important guide to affairs of state. What role should America assume in world affairs? Should we participate in international bodies such as the United Nations, or insist on our ability to act autonomously and without the consent of other nations? What is the proper role of government in economic and social life? Should the government regulate the economy? To what extent should the government enforce morality regarding religion, sexual practices, drinking and drugs, movies, TV, and other forms of mass culture? And what are our responsibilities as citizens to each other and to the nation? Americans of past generations have debated these issues with verve and conviction. Learning about these debates and how they were resolved will enrich our understanding of the policy possibilities for today and tomorrow.

History, finally, is about stories—stories that we all tell about ourselves; our families; our communities; our ethnicity, race, region, and religion; and our nation. They are stories of triumph and tragedy, of engagement and flight, and of high ideals and high comedy. When telling these stories, "American history" is often the furthest thing from our minds. But, often, an implicit sense of the past informs what we say about grandparents who immigrated many years ago; the suburb in which we live; the church, synagogue, or mosque at which we worship; or the ethnic or racial group to which we belong. How well, we might ask, do we really understand these individuals, institutions, and groups? Do our stories about them capture their history and complexity? Or do our stories wittingly or unwittingly simplify or alter what these individuals and groups experienced? A study of American history helps us first to ask these questions and then to answer them. In the process, we can embark on a journey of intellectual and personal discovery and situate ourselves more firmly than we had thought possible in relation to those who came before us. We can gain a firmer self-knowledge and a greater appreciation for the richness of our nation and, indeed, of all humanity.

Preface

We are pleased to present the fifth edition of *Liberty, Equality, Power*. Like the first four editions, this one captures the drama and excitement of America's past, from the pre-Columbian era through our own time. It integrates social and cultural history into a political story that is organized around the themes of liberty, equality, and power, and synthesizes the finest historical scholarship to create a narrative that is balanced, lively, and accessible to a broad range of students.

The *Liberty, Equality, Power* Approach

In this book, we tell many small stories, and one large one: how America transformed itself, in a relatively brief period of world history, from a land inhabited by hunter-gatherer and agricultural Native American societies into the most powerful industrial nation on earth. This story has been told many times before, and those who have told it in the past have usually emphasized the political experiment in liberty and equality that took root here in the 18th century. We, too, stress the extraordinary and transformative impact that the ideals of liberty and equality exerted on American politics, society, and economics during the American Revolution and after.

We show how the creation of a free economic environment—one in which entrepreneurial spirit, technological innovation, and industrial production have flourished—underpinned American industrial might. We have also emphasized the successful struggles for freedom that, over the course of the last 230 years, have brought—first to all white men, then to men of color, and finally to women—rights and opportunities that they had not previously known.

But we have also identified a third factor in this pantheon of American ideals—that of power. We examine power in many forms: the accumulation of vast economic fortunes and their influence on the economy and on politics; the dispossession of American Indians from land that they regarded as theirs; the enslavement of millions of Africans and their African American descendants for a period of almost 250 years; the relegation of women and of racial, ethnic, and religious minorities to subordinate places in American society; and the extension of American control over foreign peoples, such as Latin Americans and Filipinos, who would have preferred to have been free and self-governing. We do not mean to suggest that American power has always been turned to these negative purposes. Subordinate groups have also marshaled power to combat oppression, as in the abolitionist and civil-rights crusades, the campaign for woman suffrage, and the labor movement. The government has at times used its power to moderate poverty and to manage the economy in the interests of general prosperity. And it has used its military power to defeat Nazi Germany, World War II Japan, the Cold War Soviet Union, and other enemies of freedom.

The invocation of power as a variable in American history impels us to widen the lens through which we look at the past and to enrich the stories we tell. Ours has been a history of freedom and domination; of progress toward realizing a broadly democratic polity and of delays and reverses; of abundance and poverty; of wars for freedom and justice and for control of foreign markets. In complicating our master narrative in this way, we think we have rendered American history more exciting and intriguing. Progress has not been automatic, but the product of ongoing struggles.

In this book, we have tried to capture the diversity of the American past, both in terms of outcomes and in terms of the variety of groups who have participated in America's making. American Indians are not presented simply as the victims of European aggression but as peoples remarkably diverse in their own ranks, with a variety of systems of social organization and cultural expression.

We give equal treatment to the industrial titans of American history—the likes of Andrew Carnegie and John D. Rockefeller—and to those, such as small farmers and poor workers, who resisted the corporate reorganization of economic life. We celebrate the great moments of 1863, when African Americans were freed from slavery, and of 1868, when they were made full citizens of the United States. But we also note how a majority of African Americans had to wait another 100 years, until the civil-rights movement of the 1960s, to gain full access to American freedoms. We tell similarly complex stories about women, Latinos, and other groups of ethnic Americans.

Political issues are only part of America's story. Americans have always loved their leisure and have created the world's most vibrant popular culture. They have embraced technological innovations, especially those promising to make their lives easier and more fun. We have, therefore, devoted considerable space to a discussion of American popular culture, from the founding of the first newspapers in the 18th century and the rise of movies, jazz, and the comics in the early 20th century to the cable television and Internet revolutions in recent years. We have also analyzed how American industry has periodically altered home and personal life by making new products—such as clothing, cars, refrigerators, and computers—available to consumers. In such ways, we hope to give our readers a rich portrait of how Americans lived at various points in our history.

New to This Edition

The biggest change to the fifth edition was our decision to add a new author, Professor Alice Fahs of the University of California, Irvine. This is the first time in 17 years of work on this textbook that we have reached out to a new historian, and we are delighted that Professor Fahs has decided to join us. Professor Fahs is an accomplished historian of the 19th and early 20th centuries, with special expertise in cultural history and the history of gender. She has already contributed significantly to this edition by substantially reworking chapters 18 and 19, bringing to them her extraordinary knowledge of the period and her accessible and evocative writing style. We invite readers to look closely at those two revised and expanded chapters, and we think they will share our enthusiasm about adding Professor Fahs to our team. We expect her to work on this book for many years, and we are excited by the many contributions she will make.

Specific Revisions to Content and Coverage

Chapters 7 to 9 have been substantially reorganized. New titles are chapter 7, "Completing the Revolution, 1789–1815"; chapter 8, "Northern Transformations, 1800–1830"; and chapter 9, "The Old South, 1790–1850."

Chapters 11 and 12 have been reorganized to provide smoother chronology and transitions with surrounding chapters.

Chapter 18 is now titled: "A Transformed Nation: The West and the New South, 1865–1900" and includes a new introduction on experiences of homesteader Mary Abell. New material on "Industrializing West" is added, as well as a new History through Film feature on the musical *Oklahoma!*.

Chapter 19 is now titled: "The Emergence of Corporate America, 1865–1900" and includes new material on economic growth, class distinction, and culture.

Chapter 24 now includes a new History through Film feature on *Inherit the Wind*.

Chapter 26 now includes a new History through Film feature on *Casablanca*.

Chapters 30 to 32 have been revised and reorganized to include the addition of new chapter 32. New titles are chapter 30, "Power and Politics, 1974–1992"; chapter 31, "Economic, Social, and Cultural Change in the Late 20th Century"; and chapter 32, "Politics of Hope and Fear, 1993–2007."

When Old Worlds Collide:
Contact, Conquest, Catastrophe

When Christopher Columbus crossed the Atlantic, he did not know where he was going, and he died without realizing where he had been. Yet he changed history forever. In the 40 years after 1492, European navigators mastered the oceans of the world, joining together societies that had lived in isolation for thousands of years. European invaders conquered the Americas, not just with sails, gunpowder, and steel, but also with their plants and livestock and, most of all, their diseases. They brought staple crops and slavery with them as well. By 1600, they had created the first global economy in the history of humankind and had inflicted upon the native peoples of the Americas—unintentionally, for the most part—the greatest known catastrophe that human societies have ever experienced.

In the 15th century, when all of this started, the Americas were in some ways a more ancient world than Western Europe. For example, the Portuguese, Spanish, French, and English languages were only beginning to assume their modern forms during the century or two before and after Columbus's voyage. Centuries earlier, when Rome was falling into ruins and Paris and London were little more than hamlets, huge cities were thriving in the Andes and **Mesoamerica** (the area embracing Central America and southern and central Mexico). Which world was old and which was new is a matter of perspective. Each already had its own distinctive past.

Peoples in Motion

Like all other countries of North and South America, the United States is a nation of immigrants. Even the native peoples were once migrants who roamed their way through a strange new land.

Long before Europeans discovered and explored the wide world around them, many different peoples had migrated thousands of miles over thousands of years across oceans and continents. Before **Christopher Columbus** sailed west from Spain in 1492, four distinct waves of immigrants had already swept over the Americas. Three came from Asia. The last, from northern Europe, did not stay.

From Beringia to the Americas

Before the most recent Ice Age ended about 12,000 years ago, glaciers covered huge portions of the Americas, Europe, and Asia. The ice captured so much of the world's water

CHRONOLOGY

12,000 B.C.	Migration to the Americas begins
9000 B.C.	Shenandoah Valley occupied
9000–7000 B.C.	Most large American mammals become extinct
500 B.C.– A.D. 400	Adena-Hopewell mound builders emerge in Ohio River valley
874	Norsemen reach Iceland
900–1250	Toltecs dominate the Valley of Mexico • Cahokia becomes largest Mississippian mound builders' city • Anasazi culture thrives in American Southwest
982	Norse settle Greenland
1001–14	Norse found Vinland on Newfoundland
1400s	Incas begin to dominate the Andes; Aztecs begin to dominate Mesoamerica (1400–50) • Cheng Ho makes voyages of exploration for China (1405–34) • Portuguese begin to master the Atlantic coast of Africa (1434) • First Portuguese slave factory established on African coast (1448) • Dias reaches Cape of Good Hope (1487) • Columbus reaches the Caribbean (1492) • Treaty of Tordesillas divides non-Christian world between Portugal and Spain (1494) • da Gama rounds Cape of Good Hope and reaches India (1497–99)
1500s	Portuguese discover Brazil (1500) • Balboa crosses Isthmus of Panama to the Pacific (1513) • Magellan's fleet circumnavigates the globe; Cortés conquers the Aztec empire (1519–22) • de Vaca makes overland journey from Florida to Mexico (1528–36) • Pizarro conquers the Inca empire (1531–32) • de Soto's expedition explores the American Southeast (1539–43) • Coronado explores the American Southwest (1540–42) • Jesuit mission established at Chesapeake Bay (1570–71) • Philip II issues Royal Order for New Discoveries (1573) • Philip II unites Spanish and Portuguese empires (1580)

that sea level fell drastically and created a land bridge 600 miles wide across the Bering Strait between Siberia and Alaska. For more than 10,000 years after 23,000 B.C., this exposed area—geographers call it **Beringia**—was dry land on which plants, animals, and humans could live. Starting about 14,000 years ago, people drifted in small bands from Asia to North America. No doubt many generations lived on Beringia, although the harsh environment of this land on the edge of the Arctic Circle would have required unusual skills just to survive. These first humans to reach the Americas hunted animals for meat and furs and probably built small fishing vessels that could weather the Arctic storms. Faced with impassable glaciers to the north and east, they made snug homes to keep themselves warm through the fierce winters. Their numbers were, in all likelihood, quite small.

By 12,000 B.C., humans definitely were living in eastern Siberia, western Alaska, and Beringia. (Because Beringia is once again under water, it cannot be easily studied, although fossils of mammoths have been found on the ocean floor.) As the glaciers receded for the last time, these people spread throughout the Americas. By 8000 B.C., they had reached all the way to **Tierra del Fuego** at the southern tip of South America. Near the eastern coast of North America, the Thunderbird dig in Virginia's Shenandoah Valley shows signs of continuous human occupation from before 9000 B.C. until the arrival of Europeans.

These Asians probably came in three waves. Those in the first wave spread over most of the two continents and spoke **Amerind,** the forerunner of most American Indian languages on both continents. The Algonquian, Iroquoian, Muskogean, Siouan, Nahuatl (Aztec), Mayan, and all South American tongues derive from this source. Those in the middle wave, which came a few thousand years later, spoke what linguists call "Na-Déné," which eventually gave rise to the various Athapaskan languages of the Canadian Northwest as well as the Apache, Navajo, and related tongues in the American Southwest. The last to arrive, the ancestors of the Inuits (called Eskimos by other Indians), crossed after 7000 B.C., when Beringia was again under water. About 4,000 years ago, these people began to migrate from the Aleutian Islands and Alaska to roughly their present sites in the Americas. Unlike their predecessors, they found the Arctic environment to their liking and migrated across the northern rim of North America and then across the North Atlantic to Greenland, where they encountered the first Europeans migrating westward—the Norsemen. Somehow, the Inuits maintained at least limited contact with one another across 6,000 miles of bleak Arctic tundra. The Thule, or final pre-Columbian phase of Inuit culture, lasted from A.D. 1000 to 1700 and sustained similar folkways from Siberia to Greenland.

The Great Extinction and the Rise of Agriculture

As the glaciers receded and the climate warmed, the people who had wandered south and east found an attractive environment teeming with game. Imperial mammoths, huge mastodons, woolly rhinoceroses, a species of enormous bison, and giant ground sloths roamed the plains and forests, along with camels and herds of small horses. These animals had thrived in a frigid climate, but they had trouble adjusting to hot weather. They also had no instinctive fear of the two-legged intruders, who became ever more skillful at hunting them. A superior spear point, the **Clovis tip,** appeared in the area of present-day New Mexico and Texas some time before 9000 B.C., and within a thousand years its use had spread throughout North and South America. As it spread, the big game died off along with horses, which were small and valued only as food. Overhunting cannot explain the entire extinction, but it was a major factor, along with climate change. Mammoths, for example, survived until 2000 B.C. on uninhabited Wrangell Island near Alaska. Most large animals of the Americas disappeared about 9,000 years ago.

Their passing left the hemisphere with a severely depleted number of animal species. Nothing as big as the elephant survived. The largest beasts left were bears, bison, and

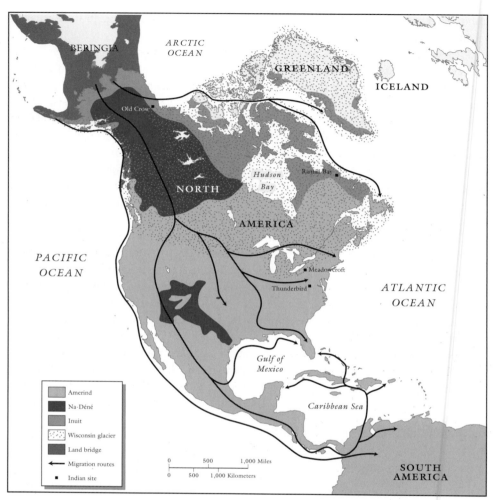

Map 1.1 Indian Settlement of America The probable routes that people followed after they left Beringia and spread throughout the Americas.

moose; the biggest cat was the jaguar. The human population had multiplied and spread with ease so long as the giant species lasted. Their extinction probably led to a decline in population as people scrambled for new sources of food. Some Indians raised guinea pigs, turkeys, or ducks, but apart from dogs on both continents, they domesticated no large animals except in South America, where they used llamas to haul light loads in mountainous terrain and raised alpacas for their wool. In Eurasia, with its numerous domesticated animals, the killer diseases such as smallpox and bubonic plague took hold first among domestic animals and then spread among humans. Disease by disease, the survivors developed immunities over a long period of time. No comparable process occurred in the Americas, where few animals could be domesticated.

Some native peoples settled down without becoming farmers. Those in the Pacific Northwest sustained themselves through fishing, hunting, and the gathering of nuts, berries, and other edible plants. Men fished and hunted; women gathered. California peoples maintained some of the densest populations north of Mexico by collecting acorns and processing them into meal, which they baked into cakes. In the rain forests of Brazil, in south and central Florida, and in the cold woodlands of northern New England, hunter-gatherers also got along without becoming farmers.

Most North Americans could not depend solely on hunting and gathering food, however. In a few places, some of them, almost certainly women, began to plant and harvest crops instead of simply gathering and eating what they found. In Asia and Africa, this practice was closely linked to the domestication of animals and happened quickly enough to be called the Neolithic (new or late Stone Age) revolution. But in the Americas the rise of farming had little to do with animals, occurred gradually, and might better be termed the **Neolithic** *evolution*. For the first 3,500 years, farming supplemented a diet that still depended mostly on fishing and hunting, although now of smaller animals. Somewhere between 4000 and 1500 B.C., permanent farm villages began to dominate parts of Peru, south-central Mexico, northeast Mexico, and the southwestern United States. Their crops were different from those of Europe, the Middle East, or East Asia. The first American farmers grew amaranth (a cereal), manioc (familiar to modern Americans as tapioca), chili peppers, pumpkins, sweet potatoes, several varieties of beans, and, above all, maize, or Indian corn, which slowly became a staple throughout most of the Americas. Indians also raised white potatoes and tomatoes. The spread of these crops launched another population surge that was great enough to support cities in some areas.

By 900 A.D. the temperature in North America and northern Europe had risen about two or three degrees Fahrenheit. Agriculture, especially an improved form of maize, became the primary means of support in most of North America. In the northeastern woodlands, peoples who spoke Algonquian and Iroquoian languages settled into semi-sedentary communities where they raised and stored their crops and erected dwellings, but then dispersed for part of the year to hunt or fish. Population again increased. Climate began to cool again in the 14th century, a trend that became more severe in the 16th and 17th centuries, which turned into a little ice age and provoked frequent droughts in both Europe and North America.

The Norsemen

Europeans also began trekking long distances. Pushed by fierce invaders from central Asia, various Germanic tribes overran the western provinces of the Roman Empire. The Norse, a Germanic people who had occupied Scandinavia, were among the most innovative of these invaders. For centuries their Viking warriors raided the coasts of the British Isles and

France. Their sleek longboats, propelled by both sails and oars, enabled them to challenge the contrary currents of the north Atlantic. Some of them began to gaze westward across the ocean.

Beginning in A.D. 874, Vikings occupied Iceland. In 982 and 983, Erik the Red, who had been accused of manslaughter in Norway and outlawed for committing more mayhem in Iceland, led his Norse followers farther west to Greenland. There the Norse made Europe's first contact with Inuits and established permanent settlements.

Leif, Erik's son, sailed west from Greenland in 1001 and began to explore the coast of North America. He made three more voyages, the last in 1014, and started a colony that he called "Vinland" on the northern coast of Newfoundland at a place now named L'Anse aux Meadows. The local Indians (called "Skrellings" by the Norse, which means "barbarians" or "weaklings") resisted vigorously, but the Norse soon quarreled among themselves and destroyed the colony by 1014. The Norse abandoned Vinland, but they continued to visit North America for another century, probably to get wood. A 12th-century Norse coin, recovered from an Indian site in Maine, gives proof of their continuing contact with North America.

About 500 years after Erik the Red's settlement, the Norse also lost Greenland. There, not long before Columbus sailed in 1492, the last Norse settler died a lonely death. In the chaos that followed the Black Death in Europe and Greenland after 1350 and the onset of the little ice age, the colony suffered a severe population decline, gradually lost regular contact with the homeland, and slowly withered away. Despite their spectacular exploits, the Norse had no impact on the later course of American history. They had reached a dead end.

Europe and the World by the 15th Century

Focus Question
What enabled relatively backward European societies to establish dominance over the oceans of the world?

Nobody in the year 1400 could have foreseen the course of European expansion that was about to begin. Europe stood at the edge, not the center, of world commerce. It desired much that others possessed but made little that those others wished to have.

China: The Rejection of Overseas Expansion

By just about every standard, China under the Ming dynasty was the world's most complex culture. In the 15th century, the government of China, staffed by well-educated bureaucrats, ruled 100 million people, a total half again as large as the combined populations of all European states west of Russia. The Chinese had invented the compass, gunpowder, and early forms of printing and paper money. Foreigners coveted the silks, teas, and other fine products available in China, but they had little to offer in exchange. Most of what Europe knew about China came from *The Travels of Marco Polo,* written by a merchant from the Italian city-state of Venice who at age 17 journeyed overland with his father and uncle to the Chinese court, which he reached in 1271, and then served the emperor, Kublai Khan, for the next 20 years. This "Great Khan is the mightiest man, whether in respect of subjects or of territory or of treasure, who is in the world today or who ever has been, from Adam our first parent down to the present moment," Marco assured Europe. The Khan's capital city (today's Beijing) was the world's largest and grandest, Marco insisted; it received 1,000 cartloads of silk a day. In brief, China outshone Europe and all other cultures.

The Chinese agreed. Between 1405 and 1434, a royal eunuch, Cheng Ho, led six large fleets from China to the East Indies and the coast of East Africa, trading and exploring along the way. His biggest ships, 400 feet long, displaced 1,500 tons and were certainly large enough to sail around the southern tip of Africa and "discover" Europe. Had China thrown its resources and talents into overseas expansion, the subsequent history of the world would have been vastly different, but most of what the Chinese learned about the outside world merely confirmed their belief that other cultures had little to offer their Celestial Kingdom. No one followed Cheng Ho's lead after he died. Instead, the emperor banned the construction of oceangoing ships and later forbade anyone to own a vessel with more than two masts. China, a self-contained economic and political system, turned inward. It did not need the rest of the world.

Europe versus Islam

Western Europe was a rather backward place in 1400. Compared with China or the Islamic world, it suffered severe disadvantages. Its location on the Atlantic rim of the Eurasian continent had always made access to Asian trade difficult and costly. Islamic societies controlled overland trade with Asia and the only known seaborne route to Asia through the Persian Gulf. As of 1400, Arab mariners were the world's best.

Europeans desired the fine silks of China. They also coveted East Indian spices to enliven their food and help preserve it through the long winters. But because Europeans produced little that Asians wished to buy, they had to pay for these imports with silver or gold, both of which were scarce. In fact, while Europe's sphere of influence was shrinking and while China seemed content with what it already had, Islamic states were well embarked on another great phase of expansion. Europe's mounted knights in heavy armor failed to stop the Ottoman Turks, who took Constantinople in 1453, overran the Balkans by the 1520s, and even threatened Vienna. The Safavid Empire in Iran (Persia) rose to new splendor at the same time. Other Moslems carried the Koran to Indonesia and northern India, where their powerful Mogul empire formed the basis for the modern states of Pakistan and Bangladesh.

Yet Europe had its own advantages. Its economy had made impressive gains in the Middle Ages, primarily because of agricultural advances, such as improved plows, that also fostered population growth. By 1300, more than 100 million people were living in Europe.

Europe's farms could not sustain further growth, however. As the climate cooled, lean years and famines ensued, leaving people undernourished. In the late 1340s, the Black Death (bubonic plague) reduced the population by more than one-third. Recurring bouts of plague kept population low until about 1500, when vigorous growth resumed. But during the long decline of the 15th century, overworked soil regained its fertility, and per capita income rose considerably among people who now had stronger immunities to disease.

By then, European metallurgy and architecture were quite advanced. The Renaissance, which revived interest in the literature and art of ancient Greece and Rome, also gave a new impetus to European culture, especially after Johannes Gutenberg invented the printing press and movable type in the 1430s. Soon information began to circulate more rapidly in Europe than anywhere else in the world. This revolution in communications permitted improvements in ship design and navigational techniques to build on each other and become a self-reinforcing process. The Arabs, by contrast, had borrowed block printing from China in the 10th century, only to give it up by 1400.

Unlike China, none of Europe's kingdoms was a self-contained economy. All had to trade with one another and with the non-Christian world. Although in 1400 this need was a drawback, between the 15th and 17th centuries it slowly became an asset. No single state had a monopoly on the manufacture of firearms or on the flow of capital, and European societies began to compete with one another in gaining access to these resources and in mastering new **maritime** and military techniques. European armies were much more formidable in 1520 than they had been in 1453, and by then European fleets could outsail and outfight all rivals.

The Legacy of the Crusades

Quite apart from the Norse explorers, Europe had a heritage of expansion that derived from the efforts of the crusaders to conquer the Holy Land from Islam. Crusaders had established their own Kingdom of Jerusalem, which survived for more than a century but was finally retaken in 1244. Thereafter, while a new wave of Islamic expansion seemed about to engulf much of the world, Christian Europe gained only a few Mediterranean and Atlantic islands before 1492 but learned some important lessons in the process. To make Palestine profitable, the crusaders had taken over sugar plantations already there and had worked them with a combination of free and slave labor. After they were driven from the Holy Land, they retreated to the Mediterranean islands of Cyprus, Malta, Crete, and Rhodes, where they used slaves to raise sugar cane or grape vines.

Long before Columbus, these planters had created the economic components of overseas expansion. They assumed that colonies should produce **a staple crop,** at least partly through slave labor, for sale in Europe. The first slaves were Moslem captives. In the 14th and 15th centuries, planters turned to pagan Slavs (hence the word *slave*) from the Black Sea area and the Adriatic. Some black Africans were also acquired from Arab merchants who controlled the caravan trade across the Sahara Desert, but these early plantations did not exploit their laborers with the intensity that would later become routine in the Americas.

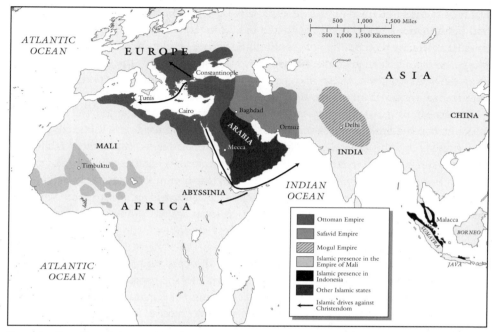

Map 1.2   Expansion of Islam   While Europeans were beginning to move overseas, Islam was also expanding into southeastern Europe, various parts of Africa, the Indian subcontinent, and the East Indies.

The Unlikely Pioneer: Portugal

It seemed highly improbable in 1400 that Europe was standing on the threshold of a dramatic expansion. That Portugal would lead the way seemed even less likely. A small kingdom of fewer than a million people, Portugal had been united for less than a century. Lisbon, with 40,000 people, was the only city of any size. Portugal's maritime traditions lagged well behind those of the Italian states, France, and England. Its merchant class was tiny, and it had little capital.

Yet Portugal had some advantages. It enjoyed internal peace and an efficient government at a time when its neighbors were beset by war and internal upheaval. Moreover, Portugal's location at the intersection of the Mediterranean and Atlantic worlds prompted its mariners to ask how they could transform the Atlantic from a barrier into a highway.

At first, they were interested in short-term gains, rather than in some all-water route to Asia. The Portuguese knew that Arab caravans crossed the Sahara to bring gold, slaves, and ivory from black Africa to Europe. Arab traders spoke of how King (or *Mansa*) Musa (d. 1332) of the Mandingo empire of Mali controlled more gold than any other ruler in the world and of how he could field an army of 100,000 men. These reports reached Europe, where Musa was described as "the richest and most noble lord of all this region on account of the abundance of gold which is gathered in his kingdom." The Portuguese believed that an Atlantic voyage to coastal points south of the Sahara would undercut Arab traders and bring large profits. The greatest problem they faced in this quest was Cape Bojador, with its treacherous shallows, awesome waves, and strong northerly winds. Several bold captains had sailed around the cape, but none had returned.

A member of the Portuguese royal family, Prince Henry, challenged this barrier. In 1420, he became head of the crusading Order of Christ and used its revenues to sponsor 15 voyages along the African coast. In 1434, one of his captains, Gil Eannes, finally succeeded. After passing the cape and exploring the coastline, Eannes sailed west into the Atlantic beyond the sight of land until he met favorable winds and currents that carried him back to Europe. Having launched Portugal's era of expansion, Henry soon lost interest in it. While he indulged in costly and futile crusades against Morocco, less exalted men pushed farther south along the African coast. Only after they made it beyond the Sahara did their efforts begin to pay off.

During the 15th century, Portugal vaulted past all rivals in two major areas—the ability to navigate the high seas beyond sight of land, and the capacity to defeat any non-European fleet on the world's oceans. Portuguese (and later Spanish) navigators mapped the prevailing winds and currents on the high seas over most of the globe. They collected geographic information from classical sources, foreigners, and modern navigators. They studied the superior designs of Arab vessels, copied them, and improved on them. They increased the ratio of length to beam (width at the broadest point of the hull) from 2:1 to 3:1, borrowed the lateen (triangular) sail from the Arabs, and combined it with square rigging in the right proportion to produce a superb oceangoing vessel, the caravel. A **caravel** could make from 3 to 12 knots and could beat closer to a head wind than any other sailing ship. Portuguese captains also used the compass and adopted the Arabs' **astrolabe,** a device that permits accurate calculation of latitude, or distances north and south. (The calculation of longitude—distances east and west—is much more difficult and was not mastered until the 18th century.) As they skirted the African coast, these Portuguese sailors made precise charts and maps that later mariners could follow.

The Portuguese also learned how to mount heavy cannon on the decks of their ships—a formidable advantage in an age when others fought naval battles by grappling and boarding enemy vessels. Portuguese ships were able to stand farther off and literally blow their opponents out of the water. As the 15th century advanced, Portuguese mariners explored ever farther along the African coast, looking for wealth and eventually a direct, cheap route to Asia. South of the Sahara they found the wealth they had been seeking—gold, ivory, and slaves. These riches kept the enterprise alive.

Africa, Colonies, and the Slave Trade

West Africa was inhabited by a mostly agricultural population that also included skilled craftsmen. West Africans probably learned how to use iron long before Europeans did, and

Don Alvar, Rix Congo (c. 1686)   King Alvare obviously derived great wealth by providing slaves to the Portuguese.

they had been supplying Europe with most of its gold for hundreds of years through indirect trade across the desert. West Africa's political history had been marked by the rise and decline of a series of large inland states. The most recent of these, the empire of Mali, was already in decline by 1450. As the Portuguese advanced past the Sahara, their commerce began to pull trade away from the desert caravans, which further weakened Mali and other interior states. By 1550, the empire had fallen apart.

The Portuguese also founded offshore colonies along the way. They began to settle the uninhabited Madeira Islands in 1418, took possession of the Azores between 1427 and 1450, occupied the Cape Verde group in the 1450s, and took over São Tomé in

1470. Like exploration, colonization turned a profit. Lacking investment capital and experience in overseas settlement, the Portuguese drew on Italian merchants for both. In this way, the plantation complex of staple crops and slavery migrated from the Mediterranean to the Atlantic. Beginning in the 1440s, Portuguese island planters produced sugar or wine, increasingly with slave labor imported from nearby Africa. Some plantations, particularly on São Tomé, kept several hundred slaves at work growing and processing sugar.

At first, the Portuguese acquired their slaves by landing on the African coast, attacking agricultural villages, and carrying off everyone they could catch, but these raids enraged coastal peoples and made other forms of trade more difficult. In the decades after 1450, the slave trade assumed its classic form. The Portuguese established small posts, or **factories**, along the coast or, ideally, on small offshore islands, such as Arguin Island near Cape Blanco, where they built their first African fort in 1448. Operating out of these bases, traders would buy slaves from the local rulers, who usually acquired them by waging war. During the long history of the **Atlantic slave trade**, nearly every African shipped overseas had first been enslaved by other Africans. **(See Map 1.3, Africa and the Mediterranean in the 15th century, in the color insert following page 96.)**

Slavery had long existed in Africa, but in a form less brutal than that which the Europeans would impose. When the Atlantic slave trade began, no African middleman could have foreseen how the enslavement of Africans by Europeans would differ from the enslavement of Africans by Africans. In Africa, slaves were not forced to toil endlessly to produce staple crops, and their descendants often became fully assimilated into the captors' society. Slaves were not isolated as a separate caste. By the time African middlemen learned about the cruel conditions of slavery under European rule, the trade had become too lucrative to stop, although several African societies tried. They discovered, however, that those who refused to participate in the trade were likely to become its victims. When the rulers of the Kongo embraced Catholicism in the 16th century, they protested against the Atlantic slave trade, only to see their own people become vulnerable to enslavement by others. The non-Christian kingdom of Benin learned the same lesson.

The Portuguese made the slave trade profitable by exploiting rivalries among the more than 200 small states of West and Central Africa, an area that was divided into more languages and small states than Europeans would find anywhere else in the world. Despite many cultural similarities among these groups, West Africans had never thought of themselves as a single people. Nor did they share a universal religion that might have restrained them from selling other Africans into slavery. Moslems believed it sinful to enslave a fellow believer. Western Europeans, although they were quite capable of waging destructive wars against one another, strongly believed that enslaving fellow Christians was immoral. Enslaving pagan or Moslem Africans was another matter. Some Europeans even persuaded themselves that they were doing Africans a favor by buying them and making their souls eligible for salvation.

Portugal's Asian Empire

Portuguese exploration continued, paying for itself through gold, ivory, and slaves. In the 1480s, the government decided to support the quest for an all-water route to Asia. In 1487, Bartolomeu Dias reached the Cape of Good Hope at the southern tip of Africa and headed east toward the Indian Ocean, but his crew rebelled in those stormy waters, and he turned back. Ten years later, Vasco da Gama led a small fleet around the Cape of Good Hope and sailed on to the Malibar Coast of southwestern India. In a voyage that lasted more than two years (1497–99), da Gama bargained and fought for spices that yielded a 20-to-1 profit for his investors.

Da Gama opened the way for Portugal's empire in the East. To secure their Asian trade, the Portuguese established a chain of naval bases that extended from East Africa to the mouth of the Persian Gulf, then to Goa on the west coast of India, and from there to the Moluccas, or East Indies. Portuguese missionaries even penetrated Japan. The Moluccas became the Asian center of the Portuguese seaborne empire, with their spices yielding most of the wealth that Portugal extracted from its eastern holdings. As early as 1515, African and Asian trade was providing two-thirds of Portugal's state revenues.

Beyond assuring its continued access to spices, Portugal made little effort to govern its holdings, and thus its eastern empire never became colonies of settlement. In all of their Asian holdings, the Portuguese remained heavily outnumbered by native peoples. Only in the Western Hemisphere—in Brazil, which was discovered accidentally by Pedro Álvares Cabral in 1500 when he was blown off course while trying to round the Cape of Good Hope—had settlement become a major goal by the late 16th century.

Early Lessons

As the Norse failure showed, the ability to navigate the high seas, although an impressive feat, gave no guarantee of lasting success. Sustained expansion overseas required the support of a home government and ready access to what other states had learned. Italian merchants in nearby Rhodes or Cyprus passed their experiences on to the Portuguese to be applied in the Atlantic islands of Madeira or the Azores. And the lessons learned there were then relayed to distant Brazil. The Portuguese drew on Italian capital and maritime skills, as well as on Arab learning and technology, in launching their ventures. Spaniards, in turn, would learn much from the Portuguese. The French, Dutch, and English would borrow from Italians, Portuguese, and Spaniards.

The economic impulse behind colonization was thus in place long before Columbus sailed west. The desire for precious metals provided the initial stimulus, but staple crops and slavery kept that impetus alive. Before the 19th century, more than two-thirds of the people who crossed the Atlantic were slaves who were brought to America to grow sugar or other staples. The Atlantic slave trade was not some unfortunate exception to a larger story of liberty. For three and a half centuries, it was the norm.

Few Europeans who crossed the ocean expected to work. Early modern Europe was a hierarchical society in which men with prestige and wealth did virtually no physical labor. Upward social mobility meant advancing toward the goal of "living nobly," without the need to labor. In both Portugal and Spain, the social barriers between aristocrats and commoners had been flexible for some time. Professional men, famous soldiers, and rich merchants could acquire titles and begin to "live nobly." The opening of the Americas offered even greater possibilities for men to succeed by forcing others to toil for them.

Spain, Columbus, and the Americas

While the Portuguese surged east, Spaniards moved more sluggishly to the west. Just as Portugal gained experience by colonizing Madeira and the Azores, the Spanish kingdom of Castile sent its first settlers to the Canary Islands shortly after 1400. They spent the last third of the 15th century conquering the local inhabitants, the Guanches, a Berber people who had left North Africa before the rise of Islam and had been almost completely cut off from Africa and Europe for a thousand years. By the 1490s, the Spanish had all but exterminated them, the first people to face virtual extinction in the wake of European expansion.

Except for seizing the Canaries, the Spaniards devoted little attention to exploration or colonization. Instead, for most of the 15th century, the Iberian kingdoms of Aragon and Castile warred with other powers, quarreled with each other, or dealt with internal unrest. But in 1469, Prince Ferdinand of Aragon married Princess Isabella of Castile. They soon inherited their respective thrones and formed the modern kingdom of Spain, which had a population of about 4.9 million by 1500. Aragon, a Mediterranean society, had made good on an old claim to the Kingdom of Naples and Sicily and thus already possessed a small imperial bureaucracy with experience in administering overseas possessions. Castile, landlocked on three sides, was larger than Aragon but in many ways more parochial. Its people, although suspicious of foreigners, had turned over much of their small overseas trade to merchants and mariners from Genoa in northern Italy who had settled in the port of Seville. Crusading Castilians, not traders, had taken the lead in expelling the Moors from the Iberian peninsula. Castilians, who were more likely than the Portuguese to identify expansion with conquest instead of trade, would lead Spain overseas.

In January 1492, Isabella and Ferdinand completed the reconquest of Spain by taking Granada, the last outpost of Islam on the Iberian peninsula. Flush with victory, they gave unconverted Jews six months to become Christians or be expelled from Spain. Just over half of Spain's 80,000 Jews fled, mostly to nearby Christian lands, including Portugal, that were more tolerant than Spain. A decade later, Ferdinand and Isabella also evicted all unconverted Moors. Spain entered the 16th century as Europe's most fiercely Catholic society, and this attitude accompanied its people overseas.

Columbus

A talented navigator from Genoa named Christopher Columbus promptly sought to benefit from the victory at Granada. He had served the Portuguese Crown for several years, had engaged in the slave trade between Africa and the Atlantic islands, had married the daughter of a prominent Madeira planter, and may even have sailed to Iceland. He had been pleading for years with the courts of Portugal, England, France, and Spain to give him the ships and men to attempt an unprecedented feat: He believed he could reach eastern Asia by sailing west across the Atlantic.

Columbus's proposed voyage was controversial, but not because he assumed the earth was round. Learned men agreed on that point, but they disagreed about the earth's size. Columbus put its circumference at only 16,000 miles. He proposed to reach Japan or China by sailing west a mere 3,000 miles. The Portuguese scoffed at his reasoning. They put the planet's circumference at about 26,000 miles, and they warned Columbus that he would perish on the vast ocean if he tried his mad scheme. Their calculations were, of course, far more accurate than those of Columbus; the circumference of the earth is about 25,000 miles at the equator. Even so, the fall of Granada gave Columbus another chance to plead his case. Isabella, who now had men and resources to spare, grew more receptive to his request. She put him in charge of a fleet of two caravels, the *Niña* and the *Pinta*, together with a larger, square-rigged vessel, the *Santa María,* which Columbus made his flagship.

Columbus's motives were both religious and practical. Like many contemporaries, he believed that the world was going to end soon but that God would make the Gospel available to all humankind before the last days. As the "Christ-bearer" (the literal meaning of his first name), Columbus was convinced that he had a role to play in bringing on the **Millennium,** the period at the end of history when Jesus would return and rule with his saints for 1,000 years; however, he was not at all averse to acquiring wealth and glory along the way.

Embarking from the port of Palos in August 1492, Columbus headed south to the Canaries, picked up provisions, and sailed west across the Atlantic. He kept two ship's logs, one to show his men, in which he underestimated the distance they had traveled, and the other for his eyes only. (Ironically, the false log turned out to be more accurate than the official one.) He promised a prize to the first sailor to sight land. Despite his assurances that they had not sailed far, the crews grew restless in early October. Columbus pushed on. When land was spotted, on October 12, he claimed the prize for himself. He said he had seen a light in the distance the previous night.

The Spaniards splashed ashore on San Salvador, now Watling's Island in the Bahamas. (A few historians argue for Samana Cay, 60 miles south of San Salvador, as the site of the first landfall.) Convinced that he was somewhere in the East Indies, near Japan or China, Columbus called the local inhabitants "Indians," a word that meant nothing to them but one that has endured. When the peaceful Tainos (or Arawaks) claimed that the Carib Indians on nearby islands were cannibals, Columbus interpreted their word for "Carib" to mean the great "Khan" or emperor of China, known to him through Marco Polo's *Travels.* Columbus set out to find the Caribs. For several months he poked about the Caribbean, mostly along the coasts of Cuba and Hispaniola. Then, on Christmas, the *Santa María* ran onto rocks and had to be abandoned. A few weeks later, Columbus sailed for Spain on the *Niña*. Some historians speculate that he had arranged the Christmas disaster as a way of forcing some of the crew to remain as a garrison on Hispaniola, but by then even the gentle Tainos had seen enough. Before Columbus returned on his second voyage in late 1493, they had killed all of those men.

The voyage had immediate consequences. In 1493, Pope Alexander VI (a Spaniard) issued a bull, *Inter Caeteras,* which divided all non-Christian lands between Spain and Portugal. A year later, in the Treaty of Tordesillas, the two kingdoms adjusted the dividing line, with Spain eventually claiming most of the Western Hemisphere, plus the Philippines, and Portugal most of the Eastern Hemisphere, including the African coast, plus Brazil. As a result, Spain never acquired direct access to the African slave trade.

Columbus made three more voyages in quest of China and also served as governor of the Spanish Indies. But Castilians never really trusted this Genoese opportunist, who spoke their language with a Portuguese accent and was a poor, and cruel, administrator to boot. The colonists often defied him, and in 1500, after his third voyage, they shipped him back to Spain in chains. Although later restored to royal favor, he died in 1506, a bitter, disappointed man.

Spain and the Caribbean

By then, overseas settlement had acquired a momentum of its own as thousands of ex-soldiers, bored **hidalgos** (minor nobles with little wealth), and assorted adventurers drifted across the Atlantic. They carried with them seeds for Europe's cereal crops and livestock, including horses, cows, sheep, goats, and pigs. On islands without fences, the animals roamed freely, eating everything in sight, and soon threatened the Tainos' food supply. Unconcerned, the Spaniards forced the increasingly malnourished Indians to work for them, mostly panning for gold. Under these pressures, even before the onset of major infectious diseases, the native population fell catastrophically throughout the Caribbean. By 1514, only 22,000 able-bodied adults remained on Hispaniola, from an initial population of perhaps one million. The native people died even more rapidly than the meager supply of placer gold disappeared. This story was soon repeated on Cuba, Jamaica, and other islands. A whole way of life all but vanished from the earth to be replaced by sugar, slaves, and livestock as the Spaniards despaired of finding other forms of wealth. African slaves, acquired from the Portuguese, soon arrived to replace the dead Indians as a labor force.

The Spaniards continued their New World explorations: Juan Ponce de León tramped through Florida in quest of a legendary fountain of youth, shrewdly calculating that such an elixir would bring a handsome price in Europe. Vasco Núñez de Balboa became the first European to reach the Pacific Ocean, after crossing the Isthmus of Panama in 1513. Even so, as late as 1519—a full generation after Columbus's first voyage—Spain had gained little wealth from these new possessions, whatever and wherever they turned out to be. One geographer concluded that Spain had found a whole new continent, which he named "America" in honor of his informant, the explorer Amerigo Vespucci. For those who doubted this claim, Ferdinand Magellan, a Portuguese mariner serving the king of Spain, settled the issue when his fleet sailed around the world between 1519 and 1522. Magellan never completed the voyage. He was killed in the Philippines.

During the same three years, **Hernán Cortés** sailed from Cuba, invaded Mexico, and found the treasure that Spaniards had been seeking. In 1519, he landed at a place he named Veracruz (The True Cross), and over the next several months he succeeded in tracking down the fabulous empire of the **Aztecs**, high in the Valley of Mexico. When his small army of 400 men first laid eyes on the Aztec capital of **Tenochtitlán** (a metropolis of 200,000, much larger than any city in Western Europe), they wondered if they were dreaming, but they marched on. Moctezuma (or Montezuma II), the Aztec "speaker," or ruler, sent rich presents to persuade the Spaniards to leave, but the gesture had the opposite effect. "They picked up the gold and fingered it like monkeys," an Aztec later recalled. "Their bodies swelled with greed, and their hunger was ravenous. . . . They snatched at the golden ensigns, waved them from side to side and examined every inch of them." Cortés had stumbled upon a wholly different world in the Americas, one with its own long and varied past.

The Emergence of Complex Societies in the Americas

The high cultures of the Americas had been developing for thousands of years before Europeans arrived. Their ways were ancient, and they were proud of their past. Their wealth fired the imagination of Europe and aroused the envy of Spain's enemies. The fabulous Aztec and Inca empires became the magnets that turned European exploration into rival empires of permanent settlement.

The Rise of Sedentary Cultures

After 4000 B.C., agriculture began to transform the lives of most Indians. As farming slowly became the principal source of food in the Americas, settled villages in a few locations grew into large cities. Most of them appeared in the Valley of Mexico, Central America, or the Andes. For centuries, however, dense settlements also thrived in Chaco Canyon in present-day New Mexico and in the Mississippi River valley. Meanwhile, farming continued to spread. As the North American climate continued to warm, it permitted the cultivation of superior strands of maize, or Indian corn, which spread from Mexico first to the Southwest, then the Mississippi and Ohio valleys, and even the northeastern seaboard by the 10th century A.D. By the time Columbus sailed, most Indians were raising crops.

Indians became completely **sedentary** (nonmigratory) only in the most advanced cultures. Most of those north of Mexico lived a **semisedentary** life—that is, they were migratory for part of each year. After a tribe chose a site, the men chopped down some trees, girded others, burned away the underbrush, and often planted tobacco, a mood-altering sacred crop grown exclusively by men. Burning the underbrush fertilized the soil with ash and gave the community years of high productivity. Meanwhile, women erected the dwellings (longhouse, wigwam, tepee) and planted and harvested food crops, especially corn. Planting beans among the corn helped maintain good crop yields. In the fall, either the men alone or entire family groups went off hunting or fishing.

Courtesy of the John Carter Brown Library at Brown University

Indian Women as Farmers   In this illustration, a French artist depicted 16th-century Indian women in southeastern North America.

Under this **slash and burn** system of agriculture, farming became women's work, beneath the dignity of men, whose role was to hunt, fish, and make war, a pattern that characterized nearly all of the peoples in the eastern woodlands. Because this system slowly depleted the soil, the whole tribe had to move to new fields after a decade or two, often because accessible firewood had been exhausted. In this semisedentary way of life, few Indians cared to acquire more personal property than the women could carry from one place to another, either during the annual hunt or when the whole community had to move. This limited interest in consumption would profoundly condition their response to capitalism after contact with Europeans.

Even sedentary Indians did not own land as individuals. Clans or families guarded their "use rights" to land that had been allocated to them by their chiefs. In sedentary societies, both men and women worked in the fields, and families accumulated surpluses for trade. Not all sedentary peoples developed monumental architecture and elaborate state forms. The Tainos of the Greater Antilles in the Caribbean were fully sedentary, for example, but they never erected massive temples or created powerful states. With a few striking exceptions, such examples of cultural complexity emerged primarily among sedentary populations. In Mesoamerica and the Andes, intensive farming, cities, states, and monumental architecture came together at several different times to produce distinctive high cultures.

The spread of farming produced another population surge among both sedentary and semisedentary peoples. Estimates vary greatly, but according to the more moderate ones, at least 50 million people were living in the Western Hemisphere by 1492—and perhaps as many as 70 million, or one-seventh of the world's population. High estimates exceed 100 million. The Valley of Mexico in 1500 was one of the most densely inhabited regions on Earth.

Despite their large populations, even the most complex societies in the Americas remained Stone Age cultures in their basic technology. The urban societies of Mesoamerica and the Andes became the largest and most complex Stone Age cultures in the history of the world. The Indians made some use of metals, although more for decorative than practical purposes. Most metalworking skills originated in South America and spread to Mesoamerica a few centuries before Columbus. By 1520, Indians had amassed enough gold and silver to provide dozens of plundering Europeans with princely fortunes. Yet as far north as the Great Lakes, copper had been discovered and fashioned into fishing tools and art objects since the first millennium B.C. Copper was traded over large areas of North America, but Indians had not learned how to make bronze (a compound of copper and tin) nor found any use for iron. Nearly all of their tools were made of stone or bone, and their sharpest weapons were made from obsidian, a hard, glassy, volcanic rock. Nor did they use the wheel or devices based on the wheel, such as pulleys or gears. Some of them knew how to make a wheel—they had wheeled toys—but they never found a practical purpose for this invention, probably because North America had no draft animals, and South Americans used llamas mostly in steep, mountainous areas where wheeled vehicles would have made no sense.

The Andes: Cycles of Complex Cultures

Despite these technological limitations, Indians accomplished a great deal. During the second millennium B.C., elaborate urban societies began to take shape both in the Andes and along Mexico's gulf coast. Because no Andean culture had become literate before the Europeans arrived, we know much less about events there than we do about Mesoamerica, but we do know that ancient Andean societies devised extremely productive agricultural systems at 12,000 feet above sea level, far above the altitude at which anyone else has ever been able to raise crops. In the 1980s, when archaeologists rebuilt part of the prehistoric Andean irrigation system according to ancient specifications, they discovered that it was far more productive than a system using modern fertilizers and machines. The Andean system could produce 10 metric tons of potatoes per hectare (about 2.4 acres), as against 1 to 4 tons on nearby modern fields. Lands using the Andean canal system never had to lie fallow. This type of irrigation took hold around Lake Titicaca about 1000 B.C. and spread throughout the region. It was abandoned around A.D. 1000, apparently in response to a monster drought that endured, with only brief intermissions, for two centuries. The same climate shift that warmed North America and encouraged the spread of agriculture produced severe droughts along the Pacific coast.

Monumental architecture and urbanization appeared in the Andes even before the canal system at Lake Titicaca was created. Between 3000 and 2100 B.C., both took hold along the Peruvian coast and in the interior. The new communities were built around a U-shaped temple about three stories high. Some of the earliest temples were pyramids, the oldest of which are as ancient as those of Egypt. In later centuries, as more people moved into the mountains, some pyramids became immense. The one at Sechin Alto near Lima, more than 10 stories high, was built between 1800 and 1500 B.C. These accomplishments gradually merged into what archaeologists call the Pre-Classic Chavin culture, which was well established by 1000 B.C., only to collapse suddenly about 300 B.C. In all probability, no single state ever dominated this culture.

Chavin culture had two offshoots: one on the coast and one in the mountains. Together they constitute the Classic phase of pre-Columbian history in South America. The Mochica culture, which emerged about A.D. 300 on the northwest coast of Peru, produced finely detailed pottery, much of it erotic, and built pyramids as centers of worship. At about the same time, another Classic culture arose in the mountains around the city of Tiwanaku, 12,000 feet above sea level. The people of this society grew a great variety of food plants, both tropical and temperate. Terraces, laid out at various altitudes on the mountainside, enabled the community to raise crops from different climatic zones, all a few hours distant from one another. At the lowest levels, Tiwanakans planted cotton in the hot, humid air. Farther up the mountain, they raised maize (corn) and other crops suitable to a temperate zone. At still higher elevations, they grew potatoes and grazed their alpacas and llamas. They even invented freeze-dried food by carrying it far up the mountains to take advantage of the frost that fell most nights of the year.

Complex Cultures of Pre-Columbian America

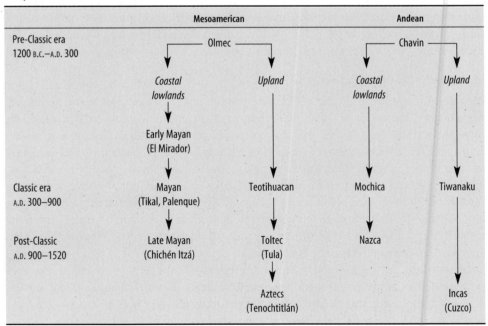

	Mesoamerican		Andean	
Pre-Classic era 1200 B.C.–A.D. 300	Olmec		Chavin	
	Coastal lowlands	Upland	Coastal lowlands	Upland
	Early Mayan (El Mirador)			
Classic era A.D. 300–900	Mayan (Tikal, Palenque)	Teotihuacan	Mochica	Tiwanaku
Post-Classic A.D. 900–1520	Late Mayan (Chichén Itzá)	Toltec (Tula)	Nazca	
		Aztecs (Tenochtitlán)		Incas (Cuzco)

The Tiwanaku Empire, with its capital on the southern shores of Lake Titicaca, flourished until even its sophisticated irrigation system could not survive the horrendous drought that began at the end of the 10th century A.D. The Classic Andean cultures collapsed between the 6th and 11th centuries A.D., possibly after a conquest of the Mochica region by the Tiwanakans, who provided water to the coastal peoples until they too were overwhelmed by the drought.

The disruption that followed this decline was temporary because complex Post-Classic cultures soon thrived both north and west of Tiwanaku. The coastal culture of the Nazca people has long fascinated both scholars and tourists because of its exquisite textiles, and above all because of a unique network of lines they etched in the desert. Some lines form the outlines of birds or animals, but others simply run straight for miles until they disappear at the horizon. Only from the air are these patterns fully visible.

Inca Civilization

Around A.D. 1400, the **Inca** (the word applied both to the ruler and to the empire's dominant nation) emerged as the new imperial power in the Andes. They built their capital at Cuzco, high in the mountains. From that upland center, the Incas controlled an empire that eventually extended more than 2,000 miles from south to north, and they bound it together with an efficient network of roads and suspension bridges. Along these roads, the Incas maintained numerous storehouses for grain. They had no written language, but high-altitude runners, who memorized the Inca's oral commands, raced along the roads to relay their ruler's decrees over vast distances. The Incas also invented a decimal system and used it to keep records of the tribute they levied upon subject peoples. They used a device they called a *quipu*. By 1500, the Inca empire ruled perhaps 8 to 12 million people. No other nonliterate culture has ever matched that feat.

Mesoamerica: Cycles of Complex Cultures

Mesoamerica experienced a similar cycle of change, but over a somewhat shorter period. Its own Pre-Classic, Classic, and Post-Classic cultures also comprised both upland and lowland societies.

The Olmecs, who appeared along the Gulf Coast about 1200 B.C., became the parent culture for the region. It centered on three cities. The oldest, San Lorenzo (names are modern, as is **Olmec**, which means "people of rubber," for the rubber trees that thrive in this tropical region), flourished from 1200 to 900 B.C., when it was conquered by invaders. Olmec influence reached its zenith during the domination of La Venta, which became an urban center about 1100 B.C., reached its peak 300 years later, and declined. After La Venta was demolished between 500 and 400 B.C., leadership passed to the city of Tres Zapotes, which thrived for another four centuries.

These three Olmec centers, with permanent populations of only about 1,000, were too small to sustain large armies. The colossal stone heads that honored their rulers were the most distinctive Olmec artifacts, but they appeared only in the homeland. Other aspects

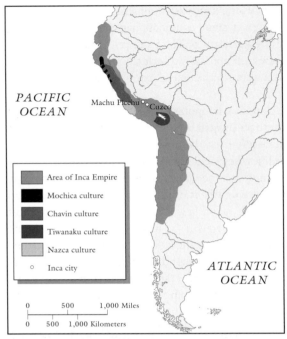

Map 1.4   Inca Empire and Principal Earlier Cultures   The Pacific coast of South America showing the location of the Mochica, Chavin, Tiwanaku, and Nazca cultures and finally the Inca empire, which covered a much larger area.

of Olmec culture became widely diffused throughout Mesoamerica. The Olmecs built the first pyramids and the first ballparks in the region. Their game, played with a heavy rubber ball, spread into what is now the southwestern United States. The losers were, at least on certain religious occasions, beheaded.

The Olmecs also learned how to write and developed a dual calendar system that endured through the Aztec era. At the end of a 52-year cycle, the first day of the "short" calendar would again coincide with the first day of the "long" one. Olmecs faced the closing days of each cycle with dread, lest the gods allow the sun and all life on earth to be destroyed—something that, Olmecs warned, had already happened several times. They believed that the sacrifice of a god had been necessary to set the sun in motion in each new creation cycle and that only the blood of human sacrifice could placate the gods and keep the sun moving.

These beliefs endured in Mesoamerica for perhaps 3,000 years, regardless of the rise and fall of empires and cities. The essentials may even be older than Olmec culture. The creation myths of both Mesoamerican and Andean peoples are similar, which may suggest a common origin in the distant past, perhaps as far back as Beringia, where the sun did disappear for part of each year. Olmec beliefs retained immense power. The arrival of the Spaniards would create a religious as well as a political crisis, because 1519 marked the end of a 52-year cycle.

The Olmecs were succeeded by two Classic cultures, both of which created great cities and studied the heavens. The city and empire of Teotihuacan emerged in the mountains not far from modern Mexico City. **Mayan** culture took shape mostly in the southern lowlands of Yucatán. Teotihuacan was already a city of 40,000 by A.D. 1 and grew to five times that size over the next three centuries. Some of its temples were enormous pyramids, but its most impressive art form was its brightly painted murals, of which only a few survive. Teotihuacan invested resources in comfortable apartment dwellings for ordinary residents, not in monuments or inscriptions to rulers. It probably had a form of senate government, not a monarchy. The city extended its influence throughout Mesoamerica and remained a powerful force until its sudden destruction in about A.D. 750, apparently by conquest, because its shrines were toppled and the city was abandoned. In all likelihood, Teotihuacan's growth had so depleted the resources of the area that the city could not have sustained itself much longer. Modern beliefs to the contrary, Indians enjoyed no mystical protection from ecological disasters.

In the lowlands, Classic Mayan culture went through a similar cycle from expansion to ecological crisis. It was also urban but less centralized than that of Teotihuacan, although some Mayan temples were just as monumental. For more than 1,000 years, Mayan culture rested on a network of competing city-states, which, as in ancient Greece, shared similar values. One of the largest Mayan cities, Tikal, arose on the plateau separating rivers flowing into the Caribbean from those emptying into the Gulf of Mexico. It controlled commerce with Teotihuacan. Tikal housed 100,000 at its peak before A.D. 800. Twenty other cities, most about one-fourth the size of Tikal, flourished throughout the region. Mayan engineers built canals to water the crops needed to support this urban system, which was well established by the first century B.C. The Danta pyramid, completed in the second century B.C. at the Pre-Classic city of El Mirador, was probably the most massive architectural structure in pre-Columbian Mesoamerica. El Mirador declined before the Classic era began. **(See Map 1.5, Ancient Mesoamerica, in the color insert following page 96.)**

The earliest Mayan writings date to 50 B.C., but few survive from the next 300 years. About A.D. 300, Mayans began to record their history in considerable detail. Since 1960, scholars have deciphered most Mayan inscriptions, which means that the Classic phase of Mayan culture is completing a shift from a prehistoric to a historic (or written) past. Mayan texts are now studied much like those of Europe. Mayan art and writings reveal the religious beliefs of these people, including the place of human sacrifice in their cosmos and the role of ritual self-mutilation in their worship, particularly among the elite. Scholars have learned, for example, about the long reign of

Inca *Quipu* The accounting device pictured here is based on a decimal system developed by the Incas.

Pacal the Great, king (or "Great Sun") of the elegant city of Palenque, who was born on March 26, 603, and died on August 31, 683. His sarcophagus lists his ancestors through six generations. Other monuments tell of the Great Suns of other cities whom Pacal vanquished and sacrificed to the gods.

Classic Mayan culture began to collapse about 50 years after the fall of Teotihuacan, which disrupted Mayan trade with the Valley of Mexico. The crisis spread rapidly. Palenque and a half-dozen other cities were abandoned between 800 and 820. The last date recorded at Tikal was in 869; the last in the southern lowlands came 40 years later. The Mayan aristocracy had grown faster than the commoners could support it, until population outstripped local resources and generated irreversible ecological decay. Frequent wars hastened the decline. Trade with the Valley of Mexico, although diminished, shifted north to other cities. With the collapse of the southern cities, the population of the region fell drastically, partly through emigration northward.

After A.D. 900, the Post-Classic era saw a kind of Mayan renaissance in the northern lowlands of the Yucatán, where many refugees from the south had fled. Chichén Itzá, a city that had existed for centuries, preserved many distinctive Mayan traits but merged them with new influences from the Valley of Mexico, where the Toltecs had become dominant in the high country and may even have conquered Chichén Itzá. The Toltecs were a fierce warrior people whose capital at Tula, with 40,000 people, was one-fifth as large as Teotihuacan at its peak. They prospered from the cocoa trade with tropical lowlands but otherwise did

© Boltin Picture Library/The Bridgeman Art Library

The Temple of the Sun at Teotihuacan   The giant, stepped pyramid shown here is one of pre-Columbian America's most elegant pyramids.

nothing to expand the region's food supply. They controlled the Valley of Mexico for almost three centuries, until about A.D. 1200, when they too declined. They left a legacy of conquest to later rulers in the valley, all of whom claimed descent from Toltec kings.

The Aztecs and Tenochtitlán

By 1400, power in the Valley of Mexico was passing to the Aztecs, a warrior people who had migrated from the north about two centuries earlier and had settled, with the bare sufferance of their neighbors, on the shore of Lake Texcoco. They built a great city, Tenochtitlán, out on the lake. Its only connection with the mainland was by several broad causeways. The Aztecs raised their agricultural productivity by creating highly productive **chinampas**, or floating gardens, right on the lake. Yet their mounting population strained the food supply. In the 1450s, the threat of famine was severe.

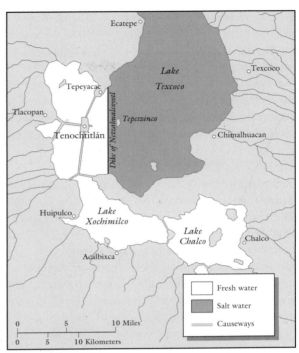

Map 1.6   Valley of Mexico, 1519   Lake Texcoco and its principal cities, especially Tenochtitlán (built on the lake) and its allies, Tlacopan and Texcoco.

Tenochtitlán, with a population of something over 200,000, had forged an alliance with Texcoco and Tlacopan, two smaller lakeside cities. Together they dominated the area, but by the second quarter of the 15th century, leadership was clearly passing to the Aztecs. As newcomers to the region, the Aztecs felt a need to prove themselves worthy heirs to Tula, Teotihuacan, and the ancient culture of the Valley of Mexico. They adopted the old religion but practiced it with a terrifying intensity. They waged perpetual war, usually with neighboring cities, to gain captives for their ceremonies. They built and constantly rebuilt and enlarged their Great Pyramid of the Sun. At its dedication in 1487, they sacrificed— if we can believe later accounts—about 14,000 people in a ritual that went on for four days until the priests dropped from exhaustion. Each captive climbed the steep steps of the pyramid and was held by his wrists and ankles over the sacrificial slab while a priest cut open his breast, ripped out his heart, held it up to the sun, placed it inside the statue of a god, and then rolled the carcass down the steps so that parts of the body could be eaten, mostly by members of the captor's family, but never by the captor. He fasted instead and mourned the death of a worthy foe.

Human sacrifice was an ancient ritual in Mesoamerica, familiar to everyone, but the Aztecs practiced it on a scale that was unparalleled anywhere else in the world. The need for thousands of victims each year created potential enemies everywhere. Although neighboring peoples shared the religious beliefs of the Aztecs, they nevertheless hated these conquerors from the north. After 1519, many Indians in Mesoamerica would help the Spaniards bring down the Aztecs. By contrast, the Spanish would find few allies in the Andes, where resistance in the name of the Inca would persist for most of the 16th century and would even revive in the late 18th century, 250 years after the conquest.

North American Mound Builders

North of Mexico, from 3000 B.C. to about A.D. 1700, three distinct cultures of "mound builders" succeeded each other and exerted a powerful influence over the interior of North America. Named for the huge earthen mounds they erected, these cultures arose near the Ohio and Mississippi rivers and their tributaries. The earliest mound builders became semi-sedentary even before learning to grow crops. Fish, game, and the lush vegetation of the river valleys sustained them for most of the year and enabled them to erect permanent dwellings.

The oldest mound-building culture appeared among a preagricultural people in what is now northeastern Louisiana about 3400 B.C., at a site called Watson Break. Later, just 40 miles away, early mound builders flourished from 1500 to 700 B.C. at Poverty Point (named for a 19th-century plantation), a center that contained perhaps 5,000 people at its peak in about 1000 B.C. The second mound-building culture, the Adena-Hopewell, emerged between 500 B.C. and A.D. 400 in the Ohio River valley. Its mounds were increasingly elaborate burial sites, indicating belief in an afterlife. Mound-building communities participated in a commerce that spanned most of the continent between the Appalachians and the Rockies, the Great Lakes and the Gulf of Mexico. Obsidian from the Yellowstone Valley in the Far West, copper from the Great Lakes basin, and shells from the Gulf of Mexico have all been found buried in the Adena-Hopewell mounds. Both the mound building and the long-distance trade largely ceased after A.D. 400, for reasons that remain unclear. The people even stopped growing corn for a few centuries. Yet the mounds were so impressive that

Theodore de Bry

Woodcut of a Queen, or the Wife of a "Great Sun" of the Mississippi Mound Builders, Being Carried on a Litter   This 16th-century engraving is by Theodore de Bry.

when American settlers found them after the Revolution, they refused to believe that "savages" could have built them.

Mound building revived in a third and final Mississippian phase between A.D. 1000 and 1700. This culture dominated the Mississippi River valley from modern St. Louis to Natchez, with the largest center at Cahokia in present-day Illinois and another important one at Moundville in Alabama. Ordinary people became "stinkards" in this culture, while some families had elite status. The "Great Sun" ruled with authority and was transported

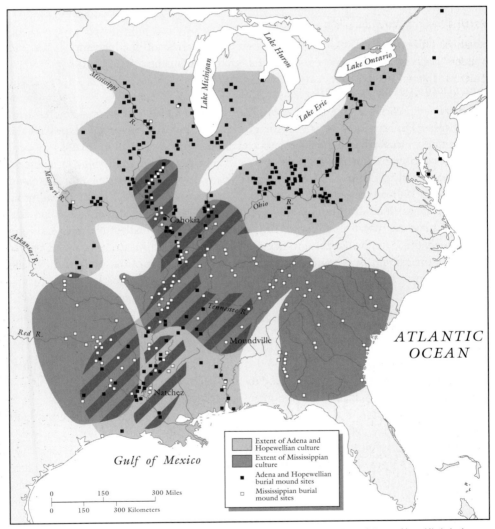

Map 1.7 Mound-Building Cultures of North America Early Adena and Hopewell burial sites and later Mississippian sites and the areas that these cultures influenced.

by litter from place to place. When he died, some of his wives, relatives, and retainers even volunteered to be sacrificed at his funeral and join him in the afterlife. Burial mounds thus became much grander in Mississippian communities. The Indians topped the mounds in which their rulers were interred with elaborate places of worship and residences for the priests and Great Suns of these highly stratified societies.

The city of **Cahokia,** near modern St. Louis, flourished from A.D. 900 to 1250 and may have had 20,000 or more residents at its peak, making it the largest city north of Mexico and half as populous as the contemporary Toltec capital at Tula. Cahokia's enormous central mound, 100 feet high, is the world's largest earthenwork. Similarities with Mesoamerican practices and artifacts have led many scholars to look for direct links between the two cultures. Yet although travel was possible between Mesoamerica and the Mississippi valley, no Mesoamerican artifacts have been found in the southeastern United States.

Urban Cultures of the Southwest

Other complex societies emerged in North America's semiarid Southwest—among them the Mogollan (perhaps best known for their beautifully painted pottery) and especially the Hohokam, the **Anasazi,** and the Pueblo. The Hohokam Indians settled in what is now central Arizona during the 600 years after 300 B.C. Their irrigation system, consisting of several hundred miles of canals, produced two harvests per year. They wove cotton cloth and made pottery with a distinctive red color. They traded with places as distant as California and Mesoamerica and even imported a version of the Mesoamerican ball game. Perhaps because unceasing irrigation increased the salinity of the soil, this culture, after enduring for more than 1,000 years, went into irreversible decline by 1450.

Even more tantalizing and mysterious is the brief flowering of the Anasazi (a Navajo word meaning "the ancient ones"), a cliff-dwelling people who have left behind some remarkable artifacts at Chaco Canyon in New Mexico, at Mesa Verde in Colorado, and at other sites. In their caves and cliffs, they constructed apartment houses five stories high with as many as 500 dwellings and with elegant and spacious *kivas,* or meeting rooms for religious functions. The Anasazi were superb astronomers. Through an arrangement of rock slabs, open to the sun and moon at the mouth of a cave, and of spirals on the interior wall that plotted the movement of the sun and moon, they created a calendar that could track the summer and winter solstices and even the 19-year cycles of the moon, an astronomical refinement Europeans had not yet achieved. They traveled to their fields and brought in lumber and other distant supplies on a network of roads that ran for scores of miles in several directions. They achieved most of these feats over a period of about two centuries, although Anasazi pottery has been found that dates from much earlier times. In the last quarter of the 13th century, apparently overwhelmed by a prolonged drought and by hostile invaders, they abandoned their principal sites. Pueblo architecture is a direct successor of that of the Anasazi, and the Pueblo Indians are descended from them.

Contact and Cultural Misunderstanding

Focus Question

Why were the native peoples of the Americas extremely vulnerable to European diseases, instead of the other way around?

After the voyage of Columbus, the peoples of Europe and America, both with ancient pasts, confronted each other. Mutual understanding was unlikely except on a superficial level. Nothing in the histories of Europeans or Indians had prepared either of them for the encounter. The humanists of Renaissance Europe, avidly studying ancient Greece and Rome, were uncovering the huge differences between those pagan cultures and the Christian values of the Middle Ages and were developing a strong sense of history—an awareness that their past had been quite different from their present. They were also used to dealing with Moslem "infidels," whom they regarded as terribly alien but whose monotheistic beliefs were not all that different from their own. They also understood that East Asia was neither classical nor Christian, not Islamic or "barbaric." Even so, none of this experience prepared them for what they found in America.

Religious Dilemmas

Christians had trouble understanding how Indians could exist at all. The Bible, they were certain, recorded the creation of all humankind, but it never mentioned the Indians. From which of the sons of Noah had they descended? Were they the "lost 10 tribes" of Israel, perhaps? This idea was first suggested by Spanish missionaries and would later appeal to British Protestants. Some theologians, such as Spaniard Juan Ginés de Sepúlveda, tried to resolve this dilemma by arguing that Indians were animals without souls, not human beings at all. The pope and the royal courts of Portugal and Spain listened instead to a Dominican missionary, Fray Bartolomé de Las Casas, who insisted on the Indians' humanity. But, asked Europeans, if Indians (and Asians) did possess immortal souls, would a compassionate God have left them in utter darkness for centuries without making the Gospel known to them? Rejecting that possibility, some early Catholic missionaries concluded that one of the apostles must have visited America (and India) and that the Indians must have rejected his message. The Portuguese announced in the 1520s that they had discovered the tomb of St. Thomas the Doubter in India, and then in 1549, a Jesuit claimed to have found Thomas's footprint in Brazil. If only to satisfy the spiritual yearnings of Europeans overseas, St. Thomas got around!

To Europeans, the sacrificial temples, skull racks, and snake motifs of Mesoamerica led to only one conclusion: The Aztecs worshiped Satan. Their statues and even their writings had to be destroyed. Human sacrifice and ritual cannibalism were widespread throughout the Americas, although nowhere else on the two continents did the scale approach that

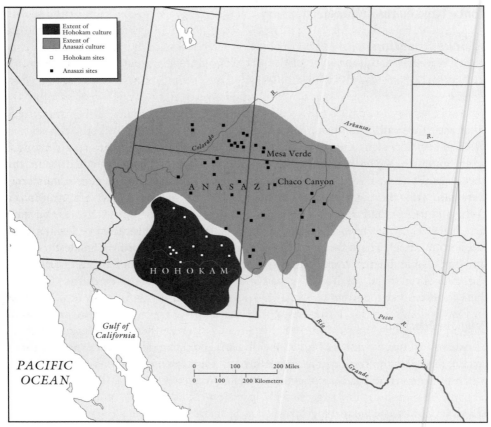

Map 1.8 Hohokam and Anasazi Sites   These cultures in the Southwest combined irrigation and road building with sophisticated architecture.

practiced by the Aztecs. The Incas, whose creation myth resembled that of Mesoamerica, offered an occasional victim to the sun or to some other god. The Indians of eastern North America frequently tortured to death their adult male captives, and every Indian warrior learned from boyhood how to endure such torments. Christians were shocked by human sacrifice and found cannibalism revolting, but Indians regarded certain European practices with equal horror. Between 1500 and 1700, Europeans burned or hanged perhaps 50,000 to 100,000 people, usually old women, for conversing with the wrong spirits—that is, for witchcraft. The Spanish Inquisition burned thousands of heretics and blasphemers. Although Indians were exempt from its jurisdiction in the Americas, they did witness many executions of Europeans. To the Indians, these incinerations looked like human sacrifices to placate an angry Christian God.

The dilemma that Indians posed for Europeans emerged almost at once. On his second voyage, Columbus brought the first missionaries to the Americas. After one of them preached to a group of Tainos and presented them with some holy images, the Indians, records relate, "left the chapel, . . . flung the images to the ground, covered them with a heap of earth, and pissed upon it." The governor, a brother of Columbus, had them burned alive. The Indians probably saw this punishment as a form of human sacrifice to a vengeful god. They had no way of grasping the Christian distinction between human sacrifice and punishment for desecration.

Even the Christians' moral message was ambiguous. Missionaries eagerly brought news of the Christ, how he had died to save humankind from sin. Catholic worship, then as now, centered on the Mass and the Eucharist, in which a priest transforms bread and wine into the literal body and blood of Christ. "Except ye eat the flesh of the Son of man, and drink his blood," Jesus told his disciples (John 6:53), "ye have no life in you." Most Protestants also accepted this sacrament but interpreted it symbolically, not literally. To the Indians, Christians seemed to be a people who ate their own god but grew outraged at the lesser matter of sacrificing a human being to please an Indian god.

When Europeans tried to convert Indians to Christianity, the Indians concluded that the converts would spend the afterlife with the souls of Europeans, separated forever from their own ancestors, whose memory they revered. Neither side fully recognized these obstacles to mutual understanding. Although early Catholic missionaries converted thousands of Indians, the results were mixed at best. Most converts adopted some Christian rites but continued many of their old rituals, often in secret.

War as Cultural Misunderstanding

Such misunderstandings multiplied as Indians and Europeans came into closer contact. Both waged war, but with different objectives. Europeans tried to settle matters on the battlefield and expected to kill many enemies. Indians fought mostly to obtain captives, whether for sacrifice (as with the Aztecs) or to replace tribal losses through adoption (as with the Iroquois). To them, massive deaths on the battlefield were almost a blasphemy, an appalling waste of life that could in no way appease the gods. Europeans and Indians also differed profoundly on what acts constituted atrocities. The torture and ritual sacrifice of captives horrified Europeans; the slaughter of women and children, which Europeans brought to America, appalled Indians.

Gender and Cultural Misunderstanding

Indian social organization also differed fundamentally from that of Europeans. European men owned almost all property, set the rules of inheritance, farmed the land, and performed nearly all public functions. Among many Indian peoples, especially those first encountered by Europeans north of Mexico, descent was **matrilineal** (traced through the maternal line), and women owned nearly all movable property. European men felt incomplete unless they acquired authority over other people, especially the other members of their households. They also expected social inferiors to obey superiors. Indian men had none of these patriarchal ambitions. Chiefs governed more through persuasion, example, and gift giving than through command. Women did the farming in semisedentary Indian cultures, and they often could demand a war or try to prevent one, although the final decision rested with men. When Europeans tried to change warriors into farmers, Indian males protested that they were being turned into women. Only over fully sedentary peoples could Europeans impose direct rule by building on the existing social hierarchy, division of labor, and system of tribute.

Conquest and Catastrophe

Focus Question
Why did the free-labor societies of Western Europe generate unfree labor systems all around their periphery?

Spanish *conquistadores,* or conquerors, led small armies that rarely exceeded 1,000 men. Yet, because they were also able to raise large Indian armies as allies, they subdued two empires much larger than Spain and then looked around for more worlds to overrun. There, beyond the great empires, Indians had more success in resisting them.

The Conquest of Mexico and Peru

When Cortés entered Tenochtitlán in 1519, he seized Moctezuma, the Aztec ruler, as prisoner and hostage. Although overwhelmingly outnumbered, Cortés and his men began to destroy Aztec religious objects, replacing them with images of the Virgin Mary or other Catholic saints. In response, while Cortés was away, the Aztecs rose against the intruders, Moctezuma was killed, and the Spaniards were driven out with heavy losses. But then the smallpox the Spaniards left behind began killing Aztecs by the thousands. Cortés found refuge with the nearby Tlaxcalans, a proudly independent people who had never submitted to Aztec rule. With thousands of their warriors, he returned the next year, built several warships armed with cannon to dominate Lake Texcoco, and destroyed Tenochtitlán. He had hoped to leave the great city intact, not wreck it, but he and the Aztecs found no common understanding that would enable them to stop fighting before the city lay in ruins. "We have chewed dry twigs and salt grasses," mourned one Aztec poet after the fall of the city; "we have filled our mouths with dust and bits of adobe; we have eaten lizards, rats and worms." With royal support from Spain, the *conquistadores* established themselves as new imperial rulers in Mesoamerica,

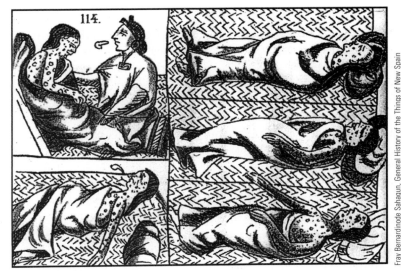

Fray Bernardino de Sahagun, General History of the Things of New Spain

The Ravages of Smallpox These drawings show the devastation of smallpox among the Aztecs, as depicted in the Aztec Codex, one of the few surviving collections of Aztec writing.

looted all the silver and gold they could find, and built Mexico City on the ruins of Tenochtitlán.

Rumors abounded about an even richer civilization far to the south, and in 1531 and 1532, Francisco Pizarro finally located the Inca empire high in the Andes. Smallpox had preceded him and killed the reigning Inca. In the civil war that followed, Atahualpa had defeated his brother to become the new Inca. Pizarro captured Atahualpa, held him hostage, and managed to win a few allies from among the Inca's recent enemies. Atahualpa filled his throne room with precious metals as a truly royal ransom, but Pizarro had him strangled anyway. Tens of thousands of angry Indians besieged the Spaniards for months in Cuzco, the Inca capital, but Pizarro, although vastly outnumbered, managed to hold out and finally prevailed. After subduing the insurgents, the Spanish established a new capital at Lima on the coast. **(See Map 1.9, Principal Spanish Explorations of North America, in the color insert following page 96.)**

In a little more than 10 years, some hundreds of Spanish soldiers with thousands of Indian allies had conquered two enormous empires with a combined population perhaps five times greater than that of all Spain. But only in the 1540s did the Spanish finally locate the bonanza they had been seeking. The fabulous silver mines at Potosí in present-day Bolivia and other smaller lodes in Mexico became the source of Spain's wealth and power for the next 100 years. So wondrous did the exploits of the *conquistadors* seem by then that anything became believable, including rumors that cities of pure gold lay somewhere in the interior of North America.

North American Conquistadores and Missionaries

Alvar Núñez Cabeza de Vaca was one of four survivors of Pánfilo de Narváez's disastrous 1528 expedition to Florida. Cabeza de Vaca made his way back to Mexico City in 1536 after an overland journey that took him from Florida through Texas and northern Mexico. In a published account of his adventures, he briefly mentioned Indian tales of great and populous cities to the north, and this reference soon became stories of "golden cities." Hernando de Soto landed in Florida in 1539 and raped and pillaged his way through much of the southeastern United States in quest of these treasures, leaving disease and mayhem in his wake. He crossed the Mississippi in 1541, wandered through the Ozarks and eastern Oklahoma, and marched back to the great river. He died there in 1542. His companions continued to explore for another year before returning to Spanish territory. Farther west, Francisco Vasquez de Coronado marched into New Mexico and Arizona, where he encountered several Pueblo towns but no golden cities. The expedition reached the Grand Canyon, then headed east into Texas and as far north as Kansas before returning to Mexico in 1542.

After the *conquistadores* departed, Spanish priests did their best to convert thousands of North American Indians to the Catholic faith. These efforts extended well north of New Spain (Mexico). In 1570, the Jesuits even established a mission in what is now Virginia, but local Indians soon wiped it out. After the failure of the Jesuit mission, Spain decided to treat the Indians of Florida and New Mexico with decency and fairness and eventually came to rely on these missions for protection against English and French intruders. The Jesuits withdrew, and Franciscans took their place. In 1573, King Philip II (1556–98) issued the Royal Orders for New Discoveries, which made it illegal to enslave Indians or even attack them. Instead, unarmed priests were to bring Indians together in missions and convert them into peaceful Catholic subjects of Spain. The Franciscans quickly discovered that, without military support, they were more likely to win martyrdom than converts. They reluctantly accepted military protection, but they tried to make sure that none of the few soldiers who accompanied them behaved like *conquistadores*.

Franciscans had no success among the nomadic residents of central and southern Florida. They had to build their missions within the permanent villages of northern Florida or the Pueblo communities of New Mexico. The Spanish incursion into New Mexico began quite badly with the slaughter of perhaps 800 Indian men, women, and children in 1599, but then relations improved. At first, Indian women willingly supplied the labor needed to build and sustain these missions. By 1630, about 86,000 Pueblo, Apache, and Navajo Indians of New Mexico had accepted baptism. They lived in a chain of missions north and south of Santa Fe, 1,500 arduous and dusty miles from the colonial capital at Mexico City. By midcentury, 30 missions in Florida contained about 26,000 baptized Indians and covered an area extending some 250 miles from the Atlantic coast of what is now Georgia westward into the Florida panhandle. The Franciscans also urged their converts, with limited success, to wear European clothing. In 1671, when a bishop counted 4,081 newly converted women in Florida who went about topless and with their lower legs exposed, he ordered them to cover up.

The Spanish Empire and Demographic Catastrophe

By the late 16th century, the Spanish Empire had emerged as a system of direct colonial rule in Mexico and Peru, where the conquerors took over and used existing systems of tribute. These core holdings were protected by a strong defensive perimeter in the Caribbean and surrounded by a series of frontier missions, extending in the north into Florida and New Mexico. The Spaniards also brought new systems of labor and new religious institutions to their overseas colonies, although in time both were altered by local conditions.

The first Spanish rulers in Mexico and Peru relied on a form of labor tribute that had helped to depopulate the West Indies. Called **encomienda,** this system permitted the holder, or *encomendero,* to claim labor from an Indian district for a stated period of time. *Encomienda* worked because it resembled the way the Aztecs and the Incas had routinely levied labor for their own massive public buildings and irrigation projects. In time, the king intervened to correct abuses and to limit labor tribute to projects that the Crown initiated, such as mining and the construction of churches or other public buildings. Spanish settlers resisted the reforms at first but slowly shifted from demanding labor to claiming land. In the countryside, the **hacienda,** a large estate with its own crops and herds, became a familiar institution.

Although the Church never had enough clergy to meet its needs, it became a massive presence during the 16th century. Yet America changed it, too. As missionaries acquired land and labor, they began to exhibit less zeal for Indian souls. The Franciscans—in Europe, the gentlest of Catholic religious orders—brutally and systematically tortured their Mayan converts in the 1560s whenever they caught them worshiping their old gods. To the Franciscans, the slightest lapse could signal a reversion to Satan worship, with human sacrifice a likely consequence. They did not dare to be kind.

Most important, the Spaniards brought deadly microbes with them. Smallpox, which could be fatal but which most Europeans survived in childhood, devastated the Indians, who had almost no immunity to it. Even measles could be fatal, and common colds easily turned into pneumonia. When Cortés arrived in 1519, the native population of Mexico probably exceeded 15 million. In the 1620s, after waves of killing epidemics, it bottomed out at 700,000 and did not regain its pre-Spanish level until the 1950s. Peru suffered nearly as horribly. Its population fell from about 10 million in 1525 to 600,000 a century later. For the hemisphere as a whole, any given region probably lost 90 or 95 percent of its population within a century of sustained contact with Europeans. Lowland tropical areas usually suffered the heaviest casualties; in some of these places, all of the Indians died. Highland areas and sparsely settled regions fared somewhat better.

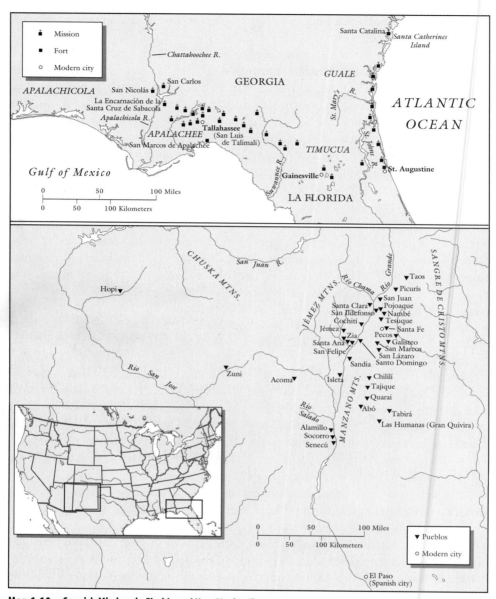

Map 1.10 Spanish Missions in Florida and New Mexico Circa 1675 Franciscan friars established missions in Florida from the Atlantic to the Gulf of Mexico and in New Mexico along the Rio Grande Valley and, in a few cases, farther inland.

The Spanish Crown spent much of the 16th century trying to keep abreast of these changes, but eventually it imposed administrative order on the unruly *conquistadores* and brought peace to its colonies. At the center of the imperial bureaucracy, in Seville, stood the Council of the Indies. The council administered the three American viceroyalties of New Spain, Peru, and eventually New Granada, which were further subdivided into smaller *audiencias,* executive and judicial jurisdictions supervised by the viceroys. The Council of the Indies appointed the viceroys and other major officials, who ruled from the new cities that the Spaniards built with local labor at Havana, Mexico City, Lima, and elsewhere. Although centralized and autocratic in theory, the Spanish Empire allowed local officials a fair degree of initiative, if only because months or even years could elapse in trying to communicate across its immense distances. "If death came from Spain," mused one official, "we should all live long lives."

Brazil

Portuguese Brazil was theoretically autocratic, too, but it was divided into 14 "captaincies," or provinces, and thus was far less centralized. The Portuguese invasion did not lead to the direct rule of native societies but to their displacement or enslavement. After the colonists on the northeast coast turned to raising sugar in the late 16th century, Brazilian frontiersmen, or **bandeirantes,** foraged deep into the continent to enslave more Indians. They even raided remote Spanish Andean missions, rounded up the converts, and dragged them thousands of miles across mountains and through the jungle to be worked to death on the sugar plantations. On several occasions, while Brazil was ruled by Spain (see the discussion that follows), outraged missionaries persuaded the king to abolish slavery altogether. Not even absolutism could achieve that goal. Slavery continued without pause, and Africans gradually replaced Indians as the dominant labor force. Brazil was the major market for African slaves until the 1640s, when Caribbean demand became even greater.

Global Colossus, Global Economy

Focus Question
How important was the establishment of an oceanic system of commerce that linked East and South Asia with Europe and the Americas?

American silver made the king of Spain the most powerful monarch in Christendom. Philip II commanded the largest army in Europe, held the Turks in check in the Mediterranean, and tried to crush the Protestant Reformation in northern Europe (see chapter 2).

He had other ambitions as well. In 1580, after the king of Portugal died with no direct heir, Philip claimed his throne, thus uniting under his own rule Portugal's Asian empire, Brazil, Spain's American possessions, and the Philippines. This colossus was the greatest empire the world had ever seen. It also sustained the first truly global economy, because the Portuguese used Spain's American silver to pay for the spices and silks they imported from Asia. The union of Spain and Portugal lasted until the 1640s, when Portugal revolted and regained its independence.

The Spanish colossus became part of an even broader economic pattern. **Serfdom,** which tied peasants to their lords and to the land, had been Europe's predominant labor system in the early Middle Ages. Although peasants could not move, neither could they be sold; they were not slaves. Serfdom had been declining in Western Europe since the 12th century and was nearly gone by 1500. A system of free labor arose in its place, and overseas expansion strengthened that trend within Western Europe. Although free labor prevailed in the Western European homeland, unfree labor systems took root all around Europe's periphery, both overseas and in Eastern Europe, and the two systems were structurally linked. In general, free labor reigned where populations were dense and still growing. Large pools of labor kept wages low, but around the periphery of Western Europe, where land was cheap and labor expensive, coercive systems became the only efficient way for Europeans to extract from those areas the products they desired.

The forms of unfree labor varied greatly across space and time, from slavery to less brutal systems. In New Spain, as the native population dwindled, the practice of *encomienda* slowly yielded to debt peonage. Unpayable debts kept Indians tied to the *haciendas* of the countryside. The mining of precious metals, on the other hand, was so dangerous and unpleasant that it almost always required a large degree of physical coercion, a system of labor tribute called *mita* in the Andes. Similarly, any colonial region that devoted itself to the production of staple crops for sale in Europe also turned to unfree labor and eventually to overt slavery. Sugar production first reduced Indians to bondage in Brazil and the Caribbean and later, as they died off, led to the importation of African slaves by the millions. Other staples—tobacco, rice, cotton, coffee—later followed similar patterns. At first these crops were considered luxuries and commanded high prices, but as they became widely available on the world market, their prices fell steeply, profit margins contracted, and planters turned overwhelmingly to coerced labor. Even in Eastern Europe, which began to specialize in producing cereal crops for sale in the more diversified West, serfdom revived. In Russia, where the Orthodox Church never condemned the enslavement of fellow Christians, the condition of a serf came to resemble that of a slave in one of the Atlantic empires. Some serfs were even bought and sold.

Spain's rise had been spectacular, but its empire was vulnerable. Although silver from the Americas vastly enhanced the Crown's ability to wage war, the costs of continuous conflict, the inflation generated by a steady influx of silver, and the need to defend a much greater perimeter absorbed Spain's new resources and a great deal more. Between 1492 and 1580, Spain's population grew from 4.9 million to 8 million, but over the course of

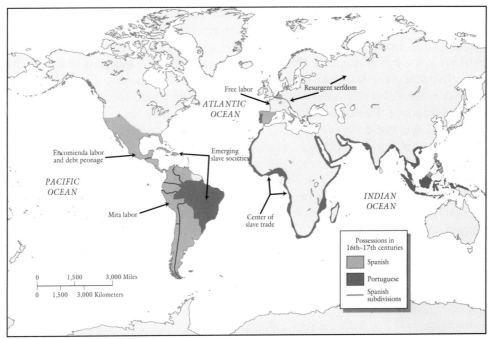

Map 1.11   Spanish Empire and Global Labor System   While Western European states were becoming free-labor societies, they created or encouraged the establishment of societies built on or providing laborers for various unfree labor systems in the Americas, the Caribbean, Africa, and Eastern Europe.

the following century, it fell by 20 percent, mostly because of the escalating costs, both financial and human, of Spain's wars. As population declined, taxes rose. Castile grew poorer, not richer, in its century and a half of imperial glory. Most of the wealth of the Indies went elsewhere to pay for goods or services that Spain failed to provide for itself— to merchants in Genoa, to manufacturers in Lombardy and the Low Countries, and to bankers in Augsburg.

Explanations: Patterns of Conquest, Submission, and Resistance

By the middle of the 18th century, Europeans who thought seriously about the discovery of America and its global implications generally agreed that the whole process had been a moral outrage, possibly the worst in history. Conquest and settlement had killed millions of Indians, had enslaved millions of Africans, and had degraded Europeans. The benefits seemed small by comparison, even though economic gains were undeniably large by 1750. If the cruelest of the conquerors had been able to foresee the results of this process, asked the Abbé Raynal, would he have proceeded? "Is it to be imagined that there exists a being infernal enough to answer this question in the affirmative!" The success of the American

Revolution, with its message of freedom and human rights, quieted such thinking for a time, but the critique has revived in recent years, especially in the developing world.

Modern historians, less moralistic than Raynal, also realize that he considerably underestimated the death toll. Even so, they are more interested in asking how and why these things happened. One major reason is geographical. The Eurasian land mass, the world's largest, follows an east-west axis that permits life forms and human inventions to travel immense distances without going through forbidding changes of climate. Chinese inventions eventually reached Europe. By contrast, the Americas, and sub-Saharan Africa, lie along north-south axes that do impose such barriers. Another compelling explanation for European success focuses on the prolonged isolation of the Americas from the rest of the world. If two communities of equal ability are kept apart, that with the larger and more varied population will be more inventive than the other, and its people will learn more rapidly from one another over time. For example, the use of iron spread gradually throughout nearly all of Asia, Africa, and Europe. And even though Europeans knew little about China, they slowly acquired Chinese inventions such as paper, the compass, and gunpowder. More than any other technological edge, far more than firearms or even horses, steel made military conquest possible. European armor stopped enemy spears and arrows, and European swords killed opponents swiftly without any need to reload.

The biological consequences of isolation were even more momentous than the technological barriers. The devastation European microbes inflicted upon the Indian population is the greatest tragedy in the history of humankind. The Indians' genetic makeup was more uniform than that of Europeans, Africans, or Asians. Indians were descended from a rather small sample of the total gene pool of Eurasia. Centuries spent in frigid Beringia had weeded out weaker people and killed the microbes that produce most diseases. The Indians first encountered by Europeans were bigger, stronger, and—at first contact—healthier than the newcomers, but they died in appalling numbers because they had almost no resistance to European diseases.

European plants also thrived at the expense of native vegetation. For example, when British settlers first crossed the Appalachians, they marveled at the lush Kentucky bluegrass. They did not realize that they were looking at an accidental European import that had conquered the landscape even faster than they had. European animals also prevailed over potential American rivals. Horses multiplied at an astonishing rate in America, and wild herds moved north from Mexico faster than the Spaniards, transforming the way of life of the Apaches and the Sioux. The lowly sparrow never had it so good until someone turned a few loose in North America. But some life forms also moved from the Americas to Europe, Asia, and Africa. Indians probably gave syphilis to the first Europeans they met. Other American exports, such as corn, potatoes, and tomatoes, were far more benign and have enriched the diet of the rest of the world. Historian Alfred W. Crosby has called this larger process "the **Columbian exchange**." It ranks as one of the most important events of all time.

Conclusion

Americans like to believe that their history is a story of progress. They are right about its European phase. After its tragic beginnings in conquest, depopulation, and enslavement, some things finally did improve.

For thousands of years, the Americas had been cut off from the rest of the world. The major cultures of Eurasia and Africa had existed in relative isolation, engaging in direct contact with only their immediate neighbors. Islamic societies that shared borders with India, the East Indies, black Africa, and Europe had been the principal mediators among these cultures and, in that era, were more tolerant than most Christian societies.

In just 40 years, daring European navigators, supported by the Crowns of Portugal and Spain, joined the world together and challenged Islam's mediating role. Between 1492 and 1532, Europe, Africa, Asia, the Spice Islands, the Philippines, the Caribbean, Aztec Mexico, Inca Peru, and other parts of the Americas came into intense and often violent contact with one another. A few individuals gained much, and Spain acquired a military advantage within Europe that endured into the 1640s. Nearly everybody else suffered, millions horribly, especially in the Americas and Africa. And Spain spent the rest of the 16th century trying to create an imperial system that could impose order on this turbulent reality. But Spain had many enemies. They too would find the lure of wealth and land overseas irresistible.

SUGGESTED READINGS

Two recent general surveys of early American history provide excellent coverage up to Independence: **Alan Taylor,** *American Colonies* (2001); and **Richard Middleton,** *Colonial America: A History, 1565–1776,* 3rd ed. (2002). For a useful collection of essays, see **Stanley N. Katz, John M. Murrin, and Douglas Greenberg, eds.,** *Colonial America: Essays in Politics and Social Development,* 5th ed. (2001).

Brian M. Fagan, *The Great Journey: The Peopling of Ancient America* (1987) is a fine introduction to pre-Columbian America. See also **David Webster,** *The Fall of the Ancient Maya: Solving the Mystery of the Maya Collapse* (2002). **Jared Diamond,** *Guns, Germs, and Steel: The Fates of Human Societies* (1997) is provocative and challenging in its global perspective. For the age of explorations, see **Peter Russell,** *Prince Henry 'the Navigator': A Life* (2000); **G. V. Scammell,** *The First Imperial Age: European Overseas Expansion c. 1400–1715* (1989); and **Alfred W. Crosby's** classic synthesis, *The Columbian Exchange: Biological and Cultural Consequences of 1492* (1972). For the slave trade, see **John Thornton,** *Africa and Africans in the Making of the Modern World, 1400–1800,* 2nd ed. (1998), which insists that Africans retained control of their affairs, including the slave trade, through the 17th century; and **Patrick Manning,** *Slavery and African Life: Occidental, Oriental, and African Slave Trades* (1990), which emphasizes the devastating impact of the slave trade in the 18th and 19th centuries. **Ira Berlin's** *Many Thousands Gone: The First Two Centuries of Slavery in North America* (1998) is an effective and comprehensive synthesis of a huge subject.

James Lockhart and Stuart B. Schwartz, *Early Latin America: A History of Colonial Latin America and Brazil* (1983) is an outstanding introduction to the Iberian empires. **J. H. Parry's**

The Spanish Seaborne Empire (1966) retains great value. **David J. Weber's** *The Spanish Frontier in North America* (1992) is easily the best introduction to its subject. For Brazil, see **John Hemming,** *Red Gold: The Conquest of the Brazilian Indians, 1500–1760* (1978).

Visit the Liberty Equality Power Companion Web site for resources specific to this textbook: http://www.thomsonedu.com/history/murrin

Also find self-tests and additional resources at ThomsonNOW. ThomsonNOW is an integrated online suite of services and resources with proven ease of use and efficient paths to success, delivering the results you want—NOW!

www.thomsonedu.com/login/

2

The Challenge to Spain and the Settlement of North America

Catholic France and two Protestant countries, the Dutch Republic and England, challenged Spanish power in Europe and overseas. None of them planted a permanent settlement in North America before 1600. In the quarter-century after 1600, they all did. Europeans, Indians, and Africans interacted in contrasting ways in this strange "New World." In Mexico and Peru, the Spaniards had set themselves up as a European ruling class over a much larger Indian population of farmers, artisans, and miners. Spain's rivals created colonies of different kinds. Some, such as Virginia and Barbados, grew staple crops with indentured servants and African slaves. New France and New Netherland developed a prosperous trade with the Indians without trying to rule them. In New England, the Puritans relied on free labor provided mostly by family members. After 1660, England conquered New Netherland, and English Quakers created another free-labor society in the Delaware valley.

The Protestant Reformation and the Challenge to Spain

By the time its enemies felt strong enough to challenge Spain overseas, the **Protestant Reformation** had shattered the religious unity of Europe. In November 1517, not long before Cortés landed in Mexico, Martin Luther nailed his 95 Theses to the cathedral door at Wittenberg in the German electorate of Saxony and touched off the Reformation. Salvation, he insisted, comes through faith alone, and God grants saving faith only to those who hear his Word preached to them, struggle to understand it, and admit that, without God's grace, they are damned. Within a generation, the states of northern Germany and Scandinavia had embraced Lutheranism.

John Calvin, a French Protestant, also embraced justification by faith alone and put his own militant principles into practice in the Swiss canton of Geneva. The Huguenot movement in France, the Dutch Reformed Church in the Netherlands, and the Presbyterian Kirk (or Church) of Scotland all embraced Calvin's principles. In England, the **Anglican** Church adopted Calvinist doctrines but kept much Catholic liturgy, a compromise that prompted the Puritan reform movement toward a more thoroughly Calvinist Church of England. After 1620 **Puritans** carried their religious vision across the Atlantic to New England.

CHRONOLOGY

1517	Luther begins the Protestant Reformation
1577–80	Drake circumnavigates the globe
1580s	Gilbert claims Newfoundland for England (1583) • Ralegh twice fails to colonize Roanoke Island (1585–87) • England repels attack by the Spanish Armada (1588)
1607	English settlement established at Jamestown
1608	Champlain founds Quebec
1609	Virginia receives sea-to-sea charter
1613–14	Rolfe grows tobacco, marries Pocahontas
1618	Sandys implements London Company reforms
1619	First Africans arrive in Virginia • House of Burgesses and headright system created
1620s	Pilgrims adopt Mayflower Compact, land at Plymouth (1620) • Dutch West India Company chartered (1621) • Opechancanough launches war of extermination in Virginia (1622) • King assumes direct control of Virginia (1624) • Minuit founds New Amsterdam (1626)
1630s	Puritans settle Massachusetts Bay (1630) • Maryland chartered (1632) • Williams founds Providence; Hooker founds Hartford (1636) • Anne Hutchinson banished to Rhode Island; Minuit founds New Sweden (1638) • New Haven Colony founded (1639)
1640s	Massachusetts "Body of Liberties" (1641) • English civil wars begin (1642) • Pavonia Massacre in New Netherland (1643) • Charles I beheaded (1649)
Mid-1650s	New Netherland conquers New Sweden • Quakers invade New England
1660s	Charles II restored to English throne (1660) • Puritans institute Half-Way Covenant (1662) • First Carolina charter granted (1663) • New Netherland surrenders to the English (1664) • New Jersey becomes a separate colony (1665) • Carolina's Fundamental Constitutions proposed (1669)
1670s	First permanent English settlement established in South Carolina (1670) • Dutch retake New York (1673–74) • West New Jersey approves Concessions and Agreements (1677)
1680s	Charleston founded (1680) • Pennsylvania charter granted (1681) • New York and Pennsylvania each adopt a Charter of Liberties (1683)
1705	Virginia adopts comprehensive slave code

Calvinists rejected the pope, all Catholic sacraments except baptism and the Lord's Supper, clerical celibacy, veneration of the saints, and the pious rituals by which Catholics strove to win salvation. They denounced these rites as "work righteousness." Calvin gave central importance to **predestination.** According to that doctrine, God decreed, even before creating the world, who will be saved and who will be damned. Christ died, not for all humankind, but only for God's elect. Because salvation and damnation were beyond human power to alter, Calvinists—especially English Puritans—felt a compelling inner need to find out whether they were saved. They struggled to recognize in themselves a conversion experience, the process by which God's elect discovered that they had received saving grace.

France, the Netherlands, and England, all with powerful Protestant movements, challenged Spanish power in Europe. Until 1559, France was the main threat, with Italy as the battleground, but Spain won that phase. In the 1560s, with France embroiled in its own Wars of Religion, a new challenge came from the 17 provinces of the Netherlands, which Spain ruled. The Dutch rebelled against the heavy taxes and severe Catholic orthodoxy imposed by Philip II. As Spanish armies put down the rebellion in the 10 southern provinces (modern Belgium), merchants and Protestants fled north. Many went to Amsterdam, which replaced Spanish-controlled Antwerp as the economic center of northern Europe. The seven northern provinces gradually took shape as the Dutch Republic, or the United Provinces of the Netherlands. The Dutch turned their resistance into a war for independence from Catholic Spain. The conflict lasted 80 years, drained Spanish resources, and spread to Asia, Africa, and America. England long remained on the edges of this struggle, only to emerge in the end as the biggest winner overseas.

New France

In 1500, France had three times the population of Spain. The French made a few stabs at oversea expansion before 1600, but with little success.

Early French Explorers

In 1524, King Francis I sent Giovanni da Verrazano, an Italian, to America in search of a northwest passage to Asia. Verrazano explored the North American coast from the Carolinas to Nova Scotia and noted Manhattan's superb potential as a harbor but found no passage to Asia. Between 1534 and 1543, Jacques Cartier made three voyages to North America. He explored the St. Lawrence valley without finding any fabulous wealth. Severe Canadian winters made him give up. For the rest of the century, the French ignored Canada, except for a few fur traders and others who descended on Newfoundland each year in growing numbers. By the 1580s, the Canadian fisheries rivaled New Spain in the volume of shipping they employed.

After 1550, the French turned to warmer climates. **Huguenots** sacked Havana, prompting Spain to turn it into a fortified, year-round naval base under the command of Admiral Pedro Menéndez de Avilés. Others planted a settlement on the Atlantic coast of Florida. Menéndez attacked them in 1565, talked them into surrendering, and then executed adult males who refused to accept the Catholic faith.

France's Wars of Religion blocked further efforts for the rest of the 16th century. King Henry IV (1589–1610), a Protestant, converted to Catholicism and granted limited toleration to Huguenots through the Edict of Nantes in 1598, thus ending the civil wars for the rest of his reign. Henry was a *politique;* he insisted that the survival of the state take precedence over religious differences. Moreover, he believed in toleration for its own sake. Another *politique* was the Catholic soldier and explorer, Samuel de Champlain.

Missions and Furs

Focus Question
Why did the number of Indians who chose to become Catholics far exceed the number that accepted Protestantifsm?

Champlain believed that Catholics and Huguenots could work together, Europeanize the Indians, convert them, and even marry them. Before his death in 1635, he made 11 voyages to Canada. During his second trip (1604–06), he planted a predominantly Huguenot settlement in Acadia (Nova Scotia). In 1608, he sailed up the St. Lawrence River, established friendly relations with the Indians, and founded Quebec. "Our sons shall wed your daughters," he told them, "and we shall be one people." Many Frenchmen cohabited with Indian women, but only 15 formal marriages took place between them in the 17th century. Champlain's friendliness toward the Indians of the St. Lawrence valley also drew him into their wars against the Iroquois Five Nations farther south. At times, Iroquois hostility almost destroyed New France.

Champlain failed to unite Catholics and Protestants in mutual harmony. Huguenots in France were eager to trade with Canada, but few settled there. Their ministers showed no interest in converting the Indians, whereas Catholic priests became zealous missionaries. In 1625, the French Crown declared that only the Catholic faith could be practiced in New France, thus ending Champlain's dream of a colony that was more tolerant than France. Acadia soon became Catholic as well. Early New France is a tale of missionaries and furs, of attempts to convert the Indians, and of efforts to trade with them. The carousing habits of the first *coureurs de bois* (roamers of the woods) did much for the fur trade but made life difficult for the missionaries.

After 1630, Jesuit missionaries made heroic efforts to bring Christ to the Indians. The Society of Jesus, or Jesuits, emerged in the 16th century as the Catholic Church's best-educated and most militant religious order. Uncompromising in their opposition to Protestants, Jesuits proved remarkably flexible in dealing with non-Christian peoples, from China to North America. Other missionaries insisted that Indians must be Europeanized before they could be converted, but the Jesuits saw nothing contradictory about a nation of Christians that retained its Indian culture. The Jesuits also tried to protect their converts from contamination by the *coureurs de bois.*

Theodore de Bry

Southeastern Indians at Work   Jacques Le Moyne, an artist who accompanied the French Huguenot expedition to Florida in 1564, painted this scene of Indians in a canoe loaded with produce. They are rowing past one of their capacious storehouses. Engraving by Theodore de Bry.

The Jesuits mastered Indian languages, lived in Indian villages, accepted most Indian customs, and converted 10,000 Indians in 40 years, most of them members of the five confederated Huron nations, but this success antagonized Indians who were still attached to their own rituals. When smallpox devastated the Hurons in the 1640s, Jesuits baptized hundreds of dying victims to ensure their salvation. Many of the Indian survivors noticed that death usually followed this mysterious rite. Suspecting witchcraft, their resistance grew stronger. A second disaster occurred when the Iroquois attacked, defeated, and scattered the Hurons. Despite these setbacks, the Jesuits' courage remained strong. They were the only Europeans who measured up to Indian standards of bravery under torture. Yet their efforts slowly lost ground to the fur trade, especially after the Crown assumed control of New France in 1663.

New France under Louis XIV

Royal intervention transformed Canada after 1663 when Louis XIV and his minister, Jean-Baptiste Colbert, took charge of the colony and tried to turn it into a model absolutist society—peaceful, orderly, deferential. Government was in the hands of two appointive officials: a **governor-general** responsible for military and diplomatic affairs, and an ***intendant*** who administered affordable justice, partly by banning lawyers. The people paid few taxes, and the church **tithe** was set at half its rate in France.

The governor appointed all **militia** officers and granted promotion through merit, not by selling commissions. When the Crown sent professional soldiers to New France after 1660, the governor put them under the command of Canadian officers, who knew the woodlands. Colbert also sent 774 young women to the St. Lawrence, to provide brides for settlers and soldiers. He offered bonuses to couples who produced large families and fined fathers whose children failed to marry while still in their teens. Between 1663 and 1700, the population of New France increased from 3,000 to about 14,000, even though close to 70 percent of 10,000 immigrants throughout the colonial era went back to France, usu-ally to claim a tiny inheritance. About one-fourth of the population concentrated in three cities—Quebec, Three Rivers, and Montreal. Montreal, the largest, became the center of the fur trade.

Farming took hold in the St. Lawrence valley, and by the 1690s, Canada was growing enough wheat to feed itself and to give its *habitants,* or settlers, a level of comfort about equal to that of contemporary New Englanders. A new class of ***seigneurs,*** or gentry, claimed most of the land between Quebec and Montreal, but they had few feudal privi-leges and never exercised the kind of power wielded by aristocrats in France. Yet when the Church was also the *seigneur,* as often happened near Quebec and Montreal, the obliga-tions imposed on farmers could be heavy.

Colbert also tried to confine the fur trade to annual fairs at Montreal and Quebec, thus bringing the Indians to the settlers, not the settlers to the Indians. He failed to abolish the *coureurs de bois,* although a stint in the forests was becoming something a man did just once or twice in his youth, before settling down. By 1700, Colbert's policies even led to a quiet rebellion in the west. Several hundred Frenchmen settled in the Mississippi River valley between the missions of Cahokia and Kaskaskia in what became the Illinois coun-try. By 1750, these communities contained 3,000 residents. The settlers rejected *seigneurs,* feudal dues, tithes, and compulsory militia service. They did, however, import African slaves from Louisiana. Most settlers prospered as wheat farmers, and many married Christian Indian women from the missions.

But Canada did not long remain the center of French overseas activity. Like other Euro-peans, most of the French who crossed the Atlantic preferred the warmer climes of the Caribbean. At first, the French in the West Indies joined with other enemies of Spain to prey upon Spanish colonies and ships, contributing the word "buccaneer" (*boucanier*) to the English language. Then they transformed the island colonies of Saint Domingue (mod-ern Haiti), Guadeloupe, and Martinique into centers of sugar or coffee production, where a small planter class prospered from the labor of thousands of slaves. The sugar islands were worth far more than Canada. By the late 18th century, Saint Domingue was generating more wealth than any other colony in the world.

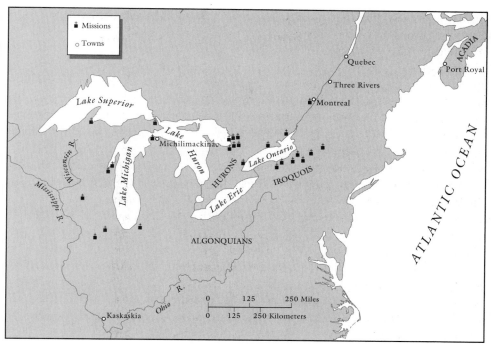

Map 2.1 New France and the Jesuit Missions The Jesuits established Indian missions near Montreal and far into the interior of North America, most of them well beyond the range of French military aid in any emergency.

The Dutch and Swedish Settlements

For most of the 17th century, the Dutch were more active overseas than the French. The Dutch Republic, whose 2 million people inhabited the most densely populated part of Europe, surpassed all rivals in finance, shipping, and trade. It offered an ideological as well as a political challenge to Spanish absolutism. In contrast to Spain, which stood for Catholic orthodoxy and the centralizing tendencies of Europe's "new monarchies," Dutch republicanism emphasized local liberties, prosperity, and, in major centers such as Amsterdam, religious toleration. Political power was decentralized to the cities and their wealthy merchants, who favored informal toleration, tried to keep trade as free as possible, and resisted the monarchical ambitions of the House of Orange. The Prince of Orange usually served as *stadholder* (captain general) of Holland, the richest province, and commanded its armies, and often those of other Dutch provinces as well.

The Dutch Republic—with Protestant dissenters from many countries, a sizable Jewish community, and a Catholic minority that exceeded 30 percent of the population—was actually a polyglot confederation. Amsterdam's merchant republicanism competed with the Dutch Reformed Church for the allegiance of the people. Only during a military crisis

Black Robe (1991)

Directed by Bruce Beresford. Starring Lothaire Bluteau (Father Laforgue), Aden Young (Daniel), Jean Brusseau (Samuel de Champlain), and Sandrine Holt (Annuka)

In *Black Robe*, director Bruce Beresford has given us the most believable film portrayal of 17th-century North America—both the landscape and its peoples—yet produced. This Canada– Australia co-production won six Genie Awards (Canada's equivalent of the Oscar), including best picture, best director, and best cinematography. The film is based on Brian Moore's novel of the same title, and Moore wrote the screenplay. It was filmed on location amid the spectacular scenery in the Lac St. Jean/Saguenay region of Quebec.

Alliance/Goldwyn/THE KOBAL COLLECTION

Black Robe, based on Brian Moore's novel of the same title, is set in 17th-century North America.

In New France in the 1630s, Father Laforgue (Lothaire Bluteau), a young Jesuit, and Daniel (Aden Young), his teenaged assistant and translator, leave on Laforgue's first mission assignment. Samuel de Champlain (Jean Brusseau), the governor of the colony, has persuaded the Algonquin tribe to convey the two to their mission site among the Hurons, far in the interior. Before long, Daniel falls in love with Annuka (Sandrine Holt), the beautiful daughter of Algonquin chief Chomina (August Schellenberg). When the priest inadvertently watches the young couple make love, he realizes that he has committed a mortal sin. From that point, his journey into the North American heartland threatens to become a descent into hell.

The Algonquins, guided by a dream quest, pursue a logic that makes no sense to the priest. Conversely, his religious message baffles them. Even so, when Chomina is wounded and Laforgue and Daniel are captured by the Iroquois, Annuka seduces their lone guard, kills him, and enables all four of them to escape. Chomina dies of his wounds, politely but firmly rejecting baptism until the end. What Indian, he asks, would want to go to the

Christian heaven, populated by many black robes but none of his own ancestors?

With the priest's approval, Daniel and Annuka go off by themselves. Laforgue reaches the mission, only to find many of the Indians dead or dying from some European disease. As the film closes, we learn that smallpox would devastate the mission in the following decade, and the Jesuits would abandon it in 1649.

Brian Moore's realism romanticizes nobody but treats both the Jesuits and the Algonquins with great respect. The screenplay drew criticism for its harsh depiction of the Iroquois, but it portrayed them through the eyes of the people they planned to torture. A smaller criticism is that Laforgue is the lone priest on the journey, during which he commits the sin of watching Daniel and Annuka make love. Jesuits, however, traveled in pairs precisely so they would always be accompanied by someone who could hear their confessions. Bruce Beresford, an Australian, directed *Breaker Morant* (1979), a highly acclaimed film set in the Boer War a century ago, and also *Driving Miss Daisy* (1989).

could the Prince of Orange mobilize the Dutch Reformed clergy and impose something like Calvinist orthodoxy, even on the cities. The **States General,** to which each province sent representatives, became a weak central government for the republic. The broader public did not vote or participate actively in public life. The tension between tolerant merchant republicanism and Calvinist orthodoxy carried over into New Netherland.

Profit was the dominant motive in Dutch expansion overseas. By 1620, Dutch foreign trade probably exceeded that of the rest of Europe combined. Even during the long war with Spain, the Dutch traded with Lisbon and Seville for products from the East Indies and America. This effrontery so annoyed Philip II that twice in the 1590s he committed a grave blunder when he confiscated all of the Dutch ships crowding his ports. The Dutch retaliated by sailing into the Atlantic and Indian oceans to acquire colonial goods at the source. The Dutch forced Spain to use expensive convoys to protect the silver fleets crossing the Atlantic. Spain's power finally crumbled under these pressures.

The East and West India Companies

In 1602, the States General chartered the Dutch East India Company, the richest corporation the world had yet seen. It pressured Spain where it was weakest, in the Portuguese East Indies. Elbowing the Portuguese out of the Spice Islands and even out of Nagasaki in Japan, the Dutch set up their own capital at Batavia (now Jakarta) on the island of Java.

The Atlantic and North America also attracted the Dutch. In 1609, during a 12-year truce between Spain and the Netherlands, Henry Hudson, an Englishman in Dutch service, sailed up what the Dutch called the North River (the English later renamed it the Hudson) and claimed the area for the Netherlands. In 1614, Lutheran refugees from Amsterdam built a fort near modern Albany to trade with the Mahicans and Iroquois for furs, but they did not create a permanent, year-round settlement.

In 1621, the States General chartered the Dutch West India Company and gave it jurisdiction over the African slave trade, Brazil, the Caribbean, and North America. The company harbored strong Orangist sympathies and even some Calvinist fervor, sustained by refugees fleeing from the Spanish army. It took over Portugal's slave-trading posts in West Africa and for a while even dominated Angola. It also occupied the richest sugar-producing region of Brazil until the Portuguese took it back, as well as Angola, in the 1640s while regaining their independence from Spain.

In North America, the Dutch claimed the Delaware, the Hudson, and the Connecticut river valleys. The company put most of its effort, and some of its religious fervor, into the Hudson valley. The first permanent settlers arrived in 1624. Two years later, Deacon Pierre Minuit, leading 30 Walloon (French-speaking) Protestant refugee families, bought Manhattan Island from the Indians, and founded the port of New Amsterdam. The Dutch established Fort Orange (modern Albany) 150 miles upriver for trade with the Iroquois. Much like New France, New Netherland depended on the goodwill of nearby Indians, and the fur trade gave the colony a similar urban flavor. But unlike New France, few Dutchmen ventured into the deep woods. There were no *coureurs de bois* and hardly any missionary effort. The Indians brought their furs to Fort Orange and exchanged them for firearms and other goods that the Dutch sold more cheaply than anyone else. New Netherland also resembled New France in other ways. In the 1630s, before the French created *seigneuries* in the St. Lawrence valley, the Dutch established **patroonships,** vast estates under a single landlord, mostly along the Hudson. But the system never thrived, largely because few Dutch settlers had much interest in becoming peasants. The one exception was Rensselaerswyck, a gigantic estate on both banks of the Hudson above and below Fort Orange, which sent wheat and flour down the river and to the Caribbean.

New Netherland as a Pluralistic Society

New Netherland became North America's first experiment in ethnic and religious pluralism. The Dutch were a mixed people with a Flemish (Dutch-speaking) majority and a Walloon minority. Both came to the colony. So did Danes, Norwegians, Swedes, Finns, Germans, and Scots. One observer in the 1640s counted 18 languages spoken by the 450 inhabitants of New Amsterdam.

The government of the colony tried to utilize this diversity by drawing on two conflicting precedents from the Netherlands. On the one hand, it appealed to religious refugees by emphasizing the company's Protestant role in the struggle against Spain. This policy, roughly speaking, reflected the Orangist position in the Netherlands. On the other hand, the West India Company sometimes recognized that acceptance of religious diversity might stimulate trade. The pursuit of prosperity through toleration was the normal role of the city of Amsterdam in Dutch politics. Minuit and Pieter Stuyvesant represented the religious formula for unity, and they resisted toleration even in the name of commerce.

After Minuit returned to Europe in 1631, the emphasis shifted rapidly from piety to trade. The Dutch sold muskets to the Iroquois to expand their own access to the fur trade. In 1643, however, Willem Kieft, a stubborn and quarrelsome governor, slaughtered a tribe of Indian refugees to whom he had granted asylum from other Indians. This Pavonia Massacre, which took place across the Hudson from Manhattan, set off a war with nearby Algonquian nations that nearly destroyed New Netherland. By the time Stuyvesant replaced Kieft in 1647, the colony's population had fallen to about 700 people. An autocrat, Stuyvesant made peace and then strengthened town governments and the Dutch Reformed Church. During his administration, the population rose to more than 6,000. Most newcomers arrived as members of healthy families who reproduced readily, enabling the population to double every 25 years.

Swedish and English Encroachments

Minuit, back in Europe, organized another refugee project, this one for Flemings who had been uprooted by the Spanish war. When Dutch authorities refused to back him, he looked for support to the Lutheran kingdom of Sweden. Financed by private Dutch capital, he returned to America in 1638 with Flemish and Swedish settlers to found New Sweden, with its capital at Fort Christina (modern Wilmington) near the mouth of the Delaware River, on land claimed by New Netherland. After Minuit died on his return trip to Europe, the colony became less Flemish and Calvinist and more Swedish and Lutheran, at a time when Stuyvesant was trying to make New Netherland an orthodox Calvinist society. In 1654, the Swedes seized Fort Casimir, a Dutch post that provided access to the Delaware. In response, Stuyvesant took over all of New Sweden the next year, and Amsterdam sent over settlers to guarantee Dutch control. Stuyvesant persecuted Lutherans (along with Jews and **Quakers**) in New Amsterdam but had to tolerate them in the Delaware Valley where they were a majority. Orthodoxy and harmony were not easily reconciled.

The English, already entrenched around Chesapeake Bay to the south and New England to the east (see following section), threatened to overwhelm the Dutch as they moved from New England onto Long Island and into what is now Westchester County, New York. Kieft welcomed them in the 1640s and gave them local privileges greater than those enjoyed by the Dutch, in the hope that their farms and herds would give the colony valuable exports. Stuyvesant regarded these **Yankees** (a Dutch word that probably meant "land pirates") as good Calvinists, English-speaking equivalents of his Dutch Reformed settlers. They agitated for a more active role in government, but their loyalty was questionable. If England attacked the colony, would these Puritans side with the Dutch Calvinists or the Anglican invaders? Which ran deeper, their religious or their ethnic loyalties? Stuyvesant learned the unpleasant answer when England attacked him in 1664.

The Challenge from Elizabethan England

England's interest in America emerged slowly. In 1497, Henry VII (1485–1509) sent Giovanni Cabato (John Cabot), an Italian mariner who had moved to Bristol, to search for a northwest passage to Asia. Cabot probably reached Newfoundland, which he took to be part of Asia. He sailed again in 1498 with five ships but was lost at sea. Only one vessel returned, but Cabot's voyages gave England a vague claim to portions of the North American coast.

The English Reformation

When interest in America revived during the reign of Elizabeth I (1558–1603), England was rapidly becoming a Protestant kingdom. Elizabeth's father, Henry VIII (1509–47), desperate for a male heir, had broken with the pope to divorce his queen and had remarried. He proclaimed himself the "Only Supreme Head" of the Church of England, confiscated monastic lands, and opened the way for serious Protestant reformers. Under Elizabeth's younger brother, Edward VI (1547–53), the government embraced Protestantism. When Edward died, Elizabeth's older sister, Mary I (1553–58), reimposed Catholicism, burned hundreds of Protestants at the stake, and drove thousands into exile. Many of them became Calvinists. Elizabeth, however, accepted Protestantism, and the exiles returned. The Church of England became Calvinist in doctrine and theology but remained largely Catholic in structure, liturgy, and ritual. By the time of Elizabeth's death, England's

Catholics were a tiny, fitfully persecuted minority, but they had powerful allies abroad, especially in Spain.

Some Protestants demanded the eradication of Catholic vestiges and the replacement of the Anglican Book of Common Prayer with sermons and psalms as the dominant mode of worship. These Puritans, also called **Non-Separatists,** insisted they were loyal to the true Church of England and resisted any relaxation of Calvinist rigor. They would play a major role in English expansion overseas. More extreme Protestants, called **Separatists,** denied that the Church of England was a true church and began to set up independent congregations of their own. Some of them would found the small colony of **Plymouth.**

Hawkins and Drake

In 1560, England was a rather backward country of 3 million people. Its chief export was woolen cloth. During the 16th century, the numbers of both people and sheep grew rapidly, and they sometimes competed for the same land. When farms were enclosed for sheep pasture, laborers were set adrift and often faced bleak prospects, creating the impression that England was overpopulated. Even without the enclosures, thousands of people headed for London, lifting the city's population from 50,000 in 1500 to 575,000 by 1700. By then London was the largest city in Western Europe. After 1600, internal migration fueled overseas settlement. Before then, interest in America centered, not in London, but in southwestern ports involved in the Newfoundland fisheries.

Taking advantage of friendly relations that still prevailed between England and Spain, John Hawkins of Plymouth made three voyages to New Spain between 1562 and 1569. On his first trip, he bought slaves in Portuguese West Africa and sold them in Hispaniola, where, by paying all legal duties, he tried to set himself up as a legitimate trader. Spanish authorities disapproved, and on his next voyage he had to trade at gunpoint. On his third trip, the Spanish viceroy, in command of a much larger fleet, trapped his six vessels in a Mexican port. After promising Hawkins quarter, he sank four of his ships. Only Hawkins and his kinsman Francis Drake escaped, vowing vengeance.

Drake even began to talk of freeing slaves from Spanish tyranny. His most dramatic exploit came between 1577 and 1580, when he rounded Cape Horn and plundered Spanish possessions along the undefended Pacific coast of Peru. Knowing that the Spaniards would be waiting for him if he returned by the same route, he sailed north, explored San Francisco Bay, and continued west around the world to England. Elizabeth rewarded him with a knighthood.

Gilbert, Ireland, and America

By the 1560s, the idea of permanent colonization intrigued several Englishmen. England had a model close at hand in Ireland, which the English Crown had claimed for centuries. After 1560, the English tried to impose their agriculture, language, local government, legal system, aristocracy, and religion upon the Irish. The Irish responded by becoming more intensely Roman Catholic than ever.

The English formed their preconceptions about American Indians largely from contact with the Irish, who, claimed one Elizabethan, are "more uncivil, more uncleanly, more barbarous and more brutish in their customs and demeanors, than in any part of the world that is known." The English tried to conquer Ulster by driving out the Catholics and replacing then with Protestants. In Munster, they ejected Catholic leaders and tried to force the remaining Catholic Irish to become tenants under Protestant landlords. Terror became an acceptable tactic, as when the English slaughtered 200 Irish at a Christmas feast in 1574.

Sir Humphrey Gilbert, a well-educated humanist, was one of the most brutal of Elizabeth's captains in the Irish wars of the 1560s. In subduing Munster in 1569, Gilbert killed nearly everyone in his path and destroyed all of the crops, a strategy that the English later employed against Indians. Massacring women and children "was the way to kill the men of war by famine," explained one admirer. Fresh from his Irish exploits, Gilbert began to think about colonizing America. He proposed that England grab control of the Newfoundland fisheries, a nursery of seamen and naval power. He urged the founding of settlements close enough to New Spain to provide bases for plundering. He obtained a royal patent in 1578 and sent out a fleet, but his ships got into a fight somewhere short of America and limped back to England. He tried again in 1583. This time his fleet sailed north to claim New-foundland. The crews of 22 Spanish and Portuguese fishing vessels and 18 French and English ships listened in astonishment as he read his royal patent to them, divided up the land among them, assigned them rents, and established the Church of England among this mostly Catholic group. He then sailed away to explore more of the American coast. His own ship went under during a storm.

Ralegh, Roanoke, and War with Spain

Gilbert's half-brother, **Sir Walter Ralegh** (or Raleigh), obtained his own patent from the queen and tried twice to plant a colony in North America. In 1585, he sent a large expe-dition to Roanoke Island in what is now North Carolina, but the settlers planted no crops and exasperated the Indians with demands for food during a drought. In June 1586, the English killed the local chief, Wingina, whose main offense was apparently a threat to reset-tle his people on the mainland and leave the colonists to starve—or work. Days later, when the expected supply vessels failed to arrive on schedule, the colonists sailed back to England on the ships of Sir Francis Drake, who had just burned the Spanish city of St. Augustine with the support of Florida Indians, whom he freed. The supply ships reached Roanoke a little later, only to find the site abandoned. They left a small garrison there and sailed off in quest of Spanish plunder. The garrison was never heard from again.

Ralegh sent a second expedition in 1587, one that included some women, a sign that he envisioned a permanent colony. When Governor John White went back to England for more supplies, his return to Roanoke was delayed by the assault of the Spanish Armada on England in 1588. By the time he reached Roanoke in 1590, the settlers had vanished, leav-ing a cryptic message—"CROATOAN"—carved on a tree. The colonists may have settled among the Chesapeake nation of Indians near the entrance to Chesapeake Bay. Sketchy evidence suggests that the Powhatans, the most powerful Indians in the area, wiped out the Chesapeakes, along with any English living with them, in spring 1607, just as the first **Jamestown** settlers were arriving in the bay.

The Spanish Armada touched off a war that lasted until 1604 and strained the resources of England. The loss of the Armada, first to nimbler English ships in the English Channel and then to fierce storms off the Irish coast, crippled Spain. By 1600, Richard Hakluyt the elder and his cousin Richard Hakluyt the younger were publishing accounts of English exploits overseas and offering advice on how to make future colonization efforts more successful. They celebrated the deeds of Hawkins, Drake, Gilbert, and Ralegh, who were all West Country men with large ambitions but limited financial resources. Although their plundering exploits continued to pay, they could not afford to sustain a colony such as Roanoke until it could return a profit. But beginning in the 1590s, London became intensely involved in American affairs by launching privateering fleets against Spain. Even though London merchants remained more interested in trade with India, the Mediterranean, and Muscovy than in North American projects, the city's growing involvement with Atlantic privateering marked a significant shift. The marriage of London capital to West Country experience would make permanent colonization possible.

The Swarming of the English

Focus Question
Why did Englishmen, crossing the Atlantic at roughly the same time, create such radically different societies in the Chesapeake, the West Indies, and New England?

In the 17th century, more than 700,000 people sailed from Europe or Africa to the English colonies in North America and the Caribbean. Most European migrants were single young men who arrived as servants. At first even some of the Africans were regarded as servants rather than slaves.

The Pattern of Settlement in the English Colonies up to 1700

Region	Who Came (in thousands)		Population in 1700 (in thousands)	
	Europeans	Africans	Europeans	Africans
West Indies	220 (29.6%)	316 (42.5%)	33 (8.3%)	115 (28.8%)
South	135 (18.1%)	30 (4.0%)	82 (20.5%)	22 (5.5%)
Mid-Atlantic	20 (2.7%)	2 (0.3%)	51 (12.8%)	3 (0.8%)
New England	20 (2.7%)	1 (0.1%)	91 (22.8%)	2 (0.5%)
Total	395 (53.1%)	349 (46.9%)	257 (64.4%)	142 (35.6%)

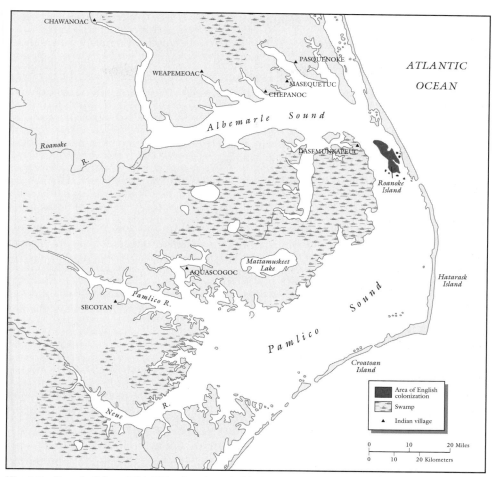

Map 2.2 Roanoke Colony, 1584-1590 Roanoke marked the first English attempt to plant a permanent colony in North America.

The Europeans who settled in New England or the Hudson and Delaware valleys were the most fortunate. Because Puritans and Quakers migrated as families into healthy regions, their population expanded at a rate far beyond anything known in Europe. The descendants of this small, idealistic minority soon became a substantial part of the total population, and they played a role in American history far out of proportion to their original numbers. As the accompanying table shows, the New England and Middle Atlantic colonies together attracted only 5.4 percent of the immigrants, but by 1700, they contained 37 percent of all the people in the English colonies and 55 percent of the Europeans.

The Chesapeake and West Indian Colonies

In 1606, King James I of England (1603–25) chartered the Virginia Company with authority to colonize North America between the 34th and 45th parallels. The company had two
headquarters. One, in the English city of Plymouth, received jurisdiction over the northern
portion of the grant. Known as the Plymouth Company, it carried on the West Country
expansionist traditions of Gilbert and Ralegh. In 1607, it planted a colony at Sagadahoc on
the coast of Maine. But the colonists found the cold winter intimidating, and when the
Abenaki Indians refused to trade with them, they abandoned the site in September 1608.
The Plymouth Company ran out of money and gave up.

The other branch, based in London, chose to colonize the Chesapeake Bay area. In
1607, the London Company sent out three ships with 104 colonists. They landed at a
defensible peninsula on what they called the James River and built a fort and other crude
buildings that they named Jamestown. Investors hoped to find gold or silver, a northwest passage to Asia, a cure for syphilis, or other valuable products for sale in Europe.
The settlers expected to persuade or compel local Indians to work for them, much as
Spain had done. If the Indians proved hostile, the settlers were told to form alliances
with more distant Indians and subdue those who resisted. Company officials did not
realize that a war chief named Powhatan ruled virtually all of the Indians below the **fall
line.** He had no rival within striking distance. The company's other expectations proved
equally skewed.

The Jamestown Disaster

The colony was a deathtrap. Every summer, the river became contaminated around
Jamestown and sent out killing waves of dysentery and typhoid fever. Before long, malaria
also set in. Only 38 of the original 104 colonists survived the first year. Of the 325 who
came before 1609, fewer than 100 were still alive in the spring of that year.

The survivors owed their good fortune to the resourcefulness of **Captain John Smith,**
a soldier and adventurer who outmaneuvered other members of the colony's ruling council and took charge. When his explorations uncovered neither gold or silver nor any quick
route to Asia, he concentrated instead on sheer survival. He tried to awe Powhatan, maintain friendly relations with him, and buy corn. Through the help of Pocahontas,
Powhatan's young daughter, he avoided war. Though Smith gave conflicting versions of
the story later on, he clearly believed that Pocahontas saved his life in December 1607, but
food remained scarce. The colony had too many gentlemen and specialized craftsmen who
considered farming beneath their dignity. Over their protests, Smith set them to work raising grain for four hours a day.

In 1609, the London Company sent out 600 more settlers under Lieutenant Governor
Thomas Gates, but his ship ran aground on Bermuda, and the crew spent a year building
another vessel. About 400 new settlers reached Virginia before Gates arrived. Smith, after
suffering a severe injury in an explosion, was shipped back to England, and the colony
lacked firm leadership for the next year. Wearying Powhatan with their endless demands

for corn at a time of severe drought, the settlers provoked the Indian war that Smith had avoided. Some escaped to the Indians, but anyone caught fleeing was executed.

When Gates finally reached Jamestown with 175 colonists in June 1610, he found only 60 settlers alive (plus a garrison at Point Comfort) and the food supply nearly exhausted. Gates despaired, packed everyone aboard ship, and started downriver. Virginia was going the way of Roanoke and Sagadahoc, despite its greater resources. Instead, the small fleet came abreast of the new governor, Thomas West, baron de la Warr, sailing up the James with 300 new colonists. They all went back to Jamestown, and the colony survived.

De la Warr and Gates found themselves in the middle of the colony's first Indian war, which lasted from 1609 to 1614. Powhatan's warriors picked off any settlers who strayed far from Jamestown. The English retaliated by slaughtering whole villages and destroying crops, as they had in Ireland. The massacre of one tribe might intimidate others. The war finally ended after the English captured Pocahontas, Powhatan's favorite daughter, and used her as a hostage to negotiate peace.

Despite the Indian war, the colony's prospects improved after 1610. The governors imposed martial law on the settlers and sent some of them to healthier locations, such as Henrico, 50 miles upstream. Through the efforts of John Rolfe, the colony began to produce a cash crop. In 1613, Rolfe imported a mild strain of tobacco from the West Indies. It brought such a good price in England that the king, who had insisted no one could build a colony "upon smoke," was proved wrong. Soon, settlers were even growing tobacco in the streets of Jamestown.

Reorganization, Reform, and Crisis

In 1609, a new royal charter extended Virginia's boundaries to the Pacific. A third charter in 1612 made the London Company a **joint-stock company.** It resembled a modern corporation except that each stockholder had only one vote regardless of how many shares he owned. The stockholders met quarterly in the company's General Court but entrusted everyday management to the company's treasurer, who until 1618 was Sir Thomas Smyth, a wealthy London merchant. The lack of profits led to turmoil among the stockholders, who replaced Smyth in 1618 with Sir Edwin Sandys, a Puritan son of the archbishop of York.

The company adopted an ambitious reform program for Virginia. It encouraged economic diversification, such as glassblowing, planting grape vines, and raising silkworms. English common law replaced martial law. The settlers were allowed to elect their own assembly, the **House of Burgesses,** to meet with the governor and his council and make local laws. Finally, the most popular reform, settlers were permitted to own land. Under this **headright** system, a colonist received 50 acres for each person whose passage to Virginia he financed. By 1623, Sandys had shipped 4,000 settlers to Virginia, but the economic diversification program failed. Only tobacco found a market. Corn still provided most of the food. Instead of growing silkworms and grapes, Virginians raised Indian crops with Indian methods, which meant using hoes instead of plows.

The flood of newcomers strained the food supply and soured relations with the Indians, especially after Powhatan died and was succeeded by his militant brother, Opechancanough. In March 1622, the new chief launched an attack that was intended to wipe out the colony. Without a last-minute warning from a friendly Indian, Jamestown might not have survived. As it turned out, 347 settlers were killed that day, and most of the outlying settlements were destroyed. Newcomers who arrived in subsequent months had nowhere to go and, with food again scarce, hundreds died over the winter.

Back in London, Smyth and his allies turned against Sandys, withdrew their capital, and asked the king to intervene. A royal commission visited the colony and found only 1,200 settlers alive out of the 6,000 sent over since 1607. In 1624, the king declared the London Company bankrupt and assumed direct control of Virginia, making it the first **royal colony,** with a governor and council appointed by the Crown. The London Company had invested some £200,000 in the enterprise, equal to more than £150 for every surviving settler, at a time when skilled English craftsmen were lucky to earn £50 per year. Such extravagance guaranteed that future colonies would be organized in different ways.

Tobacco, Servants, and Survival

Between Opechancanough's 1622 attack and the 1640s, Virginia proved that it could survive. Despite an appalling death rate, about a thousand new settlers came each year, and population grew slowly, reaching 8,100 by 1640. For 10 years, the settlers warred against Opechancanough. In 1623, they poisoned 200 Indians they had invited to a peace conference. In most years, they attacked the Indians just before harvest time, destroying their crops and villages. By the time both sides made peace in 1632, all Indians had been expelled from the peninsula between the James and York rivers below Jamestown.

The export of tobacco financed the importation of **indentured servants,** even after the price of tobacco fell sharply in the 1630s. Most servants were young men, who agreed to work for a term of years in exchange for the cost of passage, plus bed and board during their years of service, and modest freedom dues when their term expired. Those signing indentures in England usually had valuable skills and negotiated terms of four or five years. Those arriving without an indenture, most of whom were younger and less skilled, were sold by the ship captain to a planter. Those older than age 19 served five years, whereas those younger than 19 served until age 24. The system turned servants into freemen, who then hoped to prosper on their own. Most former servants became tenants for several years while they tried to save enough to buy their own land. Better tobacco prices enabled many to succeed between 1640 and 1660, but those who imported the servants were always in a stronger economic position, collecting the headright of 50 acres for each one. Because deaths still outnumbered births, the colony needed a steady flow of newcomers to survive.

In 1634, Virginia was divided into counties, each with its own justices of the peace, who sat together as the county court and, by filling their own vacancies, soon became a self-perpetuating **oligarchy.** Most counties also became Anglican **parishes,** with a church and a **vestry** of prominent laymen, usually the justices. The vestry managed temporal

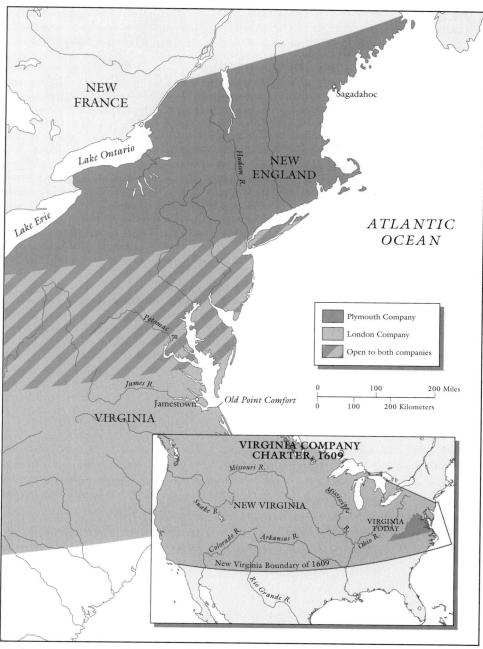

Map 2.3   Virginia Company Charter, 1606   This charter gave the Plymouth Company jurisdiction over what would become New England and New York, and the London Company jurisdiction over most of what became Virginia and North Carolina. They shared jurisdiction over the intervening area. The insert map shows Virginia's revised sea-to-sea boundaries laid out in the 1609 charter.

Book 5th

15

The Negroes Stringing & Rolling Tobacco.

Tobacco

Slaves at Work on a Tobacco Farm in Virginia   Tobacco is a demanding crop. Its cultivation required, at times, very exhausting labor.

affairs for the church and chose the minister. Although the king did not recognize the House of Burgesses until 1639, it met almost every year after 1619 and was well established by 1640. Before long, only a justice could hope to be elected as a burgess.

Until 1660, many former servants managed to acquire land, and some even served on the county courts and in the House of Burgesses. As tobacco prices fell after 1660, however, upward mobility became more difficult. Political offices usually went to the richest 15 percent of the settlers, those able to pay their own way across the Atlantic. They, and eventually their descendants, monopolized the posts of justice of the peace and vestryman, the pool from which burgesses and councilors were normally chosen. As Virginia became more oligarchic after 1660, resentments grew increasingly acute among those who were shut off from power and unable to prosper.

Maryland

Maryland arose from the social and religious vision of Sir George Calvert and his son Cecilius, both of whom became Catholics and looked to America as a refuge for persecuted English and Irish Catholics. Sir George, a prominent officeholder, had invested in the London Company. When he resigned his royal office because of his conversion, King James I made him Baron Baltimore in the Irish peerage.

The Maryland charter of 1632 made Baltimore "lord proprietor" of the colony. The most sweeping delegation of power that the Crown could make, it came close to making Baltimore king within Maryland. After 1630, most new colonial projects were **proprietary colonies,** often with the Maryland charter as a model. Many of them embodied the distinctive social ideals of their founders.

George Calvert died as the Maryland patent was being issued, and Cecilius inherited Maryland and the peerage. Like Champlain, he believed that Catholics and Protestants could live in peace in the same colony, but he expected the servants, most of whom were Protestants, to continue to serve the Catholic gentlemen of the colony after their indentures expired. Baltimore made the gentlemen manor lords, with the power to preside over feudal courts that were nearly obsolete in England.

Those plans were never fulfilled. The condition of English Catholics improved under Charles I (1625–49) and his queen, Henrietta Maria, a French Catholic for whom the colony was named. Because few Catholics emigrated, most settlers were Protestants. The civil war that erupted in England in 1642 (see later section) soon spread to Maryland. Protestants overthrew Lord Baltimore's regime several times between 1642 and 1660, but the English state always sided with him, even when the Puritans were in power. During these struggles, Baltimore conceded a **bicameral legislature** to the colony, knowing that Protestants would dominate the elective assembly and that Catholics would control the appointive council. He also sponsored the Toleration Act of 1649, which granted freedom of worship to Christians (but not officially to Maryland's tiny Jewish minority).

The manorial system did not survive these upheavals. Protestant servants, after their indentures expired, acquired their own land rather than become tenants under Catholic manor lords, most of whom died or returned to England. When Maryland's unrest ended around 1660, the colony was raising tobacco, corn, and livestock and was governed by county courts similar to those in Virginia. If anything, the proprietary family's Catholicism and its claims to special privileges made the Maryland assembly more articulate than the Virginia House of Burgesses in demanding the liberties of Englishmen. Otherwise, religion provided the biggest difference between the two colonies. Virginia was Anglican, but Maryland had no **established church** and no vestries. Most Maryland Protestants had to make do without ministers until the 1690s.

Chesapeake Family Life

At first, European men outnumbered women in Virginia by at least 5 to 1. Among new immigrant servants as late as the 1690s, the ratio was still 5 to 2. Population became self-sustaining about 1680, when live births finally began to outnumber deaths. Among adults, this transition was felt after 1700. Until then, most prominent people were immigrants.

Life expectancy slowly improved as the colonists planted orchards to provide wholesome cider to drink, but it still remained much lower than in England, where those who survived childhood could expect to live into their fifties. The Chesapeake immigrants had

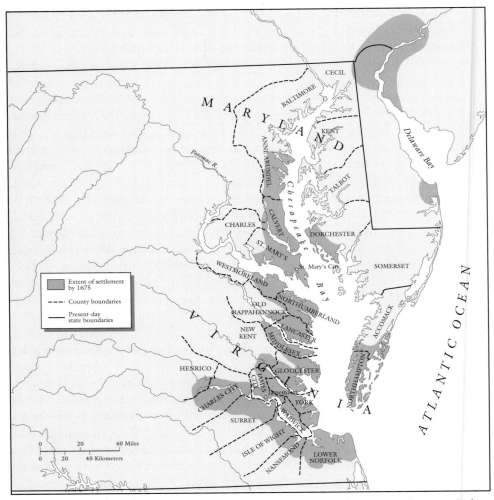

Map 2.4 Virginia and Maryland, Circa 1675 Nearly 70 years after the founding of Jamestown, settlement remained confined to the tidewater and the eastern shore.

survived childhood diseases in Europe, but men at age 20 could expect to live only to about 45, with 70 percent dead by age 50. Women died at even younger ages, especially in areas ravaged by malaria, a very dangerous disease during pregnancy. In those places, women rarely lived to age 40. England's patriarchal families found it difficult to survive in the Chesapeake. About 70 percent of the men never married or, if they did, produced no children. Most men waited years after completing their service before they could marry. Because women could not marry until they had fulfilled their indentures, most spent a good part of their childbearing years unwed. About one-fifth had illegitimate children, despite severe legal penalties, and roughly one-third were pregnant on their wedding day. Virtually all women married, most as soon as they could, usually to a landowner.

In a typical Chesapeake marriage, the groom was in his thirties and the bride eight or ten years younger. Although men outlived women, this age gap meant that the husband usually died before his wife, who then quickly remarried. In one Virginia county, three-fourths of all children lost a parent, and one-third lost both. Native-born settlers married at a much earlier age than immigrants; women were often in their middle to late teens when they wed. Orphans were a major community problem. Stepparents were common because surviving spouses with property usually remarried. Few lived long enough to become grandparents. By the time the oldest child in a household was 20, the husband and wife, because of successive remarriages, might not even be that child's blood relatives. Under these circumstances, family loyalties tended to focus on other kin—uncles, aunts, cousins, older stepbrothers or stepsisters—thus contributing to the value that Virginia and Maryland placed on hospitality. Patriarchy remained weak. Because fathers died young, even the officeholding elite that took shape after 1650 had difficulty passing on its status to its sons. Only toward the end of the 17th century were the men holding office likely to be descended from fathers of comparable distinction.

The West Indies and the Transition to Slavery

Before 1700, far more Englishmen went to the West Indies than to the Chesapeake. Between 1624 and 1640, they settled the Leeward Islands (St. Christopher, Nevis, Montserrat, and Antigua) and Barbados, tiny islands covering just over 400 square miles. In the 1650s, England seized Jamaica from Spain, increasing this total by a factor of 10. At first, English planters grew tobacco, using the labor of indentured servants, but beginning around 1645 in Barbados, sugar replaced tobacco, with dramatic social consequences. The Dutch, then being driven from Brazil by the Portuguese, provided some of the capital for this transition, showed the English how to raise sugar, introduced them to slave labor on a massive scale, and for a time dominated the exportation and marketing of the crop.

Sugar became so valuable that planters imported most of their food from North America rather than divert land and labor from the cash crop. Sugar required a heavy investment in slaves and mills, and large planters with many slaves soon dominated the islands. Ex-servants found little employment, and most of them left after their terms expired. Many joined the buccaneers or moved to the mainland. Their exodus hastened the transition to slavery. In 1660, Europeans outnumbered slaves in the English islands by 33,000 to 22,000. By 1700, the white population had stagnated, but the number of slaves had increased sixfold. By 1775, it would triple again. Planters appropriated about 80 percent of their slaves' labor for their own profit, an unprecedented rate of exploitation. They often worked slaves to death and then bought others to replace them. Of the 316,000 Africans imported before 1700, only 115,000 remained alive in that year. Observers were depressed by the moral climate on the islands, where underworked and

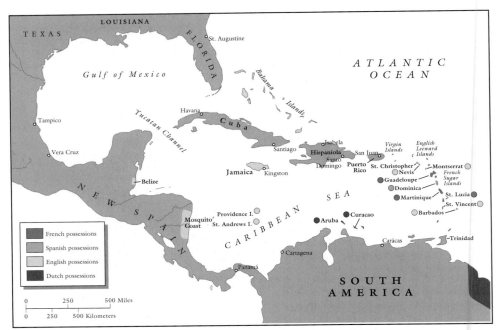

Map 2.5   Principal West Indian Colonies in the 17th Century   Spain retained control of the large islands of Cuba, Hispaniola, and Puerto Rico, while its English, French, and Dutch rivals settled the smaller but fertile islands east of Puerto Rico or south of Cuba.

overfed planters arrogantly dominated their overworked and underfed slaves. Yet the islands generated enormous wealth for the English empire, far more than the mainland colonies well into the 18th century. Around 1700, the islands sent sugar worth £710,000 per year to England at a time when Chesapeake planters were getting only £230,000 for their tobacco.

The Rise of Slavery in North America

Focus Question
In the Chesapeake colonies, why did Africans become hereditary slaves serving for life instead of indentured servants bound only for several years?

Africans reached Virginia in 1619 when, John Rolfe reported, a Dutch ship "sold us twenty Negars." Their status remained ambiguous for decades, even after slavery had been sharply defined in the West Indies. In Virginia and Maryland, many of the first Africans had Hispanic names. They were Creoles who had acquired a great deal of intercultural experience around the Atlantic world and were in a stronger position to

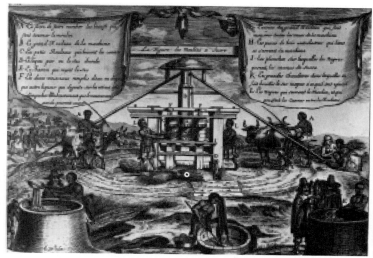

The Library Company of Philadelphia

Sugar Mill This 1665 engraving shows an animal-powered sugar mill, worked by African slaves, in one of the French West Indian Islands.

negotiate with their masters than those who came later would be. Some Africans were treated as servants and won their freedom after several years. On Virginia's eastern shore as late as the 1660s, perhaps 30 percent of African people were free, but other Africans in the early years were already serving for life, and that pattern prevailed by the end of the 17th century.

Because the English had no experience with slavery at home, a rigid caste system took time to crystallize. When Hugh Davis was whipped in 1630 "for abusing himself to the dishonor of God and shame of Christians, by defiling his body in lying with a negro," his offense may have been sodomy rather than miscegenation. The record is unclear. In 1680, when Katherine Watkins, a white woman, accused John Long, a mulatto, of raping her, the neighbors (both men and women) blamed her, not him, for engaging in seductive behavior, which they described in lurid detail. The case of Elizabeth Key, a mulatto, a Christian, and the bastard daughter of Thomas Key, shows similar ambiguity. In 1655, when she claimed her freedom, her new owner fought to keep her enslaved. William Greensted, who had fathered two children by her, sued on her behalf, won, and then married her. He had probably fallen in love with her.

In the generation after 1680, the caste structure of the Chesapeake colonies became firmly set. Fewer indentured servants reached the Chesapeake from England, as the Delaware valley and the expanding English army and navy competed more successfully for the same young men. Slaves took their place. Some of the emerging great planters, such as William Byrd I and William Fitzhugh, deliberately chose to replace indentured servants with enslaved Africans. They cost more to buy, but they served for life and could be treated more ruthlessly than English servants. In 1705, the Virginia legislature, in which slaveholders were gaining greater weight, forbade the whipping of a white servant without a court's permission, a restriction that did not apply to the punishment of slaves. To attract more whites, Virginia also promised every ex-servant 50 acres of land. The message was obvious: Every white was now superior to any black. Racial caste was replacing opportunity as the organizing principle of Chesapeake society.

The New England Colonies

Other Europeans founded colonies to engage in economic activities they could not pursue at home, but the New England settlers reproduced the mixed economy of old England, with minor variations. Their family farms raised livestock and European grains, as well as corn. They came to America, they insisted, to worship as God commanded, not as the Church of England required.

The Pilgrims and Plymouth

The **Pilgrims** were Separatists who left England for the Netherlands between 1607 and 1609, convinced that the Church of England was no true daughter of the Reformation. They hoped to worship freely in Holland. After 10 years there, they realized that their children were growing up Dutch, not English. That fear prompted a minority of the congregation to move to America. After negotiating rather harsh terms with the London Company, they sailed for Virginia on the *Mayflower*. But the ship was blown off course late in 1620, landing first on Cape Cod and then on the mainland well north of the charter boundaries of Virginia, at a place they named Plymouth. Two-thirds of the settlers were not Separatists; they had been added to the passenger list by London investors. Before landing, the 100 passengers agreed to the Mayflower Compact, which bound them all to obey the decisions of the majority, a sound precaution in a colony with uncertain legal status.

Short on supplies, the colonists suffered keenly during the first winter. Half of them died, including all but three married women and the governor. His successor was William Bradford, who would be reelected annually for all but five years until his death in 1656. The settlers fared much better when spring came. The Patuxet Indians of the area had been wiped out by disease in 1617, but their fields were ready for planting. Squanto, the only Patuxet to survive, had been kidnapped and carried to England by coastal traders in 1614. He had just made his way home and showed up at Plymouth in March 1621. He taught the settlers Indian methods of fishing and growing corn. He also introduced them to Massasoit, the powerful Wampanoag **sachem** (or chief), whose people celebrated the first thanksgiving feast with the settlers after the 1621 harvest. By 1630, the settlers numbered about 300. By paying off their London creditors, they gained political autonomy and private ownership of their flourishing farms. During the 1630s, they founded several new towns and sold their surplus crops to the colonists flooding into Massachusetts.

Covenant Theology

A much larger Puritan exodus settled Massachusetts Bay between 1630 and 1641. The best-educated English group yet to cross the Atlantic, 130 of them had attended a university, most often Cambridge, a Puritan center. Puritans distrusted Charles I and his courtiers, especially William Laud, bishop of London and then archbishop of Canterbury, whom they accused of Catholic sympathies and of Arminianism, a heresy named for a Dutch theologian who had challenged strict Calvinists a generation earlier. To Puritans, the stakes were high indeed by the late 1620s. God's wrath would visit England, they warned. During that early phase of the Thirty Years' War (1618–48), Catholic armies seemed about to crush the German Reformation. Charles I blundered into a brief war against both Spain and France, raised money by dubious means, and dissolved Parliament when it protested.

These matters were of genuine urgency to Puritans, who embraced what they called **covenant theology.** According to this system, God had made two biblical covenants with humans: the covenant of works and the covenant of grace. In the covenant of works, God had promised Adam that if he kept God's law he would never die, but Adam ate of the forbidden fruit, was expelled from the Garden of Eden, and died. All of Adam's descendants remained under the same covenant, but because of his fall would never be capable of keeping the law. All humans deserve damnation, but God was merciful and answered sin with the covenant of grace. God would save his chosen people. Everyone else would be damned. Even though the covenant of works could no longer bring eternal life, it remains in force and establishes the strict moral standards that every Christian must strive to follow, before and after conversion. A Christian's inability to keep the law usually triggered the conversion experience by demonstrating that only faith, not works, could save.

At this level, covenant theology merely restated Calvinist orthodoxy, but the Puritans gave it a novel social dimension by pairing each personal covenant with a communal counterpart. The social equivalent of the covenant of grace was the church covenant. Each congregation organized itself into a church, a community of **the elect.** The founders, or "pillars," of each church, after satisfying one another of their own conversions, agreed that within their church the Gospel would be properly preached and discipline would be strictly maintained. God, in turn, promised to bestow saving grace within that church—not to everyone, but presumably to most of the children of the elect. The communal counterpart of the covenant of works was the key to secular history. Puritans called it the "national" covenant. It determined not who was saved or damned, but the rise and fall of nations or peoples. As a people, New Englanders agreed to obey the law, and God promised to prosper them. They, in turn, covenanted with their **magistrates** to punish sinners. If magistrates enforced God's law and the people supported these efforts, God would not punish the whole community for the misdeeds of individuals. But if sinners escaped public account, God's anger would be terrible toward his chosen people of New England. God gave them much and demanded much in return.

For New Englanders, the idea of the covenant became a powerful social metaphor, explaining everything from crop failures and untimely deaths to Indian wars and political contention. Towns and militia companies used covenants to organize themselves. If only because a minister could always think of something that had missed proper correction, the covenant generated an almost automatic sense of moral crisis. It had a built-in dynamic of moral reform that was becoming obvious even before the migrants crossed the ocean. In England, the government had refused to assume a godly role. Puritans fleeing to America hoped to escape the divine wrath that threatened England and to create in America the kind of churches that God demanded.

Massachusetts Bay

In 1629, several English Puritans obtained a charter for the **Massachusetts Bay Company,** a typical joint-stock corporation except for one feature: The charter did not specify where the company was to be located. Puritan investors going to New England bought out the other stockholders. Led by Governor John Winthrop, they carried the charter to America, beyond the gaze of Charles I. They used it not to organize a business corporation, but as the constitution for the colony. The General Court created by the charter became the Massachusetts legislature. New England settlers came from the broad middle range of English society—few rich, few very poor. Most had owned property in England. When they sold it to go to America, they probably liquidated far more capital than the London Company had invested in Virginia. A godly haven was expensive to build.

An advance party that sailed in 1629 took over a fishing village on the coast and renamed it Salem. The Winthrop fleet brought 1,000 settlers in 1630. In small groups, they scattered around the bay, founding Dorchester, Roxbury, Boston, Charlestown, and Cambridge. Each town formed around a minister and a magistrate. The local congregation was the first institution to take shape. From it evolved the town meeting, as the settlers began to distinguish more sharply between religious and secular affairs. Soon the colonists were raising European livestock and growing English wheat and other grains, along with corn. Perhaps 30 percent of them perished during the first winter. A few hundred others grew discouraged and returned to England. Then conditions rapidly improved, as they had at Plymouth a decade earlier. About 13,000 settlers came to Massachusetts by 1641, most as families—a unique event in Atlantic empires to that time. **(See Map 2.6, New England in the 1640s, in the color insert following page 96.)**

Settlers did a brisk business selling grain to the newcomers arriving each year. When the flow of immigrants ceased in 1641, that trade collapsed, creating a crisis that lessened as towns improved their economic infrastructure by increasing their capacity to build ships or to raise sheep and produce woolen textiles. The region began to prosper after 1650 as Boston merchants opened up West Indian markets for New England grain, lumber, and fish. New Englanders possessed this flexibility because they had started to build ships in 1631. The very existence of colonies committed to free labor was odd. To prosper, they had to trade with more typical colonies, the societies elsewhere in the hemisphere that raised tobacco and sugar with unfree labor.

The region's economy imperiled Puritan orthodoxy. Few Boston merchants and almost no fishermen could meet the religious standards of a Puritan society. Although few of these men became church members in the first generation, the colony needed their services and had to put up with them. The fishing towns of Marblehead and Gloucester did little to implement Puritan values or even to found churches in the early decades, while Boston merchants increasingly favored toleration of Protestant dissenters because it would be good for business. Although these contrasts softened with time, strict Puritan orthodoxy was mostly a rural phenomenon.

Puritan Family Life

In rural areas, New Englanders soon observed a remarkable fact. After the first winter, deaths were rare. The place was undeniably healthy, and families grew rapidly as 6 or even 10 children reached maturity. The settlers had left most European diseases behind and had encountered no new ones in the bracing climate. For the founders and their children, life expectancy far exceeded the European norm. More than one-fifth of the men who founded Andover lived past age 80. Infant mortality fell, and few mothers died in childbirth. Because people lived so long, New England families became intensely patriarchal. Many fathers refused to grant land titles to their sons before their own deaths. In the early years, settlers often moved, looking for the richest soil, the best neighbors, and the most inspiring minister. By about 1645, most of them had found what they sought. Migration into or out of country towns became much lower than in England, and the New England town settled into a tight community that slowly became an intricate web of cousins. Once the settlers had formed a typical farming town, they grew reluctant to admit "strangers" to their midst. New Englanders largely avoided slavery, not out of sympathy for Africans or hatred of the institution, but to keep outsiders from contaminating their religion.

Conversion, Dissent, and Expansion

The vital force behind Puritanism was the quest for conversion. Probably because of John Cotton's stirring sermons in Boston, the settlers crossed an invisible boundary in the mid-1630s. As Cotton's converts described their religious experiences, their neighbors turned from analyzing the legitimacy of their own conversions to assessing the validity of someone else's. Afraid that Cotton's ecstatic converts had not scrutinized their own hearts with enough rigor, Thomas Shepard and other nearby ministers began to impose tests for regeneracy, and the standards of acceptance escalated rapidly.

The conversion experience was deeply ambiguous to a Puritan. Anyone who found no inner trace of saving grace was damned. Anyone who was absolutely certain of salvation had to be relying on personal merit and was also damned. Conversion took months, even years to achieve. It began with the discovery that one could not keep God's law and that one *deserved* damnation, not for an occasional misdeed, but for what one was at one's best—a wretched sinner. It progressed through despair to hope, which always arose from passages of scripture that spoke to that person's condition. A "saint" at last found reason to believe that God had saved him or her. The whole process involved a painful balance between assurance and doubt. A saint was sure of salvation, but never too sure.

This quest for conversion generated dissent and new colonies. The founders of Connecticut feared that Massachusetts was becoming too severe in certifying church members. The founders of the New Haven Colony worried that the Bay Colony was too lenient. The first Rhode Islanders disagreed with all of them.

In the mid-1630s, Reverend Thomas Hooker, alarmed by Cotton's preaching, led his people west to the Connecticut River, where they founded Hartford and other towns south of the charter boundary of Massachusetts. John Winthrop, Jr., built Saybrook Fort at the mouth of the river, and it soon merged with Hooker's towns into the colony of Connecticut. In 1639, an affluent group planted the New Haven Colony on Long Island Sound. The leaders were Theophilus Eaton, a wealthy London merchant, and Reverend John Davenport, who imposed the strictest requirements for church membership in New England.

The residents of most towns agreed on the kind of worship they preferred, but some settlers, such as Roger Williams and **Anne Hutchinson,** made greater demands. Williams, who served briefly as Salem's minister, was a Separatist who refused to worship with anyone who did not explicitly repudiate the Church of England. Nearly all Massachusetts Puritans were Non-Separatists who claimed only to be reforming the Anglican Church. In 1636, after Williams challenged the king's right as a Christian to grant Indian lands to anyone at all, the colony banished him. He fled to Narragansett Bay with a few disciples and founded Providence. He developed eloquent arguments for religious liberty and the complete separation of church and state.

Anne Hutchinson, a merchant's wife and an admirer of John Cotton, claimed that virtually all other ministers were preaching only the covenant of works, not the covenant of grace, and were leading people to hell. She won a large following in Boston. At her trial there, she claimed to have received direct messages from God (the Antinomian heresy). Banished in 1638, she and her followers also fled to Narragansett Bay, where they founded Newport and Portsmouth. These towns united with Providence to form the colony of Rhode Island and accepted both the religious liberty and the separation of church and state that Williams advocated.

Much of this territorial expansion reflected not just religious idealism, but also a quest for more land that threatened neighboring Indians. Connecticut and Massachusetts waged a war of terror and annihilation against the Pequot Indians, who controlled the fertile Thames River valley in eastern Connecticut. In May 1637, New England soldiers debated with their chaplain which of two Pequot forts to attack, the one held by warriors or the one with women, children, and the elderly. He probably told them to remember Saul and the Amalekites because, with horrified Narragansett Indians looking on as nominal allies of the settlers, the Puritan army chose the second fort, set fire to all the wigwams, and shot everyone who tried to flee. The godly had their own uses for terrorism.

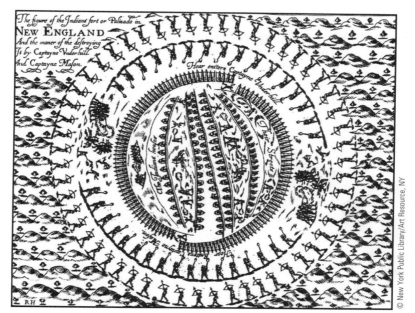

The Puritan Massacre of the Pequot Indians, 1637 The massacre took place at what is now Mystic, Connecticut. Most of the victims were women and children. The Indians shown in the outer circle were Narragansett allies of the settlers and were appalled by the carnage.

Congregations, Towns, and Colony Governments

These struggles helped shape New England's basic institutions. Congregations abandoned the Anglican Book of Common Prayer, vestments, incense, church courts, and the need to be ordained by a bishop. The sermon became the dominant rite, and each congregation chose and ordained its own minister. No singing was permitted, except of psalms. Congregations sometimes sent ministers and laymen to a synod, but its decisions were advisory, not binding. A 1648 synod issued the Cambridge Platform, which defined "Congregationalist" worship and church organization.

By then the town had become something distinct from the congregation. Some towns chose independent farms at the outset, but many adopted **open-field agriculture,** a medieval system that appeared nowhere else in colonial America. In that system, farmers owned scattered strips of land within a common field, and the town decided what crops to grow. This emphasis on communal cooperation may have appealed to the founders, but they were also short of oxen and plows at first and had to share them. The open-field system did not survive the first generation.

Town meetings decided who got how much land. It was distributed broadly but never equally. In Springfield, at one extreme, the Pynchon family controlled most of the land and most of the labor as well. In other towns, such as Dedham, the distribution was much more equitable. In some villages, town meetings occurred often, made most of the decisions, and left only the details to a board of elected "selectmen." In others, the selectmen did most of the governing. All adult males usually participated in local decisions, but Massachusetts and New Haven restricted the vote for colonywide offices to men who were full church members, a decision that greatly narrowed the electorate by the 1660s.

Massachusetts had a bicameral legislature by the 1640s. Voters in each town chose representatives who met as the Chamber of Deputies, or lower house. Voters also elected the governor and the magistrates, or upper house (the Council or, in its judicial capacity, the Court of Assistants). The magistrates also staffed the county courts. The Court of Assistants heard major criminal cases and appeals from the counties. Final appeals were heard by the General Court, with both houses sitting together to decide judicial questions.

Massachusetts defined its legal system in the "Body of Liberties" of 1641 (which may actually be history's first bill of rights) and in a comprehensive law code of 1648 that was widely imitated in other colonies. Massachusetts sharply reduced the number of capital offenses under English law and listed them in the order of the Ten Commandments. Unlike England, Massachusetts seldom executed anyone for a crime against property. Other distinctive features of the legal system included an explicit recognition of the liberties of women, children, servants, foreigners, and even "the Bruite Creature," or animals; a serious effort to ban professional lawyers; and the swift punishment of crime.

New England also transformed the traditional English jury system. New Haven abolished juries altogether because the Bible does not mention them, but the other colonies vastly expanded the role of civil (noncriminal) juries, using them even to decide appeals, something that never happened in England. Except in capital trials, however, the criminal jury—a fixture of English justice—almost disappeared in New England. The punishment of sin involved fidelity to the covenant and was too important to leave to 12 ordinary men. This system worked well because even sinners shared its values. Most offenders appeared in court and accepted their punishments. Acquittals were rare, almost unheard of in New Haven. Yet hardly anyone ran away to avoid trial or punishment.

Infant Baptism and New Dissent

Although most of the founders of the New England colonies became church members during the fervor of the 1630s, their children had trouble achieving conversion. They had never lived as part of a beleaguered minority in England, nor had they experienced the joy of joining with other holy refugees in founding their own church. They had to find God on their own and then persuade their elders—who were on guard because leniency had let Williams, Hutchinson, and other deviants through—that their conversions were authentic. Most failed. They grew up, married, and requested baptism for their children. The Cambridge Platform declared that only "saints" (the converted) and their children could be baptized. But what about the grandchildren of the saints if their own parents had not yet experienced conversion? By 1660, this problem was becoming acute.

Dissenters offered two answers, and the ministers a third. In the 1640s, some settlers became Baptists. Noting that scripture contains no mandate to baptize infants, they argued that only converted adults should receive that rite. Their position challenged the logic of a covenanted community by implying that New England was no different from Europe. The community was a mass of sinners from whom God would randomly choose a few saints. Samuel Gorton, a Baptist expelled from Massachusetts and Plymouth, founded Warwick, Rhode Island, in the 1640s. When Massachusetts arrested him, accused him of blasphemy, and put him on trial for his life, the legislature banished him instead, but Gorton appealed to Parliament in England, and Massachusetts backed down. Baptist principles also attracted Henry Dunster, the able president of Harvard College, which had been founded in 1636 to educate ministers and magistrates for a Puritan society. When the courts began to harass Baptists, Dunster left for more tolerant Plymouth.

Even more alarming to most Puritans were the Quakers, who invaded the region from England in the 1650s. Quakers found salvation within themselves—through God, the Inner Light present in all people if they will only let it shine forth. To Puritans, the Quaker answer to the conversion dilemma seemed blasphemous and Antinomian. Massachusetts hanged four Quakers who refused to stop preaching, including Mary Dyer, a former disciple of Anne Hutchinson.

The clergy's answer to the lack of conversions, worked out at a synod in 1662, became known as the **Half-Way Covenant.** Parents who had been baptized but had not yet experienced conversion could bring their children before the church, "own the covenant" (that is, subject themselves and their offspring to the doctrine and discipline of the church), and have their children baptized. In practice, women often experienced conversion before age 30, men closer to 40, but many never did. In most churches, women also began to outnumber men as full members. For 15 or 20 years after 1662, most churches were still dominated by the lay members of the founding generation. Despite the urging of the clergy (by then most ministers were young Harvard graduates, not venerable saints), aging church members resisted implementation of the Half-Way Covenant, but as the founders died off in the 1670s and 1680s, the covenant took hold and soon led to something like universal baptism. Almost every child had an ancestor who had been a full church member.

Dissent persisted anyhow. The orthodox colonies were divided over whether to persecute or to ignore their Baptist and Quaker minorities. Ministers preached "jeremiads," shrill warnings against any backsliding from the standards of the founding generation, but many laypeople disliked the persecution of conscientious Protestants.

The English Civil Wars

The 1640s were a critical decade in England and the colonies. From 1629 to 1640, Charles I governed without Parliament, but when he tried to impose the Anglican Book of Common Prayer on Presbyterian Scotland, his Scottish subjects rebelled and even invaded England. Needing revenue, Charles summoned two Parliaments in 1640 only to find that many of its members, especially the Puritans, sympathized with the Scots. The Church of England began to collapse. For two decades, no new bishops were consecrated. In 1641, Irish

Catholics launched a massive revolt against the Protestant colonizers of their land. King and Parliament agreed that the Irish must be crushed, but neither trusted the other with the resources to do the job.

Instead, they began to fight each other. In 1642, the king and Parliament raised separate armies and went to war. Parliament gradually won the military struggle and then had to govern most of England without a king. In January 1649, after its moderate members had been purged by its own New Model Army, Parliament beheaded Charles, abolished the House of Lords, and proclaimed England a Commonwealth (or republic). Within a few years, Oliver Cromwell, Parliament's most successful general, dismissed Parliament, and the army proclaimed him "Lord Protector" of England. He convened several of his own Parliaments, but these experiments failed. The army could not win legitimacy for a government that ruled without the ancient trinity of "King, Lords, and Commons."

Cromwell died in September 1658, and his regime collapsed. Part of the army invited Charles II (1660–85) back from exile to claim his throne. This "Restoration" government did its best to restore the old order. It brought back the House of Lords and reestablished the Church of England under its episcopal form of government. The English state, denying any right of dissent, persecuted both Catholics and Protestant dissenters: Presbyterians, Congregationalists, Baptists, and Quakers. This persecution drove thousands of Quakers to the Delaware valley after 1675.

The First Restoration Colonies

Focus Question
In what ways did the Restoration colonies differ from those founded earlier in the Chesapeake and New England?

England had founded 6 of the original 13 colonies before 1640. Six others were founded or came under English rule during the **Restoration era** (1660–88). The last, Georgia, was settled in the 1730s (see chapter 4). Most of the new colonies shared certain common features and also differed in some respects from earlier settlements. All were proprietary in form. A proprietary charter enabled the organizers to pursue daring social experiments. Except for Pennsylvania, the Restoration colonies were all founded by men with big ideas and small purses. The proprietors tried to attract settlers from the older colonies because importing them from Europe was expensive. The most readily available prospects were servants completing their indentures in the West Indies and being driven out by the sugar revolution. Many went to South Carolina. The most prized settlers, however, were New Englanders. Proprietors distrusted both their piety and their politics, but New Englanders had built the most thriving colonies in North America. Few of them would go farther south than New Jersey.

The Restoration colonies made it easy for settlers to acquire land, and they competed with one another by offering newcomers strong guarantees of civil and political liberties. They all promised either toleration or full religious liberty, at least for Christians. Whereas Virginia and New England (except Rhode Island) were still homogeneous societies, the Restoration colonies attracted a mix of religious and ethnic groups. They all found it difficult to create political stability out of this diversity.

Except for William Penn, the new proprietors were **Cavaliers** who had supported Charles II and his brother James, duke of York, during their long exile. Charles owed them something, and a colonial charter cost nothing to grant. Many proprietors took part in more than one project. The eight who obtained charters for Carolina in 1663 and 1665 were also prominent in organizing the Royal African Company, which soon made England a major participant in the African slave trade. Two of the Carolina proprietors obtained a charter from the duke of York for New Jersey as well.

Carolina, Harrington, and the Aristocratic Ideal

In 1663, eight courtiers obtained a charter by which they became the board of proprietors for a colony to be founded south of Virginia. Calling their province Carolina in honor of the king, they tried to colonize the region in the 1660s but achieved no success until the following decade. Most of the settlers came from two sources. Former servants from Virginia and Maryland, many in debt, hoped that they could claim land around Albemarle Sound in what eventually became North Carolina. Other former servants came from Barbados. They settled what became South Carolina.

To the proprietors in England, these scattered settlements made up a single colony called Carolina. Led by Anthony Ashley-Cooper, later the first earl of Shaftesbury and the principal organizer of England's Whig Party, the proprietors drafted the Fundamental Constitutions of Carolina in 1669, an incredibly complex plan for organizing the new colony. Philosopher John Locke, Shaftesbury's young secretary, helped write the document.

The Fundamental Constitutions drew on the work of Commonwealth England's most prominent republican thinker, James Harrington, author of *Oceana* (1656). He tried to design a republic that could endure—unlike ancient Athens or Rome, which had finally become despotic states. Harrington argued that how land was distributed ought to determine whether power should be lodged in one man (monarchy), a few men (aristocracy), or many (a republic). Where ownership of land was widespread, he insisted, absolute government could not prevail. He proposed several other republican devices, such as frequent rotation of officeholders (called "term limits" today), the secret ballot, and a bicameral legislature in which the smaller house would propose laws and the larger house approve or reject them. Harrington had greater impact on colonial governments than any other thinker of his time.

Shaftesbury believed that Harrington had uncovered the laws of history. By emphasizing Henry VIII's confiscation of monastic lands and their sale to an emerging gentry,

Harrington seemed to have an explanation for the decline of the monarchy, England's civil wars, and the execution of Charles I—an explanation that was anathema to the king because, if Harrington was correct, the monarchy was still in trouble. English writers dared not discuss these ideas openly in the 1660s, but by applying Harrington's principles at a safe distance of 3,000 miles, the Carolina proprietors could choose the kind of society they desired and devise institutions to ensure its success. Well aware that the House of Lords had been abolished for 11 years after 1649, they were not yet certain whether the English aristocracy could survive at home. In Carolina, they hoped to create a thriving aristocratic society.

They overdid it. The Fundamental Constitutions proposed a government that was far more complex than any colony could sustain. England had three supreme courts; Carolina would have eight. A legislature of commoners and nobles (called "landgraves" and "casiques") would make laws. The nobles would control 40 percent of the land. In a later version of the text, a noble who lost his land or permanently left the colony would forfeit his title, an application of Harrington's warning not to divorce power from land. A distinct group of manor lords would also have large estates. The document guaranteed religious toleration to all who believed in God, but everyone had to join a church or lose his citizenship. The document also envisioned a class of lowly whites, "leetmen," who would live on small tracts and serve the great landlords—and it accepted slavery. "Every Freeman of Carolina shall have absolute Power and Authority over his Negro Slaves," declared Article 110.

Conditions were bleak on Barbados for ex-servants, but not bleak enough to make the Fundamental Constitutions attractive to the Barbadians who settled in Carolina. Between 1670 and 1700, the proprietors tried several times, without success, to win their approval of the document. In the 1680s, weary of resistance from the predominantly Anglican Barbadians, the proprietors shipped 1,000 dissenters from England and Scotland to South Carolina. These newcomers formed the nucleus of a proprietary party in South Carolina politics and made religious diversity a social fact, but they never grew strong enough to win approval for the Fundamental Constitutions.

Carolina presented its organizers with other unanticipated obstacles to these aristocratic goals. The proprietors assumed that land ownership would be the key to everything else, including wealth and status, but many settlers prospered in other ways. Some of them, especially in Albemarle, exploited the virgin forests all around them to produce masts, turpentine, tar, and pitch for sale to English shipbuilders. Other settlers raised cattle and hogs by letting them run free on open land. Some of South Carolina's African slaves were probably America's first cowboys. The settlers also traded with the Indians, usually for deerskins, often acquired west of the Appalachians. As in New France and New Netherland, the Indian trade sustained a genuine city, Charleston, the first in the American South, founded in 1680. The Indian trade also became something more dangerous than hunting or trapping animals. Carolina traders allied themselves with some Indians to attack others and drag the captives, mostly women and children, to Charleston for sale as slaves. Until 1715, the Indian slave trade was the colony's biggest business. South Carolina exported more enslaved Indians to other colonies than it imported Africans for its emerging plantations.

In the early 18th century, South Carolina and North Carolina became separate colonies, and South Carolina's economy began to move in a new direction. For two decades, until the mid-1720s, a parliamentary subsidy sustained a boom in the naval stores industry, but Charleston merchants increasingly invested their capital, acquired in the Indian trade, in rice plantations. In the 1690s, planters learned how to grow rice from slaves who had cultivated it in West Africa. Especially after the collapse of the Indian slave trade in 1715 (see chapter 3), it became the staple export of South Carolina and triggered a sharp growth of African slavery. In 1700, more than 40 percent of the colony's population of 5,700 were African or Indian slaves engaged in a wide variety of activities. By 1730, two-thirds of the colony's 30,000 people were African slaves, most toiling on rice plantations.

New York: An Experiment in Absolutism

In 1664, James, duke of York, obtained a charter from his royal brother for a colony between the Delaware and Connecticut rivers. Charles II claimed that New Netherland was rightfully English territory because it was included in the Virginia charter of 1606. James sent a fleet to Manhattan, and the English settlers on Long Island rose to support his claim. Reluctantly, Stuyvesant surrendered without resistance. The English renamed the province New York. New Amsterdam became New York City, and Fort Orange became Albany. The Dutch ceded New Netherland with few regrets. It had never been profitable anyway. New York took over all of Long Island, most of which had been ruled by Connecticut, but never made good on its claim to the Connecticut River as its eastern boundary. New York also inherited New Netherland's role as mediator between the settlers and the Iroquois Five Nations. In effect, the duke of York's autocratic colony assumed most of the burdens of this relationship while unintentionally conferring most of the benefits on the Quakers who would begin to settle the Delaware valley a decade later. The shield provided by New York and the Iroquois would make the Quaker experiment in pacifism a viable option.

Although English soldiers abused many Dutch civilians, official policy toward the Dutch was conciliatory. Those who chose to leave could take their property with them. Those who stayed retained their property and were assured of religious toleration. Most stayed. Except in New York City and the small Dutch portion of Long Island, Dutch settlers still lived under Dutch law. Dutch inheritance practices, which were far more generous to women than English law, survived in New York well into the 18th century. England also expected to take over the colony's trade with Europe, but New York's early governors realized that a total ban on commerce with Amsterdam could ruin the colony. Under various legal subterfuges, they allowed this trade to continue.

The duke boldly tried to do in New York what he and the king did not dare attempt in England—to govern without an elective assembly. This policy upset English settlers on Long Island far more than the Dutch, who had no experience with representative government.

Map 2.7   The Duke of York's Colonial Charter   This map shows the boundary of New York as set forth in the charter of 1664, the compromise boundary the first English governor negotiated with Connecticut, and the principal manors created in the 17th century.

Governor Richard Nicolls compiled a code of laws (the Duke's Laws) that were culled mostly from New England statutes. With difficulty, he secured the consent of English settlers to this code in 1665, but thereafter he taxed and governed on his own, seeking only the advice and consent of his appointed council and of a court of assize, also appointive, that rode circuit and dispensed justice, mostly to the English settlers. Nicolls also hoped to lure New England settlers to the area west of the Hudson only to learn that James had granted it as the separate colony of New Jersey to two Carolina proprietors, Sir George Carteret and John, Lord Berkeley.

These decisions made it difficult to attract English colonists to New York, especially after New Jersey granted settlers the right to elect an assembly, which made that colony far more attractive to English settlers than New York. The creation of New Jersey also slowed the flow of Dutch settlers across the Hudson and thus helped to keep New York Dutch.

The transition from a Dutch to an English colony did not go smoothly. James expected his English invaders to assimilate the conquered Dutch, but the reverse was more common for two or three decades. Most Englishmen who settled in New York after the conquest married Dutch women (few unmarried English women were available) and sent their children to the Dutch Reformed Church. In effect, the Dutch were assimilating the English. Nor did the Dutch give up their loyalty to the Netherlands. In 1673, when a Dutch fleet threatened the colony, the Dutch refused to assist the English garrison of Fort James at the southern tip of Manhattan. Eastern Long Island showed more interest in reuniting with Connecticut than in fighting the Dutch. Much like Stuyvesant nine years earlier, the English garrison gave up without resistance. New York City now became New Orange and Fort James was renamed Fort William, both in honor of young William III of Nassau, Prince of Orange, the new *stadholder* (military leader) of the Dutch Republic in its struggle with France.

New Orange survived for 15 months, until the Dutch Republic again concluded that the colony was not worth what it cost and gave it back to England in 1674, at the end of the Third Anglo-Dutch War. The new governor, Major Edmund Andros, arrested seven prominent Dutch merchants and tried them as aliens after they refused to swear an oath of loyalty to England that might oblige them to fight other Dutchmen. Faced with the confiscation of their property, they gave in. Andros also helped secure bilingual ministers for Dutch Reformed pulpits. These preachers made a great show of their loyalty to the duke, a delicate matter now that James, in England, had openly embraced the Catholic faith. Ordinary Dutch settlers looked with suspicion on the new ministers and on wealthier Dutch families who socialized with the governor or sent their sons to New England to learn English.

English merchants in New York City resented the continuing Amsterdam trade and the staying power of the Dutch elite. They believed the colony had to become more English to attract newcomers. When Andros failed to renew the colony's revenue act before returning to England in 1680, the merchants refused to pay duties not voted by an elective assembly. The court of assize, supposedly a bastion of absolutism, supported the tax strike, convicted the duke's customs collector of usurping authority, and sent him to England for punishment, where James exonerated him. The justices also fined several Dutch officeholders for failing to respect English liberties. The English (but not Dutch) towns on Long Island joined in the demand for an elective assembly, an urgent matter now that Penn's much freer colony on the Delaware threatened to drain away the small English population of New York. Several prominent merchants did move to Philadelphia.

The duke finally relented and conceded an assembly. When it met in 1683, it adopted a Charter of Liberties that proclaimed government by consent. It also imposed English law on the Dutch parts of the province. Although the drain of English settlers to Pennsylvania declined, few immigrants came to New York at a time when thousands were going to Pennsylvania. Philadelphia's thriving trade cut into New York City's profits. New York remained a Dutch society with a Yankee enclave, governed by English intruders. In 1689, when James and William fought for the English throne, their struggle threatened to tear the colony apart.

Brotherly Love: The Quakers and America

The most fascinating social experiment of the Restoration era took place in the Delaware valley, where Quakers led another family-based, religiously motivated migration of more than 10,000 people between 1675 and 1690. Founded by George Fox during England's civil wars, the Society of Friends expanded dramatically in the 1650s as it went through a heroic phase of missionaries and martyrs, including the four executed in Massachusetts. After the Restoration, Quakers faced harsh persecution in England and finally began to seek refuge in America.

Quaker Beliefs

Quakers infuriated other Christians. They insisted that God, in the form of the Inner Light, is present in all people, who can become good—even perfect—if only they will let that light shine forth. They took literally Jesus's advice to "Turn the other cheek." They became **pacifists,** enraging Catholics and most other Protestants, nearly all of whom had found ways to justify war. Quakers also obeyed Jesus's command to "swear not." They denounced oaths as sinful. Again, other Christians reacted with horror because their judicial systems rested on oaths.

Although orderly and peaceful, Quakers struck others as dangerous radicals whose beliefs would bring anarchy. For instance, slavery made them uncomfortable, although the Friends did not embrace abolitionism until a century later (see chapter 5). Also, in what they called "the Lamb's war" against human pride, Quakers refused to doff their hats to social superiors. Hats symbolized the social hierarchy of Europe. Every man knew his place so long as he understood whom to doff to, and who should doff to him. And Quakers refused to accept or to confer titles. They called everyone "thee" or "thou," familiar terms used by superiors when addressing inferiors, especially servants.

The implications of Quaker beliefs appalled other Christians. The Inner Light seemed to obliterate predestination, original sin, maybe even the Trinity. Quakers had no sacraments, not even an organized clergy. They denounced Protestant ministers as "hireling priests." Other Protestants retorted that the Quakers were conspiring to return the world

© North Wind Picture Archives

Hexagonal Quaker Meetinghouse   This unique design emphasizes the Quaker belief in the fundamental equality of all souls under God. The interior has no altar or pulpit, no front or back. All worshippers are equally close to God.

to "popish darkness" by abolishing a learned ministry. (The terms "papists" and "popish" were abusive labels applied to Catholics by English Protestants.) Quakers also held distinctive views about revelation. If God speaks directly to Friends, that Word must be every bit as inspired as anything in the Bible. Quakers compiled books of their "sufferings," which they thought were the equal of the Acts of the Apostles in the New Testament, a claim that seemed blasphemous to others.

Contemporaries expected the Society of Friends to fall apart as each member followed the Light in some unique direction, but in the 1660s, Quakers found ways to deal with discord. The heart of Quaker worship was the "weekly meeting" of the local congregation. There was no sermon or liturgy. People spoke whenever the Light inspired them. But because a few men and women spoke often and with great effect, they became recognized as **public friends,** the closest the Quakers came to having a clergy. Public friends occupied special, elevated seats in some meetinghouses, and many went on missionary tours in Europe or America. The weekly meetings within a region sent representatives to a "monthly meeting," which resolved questions of policy and discipline. The monthly meetings sent delegates to the "yearly meeting" in London. At every level, decisions had to be unanimous. There is only one Inner Light, and it must convey the same message to every believer. This insistence on unanimity provided strong safeguards against schism.

Quaker Families

Quakers transformed the traditional family as well. Women enjoyed almost full equality, and some of them, such as Mary Dyer, became exceptional preachers, even martyrs. Women held their own formal meetings and made important decisions about discipline and betrothals. Quaker reforms also affected children, whom most Protestants saw as tiny sinners whose wills must be broken by severe discipline. But once Quakers stopped worrying about original sin, their children became innocents in whom the Light would shine if only they could be protected from worldly corruption. In America, Quakers created affectionate families, built larger houses than non-Quakers with equivalent resources, and worked hard to acquire land for all of their children. Earlier than other Christians, they began to limit family size to give more love to the children they did have. Once the missionary impulse faded, they seldom associated with non-Quakers. The needs of their own children became paramount. To marry an outsider meant expulsion from the Society, a fate more likely to befall poor Friends than rich ones.

Persecution in England helped drive Quakers across the ocean, but the need to provide for their children was another powerful motive for emigration. By 1700, about half of the Quakers in England and Wales had moved to America.

West New Jersey

In 1674, the New Jersey proprietors split their holding into two colonies. Sir George Carteret claimed what he now called East New Jersey, a province near New York City with half a dozen towns populated by Baptist, Quaker, Puritan, and Dutch Reformed settlers. Lord Berkeley claimed West New Jersey and promptly sold it to some Quakers, who then founded two colonies in America: West New Jersey and Pennsylvania. In the 1680s, Quakers bought out the proprietor of East New Jersey and also gained power in Delaware (formerly New Sweden). They seemed poised to dominate the entire region between Maryland and New York. Two of the organizers were Edward Byllinge, a social radical from the 1650s, and William Penn, an admirer of Harrington.

In 1676, Byllinge drafted a document, the West New Jersey Concessions and Agreements, which the first settlers approved in 1677. It lodged legislative power in a unicameral assembly, elected by secret ballot, and it empowered voters to instruct their representatives. In the court system, juries would decide both fact and law. Judges would merely preside over the court and, if asked by a juror, offer advice. Although the document was never fully implemented, it made West Jersey the most radical political experiment attempted in America before the Revolution. West Jersey Quakers believed that godly people could live together in love—without war, lawyers, or internal conflict. They kept government close to the people, made land easy to acquire, and promised freedom of worship to everyone. In the 1680s, lawsuits often ended with one litigant forgiving the other, and criminal trials sometimes closed with the victim embracing the perpetrator. But as social and religious diversity grew, the system broke down. Non-Quakers increasingly refused to

Library of Congress, Prints and Photographs Division

William Penn in Armor The son of an English admiral, William Penn was not always a pacifist. In the 1660s, an unknown artist painted him in this military pose. After his conversion to the Society of Friends, Penn paid a steep price for his religious convictions. Accused of blasphemy, he was imprisoned in the Tower of London from December 1668 to July 1669.

cooperate. In the 1690s, the courts became impotent, and Quaker rule collapsed. The Crown took over the colony, and East New Jersey, in 1702.

Pennsylvania

By 1681, Quaker attention was already shifting to the west bank of the Delaware River. There, **William Penn** launched a much larger, if rather more cautious, "holy experiment" in brotherly love. The son of a Commonwealth admiral, Penn grew up surrounded by privilege. He knew well both Charles II and the duke of York, attended Oxford and the **Inns of Court** (England's law schools), went on the grand tour of Europe, and began to manage his father's Irish estates. Then something happened that embarrassed his family. "Mr. William Pen," reported a neighbor in December 1667, "is a Quaker again, or some very melancholy thing." Penn often traveled to the continent on behalf of the Society of

Map 2.8 Early Pennsylvania and New Jersey, circa 1700 This map shows the first three counties of Pennsylvania and its capital of Philadelphia, the three counties of what would soon become Delaware, the colony of West New Jersey and its capital of Burlington, and the early towns of East New Jersey including its capital of Perth Amboy.

Friends, winning converts and recruiting settlers in the Netherlands and Germany. In England he was jailed several times for his beliefs.

A gentleman and a Quaker, Penn was no ordinary colonizer. Using his contacts at court, he converted an old debt (owed to his father by the king) into a charter for a proprietary colony that Charles named Pennsylvania in honor of the deceased admiral. The emerging imperial bureaucracy disliked the whole project and, after failing to block it, inserted several restrictions into the charter. Penn agreed to enforce the Navigation Acts (see chapter 3), to let the Crown approve his choice of governor, to submit all legislation to the English Privy Council for approval, and to allow appeals from Pennsylvania courts to the Privy Council in England. Contemporaries said little about the most striking innovation attempted by Quaker colonists. They entered America unarmed. Pennsylvanians did not even organize a militia until the 1740s. Friendly relations with Indians were essential to the project's success, and Penn was careful to deal fairly with the Lenni Lenape, or Delaware Indians.

More thought went into planning Pennsylvania than into the creation of any other colony. Twenty drafts survive of Penn's First Frame of Government, his 1682 constitution for the province. It evolved from what was a larger version of the West Jersey Concessions and Agreements into something more Harringtonian but still quite liberating. The settlers would elect a council of 72 men to staggered three-year terms. The council would draft all legislation and submit copies to the voters. In the early years, the voters would meet to approve or reject these bills in person. Penn anticipated that as the province expanded, such meetings would become impractical. Voters would then elect an assembly of 200, which would increase gradually to 500, about the size of the House of Commons, although for a much smaller population. Government would still remain close to the people. Penn gave up the power to veto bills but retained control of the distribution of land. Capital punishment was abolished for crimes against property and most other offenses, except murder. Religious liberty, trial by jury, and habeas corpus all received strong guarantees.

Settlers had been arriving in Pennsylvania for a year when Penn landed in 1682 with his First Frame of Government. Some lived in caves along the river. Others, imitating the nearby Swedes, built log cabins. The colonists persuaded Penn that the First Frame was too cumbersome for a small colony, and the first legislature worked with him to devise a simpler government. In what became known as the Second Frame, or the Pennsylvania Charter of Liberties of 1683, the council was reduced to 18 men and the assembly to 36. The assembly's Harrington-inspired inability to initiate legislation soon became a grievance.

Penn laid out Philadelphia as "a green country town" and organized other settlements. Although an idealist, he hoped that land sales and other revenues would provide a handsome support for his family. Then, in 1684, he returned to England to answer Lord Baltimore's complaint that Philadelphia fell within the charter boundaries of Maryland, a claim that was soon verified. This dispute troubled the Penn family until the 1760s, when the Mason-Dixon line finally established the modern boundary.

In England, persecution had kept Quaker antiauthoritarianism in check, at least in relations with other Friends. In the colony, these attitudes soon became public. Penn expected his settlers to defer to the leaders among them. He created the Free Society of Traders to control commerce with England and gave high offices to its members. From the start, however, wealth in Pennsylvania rested on trade with other colonies, especially in the Caribbean, more than with England. That trade was dominated by Quakers from Barbados, Jamaica, New York, and Boston. These men owed little to Penn and became an opposition faction in the colony. They and others demanded more land, especially in Philadelphia. They claimed that they could not afford to pay Penn's **quitrents,** and they quarreled more often than was seemly for men of brotherly love. In exasperation, Penn finally appointed John Blackwell, an old Cromwellian soldier, as governor in 1688, ordering him to end the quarrels and collect quitrents but to rule "tenderly." Boys jeered Blackwell as he tried to enter Penn's Philadelphia house, and the council refused to let him use the colony's great seal. Debate in the legislature became angrier than ever. After 13 months, Blackwell resigned. Each Quaker, he complained, "prayed for the rest on the First Day [of the week], and preyed on them the other six." Because Penn had supported James II in England, he lost control of the colony between 1691 and 1693.

In 1691, the Society of Friends suffered a brief schism in the Delaware valley. A Quaker schoolteacher, George Keith, urged all Quakers to systematize their beliefs and even wrote his own catechism, only to encounter the opposition of the public friends, who included the colony's major officeholders. When he attacked them directly, he was convicted and fined for abusing civil officers. He claimed that he was being persecuted for his religious beliefs, but the courts insisted that his only crime was his attack on public authority. In contrast to Massachusetts in the 1630s, no one was banished, and Pennsylvania remained a haven for all religions. The colony's government changed several more times before 1701, when Penn and the assembly finally agreed on the Fourth Frame, or Charter of Privileges, which gave Pennsylvania a unicameral legislature, but its politics remained turbulent and unstable into the 1720s.

Despite these controversies, Pennsylvania quickly became an economic success, well established in the Caribbean trade as an exporter of wheat and flour. Quaker families were thriving, and the colony's policy of religious liberty attracted thousands of outsiders. Some were German pacifists who shared the major goals of the Society of Friends. Others were Anglicans and Presbyterians who warned London that Quakers were unfit to rule—anywhere.

Conclusion

In the 16th century, France, the Netherlands, and England all challenged Spanish power in Europe and across the ocean. After 1600, all three founded their own colonies in North America and the Caribbean. New France became a land of missionaries and traders and developed close ties of cooperation with most nearby Indians. New Netherland also was founded to participate in the fur trade. Both colonies slowly acquired an agricultural base.

The English, by contrast, desired the land itself. They founded colonies of settlement that threatened nearby Indians, except in the Delaware valley, where Quakers insisted on peaceful relations. The southern mainland and Caribbean colonies produced staple crops for sale in Europe, first with the labor of indentured servants and then with enslaved Africans. The Puritan and Quaker colonies became smaller versions of England's mixed economy, with an emphasis on family farms. Maintaining the fervor of the founders was a problem for both. After conquering New Netherland, England controlled the Atlantic seaboard from Maine to South Carolina, and by 1700 the population of England's mainland colonies was doubling every 25 years. England was beginning to emerge as the biggest winner in the competition for empire.

SUGGESTED READINGS

W. J. Eccles, *The French in North America, 1500-1783,* rev. ed. (1998) is a concise and author-itative survey. C. R. Boxer, *The Dutch Seaborne Empire, 1600–1800* (1965) is still the best syn-thesis of Dutch activity overseas. Joyce E. Chaplin's *Subject Matter: Technology, the Body, and Science on the Anglo-American Frontier, 1500-1676* (2001), and Karen O. Kupperman, *Indians and English: Facing Off in Early America* (2000) are efforts to keep Indians and the settlers of early Virginia and New England within a common focus. Edmund S. Morgan's *American Slavery, American Freedom: The Ordeal of Colonial Virginia* (1975) has become a classic. Thad W. Tate and David L. Ammerman, eds., *The Chesapeake in the Seventeenth-Century: Essays on Anglo-American Society* (1979) is also indispensable. For the West Indies, see Richard S. Dunn, *Sugar and Slaves: The Rise of the Planter Class in the English West Indies, 1624–1713* (1972). Winthrop Jordan's *White over Black: American Attitudes toward the Negro, 1550–1812* (1968) retains its freshness and acuity.

Edmund S. Morgan's *Visible Saints: The History of a Puritan Idea* (1963) is a brief and acces-sible introduction to Puritan values in New England's first century. Michael G. Winship's *Mak-ing Heretics: Militant Protestantism and Free Grace in Massachusetts, 1636–1641* (2002) brings a challenging new perspective to the Anne Hutchinson crisis. Carla G. Pestana's *Quakers and Bap-tists in Colonial Massachusetts* (1991) deals with the principal dissenters from the New England Way. Daniel Vickers, *Farmers and Fishermen: Two Centuries of Work in Essex County, Massa-chusetts, 1630–1850* (1994) is an outstanding introduction to the New England economy.

For the Restoration colonies, see especially Robert C. Ritchie, *The Duke's Province: A Study of New York Politics and Society, 1664–1691* (1977); Gary B. Nash, *Quakers and Politics: Penn-sylvania Politics, 1681–1726* (1968); Barry J. Levy, *Quakers and the American Family: British Settlement in the Delaware Valley* (1988); Peter H. Wood, *Black Majority: Negroes in Colonial South Carolina from 1670 through the Stono Rebellion* (1974); and Alan Gallay, *The Indian Slave Trade: The Rise of the English Empire in the American South, 1670–1717* (2002).

Visit the Liberty Equality Power Companion Web site for resources specific to this textbook: http://www.thomsonedu.com/history/murrin

Also find self-tests and additional resources at ThomsonNOW. ThomsonNOW is an integrated online suite of services and resources with proven ease of use and efficient paths to success, delivering the results you want-NOW!

www.thomsonedu.com/login/

3

England Discovers Its Colonies: Empire, Liberty, and Expansion

In 1603, England was still a weak power on the fringes of Europe. By 1700, England was a global giant. It possessed 20 colonies in North America and the Caribbean, controlled much of the African slave trade, and had muscled its way into distant India. Commerce and colonies had vastly magnified England's power. This transformation occurred during a century of political and religious upheaval at home. King and Parliament fought over their respective powers—a long struggle that led to civil war and the execution of one king in 1649 and to the overthrow of another in 1688. It produced a unique constitution that rested on parliamentary supremacy and responsible government under the Crown.

By 1700, England and the colonies had begun to converge around the newly defined principles of English constitutionalism. All of them had adopted representative governments. All affirmed the values of liberty and property under the English Crown. The sheer diversity of the colonies daunted anyone who hoped to govern them. The colonies formed not a single type, but a spectrum of settlement with contrasting economies, social relationships, and institutions. Yet by 1700, England had created a system of regulation that respected colonial liberties while asserting imperial power.

The Atlantic Prism and the Spectrum of Settlement

Over thousands of years, the Indians of the Americas had become diversified into hundreds of distinct cultures and languages. The colonists of 17th-century North America and the Caribbean were following much the same course. America divided them. The Atlantic united them. Their connection with England gave them what unity they could sustain.

As long as population remained small, no colony could duplicate the complexity of England. The settlers had to choose what to bring with them and what to leave behind, what they could provide for themselves and what they would have to import—choices dictated both by their motives for crossing the ocean and by what the new environment would permit. The colonists sorted themselves out along a vast arc from the cold North to the subtropical Caribbean. If we can imagine England as a source of white light and the Atlantic as a prism refracting that light, 17th-century America becomes a spectrum of settlement, with

CHRONOLOGY

1642	Civil war erupts in England • Miantonomo abandons planned war of extermination
1643	New England Confederation created
1644	Opechancanough's second massacre in Virginia
1649	England becomes a commonwealth
1651	Parliament passes first Navigation Act
1652–54	First Anglo-Dutch War
1660	Charles II restored to English throne • Parliament passes new Navigation Act
1662	Charles II grants Rhode Island Charter
1663	Staple Act passed • Charles II grants Connecticut Charter
1664	England conquers New Netherland
1673	Plantation Duty Act passed • Dutch retake New York for 15 months
1675	Lords of Trade established • Metacom's War breaks out in New England
1676	Bacon's Rebellion breaks out in Virginia
1678	Popish Plot crisis begins in England
1680	Pueblos revolt in New Mexico
1684	Massachusetts Charter revoked
1685	Louis XIV revokes Edict of Nantes
1686	Dominion of New England established
1688–89	Glorious Revolution occurs in England
1689	Anglo-French wars begin • Glorious Revolution spreads to Massachusetts, New York, and Maryland
1691	Leisler executed in New York
1692	Nineteen people hanged for witchcraft in Salem
1696	Parliament passes comprehensive Navigation Act • Board of Trade replaces Lords of Trade
1699	French establish Louisiana • Woolens Act passed
1701	Iroquois make peace with New France
1702–04	Carolina slavers destroy Florida missions
1707	Anglo-Scottish union creates kingdom of Great Britain
1713	Britain and France make peace
1714	George I ascends British throne
1715	Yamasee War devastates South Carolina

each color merging imperceptibly into the shade next to it. Each province had much in common with its neighbors but shared few traits with more distant colonies.

Demographic Differences

The most pronounced differences involved life expectancy, the sex ratio (the ratio of men to women in any society), and family structure. At one extreme were buccaneers, the all-male, multiethnic societies in the Caribbean that lived only for plunder. In the sugar colonies, European men often died by age 40, and slaves even sooner. Because female settlers were scarce at first, even the family seemed an endangered institution. Even when the sex ratio evened out and families began to emerge, couples had few children. Life expectancy in early South Carolina was slightly better than in the islands, slightly lower than in the Chesapeake Bay area. In Virginia and Maryland, men who survived childhood diseases lived to an average age of about 45 years during the last half of the 17th century, still less than in England, where life expectancy exceeded 50. Then, as natural increase replaced immigration as the main source of population growth after 1680, women became more numerous, married much earlier, and raised larger families.

The northern colonies were much healthier. In the Delaware valley, a man who reached adulthood could expect to live past 60. In New Netherland, life expectancy and family size exceeded Europe's by 1660, and men outnumbered women among the newcomers by only 2 to 1. On Long Island in the 1680s, one woman claimed that she had more than 300 living descendants. New England was one of the healthiest places in the world. Because the sex ratio rapidly approached equality and because the thriving economy permitted couples to marry perhaps two years earlier than in England, population exploded. Canada followed a similar pattern. In the late 17th century, the birthrate in New France caught up with New England's, and population grew at a comparable pace.

These demographic differences had major consequences. For example, the Caribbean and southern colonies were youthful societies in which men with good connections could expect to achieve high office while in their 30s, or even 20s. By contrast, the New England colonies gradually became dominated by grandfathers. A man rarely became even a selectman by age 40. Despite the appalling death rate in the sugar and tobacco colonies, young men remained optimistic and upbeat, as they looked forward to challenging the world and making their fortunes. In New England, people grew more despondent as the century progressed, even though they lived much longer. After 1660, the typical sermon was a gloomy jeremiad that deplored the failings of the rising generation.

Race, Ethnicity, and Economy

The degree of racial and ethnic mixture also varied from region to region, along with economic priorities. The West Indies already had a large slave majority by 1700, when English settlers were still a clear majority in the southern mainland colonies, but African slaves became a majority in South Carolina around 1710. They would comprise 40 percent of Virginia's population

The Spectrum of Settlement: Demography, Ethnicity, Economy, 1650–1700

Category	West Indies	Lower South	Chesapeake	Mid-Atlantic	New England	New France
Life expectancy for men, age 20	40	42	45	60+	Late 60s	60s
Family size	Below replacement rate	About two children	Rising after 1680	Very large	Very large	Very large
Race and ethnicity	Black majority by circa 1670s	Black majority by circa 1710	Growing black minority	Ethnic mix, N.W. Europe, English a minority	Almost all English	Almost all French
Economy	Sugar	Rice, 1690s ff	Tobacco	Furs, farms	Farms, fishing, shipbuilding	Furs, farms

The Spectrum of Settlement: Religion and Government, Circa 1675–1700

Category	West Indies	Lower South	Chesapeake	Mid-Atlantic	New England	New France
Formal religion	Anglican Church establishment	Anglican Church establishment by circa 1710	Anglican Church establishment (after 1692 in Md.)	Competing sects, no established church	Congregational Church established	Catholic Church established
Religious tone	Irreverent	Contentious	Low-church Anglican	Family-based piety, sectarian competition	Family-based piety, intensity declining	Intensely Catholic
Local government	Parish	Parish and phantom counties (i.e., no court)	County and parish	County and township	Towns and counties; parishes after 1700	Cities
Provincial government	Royal	Proprietary	Royal (Va.), proprietary (Md.)	From proprietary to royal, except in Pa.	Corporate, with Mass. and N. H. becoming royal	Royal absolutism

by the 1730s. Africans were less numerous in the Delaware and Hudson valleys, although slavery became deeply entrenched in New York City and parts of New Jersey.

In the mid-Atlantic region, settlers from all over northwestern Europe were creating a new ethnic mosaic. English colonists were probably always a minority, outnumbered at first by the Dutch, and later by Germans, Scots, and Irish, but New England was in every sense the most English of the colonies. New France was as French as New England was English. The farther south one went, the more diverse the population; the farther north, the more uniform.

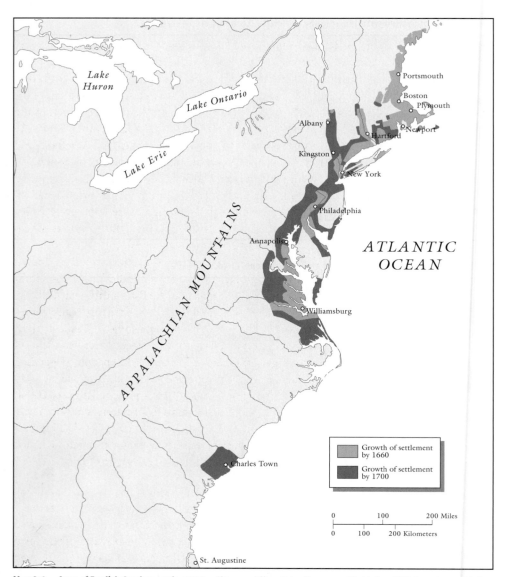

Map 3.1   Area of English Settlement by 1700   This map differentiates the areas settled before 1660 from those settled between 1660 and 1700, or roughly the Restoration era.

Slavery and staple crops went together. The slave societies raised sugar, rice, or tobacco for sale in Europe. General farming and family labor also went together. By 1700, the mid-Atlantic was the wheat belt of North America. New Englanders farmed and exported fish, livestock, and lumber to the West Indies.

Religion and Education

The intensity of religious observance varied immensely across the spectrum of settlement, ranging from irreverence and indifference in the West Indies to intense piety in New England and New France. Literacy followed a similar pattern. Colonists everywhere tried to prevent slaves from learning to read, and low literacy prevailed wherever slavery predominated. Chesapeake settlers provided almost no formal schooling for their children before the founding of the College of William and Mary in 1693 and of a Latin grammar school in Annapolis at about the same time. Even some of the justices of the peace in Maryland and Virginia were unable to write. By contrast, the Dutch maintained several good schools in New Netherland. Massachusetts founded Harvard College in 1636, and in 1642 required every town to have a writing school, and larger towns to support a Latin grammar school. In New France a seminary (now Laval University) was established in the 1660s, but lay literacy remained low in rural communities. Along the spectrum, piety, literacy, and education generally grew stronger from south to north.

Public support for the clergy followed the same pattern. By 1710, the established church of the mother country was the legally established church in the West Indies and in the southern mainland colonies. Establishment and dissent fought to a standstill in the mid-Atlantic, with toleration claiming the real victory in New York and full religious liberty in Pennsylvania. In New England, Old World dissent became the New World establishment. Public support for the clergy was much greater in the north than in the south. The sugar islands had the most wealth, but they maintained only one clergyman for every 3,000 to 9,000 people, depending on the island and the decade. In the Chesapeake, the comparable ratio was about one for every 1,500 people by 1700. It was perhaps one for every 1,000 in New York, one for every 600 in New England, and still lower in New France. Moral standards also rose from south to north. New Englanders boasted that they were far more godly than all other colonists. The Puritans "give out that they are Israelites," reported a Dutch visitor to Connecticut, "and that we in our colony are Egyptians, and that the English in the Virginias are also Egyptians."

Local and Provincial Governments

Forms of government also varied. Drawing on their English experience, settlers could choose from among parishes, boroughs (towns), and counties. The only important local institution in the sugar islands and in South Carolina was the parish, which took on many secular functions, such as poor relief. The Chesapeake colonies relied primarily on the county but also made increasing use of the parish. Few parishes were ever organized in the mid-Atlantic colonies, but county government arrived with the English conquest of New Netherland in 1664 and became a powerful institution. Townships also appeared. New England's most basic local institution was the town. Massachusetts created counties in the 1640s, followed 20 years later by Connecticut and in the 1680s by Plymouth. Rhode Island and New Hampshire waited until the 18th century before creating counties. After 1700, towns large enough to support more than one church also adopted the parish system. In local government as in its economy, New England's use of the full range of parishes, towns, and counties made the region more fully English than other colonies.

The West Indian colonies all had royal governments by the 1660s. Proprietary forms dominated the mainland south of New England, except for royal Virginia. Until the 1680s, New England relied on corporate forms of government in which all officials, even governors, were elected. This system survived in Connecticut and Rhode Island through independence.

Unifying Trends: Language, War, Law, and Inheritance

Despite this diversity, a few unifying trends emerged in the 17th century. For instance, language became more uniform in America than in England. True, the New England dialect derived mostly from East Anglia, the southern accent from southern and western England, and mid-Atlantic speech from north-central England. But Londoners went to all of the colonies (in England, people went to London), and London English affected every colony and softened the contrasts among the emerging regional dialects.

Another area of uniformity was the manner in which the settlers waged war: They did it in their own way, not with the professional armies that were just taking hold in Europe, but with short-term volunteers for whom terror against Indian women and children was often the tactic of choice. Europe was moving toward limited wars; the colonists demanded quick and total victories.

Law became a simpler version of England's complex legal system. Justice was local and uncomplicated—in fact, an organized legal profession did not emerge until the 18th century. The absence of lawyers pleased most settlers. Also, no mainland American colony rigidly followed English patterns of inheritance. Instead, the colonies were developing their own practices. Some women had a chance to acquire property, usually by inheritance from a deceased husband, particularly in the Chesapeake colonies during the long period when men greatly outnumbered women. The single women who crossed the Atlantic as servants were desperate people who had hit bottom in England. Those who survived enjoyed a fantastic chance at upward mobility. By marrying landowners, many won a respectability that was never available to them in England. In every colony, younger sons also found their situation improved. They played a huge role in settling the colonies, especially among the Chesapeake elite, and they showed little inclination to preserve institutions that had offered them no landed inheritance in England. Most families made no distinction between the eldest and other sons, except in New England, where the eldest son received a double share.

The Beginnings of Empire

In the chaotic 1640s, the English realized that their colonies overseas were bringing them few benefits. England had no coherent colonial policy.

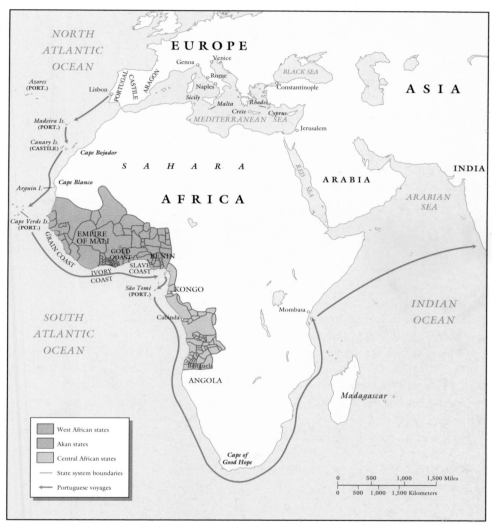

Map 1.3 Africa and the Mediterranean in the 15th Century The Mediterranean islands held by Europeans in the late Middle Ages, the Atlantic islands colonized by Portugal and Spain in the 15th century, the part of West Africa from Cape Blanco to Angola that provided the main suppliers of the Atlantic slave trade, and the Portuguese all-water route to India after 1497. View an animated version of this map or related maps at http://www.thomsonedu.com/history/murrin.

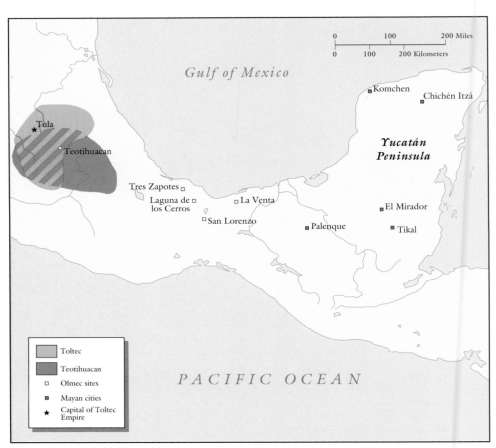

Map 1.5   Ancient Mesoamerica   The location of the three principal Olmec cities, Teotihuacan, several major Mayan cities, and the Toltec capital of Tula.

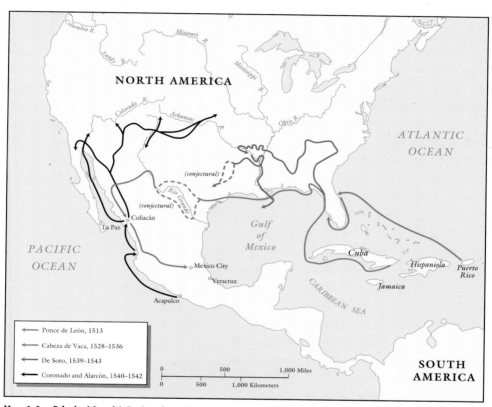

Map 1.9   Principal Spanish Explorations of North America   Four Spanish expeditions marched through much of the interior of North America between 1513 and 1543.

View an animated version of this map or related maps at http://www.thomsonedu.com/history/murrin.

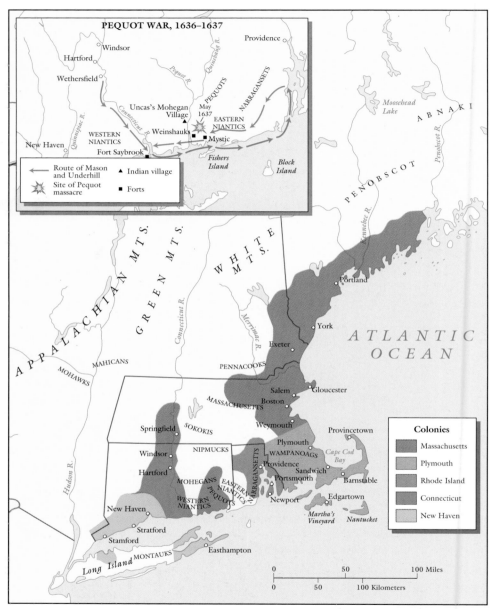

PEQUOT WAR, 1636–1637

Providence

Windsor

Hartford

Wethersfield

PEQUOTS

NARRAGANSETS

Uncas's Mohegan Village

May 1637

EASTERN NIANTICS

New Haven

WESTERN NIANTICS

Weinshauks

Mystic

Fort Saybrook

Fishers Island

Block Island

→ Route of Mason and Underhill
✶ Site of Pequot massacre
▲ Indian village
■ Forts

Moosehead Lake

ABNAKI

PENOBSCOT

Portland

WHITE MTS.

GREEN MTS.

APPALACHIAN MTS.

MAHICANS

MOHAWKS

PENNACOOKS

York

ATLANTIC OCEAN

Exeter

Salem

Gloucester

MASSACHUSETTS

Boston

Springfield

SOKOKIS

Weymouth

Windsor

NIPMUCKS

Provincetown

Plymouth

WAMPANOAGS

Cape Cod Bay

Hartford

MOHEGANS

EASTERN NIANTICS

NARRAGANSETS

Providence

Sandwich

Portsmouth

Barnstable

PEQUOTS

WESTERN NIANTICS

Newport

Edgartown

New Haven

Stratford

Stamford

Easthampton

Martha's Vineyard

Nantucket

Long Island

MONTAUKS

Colonies

- Massachusetts
- Plymouth
- Rhode Island
- Connecticut
- New Haven

0   50   100 Miles

0   50   100 Kilometers

Map 2.6 New England in the 1640s The five Puritan colonies spread over the Atlantic coast and nearby islands, the shores and islands of Narragansett Bay, both sides of Long Island Sound, and much of the Connecticut Valley. Although New Hampshire and Maine (not named as such on this map) were not founded by Puritans, Massachusetts extended its government over their settlers during the English civil wars. The insert map shows the principal military campaign of the Pequot War.

Upheaval in America: The Critical 1640s

England's civil wars rocked its emerging empire, politically and economically. As royal power collapsed in the 1640s, the West Indian colonies demanded and received elective assemblies. The Dutch took advantage of the chaos in England to finance much of the sugar revolution in Barbados and seize control of trade in and out of England's West Indian and Chesapeake colonies. By 1650, most sugar and tobacco exports were going to Amsterdam, not London.

During the civil wars, nobody in England exercised effective control over the colonies. The king had declared that their trade was to remain in English hands, but no agency existed to enforce that policy. The new elective assemblies of Barbados and the Leeward Islands preferred to trade with the Dutch, even after the English Crown took over those colonies in 1660. The mainland colonies already governed themselves. As the New England settlements expanded, the new colonies of Connecticut, Rhode Island, and New Haven did not even bother to obtain royal charters. On the mainland, only Virginia had a royal governor.

The chaos of the 1640s gave Indians a unique opportunity to resist the settlers. As civil war disrupted trade with England and threatened to cut off regular supplies of muskets and gunpowder, the Indians gained a powerful advantage over the settlements. That danger seemed so ominous that Rhode Island ordered young men to learn how to use bows and arrows. Although the Indians of the eastern woodlands never united into an effective league, many of them, such as Miantonomo in New England and Opechancanough in Virginia, began to think of driving the Europeans out altogether.

Indians greatly outnumbered settlers, except in eastern New England and the Virginia tidewater. Between 1643 and 1647, the Iroquois nearly wiped out New France, and the Hudson valley Algonquians almost destroyed New Netherland. Maryland, beset by conflicts with Susquehannock Indians and by civil war among its colonists, nearly ceased to exist. The number of settlers there may have fallen to 300 by 1648. In Virginia, the aging warrior Opechancanough staged another massacre, killing 500 settlers without warning on a holy day in 1644. This time the settlers recovered more quickly, took Opechancanough prisoner in 1646, and murdered him. They broke up his chiefdom and imposed treaties of dependency on its member tribes.

Only New England avoided war with the Indians—just barely. Miantonomo, sachem of the Narragansetts, called for a war of extermination against the settlers, to be launched by a surprise attack in 1642. He abandoned the plan after settlers got wind of it. The colonists created their own defensive alliance in 1643, the New England Confederation, which united the four orthodox colonies of Massachusetts, Plymouth, Connecticut, and New Haven. Rhode Island was not invited to join. The confederation persuaded the Mohegans to kill Miantonomo, and tensions with the Narragansett Indians remained high. The Narragansetts controlled some of the finest land in New England. Massachusetts, Plymouth, and Connecticut all wanted that land, but the Narragansetts were still too powerful to intimidate.

What happened in the colonies seemed of little interest to the English people in the turbulent 1640s. Later, as the debris of civil war was cleared away and the extent of Dutch commercial domination became obvious, the English turned their eyes westward once again. In a sense, England first discovered its colonies and their importance around 1650.

Mercantilism as a Moral Revolution

Focus Question
How important was England's mercantilistic system in gaining effective control over the colonies and in projecting English power against its European rivals?

During the 17th century, most European powers followed a set of policies now usually called **mercantilism.** Mercantilists argued that power derived ultimately from the wealth of a country, that the increase of wealth required vigorous trade, and that colonies had become essential to that growth. Clearly, a state had to control the commerce of its colonies, but mercantilists disagreed over the best ways to promote growth. The Dutch favored virtual free trade within Europe, whereas England preferred some kind of state regulation of the domestic and imperial economy.

A century of seemingly endless religious wars, driven by the quest for glory and the love of holy causes, had crippled Spain, killed one-third of the German people, and nearly destroyed the English state. As time passed, statesmen began to look more favorably upon a very different emotion—greed, a passion in which they found interesting properties. The pursuit of glory or love inspires intense but unpredictable activity, followed by relaxation or even exhaustion. Greed, because it is insatiable, fosters *predictable* behavior—namely, the pursuit of self-interest, a softer term than greed and one that most people preferred to use. By creating economic incentives, then, a state could induce its people to work to increase not only their own wealth and power but also that of the whole country. Likewise, by imposing import duties and other disincentives, the state could discourage actions detrimental to its power.

At first, these ideas were as gloomy as the world in which they arose. Early mercantilists assumed that the world contained a fixed supply of wealth. A state, to augment its own power, would have to expropriate the wealth of a rival. Trade wars would replace religious wars, although presumably they would be less destructive, which they usually were. Gradually, however, a more radical idea took hold: The growth of trade might multiply the wealth of the whole world, with all nations benefiting and becoming so interdependent that war between them would be recognized as suicidal. That vision of peace and unending growth has never been realized, but it still inspires people today.

Mercantilism marked a major breakthrough toward modernity. It gradually became associated with the emerging idea of unending progress, and it made statesmen rethink the role of legislation in their societies. Europeans were already familiar with two kinds of progress, one associated with Renaissance humanism, and the other explicitly Christian. The opening of the Americas had already reinforced both visions. Humanists knew that the distant ancestors of Europeans had all been "barbarians" who had advanced over the centuries toward "civility." Their own encounters with the indigenous peoples of Africa, Ireland, and America underscored this dualistic view by revealing new "savages" who seemed morally and culturally inferior to the "civilized" colonists. Most Christians shared these convictions, but they also believed that human society was progressing toward a future millennium in which Christ will return to earth and reign with his saints in perfect harmony for 1,000 years. To missionaries, both Catholic and Protestant, the discovery of millions of **heathens** in the Americas stimulated millennial thinking. God had chosen this moment to open a new hemisphere to Christians, they explained, because the millennium was near.

Both the humanist and the Christian notions of progress were static concepts, however. Humanity would advance to a certain level, and progress would cease. Mercantilism, by contrast, marked a revolution of the human imagination precisely because it could arouse visions of endless progress. Mercantilists also developed a more modern concept of law, which they saw as a way to change society, not merely as a means of clarifying old customs or reducing natural laws to written texts.

The First Navigation Act

English merchants began debating trade policy during a severe depression in the 1620s. They agreed that a nation's wealth depended on its **balance of trade,** that a healthy nation ought to export more than it imports, and that the difference—or balance—could be converted into military strength. They also believed that a state needed colonies to produce essential commodities unavailable at home. And they argued that a society ought to export luxuries, not import them. For England to catch up with the Dutch, Parliament would have to intervene. London merchants clamored for measures to stifle Dutch competition. Parliament listened to them, not to Oliver Cromwell and other Puritans who regarded war between two Protestant republics as an abomination. The merchants got their Navigation Act—and their naval war.

In 1650, Parliament banned foreign ships from English colonies. A year later, it passed the first comprehensive Navigation Act, aimed at Dutch competition. Under this law, Asian and African goods could be imported into the British Isles or the colonies only in English-owned ships, and the master and at least half of each crew had to be Englishmen. European goods could be imported into Britain or the colonies in either English ships or the ships of the producing country, but foreigners could not trade between one English port and another.

This new attention from the English government angered the colonists in the West Indies and North America. Mercantilists assumed that the colonies existed only to enrich the mother country. Why else had England permitted them to be founded? But the young men growing sugar in Barbados or tobacco in Virginia hoped to prosper on their own. Selling their crops to the Dutch, who offered the lowest freight rates, added to their profits. Although New England produced no staple that Europeans wanted except fish, Yankee skippers cheerfully swapped their fish or forest products in the Chesapeake for tobacco, which they then carried directly to Europe, usually to Amsterdam.

Barbados greeted the Navigation Act by proclaiming virtual independence. Virginia recognized Charles II as king and continued to welcome Dutch and Yankee traders. In 1651, Parliament dispatched a naval force to America. It compelled Barbados to submit to Parliament and then sailed to the Chesapeake, where Virginia and Maryland capitulated in 1652. But without resident officials to enforce English policy, trade with the Dutch continued.

Soon England and the Netherlands were at war, the first of three Anglo-Dutch conflicts between 1652 and 1674. For two years the English navy dealt heavy blows to the Dutch. Finally, in 1654, Cromwell sent Parliament home and made peace. A militant Protestant, he preferred to fight Catholic Spain rather than the Netherlands. He sent a fleet that failed to take Hispaniola, but it seized Jamaica in 1655.

Restoration Navigation Acts

By the Restoration era, mercantilist thinking had become widespread. Although the new royalist Parliament invalidated all legislation passed during the Commonwealth period, these Cavaliers promptly reenacted and extended the original Navigation Act in a series of new measures. The Navigation Act of 1660 required that all colonial trade be carried on English ships (a category that included colonial vessels but now excluded the Scots), but the master and *three-fourths* of the crew had to be English. The act also created a category of **enumerated commodities,** of which sugar and tobacco were the most important, permitting these products to be shipped from the colony of origin *only* to England or to another English colony—the intent being to give England a monopoly over the export of major staples from every English colony to Europe and to the rest of the world. The colonists could still export nonenumerated commodities elsewhere. New England could send fish to a French sugar island, for example, and Virginia could export wheat to Cuba, provided the French and the Spanish would let them. In a second measure, the Staple Act of 1663, Parliament regulated goods going to the colonies. With few exceptions, products from Europe or Asia had to land in England before they could be delivered to the settlements. A third measure, the Plantation Duty Act of 1673, required captains of colonial ships to post bond in the colonies that they would deliver all enumerated commodities to England, or else pay on the spot the duties that would be owed in England (the "plantation duty"). This measure, England hoped, would eliminate all incentives to smuggle. To make it effective, England for the first time sent customs officers to the colonies to collect the duty and prosecute violators. They won little compliance at first.

Parliament intended nothing less than a revolution in Atlantic trade. Properly enforced, the Navigation Acts would dislodge the Dutch and establish England's hegemony over its Atlantic trade, and that is what happened in the next half-century. In 1600, about 90 percent of England's exports consisted of woolen cloth. By 1700, colonial and Asian commerce accounted for 30 to 40 percent of England's overseas trade, and London had become the largest city in Western Europe. Its population tripled during the 17th century.

Enforcement long remained uneven, but in the 1670s, a war between France and the Netherlands diverted critical Dutch resources from trade to defense, thus helping England catch up with the Dutch. By 1700, Britain had the most powerful navy in the world. By 1710 or so, virtually all British colonial trade was carried on British ships. Sugar, tobacco, and other staple crops all passed through Britain on their way to their ultimate destination. Nearly all of the manufactured goods consumed in the colonies were made in Britain. Most products from Europe or Asia destined for the colonies passed through Britain first, although some smuggling of these goods continued.

Few government policies have ever been as successful as England's Navigation Acts, but England achieved these results without pursuing a steady course toward increased imperial control. For example, in granting charters to Rhode Island in 1662 and to Connecticut in 1663, Charles II approved elective governors and legislatures in both colonies. (The Connecticut charter also absorbed the New Haven Colony into the Hartford government.) These elective officials could not be dismissed or punished for failure to enforce the Navigation Acts. Moreover, the Crown also chartered several new Restoration colonies (see chapter 2), whose organizers had few incentives to obey the new laws. Making the empire work would take time.

Indians, Settlers, Upheaval

As time passed, the commercial possibilities and limitations of North America were becoming much clearer. The French and Dutch mastered the fur trade because they controlled the two all-water routes from the Atlantic to the interior, via the St. Lawrence system and the Hudson and Mohawk rivers. South Carolinians could go around the southern extreme of the Appalachians. They all needed Indian trading partners.

As of 1670, no sharp boundaries yet existed between Indian lands and colonial settlements. Boston, the largest city north of Mexico, was only 15 miles from an Indian village. The outposts on the Delaware River were islands in a sea of Indians. In the event of war, nearly every European settlement was vulnerable to attack.

Indian Strategies of Survival

Focus Question
Contrast the failure of New England and Virginia to preserve peaceful relations with neighboring Indians in 1675–76 with New York's success in the same decade and later.

By the 1670s, most coastal tribes had already been devastated by disease or soon would be. European diseases, by magnifying the depleted tribes' need for captives, greatly increased the intensity of wars among Indian peoples. The Iroquois, hard hit by smallpox and other ailments, acquired muskets from the Dutch and used them, first to attack other Iroquoian peoples and then Algonquians. These **mourning wars** were often initiated by the widow or bereaved mother or sister of a deceased family member. Her warrior relatives then launched a raid and brought back captives. Although adult male prisoners, who might take revenge if allowed to live, were usually tortured to death, most women and children were adopted and assimilated. Adoption worked because the captives shared the cultural values of their captors. They became Iroquois. As early as the 1660s, a majority of Indians in the Five Nations were adoptees. In this way, the confederacy remained strong while its rivals declined. In the southern **piedmont,** the warlike, Sioux-speaking Catawba Indians also assimilated thousands from other tribes, as did the Creeks farther south.

In some ways, America became as much a new world for the Indians as it did for the colonists. European cloth, muskets, hatchets, knives, and pots appealed to Indians and spread far into the interior, but Indians who learned to use them gradually abandoned traditional skills and became increasingly dependent on European goods. Alcohol, the one item always in demand, was also dangerous. Indian men drank to alter their mood and achieve visions, not for sociability. Drunkenness became a major, if intermittent, social problem.

Settlers who understood that their future depended on the fur trade tried to stay on good terms with the Indians. Pieter Stuyvesant put New Netherland on such a course, and the English governors of New York followed his lead after 1664. Edmund Andros, governor from 1674 to 1680, cultivated the friendship of the **Iroquois League,** in which the five member nations had promised not to wage war against one another. In 1677, Andros and the Five Nations agreed to make New York the easternmost link in what the English called the **Covenant Chain of Peace,** a huge defensive advantage for a lightly populated colony. Thus, while New England and Virginia fought bitter Indian wars in the 1670s, New York avoided conflict. The Covenant Chain later proved flexible enough to incorporate other Indians and colonies as well.

Where the Indian trade was slight, war became more likely. In 1675, it erupted in both New England and the Chesapeake. In the 1640s, Virginia had imposed treaties of dependency on the member nations of the Powhatan chiefdom, in the hope of keeping them loyal in the event of war with other Indians. The New England colonies had similar understandings with the large non-Christian nations of the region, but the Puritan governments placed even greater reliance on a growing number of Christianized Indians.

Puritan Indian Missions

Serious efforts to convert Indians to Protestantism began in the 1640s on the island of Martha's Vineyard under Thomas Mayhew, Sr., and Thomas Mayhew, Jr., and in Massachusetts under John Eliot, pastor of the Roxbury church. Eliot tried to make the nearby Indian town of Natick into a model mission community.

The Mayhews were more successful than Eliot, although he received most of the publicity. They worked with local sachems and challenged only the tribal **powwows** (prophets or medicine men) and even converted some of those after their rites failed to cure smallpox. The Mayhews encouraged Indian men to teach the settlers of Martha's Vineyard and Nantucket how to catch whales, an activity that made them a vital part of the settlers' economy

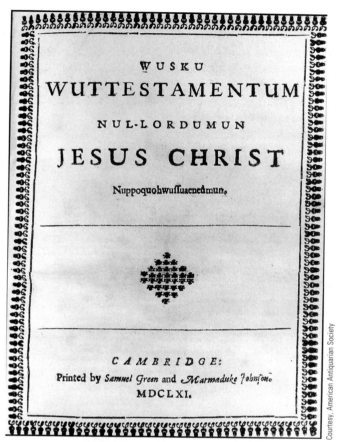

WUSKU
WUTTESTAMENTUM
NUL-LORDUMUN
JESUS CHRIST
Nuppoquohwuſſuaeneûmun,

CAMBRIDGE:
Printed by Samuel Green and Marmaduke Johnſon.
MDCLXI.

Courtesy, American Antiquarian Society

Title Page of John Eliot's Indian Bible Shown here is the New Testament (1661). Eliot's translation took many years to complete. Most copies of the Indian Bible were destroyed in Metacom's War of 1675–76.

without threatening their identity as men. Eliot, by contrast, attacked the authority of the sachems as well as the powwows, challenged the traditional tribal structure, and insisted on turning Indian men into farmers, a female role in Indian society. Yet he did translate the Bible and a few other religious works into the Massachusett language.

By the early 1670s, more than 1,000 Indians, nearly all of them survivors of coastal tribes that had been decimated by disease, lived in a string of seven "praying towns," and Eliot got busy organizing five more, mostly among the Nipmucks of the interior. By 1675, about 2,300 Indians, perhaps one-quarter of all those living in southeastern New England, were in various stages of conversion to Christianity, but only 160 of them had achieved the kind of conversion experience that Puritans required for full membership in a church. Few Indians shared the Puritan sense of sin. They could not easily grasp why their best deeds should stink in the nostrils of the Lord. The more powerful nations felt threatened by this pressure to convert, and resistance to Christianity became one cause of the war that broke out in 1675. Other causes were the settlers' lust for Indian lands, the ever-increasing intrusion of their livestock onto Indian cornfields, and the fear, especially among younger warrior-hunters, that their whole way of life was in danger of extinction. Metacom (whom the English called King Philip) was one of those Indians. He was sachem of the Wampanoags and the son of Massasoit, who had celebrated the first thanksgiving feast with the Pilgrims. Metacom once remarked that if he became "a praying sachem, I shall be a poor and weak one, and easily be trod upon."

Metacom's (or King Philip's) War

Metacom's War broke out shortly after Plymouth executed three Wampanoags accused of murdering John Sassamon, a Harvard-educated Indian preacher who may have been spying on Metacom. The fighting began in the frontier town of Swansea in June 1675, after

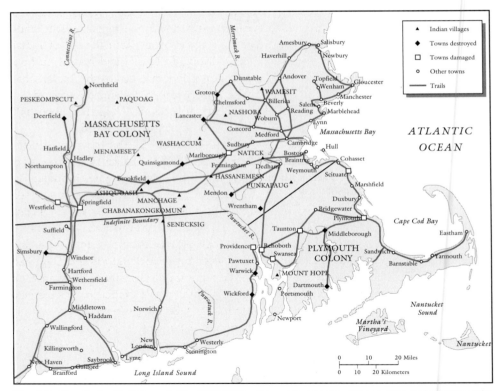

Map 3.2 New England in Metacom's War, 1675–1676 This map locates Indian villages and New England towns, and it indicates which towns were destroyed, damaged, or unscathed during the war.

settlers killed an Indian they found looting an abandoned house. When the Indians demanded satisfaction the next day, the settlers laughed in their faces. The Indians took revenge, and the violence escalated into war.

The settlers, remembering their easy triumph over the Pequots a generation earlier (see chapter 2), were confident of victory. But since the 1630s, the Indians had acquired firearms, especially flintlock muskets. They had built forges to make musket balls and repair their weapons. They had even become marksmen with the smoothbore musket by firing several smaller bullets, instead of a single shot, with each charge. The settlers, who had often paid Indians to do their hunting for them, were often armed with older firelocks and were terrible shots. In the tradition of European armies, they discharged volleys without aiming. To the shock of the colonists, Metacom won several engagements against Plymouth militia, usually by ambushing the noisy intruders. He then escaped from Plymouth Colony and headed toward the upper Connecticut valley, where the local Indians, after being ordered to disarm, joined him instead. Together they burned five Massachusetts towns in three months.

Massachusetts and Connecticut joined the fray. Rather than attack Metacom's Wampanoags, they went after the Narragansetts, who had accepted some Wampanoag refugees but were trying to remain neutral. Many prominent settlers dreamed of acquiring their fertile lands. In the Great Swamp Fight of December 1675, a Puritan army, with the aid of Indian guides, attacked an unfinished Narragansett fort during a blizzard and massacred hundreds of Indians, most of them women and children, but not before the Indians had picked off a high percentage of the officers. The surviving warriors joined Metacom and showed that they too could use terror. They torched more towns. Altogether, about 800 settlers were killed, and two dozen towns were destroyed or badly damaged.

Terrified frontier settlers demanded the annihilation of all nearby Indians, even the Christian converts. The Massachusetts government, shocked to realize that it could not win the war without Indian allies, did what it could to protect the **praying Indians.** The magistrates evacuated them to a bleak island in Boston harbor, where they spent a miserable winter of privation but then enlisted to fight against Metacom in the spring campaign.

The war nearly tore New England apart, and it did split the clergy. Increase Mather, a prominent Boston minister, saw the conflict as God's judgment on a sinful people and warned that no victory would come until New England repented and reformed. At first, the Massachusetts General Court agreed. It blamed the war on young men who wore their hair too long, on boys and girls who took leisurely horse rides together, on people who dressed above their station in life, and on blaspheming Quakers. Quakers, in turn, saw the war as divine punishment for their persecution by the Puritans. They pointed to Connecticut, which stopped hounding Quakers during the war and where only one town was destroyed. Another Boston minister, William Hubbard, insisted that the war was only a brief testing time, after which the Lord would lead his saints to victory over the heathen. To Daniel Gookin, a magistrate committed to Eliot's mission work, the war was an unspeakable tragedy for both sides.

Despite their disagreements, the settlers pulled together and won the war in 1676. Governor Andros of New York persuaded the Mohawks to attack Metacom's winter camp and disperse his people, who by then were short of gunpowder. The New Englanders, working closely with Mohegan and Christian Indian allies, then hunted down Metacom's war parties, killed hundreds of Indians, including Metacom, and sold hundreds more into West Indian slavery. Some of those enslaved had not even been party to the conflict and had actually requested asylum from it. As the tide turned, the Massachusetts government sided with Hubbard by ordering a day of thanksgiving, but Increase Mather's church observed a fast day instead. The colony had not reformed adequately, he explained. In effect, the struggle had turned into a civil war among the Indian peoples of southern New England with all the colonies supporting Metacom's enemies.

Virginia's Indian War

In Virginia, Governor Sir William Berkeley, who had led the colony to victory over Opechancanough 30 years earlier, rejoiced in the New Englanders' woes. Metacom's War was the least they deserved for the way the Puritans had ripped England apart and executed Charles I during the civil wars. Then Virginia began to have troubles of its own.

In 1675, the Doegs, a dependent Indian nation in the Potomac valley, demanded payment of an old debt from a local planter. When he refused, they ran off some of his livestock. After his overseer killed one of them, the others fled but later returned to ambush and kill the man. The county militia mustered and followed the Doegs across the Potomac into Maryland. At a fork in the trail, the militia split into two parties. Each found a group of Indians in a shack a few hundred yards up the path it was following. Both parties fired at point-blank range, killing 11 at one cabin and 14 at the other. One of the bands was indeed Doeg, but the other was not: "Susquehannock friends," blurted one Indian as he fled.

The Susquehannocks were a strong Iroquoian-speaking people with firearms; they had moved south to escape Iroquois attacks. At Maryland's invitation, they had recently occupied land north of the Potomac. Berkeley, still hoping to avoid war, sent John Washington (ancestor of George) with some Virginia militia to investigate the killings and, if possible, to set matters right.

Washington preferred vengeance. His Virginia militia joined with a Maryland force, and together they besieged a formidable Susquehannock fort on the north bank of the Potomac, too strong to take without artillery. When the Indians sent out five or six sachems to negotiate, the militia murdered them and then laid siege to the fort for the next six weeks. The Indians, short of provisions, finally broke out one night with all of their people, killing several militiamen. After hurling taunts of defiance and promises of vengeance, they disappeared into the forest. Apparently blaming Virginia more than Maryland, they killed more than 30 Virginia settlers in January 1676. The colonists began to panic.

Berkeley favored a defensive strategy against the Indians; most settlers wanted to attack. In March 1676, the governor summoned a special session of the Virginia legislature to approve the creation of a string of forts above the fall line of the major rivers, with companies of "rangers" to patrol the stretches between them. Berkeley also hoped to maintain a distinction between the clearly hostile Susquehannocks and other Indians who might still be neutral or friendly. Frontier settlers, mostly former servants frustrated by low tobacco prices and unable to acquire tidewater lands because established planters had bought them up, demanded war against all Indians. Finally, to avoid further provocation, Berkeley restricted the fur trade to a few of his close associates. To the men excluded from that circle, his actions looked like favoritism. To settlers in frontier counties, whose access to new lands was blocked by the Indians and who now had to pay higher taxes, Berkeley's strategy seemed intolerable.

In both the Second (1665–67) and Third (1672–74) Anglo-Dutch Wars, Berkeley had built costly forts to protect the colony from the Dutch navy, but Dutch warships had sailed around them and mauled the tobacco fleet anyway. Accordingly, colonists denounced the building of any more forts and demanded an offensive campaign waged by unpaid volunteers, who would take their rewards by plundering and enslaving Indians. In April, the frontier settlers found a reckless leader in Nathaniel Bacon, a young newcomer to the colony with a scandalous past and £1,800 to invest. Using his political connections (he was the governor's cousin by marriage), he managed an appointment to the council soon after his arrival in the colony in 1674. Bacon, the owner of a plantation and trading post in Henrico County at the falls of the James River (now Richmond), was one of the men excluded from the Indian trade under Berkeley's new rules.

Bacon's Rebellion

Ignoring Berkeley's orders, Bacon marched his frontiersmen south in search of the elusive Susquehannocks. After several days, his weary men reached a village of friendly Occaneechees, who offered them shelter, announced that they knew where to find a Susquehannock camp, and even offered to attack it. The Occaneechees surprised and defeated the Susquehannocks and returned with their captives to celebrate the victory with Bacon. But after they had fallen asleep, Bacon's men massacred them and seized their furs and prisoners. On their return to Henrico in May, the Baconians boasted of their prowess as Indian killers.

By then, Berkeley had outlawed Bacon, dissolved the legislature, and called the first general election since 1661. The old assembly had recently imposed a property requirement for voting, but Berkeley suspended it and asked the burgesses to bring their grievances to Jamestown for redress at the June assembly. "How miserable that man is," he complained, "that Governes a People where six parts of seaven at least are Poore Endebted Discontented and Armed."

As one measure of their resentment against elite planters, voters elected a fair number of burgesses who were not JPs, almost unheard of since midcentury. Henrico's voters elected Bacon to the assembly. Berkeley had him arrested when he reached Jamestown and made him go down on his knees before the governor and council and apologize for his disobedience. Berkeley then forgave him and restored him to his seat in the council. By then, even the governor had abandoned his effort to distinguish between hostile and friendly Indians, but he still favored a defensive war. While the burgesses were passing laws to reform the county courts, the vestries, and the tax system, Bacon slipped away to Henrico, summoned his followers again, and marched on Jamestown. At gunpoint, he forced Berkeley to commission him as general of volunteers and compelled the legislature to authorize another expedition against the Indians.

Berkeley retreated downriver to Gloucester County and mustered its militia, but they refused to follow him against Bacon. They would fight only Indians. Mortified, Berkeley fled to the eastern shore, the only part of the colony that was safe from Indian attack and thus still loyal to him. Bacon hastened to Jamestown, summoned a meeting of planters at the

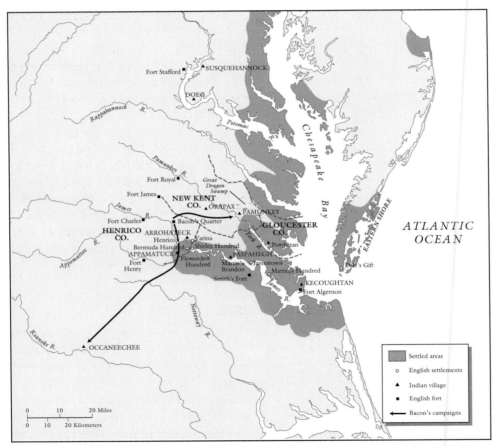

Map 3.3   Bacon's Rebellion in Virginia, 1676   Settlement had just reached the fall line by the 1670s. The map also shows Bacon's two military campaigns, against the Occaneechees and the Pamunkeys.

governor's Green Spring mansion, made them swear an oath of loyalty to him, and ordered the confiscation of the estates of Berkeley's major supporters, who were men in the process of becoming great planters. Meanwhile, Berkeley raised his own force on the eastern shore by promising the men an exemption from taxes for 21 years and the right to plunder the rebels.

Unlike the situation in New England, few Indians killed other Indians in 1676. Virginia settlers fought one another during this civil war, and royal government collapsed under the strain. During that summer, hundreds of settlers set out to make their fortunes by plundering Indians, other colonists, or both. Bacon's Rebellion was the largest upheaval in the American colonies before 1775. Despite later legends, it had little to do with liberty but a lot to do with class resentments.

Bacon never did kill a hostile Indian. While he was slaughtering and enslaving the unresisting Pamunkeys along the frontier, Berkeley assembled a small fleet and retook Jamestown in August. Bacon rushed east, exhibiting his Indian captives along the way, and laid siege to Jamestown. He captured the wives of prominent Berkeley supporters and forced them to stand in the line of fire as he dug his trenches closer to the capital. After suffering only a few casualties, the governor's men grew discouraged, and in early September, the whole force returned to the eastern shore. Bacon then burned Jamestown to the ground. He also boasted of his ability to hold off an English army, unite Virginia with Maryland and North Carolina, and win Dutch support for setting up an independent Chesapeake republic. Instead he died of dysentery in October.

Berkeley soon regained control of Virginia. Using the ships of the London tobacco fleet, he overpowered the plantations that Bacon had fortified. Then, in January 1677, a force of 1,000 redcoats arrived, too late to help but in time to strain the colony's depleted resources. Ignoring royal orders to show clemency, Berkeley hanged 23 of the rebels. A new assembly repudiated the reforms of 1676, and in many counties the governor's men used their control of the courts to continue plundering the Baconians through confiscations and fines. After the upheaval, many of the emerging great planters deliberately chose to replace their indentured servants with enslaved Africans. Summoned to England to defend himself, Berkeley died there in 1677 before he could present his case.

Crisis in England and the Redefinition of Empire

Bacon's Rebellion helped trigger a political crisis in England. Because Virginia produced little tobacco in 1676 during the uprising, English customs revenues fell sharply, and the king was obliged to ask Parliament for more money. Parliament's response was tempered by the much deeper problem of the royal succession. Charles II had fathered many bastards, but his royal marriage was childless. After the queen reached menopause in the mid-1670s, his brother James, duke of York, became his heir. By then, James had become a Catholic. When Charles dissolved the Parliament that had sat from 1661 until 1678, he knew he would have to deal with a new House of Commons that was terrified by the prospect of a Catholic king.

The Popish Plot, the Exclusion Crisis, and the Rise of Party

In this atmosphere of distrust, a cynical adventurer, Titus Oates, fabricated the sensational story that he had uncovered a "Popish Plot" to kill Charles and bring James to the throne. In the wake of these accusations, the king's ministry fell, and the parliamentary opposition won majorities in three successive elections between 1678 and 1681. Organized by Lord Shaftesbury (the Carolina proprietor), the opposition demanded that James, a Catholic, be excluded from the throne in favor of Mary and then Anne, his Protestant daughters by his first marriage. It also called for a guarantee of frequent elections and for an independent electorate not under the influence of wealthy patrons. The king's men began castigating Shaftesbury's followers as **Whigs,** the name of an obscure sect of Scottish religious extremists who favored the assassination of both Charles and James. Whigs in turn denounced Charles's courtiers as **Tories,** a term for Irish Catholic bandits who murdered Protestant landlords. Like Puritan, Quaker, Papist, and other terms of abuse, both words stuck.

England's party struggle reflected a deep rift between Court and Country forces. As of 1681, Tories were a Court party. They favored the legitimate succession, a standing army with adequate revenues to maintain it, the Anglican Church without toleration for Protestant dissenters or Catholics, and a powerful monarchy. The Whigs were a Country opposition that stood for the exclusion of James from the throne, a decentralized militia rather than a standing army, toleration of Protestant dissenters but not of Catholics, and an active role in government for a reformed Parliament. During this struggle, James fled to Scotland in virtual exile, but Charles, after getting secret financial support from King Louis XIV of France, dissolved Parliament in 1681 and ruled without one until he died in 1685.

The Lords of Trade and Imperial Reform

English politics of the 1670s and 1680s had a profound impact on the colonies. The duke of York emerged from the Third Anglo-Dutch War as the most powerful shaper of imperial policy. At his urging, the government created a new agency in 1675, the Lords Committee of Trade and Plantations, or more simply, the Lords of Trade. This agency, a permanent committee of the Privy Council, enforced the Navigation Acts and administered the colonies. Although Virginia was the oldest royal colony, the West Indies became the object of most of the new policies, simply because the Caribbean remained a much more important theater of international competition and wealth. The instruments of royal government first took shape in the islands and were then extended to the mainland.

In the 1660s, the Crown took control of the governments of Barbados, Jamaica, and the Leeward Islands. The king appointed the governor and upper house of each colony; the settlers elected an assembly. The Privy Council in England reserved to itself the power to hear appeals from colonial courts and to disallow colonial legislation after the governor had approved it. The Privy Council also issued a formal commission and a lengthy set of instructions to each royal governor. In the two or three decades after 1660, these documents became standardized. The king's commission defined a governor's powers. From the Crown's point of view, the commission *created* the constitutional structure of each colony, a claim that few settlers accepted. Most colonists believed they had an inherent right to constitutional rule even without the king's explicit warrant.

Written instructions told each royal governor how to use his broad powers. They laid out what he must do, such as command the militia, and what he must avoid, such as approving laws detrimental to English trade. Despite some confusion at first, Crown lawyers eventually agreed that these instructions were binding only on the governor, not on the colony as a whole. In other words, royal instructions never acquired the force of law.

London also insisted that each colony pay the cost of its own government. Ironically, this requirement strengthened colonial claims to self-rule. After a long struggle in Jamaica, the Crown imposed a compromise in 1681 that had broad significance for all of the colonies. The Lords of Trade threatened to make the Jamaica assembly as weak as the Irish Parliament, which could debate and approve only those bills that had first been adopted by the English Privy Council. Under the compromise, the Jamaica assembly retained its power to initiate and amend legislation, in return for agreeing to a long-term revenue act that later became permanent, a measure that freed the governor from financial dependence on the assembly.

Metacom's War and Bacon's Rebellion lent urgency to these reforms and speeded up their use in the mainland colonies. The Lords of Trade ordered soldiers to Virginia, along with a royal commission to investigate grievances there. In 1676, they also sent an aggressive customs officer, Edward Randolph, to Massachusetts. He recommended that the colony's charter be revoked. The Lords of Trade viewed New England and all proprietary colonies with deep suspicion, although they failed to block the founding of Pennsylvania as a new proprietary venture. They had reason for concern. As late as 1678, Virginia remained the only royal colony on the mainland. The Lords of Trade might enforce compliance with the Navigation Acts elsewhere, but they possessed no effective instruments for punishing violators in North America. The king could demand and reprimand, but not command.

The Jamaica model assumed that each royal governor would summon an assembly on occasion, although not often. In the 1680s, the Crown imposed a similar settlement on Virginia—an occasional assembly with full powers of legislation in exchange for a permanent revenue act. Although New York had been an experiment in autocracy since the English conquest of 1664, James conceded an assembly to that colony, too, in exchange for a permanent revenue act in 1683. The Jamaica model was becoming the norm for the Lords of Trade. James's real preference emerged after the English Court of Chancery revoked the Massachusetts Charter in 1684. Charles II died and his brother became King James II in early 1685. The possibility of a vigorous autocracy in America suddenly reappeared. James also promised to tolerate both Catholics and Protestant dissenters, a policy bound to antagonize the Anglican majority in the Parliament that he summoned.

THE CHARTER OAK.

Connecticut's Charter Oak   According to legend, when Governor Sir Edmund Andros came to Hartford in 1687 to absorb Connecticut into the Dominion of New England by taking possession of its 1663 royal charter, the lights were suddenly extinguished, and when one was relit, the charter had disappeared. It, and probably also the Fundamental Orders of 1639, which had defined the form of government until 1664, were hidden in an oak tree. When the tree fell in 1856, it was said to be more than 1,000 years old.

The Dominion of New England

Absolutist New York now became the king's model for reorganizing New England. James disallowed the New York Charter of Liberties of 1683 (see chapter 2) and abolished the colony's assembly but kept the permanent revenue act in force. In 1686, he sent Sir Edmund Andros, the autocratic governor of New York from 1674 to 1680, to Massachusetts to take over a new government called the Dominion of New England. James added New Hampshire, Plymouth, Rhode Island, Connecticut, New York, and both Jerseys to the Dominion. Andros governed this vast domain through an appointive council and a superior court that rode circuit dispensing justice. There was no elective assembly. Andros also imposed religious toleration on the Puritans, even forcing one Boston church to let Anglicans use its meetinghouse for public worship for part of each Sunday.

At first, Andros won support from merchants who had been excluded from politics by the Puritan requirement that they be full church members, but his rigorous enforcement of the Navigation Acts soon alienated them too. When he tried to compel New England

Thomas B. Macaulay, History of England from the Accession of James II, ed. by Charles H. Firth (London: Macmillan, 1914).

Le Roy de France In *Le Roy de France*, the Dutch Protestant response to the persecution of the Huguenots depicts Louis, the sun king, as death.

farmers to take out new land titles that included annual quitrents, he enraged the whole countryside. His suppression of a tax revolt in Essex County, Massachusetts, started many people thinking more highly of their rights as Englishmen than of their peculiar liberties as Puritans. By 1688, government by consent probably seemed more valuable than ever.

The Glorious Revolution

Focus Question
On what common principles did English political culture begin to converge in both the mother country and the colonies after the Glorious Revolution?

Events in England and France undermined the Dominion of New England. James II proclaimed toleration for Protestants and Catholics and began to name Catholics to high office, in violation of recent laws. In 1685, Louis XIV revoked the 1598 Edict of Nantes that had granted toleration to Protestants, and he launched a vicious persecution of the Huguenots. About 160,000 fled the kingdom, the largest forced migration of Europe's early modern era. Many went to England; several thousand settled in the English mainland colonies. James II tried to suppress the news of Louis's persecution, which made his own professions of toleration seem hypocritical, even though his commitment was probably genuine. In 1688, his queen gave birth to a son who would clearly be raised Catholic, thus imposing a Catholic *dynasty* on England. Several Whig and Tory leaders swallowed their mutual hatred and invited William of Orange, the *stadholder* of the Netherlands, to England. The husband of the king's older Protestant daughter Mary, William had become the most prominent Protestant soldier in Europe during a long war against Louis XIV.

William landed in England in November 1688. Most of the English army sided with him, and James fled to France in late December. Parliament declared that James had abdicated the throne and named William III (1689–1702) and Mary II (1689–94) as joint sovereigns. It also passed a Toleration Act that gave Protestant dissenters (but not Catholics) the right to worship publicly and a Declaration of Rights that guaranteed a Protestant succession and condemned as illegal many of the acts of James II. This Glorious Revolution also brought England and the Netherlands into war against Louis XIV, who supported James.

The Glorious Revolution in America

The Boston militia overthrew Andros on April 18 and 19, 1689, once they had learned that William had succeeded against James. Andros's attempt to suppress the news that William had landed in England convinced the Puritans that he was part of a global Popish Plot to undermine Protestant societies everywhere. After some hesitation, Massachusetts resumed the forms of its old charter government. The other New England colonies did likewise. In May and June, the New York City militia took over Fort James at the southern tip of Manhattan and renamed it Fort William. To hostile observers, this action seemed almost a replay of the events of 1673, when the Dutch had reconquered New York and renamed the fort for William. Francis Nicholson, lieutenant governor in New York under Andros, refused to proclaim William and Mary as sovereigns without direct orders from England and soon sailed for home. Most of the active rebels in New York City were Dutch Calvinists, who had little experience with traditional English liberties. Few had held high office. Their leader, Jacob Leisler, dreaded conquest by Catholics from New France and began to act like a Dutch *stadholder* in a nominally English colony.

Military defense became Leisler's highest priority, but his demands for supplies soon alienated even his Yankee supporters on Long Island. Although he summoned an elective assembly, he made no effort to revive the Charter of Liberties of 1683, while continuing to collect duties under the permanent revenue act of that year. He showed little respect for the legal rights of his opponents, most of whom were English or were Dutch merchants who had served the Dominion of New England. He jailed several Anti-Leislerians for months without bringing them to trial, and when his own assembly raised questions about the legal rights of these men, he sent it home. Loud complaints against his administration reached the Crown in London.

In Maryland, Protestants overthrew Lord Baltimore's Catholic government in 1689. The governor of Maryland had refused to proclaim William and Mary, even after all of the other colonies had done so. To Lord Baltimore's dismay, the messenger he sent from London to Maryland with orders to accept the new monarchs died en route. Had he arrived, the government might have survived the crisis.

The English Response

England responded in different ways to each of these upheavals. The Maryland rebels won the royal government they requested from England and soon established the Anglican Church in the colony. Catholics could no longer worship in public, hold office, or run their own schools, but they did receive unofficial toleration. Most prominent Catholic families braced themselves against the Protestant storm and remained loyal to their faith.

In New York, the Leislerians suffered a deadly defeat. Leisler and his Dutch followers, who had no significant contacts at the English court, watched helplessly as their enemies, working through the imperial bureaucracy that William inherited from James, manipulated the Dutch king of England into undermining his loyal Dutch supporters in New York. The new governor, Henry Sloughter, named prominent Anti-Leislerians to his council, arrested Leisler and his son-in-law in 1691, tried both for treason, denied their right to appeal to England, and had them hanged, drawn (disemboweled), and quartered. The assembly elected that year was controlled by Anti-Leislerians, most of whom were English. It passed a modified version of the Charter of Liberties of 1683, this time denying toleration to Catholics. Like its predecessor, this charter was later disallowed. Bitter struggles between Leislerians and Anti-Leislerians raged until after 1700.

Another complex struggle involved Massachusetts. In 1689, Increase Mather, acting as the colony's agent in London, failed to persuade Parliament to restore the charter of 1629.

Over the next two years, he negotiated a new charter, which gave the Crown what it had been demanding since 1664—the power to appoint governors, justices, and militia officers, and the power to veto laws and to hear judicial appeals. The 1691 charter also granted toleration to all Protestants and based voting rights on property qualifications, not church membership. In effect, liberty and property had triumphed over godliness.

While insisting on these concessions, William also accepted much of the previous history of the colony, even if it did not augur well for the emerging model of royal government. The General Court, not the governor as in other royal colonies, retained control over the distribution of land. The council remained an elective body, although it was chosen annually by the full legislature, not directly by the voters. The governor could veto any councilor. Massachusetts also absorbed the colonies of Plymouth and Maine. New Hampshire regained its autonomy, but until 1741 it usually shared the same royal governor with Massachusetts. Rhode Island and Connecticut resumed their charter governments.

The Salem Witch Trials

When Mather sailed into Boston harbor with the new charter in May 1692, he found the province besieged by witches. The accusations arose in Salem Village (modern Danvers) among a group of girls that included a young daughter and a niece of the local minister, Samuel Parris. They then spread to older girls, some of whom had been orphaned during the Indian wars. The girls howled, barked, and stretched themselves into frightful contortions. At first, Parris treated the outbursts as cases of demonic possession, but after weeks of prayer sessions brought no improvement, he accepted a diagnosis of witchcraft. With adult encouragement, the girls accused many village residents of witchcraft, mostly people who did not approve of Parris. The number of the accused escalated sharply, and the crisis spread far beyond the village after 14-year-old Abigail Hobbs confessed in April that she had made a compact with the devil in Maine at age 10 just before the outbreak of the Indian war that had since devastated northern New England. Altogether about 150 people were accused in Essex County and beyond. Satan, supported by Indian warriors on the frontier and by witches within the colony, seemed determined to destroy Massachusetts.

The trials began in Salem Town in June. The court, which included judges badly compromised by their willing service to the Andros regime, hanged 19 people, pressed one man to death because he refused to stand trial, and allowed several other people to die in jail. All of those executed insisted on their innocence. Of 50 who confessed, none was hanged. Many of the victims were grandmothers, several quite conspicuous for their piety. One was a former minister at Salem Village who had become a Baptist. The governor finally halted the trials after someone accused his wife of witchcraft. By then, public support for the trials was collapsing. The **Salem witch trials** provided a bitter finale to the era of political uncertainty that had afflicted Massachusetts since the loss of the colony's charter in 1684. Along with the new charter, the trials brought the Puritan era to a close.

© Hulton Archive/Getty Images.

Matthew Hopkins, *Discoverie of Witches* **(1647)**   This woodcut depicts activities that New Englanders associated with the behavior of witches, including flying through the air on poles or brooms.

The Completion of Empire

The Glorious Revolution killed absolutism in English America and guaranteed that royal colonies would have representative governments. Both Crown and colonists took it for granted that any colony settled by the English would elect an assembly to vote on all taxes and consent to all local laws. Governors would be appointed by the Crown or a lord proprietor. (Governors were elected in Connecticut and Rhode Island.) But royal government soon became the norm, especially after the New Jersey and Carolina proprietors surrendered their powers of government to the Crown. On the other hand, the Crown restored proprietary rule in Maryland in 1716, after the fifth Lord Baltimore converted to the Church of England. By the 1720s, Maryland and Pennsylvania (along with Delaware, which became a separate colony under the Penn proprietorship in 1704) were the only surviving proprietary provinces on the mainland, and their proprietors were usually careful to abide by the rules of imperial administration.

This transition to royal government seems smoother in retrospect than it did at the time. London almost lost control of the empire in the 1690s. Overwhelmed by the pressures of the French war, the Lords of Trade could not keep pace with events in the colonies. When French privateers disrupted the tobacco trade, Scottish smugglers stepped in and began to divert it to Glasgow in defiance of the Navigation Acts. New York became a haven for pirates. **(See Map 3.4, Government and Religion in the British colonies, 1720, in the color insert following page 288.)**

William took action in 1696. Parliament passed a new, comprehensive Navigation Act that plugged several loopholes in earlier laws and extended to America the English system of vice admiralty courts, which dispensed quick justice without juries. When the new courts settled routine maritime disputes or condemned enemy merchant ships captured by colonial privateers, their services were welcomed, but when the courts tried to assume jurisdiction over the Navigation Acts, they aroused controversy. Sometimes the common-law courts intervened and took over these cases.

William also replaced the Lords of Trade in 1696 with a new agency, the Board of Trade. Its powers were almost purely advisory. It corresponded with governors and other officials in the colonies, listened to lobbyists in England, and made policy recommendations to appropriate governmental bodies. The board tried to collect information on complex questions and to offer helpful advice. It was, in short, an early attempt at government by experts. John Locke, England's foremost philosopher and an able economist, was one of the board's first members.

Another difficult problem was resolved in 1707 when England and Scotland agreed to merge their separate parliaments and become the single kingdom of Great Britain. At a stroke, the Act of Union placed Scotland inside the Navigation Act system, legalized Scottish participation in the tobacco trade, and opened numerous colonial offices to ambitious Scots. By the middle of the 18th century, most of Scotland's growing prosperity derived from its trade with the colonies.

Imperial Federalism

The transformations that took place between 1689 and 1707 defined the structure of the British empire until the American Revolution. Although Parliament claimed full power over the colonies, in practice it seldom regulated anything colonial except Atlantic commerce. Even the Woolens Act of 1699, designed to protect the English woolens industry from Irish and colonial competition, did not prohibit the manufacture of woolen textiles in the colonies. It simply prohibited their export. The Hat Act of 1732 was similarly designed, except for a clause limiting the number of apprentices or slaves a colonial hatter could maintain. Nobody enforced that provision.

When Parliament regulated oceanic trade, its measures were usually enforceable. But compliance was minimal to nonexistent when Parliament tried to regulate inland affairs through statutes protecting white pines (needed as masts for the navy) or through the Iron Act of 1750, which prohibited the erection of certain types of new iron mills. To get things done within the colonies, the Crown had to win the settlers' agreement through their lawful assemblies and unsalaried local officials. In effect, the empire had stumbled into a system of de facto federalism, an arrangement that no one could quite explain or justify. Parliament exercised only limited powers, and the colonies controlled the rest. What seemed an arrangement of convenience in London soon acquired overtones of right in America, the right to consent to all taxes and local laws.

The Mixed and Balanced Constitution

The Glorious Revolution transformed British politics in a way that profoundly affected the colonies. To Europe's surprise, Britain, whose government had seemed wildly unstable for half a century, became a far more powerful state under its limited government after 1689 than the Stuart kings had been able to sustain with their pretensions to absolute monarchy. The British constitution, which made ministers legally responsible for their public actions, proved remarkably stable. Before long, many Englishmen were celebrating this achievement as the wonder of the age. In the ancient world, free societies had degenerated into tyrannies. Liberty had always been fragile and was easily lost. Yet England had retained its liberty and grown stronger in the process. England had defied history.

The Royal Collection ©2006 Her Majesty Queen Elizabeth II

Windsor Castle (circa 1704–05)   Like all royal palaces, Windsor was huge enough to intimidate and was a center of court culture.

The explanation, nearly everyone agreed, lay in England's "mixed and balanced" constitution. Government by King, Lords, and Commons mirrored society itself—the monarchy, aristocracy, and commonality—and literally embodied all three in its structure. As long as each freely consented to government measures, English liberty would be secure because each had voluntarily placed the public good ahead of its own interests. But if either the Crown, the Lords, or the Commons acquired the power to dominate or manipulate the other two, English liberty would be in peril. That danger fueled an unending dialogue in 18th-century Britain. The underlying drama was always the struggle of power against liberty, and liberty usually meant a limitation of governmental power. Power had to be controlled, or liberty would be lost. The real danger to liberty lay, not in a military coup, but in corruption, specifically, in the ability of Crown ministers to use patronage to undermine the independence and integrity of the House of Commons.

After 1689, England raised larger fleets and armies than it had ever mobilized before. To support them, the kingdom created for the first time a **funded national debt,** in which the state agreed to pay the interest due to its creditors ahead of all other obligations. This simple device gave Britain enormous borrowing power. In 1694, the government created the Bank of England to facilitate its own finances; the London Stock Exchange also emerged in the 1690s. Parliament levied a heavy land tax on the gentry and excises on ordinary people to meet wartime expenses. Together, debt, bank, stock market, and new sources of revenue added up to a financial revolution that enabled England to outspend France, despite having only one-fourth of France's population. By giving offices to members of Parliament, Crown ministers were almost assured of majority support for their measures.

Ever since the Popish Plot, public debates had pitted Court against Country. The Court favored policies that strengthened its war-making capabilities. The Country stood for liberty. Each of the parties, Whig and Tory, had Court and Country wings. Between 1680 and 1720, however, they reversed their polarities. Although the Tories had begun as Charles II's Court party, by 1720 most of them were a Country opposition. Whigs had defended Country positions in 1680, but by 1720 most of them were strong advocates for the Court policies of George I (1714–27). Court spokesmen defended the military buildup, the financial revolution, and the new patronage as essential to victory over France and to sustain British strength in world politics. Their Country opponents denounced standing armies, attacked the financial revolution as an engine of corruption, favored an early peace with France, demanded more frequent elections, and tried to ban placemen (officeholders who sat in Parliament) from the House of Commons.

Court Whigs emerged victorious during the long ministry of Sir Robert Walpole (1721–42), but their opponents were more eloquent and controlled more presses. By the 1720s, the opposition claimed many of the kingdom's best writers, especially Tories Alexander Pope, Jonathan Swift, John Gay, and Henry St. John, viscount Bolingbroke. Their detestation of Walpole was shared by a smaller band of radical Whigs, including John Trenchard and Thomas Gordon, who wrote *Cato's Letters,* four volumes of collected newspaper essays. The central theme of the opposition was corruption—the indirect and insidious means by which ministers threatened the independence of Parliament and thus English liberty. This debate over liberty soon reached America. *Cato's Letters* were especially popular in the northern colonies, while Bolingbroke won numerous admirers among the gentry in the southern colonies.

Contrasting Empires: Spain and France in North America

Focus Question

What enabled sparsely settled New France to resist British expansion for more than half a century, whereas Spanish Florida seemed almost helpless against a similar threat?

After 1689, Britain's enemies were France and Spain, Catholic powers with their own American empires. Until 1689, the three empires had coexisted in America without much contact among them, but Europe's wars soon engulfed them all. Spain and France shared a zeal for converting Indians that exceeded anything displayed by English Protestants, but their American empires had little else in common.

The Pueblo Revolt

In the late 17th century, the Spanish missions of North America entered a period of crisis. Franciscan zeal began to slacken, and fewer priests took the trouble to master Indian languages, insisting instead that the Indians learn Spanish. For all of their good intentions, the missionaries regarded Indians as children and often whipped or even shackled them for minor infractions. Disease also took a heavy toll. A declining Indian population led to more pressing labor demands by missionaries, and despite strong prohibitions, some Spaniards enslaved some Indians in Florida and New Mexico. After 1670, Florida also feared encroachments by English Protestants out of South Carolina, who were eager to enslave unarmed Indians, whether or not they had embraced Christianity. By 1700, the European refusal to enslave other Christians protected only white people, and yet Spain refused to trust the Indians with firearms.

The greatest challenge to the Spanish arose in New Mexico, where the Pueblo population had fallen from 80,000 to 17,000 since 1598. A prolonged drought, together with Apache and Navajo attacks, prompted many Pueblos to abandon the Christian God and resume their old forms of worship. The Spanish responded by whipping 47 medicine men for sorcery and by hanging three of them in 1675. A fourth committed suicide. Popé, a San Juan Pueblo medicine man, was one of those whipped for his beliefs. He moved north to Taos Pueblo, where he organized the most successful Indian revolt in American history. In 1680, in a carefully timed uprising, the Pueblos killed 200 of the 1,000 Spaniards in New Mexico and destroyed or plundered every Spanish building in the province (see the chapter 1 map, "Spanish Missions in Florida and New Mexico, circa 1675"). They desecrated every church and killed 21 of New Mexico's 40 priests. "Now," they exulted, "the God of the Spaniards, who was their father, is dead," but the Pueblos' own god, whom they obeyed, "[had] never died." Spanish survivors fled from Santa Fe down the Rio Grande to El Paso.

Popé lost his influence when the traditional Pueblo rites failed to end the drought or stop the attacks of hostile Indians. When the Spanish returned in the 1690s, the Pueblos were badly divided. Most villages yielded without much resistance, and Spain accepted their submission, but Santa Fe held out until December 1693. When it fell, the Spanish executed 70 men and gave 400 women and children to the returning settlers as their slaves. The Hopi Indians to the west, however, never again submitted to Spanish rule.

In both Florida and New Mexico, missionaries had often resisted the demands of Spanish governors. By 1700, the state ruled and missionaries obeyed. Spain's daring attempt to create a demilitarized Christian frontier was proving to be a tragic failure for both Indians and Franciscans.

New France and the Middle Ground

A different story unfolded along the western frontier of New France over the same decades. There the Iroquois menace made possible an unusual accommodation between the colony and the Indians of the Great Lakes region. The survival of the Iroquois Five Nations depended on their ability to assimilate captives seized from other nations through incessant warfare. Their raiders, armed with muskets, terrorized western Indians, carried away thousands of captives, and left behind grisly trophies of their cruelty to discourage revenge. The Iroquois wars depopulated nearly all of what is now the state of Ohio and much of the Ontario peninsula. The Indians around Lakes Erie and Huron either fled west to escape these horrors or were absorbed by the Iroquois. The refugees, mostly Algonquian-speaking peoples, founded new communities farther west. Most of these villages contained families from several different tribes, and village loyalties gradually supplanted older tribal (or ethnic) loyalties, which often broke down under Iroquois pressure. When the refugees disagreed with one another or came into conflict with the Sioux to their west, the absence of traditional tribal structures made it difficult to resolve their differences. Over time, French soldiers, trappers, and missionaries stepped in as mediators.

The French were not always welcome. In 1684, the only year for which we have a precise count, the Algonquians killed 39 French traders. Yet the leaders of thinly populated New France were eager to erect an Algonquian shield against the Iroquois and, in later decades, against the British. They began by easing tensions among the Algonquians while supplying them with firearms, brandy, and other European goods. In fact, to the exasperation of missionaries, brandy became the lubricant of the fur trade by keeping the warriors hunting for pelts and dependent on French traders. New France, in turn, provided the resources that the Algonquians needed to strike back against the Iroquois. By 1701, Iroquois losses had become so heavy that the Five Nations negotiated a peace treaty with the French and the western Indians. The Iroquois agreed to remain neutral in any war between France and England. France's Indian allies, supported by a new French fort erected at Detroit in 1701, began returning to the fertile lands around lakes Erie and Huron. That region became the Great Lakes Middle Ground, over which no one could wield sovereign power, although New France exercised great influence within it.

France's success in the interior rested on intelligent negotiation, not on force. Officials who gave orders instead of fostering negotiations merely alienated France's Indian allies. Blind obedience to commands, grumbled the warriors, was slavery. Hugely outnumbered, the French knew that they could not impose their will on the Indians. Indians respected those Frenchmen who honored their ways. French diplomacy followed Indian, not European rules. The governor of New France became a somewhat grander version of a traditional Indian chief. Algonquians called him **Onontio** ("Great Mountain"), the supreme alliance chief who won cooperation through persuasion and who had learned that, among the Indians, persuasion was always accompanied by gifts. The respect accorded to peacetime chiefs was roughly proportionate to how much they gave away, not to how much they accumulated. The English, by contrast, tried to "buy" land from the Indians and regarded the sale of both the land and of the Indians' right to use it as irrevocable. The French understood that this idea had no place in Indian culture. Agreements were not final contracts but required regular renewal, always with an exchange of gifts. The strongest party had to be more generous than the others.

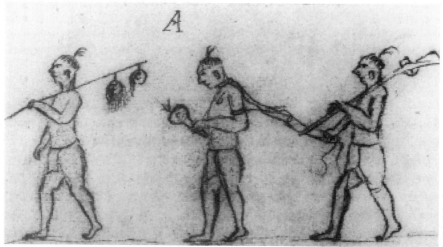

Archives Nationales

Iroquois Warriors Leading an Indian Prisoner into Captivity, 1660s   Because Indian populations had been depleted by war and disease, a tribe's survival became dependent on its ability to assimilate captives. This is a French copy of an Iroquois pictograph.

Middle Ground diplomacy came at a price. It involved New France in the Indian slave trade even though Louis XIV expressly forbade the enslavement of Indians, a command finally rescinded in 1709. Because Indians fought wars mostly to acquire captives, Onontio's western allies frequently presented captives to French traders, who realized that to refuse the gift would be an insult and could jeopardize New France's alliances with the western nations. By the 1720s, up to 5 percent of the colony's population consisted of enslaved Indians.

French Louisiana and Spanish Texas

In quest of a passage to Asia, Father Jacques Marquette and trader Louis Joliet paddled down the Mississippi to its juncture with the Arkansas River in 1673. But once they became convinced that the Mississippi flowed into the Gulf of Mexico and not the Pacific, they turned back. Then, in 1682, René-Robert Cavelier, *sieur* de La Salle traveled down the

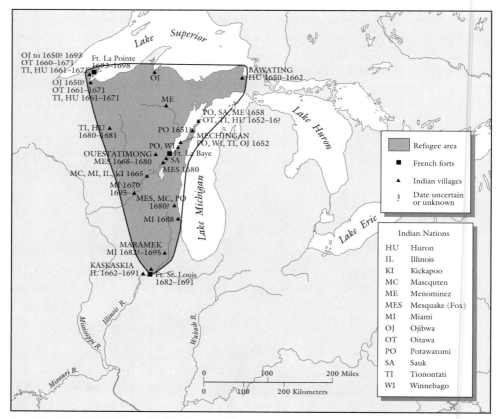

Map 3.5 French Middle Ground in North America Circa 1700 French power in North America rested mostly on the arrangements French governors worked out with refugee Algonquian Indians trying to resist Iroquois raids in the Great Lakes region.

Mississippi to its mouth, claiming possession of the entire area for France and calling it Louisiana (for Louis XIV). But when La Salle returned in 1684 by way of the Gulf of Mexico to plant a colony there, he overshot the mouth of the Mississippi, landed in Texas, and wandered around for three years in search of the great river until his exasperated men murdered him.

In 1699, during a brief lull in the wars between France and England, the French returned to the Gulf of Mexico. Pierre le Moyne d'Iberville, a Canadian, landed with 80 men at Biloxi, built a fort, and began trading with the Indians. In 1702, he moved his headquarters to Mobile, closer to the more populous nations of the interior, especially the Choctaws, who were looking for allies against the English. The Choctaws could still field 5,000 warriors but had suffered heavy losses from slaving raids organized by South Carolinians and carried out mostly by that colony's Chickasaw and Creek allies. About 1,800 Choctaws had been killed and 500 enslaved during the preceding decade. Using the Choctaws to anchor their trading system, the French created a weaker, southern version of the Great Lakes Middle Ground, acting as mediators and trading brandy, firearms, and other European products for furs and food. During the War of the Spanish Succession (1702–13), the French often received no European supplies, and they remained heavily outnumbered by the Indians. Although European diseases had been ravaging the area since the 1540s, the Indians of the lower Mississippi valley still numbered about 70,000. In 1708, the French numbered fewer than 300, including 80 Indian slaves. They were lucky to survive at all.

Spain, alarmed at any challenge to its monopoly on the Gulf of Mexico, founded Pensacola in 1698 and sent missionaries into eastern Texas in 1690, but they brought smallpox with them. Their explanation that the epidemic was God's "holy will" did not mollify the Tejas Indians, who told them to get out or be killed. They departed in 1693, leaving Texas to the Indians for another 20 years.

An Empire of Settlement: The British Colonies

By 1700, when 250,000 settlers and slaves were already living in England's mainland colonies, the population was doubling every 25 years. New France matched that pace, but with only 14,000 people in 1700, it could not close the gap. By contrast, the population of the Spanish missions continued to decline. In the struggle for empire, a growing population became Britain's greatest asset.

The Engine of British Expansion: The Colonial Household

Ordinary northern farmers and southern great planters had something in common that distinguished their households from those in England. With few exceptions, colonial families rejected the English customs of entail and primogeniture. **Entail** prohibited a landowner, or his heir, from dividing up his landed estate (that is, selling part of it) during his lifetime. **Primogeniture** obliged him to leave all of his land to his eldest surviving son. Under this system, younger sons clearly ranked below the oldest son, and daughters usually ranked behind both unless one of them could marry a man who would bring new resources into the family. Primogeniture and entail became more common in the 18th-century colonies than they had been before, but until the late colonial period, they failed to structure social relations the way they did in England. A Virginia planter, for example, might entail his home plantation (the one on which he had erected his big house) and bequeath it to his oldest son, but he would also leave land and slaves, sometimes whole plantations, to his other sons. The primacy of the eldest son was far more sentimental than structural. By contrast, the patriarchs of colonial households tried to pass on their status to all of their sons and to provide dowries that would enable all of their daughters to marry men of equal status. Until 1750 or so, these goals were usually realistic. For younger sons, then, the colonies presented a unique opportunity. Benjamin Franklin began his *Autobiography,* colonial America's greatest success story, by boasting that he was "the youngest Son of the youngest Son for 5 Generations back."

English households had become Americanized in the colonies during the earliest years of settlement, as soon as Virginia and Plymouth made land available to nearly all male settlers. By the mid-18th century, the question was whether that system could survive the pressures of a rising population. Social change began to drive American households back toward English practices. Only continual expansion onto new lands would allow the colonial household to provide equal opportunity for all sons, much less for all daughters.

Colonial households were patriarchal. The father expected to be loved and revered by his wife and children but insisted on being obeyed. A man's standing in the community depended on his success as a master at home. A mature male was expected to be the master of others. In New England and Pennsylvania, typical householders probably thought they were the rough equals of most other householders. Above all, a patriarch strove to perpetuate his household into the next generation and to preserve his own economic independence, or autonomy. Of course, complete independence was impossible. Every household owed small debts or favors to its neighbors, but these obligations seldom compromised the family's standing in the community.

Farmers tried to grow an agricultural surplus, if only as a hedge against drought, storms, and other unpredictable events. For rural Pennsylvanians, this surplus averaged about 40 percent of the total crop. With the harvest in, farmers marketed their produce, often selling it to merchants in Boston, New York, or Philadelphia for local consumption or for export to the West Indies or Europe. Farmers used the proceeds to pay taxes or their ministers' salaries and to buy British imports. Although these arrangements sometimes placed families in short-term debt to merchants, most farmers and artisans managed to avoid long-term debt. Settlers accepted temporary dependency among freemen—of sons on their parents, indentured servants on their masters, or apprentices and journeymen on master craftsmen. Sons often worked as laborers on neighboring farms, as sailors, or as journeymen craftsmen, provided that such dependence was temporary. A man who became permanently dependent on others lost the respect of his community.

The Voluntaristic Ethic and Public Life

Householders carried their quest for independence into public life. In entering politics and in waging war, their autonomy became an ethic of voluntarism. Few freemen could be coerced into doing something of which they disapproved. They had to be persuaded or induced to volunteer. Local officials serving without pay frequently ignored orders contrary to their own interests or the interests of their community.

Most young men accepted military service only if it suited their future plans. They would serve only under officers they knew, and then for only a single campaign. Few reenlisted. To the exasperation of professional British soldiers, provincials, like Indians, regarded blind obedience to commands as slavery. They did not enlist in order to become soldiers for life. After serving, they used their bonus and their pay, and often the promise of a land grant, to speed their way to becoming masters of their own households. Military service, for those who survived, could lead to land ownership and an earlier marriage. For New England women, however, war reduced the supply of eligible males and raised the median age of marriage by about two years, which meant, in effect, one fewer pregnancy per marriage.

Three Warring Empires, 1689–1716

When the three empires went to war after 1689, the Spanish and French fought mostly to survive. The British fought to expand their holdings. None of them won a decisive advantage in the first two wars, which ended with the Treaty of Utrecht in 1713.

Smart diplomacy with the Indians protected the western flank of New France, but the eastern parts of the colony were vulnerable to English invasion. The governors of New France knew that Indian attacks against English towns would keep the English colonies disorganized and make them disperse their forces. Within a year after the outbreak of war between France and England in 1689, Indians had devastated most of coastal Maine and parts of New Hampshire and had burned the Mohawk valley town of Schenectady, killing 60 and carrying off 27 captives.

In each of the four colonial wars between Britain and France, New Englanders called for the conquest of New France, usually through a naval expedition against Quebec, combined with an overland attack on Montreal. In King William's War (1689–97), Sir William Phips of Massachusetts forced Acadia to surrender in 1690 (although the French soon regained it) and later sailed up the St. Lawrence to Quebec, where he was forced to retreat with heavy losses. The overland attack on Montreal had already collapsed amid intercolonial bickering and an outbreak of smallpox. French attacks, with Indians providing most of the fighters, continued to ravage the northern frontier.

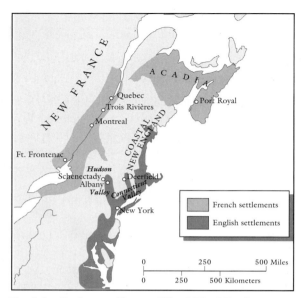

Map 3.6   Northeastern Theater of War, 1689–1713   For a quarter of a century, the colonies north of the Quaker settlements in the Delaware Valley were locked in a brutal and costly struggle against the French and Indians to their north and west.

In 1704, during Queen Anne's War (1702–13), the French and Indians destroyed Deerfield, Massachusetts, in a winter attack and marched most of its people off to captivity in Canada. Hundreds of New Englanders from Deerfield and other towns spent months or even years as captives. One of them was Eunice Williams, young daughter of John Williams, the pastor of Deerfield. Refusing to return to New England when the town's captives were released, she remained in Canada, became a Catholic, and married an Indian. Another New England woman who refused to return was Esther Wheelwright, daughter of a prominent Maine family. Captured by the Abenakis, she was taken to New France, where she also refused repatriation, converted to Catholicism, became a nun (Esther Marie Joseph de L'Enfant Jésus), and finally emerged as mother superior of the Ursuline Order in Canada—surely an unlikely career for a Puritan girl!

As the war dragged on, New Englanders twice failed to take Port Royal in Acadia, but a combined British and colonial force finally succeeded in 1710, renaming the colony Nova Scotia. An effort to subdue Quebec the following year met with disaster when many of the British ships ran aground in a treacherous stretch of the St. Lawrence River.

Farther south, the imperial struggle was grimmer and even more tragic. The Franciscan missions of Florida were already in decline, but mission Indians still attracted Carolina slavers, who invaded Florida between 1702 and 1704 with a large force of Indian allies, wrecked the

British Wars against France (and usually Spain), 1689–1763

European Name	American Name	Years	Peace
War of the League of Augsburg	King William's War	1689–1697	Ryswick
War of the Spanish Succession	Queen Anne's War	1702–1713	Utrecht
War of Jenkins' Ear, merging with		1739–1748	
War of the Austrian Succession	King George's War	1744–1748	Aix-la-Chapelle
Seven Years' War	French and Indian War	1754–1763*	Paris

*The French and Indian War began in America in 1754 and then merged with the Seven Years' War in Europe, which began in 1756.

missions, dragged off 4,000 women and children as slaves, and drove 9,000 Indians from their homes, some of whom then joined their attackers and got firearms. The invaders failed to take the Spanish fortress of St. Augustine, but slaving raids spread devastation as far west as the lands of the Choctaws and as far south as the tip of the Florida peninsula.

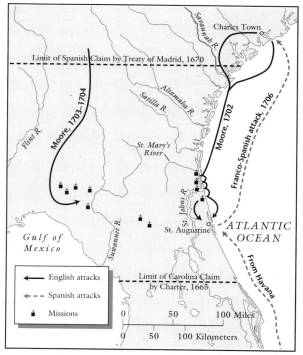

Map 3.7 Southeastern Theater of War, 1702–13 In this theater, the English and their Indian allies did most of the attacking, destroyed Spain's Florida missions, and enslaved thousands. Spain and France tried to attack Charleston, South Carolina, but their 1706 expedition failed after it was ravaged by disease.

South Carolina's greed for Indian slaves and other abuses finally alienated the colony's strongest Indian allies, the Yamasees. Traders frequently abused Indian women, including some of high status, an offense almost unknown within Indian communities. In addition, faltering Atlantic markets during wartime compelled Indian hunters to bring in more deerskins for smaller returns, and many hunters fell deeply in debt, a process that could lead to enslavement. In 1707, to resolve disputes between traders and Indians, South Carolina created the office of Indian agent, which was held first by John Wright and then Thomas Nairne. They belonged to rival factions of Indian traders, and their controversies paralyzed the colony's government. In late 1714, Wright's bloc filed so many lawsuits against Nairne that for six months he could not leave Charleston to address Yamasee grievances. When the exasperated Indians threatened war, the government sent both Nairne and Wright to resolve the crisis in April 1715. Nairne brought a message of peace; Wright privately threatened war, which would most likely lead to enslavement. Taking no chances, the Yamasees killed both men and all the other traders who had just arrived to collect their debts. Throughout the Southeast, all other Indian nations trading with South Carolina, except the Chickasaws, followed the Yamasees' example, wiping out nearly all of the colony's experienced traders and launching a war that almost destroyed the colony before the Yamasees were thrust back and nearly exterminated. Some Yamasees and some escaped African slaves fled as refugees to Spanish Florida. The war forced South Carolina to abandon the Indian slave trade, which left the production of rice as the colony's most profitable business.

The wars of 1689–1716 halted the movement of British settlers onto new lands in New England and the Carolinas. Only four Maine towns survived the wars; by 1720, after half a century, South Carolina still had only 5,200 settlers (and 11,800 slaves). In Pennsylvania, Maryland, and Virginia—colonies that had not been deeply involved in the wars—the expansive thrust continued.

Conclusion

The variety and diversity of the colonies posed a huge challenge to the English government. After 1650, it found ways to regulate colonial trade, mostly for the mutual benefit of both England and the colonies. The colonies, often beset by hostile Indians and internal discord, began to recognize that they needed protection that only England could provide. Once the Crown gave up its claims to absolute power, both sides discovered much on which they could agree.

Political values in England and the colonies began to converge during the Glorious Revolution and its aftermath. Englishmen throughout the empire insisted that the right to property was sacred, that without it liberty could never be secure. They celebrated liberty under law, government by consent, and the toleration of all Protestants. They barred Catholics from succession to the throne and loaded them with severe disabilities of other kinds. In an empire dedicated to "liberty, property, and no popery," Catholics became big losers.

So did Indians and Africans. Racism directed against Indians mostly welled up from below, taking root among ordinary settlers who competed with Indians for many of the same resources, especially land, and then bore the brunt of Indian reprisals. Colonial elites tried, often ineffectually, to contain this popular rage that nearly tore apart both New England and Virginia in 1675–76. By contrast, racism directed against enslaved Africans was typically imposed from above and increasingly enforced by law. Ordinary settlers and Africans knew one another by name, made love, sometimes even married, stole hogs together, ran away together, and even fought together under Nathaniel Bacon's leadership. The men in the process of becoming great planters used their power in the legislature to criminalize most of these activities. They were terrified by the upheaval that ex-servants could create and hoped for greater stability from a labor force serving for life. They rewarded small planters and servants with white supremacy.

By the 18th century, the British colonists, despite or perhaps even because of their growing racism, had come to believe they were the freest people on earth. They attributed this fortune to their widespread ownership of land and to the English constitutional principles they had incorporated into their own governments. When George I became king in 1714, they proudly proclaimed their loyalty to the Hanoverian dynasty that guaranteed a Protestant succession to the British throne. In their minds, the British empire had become the world's last bastion of liberty. Especially since the Glorious Revolution, it had vindicated this liberty while greatly magnifying its power.

SUGGESTED READINGS

The most comprehensive account of the Navigation Acts and England's instruments of enforcement is still **Charles M. Andrews**, *The Colonial Period of American History*, vol. 4 (1938). **Ian K. Steele's** *The English Atlantic, 1675–1740: An Exploration of Communication and Community* (1986) is careful, imaginative, and original.

Daniel K. Richter's *The Ordeal of the Longhouse: The People of the Iroquois League in the Era of European Colonization* (1992); **Richard W. Cogley's** *John Eliot's Mission to the Indians before King Philip's War* (1999); **Jill Lepore's** *The Name of War: King Philip's War and the Origins of American Identity* (1998); and **Wilcomb Washburn**, *The Governor and the Rebel: A History of Bacon's Rebellion in Virginia* (1957) are all essential to understanding the crisis of the 1670s. For the transition to slavery after Bacon's Rebellion, see **Anthony S. Parent, Jr.**, *Foul Means: The Formation of a Slave Society in Virginia, 1660–1740* (2003).

For the Dominion of New England and the Glorious Revolution in the colonies, see **Richard R. Johnson**, *Adjustment to Empire: The New England Colonies, 1675–1715* (1981); **John M. Murrin**, "The Menacing Shadow of Louis XIV and the Rage of Jacob Leisler: The Constitutional Ordeal of Seventeenth-Century New York," in **Stephen L. Schechter and Richard B. Bernstein, eds.**, *New York and the Union: Contributions to the American Constitutional Experience* (1990), pp. 29–71; and **Lois G. Carr and David W. Jordan**, *Maryland's Revolution of Government, 1689–1692* (1974). The best study of Salem witchcraft, which is also a superb introduction to the Indian wars in northern New England, is **Mary Beth Norton**, *In the Devil's Snare: The Salem Witchcraft Crisis of 1692* (2002).

For the French and Spanish colonies in these critical decades, see especially **Richard White**, *The Middle Ground: Indians, Empires, and Republics in the Great Lakes Region, 1650–1815* (1991); Ramón Gutiérrez, *When Jesus Came, the Corn Mothers Went Away: Marriage, Sexuality, and Power in New Mexico, 1500–1846* (1992), particularly on the Pueblo revolt; and **Daniel H. Usner, Jr.**, *Indians, Settlers, & Slaves in a Frontier Exchange Economy: The Lower Mississippi Valley before 1783* (1992).

On the householder economy in English North America, see **Laurel Thatcher Ulrich's** *Good Wives: Images and Reality in the Lives of Women in Northern New England* (1982), and **Mary M. Schweitzer**, *Custom and Contract: Household, Government, and the Economy in Colonial Pennsylvania* (1987).

Visit the Liberty Equality Power Companion Web site for resources specific to this textbook: http://www.thomsonedu.com/history/murrin

Also find self-tests and additional resources at ThomsonNOW. ThomsonNOW is an integrated online suite of services and resources with proven ease of use and efficient paths to success, delivering the results you want—NOW!

www.thomsonedu.com/login/

Provincial America and the Struggle for a Continent

The British colonists, who thought they were the freest people on earth, faced a growing dilemma in the 18th century. To maintain the opportunity that settlers had come to expect, the colonies had to expand onto new lands. But provincial society also increasingly emulated the cultural values of Great Britain—its architecture, polite learning, religion, and politics. Relentless expansion made this emulation difficult because the two goals often worked at cross purposes. An anglicized province would become far more hierarchical than the colonies had so far been and might not even try to provide a rough equality of opportunity. The settlers tried to sustain both, an effort that brought renewed conflict with their neighbors—the Indians, the Spanish, and the French.

When the British again went to war against Spain and France after 1739, the settlers joined in the struggle and declared that liberty itself was at stake. Less fortunate people among them disagreed. Slaves in the southern colonies saw Spain, not Britain, as their hope for liberty. In the eastern woodlands, most Indians identified France, not Britain, as the one ally genuinely committed to their survival and independence.

Expansion versus Anglicization

Focus Question
Why was it difficult to sustain both continual expansion and the anglicization of the colonies at the same time?

In the 18th century, as the British colonists sought to emulate their homeland, many of the institutions and material goods they had left behind in the 17th century began to reappear. After 1740, for example, imports of British goods grew spectacularly. The gentry, merchants, and professionals dressed in the latest London fashions and embraced that city's standards of taste and elegance. Southern planters erected "big houses," such as Mount Vernon, built by Lawrence Washington and bequeathed to his half-brother George. In Boston, on Beacon Hill, the merchant Thomas Hancock erected a stylish residence that later passed to his nephew John. Newspapers and learned professions based on English

CHRONOLOGY

1690	Massachusetts invents fiat money
1704	Boston *News-Letter* founded
1712	Slaves revolt in New York City
1716	Spanish begin to settle Texas
1718	Beginning of Scots-Irish emigration to North America
1721	Boylston introduces smallpox inoculation in Boston
1730	Three hundred slaves revolt in Virginia, and 29 are hanged
1732	Georgia charter granted by Parliament
1733	Molasses Act passed
1734	Edwards launches massive religious revival in the Connecticut valley
1735	Zenger acquitted of seditious libel in New York
1738	Spanish found Mose in Florida
1739	Slaves revolt in Stono, South Carolina
1739–41	Whitefield launches Great Awakening
1741	New York slave conspiracy trials lead to 35 executions
1745	New England volunteers take Louisbourg
1747	Ohio Company of Virginia founded • Anti-impressment rioters in Boston resist Royal Navy
1750	Massachusetts converts from paper money to silver
1754	Washington attacks French patrol near the forks of the Ohio River • Albany Congress proposes plan for colonial union
1755	Braddock suffers disaster near Fort Duquesne • British expel Acadians from Nova Scotia
1756–57	Loudoun antagonizes the colonies as commander-in-chief
1756	French take Oswego
1757	French take Fort William Henry • Pitt becomes Britain's war minister
1758	British take Fort Duquesne, Louisbourg, and Fort Frontenac • French repel British at Ticonderoga
1759	British take Ticonderoga and Crown Point • Wolfe dies taking Quebec; Montcalm also killed
1760	Montreal falls; Canada surrenders to the British
1760–61	Cherokee War devastates South Carolina backcountry
1762	Spain enters war, loses Havana and Manila
1763	Peace of Paris ends Seven Years' War

models proliferated after 1700, and colonial seaports began to resemble Bristol and other provincial cities in England.

But the population of British North America doubled every 25 years. Each new generation required twice as many colleges, ministers, lawyers, physicians, craftsmen, printers, sailors, and unskilled laborers as the preceding generation. Without them, standards of "civility" would decline. Colonial institutions could not meet these needs unless they continued to grow. As the 18th century progressed, the colonies became the scene of a contest between the unrelenting pace of raw expansion and these newer, anglicizing tendencies.

The southern colonies, which looked to England to satisfy their needs for skilled talent, could no longer attract as many people as they needed. In 1700, for example, Oxford and Cambridge universities in England had managed to meet the colonies' demand for Anglican clergymen, most of whom went to the southern colonies. By 1750, the colonial demand far exceeded what stagnant Oxford and Cambridge could supply, and the colonies were also importing Scottish and Irish clergy. Before long, those sources also proved inadequate. By contrast, northern colonies trained their own ministers, lawyers, and doctors in their own colleges, as well as their own skilled craftsmen through apprenticeships. Although still colonies, they were becoming America's first modernizing societies. They learned to do for themselves what Britain did for the southern colonies.

Much of this change occurred during prolonged periods of warfare. By midcentury, the wars were becoming a titanic struggle for control of the North American continent. Gradually, Indians realized that they would be the ultimate victims of British victory. Constant expansion for British settlers meant unending retreat for them.

Threats to Householder Autonomy

As population rose, some families acquired more prestige than others. **Gentlemen** performed no manual labor, and such men became prominent in public life. Before 1700, ordinary farmers and small planters had often sat in colonial assemblies. In the 18th century, the assemblies grew much more slowly than the overall population. In the five colonies from New York to Maryland, their size remained almost unchanged despite enormous population growth. The men who took part in public life above the local level increasingly came from a higher social status. They had greater wealth, a more impressive lineage, and a better education than ordinary farmers or craftsmen. But unlike members of Parliament, few colonial gentlemen enjoyed a patron–client relationship with the voters. In England, one or two families dominated each of the "pocket boroughs" that elected most members. In the colonies, most voters remained independent.

By midcentury, despite the high value that colonists placed on householder autonomy, patterns of dependency were beginning to emerge. In tidewater Virginia by 1760, about 80 percent of the land was **entailed.** That is, the landowner could not divide the estate but had to bequeath it intact to his heir. Younger sons had to look west for a landed inheritance. In one Maryland county, 27 percent of the householders were tenants who worked small tracts of land without slaves, or were men who owned a slave or two but had no claim to land. Such families could not satisfy the ambitions of all their children. In Pennsylvania's Chester County, a new class of married farm laborers arose. Their employers, without granting them title or lease, would let them use a small patch of land on which they could build a cottage and raise some food. Called "inmates" in Chester County records (or "cottagers" in England), such people made up 25 percent of the county population. Tenants on New York manors had to accept higher rents and shorter leases after 1750. In Chebacco Parish in Ipswich, Massachusetts, half of the farmers had land enough for only some of their sons by 1760.

Families that could not provide for all of their children reverted toward English social norms. In Connecticut, from the 1750s to the 1770s, about 75 percent of eligible sons inherited some land, but for daughters the rate fell from 44 percent to 34 percent. When a father could not support all his sons, he favored the eldest over younger sons. The younger sons, in turn, took up a trade or headed for the frontier. To increase their resources and sustain family autonomy, many New England farmers added a craft or two to the household. The 300 families of Haverhill, Massachusetts, supported 44 workshops and 19 mills by 1767. In Northampton, more than one-third of all the farming families also practiced a craft. The goal of independence continued to exercise great power, but it was under siege.

Anglicizing the Role of Women

The changing role of women provides a dramatic example of the anglicizing tendencies of the 18th century. When they married, most women received a **dowry** from their father, usually in cash or goods, not land. Under the common law doctrine of **coverture**, the legal personality of the husband "covered" the wife, and he made all legally binding decisions. If he died first, his widow was entitled to **dower rights**, usually one-third of the estate.

Women in many, perhaps most, households had to work harder to maintain the family status—at the spinning wheel, for example. New England women did virtually all of the region's weaving, which was a male occupation in Britain and in other colonies. Yet women were becoming more English in other ways, thus reversing some earlier trends. Until 1700, many Chesapeake widows inherited all of their husbands' property and administered their own estates. After 1700, such arrangements were rare. In the Hudson valley, Dutch law had been much more generous than English common law in bestowing property rights on women, but during the 18th century, English law gradually prevailed. In New England, too, as Puritan intensity waned, women suffered losses. Before 1700, courts had routinely punished men for sexual offenses, such as fornication, and many men had pleaded guilty and accepted their sentences. After 1700, almost no man would plead guilty to a sexual offense, except perhaps that of making love to his wife before their wedding day. However, to avoid a small fine, some husbands humiliated their wives by denying that charge, even if their wives had already pleaded guilty after giving birth to a child that had obviously been conceived before marriage. Courts rarely convicted men of sex offenses, not even serious crimes such as rape. The European double standard of sexual behavior, which punished women for their indiscretions while tolerating male infractions, had been in some jeopardy under the Puritan regime. It now revived.

Expansion, Immigration, and Regional Differentiation

After 1715, the settled portions of North America enjoyed their longest era of peace since the arrival of Europeans. Louis XIV's wars had emptied the borderlands of most of their inhabitants. Until midcentury, people poured into these areas, usually without provoking the strong Indian nations of the interior. As the colonies expanded, they evolved into distinct regions, although only New Englanders acquired a self-conscious sense of regional identity before independence.

Emergence of the Old South

Renewed immigration, free and unfree, drove much of the postwar expansion. After 1730, the flow became enormous. In that year, about 630,000 settlers and slaves lived in the mainland colonies. By 1775, another 248,000 Africans and 284,000 Europeans had landed, including 50,000 British convicts, shipped mostly to Maryland and Virginia, where they served long indentures. During this period, the African slave trade to North America reached its peak. Most of the 234,000 voluntary immigrants settled in the middle or southern colonies. Free migration decisively outweighed the influx of slaves only after 1763.

Almost 90 percent of the slaves went to the southern colonies. At least 84,000 slaves went to Charleston, 70,000 to Virginia, and 25,000 to Maryland. One-eighth of the slaves went to northern colonies. New England had 15,000 blacks by 1770, New York 19,000, and New Jersey, Pennsylvania, and Delaware a combined total of 16,000. About 80 percent of the slaves arrived from Africa on overcrowded, stinking, British-owned vessels. Most of the rest came, a few at a time, from the West Indies on smaller New England ships. This massive influx created the Old South, a society consisting of wealthy slaveholding planters, a much larger class of small planters, and thousands of slaves. By 1720, slaves made up 70 percent of South Carolina's population. By 1740, they were 40 percent of Virginia's and 30 percent of Maryland's populations. Slaves did most of the manual labor in the southern colonies, and their arrival transformed the social structure. In 1700, most members of Virginia's House of Burgesses were small planters who raised tobacco with a few indentured servants and perhaps a slave or two. After 1730, the typical burgess was a great planter who owned at least 20 slaves. And by 1750, the rice planters of South Carolina were richer than any other group in British North America. Tobacco and rice planters had few contacts with each other, except in North Carolina, where they did not get along. They did not yet think of themselves as "southerners."

The life of slaves in the upper South (Maryland, Virginia, and the Albemarle region of North Carolina) differed considerably from the life of slaves in the lower South (from Cape Fear in North Carolina through South Carolina and eventually Georgia). The Chesapeake tobacco planters organized their slaves into gangs, supervised them closely, and kept them in the fields all day. To make their plantations more self-sufficient, they also trained perhaps 10 percent of them as blacksmiths, carpenters, coopers, or other skilled artisans. The planters, who saw themselves as benevolent paternalists, encouraged family life among their workers, who by the 1720s were beginning to achieve a rate of reproduction that almost equaled that of the settlers. Slaveholders even explained brutal whippings as fatherly efforts to correct the behavior of members of their household.

Paternalism even extended to religion. In the 1720s, for the first time on any significant scale, many Virginia planters began to urge their slaves to convert to Christianity. At first, only adults who had a good command of the catechism, which they had to learn orally because they were not allowed to become literate, were accepted into the church, but by the 1730s, growing numbers of infants were also baptized. These efforts continued to expand despite a massive slave uprising. A rumor spread that the British government had promised emancipation to any slave who converted but that the colony was suppressing the news. On a Sunday in September 1730, about 300 slaves tried to escape through the Great Dismal Swamp. The planters hired Indians to track them, crushed the rebels, and hanged 29 of them. Yet the conversions continued to gain momentum, mostly, it seems, because planters hoped that Christian slaves would be more dutiful.

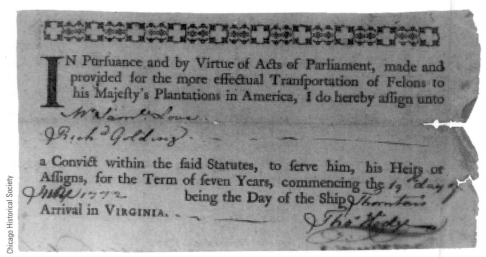

Chicago Historical Society

Contract for the Convict Trade   The convict trade, which provided long-term servants for American colonists, became quite well organized in the 18th century.

South Carolina planters began with similar paternalistic inclinations, but the rice swamps and mosquitoes defeated them. Whites who supervised slave gangs in the rice fields quickly caught malaria. Although it was seldom fatal, malaria left its victims vulnerable to other diseases that often did kill them. Many rice planters relocated their big houses to higher ground, at a safe distance from their rice fields. With few exceptions, they showed no inclination to Christianize their laborers.

Africans fared much better than whites in the marshy rice fields. (Modern medicine has shown that many Africans possess a **sickle cell** in the blood that grants them protection against malaria but can also expose their children to a deadly form of inherited anemia.) As the ability of Africans to resist malaria became evident, Carolina planters seldom ventured into the rice fields and became less paternalistic than their Virginia counterparts except toward their household servants. After midcentury, many chose to spend their summers in Charleston or in homes on high ground in the interior. Some vacationed in Newport, Rhode Island.

This situation altered work patterns. To get local manufactures, planters relied on white artisans in Charleston, many of whom bought or leased slaves, who then did most of the actual work. To produce a crop of rice, planters devised the **task system,** in which the slaves had to complete certain labor assignments each day, after which their time was their own. Slaves used their free time to raise crops, hunt, or fish, activities that enabled them to create their own largely invisible economy.

Thus, while many Chesapeake slaves were acquiring the skills of artisans, slaves on South Carolina plantations were heading in the other direction. Before rice became the colony's staple, they had performed a wide variety of tasks, but the huge profits from rice now condemned nearly all of them to demanding, monotonous labor in the marshes, even though it, in turn, freed them from the direct oversight of their masters. Rice culture also left Africans with low rates of reproduction. Yet because the task system gave them more control over their own lives, slaves preferred it to **gang labor.**

The task system also slowed assimilation into the British world. African words and customs survived longer in South Carolina than in the Chesapeake colonies. Newly imported slaves spoke **Gullah,** originally a pidgin language (that is, a simple second language for everyone who spoke it). Gullah began with phrases common to many West African languages, gradually added English words, and became the natural language of later generations, eventually evolving into modern black English.

The South Carolina slave population failed to grow by natural increase until perhaps the 1770s, a half-century later than in the tobacco colonies. Even South Carolina planters had difficulty replacing themselves before 1760. But by the Revolution, the American South was becoming the world's only self-sustaining slave society. Nowhere else could staple colonies reproduce their enslaved labor force without continuous imports from Africa.

Everywhere that slavery took hold, it required brute force to sustain it. Slaves convicted of arson were often burned at the stake, an unthinkable punishment to inflict on a white person. Whippings were frequent, with the master or overseer setting the number of stripes. In South Carolina, one overseer killed five slaves in two or three years before 1712. When one slave fell asleep and lost a parcel of rice in the river, the overseer chained him, whipped him twice a day, refused to give him food, and confined him at night in a "hellish Machine contrived by him into the Shape of a Coffin where [he] could not stir." The victim finally killed himself after obtaining a knife from one of his children.

If extreme cruelty of this sort was rare, random acts of violence were common and, from a slave's perspective, unpredictable. In Virginia, William Byrd II was one of the most refined settlers in the colony and owned its largest library. His diary reveals that when he and his wife Lucy disagreed, the slaves could suffer. "My wife and I had a terrible quarrel about whipping Eugene while Mr. Mumford was there but she had a mind to show her authority before company but I would not suffer it, which she took very ill." This time Eugene was spared, but slaves were not always so lucky. On another occasion, "My wife caused Prue to be whipped violently notwithstanding I desired not, which provoked me to have Anaka whipped likewise who had deserved it much more, on which my wife flew into such a passion she hoped she would be revenged of me." This time both slaves were whipped, apparently for minor infractions. House servants must have dreaded the days that Byrd spent in Williamsburg, leaving Lucy in charge of the plantation.

The southern colonies prospered in the 18th century by exchanging their staple crops for British imports. By midcentury, much of this trade had been taken over by Scots. Glasgow became the leading tobacco port of the Atlantic. Tobacco profits remained precarious before 1730 but then improved in later decades, partly because Virginia guaranteed a high-quality leaf by passing an inspection law in 1730 (Maryland followed suit in 1747), and partly because a tobacco contract between Britain and France brought lucrative revenues to both governments and opened up a vast continental market for Chesapeake planters. By 1770, more than 90 percent of their tobacco was reexported to Europe from Britain.

Other exports and new crafts also contributed to rising prosperity. South Carolina continued to export provisions to the sugar islands and deerskins to Britain. **Indigo,** used as a dye by the British textile industry, received a cash bounty from Parliament and emerged at midcentury as a second staple crop, pioneered by a woman planter, Eliza Lucas Pinckney. North Carolina, where the population increased fivefold between 1720 and 1760 and more than doubled again by 1775, sold **naval stores** (pitch, resin, turpentine) to British shipbuilders. Many Chesapeake planters turned to wheat as a second cash crop. It required mills to grind it into flour, barrels in which to pack it, and ships to carry it away. It did for the Chesapeake what tobacco had failed to do: It created cities. Norfolk and Baltimore had nearly 10,000 people by 1775, and smaller cities, such as Alexandria and Georgetown, also thrived. Shipbuilding, linked to the export of wheat, became a major Chesapeake industry.

The Mid-Atlantic Colonies: The "Best Poor Man's Country"

The mid-Atlantic colonies had been pluralistic societies from the start. Immigration added to this ethnic and religious diversity after 1700. The region had the most prosperous family farms in America and, by 1760, the two largest cities, Philadelphia and New York.

Pennsylvania outpaced New York in the competition for immigrants. In the 1680s and 1690s, New York governors had granted their political supporters enormous manorial estates that dominated the Hudson valley and discouraged immigration. As late as 1750, the small colony of New Jersey had as many settlers as New York but fewer slaves. Pennsylvania's growth exploded, driven by both natural increase and a huge surge of immigration. The 12th colony to be founded out of the original 13, Pennsylvania was the second most populous by 1770, surpassed only by Virginia.

After 1720, Ireland and Germany replaced England as the main source of voluntary immigrants. About 70 percent of Ireland's emigrants came from **Ulster.** They were Presbyterians whose forebears had come to Ireland from Scotland in the 17th century. (Historians now call them the Scots-Irish, a term that was seldom used at the time.) Most left for America to avoid an increase in rents and to enjoy greater trading privileges than the British Parliament allowed Ireland. Most Ulster immigrants headed for the Delaware valley. Maybe 30 percent of Irish immigrants came from southern Ireland. Most of them were Catholics, but perhaps one-fourth were Anglicans. They too headed for the mid-Atlantic colonies. Roughly 80,000 Irish reached the Delaware valley before 1776.

Perhaps 70,000 of the free immigrants were Germans. Most of them arrived as families, often as **redemptioners,** a new form of indentured service that was attractive to married couples because it allowed them to find and bind themselves to their own masters. Families could stay together. After redemptioners completed their service, most of them streamed into the interior of Pennsylvania, where Germans outnumbered the original English and Welsh settlers by 1750. Other Germans moved to the southern backcountry with the Irish.

These colonies grew excellent wheat and built their own ships to carry it abroad. At first, New York flour outsold Pennsylvania's, but Pennsylvania gained the edge in the 1720s after it instituted a new system of public inspection and quality control. When Europe's population started to surge after 1740, the middle colonies began to ship flour across the Atlantic. Around 1760, both Philadelphia and New York City overtook Boston's stagnant population of 15,000. Philadelphia, with 32,000 people, was the largest city in British North America by 1775.

The Backcountry

Many Scots-Irish, together with some Germans, pushed west into the mountains and up the river valleys into the interior parts of Virginia and the Carolinas. In South Carolina, about 100 miles of pine barrens stood between these backcountry settlements and the rice plantations along the coast. Most of the English-speaking colonists were immigrants from Ulster, northern England, or lowland Scotland, who brought their folkways with them and soon gave the region its own distinctive culture. Although most of them farmed, many turned to hunting or raising cattle. Unlike the coastal settlements, the backcountry had no newspapers, few clergymen or other professionals, and little elegance. South Carolina's backcountry had almost no government. A visiting Anglican clergyman bemoaned "the

© CORBIS

Moravian Bethlem The Moravian Brethren made Bethlehem, Pennsylvania, their main settlement in the northern colonies. They erected some of the largest structures on the mainland. This engraving is from a painting by Thomas Pownall, royal governor of New Jersey and Massachusetts in the 1750s.

abandon'd Morals and profligate Principles" of the settlers. Refined easterners found the backcountry more than a little frightening. Clannish and violent, backcountry settlers drank heavily and hated Indians. By the 1750s, the situation grew quite tense in Pennsylvania, where the Quaker assembly insisted on handling differences with the Indians through peaceful negotiations. Once war broke out with the Indians, most backcountry men demanded their extermination. Virginia and South Carolina faced similar problems.

New England: A Faltering Economy and Paper Money

New England was a land of farmers, fishermen, lumberjacks, shipwrights, and merchants and still considered itself more pious than the rest of the British Empire, but the region faced serious problems. Few immigrants, either slave or free, went there. In fact, since about 1660, more people had been leaving the region, mostly for New York and New Jersey, than had been arriving.

New England's relative isolation in the 17th century began to have negative social and economic effects after 1700. Life expectancy declined as diseases from Europe, especially smallpox and diphtheria, invaded the region. The first settlers had left these diseases behind, but lack of exposure in childhood made later generations vulnerable. When smallpox threatened to devastate Boston in 1721, Zabdiel Boylston, a self-taught doctor, began inoculating people with the disease on the theory that healthy ones would survive the injection and become immune. Although the city's leading physicians opposed the experiment as too risky, it worked and soon became a regular feature of public health in many colonies. Even so, a diphtheria epidemic in the 1730s and high military losses after 1740 reduced population growth. New England's rate of growth fell behind that of other regions.

After peace returned in 1713, New England's economy weakened. The region had prospered in the 17th century, mostly by exporting cod, grain, cattle, and barrel staves to the West Indies. After 1700, however, Yankees had trouble feeding themselves, much less others. A blight called the **wheat blast** first appeared in the 1660s and slowly spread until cultivation of wheat nearly ceased. Because Yankees preferred wheat bread to cornbread, they had to import flour from New York and Pennsylvania and, eventually, wheat from the Chesapeake colonies. Poverty became a social problem in Boston, where by the 1740s about one-third of all adult women were widows, mostly poor. Poor relief became a major public expense.

After grain exports declined, the once-profitable West Indian trade barely broke even. Yet its volume remained large, especially when enterprising Yankees opened up new markets in the lucrative French sugar islands. Within the West Indian market, competition from New York and Philadelphia grew almost too severe for New Englanders to meet, because those cities had flour to export and shorter distances over which to ship it. Mostly, the Yankees sent fish and forest products to the islands in exchange for molasses, which they used as a sweetener (cheaper than sugar) or distilled into rum. Rum joined cod and lumber as a major export. British West Indian planters, alarmed by the flood of cheap French molasses, urged Parliament to stamp out New England's trade with the French islands. Parliament passed the Molasses Act of 1733, which placed a prohibitive duty of six pence per gallon on all foreign molasses. Strictly enforced, the act would have strangled New England trade; instead, bribery and smuggling kept the molasses flowing.

Shipbuilding gave New England most of its leverage in the Atlantic economy. Yankees made more ships than all of the other colonies combined. New England ships earned enough from freight in most years to offset trade losses, but Boston merchants often had to scramble to pay for their imports. New England ran unfavorable balances with nearly every trading partner, especially England. Yankees imported many British products but produced little that anybody in Britain wanted to buy. Whale oil, used in lamps, was an exception. A prosperous whaling industry emerged on the island of Nantucket, but the grain trade with the mid-Atlantic and Chesapeake colonies was not profitable. Settlers there eagerly bought rum and a few slaves from Yankee vessels that stopped on their way back from the West Indies. Newport even became deeply involved in slave trading along the African coast. That traffic never supplied a large percentage of North America's slaves, but it contributed greatly to Newport's growth.

New England's experience with paper money illustrates these economic difficulties. In response to a military emergency in 1690, Massachusetts invented **fiat money**—that is, paper money backed, not by silver or gold, but only by the government's promise to accept it in payment of taxes. This system worked well enough until serious depreciation set in after the Treaty of Utrecht. The return of peace in 1713 meant that nearly all paper money would be retired within a few years through taxes already pledged for that purpose. To sustain its paper currency, the Massachusetts legislature created four land banks between 1714 and 1728. Settlers could borrow paper money using their land as security and pay off the debt over 10 years at 5 percent interest. But when the value of New England's currency declined steadily in relation to the British pound, most Boston merchants turned against paper money. They sold many of their wares on credit only to be repaid in depreciated paper. Farmers, who had originally been suspicious of land banks, became strong advocates after they discovered that they could benefit as debtors. When Britain forbade the governor to consent to any new public land banks, the countryside organized a private land bank that issued huge amounts of paper in 1741, provoking a major crisis. Parliament intervened to crush the bank.

The declining value of money touched off a fierce debate that raged from 1714 until 1750. Creditors attacked paper money as fraudulent: Only gold and silver, they claimed, had real value. Defenders retorted that, in most other colonies, paper was holding its value. The problem, they insisted, lay with the New England economy, which could not generate enough exports to pay for the region's imports. The elimination of paper, they warned, would only deepen New England's problems. War disrupted shipping in the 1740s, and military expenditures sent New England currency to a new low. Then, in 1748, Parliament agreed to reimburse Massachusetts for these expenses at the 1745 exchange rate. Governor William Shirley and House Speaker Thomas Hutchinson, an outspoken opponent of paper money, were barely able to persuade the legislature to use the grant to retire all paper and convert to silver money. That decision was a drastic example of anglicization. Although fiat money was the colony's own invention, Massachusetts repudiated its own offspring in 1750 in favor of orthodox British methods of public finance. But as Hutchinson's critics had warned, silver gravitated to Boston and then back to London to pay for imports. New England's economy entered a deep recession in the early 1750s. It did not revive until the next French war.

Anglicizing Provincial America

Focus Question
How were the colonists able to embrace both the Enlightenment and evangelical religion at the same time?

Forms of production made these regions diverse. What made them more alike was what they retained or acquired from Britain. Although each region exported its own distinctive products, patterns of consumption became quite similar throughout the colonies. In the mid-1740s, the mainland colonies and the West Indies consumed almost identical amounts of British imports. Just 10 years later, the mainland provinces had forged ahead by a margin of 2 to 1. Their ability to consume ever-larger quantities of British goods was beginning to make the mainland colonies more valuable to the empire than the sugar islands. They also welcomed English revivalists and absorbed much of British intellectual and political culture.

The World of Print

Few 17th-century American settlers owned books, and except in New England, even fewer engaged in the intellectual debates of the day. For most of the century, only Massachusetts had printing presses, first in Cambridge to serve Harvard College, the clergy, and the government, and then in Boston beginning in 1674. For the next century, Boston remained the print capital of North America. In the 1680s, William Bradford became Philadelphia's first printer, but he soon moved to New York. By 1740, Boston had eight printers; Philadelphia and New York each had two. No other community had more than one.

Not surprisingly, Boston also led the way in newspaper publishing. John Campbell, the city's postmaster, established the *Boston News-Letter* in 1704. By the early 1720s, two more papers had opened in Boston. Philadelphia and New York City had each acquired one. The *South Carolina Gazette* was founded in Charleston in 1732 and the *Virginia Gazette* in Williamsburg in 1736. Benjamin Franklin took charge of the *Pennsylvania Gazette* in 1729, and **John Peter Zenger** launched the controversial *New York Weekly Journal* in 1733 and won a major victory for freedom of the press when a jury acquitted him of **seditious libel,** the crime of criticizing government officials.

These papers were weeklies that devoted nearly all of their space to European affairs. Before midcentury, they rarely reported local news because they assumed their readers already knew it. At first, they merely reprinted items from the *London Gazette.* Beginning in the 1720s, however, the *New England Courant,* under James Franklin, began to reprint Richard Steele's essays from the *Spectator,* Joseph Addison's pieces from the *Tatler,* and the angry, polemical writings, mostly aimed at religious bigotry and political and financial corruption, of "Cato," a pen name used jointly by John Trenchard and Thomas Gordon. *Cato's Letters* became immensely popular among colonial printers and readers. In short, newspapers began to spread the English Enlightenment across the North American colonies.

Benjamin Franklin personified the Enlightenment values that the newspapers were spreading. As a boy, although raised in Puritan Boston, he skipped church on Sundays to read Addison and Steele and to perfect his prose style. As a young printer with his brother's *New England Courant* in the 1720s, he helped publish the writings of John Checkley, an Anglican whom the courts twice prosecuted in a vain attempt to silence him. Franklin joined the Church of England after moving to Philadelphia. After 1729, he made his *Pennsylvania Gazette* the best-edited paper in America. It reached 2,000 subscribers, four times the circulation of a Boston weekly.

An 18th-Century Printing Press   This is the printing press that James Franklin is believed to have brought to Boston from London in 1717. Benjamin, his younger brother and apprentice, used it to learn the trade of a printer.

Franklin was always looking for ways to improve society. In 1727, he and some friends founded the Junto, a working man's debating society that met Friday evenings to discuss literary and philosophical questions. It later evolved into the American Philosophical Society, which still thrives near Independence Hall. Franklin was a founder of North America's first Masonic lodge in 1730, the Library Company of Philadelphia a year later, the Union Fire Company in 1736, the Philadelphia Hospital in 1751, and an academy that became the College of Philadelphia (now the University of Pennsylvania) in the 1750s. But his greatest fame arose from his ingenious electrical experiments. He also invented the Franklin stove (much more efficient than a fireplace) and the lightning rod. By the 1760s, he had become the most celebrated North American in the world.

The Enlightenment in America

The English **Enlightenment**, which rejected a wrathful God and exalted man's capacity for knowledge and social improvement, grew out of the rational and benevolent piety favored by Low Church (Latitudinarian) Anglicans in Restoration England. They disliked rigid doctrine, scoffed at conversion experiences, attacked superstition, and rejected all "fanaticism," whether that of High Church Laudians, who had brought on England's great crisis of 1640–42, or that of the Puritans, who had executed Charles I. High Church men, a small group after 1689, stood for orthodoxy, ritual, and liturgy.

Enlightened writers celebrated Sir Isaac Newton's laws of motion as one of the greatest intellectual achievements of all time, joined the philosopher John Locke in looking for embodied this "polite and Catholick [that is, universal] spirit." He preached morality rather than dogma and had a way of defending the doctrine of eternal damnation that left his listeners wondering how a merciful God could possibly have ordained such a cruel punishment.

Enlightened ideas won an elite constituency in the mainland colonies even before newspapers began circulating these new views. Tillotson had a huge impact on America. His sermons appeared in numerous southern libraries and made a deep impression at Harvard College, beginning with two young tutors, William Brattle and John Leverett, Jr. After Leverett became Harvard's president in 1708, Tillotson's ideas became entrenched in the curriculum. For the rest of the century, most Harvard-trained ministers, although still claiming to be Calvinists, embraced Tillotson's latitudinarian piety. They stressed the similarities, not the differences, between Congregationalists and Anglicans and favored broad religious toleration. After 1800, most Harvard-educated ministers became Unitarians who no longer believed in hell or the divinity of Jesus.

In 1701, largely in reaction against this trend at Harvard, a new college was founded as a bastion of orthodoxy and finally settled in New Haven, Connecticut. It was named Yale College in honor of a wealthy English benefactor, Elihu Yale, who gave his library to the school. These Anglican books did to the Yale faculty what Tillotson's writings had done at Harvard—and more. In 1722 most of the faculty converted to the Church of England and sailed for England to be ordained by the bishop of London. Their leader, Timothy Cutler, became the principal Anglican spokesman in Boston. Samuel Johnson, another defector, became the first president of King's College (now Columbia University) in New York City in the 1750s and won a considerable reputation as a moral philosopher.

Lawyers and Doctors

The rise of the legal profession helped spread Enlightenment ideas. Before 1700, most colonists despised lawyers as men who took advantage of the misery of others and who deliberately stirred up discord. Virginia and Massachusetts briefly abolished the legal profession. Only in Maryland did it take firm hold before 1700, but then it began to spread everywhere.

In 1692, three English lawyers handled nearly all of the cases in the province of New York; by 1704, there were eight. In Boston, the legal profession seemed disreputable as late as 1720. Three British immigrants, all of them Anglicans, handled most cases. When a Congregational clergyman resigned his Connecticut pulpit and moved to Boston to practice law, he too joined Anglican King's Chapel. Benjamin Gridley, a Harvard man famous for his impiety, took up law and wrote enlightened essays for Boston newspapers in the 1730s, turned his office into an informal law school, and set up a debating society, the Sodalitas, in which students disputed legal questions within the context of contemporary oratory and philosophy. By then, a college education was almost a prerequisite to a legal career in New England.

Most Massachusetts lawyers before 1760 were either Anglicans or young men who had rejected the Congregational ministry as a career. Some were scoffers and skeptics, and most probably thought of themselves as a new learned elite. By the 1790s, American lawyers saw themselves as the cultural vanguard of the new republic. Poet John Trumbull, playwright Royall Tyler, and novelist Hugh Henry Brackenridge all continued to practice law while writing on the side. Poet William Cullen Bryant, writer Washington Irving, and novelist Charles Brockden Brown gave up law to write full time.

Medicine also became an enlightened profession, with Philadelphia setting the pace. William Shippen earned degrees at Princeton and Edinburgh, the best medical school in the world at the time, before returning to Philadelphia in 1762, where he became the first American to lecture on medicine, publish a treatise on chemistry, and dissect human cadavers, a practice that shocked the unenlightened. His student John Morgan became the first professor of medicine in North America when the College of Philadelphia established a medical faculty a few years later. Benjamin Rush, who also studied at Princeton and Edinburgh, brought the latest Scottish techniques to the newly founded Philadelphia Hospital. He too became an enlightened reformer. He attacked slavery and alcohol and supported the Revolution. Many colonial physicians embraced radical politics.

Georgia: The Failure of an Enlightenment Utopia

In the 1730s, Anglican humanitarianism and the Enlightenment belief in the possibility of social improvement converged in Britain to provide support for the founding of Georgia, named for King George II (1727–60). The sponsors of this project hoped to create a society that could make productive use of England's "worthy" poor (but not the lazy or criminal poor). They were determined to produce silk and wine, products that no other British colony had yet succeeded in making profitable. They also intended to shield South Carolina's slave society from Spanish Florida by populating Georgia with disciplined, armed free men. Appalled by what cheap English gin was doing to the sobriety and industry of England's working people, they prohibited hard liquor as well as slavery. Slaves would make Georgia just like South Carolina, with all of that colony's vulnerabilities.

A group of distinguished trustees, including members of both houses of Parliament, set themselves up as a nonprofit corporation and announced that they would give land away, not sell it. Led by James Oglethorpe, the trustees obtained a 20-year charter from Parliament in 1732, raised money from Anglican friends, and launched the colony on land claimed by both Spain and Britain. The trustees recruited foreign Protestants, including some Germans who had just been driven out of Salzburg by its Catholic bishop, a small number of Moravian Brethren (a German pacifist sect), and French Huguenots. They interviewed many prospective settlers to distinguish the worthy poor from the unworthy. They engaged silk and wine experts and recruited Scottish Highlanders as soldiers.

But the trustees refused to consult the settlers on what might be good for Georgia. As refined men, they believed they knew what the colony needed. They created no elective assembly, nor did they give the British government much chance to supervise them. Under their charter, Georgia laws had to be approved by the British Privy Council. Therefore, the trustees passed only three "laws" during their 20 years of rule. One laid out the land system, and the others prohibited slavery and hard liquor. They governed through "regulations" instead of laws. An elective assembly, they promised, would come later, after Georgia's character had been firmly set.

In 1733, the first settlers laid out Savannah, a town with spacious streets. Within 10 years, 1,800 charity cases and just over 1,000 self-supporting colonists reached Georgia. The most successful were the Salzburgers, who agreed with the prohibitions on slavery and alcohol and built a thriving settlement at Ebenezer, farther up the Savannah River. The Moravian Brethren left for North Carolina after five years rather than bear arms. A disgruntled group of Lowland Scots known as the Malcontents departed for South Carolina after Oglethorpe ignored their complaints.

The land system never worked as intended. The trustees gave 50 acres to every male settler whose passage was paid for out of charitable funds. Those who paid their own way could claim up to 500 acres. Ordinary farmers did poorly; they could not support a family on 50 acres of the sandy soil around Savannah. Because the trustees envisioned every landowner as a soldier, women could not inherit land, nor could landowners sell their **plots.**

The settlers were unable to grow grapes or to persuade the sickly worms that survived the Atlantic crossing to make silk out of mulberry leaves. They clamored for rum, smuggled it into the colony when they could, and insisted that Georgia would never thrive until it had slaves. By the mid-1740s, enough people had died or left to reduce the population by more than half, and by 1752, it had dropped below the 2,800 who had first settled the colony. Between 1750 and 1752, the trustees dropped their ban on alcohol, allowed the importation of slaves, summoned an elective assembly (but only to consult, not legislate), and finally surrendered their charter to Parliament. With the establishment of royal government in 1752, Georgia finally got an elective assembly with full powers of legislation, and the colony became what it was never meant to be, a smaller version of South Carolina, producing rice and indigo with slave labor. By then, ironically, it had done more to spread religious revivalism than to vindicate Enlightenment ideals.

The Great Awakening

Between the mid-1730s and the early 1740s, an immense religious revival swept across the Protestant world. Within the British Empire, it affected some areas more intensely than others. England, Scotland, Ulster, New England, the mid-Atlantic colonies, and for a time South Carolina, responded warmly to emotional calls for a spiritual rebirth. Southern Ireland, the West Indies, and the Chesapeake colonies remained on the margins until Virginia and Maryland were drawn into a later phase of the movement in the 1760s and 1770s. This **Great Awakening** shattered some denominational loyalties in the colonies and enabled the Methodists and the Baptists to surge ahead of all Protestant rivals in the generation after 1780.

Origins of the Revivals

Some of the earliest revivals originated in the colonies. Around 1720, Theodorus Jacobus Frelinghuysen sparked several revivals in his congregation in New Brunswick, New Jersey. The local Presbyterian pastor, Gilbert Tennent, watched and learned. Tennent was a younger son of William Tennent, Sr., an Anglican-turned-Presbyterian minister who had moved from Ulster to America. At Neshaminy, Pennsylvania, he set up his Log College, where he trained his sons and other young men as **evangelical** preachers. The Tennent family dominated the **Presbytery** of New Brunswick, used it to ordain ministers, and sent them off to any congregation that requested one, even in other presbyteries. These intrusions angered the Philadelphia **Synod**, the governing body of the Presbyterian church in the colonies. Most of its ministers emphasized orthodoxy over a personal conversion experience. In a 1740 sermon, *The Dangers of an Unconverted Ministry,* Gilbert Tennent denounced those preachers for leading their people to hell. His attack split the church. In 1741, the outnumbered revivalists withdrew and founded their own Synod of New York.

The Synod of Philadelphia by 1738

In actuality, some presbyteries had more churches than others. Arrows indicate descending lines of authority.

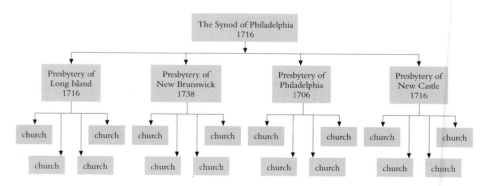

In New England, Solomon Stoddard of Northampton presided over six revivals, which he called "harvests of souls," between the 1670s and his death in 1729. Jonathan Edwards, his grandson and successor—the only member of the Yale faculty who had not defected to the Anglicans in 1722—touched off a revival in 1734 and 1735 that rocked dozens of Connecticut valley towns. It ended suddenly when a prominent man, overwhelmed by the burden of his sins, slit his own throat. Edwards's *A Faithful Narrative of the Surprising Work of God* (1737) explained what a **revival** was—an emotional response to God's Word that brought sudden conversions to scores of people. He described these conversions in acute detail and won admirers in Britain as well as in New England.

In England, John Wesley and George Whitefield set the pace. At worldly Oxford University, Wesley and his brother Charles founded the Holy Club, a High Church society whose members fasted until they could barely walk. One even lay prostrate for hours on the frigid earth, lost in prayer while his hands turned black. These methodical practices prompted scoffers to call them "Methodists." In 1735, Wesley went to Georgia as a missionary, which became an unhappy experience for him. He fell in love with a woman who did not return his affection, and the settlers rejected his ascetic piety. In 1737, on the return voyage to England, some Moravians convinced him that, for all his zeal, he had never grasped the central Protestant message, justification by faith alone. Some months later, he was deeply moved by Edwards's *Faithful Narrative*. Wesley abandoned his High Church pieties as he found his life's mission, the conversion of sinners, and it launched him on an extraordinary preaching career.

George Whitefield, who had been a talented amateur actor in his youth, joined the Holy Club at Oxford and became an Anglican minister. He followed Wesley to Georgia, founded an orphanage, and then returned to England and preached all over the kingdom to raise money for it. He had the power to move masses of people through a single sermon, and he too began to preach the "new birth"—the necessity of a conversion experience. When many pastors banned him from their pulpits, he responded by preaching in open fields to anyone who would listen. Newspapers reported the controversy, and soon Whitefield's admirers began to notify the press where he would be on any given day. Colonial newspapers, keenly sensitive to the English press, also followed his movements.

Whitefield Launches the Transatlantic Revival

In 1739, Whitefield made his second trip to America, ostensibly to raise funds for his orphanage at Bethesda, Georgia. Colonists knew who he was from newspaper accounts, and thousands flocked to hear him preach. After landing in Delaware, he preached his way northward through Philadelphia, New Jersey, and New York City, and then headed south through the Chesapeake colonies and into South Carolina. In September 1740, he sailed to Newport and for two months toured New England. During his travels, he met Benjamin Franklin, Gilbert Tennent, and Jonathan Edwards. In the cities he sometimes attracted as many as 30,000 people, double the population of Boston. His voice was so musical, claimed one observer, that he could seduce a crowd just by the way he said "Mesopotamia." Using his acting skills, he imitated Christ on the cross, shedding "pious tears" for poor sinners. Or he became God at the Last Judgment, thundering: "Depart from me ye accursed into everlasting fire!" When he wept, so did his audience. When he condemned them, they fell to the ground in agony.

Although Whitefield wore the surplice of an Anglican minister and carried the *Book of Common Prayer* when he preached, Anglicans treated him with reserve or hostility. In Charleston and New York City, the official spokesmen for the bishop of London denounced him, but Presbyterians, Congregationalists, and Baptists embraced him, at least until some of them began to fear that he was doing more harm than good. To many he embodied the old Non-Separatist ideal that all English Protestants were somehow members of the same church.

Disruptions

After Whitefield departed, other preachers tried to assume his role, but they aroused fierce controversy. In South Carolina, Hugh Bryan, a Savannah River planter, began preaching the evangelical message to his slaves. In 1742, when memories of a major slave revolt were still fresh (see later section), he denounced slavery as a sin and warned that God would pour out his wrath on the colony unless it rejected it. Proclaiming himself an American Moses, he attempted to part the waters of the Savannah River and lead the slaves to freedom in Georgia. Instead, he almost drowned. He then confessed publicly that he had been deluded. This fiasco discredited evangelicalism among the planters of the lower South for another generation, but Bryan and his family continued to convert their own slaves. African American evangelical piety, including some of the first black preachers, took root from these efforts.

Whitefield's successors also disrupted New England. Gilbert Tennent preached there for months. Lacking Whitefield's musical voice and Oxford diction, Tennent spoke with a Scottish burr and specialized in "Holy Laughter," the scornful peals of a triumphant God as sinners tumble into hell. He abandoned the usual garb of a minister for a robe and sandals and let his hair grow long, thereby proclaiming himself a new John the Baptist heralding the Second Coming of Christ. Many ecstatic followers believed that the biblical Millennium was at hand.

James Davenport succeeded Tennent. He denounced unregenerate ministers by name. He liked to preach by eerie candlelight, roaring damnation at his listeners, even grabbing Satan and wrestling him back to hell. He advised his admirers to drink rat poison rather than listen to another lifeless sermon. In 1743, he established the Shepherd's Tent in New London to train awakened preachers. This outdoor school abandoned the classical curriculum of colleges and insisted only on a valid conversion experience. He organized a book burning, in which titles by Increase Mather and other New England dignitaries went up in flames, and he threw his britches on the fire, declaring them a mark of human vanity. A New England grand jury, asked to indict him, proclaimed him mad instead. Like Bryan in South Carolina, he repented, claiming he had been deluded. The Shepherd's Tent collapsed.

Long-Term Consequences of the Revivals

The revivals had dramatic consequences. As time passed, they feminized evangelical churches. Amid the enthusiasm of Whitefield's tour, more men than usual had joined a church, but after another year or two, men became difficult to convert. The number of women church members began to soar, however, until by 1800 they often formed a majority of 3 or 4 to 1 in evangelical churches, and in some congregations they acquired an informal veto over the choice of the minister.

The revivals shattered the unity of New England's Congregational Church. Evangelicals seceded from dozens of congregations to form their own "Separate" churches. Many of those that survived went Baptist by the 1760s, thereby gaining protection under the toleration statutes of the New England colonies. In the middle colonies, the revivals strengthened denominational loyalties and energized the clergy. In the 1730s, most people in the region, particularly in New Jersey and Pennsylvania, had never joined a church. The revivals prompted many of them to become **New Side** (evangelical) Presbyterians, **Old Side** (anti-revival) Presbyterians, or non-evangelical Anglicans. Similar cleavages ran through the German population. The southern colonies were less affected, although evangelical Presbyterians made modest gains in the Virginia piedmont after 1740. Finally, in the 1760s, the Baptists began to win thousands of converts in Virginia, as did the Methodists after 1776, whose numbers surpassed the Baptists within a few decades.

The revivals created new cosmopolitan links with Britain and between colonies. Whitefield ran the most efficient publicity machine in the Atlantic world. When fervor declined in New England, Jonathan Edwards organized a Concert of Prayer with his Scottish correspondents, setting regular times for them to beseech the Lord to pour out his grace once more. As Anglicans split into Methodists and Latitudinarians, Congregationalists into **New Lights** (pro-revival) and **Old Lights** (antirevival), and Presbyterians into comparable **New Side** and **Old Side** synods, evangelicals discovered that they had more in common with revivalists in other denominations than with antirevivalists in their own. When New Side Presbyterians chose a new president of the College of New Jersey in 1757, they saw nothing strange in naming a Congregationalist, Jonathan Edwards.

Edwards was the most able apologist for revivals in Britain or America and probably the most profound theologian that North America has yet produced. When Boston's Charles Chauncy (very much a man of the Enlightenment) attacked the revivals as frauds because of their emotional excesses, Edwards replied with *A Treatise concerning Religious Affections* (1746), which displayed his own mastery of Enlightenment sources, including Newton and Locke. Although admitting that no emotional response, however intense, was proof by itself of the presence of God in a person's soul, he insisted that intense feeling must always accompany the reception of divine grace. That view upset people who believed that a rational God must have established a polite and genteel religion. For Edwards, an unemotional piety could never be the work of God. In effect, Edwards countered Chauncy's emotional defense of reason with his own rational defense of emotion.

New Colleges

The Great Awakening also created several new colleges. Each was set up primarily by a single denomination, but all admitted other Protestants. In 1740, North America had only three colleges: Harvard, William and Mary, and Yale. Although Yale eventually embraced the revivals, all three opposed them at first. In 1746, middle colony evangelicals, eager to show their commitment to classical learning after the fiasco of the Shepherd's Tent, founded the College of New Jersey. It graduated its first class in 1748 and settled in Princeton in 1756. Unlike the older colleges, it drew students from all 13 colonies and sent its graduates throughout America, especially to the middle and southern colonies. It also reshaped the Presbyterian Church. When Presbyterians healed their schism and reunited in 1758, the New Siders set the terms. Outnumbered in 1741, they held a large majority of ministers by 1758. Through control of Princeton, their numbers had increased rapidly. The Old Side, still dependent on the University of Glasgow in Scotland, could barely replace those who died.

New Light Baptists founded the College of Rhode Island (now Brown University) in the 1760s. Dutch Reformed revivalists set up Queens College (now Rutgers University) in New Jersey, mostly to train evangelical ministers who could preach in English. Eleazer Wheelock opened an evangelical school for Indians in Lebanon, Connecticut. After his first graduate, Samson Occum, raised £12,000 for the school in England, Wheelock moved to New Hampshire and used most of the money to found Dartmouth College instead, although Dartmouth did admit an occasional Indian. By 1790, Dartmouth was turning out more graduates, and far more ministers, than any other American college.

In the 1750s, Anglicans countered with two new colleges of their own: the College of Philadelphia (now the University of Pennsylvania), which also had Old Side Presbyterian support, and King's College (now Columbia University) in New York. Their undergraduate programs remained small, however, and few of their students chose a ministerial career. In the competition for student loyalties, nonevangelicals could not yet compete effectively with revivalists.

The Denominational Realignment

The revivals transformed American religious life. In 1700, the three strongest denominations had been the Congregationalists in New England, the Quakers in the Delaware valley, and the Anglicans in the South. By 1800, all three had lost ground to newcomers: the Methodists, who grew at an astonishing rate as the Church of England collapsed during the Revolution; the Baptists, who leaped into second place; and the Presbyterians. Methodists and Baptists did not expect their preachers to attend college, and they recruited ministers from a much broader segment of the population than their rivals could tap. Although they never organized their own Shepherd's Tent, they embraced similar principles, demanding only personal conversion, integrity, knowledge of the Bible, and a talent for preaching.

Antirevivalist denominations, especially Anglicans and Quakers, lost heavily. New Light Congregationalists made only slight gains because, when their people left behind the established churches of New England and moved west, they usually joined a Presbyterian church, which provided a structure and network of support that isolated congregations in a pluralistic society could not sustain.

Political Culture in the Colonies

In politics as in other activities, the colonies became more like Britain in the 18th century. A quarter-century of warfare after 1689 convinced the settlers that they needed the protection of the British state and strengthened their admiration for its parliamentary system. Provincial politics began to absorb many of the values and practices that had taken hold in Britain around the Glorious Revolution. Colonists agreed that they were free because they were British, because they were Protestants, and because they too had mixed constitutions that united monarchy, aristocracy, and democracy in almost perfect balance.

By the 1720s, every colony except Connecticut and Rhode Island had an appointive governor, plus a council and an elective assembly. The governor stood for monarchy and the council for aristocracy. In Massachusetts, Rhode Island, and Connecticut, the council, or upper house, was elected (indirectly in Massachusetts). In all other colonies except Pennsylvania an appointive council played an active legislative role. The office of councilor was not hereditary, but many councilors served for life, especially in Virginia, and some were succeeded by their sons.

The Rise of the Assembly and the Governor

Focus Question
How could both the royal governors and the assemblies grow stronger at the same time?

In all 13 colonies, once the Crown took over Georgia, the settlers elected the assembly, which embodied a colony's "democratic" elements. The right to vote in the colonies, although narrowing as population rose, was more widely shared than in England, where two-thirds of adult males were disenfranchised, a ratio that continued to rise. By contrast, something like three-fourths of free adult white men in the colonies acquired the right to vote at some point in their adult lives. The frequency of elections varied—from every seven years in New York (from the 1740s on) and Virginia, as well as in Britain, to at least once a year in five colonies. As the century advanced, legislatures sat longer and passed more laws. The lower house—the assembly—usually initiated major bills. The rise of the assembly was a major political fact of the era. It made most of its gains at the expense of the council.

Every royal colony except New York and Georgia already had an assembly with a strong sense of its own privileges when the first royal governor arrived, but governors in most colonies grew more adept over time. Because the governor's instructions usually challenged some existing practices, clashes often occurred in which the first royal governors never got all of their demands. Nevertheless, they did win concessions and became much more effective over the years. In almost every colony, the most successful governors were men who served between 1730 and 1765. Most of them had learned by then that their success depended less on their prerogatives (specific royal powers embodied in their commissions) than on their ability to win over the assembly through persuasion or **patronage.**

Early in the century, conflicts between the governor and the assembly tended to be legalistic. Each cited technical precedents to justify the governor's prerogatives or the assembly's privileges. Later on, when conflict spilled over into pamphlets and newspapers, it often pitted an aggrieved minority (unable to win a majority in the assembly) against both governor and assembly. These contests were ideological. The opposition accused the governor of corruption, of threatening the colonists' liberties, and he denounced the opposition as a "faction." Everyone condemned factions, or political parties, as self-interested and destructive. Hardly anyone claimed to be a party member; the other side was the faction.

"Country" Constitutions: The Southern Colonies

Although the colonies were well aware of the ideological currents in British politics, they reacted to them in different ways. In most southern colonies, the Country principles of the British opposition (see chapter 3) became the common assumptions of public life, acceptable to both governor and assembly, typically after a failed attempt to impose the Court alternative. When a governor, such as Virginia's Alexander Spotswood (1710–22), used his patronage to fill the assembly with his own "placemen," the voters turned them out at the next election. But just as Spotswood learned that he could not manipulate the house through patronage, the assembly discovered that it could not coerce a governor who had a permanent revenue. Accordingly, Virginia and South Carolina cultivated a **politics of harmony,** a system of ritualized mutual flattery. Governors found that they could accomplish more through persuasion than through patronage, and the assemblies responded by showing their appreciation. The planters of Virginia and South Carolina concluded that their societies embodied almost exactly what British opposition writers had been demanding. Factions disappeared, allowing the governor and the assembly to pursue the "common good" in an atmosphere free of rancor or corruption. Georgia adopted similar practices in the 1750s.

This system worked well because the planters were doing what Britain wanted them to do: growing staple crops and shipping them to Britain. Both sides could agree on measures that would make this process more efficient, such as the Virginia Tobacco Inspection Act of 1730. In Virginia, public controversy actually ceased. Between 1720 and 1765, particularly during the able administration of Sir William Gooch (1727–49), the governor and House of Burgesses engaged in only one public quarrel, an unparalleled record of political

The Spectrum of Colonial Politics

Constitutional Type	Successful	Unsuccessful
Northern "Court"	New York, circa 1710–28	New York after 1728
	New Hampshire after 1741	Pennsylvania
	Massachusetts after 1741	(successful in peace,
	New Jersey after 1750	ineffective in war)
Southern "Country"	Virginia after 1720	Maryland
	South Carolina after 1730	North Carolina
	Georgia after 1752	

Connecticut and Rhode Island never really belonged to this system.

harmony. South Carolina's politics became almost as placid from the 1730s into the 1760s, but harmony there masked serious social problems that were beginning to emerge in the unrepresented backcountry. By contrast, the politics of harmony never took hold in Maryland, where the lord proprietor always tried to seduce assemblymen with his lavish patronage, nor in factional North Carolina, where the tobacco and rice planters continually wrangled, and the growing backcountry distrusted both of them.

"Court" Constitutions: The Northern Colonies

With many economic interests and ethnic and religious groups to satisfy, the northern colonies often produced political factions. Governors with a large vision of the public welfare could win support by using patronage to reward some groups and to discipline others. William Shirley, governor of Massachusetts from 1741 to 1756, used judicial and militia appointments and war contracts to build a majority in the assembly. Like Sir Robert Walpole in Britain, he was a master of Court politics. In New Hampshire, Benning Wentworth created a political machine that rewarded just about every assemblyman between 1741 and 1767. An ineffective opposition in both colonies accused the governors of corrupting the assembly, but Shirley and Wentworth each claimed that his actions were essential to his colony's needs. Both governors remained in tight control.

The opposition, although seldom able to implement its demands at the provincial level, was important nonetheless. It kept settlers alert to any infringements on their liberties, and it dominated the town of Boston from 1720 on. Boston artisans engaged in ritualized mob activities that had a sharp political edge. Every year on Guy Fawkes Day (November 5), a North End mob and a South End mob bloodied each other for the privilege of burning effigies of the pope, the devil, and the Stuart pretender to the British throne. These men were raucously celebrating liberty, property, and no popery—the British constitution as they understood it. The violence made many wealthy merchants nervous, and by 1765 some of them would become its targets.

New York's governors, particularly Robert Hunter (1710–19), achieved great success even before 1720, mostly by playing off one faction against another in a colony that had been fiercely divided since Jacob Leisler's rebellion of 1689. Hunter's salary and perquisites became more lucrative than those attached to any other royal office in North America, and after 1716, he and his successor were so satisfied with their control of the assembly that they let 10 years pass without calling a general election. During the 25 years after 1730, later governors lost these advantages, primarily because London gave the governorship to a series of men who were eager to rebuild their tattered fortunes at New York's expense. This combination of greed and need gave new leverage to the assembly, and it attacked many royal prerogatives during the 1740s. Of the mainland colonies, only the governor of New York emerged weaker by 1760 than his predecessor had been in 1730.

Pennsylvania, by contrast, kept its proprietary governor weak well into the 1750s. After three decades of factionalism, a unified Quaker Party won undisputed control of the assembly during the 1730s. The governor, who by this time was never a Quaker, had a lot of patronage to dispense. He found it useless in controlling the Quaker assemblymen, who had lost interest in becoming judges if that meant administering oaths. Nor could he win these pacifists over with military commissions or war contracts, no matter how lucrative.

The colonists, both north and south, absorbed the ideology of the British opposition, which warned that those in power were always trying to destroy liberty and that corruption was power's most dangerous weapon. By 1776, that view would justify independence and the repudiation of a "corrupt" king and Parliament. Before the 1760s, however, it served different purposes. In the south, this ideology celebrated both Anglo-American harmony and the political success of Virginia and South Carolina. In the north, it replicated its role in Britain and became the language of frustrated minorities unable to defeat the governor or control the assembly.

The Renewal of Imperial Conflict

A new era of imperial war began in 1739 and continued, with only a brief interruption, until 1763. The British colonies, New Spain, and New France all became involved, and eventually so did all the Indians of the eastern woodlands. By 1763, France had been expelled from North America. Britain claimed the continent east of the Mississippi, Spain the land west of it.

Challenges to French Power

In the decades of peace after 1713, the French tried, with mixed results, to strengthen their position in North America. At great cost, they erected the continent's most formidable fortress, Louisbourg, on Cape Breton Island. A naval force stationed there could guard the approaches to the St. Lawrence River. The French also built Fort St. Frédéric (the British called it Crown Point) on Lake Champlain and maintained their Great Lakes posts at Forts

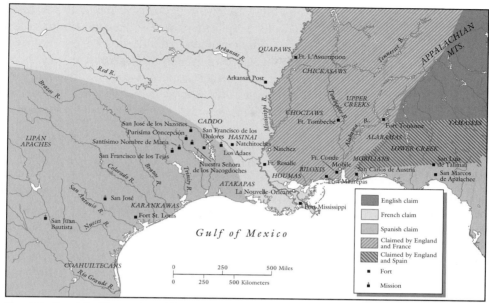

Map 4.1 French Louisiana and Spanish Texas, Circa 1730 In this part of North America, French and Spanish settlers and missionaries were spread quite thinly over a vast area and surrounded by much larger numbers of Indian peoples. View an animated version of this map or related maps at http://www.thomsonedu.com/history/murrin.

Frontenac, Michilimackinac, and Detroit. To bolster its weak hold on the Gulf of Mexico, France created the Company of the Indies, which shipped 7,000 settlers and 2,000 slaves to Louisiana between 1717 and 1721 but then failed to supply them. By 1726, half had starved to death or had fled. Another 5,000 slaves, but few settlers, reached the colony by 1730. The French founded New Orleans, which became the capital of Louisiana in 1722.

Despite these efforts, the French hold on the interior began to weaken, both north and south. From all points of the compass, Indians returned to the Ohio valley, mostly to trade with pacifist Pennsylvania or with Fort Oswego, a new British post on Lake Ontario. Compared with the French, the British were often clumsy in their dealings with Indians, but they had one advantage: British trade goods were cheaper than French goods. Many Indians founded what the French disparagingly called **republics,** villages outside the French alliance system that were willing to trade with the British. The chiefs at Venango, Logstown, and other republics accepted people from all tribes—Delawares from the east, Shawnees from the south and east, Mingoes (Iroquois who had left their homeland) from the north, and other Algonquians of the Great Lakes region to the west. Because the inhabitants of each new village had blood relatives living among all of the nearby nations, the chiefs welcomed Pennsylvania traders and hoped that none of their neighbors would endanger their own relatives by attacking these communities.

Sometimes even the French system of mediation broke down. In the northwest from 1712 to 1737, the French and their Algonquian allies fought a long, intermittent war with the Fox nation. In the southwest, an arrogant French officer decided to take over the lands of the Natchez Indians (the last of the Mississippian mound builders) and ordered them to move. While pretending to comply, the Natchez planned a counterstroke and, on November 28, 1729, killed every French male in the vicinity. In the war that followed, the French and their Choctaw allies destroyed the Natchez as a distinct people, although some Natchez refugees found homes among the Chickasaws or the Creeks.

In 1730, the French barely averted a massive slave uprising in New Orleans. To stir up hatred between Indians and Africans, the French turned over some of the African leaders of the revolt to the Choctaws to be burned alive. Unable to afford enough gifts to sustain alliances with both the Choctaws and the Chickasaws, the French encouraged hostilities between the two nations. This policy did serious damage to the French. Instead of weakening the pro-British Chickasaws, it touched off a civil war among the Choctaws, and France lost both influence and prestige.

The Danger of Slave Revolts and War with Spain

To counter the French, Spain sent missionaries and soldiers into Texas between 1716 and 1720 and founded a capital at Los Adaes, a few miles from the French trading post at Natchitoches. To prevent smuggling, Spain refused to open a seaport on the Gulf Coast. As a result, its tiny outposts had to depend on French trade goods for supplies, sometimes even for food. The Texas missions won few converts and suffered frequent depredations by Indians carrying French muskets. In 1719, the survivors of these attacks abandoned their missions in eastern Texas and fled west to San Antonio, which eventually became the capital.

The Spanish presence in Florida proved troublesome to the British, especially in South Carolina. In the 16th century, Francis Drake had proclaimed himself a liberator when he attacked St. Augustine and promised freedom to Indians and Africans who were groaning under Spanish tyranny (see chapter 2). By the 1730s, these roles had been reversed. On several occasions after 1680, Spanish Florida had promised freedom to any slaves who escaped from Carolina and were willing to accept Catholicism. In 1738, the governor established, just north of St. Augustine, a new town, Gracia Real de Santa Teresa de Mose (or Mose for short, pronounced *Moe*-shah) and made it the first community of free blacks in what is now the United States. The very existence of Mose acted as a magnet for Carolina slaves.

In 1739, the governor of Spanish Florida offered liberty to any slaves from the British colonies who could make their way to Florida. This manifesto, and rumors about Mose, touched off the Stono Rebellion in South Carolina, the most violent slave revolt in the history of the 13 colonies. Some of the rebellion's leaders were Catholics from the African Kingdom of the Kongo, where Portuguese missionaries had made numerous converts since the 16th century.

Christian Burial in the Kongo, 18th Century   At least some of the Africans who organized the Stono rebellion in South Carolina in 1739 were Catholics from the kingdom of the Kongo.

On Sunday morning, September 9, 1739, a force of 20 slaves attacked a store at Stono (south of Charleston), killed the owner, seized weapons, and moved on to assault other houses and to attract new recruits. Heading toward Florida, they killed about 25 settlers that day. When the rebels reached the Edisto River, they stopped, raised banners, and shouted "Liberty!" hoping to begin a general uprising. There the militia caught them and killed about two-thirds of the growing force. In the weeks that followed, the settlers killed another 60. None of the rebels reached Florida, but, as the founders of Georgia had foreseen, South Carolina was indeed vulnerable in any dispute with Spain.

In 1739, at almost the same moment, the War of Jenkins's Ear, derisively named for a ship captain who displayed his severed ear to Parliament as proof of Spanish cruelty, broke out between Britain and Spain. The war cost Britain dearly because Spanish defenses held everywhere. Some 3,000 men from the 13 colonies, eager for plunder, joined expeditions in 1741 and 1742 against the seaport of Cartagena in New Granada (now Colombia), and against Cuba and Panama. All were disasters. Most of the men died of disease; only 10 percent of the volunteers returned home. But one of the survivors, Lawrence Washington, so admired the British naval commander, Edward Vernon, that he named his Virginia plantation Mount Vernon. Britain also experienced a surge of patriotic fervor from the war. Both "God Save the King" and "Rule Britannia" were written during the struggle.

Georgia was supposed to protect South Carolina. General Oglethorpe, its governor, retaliated against the Spanish by invading Florida in 1740. He dispersed the black residents of Mose and occupied the site, but the Spaniards mauled his garrison in a surprise counterattack. Oglethorpe retreated without taking St. Augustine and returned to Georgia with disturbing reports. Spain, he said, was sending blacks into the British colonies to start slave uprisings, and Spanish priests in disguise were intermingled with the black conspirators and would try to destroy British fortifications. This news set off panics in the rice and tobacco colonies, but it had its biggest impact in New York City.

Back in 1712, a slave revolt had shaken the city. After setting fire to a barn one night, slaves had shot 15 settlers who rushed to put out the blaze, killing nine. Twenty-one slaves were executed, some after gruesome tortures. By 1741, New York City's 2,000 slaves were the largest concentration of blacks in British North America outside of Charleston. On March 18, Fort George burned down in what was probably an accident, but when a series of other suspicious fires broke out, the settlers grew nervous. Some of the fires probably provided cover for an interracial larceny ring that operated out of the tavern of John Hughson, a white man. When the New York Supreme Court offered freedom to Mary Burton, a 16-year-old Irish servant girl at the tavern, in exchange for her testimony, she swore that the tavern was the center of a "popish plot" to murder the city's whites, free the slaves, and make Hughson king of the Africans. Oglethorpe's warning reached New York in June, the number of the accused escalated, and John Ury, a recently arrived High Churchman and a Latin teacher, was hanged as the likely spy and priest.

The New York conspiracy trials, which continued from May into August of 1741, reminded one observer of the Salem witch frenzy of 1692, in which the testimony of several girls had led to 19 hangings. The toll in New York was worse. Four whites and 18 slaves were hanged, 13 slaves were burned alive, and 70 were banished to the West Indies. The judges spoke pompously about the sacred rights of Englishmen, again in danger from popish conspirators, and grew enraged at any African who dared to imperil what the colony would not let him share.

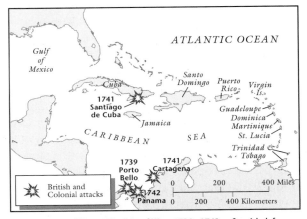

Map 4.2 Caribbean Theater of War, 1739–1742 Spanish defenses held up remarkably well against repeated and very costly British attacks.

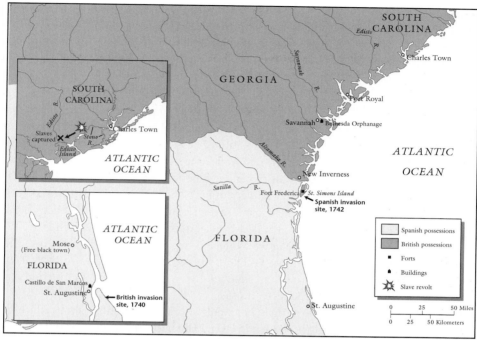

Map 4.3 Southeastern Theater of War, 1739–1742 Florida's defenders repelled a British attack led by James Oglethorpe, and then Oglethorpe turned back a much larger Spanish invasion of Georgia.

In 1742, King Philip V of Spain nearly accomplished what Oglethorpe and the New York judges dreaded. He sent 36 ships and 2,000 soldiers from Cuba with orders to devastate Georgia and South Carolina, "sacking and burning all the towns, posts, plantations, and settlements" and freeing the slaves. Although the invaders probably outnumbered the entire population of Georgia, Oglethorpe raised 900 men and met the Spaniards on St. Simons Island in July. After he ambushed two patrols, Spanish morale collapsed. When a British soldier deserted to the Spanish with word of how weak Georgia really was, Oglethorpe arranged to have the Spanish intercept a letter that implicated the deserter as a spy sent to lure them to their destruction. They departed in haste, leaving British North America as a safe haven once more for liberty, property, no popery—and slavery.

Britain did achieve one other success against Spain. Between 1740 and 1744, Commodore George Anson rounded Cape Horn, plundered and burned a small port in Peru, captured several prizes, and then sailed across the Pacific, where he captured the Manila galleon, the world's richest ship that sailed annually loaded with silver from Mexico to the Philippines. He completed his circumnavigation of the globe and returned to England with 1.3 million Spanish silver dollars and more than 35,000 ounces of unminted silver. Even though only one of Anson's six ships completed the voyage, his success alarmed the Spanish about the security of their lightly defended Pacific possessions. Spain would be reluctant to challenge Britain in the next war.

France versus Britain: King George's War

In 1744, France joined Spain in the war against Britain. The main action then shifted to the north. When the French laid siege to Annapolis Royal, the capital of Nova Scotia, Governor William Shirley of Massachusetts intervened just in time to save the small garrison, and the French withdrew. Shirley then planned his own offensive, a rash attack on Fortress Louisbourg. With only a few lightly armed Yankee vessels at his disposal, he asked the commander of the British West Indian squadron for assistance. But Shirley's expedition, which included about one-sixth of all the adult males of Massachusetts, set out before Warren could respond. With no heavy artillery of his own, Shirley ordered the expedition to take the outer batteries of the fortress, capture their guns, and use them to knock down its walls. Had the Yankees met a French fleet instead of the Royal Navy, which arrived in the nick of time, nearly every family in New England might have lost a close relative. The most amazing thing about this venture is that it worked. The British navy drove off the French, and untrained Yankee volunteers subdued the mightiest fortress in America with its own guns. Louisbourg fell on June 16, 1745.

After that, however, nothing went right. Hundreds of volunteers died of various afflictions before regular troops arrived to garrison Louisbourg. Elaborate plans to attack Quebec by sea in 1746 and 1747 came to nothing because no British fleet appeared. French and Indian raiders assaulted the weakly defended frontier, while Shirley held back most of his men for a Canada offensive that never took place. Bristol County farmers rioted against high taxes, and four Massachusetts towns seceded to Connecticut. When the Royal Navy finally docked at Boston in late 1747, its commander sent gangs of sailors ashore to **impress** anyone they could seize into serving with the fleet. An angry crowd descended on the sailors, took some officers hostage, and controlled the streets of Boston for three days before the naval commander relented and released all of the Massachusetts men he had impressed. (The rioters let him keep outsiders.) Finally, to offset losses in Europe, Britain had to return Louisbourg to France under the Treaty of Aix-la-Chapelle, which ended the war in 1748. New England had suffered enormous losses and had gained nothing except pride.

The Impending Storm

The war had driven back the frontiers of British settlement in North America, but the colonies had promised land grants to many volunteers. Thus peace touched off a frenzy of expansion that alarmed Indians and French alike. The British, aware that their hold on Nova Scotia was feeble, recruited 2,500 Protestants from the continent of Europe to populate the colony and sent four regiments of redcoats to accompany them. In 1749, they founded Halifax, which became the new capital of Nova Scotia.

In the 13 colonies, settlers eagerly pressed on to new lands. Yankees swarmed north into Maine and New Hampshire and west into the middle colonies, creating serious tensions. By refusing to pay rent to the manor lords of the Hudson valley, they sparked a tenant revolt in 1753 that the wealthy Livingston family had difficulty subduing. A year later, Connecticut's delegation to the Albany Congress (see later section) used bribes to acquire an Indian title to all of northern Pennsylvania, which Connecticut claimed on the basis of its sea-to-sea charter of 1663. Various controversies with the Mohawks west of Albany so infuriated Chief Hendrik that he bluntly told the governor of New York in 1753, "the Covenant Chain is broken between you and us [the Iroquois League]. So brother you are not to hear of me any more, and Brother we desire to hear no more of you." New York, Pennsylvania, and Virginia competed for trade with the new Indian republics between Lake Erie and the Ohio River. The expansionist thrust pitted colony against colony, as well as settler against Indian, and British against French. Virginians, whom the Indians called **long knives,** were particularly aggressive. Citing their own 1609 sea-to-sea charter (see the chapter 2 map, "Virginia Company Charter, 1606"), they organized the Ohio Company of Virginia in 1747 to settle the Ohio valley and established their first outpost where the Monongahela and Allegheny rivers converge to form the Ohio River (the site of modern Pittsburgh). The company hired George Washington as a surveyor. Farther south, encroachments upon the Cherokees almost provoked war with South Carolina in 1750.

The French response to these intrusions verged on panic. The fall of Louisbourg had interrupted the flow of French trade goods to the Ohio country for several years, and the

Collection of the New York Historical Society

Portrait of Chief Hendrik of the Mohawks　Hendrik's ultimatum to New York in 1753 precipitated the summoning of the Albany Congress a year later.

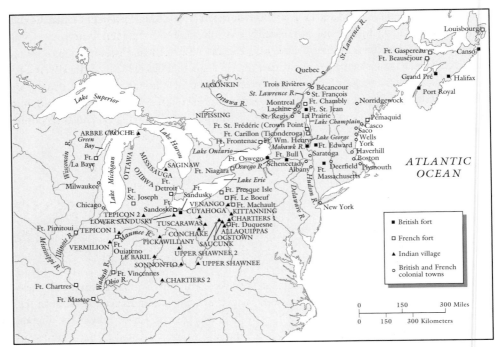

Map 4.4   France Versus Britain in North America by 1755   North of the Ohio River, much of North America was becoming a series of fortresses along the frontiers separating New France from the British colonies.

men who had long been conducting Indian diplomacy had either died or left office by the late 1740s. Authoritarian newcomers from France replaced them and began giving orders to western Indians instead of negotiating with them. The French did, however, make some constructive moves. They repaired Louisbourg and built Fort Beauséjour on the neck that connects mainland Canada to Nova Scotia. In 1755, they erected Fort Carillon (Ticonderoga to the British) on Lake Champlain to protect Crown Point.

Far more controversial was the new French policy in the area between the Great Lakes and the Ohio. Without trying to explain themselves to the Indians, they launched two expeditions into the area. In 1749, Pierre-Joseph Céloron de Blainville led several hundred men down the Allegheny and the Ohio, then up the Miami and back to Canada. He ordered western Indians to join him, but most of them refused. To the Indians, the French were acting like British settlers, intruding on their lands. Along the way, Blainville buried plaques, claiming the area for France. The Indians removed them. Marquis Duquesne sent 2,000 Canadians, with almost no Indian support, to erect a line of posts from Fort Presque Isle (now Erie, Pennsylvania) to Fort Duquesne (now Pittsburgh).

The French clearly intended to prevent British settlement west of the Alleghenies. Duquesne thought this policy so beneficial to the Indians that it needed no explanation. Yet the Mingoes warned him not to build a fort in their territory, and a delegation of Delawares and Shawnees asked the Virginians if they would be willing to expel the French from the Ohio country and then go back home. The Indians did not like the response. In 1753, Virginia sent Washington to the Ohio country to warn Duquesne to withdraw, and a small Virginia force began building its own fort at the forks of the Ohio. Duquesne ignored Washington, advanced toward the Ohio, expelled the Virginians, took over their site, and finished building the fort. Virginia sent Washington back to the Ohio in 1754. On May 28, after discovering a French patrol nearby, he launched an attack. That order set off a world war.

The War for North America

Focus Question
What made the War for North America (1754–63) so much more decisive than the three earlier Anglo-French wars?

Beginning in 1755, both France and Britain intervened in North America on an unprecedented scale in what became popularly known as the **French and Indian War.** Both discovered that their settlers and Indian allies were not living up to expectations. For France, this revelation led to disaster after French commanders tried to compel Indians to observe European rules of war. For Britain, the discovery that their anglicizing settlers had not anglicized enough provoked conflict between British army commanders and the colonists, but these differences were resolved in a manner that permitted them to cooperate effectively and finally conquer New France. At least to a modest degree, the colonists began to anglicize their way of waging war.

The Albany Congress and the Onset of War

In spring 1754, both New France and Virginia were expecting a limited clash at the forks of the Ohio River. Neither anticipated the titanic struggle that encounter would set off, nor did the French and British governments, which hoped to limit any conflict to a few strategic points in North America. New Englanders, however, saw an apocalyptic struggle in the making between "Protestant freedom" and "popish slavery," with the North American continent as the battleground. "The continent is not wide enough for us both," declared one preacher, "and they [the French] intend to have the whole."

Britain, fearful that the Six Nations (the Tuscaroras had joined the original Five Nations by the 1720s) might side with New France, ordered New York to host an intercolonial congress at Albany to redress Iroquois grievances. The governor invited every colony as far south as Virginia, except nonroyal Connecticut and Rhode Island. Virginia and New Jersey declined to attend. Governor Shirley of Massachusetts, on his own initiative, invited Connecticut and Rhode Island to participate, and the Massachusetts legislature asked its delegates to work for a plan of intercolonial union.

THE WAR THAT MADE AMERICA

A four-hour documentary that showed on PBS in January 2006 Written, produced, and directed by Eric Stange and Ben Loeterman

This ambitious documentary uses actual locations, historical reenactments, and a narrator to explore the French and Indian War in North America. The narrator is Graham Greene, an Academy Award nominee and Oneida Indian whose ancestors fought in the war. The narrative emphasizes the different roles and expectations of the British army, the settlers in the British colonies, the French army, and many of the Indian nations that fought in the conflict, mostly in an effort to guarantee that they could survive on their own native lands.

The writers begin the story with the prewar struggle between Virginia and New France for control of the Forks of the Ohio River (modern Pittsburgh), which both sides recognized as the gateway to the Great West. We watch a youthful and inexperienced George Washington, well played by Larry Nehring, open hostilities in 1754 by firing on a French patrol without realizing that it was a diplomatic mission carrying a message to the governor of Virginia. To Washington's horror, his most important Indian ally, known to the English as the Half King, then murdered the patrol's commanding officer, probably to make the breach between the French and the Virginians unbridgeable and to increase the chief's local prestige. The French retaliated by attacking Washington's force at improvised Fort Necessity. Washington had to surrender to the murdered commander's brother but, because he did not read French, he did not realize that in the document he had to sign, he took full responsibility for the murder.

Viewers then witness General Edward Braddock's disastrous defeat in 1755, the ravaging of the frontiers of Pennsylvania and Virginia, the serious quarrels between Lord Loudoun (the new British commander) and the colonists, the resurgence of British power under the leadership of William Pitt, and the fall of New France after defeats at Quebec and Montreal. Pontiac's War of 1763–64 and the atrocities committed by the Paxton Boys get major attention. The final episode argues that Britain's victory left the army and the home government so arrogant and confident of their power that they alienated the loyalties of the North American colonists. Ironically, Graham Greene tells us, the unintended consequences of the struggle proved far more important than the intended ones. Britain's victory lessened Britain's power in America by provoking a Revolution that led to the creation of the United States of America under the leadership of George Washington, whose highest ambition 20 years before independence had been to acquire a commission in the British army.

Not all viewers will accept the documentary's premise that the French and Indian War was the most important conflict ever fought on North American soil, but they will have to take that argument seriously.

Photo by Archie Carpenter/ Courtesy of WQED

In a scene from the film, Washington stands in the rain waiting for the French to close in on him at Fort Necessity in 1754 and force him to surrender.

In Philadelphia, Benjamin Franklin too was thinking about colonial union. On May 9, 1754, his *Pennsylvania Gazette* printed one of the first political cartoons in American history, with the caption "JOIN, or DIE." A month later, he drafted his "Short Hints towards a Scheme for Uniting the Northern Colonies," which he presented to the **Albany Congress** in June. His plan called for a "President General" to be appointed by the Crown as commander-in-chief and to administer the laws of the union, and for a "Grand Council" to be elected for three-year terms by the lower houses of each colony. Deputies would be apportioned according to tax receipts. The union would have the power to raise soldiers, build forts, levy taxes, regulate the Indian trade when it touched the welfare of more than a single colony, purchase land from the Indians, and supervise western settlements until the Crown organized them as new colonies. To take effect, the plan would require approval by the Crown and by each colonial legislature and presentation to Parliament for its consent. The Albany Congress adopted an amended version of Franklin's proposal.

Both Shirley and Franklin were far ahead of public opinion. Newspapers did not even discuss the Albany Plan. Every colony rejected it, most with little debate, some unanimously. The voting was close only in Massachusetts, which had borne the heaviest burden in the three earlier wars with New France. As Franklin later explained, the colonies feared that the president general might become too powerful, but they also distrusted one another. Despite the French threat, they were not ready to patch up their differences and unite. They did not yet see themselves as "Americans."

The Board of Trade responded by drafting its own plan of union. Its plan resembled Franklin's, except that the Grand Council could only requisition—instead of tax—and colonial union would not require Parliament's approval. After news arrived that Washington

The Historical Society of Pennsylvania.

Benjamin Franklin's Snake Cartoon One of the first newspaper cartoons in colonial America, this device appeared in the *Pennsylvania Gazette* in May 1754. The cartoon called for colonial union on the eve of the Albany Congress and drew on the folk legend that a snake, cut into pieces, could revive and live if it somehow joined its severed parts together before sundown.

had surrendered his small force to the French at Great Meadows in July 1754, Britain decided that the colonies were incapable of uniting in their own defense. Even if they could, the precedent would be dangerous. Instead, London sent redcoats to Virginia—two regiments, commanded by General Edward Braddock. For Britain, colonial union and direct military aid were policy *alternatives*. Although military aid would cost the British government more than the proposed union, it seemed the safer choice. By winter of 1754–55, colonial union was a dead issue on both sides of the ocean.

Yet the Albany Congress achieved one major objective. Addressing Iroquois grievances against New York, it urged the Crown to take charge of relations with all western Indians. London created two Indian superintendencies—one south of the Ohio, which went first to Edmund Atkin and then John Stuart; and one north of the Ohio, which went to William Johnson, an Irish immigrant to New York who had influence with the Mohawks. These offices would survive the war.

Britain's Years of Defeat

In 1755, London hoped that a quick victory by Braddock at the forks of the Ohio River would keep the war from spreading. Braddock's regiments landed in Virginia, a signal that London probably intended to let Virginia, rather than Quaker Pennsylvania, control the upper Ohio valley, including what is now Pittsburgh. At a council of high officials called by Braddock at Alexandria, Virginia, Governor Shirley persuaded him to accept New England's much broader war objectives. Instead of a single expedition aimed at one fort, to be followed by others if time permitted, the campaign of 1755 became four distinct offensives designed to crush the outer defenses of New France and leave it open to British invasion. Braddock was so impressed with Shirley that he named him second in command of the British army in North America, not bad for an English lawyer with no military training who had arrived in Boston almost penniless 25 years earlier.

Braddock and Shirley tried to make maximum use of both redcoats and provincials. The redcoats were highly disciplined professional soldiers who served long terms and had been trained to fight other professional armies. **Irregular war** in the forests of North America made them uneasy. Provincials, by contrast, were recruited by individual colonies. They were volunteers, often quite young, who usually enlisted only for a single campaign. They knew little about military drill, expected to serve under the officers who had recruited them, and sometimes refused to obey orders that they disliked. Provincials admired the courage of the redcoats but were shocked by their irreverence and by the brutal discipline imposed on them by their officers. Nevertheless, thousands of colonists also enlisted in the British army, providing up to 40 percent of its strength in North America by 1760.

Under the enlarged plan for 1755, the redcoats in Nova Scotia together with New England provincials would assault Fort Beauséjour, where the Acadian peninsula joins mainland Canada. New England and New York provincials would attack Crown Point, and Shirley, commissioned as a British colonel, would lead two regiments of redcoats (recently

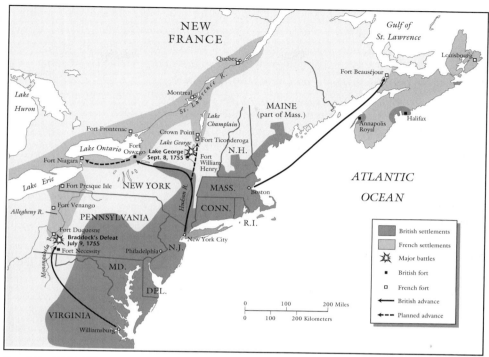

Map 4.5 **British Offenses, 1755** The British launched four major offenses against the French: in Nova Scotia, at Lake George, at Fort Oswego, and at the Forks of the Ohio River, where Edward Braddock led his men to disaster.

recruited in New England) to Niagara and cut off New France from the western Indians. Braddock would attack Fort Duquesne.

Instead, Braddock alienated the Indians and marched to disaster on the Monongahela. The western Delawares asked him whether their villages and hunting rights would be secure under the British. He replied, "No Savage Should Inherit the Land." The chiefs retorted that "if they might not have Liberty To Live on the Land they would not Fight for it." Braddock declared that he "did not need their Help." It took Braddock several months to hack a road through the forest wide enough for his artillery. He took care to prevent ambushes at two fords of the Monongahela, and as he crossed that stream on July 9, he pushed on, confident that he had overcome all obstacles.

Fort Duquesne's commander could muster only 72 French, 146 Canadians, and 637 Indians against the 1,400 regulars under Braddock and 450 Virginia provincials. The French ran into the British vanguard a few miles southeast of the fort. They clashed along a narrow path with thick forest and brush on either side. The French and Indians took cover on the British flanks. Braddock's rear elements rushed toward the sound of the guns where, massed together, they formed a gigantic bull's-eye. The Indians and the French poured round after round into them, while the British fired wild volleys at the invisible enemy. The British lost 977 killed or wounded, along with their artillery. Braddock was killed. Only 39 French and Indians were killed or wounded. The redcoats finally broke and ran. Washington, who had fought as a Virginia volunteer on Braddock's staff, reported that offensive operations would be impossible for the rest of the year. Braddock's road through the wilderness now became a highway for the enemy. For the first time in the history of Quaker Pennsylvania, its settlers faced the horrors of a frontier war.

In Nova Scotia, Fort Beauséjour fell on June 17, 1755. Then the commanders did something to indicate that this war would not be a conventional, limited struggle. When the Acadians refused to take an oath that might have obliged them to bear arms against other Frenchmen, the British and Yankees responded with an 18th-century version of ethnic cleansing. They rounded up between 6,000 and 7,000 Acadians, forced them aboard ships, and expelled them from the province, to be scattered among the 13 colonies, none of which was prepared for the influx. A second roundup in 1759 caught most of the families that had evaded the first one. The officers who organized these expulsions insisted that they had found a humane way of compelling French Catholics to assimilate with the Protestant majority. Reasoning also that the Acadians were not British subjects because they had not taken the oath, and that only British subjects could own land in a British colony, the government of Nova Scotia confiscated the land the Acadians had farmed for generations and redistributed it to Protestant settlers, mostly from New England. About 3,000 Acadian refugees, after spending miserable years as unwanted Catholic exiles in a Protestant world, finally made it to French Louisiana, where their descendants became known as Cajuns. Others went to France, and some even made their way back to Nova Scotia or what later became New Brunswick. Few remained in the 13 colonies.

In the principal northern theater of war in 1755, William Johnson led his provincials against Crown Point. The French commander, Jean-Armand, baron Dieskau, hoping to repeat the French success against Braddock, attacked a body of provincials on September 8 and drove it back in panic to its base camp, the improvised Fort William Henry near Lake George. French regulars assailed the fort but were driven off with heavy losses in a six-hour struggle. Colonial newspapers proclaimed the battle a great victory because the provincials had not only held the field but had also wounded and captured Dieskau. Johnson probably could have taken poorly defended Crown Point, but he too had been wounded and was content to hold Fort William Henry and nearby Fort Edward at the headwaters of the Hudson. It took a more professional eye than his to distinguish the carnage of victory from the carnage of defeat.

Farther west, Shirley's Niagara campaign reached Oswego on Lake Ontario and then stopped for the winter, held in check by the French at Fort Frontenac on the lake's northern shore. Oswego was soon cut off by heavy snows. Malnutrition and disease ravaged the garrison.

A World War

With the death of Braddock and the capture of Dieskau, military amateurs took over both armies: Shirley in the British colonies and Governor-General Pierre de Rigaud de Vaudreuil in New France. Vaudreuil, a Canadian, understood his colony's weakness without Indian support. The white population of the 13 colonies outnumbered that of New France by 13 to 1; Massachusetts alone had nearly three times as many settlers as New France. Vaudreuil also knew that if the redcoats and the British colonies could concentrate their resources in a few critical places, they had a good chance of overwhelming New France. Therefore, a frontier war that pitted New France primarily against ordinary settlers—horrible though it was—remained the most effective way to force the British colonies to scatter their resources over a vast area.

As long as Vaudreuil was in charge, New France kept winning. Indian attacks devastated frontier settlements, especially in Pennsylvania, a pacifist colony without a militia or any forts when the war began. Even so, the French government decided that New France needed a professional general and sent Louis-Joseph, marquis de Montcalm, in 1756. Shocked and repelled by the brutality of frontier warfare, Montcalm tried to turn the conflict into a traditional European struggle of sieges and battles in which the advantage (as Vaudreuil well understood) would pass to the British. Nevertheless, Montcalm won several major successes. Oswego fell in summer 1756. When Fort William Henry surrendered to him a year later, he promised the garrison the honors of war, which meant that it could keep its property and march unmolested to Fort Edward. But France's Indian allies considered this agreement a betrayal of their customs. They killed or carried off 308 of the 2,400 prisoners, an event that colonial newspapers called the Massacre of Fort William Henry. Most of those killed were trying to save their property, which the Indians considered their rightful plunder. Montcalm lost heavily at Fort William Henry. He never again managed to raise sizable bodies of western Indians, and because the British blamed him for the "massacre," they refused to grant the honors of war to any French force for the rest of the conflict.

Meanwhile, Braddock's defeat, combined with the British loss of Minorca in the Mediterranean, convinced the British government that the struggle with France could not be limited to a few outposts. Britain declared war on France in 1756, and the French and Indian War in the colonies merged with a general European struggle—the Seven Years' War (1756–63)—involving France, Austria, and Russia against Prussia, which was heavily subsidized by Britain. Although religion had little to do with the war in Europe, the Seven Years' War aligned coalitions of Protestant states against Catholic states in a way not seen there for a century. To many North American clergymen, a Protestant victory might herald the onset of the Millennium. The conflict spread even to India, where British forces expelled the French from nearly all of that vast subcontinent.

Reluctant to antagonize Britain, Spain remained neutral for most of the war, a choice that had huge implications within North America. In the previous war, Spain had been able to turn the slaves of South Carolina against their masters and to create unrest even in New York. At a minimum, Spanish hostilities early in the war would have forced the

British to fight in another theater of conflict. Instead, Spain's neutrality permitted Britain to concentrate its resources against New France.

Imperial Tensions: From Loudoun to Pitt

In 1755, London, to its dismay, realized that Shirley, an amateur, had taken command of the British army in North America. The government dispatched an irascible Scot, John Campbell, earl of Loudoun, to replace him and began pouring in reinforcements. Loudoun had a special talent for alienating provincials. Colonial units did not care to serve under his command and sometimes bluntly rejected his orders. Provincials believed they had a contractual relationship with *their* officers; they had never agreed to serve under Loudoun's professionals. They refused to serve beyond their term of enlistment, most of which expired on November 1 or December 1 of each year. Even when the British ordered them to stay longer, many of them defiantly marched home.

Many British officers despised the provincials, especially their officers. "The Americans are in general the dirtiest most contemptible cowardly dogs that you can conceive," snarled General James Wolfe. "They fall down dead in their own dirt and desert by battalions, officers and all." General John Forbes was usually more positive, but he too once suggested "shooting dead a Dozen of their cowardly Officers at the Head of the Line." Some British officers held more favorable opinions. Horatio Gates, Richard Montgomery, Hugh Mercer, and Arthur St. Clair all remained in America after the war and became generals in the American army during the Revolution. Colonel Isaac Barré praised American courage in the House of Commons in 1765 and even coined the phrase "Sons of Liberty" to describe them—a label instantly adopted by men who resisted Britain's postwar policies.

As the new commander-in-chief, Loudoun faced other problems: the quartering (or housing) of British soldiers, the relative rank of British and provincial officers, military discipline, revenue, and smuggling. He tried to impose authoritarian solutions on them all. When he sent redcoats into a city, he demanded that the assembly pay to quarter them, or else he would take over buildings by force. He tried to make any British senior captain superior in rank to any provincial officer, a rule that angered such experienced New England officers as General John Winslow and his six colonels. Loudoun ordered New England troops to serve directly under British officers and to accept the harsh discipline of the British army, an arrangement that New Englanders thought violated the terms of their enlistment. They refused to cooperate. When some colonial assemblies refused to vote adequate supplies, Loudoun urged Parliament to tax the colonies directly. Shocked that the molasses trade with the French West Indies was proceeding as usual, he urged the navy to stamp it out or imposed embargoes on colonial shipping, an action that punished fair traders as well as smugglers. Loudoun built up his forces but otherwise achieved little. In early 1758, Massachusetts refused to raise any men for the coming campaign, but when the afternoon mail contained letters from London that announced a more conciliatory policy, they voted to raise more men than they ever had before.

In 1757, William Pitt came to power as Britain's war minister and found workable voluntaristic solutions to the problems that had defeated Loudoun's authoritarian methods. Pitt understood that consent worked better than coercion in the colonies. Colonial assemblies built barracks to house British soldiers. Pitt declared that every provincial officer would rank immediately behind the equivalent British rank but above all lesser officers, British or provincial. He then promoted every British lieutenant colonel to the rank of "colonel in America only." That decision left only about 30 British majors vulnerable to being ordered about by a provincial colonel, but few of them had independent commands anyway. Provincial units under the command of their own officers cooperated with the British army, and the officers began to impose something close to British discipline on them, including hundreds of lashes for routine offenses. Quite a few men began to reenlist.

Rather than impose a parliamentary tax, Pitt set aside £200,000 beginning in 1758 (later reduced to £133,000) and told the colonies that they could claim a share of it in proportion to their contribution to the war effort. In effect, he persuaded the colonies to compete voluntarily in support of his stupendous war effort. The subsidies covered something less than half of the cost of fielding 20,000 provincials each year from 1758 to 1760, and rather smaller numbers in 1761 and 1762 as operations shifted to the Caribbean. Smuggling angered Pitt as much as it did anyone else, but British conquests soon reduced that problem. By 1762, Canada, Martinique, and Guadeloupe, as well as Spanish Havana, were all in British hands. Few places were any longer worth smuggling to, except Saint Domingue.

Pitt had no patience with military failure. After Loudoun called off his attack on Louisbourg in 1757, Pitt replaced him with James Abercrombie. He also put Jeffrey Amherst in charge of a new Louisbourg expedition, with James Wolfe as one of his brigadiers. By 1758, the British Empire had finally put together a military force capable of overwhelming New France and had learned how to use it. In the last years of the war, cooperation between redcoats and provincials became routine and devastatingly effective.

The Years of British Victory

By 1758, the Royal Navy had cut off Canada from reinforcements and even from routine supplies. Britain had sent more than 30 regiments to North America. Combined with 20,000 provincials, thousands of **bateau** men rowing supplies into the interior, and swarms of privateers preying on French commerce, Britain had mustered perhaps 60,000 men in North America and in nearby waters. Most of them now closed in on the 75,000 people of New France. Montcalm, who in any case was running out of goods for use in the Indian trade, refused to encourage more Indian attacks on the frontier and prepared to defend the approaches to Canada at Forts Duquesne, Niagara, Frontenac, Ticonderoga, Crown Point, and Louisbourg.

Spurred on by Quaker mediators, the British and colonial governments came to terms with the western Indians in 1758, promising not to seize their lands after the war and arranging an uneasy peace. Few settlers or officials had yet noticed a new trend that was emerging during the conflict: Before the 1750s, Indian nations had often waged terrible

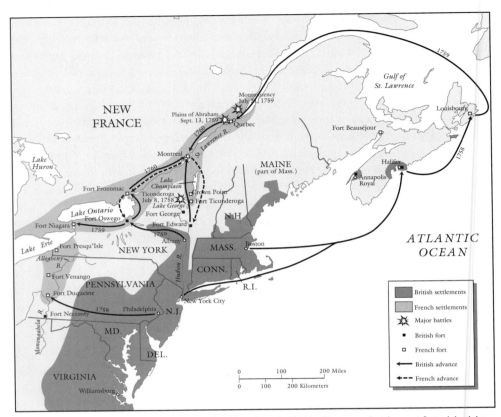

Map 4.6   Conquest of Canada, 1758–60   In three campaigns, the British with strong colonial support first subdued the outer defenses of New France, then took Quebec in 1759 and Montreal in 1760.
View an animated version of this map or related maps at http://www.thomsonedu.com/history/murrin.

wars against one another. Now, however, few Indians in the northeastern woodlands were willing to attack others. In 1755, for example, some Senecas fought with New France and some Mohawks with the British, but they maneuvered carefully to avoid confronting each other. This Iroquois sense of solidarity was beginning to spread. Iroquois and western Algonquians, once deadly enemies, saw real advantages in cooperation. A sense of pan-Indian identity was beginning to emerge.

Peace with the western Indians in 1758 permitted the British to revive the grand military plan of 1755, except that this time the overall goal was clear—the conquest of New France. Amherst and Wolfe, with 9,000 regulars and 500 provincials, besieged Louisbourg for 60 days. It fell in September, thus adding Cape Breton Island to the British province of Nova Scotia. A force of 3,000 provincials under Colonel John Bradstreet advanced to Lake Ontario, took Fort Frontenac, and began building a fleet. This victory cut off the French in the Ohio valley from their supplies. A powerful force of regulars under John Forbes and

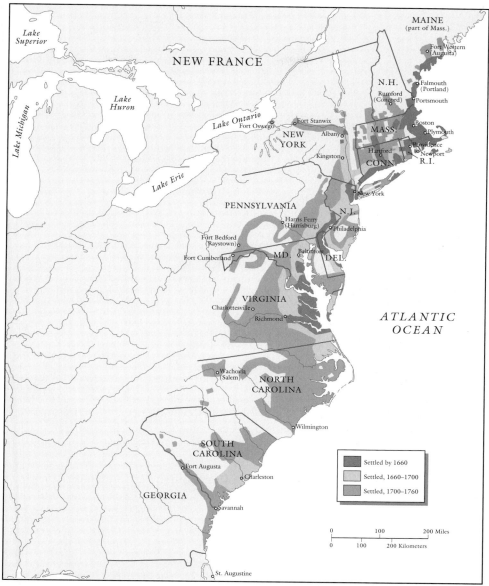

Map 4.7   Growth of Population to 1760   Between 1700 and 1760, the population of the British colonies had increased by more than a factor of six, from 250,000 to almost 1.6 million. Settlement had filled the piedmont in most areas and was beginning to cross the Appalachian watershed into the Ohio Valley.

provincials under Washington marched west, this time through Pennsylvania, to attack Fort Duquesne, but the French blew up the fort and retreated north just before they arrived. The British erected Fort Pitt on the ruins.

The only British defeat in 1758 occurred in northern New York when Abercrombie sent 6,000 regulars and 9,000 provincials against Ticonderoga (Carillon), defended by Montcalm and 3,500 troops. Instead of waiting for his artillery to arrive or trying to outflank the French, Abercrombie ordered a frontal assault against a heavily fortified position. His regulars were butchered by the withering fire, and after witnessing the carnage for several hours, the horri-fied provincials fled. Like Indians, they regarded such attacks as sheer madness. When Pitt heard the news, he sacked Abercrombie, put Amherst in charge of the New York theater of war, and left Wolfe at Louisbourg to plan an attack up the St. Lawrence River against Quebec.

In 1759, while the provincials on Lake Ontario moved west and took Niagara, Amherst spent the summer cautiously reducing Ticonderoga and Crown Point. (Pitt expected him to reach Montreal.) The most dramatic campaign occurred farther east. In June, Wolfe ascended the St. Lawrence River with 8,000 redcoats and colonial rangers and laid siege to Quebec, defended by Montcalm with 16,000 regulars, Canadian militia, and Indians. When an attack below the city failed, Wolfe mounted howitzers on high ground across the river from Quebec and began reducing most of the city to rubble. Frustrated by the French refusal to come out and fight, he turned loose his American rangers ("the worst soldiers in the universe," he boasted), who ravaged and burned more than 1,400 farms. Anyone who resisted was shot and scalped. Still the French held out.

By September, both Wolfe and Montcalm realized that the British fleet would soon have to depart or risk being frozen in during the long winter. Wolfe made a last desper-ate effort, preferring to die rather than fail. His men silently sailed up the river, climbed a formidable cliff above the city in darkness, and on the morning of September 13, 1759, deployed on the Plains of Abraham behind Quebec. Montcalm panicked. Instead of using his artillery to defend the walls from inside (Wolfe's force had been able to drag only two guns with them), he marched out of Quebec onto the plains. Both generals now had what they craved most, a set-piece European battle that lasted about 15 minutes. Wolfe and Montcalm were both mortally wounded, but the British drove the French from the field and took Quebec. After the fall of Montreal in 1760, Canada surrendered.

The Cherokee War and Spanish Intervention

In December 1759, as the British were completing their triumph over New France, the Cherokees, who had been allies and trading partners of South Carolina, reacted to a long string of violent incidents by attacking backcountry settlers. Within a year, they drove the frontier back 100 miles. South Carolina appealed to Amherst for help, and he sent regular soldiers who laid waste the Cherokee Lower Towns in the Appalachian foothills. When that expedition failed to bring peace, another one the next year devastated the Middle Towns farther west, while Virginia threatened the Overhill Towns. The Cherokees made peace in December 1761, but the backcountry settlers, left brutalized and lawless, soon became severe political problems for South Carolina's government. Only then, in January 1762, after the French and the Cherokees had been defeated, did Spain finally enter the war. British forces quickly took Havana and even Manila in the distant Philippines. France and Spain sued for peace.

The Peace of Paris

In 1763, the Peace of Paris ended the war. Britain returned Martinique and Guadeloupe to France. France surrendered to Great Britain several minor West Indian islands and all of North America east of the Mississippi, except New Orleans. In exchange for Havana, Spain ceded Florida to the British and also promised to pay a large ransom for the return of Manila. To compensate its Spanish ally, France gave all of Louisiana west of the Mississippi and New Orleans to Spain. Most of the Spanish and African occupants of Florida withdrew to other parts of the Spanish empire, but nearly all French settlers remained behind in Canada, the Illinois country, and what was now Spanish Louisiana.

The British colonists were jubilant. The age of warfare and frontier carnage seemed over at last. Britain and the colonies could now develop their vast resources in an imperial partnership and would share unprecedented prosperity. But the western Indians angrily rejected the peace settlement. No one had conquered them, and they denied the right or the power of France to surrender their lands to Great Britain. They began to plan their own war of liberation.

Conclusion

Between 1713 and 1754, expansion and renewed immigration pushed North American settlement ever farther into the interior. With a population that doubled every 25 years, many householders no longer enjoyed the opportunity to give all of their sons and daughters the level of economic success that they were enjoying. By midcentury, many families took up a trade or looked westward for what their old community could not provide. Women worked harder just to sustain levels of opportunity for their households. Many families had to favor sons over daughters and the eldest son over his younger brothers, reluctantly following practices used in England.

The colonies anglicized in other ways as well. Newspapers and the learned professions spread the English Enlightenment to the colonies. English revivalists, especially George Whitefield, had a tremendous impact in North America. The northern colonies borrowed Court politics from Walpole's Britain, while most southern colonies favored politics as envisioned by Britain's Country opposition. Both considered themselves the freest people on earth. When expansion and imperial rivalries again led to war after 1739, the colonists discovered that enslaved Africans associated Spain with liberty, whereas most eastern woodland Indians looked to New France for support. The threat of internal upheaval kept King George's War indecisive in the 1740s. Taking advantage of Spain's neutral position when Britain and France went to war after 1754, the British Empire mobilized its full resources and conquered New France.

The French and Indian War left behind vivid memories. Provincials admired the courage of the redcoats and the victories they won but hated their brutal discipline and arrogant officers. British officials greatly exaggerated what military force alone could accomplish and underestimated colonial contributions to the imperial cause. The concord and prosperity that were supposed to follow Britain's great triumph yielded instead to bitter strife.

SUGGESTED READINGS

The best study of 18th-century immigration is **Bernard Bailyn, *Voyagers to the West: A Passage in the Peopling of America on the Eve of the Revolution*** (1986). **A. Roger Ekirch, *Bound for America: The Transportation of British Convicts to the Colonies*** (1987) is also important. For gentility and the Enlightenment, excellent studies include **Richard L. Bushman, *The Refinement of America: Persons, Houses, Cities*** (1992); **Ned Landsman, *From Colonials to Provincials: Thought and Culture in America, 1680–1760*** (1998); **David S. Shields, *Civil Tongues & Polite Letters in British America*** (1997); and **Charles E. Clark, *The Public Prints: The Newspaper in Anglo-American Culture, 1665–1740*** (1994). For early Georgia, see **Harold E. Davis, *The Fledgling Province: Social and Cultural Life in Colonial Georgia, 1773–1776*** (1976); and **Larry E. Ivers, *British Drums on the Southern Frontier: The Military Colonization of Georgia, 1733–1749*** (1974). **Mark A. Noll, *The Rise of Evangelical Religion: The Age of Edwards, Whitefield, and the Wesleys*** (2003) provides a comprehensive overview of the Great Awakening. **Bernard Bailyn's *The Origins of American Politics*** (1968) touched off a considerable debate. See especially **Jack P. Greene, "Political Mimesis: A Consideration of the Historical and Cultural Roots of Legislative Behavior in the British Colonies in the Eighteenth Century,"** with a comment by Bailyn and a reply by Greene, in *American Historical Review*, 75 (1969), 333–367.

For the renewal of imperial conflict after 1739, see **Jill Lepore, *New York Burning: Liberty, Slavery, and Conspiracy in Eighteenth-Century Manhattan*** (2005); **Fred Anderson, *Crucible of War: The Seven Years War and the Fate of Empire in British North America, 1754–1766*** (2000); **Timothy J. Shannon, *Indians and Colonists at the Crossroads of Empire: The Albany Congress of 1754*** (2000); **John Mack Faragher, *A Great and Noble Scheme: The Tragic Story of the Expulsion of the French Acadians from their American Homeland*** (2005); and **Ian K. Steele, *Betrayals: Fort William Henry and the "Massacre"*** (1990).

Visit the **Liberty Equality Power** Companion Web site for resources specific to this textbook: http://www.thomsonedu.com/history/murrin

Also find self-tests and additional resources at ThomsonNOW. ThomsonNOW is an integrated online suite of services and resources with proven ease of use and efficient paths to success, delivering the results you want—NOW!

www.thomsonedu.com/login/

5

Reform, Resistance, Revolution

Britain left an army in North America after 1763 and taxed the colonies to pay part of its cost. The colonists agreed that they should contribute to their own defense but insisted that taxation without representation violated their rights as Englishmen. Three successive crises shattered Britain's North American empire by 1776.

In the Stamp Act crisis, the colonists first petitioned Parliament for a redress of grievances. When that effort failed, they nullified the Stamp Act and continued their resistance until Parliament repealed the tax in 1766. The settlers joyfully celebrated their victory. In the Townshend crisis of 1767–70, Parliament imposed new taxes on certain imported goods. The colonists petitioned and resisted simultaneously, mostly through an intercolonial nonimportation movement. The British sent troops to Boston. After several violent confrontations, the soldiers withdrew, and Parliament modified but did not repeal the Townshend Revenue Act. The duty on tea remained. Repeal of the other duties broke the back of the nonimportation movement. Nobody celebrated. The Tea Act of 1773 launched the third crisis, and it quickly escalated. Boston destroyed British tea without bothering to petition first. When Parliament responded with the Coercive Acts of 1774, the colonists created the Continental Congress to organize further resistance. Neither side dared back down, and the confrontation careened toward military violence. War broke out in April 1775. Fifteen months later, the colonies declared their independence.

Imperial Reform

In 1760, George III (1760–1820) inherited the British throne at the age of 22. The king's pronouncements on behalf of religion and virtue at first won him many admirers in North America, but the political coalition leading Britain to victory over France fell apart. The king's new ministers set out to reform the empire.

From Pitt to Grenville

The king, along with his tutor and principal adviser, John Stuart, earl of Bute, feared that the Seven Years' War would bankrupt Britain. From 1758 on, despite one victory after another, George and Bute grew increasingly despondent. When William Pitt, the king's war minister, urged a preemptive strike on Spain before Spain could attack Britain, Bute forced him to resign in October 1761, even though Pitt had become the most popular official of

CHRONOLOGY

1745–55	Land riots rock New Jersey
1760–61	Cherokee War devastates South Carolina backcountry
1760	George III becomes king of Great Britain
1761	Pitt resigns as war minister
1763	Grenville ministry takes power • Wilkes publishes *North Briton* No. 45 • Pontiac's War begins • King issues Proclamation of 1763
1764	Parliament passes Currency and Sugar Acts
1765	Parliament passes Quartering Act • Stamp Act passed and nullified • Rockingham replaces Grenville as prime minister
1766	Parliament repeals Stamp Act, passes Declaratory Act and Revenue Act of 1766 • Chatham (Pitt) ministry takes power
1767	Parliament passes New York Restraining Act and Townshend Revenue Act
1768	Massachusetts assembly dispatches Circular Letter • Wilkes elected to Parliament • Massacre of St. George's Fields occurs in England • Massachusetts refuses to rescind Circular Letter • *Liberty* riot occurs in Boston • Governors dissolve assemblies that support Circular Letter • Redcoats sent to Boston
1769	Nonimportation becomes effective • Regulators achieve major goals in South Carolina
1770	North becomes prime minister • Boston Massacre • Townshend Revenue Act partially repealed • Nonimportation collapses
1771	North Carolina regulators defeated at Alamance Creek
1772	*Gaspée* affair in Rhode Island increases tensions
1772–73	Twelve colonies create committees of correspondence
1773	Tea Act passed • Boston Tea Party protests tea duty • Wheatley's poetry published in London
1774	American Quakers prohibit slaveholding • Parliament passes Coercive Acts and Quebec Act • First Continental Congress convenes in Philadelphia
1775	Revolutionary War begins at Lexington and Concord • Second Continental Congress creates Continental Army • Olive Branch Petition fails • George III issues Proclamation of Rebellion
1775–76	Americans invade Canada
1776	Paine publishes *Common Sense* • British evacuate Boston • Continental Congress approves Declaration of Independence

the century. Bute soon learned that Pitt had been right. Spain entered the war in January 1762. In May, Bute replaced Thomas Pelham-Holles, duke of Newcastle and the most powerful politician of the previous 25 years, as first lord of the treasury. To economize, Bute next reduced Britain's subsidies to Prussia, its only major ally in Europe. So eager were the king and Bute to end the war that they gave back to France the wealthy West Indian islands of Guadeloupe and Martinique.

The British press harshly denounced Bute. As soon as Parliament approved the Treaty of Paris, Bute dismayed the king by resigning. He had had enough. In April 1763, **George Grenville** (Pitt's brother-in-law) became first lord of the treasury, although the king distrusted him and found him barely acceptable. Pitt and Newcastle, who blamed Grenville for having sided with Bute against them, would have nothing at all to do with him.

Britain's national debt had nearly doubled during the last war with France and stood at £130 million. Interest on the debt absorbed more than half of annual revenues, and Britain was already one of the most heavily taxed societies in the world. The sheer scale of Britain's victory required more revenue just to police the conquered colonies. In 1762 and 1763, Bute and Grenville decided to leave 20 battalions with about 7,000 men in America, mostly in Canada and Florida, with smaller garrisons scattered throughout Indian territory. Because the colonists would receive the benefit of this protection, Grenville argued, they ought to pay a reasonable portion of the cost, and eventually all of it. He never asked the settlers to contribute anything to Britain's national debt or to Britain's heavy domestic needs, but he did insist that the colonies begin to pay toward their own defense.

Instead of building on the voluntaristic measures that Pitt had used to win the war, Grenville reverted to the demands for coercive reforms that had crisscrossed the Atlantic during Britain's years of defeat from 1755 to 1757. London, he believed, must gain effective centralized control over the colonies. To the settlers, victory over France would mean new burdens, not relief. To Grenville, the willing cooperation of the colonies after 1758 reflected the empire's weakness, not its strength. He thought Britain had won the war, not with the cooperation of the colonies, but despite their obstruction. He believed that the British government had to act quickly to establish its authority before the colonies, with their astonishing rate of growth, slipped completely out of control. In effect, he set in motion a self-fulfilling prophecy in which the British government brought about precisely what it was trying to prevent. Nearly every step it took undermined the colonies' loyalty to Britain.

Indian Policy and Pontiac's War

The king's **Proclamation of 1763** set up governments in Canada, Florida, and other conquered colonies, and it honored wartime commitments to the western Indians. It tried to regulate the pace of western settlement by laying out the so-called Proclamation Line along the Appalachian watershed. No settlements could be planted west of that line unless Britain first purchased the land by treaty from the Indians. Settlers would be encouraged to move instead to Nova Scotia, northern New England, Georgia, or Florida. But in 1760, General Amherst stopped distributing Indian gifts, and his contempt for Indian customs deprived the government of most of its major leverage with them at a time when their ability to unite had become stronger than ever.

In 1761, Neolin, a western Delaware, reported a vision in which God commanded Indians to return to their ancestral ways. Neolin called for an end to Indian dependence on the Anglo-Americans, although he did accept Christian ideas of heaven and hell. European vices, he said, especially drinking rum, blocked the path to heaven. Neolin stopped short

Colonial Williamsburg Foundation.

Anti-Franklin Cartoon   Pontiac's War and the Paxton riots inspired this anti-Franklin cartoon in which Quakers and Franklin protect Indians from settlers instead of settlers from Indians.

of condemning the French, who were still living in the Great Lakes region. Many of his followers even hoped that their display of unity would attract the support of King Louis XV of France (1715–74), restore the friendly relations of the past, and halt British expansion. With a unity never seen before, the Indians struck in 1763. **Pontiac's War,** named for an Ottawa chief, brought together Senecas, Mingoes, Delawares, Shawnees, Wyandots, Miamis, Ottawas, and other nations. They attacked 13 British posts in the West. Between May 16 and June 20, all of the forts fell except Niagara, Pitt, Detroit, and a tiny outpost on Green Bay that the Indians did not bother to attack. For months, the Indians kept Forts Detroit and Pitt under close siege, something Indians were supposed to be incapable of doing. They hoped to drive British settlers back to the Eastern seaboard. **(See Map 5.1, Pontiac's War and the Proclamation Line of 1763, in the color insert following page 288.)**

Enraged by these successes, Amherst ordered Colonel Henry Bouquet, commander at Fort Pitt, to distribute smallpox-infested blankets among the western nations, contributing to a lethal epidemic in 1763 and 1764. "You will do well to try to Inoculate the Indians by means of Blankets," he wrote to Bouquet, "as well as to Try Every other Method that can serve to Extirpate this Execrable Race." In 1764, British and provincial forces ended resistance, restored peace, and compelled the Indians to return their hundreds of captives, many of whom preferred to stay. The British then reluctantly accepted the role that the French had played in the Great Lakes region by distributing gifts and mediating differences. On that question, the Indians won an important victory.

But 10 years of conflict had brutalized the frontiersmen. Perhaps sensing the Indians' growing revulsion against warring with one another, many settlers began to assume that all Indians must be the enemies of all whites. In December 1763, the Scots-Irish of Paxton Township, Pennsylvania, murdered six unarmed Christian Indians—two old men, three women, and a child—at nearby Conestoga. Two weeks later, the "Paxton Boys" slaughtered 14 more Christian Indians who had been brought to Lancaster for protection. After Governor John Penn removed 140 Moravian mission Indians to Philadelphia for safety, the Paxton Boys marched on the capital determined to kill them all.

Denouncing the Paxton Boys as "Christian white Savages," Benjamin Franklin led a delegation from the assembly that met the marchers at Germantown and persuaded them to go home after they presented a list of their grievances. The Moravian Indians had been spared. All efforts to bring the murderers to justice failed, however, and the frontiersmen of Pennsylvania and Virginia virtually declared an open season on Indians that continued for years. Settlers in Augusta County, Virginia, slaughtered nine Shawnees in 1765. Frederick Stump, a Pennsylvanian, murdered 10 more in 1768 but could not be convicted in his frontier county. Such atrocities kept western Indians smoldering. London had hoped that its officials would bring evenhanded justice to the frontier. Indians had won real benefits from Britain's postwar policies, such as protection from land speculators, but otherwise they found little to choose between Amherst's smallpox blankets and the murderous rage of the Paxton Boys and their imitators.

The Sugar Act

In a step that settlers found ominous, Grenville's Sugar Act of 1764 proclaimed it "just and necessary, that a revenue be raised . . . in America for defraying the expenses of defending, protecting, and securing" the colonies. The act placed duties on Madeira wine, coffee, and other products, but Grenville expected the greatest revenue to come from the molasses duty of three pence per gallon. The Molasses Act of 1733 had been designed to keep French molasses out of North America by imposing a prohibitive duty of six pence per gallon. Instead, by paying a bribe of about a penny per gallon, merchants got French molasses certified as British. By 1760, more than 90 percent of all molasses imported into New England came from the French islands. Planters in the British islands gave up, lost interest in New England markets, and turned their molasses into quality rum for sale in Britain and Ireland. Nobody, in short, had any interest in stopping the trade in French molasses. New England merchants said they were willing to pay a duty of one penny (the current cost of bribes), but Grenville insisted on three. He hoped to raise £100,000 per year from the molasses duty, although in public he seldom put the figure above £40,000.

The Sugar Act also launched Grenville's war against smugglers. It vastly increased the amount of paperwork required of ship captains and permitted seizures of ships for what owners considered to be mere technicalities. In effect, Grenville tried to make it more profitable for customs officers to hound the merchants than to accept bribes from them. The

Sugar Act encouraged them to prosecute violators in vice-admiralty courts, which did not use juries, rather than in common-law courts, which did. Prosecutors were virtually immune from any suit for damages, even when the merchant won an acquittal, so long as the judge certified "probable cause" for the seizure.

The Currency Act and the Quartering Act

Grenville passed several other imperial measures. The Currency Act of 1764 responded to wartime protests of London merchants against Virginia's paper money, which had been issued for the colony's defense but had lost almost 15 percent of its value between 1759 and 1764. The act forbade the colonies to issue any paper money as legal tender. The money question had become urgent because the Sugar Act (and, later, the Stamp Act) required that all duties be paid in **specie** (silver or gold). Supporters of those taxes argued that the new duties would keep the specie in America to pay the army, but the colonists replied that the drain of specie from some colonies would put impossible constraints on trade. Boston and Newport, for instance, would pay most of the molasses tax, but the specie collected there would follow the army to Quebec, New York, the Great Lakes, and Florida. Grenville saw "America" as a single region in which specie would circulate to the benefit of all. The colonists knew better. As of 1765, "America" existed only in British minds, not yet in colonial hearts.

Another reform measure was the Quartering Act of 1765, requested by Sir Thomas Gage, Amherst's successor as army commander. Gage asked for parliamentary authority to quarter soldiers in private homes, if necessary, when on the march and away from their barracks. Parliament ordered colonial assemblies to vote specific supplies, such as beer and candles, for the troops, which the assemblies were willingly doing already. But it also required the army to quarter its soldiers only in public buildings, such as taverns (which existed in large numbers only in cities) and not in private homes. The Quartering Act solved no problems, but it created several new ones.

The Stamp Act

In early 1764, when Parliament passed the Sugar Act, Grenville announced that a stamp tax on legal documents and on publications might also be needed. No one in the House of Commons, he declared, doubted Parliament's right to impose such a tax. Because Parliament had never levied a direct tax on the colonies, however, he also knew that he must persuade the settlers that a stamp tax would not be a constitutional innovation. This measure, his supporters insisted, did not violate the principle of no taxation without representation. Each member of Parliament, they argued, represented the entire empire, not just a local constituency. The colonists were no different from the large nonvoting majority of subjects within Great Britain. All were **virtually represented** in Parliament. Grenville also denied that there was any legal difference between external taxes (port duties, such as that on molasses) and internal (or inland) taxes, such as the proposed stamp tax.

Grenville put off passage of the Stamp Act while he collected more complete information about legal forms in the colonies. He also indicated that, if the colonies could devise a revenue plan better than a stamp tax, he would listen. His offer created confusion and became a public relations disaster for the government. All 13 colonial assemblies drafted petitions objecting to the **Stamp Act** as a form of taxation without representation. Most of them also attacked the duties imposed by the Sugar Act because they went beyond the regulation of trade. With few exceptions, they too rejected the distinction between **internal** and **external taxes.** Both kinds, they declared, violated the British constitution. While agreeing that they ought to contribute to their own defense, they urged the government to return to the traditional method of requisitions, in which the Crown asked a colony for a specific sum, and the assembly decided how (or whether) to raise it. Colonists feared that taxation by Parliament might tempt Britain to rule them without consulting their assemblies.

When these petitions began to reach London, Parliament refused to receive them, citing a standing rule that prohibited petitions against money bills and declaring that any petition challenging the right of Parliament to pass such a tax was simply inadmissible. To Grenville, requisitions were not a better idea. They had often been tried, had never worked efficiently, and never would. He rejected the petitions with a clear conscience. But to the colonists, he seemed to have acted in bad faith all along. He had asked their advice and had then refused even to consider it.

The Stamp Act passed in February 1765, to go into effect on November 1. All contracts, licenses, commissions, and most other legal documents would be void unless they were executed on officially stamped paper. Law courts would not recognize any document that lacked the proper stamp, and the colonists would quietly if grudgingly accept Parliament's power to tax them. The act would almost enforce itself. A stamp duty was also put on all newspapers and pamphlets, a requirement likely to anger every printer in the colonies. Playing cards and dice were also taxed.

When the Stamp Act became law, most colonial leaders resigned themselves to a situation that seemed beyond their power to change. Daniel Dulany, a Maryland lawyer who did more than any other colonist to refute the argument for virtual representation, drew a line short of overt resistance. "I am upon a Question of *Propriety,* not of Power," he wrote; ". . . at the same Time that I invalidate the Claim upon which [the Stamp Act] is founded, I may very consistently recommend a Submission to the Law, whilst it endures." Instead, ordinary settlers took direct action to prevent implementation of the act.

The Stamp Act Crisis

Resistance to the Stamp Act began in spring 1765 and continued for nearly a year, until it was repealed. Patrick Henry, a newcomer to the Virginia House of Burgesses, launched the first wave by introducing five resolutions on May 30 and 31. His resolves passed by margins ranging between 22 to 17 and 20 to 19; one was rescinded and expunged from the record the next day. Henry had two more in his pocket that he decided not to introduce. Over the summer, the *Newport Mercury* printed six of Henry's seven resolutions, and the *Maryland Gazette* printed all of them. Neither paper reported that some of the seven had not passed. To other colonies, Virginia seemed to have taken a far more radical position than it actually had. The last resolve printed in the *Maryland Gazette* claimed that anyone defending Parliament's right to tax Virginia "shall be Deemed, an Enemy to this his Majesty's Colony."

In their fall or winter sessions, eight colonial legislatures passed new resolutions condemning the Stamp Act. Nine colonies sent delegates to the Stamp Act Congress, which met in New York in October. It passed resolutions affirming colonial loyalty to the king and "all due subordination" to Parliament but condemned the Stamp and Sugar Acts. By 1765, nearly all colonial spokesmen agreed that the Stamp Act was unconstitutional, that colonial representation in Parliament (urged by a few writers) was impractical because of the distance and the huge expense, and that therefore the Stamp Act had to be repealed. They accepted the idea of virtual representation *within* the colonies—their assemblies, they said, represented both voters and nonvoters in each colony—but the colonists ridiculed the argument when it was applied across the Atlantic. A disenfranchised Englishman who acquired sufficient property could become a voter, pointed out Daniel Dulany, in a pamphlet that was widely admired, even in Britain. But, Dulany explained, no colonist, no matter how wealthy he became, could vote for a member of Parliament. Members of Parliament paid the taxes that they levied on others within Britain, but they would never pay any tax imposed on the colonies.

Nullification

No matter how eloquently written, resolutions and pamphlets alone could not defeat the Stamp Act. Street violence might, however, and Boston showed the way, led by men calling themselves Sons of Liberty. On August 14, the town awoke to find an effigy of Andrew Oliver, the stamp distributor, hanging on what became the town's **Liberty Tree** (the gallows on which enemies of the people deserved to be hanged). The sheriff admitted that he dared not remove the effigy. After dark, a crowd of men roamed the streets, shouted defiance at the governor and council, and demolished a new building Oliver was erecting that "they called the Stamp Office," beheaded and burned Oliver's effigy, and finally invaded Oliver's home, "declaring they would kill Him." He had already fled to a neighbor's home. Thoroughly cowed, he resigned.

On August 26, an even angrier crowd all but demolished the elegant mansion of Lt. Governor Thomas Hutchinson. Most Bostonians believed that, in letters to British friends, Hutchinson had defended and even helped to draft the Stamp Act. In fact, he had quietly opposed it. Shocked by the destruction of property, the militia finally appeared to police the streets, but when Governor Francis Bernard tried to arrest those responsible for

The Bostonian Society/Old State House Museum

Boston's Liberty Tree in 1774   The Liberty Tree, rather like the symbolism of Guy Fawkes Day riots, indicated that the enemies of the people deserved to hang from one of its limbs.

the first riot, he got nowhere. Bostonians deplored the events of August 26 but approved those of August 14. No one was punished for either event, although the whole city knew that Ebenezer McIntosh, a poor shoemaker and a leader of the annual Pope's Day (Guy Fawkes Day) processions, had organized both riots.

Everywhere except Georgia, the stamp master was forced to resign before the law took effect on November 1. With no one to distribute the stamps, the act could not be implemented. Merchants adopted **nonimportation agreements** to pressure the British into repeal. Following Boston's lead, the Sons of Liberty took control of the streets in other cities. After November 1, they agitated to open the ports and courts, which had closed down rather than operate without stamps. Neither the courts nor the customs officers had any stamps to use because nobody dared distribute them. As winter gave way to spring, most ports and some courts resumed business. Only Newport matched Boston's level of violence, but in New York City a clash between the Sons of Liberty and the British garrison grew ugly and almost escalated into an armed encounter. Violent resistance worked. The Stamp Act was nullified—even in Georgia, eventually.

Repeal

Focus Question

Why, in 1766, did the colonists stop resisting and rejoice over the repeal of the Stamp Act, even though the Revenue Act of 1766 continued to tax molasses?

The next move was up to Britain. For reasons that had nothing to do with the colonies, the king dismissed Grenville in summer 1765 and replaced his ministry with a narrow coalition organized primarily by William Augustus, duke of Cumberland, the king's uncle. An untested young nobleman, Charles Watson-Wentworth, marquess of Rockingham, took over the treasury. This "Old Whig" ministry had to deal with the riots in America, and Cumberland—the man who had sent Braddock to America in winter 1754–55—may have favored a similar use of force in late 1765. If so, he never had a chance to issue the order. On October 31, minutes before an emergency cabinet meeting on the American crisis, he died of a heart attack, leaving Rockingham in charge of the government. At first, Rockingham favored amending the Stamp Act, but by December he had decided on repeal. To win over the other ministers, the king, and Parliament, he would need great skill.

To Rockingham, the only alternative to repeal seemed to be a ruinous civil war in America, but as the king's chief minister, he could hardly tell Parliament that the world's greatest empire must yield to unruly mobs. He needed a better reason for repeal. Even before the first American nonimportation agreements reached London on December 12 (New York City's) and December 26 (Philadelphia's), he began to mobilize the British merchants and manufacturers who traded with America. They petitioned Parliament to repeal the Stamp Act. They condemned the Grenville program as an economic disaster, and their arguments gave Rockingham the leverage he needed.

Rockingham won the concurrence of the other ministers only by promising to support a Declaratory Act affirming Parliament's sovereignty over the colonies. When William Pitt eloquently demanded repeal in the House of Commons on January 14, 1766, Rockingham gained a powerful, although temporary, ally. "I rejoice that America has resisted," declared Pitt. "Three millions of people, so dead to all the feelings of liberty, as voluntarily to submit to be slaves, would have been fit instruments to make slaves of the rest." Parliament "may bind [the colonists'] trade, confine their manufactures, and exercise every power whatsoever," Pitt declared, "except that of taking their money out of their pockets without their consent."

Rockingham still faced resistance from the king, who hinted that he favored "modification" rather than repeal. George III appeared willing to repeal all the stamp duties except those on dice and playing cards, the two levies most difficult to enforce. Only Grenville, however, was ready to use the army to enforce even an amended Stamp Act. Rockingham brought the king around by threatening to resign, which would have forced the king to bring back Grenville, whom he hated. Many pro-American witnesses appeared before Parliament to urge repeal, including Benjamin Franklin, who gave a masterful performance. Slowly, Rockingham put together his majority.

Three pieces of legislation ended the crisis. The first, the Declaratory Act, affirmed that Parliament had "full power and authority to make laws and statutes of sufficient force and validity to bind the colonies and people of America . . . in all cases whatsoever." Rockingham resisted pressure to insert the word "taxes" along with "laws and statutes." That omission permitted the colonists, who drew a sharp distinction between legislation (which, they conceded, Parliament had a right to pass) and taxation (which it could not), to interpret the act as an affirmation of their position, while nearly everyone in Britain read precisely the opposite meaning into the phrase "laws and statutes." Old Whigs hoped that Parliament would never again have to proclaim its sovereign power over America. Like the royal veto of an act of Parliament, that power existed, explained Edmund Burke; and like the veto, which had not been used for almost 60 years, it should never again be invoked. The colonists agreed. They read the Declaratory Act as a face-saving gesture that made repeal of the Stamp Act possible.

The second measure repealed the Stamp Act because it had been "greatly detrimental to the commercial interests" of the empire. The third, which modern historians call the Revenue Act of 1766, even though its preamble described it as a regulation of trade, reduced the duty on molasses from three pence per gallon to one penny, but imposed the duty on all molasses, British or foreign, imported into the mainland colonies. Although the act was more favorable to the molasses trade than any other measure yet passed by Parliament, it was also, beyond any doubt, a revenue measure, and it generated more income for the empire than any other colonial tax. Few colonists attacked it for violating the principle of no taxation without representation. In Britain, it seemed that the colonists objected to internal taxes but would accept external duties.

Against the advice of British friends, the colonists greeted repeal with wild celebrations. Over the next decade, many communities observed March 18 as the anniversary of the Stamp Act's repeal. Neither side fully appreciated the misunderstandings that had made repeal possible or their significance. In the course of the struggle, both sides, British and colonial, had rejected the distinction between external and internal taxes. They could find no legal or philosophical basis for condemning the one while approving the other. Hardly anyone except Franklin noticed in 1766 that the difference was quite real and that the crisis had in fact been resolved according to that distinction. Parliament had tried to extend its authority over the internal affairs of the colonies and had failed, but it continued to collect port duties in the colonies, some to regulate trade, others for revenue. No one knew how to justify this division of authority, but the external–internal cleavage marked, even defined, the power axis of the empire, the boundary between what Parliament could do on its own and what, internally, only the Crown could do, and then only with the consent of the colonists.

Another misunderstanding was equally grave. Only the riots had created a crisis severe enough to push Parliament into repeal. Both sides, however, preferred to believe that economic pressure had been decisive. For the colonies, this conviction set the pattern of resistance for the next two imperial crises.

The Townshend Crisis

The goodwill created by repeal did not last. In 1766, the king again replaced his ministry. This time he persuaded William Pitt to form a government. He and Pitt shared a contempt for the aristocratic families that had governed Britain since 1714, most of whom were now

Rockingham Whigs. Both the king and Pitt considered factions immoral and put their faith in a government of "measures, not men." Pitt appealed to men of good will from all parties, but few responded. His ministry, which included many supporters of the Grenville program, faced serious opposition within Parliament. Pitt compounded that problem by accepting a peerage as earl of Chatham, a decision that removed his compelling oratory from the House of Commons and left Charles Townshend as his spokesman in that chamber. A witty, extemporaneous speaker, Townshend had betrayed every leader he ever served. The only point of real consistency in his political career had been his hard-line attitude toward the colonies.

The Townshend Program

New York had already created a small crisis for Chatham by objecting to the Quartering Act as a disguised form of taxation without consent. Under the old rules, the army asked for quarters and supplies and the assembly voted them. Consent was an integral part of the process. Now one legislature (Parliament) was telling others (the colonial assemblies) what they must do. New York refused. In 1767, Parliament passed the New York Restraining Act, which forbade New York's governor to sign any bill into law until the assembly complied with the Quartering Act. The crisis fizzled out when the governor bent the rules and announced that the assembly had already complied with the substance (if not all the specifics) of the Quartering Act before the Restraining Act went into effect. In the end, instead of helping the army, the Quartering Act weakened colonial loyalty to Britain.

Chatham soon learned that he could not control the House of Commons from his position in the House of Lords. During the Christmas recess of 1766–67, he saw the extent of his failure and began to slip into an acute depression that lasted more than two years. He refused to communicate with other ministers or even with the king. The colonists, who admired him more than any other Englishman of the day, expected sympathy from his administration. Instead, they got Townshend, who took charge of colonial policy in spring 1767.

A central aspect of Townshend's annual budget, the Townshend Revenue Act of 1767 imposed new duties in colonial ports on certain imports that the colonies could legally buy only from Britain: tea, paper, glass, red and white lead, and painter's colors. But Townshend also removed more duties on tea within Britain than he could offset with the new revenue collected in the colonies. Revenue, clearly, was not his object. The statute's preamble stated his real goal: To use the new American revenues to pay the salaries of governors and judges in the colonies, thereby freeing them from dependence on the assemblies. This devious strategy aroused suspicions of conspiracy in the colonies. Many sober provincials began to believe that, deep in the recesses of the British government, men really were plotting to deprive them of their liberties.

Other measures gave appellate powers to the vice-admiralty courts in Boston, Philadelphia, and Charleston and created a separate American Board of Customs Commissioners to enforce the trade and revenue laws in the colonies. The board was placed in Boston, where resistance to the Stamp Act had been fiercest, rather than in Philadelphia, which had been rather quiet in 1765 and would have been a much more convenient location. Townshend was eager for confrontation.

The British army also began to withdraw from nearly all frontier posts and concentrate near the coast. Although the primary motive was to save money, the implications were striking. It was one thing to keep an army in America to guard the frontier and then ask the colonists to pay part of its cost, but an army far distant from the frontier presumably existed only to police the colonists. Why should they pay any part of its cost if its role was to enforce policies that would deprive them of their liberties?

Townshend ridiculed the distinction between internal and external taxes, a distinction that he attributed to Chatham and the colonists, but he declared that he would honor it anyway. After winning approval for his program, he died suddenly in September 1767 and passed on to others the dilemmas he had created. Frederick, Lord North, replaced him as chancellor of the exchequer. Chatham resigned, and Augustus Henry Fitzroy, duke of Grafton, became prime minister.

Resistance: The Politics of Escalation

The external–internal distinction was troublesome for the colonists. Since 1765, they had objected to all taxes for revenue, but in 1766, they had accepted the penny duty on molasses with few complaints. Defeating the Townshend Revenue Act would prove tougher than nullifying the Stamp Act. Parliament had never been able to impose its will on the internal affairs of the colonies, as the Stamp Act fiasco demonstrated, but it did control the seas. Goods subject to duties might arrive aboard any of hundreds of ships from Britain each year, but screening the cargo of every vessel threatened to impose an enormous, perhaps impossible burden on the Sons of Liberty. A policy of general nonimportation would be easier to implement, but British trade played a bigger role in the colonial economy than North American trade did in the British economy. To hurt Britain a little, the colonies would have to harm themselves a lot.

The colonists divided over strategies of resistance. The radical *Boston Gazette* called for complete nonimportation of all British goods. The merchants' paper, the *Boston Evening Post*, disagreed. In October, the Boston town meeting encouraged greater use of home manufactures and authorized voluntary nonconsumption of British goods, but there was no organized resistance against the new measures, and the Townshend duties became operative in November 1767 with little opposition. A month later, John Dickinson, a Philadelphia lawyer, tried to rouse his fellow colonists to action through 12 urgent letters printed in nearly every colonial newspaper. These *Letters from a Farmer in Pennsylvania* denied the distinction between internal and external taxes, insisted that all parliamentary taxes for revenue violated the colonists' rights, and speculated darkly about Townshend's motives.

Massachusetts again set the pace of resistance. In February 1768, its assembly petitioned the king, not Parliament, against the new measures. Without waiting for a reply, it also sent a Circular Letter to the other assemblies, urging them to pursue "constitu-tional measures" of resistance against the Quartering Act, the new taxes, and the use of Townshend revenues to pay the salaries of governors and judges. The implication was that, because Britain responded only to resistance, the colonies had better work together.

The British ministry got the point and did not like it. Wills Hill, earl of Hillsborough and secretary of state for the American colonies (an office created in 1768), responded so sharply that he turned tepid opposition into serious resistance. He ordered the Massachusetts assem-bly to rescind the Circular Letter and instructed all governors to dissolve any assembly that dared to accept it. In June 1768, the Massachusetts House voted 92 to 17 not to rescind. Most other assemblies had shown little interest in the Townshend program, particularly in the southern colonies, where governors already had fixed salaries. Even so, they bristled at being told what they could or could not debate. All of them took up the Circular Letter or began to draft their own. One by one, the governors dissolved their assemblies until government by consent really seemed in peril.

The next escalation again came from Boston. On March 18, 1768, the town's celebra-tion of the anniversary of the Stamp Act's repeal grew so raucous that the governor and the new American Board of Customs Commissioners asked Hillsborough for troops. He ordered General Gage, based in New York, to send two regiments from Nova Scotia to Boston. On June 10, before Gage could respond, a riot broke out in Boston after customs collectors seized John Hancock's sloop *Liberty* for having smuggled Madeira wine (taxed under the Sugar Act) on its *previous* voyage. By waiting until the ship had a new cargo, informers and customs officials could split larger shares when the sloop was condemned. Terrified by the fury of the popular response, the commissioners fled to Castle William in Boston harbor and again petitioned Hillsborough for troops. He sent two more regi-ments from Ireland.

At about this time, nonimportation at last began to take hold. Two dozen Massachusetts towns adopted pacts in which they agreed not to consume British goods. Boston mer-chants drafted a nonimportation agreement on March 1, 1768, conditional on its accep-tance by New York and Philadelphia. New York agreed, but Philadelphia balked, pre-ferring to wait and see whether Parliament would make any effort to redress colonial grievances. There the matter rested until the *Liberty* riot prompted most Boston mer-chants to agree to nonimportation, effective January 1. New York again concurred, but Philadelphia held out until early 1769, when it became obvious that Parliament would make no concessions.

Spurred on by the popular but mistaken belief that the nonimportation agreements of 1765 had forced Parliament to repeal the Stamp Act, the colonists again turned to a strategy of economic sanctions. Nonimportation affected only imports from Britain. Tea, consumed mostly by women, was the most objectionable import of all. No one tried to block the importation of West Indian molasses, which was essential to the rum industry of Boston and Newport and which brought in about £30,000 a year under the Revenue Act of 1766.

Rum was consumed mostly by men. Some women resented the disproportionate sacrifices they were asked to make. On the other hand, the Sons of Liberty knew that virtually all molasses came from the French islands, and that nonimportation would injure only French planters and American manufacturers and consumers and would put no pressure on Parliament or British merchants. The only proven way to resist the penny duty was through smuggling.

Believing that he held the edge with the army on its way, Governor Bernard leaked this news in late August 1768. The public response stunned him. The Boston town meeting asked him to summon the legislature, which Bernard had dissolved in June after it stood by its Circular Letter. When Bernard refused, the Sons of Liberty asked the other towns to elect delegates to a "convention" in Boston. The convention contained most of the radical members of the House of Representatives but not the conservatives. It had no legal standing in the colony's royal government. Boston, professing alarm over the possibility of a French invasion, urged its citizens to arm themselves. When the convention met, it accepted Boston's definition of colonial grievances but refused to sanction violence. Boston had no choice but to go along. It could not call the shots for the whole colony.

An Experiment in Military Coercion

The British fleet entered Boston harbor in battle array by October 2, 1768, and landed 1,000 soldiers, sent by General Gage from Nova Scotia. Massachusetts had built public barracks—in Castle William, miles away on an island in Boston harbor, where the soldiers could hardly function as a police force. But according to the Quartering Act, any attempt to quarter soldiers on private property would expose the officer responsible to being cashiered from the army, after conviction before any two justices of the peace. And several prominent patriots, such as John Adams and James Otis, Jr., were justices. The soldiers pitched their tents on Boston Common. Seventy men deserted in the first week, about 7 percent of the force. Eventually, the soldiers took over a building that had been the Boston poorhouse. The regiments from Ireland joined them later.

To warn the public against the dangers posed by a standing army in time of peace, the patriots compiled a "Journal of the Times," describing how British soldiers were undermining public order in Boston—clashing with the town watch, endangering the virtue of young women, disturbing church services, and picking fights. The "journal" always appeared first as a newspaper column in some other city, usually New York. Only later was it reprinted in Boston, after memories of any specific incident had grown hazy. Yet violence against customs officers ceased for many months. John Mein (pronounced "mean"), loyalist editor of the *Boston Chronicle,* caricatured leading patriots (John Hancock's generosity, for example, made him "the milch-cow of the disaffected") and began to publish customs records that exposed merchants who were violating the nonimportation agreement. This information could undermine intercolonial resistance by discrediting its Boston leaders. Yet Britain's experiment in military coercion seemed successful enough to justify withdrawal of half the soldiers in summer 1769.

Meanwhile, when news of the Massachusetts convention of towns reached Britain, the House of Lords promptly escalated the crisis another notch by drafting a set of resolutions calling for the deportation of colonial political offenders to England for trial. Instead of quashing dissent, this threat to colonial political autonomy infuriated the southern colonies, which had not been deeply involved in resistance to the Townshend duties. Virginia, Maryland, and South Carolina now adopted nonimportation agreements. In the Chesapeake, the movement had more support among planters than among tobacco merchants, most of whom were Scots loyal to their parent firms. No enforcement mechanism was ever put in place. Charleston, however, took nonimportation seriously. Up and down the continent, the feeble resistance of mid-1768 was becoming formidable by 1769.

The Wilkes Crisis

John Wilkes, a member of Parliament and a radical opposition journalist, had fled into exile in 1763 and had been outlawed for publishing an attack on the king in his newspaper, *The North Briton* No. 45. In 1768, just as the Townshend Crisis was brewing, George III dissolved Parliament and issued writs for the usual septennial elections. Wilkes returned from France and won a seat for the English county of Middlesex. He then received a one-year sentence in King's Bench Prison. Hundreds of supporters gathered to chant "Wilkes and Liberty!" or even "No Wilkes? No King!" On May 10, 1768, as the new Parliament convened, Wilkites just outside the prison clashed with soldiers who fired into the crowd, killing six and wounding 15. Wilkes denounced "the massacre of St. George's Fields." The House of Commons expelled Wilkes and ordered a new election, but the voters chose him again. Two more expulsions and two more elections took place the next year, until April 1769 when, after Wilkes won again by 1,143 votes to 296, the exasperated House voted to seat the loser.

Wilkes had created a constitutional crisis. His adherents founded "the Society of Gentlemen Supporters of the Bill of Rights," which raised money to pay off his huge debts and organized a national campaign on his behalf. About one-fourth of the voters of the entire kingdom signed petitions demanding a new general election. Wilkites called for a reduction of royal patronage and major reforms of the electoral system. They also began the regular publication of parliamentary debates and sympathized openly with North American protests. Colonial Sons of Liberty began to identify strongly with Wilkes. If he lost, they warned, their own liberties would be in danger. Boston even printed a Wilkite parody of the Apostles' Creed. It began: "I believe in Wilkes, the firm patriot, maker of number 45. Who was born for our good. Suffered under arbitrary power. Was banished and imprisoned." It ended with a hope for "the resurrection of liberty, and the life of universal freedom forever. Amen." In 1769, the South Carolina assembly borrowed £1,500 sterling from the colony's treasurer and donated it to Wilkes. When the assembly passed an appropriation to cover the gift, the council rejected the bill. Because neither side would yield, the assembly voted no taxes after 1769 and passed no laws after 1771. Royal government broke down over the Wilkes question.

The Townshend crisis and the Wilkite movement became an explosive combination. For the first time, many colonists began to question the decency of the British government and its commitment to liberty. That a conspiracy existed to destroy British and colonial liberty began to seem quite credible.

The Boston Massacre

In late 1769, the Boston Sons of Liberty turned to direct confrontation with the army, and the city again faced a serious crisis. The redcoats had intimidated Boston for nearly a year. Now Boston reciprocated. The town watch clashed with the army's guard posts because the watch, when challenged by the redcoats' call "Who goes there?" refused to give the required answer: "Friends." Under English **common law,** soldiers could not fire on civilians without an order from a civil magistrate, except in self-defense when their lives were in danger. By the fall of 1769, no magistrate dared issue such a command. Clashes between soldiers and civilians grew frequent, and justices of the peace singled out the soldiers for punishment. At one point, when town officials tried to arrest a British officer who was commanding the guard at Boston Neck, Captain Ponsonby Molesworth intervened to confront a stone-throwing crowd. Molesworth ordered the soldiers to bayonet anyone throwing stones who moved too close. Later, a Boston justice told him that, under common law, a bayonet thrust was not an act of self-defense against a stone, which was not a lethal weapon. Had a soldier killed anyone, Molesworth could have been tried for his life for issuing the order.

By 1770, the soldiers often felt under siege. When rioters drove editor John Mein out of town, the army offered him no protection. "Go, Mein, to some dark corner of the world repair," mocked one poet, "And spend thy life in horror and despair." Once again the Sons of Liberty freely intimidated merchants who violated nonimportation. They nearly lynched Ebenezer Richardson, a customs informer who fired shots from his home into a stone-throwing crowd and killed an 11-year-old boy. The lad's funeral on February 26, 1770, became an enormous display of public mourning. Richardson, although convicted of murder, was pardoned by George III.

After the funeral, tensions between soldiers and citizens reached a fatal climax. Off-duty soldiers tried to supplement their meager wages with part-time employment, a practice that angered local **artisans,** who resented the competition in the city's depressed economy. On Friday, March 2, 1770, three soldiers came to John Hancock's wharf looking for work. "Soldier, will you work?" asked Samuel Gray, a ropemaker. "Yes," replied one. "Then go and clean my shit house," sneered Gray. After an ugly brawl, Gray's employer persuaded Colonel William Dalrymple to confine his men to barracks. Peace prevailed through the Puritan sabbath that ran from Saturday night to sunrise on Monday, but everyone expected trouble on Monday, March 5.

After dark on Monday, fire bells began ringing throughout the town, and civilians and soldiers clashed at several places. A crowd hurling snowballs and rocks closed in on the lone sentinel guarding the hated customs house, where the king's revenue was stored. The guard called for help. A corporal and seven soldiers, including two who had participated in the wharf brawl, rushed to his aid and loaded their weapons. Captain Thomas Preston took command and ordered the soldiers to drive the attackers slowly back with fixed bayonets. The crowd taunted the soldiers, daring them to fire. One soldier apparently slipped, discharging his musket into the air as he fell. The others then fired into the crowd, killing five and wounding six. One of the victims was Samuel Gray; another was Crispus Attucks, a man of African and Indian ancestry.

With the whole town turning out, the soldiers were withdrawn to Castle William where, the Sons of Liberty insisted, they had always belonged. Preston and six of his men stood trial for murder and were defended, brilliantly, by two radical patriot lawyers, John Adams and Josiah Quincy, Jr., who believed that every accused person ought to have a proper defense. Preston and four of the soldiers were acquitted. The other two were convicted only of manslaughter, which permitted them to plead a legal technicality called "benefit of clergy." They were branded on the thumb and released. The **Boston Massacre,** as the Sons of Liberty called this encounter, became the colonial counterpart to the Massacre of St. George's Fields in England. It marked the failure of Britain's first attempt at military coercion.

Partial Repeal

The day of the massacre marked a turning point in Britain as well, for on March 5, Lord North asked Parliament to repeal the Townshend duties, except the one on tea. North

Colonial Williamsburg Foundation.

"The Colossus of the North; or The Striding Boreas"   This print was an opposition cartoon condemning the corruption of Lord North's ministry while Britannia complains that "Those that should have been my Preservers have been my Destroyers."

Exports in £000 Sterling from England and Scotland to the American Colonies, 1766–75

Colony	1766	1767	1768	1769	1770	1771	1772	1773	1774	1775
New England	419	416	431	224	417	1,436*	844	543	577	85.0
New York	333	424	491	76	480	655*	349	296	460	1.5
Pennsylvania	334	383	442	205	140	747*	526	436	646	1.4
Chesapeake†	520	653	670	715	997*	1,224*	1,016	589	690	1.9
Lower South‡	376	292	357	385*	228	515*	575*	448	471	130.5
Totals	1,982	2,168	2,391	1,605	2,262	4,577*	3,310	2,312	2,844	220.3

Average total exports, 1766–68 = £2,180;
1769 = 73.6% of that average, or 67.1% of 1768 exports;
1770 = 103.8% of that average, or 94.6% of 1768 exports.
*These totals surpassed all previous highs.
†Chesapeake = Maryland and Virginia
‡Lower South = Carolinas and Georgia

wanted them all repealed, but the cabinet had rejected complete repeal by a 5-to-4 margin. As with the Stamp Act, Britain had three choices: enforcement, repeal, or modification. North chose the middle ground that had been rejected in 1766—modification. He claimed to be retaining only a preamble without a statute, a vestige of the Townshend Revenue Act, while repealing the substance. In fact, he did the opposite. Tea provided nearly three-fourths of the revenue under the act. North kept the substance but gave up the shadow.

This news reached the colonies just after nonimportation had achieved its greatest success in 1769. The colonies reduced imports by about one-third from what they had been in 1768, but the impact on Britain was slight, partly because Britain had found a lucrative market for textiles by selling new uniforms to the Russian army. North had hoped that partial repeal, although it would not placate all of the colonists, would at least divide them. It did. Most merchants favored renewed importation of everything but tea, while the Sons of Liberty, most of whom were artisans, still supported broad nonimportation, a policy that would increase demand for their own manufactures.

Resistance collapsed first in Newport, where smuggling had always been the preferred method of challenging British authority. It spread to New York City, where the boycott on imports had been most effective. Soon Philadelphia caved in, followed by Boston in October 1770. By contrast, nonimportation had not caused a ripple in the import trade of the Chesapeake colonies. North's repeal was followed by an orgy of importation of British goods, setting record highs everywhere.

Disaffection

Repeal in 1770 lacked the impact that it had in 1766. There was no public rejoicing, not even when Lord North's government (he had replaced Grafton as prime minister in

January 1770) took further steps to reduce tension. The Quartering Act expired quietly in 1770, some of the more objectionable features of the vice-admiralty courts were softened, and the Currency Act of 1764 was repealed in stages between 1770 and 1773, as even London began to recognize that it was harming trade. Yet North failed to restore confidence in the justice and decency of the British government. To a degree that is difficult to appreciate today, the empire ran on voluntarism, on trust, or what people at the time called "affection." Its opposite, *dis*affection, had a more literal and dangerous meaning to them than it does now.

Many colonists blamed one another for failing to win complete repeal of the duties. A Philadelphian attacked the "little dirty colony of Rhode Island" for yielding first. Bostonians lamented the "immortal shame and infamy" of New Yorkers for abandoning resistance: "Let them . . . be despised, hated, detested, and handed down to all future ages as the betrayers of their country." A New Yorker retaliated by calling Boston "the common sewer of America into which every beast that brought with it the unclean thing has disburthened itself." These recriminations, gratifying as they must have been to British officials, actually masked a vast erosion of trust in the imperial government. The colonists were angry with one another for failing to appreciate how menacing British policy still was. The tea duty continued to proclaim Parliament's sovereignty over the colonies. It remained a sliver in a wound that would not heal.

That fear sometimes broke through the surface calm of the years from 1770 to 1773. Rhode Islanders had often clashed with customs officers and had even fired on the king's ships once or twice without stirring much interest in other colonies. Then, in 1772, a predatory customs vessel, the *Gaspée*, ran aground near Providence while pursuing some peaceful coastal ships. After dark, men with blackened faces boarded the *Gaspée*, wounded its captain, and burned the ship. Britain sent a panel of dignitaries to the colony with instructions to send the perpetrators to England for trial. The inquiry failed because no one would talk.

Twelve colonial assemblies considered this threat so ominous that they created permanent **committees of correspondence** to keep in touch with one another and to *anticipate* the next assault on their liberties. Even colonial moderates now believed that the British government was conspiring to destroy liberty in America. When Governor Hutchinson announced in 1773 that, under the Townshend Act, the Massachusetts Superior Court justices would receive their salaries from the imperial treasury, Boston created its own committee of correspondence and urged other towns to do the same. Boston's role in the "patriot" cause had grown dramatically since the convention of 1768, and Bostonians such as John Adams had become the major spokesmen for the resistance movement. A plot to destroy their liberties now seemed plausible to many colonials. Hutchinson, amused at first, grew alarmed when most towns of any size followed Boston's lead. That there was a plot to destroy their liberties seemed obvious to them.

The Boston Massacre trials and the *Gaspée* affair convinced London that it was pointless to prosecute individuals for politically motivated crimes. Whole communities would have to be punished. That choice brought the government to the edge of a precipice. Was the empire held together by law and consent, or only by force? The use of force against entire communities could lead to outright war, and war is not and cannot be a system of justice. The spread of committees of correspondence within Massachusetts and throughout the colonies suggested that settlers who had been unable to unite against New France at Albany in 1754 now deemed unity against Britain essential to their liberties. By 1773, several New England newspapers were calling on the colonies to create a formal union.

In effect, the Townshend crisis never ended. With the tea duty standing as a symbol of Parliament's right to tax the colonies without their consent, genuine imperial harmony was becoming impossible. North's decision to retain the tea tax in 1770 did not guarantee that armed resistance would break out five years later, but it severely narrowed the ground on which any compromise could be built. The price of miscalculation had grown enormously.

Internal Cleavages: The Contagion of Liberty

Any challenge to British authority carried high risks for prominent families in the colonies. They depended on the Crown for their public offices, official honors, and government contracts, which in turn ratified their status at the top of society. After the Stamp Act crisis, these families faced a dilemma. The Hutchinsons of Massachusetts kept on good terms with Britain while incurring the scorn and even hatred of many of their neighbors. John Hancock, the Livingstons of New York, and most of the great planters in the southern colonies championed the grievances of their communities but alienated British authorities. The Townshend crisis was a far more accurate predictor of future behavior than response to the Stamp Act had been. Nearly everyone had denounced the Stamp Act, including such future loyalists as Daniel Dulany of Maryland. By contrast, the merchants and lawyers who resisted nonimportation in 1768 were likely to become loyalists by 1775. Artisans, merchants, and lawyers who supported the boycotts, especially those who favored continuing them past 1770, became patriots.

But the patriot leaders also faced challenges from within their own ranks. Artisans, who had mobilized to resist Britain in 1765 and 1769, demanded more power, and tenant farmers in the Hudson valley protested violently against their landlords. In Boston, where the economy had been faltering since the 1740s while taxes remained high, Britain's policies bore hard on the town and gave an angry edge to its protests. Boston's radical artisans set the pace of resistance in every imperial crisis. In New York City, Philadelphia, and Charleston, artisans began to play a much more assertive role in public affairs.

The Feudal Revival and Rural Discontent

Tensions increased in the countryside as well as in the cities. Three processes intensified discontent in rural areas: a revival of old proprietary charters, massive foreign immigration, and the settlement of the backcountry.

Between about 1730 and 1750, the men who owned 17th-century proprietary charters or manorial patents began to see, for the first time, the prospect of huge profits by enforcing these old legal claims. The great estates of the Hudson valley had attracted few settlers before the mid-18th century, and those who arrived first had received generous leases. By the 1750s, however, a typical manor lord was taking in between £1,000 and £2,000 per year, while the Livingston and Van Rensselaer families did much better. As leases became more restrictive and as New Englanders swarmed into New York, discontent increased. In 1753, the proprietor of Livingston Manor had difficulty putting down Yankee rioters, and discontent spread throughout the Hudson valley over the next decade. In 1766, several thousand angry farmers, inspired by the Stamp Act riots, took to the fields and the roads to protest the terms of their leases. They threatened to kill the lord of Livingston Manor or to pull down the New York City mansions of absentee landlords. Supported by some of the city's most prominent Sons of Liberty, the colony called in redcoats to suppress them. New York's experience exposed the difficulties of uniting urban and rural radicals in a common cause. But when New York landlords also tried to make good their claims to the upper Connecticut valley, the Yankee settlers utterly defied them, set up their own government, and, after a long struggle, ultimately became the independent state of Vermont.

The proprietors of East New Jersey claimed much of the land being worked by descendants of the original settlers of Newark and Elizabethtown, who thought they owned their farms. The proprietors, in firm control of the law courts, planned to sell or lease the land, either to the current occupants or to newcomers. After they expelled several farmers and replaced them with tenants, the farmers retaliated. A succession of land riots, in which farms were burned and jails were broken open, rocked much of northern New Jersey for 10 years after 1745. The proprietary intruders were driven out, and the riots stopped, but tensions remained high.

Maryland and Pennsylvania had brought few returns to the Calvert and Penn families before 1730, but over the next three or four decades, both families organized land sales much more carefully and began to collect quitrents. Frederick, the seventh and last Lord Baltimore, milked Maryland for the princely income of £30,000 sterling per year until his death in 1771. The Penns enjoyed similar gains in Pennsylvania, although more slowly. Their landed income rose to about £15,000 or £20,000 in the 1760s and then soared to £67,000 in 1773, only to fall sharply as the Pennsylvania government disintegrated over the next three years. With more than half of their land still unsettled, they seemed about to turn their colony into the most lucrative piece of real estate in the Atlantic world. But their reluctance to contribute to the war effort in the 1750s had so angered Benjamin Franklin that, with the assembly's support, he went to London to urge the Crown to make Pennsylvania a royal colony. This effort weakened the colony's resistance to both the Stamp Act and the Townshend Act. Meanwhile Connecticut settlers, who claimed they had bought Pennsylvania's Wyoming valley from the Indians at the Albany Congress of 1754, rejected the Penns' authority, claimed all of northern Pennsylvania on the basis of

Connecticut's sea-to-sea charter and, aided by the Paxton Boys, set off a small civil war there in the 1770s.

In Virginia, Thomas, the sixth baron Fairfax, acquired title to the entire northern neck of the colony (the land between the Potomac and the Rappahannock rivers), which Charles II had granted to two courtiers in the mid-17th century. By 1775, the Fairfax estate's 5 million acres contained 21 counties. He received £5,000 per year from his holdings, but he muted criticism by moving to the colony and setting himself up as a great planter and a patron of youthful George Washington.

In North Carolina, John Carteret, earl of Granville—the only heir of the original Carolina proprietors who refused to sell his share to the Crown in the 1720s—consolidated his claim as the Granville District after 1745. Although still living in England, he received an income of about £5,000 per year. The Granville District embraced more than half of North Carolina's land and two-thirds of its population, deprived the colony of revenue from land sales and quitrents within the district, and forced North Carolina to resort to direct taxation. For several years after Granville's death in 1763, his land office remained closed. Disgruntled settlers often rioted when they could not gain title to their lands.

Taken together, the claims of New York's manor lords, the New Jersey proprietors, and the Penn, Baltimore, Fairfax, and Granville families blanketed the colonies from New York to North Carolina. They were the biggest winners in America's feudal revival, the use of old charters to pry income from the settlers.

The Regulator Movements in the Carolinas

Massive immigration from Europe, mostly through Philadelphia, and the settlement of the backcountry created severe social tensions. Most immigrants were Scottish or Scots-Irish Presbyterians, Lutherans, or German Reformed Protestants. They were dissenters from the prevailing faith in the colonies they entered, whether it was the Quaker religion in Pennsylvania or the Church of England from Maryland to Georgia. They angered Indians by squatting on their land and, quite often, by murdering those who were in their way— behavior that the Paxton Boys' march on Philadelphia in 1763 attempted to justify. In the Carolina backcountry, the newcomers provoked the Cherokee War of 1759–61, which brutalized and demoralized the whole region.

After the Cherokee War, bands of outlaws, men who had been dislocated by the war, began roaming the countryside, plundering the more prosperous farmers and often raping their wives and daughters. As the violence peaked between 1765 and 1767, the more respectable settlers organized themselves as "regulators" (a later generation would call them "vigilantes") to impose order in the absence of any organized government. Although South Carolina claimed jurisdiction over the backcountry, the colony's law courts were located in Charleston, more than 100 miles to the east. Even though most of the white settlers now lived in the backcountry, they elected only 2 of the 48 members of South Carolina's assembly. In effect, they had no local government.

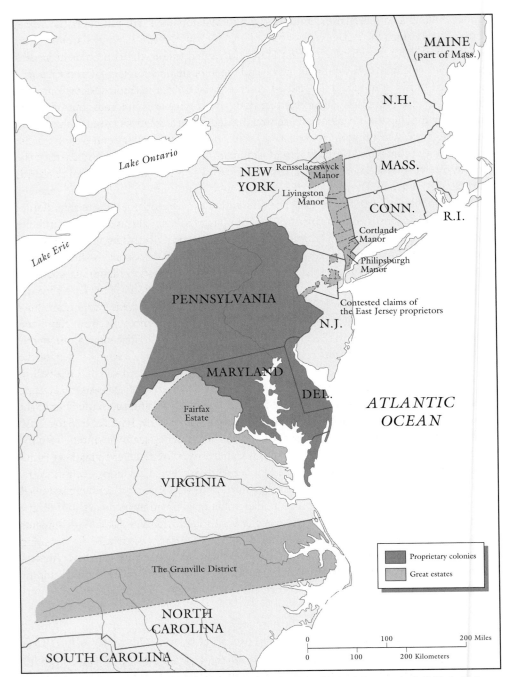

Map 5.2 Feudal Revival: Great Estates of Late Colonial America   On the eve of the Revolution, more than half of the land between the Hudson Valley and North Carolina was claimed by men who had inherited or acquired various kinds of 17th-century charters or patents.

After obtaining commissions from Charleston as militia officers and justices of the peace, the regulators chased the outlaws out of the colony, many of them into North Carolina. They then imposed order on what they called the "little people," poor settlers who often made a living as hunters, many of whom may have aided the outlaws. The discipline imposed by the regulators, typically whippings and forced labor, outraged their victims, who organized as "moderators" and got their own commissions from the governor. With both sides claiming legality, about 600 armed regulators confronted an equal force of moderators at the Saluda River in 1769. Civil war was avoided only by the timely arrival of an emissary from the governor bearing a striking message: South Carolina would finally bring government to the backcountry by providing a circuit court system for the entire colony. Violence ebbed, but tensions remained severe.

In North Carolina, the backcountry's problem was corruption, not the absence of government. The settlers, mostly immigrants pushing south from Pennsylvania, found the county courts under the control of men with strong blood or business ties to powerful families in the eastern counties. Because county officials were appointed by the governor, political success required gaining access to his circle. These justices, lawyers, and merchants seemed to regard county government as an engine for fleecing farmers through regressive poll taxes, fees, and court costs, and through suits for debt. North Carolina's regulator movement arose to reform these abuses. The backcountry counties contained more than half the colony's population, but they elected only 17 of the 78 assemblymen.

In 1768, the regulators refused to pay taxes in Orange County, which was part of the Granville District. Governor William Tryon mustered 1,300 eastern militiamen, one-sixth of whom were officers, including more than half of the assemblymen from the eastern counties. With 8 generals and 14 colonels, and led by an elite unit of Gentlemen Volunteer Light Dragoons, this force overawed the regulators for a time. Then, in a bid for a voice in the 1769 assembly, the regulators managed to capture six seats. These new assemblymen called for the secret ballot, fixed salaries (instead of fees) for justices and other officials, and a land tax rather than **poll taxes,** but they were outvoted by the eastern majority. After losing ground in the 1770 election, they stormed into Hillsborough, closed the Orange County Court, and whipped Edmund Fanning, a Yale graduate whose lust for fees had made him the most detested official in the backcountry. They also seized the court docket and scribbled unflattering comments next to many of the names of their creditors. In early 1771, Tryon responded by marching 1,000 militiamen westward, who defeated a force of more than 2,000 poorly armed regulators at the battle of Alamance Creek. Seven regulators were hanged, and many fled the colony. North Carolina entered the struggle for independence as a bitterly divided society.

Slaves and Women

Focus Question

Ever since the ancient world, Christians had insisted that sin is a form of slavery. Why did it take them over 1,500 years to conclude that enslaving others might be a grievous sin?

In Charleston, South Carolina, in 1765, the Sons of Liberty marched through the streets chanting "Liberty and No Stamps." To their amazement, slaves organized a parade of their own, shouting, "Liberty! Liberty!" Merchant Henry Laurens tried to convince himself that they probably did not know the meaning of the word.

Around the middle of the 18th century, slavery came under serious attack for the first time. An antislavery movement arose on both sides of the Atlantic and attracted both future patriots and loyalists. In the 1740s and 1750s, Benjamin Lay, John Woolman, and Anthony Benezet urged fellow Quakers to free their slaves. In the 1750s, the Quaker Yearly Meeting placed the slave trade off limits and finally, in 1774, forbade slaveholding altogether. Any Friend who did not comply by 1779 would be disowned. Britain's Methodist leader John Wesley, in almost every other respect a social conservative, also attacked slavery, as did several colonial disciples of Jonathan Edwards. Two and three decades after the Great Awakening, many evangelicals began to agree with the message of South Carolina's Hugh Bryan in 1742, that slavery was a sin.

By the 1760s, supporters of slavery found that they now had to defend the institution. Hardly anyone had bothered to do so earlier, because a social hierarchy seemed necessary and inevitable, and slavery simply marked the bottom extreme. As equal rights became a popular topic, however, some began to suggest that *all* people could claim these rights, and slavery came under attack. In Scotland, Adam Smith, the most original economist of the age, praised African slaves for their "magnanimity," which, he claimed, "the soul of the sordid master is scarce capable of conceiving." Arthur Lee, a Virginian, defended the character of his fellow planters against Smith's charge but discovered that he could not justify slavery, "always the deadly enemy to virtue and science." Patrick Henry agreed. Slavery, he wrote, "is as repugnant to humanity as it is inconsistent with the Bible and destructive of liberty." He did keep slaves, but only because of "the general inconvenience of living without them. I will not, I cannot justify it." In England, Granville Sharp, an early abolitionist, brought the Somerset case before the Court of King's Bench in 1771 and compelled a reluctant Chief Justice William Murray, baron Mansfield, to declare slavery incompatible with the "free air" of England. That decision gave England's 10,000 or 15,000 blacks a chance to claim their freedom.

New Englanders began to head in similar directions. Two women, Sarah Osborn and Phillis Wheatley, played leading roles in the movement. Osborn, an English immigrant to Newport, Rhode Island, and a widow, opened a school in 1744 to support her family. A friend of revivalist George Whitefield, she also taught women and blacks and began holding evening religious meetings, which turned into a big local revival. At one point in the 1760s, about one-sixth of Newport's Africans were attending her school. That made them the most literate African population in the colonies, although they were living in the colonial city most deeply involved in the African slave trade. Osborn's students supported abolition of the slave trade and, later, of slavery itself.

In 1761, an eight-year-old girl who would become known as Phillis Wheatley arrived in Boston from Africa and was purchased by wealthy John Wheatley as a servant for his wife, Susannah, who treated her more like a daughter than a slave and taught her to read and write. In 1767, Phillis published her first poem in Boston, and she visited London as a celebrity in 1773 after a volume of her poetry was published there. Her poems deplored slavery but rejoiced in the Christianization of Africans. Some of them supported the patriot cause, but she withheld those from the London edition.

Soon many of Boston's blacks sensed an opportunity for emancipation. On several occasions in 1773 and 1774, they petitioned the legislature or the governor for freedom, arguing that, although they had never forfeited their natural rights, they were being "held in slavery in the bowels of a free and Christian Country." When the legislature passed a bill on their behalf, Governor Hutchinson vetoed it. Boston slaves made it clear to General Gage, Hutchinson's successor, that they would serve him as a loyal militia in exchange for their freedom. In short, they offered allegiance to whichever side supported their emancipation. Many patriots began to rally to their cause. "If we would look for Liberty ourselves," the town of Medfield declared in 1773, ". . . we ought not to continue to enslave others but immediately set about some effectual method to prevent it for the future."

The patriots could look to another group of allies as well. Many women became indispensable to the broader resistance movement. They could not vote or hold office, but without their willing support, nonimportation would have been not just a failure, but a fiasco. In thousands of households, women joined the intense discussions about liberty and agreed

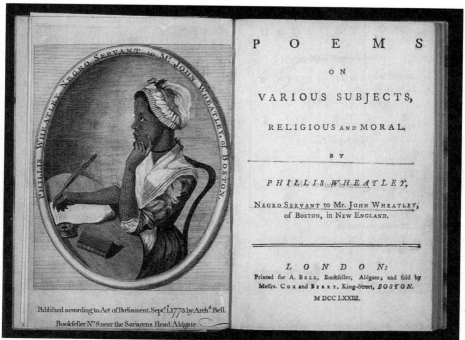

Phillis Wheatley   Engraving of Phillis Wheatley opposite the title page of her collected poems, published in 1773.

to make homespun clothing to take the place of imported British textiles. Freedom's ferment made a heady wine. After 1773, any direct challenge to British power would trigger enormous social changes within the colonies.

The Last Imperial Crisis

The surface calm between 1770 and 1773 ended when Lord North moved to save the East India Company, Britain's largest corporation, from bankruptcy. The company was being undersold in southeastern England and the colonies by low-priced, smuggled Dutch tea, which left the East India Company's warehouses bulging with millions of unsold pounds of its own. North's main concern was the company, not colonial resistance to Townshend's tea duty, but without solving the company's problems, he created a colonial crisis too big for Britain to handle.

The Tea Crisis

Focus Question
Why did the colonists start a revolution after the Tea Act of 1773 lowered the price of tea?

North decided to rescue the East India Company by empowering it to undersell its Dutch rivals. Franklin, who was still in London as a colonial agent, reminded North that he could achieve that goal in the colonies by repealing the Townshend duty for sound economic reasons. North rejected that idea. The settlers, he thought, would hardly revolt if he somehow managed to give them cheap tea. His Tea Act of 1773 repealed import duties on tea in England but retained the Townshend duty in the colonies. In both places, North estimated, legal tea would be cheaper than anyone else's. The company would be saved, and the settlers, by willingly buying legal tea, would accept Parliament's power to tax them.

Another aspect of the Tea Act antagonized most merchants in the colonies. The company had been selling tea to all comers at public auctions in London, but the Tea Act gave it a monopoly on the shipping and distribution of tea in the colonies. Only company ships could carry it, and a few consignees in each port would have the exclusive right to sell it. The combined dangers of taxation and monopoly again forged the coalition of artisans and merchants that had helped defeat the Stamp Act by 1766 and resist the Townshend Act by 1769. Patriots saw the Tea Act as a Trojan horse that would destroy liberty by seducing the settlers into accepting parliamentary sovereignty. North also unintentionally gave a tremendous advantage to those determined to resist the Tea Act. He had devised an oceanic, or external, measure that the colonists could actually nullify despite British control of the seas. No one would have to police the entire waterfront looking for tea importers. The

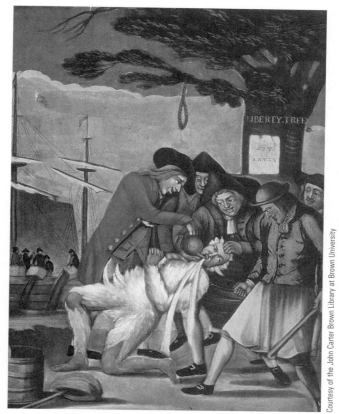

"The Bostonians Paying the Excise-Man, or Tarring and Feathering" This London cartoon of 1774 satirized the Sons of Liberty.

patriots had only to wait for the specially chartered tea ships and prevent their cargoes from landing.

Direct threats usually did the job. Most tea ships quickly departed—except in Boston. There, Governor Hutchinson, whose sons were the local tea consignees, decided to face down the radicals. He refused to grant clearance papers to three tea ships that, under the law, had to pay the Townshend duty within 21 days of arrival or face seizure. Hutchinson meant to force them to land the tea and pay the duty. This timetable led to urgent mass meetings for several weeks and generated a major crisis. Finally, convinced that they had no other way to block the landing of the tea, Boston radicals organized the **Boston Tea Party.** Disguised as Indians, they threw 342 chests of tea, worth about £11,000 sterling (more than $700,000 in 2007 dollars), into Boston harbor on the night of December 16, 1773.

Britain's Response: The Coercive Acts

This willful destruction of private property shocked both Britain and America. Convinced that severe punishment was essential to British credibility, Parliament passed four Coercive Acts during spring 1774. The Boston Port Act closed the port of Boston until Bostonians paid for the tea. A new Quartering Act allowed the army to quarter soldiers among civilians, if necessary. The Administration of Justice Act permitted a British soldier or official who was charged with a crime while carrying out his duties to be tried either in another colony or in England. Most controversial of all was the Massachusetts Government Act. It overturned the Massachusetts Charter of 1691, made the council appointive, and restricted town meetings. In effect, it made Massachusetts like other royal colonies. Before it passed, the king named General Gage, already the commander of the British army in North America, as the new governor of Massachusetts, with the clear implication that he could use military force against civilians.

Parliament also passed a fifth law, unrelated to the Coercive Acts but significant nonetheless. The Quebec Act established French civil law and the Roman Catholic Church in the Province of Quebec, provided for trial by jury in criminal but not in civil cases, gave legislative but not taxing power to an appointive governor and council, and extended the administrative boundaries of Quebec to the area between the Great Lakes and the Ohio River, saving only the legitimate charter claims of other colonies. Historians now regard the act as a farsighted measure that gave French Catholics the toleration that the empire had denied to Acadians 20 years earlier, but settlers from New England to Georgia were appalled. Instead of conciliation and toleration, they saw a deliberate revival of the power of New France and the Catholic Church on their northern border, now bolstered by Britain's naval and military might. The Quebec Act intensified the fear that evil ministers in London were conspiring to destroy British and colonial liberties. Many British colonists suspected that the autocratic government of Quebec might become a model for restructuring their own provinces. The settlers lumped the Quebec Act together with the Coercive Acts and coined their own name for all of them—the Intolerable Acts.

The Radical Explosion

The interval between passage of the Boston Port Act in March 1774 and the Massachusetts Government Act in May permits us to compare the response that each provoked. The Port Act was quite enforceable and immune to nullification by the colonists. It led to another round of nonimportation and to the summoning of the First Continental Congress, but the Government Act *was* nullified by the colonists. It led to war. The redcoats marching to Concord on April 19, 1775 were trying to enforce that act against settlers who absolutely refused to obey it.

Gage took over as governor of Massachusetts in May 1774, before passage of the Massachusetts Government Act. In June, he closed the ports of Boston and Charlestown,

Library of Congress, Prints and Photographs Division

"The Able Doctor, or America Swallowing the Bitter Draught" This 1774 engraving by Paul Revere used "The Bostonians Paying the Excise-Man" as a model but turned it into a patriot statement. In Revere's version, the British are forcing tea down the throat of America (represented by a ravished lady, Liberty). The British are also imposing martial law in Boston.

just north of Boston. The navy gave him the power to do so. At first, Boston split over the Port Act. Many merchants wanted to abolish the Boston Committee of Correspondence and pay for the tea to avoid an economic catastrophe, but they were badly outvoted in a huge town meeting. Boston then called for a colonial union and for immediate nonimportation and nonconsumption of British goods. By then, some radicals were losing patience with nonimportation as a tactic. Britain had already shut Boston down.

Discouraging news arrived from elsewhere. A mass meeting in New York City rejected immediate nonimportation in favor of an intercolonial congress. Philadelphia followed New York's lead. In both cities, cautious merchants hoped that a congress might postpone or prevent radical measures of resistance.

North assumed that the Coercive Acts would isolate Boston from the rest of the province, Massachusetts from the rest of New England, and New England from the other colonies, a goal that Britain would pursue through 1777. Instead, contributions began pouring in from all of the colonies to help Boston survive. The Stamp Act crisis and the Townshend crisis had been largely urban affairs. The Intolerable Acts politicized the countryside on a scale never seen before. When royal governors outside Massachusetts dismissed their assemblies to prevent them from joining the resistance movement, colonists elected **provincial congresses,** or conventions, to organize resistance. These bodies were much larger than the legal assemblies they displaced, and they mobilized far more people. As the congresses took hold, royal government began to collapse almost everywhere. Numerous calls for a continental congress made the movement irresistible. By June, it was also obvious that any congress would adopt nonimportation. Except for some details, that issue had been settled, even before the congress met, by mandates that the delegates brought with them.

Yet Gage remained optimistic well into the summer. Then news of the Massachusetts Government Act arrived on August 6. Gage's authority disintegrated when he tried to enforce the act, which marked the most dramatic attempt yet made by Parliament to control the internal affairs of any colony. The **mandamus** councilors whom Gage appointed to the new upper house under the act either resigned their seats or fled to Boston to seek the army's protection. The Superior Court could not hold its sessions, even in Boston under the guns of the army, because jurors refused to take an oath under the new act. At the county level (the real center of royal power in the colony), popular conventions closed the courts and took charge in August and September. Gage was beginning to realize that none of his major objectives was achievable.

Before this explosion of radical activity, Gage had called for a new General Court to meet in Salem in October. Many towns sent representatives, but others followed the lead of the Worcester County Convention, which in August urged all towns to elect delegates to a provincial congress in Concord, 17 miles inland, out of range of the navy. Although Gage revoked his call for a General Court, about 90 representatives met at Salem anyway. When Gage refused to recognize them, they adjourned to Concord in early October and joined the 200 delegates already gathered there as the Massachusetts Provincial Congress. That body became the de facto government of the colony and implemented the radical demands of the Suffolk County Convention (representing Boston and its hinterland), which included a purge of unreliable militia officers, the creation of a special force of armed "minutemen" able to respond rapidly to any emergency, and the payment of taxes to the congress in Concord, not to Gage in Boston. The Provincial Congress also collected military stores at Concord and created an executive arm, the Committee of Public Safety. North assumed that Gage's army would uphold the new Massachusetts government. Instead, Gage's government survived only where the army could protect it.

The alternative to government by consent was becoming no British authority at all in the colony. For example, in the predawn hours of September 1, Gage dispatched soldiers to confiscate 250 half-barrels of gunpowder stored a few miles outside Boston. He got the powder, but the foray started one-third of the militia of New England marching toward Boston. They turned back when they were assured that no one had been killed. In later raids on other stores, the colonists always beat the redcoats to the powder. By October, Gage's power was limited to the Boston area, which the army held. Unable to put his 3,000 soldiers to any positive use, he wrote North on October 30 that "a small Force rather encourages Resistance than terrifys." He then stunned North by asking for 20,000 redcoats, nearly as many as had been needed to conquer Canada.

The First Continental Congress

From 1769 into 1774, colonial patriots had looked to John Wilkes in London for leadership. At the **First Continental Congress,** they began relying on themselves. Twelve colonies (all but Georgia) sent delegates. In September 1774, they met at Philadelphia's Carpenters' Hall, a center of artisan strength. They scarcely even debated nonimportation. The southern colonies insisted, and the New Englanders agreed, that nonimportation finally be extended to molasses, which continued to generate revenue under the penny duty of 1766. The delegates were almost unanimous in adopting nonexportation if Britain did not redress colonial grievances by September 1775. Nonexportation was a much more radical tactic than nonimportation because it contained the implicit threat of repudiating debts to British merchants, which were normally paid off with colonial exports.

Joseph Galloway, a Pennsylvania loyalist, submitted a plan of imperial union that would have required all laws affecting the colonies to be passed by both Parliament and an intercolonial congress, but his proposal was tabled by a vote of 6 colonies to 5. The Congress spent three weeks trying to define colonial rights. Everyone agreed that the Coercive Acts, the Quebec Act, and all surviving revenue acts had to be repealed and that infringements on trial by jury had to be rejected. The delegates generally agreed on what would break the impasse, but they had trouble finding the precise language for their demands. They finally affirmed the new principle of no *legislation* without consent—but added a saving clause that affirmed colonial assent to existing acts of Parliament that regulated their trade.

Congress petitioned the king rather than Parliament because patriots no longer recognized Parliament as a legitimate legislature for the colonies. Congress explained its position in separate addresses to the people of the 13 colonies, the people of Quebec, and the people of Great Britain. It took two other radical steps: It agreed to meet again in May 1775 if the British response was unsatisfactory, and it created **the Association**—with citizen committees in every community—to enforce its trade sanctions against Britain. Most towns and counties heartily embraced the idea, and perhaps 7,000 men served on such committees during winter 1774–75. In approving the Association, Congress began to act as a central government for the United Colonies.

Toward War

The news from Boston and Philadelphia shook the North ministry. "The New England Governments are in a State of Rebellion," George III wrote North, "blows must decide whether they are to be subject to this Country or independent." Although Franklin kept assuring the British that Congress meant exactly what it said, both North and the opposition assumed that conciliation could be achieved on lesser terms. Edmund Burke, who had been out of office since 1766, urged a return to pre-1763 understandings without explaining how to restore the loyalty that had made them workable. "A great empire and little minds go ill together," he cautioned in an eloquent speech urging conciliation.

Lord Chatham (William Pitt) introduced a bill to prohibit Parliament from taxing the colonies, to recognize the Congress, and even to ask Congress to provide revenue for North American defense and to help pay down the national debt. When a spokesman for North's ministry challenged him, Chatham retorted that his plan, if implemented, "must annihilate your power . . . and at once reduce you to that state of insignificance for which God and nature designed you." Neither plan passed.

The initiative lay with Lord North, who still had vague hopes for a peaceful solution, but in January 1775, he took a step that made war inevitable. He ordered Gage to send troops to Concord, destroy the arms stored there, and arrest John Hancock and Samuel Adams. Only after sending this dispatch did he introduce his own Conciliatory Proposition. Parliament pledged that it would tax no colony that met its share of the cost of imperial defense and paid proper salaries to its royal officials, but Britain would use force against delinquent colonies. To reassure hard-liners that he was not turning soft, he introduced the New England Restraining Act on the same day. It barred New Englanders from the Atlantic fisheries and prohibited all commerce between New England and any place except Britain and the British West Indies, precisely the trade routes that Congress had resolved to block through non-importation. Both sides were now committed to economic sanctions.

North's orders to Gage arrived before his Conciliatory Proposition reached America, and Gage obeyed. He hoped to surprise Concord with another predawn march, but Boston radicals knew about the expedition almost as soon as the orders were issued. They had already made careful preparations to alert the whole countryside. Their informant, in all likelihood, was Gage's wife, Margaret Kemble Gage, a New Jerseyan by birth. At 2 A.M. on the night of April 18–19, about 700 grenadiers and light infantry began their march toward Concord. Paul Revere, a Boston silversmith who had done as much as anyone to create the information network that he now set in motion, galloped west with the news that "The redcoats are coming!" When he was captured past Lexington by a British patrol, Dr. Samuel Prescott, who was returning from a lady friend's house at the awkward hour of 1 A.M., managed to get the message through to Concord. As the British approached Lexington Green at dawn, they found 60 to 70 minutemen drawn up to face them. The outnumbered militia began to withdraw. Then somebody—probably a colonial bystander but possibly a British soldier—fired the first shot in what became the **Battle of Lexington.** Without orders, the British line opened fire, killing eight and wounding nine. From every direction, like angry hornets, the countryside surged toward them. Secrecy had become pointless, and the British broke out their regimental fifes and drums. Cheered by the tunes, they marched west toward Concord and into another world war.

The Improvised War

In April 1775, neither side had a plan for winning a major war. Gage's soldiers were trying to enforce acts of Parliament. The militia were fighting for a political regime that Parliament was determined to change. They drove the British from Concord Bridge and pursued them all the way to Boston. Suffering only 95 casualties, the militia inflicted 273 on the British. Had a relief force not met the battered British survivors east of Lexington, all of them might have been lost.

Lacking an adequate command or supply structure, the colonists besieged Boston. After two months, Gage finally declared that all settlers bearing arms, and those who aided them, were rebels and traitors. He offered to pardon anyone who returned to his allegiance, except John Hancock and Samuel Adams. Instead of complying, the besiegers escalated the struggle two days later. They fortified the high ground on Breed's Hill (next to Bunker Hill) near Charlestown and overlooking Boston. The British sent 2,400 men, one-fifth of the garrison, to take the hills on June 17. Merely by seizing Charlestown Neck, a smaller force could have cut off the Yankee militia at low risk to itself. Instead, to prove that civilians had no chance against a regular army, General William Howe launched three frontal attacks. Secure behind their defenses, the settlers shot more than 1,000 of the attackers, including 92 officers (about one-sixth of those lost in the entire war), before they ran out of ammunition and withdrew. The defenders suffered about 370 casualties, nearly all during the retreat. **(See Map 5.3, Lexington, Concord, and Boston, 1775, in the color insert following page 288.)**

For the moment at least, patriotism seemed to make colonial farmers and artisans a match for Britain's professional army, but as the war progressed, "Bunker Hillism" became a dangerous delusion. Time after time, Americans fortified a hill and then waited for the stupid frontal assault that never came. The British got the message at Bunker Hill. A few more such victories, reflected one of them, and no one would be left alive to carry the news to London.

Well into 1776, both sides fought an improvised war. In May 1775, Vermont and Massachusetts militia took Fort Ticonderoga on Lake Champlain and seized the artillery and gunpowder that would be used months later to end the siege of Boston. Crown Point also fell. With nearly all of their forces in Boston, the British were too weak to defend other positions or to intervene in the short Indian conflict, Lord Dunmore's War, that broke out in the upper Ohio valley in 1774. The collapse of royal government meant that the rebels now controlled the militia and most of the royal powder houses.

The militia became the key to political allegiance. Compulsory service with the militia politicized many waverers, who decided that they really were patriots when a redcoat shot at them or when they drove a loyalist into exile. The militia kept the countryside committed to the Revolution wherever the British army was too weak to overwhelm them.

The Second Continental Congress

When the **Second Continental Congress** met in May 1775, it inherited the war. For months it pursued the conflicting strategies of resistance and conciliation. It voted to turn the undisciplined men besieging Boston into a Continental Army. As in earlier wars, the soldiers were volunteers who expected to serve for only a few months, or a single campaign. In the absence of royal authority, they elected their officers, who tried to win their obedience through persuasion, not command. Supplying the soldiers with food and munitions became a huge problem.

Most of the men were Yankees who would have preferred to serve under their own officers, but Congress realized that a successful war effort would have to engage the other colonies as well. On June 15, at the urging of John Adams of Massachusetts, Congress made George Washington of Virginia commanding general. When Washington took charge of the Continental Army, he was appalled at the poor discipline among the soldiers and their casual familiarity with their officers. He insisted that officers behave with a dignity that would instill obedience, and as the months passed, most of them won his respect. As the year ended, however, nearly all of the men went home, and Washington had to train a new army for 1776. Regardless, enthusiasm for the cause remained strong, and fresh volunteers soon filled his camp.

In June 1775, Congress authorized an invasion of Canada, designed to win over the French before they could side with the British and attack New York or New England. Two forces of 1,000 men each moved northward. One, under General Richard Montgomery, took Montreal in November. The other, commanded by Colonel Benedict Arnold, advanced on Quebec through the Maine forests and laid siege to the city, where Montgomery joined Arnold in December. With enlistments due to expire at year's end, they decided to assault the city, partly to get maximum service out of their men and partly to inspire some of them to reenlist. Their attack in a blizzard on December 31 was a disaster. Nearly half of the 900 men still with them were killed, wounded, or captured. Montgomery was killed and Arnold wounded. Both were hailed as American heroes.

The colonial objective in this fighting was still to restore government by consent under the Crown. After rejecting Lord North's Conciliatory Proposition out of hand, Congress approved an Olive Branch Petition to George III on July 5, 1775, in the hope of ending the bloodshed. Moderates, led by John Dickinson, strongly favored the measure. The petition affirmed the colonists' loyalty to the Crown, did not even mention "rights," and implored the king to take the initiative in devising "a happy and permanent reconciliation." Another document written mostly by Virginia's Thomas Jefferson, "The Declaration of the Causes and Necessities of Taking Up Arms" set forth the colonies' grievances and justified their armed resistance. "We have counted the cost of this contest," Jefferson proclaimed, "and find nothing so dreadful as voluntary slavery." Like the Olive Branch Petition, the declaration assured the British people "that we mean not to dissolve that Union which has so long and so happily subsisted between us." It reached London along with news of Bunker (Breeds) Hill. George III replied with a formal proclamation of rebellion on August 23. The king's refusal to receive this moderate petition strengthened colonial radicals.

Congress began to function increasingly like a government, but with few exceptions, it assumed royal rather than parliamentary powers, which were taken over by the individual colonies. Congress did not tax or regulate trade, beyond encouraging nonimportation. It passed no laws. It took command of the Continental Army, printed paper money, opened diplomatic relations with Indian nations, took over the postal service, and decided which government was legitimate in individual colonies—all functions previously performed by the Crown. In short, Congress thought of itself as a temporary plural executive for the continent, not as a legislature.

War and Legitimacy, 1775–1776

Focus Question

How and why did a resistance movement, dedicated to protecting the colonists' right as Englishmen, end by proclaiming American independence instead?

Throughout 1775, the British reacted with fitful displays of violence and grim threats of turning slaves and Indians against the settlers. When the weak British forces could neither restore order nor make good on their threats, they conciliated no one, enraged thousands, and undermined British claims to legitimacy. The navy burned Falmouth (now Portland), Maine, in October. On November 7, John Murray, earl of Dunmore and governor of Virginia, offered freedom to any slaves of rebel planters who would join his 200 redcoats. About 800 slaves mustered under his banner only to fall victim to smallpox after the Virginia militia defeated them in a single action. On January 1, Dunmore bombarded Norfolk in retaliation, setting several buildings ablaze. The patriot militia, who considered Norfolk a loyalist bastion, burned the rest of the city and then blamed Dunmore for its destruction. Overall, his campaign undermined whatever loyalist sentiment survived among Virginia planters beyond Norfolk.

British efforts suffered other disasters in Boston and the Carolinas. The greatest colonial victory came at Boston, where most of the British army lay virtually imprisoned. On March 17, 1776, after Washington fortified Dorchester Heights south of the city and brought heavy artillery (from Ticonderoga) to bear on it, the British pulled out and sailed for Nova Scotia. A loyalist uprising by Highland Scots in North Carolina was crushed at Moore's Creek Bridge on February 27, and a British naval expedition sent to take Charleston was repulsed with heavy losses in June. Cherokee attacks against Virginia failed in 1776 because they occurred after Dunmore had left and did not fit into any larger general strategy. Before spring turned to summer, patriot forces had won control of the territory of all 13 colonies. Except in East and West Florida, Quebec, and Nova Scotia, the British had been driven from the continent.

Independence

George III's dismissal of the Olive Branch Petition left moderates no option but to yield or fight. In late 1775, Congress created a committee to correspond with foreign powers. By early 1776, the delegates from New England, Virginia, and Georgia already favored independence, but they knew that unless they won over all 13 colonies, the British would have the leverage to divide them. The British attack on Charleston in June nudged the Carolinas toward independence.

Resistance to independence came mostly from the mid-Atlantic colonies, from New York through Maryland. Elsewhere, provincial congresses had supplanted the colonial assemblies in 1774 and 1775. In the middle colonies, however, both assemblies and congresses met and competed for the loyalties of the people. None of the five legal assemblies in the mid-Atlantic region ever repudiated the Crown. All of them had to be overthrown along with royal (or proprietary) government itself. The last royal governor to be driven from his post was New Jersey's William Franklin, Benjamin's natural son, who was arrested on June 19, 1776, to prevent him from summoning a new session of the regular assembly.

In the struggle for middle colony loyalties, Thomas Paine's pamphlet, *Common Sense,* became a huge success. First published in Philadelphia in January 1776, it sold more than 100,000 copies within a few months and reached more people than any other colonial tract ever had. Paine, a recent immigrant from England who had waged his own contests with the British government, wasted no reverence on Britain's mixed and balanced constitution. To him, George III was "the Pharaoh of England" and "the Royal Brute of Great Britain." Paine attacked monarchy and aristocracy as degenerate institutions and urged Americans to unite under a simple republican government of their own. "Reconciliation and ruin are nearly related," he insisted. "There is something very absurd, in supposing a Continent to be perpetually governed by an island."

The British continued to alienate the colonists. The king named Lord George Germain, a hard-liner, as secretary of state for the American colonies, and thus as war minister. Germain tried to hire 20,000 Russian mercenaries, who, smirked one British official, would make "charming visitors at New York and civilize that part of America wonderfully." When that effort failed, the British bought 17,000 soldiers from Hesse and other north German states. (The colonists called them all **Hessians.**) To Jefferson, that action was "the last stab to [the] agonizing affection" that had once bound together the people of Britain and North America. Disturbing (although false) rumors suggested that Britain and France were about to sign a "partition treaty," dividing the eastern half of North America between them. Many congressmen concluded, some of them sadly, that only independence could counter these dangers by engaging Britain's European enemies on America's side. As long as conciliation was the goal, France would not participate, because American success would mean restoring the British empire to its former glory. But Louis XVI (1774–93) might well help the colonies win their independence if that meant crippling Britain.

From April to June, about 90 communities issued calls for independence. Most of them looked no further back than 1775 to justify their demand. The king had placed the colonists outside his protection, was waging war against them, and had hired foreigners to kill them. Self-defense demanded a permanent separation.

Congress finally broke the mid-Atlantic stalemate. On May 15, 1776, it voted to suppress "every kind of authority" under the British Crown, thus giving radicals an opportunity to seize power in Pennsylvania and New Jersey. Moderates remained in control in New York, Delaware, and Maryland, but they reluctantly accepted independence as inevitable. In early June, Congress postponed a vote on independence but named a committee of five, including Jefferson, John Adams, and Franklin, to prepare a declaration that would vindicate America's decision to the whole world.

On July 2, with the necessary votes in place, Congress passed Richard Henry Lee's resolution "that these United colonies are, and of right, ought to be, Free and Independent States; . . . and that all political connexion between them, and the state of Great Britain, is, and ought to be, totally dissolved." Two days later, 12 colonies, with New York abstaining for the time being, unanimously approved Jefferson's Declaration of Independence, as amended by Congress. "We hold these truths to be self-evident, that all men are created equal, that they are endowed by their Creator with certain unalienable Rights, that among these are Life, Liberty, and the pursuit of Happiness," Congress proclaimed in what is perhaps the most famous statement ever made in American public life. Whenever "any Form of Government becomes destructive of these ends, it is the Right of the People to alter or to abolish it, and to institute new Government, laying its foundation on such principles . . . as to them shall seem most likely to effect their Safety and Happiness." The longest section of the Declaration indicted George III as a tyrant.

During the three days that Congress was proclaiming American independence, the first ships of the largest armada yet sent across the Atlantic by any European state began landing British soldiers on Staten Island. Americans celebrated the creation of their new republic at the very moment that they faced a military challenge more ominous than any they had ever confronted before.

Conclusion

Between 1763 and 1776, Britain and the colonies became trapped in a series of self-fulfilling prophecies. The British feared that without major reforms to guarantee Parliament's control of the empire, the colonies would drift toward independence. Colonial resistance to the new policies convinced the British that a movement for independence really was under way, a perception that led to even sterner measures. Until a few months before it happened, nearly all colonists denied that they desired independence, but they began to fear that the British government was determined to deprive them of their rights as Englishmen. Britain's policy drove them toward a closer union with one another and finally provoked armed resistance. With the onset of war, both sides felt vindicated. The thousands of redcoats heading toward America did not bode well for colonial liberties. When the colonists did leave the empire, British ministers believed that their predictions had finally come true.

Both sides were wrong. The British had no systematic plan to destroy liberty in North America, and until winter 1775–76, hardly any colonists favored independence. But the three imperial crises undermined mutual confidence and brought about what no one had desired in 1765, or even 1774—an independent American nation. Unable to govern North America, Britain now faced the grim task of conquering it instead.

SUGGESTED READINGS

The best one-volume narrative history of the coming of the Revolution remains **Merrill Jensen's** *The Founding of a Nation: A History of the American Revolution, 1763–1776* (1968). **Bernard Bailyn's** *The Ideological Origins of the American Revolution* (1967) has had an enormous impact. **Gregory Evans Dowd** provides a fresh perspective in *War under Heaven: Pontiac, the Indian Nations, and the British Empire* (2002).

On the three imperial crises, **Edmund S. and Helen M. Morgan's** *The Stamp Act Crisis, Prologue to Revolution,* 3rd ed. (1953, 1995) has lost none of its saliency. Nor has **John Shy's** *Toward Lexington: The Role of the British Army in the Coming of the American Revolution* (1965). **Pauline Maier's** *From Resistance to Revolution: Colonial Radicals and the Development of American Opposition to Britain, 1765–1776* (1972) and **Richard D. Brown's** *Revolutionary Politics in Massachusetts: The Boston Committee of Correspondence and the Towns* (1970) are both excellent on the process of disaffection. **David Ammerman's** *In the Common Cause: American Response to the Coercive Acts of 1774* (1974) is especially strong on the First Continental Congress and its aftermath. **David Hackett Fischer's** *Paul Revere's Ride* (1994) is a rare combination of exhaustive research and stirring prose. **Pauline Maier's** *American Scripture: Making the Declaration of Independence* (1997) uses 90 local declarations of independence issued in spring 1776 to give context to Jefferson's famous text.

Important studies of internal tensions include **Gary B. Nash,** *The Urban Crucible: Social Change, Political Consciousness, and the Origins of the American Revolution* (1979); **Woody Holton's** imaginative *Forced Founders: Indians, Debtors, Slaves, and the Making of the American Revolution in Virginia* (1999); **James P. Whittenburg's** "Planters, Merchants, and Lawyers: Social Change and the Origins of the North Carolina Regulation," *William and Mary Quarterly,* 3d ser., 34 (1977): 214–38; and **Richard M. Brown,** *The South Carolina Regulators* (1963). **David Grimsted's** "Anglo-American Racism and Phillis Wheatley's 'Sable Veil,' 'Length'ned Chain,' and 'Knitted Heart,'" in **Ronald Hoffman and Peter J. Albert, eds.,** *Women in the Age of the American Revolution* (1989) is a superb study of the emerging antislavery movement and the role of women in it.

Visit the Liberty Equality Power Companion Web site for resources specific to this textbook: http://www.thomsonedu.com/history/murrin

Also find self-tests and additional resources at ThomsonNOW. ThomsonNOW is an integrated online suite of services and resources with proven ease of use and efficient paths to success, delivering the results you want—NOW!

www.thomsonedu.com/login/

6

The Revolutionary Republic

The Revolutionary War killed a higher percentage of Americans who fought in it than any other American conflict except the Civil War. It was a civil war as well. Neighbors were more likely to shoot at neighbors during the Revolution than they were between 1861 and 1865, when the geographical line separating the two sides would be much sharper. Twice, in 1776 and 1780, the British had a chance to win a decisive victory, but in both campaigns the Americans somehow rallied. The Americans won only by bringing in France as an ally, and France brought in Spain.

During the war, ever more Americans began to think in crude racial categories. Ideas about racial inferiority clashed sharply with claims of universal rights and human equality. As settlers and Indians, whites and blacks redefined their differences, they often resorted to racial stereotypes. Most Indians and enslaved Africans hoped that Britain would win the war.

Even as the war raged and the economy disintegrated, Americans drafted state constitutions and eloquent bills of rights that reached far beyond the racism many of them felt. They knew they were attempting something daring—the creation of a stable, enduring republic. Some European monarchies were 1,000 years old. No republic had lasted that long. Educated people knew a great deal about the city-states of classical Greece and about republican Rome—how they had called forth the noblest sentiments of patriotism for a time and then decayed into despotisms. Still, once Americans broke with Britain, they warmly embraced republicanism and never looked back. They were able to build viable republican governments because they grasped the voluntaristic dynamics of their society. They knew they had to restructure their governments through persuasive means. The use of force against armed fellow citizens would be self-defeating.

The war also demonstrated how weak Congress was, even after ratification of the Articles of Confederation in 1781. Congress could not pay its debts. It could not expel the British from their western military posts or defeat the Indians of the Ohio country. In the Northwest Ordinance of 1787, Congress nevertheless announced plans to create new western states and to admit them to the Union as full equals of the original 13. During that same summer, the Philadelphia Convention drafted a new Constitution for the United States. After ratification by 11 states in 1787 and 1788, it went into effect in April 1789. The federal system it created was the most distinctive achievement of the Revolutionary generation.

CHRONOLOGY

1769	Spanish found San Diego
1775	Settlement of Kentucky begins
1776	Virginia becomes first state to adopt a permanent constitution and bill of rights • British forces land on Staten Island • Declaration of Independence adopted • Pennsylvania constitution creates unicameral legislature • British win battle of Long Island; New York City falls • Washington wins at Trenton
1777	Washington wins at Princeton • Howe takes Philadelphia • Burgoyne surrenders at Saratoga • Congress completes the Articles of Confederation
1778	Franco-American alliance negotiated
1779	Indians form confederation from the Gulf to the Great Lakes • Spain declares war on Britain • Continental dollar collapses
1780	Massachusetts constitution approved • Pennsylvania adopts gradual emancipation • British take Charleston and overrun South Carolina • Gordon riots in London discredit other reformers • Arnold's treason uncovered • Americans win at King's Mountain
1781	Continental Army mutinies • Americans win at Cowpens • Congress creates executive departments • Articles of Confederation ratified • Cornwallis surrenders at Yorktown
1782	Gnadenhutten massacre leaves 100 unarmed Indians dead
1783	Peace of Paris recognizes American independence
1785	Congress passes Land Ordinance
1786	Virginia passes Statute for Religious Freedom • Annapolis convention meets
1786–87	Shays's Rebellion in Massachusetts protests taxes and economic woes
1787	Congress passes the Northwest Ordinance • Philadelphia Convention drafts a new federal Constitution
1787–88	Eleven states ratify the Constitution
1789	First federal Congress sends Bill of Rights to the states
1799	New York adopts gradual emancipation
1804	New Jersey adopts gradual emancipation

Hearts and Minds: The Northern War, 1776–1777

Because the men who ruled Britain believed that the loss of the colonies would be a fatal blow to British power, the price of patriotism escalated once independence became the goal. Britain raised more soldiers and larger fleets than ever before and more than doubled its national debt. Americans, too confident after their early successes, staggered under the onslaught.

The British Offensive

The first setback came in Canada. In May 1776, when a fresh British force sailed up the St. Lawrence River, the Americans, weakened by smallpox, had to retreat. By July, Sir Guy

Carleton drove them back into northern New York, to Fort Ticonderoga on Lake Champlain. Both sides built ships to control that strategic waterway. Largely through Benedict Arnold's efforts, the Americans held, and Carleton returned to Canada for the winter.

Farther south, Richard, viscount Howe, admiral of the British fleet, and his brother **General William Howe** prepared an awesome striking force on Staten Island. They also acted as peace commissioners, with power to restore whole colonies to the king's peace and to pardon individual rebels. They hoped to avoid using their huge army, but when they wrote **George Washington** to open negotiations, he refused to accept the letter because it did not address him as "General." To do so would have recognized the legitimacy of his appointment. Unable to negotiate, the Howes had to fight.

Washington had moved his army from Boston to New York City, where he had about 19,000 men to face more than 30,000 redcoats and Hessians. Early successes had kept morale high among American forces and helped sustain the *rage militaire* (warlike enthusiasm) that had prompted thousands to volunteer in 1775 and 1776, including 4,000 veterans of 1775 who reenlisted for 1776. Although some served in the Continental Army and others with state militia units, the difference between the two forces was still minimal. Neither of them had formal military training, and the men in both served only for short terms.

Washington was reluctant to abandon any large city. Against conventional military wisdom, he divided his inferior force and sent half of it from Manhattan to Long Island. Most of the men dug in on Brooklyn Heights, just two miles from lower Manhattan, and waited for a frontal attack. The British invaded Long Island, a loyalist stronghold, and on August 27, 1776, sent a force around the American left flank through unguarded Jamaica Pass. While Hessians feinted a frontal assault, the flanking force crushed the American left and rear and sent the survivors reeling.

The Howes did nothing to prevent the evacuation of the rest of the American army to Manhattan, which occurred under the cover of a fierce nor'easter storm. Instead, the British opened informal talks with several members of Congress on Staten Island on September 11. The talks collapsed when the Americans insisted that the British recognize their independence before discussing substantive issues. Washington evacuated lower Manhattan. The British took New York City, much of which was destroyed on September 21 by fire, probably set by Americans. The Howes then appealed directly to the people to lay down their arms and return to British allegiance within 60 days in exchange for a full pardon. In southern New York state, several thousand complied.

In October, the Howes drove Washington out of Manhattan and Westchester and then turned on two garrisons he had left behind. On November 16, at a cost of 460 casualties, the British forced 3,000 men to surrender at Fort Washington on the Manhattan side of the Hudson River. General Nathanael Greene, a lame Rhode Island Quaker who had given up pacifism for soldiering, saved his men on the New Jersey side by abandoning Fort Lee, including all of his supplies.

The Howes probably could have destroyed Washington's army on Long Island or Manhattan, but they knew what they were doing. British victories and the American reliance on short-term volunteers were destroying Washington's army. British success seemed to prove that no American force could stand before a properly organized British army. But to capture Washington's entire army would have been a political embarrassment, leading to massive treason trials, executions, and great bitterness. Instead, Britain's impressive victories demoralized Americans and encouraged them to go home, many with their muskets. In September, 27,000 Americans stood fit for duty in the northern theater (including the Canadian border); by December, only 6,000 remained, most of whom intended to leave when their enlistments expired on December 31.

The Howes' strategy nearly worked. In December, British forces swept across New Jersey as far south as Burlington. They captured Charles Lee, next in command after Washington, and Richard Stockton, a signer of the Declaration of Independence. Several thousand New Jersey residents, including Stockton, took the king's oath. To seal off Long Island Sound from both ends, the Howes also captured Newport, Rhode Island. Many observers thought the war was all but over as sad remnants of the Continental Army crossed the Delaware River into Pennsylvania, confiscating all boats along the way so that the British could not follow them. One general believed that the time had come to "bargain away the Bubble of Independency for British Liberty well secured." Even Jefferson began to think about the terms on which a restoration of the monarchy might be acceptable.

The Trenton-Princeton Campaign

Washington knew he had to do something dramatic to restore morale and encourage his soldiers to reenlist. In mid-December, the New Jersey militia, which had been silent for weeks, showed him how by harassing British outposts and patrols in the Delaware valley, pushing the Hessian garrison at Trenton toward exhaustion. On the night of December 25, 1776, Washington crossed the ice-choked Delaware and marched south, surprising the Trenton garrison at dawn in another nor'easter. At small cost to the attackers, nearly 1,000 Hessians surrendered. The British sent their most energetic general, Charles, earl Cornwallis, south with 8,000 men to "bag the fox"—Washington and the 5,000 Continentals and militia still with him. Cornwallis caught him at Trenton near sunset on January 2 but decided to wait until dawn before attacking. British patrols watched the Delaware to prevent another escape across the river, but Washington tried nothing of the kind. Leaving his campfires burning, he muffled the wheels of his wagons and guns and stole around the British left flank, heading north. At dawn, he met a British regiment just beginning its march from Princeton to Trenton. The Battle of Princeton amounted to a series of sharp clashes in which the Americans, with a 5-to-1 edge, mauled yet another outpost.

Washington's two quick victories had an enormous impact on the war, although they inspired few reenlistments. The Howes, who until January had shown a firm grasp of revolutionary warfare, blundered in not hounding Washington's remnant of an army to its destruction after Princeton, if that was still possible. Instead, afraid that Washington might pick off their outposts one at a time, they called in their garrisons and concentrated the army along the Raritan River from New Brunswick to the sea. As the British departed, the militia returned, asking who had sworn oaths to the king. Those who had taken the oath now groveled, as the price of acceptance, or fled to British lines. The Howes had encouraged **loyalists** to come forward and then abandoned them to the king's enemies. For the rest of the winter, the militia attacked and usually defeated British patrols foraging for supplies. By spring, Howe's forces were reduced to less than half the strength they had possessed in August. Many of the invaders had aroused fierce hatred by looting and raping their way across New Jersey. Together, the British and the Hessians had lost the hearts and minds of the settlers. In Howe's 1777 campaign, few would be willing to declare for the Crown. The Revolution survived.

The Campaigns of 1777 and Foreign Intervention

Britain's thoughtful strategy of 1776 gave way to incoherence in 1777. The Howes again had a plan for winning the war, but it required 20,000 reinforcements that did not exist. Instead, Lord George Germain, Britain's war minister, ordered the Howes to take Philadelphia. He also sent John Burgoyne, a poet and playwright as well as a general, to Canada with orders to march his army south and link up with the garrison of New York City, commanded by Sir Henry Clinton. A small force under Barry St. Leger was to march down the Mohawk valley and threaten Albany from the west. When few reinforcements reached the Howes, they rejected an overland march to Philadelphia as too risky and decided to invade by sea, a decision that allowed Washington to shift men north to oppose Burgoyne.

The British campaign made little sense. If the point of Burgoyne's march was to move his army to New York City, he should have gone by sea. If the point was to force a battle with New Englanders, his army should have been larger. And if Howe's army—Britain's largest—would not challenge Washington's, who would?

The Loss of Philadelphia

After Trenton and Princeton, Washington demanded stricter discipline and longer terms of enlistment. Congress responded by raising the number of lashes a soldier could receive from 39 to 100 and by promising a cash bonus to anyone enlisting for three years, and a land bounty to anyone serving for the duration. Congress never came close to raising the 75,000 men it hoped for, but these new policies did create a solid foundation for a more experienced army. Longer terms made military training a real possibility, which in turn made the Continentals much more professional than the militia.

The Continental Army acquired its own distinctive character. The men who signed up were often poor. About half of the New Jersey Line came from families that were not on the tax rolls. Some recruits were British deserters. Short-term militia, by contrast, usually held a secure place in their communities and were more likely than the Continentals to be church members. As the 1777 recruits came in, the two northern armies, swelled by militia, grew to about 28,000 men fit for duty—17,000 in northern New York and 11,000 under Washington.

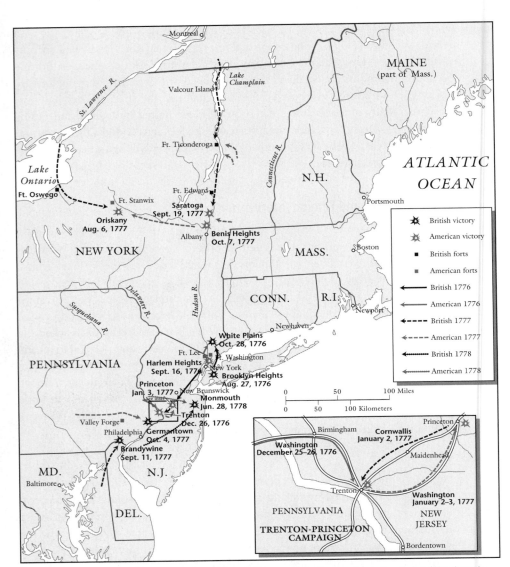

Map 6.1 Revolutionary War in the Northern States   This map shows the campaigns in New York and New Jersey in 1776–77, in northern New York and around Philadelphia in 1777, and at Monmouth, New Jersey, in 1778. The inset shows Washington's Trenton and Princeton campaigns after Christmas 1776.
View an animated version of this map or related maps at http://www.thomsonedu.com/history/murrin.

The Howes sailed south from New York with 13,000 men. When river pilots could not guarantee a safe ascent up the Delaware against American fire, the fleet sailed on to Chesapeake Bay and landed the troops at Head of Elk, Maryland, on August 24. The British marched toward Philadelphia through southeastern Pennsylvania, a region thickly populated

Mary Silliman's War (1993)

Directed by Stephen Surjik. Starring Nancy Palk (Mary Silliman), Richard Donat (Selleck Silliman), Paul Boretski (David Holly), Joanne Miller (Amelia), Elias Williams (Peter), and Allan Royal (Thomas Jones)

Strong movies about the Revolutionary War are hard to find. *Mary Silliman's War* is the rare exception. It rests on the outstanding research of Joy Day Buel and Richard Buel, Jr., on the life of an articulate woman, Mary Fish Noyes Silliman Dickinson, a woman who was widowed three times in the course of a long life (1736–1818). She left behind numerous letters and journals that make possible the reconstruction and dramatization of her life. Steven Schechter, who co-produced the film, also wrote most of the screenplay. It picks up Mary's story in 1779 when she was living in Fairfield, Connecticut, with her second husband, Gold Selleck Silliman, and their children. Selleck commanded the militia that had to respond to emergencies, and he also served as prosecuting attorney in his civilian capacity. In the northern states, the Revolutionary War had become mostly a series of destructive raids, with the British and loyalists based on Long Island and the patriots on the mainland. For good reason, both sides worried about traitors and spies in their midst.

As the film opens, Selleck is successfully prosecuting two loyalist townsmen. When they are sentenced to death, Mary objects that the war is turning neighbor against neighbor, but Selleck will not relent. In retaliation, the loyalists stage a night raid on the Silliman home, capture Selleck, and take him to New York City, which was the headquarters of the British army. The message seemed clear: If the Fairfield loyalists were to be executed, Selleck would also die. Thomas Jones, a magistrate and perhaps the most prominent loyalist living on Long Island, had known Selleck since their undergraduate days at Yale College. He acted as an intermediary. When George Washington refused to exchange a captured British officer for Selleck because he was not an officer in the Continental Army, Mary had to face an unpleasant dilemma. An American privateer, Capt. David Holly, offered to raid Long Island, capture Judge Jones, and force the British to negotiate an exchange. Mary disliked privateers and did not approve of Holly,

but after the British raided Fairfield and burned most of the town, she consented. The rest of the story explores the consequences of this decision. Mary's deep religious convictions are emphasized throughout the film.

The screenplay telescopes the chronology of these events somewhat, invents a romance between Amelia (a servant in the Silliman household) and Captain Holly, and uses the slave Peter to illustrate the dilemmas that African Americans faced during the war. But the central plot line follows a drama that is well-documented in the historical record and exposes a side of the Revolutionary War that few Americans are even vaguely aware of. The struggle was a long, brutal conflict that brought liberty to many and equality to smaller numbers but also turned some neighbors against others.

Mary Fish Silliman at age 58, four years after the death of her second husband, Gold Selleck Silliman.

with loyalists and neutral Quakers. Few militia turned out to help Washington, but most residents, aware of the atrocities committed in New Jersey in 1776, fled rather than greet the invaders as liberators. The British burned many of their abandoned farmhouses.

After his experience in New York, Washington was wary of being trapped in a city. Instead of trying to hold Philadelphia, he took up strong positions at Brandywine Creek along the British line of march. On September 11, Howe again outmaneuvered him, drove in his right flank, and forced him to retreat. Congress fled to Lancaster. The British occupied Philadelphia on September 26.

After failing to destroy a British outpost at Germantown, Washington headed west to Valley Forge, where the army endured a miserable winter. There, Frederich Wilhelm, baron von Steuben, a Prussian serving with the Continental Army who would soon become a major general, devised a drill manual for Americans based on Prussian standards. Through his efforts, the Continentals became far more soldierly. Other European volunteers also helped. From France came the marquis de Lafayette and Johann, baron de Kalb. The Poles sent Thaddeus Kosciuszko (a talented engineer) and Casimir, count Pulaski. De Kalb and Pulaski died in American service. By the last years of the war, perhaps one-fifth of all Continental officers were professional soldiers from Europe, who gave the American officer corps an aristocratic tone that sometimes alarmed civilians.

Saratoga

In northern New York, Fort Ticonderoga fell to Burgoyne on June 2, 1777, but little went right for the British after that. Colonel St. Leger, with 900 soldiers and an equal number of Indians, reached Fort Schuyler in the Mohawk valley in August and defeated 800 militia at Oriskany, but when Benedict Arnold approached with an additional 1,000 men, the Indians fled and St. Leger withdrew to Oswego.

Burgoyne's army of 7,800, advancing from Ticonderoga toward Albany, was overwhelmed in the upper Hudson valley. As his supply line to Canada grew longer, American militia swarmed behind him to cut it. When he detached 700 Hessians to forage in the Green Mountains, they ran into 2,600 militia raised by John Stark of New Hampshire. On August 16 at Bennington, Vermont, Stark killed or captured nearly all of them. A relief force of 650 Hessians was also mauled. By the time Burgoyne's surviving soldiers reached the Hudson and started toward Albany, the Americans under Horatio Gates outnumbered them 3 to 1. The British got as far as Bemis Heights, 30 miles north of Albany, but failed to break through in two costly battles, with Arnold again distinguishing himself. Burgoyne retreated 10 miles to **Saratoga,** where he surrendered his entire army on October 17.

French Intervention

In May 1776, Louis XVI authorized secret aid to the American rebels. A French dramatist, Pierre-Augustin Caron de Beaumarchais, author of *The Barber of Seville* (1775) and later *The Marriage of Figaro* (1784), set up the firm of Roderique Hortalez et Compagnie to smuggle supplies through Britain's weak blockade of the American coast. (The British navy had deployed most of its ships to transport and supply the army and had few left for blockade duty.) Without this aid, the Americans could not have continued the war.

In December 1776, Benjamin Franklin arrived in France as an agent of the American Congress. Although the French court could not officially receive him without risking a declaration of war by Britain, the 70-year-old Franklin took Parisian society by storm by adopting simple clothes, replacing his wig with a fur cap, and playing to perfection the role of an innocent man of nature that French *philosophes* associated with Pennsylvania. Through Beaumarchais, he kept the supplies flowing and organized privateering raids on British commerce, which the French court claimed it could not stop.

The fall of Philadelphia alarmed Foreign Minister Charles Gravier, comte de Vergennes. He feared that Congress might give up unless France entered the war. But Burgoyne's defeat convinced Louis that the Americans could win and that intervention was a good risk. Franklin and Vergennes signed two treaties in February 1778. One, a commercial agreement, granted Americans generous trading terms with France. In the other, France made a perpetual alliance with the United States, recognized American independence, agreed to fight until Britain conceded independence, and disavowed all territorial ambitions on the North American continent. Americans could not have hoped for more. Vergennes also brought Spain into the war a year later.

The Franco-American treaties stunned London. Lord North put together a plan of conciliation that conceded virtually everything but independence and sent a distinguished group of commissioners under Frederick Howard, earl of Carlisle, to present it to Congress and block the French alliance. In 1775, such terms would have resolved the imperial crisis, but in June 1778, Congress recognized them as signs of British desperation and rejected them out of hand.

Americans now expected a quick victory, while the British regrouped. George III declared war on France, recalled the Howe brothers, and ordered General Clinton to abandon Philadelphia. Wary of being caught at sea by the French, Clinton marched overland to New York in June 1778. Washington's newly disciplined army attacked his rear at Monmouth, New Jersey, and almost drove the British from the field, but the redcoats rallied and won a draw. Fearing a French invasion of the British Isles while most of the Royal Navy was in American waters, the British redeployed their forces on a global scale. They stood on the defensive in America through most of 1778 and 1779 and even evacuated Newport, but loyalists often raided Connecticut and New Jersey from their bases in New York City, Staten Island, and Long Island.

Spanish Expansion and Intervention

Like France, Spain was eager to avenge old defeats against Britain. The Spanish king, Charles III (1759–88), had endured the loss of Florida shortly after ascending the throne but had received Louisiana from France in compensation. Spanish rule there did not begin smoothly. In 1769, Spain suppressed a small revolt against its restrictions on trade, but in later years, when its trade policy became more favorable, Louisiana enjoyed a level of prosperity it had never before known. The province attracted 2,000 immigrants from the Canary Islands, perhaps 3,000 Acadian refugees, and other French settlers from the Illinois country, some of whom founded St. Louis in 1764.

During this time, Spaniards also moved into California, partly in response to the migration of Russian hunters into Alaska. Spain founded San Diego in 1769. In the next few years, Spaniards explored the Pacific coastline as far north as southern Alaska, set up an outpost at San Francisco Bay, and built a series of Franciscan missions under Junípero Serra. With little danger from other Europeans, Spain sent relatively few soldiers to California. In fact, its California frontier duplicated many aspects of the earlier Florida missions. For the last time in the history of North America, missionaries set the tone for a whole province. As in Florida earlier, Indians died in appalling numbers from European diseases, and many objected to the harsh discipline of the missions.

Charles III recognized the danger of one imperial power urging the subjects of another to revolt and never made a direct alliance with the United States, but in 1779, he joined France in its war against Britain, hoping to retake Gibraltar and to stabilize Spain's North American borders. Britain held Gibraltar, but Spain overran British West Florida. At the end of the war, Britain ceded East Florida as well, giving Spain, for the first time in a century, control of the entire coastline of the Gulf of Mexico.

The Reconstitution of Authority

Focus Question
How did American constitutionalism after 1776 differ from the British constitutional principles that the colonists had accepted and revered before 1776?

In 1776, the prospect of independence touched off an intense debate among Americans on constitutionalism. They agreed that every state needed a written constitution to limit the powers of government in terms more explicit than the precedents, statutes, and customs that made up Britain's unwritten constitution. They moved toward ever-fuller expressions of popular sovereignty—the theory that all power must be derived from the people. For four years, these lively debates sparked a learning process until, by 1780, Americans knew what they meant when they insisted that the people of a republic must be their own governors.

John Adams and the Separation of Powers
No one learned more from this process than John Adams. When Thomas Paine advocated a simple, unicameral legislature to carry out the people's will, Adams took alarm. He replied in *Thoughts on Government,* a tract that influenced the men drafting Virginia's constitution, which other states then imitated. In 1776, Adams was already moving away from the British notion of a "mixed and balanced" constitution, in which government by King,

Lords, and Commons embodied the distinct social orders of British society. He was grop-
ing toward quite a different notion, the **separation of powers.** Government, he affirmed,
should be divided into three branches—an executive armed with veto power, a legislature,
and a judiciary independent of both. The legislature, he insisted, must be bicameral, so
that each house could expose the failings of the other. A free government need not embody
distinct social orders to be stable. It could uphold republican values by being properly balanced within itself.

Governments exist to promote the happiness of the people, Adams declared, and happiness depends on "virtue," both public and private. **Public virtue** meant "patriotism," the
willingness of independent householders to value the common good above their personal
interests and even to die for their country. The form of government that rests entirely on
virtue, Adams argued, is a republic. Americans must elect legislatures that would mirror
the diversity of society. Britain had put the nobility in one house and the commoners in
another, but in America, everyone was a commoner. America had no social orders. In what
sense, then, could any government reflect American society? Adams came close to saying
that the legislature should represent the "interests" of its citizens, but he did not face the
implications of that argument. Should citizens enter politics to pursue selfish interests?
What then of selfless patriotism?

In 1776, Adams knew only that the legislature should mirror society. **Unicameral legislatures,** which Georgia, Pennsylvania, and Vermont all adopted, horrified him: "A single assembly, possessed of all the powers of government, would make arbitrary laws for
their own interest, execute all laws arbitrarily for their own interest, and adjudge all controversies in their own favor," he warned. Adams had not yet found a way to distinguish
between everyday legislation and the power to create a constitution. While struggling to
define what a republic ought to be, he and his admirers could not yet escape two
assumptions on which European politics rested—that government must be sovereign,
and that it alone could define the rights of the people. A few ordinary settlers had already
spotted the dangers of those assumptions. As the citizens of Concord, Massachusetts,
warned in October 1776, "A Constitution alterable by the Supreme Legislative [Power] is
no Security at all to the Subject against any Encroachment of the Governing part on . . .
their Rights and Privileges."

This concern would eventually prompt Americans, including Adams, to invent the embodiment of **popular sovereignty** in its purest form, the constitutional convention. But meanwhile, in 1776, most Americans still assumed that governments must be sovereign. In the
early state constitutions, every state lodged **sovereign power** in its legislature and let the legislature define the rights of citizens. In 1776, the American reply to Britain's sovereign Parliament was 13 sovereign state legislatures—14, with Vermont.

The Virginia Constitution

In June 1776, Virginia became the first state to adopt a permanent, republican constitution. The provincial congress (called a "convention" in Virginia), which had assumed full

legislative powers, affirmed "that the legislative and executive powers . . . should be separate and distinct from the judiciary," but then wrote a constitution that made the legislature supreme. It chose the governor, the governor's council, and all judges above the level of justice of the peace. The governor had no veto and hardly any patronage. The lower house faced annual elections, but members of the upper house served four-year terms.

George Mason drafted a declaration of rights that the Virginia delegates passed before approving the constitution, on the theory that the people should define their rights before empowering the government. The convention's amended text affirmed human equality but was carefully worded to exclude enslaved people. Mason upheld the right to life, liberty, property, and the pursuit of happiness, condemned hereditary privilege, called for rotation in office, provided guarantees for trial by jury and due process, and extolled religious liberty. Legally, Virginia's bill of rights was merely a statute, with no more authority than any other law, but it was eloquent, and many states copied it.

Other states adopted variations of the Virginia model. Because America had no aristocracy, uncertainty about the proper makeup of the upper house was widespread. Some states imposed higher property qualifications on "senators" than on "representatives." In three states, the lower house elected the upper house. Maryland chose state senators through an electoral college, but most states created separate election districts for senators. Most states also increased the number of representatives in the lower house. Inland counties, which were underrepresented in most colonial assemblies, became better represented, and men of moderate wealth won a majority of seats in most states, displacing the rich, who had been winning most colonial elections. Most states also stripped the governor of patronage and of royal prerogatives, such as the power to dissolve the legislature. At this stage, only New York empowered the governor, in conjunction with a Council of Revision, to reject bills passed by the legislature.

The Pennsylvania Constitution

In June 1776, Pennsylvania radicals overthrew Crown, proprietor, and assembly, rejected the leadership of both the old Quaker and Proprietary parties, and elected artisans to office in Philadelphia and ordinary farmers in rural areas. Until 1776, most officeholders had been either Quakers or Anglicans. Now, Scots-Irish Presbyterians and German Lutherans or Calvinists replaced most of them and drafted a new constitution in their own quest for legitimacy.

Pennsylvania also came closer than any other state to recognizing the constitutional dangers of resting sovereignty solely in the government—and government's arm, the legislature—rather than in the citizens. The radicals summoned a special convention whose only task was to write a constitution. That document established a unicameral assembly and a plural executive of 12 men, one of whom would preside and thus be called "president." All freemen who paid taxes, and their adult sons living at home, could vote. Elections were annual, voting was by secret ballot, legislative sessions were open to the public, and no representative could serve for more than four years out of any seven. All bills were to be published before passage for public discussion throughout the state. Only at the next session of the legislature could they be passed into law, except in emergencies. Pennsylvania also created a Council of Censors to meet every seven years to determine whether the constitution had been violated. It could also recommend amendments.

The Pennsylvania constitution, however, generated intense conflict in late 1776 as the British army drew near. In this emergency, the convention that drafted the constitution also began to pass laws, destroying any distinction between itself and the legislature it was creating. Likewise, the convention and the legislatures that eventually succeeded it rarely delayed the enactment of a bill until after the voters had had time to discuss it. The war lent a sense of emergency to almost every measure. Even more alarming, many residents condemned the new constitution as illegitimate. The men driven from power in 1776 never consented to it and saw no good reason why they should accept it. The radicals, calling themselves Constitutionalists, imposed an obligation on all citizens to uphold the constitution and then disenfranchised those who refused to support it, such as Quakers.

These illiberal measures gave radicals a majority in the legislature into the 1780s and kept voter turnout low in most elections, although some men (mostly leaders of the old Proprietary Party) took the new oath only to form an opposition party. Called Anticonstitutionalists at first (that is, opponents of the 1776 constitution), they soon took the name Republicans. After the war, as the disenfranchised regained the right to vote, Republicans won a solid majority in the legislature, secured ratification of the federal Constitution, and then, in 1790, replaced the 1776 state constitution with a new one that created a bicameral legislature and an elective governor with a veto that could be overridden.

Massachusetts Redefines Constitutionalism

Another bitter struggle occurred in Massachusetts. After four years of intense debate, Massachusetts found a way to lodge sovereignty with the people and not with government—that is, a way to distinguish a constitution from simple laws.

In response to the Massachusetts Government Act passed by Parliament in 1774, the colonists had prevented the royal courts from sitting. In the three western counties of Worcester, Hampshire, and Berkshire, they had ousted from office a group of wealthy, intermarried families (called "river gods" in Connecticut valley towns), most of whom became loyalists. The courts remained closed until the British withdrew from Boston in March 1776, and the provincial congress moved into the city and reestablished itself as the General Court under the royal charter of 1691. The legislature then reapportioned itself. Under the old system, most towns elected a single representative. A few (such as Salem) chose two. Only Boston could elect four. The new system let towns choose representatives in proportion to population. It rewarded the older, populous eastern towns at the expense of the lightly settled western towns.

When the General Court also revived royal practice by appointing its own members as county judges and justices of the peace, the western counties exploded. Their hatred of the river gods extended to eastern gentlemen as well. Denouncing the "antient Mode of

Government among us which we so much detest and abhor," they attacked the reapportionment act and refused to reopen the courts in Hampshire and Berkshire counties. Most of Berkshire's radicals were Baptists in religion and Lockeans in politics. They insisted on contracts or compacts as the basis of authority in both church and state and continued to use county conventions in place of the courts. To the Berkshire Constitutionalists, a **convention** was becoming the purest expression of the will of the people, superior to any legislature. These uneducated farmers set the pace in demanding a formal constitution for the state.

In fall 1776, the General Court asked the towns to authorize it to draft a constitution. By a 2-to-1 margin, the voters agreed, a result that reflected growing *distrust* of the legislature. Six months earlier, hardly anyone would have questioned such a procedure. The legislature drafted a constitution over the next year and then, in an unusual precaution, asked the towns to ratify it. The voters rejected it by the stunning margin of 5 to 1. Voters angry with a particular clause were likely to condemn the whole document. Chastened, the General Court urged the towns to postpone the question until after the war. Hampshire County reopened its courts in April 1778, but Berkshire County threatened to secede from the state unless the legislature summoned a constitutional convention. Drawing upon John Locke, these farmers insisted that they were now in a "state of nature," subject to no legitimate government. They might even join a neighboring state that had a proper constitution. At a time when Vermont was making good its secession from New York, theirs was no idle threat.

The General Court gave in, and a convention met in Boston in December 1779. John Adams drafted a constitution that the convention used as its starting point. A constitution now had to be drafted by a convention, elected for that specific purpose, and then ratified by the people. The people would then be the source of all legitimate authority.

In the four years since 1776, Adams's thoughts on the separation of powers and bicameralism had matured. Like the Virginia constitution, the Massachusetts constitution began with a bill of rights. Both houses would be elected annually. The House of Representatives would be chosen by the towns, as reapportioned in 1776. Senators would be elected by counties and apportioned according to property values, not population. The governor would be elected by the people and would have a veto that two-thirds of both houses could override. Property qualifications rose as a man's civic duties increased. For purposes of ratification only, all free adult males were eligible to vote. In accepting the basic social compact, everyone (that is, all free men) would have a chance to consent. Voters had to vote on each article separately, not on the whole document.

During spring 1780, town meetings began the ratification process. The convention tallied the results and declared that the constitution had received the required two-thirds majority, but it juggled the figures on two articles, both involving religion, to get this result. Those articles provided for the public support of ministers and required the governor to be a Christian. Baptists objected to all taxes for the support of religion, and many Protestants wanted to exclude Catholics from the governorship. The new constitution promptly went into effect and, although it has often been amended, is still in force today, making it the world's oldest written constitution. Starting with New Hampshire in 1784, other states adopted the Massachusetts model.

Confederation

Before independence, hardly anyone had given serious thought to how an American nation ought to be governed. Dozens of colonists had drafted plans for conciliation with Britain, but through 1775, only Benjamin Franklin, Connecticut's Silas Deane, and an anonymous newspaper essayist had presented plans for an American union. Franklin's was an updated version of the Albany Plan of 1754. These plans attracted no public comment. Colonists passionately debated the empire and their state governments, but not America.

Congress began discussing the American union in summer 1776. Congress had been voting by state since the First Continental Congress in 1774. Delegates from large states favored representation according to population, but no census existed to give precise numbers, and the small states insisted on being treated as equals. So long as Britain was ready to embrace any state that defected, small states had great leverage: The tail could wag the dog. In one early draft of the Articles of Confederation, John Dickinson rejected proportional representation in favor of state equality. He enumerated the powers of Congress, which did not include levying taxes or regulating trade. To raise money, Congress would have to print it or requisition specific amounts from the states. Congress then split over how to apportion these requisitions. Northern states wanted to count slaves in computing the ratios. Southern states wanted apportionment based on each state's free population. Western lands were another tough issue. States with fixed borders pressured states with boundary claims stretching into the Ohio or Mississippi valleys to surrender their claims to Congress. Many speculators favored the land cessions. Congress could not resolve these issues in 1776.

Debate resumed after Washington's victories at Trenton and Princeton. Thomas Burke of North Carolina introduced a resolution that eventually became part of the Articles of Confederation: "Each state retains its sovereignty, freedom and independence, and every power, jurisdiction, and right, which is not by this confederation expressly delegated to the United States in Congress assembled." The acceptance of Burke's resolution, with only Virginia dissenting, ensured that the Articles would contain a firm commitment to state sovereignty. Only after Saratoga, however, was Congress able to complete the Articles. In the final version, Congress was given no power over western land claims, and requisitions would be based on each state's free population. In 1781, Congress tried to change the formula so that each slave was counted as three-fifths of a person for the purpose of apportioning requisitions, but this amendment was never ratified.

In November 1777, Congress asked the states to ratify the Articles by March 10, 1778, but only Virginia met the deadline. Most states tried to attach conditions, which Congress rejected, but by midsummer, 10 had ratified. The three dissenters were Delaware, New Jersey, and Maryland—all states without western land claims who feared their giant neighbors. Maryland held out for more than three years, until Virginia agreed to cede its land claims north of the Ohio River to Congress. The Articles finally went into force on March 1, 1781.

By then, the Continental Congress had lost most of its power. Some of its most talented members, including Jefferson and Samuel Adams, had returned home to help reshape their state governments. Others, such as Washington, had taken army commands, and some, including Benjamin Franklin, John Adams, and John Jay, had departed on diplomatic assignments. The congressional effort to manage everything through committees created impossible bottlenecks. In 1776, the states had looked to Congress to confer legitimacy on their new governments, especially in the middle colonies, but as the states adopted their own constitutions, their legitimacy became more obvious than that of Congress. Even more alarming, by the late 1770s, Congress simply could not pay its bills.

The Crisis of the Revolution, 1779–1783

Americans expected a quick victory under the French alliance. Instead, the struggle turned into a grim war of **attrition**, testing which side would first exhaust its resources or lose the will to fight. Loyalists became much more important to the British war effort, both as a source of manpower and as the main justification for continuing the war. Most settlers, argued Lord North, were still loyal to Britain. They could turn the contest around. To abandon them would be dishonorable and might lead to a bloodbath. The British began to look to the Deep South as the likeliest recruiting ground for armed loyalists. The Carolinas, bitterly divided by the regulator movements and vulnerable to massive slave defections, seemed a promising source.

Courtesy, American Antiquarian Society

Extract of a letter from Monmouth county, June 12.

" Ty, with his party of about 20 blacks and whites, laft Friday afternoon took and carried off prifoners, Capt. Barns Smock and Gilbert Vanmater; at the fame time fpiked up the iron four pounder at Capt. Smock's houfe, but took no ammunition: Two of the artillery horfes, and two of Capt. Smock' horfes, were likewife taken off."

The above-mentioned Ty is a Negroe, who bears the title of Colonel, and commands a motly crew at Sandy-Hook.

An Offer of Freedom   An American newspaper reported on British efforts to gain the support of slaves by offering them freedom.

The Loyalists

Most loyalists were committed to English ideas of liberty. Many of them had objected openly to the Stamp Act and other British measures but doubted that Parliament intended to undermine government by consent in the colonies. They also thought that creating a new American union was a far riskier venture than remaining part of the British empire. For many, the choice of loyalties was painful. Some waited until the fighting reached their neighborhood before deciding which soldiers to flee from and which to shoot at. The loyalists then learned a stark truth: They could not fire at their neighbors and expect to retain their homes except under the protection of the British army. The British, in turn, were slow to take advantage of the loyalists. In the early years of the war, British officers regarded the loyalists' military potential with the same disdain that they bestowed on the patriots. As the war continued, however, loyalists, who stood to lose everything in an American victory, showed that they could be fierce soldiers.

About one-sixth of the white population chose the British side in the war, and 19,000 men joined more than 40 loyalist military units, mostly after 1778, when Britain grew desperate for soldiers. Unlike most patriots, loyalists served long terms, even for the duration, because they could not go home unless they won. By 1780, the number of loyalists under arms may have exceeded the number of Continentals by almost two to one. State governments retaliated by banishing prominent loyalists under pain of death if they returned and by confiscating their property.

Loyalist Refugees, Black and White

Focus Question

Why, given that the Declaration of Independence proclaimed that "all men are created equal," did most Indians and blacks, when given the chance, side with Britain?

When given the choice, most slaves south of New England sided with Britain. In New England, where they sensed that they could gain freedom by joining the rebels, many volunteered for military service. Elsewhere, although some fought for the Revolution, they realized that their best chance of emancipation lay with the British army. During the war, perhaps 50,000 slaves (about 10 percent) fled their owners; of that total, between 8,000 and 10,000 were evacuated by the British. The decision to flee carried risks. In South Carolina during Clinton's 1776 invasion, hundreds reached the Sea Islands in an effort to join the British, only to face their owners' wrath when the British failed to rescue them. Some approached British units only to be treated as contraband (property) and to face possible resale. But most slaves who reached British lines won their freedom, even though the British army never became an instrument of systematic emancipation. When the British withdrew after the war, blacks went with them, many to Jamaica, some to Nova Scotia, others to London. In the 1780s, the

British created a colony for former slaves at Sierra Leone in West Africa. A few even ended up in Australia.

The war, in short, created an enormous stream of refugees, black and white. In addition to 10,000 former slaves, some 60,000 to 70,000 colonists left for other parts of the British empire. The American Revolution created 30 refugees for every 1,000 people, compared with 5 per 1,000 created by the French Revolution in the 1790s. About 35,000 settlers found their way to the Maritime Provinces. Another 6,000 to 10,000 fled to Quebec, settled upriver from the older French population, and in 1791 became the new province of Upper Canada (later Ontario). A generous land policy, which required an oath of allegiance to George III, attracted thousands of new immigrants to Canada from the United States in the 1780s and 1790s. By the War of 1812, four-fifths of Upper Canada's 100,000 people were American-born. Although only one-fifth of them could be traced to the loyalist emigration, the settlers supported Britain in that war. In a real sense, the American Revolution laid the foundation for two new nations—the United States and Canada—and competition between them for settlers and loyalties continued long after the fighting stopped.

The Indian Struggle for Unity and Survival

Focus Question
Why did racist hatred of Indians reach new levels of intensity at a time when Indians were reducing their cultural differences with the settlers, as in their increasing rejection of torture?

Indians of the eastern woodlands also began to play a more active role in the war. Most of them saw that an American victory would threaten their survival as a people on their ancestral lands. Nearly all of them sided with Britain in the hope that a British victory might stem the flood of western expansion, and they achieved a level of unity without precedent in their history.

At first, most Indians tried to remain neutral. The British were rebuffed when they asked the Iroquois to fight against the colonists. The Delawares and the Shawnees, defeated in Lord Dunmore's War in 1774, also stood neutral. Only the Cherokees took up arms in 1776. Short on ammunition and other British supplies, they took heavy losses before making peace and accepting neutrality. The Chickamaugas, a splinter group, continued to resist. In the Deep South, only the Catawbas—by now much reduced in number—fought on the American side.

Burgoyne's invasion brought the Iroquois into the war in 1777. The Mohawks in the east and the Senecas in the west sided with Britain under the leadership of Joseph Brant, a literate and educated Mohawk and a Freemason. His sister, Mary Brant, emerged as a skillful diplomat in the alliance between the Iroquois and the loyalists. A minority of Oneidas and some Tuscaroras fought with the Americans. Most of them were becoming Christians under a patriot Presbyterian missionary, Samuel Kirkland. Despite severe strains during the Revolution, the Iroquois League was not shattered until after the war, when those who had fought for Britain migrated to Canada.

A minority of Shawnees, led by Cornplanter, and of Delawares, led by White Eyes and Killbuck, also pursued friendly relations with the Americans. They provided intelligence to American forces and served as wilderness guides, but they refused to fight other Indians and did their best to preserve peace along the frontier. Christian Moravian Indians in the Ohio country took a similar stance. The reluctance of Indians to kill other Indians, already evident during the Seven Years' War, became even more obvious during the Revolution. Loyalists and patriots were far more willing than Indians to kill one another.

Frontier racism, already conspicuous in Pontiac's War, intensified and made Indian neutrality all but impossible. Backcountry settlers from Carolina through New York refused to accept the neutrals on their own terms. Indian warriors, especially young men strongly influenced by nativist prophets, increasingly believed that the Great Spirit had created whites, Indians, and blacks as separate peoples who ought to remain apart. Their militancy further enraged the settlers. Young white hunters, disdained by many easterners as "near savages," secured their identity as "whites" by killing Indians.

The hatred of Indians grew so extreme that it threatened to undercut the American war effort. In 1777, a Continental officer had Cornplanter murdered. In 1778, American militia killed White Eyes. Four years later, Americans massacred 100 unarmed Moravian mission Indians at Gnadenhutten, Ohio. Nearly all of them were women and children, who knelt in prayer as, one by one, their skulls were crushed with mallets. This atrocity brutalized Indians as well as settlers. Until then, most Indians had refrained from the ritual torture of prisoners, but after Gnadenhutten they resumed the custom—selectively. They burned alive any known leaders of the massacre whom they captured.

Faced with hatred, Indians united to protect their lands. They won the frontier war north of the Ohio River. The Iroquois ravaged the Wyoming valley of Pennsylvania in 1778. When an American army devastated Iroquoia in 1779 and committed many atrocities along the way, the Indians fell back on the British post at Niagara and continued the struggle. In 1779, nearly all Indians, from the Creeks on the Gulf Coast to the nations of the Great Lakes, exchanged emissaries and planned an all-out war along the frontier. George Rogers Clark of Virginia thwarted their offensive with a daring winter raid in which he captured Vincennes and cut off the western nations from British supplies, but the Indians regrouped, and by 1782 drove the Virginia "long knives" out of the Ohio country.

Attrition

After 1778, George III's determination to continue the war bitterly divided his kingdom. Much of the British public doubted that the war could be won. Trade was disrupted, thousands of ships were lost to privateers, taxes and the national debt soared, military recruits became harder to find, and a French invasion became a serious threat. Political dissent rose and included widespread demand for the reduction of royal patronage and for electoral reforms. A proposal to abolish Lord George Germain's office, clearly an attack on the American war, failed in the House of Commons by only 208 votes to 201 in March 1780. A resolve condemning the influence of the Crown carried in April, 233 to 215. The king had great difficulty persuading North not to resign.

Desperate for men, the British army had been quietly recruiting Irish Catholics, and North supported a modest degree of toleration for English and Scottish Catholics. This leniency produced a surge of Protestant violence culminating in the Gordon riots, named for an eccentric agitator, Lord George Gordon. For a week in June 1780, crowds roared through London, smashing Catholic chapels attached to foreign embassies, liberating prisoners from city jails, and finally attacking the Bank of England. The army, supported by Lord Mayor John Wilkes, put down the rioters. This spectacular violence discredited the reformers and gave North one more chance to win the war.

Attrition also weakened the United States. Indian raids reduced harvests, and military levies kept thousands of men away from productive work. Loyalist raids into Connecticut and New Jersey wore down the defenders and destroyed a great deal of property. A 1779 raid on Virginia carried off or destroyed property worth £2 million. Merchants lost most of their European and West Indian markets, although a few of them made huge profits through blockade running or privateering. Average household income plunged by more than 40 percent. Even some American triumphs came at a high price. Burgoyne's surrender left Americans with the burden of feeding his army for the rest of the war. Provisioning a French fleet in American waters, and later a French army, also put enormous strains on American resources.

These heavy demands led to the collapse of the Continental dollar in 1779–80. Congress had been printing money to pay its bills, using the Spanish dollar as its basic monetary unit. With the French alliance bolstering American credit, this practice worked reasonably well into 1778. The money depreciated but without causing widespread dissatisfaction. As the war ground on, though, the value of Continental money fell to less than a penny on the dollar in 1779. Congress agreed to stop the printing presses and to rely instead on requisitions from the states and on foreign and domestic loans, but without paper it could not even pay the army. Congress and the army had to requisition supplies directly from farmers in exchange for certificates geared to an inflation rate of 40 to 1, well below its true rate. Many farmers, rather than lose money on their crops, simply cut back production. William Beadle, a Connecticut shopkeeper, tried to fight inflation by accepting Continental money at face value until he saw the consequences. Rather than leave his wife and children impoverished, he slit their throats and shot himself.

Continental soldiers—unpaid, ill-clothed, and often poorly fed—grew mutinous. As they became more professional through frequent drill, they also became more contemptuous of civilians. The winter of 1779–80, the worst of the century, marked a low point in morale among the main force of Continentals snowed in with Washington at Morristown, New Jersey. Many deserted. In May 1780, two Connecticut regiments of the Continental Line, without food for three days, threatened to go home, raising the danger that the whole army might dissolve. Their officers barely managed to restore control. On

Map 6.2 War on the Frontier, 1777–82   Indian unity during the Revolution exceeded even what had been achieved in Pontiac's War.

paper, Washington had 16,000 men. His real strength was 3,600 men and not even enough horses to move his artillery.

The British Offensive in the South

In 1780, the British attacked in the Deep South with great success. The Revolution entered its most critical phase and nearly collapsed. "I have almost ceased to hope," Washington confessed. In December 1778, a small British amphibious force had taken Savannah and had

The Present State of Great Britain (1779?), probably by James Gillray   The war is going badly for weary John Bull (England). America, the Indian, is stealing liberty, the Dutch are lifting Britain's purse, and the French are attacking. Only a surly Scot is defending John Bull, and he may lose his dagger.

held it through 1779. The British even restored royal government with an elective assembly in Georgia between 1780 and 1782. By early 1780, they were ready to launch a major offensive. General Clinton had finally devised a strategy for winning the war.

Much of his New York army would sail to Charleston, take it, and unleash armed loyalists to pacify the countryside. Part of the regular forces would remain in the Carolinas to deal with any other army the Americans might field. Clinton would return with the rest of the army to New York and land on the Jersey coast with a force three times larger than Washington's at Morristown. By dividing this army into two columns, Clinton could break through both passes of the Watchung Mountains leading to Morristown. Washington would either have to hold fast and be overwhelmed or else abandon his artillery for lack of horses and attack one of the invading columns on unfavorable terms. Either way, Clinton reasoned, the Continental Army would be destroyed. He was also negotiating secretly with an angry and disgruntled Benedict Arnold (he had received little recognition for his heroics in the Saratoga campaign) for the surrender of West Point, which would open the Hudson River to British ships as far north as Albany. Arnold had begun trading intelligence for cash in 1779. Finally, if the French landed in Newport, which the British had evacuated, Clinton would move against them with nearly his entire New York fleet and garrison. If he succeeded there too, he would have smashed every professional force in North America within a year's time. His remaining task would then be pacification, which he could pretty much leave to loyalists. But he told no one else about his New Jersey plan.

Clinton's invasion of South Carolina began with awesome successes. While the British navy sealed off Charleston from the sea, an army of 10,000 closed off the land approaches to the city and forced Benjamin Lincoln and 5,000 defenders to surrender on May 12. Loyalists under Banastre Tarleton caught the 350 remaining Continentals at the Waxhaws near the North Carolina border on May 29 and, in what became infamous as "Tarleton's quarter," killed them all. This calculated brutality was designed to terrorize civilians into submission. It succeeded for a time, but Thomas Sumter began to fight back after loyalists burned his plantation. His mounted raiders attacked British outposts and terrorized loyalists. At Hanging Rock on August 6, Sumter's 800 men scattered 500 loyalists, killing or wounding nearly half of them. All participants on both sides were colonists.

Leaving Cornwallis in command of 8,300 men in South Carolina, Clinton sailed north with one-third of his Carolina army, only to learn that loyalists, fearing that he would never take the initiative in the north, had persuaded Wilhelm, baron von Knyphausen, New York's temporary commander, to land in New Jersey with 6,000 men on the night of June 6–7, 1780. Even a force that small would pose a grave threat to Washington unless the militia came to his aid. Most loyalists hoped that the militia was so weary from the harsh winter and numerous raids that they would not turn out. Some companies had even begun to muster women. To the dismay of the British, however, the militia appeared in force on June 7. Only then, after an inconclusive engagement, did Knyphausen learn that Clinton was on his way with his own plan of attack. The British pulled back to the coast and waited, but they had lost the element of surprise. Clinton attacked at Springfield on June 23 while loyalists set fire to the village. The battle became America's civil war in miniature. New Jersey loyalist regiments attacked the New Jersey regiments of the Continental Line, who were assisted by New Jersey militia. A stout defense persuaded Clinton to withdraw to New York.

With Washington's army intact, Clinton ignored the French when they landed at Newport. After June 1780, the British put all of their hopes on the southern campaign. Even Arnold's attempt to betray West Point was thwarted in September. Clinton's agent, John André, was caught and hanged, but Arnold escaped to British lines and became a general in the British army.

Despite Sumter's harassment, Cornwallis's conquest of the Carolinas proceeded rapidly. Congress scraped together 900 tough Maryland and Delaware Continentals, put Horatio Gates, the hero of Saratoga, in command, and sent them south against Cornwallis. Bolstered by 2,000 Virginia and North Carolina militia, Gates rashly offered battle at Camden on August 16, even though many of his men had been up all night with diarrhea after eating half-baked bread. The militia, who lacked bayonets, fled in panic at the first British charge. The exposed Continentals fought bravely but were crushed. Gates rode an astonishing 240 miles away from the scene in three days and, from Hillsborough, North Carolina, informed Congress that he had suffered "total Defeat." Two days after Camden, Tarleton surprised Sumter's camp at Fishing Creek, near the Waxhaws, killing 150 men and wounding 300. In four months, the British had destroyed all of the Continental forces in the Deep South, mauled Sumter's band of partisans, and left North Carolina open to invasion. These victories seemed to fulfill Clinton's boast that he would strip "three stripes . . . from the detestable thirteen." Cornwallis turned the pacification of South Carolina over to his loyalists, many of whom were exiles from other states, and marched confidently on to "liberate" North Carolina.

The Partisan War

But resistance continued. In the west, frontier riflemen, led by Daniel Morgan and enraged by Britain's support of the Indians, crossed the Blue Ridge 1,800 strong to challenge Patrick Ferguson's loyalists at King's Mountain near the North Carolina border on October 7, 1780. Losing only 88 men, rebel marksmen picked off many defenders and finally overwhelmed the loyalists, killing 160 men, including Ferguson, and capturing 860. They shot many prisoners and hanged a dozen, their answer to "Tarleton's quarter." This victory, the first major British setback in the Deep South, stung Cornwallis, who halted his drive into North Carolina.

In October 1780, Congress sent **Nathanael Greene** to the Carolinas with a small Continental force. When Sumter withdrew for several months to nurse a wound, Francis Marion took his place. A much abler leader, Marion (who became known as the Swamp Fox) operated from remote bases in the marshy low country. Yet Greene's prospects seemed desperate. The ugliness of the partisan war—the mutilation of corpses, killing of prisoners, and wanton destruction of property—and the condition of his soldiers appalled him. Yet Greene and Marion devised a masterful strategy of partisan warfare that finally wore out the British.

In the face of a greatly superior enemy, Greene ignored a standard maxim of war and split up his force of 1,800 Continentals. He sent 300 men east to bolster Marion and ordered Daniel Morgan and 300 riflemen west to threaten the British outpost of Ninety-Six. Cornwallis, worried that after King's Mountain, Morgan might raise the entire backcountry against the British, divided his own army. He sent Tarleton with a mixed force of 1,100 British and loyalists after Morgan, who decided to stand with his back to a river at a place called Cowpens, where a loyalist kept cattle. Including militia, Morgan had 1,040 men.

Tarleton attacked on January 17, 1781. In another unorthodox move, Morgan sent his militia out front as skirmishers. He ordered them to fire two rounds and then redeploy in his rear as a reserve. Relieved of their fear of a bayonet charge, they obeyed. As they pulled back, the British rushed forward into the Continentals, who also retreated at first, then wheeled and discharged a lethal volley. After Morgan's cavalry charged into the British left flank, the militia returned to the fray. Although Tarleton escaped, Morgan annihilated his army.

As Morgan rejoined Greene, Cornwallis staked everything on his ability to find Greene and crush him, precisely what he had failed to do to Washington after Trenton and Princeton four years earlier. But Greene had placed flatboats at his rear at major river crossings and then lured Cornwallis into a march of exhaustion. In a race to the Dan River, Cornwallis burned his baggage in order to travel lightly. Greene escaped on his flatboats across the Yadkin River, flooded with spring rains, just ahead of Cornwallis—who had to march

Map 6.3 War in the Lower South, 1780–81   British victories in 1780 nearly restored Georgia and South Carolina to the Crown, but after Guilford Court House in March 1781, the Americans regained the advantage throughout the region. View an animated version of this map or related maps at http://www.thomsonedu.com/history/murrin.

to a ford 10 miles upstream, cross the river, and then march back while Greene rested. Greene repeated this stratagem all the way to the Dan until he judged that Cornwallis was so weak that the Americans could offer battle at Guilford Court House on March 15, 1781. With militia, he outnumbered Cornwallis 4,400 to 1,900. Even though the British retained possession of the battlefield, they lost one-quarter of their force and the strategic initiative. Cornwallis retreated to Wilmington to refit. He then marched north into Virginia—the seat of southern resistance, he told Clinton, the one place where Britain could achieve decisive results. Instead of following him, Greene returned to South Carolina, where he and Marion took the surviving British outposts one by one. After the British evacuated Ninety-Six on July 1, 1781, they held only Savannah and Charleston in the Deep South. Against heavy odds, Greene had reclaimed the region for the Revolution.

Mutiny and Reform

After the Camden disaster, army officers and state politicians demanded reforms to strengthen Congress and win the war. State legislatures sent their ablest men to Congress. Maryland, the last state to hold out, finally completed the American union by ratifying the Articles of Confederation. But before any reforms could take effect, discontent again erupted in the army. Insisting that their three-year enlistments had expired, 1,500 men of the Pennsylvania Line got drunk on New Year's Day 1781, killed three officers, and marched out of their winter quarters at Morristown. General Clinton sent agents from New York to promise them a pardon and their back pay if they defected to the British, but instead the mutineers marched south toward Princeton and turned Clinton's agents over to Pennsylvania authorities, who executed them. Congress, reassured, negotiated with the soldiers. More than half of them accepted discharges, and those who remained in service got furloughs and bonuses for reenlistment. Encouraged by this treatment, 200 New Jersey soldiers at Pompton also mutinied, but Washington used New England units to disarm them and executed two of the leaders.

Civilian violence, such as the "Fort Wilson" riot in Philadelphia, also prompted Congress to change policies. Radical artisans blamed the city's rich merchants for the rampant inflation of 1779 and demanded price controls. The merchants blamed paper money. In October, several men were killed when the antagonists exchanged shots near the fortified home of James Wilson, a wealthy lawyer. Spokesmen for the radicals deplored the violence and abandoned the quest for price controls. For all city dwellers, sound money was becoming the only solution to the devastating inflation.

Congress interpreted these disturbances as a call for reform at the national level. While armed partisans were making the war more radical, politics veered in a conservative direction, toward the creation of European state forms, such as executive departments and a bank. Patriot leaders gave up efforts at price control and allowed the market to set prices and the value of money. Congress stopped printing money, abandoned its cumbersome committee system, and created separate executive departments of foreign affairs, finance, war, and marine. Robert Morris, a Philadelphia merchant, became the first secretary of finance, helped organize the Bank of North America (America's first), and made certain that the Continental Army was clothed and well fed, although it still was not paid. Congress began to requisition revenue from the states. The states began to impose heavy taxes but never collected enough to meet both their own and national needs. Congress tried to amend the Articles of Confederation in 1781 and asked the states for a 5 percent duty on all imports. Most states quickly ratified the "impost" amendment, but Rhode Island rejected it in 1783. Amendments to the Articles needed unanimous approval by the states, and this opposition killed the impost. A new impost proposal in 1783 was defeated by New York in 1786.

The reforms of 1781 just barely kept a smaller army in the field for the rest of the war, but the new executive departments had an unforeseen effect. Congress had been a plural executive, America's answer to the imperial Crown. But once Congress created its own departments, it looked more like a national legislature, and a feeble one at that. It began to pass, not just "orders" and "resolves," but also "ordinances," which were meant to be permanent and binding. It still could not punish anyone for noncompliance, which may be why it never called any of its measures "laws."

From the Ravaging of Virginia to Yorktown and Peace

Both Cornwallis and Washington believed that events in Virginia would decide the war. When a large British force raided the state in late 1780, Governor Thomas Jefferson called up enough militia to keep the British bottled up in Portsmouth, while he continued to ship men and supplies to Greene in the Carolinas. Thereafter, the state's ability to raise men and supplies almost collapsed.

In January 1781, Clinton sent Arnold by sea from New York with 1,600 men, mostly loyalists. They sailed up the James and gutted the new capital of Richmond. When Jefferson called out the militia, few responded. Virginia had not experienced the partisan struggles that drew men to both sides in New Jersey and the Carolinas. The state provided a different kind of test for American values under stress. The voluntaristic ethic nearly failed to get the state through a long war. Most Virginia freemen had already done service, if only as short-term militia, thousands of them in response to the 1780 raid. In 1781, they thought it was now someone else's turn. For months, there was no one else. Cornwallis took command in April, and Arnold departed for New York. But the raids continued into summer, sweeping as far west as Charlottesville, where Tarleton, who had recruited a new legion since Cowpens, scattered the Virginia legislature and almost captured Jefferson. Many of Jefferson's slaves greeted the British as liberators. Washington sent Lafayette with 1,200 New England and New Jersey Continentals to contain the damage, while Cornwallis, on Clinton's orders, withdrew to Yorktown.

At last, Washington saw an opportunity to launch a major strike. He learned that a powerful French fleet under François, comte de Grasse, with 3,000 soldiers would sail from Saint-Domingue for Chesapeake Bay on August 13. Cooperating closely with the French army commander, Jean Baptiste Donatien, comte de Rochambeau, Washington sprang his trap. Rochambeau led his 5,000 soldiers from Newport to the outskirts of New York, where they joined Washington's 5,000 Continentals. After feinting an attack to freeze Clinton in place, Washington led the combined French and American armies 400 miles south to tidewater Virginia, where they linked up with Lafayette's Americans and the other

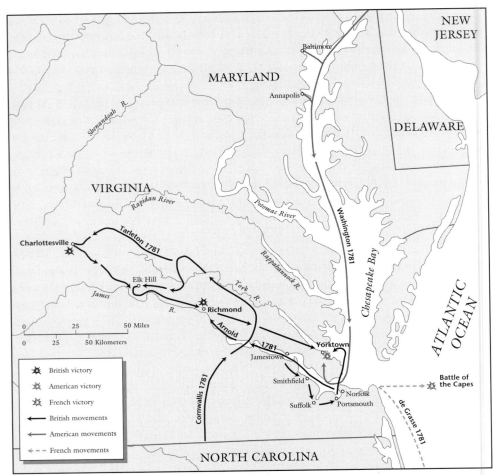

Map 6.4 Virginia and the Yorktown Campaign After the British ravaged much of Virginia, Washington and a French fleet and army were able to trap Lord Cornwallis at Yorktown, force his surrender, and guarantee American independence.

French army brought by de Grasse. After de Grasse's fleet beat off a British relief force at the Battle of the Capes on September 5, Washington cut off all retreat routes and besieged Cornwallis in **Yorktown.** On October 19, 1781, Cornwallis surrendered his entire army of 8,000 men. Many escaped slaves had died during the siege, most from smallpox, but Virginia planters hovered nearby to reclaim the survivors.

Yorktown brought down the British government in March 1782. Lord North resigned, and George III even drafted an abdication message, although he never released it. The new ministry, committed to American independence as the price of peace, continued to fight the French in the Caribbean and the Spanish at Gibraltar, but the British evacuated Savannah and Charleston and concentrated their remaining forces in New York City.

Contrary to the French Treaty of 1778, John Jay and John Adams opened secret peace negotiations in Paris with the British. They won British recognition of the Mississippi, but without New Orleans, as the western boundary of the new republic. New Englanders retained the right to fish off Newfoundland. The treaty recognized the validity of prewar transatlantic debts, and Congress promised to urge the states to restore confiscated loyalist property. These terms gave American diplomats almost everything they could have desired. After the negotiations were far advanced, the Americans told Vergennes, the French foreign minister, what they were doing. He feigned indignation, but the threat of a separate peace gave him the leverage he needed with Spain. Spain stopped demanding that France keep fighting until Gibraltar surrendered. The Treaty of Paris, although not ratified for months, ended the war in February 1783. Western Indians were appalled to learn that the treaty gave their lands to the United States. They had not been conquered, whatever European diplomats might say. Their war for survival continued with few breaks into 1795.

Congress still faced ominous problems. In March 1783, many Continental officers threatened a coup d'état unless Congress granted them generous pensions. Washington, confronting them at their encampment at Newburgh, New York, fumbled for his glasses and remarked, "I have grown old in the service of my country, and now find that I am growing blind." Tears filled the eyes of his comrades in arms, and the threat of a coup vanished.

In Philadelphia two months later, unpaid Pennsylvania soldiers marched on the statehouse, where both Congress and the state's executive council sat. Ignoring Congress, they

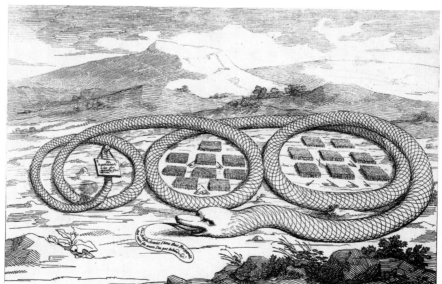

"The American Rattle Snake" This 1782 cartoon celebrated the victory of Yorktown, the second time in the war that an entire British army had surrendered to the United States.

Library of Congress, Prints and Photographs Division

demanded that Pennsylvania redress their grievances. Congress felt insulted and left the city for Princeton, where it reconvened in Nassau Hall. Its archives and administrative departments remained in Philadelphia. "I confess I have great apprehensions for the union of the states," wrote Charles Thomson, secretary to Congress since 1774. The British threat, Thomson knew, had created the American Union. He feared that the Union would dissolve with the return of peace. Congress moved on from Princeton to Annapolis and eventually settled in New York, but the Union's survival remained uncertain.

A Revolutionary Society

Focus Question
In what ways did the values shared by independent householders limit the reforms that the Revolution could offer to other Americans?

Independence transformed American life. The biggest winners were free householders, who gained enormous benefits from the democratization of politics and the chance to colonize the Great West. Besides the loyalists, the biggest losers were Indians, who continued to resist settler expansion. Many slaves won their freedom, and women struggled for greater dignity. Both succeeded only when their goals proved compatible with the ambitions of white householders.

Religious Transformations

Independence left the Anglican Church vulnerable, if only because George III was its "supreme head." Although most Anglican clergymen supported the Revolution or remained neutral, an aggressive loyalist minority stirred the wrath of patriots. Religious dissenters disestablished the Anglican Church in every southern state. They deprived it of its tax support and other privileges, such as the sole right to perform marriages. In 1786, Virginia passed Thomas Jefferson's eloquent Statute for Religious Freedom, which declared that efforts to use coercion in matters of religion "tend only to beget habits of hypocrisy and meanness." In Virginia, church attendance and the support of ministers became voluntary activities.

Other states moved more slowly. In New England, the Congregational churches had strongly supported the Revolution and were less vulnerable to attack. Ministers' salaries continued to be paid out of public taxes, although lawful dissenters, such as Baptists, could insist that their church taxes go to their own clergy. The Congregational Church exercised other public or quasi-public functions, especially on thanksgiving, fast, and election days. Disestablishment did not become complete until 1818 in Connecticut and 1833 in Massachusetts.

Although most states still restricted office-holding to Christians or Protestants, many people were coming to regard the coercion of anyone's conscience as morally wrong. Jews and Catholics both gained from the new atmosphere of tolerance. When Britain recognized the Catholic Church in the Quebec Act of 1774, most Protestants had shuddered with anxiety, but in 1790, when John Carroll of Maryland became the first Roman Catholic bishop in the United States, hardly anyone protested. Before independence, an Anglican bishop had been an explosive issue in several colonies, but in the 1780s, the Church of England reorganized itself as the Protestant Episcopal Church and quietly began to consecrate its own bishops. Both Episcopalians and Presbyterians paid homage to republican values by adopting written constitutions for their churches.

The First Emancipation

The Revolution freed tens of thousands of slaves, but it also gave new vitality to slavery in the region that people were beginning to call "the South." Within a generation, slavery was abolished in the emerging "North." Race became a defining factor in both regions. In the South, most blacks remained slaves. In the North, they became free but not equal. The independent householder and his voluntaristic ethic remained almost a white monopoly.

Many slaves freed themselves. The British army enabled more than half the slaves of Georgia and perhaps a significant fraction of those in South Carolina to win their freedom. A similar process was under way in Virginia in 1781, only to be cut off at Yorktown. Hundreds of New England slaves won their freedom through military service. They announced what they were fighting for in the surnames they chose. Jeffrey Liberty, Cuff Liberty, Dick Freeman, and Jube Freeman served in one Connecticut regiment. After the Massachusetts bill of rights proclaimed that all people were "born free and equal," Elizabeth (Bett) Freeman sued her master in 1781 and won her liberty. Thereafter, most of the slaves in Massachusetts and New Hampshire simply walked away from their masters.

Elsewhere, legislative action was necessary. Pennsylvania led the way in 1780 with the modern world's first gradual **emancipation** statute. It declared that all children born to Pennsylvania slaves after a given date would become free at age 28. The slaves,

Interior of Touro Synagogue in Newport, Rhode Island   The synagogue shown here presents the best surviving example of Jewish artistic taste in 18th-century America.

© J. Gilbert Harrington

not masters or taxpayers, thus bore the costs of their own emancipation. This requirement left them unable to compete on equal terms with free whites, who usually entered adult life with inherited property. Some masters shipped their slaves south before the moment of emancipation, and some whites kidnapped freedmen and sent them south. The Pennsylvania Abolition Society was organized largely to fight these abuses. By 1800, Philadelphia had the largest community of free blacks in America, with their own churches and other voluntary societies.

The Pennsylvania pattern took hold, with variations, in most other northern states until all of them had made provision for emancipation. Where slaves constituted more than 10 percent of the population, as in southern New York and northeastern New Jersey, slaveholders' resistance delayed legislation for years. New York yielded in 1799, New Jersey in 1804.

In the upper South, many Methodists and Baptists supported emancipation in the 1780s, only to retreat in later years. Maryland and Virginia authorized the **manumission** of individual slaves. By 1810, more than one-fifth of Maryland's slaves had been freed, as had 10,000 of Virginia's 300,000 slaves, including more than 123 freed under Washington's will after he died in 1799. But slaves were essential to the plantation economy and were usually their masters' most valuable asset. In the South, emancipation would have amounted to a social revolution and the impoverishment of the planter class. Planters supported the Christianization of their slaves and other humane reforms, but they resisted emancipation, especially with the rise of cotton as a new cash crop after the war. Cut off from British textiles during the war, South Carolina slaves insisted on growing cotton as a substitute. Their owners quickly recognized the enormous potential of that crop, which in turn guaranteed that the children and grandchildren of those slaves would remain in bondage.

Maryland and Virginia, where population growth among the slaves exceeded what the tobacco economy could absorb, banned the Atlantic slave trade, as had all states outside the Deep South. Georgia and South Carolina, to make good their losses during the war and to meet the demand for cotton after 1790, reopened the Atlantic slave trade. South Carolina imported almost 60,000 more Africans before Congress prohibited that traffic in 1808.

The Challenge to Patriarchy

Nothing as dramatic as emancipation altered relations between the sexes. With the men away fighting, many women were left in charge of the household, sometimes with interesting consequences. "I hope you will not consider yourself as commander in chief of your own house," Lucy Knox warned her soldier husband, Henry, in 1777, "but be convinced . . . that there is such a thing as equal command." Although some women acquired new authority, nearly all of them had to work harder to keep their households functioning. The war cut them off from most European consumer goods. Household manufactures, mostly the task of women, filled the gap. Women accepted these duties without demanding broader legal or political rights, but soaring food prices made many women assertive. In numerous food riots, women tried to force merchants to lower prices or stop hoarding grain.

Attitudes toward marriage were also changing. The common-law rule of coverture still denied wives any legal personality, but some of them persuaded state governments not to impoverish them by confiscating the property of their loyalist husbands. Many writers insisted that good marriages rested on mutual affection, not on property settlements. In portraits of wealthy northeastern families, husbands and wives were beginning to appear as equals. Parents were urged to respect the personalities of their children and to avoid severe discipline. Traditional reverence for the elderly was giving way to an idealization of youth and energy.

In 1780, to relieve the sufferings of Continental soldiers, Esther de Berdt Reed organized the Philadelphia Ladies Association, the first women's society in American history to take on a public role. Although few women yet demanded equal political rights, the New Jersey Constitution of 1776 let them vote if they headed a household (usually as a widow) and paid taxes. This right was revoked in 1807.

Especially in the Northeast, more women learned to read and write. Philosophers, clergymen, and even popular writers were beginning to treat women as morally superior to men, a sharp reversal of earlier teachings. The first female academies were founded in the 1790s. By 1830, nearly all native-born women in the Northeast had become literate. The ideal of the "republican wife" and the "republican mother" took hold, giving wives and mothers an expanding educational role within the family. They encouraged diligence in their husbands and patriotism in their sons. The novel became a major cultural form in the United States. Its main audience was female, as were many of the authors. Novels cast women as central characters and warned young women to beware of suitors motivated only by greed or lust.

Western Expansion, Discontent, and Conflict with Indians

Westward expansion continued during the Revolutionary War. With 30 axmen, **Daniel Boone,** a North Carolina hunter, hacked out the Wilderness Road from Cumberland Gap to the Kentucky bluegrass country in early 1775. The first settlers called Kentucky "the best poor man's country" and claimed it should belong to those who tilled its soil, not to speculators in the Transylvania Company, who claimed ownership. Although few Indians lived in Kentucky, it was the favorite hunting ground of the Shawnees and other nations. Their raids often prevented the settlers from planting crops. The settlers hunted and put up log cabins against the inside walls of large rectangular stockades, 10 feet high and built from oak logs. At each corner, a **blockhouse** with a protruding second story permitted the defenders to fire along the outside walls. Three of these "Kentucky stations" were built—at Boonesborough, St. Asaph, and Harrodsburg. Because of the constant danger, settlement grew slowly at first. Kentucky lived up to its old Indian reputation as the "dark and bloody ground." Only a few thousand settlers stuck it out until the war ended, when they were joined by swarms of newcomers. Speculators and absentees were already trying to claim the best bluegrass land. The Federal Census of 1790 listed 74,000 settlers and slaves in Kentucky and about half that many in Tennessee, where the Cherokees had ceded a large tract after their defeat in 1776. Those settlers thrived both because few Indians lived there and because British and Spanish raiders found it hard to reach them.

To the south and north of this bulge, settlement was much riskier. After the war, Spain supplied arms and trade goods to Creeks, Cherokees, Choctaws, and Chickasaws who were willing to resist Georgia's attempt to settle its western lands. North of the Ohio River, Britain refused to withdraw its garrisons and traders from Niagara, Detroit, and a few other posts, even though, according to the Treaty of Paris, those forts now lay within the boundaries of the United States. To justify their refusal, the British pointed to Congress's failure to honor America's obligations to loyalists and British creditors under the treaty. When small groups of Indians sold large tracts of land to Georgia, Pennsylvania, and New York, as well as to Congress, the Indian nations repudiated those sales and, supported by either Spain or Britain, continued to resist into the 1790s.

During the Revolutionary War, many states and Congress had recruited soldiers with promises of land after the war ended, and now they needed Indian lands to fulfill these pledges. The few Indian nations that had supported the United States suffered the most. In the 1780s, after Joseph Brant led most of the Iroquois north to Canada, New York confiscated much of the land of the friendly Iroquois who stayed. South Carolina dispossessed the Catawbas of most of their ancestral lands. The states had a harder time seizing the land of hostile Indians, who usually had Spanish or British support.

Secessionist movements arose in the 1780s when neither Congress nor eastern state governments seemed able to solve western problems. Some Tennessee settlers seceded from North Carolina and for a time maintained a separate state called Franklin. Separatist sentiment also ran strong in Kentucky. The settlers of western Pennsylvania thought of setting up on their own after Spain closed the Mississippi to American traffic in 1784. When Congress refused to recognize Vermont's independence from New York, even the radical Green Mountain Boys sounded out Canadian officials about readmission to the British empire as a separate province.

The Northwest Ordinance

After Virginia ceded its land claims north of the Ohio River to Congress in 1781, other states followed suit. Jefferson offered a resolution in 1784 that would have created 10 or more new states in this Northwest Territory. In the Land Ordinance of 1785, Congress authorized the survey of the Northwest Territory and its division into townships six miles square, each composed of 36 "sections" of 640 acres. Surveyed land would be sold at auction starting at a dollar per acre. Alternate townships would be sold in sections or as a whole, to satisfy settlers and speculators, respectively.

In July 1787, while the Constitutional Convention met in Philadelphia, Congress (sitting in New York) returned to the problem of governing the Northwest Territory. By then,

Map 6.5   Western Land Claims during the Revolution   One of the most difficult questions that Congress faced was the competing western land claims of several states. After Virginia ceded its claims north of the Ohio to Congress, other states followed suit, creating the national domain and what soon became the Northwest Territory.
View an animated version of this map or related maps at http://www.thomsonedu.com/history/murrin.

Massachusetts veterans were organizing the Ohio Company under Manassah Cutler to obtain a huge land grant from Congress. Cutler joined forces with William Duer, a New York speculator who was organizing the Scioto Company. Together they pried from Congress 1.5 million acres for the Ohio Company veterans and an option on 5 million more acres, which the Ohio Company assigned to the Scioto Company. The Ohio Company agreed to pay Congress two installments of $500,000 in depreciated securities. To meet the first payment, Duer's backers lent Cutler's $200,000. Once again, speculators, rather than settlers, seemed to be winning the West.

In the same month, Congress also passed the **Northwest Ordinance.** It authorized the creation of from 3 to 5 states, to be admitted to the Union as full equals of the original 13. The ordinance thus rejected colonialism among white people except as a temporary phase through which a "territory" would pass on its way to statehood. Congress would appoint a governor and a council to rule until population reached 5,000. At that point, the settlers could elect an assembly empowered to pass laws, although the governor (obviously modeled on earlier royal governors) had an absolute veto. When population reached 60,000, the settlers could adopt their own constitution and petition Congress for statehood. The ordinance protected civil liberties, provided for public education, and prohibited slavery in the territory.

Southern delegates all voted for the Northwest Ordinance despite its antislavery clause. They probably hoped that Ohio would become what Georgia had been in the 1730s, a society of armed freemen able to protect vulnerable slave states, such as Kentucky, from hostile invaders. Southern delegates also thought that most settlers would come from Maryland, Virginia, and Kentucky. Even if they could not bring slaves with them, they would have southern loyalties. New Englanders, by contrast, were counting on the Ohio Company to lure their own veterans to the region.

Finally, the antislavery clause may have been part of a larger Compromise of 1787, involving both the ordinance and the clauses on slavery in the federal Constitution. The Philadelphia Convention permitted states to count three-fifths of their slaves for purposes of representation and direct taxation. The antislavery concession to northerners in the ordinance was made at the same time that southern states won this concession in Philadelphia. Several congressmen were also delegates to the Constitutional Convention and traveled back and forth between the two cities while these decisions were being made. They may have struck a deal.

Congress had developed a coherent western policy, but when the first townships were offered for sale in late 1787, there were few buyers. Yet by 1789, the Ohio Company had established the town of Marietta, Kentuckians had founded a town that would soon be called Cincinnati, and tiny outposts had been set up at Columbia and Gallipolis. But without massive help from the new federal government, the settlers had little chance of overcoming stout Indian resistance. **(See Map 6.6, Advance of Settlement to 1790, in the color insert following page 288.)**

A More Perfect Union

The 1780s were difficult times. The economy failed to rebound, debtors fought creditors, and state politics became bitter and contentious. Out of this ferment arose the demand to amend or even replace the Articles of Confederation.

Commerce, Debt, and Shays's Rebellion

In 1784, British merchants flooded American markets with exports worth £3.7 million, the greatest volume since 1771, but Americans could not pay for them. Exports to Britain that year were £750,000—less than 40 percent of the £1.9 million of 1774, the last year of peace. When Britain invoked the Navigation Acts to close the British West Indies to American ships (but not to American goods), indirect returns through this once-profitable channel also faltered. Trade with France closed some of the gap, but because the French could not offer the long-term credit that the British had provided, it remained disappointing. The American economy entered a depression that lifted only slightly in 1787 and 1788 before the strong recovery of the 1790s. British imports fell by 40 percent in 1785. Exports rose to almost £900,000 but remained far below prewar levels. Private debts became a huge social problem that the states, buried under their own war debts, could not easily mitigate. Merchants, dunned by British creditors, sued their customers, many of whom could not even pay their taxes. Farmers, faced with the loss of their crops, livestock, and even their farms, resisted foreclosures and looked to their state governments for relief.

About half of the states issued paper money in the 1780s, and many passed **stay laws** to postpone the date on which a debt would come due. Massachusetts, which remembered its fierce conflicts over paper money before 1750, rejected both options and raised taxes to new highs. In 1786, many farmers in Hampshire County took matters into their own hands. Crowds gathered to prevent the courts from conducting business, much as patriots had done against the British in 1774. Governor James Bowdoin insisted that acts of resistance that had been appropriate against a tyrannical monarch were unacceptable in a government elected by the people. But in early 1787, the protestors, loosely organized under a Continental Army veteran, Captain Daniel Shays, threatened the federal arsenal at Springfield. An army of volunteers under Benjamin Lincoln marched west with artillery and scattered the Shaysites. Even so, Shaysites won enough seats in the May assembly elections to pass a stay law. In Massachusetts, **Shays's Rebellion** converted into nationalists many gentlemen and artisans who until then had opposed strengthening the central government.

Cosmopolitans versus Localists

The tensions racking Massachusetts surfaced elsewhere as well. Crowds of debtors in other states closed law courts or even besieged the legislature. State politics reflected a persistent cleavage between "cosmopolitan" and "localist" coalitions. Merchants, professional men, urban artisans, commercial farmers, southern planters, and former Continental Army officers made up the cosmopolitan bloc. They favored aggressive trade policies, hard money, payment of public debts, good salaries for executive officials and judges, and leniency to returning loyalists. Localists were farmers, rural artisans, and militia veterans who distrusted those policies. They demanded paper money, debtor relief, and generous salaries for representatives so that ordinary men could afford to serve.

In most states, localists defeated their opponents most of the time. They destroyed the feudal revival by confiscating the gigantic land claims of the Granville District, the Fairfax estate, the Calvert and Penn proprietaries, and the manorial estates of New York loyalists. (Because their owners were patriots, Rensselaerswyck and Livingston Manor survived to become the site of agrarian violence into the 1840s, when the manors were finally abolished.) Except in Vermont, localists were much less adept at blocking the claims of land speculators. Yet cosmopolitans lost so often that many of them despaired of state politics and looked to a strengthened central government for relief.

Congress also faced severe fiscal problems. Between October 1781 and February 1786, it requisitioned $15.7 million from the states but received only $2.4 million. Its annual income had fallen to $400,000 at a time when interest on its debt approached $2.5 million and when the principal on the foreign debt was about to come due. Requisitions were beginning to seem as inefficient as George Grenville had proclaimed them to be when he proposed the Stamp Act.

Foreign relations also took an ominous turn. Without British protection, American ships that entered the Mediterranean risked capture by Barbary pirates and the enslavement of their crews. In 1786, Foreign Secretary John Jay negotiated a treaty with Don Diego de Gardoqui, the Spanish minister to the United States. It offered northern merchants trading privileges with Spanish colonies in exchange for the closure of the Mississippi River to American traffic for 25 years. Seven northern states voted for the treaty, but all five southern states in Congress rejected these terms, thus defeating the treaty, which needed nine votes for ratification under the Articles of Confederation. Angry talk of disbanding the Union soon filled Congress. Delegates began haggling over which state would join what union if the breakup occurred. The quarrel became public in February 1787 when a Boston newspaper called for dissolution of the Union.

By the mid-1780s, many cosmopolitans were becoming nationalists eager to strengthen the Union. Many of them had served long, frustrating years in the army or in Congress, unable to carry out measures that they considered vital to the Confederation. In 1785, some of them tried to see what could be done outside Congress. To resolve disputes about navigation rights on the Potomac River, George Washington invited Virginia and Maryland delegates to a conference at Mount Vernon, where they drafted an agreement that was acceptable to both states and to Congress. Prompted by James Madison, a former congressman, the Virginia legislature then urged all of the states to participate in a convention at Annapolis to explore ways to improve American trade.

Four states, including Maryland, ignored the call, and the New Englanders had not yet arrived when, in September 1786, the delegates from the four middle states and Virginia accepted a report drafted by Alexander Hamilton of New York. It asked all of the states to send delegates to a convention at Philadelphia the next May "to devise such further provisions as shall appear to them necessary to render the constitution of the Federal Government adequate

"The Hero Who Defended the Mothers Will Protect the Daughters" Washington is hailed by young women near the bridge at Trenton on the way to his inauguration as first President of the United States, 1789.

to the exigencies of the Union." Seven states responded positively before Congress endorsed the convention on February 21, 1787, and five accepted later. Rhode Island refused to participate. Madison used the winter months to study the defects of classical and European confederacies and to draft a plan for a stronger American union.

The Philadelphia Convention

The convention opened in May 1787 with a plan similar to the Virginia constitution of 1776. It proposed an almost sovereign Parliament for the United States. By September, the delegates had produced a document that was much closer to the Massachusetts constitution of 1780, with a clear separation of powers. The delegates, in four months of secret sessions, repeated the constitutional learning process that had taken four years at the state level after 1776.

With Washington presiding, Governor Edmund Randolph proposed the Virginia, or "large state," plan. Drafted by Madison, it proposed a bicameral legislature, with representation in both houses apportioned according to population. The legislature would choose the executive and the judiciary. It would possess all powers currently lodged in Congress and the power "to legislate in all cases to which the separate States are incompetent." It could "negative all laws passed by the several States, contravening in [its] opinion . . . the articles of Union." Remarkably, the plan did not include specific powers to tax or regulate trade, although Madison intended to add them later on. His plan also required ratification by state conventions, not by state legislatures. Within two weeks, the delegates agreed on three-year terms for members of the lower house and seven-year terms for the upper house. The legislature would choose the executive for a single term of seven years.

In mid-June, delegates from the small states struck back. William Paterson proposed the New Jersey Plan, which gave the existing Congress the power to levy import duties and a stamp tax (as in Grenville's imperial reforms of 1764 and 1765), to regulate trade, and to use force to collect delinquent requisitions from the states (as in North's Conciliatory Proposition of 1775). As under the Articles, each state would have one vote. As another alternative, perhaps designed to terrify the small states into accepting the Virginia Plan, Hamilton suggested a government in which both the senate and the executive would serve "on good behavior"—that is, for life! To him, the British constitution still seemed the best in the world, but he never formally proposed his plan.

All of the options before the convention at that point seemed counterrevolutionary. Madison's Parliament for America (or at least what the delegates had seen of it so far), Paterson's emulation of Grenville and North, and Hamilton's enthusiasm for the British empire all challenged in major ways the principles of 1776. But as the summer progressed, the delegates asked themselves what the voters would or would not accept and relearned the hard lessons of popular sovereignty that the state constitutions had taught. The result was a federal Constitution that was truly revolutionary.

Before the Constitution took its final shape, however, the debate grew as hot as the summer weather. The small states warned that their voters would never accept a constitution that let the large states swallow them. The large states insisted on proportional representation in both houses. "The Large States dare not dissolve the Confederation," retorted Delaware's Gunning Bedford in the most inflammatory outburst of the convention. "If they do, the small ones will find some foreign ally of more honor and good faith, who will take them by the hand and do them justice." Then the Connecticut delegates announced that they would be happy with proportional representation in one house and state equality in the other.

In July, the delegates accepted this Connecticut Compromise and then completed the document by September. They finally realized that they were creating a government of laws, to be enforced on individuals through federal courts, and were not propping up a system of congressional resolutions to be carried out (or ignored) by the states. Terms for representatives were reduced to two years, and terms for senators to six, with each state legislature choosing two senators. The president would serve four years, could be reelected, and would be chosen by an **Electoral College.** Each state received as many electors as it had congressmen and senators combined, and the states were free to decide how to choose their electors. Each elector had to vote for two candidates, one of whom had to be from another state. This provision reflected the fear that localist impulses might prevent a majority vote for anyone. The delegates knew that Washington would be the first president, but there was no obvious choice after him.

In other provisions, free and slave states agreed to count only three-fifths of the slaves in apportioning both representation and direct taxes. The enumeration of congressional powers became lengthy and explicit and included taxation, the regulation of foreign and interstate commerce, and the catchall "necessary and proper" clause. Madison's negative on state laws was replaced by the gentler "supreme law of the land" clause. Over George Mason's last-minute objection, the delegates voted not to include a bill of rights.

With little debate, the convention approved a revolutionary proposal for ratifying the Constitution. This clause called for special conventions in each state and declared that the Constitution would go into force as soon as any nine states had accepted it, even though the Articles of Confederation required unanimous approval for all amendments. The delegates understood that they were proposing an illegal but peaceful overthrow of the existing legal order—that is, a revolution. They hoped that once nine or more states accepted the Constitution, the others would follow their example after the new government got under way and would make ratification unanimous. At that point, their revolution would become both peaceful and legal. The Constitution would then rest on popular sovereignty in a way that the Articles never had. The **Federalists,** as supporters of the Constitution now called themselves, were willing to risk destroying the Union in order to save and strengthen it, but they knew that they would have to use persuasion, not force, to win approval.

Ratification

When the Federalist delegates returned home, they made a powerful case for the Constitution in newspapers, most of which favored a stronger central government. Most Anti-Federalists, or opponents of the Constitution, were localists with few interstate contacts and only limited access to the press. The Federalists gave them little time to organize. The first ratifying conventions met in December. Delaware ratified unanimously on December 7, Pennsylvania by a 46-to-23 vote five days later, and New Jersey unanimously on December 18. Georgia ratified unanimously on January 2, and Connecticut soon approved, also by a lopsided margin.

Except in Pennsylvania, these victories were in small states. Ironically, although the Constitution was mostly a "large state" document, small states embraced it while large states hesitated. Small states, once they had equality in the senate, saw many advantages in a strong central government. Under the Articles, for example, New Jersey residents had to pay duties to neighboring states on foreign goods imported through New York City or Philadelphia. Under the new Constitution, import duties would go to the federal government, a clear gain for every small state but Rhode Island, which stood to lose import duties at both Providence and Newport.

By contrast, Pennsylvania was the only large state with a solid majority for ratification. But Anti-Federalists there eloquently demanded a federal bill of rights and major changes in the structure of the new government. Large states could think of going it alone. Small states could not—except for Rhode Island with its two cities and its long history of defying its neighbors.

The first hotly contested state was Massachusetts, which set a pattern for struggles in other divided states. Federalists there won by a slim margin (187 to 168) in February 1788. They blocked Anti-Federalist attempts to make ratification conditional on the adoption of specific amendments. Instead, the Federalists won their slim majority by promising to support a bill of rights by constitutional amendment after ratification. The Rhode Island legislature voted overwhelmingly not even to summon a ratifying convention. Maryland and South Carolina ratified easily in April and May, bringing the total to eight of the nine states required. Then conventions met almost simultaneously in New Hampshire, Virginia, New York, and North Carolina. In each, a majority at first opposed ratification.

As resistance stiffened, the ratification controversy turned into the first great debate about the American Union, over what kind of national government the United States ought to have. Anti-Federalists argued that the new government would be too remote from the people to be trusted with the broad powers specified in the Constitution. They warned that in a House of Representatives divided into districts of 30,000 people (twice the size of Boston), only prominent and wealthy men would be elected. The absence of a bill of rights also troubled them.

During the struggle over ratification, Hamilton, Madison, and Jay wrote a series of 85 essays, published first in New York newspapers and widely reprinted elsewhere, in which they defended the Constitution almost clause by clause. Signing themselves "Publius," they later published the collected essays as *The Federalist Papers*, the most comprehensive body of political thought produced by the Revolutionary generation. In *Federalist, no. 10*, Madison challenged 2,000 years of received wisdom when he argued that a large republic would be far more stable than a small one. Small republics were inherently unstable, he insisted, because majority factions could easily gain power within them, trample on the rights of minorities, and ignore the common good. But in a republic as huge and diverse as the United States, factions would seldom be able to forge a majority. "Publius" hoped that the new government would draw on the talents of the wisest and best-educated citizens. To those who accused him of trying to erect an American aristocracy, he pointed out that the Constitution forbade titles and hereditary rule.

Federalists won a narrow majority (57 to 46) in New Hampshire on June 21, and Madison guided Virginia to ratification (89 to 79) five days later. New York approved, by 30 votes to 27, one month later, bringing 11 states into the Union, enough to launch the new government. North Carolina rejected the Constitution in July 1788 but finally ratified in November 1789 after the first Congress had drafted the Bill of Rights and sent it to the states. Rhode Island, after voting seven times not to call a ratifying convention, finally summoned one that ratified by a vote of only 34 to 32 in May 1790.

Conclusion

Americans survived the most devastating war they had yet fought and won their independence, but only with massive aid from France. Most Indians and blacks who could do so sided with Britain. During the struggle, white Americans affirmed liberty and equality for themselves in their new state constitutions and bills of rights, but they rarely applied these values to blacks and Indians, even though every northern state adopted either immediate or gradual emancipation. The discontent of the postwar years created the Federalist coalition, which drafted and ratified a new national Constitution to replace the Articles of Confederation. Federalists endowed the new central government with more power than Parliament had ever successfully exercised over the colonies but insisted that the Constitution was fully compatible with the liberty and equality proclaimed during the Revolution. Nothing resembling the American federal system had ever been tried before. Under this new system, sovereignty was removed from government and bestowed on the people, who then empowered separate levels of government through their state and federal constitutions. As the Great Seal of the United States proclaimed, it was a *novus ordo seclorum,* a new order for the ages.

SUGGESTED READING

Stephen Conway's *The War of American Independence, 1775–1783* (1995) is a recent history that is strong and accessible. **Charles Royster's** *A Revolutionary People at War: The Continental Army and American Character, 1775–1783* (1979) is the best study of its kind. The essays in **John Shy's** *A People Numerous and Armed: Reflections on the Military Struggle for American Independence,* rev. ed. (1990) have had a tremendous influence on other historians. **David Hackett Fischer's** *Washington's Crossing* (2004) is the most important book on the Revolutionary War to appear in several decades. **Judith L. Van Buskirk,** *Generous Enemies: Patriots and Loyalists in Revolutionary New York* (2002) analyzes patterns in America's most fiercely contested state and is quite insightful about Arnold's treason and André's execution. **Walter Edgar's** *Partisans and Redcoats: The Southern Conflict That Turned the Tide of the American Revolution* (2001) is a fresh study of the bitter partisan war in the Lower South. For the war's impact on slavery, see **Sylvia R. Frey,** *Water from the Rock: Black Resistance in a Revolutionary Age* (1991) and **Arthur Zilversmit,** *The First Emancipation: The Abolition of Slavery in the North* (1967). Of the numerous studies of loyalism, **Paul H. Smith's** *Loyalists and Redcoats: A Study in British Revolutionary Policy* (1964) remains one of the best.

The single most important book on emerging American constitutionalism remains **Gordon S. Wood,** *The Creation of the American Republic, 1776–1787* (1969). **H. James Henderson's** *Party Politics in the Continental Congress* (1974) is a major contribution. **Jackson Turner Main's** *Political Parties before the Constitution* (1973) carefully investigates postwar divisions within the states. **Jack N. Rakove** won a Pulitzer Prize for *Original Meanings: Politics and Ideas in the Making of the Constitution* (1996). **Saul Cornell** provides a thoughtful approach to *The Other Founders: Anti-Federalism and the Dissenting Tradition in America* (1999). **Stuart Leibiger,** *Founding Friendship: George Washington, James Madison, and the Creation of the American Republic* (1999) is insightful and original.

Visit the Liberty Equality Power Companion Web site for resources specific to this textbook: http://www.thomsonedu.com/history/murrin

Also find self-tests and additional resources at ThomsonNOW. ThomsonNOW is an integrated online suite of services and resources with proven ease of use and efficient paths to success, delivering the results you want—NOW!

www.thomsonedu.com/login/

Completing the Revolution, 1789–1815

Almost by acclamation, George Washington became the first president under the Constitution. Washington and his closest advisers (they would soon call themselves Federalists) believed that the balance between power and liberty had tipped toward anarchy after the Revolution. "Local mischiefs," they said, had nearly destroyed the union of the states that had made independence possible. Federalists wanted the Constitution to counter democratic excesses. They were determined to make the national government powerful enough to command respect abroad and to impose order at home. For the most part, they succeeded, but in the process they aroused a determined opposition that feared the Federalists' consolidation of central power at the expense of the states and the citizenry. These self-styled Democratic Republicans (led almost from the beginning by Thomas Jefferson) were as firmly tied to revolutionary ideals of limited government and a citizenry of independent farmers as the Federalists were tied to visions of an orderly commercial republic with a powerful national state. The fight between Federalists and Democratic Republicans echoed the revolutionary contest between liberty and power—conducted this time against an ominous backdrop of international intrigue and war between France (which entered a republican revolution of its own in 1789) and Britain. Only when this Age of Democratic Revolution ended with the defeat of Napoleon in 1815 could the Americans survey the kind of society and government that their Revolution had made.

Establishing the National Government

Focus Question
What was the Federalist plan for organizing the national government and its finances? What were the Jeffersonian Republicans' principal objections to those plans?

George Washington left Mount Vernon for the temporary capital in New York City in April 1789. The way was lined with the grateful citizens of the new republic. Militia companies and local dignitaries escorted him from town to town, crowds cheered, church bells marked his progress, and lines of girls in white dresses waved demurely as he passed. At Newark Bay, he boarded a flower-bedecked barge and, surrounded by scores of boats, crossed to New York City. There he was welcomed by jubilant citizens as he made his way to the president's house. He arrived on April 23 and was inaugurated seven days later.

CHRONOLOGY

1789	George Washington inaugurated as first president of the United States • Judiciary Act establishes the Supreme Court and federal circuit courts
1790	Hamilton delivers his Report on Public Credit to Congress • Congress drafts the Bill of Rights
1794	Federalists' excise tax triggers Whiskey Rebellion
1796	Jay's Treaty and Pinckney's Treaty ratified
1798	XYZ affair results in undeclared war with France • Alien and Sedition Acts passed by Congress
1803	United States purchases Louisiana Territory from France • *Marbury v. Madison* establishes the doctrine of judicial review
1804–06	Lewis and Clark explore the Louisiana Purchase and the Columbia River Basin
1807	*Chesapeake-Leopard* affair ignites anti-British sentiment • Congress passes Embargo Act
1810	Henry Clay elected Speaker of the House
1812	War with England begins
1814	Federalists convene the Hartford Convention. Treaty of Ghent ends the War of 1812
1815	American victory at the Battle of New Orleans

The "Republican Court"

Reporting for work, President Washington found the new government embroiled in its first controversy—an argument over the dignity that would attach to his own office. Vice President John Adams had asked the Senate to create a title of honor for the president. Adams, along with many of the senators, wanted a resounding title that would reflect the power of the new executive. They rejected "His Excellency" because that was the term used for ambassadors, colonial governors, and other minor officials. Among the other titles they considered were "His Highness," "His Mightiness," "His Elective Highness," "His Most Benign Highness," "His Majesty," and "His Highness, the President of the United States, and Protector of Their Liberties." The Senate debated the question for a full month, and then gave up when it became clear that the more democratic House of Representatives disliked titles. They settled on the austere dignity of "Mr. President." A senator from Pennsylvania expressed relief that the "silly business" was over. Thomas Jefferson, who was not yet a member of the government, pronounced the whole affair "the most superlatively ridiculous thing I ever heard of."

Jefferson would learn, however, that much was at stake in the argument over titles. Although the Constitution provided a blueprint for the republic, George Washington's administration would translate the blueprint into a working state. Members of the government knew their decisions would set precedents. It mattered very much what citizens called their president, for that was part of the huge constellation of laws, customs, and forms of etiquette that would give the new government either a republican or (as many anti-Federalists feared) a courtly tone. Many of those close to Washington wanted to protect presidential power from the local-ism and democracy that, they believed, had nearly killed the republic in the 1780s. Washington's stately inaugural tour, the high salaries paid to executive appointees, the endless round of formal balls and presidential din-ners, the observance of the English custom of celebrating the execu-tive's birthday, the appearance of Washington's profile on some of the nation's coins—all were meant to bolster the power and grandeur of the new government, particularly of its executive. When Jefferson became secretary of state and attended official social functions, he often found himself the only democrat at the dinner table. Aristocratic sentiments prevailed, said Jefferson, "unless there chanced to be some [democrat] from the legislative Houses." Thus the battle

© National Portrait Gallery/Smithsonian Institution/Art Resource, NY

George Washington in 1796, Near the End of His Presidency
The artist captured the formal dignity of the first president and surrounded him with gold, red velvet, a presidential throne, and other emblems of kingly power. Only Washington's deeds and reputation suggested an attachment to liberty and equality.

over presidential titles was not "silly business." It was a revealing episode in the argument over how questions of power and liberty that Americans had debated since the 1760s would finally be answered.

The First Congress

Leadership of the First Congress fell to James Madison, the Virginia congressman who had helped write the Constitution. Under his guidance, Congress strengthened the new national government at every turn. First it passed a **tariff** on imports, which would be the government's chief source of income. Next, it turned to amendments to the Constitution demanded by the state ratifying conventions.

Madison proposed 19 constitutional amendments to the House. The 10 that survived con-gressional scrutiny and ratification by the states became the **Bill of Rights.** They reflected fears raised by a generation of struggle with centralized power. The First Amendment guaranteed the freedoms of speech, press, and religion against federal interference. The Second and Third Amendments, prompted by old fears of a standing army, guaranteed the continuation of a militia of armed citizens and stated the specific conditions under which soldiers could be quartered in citizens' households. The Fourth through Eighth Amendments protected and defined a citizen's rights in court and when under arrest—rights whose violation had been central to the Revolution's list of grievances. The Ninth Amendment stated that the enumeration of specific rights in the first eight amendments did not imply a denial of other rights. Finally, the 10th Amendment stated that powers not assigned to the national government by the Constitution remained with the states and the citizenry, though the intentional omission of the word "expressly" left room for argument.

Madison, a committed nationalist, had performed skillfully. Many doubters at the ratifying conventions had called for amendments that would change the government detailed in the Constitution. By channeling their fears into the area of civil liberties, Madison soothed their mistrust while preserving the government of the Constitution. The Bill of Rights was an important guarantee of individual liberties. In the context in which it was written and ratified, however, it was an even more important guarantee of the power of the national government.

To fill out the framework of government outlined in the Constitution, Congress created the executive departments of war, state, and treasury and guaranteed that the heads of those departments and their assistants would be appointed by the president, thus removing them from congressional control. Congress next created the federal courts which were demanded but not specified in the Constitution. The Judiciary Act of 1789 established a Supreme Court with six members, along with 13 district courts and 3 **circuit courts** of appeal. The act allowed certain cases to be appealed from state courts to federal circuit courts presided over by traveling Supreme Court justices, thus dramatizing federal power. As James Madison and other members of the intensely nationalist First Congress surveyed their handiwork, they could congratulate themselves on having strengthened national authority at every opportunity.

Hamiltonian Economics: The National Debt

Washington filled posts in what would become the cabinet with familiar faces. As secretary of war, he chose Henry Knox, an old comrade from the Revolution. The State Department went to his fellow Virginian, Thomas Jefferson. He chose **Alexander Hamilton** of New York, his trusted aide-de-camp during the Revolution, to head the Department of the Treasury.

The most single-minded nationalist in the new government, Hamilton was a brilliant economic thinker, an admirer of the British system of centralized government and finance, and a supremely arrogant and ambitious man. More than other cabinet member, and perhaps even more than Washington (he later referred to Washington's presidency as "my administration"), Hamilton directed the making of a national government.

In 1789, Congress asked Secretary of the Treasury Hamilton to report on the public debt. The debt fell into three categories, Hamilton reported. The first was the $11 million owed to foreigners—primarily debts to France incurred during the Revolution. The second and third—roughly $24 million each—were debts owed by the national and state governments to American citizens who had supplied food, arms, and other resources to the revolutionary cause. Congress agreed that both justice and the credibility of the new government dictated that the foreign debts be paid in full, but the domestic debts raised troublesome questions. Those debts consisted of notes issued during the Revolution to soldiers, and to merchants, farmers, and others who had helped the war effort. Over the years, speculators had purchased many of these notes at a fraction of their face value; when word spread that the Constitution would create a government likely to pay its debts, speculators and their agents fanned out across the countryside, buying all the notes they could find. By 1790, the government debt was concentrated in the hands of businessmen and speculators—most of them northeasterners—who had bought notes at prices only 10 percent to 30 percent of their original value. Full payment would bring them enormous windfall profits.

The Revolutionary War debts of the individual states were another source of contention. Nationalists, with Hamilton at their head, wanted to assume the debts of the states as part of a national debt—a move that would concentrate the interests of public creditors, the need for taxation, and an expanded civil service in the national government. The state debts also had been bought up by speculators, and they posed another problem as well: Many states, including all of the southern states with the exception of South Carolina, had paid off most of their notes in the 1780s; the other states still had significant outstanding debts. If the federal government assumed the state debts and paid them off at the face value of the notes, money would flow out of the southern, middle, and western states into the Northeast, whose citizens would hold fully four-fifths of the combined national debt.

That is precisely what Hamilton proposed in his Report on Public Credit, issued in January 1790. He urged Congress to assume the state debts and to combine them with the federal government's foreign and domestic debts into a consolidated national debt. He agreed that the foreign debt should be paid promptly and in full, but he insisted that the domestic debt be a permanent, tax-supported fixture of government. Under his plan, the government would issue securities to its creditors and would pay an annual rate of interest of 4 percent. Hamilton's funding and assumption plans announced to the international community and to actual and potential government creditors that the United States would pay its bills, but Hamilton had domestic plans for the debt as well. A permanent debt would attract the wealthiest financiers in the country as creditors and would render them loyal and dependent on the federal government. It would bring their economic power to the government and at the same time would require a significant enlargement of the federal civil service, national financial institutions, and increased taxes. The national debt, in short, was at the center of Alexander Hamilton's plan for a powerful national state.

Hamiltonian Economics: The Bank and the Excise

As part of that plan, Hamilton asked Congress to charter a Bank of the United States. The government would store its funds in the bank and would supervise its operations, but the bank would be controlled by directors representing private stockholders. The Bank of the United States would print and back the national currency and would regulate other banks. Hamilton's proposal also made stock in the bank payable in government securities, thus (1) adding to the value of the securities, (2) giving the bank a powerful interest in the fiscal stability of the government, and (3) binding the holders of the securities even closer to the national government. Those who looked closely saw that Hamilton's Bank of the United States was a carbon copy of the Bank of England.

To fund the national debt, Hamilton called for a federal **excise tax** on wines, coffee, tea, and spirits. The tax on spirits would fall most heavily on the whiskey produced in abundance on the frontier. Its purpose, stated openly by Hamilton, was not only to produce revenue but also to establish the government's power to create an internal tax and to collect it in the most remote regions in the republic. The result, as we shall see later in this chapter, was a **Whiskey Rebellion** in the west and an overwhelming display of federal force.

Passed in April 1791, the national bank and the federal excise measures completed Hamilton's organization of government finances. Taken separately, the consolidated government debt, the national bank, and the federal excise tax ably solved discrete problems of government finance. Taken together, however, they constituted a full-scale replica of the treasury-driven government of Great Britain.

The Rise of Opposition

In 1789, nearly everyone in government supported the Constitution. The most radical anti-Federalists took positions in state governments, or left politics altogether. Nearly everyone in the national government was committed to making the new government work. In particular, Alexander Hamilton at Treasury and James Madison in the House of Representatives expected to continue the political and personal friendship they had made while writing the Constitution and working to get it ratified. Yet in the debate over the national debt, Madison led congressional opposition to Hamilton's proposals. In 1792, Thomas Jefferson joined the opposition, insisting that Hamilton's schemes would dismantle the Revolution. Within a few short years, the consensus of 1789 had degenerated into an angry argument over what sort of government would finally result from the American Revolution. More than 25 years later, Jefferson still insisted that the battles of the 1790s had been "contests of principle between the advocates of republican and those of kingly government."

Hamilton presented his national debt proposal to Congress as a solution to specific problems of government finance, not as part of a blueprint for an English-style state. Madison and other southerners opposed it because they did not want northern speculators—many of whom had received information from government insiders—to reap fortunes from notes bought at rock-bottom prices from soldiers, widows, and orphans. He branded Hamilton's plan "public plunder."

At the urging of Jefferson and others, Madison and members of the congressional opposition compromised with Hamilton. In exchange for accepting his proposals on the debt, they won his promise to locate the permanent capital of the United States at a site on the Potomac River. The compromise went to the heart of American revolutionary republicanism. Hamilton intended to tie northeastern commercial interests to the federal government. If New York or Philadelphia became the permanent capital, political and economic power might be concentrated there as it was in Paris and London—court cities in which power, wealth, and every kind of excellence were in league against a plundered and degraded countryside. Benjamin Rush, a Philadelphian, condemned the "government which has begun so soon to ape the corruption of the British Court, conveyed to it through the impure channel of the City of New York." Madison and other agrarians considered Philadelphia just as bad and supported Hamilton's debt only on condition that the capital be moved south. The compromise would distance the commercial power of the cities from the federal government and would put an end to the "republican court" that had formed around Washington. This radically republican move ensured that the capital of the United States would be, except for purposes of government, a place of no importance.

Jefferson versus Hamilton

When Hamilton proposed the Bank of the United States, republicans in Congress immediately noted its similarity to the Bank of England and voiced deep suspicion of Hamilton's economic and governmental plans. Thomas Jefferson joined the opposition, arguing that Congress had no constitutional right to charter a bank, and that allowing Congress to do so would revive the popular fears of centralized despotism that had nearly defeated ratification of the Constitution. Hamilton responded with the first argument for expanded federal power under the clause in the Constitution empowering Congress "to make all laws which shall be necessary and proper" to the performance of its duties. President Washington and a majority in Congress ultimately sided with Hamilton.

Jefferson's strict constructionism (his insistence that the government had no powers beyond those specified in the Constitution) revealed his fears of the de facto constitution that Hamilton's system was making. Jefferson argued that the federal bank was unconstitutional, that a federal excise tax was certain to arouse public opposition, and that funding the debt would reward speculators and penalize ordinary citizens. More important, Jefferson argued, Hamilton used government securities and stock in the Bank of the United States to buy the loyalty not only of merchants and speculators but also of members of Congress. Thirty congressmen owned stock in the Bank of the United States. Many others held government securities or had close ties to men who did. Jefferson charged that this "corrupt squadron" of "papermen" in Congress was, in the classic fashion of evil ministers, enabling

Hamilton to control Congress from his nonelective seat in the executive branch. "The ultimate object of all this," insisted Jefferson, "is to prepare the way for a change, from the present republican form of government, to that of a monarchy, of which the English constitution is to be the model."

For their part, Hamilton and his supporters (who by now were calling themselves Federalists) insisted that centralization of power and a strong executive were necessary to the survival of the republic. The alternative was a return to the localism and public disorder of the 1780s and ultimately to the failure of the Revolution. The argument drew its urgency from the understanding of both Hamilton and his detractors that the United States was a small revolutionary republic in a world governed by kings and aristocrats, and that republics had a long history of failure. They all knew that Americans might yet lose their Revolution. Until late 1792, however, the argument over Hamilton's centralizing schemes were limited to government officials. Hamilton and his supporters tried to mobilize the commercial elite on the side of government, while Madison and Jefferson struggled to hold off the perceived monarchical plot until the citizens could be aroused to defend their liberties. As both sides began to mobilize popular support, events in Europe came to dominate the politics of the American republican experiment, to place that experiment in even greater jeopardy, and to increase the violence of American politics to the point at which the republic almost failed.

The Republic in a World at War, 1793–1797

Late in 1792, French revolutionaries rejected monarchy and proclaimed the French Republic. They beheaded Louis XVI in January 1793. Eleven days later, the French, who were already at war with Austria and Prussia, declared war on conservative Britain, thus launching a war between French republicanism and British-led reaction that, with periodic outbreaks of peace, would embroil the Atlantic world until the defeat of France in 1815.

Americans and the French Revolution

Americans could not have escaped involvement even if they had wanted to. Treaties signed in 1778 allied the United States with France, although Federalists and Jeffersonians would argue whether those treaties applied to the new French Republic or became void with the execution of the monarch who had signed them. Americans had overwhelmingly supported the French Revolution of 1789 and had applauded the progress of French republicanism during its first three years. Both their gratitude for French help during the American Revolution and American hopes for international republicanism faced severe tests in 1793, when the French Republic began to execute thousands of aristocrats, priests, and other "counterrevolutionaries," and when the French threatened the sovereignty of nations by declaring a war of all peoples against all monarchies. The argument between Jeffersonian republicanism and Hamiltonian centralization was no longer a squabble within the U.S.

government. National politics was now caught up and subsumed within the struggle over international republicanism.

As Britain and France went to war in 1793, President Washington declared American neutrality, thereby **abrogating** obligations made in the 1778 treaties with the French. Washington and most of his advisers realized that the United States was in no condition to fight a war. They also wanted to stay on good terms with Great Britain. Ninety percent of American imports came from Britain, and 90 percent of the federal revenue came from customs duties on those imports. Thus both the nation's commerce and the financial health of the government depended on good relations with Great Britain. Moreover, Federalists genuinely sympathized with the British in the war with France. They regarded the United States as a "perfected" England and viewed Britain as the defender of hierarchical society and ordered liberty against the homicidal anarchy of the French.

Jefferson and his friends saw things differently. They applauded the French for carrying on the republican revolution Americans had begun in 1776, and they had no affection for the monarchical politics of the Federalists or for Americans' continued neocolonial dependence on British trade. The faction led by Jefferson and Madison wanted to abandon the English mercantile system and trade freely with all nations. They did not care if that course of action hurt commercial interests (most of which supported the Federalists) or impaired the government's ability to centralize power in itself. Although they agreed that the United States should stay out of the war, the Jeffersonians sympathized as openly with the French as the Federalists did with the British.

Citizen Genêt

Throughout the war years from 1793 to 1815, both Great Britain and France, by intervening freely in the internal affairs of the United States, made American isolationism impossible.

In April 1793, the French sent Citizen Edmond Genêt as minister to the United States. Genêt's ruling Girondists were the revolutionary faction that had declared the war on all monarchies; they ordered Genêt to enlist American aid with or without the Washington administration's consent. After the president's proclamation of neutrality, Genêt openly commissioned American privateers to harass British shipping and enlisted Americans in intrigues against the Spanish outpost of New Orleans. Genêt then opened France's Caribbean colonies to American shipping, providing American shippers a choice between French free trade and British mercantilism. Genêt's mission ended abruptly in summer 1793, when Robespierre and the infamous Terror drove the Girondists from power. Learning that he would be guillotined if he returned to France, Genêt accepted the hospitality of Americans, married a daughter of George Clinton, the old anti-Federalist governor of New York, and lived out the rest of his life as an American country gentleman.

The British responded to Genêt's free-trade declaration with a promise to seize any ship trading with French colonies in the Caribbean. Word of these Orders in Council—almost certainly by design—reached the Royal Navy before American merchant seamen had learned of them, with the result that 250 American ships fell into British hands. The Royal

Navy also began searching American ships for English sailors who had deserted or who had switched to safer, better-paying work in the American merchant marine. Inevitably, some American sailors were kidnapped into the British navy in a contemptuous and infuriating assault on American sovereignty. Meanwhile, the British, operating from Canada and from their still-garrisoned forts in the Northwest, began promising military aid to the Indians north of the Ohio River. Thus, while the French ignored the neutrality of the United States, the English engaged in both overt and covert acts of war.

Western Troubles: The Whiskey Rebellion

The problems with France and on the high seas were accompanied by an intensified threat from British and Indian forces in the west, as well as from settlers in that region. The situation came to a head in summer and fall 1794. The Shawnee and allied tribes plotted with the British and talked of driving all settlers out of their territory. At the same time, frontier whites, sometimes with the encouragement of English and Spanish officials, grew increasingly contemptuous of a national government that could neither pacify the Indians nor guarantee their free use of the Mississippi River. President Washington heard that 2,000 Kentuckians were armed and ready to attack New Orleans—a move that would have started a war between the United States and Spain. Settlers in Georgia were making unauthorized forays against the Creeks, and settlers up and down the frontier refused to pay the Federalists' excise tax on whiskey—a direct challenge to federal authority. In western Pennsylvania, mobs tarred and feathered excise officers and burned the property of distillers who paid the tax. In July 1794, near Pittsburgh, 500 militiamen marched on the house of General John Neville, one of the most hated of the federal excise collectors. Neville, his family, and a few federal soldiers fought the militiamen, killing two and wounding six before they abandoned the house to be looted and burned. Two weeks later, 6,000 "Whiskey Rebels" met at Braddock's Field near Pittsburgh, threatening to attack the town.

Faced with serious international and domestic threats to his new government, Washington determined to defeat the Indians and the Whiskey Rebels by force, thus securing American control of the Northwest. He sent General "Mad Anthony" Wayne against the northwestern tribes. Wayne's decisive victory at Fallen Timbers in August 1794—fought almost in the shadow of a British fort—ended the Indian–British challenge in the Northwest for many years. In September, Washington ordered 12,000 federalized militiamen from eastern Pennsylvania, Maryland, Virginia, and New Jersey to quell the Whiskey Rebellion. The president promised amnesty to rebels who pledged to support the government and prison terms to those who did not. As the army marched west from Carlisle, they found defiant liberty poles but no armed resistance. Arriving at Pittsburgh, the army arrested 20 suspected rebels—none of them leaders—and marched them back to Philadelphia for trial. In the end, only two "rebels," both of them feebleminded, were convicted. President Washington pardoned them, and the Whiskey Rebellion was over.

Western Troubles: Indians

Focus Question

What were the principal reasons why Indian peoples between the Appalachian Mountains and the Mississippi River gave way to white settlement?

Although many of the woodland tribes were still intact and still living on their ancestral lands in 1790, they were in serious trouble. The Iroquois had been restricted to reservations in New York and Pennsylvania, and many had fled to Canada. In the Old Northwest, the Shawnee, Miami, and other tribes—with the help of the British, who still occupied seven forts within what was formally the United States—continued to trade furs and to impede white settlement. Skirmishes with settlers, however, brought reprisals, and the Indians faced not only hostile pioneers but the U.S. Army as well. In the Ohio country, punitive expeditions led by General Josiah Harmar and General Arthur St. Clair failed in 1790 and 1791—the second ending in an Indian victory in which 630 soldiers died.

In 1794, President Washington sent a third army, under General "Mad Anthony" Wayne, which defeated the Indians at Fallen Timbers, near present-day Toledo. The Treaty of Greenville forced the Native Americans to cede two-thirds of what are now Ohio and southeastern Indiana. At this point, the British decided to abandon their forts in the Old Northwest. Following their victory at Fallen Timbers, whites filtered into what remained of Indian lands. In 1796, President Washington threw up his hands and announced that "I believe scarcely any thing, short of a Chinese Wall, or a line of troops, will restrain Land Jobbers and the encroachment of settlers upon the Indian Territory." Five years later, Governor William Henry Harrison of Indiana Territory admitted that frontier whites "consider the murdering of the Indians in the highest degree meritorious."

The Jay Treaty

While he sent armies against Indians and frontiersmen, President Washington capitulated to the British on the high seas. In 1794, he sent John Jay, chief justice of the Supreme Court, to negotiate the conflicts between the United States and Britain. Armed with news of Wayne's victory, Jay extracted a promise from the British to remove their troops from American territory in the Northwest. On every other point of dispute, however, he agreed to British terms. The Jay Treaty made no mention of **impressment** or other violations of American maritime rights, nor did it refer to the old issue of British payment for slaves carried off during the Revolution. The treaty did allow small American ships back into the West Indies, but only on terms that the Senate would reject. In short, Jay's Treaty granted British trade a most-favored-nation basis in exchange for the agreement of the British to abandon their northwestern forts. Given the power of Great Britain, it was the best that Americans could expect. Washington, obliged to choose between an unpopular treaty and an unwinnable war, passed Jay's Treaty on to the Senate, which, in June 1795, ratified it by a bare two-thirds majority.

Map 7.1   The West, 1790–1796   In 1790, the United States "owned" nearly all of its present territory east of the Mississippi River, but white Americans remained concentrated east of the Appalachians (see Map 8.1 Population Density, 1790–1820, in the color insert following page 384), and independent Indian peoples controlled most of the map of the United States. The Battle of Fallen Timbers and the resultant Treaty of Greenville pushed white settlement across Ohio and into Indiana, but the Indians of the Northwest remained intact, determined, and in touch with the British in Canada. Native Americans also controlled nearly all of the Southwest, and Florida and the Gulf Coast—including all outlets from the interior to the Caribbean—remained in Spanish hands. The American west was very far from secure in the 1790s.

During the fight over Jay's Treaty, dissension within the government was first aired in public. The seaport cities and much of the Northeast reacted favorably to the treaty. It ruled out war with England and cemented an Anglo-American trade relationship that strengthened both Hamilton's national state and the established commercial interests that supported it. Moreover, northeasterners held little enthusiasm for the French Revolution, particularly in New England, with its long history of colonial wars with France. The South, on the other hand, saw Jay's Treaty as a blatant sign of the designs of Britain and the Federalists to subvert republicanism in both France and the United States. The Virginia legislature branded the treaty as unconstitutional, and Republican congressmen demanded to see all documents relating to Jay's negotiations. Washington responded by telling them that their request could be legitimate only if the House was planning to initiate **impeachment** proceedings, thus tying approval of the treaty to his enormous personal prestige.

Meanwhile, on March 3, 1796, Washington released the details of a treaty that Thomas Pinckney had negotiated with Spain. In this treaty, Spain recognized American neutrality and set the border between the United States and Spanish Florida on American terms. Most important, the Pinckney Treaty ended Spanish claims to territory in the Southwest and gave Americans the unrestricted right to navigate the Mississippi River and to trans-ship produce at the Spanish port of New Orleans. Coupled with the victory at Fallen Timbers, the British promise to abandon their posts in the Northwest, and Washington's personal popularity, Pinckney's Treaty helped turn the tide in favor of the unpopular Jay's Treaty. With a diminishing number of hotheads willing to oppose Washington, western representatives joined the Northeast and increasing numbers of southerners to ratify Jay's Treaty.

Washington's Farewell

George Washington refused to run for reelection in 1796, thus setting a two-term limit observed by every president until Franklin Roosevelt (see chapter 25). Washington could be proud of his accomplishment. He had presided over the creation of a national government. He had secured American control over the western settlements by ending British, Spanish, and Indian military threats and by securing free use of the Mississippi River for western produce. Those policies, together with the federal invasion of western Pennsylvania, had made it evident that the government could control its most distant regions. Washington had also avoided war with Great Britain, although not without overlooking assaults on American sovereignty. As he was about to leave government, he wrote, with substantial help from Hamilton, his Farewell Address. In it he warned against long-term "entangling alliances" with other countries. America, he said, should act independently in international affairs—an ideal that many felt had been betrayed in Jay's Treaty. Washington also warned against internal political divisions. Of course, he did not regard his own Federalists as a party. They were simply friends of the government. But he saw Jefferson's Democratic Republicans as a self-interested faction, thus branding them, in the language of classical republicanism, as public enemies. Washington's call for national unity and an end to partisanship was in fact a parting shot at the Democratic Republican opposition.

The Election of 1796

Washington's retirement opened the way to the competition for public office that he had feared: in 1796, Americans experienced their first contested presidential election. The Federalists chose as their candidate John Adams of Massachusetts, who had served as vice president. The Democratic Republicans nominated Thomas Jefferson. According to the gentlemanly custom of the day, neither candidate campaigned in person, but friends of the candidates, the newspaper editors who enjoyed their patronage, and even European governments ensured that the election would be hotly contested.

Adams would certainly carry New England and Jefferson would carry the South. The election would be decided in Pennsylvania and New York. Some states, most of them in the South, chose presidential electors by direct vote, but in the crucial mid-Atlantic states, state legislatures selected the presidential electors. The election of 1796 would be decided in elections to the legislatures of those states and in subsequent intriguing within those bodies. John Beckley, clerk of the House of Representatives, devised the Republican strategy in Pennsylvania. He secretly circulated a list of well-known and respected Jeffersonian candidates for the state legislature. Discovering the Republican slate only when it was too late to construct a similar list, the Federalists lost Pennsylvania. New York, however, had no John Beckley. Adams took the state's electoral votes and won the national election. The distribution of electoral votes revealed the bases of Federalist and Republican support: Adams received only 2 electoral votes south of the Potomac, and Jefferson received only 18 (all but 5 of them in Pennsylvania) north of the Potomac.

The voting was over, but the intriguing was not. Alexander Hamilton, who had retired from the Treasury in 1795, knew that he could not manipulate the independent and

© North Wind Picture Archives.

Washington, D.C.   The Americans built a capital city that had no function other than republican government. It had no mercantile or financial establishments, no theaters, and no military fortress. Broad, straight streets stretched beyond the built-up areas of the town; visually as well as politically, Washington, D.C. was dependent upon and vulnerable to the countryside—the opposite of European court cities. It was the kind of capital that American republicans wanted.

almost perversely upright John Adams. So he secretly instructed South Carolina's Federalist electors to withhold their votes from Adams. That would have given the presidency to Adams's running mate, Thomas Pinckney, relegating Adams to the vice presidency. (Before the ratification of the 12th Amendment in 1804, the candidate with a majority of the electoral votes became president, and the second-place candidate became vice president.) Like some of Hamilton's other schemes, this one backfired. New England electors heard of the plan and angrily withheld their votes from Pinckney. As a result, Adams was elected president and his opponent Thomas Jefferson became vice president. Adams narrowly won the election, but he took office with a justifiable mistrust of many members of his own party and with the head of the opposition party as his second in command. It was not an auspicious beginning.

Troubles with France, 1796–1800

As Adams entered office, an international crisis was already in full swing. France regarded Jay's Treaty as an Anglo-American alliance, and had broken off relations with the United States. The French hinted that they intended to overthrow the reactionary government of the United States but would postpone taking action in the hope that a friendlier Thomas Jefferson would replace "old man Washington" in 1797. Then, during the crucial elections in Pennsylvania, they stepped up their seizures of American ships trading with Britain, giving the Americans a taste of what would happen if they did not elect a government that was friendlier to France. When the election went to John Adams, the French gave up on the United States and set about denying Britain its new de facto ally. In 1797, the French ordered that American ships carrying "so much as a handkerchief" made in England be confiscated without compensation, and announced that American seamen serving in the British navy would be summarily hanged if captured.

President Adams wanted to protect American commerce from French depredations, but he knew that the United States might not survive a war with France. He also knew that French grievances (including Jay's Treaty and the abrogation of the French-American treaties of 1778) were legitimate. He decided to send a mission to France, made up of three respected statesmen: Charles Cotesworth Pinckney of South Carolina, John Marshall of Virginia, and Elbridge Gerry of Massachusetts. When the delegates reached Paris, however, they were left cooling their heels in the outer offices of the Directory—the revolutionary committee of five that had replaced France's beheaded king. At last, three French officials (the correspondence identified them only as "X, Y, and Z," and the incident later became known as the **XYZ affair**) discreetly hinted that France would receive them if they paid a bribe of $250,000, arranged for the United States to loan $12 million to the French government, and apologized for unpleasant remarks that John Adams had made about France. The delegates refused, saying "No, not a sixpence," and returned home. There a journalist transformed their remark into "Millions for defense, but not one cent for tribute."

President Adams asked Congress to prepare for war, and the French responded by seizing more American ships. Thus began, in April 1798, an undeclared war between France and the United States in the Caribbean. While the French navy dealt with the British in the North Atlantic, French privateers inflicted costly blows on American shipping. But after nearly a year of fighting, with the British providing powder and shot for American guns, the U.S. Navy chased the French privateers out of the Caribbean.

The Crisis at Home, 1798–1800

Focus Question
What was the nature of the governmental crisis of 1798–1800, and how was it resolved?

The troubles with France precipitated a crisis at home. Disclosure of the XYZ correspondence, together with the quasi-war in the Caribbean, produced a surge of public hostility toward the French and, to some extent, toward their Republican friends in the United States. Many Federalists, led by Alexander Hamilton, wanted to use the crisis to destroy their political opponents. Without consulting President Adams, the Federalist-dominated Congress passed several wartime measures. The first was a federal property tax—graduated, spread equally between sections of the country, and justified by military necessity, but a direct federal tax nonetheless. Congress then passed four laws known as the Alien and Sedition Acts. The first three were directed at immigrants: They extended the **naturalization** period from 5 to 14 years and empowered the president to detain enemy **aliens** during wartime and to deport those he deemed dangerous to the United States. The fourth law—the Sedition Act—set jail terms and fines for persons who advocated disobedience to federal law or who wrote, printed, or spoke "false, scandalous, and malicious" statements against "the government of the United States, or the President of the United States [note that Vice President Jefferson was not included], with intent to defame . . . or to bring them or either of them, into contempt or disrepute."

President Adams never used the powers granted under the Alien Acts, but the Sedition Act resulted in the prosecution of 14 Republicans, most of them journalists. William Duane, editor of the *Philadelphia Aurora*, was indicted when he and two Irish friends circulated a petition against the Alien Act on the grounds of a Catholic church. James Callendar, editor of a Jeffersonian newspaper in Richmond, was arrested, while another prominent Republican went to jail for statements made in a private letter. Matthew Lyon, a scurrilous Republican congressman from Vermont, had brawled with a Federalist representative in the House chamber; he went to jail for his criticisms of President Adams, Federalist militarism, and what he called the "ridiculous pomp" of the national administration.

Republicans charged that the Alien and Sedition Acts violated the First Amendment, and they turned to the states for help. Southern states, which had provided only 4 of the 44 congressional votes for the Sedition Act, took the lead. Jefferson provided the Kentucky legislature with draft resolutions, and Madison did the same for the Virginia legislature. These so-called Virginia and Kentucky Resolves restated the constitutional fundamentalism that had guided Republican opposition from the beginning. Jefferson's Kentucky Resolves reminded Congress that the Alien and Sedition Acts gave the national government powers not mentioned in the Constitution and that the 10th Amendment reserved such powers to the states. He also argued that the Constitution was a "compact" between sovereign states and that state legislatures could "nullify" federal laws they deemed unconstitutional, thus anticipating constitutional theories that states'-rights southerners would use after 1830.

The Virginia and Kentucky Resolves demonstrated the extremes to which Jefferson and Madison might go. Beyond that, however, they had few effects. Opposition to the Sedition Act ranged from popular attempts to obstruct the law to fistfights in Congress, and Virginia began calling up its militia. No other states followed the lead of Virginia and Kentucky, however, and talk of armed opposition to Federalist policies was limited to a few areas in the South.

The Politicians and the Army

Federalists took another ominous step by implementing President Adams's request that Congress create a military prepared for war. Adams wanted a stronger navy, both because the undeclared war with France was being fought on the ocean and because he agreed with other Federalists that America's future as a commercial nation required a respectable navy. Hamilton and others (who were becoming known as **"High Federalists"**) preferred a standing army. At the urging of Washington and against his own judgment, Adams appointed Hamilton inspector general. As such, Hamilton would be the de facto commander of the U.S. Army. Congress authorized a 20,000-man army, and Hamilton proceeded to raise it. Congress also provided for a much larger army to be called up in the event of a declaration of war. When Hamilton expanded the officer corps in anticipation of such an army, he excluded Republicans and commissioned only his political friends. High Federalists wanted a standing army to enforce the Alien and Sedition Acts and to put down an impending rebellion in the South. Beyond that, there was little need for such a force. The war was being fought at sea, and most Americans believed that the citizen militia could hold off any land invasion until an army was raised. The Republicans, President Adams, and many other Federalists now became convinced that Hamilton and his High Federalists were determined to destroy their political opponents, enter into an alliance with Great Britain, and impose Hamilton's statist designs on the nation by force. By 1799, Adams and many of his Federalist friends had come to see Hamilton and his supporters as dangerous, antirepublican militarists.

Adams was angry. First the Hamiltonians had tried to rob him of the presidency. Then they had passed the Alien and Sedition Acts, the direct tax, and plans for a standing army without consulting him. None of this would have been possible if not for the crisis with France.

Adams, who had resisted calls for a declaration of war, began looking for ways to declare peace. In a move that he knew would split his party and probably cost him reelection in 1800, he opened negotiations with France and stalled the creation of Hamilton's army while the talks took place. At first, the Senate refused to send an envoy to France. They relented when Adams threatened to resign and leave the presidency to Vice President Jefferson. In the agreement that followed, the French canceled the obligations that the United States had assumed under the treaties of 1778. But they refused to pay reparations for attacks on American shipping since 1793—the very point over which many Federalists had wanted war. Peace with France cut the ground from under the more militaristic and repressive Federalists and intensified discord among the Federalists in general. (Hamilton would campaign against Adams in 1800.) It also damaged Adams's chances for reelection.

The Election of 1800

Thomas Jefferson and his Democratic-Republicans approached the election of 1800 better organized and more determined than they had been four years earlier. Moreover, events in the months preceding the election worked in their favor. The Alien and Sedition Acts, the direct tax of 1798, and the Federalist military buildup were never popular. Even when peace with France was certain, the Federalists continued. The army suppressed a minor tax rebellion led by Jacob Fries in Pennsylvania, prosecutions under the Sedition Act revealed its partisan origins, and the Federalists showed no sign of repealing the tax or abandoning the Alien and Sedition Acts and the new military. Taken together, these events gave credence to the Republicans' allegation that the Federalists were using the crisis with France to consolidate their power, destroy liberty and the opposition, and overthrow the American republic. The Federalists countered by warning that the election of Jefferson and his radical allies would release the worst horrors of the French Revolution onto the streets of American towns. A Connecticut Federalist moaned that "There is scarcely a possibility that we shall escape *Civil War*" following a Republican victory, and predicted other bad results: "murder, robbery, rape, adultery, and incest will all be openly taught and practiced, the air will be rent with the cries of distress, the soil will be soaked with blood, and the nation black with crimes." Alexander Hamilton put it succinctly: the election of Jefferson would lead to the "overthrow . . . [of] the Government" by a "Revolution after the manner of Bonaparte." Each side believed that its defeat in 1800 would mean the end of the republic.

The Democratic-Republicans were strong in the South and weak in the Northeast. Jefferson knew that he had to win New York, the state that had cost him the 1796 election. Jefferson's running mate, **Aaron Burr,** arranged a truce in New York between Republican factions led by the Clinton and Livingston families and chose candidates for the state legislature who were both locally respected and committed to Jefferson. In New York City, Burr played skillfully on the interests and resentments of craftsmen and granted favors to merchants who worked outside the British trade that was dominated by Federalist insiders. The strategy succeeded. The Republicans carried New York City and won a slight majority in the legislature. New York's electoral votes belonged to Jefferson. (When it became clear that Jefferson had won the state, Hamilton suggested changing the law so that New York's electors would be chosen by popular vote; John Jay, the Federalist Governor of New York, rejected the suggestion.) The election was decided in South Carolina, which after a brisk campaign cast its votes for Jefferson.

Jefferson and Burr had won with 73 votes each. Adams had 65 votes, and his running mate Charles Cotesworth Pinckney had 64. (In order to distinguish between their presidential and vice-presidential candidates—and thus thwart yet another of Hamilton's attempts to rig the election—the Federalists of Rhode Island had withheld one vote from Pinckney.) Jefferson and Burr had tied, though everyone knew that Jefferson was the presidential candidate. But under the Constitution, a **lame-duck** Federalist Congress decided whether Jefferson or Burr was to be President. Federalists talked of choosing Burr. Jefferson wrote that Democratic Republicans had decided "to declare openly and firmly, one and all, that the day such an act passed, the Middle States would arm, and that no such usurpation, even for a single day, should be submitted to." One of his supporters put it more bluntly: anyone other than Jefferson "who should thus be appointed President by law and accept the office would instantaneously be put to death."

The Republican governors of Pennsylvania and Virginia made plans to call up the militia to prevent the expected usurpation. After six quarrelsome days and 35 ballots on which most Federalist Congressmen voted for Burr (whose part in these proceedings has never been fully uncovered), a compromise was reached: Many Federalists abandoned Burr but turned in blank ballots and thus avoided voting for the hated (but victorious) Jefferson. With that, the "Revolution of 1800" had won its first round.

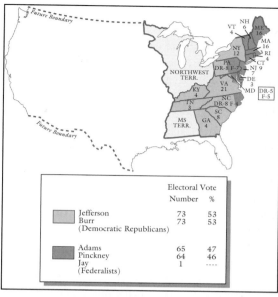

Map 7.2 Presidential Election, 1800 The electoral votes in 1800 split along starkly sectional lines. The South voted for Jefferson, New England voted for Adams, and the election was decided by close contests in Pennsylvania and New York.

The Jeffersonians in Power

Focus Question
What were the principal reforms of the national government during Thomas Jefferson's administration? What were the implications of those reforms for the nature of republican government?

On the first Tuesday of March 1801, Thomas Jefferson left his rooms at Conrad and McMunn's boardinghouse in Washington and walked up Pennsylvania Avenue. Jefferson received military salutes along the way, but he forbade the pomp and ceremony that had ushered Washington into office. Accompanied by a few friends and a company of artillery from the Maryland militia (and not by Hamilton's professional military), Jefferson walked (no carriages) up the street and into the unfinished capitol building. The central tower and the wing that would house Congress were only half completed. Jefferson joined Vice President Burr, other members of the government, and a few foreign diplomats in the newly finished Senate chamber.

The Republican Program

Jefferson took the oath of office from Chief Justice John Marshall, a distant relative and political opponent from Virginia. Then, in a small voice that was almost inaudible to those at a distance, he delivered his inaugural address. Referring to the political discord that had brought him into office, he began with a plea for unity, insisting that "every difference of opinion is not a difference of principle. We have called by different names brethren of the same principle. We are all Republicans, we are all Federalists." Jefferson did not mean that he and his opponents should forget their ideological differences. He meant only to invite moderate Federalists into a broad Republican coalition in which there was no room for the statist designs of Alexander Hamilton and his High Federalist friends.

Jefferson went on to outline the kind of government a republic should have. Grateful that the Atlantic Ocean separated the United States from "the exterminating havoc" of Europe and that America possessed "a chosen country, with room for our descendants to the thousandth and thousandth generation," he declared that Americans were a free people with no need for a national state built on European models. A people blessed with isolation, bountiful resources, and liberty needed only "a wise and frugal Government, which shall restrain men from injuring one another, shall leave them otherwise free to regulate their own pursuits of industry and improvement, and shall not take from the mouth of labor the bread it has earned. This is the sum of good government, and thus is necessary to close the circle of our felicities."

In particular, Jefferson's "wise and frugal" government would respect the powers of the states. It would also defend the liberties ensured by the Bill of Rights. It would be smaller, and it would pay its debts without incurring new ones, thus ending the need for taxation and cutting the ground from beneath the burgeoning Federalist state. It would rely for defense on "a disciplined militia" that would fight invaders while regulars were being trained, thus eliminating Hamilton's standing army. It would protect republican liberties from enemies at home and from the nations of Europe. And, Jefferson promised, it would ensure "the encouragement of agriculture, and of commerce as its handmaiden." Beyond the fostering of an agrarian republic and the maintenance of limited government, Jefferson promised little. Blessed with peace abroad and the defeat of the High Federalists at home, he believed that the United States could at last enter into its experiment with truly republican government.

The simplicity of Jefferson's inauguration set the social tone of his administration. The new president reduced the number and grandeur of formal balls, levees, and dinners. He sent his annual messages to Congress to be read by a clerk, rather than delivering them in person in the manner of English kings and Federalist presidents. He refused to ride about Washington in a carriage, preferring to carry out his errands on horseback. Abandoning grand banquets, Jefferson entertained senators and congressmen at small dinners, which were served at a round table without formal seating, thus ending the fine-tuned hierarchy of the Federalists' old arrangements. Jefferson presided over the meals without wearing a wig and dressed in old homespun clothes and a pair of worn bedroom slippers. The casualness (slovenliness, said some of his critics) did not extend to what was served at dinner, however. The food was prepared by expert chefs and accompanied by fine wines, and it was followed by brilliant conversation perfected by Jefferson while he was a diplomat and a visitor to the salons of Paris. The president's dinners set examples of the unpretentious excellence through which this cultivated country squire hoped to govern.

Cleansing the Government

Jefferson's first order of business was to reduce the size and expense of government. The Federalists, despite their elitism and their statist dispositions, had left a surprisingly small federal establishment. Jefferson found only 316 employees who were subject to presidential appointment and removal. Those employees, together with 700 clerks and assistants and 3,000 post office workers, made up the entire federal civil service. Jefferson reduced the diplomatic corps and replaced officeholders who were incompetent, corrupt, or avowedly antirepublican. Even so, the rate of turnover was only about 50 percent during his first term. The replacements were not the violent revolutionaries that Federalists had warned against but Republican gentlemen who matched or exceeded the social status of the departed Federalists. Jefferson altered the politics of the civil service, but he left its size and shape intact.

Legislation passed in March 1802 reduced the army to two regiments of infantry and one of artillery—a total of 3,350 officers and men, most of whom were assigned to western posts far from the centers of white population. Similar cutbacks reduced the navy. The goal, Jefferson explained, was to rely mainly on the militia for national defense but to maintain a small, well-trained professional army as well. (The same legislation that reduced the army created the military academy at West Point.) At Jefferson's urging, Congress also abolished the direct tax of 1798 and repealed the parts of the Alien and Sedition Acts that had not already expired. Jefferson personally pardoned the 10 victims of those acts who were still in jail and repaid their fines with interest.

Thus with a few strokes, Jefferson dismantled the repressive apparatus of the Federalist state. By reducing government expenditures, he reduced the government's debt and the

© The Granger Collection, New York

A Federalist Attack upon Jefferson   From the beginning, Federalists branded Jefferson as a friend to a French Revolution that had promised liberty and equality, then degenerated into violence and dictatorship. Here Jefferson worships at the altar of Gallic Despotism while the American eagle fights to protect the Constitution and the accomplishments of Federalist administrations.

army of civil servants and papermen gathered around it. During Jefferson's administration, the national debt fell from $80 million to $57 million, and the government built up a treasury surplus, even after paying $15 million in cash for the **Louisiana Purchase** (discussed later in this chapter). Although some doubted the wisdom of such stringent economy, no one doubted Jefferson's frugality.

The Jeffersonians and the Courts

Jefferson's demands for a "wise and frugal" government applied to the federal judiciary as well as to other branches. The Constitution had created the Supreme Court but had left the creation of lesser federal courts to Congress. The First Congress had created a system of circuit courts presided over by the justices of the Supreme Court. Only Federalists served on the Supreme Court under Washington and Adams, and Federalists on the circuit courts had extended federal authority into the hinterland—a fact that prosecutions under the Alien and Sedition Acts had made abundantly clear. Jeffersonians distrusted the federal courts. Their distrust was intensified by the Judiciary Act of 1801, passed just before Jefferson's inauguration by the lame-duck Federalist Congress. Coupled with President Adams's appointment of Federalist John Marshall as chief justice in January, the Judiciary Act ensured long-term Federalist domination of the federal courts. First, it reduced the number of associate justices of the Supreme Court from six to five when the next vacancy occurred, thus reducing Jefferson's chances of appointing a new member to the Court. The Judiciary Act also took Supreme Court justices off circuit and created a new system of circuit courts. This allowed Adams to appoint 16 new judges, along with marshals, federal attorneys, clerks, and justices of the peace. Adams worked until nine o'clock on his last night in office signing commissions for these new officers. All of them were staunch Federalists.

Republicans disagreed on what to do about the Federalists' packing of the courts. A minority distrusted the whole idea of an independent judiciary and wanted judges elected by popular vote. Jefferson and most in his party wanted the courts shielded from democratic control; at the same time, they deeply resented the Federalist **"midnight judges"** created by the Judiciary Act of 1801. Jefferson did replace the new federal marshals and attorneys with Republicans and dismissed some of the federal justices of the peace, but judges were appointed for life and could be removed only through impeachment. The Jeffersonians hit on a simple solution: They would get rid of the new judges by abolishing their jobs. Early in 1802, with some of Jefferson's supporters questioning the constitutionality of what they were doing, Congress repealed the Judiciary Act of 1801 and thus did away with the midnight appointees.

The Impeachments of Pickering and Chase

With the federal courts scaled back to their original size, Republicans in Congress, led by the Virginia agrarian John Randolph, went after High Federalists who were still acting as judges. As a first test of impeachment, they chose John Pickering, a federal attorney with the circuit court of New Hampshire. Pickering was a highly partisan Federalist. He was also a notorious alcoholic and clearly insane. The Federalists who had appointed him had long considered him an embarrassment. The House drew up articles of impeachment, and the senate removed Pickering by a strict party vote.

On the same day, Congress went after bigger game: They voted to impeach Supreme Court Justice Samuel Chase. Chase was a much more prominent public figure than Pickering, and his "crimes" were not alcoholism or insanity but mere partisanship. He hated the Jeffersonians, and he had prosecuted sedition cases with real enthusiasm. He had also delivered anti-Jeffersonian diatribes from the bench, and he had used his position and his formidable legal skills to bully young lawyers with whom he disagreed. In short, Chase was an unpleasant, overbearing, and unashamedly partisan member of the Supreme Court. Even so, his faults did not add up to the "high crimes and misdemeanors" that are the constitutional grounds for impeachment.

Moderate Republicans doubted the wisdom of the Chase impeachment, and their uneasiness grew when Congressman John Randolph took over the prosecution. Randolph led a radical states'-rights faction that violently disapproved of, among other things, the way Jefferson had settled a southern land controversy. A corrupt Georgia legislature had sold huge parcels in Mississippi and Alabama to the Yazoo Land Company, which in turn had sold them to private investors, many of them New England speculators. When a new Georgia legislature rescinded the sale and turned the land over to the federal government in 1802, Jefferson agreed to pay off the investors' claims with federal money.

As Randolph led the prosecution of Samuel Chase, he lectured in his high-pitched voice that Jefferson was double-crossing southern Republicans in an effort to win support in the Northeast. Most of the Republican senators disagreed, and some of them withdrew their support from the impeachment proceedings in order to isolate and humiliate Randolph and his friends. With Jefferson's approval, many Republicans in the Senate joined the Federalists in voting to acquit Samuel Chase.

Justice Marshall's Court

Chief Justice John Marshall probably cheered the acquittal of Justice Chase, because it was clear that Marshall was next on the list. Secretary of state under John Adams, Marshall was committed to Federalist ideas of national power, as he demonstrated with his decision in the case of **Marbury v. Madison.** William Marbury was one of the justices of the peace whom Jefferson had eliminated in his first few days in office. He sued Jefferson's secretary of state, James Madison, for his commission. Although Marbury never got his job, Marshall used the case to hand down several important rulings. The first ruling questioned the constitutionality of Jefferson's refusal to deliver Marbury's commission. It helped convince Republican moderates to repeal the Judiciary Act of 1801. The last ruling, delivered in February 1803, laid the basis for the practice of **judicial review**—that is, the Supreme Court's power to rule on the constitutionality of acts of Congress. In arguing that Congress could not alter the jurisdiction of the Supreme Court, Marshall stated that the Constitution is "fundamental and paramount law" and that it is "emphatically the province and duty of the judicial department to say what law is."

Some Republicans saw Marshall's ruling as an attempt to arrogate power to the Court, but John Marshall was not a sinister man. As secretary of state under John Adams, he had

Map 3.4   Government and Religion in the British Colonies, 1720   This map shows which colonies were royal, proprietary, or corporate in structure and whether Anglican or Congregational churches were established by law or whether, instead, the Quakers or the Dutch Reformed church predominated or numerous sects competed for the loyalties of the settlers.

Map 5.1   Pontiac's War and the Proclamation Line of 1763   Britain claimed possession of North America east of the Mississippi only to face an extraordinary challenge from the Indians of the interior, who wiped out eight garrisons but could not take Detroit, Niagara, or Fort Pitt.
View an animated version of this map or related maps at http://www.thomsonedu.com/ history/murrin.

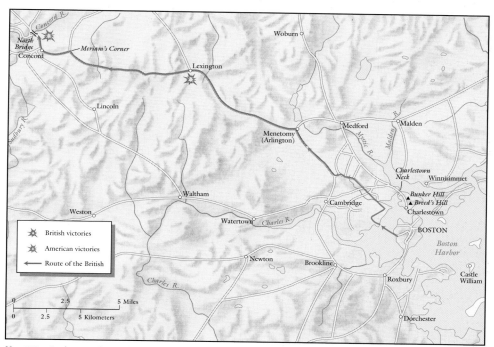

Map 5.3 Lexington, Concord, and Boston, 1775   The British march to Lexington and Concord on April 19, 1775, touched off the Revolutionary War. The colonists drove the redcoats back to Boston and then besieged the city for 11 months until the British withdrew.

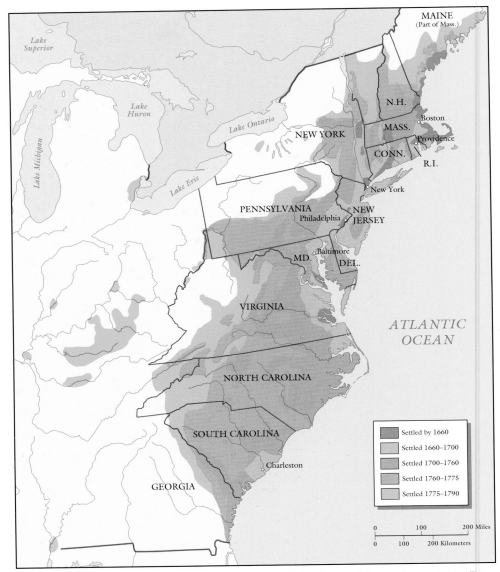

Map 6.6 Advance of Settlement to 1790   Between 1760 and 1790, America's population grew from nearly 1.6 million to almost 4 million. The area of settlement was spreading west of Pittsburgh and into much of Kentucky and parts of Tennessee. View an animated version of this map or related maps at http://www.thomsonedu.com/history/murrin.

helped end the undeclared war with France, and he had expressed doubts about the wisdom and necessity, if not the constitutionality, of the Alien and Sedition Acts. Although he disliked Congress's repeal of the 1801 legislation, he believed in Congress's right to make and unmake laws, and he accepted the situation. Jefferson and the moderate Republicans noted that Marshall was less interested in the power of the judiciary than in its independence. Ultimately, they decided they trusted Marshall more than they trusted the radicals in their own party. With the acquittal of Justice Chase, Jeffersonian attacks on the federal courts ceased.

Justice Marshall demonstrated his strict constructionism (as well as his partisanship) in the treason trial of former Vice President Aaron Burr in 1807. Following his failed attempt at the presidency in 1801, Burr's further intrigues with northern Federalists broke down—a breakdown that helped lead to a duel in which Burr killed Alexander Hamilton. The disgraced Aaron Burr headed west and organized a cloudy conspiracy that may have involved (according to varying testimonies) an invasion of Mexico or Florida or the secession of Louisiana. President Jefferson ordered his arrest. He was tried for treason at Richmond, with the Chief Justice, who was riding circuit, on the bench. Kings had frequently used the charge of treason to silence dissent. Marshall stopped what he and other Federalists considered Jefferson's attempt to do the same thing by limiting the definition of treason to overt acts of war against the United States or to adhering to the republic's foreign enemies—and by requiring two witnesses to an overt act of treason. Under these guidelines, Burr went free. At the same time, the United States had formally separated internal dissent from treason.

Louisiana

It was Jefferson's good fortune that Europe remained at peace and stayed out of American affairs during his first term. The one development that posed an international threat to the United States turned into a grand triumph: the purchase of the Louisiana Territory from France.

By 1801, a half-million Americans lived west of the Appalachians, and Republicans saw westward expansion as the best hope for the survival of the republic. Social inequality and the erosion of **yeoman** independence would almost inevitably take root in the East, but in the vast lands west of the mountains, the republic could renew itself for many generations to come. To serve that purpose, however, the West needed ready access to markets through the river system that emptied into the Gulf of Mexico at New Orleans. "There is on the globe," wrote President Jefferson, "one single spot, the possessor of which is our natural and habitual enemy. It is New Orleans."

In 1801, Spain owned New Orleans and under Pinckney's Treaty allowed Americans to trans-ship produce from the interior. The year before, however, Spain had secretly ceded the Louisiana Territory (roughly, all the land west of the Mississippi drained by the Missouri and Arkansas rivers) to France. Napoleon Bonaparte had plans for a new French empire in

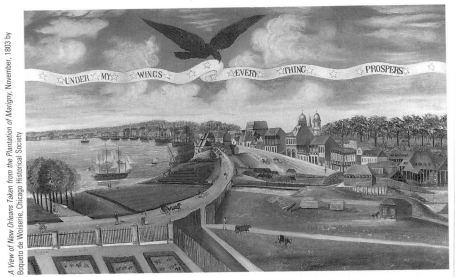

A View of New Orleans Taken from the Plantation of Marigny, November, 1803 by Boqueto de Woiserie, Chicago Historical Society

The Louisiana Purchase This panorama of New Orleans celebrates the Louisiana Purchase of 1803. The patriotic caption promises prosperity for the city and (by inference) for the American settlements upriver. Here the power of the central government (in the form of money and the purchase of land) is shown to serve the spread of liberty.

America with the sugar island of Hispaniola (present-day Haiti and Dominican Republic) at its center, and with mainland colonies feeding the islands and thus making the empire self-sufficient. Late in 1802, the Spanish, who had retained control of New Orleans, closed the port to American commerce, creating rumors that they would soon transfer the city to France. That would threaten the existence of American settlements west of the Appalachians. President Jefferson sent a delegation to Paris early in 1803 with authorization to buy New Orleans for the United States.

By the time the delegates reached Paris, events had dissolved French plans for a new American empire. The slaves of Saint-Domingue (the French colony on Hispaniola) had revolted and had defeated French attempts to regain control of the island. At the same time, another war between Britain and France seemed imminent. Napoleon—reputedly chanting "Damn sugar, damn coffee, damn colonies"—decided to bail out of America and concentrate his resources in Europe. He astonished Jefferson's delegation by offering to sell not only New Orleans but the whole Louisiana Territory—which would double the size of the United States—for the bargain price of $15 million. **(See Map 7.3, Louisiana Purchase, in the color insert following page 384.)**

Jefferson, who had criticized Federalists when they violated the letter of the Constitution, faced a dilemma: The president lacked the constitutional power to buy territory, but the chance to buy Louisiana was too good to refuse. It would ensure Americans access to the rivers of the interior; it would eliminate a serious foreign threat on America's western border; and it would give American farmers enough land to sustain the agrarian republic for a long time to come. Swallowing his constitutional scruples (and at the same time half-heartedly asking for a constitutional amendment to legalize the purchase), Jefferson told the American delegates to buy Louisiana. Republican senators quickly ratified the Louisiana treaty over Federalist objections that the purchase would encourage rapid settlement and add to backcountry barbarism and Republican strength. Most Americans agreed that the accidents of French and Haitian history had given the United States a grand opportunity, and Congress's ratification of the Louisiana Purchase met with overwhelming public approval. For his part, Jefferson was certain that the republic had gained the means of renewing itself through time. As he claimed in his second inaugural address, he had bought a great "empire of liberty."

Lewis and Clark

The Americans knew almost nothing about the land they had bought. Only a few French trappers and traders had traveled the plains between the Mississippi and the Rocky Mountains, and no white person had seen the territory drained by the Columbia River. In 1804, Jefferson sent an expedition under Meriwether Lewis, his private secretary, and William Clark, brother of the Indian fighter George Rogers Clark, to explore the new land. To prepare for the expedition, Lewis studied astronomy, zoology, and botany; Clark was already an accomplished mapmaker. The two kept meticulous journals of one of the epic adventures in American history.

In May 1804, Lewis and Clark and 41 companions boarded a keelboat and two large canoes at the village of St. Louis. They poled and paddled 1,600 miles up the Missouri River, passing through rolling plains dotted by the farm villages of the Pawnee, Oto, Missouri, Crow, Omaha, Hidatsa, and Mandan peoples. The villages of the lower Missouri had been cut off from the western buffalo herds and reduced to dependence by mounted Sioux warriors, who had begun to establish their hegemony over the northern plains.

Lewis and Clark traveled through Sioux territory and stopped for the winter at the heavily fortified Mandan villages at the big bend of the Missouri River in Dakota country. In the spring they hired Toussaint Charbonneau, a French fur trader, to guide them to the Pacific. Charbonneau was useless, but his wife, a teenaged Shoshone girl named Sacajawea, was an indispensable guide, interpreter, and diplomat. With her help, Lewis and Clark navigated the upper Missouri, crossed the Rockies to the Snake River, and followed that stream to the Columbia River. They reached the Pacific in November 1805 and spent the winter at what is now Astoria, Oregon. Retracing their steps the following spring and summer, they returned to St. Louis in September 1806. They brought with them many volumes of drawings and notes, along with assurances that the Louisiana Purchase had been worth many, many times its price.

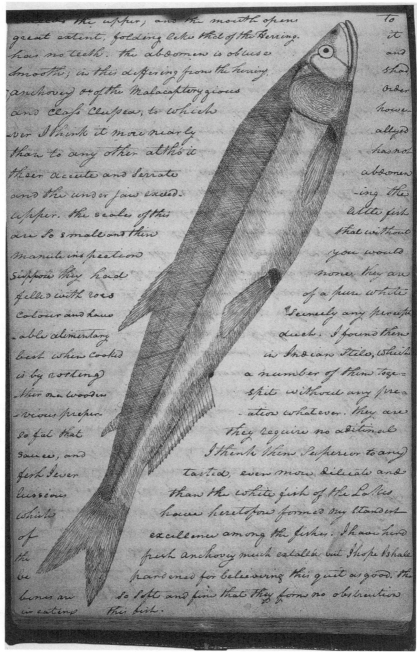

A page from the journals of Lewis and Clark Lewis and Clark traveled among peoples, flora, and wildlife that no American white person had ever seen. Their journals reveal both meticulous observation and a sense of wonder.

As Jefferson stood for reelection in 1804, he could look back on an astonishingly successful first term. He had dismantled the government's power to coerce its citizens, and he had begun to wipe out the national debt. The Louisiana Purchase had doubled the size of the republic at remarkably little cost. Moreover, by eliminating France from North America, it had strengthened the argument for reducing the military and the debts and taxes that went with it. Jefferson was more certain than ever that the republic could preserve itself through peaceful expansion. The "wise and frugal" government he had promised in 1801 was becoming a reality.

The combination of international peace, territorial expansion, and inexpensive, unobtrusive government left the Federalists without an issue in the 1804 election. They went through the motions of nominating Charles Pinckney of South Carolina as their presidential candidate and then watched Jefferson capture the electoral votes of every state but Delaware and Connecticut. As he began his second term in 1805, Jefferson could assume that he had ended the Federalist threat to the republic.

The Republic and the Napoleonic Wars, 1804–1815

Focus Question
What was the situation of the United States within the international politics created by the Napoleonic Wars, and how did that situation degenerate into a second war with Great Britain?

In spring 1803, a few weeks after closing the deal for Louisiana, Napoleon declared war on Great Britain. This 11-year war, like the wars of the 1790s, dominated the national politics of the United States. Most Americans wanted to remain neutral. Few Republicans supported Bonaparte as they had supported the French revolutionaries of 1789, and none but the most rabid Federalists wanted to intervene on the side of Great Britain. Neither France nor Britain, however, would permit American neutrality.

The Dilemmas of Neutrality

At the beginning, both Britain and France, whose rural economies were disrupted by war, encouraged the Americans to resume their role as neutral carriers and suppliers of food. For a time, Americans made huge profits. Between 1803 and 1807, U.S. exports—mostly foodstuffs and plantation staples—rose from $66.5 million to $102.2 million. Re-exports—goods produced in the British, Spanish, and French islands of the Caribbean, picked up by American vessels, and then reloaded in American ports onto American ships bound for Europe—rose even faster, from $13.5 million to $58.4 million.

In 1805, the Royal Navy under Lord Nelson destroyed the French and Spanish fleets at the Battle of Trafalgar. Later that year, Napoleon's armies won a decisive victory over Austria and Russia at the Battle of Austerlitz and won effective control of Europe. The war reached a stalemate: Napoleon's army occupied Europe, and the British navy controlled the seas.

Britain decided to use its naval supremacy to blockade Europe and starve the French into submission. The Essex Decision of 1805 empowered the Royal Navy to seize American ships engaged in the re-export trade with France. In spring 1806, Congress, angered by British seizures of American ships, passed the Non-Importation Act forbidding the importation of British goods that could be bought elsewhere or that could be manufactured in the United States. A month after that, Britain blockaded long stretches of the European coast. Napoleon responded with the Berlin Decree, which outlawed all trade with the British Isles. The British answered with an Order in Council that demanded that neutral ships trading with Europe stop first for inspection and licensing in a British port. Napoleon responded with the Milan Decree, which stated that any vessel that obeyed the British decrees or allowed itself to be searched by the Royal Navy was subject to seizure by France. Beginning in 1805 and ending with the Milan Decree in December 1807, the barrage of European decrees and counter-decrees meant that virtually all American commerce with Europe was outlawed by one or the other of the warring powers.

Trouble on the High Seas

Given British naval supremacy, French decrees were effective only against American ships that entered ports controlled by France. The Royal Navy, on the other hand, maintained a loose blockade of the North American coast and stopped and searched American ships as they left the major seaports. Hundreds of ships were seized, along with their cargoes and crews. Under British law, the Royal Navy could impress any British subject into service during wartime. Many British subjects, including legions of deserters from the Royal Navy, were hiding in the American merchant marine, where they avoided the danger, low pay, bad food, and draconian discipline of the British navy. British ships commandeered those men. They also took Englishmen who had taken out U.S. citizenship (an act the British did not recognize) and, inevitably, native-born Americans. An estimated 6,000 American citizens were impressed into the Royal Navy between 1803 and 1812.

The kidnapping of American sailors enraged the citizens of the United States and brought the country close to war in summer 1807. In June, the American naval frigate *Chesapeake* signed on four English deserters from the British navy, along with some Americans who had joined the British navy and then deserted. Some of the deserters spotted their old officers from *H.M.S. Leopard* in Norfolk, Virginia, and taunted them on the streets. The *Leopard* left port and resumed its patrol of the American coast. On June 21, the *Leopard* caught the *Chesapeake* off Hampton Roads and demanded the return of the British deserters. When the American captain refused, the British fired on the *Chesapeake,* killing 3 Americans and wounding 18. The British then boarded the *Chesapeake,* seized the four deserters, and later hanged one of them.

The *Chesapeake* affair set off huge anti-British demonstrations in the seaport towns and angry cries for war throughout the country. President Jefferson responded by barring British ships from American ports and American territorial waters and by ordering state governors to prepare to call up as many as 100,000 militiamen. The United States in 1807 stood at the brink of full-scale war with the most powerful nation in the world.

Embargo

Jefferson wanted to avoid war, which would inevitably bring high taxes, government debt, a bloated military and civil service, and the repression of dissent—precisely the evils that Jefferson had vowed to eliminate. Worse, war carried the danger of defeat and thus the possible failure of America's republican experiment.

Jefferson had one more card to play: He could suspend trade with Europe altogether and thus keep American ships out of harm's way. For many years, Jefferson had assumed that U.S. farm products and the U.S. market for imported goods had become crucial to the European economies. He could use trade as a means of "peaceable coercion" that would both ensure respect for American neutral rights and keep the country out of war. "Our commerce," he wrote just before taking office, "is so valuable to them, that they will be glad to purchase it, when the only price we ask is to do us justice." Convinced that America's yeoman republic could survive without European luxuries more easily than Europe could survive without American food, Jefferson decided to give "peaceable coercion" a serious test. Late in 1807, he asked Congress to suspend all U.S. trade with foreign countries.

Congress passed the Embargo Act on December 22. Within a few months, it was clear that peaceable coercion would not work. The British found other markets and other sources of food. They encouraged the smuggling of American goods into Canada, and American merchantmen who had been at sea when the **embargo** went into effect stayed away from their home ports and functioned as part of the British merchant marine. A loophole in the Embargo Act allowed U.S. ships to leave port in order to pick up American property stranded in other countries. An estimated 6,000 ships set sail under that excuse. Hundreds of others, plying the coastal trade, were "blown off course" and found themselves thrust into international commerce. For his part, Napoleon seized American ships in European ports, explaining that, because the embargo kept all American ships in port, those trading under American flags must be British ships in disguise.

The embargo hurt American commerce badly. Its 1807 exports of $108 million dropped to $22 million in 1808. The economy slowed in every section of the country, but it ground to a halt in the cities of the Northeast. While the oceangoing merchant fleet rotted at anchor, unemployed sailors, dockworkers, and other maritime workers and their families sank to levels of economic despair seldom seen in British North America. Northeastern Federalists branded Jefferson's embargo a "Chinese" (i.e., isolationist) solution to the problems of commerce and diplomacy. Commerce, they argued, was the great civilizer: "Her victories are over ferocious passions, savage manners, deep rooted prejudices, blind superstition and delusive theory." Federalists accused Jefferson of plotting an end to commerce and a reversion to rural barbarism, and they often took the lead in trying to subvert the embargo through smuggling and other means. In Connecticut, the Federalist governor flatly refused Jefferson's request to mobilize the militia to enforce the embargo.

The Federalists gained ground in the elections of 1808. James Madison, Jefferson's old ally and chosen successor, was elected president with 122 electoral votes to 47 for his Federalist opponent, C. C. Pinckney. Although Republicans retained control of both houses of Congress, Federalists made significant gains in Congress and won control of several state legislatures. Federalist opposition to the embargo, and to the supposed southern, agrarian strangle-hold on national power, was gaining ground.

The Road to War

When President Madison took office in spring 1809, it was clear that the embargo had failed. On the contrary, the embargo had created misery in the seaport cities, choked off the imports that provided 90 percent of federal revenue, and revived Federalist opposition to Republican dominance. Early in 1809, Congress passed the Non-Intercourse Act, which retained the ban on trade with Britain and France but reopened trade with other nations. It also gave President Madison the power to reopen trade with either Britain or France once they had agreed to respect American rights. Neither complied, and the Non-Intercourse Act proved nearly as ineffective as the embargo.

In 1810, Congress passed Macon's Bill No. 2, a strange piece of legislation that rescinded the ban on trade with France and Britain but also authorized the president to reimpose the Non-Intercourse Act on either belligerent if the other agreed to end its restrictions on U.S. trade. Napoleon decided to test the Americans. In September 1810, the French promised, with vague conditions, that France would repeal the Berlin and Milan Decrees. Although the proposal was a clear attempt to lead the United States into conflict with Great Britain, Madison saw no choice but to go along with it. He accepted the French promise and proclaimed in November 1810 that the British had three months to follow suit. "It promises us," he said of his proclamation, "at least an extrication from the dilemma, of a mortifying peace, or a war with both the great belligerents."

In the end, Madison's proclamation led to war. The French repealed only those sections of the Berlin and Milan Decrees that applied to the neutral rights of the United States. The British refused to revoke their Orders in Council and told the Americans to withdraw their restrictions on British trade until the French had repealed theirs. The United States would either have to obey British orders (thus making American exports and the American merchant marine a part of the British war effort—a neo-colonial situation that was utterly repugnant to most Americans) or go to war. When Congress reconvened in November 1811, it voted military measures in preparation for war with Great Britain.

The War Hawk Congress, 1811–1812

Republicans controlled both houses of congress in 1811–12 by 75 percent of the House and 82 percent of the Senate, but they were a divided majority. The Federalist minority was united in opposition to Madison. They were often joined by northeastern Republicans who followed the pro-British, Federalist line on international trade, and by Republicans who wanted a more powerful military than other Republicans would allow. Also opposed to Madison were the self-styled Old Republicans of the South, led by John Randolph. Thus it was a deeply divided Congress that met the war crisis.

In this confused situation, a group of talented young congressmen took control. Nearly all of them were Republicans from the South or the West: Richard M. Johnson and Henry Clay of Kentucky, John C. Calhoun and William Lowndes of South Carolina, George M. Troup of Georgia, Peter B. Porter from the Niagara district of New York, and others. Called the **War Hawks,** these ardent nationalists wanted to declare war on England to protect U.S. rights. Through their organizational, oratorical, and intellectual power, they won control of Congress. Henry Clay, only 34 years old and serving his first term in Congress, was elected Speaker of the House. More vigorous than his predecessors, Clay controlled debate, packed key committees, worked tirelessly behind the scenes, and imposed order on his fellow congressmen. When John Randolph, one of the most feared members of the House, brought his dog into the House chamber, Speaker Clay pointedly ordered the dog removed. Earlier speakers had not dared give such an order.

In the winter and spring of 1811–12, the War Hawks led Congress into a declaration of war. In November they voted military preparations, and in April they enacted a 90-day embargo—not to coerce the British but to return American ships safely to port before war began. (As in 1807, the embargo prompted seaport merchants to rush their ships to sea.) On June 1, Madison sent a war message to Congress. This was to be the first war declared under the Constitution, and the president stayed out of congressional territory by not asking explicitly for a declaration of war. He did, however, present a list of British crimes that could be interpreted in no other way: (1) the enforcement of the Orders in Council, even within the territorial waters of the United States; (2) the impressment of American seamen; (3) the use of spies and provocateurs within the United States; and (4) the wielding of "a malicious influence over the Indians of the Northwest Territory." Madison concluded that war had in fact begun: "We behold . . . on the side of Great Britain a state of war against the United States; and on the side of the United States, a state of peace toward Great Britain."

Congress declared war on June 18. The vote was far from unanimous: 79 to 49 in the House of Representatives, 19 to 13 in the Senate. All 30 Federalists voted against the declaration, as did one in five Republicans, nearly all of them from the Northeast. Thus the war was declared by the Democratic Republican Party, more particularly by the Republicans of the South and the West. The Northeast, whose commercial rights were supposedly the issue at stake, opposed the declaration.

***We Owe Allegiance To No Crown,* a Patriotic Painting from the War of 1812**   Liberty—portrayed, as always, by a pure and determined woman—holds a Liberty Cap on a staff (the old symbol of international republicanism) and crowns an embattled American seaman with a classical wreath. Here the war is portrayed not only as a conflict between Britain and America but also as a contest between monarchy and republicanism—between despotism and liberty.

American Strategy in 1812

The War Hawks declared a war to defend the sovereignty, the western territory, and the maritime rights of the United States. The war they planned and fought, however, bore the stamp of southern and western Republicanism. Federalists and many northeastern Republicans expected a naval war. After all, the British had committed their atrocities on the ocean, and some, remembering U.S. naval successes against France in the quasi-war of 1798–1800, predicted similar successes against Great Britain. Yet when Madison asked Congress to prepare for war, the War Hawks led a majority that strengthened the U.S. Army and left the navy weak. Reasoning that no U.S. naval force could challenge British control of the seas, they prepared instead for a land invasion of British Canada.

The decision to invade Canada led the Federalists, along with many of Randolph's Old Republicans, to accuse Madison and the congressional majority of planning a war of territorial aggression. Some members of Congress did want to annex Canada to the United States, but most saw the decision to invade Canada as a matter of strategy. Lightly garrisoned and with a population of only one-half million (many of them French, and most of the others American émigrés of doubtful loyalties), Canada seemed the easiest and most logical place in which to damage the British. It was also from bases in Canada that the British armed the Indians of the Northwest, and western Republicans were determined to end that threat decisively. Finally, Canada was a valuable colony of Great Britain. The American embargoes, coupled with Napoleon's control of Europe, had impaired Britain's ability to supply her plantation colonies in the West Indies, and Canadian farmers had begun to fill the gap. Thus Canada was both valuable and vulnerable, and American policy makers reasoned that they could take it and hold it hostage while demanding that the British back down on other issues. Although U.S. military strategy focused on Canada, maritime rights and national honor, along with the British-fed Indian threat west of the Appalachians, were the central issues in 1812. As John C. Calhoun, who was instrumental in taking the nation to war, concluded: "The mad ambition, the lust of power, and commercial avarice of Great Britain have left to neutral nations an alternative only between the base surrender of their rights, and a manly vindication of them."

The Rise of Tecumseh

Native peoples east of the Mississippi River recognized alliances with Britain as a final chance to hold back American settlers. Northwestern Indians had lost much of their land at the Battle of Fallen Timbers and the Treaty of Greenville. Relegated to smaller territory but still dependent on the European fur trade, they fell into competition with settlers and other Indians for the diminishing supply of game. The Creeks, Choctaws, and other tribes of the Old Southwest faced the same problem: Even when they chased settlers out of their territory, the settlers managed to kill or scare off the deer and other wildlife, thus ruining the old hunting grounds. When the Shawnee sent hunting parties farther west, they met irate western Indians. The Choctaws also sent hunters across the Mississippi, where they found both new sources of furs and angry warriors of the Osage and other peoples of Louisiana and Arkansas. The Indians of the interior now realized that the days of the fur trade, on which they depended for survival, were numbered. **(See Map 7.4, Native America, 1783–1812, in the color insert following page 384.)**

Faced with shrinking territories, the disappearance of wildlife, and diminished opportunities to be traditional hunters and warriors, many Indian societies sank into despair. Epidemics of European diseases (smallpox, influenza, measles) attacked peoples who were increasingly sedentary and vulnerable. Old internal frictions grew nastier. In the Old Southwest, full-blooded Indians came into conflict with mixed-blood Indians, who often no longer spoke the native language and who wanted their people to adopt white ways. Murder and clan revenge plagued the tribes, and depression and suicide became more common. The use of alcohol, which had been a scourge on Indian societies for two centuries, increased. Indian males spent more time in their villages and less on the hunt, and by most accounts they drank more and grew more violent when they drank.

Out of this cultural wreckage emerged visionary leaders who spoke of a regenerated native society and the expulsion of all whites from the old tribal lands. The prophet who came closest to military success was Tenskwatawa, a fat, one-eyed, alcoholic Shawnee who had failed as a warrior and medicine man. He went into a deep trance in 1805, and the people thought he was dead. During preparations for his funeral, he awoke and told them he had visited heaven and hell and had received a prophetic vision. First, all Indians must stop drinking and fighting among themselves. They must also return to their traditional food, clothing, tools, and hairstyles, and must extinguish all of their fires and start new ones without using European tools. All who opposed the new order (including local chiefs, medicine men, shamans, and witches) must be put down by force. When all of that had been done, God (a monotheistic, punishing God borrowed from the Christians) would restore the world that Indians had known before the whites came over the mountains.

Tenskwatawa's message soon found its way to the Delawares (who attacked the Christians among their people as witches) and other native peoples of the Northwest. When converts flooded into the prophet's home village, he moved to Prophetstown (Tippecanoe) in what is now Indiana. There, with the help of his brother Tecumseh, he created an army estimated by the whites at anywhere between 650 and 3,000 warriors and pledged to end further encroachment by whites. Tecumseh, who took control of the movement, announced to the whites that he was the sole chief of all the Indians north of the Ohio River. Land cessions by anyone else would be invalid. Tenskwatawa's prophecy and Tecumseh's leadership had united the Indians of the Old Northwest in an unprecedented stand against white encroachment.

Tecumseh's confederacy posed a threat to the United States. A second war with England was looming, and Tecumseh was receiving supplies and encouragement from the British in Canada. He was also planning to visit the southern tribes in an attempt to bring them into his confederacy. The prospect of unified resistance by the western tribes in league with the British jeopardized every settler west of the Appalachians. In 1811, William Henry Harrison led an army toward Prophetstown. With Tecumseh away, Tenskwatawa ordered an unwise attack on Harrison's army and was beaten at the Battle of Tippecanoe. But Tecumseh's confederacy remained a formidable opponent of the United States.

The War with Canada, 1812–1813

The United States attacked Canada in 1812, with disastrous results. The plan was to invade Upper Canada (Ontario) from the Northwest, thus cutting off the Shawnee, Potawatomi, and other pro-British Indian tribes from their British support. When General William Hull, governor of Michigan Territory, took a poorly supplied, badly led army of militiamen and volunteers into Canada from a base in Detroit, he found that the British had outguessed him. The area was crawling with British troops and their Indian allies. With detachments of his army overrun and his supply lines cut, he retreated to the garrison at Detroit. Under siege, he heard that an Indian force had captured the garrison at Fort Dearborn. British General Isaac Brock, who knew that Hull was afraid of Indians, sent a note into the fort telling him that "the numerous body of Indians who have attached themselves to my troops, will be beyond my controul the moment the contest commences." Without consulting his officers, Hull surrendered his army of 2,000 to the smaller British force. Although Hull was later court-martialed for cowardice, the damage had been done: The British and Indians occupied many of the remaining American garrisons in the Northwest and transformed the U.S. invasion of Upper Canada into a British occupation of much of the Northwest.

The invasion of Canada from the east went no better. In October a U.S. force of 6,000 faced 2,000 British and Indians across the Niagara River separating Ontario from western New York. The U.S. regular army crossed the river, surprised the British, and established a toehold at Queenston Heights. While the British prepared a counterattack, New York militiamen refused to cross the river to reinforce the regulars. Ohio militiamen had behaved the same way when Hull invaded Canada, and similar problems had arisen with the New York militia near Lake Champlain. Throughout the war, citizen-soldiers proved that Jefferson's confidence in the militia could not be extended to the invasion of other countries. The British regrouped and slaughtered the outnumbered, exhausted U.S. regulars at Queenston Heights.

As winter set in, it was clear that Canada would not fall as easily as the Americans had assumed. The invasion, which U.S. commanders had thought would knife through an apathetic Canadian population, had the opposite effect: The attacks by the United States turned the ragtag assortment of American loyalist émigrés, discharged British soldiers, and American-born settlers into a self-consciously British Canadian people. Years later, an Englishwoman touring Niagara Falls asked a Canadian ferryman if it was true that Canadians had thrown Americans off Queenston Heights to their death on the rocky banks of the Niagara River. "Why yes," he replied, "there was a good many of them; but it was right to show them that there was water between us, and you know it might help to keep the rest of them from coming to trouble us on our own ground."

Tecumseh's Last Stand

Tecumseh's confederacy, bruised but not broken in the Battle of Tippecanoe, allied itself with the British in 1812. On a trip to the southern tribes, Tecumseh found the traditionalist wing of the Creeks—led by prophets who called themselves Red Sticks—willing to join him.

Map 7.5 War of 1812 Early in the war, Americans chose to fight the British in Canada, with costly and inconclusive results. Later, the British determined to blockade the whole coast of the United States and, late in the war, to raid important coastal towns. The results were equally inconclusive: Both sides could inflict serious damage, but neither could conquer the other. The one clear military outcome—one that the Americans were determined to accomplish—was the destruction of Indian resistance east of the Mississippi.

The augmented confederacy provided stiff resistance to the United States throughout the war. The Red Sticks chased settlers from much of Tennessee. They then attacked a group of settlers who had taken refuge in a stockade surrounding the house of an Alabama trader named George Mims. In what whites called the Massacre at Fort Mims, the Red Sticks (reputedly with the collusion of black slaves within the fort) killed at least 247 men, women, and children. In the Northwest, Tecumseh's warriors, fighting alongside the British, spread terror throughout the white settlements.

A wiser U.S. army returned to Canada in 1813. They raided and burned the Canadian capital at York (Toronto) in April, and then fought inconclusively throughout the summer. An autumn offensive toward Montreal failed, but the Americans had better luck on Lake Erie. The barrier of Niagara Falls kept Britain's saltwater navy out of the upper Great Lakes, and on Lake Erie, the British and Americans engaged in a frenzied shipbuilding contest throughout the first year of the war. The Americans won. In September 1813, Commodore Oliver Hazard Perry cornered and destroyed the British fleet at Put-in-Bay. Control of Lake Erie enabled the United States to cut off supplies to the British in the Northwest, and a U.S. army under William Henry Harrison retook the area and continued on into Canada. On October 5, Harrison caught up with a force of British and Indians at the Thames River and beat them badly. In the course of that battle, Richard M. Johnson, a War Hawk congressman acting as commander of the Kentucky militia, killed Tecumseh. Proud militiamen returned to Kentucky with pieces of hair and clothing and even swatches of skin torn from Tecumseh's corpse. Their officers reaped huge political rewards: The Battle of the Thames would eventually produce a president of the United States (Harrison), a vice president (Johnson), 3 governors of Kentucky, 3 lieutenant governors, 4 U.S. senators, and about 20 congressmen— telling evidence of how seriously the settlers of the interior had taken Tecumseh.

The following spring, General Andrew Jackson's Tennessee militia, aided by Choctaw, Creek, and Cherokee allies, attacked and slaughtered the Red Sticks, who had fortified themselves at Horseshoe Bend in Alabama. With the Battle of the Thames and the Battle of Horse Shoe Bend, the military power of the Indian peoples east of the Mississippi River was broken.

The British Offensive, 1814

The British defeated Napoleon in April 1814, thus ending the larger war from which the War of 1812 erupted. They then turned their attention to the American war and went on the offensive. They had already blockaded much of the American coast from Georgia to Maine. During summer 1814, they raided Chesapeake Bay and marched on Washington, D.C. As retribution for the torching of the Canadian capital at York, they chased the army and politicians out of town and burned down the capitol building and the president's mansion. In September, the British attacked Baltimore, but could not blast their way past the determined garrison that commanded the harbor from Fort McHenry. This was the battle that inspired Francis Scott Key to write "The Star-Spangled Banner," which was set to music and chosen as the national anthem in the 1930s. When a British offensive on Lake Champlain stalled during the autumn, the war reached a stalemate: Britain had prevented the invasion of Canada and had blockaded the American coast, but neither side could take and hold the other's territory.

The British now shifted their attention to the Gulf Coast, particularly to New Orleans, a city of vital importance to U.S. trans-Appalachian trade and communications. Peace negotiations had begun in August, and the British wanted to capture and hold New Orleans as a bargaining chip. A large British amphibious force landed and camped eight miles south of New Orleans. There they met an American army made up of U.S. regulars, Kentucky and Tennessee militiamen, clerks, workingmen, free blacks from the city, and about a thousand French pirates—all under the command of Andrew Jackson of Tennessee. Throughout late December and early January, unaware that a peace treaty had been signed on December 24, the armies exchanged artillery barrages and the British probed and attacked American lines. On January 8, they launched a frontal assault. A formation of 6,000 British soldiers marched across open ground toward 4,000 Americans concealed behind breastworks. With the first American volley, it was clear that the British had made a mistake. Veterans of the bloodiest battles of the Napoleonic wars swore that they had never seen such withering fire; soldiers in the front ranks who were not cut down threw themselves to the ground and surrendered when the shooting stopped. The charge lasted half an hour. At the end, 2,000 British soldiers lay dead or wounded. American casualties numbered only 70. Fought nearly two weeks after the peace treaty, the Battle of New Orleans had no effect on the outcome of the war or on the peace terms, but it salved the injured pride of Americans and made a national hero and a political power of Andrew Jackson.

The Hartford Convention

While most of the nation celebrated Jackson's victory, events in Federalist New England went differently. New Englanders had disliked Republican trade policies, and their congressmen had voted overwhelmingly against going to war. The New England states seldom met their quotas of militiamen for the war effort, and some Federalist leaders had openly urged resistance to the war. The British had encouraged that resistance by not extending their naval blockade to the New England coast, and throughout the first two years of the war, New England merchants and farmers had traded freely with the enemy. In 1814, after the Royal Navy had extended its blockade northward and had begun to raid the towns of coastal Maine, some Federalists talked openly about seceding and making a separate peace with Britain.

In an attempt to undercut the secessionists, moderate Federalists called a convention at Hartford to air the region's grievances. The Hartford Convention, which met in late December 1814, proposed amendments to the Constitution that indicated New England's position as a self-conscious minority within the Union. First, the convention delegates wanted the "three-fifths" clause, which led to overrepresentation of the South in Congress and the electoral college (see chapter 6), stricken from the Constitution. They also wanted to deny naturalized citizens—who were strongly Republican—the right to hold office. They wanted to make it more difficult for new states, all of which sided with the Republicans and their southern leadership, to enter the Union. Finally, they wanted to require a two-thirds majority of both houses for a declaration of war—a requirement that would have prevented the War of 1812.

The Federalist leaders of the Hartford Convention, satisfied that they had headed off the secessionists, took their proposals to Washington in mid-January. They arrived to find the capital celebrating news of the peace treaty and Jackson's victory at New Orleans. When they aired their sectional complaints, they were branded as negative and unpatriotic. Although Federalists continued for a few years to wield power in southern New England, the Hartford debacle ruined any chance of a nationwide Federalist resurgence after the war. Andrew Jackson had stolen control of American history from New England. He would do so again in the years ahead.

The Treaty of Ghent

Britain's defeat of Napoleon had spurred British and American efforts to end a war that neither wanted. In August 1814, they opened peace talks in the Belgian city of Ghent. Perhaps waiting for the results of their 1814 offensive, the British opened with proposals that the Americans were certain to reject. They demanded the right to navigate the Mississippi. Moreover, they wanted territorial concessions and the creation of the permanent, independent Indian buffer state in the Northwest that they had promised their Indian allies. The Americans ignored these proposals and talked instead about impressment and maritime rights. As the autumn wore on and the war reached stalemate, both sides began to compromise. The British knew that the Americans would grant concessions in the interior only if they were thoroughly defeated, an outcome that most British commanders thought impossible. For their part, the Americans realized that the British maritime depredations were by-products of the struggle with Napoleonic France. Faced with peace in Europe and a senseless military stalemate in North America, negotiators on both sides began to withdraw their demands. The Treaty of Ghent, signed on Christmas Eve 1814, simply ended the war. The border between Canada and the United States remained where it had been in 1812; Indians south of that border—defeated and without allies—were left to the mercy of the United States; and British maritime violations were not mentioned. The makers of the treaty stopped a war that neither side could win, trusting that a period of peace would resolve the problems created by two decades of world war.

Conclusion

In 1816, Thomas Jefferson was in retirement at Monticello, satisfied that he had defended liberty against the Federalists' love of power. The High Federalist attempt to consolidate power, militarize government, and jail their enemies had failed. Their direct taxes were repealed. Their debt and their national bank remained in place, but only under the watchful eyes of true republicans. And their attempt to ally the United States with the antirepublican designs of Great Britain had ended in what many called the Second War of American Independence. American independence was truly won, and Jefferson's vision of a union of independent republican states seemed to have been realized.

Yet for all his successes, Jefferson saw that he must sacrifice some of his longest-held dreams. Jefferson's republican ideal was grounded in farmer-citizens whose vision was local and who wanted nothing more from government than protection of their property and rights. Jefferson's imagined yeomen traded farm surpluses for European manufactured goods—a system that encouraged rural prosperity, prevented the growth of cities and factories (the much-feared nurseries of corruption and dependence), and thus sustained the landed independence on which republican citizenship rested. Westward expansion, Jefferson had believed, would ensure the yeoman republic for generations to come. By 1816, that dream was ended. The British and French had "cover[ed] the earth and sea with robberies and piracies," disrupting America's vital export economy whenever it suited their whims. Arguing as Hamilton had argued in 1790, Jefferson insisted that "we must now place the manufacturer by the side of the agriculturalist."

SUGGESTED READINGS

Stanley Elkins and Eric McKitrick, *The Age of Federalism: The Early American Republic, 1788–1800* (1993) is definitive, while Henry Adams, *History of the United States of America during the Administrations of Thomas Jefferson and James Madison,* 9 vols. (1889–1891; reprint, 2 vols., 1986) remains the fullest introduction to the Republican presidencies. Thomas G. Slaughter, *The Whiskey Rebellion: Frontier Epilogue to the American Revolution* (1986) is good on its subject. Lance Banning, *The Jeffersonian Persuasion: Evolution of a Party Ideology* (1980); Drew R. McCoy, *The Elusive Republic: Political Economy in Jeffersonian America* (1980); and Peter Onuf, *Jefferson's Empire: The Language of American Nationhood* (2001) are insightful studies of Jeffersonianism. On relations with other countries, see Lawrence Kaplan, *"Entangling Alliances with None": American Foreign Policy in the Age of Jefferson* (1987) and Donald R. Hickey, *The War of 1812: A Forgotten Conflict* (1989). Joseph J. Ellis, *Founding Brothers: The Revolutionary Generation* (2000) and Joanne B. Freeman, *Affairs of Honor: National Politics in the New Republic* (2001) discuss the political culture of the founding generation.

Visit the Liberty Equality Power Companion Web site for resources specific to this textbook: http://www.thomsonedu.com/history/murrin

Also find self-tests and additional resources at ThomsonNOW. ThomsonNOW is an integrated online suite of services and resources with proven ease of use and efficient paths to success, delivering the results you want—NOW!

www.thomsonedu.com/login/

8

Northern Transformations, 1790–1850

In 1790, American society approximated Jefferson's ideal: the United States was a nation of farmers who provided for themselves and sent surpluses overseas to be traded for manufactured goods. To put it in a less bucolic way, Americans remained on the colonial periphery of North Atlantic capitalism. They sent timber, cured fish, wheat, tobacco, rice, and money to Europe (primarily Great Britain), and Europe (again, Britain was the big player) sent manufactured goods—along with bills for shipping, insurance, banking, and tariff duties—back to America. In the 25 years following adoption of the Constitution, this old relationship fed significant economic growth in the United States, as European wars increased the demand for American produce and American shipping. Americans sent growing mountains of food and raw materials overseas, and they decorated their homes with comforts and small luxuries produced in British factories.

Beginning in the 1790s and accelerating dramatically with the peace of 1815, northern farmers changed that relationship: by 1830, the primary engine of northern economic development was no longer the North Atlantic trade; it was the self-sustained internal development of the northern United States. Northeastern businessmen noted that rural markets were expanding, that imports were unreliable, and that a crowded countryside produced people eager to work for wages. They began to invest in factories. New factory towns, together with the old seaports and new inland towns that served a commercializing agriculture, provided the country's first significant domestic market for food. Governments of the northern states built roads and canals that linked farmers to distant markets, and farmers turned to cash-crop agriculture and bought necessary goods (and paid mortgages and crop loans) with the money they made. By 1830, a large and growing portion of New England, the mid-Atlantic, and the Northwest had transcended colonial economics to become an interdependent, self-sustaining market society.

The pioneering sociologist Max Weber made a distinction between capitalism and the *spirit* of capitalism. Economic exchange and the desire for profit, Weber noted, have existed in all societies. Only a few, however, have organized capitalism into an everyday culture. Historians have coined the term "market revolution" to describe the transformation of the North from a society with markets to a market society—a society in which the market was implicated in the ways in which northerners saw the world and dealt with it. This chapter describes that revolution in the North up to 1830. The succeeding chapter describes the very different patterns of change in the South in the same years.

CHRONOLOGY

1789	National government under the Constitution begins
1790	Samuel Slater builds his first Arkwright spinning mill at Pawtucket, Rhode Island
1791	Vermont enters the union as the 14th state
1793	Beginning of Anglo-French War • Ohio enters the union as the 17th state
1807	Robert Fulton launches first steamboat
1812	Second war with Britain begins
1813	Boston Associates erect their first textile mill at Waltham, Massachusetts
1815	War of 1812 ends
1818	National Road completed to Ohio River at Wheeling, Virginia
1822	President Monroe vetoes National Road reparations bill
1825	New York completes the Erie Canal between Buffalo and Albany
1828	Baltimore and Ohio Railroad (America's first) completed
1835	Main Line Canal connects Philadelphia and Pittsburgh

Postcolonial Society, 1790–1815

Focus Question
What was the nature of the northern agricultural economy and of agricultural society in the years 1790–1820?

Farms

In 1782, J. Hector St. John de Crèvecoeur, a French soldier who had settled in rural New York, explained America's agrarian republic through the words of a fictionalized farmer. First of all, he said, the American farmer owns his own land and bases his claim to dignity and citizenship on that fact. He spoke of "the bright idea of property," and went on: "This formerly rude soil has been converted by my father into a pleasant farm, and in return, it has established all our rights; on it is founded our rank, our freedom, our power as citizens, our importance as inhabitants of [a rural neighborhood]. . . ." Second, he said, farm ownership endows the American farmer with the powers and responsibilities of fatherhood. "Often when I plant my low ground," he said, "I place my little boy on a chair which screws to the beam of the plough—its motion and that of the horses please him; he is perfectly happy and begins to chat. As I lean over the handle, various are the thoughts which crowd into my mind. I am now doing for him, I say, what my father did for me; may God enable him to live that he may perform the same operations for the same purposes when I am worn out and old!"

Crèvecoeur's farmer, musing on liberty and property, working the ancestral fields with his male heir strapped to the plough, was concerned with proprietorship and fatherhood, not with making money. He shared those concerns with most northern farmers. Their first concern was to provide food and common comforts for their households. Their second was to achieve long-term security and the ability to pass their farms on to their sons. The goal was to create what rural folks called a **"competence"**: the ability to live up to neighborhood standards of material decency while protecting the long-term independence of the household. Farmers thought of themselves first as fathers, neighbors, and stewards of family resources, and they avoided financial risk. Weather, bad crop years, pests, and unexpected injuries or deaths provided enough of that without adding the uncertainties of cash-crop agriculture and international commodity prices. In this situation, most farmers practiced what scholars call "safety-first," **"subsistence-plus,"** or simply **"mixed" agriculture.** They raised a variety of animals and plants, and did not concentrate on a single cash crop. Most farms in New England and the middle states were divided into corn and grain fields, pasturage for animals, woodlands for fuel, a vegetable garden, and perhaps a dairy cow. These complicated farms were a hedge against the uncertainties of rural life. Farm families ate most of what they grew, bartered much of the rest within their neighborhoods, and gambled surpluses on long-distance trade.

West Indian and European markets for American meat, grain, and corn had been growing since the mid-18th century. They expanded dramatically between 1793 and 1815, when war disrupted farming in Europe. Many northern farmers, although they seldom abandoned mixed agriculture, expanded production to take advantage of these overseas markets. The prosperity and aspirations of hundreds of thousands of farmers rose, and their houses were sprinkled with tokens of comfort and gentility. The same markets, however, sustained traditions of household independence and neighborly cooperation. Farmers continued to provide for their families from their own farms and neighborhoods, and they risked little by increasing their surpluses and sending them overseas. They profited from world markets without becoming dependent on them.

Production for overseas markets after 1790 did, however, alter relationships within farm families—usually in ways that reinforced the independence of the household and the power of its male head. Farm labor in post-revolutionary America was carefully divided by sex. Men worked in the fields, and production for markets both intensified that labor and made it more exclusively male. In the grain fields of the middle states, for instance, the long-handled scythe was replacing the sickle as the principal harvest tool. Women could use the sickle efficiently, but the long, heavy scythe was designed to be wielded by men. At the same time, farmers completed the substitution of ploughs for hoes as the principal cultivating tools—not only because ploughs worked better, but also because rural Americans had developed a prejudice against women working in the fields, and ploughs were male tools. By the early 19th century, visitors to the long-settled farming areas (with the exception of some mid-Atlantic German communities) seldom saw women in the fields. In his travels throughout France, Thomas Jefferson spoke harshly of peasant communities where he saw women doing field labor.

At the same time, household responsibilities multiplied and fell more exclusively to women. Farm women's labor and ingenuity helped create a more varied and nutritious rural diet in these years. Bread and salted meat were still the staples. The bread was the old mix of Indian corn and coarse wheat ("rye and Injun," the farmers called it), with crust so thick that it was used as a scoop for soups and stews. Though improved brines and pickling techniques augmented the supply of salt meat that could be laid by, farmers' palates doubtless told them that it was the same old salt meat. A variety of other foods were now available, however.

By the 1790s, improved winter feeding for cattle and better techniques for making and storing butter and cheese kept dairy products on the tables of the more prosperous farm families throughout the year. Chickens became more common, and farm women began to fence and manure their kitchen gardens, planting them with potatoes, turnips, cabbages, squashes, beans, and other vegetables that could be stored in the root cellars that were becoming standard features of farmhouses. By the 1830s, a resident of Weymouth, Massachusetts, claimed that "a man who did not have a large garden of potatoes, crooked-necked squashes, and other vegetables . . . was regarded [as] improvident." He might have added poultry and dairy cattle to the list, and he might have noted—as he did not—that all were more likely to result from the labor of women than from the labor of men.

Lewis Miller (1796-1882). The Historical Society of York County, The York County Heritage Trust, PA.

Old Mrs. Hansman Killing a Hog   This Pennsylvania farm wife seldom if ever worked in the fields, but her daily round of work was no dainty business. Along with other arduous and dirty labors, she killed and butchered hogs not only for her family but for some of her neighbors as well.

Neighborhoods

Rural communities were far more than accumulations of independent farm-owning house-holds. The struggle to maintain household independence involved most farm families in elaborate networks of neighborly cooperation, and long-term, give-and-take relationships with neighbors were essential economic and social assets. Few farmers possessed the tools, the labor, and the food they would have needed to be truly self-sufficient. They regularly worked for one another, borrowed oxen and plows, and swapped one kind of food crop for another. Women traded ashes, herbs, butter and eggs, vegetables, seedlings, baby chicks, goose feathers, and the products of their spinning wheels and looms. The regular exchange of such goods and services was crucial to the workings of rural neighborhoods. Some undertakings—house and barn raisings and husking bees, for example—brought the whole neighborhood together, transforming a necessary chore into a pleasant social event. The gossip, drinking, and dancing that took place on such occasions were fun. They were also—like the exchanges of goods and labor—social rituals that strengthened the neigh-borly relations within which farmers created a livelihood and passed it on to their sons.

Few of these neighborhood transactions involved money. In 1790, no paper money had yet been issued by the states or the federal government, and the widespread use of Span-ish, English, and French coins testified to the shortage of specie. In New England, farmers kept careful accounts of neighborhood debts. In the South and West, farmers used a **"changing system"** in which they simply remembered what they owed; they regarded the New England practice as a sign of Yankee greed and lack of character. Yet farmers every-where relied more on barter than on cash. "Instead of money going incessantly backwards and forwards into the same hands," observed a French traveler in Massachusetts in 1790, Americans "supply their needs in the countryside by direct reciprocal exchanges. The tai-lor and the bootmaker go and do their work at the home of the farmer . . . who most fre-quently provides the raw material for it and pays for the work in goods. They write down what they give and receive on both sides, and at the end of the year they settle a large vari-ety of exchanges with a very small quantity of coin."

George Holcomb, a farmer in New York's Hudson Valley, left a record of his neighborly transactions over a few days in 1812: "Today Wm. Dixon paid me eight dollars and I lent the same to Samuel Holcomb and today I wanted about two thirds of it for Wm. Dixon and he paid me in three trees of timber that I went and chopped and got home at night . . . this evening I went to Mr. Zach Chapman to a party, Mr. Foley came and dressed flax for half a cord of wood I drew him last winter to the school house." In a short time, George Holcomb dealt with neighbors and relatives, with cash and bartering, and with a local economy that mixed cut wood, schoolhouse provisions, dressed flax, and a party. He conducted his eco-nomic life within an elaborate network of neighborly and family obligations, and not by buying, selling, and calculating.

Country storekeepers and village merchants handled relationships between farmers and long-distance markets, and they were as much a part of their neighborhoods as of the wider world. In most areas, farmers brought produce—often a mixed batch of grain, vegetables, ashes, goose down, and so on—to the storekeeper, who arranged its shipment to a seaport town. Some paid cash for produce, but most simply credited the farmer's account. Farmers also bought store goods on credit, and when bad crop years or bad luck made them unable to pay, storekeepers tended to wait for payment without charging interest. In many instances, the store was incorporated into the relations of local exchange. Hudson River merchants paid the same prices for local goods that were to be sold locally over long periods of time—a price that reflected their relative value within the local barter economy. When sent to New York City, the prices of the same goods floated up and down with their value on international markets. Storekeepers also played a role in local networks of debt, for it was common for farmers to bring their grain, ashes, butter, and eggs to the store, and to have them credited to the accounts of neighbors to whom they were in debt, thus turning the storekeeper into a broker within the complicated web of neighborhood obligations.

Standards of Living

In 1790, most farmhouses in the older rural areas were small, one-story structures, and few farmers bothered to keep their surroundings clean or attractive. They repaired their fences only when they became too dilapidated to function. They rarely planted trees or shrubs, and housewives threw out garbage for chickens and pigs that foraged near the house.

Inside, there were few rooms and many people. Beds stood in every room, and few family members slept alone. Growing up in Bethel, Connecticut, the future show-business entrepreneur P. T. Barnum shared a bed with his brother and an Irish servant. Guests shared beds in New England taverns until the 1820s. The hearth remained the source of heat and light in most farmhouses. Between 1790 and 1810, over half the households in central Massachusetts, an old and relatively prosperous area, owned only one or two candlesticks, suggesting that one of the great disparities between wealthy families and their less affluent neighbors was that the wealthy could light their houses at night. Another disparity was in the outward appearance of houses. The better-off families painted their houses white as a token of pristine republicanism, but their bright houses stood apart from the weathered greybrown clapboard siding of their neighbors in stark and unrepublican contrast.

Increased income from foreign markets did result in improvement. Farmers bought traditional necessities such as salt and pepper, gunpowder, tools, and coffee and tea, but these were now supplemented with an increasingly alluring array of little luxuries such as crockery, flatware, finished cloth, mirrors, clocks and watches, wallpaper, and the occasional book. At mealtimes, only the poorest families continued to eat with their fingers or with spoons from a common bowl. By 1800, individual place settings with knives and forks and china plates, along with individual chairs instead of benches, had become common in rural America.

Inheritance

Northern farmers between 1790 and 1815 were remarkably like Jefferson's yeoman-citizen ideal: prosperous, independent, living in rough equality with neighbors who shared the same status. Yet even as rural Americans acted out that vision, its social base was disintegrating. Overcrowding and the growth of markets caused the price of good farmland to rise sharply throughout the older settlements. Most young men could expect to inherit only a few acres of exhausted land, or to move to wilderness land in the **back-country**. Failing those, they could expect to quit farming altogether. Crèvecoeur's baby boy—who in fact ended up living in Boston—was in a more precarious position than his seat on his father's plough might have indicated.

In Revolutionary America, fathers had been judged by their ability to support and govern their households, to serve as good neighbors, and to pass land on to their sons. After the war, fewer farm fathers were able to do that. Those in the old settlements had small farms and large families, which made it impossible for them to provide a competence for all of their offspring. Fathers felt that they had failed as fathers, and their sons, with no prospect of an adequate inheritance, were obliged to leave home. Most fathers tried to provide for all of their heirs (generally by leaving land to their sons and personal property to their daughters.) Few left all of their land to one son, and many stated in their wills that the sons to whom they left the land must share barns and cider mills—even houses—on farms that could be subdivided no further. Such provisions fitted a social system that guaranteed the independence of the household head through complex relations with kin and neighbors, but they were also an indication that that system had reached the end of the line.

Outside New England, farm **tenancy** was on the increase. In parts of Pennsylvania and in other areas as well, farmers often bought farms when they became available in the neighborhood, rented them to tenants to augment the household income, and gave them to their sons when they reached adulthood. The sons of poorer farmers often rented a farm in the hope of saving enough money to buy it. Some fathers bought tracts of unimproved land in the backcountry—sometimes on speculation, more often to provide their sons with land they could make into a farm. Others paid to have their sons educated, or arranged an apprenticeship to provide them with an avenue of escape from a crowded countryside. As a result, more and more young men left home. The populations of the old farming communities grew older and more female, while the populations of the rising frontier settlements and seaport cities became younger and more male. The young men who stayed home often had nothing to look forward to but a lifetime as tenants or hired hands.

The Seaport Cities

When the first federal census takers made their rounds in 1790, they found 94 percent of Americans living on farms and in rural villages. The remaining 6 percent lived in 24 towns with a population of more than 2,500 (a census definition of "urban" that included many communities that were, by modern standards, very small). Only five places had populations over 10,000: Boston (18,038), New York (33,131), Philadelphia (42,444), Baltimore (13,503), and Charleston (16,359). All five were seaports, which is testimony to the key role of international commerce in the economy of the early republic.

The little streams of produce that left farm neighborhoods joined with others on the rivers and the coastal shipping lanes, and they piled up as a significant national surplus on the docks of the seaport towns. When war broke out between Britain and France in 1793, the overseas demand for American foodstuffs, and thus the production of American farms, increased. The warring European powers also needed shipping to carry products from the Caribbean islands to Europe. America's saltwater merchants, free from the old colonial restrictions, responded by building one of the great merchant fleets in the world, and American overseas trade entered a period of unprecedented growth. Ocean trade during these years was risky and uneven, subject to the tides of war and the strategies of the belligerents. French seizures of American shipping and the resulting undeclared war of 1798–1800, the British ban on America's re-export trade in 1805, Jefferson's nonimportation of 1806 and his embargo of 1807, and America's entry into the war in 1812 all disrupted the maritime economy and threw the seaports into periods of economic collapse. But by 1815, wartime commerce had transformed the seaports and the institutions of American business. New York City had become the nation's largest city, with a population that grew from 33,131 in 1790 to 96,373 in 1810. Philadelphia's population had risen to 53,722 by 1810; Boston's to 34,322; and Baltimore's to 46,555. Economic growth in the years 1790 to 1815 was most palpably concentrated in these cities.

The Historical Society of Pennsylvania, *Procession of the Victuallers*, by John Lewis Krimmel (Bc85 K89)

Procession of Victuallers, 1815 The frequent and festive parades in the seaport cities included militia companies, political officials, clergymen, and artisans organized by trade. In this Philadelphia parade celebrating the end of the War of 1812, the victuallers, preceded by militia cavalrymen, carry a penned steer and a craft flag high atop a wagon, while butchers in top hats and clean aprons ride below. Behind them, shipbuilders drag a ship through the streets. Such parades were vivid displays of the system of interlocking labors that made up the city and of the value of artisans within that system.

Seaport merchants in these years amassed the private fortunes and built the financial infrastructure that would soon take up the task of commercializing and industrializing the northern United States. Old merchants like the Brown brothers of Providence and Elias Hasket Darby of Salem grew richer, and newcomers like the immigrant John Jacob Astor of New York City built huge personal fortunes. To manage those fortunes, new institutions emerged. Docking and warehousing facilities improved dramatically. Bookkeepers were replaced by accountants who were familiar with the new double-entry system of accounting, and insurance and banking companies were formed to handle the risks and rewards of wartime commerce.

The cities prospered in these years. The main thoroughfares and a few of the side streets were paved with cobblestones and lined with fine shops and townhouses. But in other parts of the cities, visitors learned that the boom was creating poverty as well as wealth. There had been poor people and depressed neighborhoods in the 18th-century seaports, but not on the scale that prevailed between 1790 and 1820. A few steps off the handsome avenues were narrow streets crowded with ragged children, browsing dogs and pigs, with garbage and waste filling the open sewers. Epidemics became more frequent and deadly. New York City, for example, experienced six severe bouts of yellow fever between 1791 and 1822. Each time, the disease entered through the seaport and settled in the slums. Life expectancy in Boston, reputedly the healthiest city in America, was three to five years lower than in the surrounding countryside.

The slums were evidence that money created by commerce was being distributed in undemocratic ways. Per capita wealth in New York rose 60 percent between 1790 and 1825, but the wealthiest 4 percent of the population owned over half of that wealth. The wages of skilled and unskilled labor rose in these years, but the increase in seasonal and temporary employment, together with the recurring interruptions of foreign commerce, cut deeply into the security and prosperity of ordinary women and men. Added to the old insecurities of sickness, fire, accident, aging, and any number of personal misfortunes, these ate up the gains made by laborers, sailors, and most artisans and their families.

Meanwhile, the status of artisans in the big cities was undergoing change. In 1790, artisans were the self-proclaimed "middling classes" of the towns. They demanded and usually received the respect of their fellow citizens. When a clerk in Boston refused to attend dancing classes that one of the town's master saddlers had joined, a newspaper scolded him (a mere "stockjobber's lackey") for considering himself the social superior of the saddler and other "reputable mechanics." Skilled manual workers constituted about half the male workforce of the seaport cities, and their respectability and usefulness, together with the role they had played in the Revolution, had earned them an honorable status.

That status rested in large part on their independence. In 1790, most artisan workshops were household operations with at most one or two apprentices and hired journeymen—wage earners who looked forward to owning their own shops one day. Timothy Dwight, the conservative president of Yale College, observed that there were few of those "amphibious beings" in America who remained journeymen (wage earners) for life. Most master craftsmen lived modestly (on the borderline of poverty in many cases) and aspired only to support their household in security and decency, and to do so by performing useful work. They identified their way of life with republican virtue. Jefferson proclaimed them "the yeomen of the cities."

The patriarchal base of that republicanism, however, was eroding. With the growth of the maritime economy, the nature of construction work, shipbuilding, the clothing trades, and other specialized crafts changed. Artisans were being replaced by cheaper labor and undercut by subcontracted "slop work" performed by semiskilled rural outworkers. Perhaps one in five master craftsmen entered the newly emerging business class. The others took work as laborers or wage-earning craftsmen. By 1815, most young craftsmen in the seaports could not hope to own their own shops. About half of New York City's journeymen that year were over 30 years old; nearly a quarter were over 40. Most were married, and half headed a household that included four or more dependents. In short, they had become wage earners for life. In the seaports between 1790 and 1815, the world of artisans like Paul Revere, Benjamin Franklin, and Thomas Paine was passing out of existence. Wage labor was taking its place.

The loss of independence undermined artisan husbands and fathers. Few wage earners could support a family without the earnings of a wife and children. Working-class women took in boarders and did laundry and found work as domestic servants or as peddlers of fruit, candy, vegetables, cakes, or hot corn. They sent their children out to scavenge in the streets. The descent into wage labor and the reliance on the earnings of women and children were at variance with the republican, patriarchal assumptions of fathers.

From Backcountry to Frontier: The Northwest

The United States was a huge country in 1790, at least on paper. In the treaty that ended the War of Independence in 1783, the British ignored Indian claims and ceded all of the land from the Atlantic Ocean to the Mississippi River to the new republic, with the exceptions of Spanish Florida and New Orleans. The states then surrendered their individual claims to the federal government, and in 1790, George Washington became president of a nation that stretched nearly 1,500 miles inland. Still, most white Americans lived on thin strips of settlement on the Atlantic coast and along the few navigable rivers that emptied into the Atlantic. Some were pushing their way into the wilds of Maine and northern Vermont, and in New York others set up communities as far west as the Mohawk Valley. Pittsburgh was a struggling new settlement, and two outposts had been established on the Ohio River: at Marietta and at what would become Cincinnati.

The Backcountry, 1790–1815

To easterners, the backcountry whites who were displacing the Indians seemed no different from the defeated aborigines. In fact, in accommodating themselves to a borderless forest used by both Indians and whites, many settlers—like many Indians—had melded Indian and white ways. To clear the land, backcountry farmers simply girdled the trees and left them to die and fall down by themselves. They plowed the land by navigating between the stumps. To easterners' minds, the worst offense was that women often worked the fields, particularly while their men, as did Indians, spent long periods away on hunting trips for food game and animal skins for trade. The arch-pioneer Daniel Boone, for instance, braided his hair, dressed himself in Indian leggings, and, with only his dogs for company, disappeared for months at a time on "long hunts." When easterners began to "civilize" his neighborhood, Boone moved farther west.

Eastern visitors were appalled not only by the poverty, lice, and filth of frontier life but also by the drunkenness and violence of the frontiersmen. Americans everywhere drank heavily in the early years of the 19th century, but everyone agreed that westerners drank more and were more violent when drunk than men anywhere else. Travelers told of no-holds-barred fights in which men gouged the eyes and bit off the noses and ears of their opponents. No account was complete without a reckoning of the number of one-eyed, one-eared men the traveler had met on the frontier. Stories arose of half-legendary heroes such as Davy Crockett of Tennessee, who wrestled bears and alligators and had a recipe for Indian stew, and Mike Fink, a Pennsylvania boatman who brawled and drank his way along the rivers of the interior until he was shot and killed in a drunken episode that none of the participants could clearly remember. Samuel Holden Parsons, a New Englander serving as a judge in the Northwest Territory, called the frontiersmen "our white savages." Massachusetts conservative Timothy Pickering branded them "the least worthy subjects of the United States. They are little less savage than the Indians."

Settlement

After 1789, settlers of the backcountry made two demands of the new national government: protection from the Indians and a guarantee of the right to navigate the Ohio and Mississippi rivers. The Indians were pushed back in the 1790s and finished off in the War of 1812, and in 1803, Jefferson's Louisiana Purchase ended the European presence on the rivers and at the crucial chokepoint at New Orleans. Over these years, the pace of settlement quickened. In 1790, only 10,000 settlers lived west of the Appalachians—about 1 American in 40. By 1800, the number of settlers had risen to nearly 1 million. By 1820, 2 million Americans were westerners—one in five. **(See Map 8.1, Population Density, 1790–1820, in the color insert following page 384.)**

The new settlers bought land from speculators who had acquired tracts under the Northwest Ordinance in the Northwest; from English, Dutch, and American land companies in western New York; and from land dealers in the Southwest and in northern New England. They built frame houses surrounded by cleared fields, planted marketable crops, and settled into the struggle to make farms out of the wilderness and to meet mortgage payments along the way. Ohio entered the union in 1803, followed by Indiana (1816) and Illinois (1818). As time passed, the term *backcountry,* which easterners had used to refer to the wilderness and the dangerous misfits who lived in it, fell into disuse. By 1820, the term *frontier* had replaced it. The new settlements no longer represented the backwash of American civilization. They were its cutting edge.

The Decline of Patriarchy

In the 50 years following the Declaration of Independence, the patriarchal republic created by the Founding Fathers became a democracy. The decline of authority and deference and the rise of individualistic, democratic social and political forms had many roots—most obviously in rural overcrowding, the movement of young people west and into the towns, and, more happily, in the increasingly democratic implications of American Revolutionary ideology. Most Americans witnessed the initial stirrings of change as a withering of paternal authority in their own households. Some—slaves and many women in particular—welcomed the decline of **patriarchy.** Others (the fathers, disinherited sons, and women who looked to the security of old ways) considered it a disaster of unmeasured proportions. Whether they experienced the transformation as a personal rise or fall, northerners had entered a world where received authority and past experience had lost their power. A new democratic faith emerged, grounded in the experience, intellect, and intuition of ordinary people.

Paternal Power in Decline

The philosopher Ralph Waldo Emerson, who reached adulthood in the 1830s, mused that he had had the misfortune to be young when age was respected and to have grown old when youth counted for everything. Arriving in America at about the time Emerson came of age, the French visitor Alexis de Tocqueville observed that paternal power was largely absent in American families. "All that remains of it," he said, "are a few vestiges in the first years of childhood. . . . But as soon as the young American approaches manhood, the ties of filial obedience are relaxed day by day; master of his thoughts, he is soon master of his conduct. . . . At the close of boyhood the man appears and begins to trace out his own path."

From the mid-18th century onward, and especially after the Revolution, many young people grew up knowing that their fathers would be unable to help them and that they would have to make their own way in the world. The consequent decline of parental power became evident in many ways, perhaps most poignantly in changing patterns of courtship and marriage. In the countryside, young men knew that they would not inherit the family farm, and young women knew that their father would be able to provide only a small dowry. As a result, fathers exerted less control over marriage choices than when marriage entailed a significant transfer of property. Young people now courted away from parental scrutiny and made choices based on affection and personal attraction more than on property or parental pressure. In 18th-century America, rural marriages had united families; now they united individuals. One sign of youthful independence (and of young people's lack of faith in their future) was the high number of pregnancies outside of marriage. Such incidents had been few in the 17th-century

North, but in the second half of the 18th century and in the first decades of the 19th, the number of first births that occurred within eight months of marriage averaged between 25 percent and 30 percent, with the rates running much higher among poor couples. Apparently, fathers who could not provide for their children could not control them either.

The Alcoholic Republic

The erosion of the old family economy was paralleled by a dramatic rise in alcohol consumption. Americans had been drinking alcohol since the time of the first settlements. (The Puritan flagship *Arabella* had carried three times as much beer as water.) But drinking, like all other "normal" behaviors, took place within a structure of paternal authority. Americans tippled every day in the course of their ordinary activities: at family meals and around the fireside, at work, and at barn-raisings, militia musters, dances, court days (even judges and juries passed the bottle), weddings, funerals, corn-huskings—even at the ordination of ministers. Under such circumstances, drinking—even drunkenness—seldom posed a threat to authority or to the social order.

That old pattern of communal drinking persisted into the 19th century, but during the 50 years following the Revolution, it gradually gave way to a new pattern. Farmers, particularly those in newly settled areas, regularly produced a surplus of grain that they turned into whiskey. In Washington County in western Pennsylvania, for example, 1 family in 10 operated a distillery in the 1790s. Whiskey was safer than water and milk, which were often tainted, and it was cheaper than coffee or tea. It was also cheaper than imported rum, so Americans embraced whiskey as their national drink and consumed extraordinary quantities of it. Per capita consumption of pure alcohol in all its forms increased by three to four gallons annually between 1790 and 1830. Most of the increase was in consumption of cheap and potent whiskey. By 1830, per capita consumption of distilled spirits was more than five gallons per year—the highest it has ever been, and three times what it is in the United States today. The United States had become, as one historian has said, an **"alcoholic republic."**

The nation's growing thirst was driven not by conviviality or neighborliness but by a desire to get drunk. Most Americans drank regularly, although with wide variations. Men drank far more than women, the poor and the rich drank more than the emerging middle class, city dwellers drank more than farmers, westerners drank more than easterners, and southerners drank a bit more than northerners. Throughout the nation, the heaviest drinking took place among the increasing numbers of young men who lived away from their families and outside the old social controls: soldiers and sailors, boatmen and other transport workers, lumberjacks, schoolmasters, **journeyman** craftsmen, college students. Among such men, the controlled tippling of the 18th century gave way to the binge and to solitary drinking. By the 1820s, American physicians were learning to diagnose delirium tremens—the trembling and the paranoid delusions brought on by withdrawal from physical addiction to alcohol. By that decade, social reformers branded alcohol as a threat to individual well-being, domestic peace, public order, and the republic itself. (See chapter 12.)

Transportation Revolution, 1815–1860

Focus Question
How did improvements in transportation actually channel commerce within and between sections?

After 1815, dramatic improvements in transportation—more and better roads, steamboats, canals, and railroads—tied old communities together and penetrated previously isolated neighborhoods and transformed them. Most of these improvements were the work of state governments. They made the transition to a market society physically possible.

Transportation in 1815

In 1815, the United States was a rural nation stretching from the old settlements on the Atlantic coast to the trans-Appalachian west, with transportation facilities that ranged from primitive to nonexistent. Americans despaired of communicating, to say nothing of doing business on a national scale. In 1816, a Senate committee reported that $9 would move a ton of goods across the 3,000-mile expanse of the North Atlantic. The same $9 would move the same ton of goods only 30 miles inland. A year later, the cost of transporting wheat from the new settlement of Buffalo to New York City was three times greater than the selling price of wheat in New York. Farming for profit made sense only for farmers near urban markets or with easy river access to the coast.

West of the Appalachians, transportation was almost entirely undeveloped. Until the 1820s, most northwesterners were southern yeomen who settled near tributaries of the Ohio–Mississippi River Valley, which reached the sea at New Orleans. Farmers floated their produce downriver on jerry-built flatboats. Boatmen making the trip from Louisville to New Orleans spent a full month navigating dangerous rivers through unsettled territory. At New Orleans, northwestern produce was trans-shipped to New York and other eastern ports. Most boatmen knocked down their flatboats, sold the lumber, then walked home to Kentucky or Ohio over the difficult and dangerous Natchez Trace.

Transporting goods *into* the western settlements was even more difficult. Keel boatmen like the legendary Mike Fink could navigate upstream—using eddies and back currents, sailing when the wind was right, but usually poling their boats against the current. Skilled crews averaged only 15 miles a day, and the trip from New Orleans to Louisville took three to four months. Looking for better routes, some merchants dragged finished goods across Pennsylvania and into the West at Pittsburgh, but transport costs made these goods prohibitively expensive. Consequently, the trans-Appalachian settlements—home to one in five Americans by 1820—remained marginal to the market economy. By 1815, New Orleans was shipping about $5 million of western produce annually—an average of only $15 per farm family in the interior.

Improvements

In 1816, Congress resumed construction of the **National Road** (first authorized in 1802) that linked the Potomac River with the Ohio River at Wheeling, Virginia—an attempt to link west and east through the Chesapeake. The smooth, crushed-rock thoroughfare reached Wheeling in 1818. At about the same time, Pennsylvania extended the Lancaster Turnpike to make it run from Philadelphia to the Ohio River at Pittsburgh. These ambitious roads into the West, however, had limited effects. The National Road made it easier for settlers and a few merchants' wagons to reach the West, but the cost of moving bulky farm produce over the road remained high. Eastbound traffic on the National Road consisted largely of cattle and pigs, which carried themselves to market. Farmers continued to float their corn, **cotton,** wheat, salt pork, and whiskey south by riverboat and thence to eastern markets.

It was the steamboat that first made commercial agriculture feasible in the Northwest. Tinkerers and mechanics had been experimenting with steam-powered boats for a generation or more when an entrepreneur named **Robert Fulton** launched the *Clermont* on an upriver trip from New York City to Albany in 1807. Over the next few years, Americans

Thomas L. McKenney, *Sketches of a Tour to the Lakes* (1827)

A River Steamboat in 1826   By the mid-1820s, steamboats regularly plied the river systems of the United States. Businessmen and elite travelers rented nicely appointed cabins on the steamer and viewed the scenery as they strolled the comfortable (and usually uncrowded) passenger deck. Poorer passengers bought passage on the "Safety Barge" that was dragged behind the steamer.

developed flat-bottomed steamboats that could navigate rivers even at low water. The first steamboat reached Louisville from New Orleans in 1815. Two years later, with 17 steamboats already working western rivers, the *Washington* made the New Orleans–Louisville run in 25 days, a feat that convinced westerners that two-way river trade was possible. By 1820, 69 steamboats were operating on western rivers. The 60,000 tons of produce that farmers and planters had shipped out of the interior in 1810 grew to 500,000 tons in 1840. The steamboat had transformed the interior from an isolated frontier into a busy commercial region that traded farm and plantation products for manufactured goods.

In the East, state governments created rivers where nature had made none. In 1817, Governor DeWitt Clinton, after failing to get federal support, talked the New York legislature into building a canal linking the Hudson River with Lake Erie, thus opening a continuous water route between the Northwest and New York City. The **Erie Canal** was a near-visionary feat of engineering. Designed by self-taught engineers and built by gangs of Irish immigrants, local farm boys, and convict laborers, it stretched 364 miles from Albany to Buffalo. Although "Clinton's Ditch" passed through carefully chosen level ground, it required a complex system of 83 locks, and it passed over 18 rivers on stone aqueducts. Construction began in 1819, and the canal reached Buffalo in 1825. It was clear even before then that the canal would repay New York state's investment of $7.5 million many times over, and that it would transform the territory that it served. **(See Map 8.2, Rivers, Roads, and Canals, 1825–1860, in the color insert following page 384.)**

The Erie Canal would direct the trade of the whole Great Lakes watershed into New York City, but its first and most powerful effects were on western New York, which had been a raw frontier accessible to the East only over a notoriously bad state road. By 1830, the New York corridor of the Erie Canal, settled largely from hill-country New England, was one of the world's great grain-growing regions, dotted with market towns and new cities like Syracuse, Rochester, and Buffalo.

The Erie Canal was an immense success, and legislators and entrepreneurs in other states joined a canal boom that lasted for 20 years. When construction began on the Erie Canal, there were fewer then 100 miles of canal in the United States. By 1840, there were 3,300 miles, nearly all of it in the Northeast and Northwest. Northwestern states, Ohio in particular, built ambitious canal systems that linked isolated areas to the Great Lakes and thus to the Erie Canal. Northeastern states followed suit. A canal between Worcester and Providence linked the farms of central Massachusetts with Narragansett Bay. Another canal linked the coal mines of northeastern Pennsylvania with the Hudson River at Kingston, New York. In 1835, Pennsylvania completed a canal from Philadelphia to Pittsburgh.

The canal boom was followed quickly by a boom in railroads. The first of them connected burgeoning cities to rivers and canals. The Baltimore and Ohio Railroad, for example, linked Baltimore to the rivers of the West. Although the approximately 3,000 miles of railroads built between the late 1820s and 1840 helped the market positions of some cities, they did not constitute a national or even a regional rail network. A national system developed with the 5,000 miles of track laid in the 1840s and with the flurry of railroad building that gave the United States a rail network of 30,000 miles by 1860—a continuous, integrated system that created massive links between the East and the Northwest and that threatened to put canals out of business. In fact, the New York Central, which paralleled the Erie Canal, rendered that canal obsolete. Other railroads, particularly in the northwestern states, replaced canal and river transport almost completely, even though water transport remained cheaper. By 1860, few farmers in the North and West lived more than 20 road miles from railroads, canals, or rivers that could deliver their produce to regional, national, and international markets.

Time and Money

The transportation revolution brought a dramatic reduction in the time and money that it took to move heavy goods. Turnpikes cut the cost of wagon transport, but goods traveled most cheaply on water. In 1816, freight rates on the Ohio–Mississippi system had been 1.3 cents per ton-mile for downriver travel and 5.8 cents for upriver travel. Steamboats cut both costs to a bit more than a third of a cent. The Erie Canal and the Ohio canals reduced the distance between East and West and carried goods at about a cent per ton-mile. By 1830, farmers in the Northwest and western New York could grow wheat and sell it at a profit on the New York market.

Improvements in speed were nearly as dramatic. The overland trip from Cincinnati to New York in 1815 (by keelboat upriver to Pittsburgh, then by wagon the rest of the way) had taken a minimum of 52 days. Steamboats traveled from Cincinnati to New Orleans, then passed goods on to coasting ships that finished the trip to New York City in a total of 28 days. By 1840, upriver steamboats carried goods to the terminus of the Main Line Canal at Pittsburgh, which delivered them to Philadelphia, which sent them on to New York City for a total transit time of 18 to 20 days. At about the same time, the Ohio canal system enabled Cincinnati to send goods north through Ohio, across Lake Erie, over the Erie Canal, and down the Hudson to New York City—an all-water route that reduced costs and made the trip in 18 days. Similar improvements occurred in the densely settled and increasingly urbanized Northeast. By 1840, travel time between the big northeastern cities had been reduced to from one-fourth to one-eleventh of what it had been in 1790. These improvements in speed and economy made a northern market economy possible.

By 1840, improved transportation had made a market revolution. Foreign trade, which had driven American economic growth up until 1815, continued to expand. The value of American exports in 1815 had stood at $52.6 million, while imports totaled $113 million. Both rose dramatically in the years of the market revolution: exports (now consisting more of southern cotton than of northern food crops) continued to increase, and the flow of imported manufactured goods increased as well. Yet foreign trade now accounted for a smaller *proportion* of American—particularly northern—market activity. Before 1815, Americans had exported about 15 percent of their total national product. By 1830, exports accounted for only 6 percent of a vastly increased national production. The reason for this

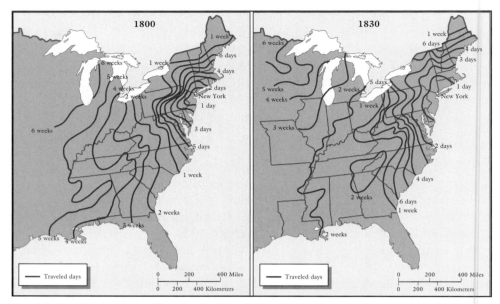

Map 8.3 Time Required to Travel from New York City, 1800 and 1830 These maps illustrate the increasing ease of travel in the first third of the 19th century. In general, travelers could cover nearly twice as much territory in a day in 1830 than in 1800, although in both cases travel became more difficult as one left the densely settled east.

shift was that after 1815, the United States developed self-sustaining domestic markets for farm produce and manufactured goods. The great engine of economic growth in the North and West was not the old colonial relationship with Europe but a self-sustaining domestic market.

Markets and Regions

Henry Clay and other proponents of the **American System** (see chapter 11) dreamed of a market-driven economy that would transcend sectionalism and create a unified United States. But until at least 1840, the market revolution produced greater results within regions than between them. The farmers of New England traded food for finished goods from Boston, Lynn, Lowell, and other towns in what was becoming an urban, industrial region. Philadelphia traded manufactures for food from the farmers of the Delaware Valley. Although the **Erie Canal** created a huge potential for interregional trade, until 1839 most of its eastbound tonnage originated in western New York. In the West, market-oriented farmers fed such rapidly growing cities as Rochester, Pittsburgh, and Cincinnati, which in turn supplied the farmers with locally manufactured farm tools, furniture, shoes, and other goods. Thus until about 1840, the market revolution was more a regional than an interregional phenomenon. Yet it was clear to politicians, and to anyone else who looked at a map, that the New England, mid-Atlantic, and Northwestern states were on their way to becoming an integrated market society—one

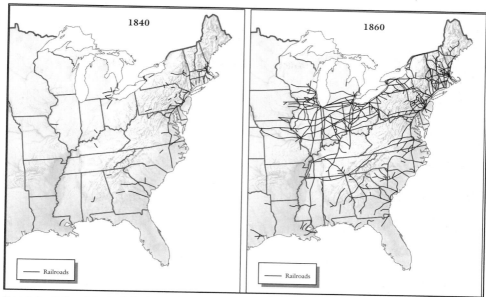

Map 8.4   Railroads in the United States, 1840 and 1860   In these 20 years, both the North and South built railway systems. Northerners built rail lines that integrated the market economies of the Midwest and the East—both within sections and between them. For the most part, Southern railroads linked the plantation belt with the ocean. Revealingly, only a few lines connected the North and South.

that did not include southern plantations that grew for export (see chapter 9). It was not what Henry Clay had had in mind.

Northeastern Farms, 1815–1860

In the old farming communities of the Northeast, the transformations of the early 19th century sent many young people off to cities and factory towns and others to the West. Those who remained at home engaged in new forms of agriculture on a transformed rural landscape, while their cousins in the Northwest turned a wilderness into cash-producing farms. In both regions, farmers abandoned the old mixed, safety-first agriculture and began to raise a single crop intended for distant markets. That decision committed them to buying things that their forebears had grown or made, and thus to participate as both producers and consumers in a new market economy.

An early 19th-century New England farm geared toward family subsistence required only 3 acres of cultivated land, 12 acres of pasture and meadow, another acre for the house, outbuildings, and vegetable garden, and a 30-acre woodlot to stoke the hearth that cooked the food and heated the house. Visitors to even the oldest towns found farmsteads, tilled fields, and pastures scattered across a heavily wooded landscape. Overcrowding had encouraged some farmers to turn woodlots into poor farmland, but New Englanders who tried to grow grain on their rocky, worn-out soil could not compete with the farmers of western New York and the Northwest. At the same time, however, the factories and cities of the Northeast provided Yankee farmers with a market for meat and other perishables. Beef became the great New England cash crop. Dairy products were not far behind, and the proximity to city markets encouraged the spread of poultry and egg farms, fruit orchards, and truck gardens. The burgeoning shoe industry bought leather from the farmers, and woolen mills created a demand for wool, and thus for great flocks of New England sheep. As a result, millions of trees were stripped from the New England landscape to make way for pastureland.

The rise of livestock specialization reduced the amount of land under cultivation. Early in the century, New Englanders still tilled their few acres in the old three-year rotation: corn the first year, rye the second, fallow the third. By the 1820s and 1830s, as farmers raised more livestock and less grain, the land that remained in cultivation was farmed more intensively. Farmers saved manure and ashes for fertilizer, plowed more deeply and systematically, and tended their crops more carefully. These improved techniques, along with cash from the sale of their livestock and the availability of food at stores, encouraged Yankee farmers to allocate less and less land to the growing of food crops. In Concord, Massachusetts—the home town of the agrarian republic—the portion of town land in tillage dropped from 20 percent to 7 percent between 1771 and 1850.

The transition to livestock-raising transformed woodlands into open pastures. As farmers leveled the forests, they sold the wood to fuel-hungry cities. It was a lucrative, although short-term, market: in 1829, a cord of wood sold for $1.50 in Maine and for $7 in Boston. In the 1820s, manufacturers began marketing cast-iron stoves that heated houses more cheaply and more efficiently than open hearths, and canals brought cheap Pennsylvania anthracite to the Northeast. Farmers who needed pastureland could gain substantial one-time profits from the sale of cut wood. The result was massive deforestation. In 1790, in the central Massachusetts town of Petersham, forest covered 85 percent of the town lands. By 1830, the creation of pastureland through commercial woodcutting had reduced the forested area to 30 percent. (By 1850, woods covered only 10 percent of the town, the pasturelands were overgrazed and ruined, and the landscape was dotted with abandoned farms.)

With the shift to specialized market agriculture, New England farmers became customers for necessities that their forebears had produced themselves or had acquired through barter. They heated their houses with coal dug by Pennsylvania miners. They wore cotton cloth made by the factory women at Lowell. New Hampshire farm girls made straw hats for them, and the craftsmen of Lynn made their shoes. By 1830 or so, many farmers were even buying food. The Erie Canal and the western grain belt sent flour from Rochester into eastern neighborhoods where grain was no longer grown. Many farmers found it easier to produce specialized crops for market, and to buy butter, cheese, eggs, and vegetables at country stores.

The turning point came in the 1820s. The storekeepers of Northampton, Massachusetts, for instance, had been increasing their stock in trade by about 7 percent per decade since the late 18th century. In the 1820s, they increased it 45 percent and now carried not only local farm products and sugar, salt, and coffee, but also bolts of New England cloth, sacks of western flour, a variety of necessities and little luxuries from the wholesale houses of New York City and Boston, and pattern samples from which to order silverware, dishes, wallpaper, and other household goods. Those goods were better than what could be made at home, and for the most part they were cheaper. The price of factory-made cloth, for instance, declined sixfold between 1815 and 1830.

As a result, spinning wheels and handlooms disappeared from the farmhouses of New England. Farm families that bought the new cast-iron stoves enjoyed pies and bread baked from western white flour; the old "Rye and Injun" disappeared. All of these things cost money and committed farm families to increasing their cash incomes. Standards of living rose dramatically. At the same time, northeastern farmers depended on markets in ways that their fathers and grandfathers would have considered dangerous not only to family welfare but to the welfare of the republic itself.

The Northwest

One reason the market revolution in the Northeast went as smoothly as it did was that young people with little hope of inheriting land in the old settlements moved to towns and cities or to the new farmlands of the Northwest. Between 1815 and 1840—precisely the years in which northeastern agriculture became a cash-crop business—migrants from the older areas transformed the Northwest Territory into a working agricultural landscape.

Southern Settlers

In the Northwest until the 1820s, most settlers were yeomen from Kentucky and Tennessee, usually a generation removed from Virginia, the Carolinas, and western Maryland. They moved along the Ohio and up the Muskingum, Miami, Scioto, Wabash, and Illinois rivers to set up farms in the southern and central counties of Ohio, Indiana, and Illinois. When southerners moved north of the Ohio River into territory that banned slavery, they often did so saying that slavery blocked opportunities for poor whites. The Methodist preacher Peter Cartwright left Kentucky thinking, "I would get entirely clear of the evil of slavery," and "could raise my children to work where work was not thought a degradation." Similar hopes drew thousands of other southern yeomen north of the Ohio.

But even those who rejected slavery seldom rejected southern folkways. Like their kinfolk in Kentucky and Tennessee, the farmers of southern and central Ohio, Indiana, and Illinois remained tied to the river trade and to a mode of agriculture that favored free-ranging livestock over cultivated fields. The typical farmer fenced in a few acres of corn and left the rest of his land in woods to be roamed by hogs known as "razorbacks" and "land sharks." These animals were thin and tough (they seldom grew to over 200 pounds), and they could run long distances, leap fences, and fend for themselves in the woods. They were notoriously fierce; more settlers were injured by their own hogs than by wild animals. When it was time to gather the hogs for slaughter, many settlers played it safe and hunted them with guns.

The southern-born pioneers of the Northwest, like their cousins across the Ohio River, depended more on their families and neighbors than on distant markets. Newcomers found that they could neither rent tools from their southern neighbors nor present them with "gifts" during hard times. Southerners insisted on repaying debts in kind and on lending tools rather than renting them, thus engaging outsiders in the elaborate network of "neighboring" through which transplanted southerners made their livings. As late as the 1840s, in the bustling town of Springfield, Illinois, barter was the preferred system of exchange. "In no part of the world," said a Scotsman in southern Illinois, "is good neighborship found in greater perfection than in the western territory."

Northern Farmers

In the 1820s, with improved transportation and with the wars with Indians and Canadians at an end, northeastern migrants entered the Northwest. They settled near the Great Lakes, filling the new lands of Michigan and the northern counties of the older northwestern states. Most of them were New Englanders who had spent a generation in western New York (such settlers accounted for three-fourths of the early population of Michigan). The rest came directly from New England. Arriving in the Northwest along the market's busiest arteries, they practiced an intensive, market-oriented agriculture. They penned their cattle and hogs and fattened them up, making them bigger and worth more than those farther south. They planted their land in grain and transformed the region—beginning with western New York's Genesee Country in the 1820s and rolling through the Northwest—into one of the world's great wheat-producing regions. In 1820, the Northwest had exported only 12 percent of its agricultural produce. By 1840, that figure had risen to 27 percent, and it stood much higher among northern-born grain farmers.

The new settlers were notably receptive to improvements in farming techniques. While there were plenty of southern proponents of progress and plenty of backward northerners, the line between new and old agricultural ways separated northern grain farmers from corn, hogs, and southern settlers. In breaking new land, for instance, southerners still used the old shovel plow, which dug a shallow furrow and skipped over roots. Northerners preferred newer, more expensive cast-iron plows, which cut cleanly through oak roots four inches thick. By the 1830s, the efficient, expensive grain cradle had replaced the age-old sickle as the principal harvest tool in northwestern wheat fields. Instead of threshing their grain by driving cattle and horses over it, farmers bought new horse-powered and treadmill threshers and used hand-cranked fanning mills to speed the process of cleaning the grain.

Most agricultural improvements were tailored to grain and dairy farming and were taken up most avidly by the northern farmers. Others rejected them as expensive and unnatural. They thought that cast-iron plows poisoned the soil and that fanning mills made a "wind contrary to nater," and thus offended God. John Chapman, an eccentric Yankee who earned the nickname "Johnny Appleseed" by planting apple tree cuttings in southern Ohio and Indiana before the settlers arrived, planted only low-yield, common trees. He regarded grafting, which farmers farther north and east were using to improve the quality of their apples, as "against nature." Southerners scoffed at the Yankee fondness for mechanical improvements, the systematic breeding of animals and plants, careful bookkeeping, and farm techniques learned from books. "I reckon," said one, "I know as much about farming as the printers do."

Conflict between intensive agriculture and older, less market-oriented ways reached comic proportions when the Illinois legislature imposed stiff penalties on farmers who allowed their small, poorly bred bulls to run loose and impregnate cows with questionable sperm, thereby depriving the owners of high-bred bulls of their breeding fees and rendering the systematic breeding of cattle impossible. When the poorer farmers refused to pen their bulls, the law was rescinded. A local historian explained that "there was a generous feeling in the hearts of the people in favor of an equality of privileges, even among bulls."

Farm Families

> ### Focus Question
> How did northern farm families experience the transition into commercial agriculture between 1815 and 1850?

Households

The market revolution transformed 18th-century households into 19th-century homes. For one thing, Americans began to limit the size of their families. White women who married in 1800 had given birth to an average of 6.4 children. Those who married between 1800 and 1849 averaged 4.9 children. The decline was most pronounced in the North, particularly in commercialized areas. Rural birthrates remained at 18th-century levels in the southern uplands, in the poorest and most isolated communities of the North, and on the frontier. (As New Yorker Washington Irving passed through the Northwest in the 1830s, he noted in his journal: "Illinois—famous for children and dogs—in house with nineteen children and thirty-seven dogs.") These communities practiced the old labor-intensive agriculture and relied on the labor of large families. For farmers who used newer techniques or switched to livestock or grain, large families made less sense. Moreover, large broods hampered the ability of future-minded parents to provide for their children and conflicted with new notions of privacy and domesticity that were taking shape among an emerging rural middle class.

Before 1815, farm wives had labored in the house, the barnyard, and the garden while their husbands and sons worked in the fields. With the market revolution came a sharper distinction between male work that was part of the cash economy and female work that was not. Even such traditional women's tasks as dairying, vegetable gardening, and poultry raising became men's work once they became cash-producing specialties. A Pennsylvanian who lived among businesslike New Englanders in the Northwest was appalled at such tampering with hallowed gender roles and wrote the Yankees off as "a shrewd, selfish, enterprising, cow-milking set of men."

At the same time, new kinds of women's work emerged within households. Though there were fewer children to care for, the culture began to demand forms of child-rearing that were more intensive, individualized, and mother-centered. Store-bought white flour, butter, and eggs and the new iron stoves eased the burdens of food preparation, but they also created demands for pies, cakes, and other fancy foods that earlier generations had

A Soap Advertisement from the 1850s   The rigors of "Old Washing Day" lead the mother in this advertisement to abuse the children and house pets, while her husband leaves the house. With American Cream Soap, domestic bliss returns: The children and cats are happy, the husband returns, and the wife has time to sew.

only dreamed of. And while farm women no longer spun and wove their own cloth, the availability of manufactured cloth created the expectation that their families would dress more neatly and with greater variety than they had in the past, and women spent more time sewing, washing, and ironing. Similar expectations demanded greater personal and domestic cleanliness and taste, and farm women worked at planting flower beds, cleaning and maintaining prized furniture, mirrors, rugs, and ceramics, and scrubbing floors and children. The market and housework grew hand in hand: among the first mass-produced commodities in the United States was the household broom.

Housework was tied to new notions of privacy, decency, and domestic comfort. Before 1820, farmers cared little about how their houses looked, often tossing trash and garbage out the door for pigs and chickens that foraged near the house. In the 1820s and 1830s, as farmers began to grow cash crops and adopt middle-class ways, they began to plant shade trees and to keep their yards free of trash. They painted their houses and sometimes their fences and outbuildings, arranged their woodpiles into neat stacks, surrounded their houses with flowers and ornamental shrubs, and tried to hide their privies from view. The new sense of refinement extended into other aspects of country life. The practice of chewing (and spitting) tobacco was gradually banned in churches and meeting halls, and in 1823, the minister in Shrewsbury, Massachusetts, ordered dogs out of the meetinghouse.

Inside, prosperous farmhouses took on an air of privacy and comfort. Separate kitchens and iron stoves replaced open hearths. Many families used a set of matched dishes for individual place settings, and the availability of finished cloth permitted the regular use of tablecloths, napkins, doilies, curtains, bedspreads, and quilts. Oil lamps replaced homemade candles, and the more prosperous families began to decorate their homes with wallpaper and upholstered furniture. Farm couples moved their beds away from the hearth and (along with the children's beds that had been scattered throughout the house) put them into spaces designated as bedrooms. They took wash stands and basins out of the kitchen and put them into the bedroom, thus making sleeping, bathing, and sex more private than they had been in the past. At the center of this new house stood the farm wife, apart from the bustling world of commerce but decorating and caring for the amenities that commerce bought, and demanding that men respect the new domestic world that commerce had made possible.

Neighborhoods

By 1830, the market revolution was transforming the rural landscape of the North. The forests had been reduced, the swamps had been drained, and most of the streams and rivers were interrupted by mill dams. Bears, panthers, and wolves had disappeared, along with the beaver and many of the fish. Now there were extensive pastures where English cattle and sheep browsed on English grasses dotted with English wildflowers like buttercups, daisies, and dandelions. Next to the pastures were neatly cultivated croplands that were regularly fertilized and seldom allowed to lie fallow. And at the center stood painted houses and outbuildings surrounded by flowers and shrubs and vegetable gardens. Many towns, particularly in New England, had planted shade trees along the country roads, completing a rural landscape of straight lines and human cultivation—a landscape that looked both settled and comfortable, and that made it easy to think of nature as a commodity to be altered and controlled.

Within that landscape, old practices and old forms of neighborliness fell into disuse. Neighbors continued to exchange goods and labor and to contract debts that might be left unpaid for years, but debts were more likely to be owed to profit-minded storekeepers and creditors, and even debts between neighbors were often paid in cash. Traditionally, storekeepers had allowed farmers to bring in produce and have it credited to a neighbor/creditor's account—a practice that made the storekeeper an agent of neighborhood bartering. In 1830, half of all the stores in rural New England still carried accounts of this sort, but storekeepers increasingly demanded cash payment or charged lower prices to those who paid cash.

The farm newspapers that appeared in these years urged farmers to keep careful records of the amount of fertilizer used, labor costs, and per-acre yields, and discouraged them from relying on the old system of neighboring. Neighborly rituals like parties, husking bees, and barn-raisings—with their drinking and socializing—were scorned as inefficient and morally suspect wastes of time. The *Farmer's Almanac* of 1833 warned New England farmers: "If you love fun, frolic, and waste and slovenliness more than economy and profit, then make a husking."

By 1830, the efficient northern farmer concentrated on producing commodities that could be marketed outside the neighborhood, and used his cash income to buy material comforts for his family, to pay debts, and to provide a cash inheritance for his children. Although much of the old world of household and neighborhood survived, farmers created a subsistence and maintained the independence of their households not through those spheres but through unprecedented levels of dependence on the outside world.

The Beginnings of the Industrial Revolution

Focus Question
What was the relationship between urban-industrial growth and the commercialization of the northern countryside?

In the 50 years following 1820, American cities grew faster than ever before or since. The old seaports—New York City in particular—grew rapidly in these years, but the fastest growth was in new cities that served commercial agriculture and in factory towns that produced for a largely rural domestic market. Even in the seaports, growth derived more from commerce with the hinterland than from international trade. Paradoxically, the market revolution in the countryside had produced the beginnings of industry and the greatest period of urban growth in U.S. history.

Factory Towns: The Rhode Island System

Jeffersonians held that the United States must always remain rural. Americans, they insisted, could expand into the West, trade their farm surpluses for European finished goods, and thus avoid creating cities with their dependent social classes. Some Federalists argued that Americans, in order to retain their independence, must produce their own manufactured necessities. Proponents of domestic manufactures argued that Americans could enjoy the benefits of factory production without the troublesome blight of industrial cities. They assured Americans that abundant water power—particularly the fast-running streams of the Northeast—would enable Americans to build their factories in the countryside. Such a decentralized factory system would provide employment for country women and children and thus subsidize the independence of struggling farmers. It was on those premises that the first American factories were built.

The American textile industry originated in industrial espionage. The key to the mass production of cotton and woolen textiles was a water-powered machine that spun yarn and thread. The machine had been invented and patented by the Englishman Richard Arkwright in 1769, and the British government forbade the machinery or the people who worked with it to leave the country. Scores of textile workers, however, defied the law and made their way to North America. One of them was Samuel Slater, who had served an apprenticeship under Jedediah Strutt, a partner of Arkwright who had improved on the original machine. Working from memory while employed by Moses Brown, a Providence merchant, Slater built the first Arkwright spinning mill in America at Pawtucket, Rhode Island, in 1790.

Slater's first mill was a small frame building tucked among the town's houses and craftsmen's shops. Although its capacity was limited to the spinning of cotton yarn, it provided work for children in the mill and for women who wove yarn into cloth in their homes. Thus this first mill satisfied American requirements: it did not require the creation of a factory town, and it supplemented the household incomes of farmers and artisans. As his business grew and he advertised for widows with children, however, Slater was greeted by families headed by landless, impoverished men. Slater's use of children from these families prompted respectable farmers and craftsmen to pull their children out of Slater's growing complex of mills. More poor families arrived to take their places, and during the first years of the 19th century, Pawtucket became a disorderly mill town.

Soon Slater and other mill owners built factory villages in the countryside where they could exert better control over their operations and their workers. The practice became known as the Rhode Island or "family" system. At Slatersville, Rhode Island, at Oxford, Massachusetts, and at other locations in southern New England, mill owners built whole villages surrounded by company-owned farmland that they rented to the husbands and fathers of their mill workers. The workplace was closely supervised, and drinking and other troublesome practices were forbidden in the villages. Fathers and older sons worked either on rented farms or as laborers at the mills. By the late 1820s, Slater and most of the other owners were getting rid of the outworkers and were buying power looms, thus transforming the villages into self-contained factory towns that turned raw cotton into finished cloth, but at great cost to old forms of household independence. When President Andrew Jackson visited Pawtucket in 1829, he remarked to Samuel Slater, "I understand you taught us how to spin, so as to rival Great Britain in her manufactures; you set all these thousands of spindles to work, which I have been delighted in viewing, and which have made so many happy, by a lucrative employment." "Yes sir," replied Slater. "I suppose that I gave out the psalm and they have been singing to the tune ever since."

Factory Towns: The Waltham System

A second act of industrial espionage was committed by a Boston merchant named Francis Cabot Lowell. Touring English factory districts in 1811, Lowell asked questions and made secret drawings of the machines. He also experienced a genteel distaste for the squalor of the English textile towns. Returning home, Lowell joined with wealthy friends to form the

Pawtucket in 1817   Here is America's first textile milling town. It is set beside a waterfall that provides power for the mills. A bridge runs directly over the brink of the falls, and men and boys fish and play in the pool below them. It is a pastoral scene, the combination of nature and human artifice that early factory promoters held up as the ideal and attainable industrial landscape for the United States. But it is the factories and poor houses in the background, and not the river and its charms, that have a future.

Boston Manufacturing Company—soon known as the Boston Associates. In 1813, they built their first mill at **Waltham**, Massachusetts, and then expanded into Lowell, Lawrence, and other new towns near Boston during the 1820s. The company built mills that differed from the early Rhode Island mills in two ways: (1) they were heavily capitalized and as fully mechanized as possible; they turned raw cotton into finished cloth with little need for skilled workers; and (2) their workers were young, single women recruited from the farms of northern New England—farms that were switching to livestock raising, and thus had little need for the labor of daughters. The company provided boardinghouses for them and enforced rules of conduct both on and off the job. The young women worked steadily, never drank, seldom stayed out late, and attended church faithfully. They dressed neatly—often stylishly—and read newspapers and attended lectures. They impressed visitors, particularly those who had seen factory workers in other places, as a dignified and self-respecting workforce.

The brick mills and prim boardinghouses set within landscaped towns and occupied by sober, well-behaved farm girls signified the Boston Associates' desire to build a profitable textile industry without creating a permanent working class. The women would work for a few years in a carefully controlled environment, send their wages back to their families, and return home to live as country housewives. These young farm women did in fact form an efficient, decorous workforce, but the decorum was imposed less by the owners than by the women themselves. In order to protect their own reputations, they punished transgressions and shunned fellow workers who misbehaved. Nor did they send their wages home or, as was popularly believed, use them to pay for their brothers' college educations. Some saved their money to use as dowries that their fathers could not afford. More, however, spent their wages on themselves, particularly on clothes and books.

The owners of the factories expected that the young women's sojourn would reinforce their own paternalism and that of the girls' fathers. Instead, it produced a self-respecting sisterhood of wage-earning women. Twice in the 1830s, the women of Lowell went on strike, proclaiming that they were not wage slaves but "the daughters of freemen." After finishing their stint in the mills, many Lowell women entered public life as reformers. Most of them married and became housewives, but not on the terms their mothers had known. One in three of them married Lowell men and became city dwellers. Those who returned home remained unmarried longer than their sisters who had stayed on the farm, and then married men about their own age who worked at something other than farming. Thus the Boston Associates kept their promise to produce cotton cloth profitably without creating a permanent working class, but they did not succeed in shuttling young women between rural and urban paternalism and back again. Wage labor, the ultimate degradation for agrarian-republican men, opened a road to independence for thousands of young women.

Cities

The market revolution hit American cities—the old seaports as well as the new marketing and manufacturing towns—with particular force. Here there was little concern for creating a classless industrial society: Vastly wealthy men of finance, a new middle class that bought and sold an ever-growing variety of consumer goods, and the impoverished women and men who made those goods lived together in communities that unabashedly recognized the reality of social class.

The richest men were seaport merchants who had survived and prospered during the world wars that ended in 1815. They carried on as importers and exporters, took control of banks and insurance companies, and made great fortunes in urban real estate. Those in Boston constituted an urbane and responsible cluster of families known as the Boston Brahmins. The elite of Philadelphia was less unified and perhaps less responsible, and that of New York even less. These families continued in international commerce, profiting mainly from cotton exports and from a vastly expanded range of imports, they speculated in urban real estate, and they sometimes invested in manufacturing ventures.

Below the old mercantile elite (or, in the case of the new cities of the interior, at the top of society) stood a growing middle class of wholesale and retail merchants, small manufacturers, and an army of lawyers, salesmen, auctioneers, clerks, bookkeepers, and accountants who handled the paperwork for a new market society. At the head of this new middle class were the wholesale merchants of the seaports who bought hardware, crockery, and other commodities from importers (and increasingly from American manufacturers) and then sold them in smaller lots to storekeepers from the interior. The greatest concentration of wholesale firms was on Pearl Street in New York City. Slightly below them were the large processors of farm products, including the meat packers of Cincinnati and the flour millers of Rochester, and large merchants and real estate dealers in the new inland cities.

Another step down were specialized retail merchants who dealt in books, furniture, crockery, and other consumer goods. In Hartford, Connecticut, for instance, the proportion of retailers who specialized in specific commodities rose from 24 percent to 60 percent between 1792 and 1845. Alongside the merchants stood master craftsmen who had become manufacturers. With their workers busy in backrooms or in household workshops, they now called themselves shoe dealers and merchant tailors. At the bottom of this new commercial world were hordes of clerks, most of them young men who hoped to rise in the world. Many of them—one study puts the figure at between 25 percent and 38 percent—did move up in society. Both in numbers and in the nature of the work, this white-collar army formed a new class created by the market revolution, particularly by the emergence of a huge consumer market in the countryside.

In the 1820s and 1830s, the commercial classes transformed the look and feel of American cities. As retailing and manufacturing became separate activities (even in firms that did both), the merchants, salesmen, and clerks now worked in quiet offices on downtown business streets. The seaport merchants built counting rooms and decorated their warehouses in the "new counting house style." Both in the seaports and the new towns of the interior, impressive brick-and-glass storefronts appeared on the main streets. Perhaps the most telling monuments of the new business society were the handsome retail arcades that began going up in the 1820s. Boston's Quincy Market (1825), a two-story arcade on Philadelphia's Chestnut Street (1827), and Rochester's four-story Reynolds Arcade (1828) provided consumers with comfortable, gracious space in which to shop.

Metropolitan Industrialization

While businessmen were developing a new middle-class ethos, and while their families were flocking to the new retail stores to buy emblems of their status, the people who made the consumer goods were growing more numerous and subsequently were disappearing from view. With the exception of textiles and a few other commodities, few goods were made in mechanized factories before the 1850s. Most of the clothes and shoes, brooms, hats, books, furniture, candy, and other goods available in country stores and city shops were made by hand. City merchants and master craftsmen met the growing demand by hiring more workers. The largest handicrafts—shoemaking, tailoring, and the building trades—were divided into skilled and semiskilled segments and farmed out to subcontractors who could turn a profit only by cutting labor costs. The result was the creation of an urban working class, not only in the big seaports and factory towns but in scores of milling and manufacturing towns throughout the North and the West as well.

The rise of New York City's ready-made clothing trade provides an example. In 1815, wealthy Americans wore tailor-made clothing. Everyone else wore clothes sewn by women at home. In the 1820s, the availability of cheap manufactured cloth and an expanding pool of cheap—largely female—labor, along with the creation of the southern and western markets, transformed New York City into the center of a national market in ready-made clothes. The first big market was in "Negro cottons"—graceless shirts, pants, and sack dresses in which southern planters clothed their slaves. Within a few years, New York manufacturers were sending dungarees and hickory shirts to western farmers and supplying inexpensive clothing to urban workers. By the 1830s, many New York tailoring houses, including the storied Brooks Brothers, offered fancier ready-made clothes to the new middle class.

High rents and costly real estate, together with the absence of water power, prohibited locating large factories in cities, but the nature of the clothing trade and the availability of cheap labor gave rise to a system of subcontracting that transformed needlework into the first "sweated" trade in America. Merchants kept a few skilled male tailors to take care of the custom trade and to cut cloth into patterned pieces for ready-made clothing. The pieces were sent out, often by way of subcontractors, to needleworkers who sewed them together in their homes. Male tailors continued to do the finishing work on men's suits, but most of the work—on cheap goods destined for the countryside—was done by women who worked for piece rates that ranged from 75 cents to $1.50 per week. Along with clothing, women in garrets and tenements manufactured the items with which the middle class decorated itself and its homes: embroidery, doilies, artificial flowers, fringe, tassels, fancy-bound books, and parasols. All provided work for ill-paid legions of female workers.

Other trades followed similar patterns. For example, northeastern shoes were made in uniform sizes and sent in barrels all over the country. Like tailoring, shoemaking was

A MIDWIFE'S TALE

Directed by Richard D. Rodgers (PBS).

The historian Laurel Thatcher Ulrich's *A Midwife's Tale* won the Pulitzer Prize for history and biography in 1991. Shortly thereafter, the Public Broadcasting System (PBS) turned the book into a documentary movie—a close and imaginative analysis of the diary of Martha Ballard, a Maine farm woman and midwife of the late 18th and early 19th centuries. Events are acted out on screen, and period modes of dress, housing, gardening, washing, coffin-making, spinning and weaving, and other details are reconstructed with labored accuracy.

The viewer hears the sounds of footfalls, horses, hand-looms, and dishes, but the only human sounds are an occasional cough, exclamation, or drinking song. The principal narrative is carried by an actress who reads passages from the diary, and Thatcher occasionally breaks in to explain her own experiences with the diary and its interpretation. The result is a documentary film that knows the difference between dramatizing history and making it up. It also dramatizes the ways in which a skilled and sensitive historian goes about her work.

Martha Ballard was a midwife in a town on the Kennebec River. She began keeping a daily diary at the age of 50 in 1785, and continued until 1812. Most of the film is about her daily life: delivering babies, nursing the sick, helping neighbors, keeping house, raising and supervising the labor of her daughters and niece, gardening, and tending cattle and turkeys. In both the book and the film, the busyness of an ordinary woman's days—and a sense of her possibilities and limits—in the early republic comes through in exhausting detail. The dailiness of her life is interrupted only occasionally by an event: a fire at her husband's sawmill, an epidemic of scarlet fever, a parade organized to honor the death of George Washington, the rape of a minister's wife by his enemies (including the local judge, who is set free), and a neighbor's inexplicable murder of his wife and six children.

divided into skilled operations and time-consuming unskilled tasks. Men performed the skilled work of cutting and shaping the uppers. The drudgery of sewing the pieces together went to low-paid women. In the shops of Lynn, Massachusetts, in the shoemakers' boardinghouses in Rochester and other new manufacturing cities of the interior, and in the cellars and garrets of New York City, skilled shoemakers performed the most difficult work for taskmasters who passed the work along to subcontractors who controlled poorly paid, unskilled workers. Skilled craftsmen could earn as much as $2 per day making custom boots and shoes. Men shaping uppers in boardinghouses earned a little more than half of that. Women binders could work a full week and earn as little as 50 cents. In this as in other trades, wage rates and gendered tasks reflected the old family division of labor, which was based on the assumption that female workers lived with an income-earning husband or father. In fact, increasing numbers of them were young

"...a film of almost tactile pleasure and keen intelligence." *The Boston Globe*

The PBS documentary movie *A Midwife's Tale* is based on the Pulitzer Prize–winning book of the same name by historian Laurel Thatcher Ulrich.

There is also the process of getting old. At the beginning, Martha Ballard is the busy wife in a well-run household. As she ages and her children leave to set up households of their own, Ballard hires local girls who—perhaps because an increasingly democratic culture has made them less subservient than Ballard would like, perhaps because Ballard is growing old and impatient, perhaps both—tend to be surly. Her husband, a surveyor who works for merchants speculating in local land, is attacked twice in the woods by squatters and spends a year and a half in debtor's jail—not for his own debts but because, as tax collector, he failed to collect enough. While the husband is in jail and his aging wife struggles to keep the house going, their son moves his own family into the house and Martha is moved into a single room and is made to feel unwanted—a poignant and unsentimental case of the strained relations between generations that historians have discovered in the early republic.

A Midwife's Tale is a modest film that comes as close as a thorough and imaginative historian and a good film-maker can to re-creating the texture of lived experience in the northeastern countryside at the beginning of the 19th century. Students who enjoy the movie should go immediately to the book.

women living alone or older women who had been widowed, divorced, or abandoned—often with small children.

In their shops and counting rooms, the new middle class entertained notions of gentility based on the distinction between manual and nonmanual work. Lowly clerks and wealthy merchants prided themselves on the fact that they worked with their heads and not their hands. They fancied that their entrepreneurial and managerial skills were making the market revolution happen, while manual workers simply performed tasks thought up by the middle class. The old distinction between proprietorship and dependence, which had placed master craftsmen and independent tradesmen, along with farm-owning yeomen, among the respectable "middling sort," disappeared. The men and women of an emerging working class struggled to make dignity and a sense of public worth in a society that hid them from view and defined them as "hands."

Conclusion

In the first half of the 19th century, northern society became based in buying and selling. The Northeast—New York City in particular—sloughed off its old colonial status and moved from the periphery to the industrial and financial core of the world market economy. Other countries have made that transition: England was first, Japan was the most recent. Both of those countries, however, deemphasized agriculture, drew their populations into cities, and relied on the export of manufactured goods as their principal source of income. The American North, on the other hand, built factories and commercial farms at the same time and as parts of the same process. The market for American manufactures was in the American countryside. (Industrial exports from the United States were insignificant until the end of the 19th century.) The principal market for American food was in American towns and cities, and even on farms whose proprietors were too busy with staple crops to grow the old array of food. The result was a massive commercialization of the Northwestern, mid-Atlantic, and New England states, and the beginnings of their integration into a unified northern capitalist democracy.

SUGGESTED READINGS

Douglas C. North, *The Economic Growth of the United States, 1790–1860* (1961) is an economic overview of these years, while **George Rogers Taylor**, *The Transportation Revolution, 1815–1860* (1951) remains the best single book on its subject. On rural society in the North, see **Christopher Clark**, *The Roots of Rural Capitalism: Western Massachusetts, 1780–1860* (1990); **Laurel Thatcher Ulrich**, *A Midwife's Tale: The Life of Martha Ballard, Based on Her Diary, 1785–1812* (1990); **Martin Bruegel**, *Farm, Shop, Landing: The Rise of a Market Society in the Hudson Valley, 1780–1860* (2002); **Jack Larkin**, *The Reshaping of Everyday Life, 1790–1840* (1988); **Carolyn Merchant**, *Ecological Revolutions: Nature, Gender, and Science in New England* (1989); **John Mack Faragher**, *Sugar Creek: Life on the Illinois Prairie* (1986) treats settler societies.

Solid studies of industrial communities include **Thomas Dublin**, *Women at Work: The Transformation of Work and Community in Lowell, Massachusetts, 1810–1860* (1979); and **Anthony F. C. Wallace**, *Rockdale: The Growth of an American Village in the Early Industrial Revolution* (1978). The best introduction to the seaports in these years is **Edwin G. Burrows and Mike Wallace**, *Gotham: A History of New York City to 1898* (1999). **Sean Wilentz**, *Chants Democratic: New York City and the Rise of the American Working Class* (1984) remains essential.

Visit the Liberty Equality Power Companion Web site for resources specific to this textbook: http://www.thomsonedu.com/history/murrin
Also find self-tests and additional resources at ThomsonNOW. ThomsonNOW is an integrated online suite of services and resources with proven ease of use and efficient paths to success, delivering the results you want—NOW!
www.thomsonedu.com/login/

The Old South, 1790–1850

In the 18th century, the southern plantation colonies had been Britain's most valuable mainland possessions. In 1790, the great planters of Virginia and South Carolina remained among the richest and most powerful men in the new republic, but world markets for their tobacco and rice were in a long-term decline, and their long-term future was uncertain.

Their position improved after the 1790s, when international markets and technological innovation encouraged them to grow short-staple cotton. Cotton became the great southern cash crop, and the planters spread cotton culture across an expanding deep south. The planters sent mountains of cotton to Great Britain, made a lot of money, and bought a lot of nice things. Other southerners, however, were not as fortunate. Enslaved workers experienced longer hours and tighter discipline than in the past. They lost their families and friends to a burgeoning interstate slave trade, and they watched their masters' commitment to slavery harden into an unmovable political axiom. In addition, most white farmers moved to the edges of the cotton economy. They continued in the old-style mixed agriculture, and traded relatively little beyond their neighborhoods. In the North, country people became the great consumer market that drove much of regional economic development. In the South, slaves and most whites bought little, and what they bought was manufactured outside of the region.

The South experienced stupendous economic growth between 1790 and 1850, but most southern investment and entrepreneurial talent went into producing cotton for export, an activity that produced wealth for the planters, but that strengthened the South's neocolonial dependence upon Great Britain and, increasingly, the northeastern United States. In addition, it gave the South a labor system, a leadership class, and an economic and political culture that set the region apart from the burgeoning capitalist democracy of the North and from dominant ideological trends in the North Atlantic world.

Old Farms: The Southeast

The Chesapeake, 1790–1820

In 1790, the future of plantation agriculture in the Chesapeake (the states of Virginia, Maryland, and Delaware, where slavery first took root in North America) was precarious. The market for tobacco, their principal crop, had been falling since before the Revolution, and it continued to decline after 1790. Tobacco also depleted the soil, and by the late 18th century, tidewater farms and plantations were giving out. As lands west of the Appalachians

CHRONOLOGY

1792	Kentucky enters the union as the 15th state
1793	Eli Whitney invents the cotton gin
1796	Tennessee enters the union as the 16th state
1799	Successful slave revolution in Haiti
1800	Gabriel's Rebellion in Virginia
1808	International slave trade ends
1803	Jefferson purchases the Louisiana Territory from France
1812	Second war with Britain begins
1817	Mississippi enters the union
1819	Alabama enters the union • Adams-Onis Treaty conveys Florida and the Gulf Coast to the United States
1822	Denmark Vesey's slave conspiracy in South Carolina
1831	Nat Turner's rebellion in Virginia

opened to settlement, white tenants, laborers, and small farmers left the Chesapeake in droves. Many of them moved to Kentucky, Tennessee, or the western reaches of Virginia. Many others found new homes in nonslave states north of the Ohio River. Faced with declining opportunities within the slave societies of the Chesapeake, thousands of the poorer whites had voted with their feet.

With tobacco profits falling, many Chesapeake planters were switching to wheat, corn, and livestock. They did it on a large scale. In many parts of the region, the old tobacco lands gave way to grain fields and pastures, and by 1830, Richmond rivaled Rochester, New York, as the nation's leading flour milling center. It was a sensible move, but it left the Chesapeake with a huge investment in slaves who were less and less necessary. Grazing animals and raising wheat required less labor than tobacco. Enslaved workers planted individual tobacco plants and pruned and weeded them and picked worms off of them by hand. At harvest time they picked the leaves one at a time, then hung them to cure, packed them, and shipped them off to market. In sharp contrast, grain and livestock took care of themselves through most of the year. Planters with large numbers of slaves had to think up new uses for them. Some divided their land into small plots and rented both the plots and their slaves to white tenant farmers. Others, particularly in Maryland, recruited tenants from the growing ranks of free blacks. Still others hired out their slaves as artisans and urban laborers.

Race, Gender, and Chesapeake Labor

The increasing diversification of the Chesapeake economy involved assigning new chores to slave women and men. Wheat cultivation, for example, meant a switch from the hoes used for tobacco to the plow and grain cradle, both of which called for the upper-body

An Overseer Doing His Duty   In 1798, the architect and engineer Benjamin Latrobe sketched a white overseer smoking a cigar and supervising slave women as they hoed newly cleared farmland near Fredericksburg, Virginia. A critic of slavery, Latrobe sarcastically entitled the sketch *An Overseer Doing His Duty*.

strength of adult men. The grain economy also required carts, wagons, mills, and good roads, and thus created a need for greater numbers of slave artisans, nearly all of whom were men. Many of these artisans were hired out to urban employers, and lived as a semi-free caste in cities and towns. In the new economy of the Chesapeake, male slaves did the plowing, mowing, sowing, ditching, and carting and performed most of the tasks requiring artisanal skills. All of this work demanded high levels of training and could be performed by someone working either by himself or in a small group with little need for supervision.

Slave women were left with the lesser tasks. Contrary to legend, few slave women in the Chesapeake worked as domestic servants in the planter's houses. Some were assigned to such chores as cloth manufacture, sewing, candle molding, and the preparation of salt meat, but most female slaves still did farm work—hoeing, weeding, spreading manure, cleaning stables—that was monotonous, called for little skill, and was closely supervised. This new division of labor was clearly evident during the wheat harvest. On George Washington's farm, for example, male slaves, often working beside temporary white laborers, moved in a broad line as they mowed the grain. Following them came a gang of children and women bent over and moving along on their hands and knees as they bound wheat into shocks. Thomas Jefferson, who had been shocked to see French women working in the fields, abandoned his concern for female delicacy when his own slaves were involved. At the grain harvest, he instructed his overseers to organize "gangs of half men and half women."

Flirting with Emancipation

Neither new crops nor new employments, however, erased the growing fact that Chesapeake proprietors needed less slave labor than they had in the past—or the parallel fact that their slaves reproduced at a higher rate than almost any other Americans. Nothing, it seemed, could employ the great mass of enslaved people or repay the planters' huge investment in slaves. In this situation, some Chesapeake planters (who had, after all, fought a revolution in the name of natural rights) began to manumit their slaves. The farmers of Maryland and Delaware in particular set their slaves free. By 1810, 76 percent of Delaware blacks and 23 percent of Maryland blacks were free. (In 1790, these figures had stood at 31 percent and 7 percent, respectively.) Virginia's economic and cultural commitment to the plantation was stronger, but even in the Old Dominion there was a movement to manumit slaves. George Washington stated that he wished "to liberate a certain species of property," and manumitted his slaves by will. (The manumissions were to take place at the death of his widow, thus, as one wag declared, surrounding Mrs. Washington with 100 people who wanted her dead.) Robert Carter, reputedly the largest slaveholder in Virginia, also freed his slaves, as did many others. The free black population of Virginia stood at 3,000 in 1782, when the state passed a law permitting manumission. The number of free blacks rose to 12,766 in 1790, to 20,124 in 1800, and to 30,570 in 1810. These were impressive numbers, but the birthrate of Virginia slaves erased them. Between 1780 and 1810, the slave population of the state rose, despite the manumissions, from 250,000 to 400,000.

Emancipation moved slowly in Virginia for several reasons. First, few Virginia planters could afford to free their slaves without compensation. Second, white Virginians feared the social consequences of black freedom. Thomas Jefferson, for instance, owned 175 slaves when he penned the phrase that "all men are created equal." He lived off their labor, sold them to pay his debts, gave them away as gifts, sold them away from their families as a punishment, and kept one of them as a mistress. Through it all he insisted that slavery was wrong. He could not imagine emancipation, however, without the colonization of freed slaves far from Virginia. A society of free blacks and whites, Jefferson insisted, would end in disaster: "Deep rooted prejudices entertained by the whites; ten thousand recollections, by the blacks, of the injuries they have sustained; new provocations; the real distinctions which nature has made . . . [will] produce convulsions which will probably never end but in the extermination of the one or the other race." Jefferson went on to a virulently racist argument for black inferiority and to the insistence that "When freed, [blacks are] to be removed beyond the reach of mixture." Near the end of an adult lifetime of condemning slavery but doing nothing to end it, Jefferson cried out that white Virginians held "a wolf by the ears": they could not hold onto slavery forever, and they could never let it go.

The Lowcountry, 1790–1820

The other region that had been a center of plantation slavery during the 18th century— lowcountry South Carolina and Georgia—made a massive recommitment to slave labor in the years after the Revolution. Here the principal crop was rice, which, along with other

American foodstuffs, enjoyed a rise in international demand during the European wars between 1793 and 1815. But lowcountry planters faced increasing competition from rice farmers in India, Java, Burma, and Europe. The rice coast—one of the great sources of American wealth in the 18th century—remained profitable, but it was losing relative position to faster-growing regions. The planters of the lowcountry, like those in Virginia, remained wealthy men. Their long-term future, however, was in doubt.

Thousands of slaves in this region had either run away or had been carried off by the British in the Revolution, and planters knew that the African slave trade was scheduled to end in 1808. Lowcountry planters, unlike their Chesapeake counterparts, could not imagine emancipating their slaves. They rushed to import as many Africans as they could in the time remaining. Between 1788 and 1808, 250,000 captive people were brought directly from Africa to the United States, nearly all of them to Charleston and Savannah. That figure equaled the number of Africans who had been brought to North America during the whole colonial period.

The Task System

In the plantation counties of coastal South Carolina and Georgia, slaves made up 80 percent of the population, and more than 90 percent in many parishes. Farms and slave labor forces were big, and rice cultivation demanded intensive labor, often performed by workers who stood knee-deep in water. The work and the hot, sticky climate encouraged deadly summer diseases and kept white owners and overseers out of the fields. Many of the wealthiest planters built homes in Charleston and Savannah and hired others to manage their plantations. Both they and planters who stayed on their farms organized enslaved workers according to the so-called task system. Each morning the owner or manager assigned a specific task to each slave. When the task was done, the rest of the day belonged to the slave. Slaves who did not finish their task were punished, and when too many slaves finished early, the owners assigned heavier tasks. In the 18th century, each slave had been expected to tend three to four acres of rice each day. In the early 19th century, with the growth of a competitive rice market, the assignment was raised to five acres.

The task system encouraged slaves to work hard without supervision, and slaves turned the system to their own uses. Often several slaves would work together until all of their tasks were completed, and strong young slaves often helped older and weaker slaves after they had finished their own tasks. Once the day's work was done, the slaves shared their hard-earned leisure out of sight of the owner. A Jamaican visitor remarked that South Carolina and Georgia planters were "very particular in employing a negro, without his consent, after his task is finished, and agreeing with him for the payment which he is to receive."

Slaves under the task system won the right to cultivate land as **"private fields,"** not the little garden plots common in the Chesapeake but farms of up to five acres on which they grew produce and raised livestock for market. There was a lively trade in slave-produced goods, and eventually slaves in the low country not only produced and exchanged property but also passed it on to their children. The owners tolerated such activity because slaves on the task system worked hard, required minimal supervision, produced much of their own subsistence, and made money for their owners. The rice planters in South Carolina and Georgia were among the richest men in the United States.

New Farms: The Rise of the Deep South

While the old centers of slavery and southern power stagnated or declined, planters discovered a new and promising cash crop. British textile factories had been buying raw cotton since the mid-18th century. Southern planters knew they could sell all of the cotton they could grow. But long-staple cotton, the only variety that could be profitably grown, was a delicate plant that thrived only on the Sea Islands off the coasts of Georgia and South Carolina. The short-staple variety was hardier, but its sticky seeds had to be removed by hand before the cotton could be milled. It took a full day for an adult slave to clean a single pound of short-staple cotton—an expenditure of labor that took the profit out of cotton. In 1790, the United States produced only 3,000 bales of cotton, nearly all of it on the long-staple plantations of the Sea Islands.

In 1793, **Eli Whitney**, a Connecticut Yankee who had come south to work as a tutor, set his mind to the problem of cleaning short-staple cotton. Within a few days he had made a model of a cotton "gin" (a southern contraction of "engine") that combed the seeds from the fiber with metal pins fitted into rollers. Working with Whitney's machine, a slave could clean 50 pounds of short-staple cotton in a day. Within a very few years, cotton became the great southern cash crop, and slavery and plantation agriculture had a new lease on life.

The Rise of the Cotton Belt

Beginning in the late 1790s, planters and their slaves moved into upland South Carolina and Georgia, transforming a sparsely settled farm country into the first great short-staple cotton region. With the end of war in 1815, the cotton belt expanded dramatically. The defeat of native peoples and the expropriation of their land in the Southwest, the resumption of international trade, and the revival of textile production encouraged planters to extend the cotton lands of South Carolina and Georgia into a Deep South cotton belt that stretched beyond the Mississippi River.

The national government dominated by Jeffersonian Republicans made the cotton belt possible. Planters did not take their money and slaves into the interior until the government had ended Indian resistance and secured access to international markets through the system of rivers. Early settlers had demanded not only help against the Indians but also the free use of the Mississippi River. The Tennessee constitution of 1796, for instance, declared that "An equal participation of the free navigation of the Mississippi is one of the inherent rights of the citizens of this state." (This at a time when Spain held sovereignty over the west bank of the river, the mouth of the river at New Orleans, and the gulf coast from Florida to Louisiana, and when independent Indian peoples controlled nearly all of the interior.) Jefferson's Louisiana Purchase of 1803 secured free navigation of the Mississippi Valley for the United States. The Adams-Onis Treaty of 1819 bought Florida and the Gulf Coast. A Mississippi editor praised the latter: "It rounds off our southern possessions, and for ever precludes foreign immisaries from stirring up Indians to war and negroes to rebellion, whilst it gives the southern country important outlets to the sea." With the final defeat of the southwestern Indians in the War of 1812, western Georgia, Alabama, Mississippi, and northern Louisiana were opened to large-scale cotton cultivation.

Jefferson had proclaimed the west a great "Empire for Liberty," but it was liberty on southern terms. The Southwest was secured for the plantation, and until 1830 or so, the Northwest, which banned slavery, was settled by southern yeomen. Western settlement promised long-term southern political majorities and the protection of southern interests, and few imagined that the situation would change in the foreseeable future. Jefferson's Empire for Liberty was emerging as an empire for slavery.

The cotton belt grew quickly: by 1834, the new southwestern states of Alabama, Mississippi, and Louisiana grew more than half of a vastly increased U.S. cotton crop. In 1810, the South produced 178,000 bales of ginned cotton, more than 59 times the 3,000 bales it had produced in 1790. With the opening of southwestern cotton lands, production jumped to 334,000 bales in 1820 and to 1,350,000 bales in 1840. In these years, cotton made up from one-half to two-thirds of the value of all U.S. exports. The South produced three-fourths of the world supply of cotton—a commodity that, more than any other, was the raw material of industrialization in Britain and Europe and, increasingly, in the northeastern United States. Cotton, in short, was a very big business.

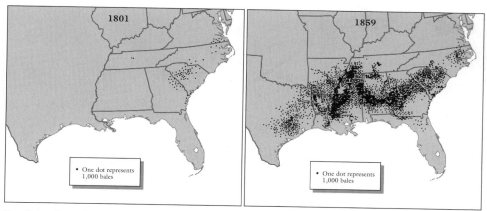

Map 9.1   Cotton Production, 1801 and 1859   Short-staple cotton thrived wherever there was fertile soil, heat and humidity, low altitude, and a long growing season. As a result, a great belt of cotton and slavery took shape in the Lower South, from the midlands of South Carolina through East Texas.

The Interstate Slave Trade

The international slave trade ended in 1808. Even before that date, the principal source of slaves for the emerging cotton belt was the old seaboard states—those with a growing population of slaves and a diminishing need for them. As early as the 1790s, the Chesapeake states of Virginia, Delaware, and Maryland were net exporters of slaves. Those states sent 40,000 to 50,000 enslaved workers south and west in that decade. The number rose to 120,000 in the 1810s. The slave families and slave communities of the Chesapeake lost 1 in 12 of their members in the 1790s, 1 in 10 between 1800 and 1810, and 1 in 5 between 1810 and 1820. In the 1820s, South Carolina and Kentucky joined the slave-exporting states (although South Carolina sent many thousands out of the low country and into its new upcountry cotton belt), and 150,000 slaves left their homes and crossed state lines. The trade in slaves reordered the human geography of the South. In 1790, planters in Virginia and Maryland had owned 56 percent of all American slaves. By 1860, they owned only 15 percent.

Some enslaved migrants—estimates run as high as 30 percent—left their old neighborhoods in the company of masters (or masters' sons) and familiar fellow slaves. These slaves made new plantations and new lives in the Southwest surrounded by some of the people they had known at home, but most were sold and resold as individuals in an organized interstate

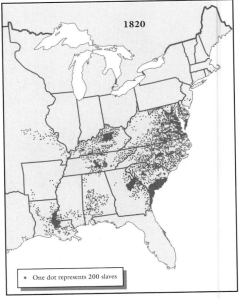

Map 9.2   Distribution of Slave Population, 1790, 1820, and 1860   In 1790, slaves were concentrated in the Chesapeake and in the South Carolina and Georgia low country. Over the next 70 years, Chesapeake planters put thousands of slaves into the interstate trade, which sold them into a Black Belt that stretched from the interior of the Carolinas to East Texas. View an animated version of this map or related maps at http://www.thomsonedu.com/history/murrin.

slave market. Soon after the Revolution, men known as "Georgia Traders" appeared in the Upper South, buying slaves on speculation and selling them farther south. By 1820, the slave trade had become an organized business with sophisticated financing, sellers who had an accurate knowledge of slave prices in various southern markets, a well-traveled shipping route between Norfolk and New Orleans, and systems of slave pens and safe houses along the roads of the interior. The domestic slave trade was the biggest and most modern business in the South, with the single exception of the plantation. The centrality of that trade advertised the nature of southern economic development: while northerners exchanged wheat, furniture, books, and shoes with each other, Southerners exchanged slaves.

Most slaves moved into the cotton belt with other slaves who were strangers and under the temporary ownership of traders who knew them only as merchandise. Those who were transported by ship experienced some of the horrors of the old Middle Passage from Africa: cramped quarters, minimal food, discipline at the hands of nervous white

Abby Aldrich Rockefeller Folk Art Center, Williamsburg, VA

Going to Tennessee   The Pennsylvanian Lewis Miller met with this group of slaves near Staunton, Virginia, in 1853. They were being sent from their old farms in Virginia to the slave markets of Tennessee and from there to the cotton fields of the newer southern states. In the years after 1820, hundreds of thousands of Upper South slaves suffered this migration.

crewmen, and the odd murder or casual rape. Those who walked from the old plantations to the Southwest had their own share of terrors. The journey could take as long as
seven weeks, and traders organized it with military precision. An old slave remembered
the order of march: "them speculators would put the chillens in a wagon usually pulled
by oxens and the older folks was chained or tied together sos dey could not run off."
The slave Charles Ball remembered the same thing in poignant detail: he went south in
an unwilling parade of about 50, in which the women

> were tied together with a rope, about the size of a bed cord, which was tied like a hal-
> ter round the neck of each; but the men . . . were very differently caparisoned. A
> strong iron collar was closely fitted by means of a padlock round each of our necks.
> A chain of iron about a hundred feet long was passed through the hasp of each pad-
> lock, except at the two ends, where the hasps of the padlocks passed through a link
> of the chain. In addition to this, we were handcuffed in pairs. . . .
>
> The poor man to whom I was ironed, wept like an infant when the blacksmith, with
> his heavy hammer, fastened the ends of the bolts that kept the staples from slipping
> from our arms.

Traders and slaves camped along the roads or spent nights crammed into public houses
and slave pens. Beatings, rapes, and other abuses along the road entered black folk memory
and stayed there. One often-repeated (and apparently true) story told of a small boy taken
from his mother's arms and left with a tavern keeper to pay a bar bill.

Cotton and Slave Labor

The cotton plantations returned a rate of profit equal to northeastern banks and factories,
and they were operated in a more calculating and businesslike way than the old estates on
the Chesapeake and in the low country.

Most obviously, cotton planters exerted a more disciplined and direct control over their
enslaved workers. Masters in the old settlements had encouraged slaves to create their own
livelihoods—by hiring them out, giving them time and land with which to grow their own
food, and working them by the task system or under slave overseers—all of which reduced
the costs of supervising and providing for slaves while allowing them pockets of autonomy
within slavery. On the cotton frontier, good land and slave labor were too valuable to be
worked in casual ways, and new farms had to become profitable in a short time. Enslaved
men and women who had grown up with the relatively loose work routines of the low
country and the Chesapeake now performed the back-breaking labor of turning forests
into farms. (They had to "whittle a plantation right out of the woods," recalled one slave.)
Slaves worked in gangs, usually under white owners or overseers. Clearing trees, rolling
logs, pulling stumps, clearing and burning brush, and building cabins, fences, and outbuildings was hard labor. The planters preferred crews of young men for these tasks, but
such slaves were expensive, and everyone was put to work. A teenaged boy sold from the
Chesapeake to Mississippi saw women clearing brush from new land, and remarked that
"such work was not done by women slaves in Virginia." Another slave recalled that her

mother labored with a two-horse plow "when she warn't cleanin' new ground or diggin' ditches." The labor of making new farms lasted from dawn to dusk, and enslaved men and women worked under the eyes of owners who knew that they must turn the forest into cash-producing farms or go broke.

Once established, the plantations of the cotton belt were among the most intensely commercialized farms in the world. Many of them grew nothing but cotton, buying food from their neighbors or from merchants who sold corn meal and salt pork in bulk. Others grew supplementary crops and produced their own food. But nearly all of the plantation owners, from the proudest grandee to the ambitious farmer with a few slaves, organized labor in ways that maximized production and reinforced the dominance of the white men who owned the farms.

Slaves from the Chesapeake and the rice coast experienced cotton cultivation as a difficult step down. Cotton required a long growing season and a lot of attention, but it did not demand much skill. Early in the spring, the land was cleared and ploughed, and gangs of slaves walked the furrows dropping seeds. During the growing season, black laborers constantly thinned the plants and cleared the fields of weeds, "chopping" the fields with hoes in the hot, humid Deep South summer. The cotton ripened unevenly. In a harvest season that could last long past Christmas, pickers swept through the fields selecting only the ripe bolls, then repeated the task until the full crop was harvested. Cotton, in short, required constant unskilled labor. Slaves in the diversifying Chesapeake had made barrels and crates, boats, wagons, barns and storage sheds; slaves on the rice coast farther south had built complex systems of dikes and levees and had mastered the science of moving and controlling large amounts of water. In the cotton belt, they gave up those skills and went to work with axes, hoes, and their hands.

The work was relentless. Planters in the east had found it economical to allow slaves to work at varied tasks, at irregular times, or under the tasking system. They gave slaves only part of their food (often cornmeal and nothing else), then provided time and land with which slaves grew their own vegetables, chickens, and pigs. Planters on the cotton frontier did away with all that. Only a few cotton-belt planters retained the task system, and these were looked upon as eccentrics by their neighbors, who worked their slaves in gangs from dawn to dusk six days a week. Cotton land was too valuable to permit slave gardens. It made more sense to keep the slaves constantly at cotton cultivation and to supply them with all of their food. It was a more efficient and productive way of growing cotton. It was also a way of reducing the slaves' customary privileges within slavery, and of enforcing the master's role as the giver and taker of all things. Even slaves who grew their own food did so in white-supervised fields and not in family plots. An Alabama planter put it bluntly: "Allow it once to be understood by a Negro that he is to provide for himself, and you that moment give him an undeniable claim on you for a portion of his time to make this provision; and should you from necessity, or any other cause, encroach upon his time, disappointment and discontent are seriously felt." In order to create "a perfect dependence," this master insisted that "my Negroes have no time whatever." The Louisiana planter Bennet H. Barrow explained that the master must make the slave "as comfortable at home as possible, affording him what is essentially necessary for his happiness—you must provide for him your self and by that means creat[e] in him a habit of perfect dependence on you."

The masters set harsher working conditions and longer hours than slaves had known in their old homes. Slaves could not hope to reinstitute the task system, the family gardens and little farms, the varied tasks, or the uneven hours of labor that they had known on the coast. Yet despite masters' lack of encouragement, gardens—some of them large and profitable—quickly appeared in the new slave quarters, and enslaved workers found that they could hold masters to agreed-upon standards of time and work. Masters who demanded longer than customary hours or labor on Sunday found the work going slower. In the 1840s, a Mississippi planter noted that slaves had adapted to the long hours, close supervision, and pace of work under the gang system, but would perform the new customary workload and nothing more. "All of them know what their duty is upon a plantation, and that they are generally willing to do, and nothing more." When asked to work harder or longer "they will not submit to it, but become turbulent and impatient of control, and all the whips in Christendom cannot drive them to perform more than they think they ought to do, or have been in the long habit of doing."

On the whole, the exploitation of slave labor after 1820 became both more rigorous and more humane. Planters imposed a new and more total control over their slaves, but they clothed it within a larger attempt to make North American slavery into a system that was both paternalistic and humane, and to portray themselves as gentlemen and not as heartless slave-drivers. Food and clothing seems to have improved, and individual cabins for slave families became standard. State laws often forbade the more brutal forms of discipline, and they uniformly demanded that slaves be given Sunday off.

Material standards seem to have risen. One rough indicator is physical height. On the eve of the Civil War, southern slaves averaged about an inch shorter than northern whites, but they were fully three inches taller than newly imported Africans, two inches taller than slaves on the Caribbean island of Trinidad, and an inch taller than British Marines. Slaves suffered greater infant mortality than whites, but those who survived infancy lived out "normal" life spans. Brazil, Cuba, and other slave societies had to import Africans to make up for the deaths of slaves, but the slave population of the southern states increased three-fold—from 657,000 to 1,981,000—between 1790 and 1830. With the importation of new Africans banned after 1808 (and with runaways outnumbering new Africans who were smuggled into the country), the increase was due entirely to the fact that—alone among the slave societies of the Western Hemisphere—the American slave population was healthy enough to reproduce itself.

Material conditions on the plantations sprang from both planter self-interest and an attempt to exert a kindly, paternal control over slaves that planters often called "our people" or "our family, black and white." But humane treatment came at a high price. At the same time that they granted slaves protection from the worst kinds of brutality, cotton-belt states enacted slave codes that defined slaves as persons without rights. The Louisiana code of 1824, for instance, stated that "[The slave] is incapable of making any kind of contract. . . . They can transmit nothing by succession. . . . The slave is incapable of exercising any public office, or private trust. . . . He cannot be a party in any civil action. . . . Slaves cannot marry without the consent of their masters, and their marriages do not produce any of the civil effects which result from such contract." It was an exact negative image of the rights enjoyed by the white men who owned the plantations, controlled the slaves, and wrote the laws.

Mastery as a Way of Life

Plantation masters, both the old southeastern nabobs and the cotton planters of newer regions, were the acknowledged economic, social, cultural, and political elite of the South. Their authority rested on economic power and on their connections—often family relationships—with each other. But they dressed their power in gentility and an aura of mastery, a visible "right to rule" that few others, North or South, could match. That power and authority was tied intimately to the ownership of slaves. When assessing a planter's standing, contemporaries seldom added up his acreage or the money that made up his family's fortune. Instead, they counted slaves. In the most common calculation, the ownership of 20 slaves separated planters from farmers. It was a good enough measure, for the planter class made itself out of slaves. Most obviously, the labor of enslaved persons bought the carpets, chandeliers, fine clothes, English chivalric novels, and race horses with which planters displayed their social mastery.

Southern ladies and gentlemen marked themselves off from others most clearly by the fact that they did not work. That too was a result of owning slaves. An observer of one plantation mistress noted that "She has a faithful nurse (Negro) to whose care she abandons her babes entirely, only when she has a fancy to caress them does she see them. Eight children and cannot lay to their charge the loss of a single night's rest." In short, the ownership of a slave transformed a harried housewife into a lady. A southern publicist boasted that "The non-slaveholder knows that as soon as his saving will admit, he can become a slaveholder, and thus relieve his wife from the necessities of the kitchen and the laundry and his children from the labors of the field." Southern farmers without slaves tended to sire very large families and to keep their children in the fields. The women worked outdoors as well. Southerners who owned slaves had fewer children, sent them to school, and moved their wives indoors. The skin of farm women was weathered, cracked, and darkened by the sun; plantation mistresses were smoother and less exhausted, and their skin was literally whiter. "Laborers was respected," recalled a small farmer, "but the men that owned slaves did not work and did not have there children do any work."

The opposite of gentility was the South Carolina farmer who, according to a neighbor, "used to work [his daughters] in the fields like Negroes." According to northern visitors, this association of labor with slavery encouraged laziness among southern whites and robbed work of the dignity it enjoyed in other parts of the country. Most southern white farmers would have disagreed, but the association of black labor, white leisure, and white gentility was central to the plantation regime. The South would not have been the South without it.

Southern Families

Antebellum white southerners remained localistic and culturally conservative. Farm and plantation labor and the routines of daily life still centered in the household, and prospects for most whites remained rooted in inherited land and family help. While the new northern **middle class** nourished a cosmopolitan culture and a domestic sentimentalism that subverted traditional authority, southerners—planters and yeomen alike—distrusted outsiders and defended rural neighborhoods grounded in the authority of fathers and the integrity of families.

Most southern whites regarded themselves less as individuals than as representatives of families that extended through time from the distant past to unborn generations. Southern boys often received the family names of heroes as their first names: Jefferson Davis, for example, or Thomas Jefferson (later, "Stonewall") Jackson. More often, however, they took the name of a related family—Peyton Randolph, Preston Brooks, Langdon Cheves—and carried them as proud and often burdensome badges of who they were. Children learned early that their first duty was to their family's reputation. When young Benjamin Tillman of South Carolina was away at school, his sister wrote, "Don't relax in your efforts to gain a good education. . . . I want you to be an ornament to your family." Two years later, another sister wrote, "Do, Bud, study hard and make good use of your time. . . . I want you to do something for the Tillman name."

In the white South, reputation and the defense of family honor were everything. Boys and girls were taught to act as though everyone were watching them, ready to note any hint of inadequacy. A boy with a reputation for cowardice, for ineptness at riding or fighting, or for failure to control his emotions or hold his liquor was an embarrassment to his family. An "unsullied reputation," insisted Albert Gallatin Brown of Mississippi, placed a man "on a social level with all his fellows." As John Horry Dent, an Alabama slave-holder and bad amateur poet, put it:

> Honor and shame from all conditions rise;
> Act well your part and there the honor lies.

Among southern white men, wealth generally counted for less than did maintaining one's personal and family honor and thus winning membership in the democracy of honorable males.

The code of honor, although it forged ties of equality and respect among white men, made rigid distinctions between men and women and whites and blacks. Women and girls who misbehaved—with transgressions ranging from simple gossip to poor housekeeping to adultery—damaged not only their own reputation but also the honor of the fathers, brothers, or husbands who could not control them. Such a charge could mean social death in a rural community made up of patriarchal households and watchful neighbors. In 1813, Bolling Hall of Alabama advised his daughter, "If you learn to restrain every thought, action, and word by virtue and religion, you will become an ornament." A "good man" or a "good woman" was someone who upheld the family by acting within a prescribed social role ("Act well your part"), and not, as the children of the northern middle class were being taught, by acting as an autonomous, self-governing individual.

When northerners attacked slavery because it denied the freedom of the individual, one southerner responded in a way that was meant to end the argument: "Do you say that the slave is held to involuntary service? So is the wife, [whose] relation to her husband, in the great majority of cases, is made for her and not by her." Few white southerners would have questioned the good sense of that response. Southern life was not about freedom, individual fulfillment, or social progress. It was about honoring the obligations to which one was born.

The Southern Yeomanry

Yeomen and Planters

Some southern boosters advertised cotton as a "democratic" crop that could be cultivated at a profit by almost any southern farmer, but that is not how it worked. Cotton, like other plantation crops, rewarded economies of scale: planters with big farms and many slaves operated more efficiently and more profitably than farmers with fewer resources. The wealthier planter families bought up good cotton land with ready access to markets and turned it into large plantations. They also bought up the majority of slaves. Only 30 percent to 35 percent of southern white families owned at least one slave in 1830, and that percentage dropped as time passed. On the eve of the Civil War, only one white family in four owned a slave. Among the minority of southerners who were slaveowners, half owned fewer than five, and less than 5 percent of white southerners owned 20 or more slaves— the roughly agreed-upon number that separated planters from farmers. Cotton, it turned out, was not democratic: among southern whites it produced not only an unequal distribution of wealth but a dual economy: plantations at the commercial center and a marginally commercial yeomanry on the fringes.

As land prices and local taxes rose in the plantation counties, many of the poorer whites moved out. Those who stayed subsisted on poor, hilly land far from navigable rivers. They tended to be commercial farmers, growing a few bales of cotton with family labor and perhaps a slave or two. Many of them were poor relatives of prosperous plantation owners. They voted the great planters into office and used their cotton gins and tapped into their marketing networks. Some of them worked as overseers for their wealthy neighbors, sold them food, and served on local slave patrols. Economic disparities between planters and farmers in the plantation belt continued to widen, but the farmers remained tied to the cotton economy and its economic and social imperatives.

Most yeomen, however, lived away from the plantations in neighborhoods with few slaves and limited commercial activities. Large numbers of them moved into nonslave territory north of the Ohio River, but most of them stayerd in the South: in the upcountry and the eastern slopes of the Appalachians from the Chesapeake through Georgia, the western slopes of the mountains in Kentucky and Tennessee, the pine-covered hill country of northern Mississippi and Alabama, and in swampy, hilly, heavily wooded lands throughout the

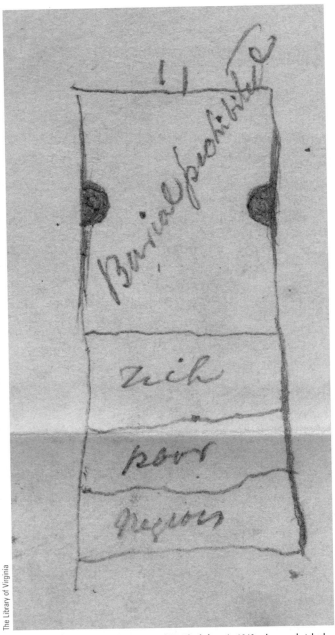

A Map of the Burial Ground in Farmville, Virginia   In 1840, a lawyer sketched the map of a graveyard in slaveholding country near the Appomattox River to make a point in a court case. It was a map of the living as well: rich whites at the top, poor whites in the middle, blacks at the bottom, yet all occupying the same ground.

southern states. All of these areas were unsuitable for plantation crops. Here the farmers built a yeoman society that retained many of the characteristics of the 18th-century countryside, North and South. But while northern farmers commercialized in the 19th century, their southern cousins continued in a household- and neighborhood-centered agriculture until the Civil War and beyond.

Many southern farmers stayed outside the market almost entirely. The mountaineers of the southern Appalachians sent a trickle of livestock and timber out of their neighborhoods, but the mountains remained largely outside the market until the coming of big-business coal mines in the late 19th century. Moreover, farmers in large parts of the upcountry South preferred raising livestock to growing cotton or tobacco. They planted cornfields and let their pigs run loose in the woods and on unfenced private land. In late summer and fall, they rounded up the animals and sold them to drovers who herded them cross-country and sold them to flatland merchants and planters. Thus these hill-country yeomen lived off a market with which they had little firsthand experience. It was a way of life that sustained some of the most fiercely independent neighborhoods in the country.

A larger group of southern yeomen practiced mixed farming for household subsistence and neighborhood exchange, with the surplus sent to market. Most of them owned their own land. The settlement of new lands in the old backcountry and the southwestern states reversed the 18th-century drift toward white tenancy. Few of these farmers kept slaves. In the counties of upland Georgia, for instance, between 7 in 10 and 9 in 10 households were without slaves. These farmers practiced a "subsistence plus" agriculture that was complicated by the nature of southern cash crops. Northern yeomen before 1815 had grown grain and livestock with which they fed their families and traded with neighbors. Whatever was left over, they sent to market. But cotton, like tobacco and other southern cash crops, was not a food. It could be turned into clothing, and often was: farm women in the South spun and wove small cotton crops into clothes for their families. (This at a time when cards, spinning wheels, and looms were disappearing from northern farmhouses.) Most middling and poor southern farmers played it safe: they put their improved land into corn and sweet potatoes, and set pigs and cattle loose to browse the remaining land. The more substantial and ambitious of them cultivated a few acres of cotton. They grew more cotton as transportation made markets more accessible, but few southern yeomen became wholly dependent on the market. With the income from a few bales of cotton, they could pay their debts and taxes and buy coffee, tea, sugar, tobacco, cloth, and shoes. But they continued to enter and leave the market at will, and to retain the ability to subsist within their neighborhoods. In the yeoman neighborhoods of the southern states, the economic and social practices of the 18th century were alive and well.

Yeoman Neighborhoods

The way of life in most southern farm neighborhoods discouraged business-like farming and individual ambition. Because few farms were self-sufficient, farmers routinely traded labor and goods with each other. In the plantation counties, such cooperation tended to reinforce the power of planters, who put some of their resources at the disposal of their poorer neighbors. In the upcountry, cooperation reinforced neighborliness. As one upland Georgian remarked, "Borrowing . . . was neighboring." Debts contracted within the network of kin and neighbors were generally paid in kind or in labor, and creditors often allowed their neighbors' debts to go unpaid for years.

Among southern neighborly restraints on entrepreneurialism, none was more distinctive than the region's attitude toward fences. Northerners never tired of comparing their neatly fenced farms with the dilapidated or absent fences of the South. In the capitalist North, well-maintained fences were a sign of ambitious, hardworking farmers. The poor fences of the South, they said, were a sign of laziness. Actually, the scarcity of fences in most southern neighborhoods was the result of local custom and state law. Georgia, for instance, required farmers to fence their planted fields but not the rest of their land. In country neighborhoods where families fished and hunted for food, and where livestock roamed freely, fences conflicted with a local economy that required neighborhood use of privately owned land. In this sense, the northerners were right: the absence of fences in the South reflected neighborhood constraints on the private use of private property, and thus on individual acquisitiveness and ambition. Such constraints, however, were necessary to the subsistence of families and neighborhoods as they were organized in the upland South.

Southern farmers marketed their cotton and food surpluses at country stores, and again the patterns of the 18th and early 19th centuries persisted. Northern stores, particularly in the more commercializing regions, were stocking their shelves with a wider variety of imported and domestic goods to serve farm families that no longer produced for themselves and that had money in their pockets. Southern yeomen, on the other hand, bought very little. A relatively prosperous backwoods farmer in South Carolina recalled that "My farm gave me and my whole family a good living on the produce of it, and left me, one year after another, one hundred and fifty silver dollars, *for I never spent more than ten dollars a year*, which was for salt, nails and the like. Nothing to wear, eat or drink was purchased, as my farm provided all."

Families such as these continued to live without carpets or curtains, to eat homegrown food from wooden or pewter plates, and to wear everyday cloth spun and woven by the women of the family, although many who could afford it wore clothing fashioned from machine-made cloth on Sunday. And like the rest of their transactions, yeomen seldom bought items or settled transactions in cash. The store of Leach Carrigan and Samuel Carrigan in South Carolina, for instance, traded 85 percent of its merchandise for cotton. While the northern countryside and the lowland plantation districts functioned in businesslike ways, the old barter economy—and the forms of family independence and neighborly cooperation on which it rested—persisted in the southern upcountry.

Unlike the plantations, the farm neighborhoods of the South were places in which white people worked. Most farmers relied solely on family labor. They sired many children and put them to work at an early age. Farm wives often labored in the fields, particularly at peak times. Even those who were spared from field work took up heavy burdens.

A southern yeoman remembered that his mother worked "in the house sutch as cooking carding spinning and weaving and washing. Thare [were] 14 in the family," and "she did not have any servant to help her." George Washington Lewis, who grew up on his father's southern farm, recalled a boyhood filled with hard labor. He "chopped, plowed, hoed, carded, reaped, mowed and bound sheaves, in fact all kinds of work necessary on a farm and lots of it. Split rails, built fences, log roled and danced with the girls at quiltings." We may be happy to learn that this boy found time for fun, but we must note—as northern critics did not—that he spent most of his waking hours at hard physical labor.

The Private Lives of Slaves

Focus Question
Describe the cultural life that slaves made for themselves within the limits of slavery.

In 1790, slaves in the Chesapeake had lived for generations in the same neighborhoods— old communities filled with kinfolk, ancestral graveyards, family gardens, and familiarity with each other and with local whites. They had made a distinctively African American way of life within the boundaries of slavery. Slaves along the South Carolina–Georgia rice coast, living and working in large groups under minimal white supervision, had made their own African American ways. In the first half of the 19th century, hundreds of thousands of these people were torn from their communities and sold into the cotton states. It began a period of cultural destruction and reconstruction equaled only by the process of enslavement. We can view that process intimately by looking into the most vital of slave institutions: the slave family and slave religion.

Slave Families

In law, in the census, and in the minds of planters, slaves were members of a plantation household over which the owner exercised absolute authority as owner, paternal protector, and lawgiver. Yet both slaveholders and slaves knew that slaves could not be treated like farm animals or little children. Wise slaveholders learned that the success of a plantation depended less on terror and draconian discipline (though whippings—and worse— were common) than on the accommodations by which slaves traded labor and obedience for privileges and some measure of autonomy within the bonds of slavery. After achieving privileges, the slaves called them their own: holidays, garden plots, friendships and social gatherings both on and off the plantation, hunting and fishing rights, the right to trade slave-made goods, and—most vitally—the right to live in families of their own. These hard-won privileges provided some of the ground on which slaves in the old plantation states had made their own lives within slavery. The domestic slave trade and the movement onto the cotton frontier cut that ground from beneath their feet. Slaves learned painfully that they were not members of families or communities—either the masters' or their own. They were property, and they could be bought and sold.

The most precious privilege on Chesapeake plantations had been the right to make and maintain families. As early as the Revolutionary era, most Chesapeake slaves lived in units consisting of a mother, a father, and their small children. On Charles Carroll's Maryland farms in 1773, for example, 325 of the 400 slaves lived in such families. At Thomas Jefferson's Monticello, most slave marriages were for life, and small children almost always lived with both parents. The most common exceptions to this practice were fathers who had married away from their own plantations and who visited "broad wives" and children during their off hours. Owners encouraged stable marriages because they made farms more peaceful and productive and because they flattered the owners' own religious and paternalistic sensibilities. For their part, slaves demanded families as part of the price of their labor.

Yet slave families had always been vulnerable. Many slaveholders assumed that they had the right to coerce sex from female slaves. Some (including Thomas Jefferson) kept slaves as mistresses. The planters tended, however, to keep these liaisons within bounds. While the slave community seldom punished sex before marriage, it took adultery seriously. Slaveholders knew that violations of married slave women could be enormously disruptive and strongly discouraged them. Slave sales also threatened families, but most sales before 1800 or so took place within neighborhoods, damaging slave families and communities without destroying them. The most serious threat was the death or bankruptcy of the

Library of Congress, Prints and Photographs Division

Five Generations of a Slave Family on a South Carolina Sea Island Plantation, 1862 Complex family ties such as those of the family shown here were among the most hard-won and vulnerable cultural accomplishments of enslaved blacks.

slaveholder, which led to the liquidation of estates and the division of property among heirs. Yet even these events, in comparison to what came later, tended to keep slaves in the same extended neighborhood.

The Slave Trade and the Slave Family

That changed with the growth of the cotton belt and the interstate slave trade. Masters in the seaboard states claimed (often truthfully) that they tried to keep slave families together and that they sold slaves to traders only out of dire necessity or as a means of getting rid of troublesome individuals. The latter category could be used as a threat. One slave remembered that "Slaves usually got scared when it became clear that Negro-Trader [John] White was in the community. The owners used White's name as a threat to scare the slaves when they had violated some rule." "If a man did anything out of the way," recalled another slave, "he was in more danger of being sold than being whipped." Thomas Jefferson, reputedly the kindest of masters, punished a troublesome slave by selling him in 1803, declaring that he would be sent into "so distant an exile . . . as to cut him off completely from ever being heard of [again]."

Chesapeake planters and slaves knew, however, that the slave trade was more than a means of settling debts or punishing individuals. It had become an important source of income. Myths of slave "breeding farms" in the Chesapeake are just that—myths. Slaves in the exporting states continued to live in families that produced and nurtured their own children, but the children could expect to be sold into long-distance markets when they came of age. The systematic selling of teenaged and young adult slaves, who commanded the highest prices, became a standard way in which Chesapeake gentlemen maintained their status. John Randolph of Roanoke, one of the great planter-politicians of Virginia, routinely translated younger members of his "plantation family" into cash. In 1823, he traveled to New York to see the great match race between the northern horse American Eclipse and the southern horse Henry. In a moment of pride and exuberance, he shouted from the grandstand that he would bet "a year's crop of negroes" on the southern champion.

Professional slave traders made no effort to hide their willingness to break slave families. Neither did the southwestern planters who bought slaves from the older states. One planter insisted that "it is better to buy *none in families,* but *to select only choice, first rate, young hands from 14 to 25 years of age,* (buying no children or aged negroes.)" Seaboard planters, trying to convince themselves and anyone who would listen that they were responsible paternalists, made a sharp division between the plantation "family" and the well-known horrors of the domestic slave trade, but the slaves knew better. A Virginia slave woman had this to say of the planter who had sold her daughters: "he was a mean dirty slave trader."

Separated from their kinfolk and communities, cotton-belt slaves began the old process of negotiation with their masters, and they reconstructed families. Cotton planters preferred young men for the labor of clearing the land, but they soon began importing nearly equal numbers of women, encouraging marriage, and providing cabins for slave families. Families made for greater peace and quiet on the plantations, and they were a good long-term investment in the production of new slaves. The slaves grasped the opportunity. As early as the 1820s, 51 percent of rural Louisiana slaves lived in families composed of two parents and their children. That figure was smaller than it had been on the old farms, but in view of what the slaves had been through, it was surprisingly large.

Slaveholders who encouraged slave marriages—perhaps even solemnizing them with a religious ceremony—knew that marriage implied a form of self-ownership that conflicted with the slaves' status as property. Some conducted ceremonies in which couples "married" by jumping over a broomstick. Others had the preacher omit the phrases "let no man put asunder" and "till death do you part" from the ceremony. Slaves knew that such ceremonies had no legal force. A Virginia slave remarked, "We slaves knowed that them words wasn't bindin'. Don't mean nothin' lessen you say, 'What God has jined, caint no man pull asunder.' But dey never would say dat. Jus' say 'Now you married.'" A South Carolina slave preacher routinely ended the ceremony with "Till death or buckra [whites] part you."

Slaves built their sense of family and kinship around such uncertainties. Because separation from father or mother was common, children spread their affection among adult relatives, treating grandparents, aunts, and uncles almost as though they were parents. In fact, slaves often referred to all of their adult relatives as "parents." They also called nonrelatives "brother," "sister," "aunt," and "uncle," thus extending a sense of kinship to the slave community at large. Slaves chose as surnames for themselves the names of former owners, Anglicized versions of African names, or names that simply sounded good. They rarely chose the name of their current owner. Families tended to use the same given names over and over, naming boys after their father or grandfather, perhaps to preserve the memory of fathers who might be taken away. They seldom named girls after their mothers, however. Unlike Southern whites, slaves never married a first cousin, even though many members of their community were close relatives. The origins and functions of some of these customs are unknown. We know only that slaves practiced them consistently, often without the knowledge of the slaveholders.

The Beginnings of African American Christianity in the Chesapeake

Until the mid-18th century, neither enslaved Africans nor their masters showed much interest in christianizing slaves. That changed with the rise of evangelical Christianity in the South (see chapter 10). Blacks participated in the revivals of the southern Great Awakening, and the number of Christian slaves increased steadily in the second half of the 18th century. In the slave communities of the Upper South, as well as the burgeoning free and semifree black populations in the towns, the evangelical revivals of the late 18th and early 19th centuries appealed powerfully to African Americans, who sensed that the bonds of slavery were loosening. By 1820, most blacks in the Chesapeake considered themselves Christians. They would take their religion with them when they went farther south.

Between the Revolution and 1820, Chesapeake slaves embraced Christianity and began to turn it into a religion of their own. Slaves attended camp meetings, listened to **itinerant preachers,** and joined the Baptist and Methodist congregations of the southern revival.

The revivalists, in turn, welcomed slaves and free blacks to their meetings and sometimes recruited them as preachers. Evangelical preaching, singing, and spiritual exercises were much more attractive than the cold, high-toned lectures of the Anglicans. So were the humility and suffering of evangelical whites, most of whom where poor men and outsiders. Finally, the slaves gloried in the evangelicals' assault on the slaveholders' culture and in the antislavery sentiments of many white evangelicals (see chapter 10). The result was a huge increase in the number of African American Christians. Methodists, who counted converts more carefully than some others, claimed 20,000 black members in 1800—one in three American Methodists.

The integrated congregations, however, did not last. There were exceptions, but most congregations were in fact internally segregated, with blacks sitting in the back of the church or upstairs in the gallery, and with only whites serving in positions of authority. Blacks, with both positive and negative encouragement from whites, organized independent churches in Baltimore, Wilmington, Richmond, Norfolk, and the scattered villages that had risen to serve the Chesapeake's new mixed economy. Even Charleston boasted an independent Methodist conference made up of 4,000 slaves and free blacks in 1815. By 1820, roughly 700 independent black churches operated in the United States. There had been none at all 30 years earlier. And on the plantations, slaves met informally—sometimes with the masters' permission, sometimes without it—to preach and pray.

Slave Theology

Slaves understood and used the message of Christianity in their own ways. The biblical notion that slavery could be punishment for sin and the white southern notion that God intended blacks to be slaves never took root among enslaved Christians. Hannah Scott, a slave in Arkansas, remarked on what she heard a white preacher say: "But all he say is 'bedience to de white folks, and we hears 'nough of dat without him telling us." One slave asked a white preacher, "Is us slaves gonna be free in heaven?" The preacher had no answer. As one maid boldly told her mistress, "God never made us to be slaves for white people."

Another way in which slave religion differed from what was preached to them by whites was in the practice of conjuring, folk magic, root medicine, and other occult knowledge, most of it passed down from West Africa. Such practices provided help in areas in which Christianity was useless. They could reputedly cure illnesses, make people fall in love, ensure a good day's fishing, or bring harm to one's enemies. Sometimes African magic was in competition with plantation Christianity. Just as often, however, slaves combined the two. For instance, slaves sometimes determined the guilt or innocence of a person accused of stealing by hanging a Bible by a thread, then watching the way it turned. The form was West African; the Bible was not. The slave root doctor George White boasted that he could "cure most anything," but added that "you got to talk wid God an' ask him to help out." "Maum Addie," a slave in coastal South Carolina, dealt with the malevolent African spirits called plat-eyes with a combination of African potions, the Christian God, and a stout stick: "So I totes mah powder en sulphur en I carries mah stick in mah han en puts mah truss in Gawd."

While Christianity could not cure sick babies or identify thieves, it gave slaves something more important: a sense of themselves as a historical people with a role to play in God's cosmic drama. In slave Christianity, Moses the liberator (and not the slaveholders' Abraham) stood beside Jesus. The slaves' appropriation of the book of Exodus denied the smug assumption of the whites that they were God's chosen people who had escaped the bondage of despotic Europe to enter the promised land of America. To the slaves, America was Egypt, they were the chosen people, and the slaveholders were Pharaoh. Thomas Wentworth Higginson, a Boston abolitionist who went south during the Civil War to lead a Union regiment of freed South Carolina slaves, wrote that his men knew the Old Testament books of Moses and the New Testament book of Revelation. "All that lies between," he said, "even the life of Jesus, they hardly cared to read or to hear." He found their minds "a vast bewildered chaos of Jewish history and biography; and most of the events of the past, down to the period of the American Revolution, they instinctively attribute to Moses."

The slaves' religious songs, which became known as spirituals, told of God's people, their travails, and their ultimate deliverance. In songs and sermons, the figures of Jesus and Moses were often blurred, and it was not always clear whether deliverance—accompanied by divine retribution—would take place in this world or the next. But deliverance always meant an end to slavery, with the possibility that it might bring a reversal of relations between slaves and masters. "The idea of a revolution in the conditions of the whites and blacks," said the escaped slave Charles Ball, "is the cornerstone of the religion of the latter."

Religion and Revolt

In comparison with slaves in Cuba, Jamaica, Brazil, and other New World plantation societies, North American slaves seldom went into organized, armed revolt. The environment of the United States was unfriendly to such events. American plantations were relatively small and dispersed, and the southern white population was large, vigilant, and very well-armed. Whites also enjoyed—until the cataclysm of the Civil War—internal political stability. There were thus few situations in which slaves could hope to win their freedom by violent means. Thousands of slaves demonstrated their hatred of the system by running away. Others fought masters or overseers, sabotaged equipment and animals, stole from planters, and found other ways to oppose slavery, but most knew that open revolt was suicide.

Christianity convinced slaves that history was headed toward an apocalypse that would result in divine justice and their own deliverance. It thus contained the possibility of revolt. But slave preachers seldom indulged in prophecy and almost never told their congregations to become actively engaged in God's divine plan, for they knew that open resistance was hopeless. Slave Christians believed that God hated slavery and would end it, but that their role was to have faith in God, to take care of one another, to preserve their identity as a people, and to await deliverance. Only occasionally did slaves take retribution and deliverance into their own hands, and each time they were armed with some mix of republican equalitarianism and evangelical Christianity.

Gabriel's Rebellion

Masters who talked of liberty, natural rights, and equality before God sometimes worried that slaves might imagine that such language could apply to themselves. The Age of Democratic Revolution took a huge step in that direction in 1789, when the French Revolution—fought in the name of "Liberty, Equality, and Fraternity"—went beyond American notions of restored English liberties and into the heady regions of universal natural rights. Among the first repercussions outside of France was a revolution in the French Caribbean colony of Saint-Domingue. That island's half-million slaves fought out a complicated political and military revolt that began with the events in Paris in 1789 and resulted—after the defeats of Spanish, English, and French armies—with the creation of the independent black republic of Haiti on the western one-third of the island. Slave societies throughout the hemisphere heard tales of terror from refugee French planters and stories of hope from the slaves they brought with them (12,000 of these entered South Carolina and Louisiana alone). In 1800, a conservative Virginia white complained that "Liberty and Equality has been infused into the minds of the negroes." A South Carolina congressman agreed that "this newfangled French philosophy of liberty and equality" was stirring up the slaves. Even Thomas Jefferson, who applauded the spread of French republicanism, conceded that "the West Indies appears to have given considerable impulse to the minds of the slaves . . . in the United States."

Slaves from the 1790s onward whispered of natural rights and imagined themselves as part of the Democratic Revolution. This covert republic of the slaves sometimes came into the open. In Richmond in 1800, a slave blacksmith named **Gabriel** hatched a conspiracy to overthrow Virginia's slave regime. Gabriel had been hired out to Richmond employers for most of his adult life; he was shaped less by plantation slavery than by the democratic, loosely interracial underworld of urban artisans. In the late 1790s, the repressive acts of the Federalist national government and the angry responses of the Jeffersonian opposition (see chapter 7), along with the news from Haiti, drove the democratic sensibilities of that world to new heights.

Gabriel, working with his brother and other hired-out slave artisans, planned his revolt with military precision. Working at religious meetings, barbecues, and the grog shops of Richmond, they recruited soldiers among slave artisans, adding plantation slaves only at the last moment. Gabriel planned to march an army of 1,000 men on Richmond in three columns. The outside columns would set diversionary fires in the warehouse district and prevent the militia from entering the town. The center would seize Capitol Square, including the treasury, the arsenal, and Governor James Monroe.

Although his army would be made up of slaves, and although his victory would end slavery in Virginia, Gabriel hoped to make a republican revolution, not a slave revolt. His chosen enemies were the Richmond "merchants" who had controlled his labor. Later, a co-conspirator divulged the plan: The rebels would hold Governor Monroe hostage and split the state treasury among themselves, and "if the white people agreed to their freedom they would then hoist a white flag, and [Gabriel] would dine and drink with the merchants of the city on the day when it would be agreed to." Gabriel expected what he called "the poor white people" and "the most redoubtable republicans" to join him. He in fact had the shadowy support of two Frenchmen, and rumors indicated that other whites were involved, although never at levels that matched the delusions of the conspirators or of worried whites. Gabriel planned to kill anyone who opposed him, but he would spare Quakers, Methodists, and Frenchmen, for they were "friendly to liberty." Unlike earlier slave insurgents, Gabriel did not plot violent retribution or a return to or reconstruction of West Africa. He was an American revolutionary, and he dreamed of a truly democratic republic for Virginia. His army would march into Richmond under the banner "Death or Liberty."

Gabriel recruited at least 150 soldiers who agreed to gather near Richmond on August 30, 1800. The leaders expected 500 to 600 more to join them as they marched upon the town. On the appointed day, however, it rained heavily, washing out bridges and making roads impassable. Rebels could not reach the meeting point, and amid white terror and black betrayals, Gabriel and his henchmen were hunted down, tried, and sentenced to death. In all, the state hanged 27 supposed conspirators, while others were sold and transported out of Virginia. The condemned carried their republican dreams to their graves. A white Virginian marveled that the rebels on the gallows displayed a "sense of their [natural] rights, [and] a contempt of danger." When asked to explain the revolt, one condemned man replied in terms that could only have disturbed the white republicans of Virginia: "I have nothing more to offer than what General Washington would have had to offer, had he been taken by the British and put to trial by them. I have adventured my life in endeavoring to obtain the liberty of my countrymen, and am a willing sacrifice in their cause."

Denmark Vesey

Denmark Vesey, a free black of Charleston, South Carolina, hatched the most ambitious conspiracy. Vesey was a leading member of an African Methodist congregation that had seceded from the white Methodists and had been independent from 1817 to 1821. At its height, the church had 6,000 members, most of them slaves. Vesey and some of the other members read widely in political tracts, including the antislavery arguments in the Missouri debates (see chapter 11) and in the Bible. They talked about their delivery out of Egypt, with all white men, women, and children being cut off. They identified Charleston as Jericho and planned its destruction in 1822. A few dozen Charleston blacks would take the state armory, then arm rural slaves who would rise up to help them. They would kill the whites and commandeer ships in the harbor and make their getaway, presumably to black-controlled Haiti. Word of the conspiracy spread secretly into the countryside, largely through the efforts of Gullah Jack, who was both a Methodist and an African conjurer. Jack recruited African-born slaves as soldiers, provided them with charms as protection against whites, and used his spiritual powers to terrify others into keeping silent.

In the end, the Vesey plot was betrayed by slaves. As one coerced confession followed another, white authorities hanged Vesey, Gullah Jack, and 34 other accused conspirators— 22 of them in one day. But frightened whites knew that most of the conspirators (estimates ranged from 600 to 9,000) remained at large and unidentified.

Nat Turner This contemporary woodcut depicts scenes from Nat Turner's rebellion. In this bloodiest of all North American slave revolts, 55 whites, most of them women and children, were shot and hacked to death.

Nat Turner

In August 1831, in a revolt in Southampton County, Virginia, some 60 slaves shot and hacked to death 55 white men, women, and children. Their leader was **Nat Turner,** a Baptist lay preacher. Turner was neither a conjurer like Gullah Jack (he violently opposed plantation conjurers) nor a republican revolutionary like Denmark Vesey or the Richmond slave Gabriel. He was, he told his captors, a Christian prophet and an instrument of God's wrath. As a child, he had prayed and fasted often, and the spirit—the same spirit that had spoken to the prophets of the Bible—had spoken to him. When he was a young man, he had run away to escape a cruel overseer, but God said that He had not chosen him merely to have him run away, and Nat had returned. He justified his return with one of the slaveowners' favorite verses of scripture: "He who knoweth his master's will and doeth it not, shall be beaten with many stripes." But Turner knew that his Master was God, not a slaveowner.

Around 1830, Turner received visions of the final battle in Revelation, recast as a war between white and black spirits. He saw Christ crucified against the night sky, and the next morning he saw Christ's blood in a cornfield. Convinced by a solar eclipse in February 1831 that the time had come, Turner began telling other slaves about his visions, recruited his force, and launched his bloody and hopeless revolt.

The revolts of Gabriel, Turner, and Vesey, along with scores of more limited conspiracies, deeply troubled southern whites. Slaveholders were committed to a paternalism that was increasingly tied to the South's attempt to make slavery both domestic and Christian. For their part, slaves recognized that they could receive decent treatment and pockets of autonomy in return for outward docility. Gabriel, Vesey, and Turner opened wide cracks in that mutual charade. During the Turner revolt, slaves whose masters had been murdered joined the rebels without a second thought. A plantation mistress who survived by hiding in a closet listened to the murders of her husband and children, then heard her house servants arguing over possession of her clothes. A Charleston grandee named Elias Horry, upon finding that his coachman was among the Vesey conspirators, asked him, "What were your intentions?" The formerly docile slave replied that he had intended "to kill you, rip open your belly, and throw your guts in your face."

A Balance Sheet: The Plantation and Southern Growth

Focus Question
What were the nature and limits of the market revolution in the South? Why?

The cotton plantation was a profitable business. In 1860, the cash value of the southern slave population was $3 billion. That was more than the value of investments in banking, railroads, and manufacturing combined. The best estimates put the annual rate of return on the larger plantations at 10 percent—higher than factories, banks, and other more modern enterprises. Land and slaves produced wealth and social esteem in the South, and planters invested their profits in more slaves and more land. The result was a lack of diversification and an increasing concentration of resources in the hands of the planter class. There was significant economic growth in the South, but most of it happened on the largest farms.

The commercialization of the northern family farm created a rural demand for credit, banking facilities, farm tools, clothing, and other consumer goods and services, spurring a revolution in commerce, finance, and industry. The South, on the other hand, was a poor

The Historic New Orleans Collection, Accension #1977. 13734311

A Cotton Press Mule-driven presses such as the one shown here packed southern cotton into bales for easier transport to market. The cotton was pressed into a frame by a wooden screw carved from a whole tree.

Beloved (1998)

Directed by Jonathan Demme. Starring Danny Glover (Paul D), Oprah Winfrey (Sethe), Beah Richards (Baby Suggs).

Oprah Winfrey produced and starred in this adaptation of Toni Morrison's Pulitzer Prize–winning novel. It is a story of persisting personal and communal wounds inflicted by slavery, told from within a damaged black household near Cincinnati in 1873.

The action begins when Paul D (Danny Glover) walks up to the house of Sethe (Oprah Winfrey) and her daughter, Denver. As he enters, the house fills with a red glow and shakes itself into a storm of furniture and kitchen implements. The house is haunted by the ghost of Sethe's baby girl. Paul D is a former slave from Sweet Home, the horrific Kentucky plantation from which Sethe escaped. He moves in, the ghost moves out, and the film follows this household through the next year.

Peace lasts only a short time. A strange young woman named Beloved moves in and becomes Denver's sister, Sethe's daughter, and Paul D's mystical seducer. (The camera pans back from the seduction scene in the red glow that we remember from the initial haunting.) Paul D discovers that Sethe had killed her own baby in 1856 and he leaves. Beloved, now pregnant, demands (and gets) Sethe's time, money, and affection. Sethe loses her job and runs out of food and money, serving Beloved all the while. Denver begs work from an old teacher, and the community of black women, who have shunned Sethe and her family throughout the movie, begin leaving food.

In the climactic scene, Denver waits on the porch for her new white employer (a former abolitionist), when the black women arrive to sing and chant in an effort to exorcise ghosts from the house. Sethe, crazed, followed by naked and pregnant Beloved, comes onto the porch and attacks the employer with an ice pick. The women subdue her, Denver rides off (like her brothers before her) to another life, and Beloved disappears. The film ends with the return of Paul D, and we are left with the hope that Sethe may outlive her ghosts.

Although the action occurs in 1873, the explanation lies in slavery and in the 1856 escape attempt told—in conversation, dreams, and flashbacks—as memory. Love scenes between Sethe and Paul D display the scars of whippings, particularly on Sethe. She saw her mother hanged, she was whipped and beaten while pregnant, and her owner's sons held her down and sucked the milk from her. (Sethe learns later that her husband, whom she thought had abandoned her, witnessed this scene from a hayloft and went hopelessly insane.) Her escape is botched and violent. Sethe secretly sends her two sons ahead to Baby Suggs (Beah Richards), her mother-in-law in Ohio. Sethe sets off alone, gives birth to Denver on the banks of the Ohio River, crosses the river, and spends one perfect month tending her children and going to Baby Suggs's church meetings in the woods—meetings at which Suggs demands that her people love themselves. Then the old master arrives to take them back to Kentucky. Sethe grabs the children, takes them into an outbuilding, and tries to kill them, succeeding only with Denver's infant older sister.

It all works better in Morrison's novel than in Oprah Winfrey's movie, but both are terrible and disturbing dramatizations of the injury slavery inflicted and of African American attempts to both absorb and transcend the crimes committed against them.

© CORBIS SYGMA

Beloved (1998) stars Danny Glover and Oprah Winfrey and is based on Toni Morrison's Pulitzer Prize–winning novel.

market for manufactured goods. Most white farmers relied on the production of their households and neighbors, and they remained marginal to the market economy. They bought finished goods from the outside, but at a rate that was far lower than their northern counterparts. The slaves wore cheap cloth made in the Northeast and bought by their masters, and their trade in slave-made goods, while it was crucial to subsistence and a valued form of "independence" within slavery, resulted in only low-level (often furtive) entry into the market. For their part, the larger planters furnished themselves and their homes with finery from Europe. The South continued to export its plantation staples and to pay outsiders for shipping, financial services, and finished goods. A market revolution produced commercial agriculture, urbanization, a specialized labor force, and technological innovation in the North. In the South, it simply produced more cotton and more slavery.

Not that the South neglected technological change and agricultural improvement. Southerners developed Eli Whitney's table-top cotton gin into big machines capable of performing complex milling operations. They improved steamboat design as well, creating flat-bottomed boats that could travel far up shallow rivers. They also developed, among others, a machine with a huge wooden screw powered by horses or mules to press ginned cotton into tight bales for shipping. Jordan Goree, a slave craftsman in Huntsville, Texas, won a reputation for being able to carve whole trees into perfect screws for these machines. There were, however, few such innovations, and they had to do with the processing and shipping of cotton. Despite the experiments of a few gentleman-planters, there were almost no improvements in the *cultivation* of cotton. The truth is that cotton was a labor-intensive crop that discouraged innovation. Moreover, plantation workers often resisted their enslavement by sabotaging expensive tools and draft animals, scattering manure in haphazard ways, and passively resisting innovations that would have added to their drudgery. So the cotton fields continued to be cultivated by enslaved people working with clumsy, mule-drawn plows that barely scratched the soil, by women wielding heavy hoes, and by gangs who harvested the crop by hand.

Southern state governments spent little on **internal improvements.** A Virginia canal linked the flour mills at Richmond with inland grain fields, and another would connect Chesapeake Bay with the National Road, thus realizing—too late—Washington's and Jefferson's dreams of a thoroughfare between the Chesapeake and the Ohio Valley. But cotton-belt planters built their farms on alluvial land with ready access to the South's magnificent system of navigable rivers. They had little interest in expensive, state-supported internal improvements that their own neighborhoods did not need. Upcountry whites, particularly in the Upper South, sometimes campaigned for roads and canals, but they seldom got such measures through planter-dominated legislatures.

Nor did the South build cities, much less a regional *system* of cities. In 1800, about 82 percent of the southern workforce and about 70 percent of the northern workforce were employed in agriculture. By 1860, only 40 percent of the northern workforce was so employed. In the South, the proportion had risen to 84 percent. The old northern seaports grew dramatically in the early 19th century, and they extended their sway over systems of satellite cities. New York, which became America's great city in the first third of the 19th century, exercised not only commercial but also cultural power over the old capital at Albany, as well as new Erie Canal cities such as Utica, Syracuse, Rochester, and Buffalo. Between 1800 and 1840, the urban population of New York State rose from 12.7 percent to 19.4 percent, despite the settlement of huge tracts of new agricultural land. In Massachusetts, the urban population rose from 15.4 percent to 37.9 percent in these years. By 1840, every northeastern and mid-Atlantic state with the exceptions of Maine and Vermont had at least 10 percent of their people living in cities. No southern state urbanized at that level. Virginia, at 6.9 percent, had the largest urban population of any of the future Confederate states.

Commercial and manufacturing cities sprouted up throughout the interior of the North. The few southern cities were located on the periphery of the region and served as transportation depots for plantation crops. River cities like Louisville, Memphis, and St. Louis were little more than stopping places for steamboats. The great seaports of New Orleans, Charleston, and Baltimore had in the past shipped plantation staples directly to British and European markets. But as the 19th century progressed, they sent more and more of their goods by coasting vessel to New York City, where they were trans-shipped to foreign ports. In turn, Europe's manufactured goods were funneled into New York, then sold off to the southern (and northern) countryside. The commercial metropolis of the southern United States was becoming less London and more New York. What had *not* changed was the colonial status of the South.

Thus while the North and the Northwest developed towns and cities throughout their regions, southern cities continued to be few and to perform the colonial functions of 18th-century seaport towns. Southern businessmen turned to New York City for credit, insurance, and coastal and export shipping. From New York they ordered finished goods for the southern market. *De Bow's Review,* the principal business journal of the South, reported that South Carolina storekeepers who bought goods from Charleston wholesalers concealed that fact and claimed they had bought them directly from New York City, for it was well known that New York provided better goods at lower prices than any supplier in the South. De Bow testified to the superior skill and diversification of the North when, after trying several New Orleans sources, he awarded the publishing contract for his *Review* to a northern printer. That was not surprising in any case, because De Bow received three-fourths of his income from northern advertisers. In all, southerners estimated that 40 cents of every dollar produced by cotton remained in the Northeast.

Conclusion

On the eve of the Civil War, James H. Hammond, a slaveholding senator from South Carolina, asked, "What would happen if no cotton was furnished for three years. . . . England would topple headlong and carry the whole civilized world with her save the south. No, you dare not make war on cotton. No power on earth dares to make war on cotton. Cotton is king." Hammond was arguing, as Jefferson had argued in 1807, that farmers at the fringes of the world market economy could coerce the commercial-industrial center. He was wrong. The commitment to cotton and slavery had isolated the South politically. It had also deepened the South's dependence on the world's financial and industrial centers. The North transformed itself from a part of the old colonial periphery (the suppliers of food and raw materials) into a part of the core (the suppliers of manufactured goods and financing) of the world market economy, while the South continued to export plantation staples in exchange for imported goods. In the process, the South worked itself deeper and deeper into dependence, now as much upon the American Northeast as upon the old colonial rulers in London.

SUGGESTED READINGS

On the plantation economy, see **Eugene D. Genovese, *The Political Economy of Slavery: Studies in the Economy and Society of the Slave South,*** 2d ed. (1989) and **R.W. Fogel, *Without Consent or Contract: The Rise and Fall of American Slavery*** (1994). **Walter Johnson, *Soul by Soul: Life Inside the Antebellum Slave Market*** (1999) analyzes ways in which planters made a white culture out of slavery. **Bertram Wyatt-Brown, *Southern Honor: Ethics & Behavior in the Old South*** (1982) is essential.

On the southern yeomanry, see **Stephanie McCurry, *Masters of Small Worlds: Yeoman Households, Gender Relations, & the Political Culture of the South Carolina Lowcountry*** (1995) and **Steven Hahn, *The Roots of Southern Populism: Yeoman Farmers and the Transformation of the Georgia Upcountry, 1850–1890*** (1983). The social history of colonial and early national slavery is ably covered in **Ira Berlin, *Many Thousands Gone: The First Two Centuries of Slavery in North America*** (1998). Two pioneering works on slave culture are **Eugene D. Genovese, *Roll, Jordan, Roll: The World the Slaves Made*** (1974); and **Lawrence W. Levine, *Black Culture and Black Consciousness: Afro-American Folk Thought from Slavery to Freedom*** (1977).

Visit the Liberty Equality Power Companion Web site for resources specific to this textbook: http://www.thomsonedu.com/history/murrin

Also find self-tests and additional resources at ThomsonNOW. ThomsonNOW is an integrated online suite of services and resources with proven ease of use and efficient paths to success, delivering the results you want—NOW!

www.thomsonedu.com/login/

Toward an American Culture

Americans after 1815 experienced wave after wave of social and cultural change. Territorial expansion, the growth of the market, and the spread of plantation slavery uprooted Americans and broke old social patterns. Americans in these years reinvented family life. They created distinctively American forms of popular literature and art, and they found new ways of having fun. They flocked to evangelical churches that expanded and remade American religious life. They began, in short, to make a distinctively American culture.

The emerging American culture was more or less uniformly republican, capitalist, and Protestant. But different kinds of Americans made different cultures out of the revolutionary inheritance, market expansion, and revival religion. Southern farmers and their northern cousins thought differently about fatherhood and the proper way to make a family. Northeastern businessmen and southern planters agreed that economic progress was indeed progress, but they differed radically on its moral implications. Slaveholders, factory hands, rich and poor farmers, and middle-class women all heard the same Bible stories and learned different lessons. The result, visible from the 1830s onward, was an American national culture that was (and is) less an accepted body of rules than an ongoing conversation. This chapter identifies the ways in which various groups of Americans thought and felt about four of the hot spots in that conversation: family life and personal identity, the Christian inheritance, the emerging question of race, and the nature of republican citizenship.

The Democratization of Culture

The weakening of traditional authority created spaces that Americans filled in their own ways. Important pillars of old cultures remained: the Bible and revolutionary ideas of liberty and equality were fundamental to the new cultural forms. But the transportation network that carried wheat and cotton out of rural neighborhoods brought new things in: furniture and ways of arranging it, new clothing styles, new forms of entertainment, new information, new aspirations. In part, Americans made new ways of thinking and living as consumers of these cultural goods.

Among the items reaching Americans was information—newspapers, books, magazines, business communications, personal letters, and travelers who carried news. The information circulated among a public that was remarkably literate and well-informed.

CHRONOLOGY

1830	Charles Grandison Finney leads religious revival in Rochester • Joseph Smith founds the Church of Jesus Christ of Latter-Day Saints
1831	First minstrel show is presented
1843	William Miller's Adventists expect the world to end
1845	George Lippard's lurid novel *Quaker City* becomes a best seller
1849	Astor Place theater riot in New York City leaves 20 dead
1852	Harriet Beecher Stowe publishes *Uncle Tom's Cabin*

The literacy rate in the preindustrial United States was among the highest ever recorded. In 1790, approximately 85 percent of adult men in New England and 60 percent of those in Pennsylvania and the Chesapeake could read and write. The literacy rate among women was lower—about 45 percent in New England—but on the rise. By 1820, all but the poorest white Americans, particularly in the North, could read and write. The United States, more than perhaps any other country, was a nation of readers.

A Revolution in Print

The rise of a reading public was accompanied by a print revolution: enterprising men (and a few women) learned how to make their livings by providing cheap Bibles and English novels, almanacs, newspapers, and other printed matter to a public that not only could but did read. Readers were encouraged by their republican governments. The states provided common schools, and the national government helped the flow of print in ways that were unprecedented. The governments of Great Britain and the European powers tried to control the circulation of information: they established few post offices, taxed newspapers, monitored what was said in the newspapers and even in the mail, and prosecuted people who said the wrong things in print.

There were attempts to do such things in America. The Stamp Tax of 1765 had included a tax on newspapers, which many Americans considered an attempt not only at direct taxation but at controlling the news. And in 1798, Federalists had jailed editors with whom they disagreed. Americans defeated both of these attempts. The First Amendment guaranteed freedom of the press, and the U.S. government (with that brief Federalist exception) did not interfere with newspapers. Just the opposite: newspapers enjoyed discounted postal rates and circulated far beyond their points of publication. A law of 1792 allowed newspapers to mail copies to each other without cost, and the editors of country weeklies cut national and international news from the New York, Baltimore, and Philadelphia papers, combined them with local advertising and legal notices, and provided their readers with cheap sources of information that were remarkably uniform throughout the North and

West and much of the South. The rise of a democratic and national reading public, then, was directly and knowingly subsidized by the national government.

Newspapers were the most widely distributed form of print in the new republic. In 1790, 106 newspapers were being published in the United States. In 1835, 1,258 were in publication, 90 of which were dailies. In the latter year, the number of newspapers per capita in the United States was two to three times greater than in Great Britain. Still, even in New England, only about 1 household in 10 subscribed to a newspaper. Yet most members of the new democratic public knew what was in them, for the papers were passed from hand to hand, read aloud in groups, and made available at taverns and public houses. Timothy Dwight, Federalist president of Yale College, hated newspapers and associated them with gambling, tavern-haunting, drinking, and democracy.

Improvements in distribution and printing technology encouraged other forms of popular literature as well. The emerging evangelical crusade (see later section) made full and innovative use of print. Sunday school tracts, temperance pamphlets, and other religious materials were printed in huge numbers in New York and distributed efficiently and cheaply through the mails—so cheaply that the American Bible Society devised a realistic plan to provide every household in America with a free Bible. While newspapers were men's reading, the religious tracts tended to find their way into the hands of women. Women also were the principal readers of novels, a new form of reading matter that Thomas Jefferson and other authorities denounced as frivolous and aberrant. The first best-selling novel in the United States was *The Power of Sympathy,* a morally ambiguous tale of seduction and betrayal that exposed hypocrisy in male authorities who punished (generally poor and vulnerable) women for their own seductions. Such tales were seen as dangerous not only because they contained questionable subject matter but also because girls and women read them silently and in private. Printed matter provided information and opinion for the men who exercised power and conducted the public life of democracy, but it could also provide sustenance for the spirits and imaginations of Americans who were excluded from power and the public.

The increase in literacy and in printed matter accelerated both the market and democratic individualism. Books and newspapers were scarce in the 18th century, and most Americans had experienced the written word only as it was read aloud by fathers, ministers, or teachers. After 1790, private, silent reading of new kinds of texts became common. No longer were adult male authorities the sole interpreters of the world for families and neighborhoods. The new print culture encouraged Americans to read, think, and interpret information for themselves.

The Northern Middle Class

Focus Question
What were the central cultural maxims of the emerging northern middle class?

A New Middle Class

"The most valuable class in any community," declared the poet-journalist Walt Whitman in 1858, "is the middle class." At that time, the term *middle class* (and the social group that it described) was no more than 30 or 40 years old. The Market Revolution had created new towns and cities and transformed the old ones, and it had turned the rural North into a landscape of family-owned commercial farms. Those who claimed the title "middle class" were largely the new kinds of proprietors made by the market revolution—city and country merchants, master craftsmen who had turned themselves into manufacturers, and the mass of market-oriented farmers. They lived at the centers of the new marketing and communications networks, and they developed a self-conscious middle-class identity that was remarkably uniform throughout the North.

A disproportionate number of them were New Englanders. New England was the first center of factory production, and southern New England farms were thoroughly commercialized by the 1830s. Yankee migrants dominated the commercial heartland of western New York and the northern regions of the Northwest. Even in the seaport cities (New York's Pearl Street wholesale houses are a prime example), businessmen from New England were often at the center of economic innovation. This Yankee middle class invented cultural forms that became the core of an emerging business civilization. Liberty for them meant self-ownership and the freedom of action and ambition. Equality meant equality of opportunity. They upheld the autonomous and morally accountable individual against the claims of traditional neighborhoods and traditional families. They devised an intensely private, mother-centered domestic life. Most of all, they adhered to a reformed Yankee Protestantism whose moral imperatives became the foundation of American middle-class culture.

The Evangelical Base

In November 1830, the evangelist Charles Grandison Finney preached in Rochester, New York. Most in his audience were transplanted New Englanders, the heirs of what was left of Yankee Calvinism. In their ministers' weekly sermons and in the set prayers their children memorized, they reaffirmed the old Puritan beliefs in providence and original sin. The earthly social order (the fixed relations of power and submission between men and women, rich and poor, children and parents, and so on) was necessary because humankind was innately sinful and prone to selfishness and disorder. Christians must obey the rules governing their station in life; attempts to rearrange the social order were both sinful and doomed to failure.

Yet while they reaffirmed those conservative Puritan beliefs in church, the men and women in Finney's audience routinely ignored them in their daily lives. Market expansion was clearly the result of human effort. Just as clearly, it added up to "improvement" and "progress." And as middle-class Christians built an improved material and social world, the doctrines of human inability and natural depravity, along with faith in divine providence, made less sense.

© Bettmann/CORBIS

Charles Finney   The evangelist, pictured here at the height of his preaching power in the 1830s, was remarkably successful at organizing the new middle-class culture into a millennial crusade.

To such an audience, Charles Finney preached the organizing principle of northern middle-class evangelicalism: "God," he insisted, "has made man a moral free agent." Neither the social order, the troubles of this world, nor the spiritual state of individuals were divinely ordained. People would make themselves and the world better by choosing right over wrong—though they would choose right only after submitting their rebellious wills to the will of God. It was a religion that valued individual holiness over a permanent and sacred social order. It made the spiritual nature of individuals a matter of prayer, submission, and choice. Thus it gave Christians the means—through the spread of revivals—to bring on the thousand-year reign of Christianity that they believed would precede the Second Coming of Christ. As Charles Finney told his Rochester audience,

"If [Christians] were united all over the world the Millennium might be brought about in three months."

Charles Finney's Rochester revival—a six-month marathon of preaching and praying—was no isolated event. Yankee evangelists had been moving toward Finney's formulation since the turn of the 19th century. Like Finney, they borrowed revival techniques from the Methodists (weeklong meetings, meetings in which women prayed in public, an **"anxious bench"** for the most likely converts), but toned them down for their own more "respectable" and affluent audience. At the same time, middle-class evangelicals retained the Puritans' Old Testament sense of cosmic history. They enlisted personal holiness and spiritual democracy in a fight to the finish between the forces of good and evil in this world. Building on these imperatives, the entrepreneurial families of the East and Northwest constructed an American middle-class culture after 1825. It was based, paradoxically, on an intensely private and emotionally loaded family life and an aggressively reformist stance toward the world at large.

Domesticity

The Yankee middle class made crucial distinctions between the home and the world—distinctions that grew from the disintegration of the old patriarchal household economy. Men in cities and towns now went off to work, leaving wives and children to spend the day at home. Even commercializing farmers made a clear distinction between (male) work that was oriented toward markets and (female) work that was tied to household maintenance (see chapter 8). The new middle-class evangelicalism encouraged this division of domestic labor. The public world of politics and economic exchange, said the preachers, was the proper sphere of men; women, on the other hand, were to exercise new kinds of moral influence within households. As one evangelical put it, "Each has a distinct sphere of duty—the husband to go out into the world—the wife to superintend the household. . . . Man profits from connection with the world, but women never; their constituents [sic] of mind are different. The one is raised and exalted by mingled association. The purity of the other is maintained in silence and seclusion."

The result was a feminization of domestic life. In the old yeoman-artisan republic, the fathers who owned property and headed households were God's delegated authorities on earth, assigned the task of governing women, children, and other underlings. Middle-class evangelicals raised new spiritual possibilities for women and children. Mothers replaced fathers as the principal child-rearers, and they enlisted the doctrines of free agency and individual moral responsibility in that task. Middle-class mothers raised their children with love and reason, not fear. They sought to develop the children's conscience and their capacity to love, to teach them to make good moral choices, and to prepare themselves for conversion and a lifetime of Christian service.

Middle-class mothers could take up these tasks because they could concentrate their efforts on household duties and because they had fewer children than their mothers or grandmothers had had. In Utica, New York, for example, women who entered their childbearing years in the 1830s averaged only 3.6 births apiece; those who had started families only 10 years earlier averaged 5.1 births. Housewives also spaced their pregnancies differently. Unlike their forebears, who gave birth to a child about once every two years throughout their childbearing years, Utica's middle-class housewives had their children at five-year intervals, which meant that they could give each child close attention. As a result, households were quieter and less crowded; children learned from their mothers how to govern themselves and seldom experienced the rigors of patriarchal family government. Thus mothers assumed responsibility for nurturing the children who would be carriers of the new middle-class culture, and fathers, ministers, and other authorities recognized the importance of that job. Edward Kirk, a minister in Albany, insisted that "the hopes of human society are to be found in the character, in the views, and in the conduct of mothers."

The new ethos of moral free agency was mirrored in the **Sunday schools.** When Sunday schools first appeared in the 1790s, their purpose was to teach working-class children to read and write by having them copy long passages from the Bible. Their most heavily publicized accomplishments were feats of memory. In 1823, Jane Wilson, a 13-year-old in Rochester, memorized 1,650 verses of scripture. Pawtucket, Rhode Island, claimed a mill girl who could recite the entire New Testament.

After the revivals of the 1820s and 1830s, the emphasis shifted from promoting feats of memory to preparing children's souls for conversion. Middle-class children were now included in the schools, corporal punishment was forbidden, and Sunday school teachers now tried to develop the moral sensibilities of their charges. They had the children read a few Bible verses each week and led them in a discussion of the moral lessons conveyed by the text. The proudest achievements of the new schools were children who made good moral choices. Thus Sunday schools became training grounds in free agency and moral accountability—a transformation that made sense only in a world where children could be trusted to make moral choices.

Sentimentality

Improvements in the printing, distribution, and marketing of books led to an outpouring of popular literature, much of it directed at the middle class. There were cookbooks, etiquette books, manuals on housekeeping, sermons, and sentimental novels, many of them written and most of them read by women. The works of popular religious writers such as Lydia Sigourney, Lydia Maria Child, and Timothy Shay Arthur found their way into thousands of middle-class homes. **Sarah Josepha Hale**, whose *Godey's Lady's Book* was the first mass-circulation magazine for women, acted as an arbiter of taste not only in furniture, clothing, and food but also in sentiments and ideas. Upon reviewing the sentimental literature read in middle-class homes, Nathaniel Hawthorne was not the only "serious" writer to deplore a literary marketplace dominated by "a damned mob of scribbling women."

Hawthorne certainly had economic reason for complaint. Sentimental novels written by women outsold by wide margins his *Scarlet Letter* and *House of Seven Gables*, Ralph

Waldo Emerson's essays, Henry David Thoreau's *Walden,* Herman Melville's *Moby Dick,* Walt Whitman's *Leaves of Grass,* and other works of the American Renaissance of the 1850s. Susan Warner's *The Wide, Wide World* broke all sales records when it appeared in 1850. Harriet Beecher Stowe's **Uncle Tom's Cabin** (1852) broke the records set by Warner. In 1854, Maria Cummin's *The Lamplighter* (the direct target of Hawthorne's lament about scribbling women) took its place as the third of the monster best sellers of the early 1850s.

These sentimental novels upheld the new middle-class domesticity. They sacralized the middle-class home and the trials and triumphs of Christian women. The action in each takes place indoors, usually in the kitchen or parlor, and the heroines are women (in Stowe's book, docile slave Christians are included) who live under worldly patriarchy but who triumph through submission to God. The stories embody spiritual struggle, the renunciation of greed and desire, and mother love. The home is a shrine that is juxtaposed to the marketplace and the world of competition and power. Unlike the female characters in British and European novels of the time, the women in these American novels are intelligent, generous persons who grow in strength and independence. (The French visitor Alexis de Tocqueville commented that European women "almost think it a privilege to appear futile, weak, and timid. The women of America never lay claim to rights of that sort.")

In sentimental **domestic fiction,** women assume the role of evangelical ministers, demonstrating Christian living by precept, example, and moral persuasion. Female moral influence, wielded by women who had given themselves to God, is at war with the male world of politics and the marketplace—areas of power, greed, and moral compromise. Although few sentimental writers shared the views of the feminist Margaret Fuller, they would have agreed with her on the place of religion in women's lives. "I wish women to live first for God's sake," she wrote. "Then she will not make an imperfect man her God, and thus sink to idolatry."

The most successful sentimental novel of the 1850s was Harriet Beecher Stowe's *Uncle Tom's Cabin.* Stowe's book was also the most powerful antislavery tract of these years, in part because it successfully dramatized the moral and political imperatives of the northern middle class. At its core, *Uncle Tom's Cabin* indicts slavery as a system of absolute power at odds with domesticity and Christian love. The novel reverses the power relations of this world: In it, the home, and particularly the kitchen, is the ultimate locus of good, whereas law, politics, and the marketplace—the whole realm of men—are moved to the periphery and defined as unfeeling destroyers. Based solidly in revival Christianity, the novel lambastes the rational calculation, greed, and power-hunger of the "real world" that was made and governed by white men and upholds domestic space filled with women, slaves, and children who gain spiritual power through submission to Christ. The two most telling scenes—the deaths of the Christian slave Uncle Tom and the perfect child Eva St. Claire—reenact the crucifixion of Jesus. Uncle Tom prays for his tormentors as he is beaten to death, and little Eva extracts promises of Christian behavior from her deathbed. Both are powerless, submissive characters who die in order to redeem a fallen humankind. Their deaths are thus Christian triumphs that convert the powerful and hasten the millennial day when the world will be governed by a feminized Christian love and not by male power.

Uncle Tom's Cabin and other popular sentimental novels were not, as Hawthorne and his friends believed, frivolous fairytales into which housewives retreated from the real world. They were subversive depictions of a higher spiritual reality that would move the feminine ethos of the Christian home to the center of civilization. That vision drove an organized public assault on irreligion, drunkenness, prostitution, slavery, and other practices and institutions that substituted passion and force for Christian love (see chapter 12), an assault that tried to "domesticate" the world and shape it in the image of the middle-class evangelical home.

The Plain People of the North

Focus Question
Within the North, what were the alternatives to middle-class culture?

From the 1830s onward, northern middle-class evangelicals proposed their religious and domestic values as a national culture for the United States. But even in their own region they were outnumbered by Americans who rejected their cultural leadership. The plain people of the North were a varied lot: settlers in the lower Northwest who remained culturally southern; hill-country northerners who had experienced little of what their middle-class cousins called "progress"; refugees from the countryside who had taken up urban wage labor; and increasing thousands of Irish and German immigrants. They did share a cultural conservatism—often grounded in the traditional, father-centered family—that rejected sentimentalism and reformist religion out of hand. As often as not, that conservatism was grounded in religious revivals (very different from those of the new middle class) that showered on the northern plain folk in the early 19th century.

The Decline of the Established Churches

The Founding Fathers had been largely indifferent to organized religion. A few were pious men, and some, like George Washington, attended church out of a sense of obligation. Many of the better educated, including Thomas Jefferson, subscribed to **deism**, the belief that God had created the universe but did not intervene in its affairs. Many simply did not bother themselves with thoughts about religion. When asked why the Constitution mentioned neither God nor religion, Alexander Hamilton is reported to have smiled and answered, "We forgot."

In state after state, post-revolutionary constitutions withdrew government support from religion, and the First Amendment to the U.S. Constitution clearly prescribed the separation of church and the national state. Reduced to their own sources of support, the established churches—Congregationalism in New England, the Church of England (renamed Episcopalians) in the South and much of the mid-Atlantic) went into decline. The Connecticut Congregationalist Ezra Stiles reported in 1780 that 60 parishes in Vermont and an equal number in New Hampshire were without a minister. In Massachusetts, according to Stiles's reports, 80 parishes lacked a minister. In all, about one-third of New England's Congregational pulpits were vacant in 1780, and the situation was worse to the north and west. In Vermont between 1763 and 1820, the founding of churches followed the incorporation of towns by an average of 15 years, indicating that settlement in that state proceeded almost entirely without the benefit of organized religion. In 1780, nearly all of the 750 Congregational churches in the United States were in New England. In the next 40 years, although the nation's population rose from 4 to 10 million, the number of Congregational churches rose only to 1100. Ordinary women and men were leaving the churches that had dominated the religious life of colonial America, sometimes ridiculing the learned clergy as they departed. To Ezra Stiles and other conservatives, it seemed that the republic was plunging into atheism.

The Rise of the Democratic Sects

They were wrong. The collapse of the established churches, the social dislocations of the post-revolutionary years, and the increasingly antiauthoritarian, democratic sensibilities of ordinary northerners provided fertile ground for the growth of new democratic sects. These were the years of **camp-meeting** revivalism, years in which Methodists and Baptists grew from small, half-organized sects into the great popular denominations they have been ever since. They were also years in which fiercely independent dropouts from older churches were putting together a loosely organized movement that would become the Disciples of Christ. At the same time, ragged, half-educated preachers were spreading the Universalist and Freewill Baptist messages in upcountry New England, while in western New York young **Joseph Smith** was receiving the visions that would lead to Mormonism.

The result was, first of all, a vast increase in the variety of choices on the Northern religious landscape, but within that welter of new churches there was a roughly uniform democratic style shared by the fastest-growing sects. First, they renounced the need for an educated, formally authorized clergy. Religion was now a matter of the heart and not the head. **Crisis conversion** (understood in most churches as personal transformation that resulted from direct experience of the Holy Spirit) was a necessary credential for preachers; a college degree was not. The new preachers substituted emotionalism and storytelling for Episcopal ritual and Congregational theological lectures. Stories attracted listeners, and they were harder for the learned clergy to refute. The new churches also held up the Bible as the one source of religious knowledge, thus undercutting all theological knowledge and

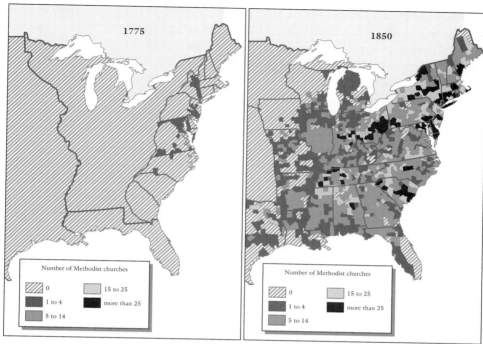

Map 10.1 **Growth of American Methodism, 1775–1850** This is a county-by-county map of the rise of American Methodism from the Revolution through the eve of the Civil War. In 1775, Methodism was almost nonexistent in British North America. By 1850, the Methodists were the largest Protestant denomination in the United States, and they were truly a national faith: There were Methodist churches in almost every county in the country.

placing every literate Christian on a level with the best-educated minister. These tendencies often ended in **Restorationism**—the belief that all theological and institutional changes since the end of biblical times were man-made mistakes, and that religious organizations must restore themselves to the purity and simplicity of the church of the Apostles. In sum, this loose democratic creed rejected learning and tradition and raised up the priesthood of all believers.

Baptists and Methodists were by far the most successful at preaching to the new democratic audience. The United States had only 50 Methodist churches in 1783; by 1820 it had 2,700. Over those same years, the number of Baptist churches rose from 400 to 2,700. Together, in 1820, these two denominations outnumbered Episcopalians and Congregationalists by 3 to 1, almost a reversal of their relative standings 40 years earlier. Baptists based much of their appeal in localism and congregational democracy. Methodist success, on the other hand, entailed skillful national organization. Bishop Francis Asbury, the head of the church in its fastest-growing years, built an episcopal bureaucracy that seeded churches throughout the republic and sent **circuit-riding preachers** to places that had none. These early Methodist missions were grounded in self-sacrifice to the point of martyrdom. Asbury demanded much of his **itinerant preachers,** and until 1810, he strongly suggested that they remain celibate. "To marry," he said, "is to locate." Asbury also knew that married circuit riders would leave many widows and orphans behind, for hundreds of them worked themselves to death. Of the men who served as Methodist itinerants before 1819, at least 60 percent died before the age of 40.

From seaport cities to frontier settlements, few Americans escaped the sound of Methodist preaching in the early 19th century. The Methodist preachers were common men who spoke plainly, listened carefully to others, and carried hymnbooks with simple tunes that anyone could sing. They also, particularly in the early years, shared traditional folk beliefs with their humble flocks. Some of the early circuit riders relied heavily on dreams; some could predict the future; many visited heaven and hell and returned with full descriptions. In the end, however, it was the hopefulness and simplicity of the Methodist message that attracted ordinary Americans. The Methodists rejected the old terrors of Calvinist determinism and taught that although salvation comes only through God, men and women can decide to open themselves to divine grace and thus play a decisive role in their own salvation. They also taught that a godly life is a gradual, lifetime growth in grace, thus allowing for repentance for minor, and sometimes even major, lapses of faith and behavior. By granting responsibility (one might say sovereignty) to the individual believer, the Methodists established their democratic credentials and drew hundreds of thousands of Americans into their fold.

The Providential Worldview

Northern plain folk favored churches as doctrinally varied as the people themselves. These ranged from the voluntaristic "free grace" doctrines of the Methodists to the iron-bound Calvinism of most Baptists, from the fine-tuned hierarchy of the Mormons to the near-anarchy of the Disciples of Christ. They included the most popular faiths (Baptists and Methodists came to contain two-thirds of America's professing Protestants) as well as such smaller sects as Hicksite Quakers, Universalists, Adventists, Moravians, and Freewill Baptists. Yet for all their diversity, these churches had important points in common. Most shared an evangelical emphasis on individual experience over churchly authority. Most favored democratic, local control of religious life and distrusted outside organization and religious professionalism—not only the declining colonial establishments but also the emerging missionary network created by middle-class evangelicals. They also rejected middle-class optimism and reformism, reaffirming God's providence and humankind's duty to accept an imperfect world even while waging war against it.

The most pervasive strain was a belief in providence—the conviction that human history is part of God's vast and unknowable plan, and that all events are willed or allowed by God. Middle-class evangelicals spoke of providence, too, but they seemed to assume that God's plan was manifest in the progress of market society and middle-class religion.

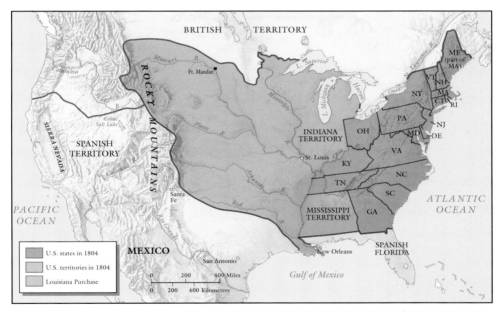

Map 7.3 **Louisiana Purchase** Jefferson's Louisiana Purchase nearly doubled the geographic size of the United States. It ended European competition for control of the North American interior and granted the United States the mouth of the Mississippi River, thus strengthening white settlements between the Appalachians and the Mississippi and increasing American control over those settlements.

Map 7.4 Native America, 1783–1812   Native Americans had lost a lot before the American Revolution, but the losses grew worse as British, French, and Spanish traders, missionaries, and soldiers were replaced by a democratic republic of farmers who wanted Indian land. By 1812, Indian peoples in the Northwest were battered and increasingly threatened by settlement; Indians of the Southwest continued to occupy most of their old lands, but they would lose everything within the next generation.

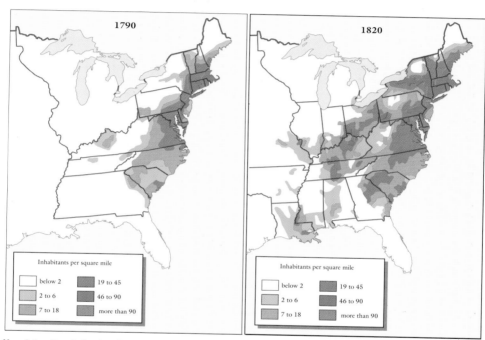

Map 8.1   Population Density, 1790–1820   The population of the United States nearly doubled between 1790 and 1820, growing from 5.2 million to 9.6 million persons. In the South, an overwhelmingly rural population spread rapidly across space. The population of the Northeast and mid-Atlantic also occupied new territory over these years, but the rise of seaport towns and intensely commercialized (and often overcrowded) farming areas were turning the North into a much more densely settled region.

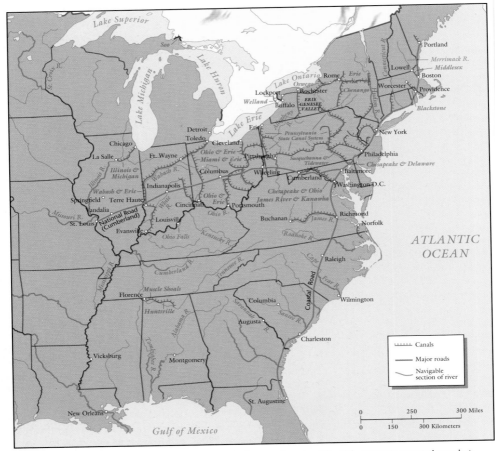

Map 8.2   Rivers, Roads, and Canals, 1825–1860   In the second quarter of the 19th century, transportation projects linked the North and Northwest into an integrated economic and social system. There were fewer improvements in the South: farm produce traveled down navigable rivers from bottomland plantations to river and seaport towns, thence to New York for shipment overseas; southern legislatures and entrepreneurs saw little use for further improvements.

Humbler evangelicals held to the older notion that providence is immediate, mysterious, and unknowable. They believed that the events of everyday life are parts of a vast blueprint that exists only in the mind of God—and not in the vain aspirations of women and men. When making plans, they added the caveat "the Lord willing," and they learned to accept misfortune with fortitude. They responded to epidemics, bad crop years, aches and pains, illness, and early death by praying for the strength to endure. As a minister told the Scots Covenanters of Cambridge, New York, "It is through tribulation that all the saints enter into the kingdom of God. . . . The tempest sometimes ceases, the sky is clear, and the prospect is desirable, but by the by the gathering clouds threaten a new storm; here we must watch, and labor, and fight, expecting rest with Christ in glory, not on the way to it."

The providential worldview and the notion that God granted spiritual progress only through affliction came directly into play when a member of a poor Protestant family died. Country Baptists and working-class Methodists mourned their dead but took care not to "murmur" against God. In a world governed by providence, the death of a loved one was a test of faith. The death of children in particular called for heroic acts of submission to God's will. Parents mourned the loss but stopped short of displaying grief that would suggest selfishness and lack of faith. Poor families washed and dressed the dead body themselves and buried it in a churchyard or on a hilltop plot on the family farm. Whereas the urban middle class preferred formal funerals and carefully tended cemeteries, humbler people regarded death as a lesson in the futility of pursuing worldly goals and in the need to submit to God's will.

Popular Millennialism

Middle-class evangelicals were **postmillennialists.** They believed that Christ's Second Coming would occur at the end of 1,000 years of social perfection brought about by the missionary conversion of the world. Ordinary Baptists, Methodists, and Disciples of Christ, however, assumed that the millennium would arrive with world-destroying violence, followed by 1,000 years of Christ's rule on earth. Few, however, dwelled on this terrifying *premillennialism,* assuming that God would end the world in his own time. Now and then, however, the ordinary evangelicals of the North predicted the fiery end of the world. Prophets rose and fell, and thousands of people looked for signs of the approaching millennium in thunderstorms, shooting stars, eclipses, economic panics and depressions, and—especially—in hints that God had placed in the Bible.

One avid student of those hints was William Miller, a Vermont Baptist who, after years of systematic study, concluded that God would destroy the world during the year following March 1843. Miller publicized his predictions throughout the 1830s, and near the end of the decade the Millerites (as his followers were called) accumulated thousands of believers—most of them conservative Baptists, Methodists, and Disciples in hill-country New England and in poor neighborhoods in New York, Ohio, and Michigan. As the end approached, the believers read the Bible, prayed, and attended meeting after meeting. A publicist

Courtesy, American Antiquarian Society

Prophetic Chart A fixture at Millerite Adventist meetings, prophetic charts such as the one shown here displayed the succession of Biblical kingdoms and the prophecies of Daniel and John. Millerites revised their charts when the world failed to end in 1843.

named Henry Jones reported that a shower of meat and blood had fallen on Jersey City, and newspapers published stories alleging that the Millerites were insane and sexually licentious. Some, the press reported, were sewing "ascension robes" in which they would rise straight to heaven without passing through death.

When the end of the year—March 23, 1844—came and went, most of the believers quietly returned to their churches. A committed remnant, however, kept the faith, and by the 1860s founded the Seventh-Day Adventist Church. The Millerite movement was a reminder that hundreds of thousands of northern Protestants continued to believe that the God of the Old Testament governed everything from bee stings to the course of human history, and that one day he would destroy the world in fire and blood.

Family and Society

Baptists, Methodists, Disciples of Christ, and the smaller popular sects evangelized primarily among persons who had been bypassed or hurt by the Market Revolution. Many had been reduced to dependent, wage-earning status. Others had become market farmers or urban storekeepers or master workmen; few had become rich. Their churches taught them that the attractions and temptations of market society were at the center of the world they must reject.

Often their rhetoric turned to criticism of market society, its institutions, and its centers of power. The Quaker schismatic Elias Hicks, a Long Island farmer who fought the worldliness and pride of wealthy urban Quakers, listed the following among the mistakes of the early 19th century: railroads, the Erie Canal, fancy food and other luxuries, banks and the credit system, the city of Philadelphia, and the study of chemistry. The Baptist millenarian William Miller expressed his hatred of banks, insurance companies, stock-jobbing, chartered monopolies, personal greed, and the city of New York. In short, what the evangelical middle class identified as the march of progress, poorer and more conservative evangelicals often condemned as a descent into worldliness that would almost certainly provoke God's wrath.

Along with doubts about economic change and the middle-class churches that embraced it, members of the popular sects often held to the patriarchal family form in which they had been raised, and with which both the Market Revolution and middle-class domesticity seemed at war. Hundreds of thousands of northern Protestants considered the erosion of domestic patriarchy a profound cultural loss and not, as it seemed to the middle class, an avenue to personal liberation. Their cultural conservatism was apparent in their efforts to sustain the father-centered family of the old rural North or to revive it in new forms.

For some, religious conversion came at a point of crisis in the traditional family. William Miller, for example, had a strict Calvinist upbringing in a family in which his father, an uncle, and his grandfather were all Baptist ministers. As a young man he rejected his family, set about making money, and became a deist—actions that deeply wounded his parents. When his father died, Miller was stricken with guilt. He moved back to his hometown, took up his family duties, became a leader of the Baptist church, and (after reading a sermon entitled "Parental Duties") began the years of Bible study that resulted in his world-ending prophecies. Alexander Campbell, one of the founders of the Disciples of Christ, dramatized his filial piety when he debated the free-thinking socialist Robert Owen before a large audience in the Methodist meetinghouse in Cincinnati in 1828. He insisted that his white-haired father (a Scots Presbyterian minister) stand in the pulpit above the debaters.

The Prophet Joseph Smith

The weakening of patriarchal authority and attempts to shore it up were central to the life and work of one of the most unique and successful religious leaders of the period: the Mormon prophet Joseph Smith (see also chapter 13). Smith's father was a landless Vermont Baptist who moved his wife and nine children to seven rented farms within 20 years. Around 1820, when young Joseph was approaching manhood, the family was struggling to make mortgage payments on a small farm outside Palmyra, New York. That farm—Joseph referred to it as "my father's house"—was a desperate token of the Smith family's commitment to yeoman independence and an endangered rural patriarchy. Despite the efforts of Joseph and his brothers, a merchant cheated the Smith family out of the farm. With that, both generations of the Smiths faced lifetimes as propertyless workers. To make matters worse, Joseph's mother and some of his siblings began to attend an evangelical Presbyterian church in Palmyra, apparently against the father's wishes.

Before the loss of the farm, Joseph had received two visions warning him away from existing churches and telling him to await further instructions. In 1827, the Angel Moroni appeared to him and led him to golden plates that translated into *The Book of Mormon*. It told of a light-skinned people, descendants of the Hebrews, who had sailed to North America long before Columbus. They had had an epic, violent history, a covenanted relationship with God, and had been visited by Jesus following his crucifixion and resurrection.

Joseph Smith later declared that his discovery of *The Book of Mormon* had "brought salvation to my father's house" by unifying the family. It eventually unified thousands of others under a patriarchal faith based on restored theocratic government, male dominance, and a democracy among fathers. The good priests and secular leaders of *The Book of Mormon* are farmers who labor alongside their neighbors; the villains are self-seeking merchants, lawyers, and bad priests. The account alternates between periods when the people obey God's laws and periods when they do not, each period accompanied by the blessings or punishments of a wrathful God. Smith carried that model of brotherly cooperation and patriarchal authority into the Church of Jesus Christ of Latter-Day Saints, which he founded in 1830.

The new church was ruled, not by professional clergy, but by an elaborate lay hierarchy of adult males. On top sat the father of Joseph Smith, rescued from destitution and shame, who was appointed Patriarch of the Church. Below him were Joseph Smith and his brother Hyrum, who were called First and Second Elders. The hierarchy descended through a succession of male authorities that finally reached the fathers of households. Smith claimed that this hierarchy restored the ancient priesthood that had disappeared over the 18 centuries of greed and error that he labeled the Great Apostasy of the Christian churches. Americans who knew the history of the Market Revolution and the Smith family's travails within it, however, might have noted similarities between the restored ancient order and a poor man's visionary retrieval of the social order of the 18th-century North.

A New Popular Culture

Not all of the northern plain folk spent their time in church. Particularly in cities and towns, they became both producers and consumers of a nonreligious (sometimes irreligious) commercial popular culture. The sports and shows attended by northern plain folk, like the churches they attended, were often grounded in an antisentimental view of the world and in traditional forms of patriarchy and masculinity.

P. T. Barnum and Tom Thumb   Here is Phineas Taylor Barnum, America's greatest showman, together with the sprightly midget Tom Thumb, his first hugely successful attraction. The photograph conveys the combination of chicanery, farce, strangeness, and straight-faced respectability that made Barnum (but not Tom Thumb) a rich man.

Blood Sports

Urban working-class neighborhoods were particularly fertile ground for popular amusements. Young working men formed a bachelor subculture that contrasted with the piety and self-restraint of the middle class. They organized volunteer fire companies and militia

Prizefighter The Irishman James "Yankee" Sullivan (shown above) was an immensely popular hero of native and Irish workingmen, as well as of the street gangs and political factions of Irish descent.

units that spent more time drinking and fighting rival groups than drilling or putting out fires. Gathering at firehouses, saloons, and street corners, they drank, joked, boasted, and nurtured notions of manliness based on physical prowess and coolness under pressure.

They also engaged in such **"blood sports"** as cock fighting, ratting, and dog fighting, even though many states had laws forbidding such activities. In 1823, an English tourist in New York City noted that "it is perfectly common for two or three cockfights to regularly take place every week." Such contests grew increasingly popular during the 1850s and often were staged by saloonkeepers doubling as sports impresarios. One of the best known was Kit Burns of New York City, who ran Sportsman Hall, a saloon frequented by prizefighters, criminals, and their hangers-on. Behind the saloon was a space—reached through a narrow doorway that could be defended against the police—with animal pits and a small amphitheater that seated 250 but that regularly held 400 yelling spectators.

Although most of the spectators were working men, a few members of the old aristocracy who rejected middle-class ways also attended these events. In 1861, for instance, 250 spectators paid as much as $3 each to witness a fight between roosters belonging to the prizefighter John Morrissey and Mr. Genet, president of the New York City board of aldermen. A newspaper estimated bets on the event at $50,000. Frederick Van Wyck, scion of a wealthy old New York family, remembered an evening spent at Tommy Norris's livery stable, where he witnessed a fight between billy goats, a rat baiting, a cockfight, and a boxing match between bare-breasted women. "Certainly for a lad of 17, such as I," he recalled, "a night with Tommy Norris and his attraction was quite a night."

Boxing

Prizefighting emerged from the same subterranean culture that sustained cockfights and other blood sports. This sport, imported from Britain, called for an enclosed ring, clear rules, cornermen, a referee, and a paying audience. Boxing's popularity rose during the 1840s and 1850s, a time of increasing immigration and violence in poor city neighborhoods. Many of the fighters had close ties with ethnic-based saloons, militia units, fire companies, and street gangs such as New York's (Irish) Dead Rabbits and (native) Bowery B'hoys, and many labored at occupations with a peculiarly ethnic base. Some of the best American-born fighters were New York City butchers—a licensed, privileged trade from which cheap immigrant labor was systematically excluded. Butchers usually finished work by 10 A.M. They could then spend the rest of the day idling at a firehouse or a bar and often were prominent figures in neighborhood gangs. A prizefight between an American-born butcher and an Irish day laborer would attract a spirited audience that understood its class and ethnic meaning.

Prizefighting was a way of rewarding courage and skill and, sometimes, of settling scores through fair contests limited to two combatants. Nonetheless, the fights were brutal. Boxers fought with bare knuckles, and a bout ended only when one of the fighters was unable to continue. In an infamous match in 1842, for instance, the Englishman Christopher Lilly knocked down his Irish opponent Thomas McCoy 80 times; the fight ended with round 119, when McCoy died in his corner.

Although boxing had close ties to ethnic rivalries, the contestants often exhibited a respect for one another that crossed ethnic lines. For example, native-born Tom Hyer, who had defeated Irishman James "Yankee" Sullivan in one of the great early fights, later bailed Sullivan out of jail. In 1859, when Bill Harrington, a retired native-born boxer, disappeared and left a wife and children, his former Irish-born opponent, John Morrissey, arranged a sparring match and sent the proceeds to Mrs. Harrington.

An American Theater

In the 18th and early 19th centuries, all American theaters were in the large seaport cities. Those who attended were members of the urban elite, and nearly all of the plays, managers, and actors were English. After 1815, however, improvements in transportation and communication, along with the rapid growth of cities, created a much broader audience. Theaters and theater companies sprang up not only in New York and Philadelphia but also in Cincinnati, St. Louis, San Francisco, Rochester, and dozens of other new towns west of the Appalachians, and traveling troupes carried theatrical performances to the smallest hamlets. Most of them catered to male, largely plebeian audiences. Before 1830, the poorer theatergoers—nearly all of them men—occupied the cheap balcony seats (with the exception of the second balcony, which was reserved for prostitutes); artisans and other workingmen filled benches in the ground-floor area known as "the pit"; wealthier and more genteel patrons sat in the boxes. Those sitting in the pit and balcony joined in the performance: They ate and drank, talked, and shouted encouragement and threats to the actors. The genteel New Yorker Washington Irving lamented the "discharge of apples, nuts, and gingerbread" flying out of the balconies "on the heads of honest folks" in the pit.

As time passed, however, rowdyism turned into violence. The less genteel members of theater audiences protested the elegant speech, gentlemanly bearing, and understated performances of the English actors, which happened to match the speech, manners, and bearing of the American urban elite. Thus the protests were directed not only at the English actors but also at the ladies and gentlemen in the orchestra who were seen as adherents of an aristocratic English culture unsuitable in a democratic republic.

The first theater riot occurred in 1817, when the English actor Charles Incledon refused a New York audience's demand that he stop what he was doing and sing "Black-Eyed Susan." Such assaults grew more common during the 1820s. By the 1830s, separate theaters offered separate kinds of performances for rich and poor, but violence continued. It culminated in the rivalry between the American actor Edwin Forrest and the English actor William Charles Macready. Macready was a trained Shakespearean actor, and his restrained style and attention to the subtleties of the text had won him acclaim both in Britain and in the United States. Forrest, on the other hand, played to the cheap seats. With his bombast and histrionics, he transformed Shakespeare's tragedies into melodramas. Forrest and Macready carried out a well-publicized feud that led to a mob attack on Macready in 1849. Led by E. Z. C. Judson (who, under the pen name Ned Buntline, wrote scores of dime novels), the mob descended on Macready's performance at the exclusive Astor Place Opera House. The militia was waiting for them, and 20 people died in the ensuing riot and gunfight.

Playhouses that catered to working-class audiences continued to feature Shakespearean tragedies (*Richard III,* played broadly and with a lot of swordplay, was the favorite), but they now shared the stage with works written in the American vernacular. The stage "Yankee," rustic but shrewd, appeared at this time, and so did Mose the Bowery B'hoy, a New York volunteer fireman who performed feats of derring-do. Both frequently appeared in opposition to well-dressed characters with English accents. The Yankee outsmarted them; Mose beat them up.

Minstrelsy

The most popular form of theater was the blackface **minstrel show.** These shows were blatantly racist, and they were the preferred entertainment of working men (again, the audience was overwhelmingly working class and male) in northern cities from 1840 to 1880. The first minstrel show was presented in 1831 when a white showman named Thomas Rice blacked his face and "jumped Jim Crow," imitating a shuffle-dance he had seen on the Cincinnati docks. Within a few years, a formula for these shows had emerged that every theatergoer knew by heart.

The minstrel shows lasted an hour and a half and were presented in three sections. The first consisted of songs and dances performed in a walkaround, in which the audience was encouraged to clap and sing along. This was followed by a longer middle section in which the company sat in a row with a character named Tambo at one end and a character named Bones at the other (named for the tambourine and bones, the instruments they played), with an interlocutor in the middle. The Tambo character, often called Uncle Ned, was a simple-minded plantation slave dressed in plain clothing. The Bones character, usually called Zip Coon, was a dandified, oversexed free black dressed in top hat and tails. The interlocutor was the straight man—fashionably dressed, slightly pretentious, with an English accent. This middle portion of the show consisted of a conversation among the three, which included pointed political satire, skits ridiculing the wealthy and the educated, and sexual jokes that bordered on obscenity. The third section featured songs, dances, and jokes, most of them familiar enough so that the audience could sing along and laugh at the right places.

The minstrel shows introduced African American song and dance—in toned-down, Europeanized form—to audiences who would not have permitted black performers on the stage. They also reinforced racial stereotypes that were near the center of American popular culture. Finally, hiding behind black masks, minstrel performers dealt broadly with aspects of social and political life that other performers avoided.

Minstrel shows and other theatrical entertainments traveled the new transportation network to rural America. The Grecian Dog Apollo, for example, arrived in New York from London in 1827. Appearing at theaters and lecture halls, he played cards, solved problems in arithmetic, and answered questions on astronomy and geography. Apollo traveled the Erie Canal circuit, playing at Albany, Saratoga Springs, Utica, Rochester, Buffalo, and Niagara Falls before returning to Peale's Museum in New York for the 1828 season. Many actors traveled well-established circuits, calling on local amateurs for their supporting casts. Minstrel companies traveled the river system of the interior and played to enthusiastic audiences wherever the riverboats docked. Mark Twain recalled them fondly: "I remember the first Negro musical show I ever saw. It must have been in the early forties. It was a new institution. In our village of Hannibal [Missouri] . . . it burst upon us as a glad and stunning surprise." Among Americans who had been taught to distrust cities by cultural leaders ranging from Thomas Jefferson to Emerson and Thoreau to the evangelical preachers in their own neighborhoods, minstrel shows and other urban entertainments gave rural folk a sense of the variety and excitement of city life.

Novels and the Penny Press

Few of the commodities made widely available by the market revolution were more ubiquitous than newspapers and inexpensive books. Improvements in printing and papermaking enabled entrepreneurs to sell daily newspapers for a penny. Cheap "story papers" became available in the 1830s, "yellow-back" fiction in the 1840s, and dime novels from the 1850s onward. Although these offerings were distributed throughout the North and the West, they found their first and largest audience among city workers.

Mass-audience newspapers carried political news and local advertisements, but they were heavily spiced with sensationalism. The *Philadelphia Gazette* in late summer 1829, for instance, treated its eager readers to the following: "Female Child with Two Heads," "Bats," "Another Shark," "More Stabbing," "Fishes Travelling on Land," "Dreadful Steam Boat Disaster," "Raffling for Babies," "Combat with a Bear," "Lake Serpent," "Atrocious Murder," and much more. Henry David Thoreau commented on the "startling and monstrous events as fill the family papers," while his friend Ralph Waldo Emerson reported that Americans were "reading all day murders & railroad accidents." Even though such sensational stories are most remarkable for their variety, they all portrayed a haunted, often

THE

FEMALE LAND PIRATE:

OR

AWFUL, MYSTERIOUS, AND HORRIBLE DISCLOSURES

OF

AMANDA BANNORRIS,

WIFE AND ACCOMPLICE OF RICHARD BANNORRIS, A LEADER IN THAT TERRIBLE BAND OF ROBBERS AND MUR-DERERS, KNOWN FAR AND WIDE AS THE

MURRELL MEN.

At length the door opened, and two large fellows, with masks on their faces, carrying a dark lantern, entered, and in a gruff voice said I must go with them. Their first operation was to blindfold me—which done, one of them seized me in his brawny arms, bore me out, mounted me on a horse, and rode swiftly away—the other following. *(See page 17.)*

CINCINNATI.

PRINTED FOR, AND PUBLISHED BY E. E. BARCLAY.

1847.

Yellow-Back Novels A pulp fiction hit of the 1840s: a crime story about robberies and murders committed by the "Female Land Pirate"—not the kind of woman encountered in middle-class sentimental fiction.

Courtesy, American Antiquarian Society

demonic nature that regularly produced monstrosities and ruined the works of humankind, as well as a human nature that, despite appearances, was often deceptive and depraved.

Working-class readers discovered a similarly untrustworthy world in cheap fiction. George Lippard's *Quaker City* (1845) sold 60,000 copies in its first year and 30,000 in each of the next five years, making it the best-selling American book before the sentimental blockbusters of the 1850s. Lippard's book was a fictional exposé of the hypocrisy, lust, and cruelty of Philadelphia's outwardly genteel and Christian elite. Lippard and other adventure writers (whose works accounted for 60 percent of all American fiction titles published between 1831 and 1860) indulged in a pornography of violence that included cannibalism, blood drinking, and murder by every imaginable means. They also dealt with sex in unprecedentedly explicit ways. The yellow-back novels of the 1840s introduced readers not only to seduction and rape but also to transvestitism, child pornography, necrophilia, miscegenation, group sex, homosexuality, and—perhaps most shocking of all—women with criminal minds and insatiable sexual appetites. The scenes of gore and sexual depravity were presented voyeuristically—as self-righteous exposés of the perversions of the rich and powerful and stories of the Founders' Republic trampled upon by a vicious elite that pretended virtue but lived only for its appetites.

Popular fictions—like most popular plays, Edwin Forrest's Shakespeare, and much of what went on in blood sports, the prize ring, and the penny press—were melodramatic contests between good and evil. Evil was described in terms reminiscent of original sin: It provided the background of all human action, and heroes met a demonic world with courage and guile without hoping to change it. Melodramatic heroes frequently acknowledged evil in themselves while claiming moral superiority over the hypocrites and frauds who governed the world. A murderer in Ned Buntline's *G'hals of New York* (1850) remarks, "There isn't no *real* witue [virtue] and honesty nowhere, 'cept among the perfessional *dis*-honest." By contrast, in middle-class sentimental novels, the universe was benign; good could be nurtured, and evil could be defeated and transformed. Harriet Beecher Stowe's slave driver Simon Legree—the best-known villain in American literature—is evil not because of a natural disposition toward evil, but because he had been deprived of a mother's love during childhood. The world, in Stowe's view, could be nurtured into being good. Most northern plain folk (whether they favored church or popular entertainments) did not want to fix an imperfect and often chaotic world. They wanted only to live decently and bravely within it.

Family, Church, and Neighborhood: The White South

Focus Question

In what specific ways did evangelical Protestantism act as a conservative force within southern culture?

The Beginnings of the Bible Belt

In the first third of the 19th century, evangelical Protestantism transformed the South into what it has been ever since: the Bible Belt. That transformation began when poor and middling whites found spiritual alternatives to the culture of the gentry—to their formalistic Episcopalianism, their love of luxury and display, and their enjoyment of money and power. Early southern Baptists and Methodists demanded a crisis conversion followed by a life of piety and a rejection of what they called "the world." To no small degree, the world was the economic, cultural, and political world controlled by the planters. James McGready, who preached in rural North Carolina in the 1790s, openly condemned the gentry: "The world is in all their thoughts day and night. All their talk is of corn and tobacco, of land and stock. The price of merchandise and negroes are inexhaustible themes of conversation. But for them, the name of Jesus has no charms; it is rarely mentioned unless to be profaned." This was dangerous talk, as McGready learned when young rakes rode their horses through one of his outdoor meetings, tipped over the benches, set the altar on fire, and threatened to kill McGready.

Southern Baptists, Methodists, and Presbyterians spread their message in the early 19th century through the camp meeting, and this too was subversive of southern social distinctions. Though its origins stretched back into the 18th century, the first full-blown camp meeting took place at Cane Ridge, Kentucky, in 1801. Here the annual "Holy Feast," a three-day communion service of Scotch-Irish Presbyterians, was transformed into an outdoor, interdenominational revival at which hundreds experienced conversion under Presbyterian, Methodist, and Baptist preaching. Estimates of the crowd at Cane Ridge ranged from 10,000 to 20,000 persons, and by all accounts the enthusiasm was unprecedented. Some converts fainted, others jerked uncontrollably, and a few barked like dogs, all of them visibly taken by the Holy Spirit. These exercises fell upon women and men, whites and blacks, rich and poor, momentarily blurring social hierarchy in moments of profound and very public religious ecstasy. A witness to a later camp meeting recounted that "to see a bold and courageous Kentuckian (undaunted by the horrors of war) turn pale and tremble at the reproof of a weak woman, a little boy, or a poor African; to see him sink down in deep remorse, roll and toss, and gnash his teeth, till black in the face, entreat the prayers of those he came to devour . . . who can say the change was not supernatural?" (Southern white men, even when under religious conviction, sometimes resisted this loss of mastery and self-control. One preacher remembered a "fine, strong, good-looking young man" who felt himself giving in to camp-meeting preaching. He "found no relief until he drew a large pistole out of his pocket, with which he intended to defend himself if any one should offer to speak to him on the subject of religion.")

The early southern evangelicals irritated and angered the elite and white men generally, for they seemed to question not only worldliness but the white male dominance that held the southern world together. The conversion of wives and children (not to mention slaves) could trouble southern families; the conversion of white men could "unman" them and render them "womanish. But the governors of southern farms and southern families found that they had little to worry about. The Baptists, Methodists, and Presbyterians of the South, though they never stopped railing against greed and pride, found that they could conquer the South and live comfortably with a system of fixed hierarchy and God-given social roles—with slavery and father-dominated families in particular.

Slavery and Southern Evangelicals

Slavery became a major case in point. For a brief period after the Revolution, evangelicals joined with an elite minority of slaveholders (see chapter 9) to oppose slavery. Methodists and Baptists preached to slaves as well as to whites, and Bishop Francis Asbury, the principal architect of American Methodism, admired John Wesley's statement that slavery was against "all the laws of Justice, Mercy, and Truth." In 1780, a conference of Methodist preachers ordered circuit riders to free their slaves and advised all Methodists to do the same. In 1784, the Methodists declared that they would excommunicate members who failed to free their slaves within two years. Many lay Methodists took the order seriously. On the Delmarva Peninsula (Delaware and the Eastern Shore of Maryland and Virginia), for instance, Methodist converts freed thousands of slaves in the late 18th century. Other evangelicals shared their views. As early as 1787, southern Presbyterians prayed for "final abolition," and two years later, Baptists condemned slavery as "a violent deprivation of the rights of nature and inconsistent with a republican government."

The period of greatest evangelical growth, however, came during the years in which the South committed irrevocably to plantation slavery. As increasing numbers of both slaves and slave owners came within the evangelical fold, the southern churches had to rethink their position on human bondage. The Methodists never carried out their threat to excommunicate slaveholders, confessing in 1816 that southerners were so committed to slavery that "little can be done to abolish the practice so contrary to moral justice." Similarly, the Baptists and Presbyterians never translated their antislavery rhetoric into action. By 1820, evangelicals were coming to terms with slavery. Instead of demanding freedom for slaves, they suggested, as the Methodist James O'Kelly put it, that slave owners remember that slaves were "dear brethren in Christ" who should not be treated cruelly and who should be allowed to attend religious services. After 1830, with large numbers of the planter elite converted to evangelicalism, this would evolve into a full-scale effort to Christianize the institution of slavery.

Gender, Power, and the Evangelicals

Southern men, yeomen as well as planters, distrusted the early evangelicals for more than their views on slavery. The preachers seemed even more grievously mistaken about white manhood and the integrity of white families. Southerners were localistic and culturally conservative. While the new northern middle class nourished a cosmopolitan culture, an individualism, and a domestic sentimentalism that subverted traditional authority, southerners distrusted outsiders and defended rural neighborhoods grounded in the sovereignty of fathers over their property and families, and in the power, judgment, skills, and physical prowess of those fathers.

The early evangelicals seemed to threaten southern patriarchy. They preached individual salvation to women, children, and slaves—often hinting that the "family" of believers could replace blood ties. Churches sometimes intervened in family disputes or disciplined family members in ways that subverted patriarchal control. Perhaps worse, many of the preachers failed to act out the standards of southern manhood in their own lives. James McGready and other camp-meeting preachers often faced hecklers and rowdies. When attacked, they either ran off or quietly took their beatings. White men often met the turn-the-other-cheek meekness of the preachers (not to mention the celibacy of the Methodists) with suspicion and contempt. They felt the same about the hugging, kissing, crying, and bodily "exercises" acted out in evangelical meetings.

As they had with slavery, southern evangelicals came to terms with the notions of manhood and the father-centered families of the South. The preachers learned to assert traditional forms of manhood. Their fathers and often themselves, they said, had fought the British and Indians heroically. They revealed that they had often been great drinkers, gamblers, fighters, and fornicators before submitting to God, and they also began fighting back when attacked. Peter Cartwright, who conquered much of Kentucky and southern Illinois for Methodism, told numerous stories of how he outwitted and often outfought rowdies who attacked his meetings. On many occasions, he walked out of the pulpit to confront hecklers, and punched more than a few of them. The preachers also made it clear that they would pose no threat to the authority of fathers. They discouraged the excesses of female and juvenile piety. At the same time, church disciplinary cases involving adultery, wife-beating, private drunkenness, and other offenses committed within families became more and more rare.

Religious Conservatism

More fundamentally, evangelicals upheld the southern world of fixed hierarchy and God-given social roles, and their churches reinforced localistic neighborhoods and the patriarchal family. Some southern communities began when a whole congregation moved onto new land. Others were settled by the chain migration of brothers and cousins, and subsequent revivals spread through family networks. Rural isolation limited most households to their own company during the week, but on Sundays church meetings united the neighborhood's cluster of extended families into a community of believers. In most neighborhoods, social connections seldom extended beyond that. The word "church" referred ultimately to the worldwide community of Christians, and the war between the "church" and the "world" referred to a cosmic history that would end in millennial fire. But in the day-to-day understandings of southern evangelicals, the church was the local congregation and the world was local sins and local sinners. Churches disciplined members for such worldly practices as drinking, gambling, dancing, swearing, fornication, and adultery, and even for giving the *impression* of sinful behavior. Mount Olive Baptist Church in North Carolina, for example, expelled Mary Bivens because she was "too thick with young men." While they patrolled their own congregations, however, southern evangelicals seldom thought about changing the world.

Southern evangelicalism rested on the sovereignty of God, a conviction of human imperfection, and an acceptance of disappointment and pain as part of God's grand and unknowable design. When the young son of a planter family died, the mother was certain that God had killed the child because the parents had loved him more than God: "But God took him for he saw he was our idol." A grieving South Carolinian received this consolation from a relative: "Hope you are quite reconciled to the loss of your darling babe. As it was the will of God to take him, we must obey, and He will be angry at us if we go past moderate grief." Francis Pickens, another South Carolinian, wrote after losing his wife and child, "I had almost forgot there was a God, and now I stand the scattered . . . and blasted monument of his just wrath." It was a far cry from the middle-class North's sentimentalism and the romantic, redemptive deaths of children in sentimental fiction.

Within this flawed and dangerous world, patriarchal social relations were crucial to Christian living. Southerners revered the patriarch and slaveholder Abraham more than any other figure in the Bible, and John C. Calhoun would proclaim "Hebrew Theocracy" the best government ever experienced by humankind. The father must—like Abraham—govern and protect his household, the mother must assist the father, and the women, children, and slaves must faithfully act out the duties of their stations. Eternal salvation was possible for everyone, but the saved lived out their godliness by striving to be a good mother, a good father, a good slave. By the same token, a Christian never questioned his or her God-given social role.

Pro-Slavery Christianity

In revolutionary and early national America, white southerners had been the most radical of republicans. Jeffersonian planter-politicians led the fights for equal rights and the absolute separation of church and state, and southern evangelicals were the early republic's staunchest opponents of slavery. By 1830, however, the South was an increasingly conscious minority within a democratic and capitalist nation. The northern middle classes proclaimed a link between material and moral progress, identifying both with individual autonomy and universal rights. A radical northern minority was agitating for the immediate abolition of slavery (chapter 12).

Southerners met this challenge with an "intellectual blockade" against outside publications and ideas and with a moral and religious defense of slavery. The Bible provided plenty of ammunition. Southerners preached that the Chosen People of the Old Testament had been patriarchs and slaveholders, and that Jesus had lived in a society that sanctioned slavery and never criticized the institution. Some ministers claimed that blacks were the descendants of Ham and thus deserved enslavement. The most common religious argument, however, was that slavery had given millions of heathen Africans the priceless opportunity to become Christians and to live in a Christian society. Thornton Stringfellow, a Virginia Baptist minister, insisted that "their condition . . . is now better than that of any equal number of laborers on earth, and is daily improving."

Like their northern counterparts, southern clergymen applauded the material improvements of the age, but they insisted that moral improvement occurred only when people embraced the timeless truths of the Bible. The South Carolinian William F. Hutson put it simply: "In religion and morals, we doubt all improvements, not known to certain fishermen who lived eighteen hundred years ago." Northern notions of progress through individual liberation, equal rights, and universal Christian love were wrong-headed and dangerous. The Presbyterian John Adger asserted that relations of dominance and submission (and not "barbarism and personal savage independence") were utterly necessary to both social and individual fulfillment, and that the distribution of rights and responsibilities was unequal and God-given. "The rights of the father are natural, but they belong only to the fathers. Rights of property are natural, but they belong only to those who have property," and such natural rights were coupled with the awesome duties of fatherhood and proprietorship. In the end, southern pro-slavery intellectuals rejected Jefferson's "self-evident" equality of man; Edmund Ruffin, for instance, branded that passage of the Declaration of Independence as "indefensible" as well as "false and foolish."

The Mission to the Slaves

By the 1820s, southern evangelicalism had long since abandoned its hostility toward slavery, and slaveholders commonly attended camp meetings and revivals. These prosperous converts faced conflicting duties. Their churches taught them that slaves had immortal souls and that planters were as responsible for the spiritual welfare of their slaves as they were for the spiritual welfare of their own children. One preacher remarked that it was difficult "to treat them as property, and at the same time render to them that which is just and equal as immortal and accountable beings, and as heirs of the grace of life, equally with ourselves." A planter on his deathbed told his children that humane treatment and religious instruction for slaves was the duty of slave owners; if these were neglected, "we will have to answer for the loss of their souls." After Nat Turner's bloody slave revolt in 1831 (chapter 9), missions to the slaves took on new urgency: If the churches were to help create a patriarchal Christian society in the South, that society would have to include the slaves. The result after 1830 was a concerted attempt to Christianize the slaves.

To this end, Charles Colcock Jones, a Presbyterian minister from Georgia, spent much of his career writing manuals on how to preach to slaves. He taught that no necessary connection linked social position and spiritual worth: there were good and bad slaveholders and good and bad slaves. He also taught, preaching from the Epistles of Paul ("Servants, obey your masters"), that slaves must accept the master's authority as God's, and that obedience was their prime religious virtue. Jones warned white preachers never to become personally involved with their slave listeners—to pay no attention to their quarrels, their complaints about their master or about their fellow slaves, or about working conditions on the plantation. "We separate entirely their religious from their civil condition," he said, "and contend that one may be attended to without interfering with the other." The catechism Jones prepared for slaves included the question, "What did God make you for?" The answer was, "To make a crop."

The evangelical mission to the slaves was not as completely self-serving as it may seem. For to accept one's worldly station, to be obedient and dutiful within that station, and to seek salvation outside of this world were precisely what the planters demanded of themselves and their own families. An important goal of plantation missions was to create safe and profitable plantations. Yet that goal was to be achieved by Christianizing both slaveholders and slaves—a lesson that some slaveholders learned when they were expelled from their churches for mistreating their slaves. As for the slaves, we have seen that they listened selectively to what white missionaries preached, and turned evangelical Christianity into a religion of their own (chapter 9.)

Southern Entertainments

Southerners of all classes and races were leisure-loving people, but the rural character of the South threw them upon their own resources rather than on commercial entertainments. They drank, told stories, engaged in wrestling and boxing matches, and danced. For evangelicals who withdrew from such entertainments, church socials and camp meetings filled the gap. Books were not as readily available as they were in the North. Whereas the big publishing houses produced many titles aimed at northern and western readers and at such specialized constituencies as dairy farmers or middle-class housewives, the southern literary market was too small to justify such special attention. Most southern families owned a Bible, and wealthier families often read histories, religious and political tracts, and English (seldom American) literature, with Shakespeare leading the way and Sir Walter Scott's tales of medieval chivalry not far behind. English rural sports persisted in the South. Hunting and fishing were southern passions. Fox and deer hunts provided the gentry with an opportunity to display their skill with horses and guns, while the hunts of poorer whites and slaves both provided sport and enhanced their threatened roles as providers. Although state laws forbade slaves to own guns or dogs, thousands of slave owners overlooked the laws. Thoroughbred horse racing was concentrated in the South, with prominent planters—Andrew Jackson and Henry Clay among them—leading the way.

Commercial entertainments in the South were concentrated in the larger towns and along the major rivers. Showboats brought theatrical troupes, minstrel shows, animal acts, and other entertainment to the river towns. New Orleans, the great market town of the Southwest, was a center of theater, music, and other entertainments. It was also the only southern city where one could watch a professional prizefight, and violent contests seem to have appealed to New Orleans audiences. In 1819, a New Orleans impresario pitted a bull against six "of the strongest dogs in the country"; six bulldogs versus a Canadian bear; a "beautiful Tiger" versus a black bear; and 12 dogs versus a "strong and furious Opeloussas Bull." The advertisement further promised: "If the tiger is not vanquished in his fight with the Bear, he will be sent alone against the last Bull; and if the latter conquers all his enemies, several pieces of fireworks will be placed on his back, which will produce a very entertaining amusement." The impresario also stated that the premises had been inspected by the mayor of New Orleans, and that children would be admitted at half price. Although such events were outlawed in later years, they continued on the sly. In 1852, a crowd of 5,000 gathered outside New Orleans to watch a bull and a grizzly bear fight to the death.

Race

Americans in the first half of the 19th century revised the racial order as well as the religious and domestic order of their society. White Americans had long assumed that Africans belonged at the bottom of society, but they assumed that others belonged there as well. In a colonial world in which many whites were indentured servants, tenants, apprentices, and workers who lived in their employers' homes, where increasing numbers of blacks were formally free and many others were hired out as semi-free, few Americans made rigid distinctions concerning the "natural" independence of whites and the "natural" dependence of blacks. (All Americans, after all, were colonial subjects of the British king.) The language of colonial social division separated gentlemen from the "middling sort," and relegated the propertyless and dependent to the "lower orders" or the "lower sort." While the better-off whites were far from color blind, they wrote off poverty, disorder, drunkenness, and rioting as the work not of blacks but of an undifferentiated substratum of "Negroes, sailors, servants, and boys."

Modern racism—the notion that blacks were a separate and hopelessly inferior order of humankind—emerged from developments in the early 19th century: national independence and the crucial new distinction between Americans who were citizens and those who were not, the recommitment to slavery in the South, and the making of what would be called "free labor" in the North. Whites who faced lifetimes of wage labor and dependence struggled to make dignity and self-respect out of that situation. At the same time, freed slaves entered the bottom of a newly defined "free labor" society and tried to do the same. With plenty of help from the wealthy and powerful, whites succeeded in making white democracy out of the rubble of the old patriarchal republic. In the process, they defined nonwhites as constitutionally incapable of self-discipline, personal independence, and political participation.

Free Blacks

There had been sizable pockets of slavery in the northern colonies, but revolutionary idealism, coupled with the growing belief that slavery was inefficient, led one northern state after another to abolish it. Vermont, where there were almost no slaves, outlawed slavery in its revolutionary constitution. By 1804, every northern state had taken some action, usually by passing laws that called for gradual emancipation. The first of such laws, and the model for others, was passed in Pennsylvania in 1780. This law freed slaves born after 1780 when they reached their 28th birthday. Slaves born before 1780 would remain slaves, and slave children would remain slaves through their prime working years. By 1830, only a handful of aging blacks remained slaves in the North.

Gradual emancipation did not stop at the Mason-Dixon Line. We have seen (chapter 9) that thousands of Chesapeake slaveholders freed their slaves in the decades following the Revolution. Virginia seriously considered abolishing slavery outright. In 1832, a Virginia constitutional convention argued the question of immediate emancipation by state law. With the western counties supporting abolition (but insisting that freed blacks be transported from the state) and some of the eastern, slaveholding counties threatening to secede from the state if abolition won, the legislature rejected emancipation by a vote of 73–58. In the Deep South, where slavery was a big and growing business, whites did not talk about emancipation. They assumed that slavery was permanent, and that the only proper status for blacks was bondage and submission to whites.

From Virginia on north, the rising population of free blacks gravitated to the cities and towns. Despite the flood of white immigrants from Europe and the American countryside, African Americans constituted a sizable minority in the rapidly expanding cities. New York City's black population, 10.5 percent in 1800, was still 8.8 percent in 1820. Philadelphia, the haven of thousands of southern refugees, was 10.3 percent African American in 1800 and 11.9 percent in 1820.

Blacks in the seaports tended to take stable, low-paying jobs. A few became successful (occasionally wealthy) entrepreneurs, while some others practiced skilled trades. Many of the others took jobs as waiters or porters in hotels, as merchant seamen, as barbers, and as butlers, maids, cooks, washerwomen, and coachmen for wealthy families. Others worked as dockworkers and laborers. Still others became dealers in used clothing, or draymen with their own carts and horses, or food vendors in the streets and in basement shops. (In New York, oysters were a black monopoly.) As never before, free black faces and voices became parts of the landscape and soundscape of cities and towns—hawking buttermilk, hot corn, and oysters, talking and laughing in the streets, jostling their way through city crowds. More than a few whites were disturbed. The New York journalist Mordecai Noah, like many other elite whites, had expected freed slaves to be grateful and deferential to their former masters, but "instead of thankfulness for their redemption, they have become impudent and offensive beyond all precedent."

African Americans with money established businesses and institutions of their own. At one end were black-owned gambling houses, saloons, brothels, oyster cellars, and dance halls, which often served a mixed clientele. At the other end were institutions built by self-consciously "respectable" free blacks to assert their dignity and to "uplift" their once-dependent people. Most prominent among these were churches, which sprang up wherever African Americans lived. In Philadelphia, black preachers Richard Allen and Absalom Jones rebelled against segregated seating in St. George's Methodist Church and, in 1794, founded two separate black congregations; by 1800, about 40 percent of Philadelphia's blacks belonged to one of those two churches. The African Methodist Episcopal Church grew from Allen's church, and established itself as a national denomination in 1816.

Schools and relief societies, usually associated with churches, grew quickly. Black Masonic lodges attracted hundreds of members. Many of the churches and social organizations took names that proudly called up the blacks' African origins. In Philadelphia, for instance, there were African Methodists, Abyssinian Baptists, the Daughters of Ethiopia, the African Dorcas Society—to name only a few. Not only their names and activities, but their presence as black-owned buildings filled with respectable former slaves caught the attention of their white and black neighbors. It was from this matrix of black businesses and institutions that black abolitionists—David Walker in Boston, Fredrick Douglass in New Bedford and Rochester, the itinerant Sojourner Truth, and many others—would emerge to demand abolition of slavery and equal rights for black citizens.

The Beginnings of Modern Racism

In post-revolutionary America, the most important social and political distinction was not between black and white or rich and poor. It was between the heads of independent households and the women, slaves, servants, apprentices, and others who were their dependents. Wage labor and tenancy reduced the number of northern whites who were, by traditional measures, independent. They fought that threat in a number of ways: their skills and labor, they said, constituted a kind of property; their manhood conferred judgment and strength and thus independence. These were assertions of worth and independence that had little to do with the ownership of property. In ways that were sometimes subtle but just as often brutal, they often made those assertions at the expense of African Americans. Along with the value of their labor and their manhood, white men discovered the decisive value of white skin.

Whites in the early 19th century began refusing to work alongside blacks, and some of the earliest and most decisive racist assaults came when whites asserted their control over some occupations and relegated blacks to others. They chased blacks out of skilled jobs by pressuring employers to discriminate, and often by outright violence. As a result, African Americans were almost completely eliminated from the skilled trades, and many unskilled and semiskilled blacks lost their jobs on the docks and in warehouses. In 1834, a Philadelphian reported that "colored persons, when engaged in their usual occupations, were repeatedly assailed and maltreated, usually on the [waterfront]. Parties of white men have insisted that no blacks shall be employed in certain departments of labor." And as their old jobs disappeared, blacks were systematically excluded from the new jobs that were opening up in factories.

Even whites who remained in positions of personal dependence (servants, waiters, and other jobs that were coming to be defined as "black" work) refused the signs and language of servility. White servants refused to wear livery, which became the uniform of black servants of the rich. Whites also refused to be called servants. As early as 1807, when an English visitor asked a New England servant for her master, the woman replied that she had no master. "I am Mr. ___'s *help*," she said. "I'd have you know, *man,* that I am no *sarvant,* none but *negars* are *sarvants.*" The Englishwoman Frances Trollope, who spent the late

1820s in the United States, explained: "It is more than petty treason to the republic to call a free citizen a *servant*."

There was trouble off the job as well. As early as the 1790s, whites had disrupted African American church meetings, and they frequently attacked black celebrations of northern emancipation and Haitian independence. Black neighborhoods and institutions came under increasing attack. In the late 1820s and early 1830s, every northern city experienced antiblack rioting. In 1829, white mobs destroyed black homes and businesses in Cincinnati. Hundreds of blacks fled that city for Canada; many others sought refuge in slaveholding Kentucky. Another major race riot would break out in Philadelphia in 1834 between working-class whites and blacks at a street carnival. While blacks seem to have won the first round, the whites refused to accept defeat. Over the next few nights, they wrecked a black-owned tavern, broke into black households to terrorize families and steal their property, attacked whites who lived with, socialized with, or operated businesses catering to blacks, wrecked the African Presbyterian Church, and destroyed a black church on Wharton Street by sawing through its timbers and pulling it down.

Sporadic racial violence wracked the city throughout the 1830s and 1840s, reaching its height in 1849. That summer a firehouse gang of Irish immigrants calling themselves "the Killers" attacked the California House, a black-owned tavern and gambling hall. The black patrons had anticipated the attack and had armed themselves, and in the melee five Killers were shot. For two months, tempers simmered. Finally, the Killers set a fire at the California House that spread to nearby houses. They fought off neighborhood blacks, rival firemen, and the police. The riot ended only when the city sent in four companies of militia.

Mobs often targeted whites who socialized or cooperated with blacks. Integrated taverns, dance halls, brothels, and boarding houses were burned in city after city, and whites who helped blacks became special targets. Free blacks who built churches, schools, and other institutions of respectability often had the assistance of whites (usually middle-class evangelicals) in their attempts to "uplift" the survivors of slavery. Black leaders and a small number of white reformers dreamed of an America in which godly behavior—and not skin color—would win entrance into the American community of respect. By the early 1830s, they formed antislavery societies that called not only for immediate and universal emancipation but for equal rights as well. (see chapter 12). These became the targets of some of the most vicious mobs. In July 1834, for instance, a New York City mob sacked the house of the white abolitionist merchant Lewis Tappan, moved on to the Rev. Charles Finney's Chatham Street Chapel, where abolitionists were said to be meeting, and finished the evening by attacking a British (and thus supposedly aristocratic) actor at the Bowery theater. The manager saved his theater by waving two American flags and ordering an American actor to perform popular minstrel routines for the mob. Democracy and working-class aspirations, it seemed, were in league with racism.

Above all, white populists pronounced blacks unfit to be citizens of the republic. Federalists and other upper-class whites had often supported various forms of black suffrage; less-privileged whites opposed it. The insistence that blacks were incapable of citizenship

The Library Company of Philadelphia

The Attack on the California House   In the big antebellum cities, volunteer fire companies were often ethnic clubs, and many were tied to street gangs. In 1849, a Philadelphia Irish gang called the Killers, some of them wearing their fire hats and carrying their fire horns, attacked a black-owned gambling and drinking establishment called the California House. The blacks (and apparently some of their white patrons) fought back with guns.

reinforced an equally natural white male political capacity. The most vicious racist assaults were often carried out beneath symbols of the revolutionary republic. Antiblack mobs in Baltimore, Cincinnati, and Toledo called themselves Minute Men and Sons of Liberty. Philadelphia blacks who gathered to hear the Declaration of Independence read on the Fourth of July were attacked for "defiling the government." The antiabolitionist mob that sacked Lewis Tappan's house destroyed his furniture, but they rescued a portrait of George Washington and carried it as a banner during their later attacks on Finneyite evangelicals and English actors.

The more respectable and powerful whites had long been worried about the mixed-race underclass of the cities and towns. Now, as the disorder that they expected of the lower orders took the form of race riots, the authorities responded. But rather than protect the jobs, churches, schools, businesses, friends, and political rights of African Americans from criminal attack, they determined to stop the trouble by removing black people—from employment, from public festivities, from their already-limited citizenship, and, ultimately, from the United States.

Wealthier and better-educated whites shared their compatriots' belief that the United States would never be a racially integrated democracy. By far the largest organization that addressed itself to problems of slavery and race in these years was the **American Colonization Society,** which envisioned sending freed blacks (but not slaves) "back" to Africa. The Society held its first meeting at the end of 1816—in the chamber of the House of Representatives, with Bushrod Washington, stepson of George Washington, as president. Early members included Henry Clay, John Taylor of Caroline, Andrew Jackson, and other political and social leaders of the West, the Middle States, and the Upper South. The Colonizationists did not see slavery as the problem. Like white rioters, they saw the problem as black freedom. African Americans, they said, would continue to suffer from white prejudice and their own deficiencies as long as they stayed in the United States. They would exercise freedom and learn Christian and republican ways only if exported to Liberia, on the west coast of Africa.

A few free blacks took them up on the offer, but most adamantly refused, insisting that colonization was not an offer of freedom but an attempt to round up native-born citizens who were not white and make them disappear. Colonizationists frequently denounced white violence against free blacks. Just as often, however, they blamed the "degradation" of blacks as the root of the problem. Colonization remained the principal racial doctrine of white respectables—in a chronological line running from Henry Clay to Abraham Lincoln—north of the Lower South until the end of slavery.

Citizenship

The transition from republic to democracy—and the relation of that transition to the decline of patriarchy and efforts to shore up white manhood—took on formal, institutional shape in a redefinition of republican citizenship. The revolutionary constitutions of most states retained colonial freehold (property) qualifications for voting. In the yeoman societies of the late 18th century, freehold qualifications granted the vote to between one-half and three-quarters of adult white men. Many of the disfranchised were dependent sons who expected to inherit citizenship along with land. Some states dropped the freehold clause and gave the vote to all adult men who paid taxes, but with little effect on the voting population. Both the freehold and taxpaying qualifications tended to give political rights to adult men who headed households, thus reinforcing republican notions that granted full citizenship to independent fathers and not to their dependents. Arthur St. Clair, the territorial governor of Ohio, argued for retention of the Northwest Ordinance's 50-acre freehold qualification for voting in territorial elections in set-piece republican language: "I do not count independence and wealth always together," he said, "but I pronounce poverty and dependence inseparable." When Nathaniel Macon, a respected old revolutionary from North Carolina, saw that his state would abolish property qualifications in 1802, he suggested that the suffrage be limited to married men. Like St. Clair's proposition, it was an attempt to maintain the old distinction between citizen-householders and disfranchised dependents.

Between 1790 and 1820, republican notions of citizenship grounded in fatherhood and proprietorship gave way to a democratic insistence on equal rights for all white men. There were several reasons for that development. First, the proportion of adult white men who could not meet property qualifications multiplied at an alarming rate. In the new towns and cities, artisans and laborers and even many merchants and professionals did not own real estate. And in the west, new farms were often valued at below property qualifications. This became particularly troublesome after the War of 1812, when a large proportion of veterans could not vote. In Shenandoah County, Virginia, for instance, 700 of 1000 men at a militia muster claimed that they were disfranchised. In 1829, the "Non-Freeholders of the City of Richmond" petitioned for the right to vote, arguing that the ownership of property did not make a man "wiser and better." "Virtue" and "intelligence," they insisted, were "not among the products of the soil." Even the aging Thomas Jefferson had come to believe, by 1824, that property restrictions violated "the principal of equal political rights."

Under the impetus of growing disenfranchisement (and of Jeffersonian legislatures and state conventions eager to increase their constituencies), state after state extended the vote to include all adult white men. In 1790, only Vermont granted the vote to all free men. Kentucky entered the Union in 1792 without property or taxpaying qualifications. Tennessee followed with a freehold qualification, but only for newcomers who had resided in their counties for less than six months. The federal government dropped the 50-acre freehold qualification in the territories in 1812. Of the eight territories that became states between 1796 and 1821 none kept a property qualification, only three maintained a taxpaying qualification, and five explicitly granted the vote to all white men. In the same years, one eastern state after another widened the franchise. By 1840, only Rhode Island retained a propertied electorate, primarily because Yankee farmers in that state wanted to retain power in a society made up increasingly of urban, immigrant wage earners. (When Rhode Island finally reformed the franchise in 1843, the new law included a freehold requirement that applied only to the foreign-born, and explicitly withheld the franchise from blacks.) With that exception, the white men of every state held the vote.

Early 19th-century suffrage reform gave political rights to propertyless men, and thus took a long step away from the Founders' republic and toward mass democracy. At the same time, however, reformers explicitly limited the democratic franchise to those who were white and male. New Jersey's revolutionary constitution, for instance, had granted the vote to "persons" who met a freehold qualification. This loophole enfranchised property-holding widows, many of whom exercised their rights. A law of 1807 abolished property restrictions and gave the vote to all white men. The same law closed the loophole that had allowed propertied women to vote. The question of woman suffrage would not be considered again until women raised it in 1848. It would not be settled until well into the 20th century.

New restrictions also applied to African Americans. The revolutionary constitutions of Massachusetts, New Hampshire, Vermont, and Maine—northeastern states with tiny black minorities—granted the vote to free blacks. New York and North Carolina laws gave the vote to "all men" who met the qualifications, and propertied African Americans (a tiny but symbolically crucial minority) in many states routinely exercised the vote. Post-revolutionary laws that extended voting rights to all white men often specifically excluded or severely restricted votes for blacks. Free blacks lost the suffrage in New York, New Jersey, Pennsylvania, Connecticut, Maryland, Tennessee, and North Carolina—all states in which they had previously voted. By 1840, fully 93 percent of blacks in the North lived in states that either banned or severely restricted their right to vote, and the restrictions were explicitly about race. A delegate to the New York constitutional convention of 1821, noting the movement of freed slaves into New York City, argued against allowing them to vote: "The whole host of Africans that now deluge our city (already too impertinent to be borne), would be placed upon an equal with the citizens." At the Tennessee convention that eliminated property and residence requirements for whites while it stripped the vote from free blacks in 1834, delegate G. W. L. Marr declared that "We the People" meant "we the free white people of the United States and the free white people only." The convention declared blacks "outside the social compact." A year later, the old republican Nathaniel Macon told a North Carolina convention that in 1776, free blacks had been "no part of the then political family."

Thus the "universal" suffrage of which many Americans boasted was far from universal. New laws dissolved the old republican connections between political rights and property, and thus saved the citizenship of thousands who were becoming propertyless tenants and wage earners. The same laws that gave the vote to all white men, however, explicitly barred other Americans from political participation. Faced with the disintegration of Jefferson's republic of proprietor-patriarchs, the wielders of power had chosen to blur the emerging distinctions of social class while they hardened the boundaries of sex and race. In 1790, citizenship had belonged to men who were fathers and farm owners. Forty years later, the citizenry was made up of those who were (the phrase came into use at this time) "free, white, and twenty-one." Much more explicitly and completely than had been the case at the founding, America in 1830 was a white man's republic.

Conclusion

By the second quarter of the 19th century, Americans had made a patchwork of regional, class, and ethnic cultures. The new middle classes of the North and West compounded their Protestant and republican inheritance with a new entrepreneurial faith in progress. The result was a way of life grounded in the self-made and morally accountable individual and the sentimentalized (often feminized) domestic unit.

Their means of proposing that way of life as a national culture for the United States often offended others. The middle class met resistance, first of all, from poorer urban dwellers and the less prosperous farmers in their own sections—a northern and western majority that remained grimly loyal to the unsentimental, male-dominated families of their fathers and grandfathers, to new and old religious sects that continued to believe in human depravity and the mysterious workings of providence, and to the suspicion that perfidy and disorder lurked behind the smiling moral order of market economics and sentimental culture.

In the South, most white farmers persisted in a neighborhood-based, intensely evangelical, and socially conservative way of life; when asked their opinions, they often talked like classic Jeffersonian yeomen. Southern planters, although they shared in the northern elite's belief in material progress and the magic of the market, were bound by family values, a system of slave labor, and a code of honor that was strikingly at variance with middle-class faith in an orderly universe and perfectible individuals. And we have seen (chapter 9) that slaves in these years continued to make cultural forms of their own. Despite their exclusion from the white world of liberty and equality, they tied their aspirations to the family, to an evangelical Protestant God, and to the individual and collective dignity that republics promise to their citizens.

SUGGESTED READINGS

The early chapters of **Paul Starr, The Creation of the Media: Political Origins of Modern Communications** (2004) provide valuable introduction to the communications revolution. **Stuart M. Blumin, The Emergence of the Middle Class: Social Experience in the American City, 1760–1900** (1989) is a thorough study of work and material life among the urban middle class. Studies that treat religion, family, and sentimental culture include **Paul E. Johnson, A Shopkeeper's Millennium: Society and Revivals in Rochester New York, 1815–1837** (1978); **Mary P. Ryan, Cradle of the Middle Class: The Family in Oneida County, New York, 1790–1865** (1981); and **Jane Tompkins, Sensational Designs: The Cultural Work of American Fiction, 1790–1860** (1985). **Nathan O. Hatch, The Democratization of American Christianity** (1989) is a good introduction to plain-folk religion in these years.

Studies of popular literature and entertainments include **Elliott J. Gorn, The Manly Art: Bare-Knuckle Prize Fighting in America** (1986); **Eric Lott, Love & Theft: Blackface Minstrelsy and the American Working Class** (1993); **David S. Reynolds, Beneath the American Renaissance: The Subversive Imagination in the Age of Emerson and Melville** (1988); and **Paul E. Johnson, Sam Patch, the Famous Jumper** (2003.) Essential books on the culture of southern whites are **Bertram Wyatt-Brown, Southern Honor: Ethics & Behavior in the Old South** (1982); **Christine Leigh Heyerman, Southern Cross: The Beginnings of the Bible Belt** (1997); and **Elizabeth Fox-Genovese and Eugene D. Genovese, The Mind of the Master Class: History and Faith in the Southern Slaveholders' Worldview** (2005). An enlightening counterpoint between black and white understandings of the slave trade (and, by extension, of the slave South generally) is presented in **Walter Johnson, Soul by Soul: Life Inside the Antebellum Slave Market** (1999).

Visit the Liberty Equality Power Companion Web site for resources specific to this textbook: http://www.thomsonedu.com/history/murrin

Also find self-tests and additional resources at ThomsonNOW. ThomsonNOW is an integrated online suite of services and resources with proven ease of use and efficient paths to success, delivering the results you want—NOW!

www.thomsonedu.com/login

Democrats and Whigs

National political leaders from the 1820s until the outbreak of the Civil War faced two persistent questions. First, a deepening rift between slave and free states threatened the very existence of the nation. Second, explosive economic development and territorial expansion made new demands on the political system—demands that raised the question of government participation in economic life.

The Whig Party proposed the American System as the answer to both questions. The national government, said the Whigs, should subsidize roads and canals, foster industry with protective tariffs, and maintain a national bank capable of exercising centralized control over credit and currency. The result would be a peaceful, prosperous, and truly national market society. If the South, the West, and the Northeast were profiting by doing business with each other, the argument went, sectional fears and jealousies would quiet down. Jacksonian Democrats, on the other hand, argued that the American System was unconstitutional, that it violated the rights of states and localities, and that it would tax honest citizens in order to benefit corrupt and wealthy insiders. Most dangerous of all, argued the Democrats, Whig economic nationalism would create an activist, interventionist national government that would anger and frighten the slaveholding South. To counter both threats, the Jacksonians resurrected Jefferson's agrarian republic of states' rights and inactive, inexpensive government—all of it deeply inflected in the code of white male equality, domestic patriarchy, and racial slavery that was being acted out in families, neighborhoods, and state legislatures.

The American System

President James Madison delivered his annual message to the 14th Congress in December 1815. He asked for legislation to create a new national bank, a tariff to protect American manufacturers, and congressional support for those canals and roads "which can best be executed under national authority." Congress agreed. Made up overwhelmingly of Jeffersonian Republicans and led by the young southern and western nationalists who had favored the war, this Congress reversed many of the positions taken by Jefferson's old party. It chartered a national bank, enacted a protective tariff, and debated a national system of roads and canals at federal expense. Most prewar Republicans had viewed such programs as heresy. But by 1815, the Republican majority in Congress had come to accept them as orthodox and necessary. Secretary of the Treasury Albert Gallatin explained: "The War has renewed and reinstated the national feelings which the Revolution had given and which

CHRONOLOGY

1816	Congress charters a Second Bank of the United States and the first avowedly protective tariff • *Dartmouth College* v. *Woodward* defines a private charter as a contract that cannot be altered by a state legislature
1819	Controversy arises over Missouri's admission to the Union as a slave state • Panic of 1819 marks the first failure of the national market economy
1820	Missouri Compromise adopted
1823	Monroe Doctrine written by Secretary of State John Quincy Adams
1824	*Gibbons* v. *Ogden* asserts federal control of interstate commerce
1824–25	Adams wins the presidency over Andrew Jackson • Adams appoints Henry Clay as secretary of state • Jacksonians charge a "Corrupt Bargain" between Adams and Clay
1827	Cherokees in Georgia declare themselves a republic
1828	Jackson defeats Adams for the presidency • "Tariff of Abominations" passed by Congress • John C. Calhoun's *Exposition and Protest* presents doctrine of nullification
1830	Congress passes the Indian Removal Act
1832	Jackson reelected over Henry Clay • *Worcester* v. *Georgia* exempts the Cherokee from Georgia law • Jackson vetoes recharter of the Bank of the United States
1833	Force Bill and Tariff of 1833 end the nullification crisis
1834	Whig Party formed in opposition to Jacksonians
1836	Congress adopts "gag rule" to table antislavery petitions • Van Buren elected president
1837	Financial panic ushers in a severe economic depression
1838	U.S. Army marches the remaining Cherokee to Indian Territory
1840	Whig William Henry Harrison defeats Van Buren for presidency

were daily lessened. The people have now more general objects of attachment with which their pride and political opinions are connected. They are more American."

Even as they convinced themselves that they had won the war, Republicans were painfully aware of the weaknesses that the war had displayed. Put simply, the United States had been unable to coordinate a national fiscal and military effort: bad roads, local jealousies, and a bankrupt treasury had nearly lost the war. In addition, the war and the years leading up to it convinced many Republicans, including Jefferson and Madison, that the export economy rendered the United States dangerously dependent on Europe (and especially Great Britain) which were not dependable. Finally, many of the younger Republicans in Congress were interested less in ideological purity than in bringing commerce into new regions. The nation, they said, must abandon Jefferson's export-oriented agrarianism and encourage prosperity and national independence through subsidies to commerce, manufactures, and internal improvements.

National Republicans

The man most closely associated with this shift in Republicanism was Henry Clay of Kentucky. Retaining his power in the postwar Congress, Clay headed the drive for protective tariffs, the bank, and internal improvements. He would call his program the "American System," arguing that it would foster national economic growth and a salutary harmony between geographic sections, thus a happy and prosperous republic.

In 1816, Congress chartered a Second Bank of the United States, headquartered in Philadelphia and empowered to establish branches wherever it saw fit. The government agreed to deposit its funds in the Bank, to accept the Bank's notes as payment for government land, taxes, and other transactions, and to buy one-fifth of the Bank's stock. The Bank of the United States was more powerful than the one that had been rejected (by one vote) by a Republican Congress in 1811. The fiscal horrors of the War of 1812, however, had convinced most representatives that it would be a good idea to move toward a national currency and centralized control of money and credit. The alternative was to allow state banks—which had increased in number from 88 to 208 between 1813 and 1815—to issue the unregulated and grossly inflated notes that had weakened the war effort and that promised to throw the anticipated postwar boom into chaos.

With no discussion of the constitutionality of what it was doing, Congress chartered the Bank of the United States as the sole banking institution empowered to do business throughout the country. Notes issued by the Bank would be the first semblance of a national currency (they would soon constitute from one-tenth to one-third of the value of notes in circulation). Moreover, the Bank could regulate the currency by demanding that state banknotes used in transactions with the federal government be redeemable in gold. In 1816, the Bank set up shop in Philadelphia's Carpenter's Hall, and in 1824, it moved around the corner to a Greek Revival edifice modeled after the Parthenon—a marble embodiment of the republican conservatism that directors of the Bank of the United States promised as their fiscal stance. From that vantage point they would fight (with a few huge lapses) a running battle with state banks and local interests in an effort to impose fiscal discipline and centralized control over an exploding market economy.

The same Congress drew up the nation's first overtly protective tariff in 1816. Shut off from British imports during the war, the Americans had built their first factories, almost entirely in southern New England and the mid-Atlantic. The British planned to flood the postwar market with cheap goods and kill American manufactures, and Congress determined to stop them. Shepherded through the House by Clay and his fellow nationalist John C. Calhoun of South Carolina, the Tariff of 1816 raised import duties an average of 25 percent, extending protection to the nation's infant industries at the expense of foreign trade and American consumers. Again, wartime difficulties and wartime nationalism had paved the way: since Americans could not depend on imported manufactures, Congress saw domestic manufactures as a patriotic necessity and a spur to commerce between the sections. The tariff was supported by the Northeast and the West, with enough southern support to ensure its passage. Tariffs would rise and fall between 1816 and the Civil War, but the principle of protectionism would persist.

Many of the Founders had seen a national transportation system as essential to the prosperity and safety of the union. George Washington had urged roads and canals linking the Atlantic states with the interior—both to provide western farmers with the civilizing benefits of commerce and to secure their loyalty to the United States. Thomas Jefferson shared Washington's views, and like his fellow Virginian, he favored improvements that would channel western commerce through Chesapeake Bay. He and Washington both insisted that the most sensible route would link the Potomac River with the Ohio. In 1802, President Jefferson signed a bill that began construction of the Cumberland Road (often called the National Road) from Cumberland, Maryland, to the Ohio River at Wheeling. In 1811, Secretary of the Treasury Albert Gallatin issued a report outlining a vast system of canals and roads that would tie the country together.

These early dreams and projects were meant to serve the postcolonial economy: they would deliver farm produce to the coast and then to international markets; the coastal towns would receive imported goods and ship them back into the countryside. As early as 1770, George Washington had dreamed of making the Potomac River a busy "Channel of Commerce between Great Britain" and the farmers of the interior. Others dreamed of other routes and rivers, but nearly all proponents of transportation into the west (with the partial exception of Gallatin) shared the great assumption of Washington's early vision: the export economy would remain dominant; the United States would be an independent, unified, and prosperous economic colony of the Old World.

Henry Clay's American System grew into a new vision: a national transportation network that would make the United States economically independent of Europe and geographically interdependent within itself. The Bank of the United States would supply fiscal stability and a uniform, trustworthy currency. The tariff would encourage Northeasterners to build factories and citizens in other parts of the country to buy what American manufacturers made, and agriculturalists would enjoy expanded internal markets: the West would sell food to the cities and to the plantation South, and the South would supply the burgeoning textile industry with cotton. The system would not deny international trade, but it would make the United States an economically integrated and independent nation.

The need for internal improvements was widely acknowledged in 1816. The British wartime blockade had hampered coastal shipping and had made Americans dependent on the wretched roads of the interior. Many members of the 14th Congress, after spending days of bruising travel on their way to Washington, were determined to give the United States an efficient transportation network. Some urged completion of the National Road linking the Chesapeake with the trans-Appalachian west. Some talked of an inland canal system to link the northern and southern coastal states. Others wanted a federally subsidized turnpike from Maine to Georgia.

Bills to provide such public works, however, did not get through Congress. Internal improvements were subject to local ambitions: canals and roads that helped one place hurt another. Some areas—southern New England and eastern Pennsylvania are examples—had already built good roads and did not want to subsidize the competition. There were also objections based in old Republican ideals. Roads and canals were big public works projects with scores of contractors and subcontractors—all dependent on government subsidies, with the potential for becoming a system of corruption that was impossible to stop. Finally, federally sponsored improvements, however beneficial, were constitutionally doubtful. In the Constitutional Convention, Benjamin Franklin had proposed that the power to build roads and cut canals within the states be written into the Constitution, and his proposal had been voted down. National support for internal improvements could be justified only by the "necessary and proper" and "general welfare" clauses. The Republicans could charter a Second Bank of the United States because Hamilton's bank had established the precedent. Roads and canals—extensive local projects at national expense—would stretch those clauses much further, worrying many Republicans that future legislatures would justify whatever struck them as necessary and proper at any given time.

When Congress agreed to complete the National Road—the one federal internal improvement already underway—President Madison and his Republican successor James Monroe vetoed the bills, refusing to support further internal improvements without a constitutional amendment. In 1822, Monroe even vetoed a bill authorizing repairs on the National Road, stating once again that the Constitution did not empower the federal government to build roads within the states. As a result, the financing and construction of roads and canals fell to the states, overwhelmingly the *northern* states. Henry Clay watched his vision of transportation as a nationalizing force turn into southern inaction and northern regionalization, a dangerous trend that continued throughout his long political life.

Commerce and the Law

The courts after 1815 played an important nationalizing and commercializing role. John Marshall, who presided over the Supreme Court from 1801 to 1835, took the lead. From the beginning he saw the Court as a conservative hedge against the excesses of provincialism and democratic legislatures. His early decisions protected the independence of the courts and their right to review legislation (see chapter 7). From 1816 onward, his decisions encouraged business and strengthened the national government at the expense of the states.

Marshall's most important decisions protected the sanctity of contracts and corporate charters against state legislatures. For example, in *Dartmouth College* v. *Woodward* (1816), Dartmouth defended a royal charter granted in the 1760s against changes introduced by a Republican legislature that wanted to transform Dartmouth from a privileged bastion of Federalism into a state college. Daniel Webster, who was a Dartmouth alumnus, the school's highly paid lawyer, and one of the few avowed Federalists left in Congress, finished his argument before the Supreme Court on a histrionic note: "It is, sir, as I have said, a small college. And yet there are those who love it—." Reputedly moved to tears, Marshall ruled that Dartmouth's original corporate charter could not be altered by legislation. Though in this case the Supreme Court was protecting Dartmouth's independence and its chartered privileges, Marshall and Webster knew that the decision also protected the hundreds of turnpike and canal companies, manufacturing corporations, and other ventures that held privileges under corporate charters granted by state governments. Once the charters had been granted, the states could neither regulate the corporations nor cancel their privileges. Thus corporate charters acquired the legal status of contracts, beyond the reach of democratic politics.

Two weeks after deciding the *Dartmouth* case, Marshall handed down the majority decision in *McCulloch* v. *Maryland*. The Maryland legislature, nurturing old Jeffersonian doubts about the constitutionality of the Bank of the United States, had attempted to tax the Bank's Baltimore branch, which in fact was a corrupt and ruinous institution (see later section). The Bank had challenged the legislature's right to do so, and the Court decided in favor of the Bank. Marshall stated, first, that the Constitution granted the federal government "implied powers" that included chartering the Bank, and he denied Maryland's right to tax the Bank or any other federal agency: "The power to tax," he said, "involves the power to destroy." It was Marshall's most explicit blow against Jeffersonian strict construction. Americans, he said, "did not design to make their government dependent on the states." And yet there were many, particularly in Marshall's native South, who remained certain that that was precisely what the Founders had intended.

In *Gibbons* v. *Ogden* (1824), the Marshall Court broke a state-granted steamship monopoly in New York harbor. The monopoly, Marshall argued, interfered with federal jurisdiction over interstate commerce. Like the *Dartmouth* case and *McCulloch* v. *Maryland*, this decision empowered the national government in relation to the states, and like them, it encouraged private entrepreneurs. As surely as Congressmen who supported the American System, John Marshall's Supreme Court assumed a natural and beneficial link between federal power and market society.

Meanwhile, the state courts were working quieter but equally profound transformations of American law. In the early republic, state courts had often viewed property not only as a private possession but as part of a neighborhood. Thus when a miller built a dam that flooded upriver farms or impaired the fishery, the courts might make him take those interests into account, often in ways that reduced the business uses of his property. By 1830, New England courts routinely granted the owners of industrial mill sites unrestricted water rights, even when the exercise of those rights inflicted damage on their neighbors. As early as 1805, the New York Supreme Court in *Palmer* v. *Mulligan* had asserted that the right to develop property for business purposes was inherent in the ownership of property. In the courts of northern and western states, what was coming to be called "progress" demanded legal protection for the business uses of private property, even when such uses conflicted with old common-law restraints.

1819

Focus Question

What enduring political issues were raised by the Missouri controversy and the Panic of 1819?

Many traditionalist Jeffersonians disliked these developments, but they could not stop them. That changed in 1819. First, the debate that surrounded Missouri's admission as a slave state revealed the centrality and vulnerability of slavery within the national Union. Second, a severe financial collapse led many Americans to doubt the Market Revolution's compatibility with the Jeffersonian republic. By 1820, politicians were determined to reconstruct the limited-government, states'-rights coalition that had elected Thomas Jefferson. By 1828, they had formed the Democratic Party, with **Andrew Jackson** at its head.

The Argument over Missouri

Early in 1819, slaveholding Missouri applied for admission to the Union as the first new state to be carved out of the Louisiana Purchase. New York Congressman James Tallmadge, Jr., quickly proposed two amendments to the Missouri statehood bill. The first would bar additional slaves from being brought into Missouri (16 percent of Missouri's people were already slaves). The second would emancipate Missouri slaves born after admission when they reached their 25th birthday. Put simply, the Tallmadge amendments would admit Missouri only if Missouri agreed to become a free state.

The congressional debates on the Missouri question had little to do with humanitarian objections to slavery and everything to do with political power. Rufus King of New York, an old Federalist who led the northerners in the Senate, insisted that he opposed the admission of a new slave state "solely in its bearing and effects upon great political interests, and upon the just and equal rights of the freemen of the nation." Northerners had long chafed at the added representation in Congress and in the electoral college that the "three-fifths" rule granted to the slave states (see chapter 6). The rule had, in fact, added significantly to southern power: In 1790, the South, with 40 percent of the white population, controlled 47 percent of the votes in Congress—enough to decide close votes both in Congress and in presidential elections. Federalists pointed out that of the 12 additional electoral votes the three-fifths rule gave to the South, 10 had gone to Thomas Jefferson in 1800 and had given him the election. Without the bogus votes provided by slavery, they argued, Virginia's stranglehold on the presidency would have been broken with Washington's departure in 1796.

In 1819, the North held a majority in the House of Representatives. The South, thanks to the recent admissions of Alabama and southern-oriented Illinois, controlled a bare majority in the Senate. Voting on the Tallmadge amendments in the House of Representatives was starkly sectional: a northern majority passed them on to the Senate. There, a unanimous South defeated the Tallmadge amendments with the help of the two Illinois senators and three northerners. Deadlocked between a Senate in favor of admitting Missouri as a slave state and a House dead set against it, Congress broke off one of the angriest sessions in its history and went home.

The Missouri Compromise

The new Congress that convened in the winter of 1819–20 passed the legislative package that became known as the **Missouri Compromise.** Massachusetts offered its northern counties as the new free state of Maine, thus neutralizing fears that the South would gain votes in the Senate with the admission of Missouri. Senator Jesse Thomas of Illinois proposed the so-called Thomas Proviso: If the North would admit Missouri as a slave state, the South would agree to outlaw slavery in territories above 36°30' N latitude—a line extending from the southern border of Missouri to Spanish (within a year, Mexican) territory. That line would open Arkansas Territory (present-day Arkansas and Oklahoma) to slavery and would ban slavery from the remainder of the Louisiana Territory—land that would subsequently become all or part of nine states.

Congress admitted Maine with little debate, but the Thomas Proviso met northern opposition. A joint Senate–House committee finally decided to separate the two bills. With half of the southern representatives and nearly all of the northerners supporting it, the Thomas Proviso passed. Congress next took up the admission of Missouri. With the votes of a solid South and 14 compromise-minded northerners, Missouri entered the Union as a slave state. President James Monroe applauded the "patriotic devotion" of the northern representatives "who preferr'd the sacrifice of themselves at home" to endangering the Union. His words were prophetic: Nearly all of the 14 were voted out of office in the next election.

The Missouri crisis brought the South's commitment to slavery and the North's resentment of southern political power into collision, revealing an angry gulf between slave and free states. While northerners vowed to relinquish no more territory to slavery, southerners talked openly of disunion and civil war. A Georgia politician announced that the Missouri debates had lit a fire that "seas of blood can only extinguish." President Monroe's secretary of state, John Quincy Adams, saw the debates as an omen: Northerners would unanimously oppose the extension of slavery whenever the question came to a vote. Adams confided in his diary: "Here was a new party ready formed, . . . terrible to the whole Union, but portentiously terrible to the South—threatening in its progress the emancipation of all their slaves, threatening in its immediate effect that Southern domination which has swayed the Union for the last twenty years."

Viewing the crisis from Monticello, the aging Thomas Jefferson was distraught: "A geographical line, coinciding with a marked principle, moral and political, once conceived and held up to the angry passions of men, will never be obliterated; every new irritation will mark it deeper and deeper. . . . This momentous question, like a fire-bell in the night, awakened and filled me with terror. I considered it at once the knell of the Union." The Missouri question underlined a basic fact of American national politics: if politicians argued about slavery they would split along North-South lines and the Union would be endangered.

The Panic of 1819

Politicians debated the Missouri question against a darkening backdrop of economic depression—a downturn that would shape political alignments as much as the slavery question. The origins of the Panic of 1819 were international and numerous: European agriculture was recovering from the Napoleonic wars, thereby reducing the demand for American foodstuffs; war and revolution in Latin America had cut off the supply of precious metals (the base of the international money supply); debt-ridden European governments hoarded the available specie; and American bankers and businessmen met the situation by expanding credit and issuing banknotes that were mere dreams of real money. Coming in the first years of the Market Revolution, this speculative boom was encouraged by American bankers who had little experience with corporate charters, promissory notes, bills of exchange, or stocks and bonds.

Congress had in part chartered the Second Bank of the United States in 1816 to impose order on this situation, but the Bank under the presidency of the genial Republican politician William Jones became part of the problem. The western branch offices in Cincinnati and Lexington became embroiled in the speculative boom, and insiders at the Baltimore branch hatched criminal schemes to enrich themselves. With matters spinning out of control, Jones resigned early in 1819. The new president, Langdon Cheves of South Carolina, curtailed credit and demanded that state banknotes received by the Bank of the United States be redeemed in specie (precious metals). By doing so, Cheves rescued the Bank from the paper economy created by state-chartered banks, but at huge expense: When the state banks were forced to redeem their notes in specie, they demanded payment from their own borrowers, and the national money and credit system collapsed.

The depression that followed the Panic of 1819 was the first failure of the market economy. Local ups and downs had occurred since the 1790s, but this collapse was nationwide. Employers who could not meet their debts went out of business, and hundreds of thousands of workers lost their jobs. In Philadelphia, unemployment reached 75 percent. A tent city of the unemployed sprang up on the outskirts of Baltimore. Other cities and towns were hit as hard, and the situation was no better in the countryside. Thomas Jefferson reported that farms in his neighborhood were selling for what had earlier been a year's rent, and a single session of the county court at Nashville handled more than 500 lawsuits for debt.

Faced with a collapse that none could control and that few understood, many Americans directed their resentment onto the Bank of the United States. John Jacob Astor, a New York merchant and possibly the richest man in America at that time, admitted that "there has been too much Speculation and too much assumption of Power on the Part of the Bank Directors which has caused [sic] the institution to become unpopular." William Gouge, who would become the Jacksonian Democrats' favorite economist, put it more bluntly: When the Bank demanded that state banknotes be redeemed in specie, he said, "the Bank was saved and the people were ruined." By the end of 1819, the Bank of the United States had won the name that it would carry to its death in the 1830s: the Monster.

Republican Revival

The crises during 1819 and 1820 prompted demands for a return to Jeffersonian principles. President Monroe's happily proclaimed Era of Good Feelings—a new era of partyless politics created by the collapse of Federalism—was, according to worried Republicans, a disaster. Without opposition, Jefferson's dominant Republican Party had lost its way. The nationalist Congress of 1816 had enacted much of the Federalist program under the name of Republicanism; the result, said the old Republicans, was an aggressive government that helped bring on the Panic of 1819. At the same time, the collapse of Republican Party discipline in Congress had allowed the Missouri question to degenerate into a sectional free-for-all. By 1820, many Republicans were calling for a Jeffersonian revival that would limit government power and guarantee southern rights within the Union.

Martin Van Buren Leads the Way

The busiest and the most astute of those Republicans was Martin Van Buren, leader of New York's Bucktail Republican faction, who took his seat in the Senate in 1821. An immensely talented man with no influential family connections (his father was a Hudson valley tavern keeper) and little formal education, Van Buren had built his political career out of a commitment to Jeffersonian principles, personal charm, and party discipline. He and his colleagues in New York, deploying group discipline oiled by the partisan use of government patronage, had begun to invent the modern political party, arguing that it was a necessary weapon in democracy's contests with the well-placed, well-educated gentlemen who had monopolized public office. Arriving in Washington in the aftermath of the Missouri debates and the Panic of 1819, he hoped to apply his new politics to what he perceived as a dangerous turning point in national public life.

Van Buren's New York experience, along with his reading of national politics, told him that disciplined political parties were necessary democratic tools. The Founding Fathers had denounced parties, claiming that republics rested on civic virtue, not competition. Van Buren claimed that the Era of Good Feelings had turned public attention away from politics, allowing privileged insiders to create a big national state and to reorganize politics along sectional lines. Van Buren insisted that competition and party divisions were inevitable and good, but that they must be made to serve the republic. He wrote: "We must always have party distinctions, and the old ones are the best. . . . If the old ones are suppressed, geographical differences founded on local instincts or what is worse, prejudices between free & slave holding states will inevitably take their place." Working with like-minded politicians, Van Buren reconstructed the coalition of northern and southern agrarians that had elected Thomas Jefferson. The result was the Democratic Party and, ultimately, a national two-party system that persisted until the eve of the Civil War.

The Election of 1824

With the approach of the 1824 presidential election, Van Buren and his friends supported William H. Crawford, Monroe's secretary of war and a staunch Georgia Republican. The Van Burenites controlled the Republican **congressional caucus,** the body that traditionally chose the party's presidential candidates. The public distrusted the caucus as undemocratic because it represented the only party in government and thus could dictate the choice of a president. Van Buren, however, continued to regard it as a necessary tool of party discipline. With most congressmen fearing their constituents, only a minority showed up for the caucus vote. They dutifully nominated Crawford.

With Republican Party unity broken, the list of sectional candidates grew. John Quincy Adams was the son of a Federalist president, successful secretary of state under Monroe, and one of the northeastern Federalist converts to Republicanism who, according to people like Van Buren and Crawford, had blunted the republican thrust of Jefferson's old party. He entered the contest as New England's **favorite son.** Henry Clay of Kentucky, chief proponent of the American System, expected to carry the West. John C. Calhoun of South Carolina announced his candidacy, but when he saw the swarm of candidates, he dropped out and put himself up as the sole candidate for vice president.

The wild card was Andrew Jackson of Tennessee, who in 1824 was known only as a military hero—scourge of the southern Indians and victor over the British at New Orleans (see chapter 8). He was also a frontier nabob with a reputation for violence: He had killed a rival in a duel, had engaged in a shoot-out in a Nashville tavern, and had reputedly stolen his wife from her estranged husband. According to Jackson's detractors, such impetuosity marked his public life as well. As commander of U.S. military forces in the South in 1818, Jackson had led an unauthorized invasion of Spanish Florida, claiming that it was a hideout for Seminole warriors who raided into the United States and a sanctuary for runaway Georgia slaves. During the action, he had occupied Spanish forts, summarily executed Seminoles, and hanged two British subjects. Secretary of State John Quincy Adams had belatedly approved the raid, knowing that the show of American force would encourage the Spanish to sell Florida to the United States. Secretary of War Crawford, on the other hand, as an "economy" measure, had reduced the number of major generals in the U.S. Army from two to one, thus eliminating Jackson's job. After being appointed governor of newly acquired Florida in 1821, Jackson retired from public life later that year. In 1824, eastern politicians knew Jackson only as a "military chieftain," "the Napoleon of the woods," a frontier hothead, and, possibly, a robber-bridegroom.

Jackson may have been all of those things, but the easterners failed to recognize his immense popularity, particularly in the new states of the South and West. In the election of 1824, in the 16 states that chose presidential electors by popular vote (six states still left the choice to their legislatures), Jackson polled 152,901 votes to Adams's 114,023 and Clay's 47,217. Crawford, who suffered a crippling stroke during the campaign, won 46,979 votes. Jackson's support was not only larger but also more nearly national than that of his opponents. Adams carried only his native New England and a

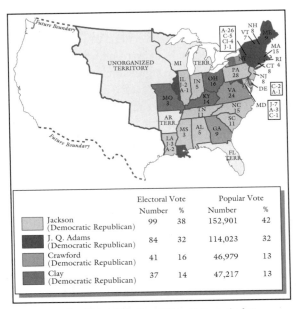

Map 11.1   Presidential Election, 1824   Voting in the four-cornered contest of 1824 was starkly sectional. John Quincy Adams carried his native New England, while Crawford and Clay carried only a few states in their own sections. Only Andrew Jackson enjoyed national support: He carried states in every section but New England, and he ran a strong second in many of the states that were awarded to other candidates.

portion of New York. Clay's meager support was limited to the Northwest, and Crawford's to the Southeast and to the portions of New York that Van Buren was able to deliver. Jackson carried 84 percent of the votes of his own Southwest, and won victories in Pennsylvania, New Jersey, North Carolina, Indiana, and Illinois, and ran a close second in several other states.

"A Corrupt Bargain"

Jackson assumed that he had won the election: He had received 42 percent of the popular vote to his nearest rival's 33 percent, and he was clearly the nation's choice, but his 99 electoral votes were 32 shy of the plurality demanded by the Constitution. And so, acting under the 12th Amendment, the House of Representatives selected a president from among the top three candidates. As the candidate with the fewest electoral votes, Henry Clay was eliminated, but he remained Speaker of the House and had enough support to throw the election to either Jackson or Adams. Years later, Jackson told a dinner guest that Clay had offered to support him in exchange for Clay's appointment as secretary of state—an office that traditionally led to the presidency. When Jackson turned him down, according to Jacksonian legend, Clay went to Adams and made the same offer. Adams accepted what became known as the **"Corrupt Bargain"** in January 1825. During the House vote, Clay's supporters, joined by several old Federalists, switched to Adams, giving him a one-vote victory. The new president appointed Henry Clay as his secretary of state.

Reaction to the alleged Corrupt Bargain dominated the Adams administration and created a rhetoric of intrigue and betrayal that nourished a rising democratic movement. Before the vote took place in the House of Representatives, Andrew Jackson predicted a "bargain & sale" of the presidency. Afterward, Jackson declared that "the rights of the people have been bartered for promises of office." "So you see," Jackson said, "the *Judas* of the West has closed the contract and will receive the thirty pieces of silver. His end will be the same." Others in Washington were equally appalled. Robert Y. Hayne of South Carolina denounced the "monstrous union between Clay & Adams," and Louis McLane of Delaware declared the coalition of Clay and Adams utterly "unnatural & preposterous." Eventually, Clay challenged Virginia Senator John Randolph, one of his nastiest critics, to a duel. Clay's shot passed harmlessly

Library of Congress, Prints and Photographs Division

"The Symptoms of a Locked Jaw" In 1827, Henry Clay published a rebuttal of Jacksonian charges that he had participated in a Corrupt Bargain to deliver the presidency to John Quincy Adams. Here, a pro-Clay cartoonist displays Clay as a tailor in the act of sewing Andrew Jackson's mouth shut. Neither the rebuttal nor the cartoon worked: the long-term suspicions of the bargain with Adams ruined Clay's chances to become president.

through Randolph's flowing coat, and Randolph fired a gentlemanly shot into the air. But the charge of corruption would follow Clay for the rest of his political life.

Jacksonian Melodrama

Andrew Jackson regarded the intrigues that robbed him of the presidency in 1825 as the culmination of a long train of corruption that the nation had suffered over the previous 10 years. Although in the campaign he had made only vague policy statements, he had firm ideas of what had gone wrong with the republic. In 1821, after having been "betrayed" by members of Monroe's cabinet over his raid into Florida, Jackson had retired to his plantation near Nashville to ponder the state of the nation and fill page after page with what he called "memorandums." (This was the kind of gaffe that appalled his educated eastern opponents and pleased nearly everyone else.)

A frontier planter with a deep distrust of banks, Jackson claimed that the Panic of 1819 had been brought on by self-serving miscreants in the Bank of the United States. He insisted that the national debt was another source of corruption; it must be paid off and never allowed to recur. The federal government under James Monroe was filled with swindlers, and in the name of a vague nationalism they were taking power for themselves and scheming against the liberties of the people. The politicians had been bought off, said Jackson, and had attempted—through "King Caucus"—to select a president by backstairs deals rather than by popular election. Finally, in 1825, they had stolen the presidency outright.

Like hundreds of thousands of other Americans, Jackson sensed that something had gone wrong with the republic—that selfishness and intrigue had corrupted the government. In the language of revolutionary republicanism, which Jackson had learned as a boy in the Carolina backwoods and would speak throughout his life, a corrupt power once again threatened to snuff out liberty.

In his memorandums, Jackson set against the designs of that power the classic republican safeguard: a virtuous citizenry. Unlike most of his revolutionary forebears, however, he believed that government should follow the will of popular majorities. An aroused public, he said, was the republic's best hope: "My fervent prayers are that our republican government may be perpetual, and the people alone by their virtue, and independent exercise of their free suffrage can make it perpetual."

More completely than any of his rivals, Jackson had captured the rhetoric of the revolutionary republic. And, with his fixation on secrecy, corruption, and intrigues, he transformed both that rhetoric and his own biography into popular melodrama. Finally, with a political alchemy that his rivals never understood, Jackson submerged old notions of republican citizenship into a firm faith in majoritarian democracy: Individuals might become selfish and corrupt, he believed, but a democratic majority was, by its very nature, opposed to corruption and governmental excess. Thus the republic was safe only when governed by the will of the majority. The Corrupt Bargain of 1825 had made that clear: Either the people or political schemers would rule.

Adams *versus* Jackson

While Jackson plotted revenge, John Quincy Adams assumed the duties of the presidency. He was well prepared. The son of a Federalist president, he had been an extraordinarily successful secretary of state under Monroe, guiding American diplomacy in the postwar world.

Nationalism in an International Arena

In the Rush-Bagot Treaty of 1817 and the British-American Convention of 1818, Secretary of State John Quincy Adams helped pacify the Great Lakes, restore American fishing rights off the coast of Canada, and draw the U.S.–Canadian boundary west to the Rocky Mountains—actions that transformed the Canadian–American frontier from a battleground into the peaceful border that it has been ever since. He pacified the southern border as well. In 1819, following Jackson's raid into Florida, the Adams-Onis Treaty procured Florida for the United States and defined the U.S.–Spanish border west of the Mississippi in ways that gave the Americans claims to the Pacific Coast in the Northwest.

Trickier problems had arisen when Spanish colonies in the Americas declared their independence. Spain could not prevent this, and the powers of Europe, victorious over Napoleon and determined to roll back the republican revolution, talked openly of helping Spain or of annexing South American territory for themselves. Both the Americans and the British opposed such a move, and the British proposed a joint statement outlawing the interference of any outside power (including themselves) in Latin America. Adams had thought it better for the United States to make its own policy than to "come in as cockboat in the wake of the British man-of-war." In 1823, he wrote what became known as the **Monroe Doctrine.** Propounded at the same time that the United States recognized the new Latin American republics, it declared American opposition to any European attempt at colonization in the New World without (as the British had wanted) denying the right of the United States to annex new territory. Although the international community knew that the British navy, and not the Monroe Doctrine, kept the European powers out of the Americas, Adams had announced that the United States was determined to become the preeminent power in the Western Hemisphere.

Nationalism at Home

As president, Adams tried to translate his fervent nationalism into domestic policy. Although the brilliant, genteel Adams had dealt smoothly with European diplomats, as president of a democratic republic he went out of his way to isolate himself and to offend popular democracy. In his first annual message to Congress, Adams outlined an ambitious program for national development under the auspices of the federal government: roads, canals, a national university, a national astronomical observatory ("lighthouses of the skies"), and other costly initiatives:

> The spirit of improvement is abroad upon the earth. . . . While foreign nations less blessed with . . . freedom . . . than ourselves are advancing with gigantic strides in the career of

public improvement, were we to slumber in indolence or fold up our arms and proclaim to the world that we are palsied by the will of our constituents, would it not . . . doom ourselves to perpetual inferiority?

Congressmen could not believe their ears. Here was a president who had received only one in three votes and who had entered office accused of intrigues against the democratic will. And yet at the first opportunity he was telling Congress to pass an ambitious program and not to be "palsied" by the will of the electorate. Even the many members of Congress who favored Adams's program were afraid to vote for it.

Adding to his reputation as an enemy of democracy whenever opportunity presented itself, Adams heaped popular suspicions not only on himself but on his program as well. Hostile politicians and journalists never tired of joking about Adams's "lighthouses to the skies." More lasting, however, was the connection they drew between federal public works projects and high taxes, intrusive government, the denial of democratic majorities, and expanded opportunities for corruption, secret deals, and special favors. Congress never acted on the president's proposals, and the Adams administration emerged as little more than a long prelude to the election of 1828.

The Birth of the Democratic Party

As early as 1825, it was clear that the election of 1828 would pit Adams against Andrew Jackson. Van Buren and like-minded Republicans (with their candidate Crawford hopelessly incapacitated) switched their allegiance to Jackson. They wanted Jackson elected, however, not only as a popular hero but as head of a disciplined and committed Democratic Party that would continue the states'-rights, limited-government positions of the old Jeffersonian Republicans.

The new Democratic Party linked popular democracy with the defense of southern slavery. Van Buren began preparations for 1828 with a visit to John C. Calhoun of South Carolina. Calhoun was moving along the road from postwar nationalism to states'-rights conservatism. He also wanted to stay on as vice president and thus keep his presidential hopes alive. After convincing Calhoun to support Jackson, Van Buren wrote to Thomas Ritchie, editor of the *Enquirer* and leader of Virginia's Republicans. Ritchie could deliver Crawford's southern supporters to Jackson. In his letter, Van Buren proposed to revive the alliance of "the planters of the South and the plain Republicans of the North" that had won Jefferson the presidency. Reminding Ritchie of how one-party government had allowed the Missouri question to get out of hand, Van Buren insisted that "if the old [party loyalties] are suppressed, prejudices between free and slave holding states will inevitably take their place."

Thus a new Democratic Party, committed to an agrarian program of states' rights and minimal government and dependent on the votes of both slaveholding and nonslaveholding states (beginning, much like Jefferson's old party, with Van Buren's New York and Ritchie's Virginia), would ensure democracy, the continuation of slavery, and the preservation of the Union. The alternative, Van Buren firmly believed, was an expensive and invasive national state (Adams's "lighthouses to the skies"), the isolation of the slaveholding South, and thus mortal danger to the republic.

The Election of 1828

The presidential campaign of 1828 was an exercise in slander rather than a debate on public issues. Adhering to custom, neither Adams nor Jackson campaigned directly, but their henchmen viciously personalized the campaign. Jacksonians hammered away at the Corrupt Bargain of 1825, while the Adams forces attacked Jackson's character. They reminded voters of his duels and tavern brawls and circulated a "coffin handbill" describing Jackson's execution of militiamen during the Creek War. One of Henry Clay's newspaper friends circulated the rumor that Jackson was a bastard and that his mother was a prostitute, but the most egregious slander of the campaign centered on Andrew Jackson's marriage. In 1790, Jackson had married Rachel Donelson, probably aware that she was estranged but not formally divorced from a man named Robards. Branding the marriage an "abduction," the Adams team screamed that Jackson had "torn from a husband the wife of his bosom," and had lived with her in a state of "open and notorious lewdness." They branded Rachel Jackson (now a deeply pious plantation housewife) an "American Jezebel," a "profligate woman," and a "convicted adulteress" whose ungoverned passions made her unfit to be First Lady of a "Christian nation."

   The Adams strategy backfired. Many voters did agree that only a man who strictly obeyed the law was fit to be president and that Jackson's "passionate" nature disqualified him, but many others criticized Adams for making Jackson's private life a public issue. Some claimed that Adams's rigid legalism left no room for privacy or for local notions of justice. Whatever the legality of their marriage, Andrew and Rachel Jackson had lived as models of marital fidelity for nearly 40 years. Their neighbors had long ago forgiven whatever transgressions they may have committed. Thus, on the one hand, Jackson's supporters accused the Adams campaign of a gross violation of privacy and honor. On the other, they defended Jackson's marriage—and his duels, brawls, executions, and unauthorized military forays—as a triumph of what was right and just over what was narrowly legal. The attempt to brand Jackson as a lawless man, in fact, enhanced his image as a melodramatic hero who battled shrewd, unscrupulous, legalistic enemies by drawing on his natural nobility and force of will.

   The campaign caught the public imagination. Voter turnout was double what it had been in 1824, totaling 56.3 percent. Jackson won the election with 56 percent of the popular vote (a landslide unmatched until the 20th century) and with a margin of 178 to 83 in electoral votes. Adams carried New England, Delaware, and most of Maryland, and took 16 of New York's 36 electoral votes. Jackson carried every other state. It was a clear triumph of democracy over genteel statesmanship, of limited government over expansive nationalism, and of the South and the West over New England. Just as clearly, it was a victory of popular melodrama over old forms of cultural gentility.

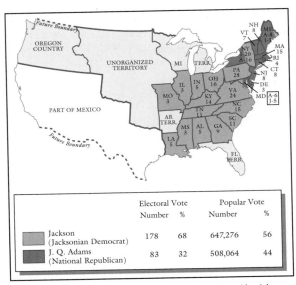

	Electoral Vote		Popular Vote	
	Number	%	Number	%
Jackson (Jacksonian Democrat)	178	68	647,276	56
J. Q. Adams (National Republican)	83	32	508,064	44

Map 11.2 Presidential Election, 1828 The 1828 presidential contest was a clear result of the organizing efforts that were building a national Democratic party under the name of Andrew Jackson. Jackson picked up all of the states that had gone for Crawford or Clay in 1824, leaving only New England and small portions of the mid-Atlantic for John Quincy Adams.

A People's Inauguration

Newspapers estimated that from 15,000 to 20,000 citizens (Duff Green's *United States Telegraph,* a Jackson paper, claimed 30,000) came to Washington to witness Jackson's inauguration on March 4, 1829. They were "like the inundation of the northern barbarians into Rome," remarked Senator Daniel Webster. Many had traveled as much as 500 miles, and "they really seem to think that the country is rescued from some dreadful danger." As members of the Washington establishment watched uneasily, the crowd filled the open spaces and the streets near the east portico of the Capitol Building, where Jackson was to deliver his inaugural address.

Jackson arrived at the Capitol in deep mourning. In December, his wife Rachel had gone to Nashville to shop and had stopped to rest in a newspaper office. There, for the first time, she read the accusations that had been made against her. She fainted on the spot. Although she had been in poor health, no one would ever convince Jackson that her death in January was not caused by his political enemies. As he arrived to assume the presidency, he wore a black suit and black tie, a black armband, and a black hatband that trailed down his neck in what was called a weeper.

Jackson's inaugural address was vague. He promised "proper respect" for states' rights and a "spirit of equity, caution, and compromise" on the question of the tariff, which was beginning to cause sectional controversy. He promised to reform the civil service by replacing "unfaithful or incompetent" officers, and he vowed to retire the national debt through "a strict and faithful economy." Beyond that, he said little, although he took every opportunity to flatter the popular majority. He had been elected "by the choice of a free people" (and not by King Caucus or Corrupt Bargains), and he pledged "the zealous dedication of my humble abilities to their service and their good." He finished—as he often finished an important statement—by reminding Americans that a benign providence looked over them. He then looked up to a roar of applause.

The new president traveled slowly from the Capitol to the White House, with the throng following. Soon Jackson's well-wishers were ranging through the mansion, muddying the carpets, tipping things over, breaking dishes, and standing in dirty boots on upholstered chairs. Jackson had to retreat to avoid being crushed. The White House staff lured much of the crowd outside by moving the punch bowls and liquor to the lawn. A wealthy Washington matron who had admired the well-behaved crowd at the inaugural address exclaimed, "What a scene did we witness! *The Majesty of the People* had disappeared, and a rabble, a mob, of boys, negros, women, children, scrambling, fighting, romping. What a pity, what a pity." Another guest pronounced the occasion a "Saturnalia . . . of mud and filth." A Democratic newspaper reported more favorably: "General Jackson is *their own* President. . . . He was greeted by them with an enthusiasm which bespoke him the Hero of a popular triumph."

The Spoils System

Jackson had begun to assemble his administration months before he took office. Martin Van Buren, who had mobilized much of the support Jackson gained between 1824 and 1828, was the new secretary of state—positioned to succeed Jackson as president. He became Jackson's most valued adviser. Other appointments were less promising, for Jackson filled cabinet posts with old friends and political supporters who, in many cases, proved unfit for their jobs. A critic looked at Jackson's cabinet and pronounced it—with the exception of Van Buren— "the Millennium of the Minnows."

Others were more concerned about what Jackson would do to the civil service than about whom he named to his cabinet. During the campaign, Jackson had vowed to fire corrupt officeholders—a term he applied to grafters, incompetents, long-term officeholders who considered their jobs personal property, and those who supported John Quincy Adams. Opponents soon complained that Jackson was replacing able, educated, patriotic public servants with political hacks. They soon had convincing evidence: Samuel Swarthout, whom Jackson had appointed collector of the Port of New York (an office that handled $15 million in tariff revenue annually), stole $1.2 million and took off for Europe.

Actually, much of the furor over Jackson's **"spoils system"** was overwrought and misdirected. He aimed, Jackson claimed, only to institute "rotation in office" and to eject officeholders who expected to hold lifetime appointments. Arguing that government jobs could be performed by any honest, reasonably intelligent citizen, Jackson proposed ending the long tenures that, he said, turned the civil service into "support of the few at the expense of the many." Jackson removed about 1 in 10 executive appointees during his eight years in office, and his replacements (at least at the level of ambassadors, federal judges and attorneys, and cabinet members) were as wealthy and well-educated as their predecessors. They were, however, most decidedly *political* appointees. Acting out of his own need for personal loyalty and on the advice of Van Buren and other architects of the Democratic Party, Jackson filled vacancies—down to postmasters in the smallest towns— with Democrats who had worked for his election.

Jackson sought Van Buren's advice on appointments. Van Buren knew the political value of dispensing government jobs; one of his henchmen coined the phrase "To the victor belongs the spoils." In resorting to patronage to build the party, however, Jackson gave his opponents an important issue. Revolutionary republicans feared a government of lackeys dependent on a powerful executive, and congressional opponents argued that Jackson was using appointments to "convert the entire body of those in office into corrupt and supple instruments of power." "A standing army," railed Henry Clay in the Senate, "has been, in all free countries, a just object of jealousy and suspicion. But is not a corps of one hundred thousand dependents upon government, actuated by one spirit, obeying one will, and aiming at one end, more dangerous than a standing army?" It became an anti-Jacksonian axiom that Jackson had made the federal civil service an arm of the Democratic Party and of despotic executive power.

Jacksonian Democracy and the South

Focus Question
At the national level, how did Jacksonian Democrats and their rivals deal with widening differences between North and South during these years?

Andrew Jackson was a national figure, but his base of support was in the South, where he won 8 of every 10 votes in 1828. Southerners had grown wary of an activist government in which they were in the minority. They looked to Jackson not only as a military hero but also as a Tennessee planter who talked about returning to republican fundamentals. Although southerners expected Jackson to look after southern interests, disagreement arose within the administration about how those interests should be protected. Some sided with Vice President Calhoun, who believed that any state had the right to veto federal legislation and even in extreme cases to secede from the Union. Others agreed with Secretary of State Van Buren that the Union was inviolable and that the South's best safeguard was in a political party committed to states' rights within the Union. The differences were

HISTORY THROUGH FILM

AMISTAD (1997)

Directed by Steven Spielberg. Starring Matthew McConaughey (Roger Baldwin), Morgan Freeman (Theodore Joadson), Anthony Hopkins (John Quincy Adams), Djimon Hounsou (Cinque).

In 1839, an American cruiser seized the Cuban slave ship *Amistad* off the shore of Long Island. The ship carried 41 Africans who had revolted, killed the captain and crew, and commandeered the ship—along with two Spanish slave dealers who bargained for their lives by promising to sail the ship east to Africa, then steered for North America. The Africans were imprisoned at New Haven and tried for piracy and murder in federal court. The government of Spain demanded their return, and southern leaders pressured President Van Buren for a "friendly" decision. The legal case centered on whether the Africans were Cuban slaves or kidnapped Africans. (The international slave trade was by then illegal.) The New Haven court acquitted them, the federal government appealed the case, and the Supreme Court freed them again. The Africans were returned to Sierra Leone.

The Africans spend most of the movie in a dark jail or in court, and the film centers on them and their experiences with two groups of Americans: the abolitionists who are trying to free them, and the political and legal officials who want to hang them—largely to keep their own political system intact. Spielberg's abolitionists are Lewis Tappan, a black activist (Morgan Freeman), an obscure young white lawyer (Matthew McConaughey), and, in the grand finale, Congressman and former President John Quincy Adams (played wonderfully by Anthony Hopkins). In the historical case, the defense was handled by veteran abolitionists or by persons who had been working with abolitionists for a long time. Spielberg shaped this group to tell his own story, beginning with reluctant and confused reformers and politicians who, along with the audience, gradually realize the moral imperatives of the case.

In one of the film's more powerful sequences, the Africans' leader, Cinque (Djimon Hounsou), through a translator, tells his story to the lawyer: his village life in Sierra Leone (the one scene filmed in bright sunlight), his capture by Africans, his transportation to the slave fort of Lomboko, the horrors of the passage on the Portuguese slaver *Tecora*, the slave market in Havana, and the bloody revolt on the *Amistad*—all of it portrayed wrenchingly on the screen. The Africans' story continues in jail, as they study pictures in a Bible and try to figure out the American legal, political, and moral system. In court, they finally cut through the mumbo-jumbo by standing and chanting "Give Us Free!"

In a fictive interview on the eve of the Supreme Court case, Cinque tells Adams that he is optimistic because he has called on the spirits of his ancestors to join him in court. This moment, he says, is the whole reason for their having existed at all. Adams, whose own father had helped lead the Revolution, speaks for his and Cinque's ancestors before the Supreme Court: to the prosecution's argument that the Africans are pirates and murderers and to southern arguments that slavery is a natural state, he answers that America is founded on the "self-evident truth" that the one natural state is freedom. It is a fine Hollywood courtroom speech: Adams has honored his ancestors, the justices and the audience see the moral rightness of his case, and the Africans are returned to Sierra Leone. (In a subscript, Spielberg tells us that Cinque returns to a village that had been destroyed in civil war, but the final ironic note is overwhelmed by the moral triumphalism of the rest of the movie.)

Amistad (1997) tells the story of 41 Africans who stage a revolt on the slave ship carrying them to Cuba and the trial that follows.

fought out in the contest between Calhoun and Van Buren for the right to succeed Jackson as president, a contest that shaped every major issue of Jackson's first term.

Southerners and Indians

When Jackson entered office, a final crisis between frontier whites and the native peoples of the eastern woodlands was under way. By the 1820s, few Native Americans were left east of the Appalachians. The Iroquois of New York were penned into tiny reservations, and the tribes of the Old Northwest were broken and scattered. But in the Old Southwest, 60,000 Cherokees, Creeks, Choctaws, Chickasaws, and Seminoles were still living on their ancestral lands, with tenure guaranteed by federal treaties that (at least implicitly) recognized them as sovereign peoples. Congress had appropriated funds for schools, tools, seeds, and training to help these Civilized Tribes make the transition to farming. Most government officials assumed that the tribes would eventually trade their old lands and use their farming skills on new land west of the Mississippi.

Southwestern whites resented federal Indian policy as an affront to both white democracy and states' rights. The poorer farmers coveted the Indians' land, and states'-rights southerners denied that the federal government had the authority to make treaties or to recognize sovereign peoples within their states. Resistance centered in Georgia, where Governor George Troup brought native lands under the state's jurisdiction and then turned them over to poor whites by way of lotteries, thus tying states' rights to white hunger for Indian land. At one point, Troup sent state surveyors onto Creek territory before federal purchase from the Indians was complete, telling President Adams that if he resisted state authority he would be considered a "public enemy."

The Cherokees in Georgia pressed the issue in 1827 by declaring themselves a republic with its own constitution, government, courts, and police. The Georgia legislature promptly declared Cherokee law null and void, extended Georgia's authority into Cherokee country, and began surveying the lands for sale. Hinting at the old connection between state sovereignty and the protection of slavery, Governor Troup warned that the federal "jurisdiction claimed over one portion of our population may very soon be asserted over *another*." Alabama and Mississippi quickly followed Georgia's lead by extending state authority over Indian lands and denying federal jurisdiction.

Indian Removal

President Jackson agreed that the federal government lacked the authority to recognize native sovereignty within a state and declared that he could not protect the Cherokees and the other Civilized Tribes from state governments. Instead, he offered to remove them to federal land west of the Mississippi, where they would be under the authority of the benevolent federal government. Congress made that offer official in the **Indian Removal Act** of 1830.

The Cherokees, with the help of New England missionaries, had taken their claims of sovereignty to court in the late 1820s. In 1830, John Marshall's Supreme Court ruled in

Cherokee Nation v. *Georgia* that the Cherokees could not sue Georgia because they were not a sovereign people but "domestic dependent nations," thus dependents of the federal government, and not of the state of Georgia, although somehow "nations" as well. The Court's decision in *Worcester* v. *Georgia* (1832) declared that Georgia's extension of state law over Cherokee land was unconstitutional. President Jackson ignored the decision, however, reportedly telling a congressman, "John Marshall has made his decision: *now let him enforce it!*" In the end, Jackson sat back as the southwestern states encroached on the Civilized Tribes. In 1838, his successor, Martin Van Buren, sent the army to march the 18,000 remaining Cherokee to Oklahoma. Four thousand of them died along this Trail of Tears of exposure, disease, starvation, and white depredation.

Indian removal had profound political consequences. It violated Supreme Court decisions and thus strengthened Jackson's reputation as an enemy of the rule of law and a friend of local, "democratic" solutions. At the same time, it reaffirmed the link between racism and white democracy in the South and announced Jackson's commitment to state sovereignty and limited federal authority.

Southerners and the Tariff

In 1828, the Democratic Congress, acting under the direction of Van Buren and his congressional sidekick Silas Wright, set about writing a tariff that would win votes for Jackson

Trail of Tears In 1838, the U.S. Army marched 18,000 Cherokee men, women, and children, along with their animals and whatever they could carry, out of their home territory and into Oklahoma. At least 4,000—most of them old or very young— died during the march.

Woolaroc Museum

in the upcoming presidential election. Assured of support in the South, the creators of the tariff bill fished for votes in the mid-Atlantic states and in the Old Northwest by including protective levies on raw wool, flax, molasses, hemp, and distilled spirits. The result was a patchwork tariff that pleased northern and western farmers but that worried the South and violated Jackson's own ideas of what a "judicious" tariff should be. Protective tariffs hurt the South by diminishing exports of cotton and other staples and by raising the price of manufactured goods. More ominous, they demonstrated the power of other sections to write laws that helped them and hurt the outnumbered South—a power, as southerners constantly reminded themselves, that might someday be used to attack slavery. Calling the new bill a Tariff of Abominations, the legislature of one southern state after another denounced it as (this was Virginia's formulation) "unconstitutional, unwise, unjust, unequal, and oppressive."

South Carolina, guided by Vice President Calhoun, took the lead in opposing the Tariff of 1828. During the War of 1812 and the ensuing Era of Good Feelings, Calhoun's South Carolina—confident of its future and deeply engaged in international markets for its rice and cotton—had favored the economic nationalism of the American System, but the Missouri debates had sent Carolinians looking for ways to safeguard slavery. The Denmark Vesey slave conspiracy of 1822 (see chapter 9) had stirred fears among the outnumbered whites of coastal South Carolina. Their fears grew more intense when federal courts shot down a state law forbidding black merchant seamen from moving about freely while their ships were docked at Charleston. Carolinians were disturbed too by persistent talk of gradual emancipation—at a time when their own commitment to slavery was growing stronger. Finally, southerners noted that in the congressional logrolling that made the Tariff of 1828, many western representatives had abandoned their old Jeffersonian alliance with the South to trade favors with the Northeast.

With the growth in the Northeast of urban markets for western produce, the American System's promise of interdependence among regions was beginning to work, but in ways that united the Northwest and Northeast against the export-oriented South. The Tariff of 1828 was the last straw: It benefited the city and commercial food producers at the expense of the plantation, and it demonstrated that the South could do nothing to block the passage of such laws.

Nullification

As early as 1827, Calhoun concluded that southern states could protect themselves from national majorities only if they possessed the power to veto federal legislation within their boundaries. In 1828, in his anonymously published essay *Exposition and Protest*, he argued that the Constitution was a compact between sovereign states and that the states (not the federal courts) could decide the constitutionality of federal laws. A state convention (like the conventions that had ratified the Constitution) could nullify any federal law within state borders. "Constitutional government and the government of a majority," Calhoun argued, "are utterly incompatible." *Exposition and Protest* echoed the Virginia and Kentucky

Resolves of 1798 and 1799 and anticipated the secessionist arguments of 1861: The Union was a voluntary compact between sovereign states, states were the ultimate judges of the validity of federal law, and states could break the compact if they wished.

Nullification was extreme, and Calhoun and his friends tried to avoid using it. They knew that President Jackson was a states'-rights slaveholder who disliked the Tariff of 1828, and they assumed that Vice President Calhoun would succeed to the presidency and would protect southern interests. They were wrong on both counts. Jackson favored states' rights, but only within a perpetual and inviolable Union. His Indian policy, which had emboldened some southerners, was simply an acknowledgment of state jurisdiction over institutions within state boundaries. A tariff, on the other hand, was ultimately a matter of foreign policy, clearly within the jurisdiction of the federal government. To allow a state to veto a tariff would be to deny the legal existence of the United States.

Jackson revealed his views at a celebration of Jefferson's birthday on April 13, 1830. Calhoun's southern friends dominated the speechmaking, and Jackson listened quietly as speaker after speaker defended the extreme states'-rights position. After the formal speeches were over, the president rose to propose an after-dinner toast: "Our Federal Union," he said, *"It must be preserved."* Isaac Hill, a New Hampshire Democrat and a supporter of Van Buren, reported that "an order to arrest Calhoun where he sat would not have come with more blinding, staggering force." Dumb-struck, the southerners looked to Calhoun, who as vice president was to propose the second toast. Obviously shaken by Jackson's unqualified defense of the Union, Calhoun offered this toast: "The Union. Next to our liberties the most dear." They were strong words, but they had little meaning after Jackson's affirmation of the Union. A few days later, a South Carolina congressman on his way home asked the president if he had any message for him to take back. "Yes, I have," replied Jackson. "Please give my compliments to my friends in your state, and say to them, that if a single drop of blood shall be shed there in opposition to the laws of the United States, I will hang the first man I can lay my hand on engaged in such treasonable conduct, upon the first tree I can reach."

Having reaffirmed the Union and rejected nullification, Jackson asked Congress to reduce the tariff rates in the hope that he could isolate the nullifiers from southerners who simply hated the tariff. The resulting Tariff of 1832 lowered the rates on many items but still affirmed the principle of protectionism. That, along with the Boston abolitionist William Lloyd Garrison's declaration of war on slavery in 1831, followed by Nat Turner's bloody slave uprising in Virginia that same year (see chapter 9), led the whites of South Carolina and Georgia to intensify their distrust of outside authority and their insistence on the right to govern their own neighborhoods. South Carolina, now with Calhoun's open leadership and support, called a state convention that nullified the Tariffs of 1828 and 1832.

In Washington, President Jackson raged that nullification (not to mention the right of secession that followed logically from it) was illegal. Insisting that "Disunion . . . is *treason*," he asked Congress for a Force Bill empowering him to personally lead a federal army into South Carolina. At the same time, however, he supported the rapid reduction of tariffs.

When Democratic attempts at reduction bogged down, Henry Clay, who was now back in the Senate, took on the tricky legislative task of rescuing his beloved protective tariff while quieting southern fears. The result was the Compromise Tariff of 1833, which by lowering tariffs over the course of several years, gave southern planters the relief they demanded while maintaining moderate protectionism and allowing northern manufacturers time to adjust to the lower rates. Congress also passed the Force Bill. Jackson signed both into law on March 2, 1833.

With that, the nullification crisis came to a quiet end. No other southern state had joined South Carolina in nullifying the tariff, although some states had made vague pledges of support in the event that Jackson led his army to Charleston. The Compromise Tariff of 1833 isolated the South Carolina nullifiers. Deprived of their issue and most of their support, they declared victory and disbanded their convention, but not before nullifying the Force Bill. Jackson chose to overlook that last defiant gesture because he had accomplished what he wanted: He had asserted a perpetual Union, and he had protected southern interests within it.

The "Petticoat Wars"

The spoils system, Indian removal, nullification, and other heated questions of Jackson's first term were fought out against a backdrop of gossip, intrigue, and angry division within the inner circles of Jackson's government. The talk centered on Peggy O'Neal Timberlake, a Washington tavern keeper's daughter who, in January 1829, had married John Henry Eaton, Jackson's old friend and soon to be his secretary of war. Eaton was middle-aged; his bride was 29, pretty, flirtatious, and, according to Washington gossip, "frivolous, wayward, [and] passionate." Knowing that his marriage might cause trouble for the new administration, Eaton had asked for and received Jackson's blessings—and, by strong implication, his protection.

The marriage of John and Peggy Eaton came at a turning point in the history of both Washington society and elite sexual mores. Until the 1820s, most officeholders had left their families at home. They took lodgings at taverns and boardinghouses and lived in a bachelor world of shirtsleeves, tobacco, card-playing, and occasional liaisons with local women. But in the 1820s, the boardinghouse world was giving way to high society. Cabinet members, senators, congressmen, and other officials moved into Washington houses, and their wives presided over the round of dinner parties through which much of the government's business was done. As in other wealthy families, political wives imposed new forms of gentility and politeness on these affairs, and they assumed the responsibility of drawing up the guest lists. Many of them determined to exclude Peggy Eaton from polite society.

The shunning of Peggy Eaton split the Jackson administration in half. Jackson was committed to protect her. He had met his own beloved Rachel while boarding at her father's Nashville tavern, and their grand romance (as well as the gossip that surrounded it) was a striking parallel to the affair of John and Peggy Eaton. That, coupled with Jackson's honor-bound agreement to the Eaton marriage, ensured that he would protect the Eatons to the

An Opposition Cartoon on the Cabinet Shuffle of 1831 The cabinet rats run from the falling house of government, while a bewildered Jackson retains Van Buren by standing on his tail.

bitter end. Always suspicious of intrigues, Jackson labeled the "dark and sly insinuations" about Peggy Eaton part of a "conspiracy" against his presidency. Jackson noted that the rumor-mongers were not only politicians' wives but also prominent clergymen. Most prominent among the latter was Ezra Styles Ely of Philadelphia, who had recently called for an evangelical "Christian Party in politics." Jackson blamed the conspiracy on "females with clergymen at their head."

In fact, Mrs. Eaton's tormentors included most of the cabinet members as well as Jackson's own White House "family." Widowed and without children, Jackson had invited his nephew and private secretary, Andrew Jackson Donelson, along with his wife and her sister, to live in the White House. Donelson's wife, serving as official hostess, shunned Peggy Eaton. Jackson valued domestic harmony and personal loyalty. He assumed that schemers had invaded and subverted his own household. Before long, his suspicions centered on Vice President Calhoun, whose wife, Floride Bonneau Calhoun, a powerful Washington matron, was a leader of the assault on Peggy Eaton. Only Secretary of State Van Buren, a widower and an eminently decent man, included the Eatons in official functions. Sensing that Jackson was losing his patience with Calhoun, Van Buren's friends, soon after the Jefferson birthday banquet in spring 1830, showed Jackson a letter from William H. Crawford revealing that while serving in Monroe's cabinet, Calhoun, contrary to his protestations, had favored censuring Jackson for his unauthorized invasion of Florida in 1818. An open break with Calhoun became inevitable.

The Fall of Calhoun

Jackson resolved the Peggy Eaton controversy, as he would resolve nullification, in ways that favored Van Buren in his contest with Calhoun. He sent Donelson, his wife, and his sister-in-law back to Tennessee and invited his friend W. B. Lewis and his daughter to take their place, but he pointedly made Peggy Eaton the official hostess at the White House. In spring 1831, Van Buren gave Jackson a free hand to reconstruct his tangled administration. He offered to resign his cabinet post and engineered the resignations of nearly all other members of the cabinet, thus allowing Jackson to remake his administration without firing anyone. Many of those who left were southern supporters of Calhoun. Jackson replaced them with a mixed cabinet that included political allies of Van Buren. Also at this time, President Jackson began to consult with an informal Kitchen Cabinet that included journalists Amos Kendall and Francis Preston Blair, along with Van Buren and a few others. The Peggy Eaton controversy and the resulting shakeup in the administration were contributing mightily to the success of Van Buren's southern strategy.

Van Buren's victory over Calhoun came to a quick conclusion. As part of his cabinet reorganization, Jackson appointed Van Buren minister to Great Britain—an important post that would remove him from the heat of Washington politics. Vice President Calhoun, sitting as president of the Senate, rigged the confirmation so that he cast the deciding vote against Van Buren's appointment—a petty act that turned out to be his last exercise of national power. Jackson replaced Calhoun with Van Buren as the vice presidential candidate in 1832 and let it be known that he wanted Van Buren to succeed him as president.

Petitions, the Gag Rule, and the Southern Mails

Van Buren and other architects of the Democratic Party promised to protect slavery with a disciplined national coalition committed to states' rights within an inviolable Union. The rise of a northern antislavery movement (see chapter 12) posed a direct challenge to that formulation. Middle-class evangelicals, who were emerging as the reformist core of the northern Whig Party, had learned early on that Jacksonian Democrats wanted to keep moral issues out of politics. In 1828 and 1829, when they petitioned the government to stop movement of the mail on Sundays, Jackson had turned them down. They next petitioned the government for humane treatment of the Civilized Tribes, whose conversion to Christianity had been accomplished largely by New England missionaries; again, the Jackson administration had refused. Northern evangelicals suspected Jackson of immorality, and they were appalled by his defense of Peggy Eaton and his attack on gentlewomen and preachers. Most of all, reformist evangelicals disliked the Democrats' rigid party discipline, which in each case had kept questions of morality from shaping politics.

In the early 1830s, a radical minority of evangelicals formed societies committed to the immediate abolition of slavery, and they devised ways of making the national government confront the slavery question. In 1835, abolitionists launched a "postal campaign," flooding the mail—both North and South—with antislavery tracts that southerners and most northerners considered incendiary. From 1836 onward, they bombarded Congress with petitions, most of them for the abolition of slavery and the slave trade in the District of Columbia (where Congress had undisputed jurisdiction), others against the interstate slave trade, slavery in the federal territories, and the admission of new slave states.

Some Jacksonians, including Jackson, wanted to stop the postal campaign with a federal censorship law. Calhoun and other southerners, however, argued that the states had the right to censor mail crossing their borders. Knowing that state censorship of the mail was unconstitutional and that federal censorship of the mail would be a political disaster, Amos Kendall, a Van Burenite who had become postmaster general in the cabinet shuffle, proposed an informal solution. Without changing the law, he would simply look the other way as local postmasters removed abolitionist materials from the mail. Almost all such materials were published in New York City and mailed from there. The New York postmaster, a loyal appointee, proceeded to sift them out of the mail and thus cut off the postal campaign at its source. The few tracts that made it to the South were destroyed by local postmasters. Calhoun and his supporters continued to demand state censorship, but the Democrats had no intention of relinquishing federal control over the federal mail. They made it clear, however, that no abolitionist literature would reach the South as long as Democrats controlled the U.S. Post Office.

The Democrats dealt in a similar manner with antislavery petitions to Congress. Southern extremists demanded that Congress disavow its power to legislate on slavery in the District of Columbia, but Van Buren, who was preparing to run for president, declared that Congress did have that power but should never use it. In dealing with the petitions, Congress simply voted at each session from 1836 to 1844 to **table** them without reading them, thus acknowledging that they had been received but sidestepping any debate on them. This procedure, which became known as the "gag rule," was passed by southern Whigs and southern Democrats with the help of most (usually 80 percent or more) of the northern Democrats. Increasingly, abolitionists sent their petitions to ex-President John Quincy Adams, who had returned to Washington as a Whig congressman from Massachusetts. Like other northern Whigs, Adams openly opposed both slavery and the gag rule in Congress. Northern Whigs began calling him Old Man Eloquent, while Calhoun dubbed him "a mischievous, bad old man." But most southerners saw what the Democrats wanted them to see: that their surest guarantee of safety within the Union was a disciplined Democratic Party determined to avoid arguments about slavery.

Thus the Jacksonians answered the question that had arisen with the Missouri debates: how to protect the slaveholding South within the federal Union. Whereas Calhoun and other southern radicals found the answer in nullification and other forms of state sovereignty, Jackson and the Democratic coalition insisted that the Union was inviolable and that any attempt to dissolve it would be met with force. At the same time, a Democratic Party uniting northern and southern agrarians into a states'-rights, limited-government majority could guarantee southern rights within the Union. This answer to the southern question stayed in place until the breakup of the Democratic Party on the eve of the Civil War.

Jacksonian Democracy and the Market Revolution

> ### *Focus Question*
> How did Democrats and Whigs in the national government argue questions raised by economic development?

Jacksonian Democrats cherished the simplicity of Jefferson's agrarian republic. They assumed power at the height of the Market Revolution, and they spent much of the 1830s and 1840s trying to reconcile the market and the republic. Like the Jeffersonians before them, Jacksonian Democrats welcomed commerce as long as it served the liberties and rough equality of white men, but paper currency and the dependence on credit that came with the Market Revolution posed problems. The so-called paper economy separated wealth from "real work" and encouraged an unrepublican spirit of luxury and greed. Worst of all, the new paper economy required government-granted privileges that the Jacksonians, still speaking the language of revolutionary republicanism, branded "corruption." For the same reasons, the protective tariffs and government-sponsored roads and canals of the American System were unacceptable. The Jackson presidency aimed to curtail government involvement in the economy, to end special privilege, and thus to rescue the republic from the Money Power.

The opposition to the Democrats (by 1834 they called themselves Whigs) favored an activist central government that would encourage orderly economic development through the American System of protective tariffs, a federally subsidized transportation network, and a national bank. This system, they argued, would encourage national prosperity. At the same time, it would create a truly national market economy that would soften sectional divisions. Jacksonian rhetoric about the Money Power and the Old Republic, they argued, was little more than the demagoguery of unqualified, self-seeking politicians.

The Second Bank of the United States

The argument between Jacksonians and their detractors came to focus on the Second Bank of the United States, chartered by Congress in 1816. The national government deposited its revenue in the bank, thus giving it an enormous capital base. The government deposits also included state banknotes that had been used to pay customs duties or to buy public land; the Bank of the United States had the power to demand redemption of these notes in specie (gold and silver), thus discouraging state banks from issuing inflationary notes that they could not back up. The bank also issued notes of its own, which served as the beginnings of a national paper currency. Thus with powers granted under its federal charter, the Bank of the United States exercised central control over the nation's monetary and credit systems.

Most members of the business community valued the Bank of the United States because it promised a stable, uniform paper currency and competent, centralized control over the banking system. But millions of Americans resented and distrusted the national bank, citing its role in the Panic of 1819 as evidence of the dangers posed by privileged, powerful institutions. President Jackson agreed with the latter opinion. A southwestern agrarian who had lost money in an early speculation, he was leery of paper money, banks, and the credit system. He insisted that both the bank and paper money were unconstitutional and that the only safe, natural, republican currencies were gold and silver. Above all, Jackson saw the Bank of the United States as a government-sponsored concentration of power that threatened American liberty.

The Bank War

The charter of the Bank of the United States ran through 1836, but Senators Henry Clay and Daniel Webster encouraged Nicholas Biddle, the Bank's brilliant, aristocratic president, to apply for recharter in 1832. Clay planned to oppose Jackson in the presidential election later that year, and he knew that Jackson hated the bank. He and his friends hoped to provoke the hot-tempered Jackson into a response they could use against him in the election. Biddle applied to Congress for a recharter of the Bank of the United States in January 1832. Congress passed the recharter bill in early July and sent it on to the president. Jackson understood the early request for recharter as a political ploy. On July 4, Van Buren visited the White House and found Jackson sick in bed; Jackson took Van Buren's hand and said, "The bank, Mr. Van Buren, is trying to kill me, *but I will kill it!*" Jackson vetoed the bill.

Jackson's Bank Veto Message, sent to Congress on July 10, was a manifesto of Jacksonian Democracy. Written by Amos Kendall, Francis Preston Blair, and Roger B. Taney—republican fundamentalists who both hated the bank and understood the popular culture that shared their hatred—the message combined Jeffersonian verities with appeals to the public's prejudice. Jackson declared that the bank was "unauthorized by the Constitution, subversive of the rights of the states, and dangerous to the liberties of the people." Its charter,

Jackson complained, bestowed special privilege on the bank and its stockholders, almost all of whom were northeastern businessmen or, worse, British investors. Having made most of its loans to southerners and westerners, the bank was a huge monster that sucked resources out of the agrarian South and West and poured them into the pockets of northeastern gentlemen and their English friends.

The granting of special privilege to such people (or to any others) threatened the system of equal rights that was essential in a republic. Jackson granted that differences in talents and resources inevitably created social distinctions, but he stood firm against "any prostitution of our Government to the advancement of the few at the expense of the many." He concluded with a call to the civic virtue and the conservative, God-centered Protestantism in which he and most of his agrarian constituency had been raised: "Let us firmly rely on that kind Providence which I am sure watches with peculiar care over the destinies of our Republic, and on the intelligence and wisdom of our countrymen. Through *His* abundant goodness and *their* patriotic devotion our liberty and Union will be preserved."

The Bank Veto Message was a long, rambling attack that, in their opinion of the Bank's supporters, demonstrated Jackson's unfitness for office. "It has all the fury of a chained

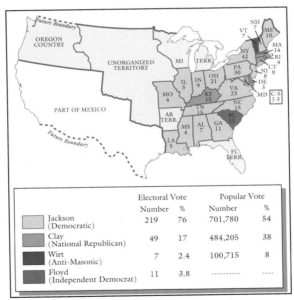

	Electoral Vote		Popular Vote	
	Number	%	Number	%
Jackson (Democratic)	219	76	701,780	54
Clay (National Republican)	49	17	484,205	38
Wirt (Anti-Masonic)	7	2.4	100,715	8
Floyd (Independent Democrat)	11	3.8	----------	----

Map 11.3 Presidential Election, 1832   The election of 1832 was a landslide victory for Andrew Jackson. The National Republican Henry Clay carried only his native Kentucky, along with Delaware and southern New England. A defeated and resentful South Carolina ran its own candidate. Jackson, on the other hand, won in the regions in which he had been strong in 1828 and added support in New York and northern New England.

panther biting the bars of its cage," said Nicholas Biddle. "It really is," he concluded, "a manifesto of anarchy." So certain were they that the public shared their views that Clay's supporters distributed Jackson's Bank Veto Message as *anti*-Jackson propaganda during the 1832 campaign. They were wrong. A majority of the voters shared Jackson's attachment to a society of virtuous, independent producers and to pristine republican government. They also agreed that the republic was being subverted by parasites who grew rich by manipulating credit, prices, paper money, and government-bestowed privileges. Jackson portrayed himself as both the protector of the Old Republic and a melodramatic hero contending with illegitimate, aristocratic, privileged, secretive powers. With the bank and Jackson's veto as the principal issues, Jackson won reelection by a landslide in 1832.

Jackson began his second term determined to kill the Bank of the United States before Congress could reverse his veto. The bank would be able to operate under its old charter until 1836, but Jackson hurried its death by withdrawing government deposits as they were needed and by depositing new government revenues in carefully selected state banks—soon to be called Pet Banks by the opposition. By law, the decision to remove the deposits had to be made by the secretary of the treasury, and Treasury Secretary Louis McLane, along with most of the cabinet, doubted the wisdom, if not the legality, of withdrawing these funds. Jackson in response transferred McLane to the vacant post of secretary of state and named William J. Duane as treasury secretary. Duane, too, refused to withdraw the deposits. Jackson fired him and appointed Roger B. Taney, the attorney general and a close adviser who had helped write the Bank Veto Message. A loyal Democrat, Taney withdrew the deposits. In 1835, when the old Federalist John Marshall died, Jackson rewarded Taney by making him Chief Justice of the Supreme Court, a post from which he continued to serve the Democratic Party.

The Beginnings of the Whig Party

Conflict over deposit removal and related questions of presidential power united anti-Jacksonians—most of them committed advocates of the American System—into the Whig Party in 1834. The name of the party, as everyone who knew the language of the republic knew, stood for legislative opposition to a power-mad executive. Jackson, argued the Whigs, had transformed himself from the limited executive described in the Constitution into King Andrew I. This had begun with Jackson's arbitrary uses of the executive patronage. It had become worse when Jackson began to veto congressional legislation. Earlier presidents had exercised the veto only nine times, usually on unimportant bills and always on the grounds that the proposed legislation was unconstitutional. Jackson used the veto often—too often, said the Whigs, when a key component of the American System was at stake. In May 1830, for instance, Jackson vetoed an attempt by Congress to buy stock in a turnpike to run from the terminus of the National Road at Louisville to Maysville, Kentucky. Jackson argued that because the road would be entirely in Kentucky, it was "partial" legislation that would take money from the whole people to benefit just one locality. He also questioned whether such federal subsidies were constitutional. Most important, however, Jackson announced that he was determined to reduce federal expenditures in order to retire the national debt, hinting strongly that he would oppose all federal public works.

The bank veto conveyed the same message even more strongly, and the withdrawal of the government deposits brought the question of "executive usurpation" to a head in 1834. Withdrawal of the deposits, together with Jackson's high-handed treatment of his treasury secretaries, caused uneasiness even among the president's supporters, and his enemies took extreme measures. Nicholas Biddle, announcing that he must clean up the affairs of the Bank of the United States before closing its doors, demanded that all its loans be repaid—a demand that undermined the credit system and produced a sharp financial panic. No doubt one reason for Biddle's action was to punish Andrew Jackson. While Congress received a well-orchestrated petition campaign to restore the deposits, Henry Clay led an effort in the Senate to censure the president, which it did in March 1834. Daniel Webster, the Bank's best friend in government, and Clay, who had watched as Jackson denied one component after another of his American System, led the old National Republican coalition (the name that anti-Jacksonians had assumed since 1824) into the new Whig Party. They were joined by southerners (including Calhoun) who resented Jackson's treatment of the South Carolina nullifiers and Biddle's bank, and who distrusted his assurances on slavery. But Jackson's war on the Bank of the United States did the most to separate parties. His withdrawal of the deposits chased lukewarm supporters into the opposition, while Democrats who closed ranks behind him could point to an increasingly sharp division between the Money Power and the Old Republic. Referring to Biddle's panic of 1834, James K. Polk of Tennessee, who led the Democrats in the House of Representatives, declared that "the question is in fact whether we shall have the Republic without the Bank or the Bank without the Republic."

A Balanced Budget

In part, Jackson removed the deposits because he anticipated a federal surplus revenue that, if handed over to Biddle's Bank of the United States, would have made it stronger than ever. The Tariffs of 1828 and 1832 produced substantial government revenue, and Jackson's frugal administration spent little of it. Even the Compromise Tariff of 1833 left rates temporarily high, and the brisk sale of public lands was adding to the surplus. In 1833, for the only time in its history, the United States paid off its national debt. Without Jackson's removal of the deposits, a growing federal treasury would have gone into the bank and would have found its way into the hated paper economy.

Early in his administration, Jackson had favored distributing surplus revenue to the states to be used for internal improvements, but he came to distrust even that minimal federal intervention in the economy, fearing that redistribution would encourage Congress to keep land prices and tariff rates high. Whigs, who by now despaired of ever creating a federally subsidized, coordinated transportation system, picked up the idea of redistribution. With some help from the Democrats, they passed the Deposit Act of 1836, which increased the number of banks receiving federal deposits (thus removing power from Jackson's Pet

King Andrew   In this widely distributed opposition cartoon, King Andrew, with a scepter in one hand and a vetoed bill in the other, tramples on internal improvements, the Bank of the United States, and the Constitution.

Banks) and distributed the federal surplus to the states to be spent on roads, canals, and schools. Jackson, who distrusted state-chartered banks as much as he distrusted the Bank of the United States, feared that the new deposit banks would use their power to issue mountains of new banknotes. He demanded a provision limiting their right to print banknotes. With that provision, he reluctantly signed the Deposit Act.

Jackson and many members of his administration had deep fiscal and moral concerns about the inflationary boom that accompanied the rapid growth of commerce, credit, roads, canals, new farms, and the other manifestations of the Market Revolution in the 1830s. After insisting that his hard-money, anti-inflationary provision be added to the Deposit Act, Jackson issued a Specie Circular in 1836. This provided that speculators could buy large parcels of public land only with silver and gold coins, while settlers could continue to buy farm-sized plots with banknotes. Henceforth, speculators would have to bring wagonloads of coins from eastern banks to frontier land offices. With this provision, Jackson hoped to curtail speculation and to reverse the flow of specie out of the South and West. The Specie Circular was Jackson's final assault on the paper economy. It repeated familiar themes: It favored hard currency over paper, settlers over speculators, and the South and West over the Northeast.

The Second American Party System

Focus Question
What was peculiarly national about the Second Party System?

In his farewell address in 1837, Jackson spoke once again of the incompatibility between the republic and the Money Power. He warned against a revival of the Bank of the United States and against all banks, paper money, the spirit of speculation, and every aspect of the "paper system." That system encouraged greed and luxury, which were at odds with republican virtue, he said. Worse, it thrived on special privilege, creating a world in which insiders meeting in "secret conclaves" could buy and sell elections. The solution, as always, was an arcadian society of small producers, a vigilant democratic electorate, and a chaste republican government that granted no special privileges.

"Martin Van Ruin"

Sitting beside Jackson as he delivered his farewell address was his chosen successor, Martin Van Buren. In the election of 1836, the Whigs had acknowledged that Henry Clay, the leader of their party, could not win a national election. Instead, they ran three sectional candidates: Daniel Webster in the Northeast, the old Indian fighter William Henry Harrison in the West, and Hugh Lawson White of Tennessee, a turncoat Jacksonian, in the South. With this ploy, the Whigs hoped to deprive Van Buren of a majority and throw the election into the Whig-controlled House of Representatives.

The strategy failed. Van Buren had engineered a national Democratic Party that could avert the dangers of sectionalism, and he questioned the patriotism of the Whigs and their sectional candidates, asserting that "true republicans can never lend their aid and influence in creating geographical parties." That, along with his association with Jackson's popular presidency, won him the election. Van Buren carried 15 of the 26 states and received 170 electoral votes against 124 for his combined opposition. His popular plurality, however, was less than 51 percent.

Van Buren had barely taken office when the inflationary boom of the mid-1830s collapsed. Economic historians ascribe the Panic of 1837 and the ensuing depression largely to events outside the country. The Bank of England, concerned over the flow of British gold to American speculators, cut off credit to firms that did business in the United States. As a result, British demand for American cotton fell sharply, and the price of cotton dropped by half. With much of the speculative boom tied to cotton grown in the Southwest, the economy collapsed. The first business failures came in March 1837, just as Van Buren took office. By May, New York banks, unable to accommodate people who were demanding hard coin for their notes, suspended specie payments. Other banks followed suit, and soon banks all over the country,

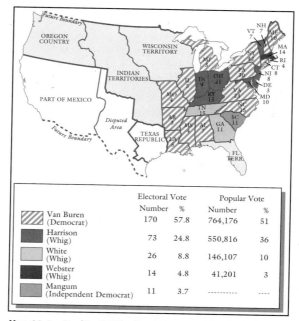

		Electoral Vote		Popular Vote	
		Number	%	Number	%
	Van Buren (Democrat)	170	57.8	764,176	51
	Harrison (Whig)	73	24.8	550,816	36
	White (Whig)	26	8.8	146,107	10
	Webster (Whig)	14	4.8	41,201	3
	Mangum (Independent Democrat)	11	3.7	----------	----

Map 11.4 Presidential Election, 1836 In 1836, the Whigs tried to beat the Democrats' national organization with an array of sectional candidates, hoping to throw the election into the House of Representatives. The strategy failed. Martin Van Buren, with significant support in every section of the country, defeated the three Whig candidates combined.

including Nicholas Biddle's newly renamed Bank of the United States of Pennsylvania, went out of business. The commercial and export sectors of the economy suffered most. In the seaport cities, one firm after another closed its doors, and about one-third of the workforce was unemployed. Wages for those who kept their jobs declined by 30 to 50 percent. It was the deepest, most widespread, and longest economic depression Americans had ever faced.

Whigs blamed the depression on Jackson's hard-money policies, particularly his destruction of the Bank of the United States and his Specie Circular. With economic distress the main issue, Whigs scored huge gains in the midterm elections of 1838, even winning control of Van Buren's New York with a campaign that castigated the president as "Martin Van Ruin." Democrats blamed the crash on speculation, luxury, and Whig paper money. Whigs demanded a new national bank, but Van Buren proposed the complete divorce of government from the banking system. Under his plan, the federal government would simply hold and dispense its money without depositing it in banks. He also required that customs and land purchases be paid in gold and silver coins or in notes from specie-paying banks, a provision that allowed government to regulate state banknotes without resorting to a central bank. Van Buren asked Congress to set up the Independent Treasury in 1837, and Congress spent the rest of Van Buren's time in office arguing about it. The Independent Treasury Bill finally passed in 1840, completing the Jacksonian separation of bank and state.

The Election of 1840

Whigs were confident that they could take the presidency away from Van Buren in the election of 1840. Trying to offend as few voters as possible, they passed over their best-known leaders, Senators Henry Clay and Daniel Webster, and nominated William Henry Harrison of Ohio as their presidential candidate. Harrison was the hero of the Battle of Tippecanoe (see chapter 7) and a westerner whose Virginia origins made him palatable in the South. He was also a proven vote-getter: As the Whigs' "western" candidate in 1836, he had carried seven states scattered across the Northwest, the mid-Atlantic, New England, and the Upper South. Best of all, he was a military hero who had expressed few opinions on national issues and who had no political record to defend. As his running mate, the Whigs chose John Tyler, a states'-rights Virginian who had joined the Whigs out of hatred for Jackson. To promote this baldly pragmatic ticket, the Whigs came up with a catchy slogan: "Tippecanoe and Tyler Too." Philip Hone, a wealthy New York City Whig, admitted that the slogan (and the ticket) had "rhyme, but no reason in it."

Early in the campaign, a Democratic journalist, commenting on Harrison's political inexperience and alleged unfitness for the presidency, wrote, "Give [Harrison] a barrel of hard cider, and settle a pension of two thousand a year on him, and my word for it, he will sit out the remainder of his days in his log cabin." Whigs who had been trying to shake their elitist image seized on the statement and launched what was known as the Log Cabin Campaign. The log cabin, the cider barrel, and Harrison's folksiness and heroism constituted the

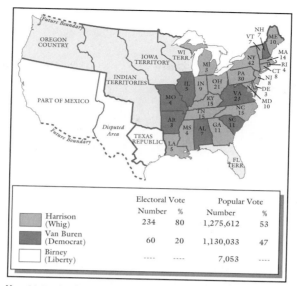

Map 11.5 columns:

	Electoral Vote		Popular Vote	
	Number	%	Number	%
Harrison (Whig)	234	80	1,275,612	53
Van Buren (Democrat)	60	20	1,130,033	47
Birney (Liberty)	----	----	7,053	----

Map 11.5 Presidential Election, 1840 In 1840, the Whigs united under William Henry Harrison, the one Whig candidate who had won national support four years earlier. Borrowing campaign tactics from the Democrats and inventing many of their own, Whigs campaigned hard in every state. The result was a Whig victory and a truly national two-party system.

entire Whig campaign, while Van Buren was pictured as living in luxury at the public's expense. The Whigs conjured up an image of a nattily dressed President "Van Ruin" sitting on silk chairs and dining on gold and silver dishes while farmers and workingmen struggled to make ends meet. Whig doggerel contrasted Harrison the hero with Van Buren the professional politician:

> The knapsack pillow'd Harry's head
> The hard ground eas'd his toils;
> While Martin on his downy bed
> Could dream of naught but spoils.

Democrats howled that Whigs were peddling lies and refusing to discuss issues, but they knew they had been beaten at their own game. Harrison won only a narrow majority of the popular vote, but a landslide of 234 to 60 votes in the electoral college.

Two Parties

The election of 1840 signaled the completion of the second party system—the most fully national alignment of parties in U.S. history. Andrew Jackson had won in 1828 with Jefferson's old southern and western agrarian constituency; in 1832, he had carried his old

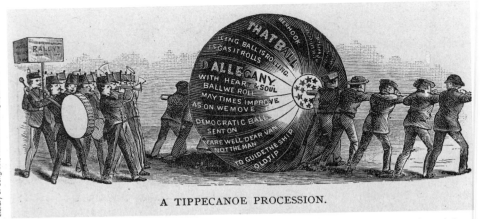

A TIPPECANOE PROCESSION.

"A Tippecanoe Procession"   In 1840, the Whigs, who had earlier been repelled by the boisterous electioneering techniques of the Democrats, filled the campaign with humor and noise, beating the Democrats at their own game. Among many other things, the Whigs covered a great paper ball with slogans (none of which had anything to do with national issues) and rolled it across the midwestern and northeastern states—accompanied by brass bands and shouts of "Keep the ball rolling!"

voters and had won added support in the mid-Atlantic states and in northern New England. In 1836, Whigs capitalized on southern resentment of Jackson's defeat of nullification and on southern mistrust of the New Yorker Van Buren. They broke the Democratic hold on the South. Whigs came out of their old northeastern strongholds to carry Ohio, Illinois, Kentucky, Georgia, South Carolina, and even Jackson's Tennessee. Jackson had won 8 in 10 southern votes; Van Buren carried barely half, but won majorities in old anti-Jackson neighborhoods in New England. The election of 1840 completed the transition: Harrison and Van Buren contested the election in nearly every state; perhaps most significantly, they received nearly equal levels of support in the slave and free states. Van Buren's dream of a national party system that transcended sectional differences was realized. Ironically, the final pieces fell into place in an election that cost him the presidency.

The election of 1840 also witnessed the high-water mark of voter turnout. Whig and Democratic organizations focused on presidential elections, and prospective voters met a quadrennial avalanche of oratory, door-to-door canvassing, torchlight parades, and party propaganda. As the contests became national, Democrats or Whigs could take no state in the Union for granted. (In 1828, winning candidates carried individual states by an average of 36 percent; by 1840, that figure had dropped to 11 percent.) Both Whigs and Democrats maintained organizations and contested elections in nearly every neighborhood in the country, and the result was increased popular interest in politics. In 1824, about one in four adult white men had voted in the presidential election. Jackson's vengeful campaign of 1828 lifted the turnout to 56.3 percent, and it stayed at about that level in 1832 and 1836. The campaign of 1840 brought out 78 percent of the eligible voters, and the turnout remained at that high level throughout the 1840s and 1850s.

Conclusion

By 1840, American politics operated within a stable, national system of two parties, both of which depended on support in every section of the country. Whigs argued for the economic nationalism of the American System. Democrats argued for the limited, inexpensive government that since Jefferson's day had been a bulwark of both republicanism and slavery. The party system provided answers to the questions of sectionalism and economic development that had helped bring it into being. Democrats successfully fought off the American System: They dismantled the Bank of the United States, refused federal support for roads and canals, and revised the tariff in ways that mollified the export-oriented South. The result, however, was not the return to Jeffersonian agrarianism that many Democrats had wanted but an inadvertent experiment in laissez-faire capitalism. The stupendous growth of the American economy between 1830 and 1860 became a question of state and local—not national—government action. On the growing political problems surrounding slavery, the two-party system did what Van Buren had hoped it would do: Because the Whig and (especially) Democratic Parties needed both northern and southern support, they were careful to focus national political debates on economic development, avoiding any discussion of sectional questions. It worked that way until the party system disintegrated on the eve of the Civil War.

SUGGESTED READINGS

Sean Wilentz, *The Rise of American Democracy: Jefferson to Lincoln* (2006) is a comprehensive and definitive political history, while **Harry L. Watson,** *Liberty and Power: The Politics of Jacksonian America* (1990) is an excellent shorter synthesis. **John Lauritz Larson,** *Internal Improvement: National Public Works and the Promise of Popular Government in the Early United States* (2001) is essential. On legal and constitutional issues, see **R. Kent Newmeyer,** *The Supreme Court under Marshall and Taney* (1968); and **Morton J. Horwitz,** *The Transformation of American Law, 1780–1860* (1977). *George Dangerfield, The Era of Good Feelings* (1953) and **Glover Moore,** *The Missouri Controversy, 1819–1821* (1953) are standard treatments of their subjects. On nullification, see **William W. Freehling,** *Prelude to Civil War: The Nullification Controversy in South Carolina, 1816–1836* (1965) and **Richard E. Ellis,** *The Union at Risk: Jacksonian Democracy, States' Rights and the Nullification Crisis* (1987).

Two important accounts of slavery in national politics are **William Lee Miller,** *Arguing About Slavery: The Great Battle in the United States Congress* (1996) and **Don E. Fehrenbacher,** *The Slaveholding Republic: An Account of the United States Government's Relations to Slavery* (2001). On Jackson and Indian Removal, a good introduction is **Robert V. Remini,** *Andrew Jackson and His Indian Wars* (2001). On the Bank War, see **Peter Temin,** *The Jacksonian Economy* (1967). The making of the party system is the subject of **Richard Hofstadter**, *The Idea of a Party System: The Rise of Legitimate Opposition in the United States, 1780–1840* (1969) and **Richard P. McCormick**, *The Second American Party System: Party Formation in the Jacksonian Era* (1966).

Visit the Liberty Equality Power Companion Web site for resources specific to this textbook: http://www.thomsonedu.com/history/murrin

Also find self-tests and additional resources at ThomsonNOW. ThomsonNOW is an integrated online suite of services and resources with proven ease of use and efficient paths to success, delivering the results you want—NOW!

www.thomsonedu.com/login/

12

Whigs, Democrats, and the Shaping of Society

Between 1820 and 1845, Thomas Jefferson's agrarian republic became Andrew Jackson's mass democracy. Politicians who built the Whig and Democratic parties participated in the economic and social transformations of those years. They were also consumers and producers of the new forms of popular culture. In making their political appeals, they tapped skillfully into the national patchwork of aspiration, fear, and resentment. John Quincy Adams, Henry Clay, and their National Republican and Whig allies envisioned smooth-running, government-sponsored transportation and monetary systems. Such visions echoed the faith in cosmic order, material progress, and moral improvement that had become cultural axioms for the more prosperous and cosmopolitan Americans. Democrats, on the other hand, defended Jefferson's republic of limited government and widespread equality and liberty. They portrayed a haunted political universe in which trickery, deceit, and special privilege lurked behind the promises of the Whigs.

Politicians constructed the Whig and Democratic coalitions largely at the neighborhood and state levels. Their arguments for and against state-supported internal improvements and state-chartered banks and corporations mirrored the national debate. But local cultural battles—arguments on race, alcohol, sexual morality, education, crime, and much more—sharpened Democratic and Whig attitudes, making national coalitions out of local issues. Cultural politics from the 1820s through the 1840s is the subject of this chapter.

Constituencies

Focus Question
Which Americans were likely to support the Democratic Party in the 1830s and 1840s? Which Americans were likely to support the Whigs?

By the 1830s, support for the Democratic or Whig Party was a matter of personal identity as much as of political preference: A man's vote demonstrated his personal history, his cultural values, and his vision of the good society as clearly as it demonstrated his opinion on any particular political issue. Voters remained loyal to their parties in selecting officeholders

CHRONOLOGY

1819	New York state builds the first prison under the Auburn system
1826	Reformers found the American Society for the Promotion of Temperance
1831	William Lloyd Garrison begins publication of the antislavery *Liberator* • New York *Magdalen* Society publishes its first annual report
1833	Abolitionists found the American Anti-Slavery Society
1840	Working-class drinkers found the Washington Temperance Society
1848	First Women's Rights Convention held in Seneca Falls, New York
1851	Maine becomes the first of 17 states to enact statewide prohibition
1860	New York enacts the Married Women's Property Act

ranging from local coroners and school board members to state legislators and presidents of the United States. Thus political parties reduced the stupendous diversity of American society to two political choices. Of course, limiting citizenship to white men narrowed diversity, but even with the deck stacked in favor of a homogeneous electorate, the Whig and Democratic parties were national coalitions of ill-matched regional, economic, ethnic, and religious groups. They were united by Whig and Democratic political cultures—consistent attitudes toward government and politics embedded in religion, family, and economic life. For all their patchwork diversity, the Democratic and Whig parties appealed to coherent constituencies and proposed coherent programs in every corner of the republic.

The North and West

In the North and West, the makers of what would become the Whig Party found their core support at the centers of the Market Revolution and the Finneyite revival. The broad band of Yankee commercial farms stretching across southern New England, western New York, and the Old Northwest was the northern Whig heartland. Whigs also enjoyed support in northern cities and towns. The wealthiest men in cities were Whigs; more than 8 in 10 among the merchant elite of Boston and New York, for instance, supported them. The new urban commercial classes created in the Market Revolution also tended to support the Whigs. Factory owners were solidly Whig, and native-born factory workers often joined them—partly because Whigs promised opportunities to rise in the world, partly because Whigs protected their jobs by encouraging domestic markets for what they made, and, increasingly, because Whigs pandered to their fears of immigrant labor. For similar reasons, many skilled urban artisans supported the Whigs, as did smaller numbers of dockworkers, day laborers, and others among the unskilled.

Northern Whiggery was grounded in the Market Revolution, but the Whig political agenda ranged far beyond economic life. The strongholds of Whiggery and the market were also the strongholds of the Finneyite revival. Among the urban middle class and in the more market-oriented rural neighborhoods, the inheritors of Puritan theocracy translated the spirit of the late 1820s and early 1830s revivals into an avowedly Christian Whig politics. Northern and western Whigs demanded that government actively encourage the transition to market society. At the same time, they called for moral legislation on such issues as Sabbath observance, temperance, and Bible-based public schools. Marching under the banner of activist government, economic development, and moral progress, Whigs set the political agenda in most northern states.

They met a determined Democratic opposition. Campaigning as defenders of the Jeffersonian republic, autonomous neighborhoods, and private conscience, Democrats found supporters among cultural traditionalists who had gained little from the expansion of national markets and who had no use for the moral agenda of the Whigs. The **Butternuts** (so named for the yellow vegetable dye with which they colored their homespun clothing) of the southern, river-oriented counties of the Northwest joined the Democratic Party. Farmers in the Allegheny Mountains of southern New York and northern Pennsylvania, in the declining (and non-Yankee) countryside of the Hudson River valley, and in the poor and isolated hill towns of northern and western New England also supported the Democrats.

In cities and towns, Democrats made up substantial minorities among businessmen, master craftsmen, and professionals, but most urban Democrats were wage earners. Perhaps the most overwhelmingly Democratic group in the country was immigrant Irish Catholics, who were filling the lower ranks of the urban workforce. Their presence in the Democratic Party pushed increasing numbers of native Protestant workers into the Whig ranks—a division that appeared in New York City in the early 1830s, in most cities and towns by the 1840s, and that pervaded the North and West in the 1850s.

When confronted with opposition to evangelical legislation, Whigs labeled the Democrats the party of atheism and immorality. Democrats responded that they opposed theocracy, not religion. True, most free-thinkers, atheists, and persons who simply did not care about religion supported the Democratic Party. So did immigrant Catholics, who rightfully feared the militant Protestantism of the Whigs. Democrats, however, won the support of hundreds of thousands of evangelical Protestants as well. At least half of Methodists, Baptists, Disciples of Christ, Old School Presbyterians, and members of Reformed churches put their faith in providence and individual piety, and deeply distrusted what they called "church and state" Whiggery and the mixing of politics and religion. "I am myself a candidate," said a Methodist Democrat in 1840, "but it is for eternal life. I aspire to a throne, but I must have one which will not perish." Evangelical Democrats were joined by sectarian Christians who looked to the Democrats for protection: Freewill Baptists, Universalists, Lutherans, Scots Covenanters, many Quakers, Mormons, and others. These Democratic churchgoers rejected Whig moral legislation as antirepublican and as Yankee cultural imperialism. George Washington Bethune, a Dutch Reformed minister and a New York Democrat, put the Democratic creed succinctly: "Religion is not to be advanced by civil power."

The South

Throughout the 1830s and 1840s, the southern states divided their votes equally between Whigs and Democrats, but most southern neighborhoods were either solidly Democratic or solidly Whig. In the 1844 elections, for instance, the counties of Virginia and Alabama supported their favored candidates by margins of 23 and 27 percent, respectively, landslide margins by the standards of two-party politics. (The comparable figure for New York counties was 9 percent.)

Isolated southern neighborhoods tended to support the Democrats. Thus Democrats ran strongest in yeoman neighborhoods with few slaves and relatively little market activity—upcountry communities that valued household independence and the society of neighbors and that deeply distrusted intrusions from the outside. The more cosmopolitan southern communities tended to support the Whigs. In general, this meant that Whigs were strongest in plantation counties, where they commanded the votes not only of planters but also of smaller farmers, and of lawyers, storekeepers, and craftsmen in county-seat towns. Upland, nonplantation neighborhoods in which Whigs ran well (eastern Tennessee, western North Carolina, and parts of Virginia are examples) were places where Whigs promised state-sponsored internal improvements that would link ambitious but isolated farmers to outside markets. On the other hand, some plantation districts with easy access to markets, such as the South Carolina low-country, opposed expensive Whig projects that would benefit other areas.

Many other southern exceptions to the link between commerce and the Whig Party were grounded in the prestige and power of local leaders. Southern statesmen who broke with the Jacksonians in the 1830s—John C. Calhoun in South Carolina, Hugh Lawson White in Tennessee, and others—took personal and regional followings with them (see chapter 11). Political campaigners also had to contend with southerners such as George Reynolds of Pickens County, Alabama. Reynolds was a half-literate yeoman who fathered 17 children and had 234 direct descendants living in his neighborhood. He delivered them as a bloc to politicians who pleased him. Despite the vagaries of southern kinship and community, Whigs knew that their core constituency in the South was in communities that were or wanted to be linked to commercial society.

In sharp contrast with the North and West, southern political divisions had little to do with religion. The South was thoroughly evangelized by 1830, but southern Baptists, Methodists, and Presbyterians seldom combined religion and politics. The southern evangelical churches had begun as marginal movements that opposed the Anglican establishment. They continued to distrust ties between church and state. Although they enforced morality within their own households and congregations, southern evangelicals seldom asked state legislatures to pass moral legislation. In extreme cases, southern premillennialists rejected politics altogether, insisting that Jesus would soon return to take the reins of government. (One political canvasser faced with that argument responded, "I will bet one hundred dollars he can't carry Kentucky.") Southern evangelicals who embraced the world of the market assumed, along with their northern Whig counterparts, that the new economy encouraged a Christian, civilized life. Other southern churchgoers responded to the Jacksonians' denunciations of greed, pride, and the spirit of speculation. Thus, even though many southern communities were bitterly divided over religion, the divisions seldom shaped party politics.

The social, religious, cultural, and economic bases of party divisions formed coherent Whig and Democratic political cultures. Whig voters in the North and South either were or hoped to become beneficiaries of the Market Revolution and wanted government to subsidize economic development. In the North, they also demanded that government help shape market society into a prosperous, orderly, and homogeneous Christian republic. Democrats, North and South, demanded a minimal government that kept taxes low and that left citizens, their families, and their neighborhoods alone.

The Politics of Economic Development

Focus Question

What were Whig and Democratic conceptions of the duties and limits of government?

Both Whigs and Democrats accepted the transition to market society, but they wanted to direct it into different channels. Whigs wanted to use government and the market to make an economically and morally progressive—albeit hierarchical—republic. Democrats viewed both government and the new institutions of market society with suspicion and vowed to allow neither to subvert the equal rights and rough equality of condition that were, in their view, the preconditions of republican citizenship. In language that echoed their Jeffersonian forebears, Jacksonian Democrats demanded that the market remain subservient to the republic.

Government and Its Limits

"The government," remarked a New York City Whig in 1848, "is not merely a machine for making wars and punishing felons, but is bound to do all that is within its power to promote the welfare of the People—its legitimate scope is not merely negative, representative, defensive, but also affirmative, creative, constructive, beneficent." *The American Review,* a Whig periodical, agreed: "Forms of government are instituted for the protection and fostering of virtue, and are valuable only as they accomplish this."

The Whigs insisted that economic development, moral progress, and social harmony were linked and that government should foster them. Market society, they argued, opened up opportunities for individual Americans. As long as people developed the work habits and moral discipline required for success, they would be rewarded. To poor farmers and city workers who believed that the Market Revolution undermined their independence, Whigs promised social mobility within a new system of interdependence, but only to deserving individuals. According to the New York *Herald* in 1836, "The mechanic who attends quietly to his business—is industrious and attentive—belongs to no club—never visits the porter-house—is always at work or with his family—such a man gradually rises in society and becomes an honor to himself, his friends, and to human nature." The *Herald* editor continued, "On the contrary, look at the Trade Unionist—the pot-house agitator—the stirrer-up of sedition—the clamorer for higher wages—After a short time, he ends his career in the Pen or State Prison." Whigs believed that the United States exhibited a harmony of class interests and an equality of opportunity that every virtuous person would recognize and that only resentful, mean-spirited, unworthy people would doubt. Pointing to self-made Whigs such as Daniel Webster and Abraham Lincoln, they demanded activist government that nurtured the economic, cultural, and moral opportunities provided by market society.

Democrats seldom praised or condemned market society per se. Instead, they argued for the primacy of citizenship: Neither government nor the market, they said, should be allowed to subvert the civil and legal equality among independent men on which the republic rested. Often sharing a view of human nature that was (in contrast to the Whigs' more optimistic views) a grim combination of classical republicanism and gothic romance, Democrats saw government not as a tool of progress but as a dangerous—although regrettably necessary—concentration of power in the hands of imperfect, self-interested men. The only safe course was to limit its power. In 1837, the *United States Magazine and Democratic Review* declared: "The best government is that which governs least," and went on to denounce the "natural imperfection, both in wisdom and judgment and purity of purpose, of all human legislation, exposed constantly to the pressure of partial interest; interests which, at the same time that they are essentially selfish and tyrannical, are ever vigilant, persevering, and subtle in all the arts of deception and corruption."

Democrats argued that the Whig belief in benign government and social harmony was absurd. Corporate charters, privileged banks, and subsidies to turnpike, canal, and railroad companies, they said, benefited privileged insiders and transformed republican government into an engine of inequality. Granting such privileges, warned one Democrat, was sure "to break up that social equality which is the legitimate foundation of our institutions, and the destruction of which would render our boasted freedom a mere phantom." George Bancroft, a radical Democrat from Massachusetts, concurred: "A republican people," he said, "should be in an equality in their social and political condition; . . . pure democracy inculcates equal rights—equal laws—equal means of education—and *equal means* of wealth also." By contrast, the government favored by the Whigs would enrich a favored few. Bancroft and other Democrats demanded limited government that was deaf to the demands of special interests.

Banks

Andrew Jackson's national administration destroyed the Bank of the United States (see chapter 11). As a result, regulation of banking, credit, and currency fell to the state governments. Banks emerged as a central political issue in nearly every state, particularly after the widespread bank failures following the crash of 1837. Whigs defended banks as agents of economic progress, arguing that they provided credit for roads and canals, loans to businessmen and commercial farmers, and the banknotes that served as the chief medium of exchange. Democrats branded banks as agents of inequality dominated by insiders who controlled artificial concentrations of money, who enjoyed chartered privileges, and who issued banknotes and expanded or contracted credit to their own advantage. In short, they regarded banks as government-protected institutions that enabled a privileged few to make themselves rich at the public's expense.

The economic boom of the 1830s and the destruction of the national bank created a dramatic expansion in the number of state-chartered banks—from 329 in 1830 to 788 in 1837. Systems varied from state to state. South Carolina, Georgia, Tennessee, Kentucky, and Arkansas had state-owned banks. Many banks in the Old Northwest were also partially state-owned. Such banks often operated as public-service institutions. Georgia's Central Bank, for example, served farmers who could not qualify for private loans, as did other state-owned banks in the South. The charter of the Agricultural Bank of Mississippi (1833) stipulated that at least half of the bank's capital be in long-term loans (farm mortgages) rather than in short-term loans to merchants.

Beginning in the 1820s, many states introduced uniform banking laws to replace the unique charters previously granted to individual banks. The new laws tried to stabilize currency and credit. In New York, the **Safety-Fund Law** of 1829 required banks to pool a fraction of their resources to protect both bankers and small noteholders in the case of bank failures. The result was a self-regulating and conservative community of state banks. Laws in other states required that banks maintain a high ratio of specie (precious metals) to notes in circulation. Such laws, however, were often evaded. Michigan's bank inspectors, for instance, complained that the same cache of silver and gold was taken from bank

A Three-Dollar Bill This three-dollar bill was no joke. It was one of the small private banknotes that Democrats wanted to take out of circulation.

to bank one step ahead of them. At one bank, an inspector encountered a bank teller who had 10 metal boxes behind his counter. The teller opened one of the boxes and showed that it was full of federal silver dollars. The wary inspector picked up another one and found that it was full of nails covered with a thin layer of silver dollars. All of the other boxes were the same, except for one that was filled with broken glass. Many Americans greeted such stories with a knowing wink until the Panic of 1837, when they presented state banknotes for redemption in specie and were turned down.

"Hard Money" Democrats (those who wanted to get rid of paper money altogether) regarded banks as centers of trickery and privilege and proposed that they be abolished. Banks, they claimed, with their manipulation of credit and currency, encouraged speculation, luxury, inequality, and the separation of wealth from real work. Jackson branded banks "a perfect humbug." An Alabama Democrat declared that banking was "in conflict with justice, equity, morality and religion" and that there was "nothing evil that it does not aid—nothing good that it is not averse to." Senator Bedford Brown of North Carolina doubted "whether banking institutions were at all compatible with the existence of a truly republican government," and Richard Swinton of Iowa dismissed banks as "a set of swindling machines." Samuel Medary of Ohio cast banks as the villains of Democratic melodrama. Banks possess, Medary wrote, "every inducement to attract the confidence of the unwary and seduce into their grasp the most watchful and shrewd, by the convenience and safety they hold out to the public through a thousand pretenses of being the exclusive friends and engines of trade and commerce."

In state legislatures, Whigs defended what had become a roughly standard system of private banks chartered by state governments. They had the right to circulate banknotes and had **limited liability** to protect directors and stockholders from debts incurred by their bank. Many Democrats proposed abolishing all banks. Others proposed reforms. They demanded a high ratio of specie reserves to banknotes as a guard against inflationary paper money. They proposed eliminating the issuance of banknotes in small denominations, thus ensuring that day-to-day business would be conducted in hard coin and protecting wage earners and small farmers from speculative ups and downs. Democrats also wanted to hold bank directors and stockholders responsible for corporate debts and bankruptcies; some proposed banning corporate charters altogether.

By these and other means, Democrats in the states protected currency and credit from the government favoritism, dishonesty, and elitism that, they argued, enriched Whig insiders and impoverished honest Democrats. Whigs responded that corporate privileges and immunities and an abundant, elastic currency were keys to economic development, and they fought Democrats every step of the way.

Internal Improvements

Democrats in Congress and the White House blocked federally funded roads and canals (see chapter 11). In response, the states launched the transportation revolution themselves, either by taking direct action or by chartering private corporations to do the work.

State legislatures everywhere debated the wisdom of direct state action, of corporate privileges, of subsidies to canals and railroads, and of the accumulation of government debt. Whigs, predictably, favored direct action by state governments. Democrats were lukewarm toward the whole idea of internal improvements, convinced that debt, favoritism, and corruption would inevitably result from government involvement in the economy.

Whigs assumed a connection between market society and moral progress, and they used that relationship as a basis of their argument for internal improvements. William H. Seward, the Whig governor of New York, supported transportation projects because they broke down neighborhood isolation and hastened the emergence of a market society with "all the consequent advantages of morality, piety, and knowledge." The historian Henry Adams, who grew up in a wealthy Whig household in Boston, later recalled that his father had taught him about a strong connection between good roads and good morals. In the minds of Whig legislators, a vote for internal improvements was a vote for moral progress and for individual opportunity within a prosperous and happily interdependent market society.

Democratic state legislators, although with less enthusiasm, supported at least some internal improvements, but they opposed "partial" legislation that would benefit part of their state at the expense of the rest. They also opposed projects that would lead to higher taxes and put state governments into debt—arguments that gathered force after the crash of 1837 bankrupted states that had overextended themselves in the canal boom of the 1830s. The Democrats made the same argument in every state: Beneath Whig plans for extensive improvements lay schemes to create special privilege, inequality, debt, and corruption—all at the expense of a hoodwinked people.

The Politics of Social Reform

Focus Question

What were the principal social reform movements of these years, and how did the political parties react to them?

In the North, the churchgoing middle class provided the Whig Party with a political culture, a reform-oriented social agenda, and most of its electoral support. Whig evangelicals believed that with God's help they could improve the world by improving the individuals within it, and they enlisted the Whig Party in that campaign. On a variety of issues, including prostitution, temperance, public education, and state-supported insane asylums and penitentiaries, Whigs used government to improve individual morality and discipline. Democrats argued that attempts to dictate morality through legislation were both antirepublican and wrong. Questions of social reform provoked the angriest differences between Democrats and Whigs, particularly in the North.

Public Schools

During the second quarter of the 19th century, local and state governments built systems of tax-supported public schools, known as **"common" schools.** Before that time, most children learned reading, writing, and arithmetic at home, in poorly staffed town schools, in private schools, or in charity schools run by churches or other benevolent organizations. Despite the lack of any system of education, most children learned to read and write. That was, however, more likely among boys than among girls, among whites than among blacks, and among northeasterners than among westerners or southerners.

By the 1830s, Whigs and Democrats agreed that providing common schools was a proper function of government, and Democrats often agreed with Whigs that schools could equalize opportunity. Massachusetts Democrat Robert Rantoul, for example, believed that rich and poor children should "be brought equally and together up to the starting point at the public expense; after that we must shift for ourselves." More radical Democrats, however, wanted public schooling that would erase snobbery. A newspaper declared in 1828 that "the children of the rich and the poor shall receive a national education, calculated to make republicans and banish aristocrats." Marcus Morton, Democratic governor of Massachusetts, agreed that it was the job of the common schools to democratize children "before the pride of family or wealth, or other adventitious distinction has taken a deep root in the young heart."

The reformers who created the most advanced, expensive, and centralized state school systems were Whigs: Horace Mann of Massachusetts, Henry Barnard of Connecticut, Calvin Stowe (husband of Harriet Beecher) of Ohio, and others. These reformers talked more about character building and Whig Protestant culture than about the three R's. They wanted schools that would downplay class divisions, but they were interested less in democratizing wealthy children than in civilizing the poor. Calvin H.Wiley, the Whig superintendent of schools in North Carolina, promised that proper schools would make Americans "homogeneous . . . intelligent, eminently republican, sober, calculating, moral and conservative." A Whig newspaper in Ohio declared in 1836 that character-building schools were essential in a democracy: "Other nations have hereditary sovereigns, and one of the most important duties of their governments is to take care of the education of the heir to their throne; these children all about your streets . . . are your future sovereigns." William Seward, the Whig governor of New York, insisted that "education tends to produce equality, not by leveling all to the condition of the base, but by elevating all to the association of the wise and good."

The schools taught a basic Whig axiom: that social questions could be reduced to questions of individual character. A textbook entitled *The Thinker, A Moral Reader* (1855) told children to "remember that all the ignorance, degradation, and misery in the world, is the result of indolence and vice." To teach that lesson, the schools had children read from the King James Bible and recite prayers acceptable to all of the Protestant sects. Such texts reaffirmed a common Protestant morality while avoiding divisive doctrinal matters. Until the arrival of significant numbers of Catholic immigrants in the 1840s and 1850s, few parents complained about Protestant religious instruction in the public schools.

Political differences centered less on curriculum than on organization. Whigs wanted state-level centralization and proposed state superintendents and state boards of education, **normal schools** (state teachers' colleges), texts chosen at the state level and used throughout the state, and uniform school terms. They also (often with the help of economy-minded Democrats) recruited young women as teachers. In addition to fostering Protestant morality in the schools, these women were a source of cheap labor. Salaries for female teachers in the northern states ranged from 40 percent to 60 percent lower than the salaries of their male coworkers. Largely as a result, the proportion of women among Massachusetts teachers rose from 56 percent in 1834 to 78 percent in 1860.

Democrats objected to the Whigs' insistence on centralization as elitist, intrusive, and expensive. They preferred to give power to individual school districts, thus enabling local school committees to tailor the curriculum, the length of the school year, and the choice of teachers and texts to local needs. Centralization, they argued, would create a metropolitan educational culture that served the purposes of the rich but ignored the preferences of farmers and working people. It was standard Democratic social policy: inexpensive government and local control. Henry Barnard, Connecticut's superintendent of schools, called his Democratic opponents "ignorant demagogues" and "a set of blockheads." Horace Mann denounced them as "political madmen." As early as 1826, Thaddeus Stevens, who would become a prominent Pennsylvania Whig, argued that voters must "learn to dread ignorance more than taxation."

Ethnicity, Religion, and the Schools

The argument between Whig centralism and Democratic parsimony dominated the debate over public education until the children of Irish and German immigrants began to enter schools by the thousands in the mid-1840s. Most immigrant families were poor and relied on their children to work and supplement the family income. Consequently, their children's attendance at school was irregular at best. Moreover, most immigrants were Catholics. The Irish regarded Protestant prayers and the King James Bible as heresies and as hated tools of British oppression. Some of the textbooks were worse. Olney's *Practical System of Modern Geography,* a standard textbook, declared that "the Irish in general are quick of apprehension, active, brave and hospitable; but passionate, ignorant, vain, and superstitious." A nun in Connecticut complained that Irish children in the public schools "see their parents looked upon as an inferior race."

Many Catholic parents simply refused to send their children to school. Others demanded changes in textbooks, the elimination of the King James Bible (perhaps to be replaced by the Douay Bible), tax-supported Catholic schools, or at least tax relief for parents who sent their children to parish schools. Whigs, joined by many native-born Democrats, saw Catholic complaints as popish assaults on the Protantism that they insisted was at the heart of American republicanism.

Some school districts, particularly in the rural areas to which many Scandinavian and German immigrants found their way, created foreign-language schools and provided bilingual instruction. In other places, state support for church-run charity schools persisted. For example, both Catholic and Protestant schools received such assistance in New York City until 1825. So did Lowell, Massachusetts; Hartford and Middletown, Connecticut; and Milwaukee, Wisconsin, at various times from the 1830s through the 1860s. New Jersey provided state support to Catholic as well as other church schools until 1866. In northeastern cities, however, where immigrant Catholics often formed militant local majorities, such demands led to violence and to organized nativist (anti-immigrant) politics. In 1844, the Native American Party, with the endorsement of the Whigs, won the New York City elections. That same year in Philadelphia, riots that pitted avowedly Whig Protestants against Catholic immigrants, ostensibly over the issue of Bible reading in schools, killed 13 people. Such conflicts would severely damage the northern Democratic coalition in the 1850s.

Prisons

From the 1820s onward, state governments built institutions to house orphans, the dependent poor, the insane, and criminals. The Market Revolution increased the numbers of such persons and made them more visible, more anonymous, and more separated from family and community resources. Americans in the 18th century (and many in the 19th century as well) had assumed that poverty, crime, insanity, and other social ills were among God's ways of punishing sin and testing the human capacity for both suffering and charity. By the 1820s, however, reformers were arguing that deviance was the result of childhood deprivation. "Normal" people, they argued, learned discipline and respect for work, property, laws, and other people from their parents. Deviants were the products of brutal, often drunken households devoid of parental love and discipline. The cure was to place them in a controlled setting, teach them work and discipline, and turn them into useful citizens.

In state legislatures, Whigs favored putting deviants into institutions for rehabilitation. Democrats, although they agreed that the states should incarcerate criminals and deviants, regarded attempts at rehabilitation as wrong-headed and expensive. They favored institutions that isolated the insane, warehoused the dependent poor, and punished criminals. Most state systems were a compromise between the two positions.

Pennsylvania built prisons at Pittsburgh (1826) and Philadelphia (1829) that put solitary prisoners into cells to contemplate their misdeeds and to plot a new life. The results of such solitary confinement included few reformations and numerous attempts at suicide. Only New Jersey imitated the Pennsylvania system. Far more common were institutions based on the model developed in New York at Auburn (1819) and Sing Sing (1825). In the **Auburn system,** prisoners slept in solitary cells and marched in military formation to meals and workshops. They were forbidden to speak to one another at any time. The rule of silence, it was believed, encouraged both discipline and contemplation. The French writer Alexis de Tocqueville, visiting a New York prison in 1830, remarked that "the silence within these vast walls . . . is that of death. . . . There were a thousand living beings, and yet it was a vast desert solitude."

The Auburn system was designed both to reform criminals and to reduce expenses, for the prisons sold workshop products to the outside. Between these two goals, Whigs favored rehabilitation. Democrats favored profit-making workshops, and thus lower operating costs and lower taxes. Robert Wiltse, named by the Democrats to run Sing Sing prison in the 1830s, used harsh punishments (including flogging and starving), sparse meals, and forced labor to punish criminals and make the prison pay for itself. In 1839, William Seward, as the newly elected Whig governor of New York, fired Wiltse and appointed administrators who substituted privileges and rewards for punishment and emphasized rehabilitation over profit making. They provided religious instruction; they improved food and working conditions; and they cut back on the use of flogging. When Democrats took back the statehouse in the 1842 elections, they discovered that the Whigs' brief experiment in kindness had produced a $50,000 deficit, so they swiftly reinstated the old regime.

Asylums

The leading advocate of humane treatment of the insane was **Dorothea Dix,** a Boston humanitarian who was shocked by the incarceration and abuse of the insane in common jails. She traveled throughout the country, urging citizens to pressure their state legislatures into building asylums committed to what reformers called "moral treatment." The asylums were to be clean and pleasant places, preferably outside the cities, and the inmates were to be treated humanely. Attendants were not to beat inmates or tie them up, although they could use cold showers as a form of discipline. Dix and other reformers wanted the asylums to be safe, nurturing environments in which people with mental illness could be made well.

By 1860, the legislatures of 28 of the 33 states had established state-run insane asylums. Whig legislators, with minimal support from Democrats, approved appropriations for the more expensive and humane moral treatment facilities. Occasionally, however, Dorothea Dix won Democratic support as well. In North Carolina, she befriended the wife of a powerful Democratic legislator as the woman lay on her deathbed. The dying woman convinced her husband to support building an asylum. His impassioned speech won the approval of the lower house for a state asylum to be named Dix Hill. In the North Carolina senate, however, the proposal won the votes of 91 percent of the Whigs and only 14 percent of the Democrats—a partisan division that held in state after state.

The South and Social Reform

On most economic issues, southern state legislatures divided along the same lines as northern legislatures: Whigs wanted government participation in the economy, Demo-crats did not. On social questions, however, southern Whigs and Democrats responded in distinctly southern ways. The South was a rural, culturally conservative region of patriarchal households that viewed every attempt at government intervention as a threat to independence. Most southern voters, Whigs as well as Democrats, perceived attempts at "social improvement" as expensive and wrong-headed.

The southern states enacted school laws and drew up blueprints for state school systems, but the culturally homogeneous white South had little need for schools to enforce a common culture. Moreover, the South had less money and less faith in government. Consequently, southern schools tended to be locally controlled, to be infused with southern evangelical culture, and to have a limited curriculum and a short school year. In 1860, northern children attended school for an average of more than 50 days a year; white children in the South attended school for an average of 10 days annually.

By 1860, every slave state except Florida and the Carolinas operated prisons modeled on the Auburn system. Here, however, prisons stressed punishment and profits over rehabilitation. Although some southerners favored northern-style reforms, they knew that southern voters would reject them. Popular votes in Alabama in 1834 and in North Carolina in 1846 brought in resounding defeats for proposals to build or reform

North Wind Picture Archives

The Whipping Post and Pillory at New Castle, Delaware   Delaware was a slave state that continued to inflict public, corporal punishment on lawbreakers. Many of the witnesses to the whipping depicted here are small children, who are supposedly learning a lesson.

penitentiaries in those states. While northern evangelicals were preaching that criminals could be rescued, southern preachers demanded Old Testament vengeance, arguing that hanging, whipping, and branding were sanctioned by the Bible, inexpensive, and more effective than mere incarceration. Other southerners, defending the code of honor, charged that victims and their relatives would be denied vengeance if criminals were tucked away in prisons. Some southern prisons leased prison labor (and sometimes whole prisons) to private entrepreneurs, and dreams of reforming southern criminals were forgotten.

The South did participate in temperance—the all-consuming reform that is discussed in the next section. By the 1820s, Baptists and Methodists had made deep inroads into southern society. Southern ministers preached against dueling, fighting, dancing, gambling, and drinking, while churchgoing women discouraged their husbands, sons, and suitors from drinking. Many southern men either stopped drinking altogether or sharply reduced their consumption. Accordingly, the South contributed its share to the national drop in alcohol consumption. During the 1840s, the Washington Temperance Society and other voluntary temperance groups won a solid footing in southern towns, but southern religious and temperance organizations were based on individual decisions to abstain. Legal prohibition, which became dominant in the North, got nowhere in the South. In the 1850s, when one northern legislature after another passed statewide prohibition, the only slave state to follow was tiny, northern-oriented Delaware.

At bottom, southern resistance to social reform stemmed from a conservative, Bible-based acceptance of suffering and human imperfection and a commitment to the power and independence of white men who headed families. Any proposal that sounded like social tinkering or the invasion of paternal rights was doomed to failure. To make matters worse, many reforms—public schools, Sunday schools, prohibitionism, humane asylums—were seen as the work of well-funded and well-organized missionaries from the Northeast who wanted to fashion society in their own image. The southern distrust of reform was powerfully reinforced after 1830, when northern reformers began to call for abolition of slavery and equality of the sexes—reforms most white southerners found unthinkable.

Excursus: The Politics of Alcohol

Central to party formation in the North was the fight between evangelical Whigs who demanded that government regulate public (and often private) morality and Democrats who feared both big government and the Whig cultural agenda. The most persistent issue in the argument was the question of alcohol—so much so that in many places the temperance question defined the differences between Democrats and Whigs.

Ardent Spirits

Drinking had been a part of social life since the beginning of English settlement, but the withering of authority and the disruptions of the Market Revolution led to increased consumption, increased public drunkenness, and a perceived increase in alcohol-led violence

and social problems (see chapter 8). Beginning in the 1790s, physicians and a few clergymen attacked not only habitual drunkenness but also alcohol. And for a short time after
1812, Federalist politicians and Congregational clergymen formed "moral societies" in
New England that discouraged strong drink. Their imperious tone and their association
with the old seats of authority, however, doomed them to failure.

The temperance crusade began in earnest in 1826, when northeastern evangelicals founded
the American Society for the Promotion of Temperance (soon renamed the American Temperance Society). The movement's manifesto was Lyman Beecher's *Six Sermons on the
Nature, Occasions, Signs, Evils, and Remedy of Intemperance* (1826). Addressing the churchgoing middle class, Beecher declared alcohol an addictive drug and warned that even moderate drinkers risked becoming hopeless drunkards. Thus temperance, like other evangelical reforms, was presented as a contest between self-control and slavery to one's appetites.
By encouraging total abstinence, reformers hoped to halt the creation of new drunkards
while the old ones died out. Even though Beecher pinned his hopes on self-discipline, he
wanted middle-class abstainers to spread reform through both example and coercion. As
middle-class evangelicals eliminated alcohol from their own lives, they also ceased to offer
it to their guests, buy or sell it, or provide it to their employees, and they encouraged their
friends to do the same.

The Drunkard's Progress   This popular print describes the drunkard's progression from social drinking to alcoholism, isolation,
crime, and death by suicide. His desolate wife and daughter and his burning house are at bottom.

Beecher's crusade gathered strength in the middle-class revivals of the 1820s and 1830s. Charles Grandison Finney (see chapter 10), in his revival at Rochester, made total abstinence a condition of conversion. Many other ministers and churches followed suit, and by the mid-1830s, members of the middle class had largely disengaged themselves from alcohol and from the people who drank it. Following a temperance lecture by Finney's coworker Theodore Dwight Weld, for instance, Rochester grocers Elijah and Albert Smith rolled their stock of whiskey out on the sidewalk, smashed the barrels, and let the liquor spill into the street. Other Rochester merchants threw their liquor into the Erie Canal or sold it off at cost. Hundreds of evangelical businessmen pledged that they would refuse to rent to merchants who sold liquor, sell grain to distillers, or enter a store that sold alcohol. Many of them made abstinence a condition of employment, placing ads that carried the line "None But Temperate Men Need Apply." Abstinence and opposition to the use of distilled spirits (people continued to argue about wine and beer) had become a badge of middle-class respectability.

Among themselves, the reformers achieved considerable success. By 1835, the American Temperance Society claimed 1.5 million members and estimated that 2 million Americans had renounced ardent spirits (whiskey, rum, and other distilled liquors); 250,000 had formally pledged to completely abstain from alcohol. The society further estimated that 4,000 distilleries had gone out of business, and that many of the survivors had cut back their production. Many politicians no longer bought drinks to win voters to their cause. The Kentucky Whig Henry Clay, once known for keeping late hours, began to serve only cold water when he entertained at dinner. And in 1833, members of Congress formed the American Congressional Temperance Society. The U.S. Army put an end to the age-old liquor ration in 1832, and increasing numbers of militia officers stopped supplying their men with whiskey. The annual consumption of alcohol, which had reached an all-time high in the 1820s, dropped by more than half in the 1830s (from 3.9 gallons of pure alcohol per adult in 1830 to 1.8 gallons in 1840).

The Origins of Prohibition

In the middle 1830s, Whigs made temperance a political issue. Realizing that voluntary abstinence would not end drunkenness, Whig evangelicals drafted coercive, prohibitionist legislation. First, they attacked the licenses granting grocery stores and taverns the right to sell liquor by the drink and to permit it to be consumed on the premises. The licenses were important sources of revenue for local governments. They also gave local authorities the power to cancel the licenses of troublesome establishments. Militant temperance advocates, usually in association with local Whigs, demanded that the authorities use that power to outlaw all public drinking places. In communities throughout the North, the licensing issue, always freighted with divisions over religion and social class, became the issue around which local parties organized. The question first reached the state level in Massachusetts, when in 1838 a Whig legislature passed the Fifteen-Gallon Law, which decreed that merchants could sell ardent spirits only in quantities of 15 gallons or more, thus outlawing every public drinking place in the state. In 1839, Massachusetts voters sent enough Democrats to the legislature to rescind the law.

The Whig attempt to cancel tavern licenses proved unenforceable because proprietors simply operated without licenses or found ways to get around the laws. While the Massachusetts Fifteen-Gallon Law was in effect, one Boston tavern keeper painted stripes on a pig and charged patrons an admission fee of six cents (the old price of a drink) to view the "exhibition." He then provided customers—who paid over and over to see the pig—with a "complimentary" glass of whiskey.

Leading Democrats agreed with Whigs that Americans drank too much, but whereas Whigs insisted that regulating morality was a proper function of government, Democrats warned that government intrusion into areas of private choice would violate republican liberties. The Democrats of Rochester, New York, responding to the license issue, made the following declaration:

> Anything which savours of restraint in what men deem their natural rights is sure to meet with opposition, and men convinced of error by force will most likely continue all their lives unconvinced in their reason. Whatever shall be done to stay the tide of intemperance, and roll back its destroying wave, must be done by suasive appeals to the reason, the interest, or the pride of men; but not by force.

In many communities, alcohol became the defining difference between Democrats and Whigs. In 1834, for instance, a Whig campaign worker ventured into a poor neighborhood in Rochester and asked a woman how her husband planned to vote. "Why, he has always been Jackson," she said, "and I don't think he's joined the Cold Water."

The Democratization of Temperance

Democratic voters held ambiguous attitudes toward temperance. Many of them continued to drink, while many others voluntarily abstained or cut down. Yet almost without exception they resented the coercive tactics of the Whigs and supported their party's pledge to stop evangelical meddling in private matters. In 1830, when Lyman Beecher's Hanover Street Church in Boston caught fire, the volunteer fire companies (which doubled as working-class drinking clubs) arrived, noted that it was the hated Beecher's church, and made no effort to put out the fire. Unbeknownst to the Reverend Beecher, the church had rented basement space to a merchant who used it to store barrels of rum. According to a contemporary report, the crowd that gathered to watch the church burn to the ground cheered as the barrels exploded one by one.

Democrats, despite their opposition to prohibition, often spoke out against drunkenness. Many craft unions denied membership to heavy drinkers, and hundreds of thousands of rural and urban Democrats quietly stopped drinking. Then, in the late 1830s, former antiprohibitionists launched a temperance movement of their own.

One evening in 1840—in the depths of a devastating economic depression—six craftsmen were drinking at Chase's Tavern in Baltimore. More or less as a joke, they sent one of their number to a nearby temperance lecture. He came back a teetotaler and converted the

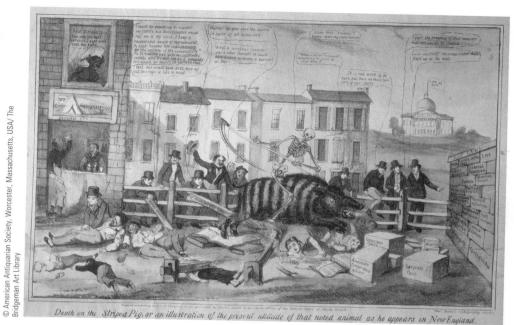

Striped Pig This cartoon, filled with the individual sin and misery and the social destruction caused by alcohol, portrays the Massachusetts' tavernkeeper's famous striped pig as an instrument of the devil.

others. They then drew up a total abstinence pledge and promised to devote themselves to the reform of other drinkers. Within months, from this beginning a national movement had emerged, called the Washington Temperance Society. With a core membership of men who had opposed temperance in the 1830s, the Washingtonians differed from older temperance societies in several ways. First, they identified themselves as members of the laboring classes. Second, they were separated from the churches. Although many of them were churchgoers (usually Methodist or Baptist), many were not, and the Washingtonians avoided religious controversy by avoiding religion. Third, the Washingtonians—at least those who called themselves True Washingtonians—rejected recourse to politics and legislation and concentrated instead on the conversion of drinkers through compassion and persuasion. Finally, they welcomed "hopeless" drunkards—who accounted for about 10 percent of the membership—and hailed them as heroes when they sobered up.

Temperance Schisms

Whig reformers welcomed the Washingtonians at first, but they soon had second thoughts. The nonreligious character of the movement disturbed those who saw temperance as an arm of evangelical reform. Previous advocates of temperance had assumed that sobriety would be accompanied by evangelical decorum. Instead, the meetings, picnics, and parades held by the Washingtonians were continuous with a popular culture that Whig evangelicals opposed. While the temperance regulars read pamphlets and listened to lectures by clergymen, lawyers, and doctors, the Washingtonians enjoyed raucous sing-alongs, comedy routines, barnyard imitations, dramatic skits, and even full-dress minstrel shows geared to temperance themes. Meetings featured experience speeches by reformed drunkards. Speaking extemporaneously, they omitted none of the horrors of an alcoholic life—attempts at suicide, friendships betrayed, fathers and mothers desolated, wives beaten and abandoned, children dead of starvation. Although Washingtonians had given up alcohol, their melodramatic tales, street parades, song books, and minstrel shows—even when presented with a Methodist or Baptist accent—were not the temperance reformation that Lyman Beecher and the Whigs had had in mind.

Nowhere did the Washingtonians differ more sharply from the temperance regulars than in their visions of the reformed life. The Whig reformers tied abstinence to individual ambition and middle-class domesticity. They expected men who quit drinking to withdraw from the male world in which drinking was common and retreat into the comfort of the newly feminized middle-class family. Washingtonians, on the other hand, translated traditional male sociability into sober forms. Moreover, they called former drinkers back to the responsibilities of traditional fatherhood. Their experience stories began with the hurt drunkards had caused their wives and children and ended with their transformation into dependable providers and authoritative fathers. While the Whig temperance regulars tried to extend the ethos of individual ambition and the new middle-class domesticity into society at large, Washingtonians sought to rescue the self-respect and moral authority of working-class fathers.

The Washington Temperance Society collapsed toward the end of the 1840s, but its legacy survived. Among former drinkers in the North, it had introduced a new sense of domestic responsibility and a healthy fear of drunkenness. Consumption of pure alcohol dropped from 1.8 to 1.0 gallons annually in the 1840s. Along the way, the Washingtonians and related groups created a self-consciously respectable native Protestant working class in American cities.

Ethnicity and Alcohol

In the 1840s and 1850s, millions of Irish and German immigrants poured into neighborhoods recently stirred by working-class revivals and temperance agitation. The newcomers had their own time-honored relations to alcohol. The Germans introduced lager beer to the United States, thus providing a wholesome alternative for Americans who wished to give up spirits without joining the teetotalers. The Germans also built old-country beer halls in American cities, complete with sausage counters, oompah bands, group singing, and other family attractions. For their part, the Irish reaffirmed their love of whiskey—a love forged in colonial oppression and in a culture that accepted trouble with resignation—a love that legitimized levels of male drunkenness and violence that Americans, particularly the temperance forces, found appalling. (Differences in immigrant drinking were given architectural expression. German beer halls provided seating arrangements for whole families. Irish bars, on the other hand, provided a bar but no tables or chairs. If a drinker had to sit down, they reasoned, it was time for him to go home.)

In the 1850s, native resentment of Catholic immigrants drove thousands of Baptist and Methodist "respectables" out of the Democratic coalition and into nativist Whig majorities that—beginning with Maine in 1851—established legal prohibition throughout New England, in the middle states, and in the Old Northwest. Many of these Democrats became part of the North's Republican majority on the eve of the Civil War.

The Politics of Race

Focus Question
How did Whigs and Democrats differ on questions of gender and race?

Most whites in antebellum America believed in "natural" differences based on sex and race. God, they said, had given women and men and whites and blacks different mental, emotional, and physical capacities. Because humankind (female and nonwhite more than others) was innately sinful and prone to disorder, God ordained a fixed social hierarchy in which white men exercised power over others. Slaves and free blacks accepted their subordinate status only as a fact of life, not as something that was natural and just. Some women also questioned patriarchy, but before 1830, hierarchy based on sex and race was seldom questioned in public, particularly by persons who were in a position to change it.

In the antebellum years, as southerners and most northerners stiffened their defense of white paternalism (see chapter 10), a radical minority of Whig evangelicals began to envision a world based on Christian love and individual worth, not inherited status. They transformed marriage from rank domination into a sentimental partnership—unequal, but a partnership nonetheless. They also questioned the more virulent forms of racism. While conservative Christians insisted that relations based on dominance and submission were the lot of a sinful humankind, reformers argued that such relations interposed human power, too often in the form of brute force, between God and the individual spirit. They called for a world that substituted spiritual freedom and Christian love for every form of worldly domination. The result was a community of uncompromising radical reformers who attacked slavery and patriarchy as national sins.

The growth of modern racism (see chapter 10) was accompanied by official discrimination against African Americans. Cities either excluded black children from public schools or set up segregated schools. In 1845, when Massachusetts passed a law declaring that all children had the right to attend neighborhood schools, the Boston School Committee blithely ruled that the law did not apply to blacks. Blacks were also excluded from white churches or sat in segregated pews. Even the Quakers seated blacks and whites separately.

Democratic Racism

Neither the Whigs nor the Democrats encouraged the aspirations of slaves or free blacks, but the Democrats, from their beginnings in the 1820s, incorporated racism into their political agenda. Minstrel shows, for example, often reflected the Democratic line on current events, and Democratic cartoonists often featured minstrelsy's bug-eyed, woolly-haired caricatures of blacks. By the time of the Civil War, Democrats mobilized voters almost solely with threats of "amalgamation" and "Negro rule." In Jackson, Michigan, in 1839, after the local Sunday schools announced an outdoor meeting featuring temperance and antislavery speakers, antievangelical rowdies removed the benches from the meeting ground the night before and burned them in the town square. They then dug up the corpse of a black man who had been buried a few days earlier and propped him up in the pulpit of the Presbyterian church, where he greeted the Sunday school the next morning.

Meanwhile, educated Democrats were being taught to think in racist terms. Among most scientists, biological determinism replaced historical and environmental explanations of racial differences; many argued that whites and blacks were separate species. Democrats welcomed that "discovery." John Van Evrie, a New York doctor and Democratic pamphleteer, declared that "it is a palpable and unavoidable fact that Negroes are a different species," and that the story of Adam and Eve referred only to the origin of white people. In 1850, the *Democratic Review* confided, "Few or none now seriously adhere to the theory of the unity of the races. The whole state of the science at this moment seems to indicate that there are several distinct races of men on the earth, with entirely different capacities, physical and mental."

As whites came to perceive racial differences as God-given and immutable, they changed the nature of those differences as well. In the 18th and early 19th centuries, whites had stereotyped blacks as ignorant and prone to drunkenness and thievery, but they had also maintained a parallel stereotype of blacks as loyal and self-sacrificing servants. From the 1820s onward, racists continued to regard blacks as incompetent, but they found it harder to distinguish mere carelessness from dishonesty. Now they saw blacks as treacherous, shrewd, and secretive—individuals who only *pretended* to feel loyalty to white families and affection for the white children they took care of, while awaiting the chance to steal from them or poison them. The writer Herman Melville, a lifelong Democrat who shared little of his compatriots' racism but who helped codify their fascination with duplicity and deceit, dramatized these fears in *Benito Cereno,* a novel about slaves who commandeer a sailing ship and its captain and crew, then (with knives secretly at the throats of their captives) act out a servile charade for unsuspecting visitors who come aboard.

Before 1820, few whites considered slavery a moral issue. Quakers, at their annual meeting in 1758, had condemned both the slave trade and slavery, and Methodists and some Baptists had done the same late in the century. Washington, Jefferson, and other

Chesapeake gentlemen doubted the wisdom, if not the morality, of holding slaves; New England Federalists had condemned slavery in the course of condemning Jeffersonian masters. But there were too few Quakers to make a difference, and the movement to free slaves in the Upper South and the antislavery sentiments of southern evangelicals both died out early in the 19th century. Southerners and most northerners—when they bothered to think about it at all—tended to accept slavery as the result of human (read "black") depravity and God's unknowable plan. Organized opposition to slavery was mostly limited to the aristocratic and half-hearted American Colonization Society (see chapter 10).

Abolitionists

Although few white Americans actively opposed slavery before 1830, the writing was on the wall. Emancipation in the North, although it came about quietly, constituted an implicit condemnation of slavery in the South; so did events outside the United States. Toussaint L'Ouverture's successful slave revolution in Haiti in 1804 threatened slavery everywhere (see chapter 7). The British, whose navy could enforce their dictates on the seas, outlawed the Atlantic slave trade in 1808. Mexico, Peru, Chile, Gran Colombia (present-day Colombia, Venezuela, Ecuador, and Panama), and other new republics carved out of the Spanish empire emancipated their slaves. The most powerful blow came in 1830, when the British Parliament emancipated the slaves of Jamaica, Bermuda, and other Caribbean islands ruled by Britain.

Religious revivals during the late 1820s and early 1830s created a reform-minded evangelical culture in the northern United States. Radical **abolitionism** dates from 1831, when William Lloyd Garrison published the first issue of the *Liberator*. Already a veteran reformer, Garrison condemned slavery as a national sin and demanded immediate emancipation—or at least an immediate start toward emancipation. "I am in earnest," he declared in his first editorial; "I will not equivocate—I will not excuse—I will not retreat a single inch—and I will be heard!" In 1833, Garrison and like-minded abolitionists formed the **American Anti-Slavery Society.** Some of them—Wendell Phillips, Thomas Wentworth Higginson, Theodore Parker—were Unitarians who opposed slavery as an affront to both humanity and rationality. Others—most notably the poet John Greenleaf Whittier—were Quakers who were happy to join the movement. But abolitionists found their greatest support in southern New England, western New York, northern Ohio, and among the new middle classes of the northeastern cities—ground that Yankee settlement, the Market Revolution, and Finneyite revivals had turned into the heartland of the northern Whig Party.

Opposition to slavery was a logical extension of middle-class evangelicalism. Charles Finney, Lyman Beecher, and other Whig evangelicals retained a Puritan inheritance that demanded that God's people legislate the behavior of others. The new evangelicalism, however, was grounded in the morally accountable individual, and not in coercive institutions. Whig evangelicals posed a contest between Christian love and moral free agency on the one hand and every kind of passion, brutality, and force on the other. They often promised that their reforms would liberate the individual spirit from "slavery" to alcohol, lust, or ignorance, thus phrasing moral legislation as liberation, not coercion. Before long, some discovered that slavery, an institution that obliterated moral choice and encouraged the worst human passions, was America's great national sin.

The American Anti-Slavery Society demanded immediate emancipation of slaves and full civil and legal rights for blacks. Assuming that God had created blacks and whites as members of one human family, abolitionists opposed the "scientific" racism spouted by Democrats and many Whigs. Moderates and latecomers to abolitionism spoke of inherent racial characteristics but still tended to view blacks in benign (if condescending) ways. Harriet Beecher Stowe, for instance, portrayed blacks as simple, innocent, loving people who possessed a capacity for sentiment and emotionalism that most whites had lost. In 1852, Horace Mann told an audience of blacks in Ohio that "in intellect, the blacks are inferior to the whites, while in sentiment and affections, the whites are inferior to the blacks." Radical abolitionists, however, remained committed environmentalists. Lydia Maria Child of New York City declared, "In the United States, colored persons have scarcely any chance to rise. But if colored persons are well treated, and have the same inducements to industry as others, they [will] work as well and behave as well."

Old Sturbridge Village

An Abolitionist View of Slave Society   This provocative woodcut appeared in the *Anti-Slavery Almanac for 1840* (Boston, 1839). It pictures the lynching of slaves and their abolitionist allies by a southern mob. Surrounding the hanging tree are men (no women appear in the picture) engaged in other activities that northern reformers insisted grew from the brutal patriarchy of slave society. Men duel with pistols and knives, others engage in an eye-gouging wrestling match, others gamble and drink, and still others cheer for cockfights and horse races. The enemy here is not simply slavery but the debauchery and unbridled passions that abolitionists associated with it.

Agitation

Antislavery, unlike other reforms, was a radical attack on one of the nation's central institutions, and the movement attracted a minority even among middle-class evangelicals. Both Lyman Beecher and Charles Finney opposed the abolitionists in the 1830s, arguing that emancipation would come about sooner or later through the religious conversion of slave owners; antislavery agitation and the denunciation of slaveholders, they argued, would divide Christians, slow the revival movement, and thus actually delay emancipation. Finney warned his abolitionist friend Theodore Dwight Weld that the logical end of antislavery was civil war.

Savoring its role as a beleaguered minority, the American Anti-Slavery Society staged a series of campaigns to force government and the public at large to confront the question of slavery. In 1835, the society launched its **Postal Campaign,** flooding the nation's postal system with abolitionist tracts that southerners and most northerners regarded as "incendiary." From 1836 onward, they petitioned Congress to abolish slavery and the slave trade in the District of Columbia and to deny the slaveholding Republic of Texas admission to the Union. These tactics forced President Andrew Jackson to permit southern postal workers to censor the mails. They also forced Democrats and southern Whigs to abridge the right of petition to avoid discussion of slavery in Congress (see chapter 11).

In these ways, a radical minority forced politicians to demonstrate the complicity of the party system (and the Democrats in particular) in the institution of slavery. They brought the slavery question to public attention and tied it to questions of civil liberties in the North and political power in the South. They were a dangerous minority indeed.

The Politics of Gender and Sex

Whigs valued a reformed masculinity that was lived out in the sentimentalized homes of the northern business classes or in the Christian gentility of the Whig plantation and farm. Jacksonian voters defended domestic patriarchy. Whereas most were unimaginative paternalists, Democrats often made heroes of men whose flamboyant, rakish lives directly challenged Whig domesticity. Whigs denounced Andrew Jackson for allegedly stealing his wife from her lawful husband; Democrats often admired him for the same reason. Richard M. Johnson of Kentucky, who was vice president under Martin Van Buren, openly kept a mulatto mistress and had two daughters by her; with his pistols always at hand, he accompanied her around Washington, D.C. "Prince" John Van Buren, the president's son and a prominent New York Democrat, met a "dark-eyed, well-formed Italian lady," who called herself Amerigo Vespucci and claimed to be a direct descendant of the man for whom America was named. She became young Van Buren's "fancy lady," remaining with him until he lost her in a high-stakes card game.

Whigs made Democratic contempt for sentimental domesticity a political issue. William Crane, a Michigan Whig, claimed that Democrats "despised no man for his sins," and went on to say that "brothel-haunters flocked to this party, because here in all political circles, and political movements, they were treated as nobility." Much of the Whig cultural agenda (and much of Democratic hatred of that agenda) was rooted in contests between Whig and Democratic masculine styles.

Appetites

Many of the reforms urged by Whig evangelicals had to do with domestic and personal life rather than with politics. Their hopes for the perfection of the world hinged more on the character of individuals than on the role of institutions. Calvinism had taught that because human beings were innately selfish and subject to animal appetites, they must submit to godly authority. Whig evangelicals defined original sin as a *tendency* toward selfishness and sin that could be fought off, with God's help, through prayer and personal discipline. They hoped to perfect the world by filling it with godly, self-governing individuals.

It was not an easy task, for opportunities to indulge in vanity, luxury, and sensuality were on the rise. Charles Finney, for instance, preached long and hard against vanity. "A self-indulgent Christian," he said, "is a contradiction. You might as well write on your clothes 'NO TRUTH IN RELIGION,'" he told fashionably dressed women, for their dress proclaimed "GIVE ME DRESS, GIVE ME FASHION, GIVE ME FLATTERY, AND I AM HAPPY." Finney also worried about the effect of money, leisure time, and cheap novels on middle-class homes. He could not, he said, "believe that a person who has ever known the love of God can relish a secular novel" or open his or her home to "Byron, Scott, Shakespeare, and a host of triflers and blasphemers of God." Evangelicals also disdained luxury in home furnishings; they discouraged the use of silks and velvets and questioned the propriety of decorating the home with mahogany, mirrors, brass furnishings, and upholstered chairs and sofas.

The evangelical middle class tried to define levels of material comfort that would distinguish them from the indulgences of those above and below them. They made similar attempts in the areas of food and sex. Sylvester Graham (now remembered for the cracker that bears his name) gave up the ministry in 1830 to become a full-time temperance lecturer. Before long, he was lecturing on the dangers of excess in diet and sex. He claimed that the consumption of red meat, spiced foods, and alcohol produced bodily excitement that resulted in weakness and disease. Sex—including fornication, fantasizing, masturbation, and bestiality—affected the body in even more destructive ways, and the two appetites reinforced each other. (Graham admitted that marital sex, although it was physiologically no different from other forms of sex, was preferable, for it was the least exciting.)

Acting on Graham's concerns, reformers established a system of Grahamite boarding-houses in which young men who were living away from home were provided with diets that helped them control their other appetites. Oberlin College, when it was founded by evangelicals in 1832, banned "tea and coffee, highly seasoned meats, rich pastries, and all unholsome [sic] and expensive foods." Among others who heeded Graham's advice were such future feminists as Lucy Stone, Susan B. Anthony, and Amelia Bloomer. Reformers who did not actually adopt Graham's system shared his concern over the twin evils of rich food and sexual excess. John R. McDowall, a divinity student who headed a mission to New York City prostitutes, admitted, "Having eaten until I am full, lust gets the control of me." John Humphrey Noyes (another divinity student who turned to reform) set up a community in Oneida, New York, that indulged in plural marriage but at the same time urged sexual self-control; he also believed that a perfect Christian world would not allow meat eating.

Moral Reform

Sexual self-control became a badge of middle-class status. Men supposedly had the greatest difficulty taming their appetites. The old image—beginning with Eve and including Delilah and Jezebel and other dangerous women of the Old Testament—of woman as seductress persisted in the more traditionalist churches and in the pulp fiction from which middle-class mothers tried to protect their sons (see chapter 10). Whig evangelicals, on the other hand, discovered that women were naturally free of desire and that only men were subject to the animal passions. "What terrible temptations lie in the way of your sex," wrote Harriet Beecher Stowe to her husband. "Tho I did love you with an almost insane love before I married you, I never knew yet or felt the pulsation which showed me that I could be tempted in that way. I loved you as I now love God." The middle-class ideal combined female purity and male self-control. For the most part, it was a private reform, contained within the home. Sometimes, however, evangelical domesticity produced moral crusades to impose that ethos on the world at large. Many of these crusades were led by women from Whig families.

In 1828, a band of Sunday school teachers, most of them women, initiated an informal mission to prostitutes that grew into the New York Magdalen Society. Taking a novel approach to an age-old question, the society argued that prostitution was created by brutal fathers and husbands who abandoned their young daughters or wives, by dandies who seduced them and turned them into prostitutes, and by lustful men who bought their services. Prostitution, in other words, was not the result of the innate sinfulness of prostitutes; it was the result of the brutality and lust of men. The solution was to separate prostitutes from bad male power, pray with them, and convert them to middle-class morality.

The Magdalen Society's *First Annual Report* (1831) inveighed against male lust and printed shocking life histories of prostitutes. Some men, however, read it as pornography. Others used it as a guidebook to the seamier side of New York City. The wealthy male evangelicals who had bankrolled the Magdalen Society withdrew their support, and the organization fell apart. Thereupon many of the women reformers set up the Female Moral Reform Society, with a House of Industry in which prostitutes were taught morality and household skills to prepare them for new lives as domestic servants in pious middle-class homes. This effort also failed, largely because few prostitutes were interested in domestic service or evangelical religion. That fact became distressingly clear when in 1836 the society was obliged to close its House of Industry after the residents had taken it over during the caretaker's absence.

The Female Moral Reform Society was more successful with members of its own class. Its newspaper, the *Advocate of Moral Reform,* circulated throughout the evangelical North, eventually reaching 555 auxiliary societies with 20,000 readers. Now evangelical women fought prostitution by publishing the names of customers. They campaigned against pornography, obscenity, lewdness, and seduction and taught their sons to be pure, even when it meant dragging them out of brothels. Occasionally, they prosecuted men who took advantage of servant girls. They also publicized the names of adulterers, and they had seducers brought into court. In the process, women reformers fought the sexual double standard and assumed the power to define what was respectable and what was not.

Women's Rights

From the late 1820s onward, middle-class women in the North assumed roles that would have been unthinkable to their mothers and grandmothers. Evangelical domesticity made loving mothers (and not stern fathers) the principal rearers of children. Housewives saw themselves as missionaries to their families, influencing the moral choices their children and husbands made. In that role, women became arbiters of fashion, diet, and sexual behavior. Many joined the temperance movement and moral reform societies, where they became public reformers while posing as mothers protecting their sons from rum sellers and seducers. Such experiences gave them a sense of spiritual empowerment that led some to question their own subordinate status within a system of gendered social roles. Lydia Maria Child, a writer of sentimental fiction and manuals on household economy as well as a leading abolitionist and moral reformer, proclaimed, "Those who urged women to become missionaries and form tract societies . . . have changed the household utensil to a living, energetic being, and they have no spell to turn it into a broom again."

The antislavery movement turned many women into advocates of women's rights. Abolitionists, following the perfectionist implications of Whig evangelicalism to their logical ends, called for absolute human equality and a near-anarchist rejection of impersonal institutions and prescribed social roles. It became clear to some female abolitionists that the critique of slavery (a root-and-branch denunciation of patriarchy and prescribed hierarchy) applied as well to inequality based on sex.

Radical female abolitionists reached the conclusion that they were human beings first and women second. In 1837, **Sarah Grimke** announced, "The Lord Jesus defines the duties of

REPORT

OF THE

WOMAN'S RIGHTS

CONVENTION,

Held at SENECA FALLS, N. Y., July 19th and 20th, 1848.

ROCHESTER:

PRINTED BY JOHN DICK

AT THE NORTH STAR OFFICE.

The Declaration of Sentiments Published by the First Woman's Rights Convention in 1848 This account of the proceedings and list of resolutions announced that there was an organized women's rights movement in the United States. It also announced that women's rights activists knew how to organize a convention and how to publicize their activities in print. (Ties between the women's and antislavery movements led the women to have their report printed at the offices of the *North Star*, an antislavery paper published by the black abolitionist Frederick Douglass—the only male member of the convention—in Rochester.)

his followers in his Sermon on the Mount . . . without any reference to sex or condition . . . never even referring to the distinction now so strenuously insisted upon between masculine and feminine virtues. . . . Men and women are CREATED EQUAL! They are both moral and accountable beings, and whatever is right for a man to do is right for woman." A women's rights convention put it just as bluntly in 1851: "We deny the right of any portion of the species to decide for another portion . . . what is and what is not their 'proper sphere'; that the proper sphere for all human beings is the largest and highest to which they are able to attain."

Beginning about 1840, women lobbied state legislatures and won significant changes in the laws governing women's rights to property, to the wages of their own labor, and to custody of children in cases of divorce. Fourteen states passed such legislation, culminating in New York's Married Women's Property Act in 1860.

The first Woman's Rights Convention met in Seneca Falls, New York, in 1848, and its ties to antislavery were clear. An argument over the right of women to deliver speeches and engage in other forms of public agitation had already split the American Anti-Slavery Society in 1840. Feminist abolitionists organized the **Seneca Falls Convention.** The only male delegate was the black abolitionist Frederick Douglass. Sojourner Truth, another prominent black opponent of slavery, also attended. Nearly all of the other delegates were white women who had worked within the abolition movement. Both as abolitionists and as feminists, they based their demands for equality not only on legal and moral arguments but also on the spirit of republican institutions. The principal formal document issued by the convention, a Declaration of Sentiments and Resolutions based on the Declaration of Independence, denounced "the repeated injuries and usurpations on the part of man toward woman."

Most of those "injuries and usurpations" were political. The central issue was the right to vote, for citizenship was central to the "democratic" pattern that granted liberty and equality to white men regardless of class and excluded Americans who were not white and male. Thus female participation in politics was a direct challenge to a male-ordained women's place. A distraught New York legislator agreed: "It is well known that the object of these unsexed women is to overthrow the most sacred of our institutions. . . . Are we to put the stamp of truth upon the libel here set forth, that men and women, in the matrimonial relation, are to be equal?" Later, feminist Elizabeth Cady Stanton recalled such reactions: "Political rights," she said, "involving in their last results equality everywhere, roused all the antagonism of a dominant power, against the self-assertion of a class hitherto subservient."

Conclusion

By the 1830s, most citizens in every corner of the republic firmly identified with either the Whig or Democratic Party, so much so that party affiliation was a big part of personal identity. In the states and neighborhoods, Whigs embraced commerce and activist government, arguing that both would foster prosperity, social harmony, and moral progress. Faith in progress and improvement led Northern and western Whigs, primarily the more radical evangelicals among them. to imagine that liberty and equality might apply to women and blacks. Democrats were generally more localistic and culturally conservative. Like the Whigs, they seldom doubted the value of commerce, but they worried that the market and its organization of banking, credit, and monetary supply was creating unprecedented levels of inequality and personal dependence among the republic's white male citizenry; they were certain that Whig public works projects and Whig taxation increased inequality and corrupted the republic. Democrats also looked with angry disbelief at attempts of Whigs (and rebellious members of Whig families) to govern the private and public behavior of their neighbors, and sometimes even to tinker with the "natural" distinctions of gender and race.

In sum, Whigs reformulated the revolutionary legacy of liberty and equality, moving away from classical notions of citizenship and toward liberty of conscience and equality of opportunity within a market-driven democracy. They often attempted to civilize that new world by using government power to encourage commerce, social interdependence, and cultural homogeneity. When Democrats argued that Whig "interdependence" in fact meant dependence and inequality, Whigs countered with promises of individual success for those who were morally worthy of it. Democrats trusted none of that. Theirs was a Jeffersonian formulation grounded in a fierce defense of the liberty and equality of white men, and in a minimal, inexpensive, decentralized government that protected the liberties of those men without threatening their independence or their power over their households and within their neighborhoods.

SUGGESTED READINGS

On party ideologies, see **John Ashworth, *'Agrarians & Aristocrats': Party Political Ideology in the United States, 1837–1846*** (1983), and **Daniel Walker Howe, *The Political Culture of the American Whigs*** (1979). Constituencies and state-level issues are addressed in **Lee Benson, *The Concept of Jacksonian Democracy: New York as a Test Case*** (1961); **Ronald P. Formisano, *The Transformation of Political Culture: Massachusetts Parties, 1790s–1840s*** (1983); and **Lacy K. Ford, Jr., *Origins of Southern Radicalism: The South Carolina Upcountry, 1800–1860*** (1988). **Richard J. Carwardine, *Evangelicals and Politics in Antebellum America*** (1993) is an insightful study of religion and politics in these years. On the politics of schools, see **Carl F. Kaestle, *Pillars of the Republic: Common Schools and American Society, 1780–1860*** (1983).

Influential studies of prisons and asylums include **David J. Rothman, *The Discovery of the Asylum: Social Order and Disorder in the New Republic*** (1971) and **Michael Meranze, *Laboratories of Virtue: Punishment, Revolution, and Authority in Philadelphia, 1760–1835*** (1996). Drinking and temperance are the subjects of **W. J. Rorabaugh, *The Alcoholic Republic: An American Tradition*** (1979). The literature on reform movements is synthesized in **Steven Mintz, *Moralists & Modernizers: America's Pre–Civil War Reformers*** (1995). Students might also consult **Robert H. Abzug, *Cosmos Crumbling: American Reform and the Religious Imagination*** (1994); **Jean Fagan Yellin, *Women & Sisters: The Antislavery Feminists in American Culture*** (1989); and **Lori D. Ginzberg, *Women and the Work of Benevolence: Morality, Politics, and Class in the 19th-Century***

United States (1990). The cultural and moral underpinnings of reform are a subtext of **Karen Halttunen's** subtle and important *Murder Most Foul: The Killer and the American Gothic Imagination* (1998).

Visit the Liberty Equality Power Companion Web site for resources specific to this textbook: http://www.thomsonedu.com/history/murrin

Also find self-tests and additional resources at ThomsonNOW. ThomsonNOW is an integrated online suite of services and resources with proven ease of use and efficient paths to success, delivering the results you want—NOW!

www.thomsonedu.com/login/

13

Manifest Destiny:
An Empire for Liberty—or Slavery?

When William Henry Harrison took the oath as the first Whig president on March 4, 1841, the stage seemed set for the enactment of Henry Clay's American System. Instead, Harrison contracted pneumonia after he delivered an interminable inaugural address outdoors in a sleet and snow storm. He died a month later, and John Tyler, a states-rights Virginian, became president. Tyler had become a nominal Whig only because of his hatred of Andrew Jackson. He proceeded to read himself out of the Whig Party by vetoing two bills to create a new national bank. Their domestic program a shambles, the Whigs lost control of the House in the 1842 midterm elections. Thereafter, the political agenda shifted to the Democratic program of territorial expansion. Through annexation, negotiation, and war, the United States increased its size by 50 percent in the years between 1845 and 1848, but this achievement reopened the issue of slavery's expansion and planted the bitter seeds of civil war.

Growth as the American Way

Focus Question
What impulses lay behind the Manifest Destiny of America's westward expansion?

By 1850, older Americans had seen the area of the United States quadruple in their lifetime. During the 47 years since the Louisiana Purchase of 1803, the American population had also quadrupled. If those rates of growth had continued after 1850, the United States would have contained 1.9 *billion* people at the beginning of the 21st century and would have occupied every square foot of land on the globe. If the sevenfold increase in the gross national product that Americans enjoyed from 1800 to 1850 had persisted, today's U.S. economy would be larger than that of today's entire world economy.

Many Americans in 1850 took this prodigious growth for granted. They considered it evidence of God's beneficence to this virtuous republic. During the 1840s, a group of expansionists affiliated with the Democratic Party began to call themselves the **Young America movement.** They proclaimed that it was the **Manifest Destiny** of the United States "to overspread and to possess the whole of the continent which Providence has

CHRONOLOGY

1844	Senate rejects Texas annexation • James K. Polk elected president
1845	Congress annexes Texas • Mexico spurns U.S. bid to buy California and New Mexico
1846	U.S. declares war on Mexico • U.S. forces under Zachary Taylor win battles of Palo Alto and Resaca de la Palma • U.S. and Britain settle Oregon boundary dispute • U.S. occupies California and New Mexico • House passes Wilmot Proviso • U.S. forces capture Monterrey, Mexico
1847	Americans win battle of Buena Vista • U.S. Army under Winfield Scott lands at Veracruz • Americans win battles of Contreras, Churubusco, Molino del Rey, and Chapultepec • Mexico City falls
1848	Treaty of Guadalupe Hidalgo ends Mexican War, fixes Rio Grande as border, cedes New Mexico and California to U.S. • Gold discovered in California • Spain spurns Polk's offer of $100 million for Cuba • Zachary Taylor elected president
1849	John C. Calhoun pens "Address of the Southern Delegates" • California seeks admission as a free state
1850	Taylor dies, Millard Fillmore becomes president • Bitter sectional debate culminates in Compromise of 1850 • Fugitive Slave Law empowers federal commissioners to recover escaped slaves
1851	Fugitive Slave Law provokes rescues and violent conflict in North • American filibusters executed in Cuba
1852	*Uncle Tom's Cabin* becomes best seller • Franklin Pierce elected president
1854	Anthony Burns returned from Boston to slavery • William Walker's filibusters invade Nicaragua • Pierce tries to buy Cuba • Ostend Manifesto issued
1856	William Walker legalizes slavery in Nicaragua
1860	William Walker executed in Honduras

given us for the development of the great experiment of liberty," wrote John L. O'Sullivan, editor of the *Democratic Review*, in 1845.

Not all Americans considered this unbridled expansion good. For the earliest Americans, whose ancestors had arrived on the continent thousands of years before the Europeans, it was a story of defeat and contraction rather than of conquest and growth. By 1850, the white man's diseases and guns had reduced the Indian population north of the Rio Grande to fewer than half a million, a fraction of the population of two or three centuries earlier. The relentless westward march of white settlements had pushed all but a few thousand Indians beyond the Mississippi. In the 1840s, the U.S. government decided to create a "permanent Indian frontier" at about the 95th meridian (roughly the western borders of Iowa, Missouri, and Arkansas). But white emigrants were already violating that frontier on the overland trails to the Pacific, and settlers were pressing against the borders of Indian territory. In little more than a decade, the idea of "one big reservation" in the West would give way to the policy of forcing Indians onto small reservations. The government "negotiated" with Indian chiefs for vast cessions of land in return for annuity payments that were soon spent on the white man's fire-water and other purchases from shrewd or corrupt traders. Required to learn the white man's ways or perish, many Indians perished—of disease, malnutrition, and alcohol, and in futile efforts to break out of the reservations and regain their land.

Manifest Destiny and Slavery

If the Manifest Destiny of white Americans spelled doom for red Americans, it also presaged a crisis in the history of black Americans. By 1846, the Empire for Liberty that Thomas Jefferson had envisioned for the Louisiana Purchase seemed more an empire for slavery: Territorial acquisitions since 1803 had brought into the republic the slave states of Louisiana, Missouri, Arkansas, Florida, Texas, and parts of Alabama and Mississippi. Only Iowa, admitted in 1846, had joined the ranks of the free states. (**See Map 13.1, Free and Slave States and Territories, 1848, in the color insert following page 624.**)

The division between slavery and freedom in the rest of the Louisiana Purchase had supposedly been settled by the Compromise of 1820. Although the issue frequently disturbed public tranquility for a quarter-century thereafter, as long as the controversy focused on the morality of slavery where it already existed, the two-party system—in which both major parties did their best to evade the issue—managed to contain its explosive potential. When the issue became the expansion of slavery into new territories, however, evasion and containment no longer sufficed. The issue first arose with the annexation of Texas, which helped provoke war with Mexico in 1846—a war that many antislavery northerners considered an ugly effort to expand slavery.

The Westering Impulse

Many Americans of European descent saw their future in the West. In the 1840s, **Horace Greeley** urged, "Go west, young man." And to the West they went in unprecedented numbers, driven in part by the depression of 1837–43 that prompted thousands to search for cheap land and better opportunity. "The West is our object, there is no other hope left for us," declared one farmer as he and his family set out on the Oregon Trail. "There is nothing like a new country for poor folks."

An earlier wave of migration had populated the region between the Appalachians and the Missouri River, bringing a new state into the Union on an average of every three years. During those years, reports from explorers, fur traders, missionaries, and sailors filtered back from California and the Pacific Northwest, describing the bounteous resources and benign climates of those wondrous regions. Richard Henry Dana's *Two Years before the Mast* (1840), the story of his experience in the cowhide and tallow trade between California and Boston, alerted thousands of Americans to this new Eden on the Pacific. Guidebooks rolled off the presses describing the boundless prospects that awaited settlers who would turn "those wild forests, trackless plains, untrodden valleys" into "one grand scene of continuous improvements, universal enterprise, and unparalleled commerce."

The Hispanic Southwest

Another people of partial European descent already lived in portions of the region west of the 98th meridian. The frontier of New Spain had pushed north of the Rio Grande early in the 17th century. By the time Mexico won its independence from Spain in 1821, some 80,000 Mexicans lived in this region. Three-fourths of them had settled in the Rio Grande Valley of New Mexico and most of the rest in California. Centuries earlier, the Spaniards had introduced horses, cattle, and sheep to the New World. These animals became the economic mainstay of Hispanic society along New Spain's northern frontier. Later, Anglo-Americans would adopt Hispanic ranching methods to invade and subdue the lands of the arid western plains. Spanish words still describe the tools of the trade and the land: *bronco, mustang, lasso, rodeo, stampede, canyon, arroyo, mesa.*

Colonial society on New Spain's northern frontier had centered on the **missions** and the **presidios.** Intended to Christianize Indians, the missions also became an instrument to exploit their labor, while the presidios (military posts) protected the settlers from hostile Indians. By the late 18th century, the mission system had fallen into decline, and 15 years after Mexican independence in 1821, it collapsed entirely. The presidios, underfunded and understaffed, also declined after Mexican independence, so that the defense of Mexico's far northern provinces increasingly fell to the residents. But by the 1830s, many residents of New Mexico and California were more interested in bringing American traders in than in keeping American settlers out. A flourishing trade over the Santa Fe Trail from Independence, Missouri, brought American manufactured goods to Santa Fe, New Mexico (and points south), in exchange for Mexican horses, mules, beaver pelts, and silver. New England ships carried American goods all the way around the horn of South America to San Francisco and other California ports in exchange for tallow and hides produced by *californio* ranchers. This trade linked the economies of New Mexico and California more closely to the United States than to the Mexican heartland. The trickle of Americans into California and New Mexico in the 1820s foreshadowed the flood that would engulf these regions two decades later.

The Oregon and California Trails

In 1842 and 1843, Oregon fever swept the Mississippi Valley. Thousands of farm families sold their land, packed their worldly goods in covered wagons along with supplies for five or six months on the trail, hitched up their oxen, and headed out from Independence or St. Joseph, Missouri, for the trek of almost 2,000 miles to the river valleys of Oregon or California. On the way, they passed through regions claimed by three nations—the United States, Mexico, and Britain—and they settled on land owned by Mexico (California) or

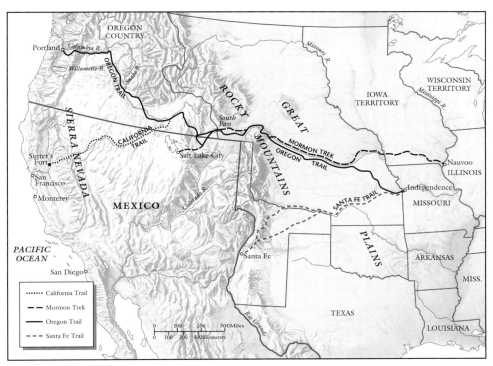

Map 13.2 **Overland Trails, 1846** The Santa Fe Trail was mainly a route for trade between the United States and the Mexican province (before 1848) of New Mexico. The other three trails carried hundreds of thousands of Americans to new homes in the West.

claimed jointly by the United States and Britain (Oregon, which then stretched north to the border of Russian Alaska). But no matter who claimed it, the land was occupied mostly by Indians, who viewed this latest intrusion with wary eyes. Few of the emigrants thought about settling down along the way, for this vast reach of arid plains, forbidding mountains, and burning wastelands was then known as the **Great American Desert.** White men considered it suitable only for Indians and the disappearing breed of mountain men who had roamed the region trapping beaver.

During the next quarter-century, half a million men, women, and children crossed a half-continent in one of the great sagas of American history. After the migration of farm families to Oregon and California came the 1847 exodus of the **Mormons** to a new **Zion** in the basin of the Great Salt Lake and the 1849 gold rush to California. The stories of these migrants were of triumph and tragedy, survival and death, courage and despair, success and failure. Most of them reached their destinations; some died on the way—victims of disease, exposure, starvation, suicide, or homicide by Indians or by fellow emigrants. Of those who arrived safely, a few struck it rich, most carved out a modest although hard living, and some drifted on, still looking for the pot of gold that had thus far eluded them. Together, they generated pressures that helped bring a vast new empire—more than 1 million square miles—into the United States by 1848.

Migration was mostly a male enterprise. Adult men outnumbered women on the Oregon Trail and on the California Trail before the gold rush by more than 2 to 1, and in the gold rush by more than 10 to 1. The quest for new land, a new start, and a chance to make a big strike represented primarily masculine ideals. Women felt more rooted in family, home, and community, and were less willing to pull up stakes to march into the wilderness. Yet even on the rough mining frontier of the West, men sought to replicate as soon as possible the homes and communities they had left behind. "We want families," wrote a Californian in 1858, "because their homes and hearth stones everywhere, are the only true and reliable basis of any nation." Most of the migrants, except during the gold rush, were family groups.

Many of the women were reluctant migrants. Although middle-class urban families had made some small beginnings toward equal partnership in marriage, men still ruled the family on the midwestern farms from which most of the migrants came. Men made the decision to go; women obeyed. Diaries kept by women on the trail testify to their unhappiness:

> What had possessed my husband, anyway, that he should have thought of bringing us away out through this God-forsaken country? . . . Oh, how I wish we never had started for the Golden Land. . . . I would make a brave effort to be cheerful and patient until the camp work was done. Then . . . I would throw myself down on the ground and shed tears, wishing myself back home with my friends and chiding myself for consenting to take this wild goose chase.

For some families it did turn out to be a wild goose chase, but for many of those who stayed the course and settled in the far West, it was a success story, made so in great measure by the women. They turned houses into homes, settlements into communities. The frontier did not break down the separate spheres of men and women. Woman's sphere in the West was still the home and the family, the bearing and nurturing of children, the management of the household economy. Man's sphere remained the world of public events and economic production.

The Mormon Migration

Patriarchal rule was strongest among those migrants with the most nearly equal sex ratio—the Mormons. Subjected to persecution that drove them from their original home in western New York to Ohio, Missouri, and eventually to Illinois, the Mormons established Nauvoo, Illinois, a thriving community of 15,000 souls, based on collective economic effort and theocratic discipline imposed by their founder and prophet, Joseph Smith. But the people of Illinois proved no more hospitable to the Mormons than the sect's previous neighbors had been. Smith did not make matters any easier. His insistence that God spoke through him, his autocratic suppression of dissent, and his assertion that the Mormons were the only true Christians and would inherit the earth provoked hostility. When a dissident faction of

Courtesy of the Church Archives, The Church of Jesus Christ of Latter-day Saints

Mormon Emigrants on Their Way West   This rare photograph depicts a Mormon wagon train snaking through a narrow mountain pass on its way to Salt Lake City. Beleaguered by neighbors in Illinois, the Mormons decided after Joseph Smith's murder in 1844 to emigrate to what was then Mexican territory—but would soon become part of the United States.

Mormons published Smith's latest revelation, which sanctioned **polygamy**, he ordered their printing press destroyed. The county sheriff arrested him, and in June 1844, a mob broke into the jail and killed him.

Smith's martyrdom prompted yet another exodus. Under the leadership of Smith's successor, Brigham Young, the Mormons began the long trek westward that would eventually lead them to the Great Salt Lake basin in a part of Mexican territory that soon was ceded to the United States in the wake of the Mexican War. A man of iron will and administrative genius, Young organized the migration down to the last detail. Arriving with the advance guard of Mormon pioneers at a pass overlooking the Great Basin on July 24, 1847, Young, who was ill with tick fever, struggled from his wagon and stared at the barren desert and mountains surrounding the lake. "This is the right place," he declared. Here the Mormons could create their Zion undisturbed.

They built a flourishing community, making the desert bloom with grain and vegetables irrigated by water they ingeniously diverted from mountain streams. Organizing the economy and the civil society as he had organized the exodus, Young reigned as leader of the church, and from 1850 to 1857 as governor of the newly created Utah Territory.

Zion, however, did not remain undisturbed. Relations with the government in Washington, D.C., and with those sent out as territorial officials were never smooth, especially after Young's proclamation in 1852 that authorized polygamy. (Although Young married a total of 55 women, most Mormon men could afford to support no more than one wife and her children; only about one-sixth of Mormon marriages were polygamous.) When conflict between the Mormons and the U.S. Army broke out in 1857, Young surrendered his civil authority and made an uneasy peace with the government.

The Republic of Texas

As the Mormons were starting west, a crisis between Mexico and the United States was coming to a boil. Although the United States had renounced any claim to **Texas** in a treaty with Spain negotiated in 1819, many Americans believed that Texas had been part of the Louisiana Purchase. By the time the treaty was ratified in 1821, Mexico had won its independence from Spain. The new Republic of Mexico wanted to develop its northern borderlands in Texas by encouraging immigration and settlement there. Thus, Stephen F. Austin, a Missouri businessman, secured a large land grant from Mexico to settle 300 families from the United States. Despite their pledge to become Roman Catholics and Mexican citizens, these immigrants and many who followed remained Protestants and Americans at heart. They also brought in slaves, in defiance of a recent Mexican law abolishing slavery. Despite Mexican efforts to ban any further immigration, 30,000 Americans lived in Texas by 1835, outnumbering Mexicans 6 to 1.

American settlers, concentrated in east Texas, initially had little contact with Mexican *tejanos* (Texans), whose settlements were farther south and west. But political events in Mexico City in 1835 had repercussions on the northern frontier. A new conservative national government seemed intent on consolidating its authority over the northern territories, including Coahuila-Texas. In response, the Anglo-American settlers and the *tejanos* forged a political alliance to protest any further loss of autonomy in their province. When the Mexican government responded militarily, many Texans—both Anglo and Mexican—fought back. Then, in March 1836, delegates from across Texas met at a village appropriately called Washington. They declared Texas an independent republic and adopted a constitution based on the U.S. model.

The American Revolution had lasted seven years; it took the Texans less than seven months to win and consolidate their independence. Mexican General Antonio López de Santa Anna led the Mexican army that captured the **Alamo** (a former mission converted to a fort) in San Antonio on March 6, 1836, killing all 187 of its defenders, including the legendary Americans Davy Crockett and Jim Bowie. Rallying to the cry "Remember the Alamo!" Texans swarmed to the revolutionary army commanded by Sam Houston. When the Mexican army slaughtered another force of more than 300 men after they had surrendered at Goliad on March 19, the Texans were further inflamed. A month later, Houston's army, aided by volunteers from southern U.S. states, routed a larger Mexican force on the San Jacinto River (near present-day

Houston) and captured Santa Anna. Under duress, he signed a treaty granting Texas its independence. The Mexican congress later repudiated the treaty but could not muster enough strength to reestablish its authority north of the Nueces River. The victorious Texans elected Sam Houston president of their new republic and petitioned for annexation to the United States.

The Annexation Controversy

Focus Question
How did westward expansion relate to the issue of slavery?

President Andrew Jackson, wary of provoking war with Mexico or quarrels with antislavery northerners, rebuffed the annexationists. So did his successor, **Martin Van Buren.** Although disappointed, the Texans turned their energies to building their republic. The British government encouraged the Texans, in the hope that they would stand as a buffer against further U.S. expansion. **Abolitionists** in England even cherished the notion that Britain might persuade the Texans to abolish slavery. Texas leaders made friendly responses to some of the British overtures, probably in the hope of provoking American annexationists to take action. They did.

Soon after Vice President John Tyler became president on the death of William Henry Harrison in 1841, he broke with the Whig Party that had elected him. Seeking to create a new coalition to reelect him in 1844, Tyler seized on the annexation of Texas as "the only matter that will take sufficient hold of the feelings of the South to rally it on a southern candidate."

Tyler named John C. Calhoun of South Carolina as secretary of state to negotiate a treaty of annexation. The southern press ran scare stories about a British plot to use Texas as a beachhead for an assault on slavery, and annexation became a popular issue in the South. Calhoun concluded a treaty with the eager Texans, but then he made a mistake: He released to the press a letter he had written to the British minister to the United States, informing him that, together with other reasons, Americans wanted to annex Texas in order to protect slavery, an institution "essential to the peace, safety, and prosperity" of the United States. This seemed to confirm abolitionist charges that annexation was a pro-slavery plot. Northern senators of both parties provided more than enough votes to defeat the treaty in June 1844.

By then, Texas had become the main issue in the forthcoming presidential election. Whig candidate Henry Clay had come out against annexation, as had the leading contender for the Democratic nomination, former president Martin Van Buren. Van Buren's stand ran counter to the rising tide of Manifest Destiny sentiment within the Democratic Party. It also angered southern Democrats, who were determined to have Texas. Through eight ballots at the Democratic national convention, they blocked Van Buren's nomination; on the ninth, the southerners broke the stalemate by nominating one of their own, James K. Polk of Tennessee. Polk, a staunch Jacksonian who had served as Speaker of the House of Representatives during Jackson's presidency, was the first "dark horse" candidate (not having been a contender before the convention). Southerners exulted in their victory. "We have triumphed," wrote one of Calhoun's lieutenants. "Polk is nearer to *us* than any public man who was named. He is a large Slave holder and [is for] Texas—States rights *out & out*." Polk's nomination undercut President Tyler's forlorn hope of being reelected on the Texas issue, so he bowed out of the race.

Polk ran on a platform that called for not only the annexation of Texas but also the acquisition of all of Oregon up to 54°40' (the Alaskan border). That demand was aimed at voters in the western free states, who believed that bringing Oregon into the Union would balance the expansion of slavery into Texas with the expansion of free territory in the Northwest. Polk was more than comfortable with this platform. In fact, he wanted not only Texas and Oregon, but California and New Mexico as well.

Texas fever swept the South during the campaign. So powerful was the issue that Clay began to waver, stating that he would support annexation if it could be done without starting a war with Mexico. This concession won him a few southern votes but angered northern antislavery Whigs. Many of them voted for James G. Birney, candidate of the Liberty Party, which opposed any more slave territory. Birney probably took enough Whig votes from Clay in New York to give Polk victory there and in the electoral college.

Acquisition of Texas and Oregon

Although the election was extremely close (Polk won only a plurality of 49.5 percent of the popular vote), Democrats regarded it as a mandate for annexation. Eager to leave office in triumph, lame-duck President Tyler submitted to Congress a **joint resolution** of annexation, which required only a simple majority in both houses instead of the two-thirds majority in the Senate that a treaty would have required. Congress passed the resolution in March 1845. Texas thus bypassed the territorial stage and came in as the 15th slave state in December 1845. Backed now by the United States, Texans claimed a southern and western border beyond the Nueces River all the way to the Rio Grande, which nearly tripled the area that Mexico had formerly defined as Texas. Mexico responded by breaking off diplomatic relations with the United States. The stage was set for five years of bitter controversy that included a shooting war with Mexico and political warfare in the United States over the issue of slavery expansion.

Meanwhile, Polk lost no time in addressing his promise to annex Oregon. "Our title to the country of the Oregon is 'clear and unquestionable,'" he said in his inaugural address. "Already our people are preparing to perfect that title by occupying it with their wives and children." The problem was to persuade Britain to recognize the title. Both countries had jointly "occupied" Oregon since 1818, overseeing the fur trade carried on by British and

American companies. Chanting the slogan "Fifty-four forty or fight!" many Americans in 1845 demanded all of Oregon, as pledged in the Democratic platform. But Polk proved unwilling to fight for 54°40'. So far, Americans had settled only in the region south of the Columbia River, at roughly the 46th parallel. In June 1846, Polk accepted a compromise treaty that split the Oregon country between the United States and Britain at the 49th parallel. Several Democratic senators from the **Old Northwest** (states north of the Ohio River and west of Pennsylvania) accused Polk of betrayal and voted against the treaty. They had supported Texas to the Rio Grande, and they had expected Polk to support Oregon to 54°40'. A sectional breach had opened in the Democratic Party that would soon grow wider.

The Mexican War

Focus Question
What were the causes and consequences of the Mexican-American War?

Having avoided a war with Britain, Polk provoked one with Mexico in order to gain California and New Mexico. In 1845, he sent a special envoy to Mexico City with an offer to buy California and New Mexico for $30 million. To help Mexico make the right response, he ordered federal troops to the disputed border area between Mexico and Texas, dispatched a naval squadron to patrol the Gulf Coast of Mexico, and instructed the American consul at Monterrey (the Mexican capital of California) to stir up annexation sentiment among settlers there. These strong-arm tactics provoked a political revolt in Mexico City that brought a militant anti-American regime to power.

Polk responded in January 1846 by ordering 4,000 soldiers under General Zachary Taylor to advance all the way to the Rio Grande. Recognizing that he could achieve his goals only through armed conflict, Polk waited for news from Texas that would justify a declaration of war, but none came. His patience having run out, on May 9, 1846, he began to draft a message to Congress asking for a declaration of war on general grounds of Mexican defiance. That evening, word finally arrived that two weeks earlier Mexican troops had crossed the Rio Grande and attacked an American patrol, killing 11 soldiers. Polk had what he wanted. He quickly revised his message and sent it to Congress on May 11.

Most Whigs opposed war with Mexico, but in the end, not wanting to be branded unpatriotic, all but a handful of them voted for the final declaration of war, which passed the House by 174 to 14 and the Senate by 40 to 2. Despite their continuing opposition to what they called "Mr. Polk's War," most Whigs voted supplies for the army. Having witnessed the demise of the Federalist Party after it had opposed the war in 1812, one Whig congressman said sarcastically that from then on he had decided to vote for "war, pestilence, and famine."

The United States went to war with a tiny regular army of fewer than 8,000 men, supplemented by 60,000 volunteers in state regiments, and an efficient navy that quickly established domination of the sea lanes. Mexican soldiers outnumbered American in most of the battles, but the Americans had higher morale, better leadership, and better weapons (especially artillery). They also enjoyed the backing of a more determined, stable government and a far richer, stronger economy. The U.S. forces won every battle—and the war—in a fashion that humiliated the proud Mexicans and left a legacy of national hostility and border violence. Especially remarkable was the prominent role played by junior American officers trained at West Point, for whom the Mexican War was a rehearsal for a larger conflict that would take place 15 years later: Robert E. Lee, Ulysses S. Grant, Pierre G. T. Beauregard, George B. McClellan, Braxton Bragg, George H. Thomas, Thomas J. Jackson, George G. Meade, Jefferson Davis, and others, whose names would become household words during the Civil War.

Military Campaigns of 1846

The Mexican War proceeded through three phases. The first phase was carried out by Zachary Taylor's 4,000 regulars on the Rio Grande. In two small battles on May 8 and 9, at Palo Alto and Resaca de la Palma, they routed numerically superior Mexican forces even before Congress had declared war. Those victories made "Old Rough and Ready" Taylor a hero, a reputation he rode to the presidency two years later. Reinforced by several thousand volunteers, Taylor pursued the retreating Mexicans 100 miles south of the Rio Grande to the heavily fortified Mexican city of Monterrey, and took the city after four days of fighting in September 1846. Mexican resistance in the area crumbled, and Taylor's force settled down as an army of occupation.

Meanwhile, the second phase of American strategy had gone forward in New Mexico and California. In June 1846, General Stephen Watts Kearny led an army of 1,500 tough frontiersmen and regulars west from Fort Leavenworth toward Santa Fe. Kearny bluffed and intimidated the New Mexico governor, who fled southward without ever ordering the local 3,000-man militia into action. Kearny's army occupied Santa Fe on August 18 without firing a shot. With closer economic

American Forces in Saltillo, Mexico This posed photograph of General John E. Wool and his staff of Zachary Taylor's army on its march southward from Monterrey through Saltillo in November 1846 is the earliest known photograph of an American military force. Photography had recently been invented, and pictures such as this one were extremely rare before the 1850s.

Yale Collection of Western Americana, Beinecke Rare Book and Manuscript Library ties to the United States than to their own country, which taxed them well but governed them poorly, many New Mexicans seemed willing to accept American rule.

After receiving reinforcements, Kearny left a small occupation force and divided his remaining troops into two contingents, one of which he sent under Colonel Alexander Doniphan into the Mexican province of Chihuahua. In the most extraordinary campaign of the war, these 800 Missourians marched 1,500 miles, foraging supplies along the way, fought and beat two much larger enemy forces, and finally linked up with Zachary Taylor's army near Monterrey in spring 1847.

Kearny led the other contingent across deserts and mountains to California. Events there had anticipated his arrival. In June 1846, a group of American settlers backed by Captain John C. Frémont, a renowned western explorer with the army topographical corps, captured Sonoma and raised the flag of an independent California, displaying the silhouette of a grizzly bear. Marked by exploits both courageous and comic, this "bear-flag revolt" paved the way for the conquest of California by the *americanos.* The U.S. Pacific Fleet seized California's ports and the capital at Monterrey; sailors from the fleet and volunteer soldiers under Frémont subdued Mexican resistance. Kearny's weary and battered force arrived in December 1846, barely in time to help with the mopping up.

Military Campaigns of 1847

New Mexico and California had fallen into American hands, and Mexican armies had experienced nothing but defeat, but the Mexican government refused to admit that the war was lost. A political maneuver by President Polk to secure a more tractable government in Mexico had backfired. In one of Mexico's many palace revolts, Santa Anna had been overthrown and forced into exile in Cuba in 1844. A shadowy intermediary convinced Polk in July 1846 that if Santa Anna returned to power, he would make peace on American terms in return for $30 million. Polk instructed the navy to pass Santa Anna through its blockade of Mexican ports. The wily Mexican general then rode in triumph to Mexico City, where yet another new government named him supreme commander of the army and president of the republic. Breathing fire, Santa Anna spoke no more of peace. Instead, he raised new levies and marched north early in 1847 to attack Taylor's army near Monterrey.

Taylor, 62 years old, was still rough but not as ready to withstand a counteroffensive as he had been a few weeks earlier. After capturing Monterrey in September 1846, he had let the defeated Mexican army go and had granted an eight-week **armistice** in the hope that it would allow time for peace negotiations. Angry at Taylor's presumption in making such a decision and suspicious of the general's political ambitions, Polk canceled the armistice and named General-in-Chief Winfield Scott to command the third phase of the war, a campaign against Mexico City. A large, punctilious man, Scott acquired the nickname "Old Fuss and Feathers" for a military professionalism that contrasted with the homespun manner of "Rough and Ready" Zach Taylor. Scott decided to lead an invasion of Mexico's heartland from a beachhead at Veracruz, and in January 1847 ordered the transfer of more than half of Taylor's troops to his own expeditionary force.

Left with fewer than 5,000 men, most of them untried volunteers, Taylor complained bitterly of political intrigue and military favoritism. Nevertheless, he marched out to meet Santa Anna's army of 18,000. In a two-day battle on February 22 and 23 at Buena Vista, Taylor's little force bent but never broke. They inflicted twice as many casualties as they suffered in a fierce struggle highlighted by the brilliant counterattack of a Mississippi regiment commanded by Jefferson Davis. The bloodied Mexican army retreated toward the capital. When news of the victory reached the East, Taylor's popularity soared to new heights. If Polk had wanted to quash a political rival by taking away most of his troops— as Taylor believed—he had achieved just the opposite.

But it was General Scott who actually won the war. With a combined army-navy force, he took the coastal fortress at Veracruz in March 1847. Over the next five months, his army, which never totaled more than 14,000 men (with considerable turnover because of expiring one-year enlistments), marched and fought its way over more than 200 miles of mountains and plains to Mexico City. It was a bold, high-risk action. When Scott's forces reached the fortifications of Mexico City, held by three times their numbers, the Duke of Wellington, who was following the campaign closely, predicted, "Scott is lost—he cannot capture the city, and he cannot fall back upon his base." But capture it he did, on September 14, after fierce hand-to-hand combat in the battles of Contreras, Churubusco, Molino del Rey, and Chapultepec. It was a brilliant success, even though it owed much to wrangling among Mexican leaders that forced Santa Anna to spend almost as much time facing down his internal enemies as fighting the Americans.

Antiwar Sentiment

The string of military victories prevented the significant U.S. antiwar sentiment from winning even wider support. The war had enthusiastic support in the South and West and among Democrats, but the Whigs and many people in the Northeast, especially in New England, considered it "a wicked and disgraceful war." Democrats and Whigs had different notions of progress. Democrats believed in expanding American institutions over *space*—in particular, the space occupied by Mexicans and Indians. Whigs, on the other hand, believed in improving American institutions over *time*. "Opposed to the instinct of boundless acquisition stands that of Internal Improvement," said Horace Greeley. "A nation cannot simultaneously devote its energies to the absorption of others' territories and the improvement of its own."

Antislavery people raised their eyebrows when they heard Manifest Destiny rhetoric about "extending the blessings of American liberty" to benighted regions. They suspected that the real reason was the desire to extend slavery. Hosea Biglow, the rustic Yankee philosopher created by the abolitionist poet James Russell Lowell, observed:

They jest want this Californy
So's to lug new slave-states in
To abuse ye an' to scorn ye,
And to plunder ye like sin.

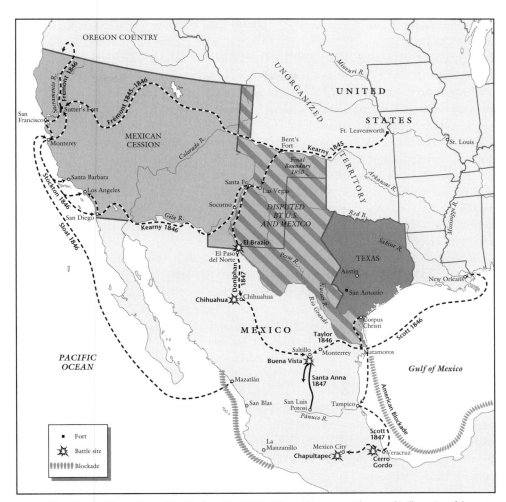

Map 13.3   Principal Campaigns of the Mexican War, 1846–1847   This map provides a graphic illustration of the vast territory over which the Mexican War was fought; the distance from Veracruz to San Francisco is 2,500 miles.
View an animated version of this map or related maps at http://www.thomsonedu.com/history/murrin.

The Wilmot Proviso

The slavery issue overshadowed all others in the debate over the Mexican War. President Polk could not understand the reason for the fuss. "There is no probability," he wrote in his diary, "that any territory will ever be acquired from Mexico in which slavery would ever exist." But other Americans were less sure. Many southerners hoped that slavery would spread into the fertile lowlands of Mexican territory. Many northerners feared that it might. Their fear was strengthened by an editorial in a Charleston newspaper: "California is peculiarly adapted for slave labor. The right to have [slave] property protected there is not a mere abstraction." The issue came to a head early in the war. On August 8, 1846, Pennsylvania Democratic Congressman David Wilmot offered an amendment to an army appropriations bill: ". . . that, as an express and fundamental condition of the acquisition of any territory from the Republic of Mexico . . . neither slavery nor involuntary servitude shall ever exist in any part of said territory."

This famous Wilmot Proviso framed the national debate over slavery for the next 15 years. The House passed the amendment. Nearly all northern Democrats joined all northern Whigs in the majority, while southern Democrats and southern Whigs voted almost unanimously against it. (In the Senate, greater southern strength defeated the proviso.) This outcome marked an ominous wrenching of the party division between Whigs and Democrats into a *sectional* division between free and slave states. It was a sign that the two-party system might not successfully contain the convulsive question of slavery expansion.

Several factors underlay the split of northern Democrats from their own president on this issue. Ever since southern Democrats had blocked Van Buren's nomination in 1844, resentment had been growing in the party's northern wing. Polk's acceptance of 49° latitude for Oregon's northern boundary exacerbated this feeling. "Our rights to Oregon have been shamefully compromised," fumed an Ohio Democrat. "The administration is Southern, Southern, Southern! . . . Since the South have fixed boundaries for free territory, let the North fix boundaries for slave territories." The reduced rates of the Walker tariff in 1846 (sponsored by Robert J. Walker of Mississippi, Polk's secretary of the treasury) dismayed Democrats from Pennsylvania's industrial districts. Polk further angered Democrats from the Old Northwest by vetoing a rivers and harbors bill that would have provided federal aid for transportation improvements in their districts. The Wilmot Proviso was in part the product of these pent-up frustrations over what northerners were increasingly calling "the slave power." "The time has come," said a Democratic congressman in 1846, "when the Northern Democracy should make a stand. Every thing has taken a Southern shape and been controlled by Southern caprice for years. . . . We must satisfy the Northern people . . . that we are not to extend the institution of slavery as a result of this war."

The slavery issue hung like the sword of Damocles over Polk's efforts to negotiate peace with Mexico. Polk also came under pressure from expansionist Democrats who, excited by military victory, wanted more Mexican territory, perhaps even "all Mexico." Polk had sent diplomat Nicholas Trist with Scott's army to negotiate the terms of Mexican surrender. Authorized to pay Mexico $15 million for California, New Mexico, and a Texas border on the Rio Grande, Trist worked out such a treaty. In the meantime, though, Polk had succumbed to the "all Mexico" clamor. He ordered Trist back to Washington, intending to replace him with someone who would exact greater concessions from Mexico. Trist ignored the recall, signed the treaty of Guadalupe Hidalgo on February 2, 1848, and sent it to Washington. Although angered by Trist's defiance, Polk nonetheless decided to end the controversy by submitting the treaty to the Senate, which approved it on March 10 by a vote of 38 to 14.

Half the opposition came from Democrats who wanted more Mexican territory and half from Whigs who wanted none. As it was, the treaty sheared off half of Mexico and increased the size of the United States by one-fourth.

The Election of 1848

The treaty did nothing to settle the question of slavery in the new territory, however. Mexico had abolished the institution two decades earlier; would the United States reintroduce it? Many Americans looked to the election of 1848 to decide the matter. Four positions on the issue emerged, each identified with a candidate for the presidential nomination.

The Wilmot Proviso represented the position of those determined to bar slavery from all territories. The Liberty Party endorsed the proviso and nominated Senator John P. Hale of New Hampshire for president. Southern Democrat John C. Calhoun formulated the "southern-rights" position. Directly challenging the Wilmot Proviso, Calhoun introduced resolutions in the Senate in February 1847 affirming the right of slave owners to take their human property into any territory. The Constitution protected the right of property, Calhoun pointed out; Congress could no more prevent a settler from taking his slaves to California than it could prevent him from taking his horses there.

Although most southerners agreed with Calhoun, the Democratic Party sought a middle ground. The Polk administration endorsed the idea of extending the old Missouri Compromise line of 36°30' to the Pacific. This would have excluded slavery from present-day Washington, Oregon, Idaho, Utah, Nevada, and the northern half of California, but would have allowed it in present-day New Mexico, Arizona, and southern California. Secretary of State James Buchanan, also a candidate for the Democratic presidential nomination (Polk did not seek renomination), embraced this position.

Another compromise position became known as **"popular sovereignty."** Identified with Senator Lewis Cass of Michigan, yet another contender for the Democratic nomination, this concept proposed to let the settlers of each territory decide for themselves whether to permit slavery. This solution contained a crucial ambiguity: It did not specify *at what stage* the settlers of a territory could decide on slavery. Most northern Democrats assumed that a territorial legislature would make that decision as soon as it was organized. Most southerners assumed that the decision would not be made until the settlers had drawn up a state constitution. That would normally happen only after several years as a territory, during which time slavery might well have taken deep enough root to be implanted in the state constitution. So long as neither assumption was tested, each faction could support popular sovereignty.

The Democratic convention nominated Cass for president, thereby seeming to endorse popular sovereignty. In an attempt to maintain party unity, however, the platform made no mention of the matter. The attempt was not entirely successful: Two Alabama delegates walked out when the convention refused to endorse Calhoun's southern-rights position, and an antislavery faction from New York walked out when it failed to win a credentials fight.

The Whig convention tried to avoid a similar schism by adopting no platform at all, but the slavery issue would not die. In the eyes of many antislavery delegates who styled themselves **Conscience Whigs,** the party made itself ridiculous by nominating Zachary Taylor for president. Desperate for victory, the Whigs chose a hero from a war that most of them had opposed. But the fact that Taylor was also a large slaveholder who owned several plantations in Louisiana and Mississippi was too much for the Conscience Whigs. They bolted from the party and formed a coalition with the Liberty Party and antislavery Democrats.

The Free Soil Party

The **Free-Soilers** met in convention in August 1848. The meeting resembled a religious camp meeting more than a political gathering. Speakers proclaimed slavery "a great moral, social, and political evil—a relic of barbarism which must necessarily be swept away in the progress of Christian civilization." The convention did not say how that would be done, but it did adopt a platform calling for "no more Slave States and no more Slave Territories." The Free Soil Party nominated former president Martin Van Buren, with Charles Francis Adams, the son and grandson of presidents, as his running mate.

The campaign was marked by the futile efforts of both major parties to bury the slavery issue. Free Soil pressure compelled both northern Democrats and Whigs to take a stand against slavery in the territories. Whigs pointed to their earlier support of the Wilmot Proviso, while Democrats said popular sovereignty would keep the territories free. In the South, though, the two parties presented other faces. There, the Democrats pointed with pride to their expansionist record that had brought to the nation hundreds of thousands of square miles of territory—into which slavery might expand. But Taylor proved the strongest candidate in the South because he was a southerner and a slaveholder. "Will the people of [the South] vote for a Southern President or a Northern one?" asked southern newspapers. "We prefer Old Zack with his sugar and cotton plantations and four hundred negroes to all their compromises."

Taylor carried 8 of the 15 slave states and increased the Whig vote in the South by 10 percent over 1844, while the Democratic vote declined by 4 percent. Although he did less well in the North, he carried New York and enough other states to win the election. The Free-Soilers won no electoral votes but polled 14 percent of the popular vote in the North. They also elected nine congressmen along with two senators who would be heard from in the future: Salmon P. Chase of Ohio, architect of the Free Soil coalition in 1848, and Charles Sumner of Massachusetts, leader of the Conscience Whigs.

The Gold Rush and California Statehood

About the time Nicholas Trist was putting the finishing touches on the treaty to make California part of the United States, workers building a sawmill on the American River near Sacramento discovered flecks of gold in the riverbed. The word gradually leaked out, reaching the East in August 1848, where a public that had been surfeited with tall tales out of the West greeted this news with skepticism. But in December, Polk's final message to Congress confirmed the "extraordinary" discoveries of gold. Two days later, a tea caddy containing 320 ounces of pure gold from California arrived in Washington. Now all doubts disappeared. By spring 1849, 100,000 gold-seekers were poised to take off by foot on the overland trail or by ship—either around Cape Horn or to the isthmus of Central America, where after a land crossing, they could board another ship to take them up the Pacific Coast to the new boomtown of San Francisco. Eighty thousand actually made it that first year (5,000 succumbed to a cholera epidemic). Some of them struck it rich, most kept hoping to, and more came by the scores of thousands every year from all over the world, including China.

Political organization of California could not be postponed. The mining camps needed law and order; the settlers needed courts, land and water laws, mail service, and other amenities of established government. In New Mexico, the 60,000 former Mexican citizens,

Courtesy of the California History Room, California State Library, Sacramento, California

The California Gold Rush Prospectors for gold in the foothills of California's Sierra Nevada came from all over the world, including China. This photograph shows American-born and Chinese miners near Auburn, California, a year or two after the initial gold rush of 1849. It illustrates the original technology of separating gravel from gold by panning or by washing the gravel away in a sluice box, leaving the heavier gold flakes behind.

now Americans, also needed a governmental structure for their new allegiance. Nor could the growing Mormon community at Salt Lake be ignored.

Still, the slavery question paralyzed Congress. In December 1848, lame-duck president Polk recommended extension of the Missouri Compromise 36°30' line to the Pacific. The Whig-controlled House defied him, reaffirmed the Wilmot Proviso, drafted a bill to organize California as a free territory, and debated abolishing the slave trade and even slavery itself in the District of Columbia. Fistfights flared in Congress; southerners declared that they would secede if any of those measures became law; the Democratic Senate quashed all the bills. A southern caucus asked Calhoun to draft an address setting forth its position. He eagerly complied, producing in January 1849 a document that breathed fire against "unconstitutional" northern efforts to keep slavery out of the territories. Calhoun reminded southerners that their "property, prosperity, equality, liberty, and safety" were at stake and prophesied secession if the South did not prevail.

But Calhoun's firebomb fizzled. Only two-fifths of the southern congressmen and senators signed it. The Whigs wanted nothing to do with it. They looked forward to good times in the Taylor administration and opposed rocking the boat. "We do not expect an administration which we have brought into power [to] do any act or permit any act to be done [against] our safety," said Robert Toombs of Georgia, a leading Whig congressman. "We feel *secure* under General Taylor," added his fellow Georgian Alexander H. Stephens.

They were in for a rude shock. Taylor viewed matters as a nationalist, not as a southerner. New York's antislavery Senator William H. Seward became one of his principal advisers. A novice in politics, Taylor was willing to be guided by Seward. As a military man, he was attracted to the idea of vanquishing the territorial problem by outflanking it. He proposed to admit California and New Mexico (the latter comprising present-day New Mexico, Arizona, Nevada, Utah, and part of Colorado) immediately as *states,* skipping the territorial stage.

From the South came cries of outrage. Immediate admission would bring in two more free states because slavery had not existed under Mexican law, and most of the 49ers were Free Soil in sentiment. With the administration's support, Californians held a convention in October 1849, drew up a constitution excluding slavery, and applied to Congress for admission as a state. Taylor's end run would tip the existing balance of 15 slave and 15 free states in favor of the North, probably forever. The South would lose its de facto veto in the Senate. "For the first time," said freshman Senator Jefferson Davis of Mississippi, "we are about permanently to destroy the balance of power between the sections." Davis insisted that slave labor was suitable to mining and that slavery should be permitted in California. Southerners vowed never to "consent to be thus degraded and enslaved" by such a "monstrous trick and injustice" as admission of California as a free state.

The Compromise of 1850

Focus Question
What issues were at stake in the congressional debates that led to the Compromise of 1850? How successfully did the compromise resolve these issues?

California and New Mexico became the focal points of a cluster of slavery issues that faced the Congress of 1849–50. An earlier Supreme Court decision (*Prigg* v. *Pennsylvania,* 1842) had relieved state officials of any obligation to enforce the return of **fugitive slaves** who had escaped into free states, declaring that this was a federal responsibility. Southerners therefore demanded a strong national fugitive slave law (in utter disregard of their oft-stated commitment to states' rights); antislavery northerners, on the other hand, were calling for an end to the disgraceful buying and selling of slaves in the national capital; and in the Southwest, a shooting war threatened to break out between Texas and New Mexico. Having won the Rio Grande as their southern border with Mexico, Texans insisted that the river must also mark their western border with New Mexico. (That would have given Texas more than half of the present state of New Mexico.) This dispute also involved slavery because the terms of Texas's annexation authorized the state to split into as many as five states, and the territory it carved out of New Mexico would create the potential for still another slave state.

These problems produced both a crisis and an opportunity. The crisis lay in the threat to break up the Union. From Mississippi had gone forth a call for a convention of southern states at Nashville in June 1850 "to devise and adopt some mode of resistance to northern aggression." Few doubted that the mode would be secession unless Congress met southern demands at least halfway, but Congress got off to an unpromising start. Sectional disputes prevented either major party from commanding a majority in electing a Speaker of the House. Through three weeks and 62 ballots, the contest went on while tempers shortened. Northerners and southerners shouted insults at each other, fistfights broke out, and a Mississippian drew a revolver during one heated debate. Southern warnings of secession became a litany: "If, by your legislation, you seek to drive us from the territories of California and New Mexico," thundered Toombs of Georgia, "*I am for disunion.*" On the 63rd ballot, the exhausted legislators finally elected Howell Cobb of Georgia as Speaker by a plurality rather than a majority.

The Senate Debates

As he had in 1820 and 1833, Henry Clay hoped to turn the crisis into an opportunity. Seventy-two years old, a veteran of 30 years in Congress, three times an unsuccessful candidate for president, Clay was the most respected and still the most magnetic figure in the Senate. A nationalist from the border state of Kentucky, he hoped to unite North and South in a compromise. On January 29, 1850, he presented eight proposals to the Senate and supported them with an eloquent speech, the first of many to be heard in that body during what turned out to be the most famous congressional debate in U.S. history. Clay grouped the first six of his proposals into three pairs, each pair offering one concession to the North and one to the South. The first pair would admit California as a free state but would organize the rest of the Mexican cession without restrictions against slavery. The second would settle the Texas boundary dispute in favor of New Mexico but would compensate Texas to enable the state to pay off bonds it had sold when it was an independent republic. (Many holders of the Texas bonds were southerners.) The third pair of proposals would abolish the slave trade in the District of Columbia but would guarantee the continued existence of slavery there unless both Maryland and Virginia consented to abolition. Of Clay's final two proposals, one affirmed that Congress had no jurisdiction over the interstate slave trade; the other called for a strong national fugitive slave law.

At the end of a long, grueling bargaining process, the final shape of the **Compromise of 1850** closely resembled Clay's package. The public face of this process featured set speeches in the Senate, the most notable of which were those of John C. Calhoun, Daniel Webster, and William H. Seward. Calhoun and Webster (along with Clay) represented the grand Senate triumvirate of the previous generation; Seward was the rising star of a new generation, whose speech catapulted him into renown. Each senator spoke for one of the three principal viewpoints on the issues.

Calhoun went first, on March 4. Suffering from consumption (he would die within a month), Calhoun sat shrouded in flannel as a colleague read his speech to a rapt audience. Unless northerners returned fugitive slaves in good faith, Calhoun warned, unless they consented to the expansion of slavery into the territories and accepted a constitutional amendment, "which will restore to the South, in substance, the power she possessed of protecting herself before the equilibrium between the two sections was destroyed," southern states could not "remain in the Union consistently with their honor and safety." Calhoun wanted to give slave states a veto power over any national legislation concerning slavery.

Webster's famous "seventh of March" speech three days later was both a reply to Calhoun and an appeal to the North for compromise. In words that would be memorized by generations of schoolchildren, Webster announced his theme: "I wish to speak to-day, not as a Massachusetts man, nor as a Northern man, but as an American. I speak to-day for the preservation of the Union. Hear me for my cause." Although Webster had voted for the Wilmot Proviso, he now urged Yankees to forgo "taunt or reproach" of the South by insisting on the proviso. Nature would exclude slavery from New Mexico. "I would not take pains uselessly to reaffirm an ordinance of nature, nor to reenact the will of God." Believing that God helped those who helped themselves, many of Webster's former antislavery admirers repudiated his leadership, especially because he also endorsed a fugitive slave law.

On March 11, Seward expressed the antislavery position in what came to be known as his "higher law" speech. Both slavery and compromise were "radically wrong and essentially vicious," he said. In reply to Calhoun's arguments for the constitutional protection of slavery in the territories, Seward invoked "a higher law than the Constitution," the law of God in whose sight all persons were equal. Instead of legislating the expansion of slavery or the return of fugitive slaves, the country should be considering how to bring slavery peacefully to an end, for "you cannot roll back the tide of social progress."

Passage of the Compromise

While these speeches were being delivered, committee members worked ceaselessly behind the scenes to fashion compromise legislation. They were aided by lobbyists for Texas bondholders and for business interests that wanted an end to this distracting crisis. But, in reaching for a compromise, Clay chose what turned out to be the wrong tactic. He lumped most of his proposals together in a single bill, hoping that supporters of any given part of the compromise would vote for the whole in order to win the part they liked. Instead, most senators and representatives voted against the package in order to defeat the parts they disliked. President Taylor continued to insist on the immediate admission of California (and New Mexico, when it was ready) with no quid pro quo for the South. Exhausted and discouraged, Clay fled Washington's summer heat, leaving a young senator from Illinois, **Stephen A. Douglas,** to lead the forces of compromise.

Another rising star of the new generation, Douglas reversed Clay's tactics. Starting with a core of supporters made up of Democrats from the Old Northwest and Whigs from the upper South, he built a majority for each part of the compromise by submitting it separately and adding its supporters to his core: northerners for a free California, southerners for a fugitive slave law, and so on. This effort benefited from Taylor's sudden death on July 9 (of gastroenteritis, after consuming large quantities of iced milk and cherries on a hot Fourth of July). The new president, Millard Fillmore, was a conservative Whig from New York who gave his support to the compromise. One after another, in August and September, the separate measures became law: the admission of California as a free state; the organization of the rest of the Mexican cession into the two territories of New Mexico and Utah without restrictions against slavery; the settlement of the Texas–New Mexico border dispute in favor of New Mexico and the compensation of Texas with $10 million; the abolition of the slave trade in the District of Columbia and the guarantee of slavery there; and the passage of a new fugitive slave law. When it was over, most Americans breathed a sigh of relief, the Nashville convention adjourned tamely, and President Fillmore christened the Compromise of 1850 "a final settlement" of all sectional problems. Calhounites in the South and antislavery activists in the North branded the compromise a betrayal of principle, but, for the time being, they seemed to be in a minority.

The compromise produced consequences different from what many anticipated. California came in as the 16th free state, but its senators during the 1850s were in fact conservative Democrats who voted with the South on most issues. California law even allowed slave owners to keep their slaves while sojourning in the state. The territorial legislatures of Utah and New Mexico legalized slavery, but few slaves were brought there. And the fugitive slave law generated more trouble and controversy than all the other parts of this final settlement combined.

The Fugitive Slave Law

The Constitution required that a slave who escaped into a free state must be returned to his or her owner, but failed to specify how that should be done. Under a 1793 law, slave owners could take their recaptured property before any state or federal court to prove ownership. This procedure worked well enough so long as officials in free states were willing to cooperate. As the antislavery movement gained momentum in the 1830s, however, some officials proved uncooperative. And professional slave-catchers sometimes went too far—kidnapping free blacks, forging false affidavits to "prove" they were slaves, and selling them south into bondage. Several northern states responded by passing antikidnapping laws that gave alleged fugitives the right of trial by jury. The laws also prescribed criminal penalties for kidnapping. In *Prigg* v. *Pennsylvania* (1842), the U.S. Supreme Court declared Pennsylvania's antikidnapping law unconstitutional. But the Court also ruled that enforcing the Constitution's fugitive slave clause was entirely a federal responsibility, thereby absolving the states of any need to cooperate in enforcing it. Nine northern states thereupon passed **personal liberty laws** prohibiting the use of state facilities (courts, jails, police or sheriffs, and so on) in the recapture of fugitives.

Fugitive slaves dramatized the poignancy and cruelties of bondage more vividly than anything else. A man or woman risking all for freedom was not an abstract issue but a real human being whose plight invited sympathy and help. Consequently,

Kidnapping Again! This is a typical poster printed by abolitionist opponents of the Fugitive Slave Law. It was intended to rally the citizens of Boston against the recapture and reenslavement of Anthony Burns, a fugitive slave from Virginia seized in Boston in May 1854.

many northerners who were not necessarily opposed to slavery in the South nonetheless felt outrage at the idea of fugitives being seized in a land of freedom and returned to slavery. The **"underground railroad"** that helped spirit slaves out of bondage took on legendary status. Stories of secret chambers where fugitives were hidden, dramatic trips in the dark of the moon between stations on the underground, and clever or heroic measures to foil pursuing bloodhounds exaggerated the legend.

Probably fewer than 1,000 of a total 3 million slaves actually escaped to freedom each year. But to southerners the return of those fugitives—like the question of the legality of slavery in California or New Mexico—was a matter of *honor* and *rights*. "Although the loss of property is felt," said Senator James Mason of Virginia, sponsor of the Fugitive Slave Act, "the loss of honor is felt still more." The fugitive slave law, said another southern politician, was "the only measure of the Compromise [of 1850] calculated to secure the rights of the South." Southerners therefore regarded obedience to the law as a test of the North's good faith in carrying out the compromise.

The law's provisions were extraordinary. It created federal commissioners who could issue warrants for arrests of fugitives and before whom a slaveholder would bring a captured fugitive to prove ownership. All the slaveholder needed for proof was an affidavit from a slave-state court or the testimony of white witnesses. The fugitive had no right to testify on his or her own behalf. The commissioner received a fee of $10 if he found the owner's claim valid, but only $5 if he let the fugitive go. (The difference was supposedly justified by the larger amount of paperwork required to return the fugitive to slavery.) The federal treasury would pay all costs of enforcement. The commissioner could call on federal marshals to apprehend fugitives, and the marshals in turn could deputize any citizen to help. A citizen who refused could be fined up to $1,000, and anyone who harbored a fugitive or obstructed his or her capture would be subject to imprisonment. Northern senators had tried in vain to weaken some of these provisions and to amend the law to give alleged fugitives the rights to testify, to habeas corpus, and to a jury trial.

The Slave-Catchers

Abolitionists denounced the law as draconian, immoral, and unconstitutional. They vowed to resist it. Opportunities soon came, as slave owners sent agents north to recapture fugitives, some of whom had escaped years earlier (the act set no statute of limitations). In February 1851, slave-catchers arrested a black man living with his family in Indiana and returned him to an owner who said he had run away 19 years before. A Maryland man tried to claim ownership of a Philadelphia woman who he said had escaped 22 years earlier; he also wanted her six children, all of whom were born in Philadelphia. In this case, the commissioner disallowed his claim to both mother and children, but statistics show that the law was rigged in favor of the claimants. In the first 15 months of its operation, 84 fugitives were returned to slavery and only 5 were released. (For the entire decade of the 1850s, the ratio was 332 to 11.)

Unable to protect their freedom through legal means, many blacks, with the support of white allies, resorted to flight and resistance. Thousands of northern blacks fled to Canada—3,000 in the last three months of 1850 alone. In February 1851, slave-catchers arrested a fugitive who had taken the name Shadrach when he escaped from Virginia a year earlier. They rushed him to the federal courthouse, where a few deputy marshals held him, pending a hearing. But a group of black men broke into the courtroom, overpowered the deputies, and spirited Shadrach out of the country to Canada. This was too much for the Fillmore administration. In April 1851, another fugitive, Thomas Sims, was arrested in Boston, and the president sent 250 soldiers to help 300 armed deputies enforce the law and return Sims to slavery.

Continued rescues and escapes kept matters at fever pitch for the rest of the decade. In the fall of 1851, a Maryland slave owner and his son accompanied federal marshals to Christiana, Pennsylvania, a Quaker village, where two of the man's slaves had taken refuge. The hunters ran into a fusillade of gunfire from a house where a dozen black men were protecting the fugitives. When the shooting stopped, the slave owner was dead and his son was seriously wounded. Three of the blacks fled to Canada. This time Fillmore sent in the marines. They helped marshals arrest 30 black men and a half-dozen whites, who were indicted for treason. But the U.S. attorney dropped charges after a jury acquitted the first defendant, a Quaker.

Another white man who aided slaves was not so lucky. Sherman Booth was an abolitionist editor in Wisconsin who led a raid in 1854 to free a fugitive from custody. Convicted in a federal court, Booth appealed for a writ of habeas corpus from the Wisconsin Supreme Court. The court freed him and declared the Fugitive Slave Law unconstitutional. That assertion of states' rights prompted the southern majority on the U.S. Supreme Court to overrule the Wisconsin court, assert the supremacy of federal law, and order Booth back to prison.

Two of the most famous fugitive slave cases of the 1850s ended in deeper tragedy. In spring 1854, federal marshals in Boston arrested a Virginia fugitive, Anthony Burns. Angry abolitionists poured into Boston to save him. Some of them tried to attack the federal courthouse, where a deputy was killed in an exchange of gunfire. But the new president, Franklin Pierce, was determined not to back down. "Incur any expense," he wired the district attorney in Boston, "to enforce the law." After every legal move to free Burns had failed, Pierce sent a U.S. revenue cutter to carry Burns back to Virginia. While thousands of angry Yankees lined the streets under American flags hanging upside down to signify the loss of liberty in the cradle of the Revolution, 200 marines and soldiers marched this lone black man back into bondage.

Two years later, Margaret Garner escaped from Kentucky to Ohio with her husband and four children. When a posse of marshals and deputies caught up with them, Margaret seized a kitchen knife and tried to kill her children and herself rather than return to slavery. She managed to cut her three-year-old daughter's throat before she was overpowered.

After complicated legal maneuvers, the federal commissioner remanded the fugitives to their Kentucky owner. He promptly sold them down the river to Arkansas, and, in a steamboat accident along the way, one of Margaret Garner's sons drowned in the Mississippi.

Such events had a profound impact on public emotions. Most northerners were not abolitionists, and few of them regarded black people as equals, but millions of them moved closer to an antislavery—or perhaps it would be more accurate to say anti-Southern—position in response to the shock of seeing armed slave-catchers on their streets. "When it was all over," agreed two previously conservative Whigs in Boston after the Anthony Burns affair, "I put my face in my hands and wept. I could do nothing less. . . . We went to bed one night old-fashioned, conservative, compromise Union Whigs and waked up stark mad Abolitionists."

Several northern states passed new personal liberty laws in defiance of the South. Although those laws did not make it impossible to recover fugitives, they made it so difficult, expensive, and time consuming that many slave owners gave up trying. The failure of the North to honor the Fugitive Slave Law, part of the Compromise of 1850, was one of the South's bitter grievances in the 1850s. Several southern states cited it as one of their reasons for seceding in 1861.

Owen ♡ Danny

Uncle Tom's Cabin

A novel inspired by the plight of fugitive slaves further intensified public sentiment. Harriet Beecher Stowe, author of *Uncle Tom's Cabin,* was the daughter of Lyman Beecher, the most famous clergyman-theologian of his generation, and the sister of Henry Ward Beecher, the foremost preacher of the next generation. Writing this book made her more famous than either of them. Having grown up in the doctrinal air of New England Calvinist notions of sin, guilt, and atonement, Harriet lived for 18 years in Cincinnati, where she became acquainted with fugitive slaves who had escaped across the Ohio River. During the 1840s, in spare moments that she carved out from the duties of bearing and nurturing seven children, Stowe wrote numerous short stories. Outraged by the Fugitive Slave Law in 1850, she responded to her sister-in-law's suggestion: "Hattie, if I could use a pen as you can, I would write something that will make this nation feel what an accursed thing slavery is."

In 1851, writing by candlelight after putting the children to bed, Stowe turned out a chapter a week for serial publication in an antislavery newspaper. When the installments were published as a book in spring 1852, *Uncle Tom's Cabin* became a runaway best seller and was eventually translated into 20 languages. Contrived in plot, didactic in style, steeped in sentiment, *Uncle Tom's Cabin* is nevertheless a powerful novel with unforgettable characters. Uncle Tom is not the fawning, servile Sambo of later caricature, but a Christlike figure who bears the sins of white people and carries the salvation of black people on his shoulders. The novel's central theme is the tragedy of the breakup of families by slavery—the theme most likely to pluck at the heartstrings of middle-class Americans of that generation. Few eyes remained dry as they read about Eliza fleeing across the ice-choked

Ohio River to save her son from the slave trader, or about Tom grieving for the wife and children he had left behind in Kentucky when he was sold.

Although banned in some parts of the South, *Uncle Tom's Cabin* found a wide but hostile readership there. A measure of the defensiveness of southerners toward the book is the tone of the reviews that appeared in southern journals. The editor of the South's leading literary periodical instructed the reviewer: "I would have the review as hot as hellfire, blasting and searing the reputation of [this] vile wretch in petticoats." Pro-slavery authors rushed into print with more than a dozen novels challenging Stowe's themes, but all of them together made nothing like the impact of *Uncle Tom's Cabin*. The book helped shape a whole generation's view of slavery.

Filibustering

If the prospects for slavery in New Mexico appeared unpromising, southerners could contemplate a closer region where slavery already existed—Cuba. Enjoying an economic boom based on slave-grown sugar, this Spanish colony only 90 miles from American shores had nearly 400,000 slaves in 1850—more than any American state except Virginia. President Polk, his appetite for territory not yet sated by the acquisition of Texas, Oregon, and half of Mexico, offered Spain $100 million for Cuba in 1848. The Spanish foreign minister spurned the offer, stating that he would rather see the island sunk in the sea than sold.

If money did not work, revolution might. Cuban planters, restive under Spanish rule, intrigued with American expansionists in the hope of fomenting an uprising on the island. Their leader was Narciso López, a Venezuelan-born Cuban soldier of fortune. In 1849, López recruited several hundred American adventurers for the first **"filibustering"** expedition against Cuba (from the Spanish *filibustero*, a freebooter or pirate). When President Taylor ordered the navy to prevent López's ships from leaving New York, López shifted his operations to the friendlier environs of New Orleans, where he raised a new force of filibusters, many of them Mexican War veterans. Port officials in New Orleans looked the other way when the expedition sailed in May 1850, but Spanish troops drove the filibusters into the sea after they had established a beachhead in Cuba.

Undaunted, López escaped and returned to a hero's welcome in the South, where he raised men and money for a third try in 1851. This time, William Crittenden of Kentucky, nephew of the U.S. attorney general, commanded the 420 Americans in the expedition, but the invasion ended in fiasco and tragedy. Spanish soldiers suppressed a local uprising timed to coincide with the invasion and then defeated the filibusters, killing 200 and capturing the rest. López was garroted in the public square of Havana, after which 50 American prisoners, including Crittenden, were lined up and executed by firing squad.

These events dampened southerners' enthusiasm for Cuba, but only for a time. "Cuba must be ours," declared Jefferson Davis, in order to "increase the number of slave-holding constituencies." In 1852, the Democrats nominated Franklin Pierce of New Hampshire for president. Although a Yankee, Pierce had a reputation as a "doughface"—a northern man with southern principles. Southern Democrats were delighted with his nomination. Pierce was "as reliable as Calhoun himself," wrote one, while another said that "a nomination so favorable to the South had not been anticipated." Especially gratifying was Pierce's support for annexing Cuba, which he made one of the top priorities of his new administration after winning a landslide victory over a demoralized Whig Party weakened by schism between its northern and southern wings.

Pierce covertly encouraged a new filibustering expedition to Cuba. This one was to be led by former Governor John Quitman of Mississippi. While Quitman was recruiting hundreds of volunteers, southerners in Congress introduced a resolution to suspend the neutrality law that prohibited American interference in the internal affairs of other countries. But at the last moment Pierce backed off, fearful of political damage in the North if his administration became openly identified with filibustering. The Quitman expedition never sailed.

Pierce again tried to buy Cuba, instructing the American minister in Madrid to offer Spain $130 million. The minister was Pierre Soulé, a flamboyant Louisianian who managed to alienate most Spaniards by his clumsy intriguing. Soulé's crowning act came in October 1854 at a meeting with the American ministers to Britain and France in Ostend, Belgium. He persuaded them to sign what came to be known as the Ostend Manifesto. "Cuba is as necessary to the North American republic as any of its present . . . family of states," declared this document. If Spain persisted in refusing to sell, then "by every law, human and divine, we shall be justified in wresting it from Spain."

This "manifesto of the brigands," as antislavery Americans called it, caused an international uproar. The administration repudiated the Ostend Manifesto and recalled Soulé. Nevertheless, acquisition of Cuba remained an objective of the Democratic Party. The issue played a role in both the 1860 presidential election and the secession controversy during 1860 and 1861. Meanwhile, American filibustering shifted its focus 750 miles south of Havana to Nicaragua. There, the most remarkable of the *filibusteros*, William Walker, had proclaimed himself president and restored the institution of slavery.

The Gray-Eyed Man of Destiny

A native of Tennessee and a brilliant, restless man, Walker had earned a medical degree from the University of Pennsylvania and studied and practiced law in New Orleans before joining the 1849 rush to California. Weighing less than 120 pounds, Walker seemed an unlikely fighter or leader of men, but he fought three duels, and his luminous eyes, which seemed to transfix his fellows, won him the sobriquet "gray-eyed man of destiny."

Walker found his true calling in filibustering. At the time, numerous raids were taking place back and forth across the border with Mexico, some of them staged to seize more of that country for the United States. In 1853, Walker led a ragged "army" of footloose 49ers into Baja California and Sonora and declared the region an independent republic. Exhaustion and desertion depleted his troops, however, and the Mexicans drove the survivors back to California.

Walker decided to try again, with another goal. Many southerners eyed Nicaragua's potential for growing cotton, sugar, coffee, and other crops. The unstable Nicaraguan government offered a tempting target. In 1854, Walker signed a contract with rebel leaders in the civil war of the moment. The following spring, he led an advance guard of filibusters to Nicaragua and proclaimed himself commander-in-chief of the rebel forces. At the head of 2,000 American volunteers, he gained control of the country and named himself president in 1856. The Pierce administration extended diplomatic recognition to Walker's regime.

But things soon turned sour. The other Central American republics formed an alliance to invade Nicaragua and overthrow Walker. To win greater support from the southern states, Walker issued a decree in September 1856 reinstituting slavery in Nicaragua. A convention of southern economic promoters meeting in Savannah praised Walker's efforts "to introduce civilization in the States of Central America, and to develop these rich and productive regions by slave labor." Boatloads of new recruits arrived in Nicaragua from New Orleans, but in spring 1857, they succumbed to disease and to the Central American armies.

Walker escaped to New Orleans, where he was welcomed as a hero. He had no trouble recruiting men for another attempt, but the navy stopped him in November 1857. Southern congressmen condemned the naval commander and encouraged Walker to try again. He did, in December 1858, after a New Orleans jury refused to convict him of violating the neutrality law. On this third expedition, Walker's ship struck a reef and sank. Undaunted, he tried yet again. He wrote a book to raise funds for another invasion of Nicaragua, urging "the hearts of Southern youth to answer the call of honor. . . . The true field for the expansion of slavery is in tropical America." A few more southern youths answered the call, but they were stopped in Honduras. There, on September 12, 1860, the gray-eyed man met his destiny before a firing squad.

Conclusion

Within the three-year period from 1845 to 1848, the annexation of Texas, the settlement of the Oregon boundary dispute with Britain, and the acquisition by force of New Mexico and California from Mexico added 1,150,000 square miles to the United States. This expansion was America's "manifest destiny," according to Senator Stephen A. Douglas of Illinois. He further proclaimed:

> Increase, and multiply, and expand, is the law of this nation's existence. You cannot limit this great republic by mere boundary lines. Any one of you gentlemen might as well say to a son twelve years old that he is big enough, and must not grow any larger, and in order

to prevent his growth put a hoop around him and keep him to his present size. Either the hoop must burst and be rent asunder, or the child must die. So it would be with this great nation.

But other Americans feared that the country could not absorb such rapid growth without strains that might break it apart. At the outbreak of the war with Mexico, Ralph Waldo Emerson predicted that "the United States will conquer Mexico, but it will be as the man swallows the arsenic, which brings him down in turn. Mexico will poison us." Emerson proved correct. The poison was the reopening of the question of slavery's expansion, which had supposedly been settled by the Missouri Compromise in 1820. The admission of Texas as a huge new slave state and the possibility that more slave states might be carved out of the territory acquired from Mexico provoked northern congressmen to pass the Wilmot Proviso. Southerners bristled at this attempt to prevent the further expansion of slavery. Threats of secession and civil war poisoned the atmosphere in 1849 and 1850.

The Compromise of 1850 defused the crisis and appeared to settle the issue once again, but events would soon prove that this compromise had merely postponed the crisis. The fugitive slave issue and filibustering expeditions to acquire more slave territory kept sectional controversies smoldering. In 1854, the Kansas-Nebraska Act would cause them to burst into a hotter flame than ever.

SUGGESTED READINGS

For the theme of Manifest Destiny, the best introduction is **Frederick Merk, *Manifest Destiny and Mission in American History*** (1963). See also the essays in **Samuel W. Haynes and Christopher Morris, eds., *Manifest Destiny and Empire*** (1997). Two good studies of the overland trails to California and Oregon and other points West are **John D. Unruh, Jr., *The Plains Across: The Overland Emigrants and the Trans-Mississippi West, 1840–1860*** (1979), and **John Mack Faragher, *Women and Men on the Overland Trail*** (1978). A fine introduction to the impact of American expansion on the Indians of the West is **Philip Weeks, *Farewell, My Nation: The American Indian and the United States 1820–1890*** (rev. ed., 2000). The political polarization produced by the controversy over the annexation of Texas is clearly laid out by **Joel H. Silbey, *Storm Over Texas: The Annexation Controversy and the Road to Civil War*** (2005). A good study of the relationship between American expansion and the coming of war with Mexico is **David Pletcher, *The Diplomacy of Annexation: Texas, Oregon, and the Mexican War*** (1973). For the Mexican War, a good narrative is **John S. D. Eisenhower, *So Far from God: The U.S. War with Mexico 1846–1848*** (1989). Opposition to and support for the war by different elements of the public are chronicled in **John H. Schroeder, *Mr. Polk's War: American Opposition and Dissent, 1846–1848*** (1973), and **Robert W. Johannsen, *To the Halls of the Montezumas: The Mexican War in the American Imagination*** (1985). For the conflict provoked by the issue of slavery's expansion into territory acquired from Mexico, see **David M. Potter, *The Impending Crisis 1848–1861*** (1976); **Richard H. Sewell, *Ballots for Freedom: Antislavery Politics in the United States 1837–1860*** (1976); **Michael A. Morrison, *Slavery and the American West: The Eclipse of Manifest Destiny and the Coming of the Civil War*** (1997); and **Leonard D. Richards, *The Slave Power: The Free North and Southern Domination, 1780–1860*** (2000). The partisan roots of sectional conflict are emphasized in **Michael F. Holt,**

The Fate of Their Country: Politicians, Slavery Extension, and the Coming of the Civil War (2004). The best study of the Compromise of 1850 is **Holman Hamilton**, *Prologue to Conflict: The Crisis and Compromise of 1850* (1964). The passage and enforcement of the Fugitive Slave Act is the subject of **Stanley W. Campbell**, *The Slave Catchers* (1970). Still the best book on filibustering is **Robert E. May**, *The Southern Dream of a Caribbean Empire 1854–1861* (1971).

Visit the **Liberty Equality Power** Companion Web site for resources specific to this textbook: http://www.thomsonedu.com/history/murrin
Also find self-tests and additional resources at ThomsonNOW. ThomsonNOW is an integrated online suite of services and resources with proven ease of use and efficient paths to success, delivering the results you want—NOW!
www.thomsonedu.com/login/

The Gathering Tempest, 1853–1860

The wounds caused by the 1850 battle over slavery in the territories had barely healed when they were reopened. This time the strife concerned the question of slavery in the Louisiana Purchase territory, an issue presumably settled 34 years earlier by the Missouri Compromise of 1820.

The Compromise of 1820 had admitted Missouri as a slave state but had banned slavery from the rest of the Purchase north of 36°30'. Senator Stephen Douglas, in search of southern support for organizing Kansas and Nebraska as territories, consented to the repeal of this provision of the Missouri Compromise. Northern outrage at this repudiation of a "sacred contract" killed the Whig Party and gave birth to the antislavery Republican Party. In 1857, the Supreme Court added insult to injury with the **Dred Scott** decision, which denied Congress the power to restrict slavery from the territories. The ominous reorientation of national politics along sectional lines was accompanied by a bloody civil war in Kansas and a raid on the federal arsenal at **Harpers Ferry**, Virginia, by **John Brown** and his followers.

Kansas and the Rise of the Republican Party

Focus Question
Why did the Whig party die, and why did the Republican rather than the American party emerge as the new majority party in the North?

By 1853, land-hungry settlers had pushed up the Missouri River to its confluences with the Kansas and Platte rivers, and entrepreneurs were talking about a railroad across the continent to San Francisco. But settlement of the country west of Missouri and land surveys for a railroad through it would require its organization as a territory. Accordingly, in 1853, the House passed a bill creating the Nebraska Territory, embracing the area north of Indian Territory (present-day Oklahoma) up to the Canadian border. But the House bill ran into trouble in the Senate. Under the Missouri Compromise, slavery would be excluded from the new territory. Having lost California, the pro-slavery forces were determined to salvage something from Nebraska. Missourians were particularly adamant, because a free Nebraska would leave them almost surrounded on three sides by free soil. Senator David R. Atchison of Missouri vowed to see Nebraska "sink in hell" before having it become free soil.

CHRONOLOGY

1852	Plenary Council of Catholic Church seeks tax support for parochial schools
1853	American Party emerges
1854	Crimean War begins • Congress passes Kansas-Nebraska Act • Republican Party organized • Antebellum immigration reaches peak
1855	Ethnic riots in several cities • "Border Ruffian" legislature in Kansas legalizes slavery
1856	Civil war in Kansas • Preston Brooks canes Charles Sumner on Senate floor • Crimean War ends • Buchanan wins three-way presidential election
1857	Supreme Court issues Dred Scott decision • Lecompton constitution written in Kansas • Congress enacts lower tariff • Panic of 1857 • Helper's Impending Crisis published
1858	Kansas voters reject Lecompton constitution • Lincoln-Douglas debates
1859	Congress defeats federal slave code for territories • John Brown's raid at Harpers Ferry
1860	Shoemakers' strike in New England • Buchanan vetoes Homestead Act

As president pro tem of the Senate, Atchison wielded great influence. A profane, gregarious man, he had inherited Calhoun's mantle as leader of the southern-rights faction. In the 1853–54 session of Congress, he kept raising the asking price for southern support of a bill to organize the Nebraska Territory. The sponsor of the Senate bill was Stephen A. Douglas, chairman of the Senate Committee on Territories. Only 5 feet 4 inches tall, Douglas had earned the nickname Little Giant for his parliamentary skill, which he had demonstrated most dramatically in helping pass the Compromise of 1850 through Congress. In Douglas's opinion, the application of popular sovereignty to the slavery question in New Mexico and Utah had been the centerpiece of the compromise. The initial draft of his Nebraska bill merely repeated the language used for those territories, specifying that when any portion of the Nebraska Territory came in as a state, it could do so "with or without slavery, as its constitution may provide."

This was not good enough for Atchison and his southern colleagues. After talking with them, Douglas announced that because of a "clerical error," a provision calling for the territorial legislature to decide on slavery had been omitted from the draft. But Atchison raised the price once again, insisting on an explicit repeal of the Missouri Compromise. Sighing in response, Douglas stated that this action "will raise a hell of a storm," but he nevertheless agreed. He further agreed to divide the area in question into two territories: Kansas west of Missouri and Nebraska west of Iowa and Minnesota. To many northerners this looked suspiciously like a scheme to mark Kansas out for slavery and Nebraska for freedom. Douglas then joined **Jefferson Davis**, Atchison, and other southern senators on a visit to the White House, where they twisted President Pierce's arm to give the revised Kansas-Nebraska bill the administration's support and to make its approval "a test of [Democratic] party orthodoxy."

The Kansas-Nebraska Act

The bill did "raise a hell of a storm." Contemporaries and historians have speculated endlessly on Douglas's motives. Some thought he wanted to win southern support for the presidential nomination in 1856. Perhaps, but he risked losing northern support. Others point out that Douglas's real estate holdings in Illinois would have risen in value if a transcontinental railroad were to traverse the Nebraska Territory and that southern opposition could block this route. The most likely reason, however, was Douglas's passionate belief in Manifest Destiny, in filling up the continent with American settlers and institutions. "The tide of immigration and civilization must be permitted to roll onward," he proclaimed. For this, he was willing to pay the South's price for support of his Kansas-Nebraska bill. He failed to recognize the depth of northern opposition to the "slave power" and to the expansion of slavery. Douglas had no firm moral convictions about slavery. He said that he cared not whether the settlers voted slavery up or down; the important thing was to give them a chance to vote.

But many Americans did care. They regarded the expansion of slavery as a national question, and one that was too important to be left to territorial voters. One of them was an old acquaintance of Douglas, **Abraham Lincoln.** An antislavery Whig who had served four terms in the Illinois legislature and one term in Congress, Lincoln was propelled back into politics by the shock of the Kansas-Nebraska bill. He acknowledged the constitutional right to hold slave property in the states where it already existed, but he believed slavery was "an unqualified evil to the negro, the white man, and to the state. . . . There can be no moral right in connection with one man's making a slave of another." Lincoln admitted he did not know how to bring this deeply entrenched institution to an end. He understood that race prejudice was a powerful obstacle to emancipation. Still, he believed that the country must face up to the problem. It must stop any further expansion of slavery as the first step on the long road to its "ultimate extinction."

Lincoln excoriated Douglas's "care not" attitude toward whether slavery was voted up or down: "I can not but hate [this] *declared* indifference, but as I must think, covert *real* zeal for the spread of [slavery]." The assertion that slavery would never be imported into Kansas anyway, because of the region's unsuitable climate, Lincoln branded as a "LULLABY argument." The climate of eastern Kansas was similar to that of the Missouri River Valley in Missouri, where slaves were busily raising hemp and tobacco. Missouri slaveholders were already poised to take their slaves into the Kansas River valley. "Climate will not . . . keep slavery out of these territories," said Lincoln. "Nothing in *nature* will." Many of the founding fathers had looked forward to the day when slavery would no longer exist in republican America. Instead, the United States had become the world's largest slaveholding society, and Douglas's bill would permit slavery to expand even further. In a political speech at Peoria, Illinois, in October 1854, Lincoln insisted that

> The monstrous injustice of slavery deprives our republican example of its just influence in the world—enables the enemies of free institutions, with plausibility, to taunt us as hypocrites. . . . Let us re-adopt the Declaration of Independence, and with it, the practices, and policy, which harmonize with it. . . . If we do this, we shall not only have saved the Union; but we shall have so saved it, as to make, and to keep it, forever worthy of the saving.

With these eloquent words, Lincoln voiced the feelings that fostered an uprising against the Kansas-Nebraska bill. Abolitionists, Free-Soilers, northern Whigs, and even many northern Democrats held impassioned meetings to form anti-Nebraska coalitions, but they could not stop passage of the bill. It cleared the Senate easily, supported by a solid South and 15 of the 20 northern Democrats. In the House, where all of the northern Democrats would have to face the voters in the fall elections, the Pierce administration and the Democratic leadership still managed to wield the whip of patronage and party pressure and force half of them to vote for the bill, which passed by a vote of 113 to 100.

Death of the Whig Party

These proceedings completed the destruction of the Whigs as a national party. Southern Whigs had been disappearing ever since Zachary Taylor had "betrayed" them on the issue of a free California. After the presidential election of 1852, few Whigs remained in the cotton South. In that year, the Whig Party nominated General Winfield Scott for president. Although he was a Virginian, Scott, like Taylor, took a national rather than a southern view. He was the candidate of the northern Whigs in the national convention, which nominated him on the 53rd ballot after a bitter contest between the northern and southern wings of the party. A mass exodus of southern Whigs into the Democratic Party enabled Franklin Pierce to carry all but two slave states in the election. The unanimous vote of northern Whigs in Congress against the Kansas-Nebraska bill was the final straw. The Whig Party never recovered its influence in the South.

Whig strength seemed to be on its last legs in the North as well. Antislavery Whig leaders such as Seward and Lincoln hoped to channel the flood of anti-Nebraska sentiment through the Whig Party, an effort akin to containing Niagara Falls. Free-Soilers and antislavery Democrats spurned the Whig label. Political coalitions arose spontaneously in the North under various names: anti-Nebraska, Fusion, People's, Independent. The name that caught on evoked memories of America's first fight for freedom in 1776: Republican. The first use of this name seems to have occurred at an anti-Nebraska rally in a Congregational church at Ripon, Wisconsin, in May 1854. Soon, most of the congressional candidates fielded by anti-Nebraska coalitions ran their campaigns under the Republican banner.

The 1854 elections were disastrous for northern Democrats. One-fourth of Democratic voters deserted the party. The Democrats lost control of the House of Representatives when 66 of 91 incumbent free-state Democratic congressmen (including 37 of the 44 who had voted for the Kansas-Nebraska bill) went down to defeat. Combined with the increase in the number of Democratic congressmen from the South, where the party had picked up the pieces of the shattered Whig organization, this rout brought the party under southern domination more than ever.

But who would pick up the pieces of old parties in the North? The new Republican Party hoped to do so, but it suffered a shock in urban areas of the Northeast. Hostility toward immigrants created a tidal wave of **nativism** that threatened to swamp the anti-Nebraska movement. "Nearly everybody appears to have gone deranged on Nativism," reported a Pennsylvania Democrat, while a Whig in upstate New York warned that his district was "very badly infected with Knownothingism." Described as a "tornado," a "hurricane," a "freak of political insanity," the **Know-Nothings** won landslide victories in Massachusetts and Delaware, polled an estimated 40 percent of the vote in Pennsylvania, and did well elsewhere in the Northeast and border states. Who were these mysterious Know-Nothings? What did they stand for? What part did they play in the political upheaval of 1854?

Immigration and Nativism

Focus Question
What were the origins of Nativism, and how did this movement relate to the slavery issue?

During the early 19th century, immigration was less pronounced than in most other periods of U.S. history. The volume of immigration (expressed as the number of immigrants during a decade in proportion to the whole population at its beginning) was little more than 1 percent in the 1820s, increasing to 4 percent in the 1830s. Three-quarters of the newcomers were Protestants, mainly from Britain. Most of them were skilled workers, farmers, or members of white-collar occupations.

In the 1840s, a combination of factors abruptly quadrupled the volume of immigration and changed its ethnic and occupational makeup. The pressure of expanding population on limited land in Germany and successive failures of the potato crop in Ireland impelled millions of German and Irish peasants to emigrate. A majority came to the United States, where recovery from the depression of the early 1840s brought an economic boom with its insatiable demand for labor. During the decade after 1845, three million immigrants entered the United States—15 percent of the total American population in 1845, the highest proportional volume of immigration in American history. Many of them, especially the Irish, joined the unskilled and semiskilled labor force in the rapidly growing eastern cities and in the construction of railroads that proliferated to all points of the compass.

Most of them were also Roman Catholics. Anti-Catholicism had centuries-deep roots in Anglo-American Protestantism. Fear of the pope and of the Roman Church as autocratic and antirepublican was never far from the surface of American political culture, and scurrilous

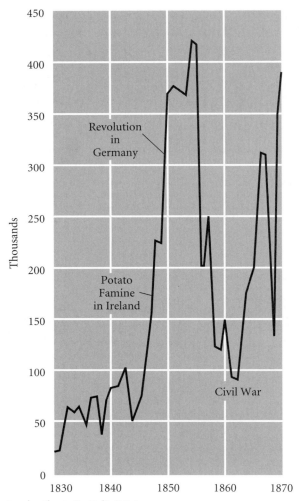

Immigration to the United States

Source: From *Division and the Stresses of Reunion 1845–1876,* by David M. Potter. Copyright © 1973 Scott, Foresman and Company. Reprinted by permission.

anti-Catholic literature circulated during the 1830s. Several ethnic riots between Protestant and Catholic workers over the years culminated in pitched battles and numerous deaths in Philadelphia in 1844. Short-lived nativist political parties that sprang up in several eastern cities in the early 1840s called for curbing the political rights of immigrants. Some of the nativists were actually immigrants from Britain and Northern Ireland who brought their anti-Catholicism with them.

Nativism appeared to subside with the revival of prosperity after 1844, but the decline was temporary because the vast increase of immigration proved too much for the country to absorb. Not only were most of the new immigrants Catholics, but many of them also spoke a foreign language and had alien cultural values. The **temperance** crusade had sharply curtailed drinking among native-born Protestants but had made little impact on the Irish and Germans, much of whose social and political life revolved around taverns and beer parlors (see chapter 11). Established Americans perceived more recent arrivals as responsible for an increase of crime and poverty in the cities. Cincinnati's overall crime rate tripled between 1846 and 1853; its murder rate increased sevenfold. Boston's expenditures for poor relief tripled during the same period.

Immigrants in Politics

The political power of immigrants also grew. In Boston, for example, the number of foreign-born voters (mostly Irish) increased by 200 percent from 1850 to 1855, whereas the number of native-born voters grew by only 14 percent. Most of the immigrants became Democrats, because that party welcomed or at least tolerated them and many Whigs did not. Foreign-born voters leaned toward the pro-slavery wing of the Democratic Party, even though seven-eighths of them settled in free states. Mostly working-class and poor, they rubbed shoulders against the small northern black population; Irish American mobs sometimes attacked black neighborhoods and rioted against black workers. They supported the Democratic Party as the best means of keeping blacks in slavery and out of the North. These attitudes sparked hostility toward immigrants among many antislavery people, some of whom equated slavery with Catholicism as a backward, despotic, repressive institution.

The Roman Catholic hierarchy did little to allay that hostility. Pope Pius IX (1846–78) led the Church into a period of reaction against secular liberalism. The Church sided with the counterrevolutionary forces that crushed the European uprisings of 1848, which sought greater political and social democracy. In the United States, the leading Catholic prelate, Archbishop John Hughes of New York, taking his cue from the pope, attacked abolitionists, Free-Soilers, and various Protestant reform movements as akin to the Red Republicanism of Europe. In 1850, in a widely publicized address titled "The Decline of Protestantism and Its Causes," Hughes noted proudly that Catholic Church membership in the United States had grown three times faster than Protestant membership over the previous decade, and he predicted an eventual Catholic majority. "Protestantism is effete, powerless, dying out . . . and conscious that its last moment is come when it is fairly set, face to face, with Catholic truth."

Attitudes toward immigrants had political repercussions. Two of the hottest issues in state and local politics during the early 1850s were temperance and schools. The temperance crusaders had grown confident and aggressive enough to go into politics. The drunkenness and rowdiness they associated with Irish immigrants became one of their particular targets. Beginning with Maine in 1851, 12 states had enacted prohibition laws by 1855.

Although several of the laws were soon weakened by the courts or repealed by legislatures, they exacerbated ethnic tensions.

So too did battles over public schools versus **parochial schools** increase. Catholics resented the Protestant domination of public education and the reading of the King James Bible in schools. Archbishop Hughes flayed the public schools as purveyors of "Socialism, Red Republicanism, Universalism, Infidelity, Deism, Atheism, and Pantheism." The Church began to build parochial schools for the faithful, and in 1852, the first Plenary Council of American bishops decided to seek tax support for these schools or tax relief for Catholic parents who sent their children to them. This effort set off heated election contests in numerous northern cities and states. Anti-Catholic "free school" tickets won most of these elections on a platform of defending public schools against the "bold effort" of this "despotic faith" to "uproot the tree of Liberty."

The Rise of the Know-Nothings

It was in this context that the Know-Nothings (their formal name was the American Party) burst onto the political scene. This party was the result of the merger in 1852 of two secret fraternal societies that limited their membership to native-born Protestants: the Order of the Star-Spangled Banner and the Order of United Americans. Recruiting mainly young men in skilled blue-collar and lower white-collar occupations, the merged Order had a membership of 1 million or more by 1854. The Order supported temperance and opposed tax support for parochial schools. They wanted public office restricted to native-born men and sought to lengthen the naturalization period before immigrants could become citizens and voters from 5 to 21 years. Members were pledged to secrecy about the Order; if asked, they were to reply "I know nothing."

This movement swept through the Northeast in the 1854 elections, doing to the Whig Party in the Northeast what the slavery issue had done to it in the South. Although the American Party drew voters from both major parties, it cut more heavily into the Whig constituency. As a cultural force, nativism had found a more congenial home in the Whig Party than in the Democratic Party. When the American Party raised its banner in 1854, many northern Whigs who had not already gone over to the Republicans flocked to the Know-Nothings.

When the dust of the 1854 elections settled, it was clear that those who opposed the Democrats would control the next House of Representatives. But who would control the opposition—antislavery Republicans or nativist Americans? In truth, some northern voters and the congressmen they elected adhered to both political faiths. A Know-Nothing convention in Massachusetts resolved that "there can exist no real hostility to Roman Catholicism which does not also abhor slavery." In New England, several Know-Nothing leaders were actually Republicans in disguise who had jumped on the nativist bandwagon with the intention of steering it in an antislavery direction.

Many Republicans, however, warned against flirting with religious **bigotry.** "How can any one who abhors the oppression of negroes, be in favor of degrading classes of white people?" asked Abraham Lincoln in a letter to a friend. He further stated:

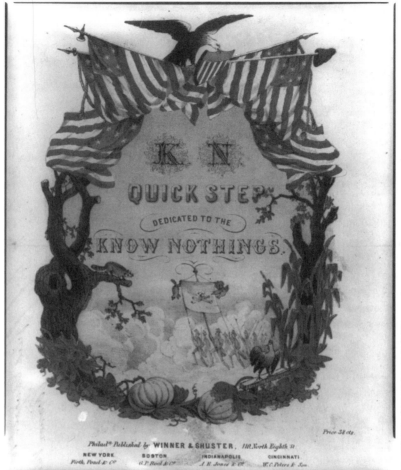

Know Nothing Sheet Music   Composers of popular music produced songs for political parties and movements of every stripe, and the Know Nothing movement was no exception. Note the symbolism of the eagle and the flags for this anti-immigrant party. The pumpkins, chicken, and corn seem to symbolize rural America threatened by cities with a growing foreign-born population. The symbolic purpose of the raccoons is not clear.

As a nation, we began by declaring that "all men are created equal." We now practically read it "all men are created equal, except negroes." When the Know Nothings get control, it will read "all men are created equal, except negroes, and foreigners, and catholics." When it comes to this I should prefer emigrating to some country where they make no pretense of loving liberty—to Russia, for instance, where despotism can be taken pure, and without the base alloy of hypocrisy.

Other Republicans echoed Lincoln. Because "we are against Black Slavery, because the slaves are deprived of human rights," they declared, "we are also against . . . [this] system of Northern Slavery to be created by disfranchising the Irish and Germans." Many Republicans also considered nativism a red herring that diverted attention from the true danger confronting the country. "Neither the Pope nor the foreigners ever can govern the country or endanger its liberties," wrote the managing editor of the *New York Tribune,* "but the slavebreeders and slavetraders *do* govern it."

The Decline of Nativism

In 1855, Republican leaders maneuvered skillfully to divert the energies of northern Know-Nothings from their crusade against the pope to a crusade against the slave power. Two developments helped them. The first was turmoil in Kansas, which convinced many northerners that the slave power was a greater threat than the pope. The second was a significant shift southward in the center of nativist gravity. The American Party continued to do well in off-year elections in New England during 1855, but it also won elections in Maryland, Kentucky, and Tennessee and polled at least 45 percent of the votes in five other southern states. Violence in several southern cities with large immigrant populations preceded or accompanied these elections. Riots left 10 dead in St. Louis, 17 in Baltimore, and 22 in Louisville, showing a significant streak of nativism in the South. But the American Party's success there probably owed a great deal to the search by former Whigs for a new political home outside the Democratic Party. Areas of American Party strength in seven or eight southern states more or less coincided with areas of former Whig strength.

These developments had important implications at the national level. Southern Know-Nothings were pro-slavery, whereas many of their Yankee counterparts were antislavery. Similar to the national Whig Party, so did the American Party founder on the slavery issue during 1855 and 1856. At the party's first national council in June 1855, most of the northern delegates walked out when southerners and northern conservatives joined forces to pass a resolution endorsing the **Kansas-Nebraska Act.** A similar scene occurred at an American Party convention in 1856. By that time, most northern members of the party had, in effect, become Republicans. When the House of Representatives elected in 1854 convened in December 1855, a protracted fight for the speakership again took place. The Republican candidate was Nathaniel P. Banks of Massachusetts, a former Know-Nothing who now considered himself a Republican. Banks finally won on the 133rd ballot with the support of about 30 Know-Nothings who thereby declared themselves Republicans. This marriage was consummated in summer 1856, when the "North Americans" endorsed the Republican candidate for president.

By that time, nativism had faded. The volume of immigration suddenly dropped by more than half in 1855 and stayed low for the next several years. Ethnic tensions eased, and cultural issues such as temperance and schools receded. Although the Republican Party took on some of the cultural baggage of nativism when it absorbed many northern Know-Nothings, party leaders shoved the baggage into dark corners. The real conflict was not the struggle between native and immigrant, or between Protestant and Catholic, but between North and South over the extension of slavery. That conflict led to civil war—and the war seemed already to have begun in the territory of Kansas.

Bleeding Kansas

When it became clear that southerners had the votes to pass the Kansas-Nebraska Act, William H. Seward stood up in the Senate and told his southern colleagues: "Since there is no escaping your challenge, I accept it in behalf of the cause of freedom. We will engage in competition for the virgin soil of Kansas, and God give victory to the side which is stronger in numbers as it is in right." Senator David Atchison of Missouri was ready for the expected influx of Free Soil settlers to the new Kansas Territory. "We are playing for a mighty stake," he wrote. "If we win we carry slavery to the Pacific Ocean; if we fail we lose Missouri, Arkansas, Texas and all the territories; the game must be played boldly."

Atchison did play boldly. At first, Missouri settlers in Kansas posted the stronger numbers. As the year 1854 progressed, however, settlers from the North came pouring in. Alarmed by this influx, bands of Missourians, labeled **"border ruffians"** by the Republican press, rode into Kansas prepared to vote as many times as necessary to install a pro-slavery

Kansas State Historical Society, #FK2.83*15

Free-State Men Ready to Defend Lawrence, Kansas, in 1856   After pro-slavery forces sacked the free-state capital of Lawrence in 1856, Northern settlers decided they needed more firepower to defend themselves. Somehow they got hold of a six-pound howitzer. This cannon did not fire a shot in anger during the Kansas troubles, but its existence may have deterred the "border ruffians."

government. In fall 1854, they cast at least 1,700 illegal ballots and sent a pro-slavery territorial delegate to Congress.

The following spring, when the time came to elect a territorial legislature, even greater efforts were needed because numerous Free Soil settlers had taken up claims during the winter. Atchison was equal to the task. He led a contingent of border ruffians to Kansas for the election. "There are eleven hundred coming over from Platte County to vote," he told his followers, "and if that ain't enough, we can send five thousand—enough to kill every God-damned abolitionist in the Territory."

His count was accurate. Nearly five thousand came—4,968 as determined by a congressional investigation—and voted illegally to elect a pro-slavery territorial legislature. The territorial governor pleaded with President Pierce to nullify the election. Pierce instead listened to Atchison and removed the governor. Meanwhile, the new territorial legislature legalized slavery and adopted a slave code that even authorized the death penalty for helping a slave to escape.

The so-called Free State party, outraged by these proceedings, had no intention of obeying laws enacted by this "bogus legislature." By fall 1855, they constituted a majority of bona fide settlers in Kansas. They called a convention, adopted a free-state constitution, and elected their own legislature and governor. By January 1856, two territorial governments in Kansas stood with their hands at each other's throats.

Kansas now became the leading issue in national politics. The Democratic Senate and President Pierce recognized the pro-slavery legislature meeting in the town of Lecompton, while the Republican House of Representatives recognized the antislavery legislature in the town of Lawrence. Southerners saw the struggle as crucial to their future. "The admission of Kansas into the Union as a slave state is now a point of honor," wrote Congressman Preston Brooks of South Carolina. "The fate of the South is to be decided with the Kansas issue." On the other side, Charles Sumner of Massachusetts gave a well-publicized speech in the Senate on May 19 and 20 entitled "The Crime against Kansas." "Murderous robbers from Missouri," charged Sumner, "from the drunken spew and vomit of an uneasy civilization" had committed the "rape of a virgin territory, compelling it to the hateful embrace of slavery." Among the southern senators whom Sumner singled out for special condemnation and ridicule was Andrew Butler of South Carolina, a cousin of Congressman Brooks. Butler was a "Don Quixote," said Sumner, "who had chosen a mistress to whom he has made his vows . . . the harlot, Slavery."

The Caning of Sumner

Sumner's speech incensed southerners, none more than Preston Brooks, who decided to avenge his cousin. He knew that Sumner would never accept a challenge to a duel. Anyway, dueling was for gentlemen, and even horse-whipping was too good for this Yankee blackguard. Two days after the speech, Brooks walked into the Senate chamber and began beating Sumner with a heavy cane. His legs trapped beneath the desk that was bolted to the floor, Sumner wrenched the desk loose as he stood up to try to defend

SOUTHERN CHIVALRY — ARGUMENT versus CLUB'S.

The Caning of Sumner   This drawing by an antislavery Northerner shows pro-slavery Congressman Preston Brooks of South Carolina beating Senator Charles Sumner of Massachusetts with a heavy cane on the floor of the Senate on May 22, 1856. It portrays the inability of the South to respond to the power of Northern arguments, symbolized by the pen in Sumner's right hand and a speech in his left hand, except with the unthinking power of the club. Note other Southern senators in the background smiling on the scene or preventing Northern senators from coming to Sumner's aid. The caning of Sumner was the worst of several instances of North–South violence or threatened violence on the floor of Congress in the 1850s, presaging the violence on the battlefields of the 1860s.

himself, whereupon Brooks clubbed him so ferociously that Sumner slumped forward, bloody and unconscious.

News of the incident sent a thrill of pride through the South and a rush of rage through the North. Charleston newspapers praised Brooks for "standing forth so nobly in defense of . . . the honor of South Carolinians." Brooks resigned from Congress after censure by the House and was unanimously reelected. From all over the South came gifts of new canes, some inscribed with such mottoes as "Hit Him Again" and "Use Knock-Down Arguments." But, in the North, the Republicans gained thousands of voters as a result of the affair. It seemed to prove their contentions about "the barbarism of slavery." "Has it come to this," asked the poet William Cullen Bryant, editor of the *New York Evening Post,* "that we must speak with bated breath in the presence of our Southern masters? . . . Are we to be chastised as they chastise their slaves?" A veteran New York politician reported that he had "never before seen anything at all like the present state of deep, determined, & desperate feelings of hatred, & hostility to the further extension of slavery, & its political power."

Republicans were soon able to add "Bleeding Kansas" to "Bleeding Sumner" in their repertoire of winning issues. Even as Sumner was delivering his speech in Washington, an "army" of pro-slavery Missourians, complete with artillery, marched on the free-state capital of Lawrence, Kansas. On May 21, they shelled and sacked the town, burning several buildings. A rival force of free-state men arrived too late to intercept them. One of the free-state "captains" was John Brown, an abolitionist zealot who considered himself anointed by the Lord to avenge the sins of slaveholders. When he learned of the murder of several free-state settlers and the sack of Lawrence, he "went crazy—crazy," according to one of his followers. We must "fight fire with fire," Brown declared. "Something must be done to show these barbarians that we, too, have rights." Leading four of his sons and three other men to a pro-slavery settlement at Pottawatomie Creek on the night of May 24–25, 1856, Brown dragged five men from their cabins and split open their heads with broadswords.

Here was the Old Testament retribution of an eye for an eye. Brown's murderous act set off a veritable civil war in Kansas. One of Brown's sons was among the estimated 200 men killed in the bushwhackings and raids. Not until President Pierce sent a tough new territorial governor and 1,300 federal troops to Kansas in September 1856 did the violence subside—just in time to save the Democrats from possible defeat in the presidential election.

The Election of 1856

By 1856, the Republicans had become the largest party in the North. With the old Free-Soilers as their radical core, they had recruited about three-fourths of the former Whigs and one-fifth of the Democrats. They were also the first truly sectional party in American history because they had little prospect of carrying a single county in the slave states. At their first national convention, the Republicans wrote a platform that focused mainly on that "relic of barbarism," slavery. The platform also incorporated the old Whig program of federal aid to internal improvements, including a railroad to California. For its presidential nominee, the party steered away from its most prominent leaders, who were identified with the old parties, and turned instead to John C. Frémont. This "Pathfinder of the West" had a dashing image as an explorer and for his role in the acquisition of California. With little political experience, he had few political enemies, and his antislavery credentials were satisfactory.

The Democrats chose as their candidate James Buchanan, a veteran of 30 years in various public offices. He had been minister to Britain during the Kansas-Nebraska controversy and so was not tainted with its unpopularity in the North, as were Pierce and Douglas, the

Popular and Electoral Votes in the 1856 Presidential Election

Candidate	Free States		Slave States		Total	
	Popular	Electoral	Popular	Electoral	Popular	Electoral
Buchanan (Democrat)	1,227,000	62	607,000	112	1,833,000	174
Frémont (Republican)	1,338,000	114	0	0	1,338,000	114
Fillmore (American)	396,000	0	476,000	8	872,000	8

other aspirants for nomination. The Democratic platform endorsed popular sovereignty and condemned the Republicans as a "sectional party" that incited "treason and armed resistance in the Territories."

This would be a three-party election because the American Party was still in the field. Having become mainly a waystation for former southern Whigs, the party nominated ex-Whig Millard Fillmore. The three-party campaign sifted out into a pair of two-party contests: Democrats versus Americans in the South; Democrats versus Republicans in the North. Fillmore, despite a good showing of 44 percent of the popular vote in the South, carried only Maryland. Considering Buchanan colorless but safe, the rest of the South gave him three-fourths of the electoral votes he needed for victory.

The real excitement in this election showed itself in the North. For many Republicans, the campaign was a moral cause, an evangelical crusade against the sin of slavery. Republican "Wide Awake" clubs marched in torch-light parades chanting "Free Soil, Free Speech, Free Men, Frémont!" A veteran politician in Indiana marveled: "Men, Women & Children all seemed to be out, with a kind of fervor I have never witnessed before in six Pres. Elections in which I have taken an active part." The turnout of eligible voters in the North was a remarkable 83 percent. One awestruck journalist, anticipating a Republican victory, wrote that "the process now going on in the United States is a *Revolution.*"

Not quite. Although the Republicans swept New England and the upper parts of New York state and the Old Northwest—both settled by New Englanders, where evangelical and antislavery reform movements had taken hold—the contest in the lower North was close. Buchanan needed only to carry Pennsylvania and either Indiana or Illinois to win the presidency, and the campaign focused on those states. The immigrant and working-class voters of the eastern cities and the rural voters of the lower Midwest, descendants of upland southerners who had settled there, were antiblack and antiabolitionist in sentiment. They were ripe for Democratic propaganda that accused Republicans of favoring racial equality. **"Black Republicans,"** declared an Ohio Democratic newspaper, intended to "turn loose . . . millions of negroes, to elbow you in the workshops, and compete with you in fields of honest labor." A Democrat in Pennsylvania told voters that "the one aim" of the Republicans was "to elevate the African race in this country to complete equality of political and economic condition with the white man." Indiana Democrats organized parades, with young girls in white dresses carrying banners inscribed "Fathers, save us from nigger husbands."

The Republicans in these areas denied that they favored racial equality. They insisted that the main reason for keeping slavery out of the territories was to enable white farmers and workers to make a living there without competition from black labor. But their denials were in vain. Support for the Republican Party by prominent black leaders, including Frederick Douglass, convinced hundreds of thousands of voters that the Black Republicans were racial egalitarians. For the next two decades, that sentiment would be one of the most potent weapons in the Democratic arsenal.

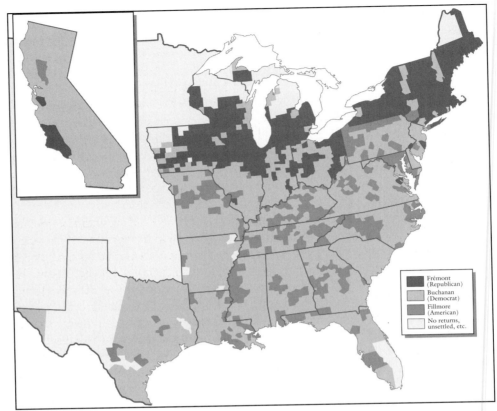

Map 14.1   Counties Carried by Candidates in the 1856 Presidential Election   This map illustrates the sharp geographical division of the vote in 1856. The pattern of Republican counties coincided almost exactly with New England and the portions of other states settled by New England migrants during the two preceding generations. View an animated version of this map or related maps at http://www.thomsonedu.com/history/murrin.

In 1856, though, the charge that a Republican victory would destroy the Union was even more effective. Buchanan set the tone in his instructions to Democratic Party leaders: "The Black Republicans must be . . . boldly assailed as disunionists, and the charge must be re-iterated again and again." It was. And southerners helped the cause by threatening to secede if Frémont won. We "should not pause," said Senator James Mason of Virginia, "but proceed at once to 'immediate, absolute, and eternal separation.'" Fears of disruption caused many conservative ex-Whigs in the North to support Buchanan, who carried Pennsylvania, New Jersey, Indiana, Illinois, and California and won the presidency.

But southerners did not intend to let Buchanan forget that he owed his election mainly to the South. "Mr. Buchanan and the Northern Democracy are dependent on the South," wrote a Virginian after the election. "If we can succeed in Kansas . . . and add a little more slave territory, we may yet live free men under the Stars and Stripes."

The Dred Scott Case

The South took the offensive at the outset of the Buchanan administration. Its instrument was the Supreme Court, which had a majority of five justices from slave states led by Chief Justice Roger B. Taney of Maryland. Those justices saw the Dred Scott case as an opportunity to settle once and for all the question of slavery in the territories.

Dred Scott was a slave whose owner, an army surgeon, had kept him at military posts in Illinois and in Wisconsin Territory for several years before taking him back to Missouri. After the owner's death, Scott sued for his freedom on the grounds of his prolonged stay in the Wisconsin Territory, where slavery had been outlawed by the Missouri Compromise. The case worked its way up from Missouri courts through a federal circuit court to the U.S. Supreme Court. There it began to attract attention as a test case of Congress's power to prohibit slavery in the territories.

The southern Supreme Court justices decided to declare that the Missouri Compromise ban on slavery in the territories was unconstitutional. To avoid the appearance of a purely sectional decision, they sought the concurrence of a northern Democratic justice, Robert Grier of Pennsylvania. President-elect Buchanan played an improper role by pressing his fellow Pennsylvanian to go along with the southern majority. Having obtained Justice Grier's concurrence, Chief Justice Taney issued the Court's ruling stating that Congress lacked the power to keep slavery out of a territory, because slaves were property and the Constitution protects the right of property. For good measure, Taney also wrote that the circuit court should not have accepted the Scott case in the first place because black men were not citizens of the United States and therefore had no standing in its courts. Five other justices wrote concurring opinions. The two non-Democratic northern justices (both former Whigs, one of them now a Republican) dissented vigorously. They stated that blacks were legal citizens in several northern states and were therefore citizens of the United States. To buttress their opinion that Congress could prohibit slavery in the territories, they cited Congress's Constitutional power to make "all needful rules and regulations" for the territories.

Modern scholars agree with the **dissenters.** In 1857, however, Taney had a majority, and his ruling became law. Modern scholars have also demonstrated that Taney was motivated by his passionate commitment "to southern life and values" and by his determination to stop "northern aggression" by cutting the ground out from under the hated Republicans. His ruling that their program to exclude slavery from the territories was unconstitutional was designed to do just that.

Republicans denounced Taney's "jesuitical decision" as based on "gross perversion" of the Constitution. The New York Tribune sneered that the Dred Scott decision was "entitled to just as much moral weight as would be the judgment of a majority of those congregated in any Washington bar-room." Several Republican state legislatures resolved that the ruling was "not binding in law and conscience." They looked forward to the election of a Republican president who could "reconstitute" the Court and secure a reversal of the decision. "The remedy," said the Chicago Tribune, "is the ballot box. . . . Let the next President be Republican, and 1860 will mark an era kindred with that of 1776."

The Lecompton Constitution

Instead of settling the slavery controversy, the Dred Scott decision intensified it. Meanwhile, pro-slavery advocates, having won legalization of slavery in the territories, moved to ensure that it would remain legal when Kansas became a state. That required deft maneuvering, because legitimate antislavery settlers outnumbered pro-slavery settlers by more than two to one. In 1857, the pro-slavery legislature (elected by the fraudulent votes of border ruffians two years earlier) called for a constitutional convention at Lecompton to prepare Kansas for statehood. Because the election for delegates was rigged, Free Soil voters refused to participate. One-fifth of the registered voters thereupon elected convention delegates, who met at Lecompton and wrote a state constitution that made slavery legal.

Then a nagging problem arose. Buchanan had promised that the Lecompton constitution would be presented to voters in a fair **referendum.** The problem was how to pass the pro-slavery constitution given the antislavery majority of voters. The convention came up with an ingenious solution. Instead of a referendum on the whole constitution, it would allow the voters to choose between a constitution "with slavery" and one "with no slavery." The catch was that the constitution "with no slavery" guaranteed slave owners' "inviolable" right of property in the 200 slaves already in Kansas and their progeny. It also did nothing to prevent future smuggling of slaves across the 200-mile border with Missouri. Once in Kansas, they, too, would become "inviolable" property.

Free-state voters branded the referendum a farce and boycotted it. One-quarter of the eligible voters went to the polls in December 1857 and approved the constitution "with slavery." Meanwhile, in a fair election policed by federal troops, the antislavery party won control of the new territorial legislature and promptly submitted both constitutions to a referendum that was boycotted by pro-slavery voters. This time, 70 percent of the eligible voters went to the polls and overwhelmingly rejected both constitutions.

Which referendum would the federal government recognize? That question proved even more divisive than the Kansas-Nebraska debate four years earlier. President Buchanan faced a dilemma. He had promised a fair referendum. But southerners, who dominated both the Democratic Party and the administration (the vice president and four of the seven cabinet members were from slave states), threatened secession if Kansas was not admitted to statehood under the Lecompton constitution "with slavery." "If Kansas is *driven out of the Union for being a Slave State,*" thundered Senator James Hammond of South Carolina, "can any Slave State remain in it with honor?" Buchanan caved in. He explained to a shocked northern Democrat that if he did not accept the Lecompton constitution, southern states would "secede from the Union or take up arms against us." Buchanan sent the Lecompton constitution to Congress with a message recommending statehood. Kansas, said the president, "is at this moment as much a slave state as Georgia or South Carolina."

What would Stephen Douglas do? If he endorsed the Lecompton constitution, he would undoubtedly be defeated in his bid for reelection to the Senate in 1858. And he regarded the Lecompton constitution as a travesty of popular sovereignty. He broke with the administration on the issue. He could not vote to "force this constitution down the throats of the people of Kansas," he told the Senate, "in opposition to their wishes and in violation of our pledges."

The fight in Congress was long and bitter. The South and the administration had the votes they needed in the Senate and won handily there, but the Democratic majority in the House was so small that the defection of even a few northern Democrats would defeat the Lecompton constitution. The House debate at one point got out of hand, and a wild fistfight erupted between Republicans and southern Democrats. "There were some fifty middle-aged and elderly gentlemen pitching into each other like so many Tipperary savages," wrote a bemused reporter, "most of them incapable, from want of wind and muscle, from doing each other any serious harm."

When the vote was finally taken, two dozen northern Democrats defected, providing enough votes to defeat Lecompton. Both sides then accepted a compromise proposal to resubmit the constitution to Kansas voters, who decisively rejected it. This meant that while Kansas would not come in as a slave state, neither would it come in as a free state for some time yet. Nevertheless, the Lecompton debate had split the Democratic Party, leaving a legacy of undying enmity between southerners and Douglas. The election of a Republican president in 1860 was now all but assured.

The Economy in the 1850s

Focus Question
How did economic developments in the 1840s and 1850s widen the breach between North and South?

Beginning in the mid-1840s, the American economy enjoyed a dozen years of unprecedented growth and prosperity, particularly for the railroads. The number of miles in operation quintupled during those years. Railroad construction provided employment for many immigrants and spurred growth in industries that produced rails, rolling stock, and other railroad equipment. Most railroad construction took place in the Old Northwest, linking the region more closely to the Northeast and continuing the reorientation of transportation networks from a north-south river pattern to an east-west canal and rail pattern. By the mid-1850s, the east-west rail and water routes carried more than twice as much freight tonnage as the north-south river routes. This closer binding of the western and eastern states reinforced the effect of slavery in creating a self-conscious "North" and "South."

Although the Old Northwest remained predominantly agricultural, rapid expansion of railroads there laid the basis for its industrialization. During the 1850s, industrial output in the free states west of Pennsylvania grew at twice the rate of Northeast industrial output and three times as great as the rate in the South. The Northwest urban growth rate tripled that of the Northeast and quadrupled that of the South. Chicago became the terminus for 15 rail lines in the 1850s, during which its population grew by 375 percent. In 1847, two companies that contributed to the rapid growth of agriculture during this era built their plants in Illinois: the McCormick reaper works at Chicago and the John Deere steel-plow works at Moline.

According to almost every statistical index available from that period, economic expansion considerably outstripped even the prodigious pace of population increase. While the number of Americans grew by 44 percent during these 12 years (1844–56), the value of both exports and imports increased by 200 percent; mined coal tonnage by 270 percent; banking capital, industrial capital, and industrial output by approximately 100 percent; farmland value by 100 percent; and cotton, wheat, and corn harvests by about 70 percent. These advances meant a significant increase of **per capita** production and income, although the distance between rich and poor was widening—a phenomenon that has characterized all capitalist economies during stages of rapid industrial growth.

By the later 1850s, the United States had forged ahead of most other countries to become the second-leading industrial producer in the world, behind only Britain. But the country was still in the early stages of industrial development. Agricultural product processing and raw materials still played the dominant role. By 1860, the four leading industries, measured by value added in manufacturing, were cotton textiles, lumber products, boots and shoes, and flour milling. Iron and machinery, industries typical of a more mature manufacturing economy, ranked sixth and seventh.

"The American System of Manufactures"

The United States had pioneered in one crucial feature of modern industry: the mass production of **interchangeable parts.** This revolutionary concept had begun with the manufacture of firearms earlier in the 19th century and had spread to many products by the 1850s. High wages and a shortage of the skilled craftsmen who had traditionally fashioned guns, furniture, locks, watches, and other products had compelled American entrepreneurs to seek alternative methods. "Yankee ingenuity," already world-famous, came up with an answer: special-purpose machine tools that would cut and shape an endless number of parts that could be fitted together with other similarly produced parts to make whole guns, locks, clocks, and sewing machines in mass quantities. These products were less elegant and less durable than products made by skilled craftsmen, but they were also less expensive and thus more widely available to the "middling classes" of a society that professed to be more democratic than Europe in its consumer economy as well as in its politics.

Such American-made products were the hit of the first World's Fair, the Crystal Palace Exhibition at London in 1851. British manufacturers were so impressed by Yankee techniques, which they dubbed "the American system of manufactures," that they sent two commissions to the United States to study them. "The labouring classes are comparatively

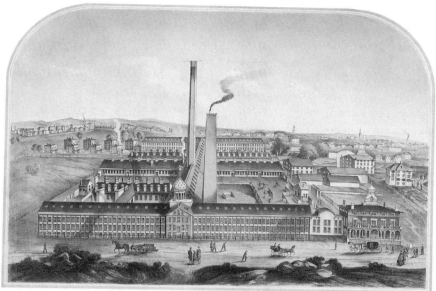

Colt Arms Plant in Hartford, Connecticut   Samuel Colt's factory for manufacturing firearms was a showpiece for the American system of manufactures in the 1850s. All of the processes for production of the famous Colt revolver were housed under one roof, with power-driven machinery cutting the metal and shaping the interchangeable parts. Hand filing was necessary, however, for a perfect fit of the parts, because the tolerances of machine tools were not yet as finely calibrated as they later became.

few," reported one commission in 1854, "and to this very want . . . may be attributed the extraordinary ingenuity displayed in many of these labour-saving machines." The British firearms industry imported American experts to help set up the Enfield Armoury in London to manufacture the new British army rifle.

The British also invited Samuel Colt of Connecticut, inventor of the famous six-shooting revolver, to set up a factory in England stocked with machinery from Connecticut. In testimony before a parliamentary committee in 1854, Colt summed up the American system of manufactures in a single sentence: "There is nothing that cannot be produced by machinery." Although the British had a half-century head start over Americans in the Industrial Revolution, Colt's testimony expressed a philosophy that would enable the United States to surpass Britain as the leading industrial nation by 1880.

The British industrial commissions also cited the American educational system as an important reason for the country's technological proficiency. "Educated up to a far higher standard than those of a much superior grade in the Old World," reported the 1854 commission, "every [American] workman seems to be continually devising some new thing to assist him in his work, and there is a strong desire . . . to be 'posted up' in every new improvement." By contrast, the British workman, trained by long apprenticeship "in the trade," rather than in school, lacked "the ductility of mind and the readiness of apprehension for a new thing" and was therefore "unwilling to change the methods he has been used to."

Whether this British commission was right in its belief that American schooling encouraged the "adaptive versatility" of Yankee workers, it was certainly true that public education and literacy were more widespread in the United States than in Europe. Almost 95 percent of adults in the free states were literate in 1860, compared with 65 percent in England and 55 percent in France. The standardization and expansion of public school systems that had begun earlier in New England had spread to the mid-Atlantic states and into the Old Northwest by the 1850s. Nearly all children received a few years of schooling, and most completed at least six or seven years.

This improvement in education coincided with the feminization of the teaching profession, which opened up new career opportunities for young women. The notion that the "woman's sphere" was in the home, rearing and nurturing children, ironically projected that sphere outside the home into the schoolroom when schools took over part of the responsibility of socializing and educating children. By the 1850s, nearly three-quarters of the public school teachers in New England were women (who worked for lower salaries than male teachers), a trend that was spreading to the mid-Atlantic states and the Old Northwest as well.

The Southern Economy

The feminization of teaching had not yet reached the South. Nor had the idea of universal public education taken deep root in the slave states. In contrast to the North, where 94 percent of the entire population could read and write, 80 percent of the free population and only 10 percent of the slaves in the South were literate. This was one of several differences between North and South that antislavery people pointed to as evidence of the backward, repressive, and pernicious nature of a slave society.

Still, the South shared in the economy's rapid growth following recovery from the depression of 1837–43. Cotton prices and production both doubled between 1845 and 1855. Similar increases in price and output emerged in tobacco and sugar. The price of slaves, a significant index of prosperity in the southern economy, also doubled during this decade. Southern crops provided three-fifths of all U.S. exports, with cotton alone supplying more than half.

But a growing number of southerners deplored the fact that the **"colonial" economy** of the South was so dependent on the export of agricultural products and the import of manufactured goods. The ships that carried southern cotton were owned by northern or British firms; financial and commercial services were provided mostly by Yankees or Englishmen. In the years of rising sectional tensions around 1850, many southerners began calling for economic independence from the North. How could they obtain their rights, they asked, if they were "financially more enslaved than our negroes?" Yankees "abuse and denounce slavery and slaveholders," declared a southern newspaper in 1851, yet "we purchase all our luxuries and necessaries from the North. . . . Our slaves are clothed with Northern manufactured goods and work with Northern hoes, ploughs, and other implements. . . . The slaveholder dresses in Northern goods . . . and on Northern-made paper, with a Northern pen, with Northern ink, he resolves and re-resolves in regard to his rights."

Southerners must "throw off this humiliating dependence," declared James D. B. De Bow, the young champion of economic diversification in the South. In 1846, De Bow had founded in New Orleans a periodical eventually known as *De Bow's Review*. Proclaiming on its cover that "Commerce is King," the *Review* set out to make this slogan a southern reality. De Bow took the lead in organizing annual commercial conventions that met in various southern cities during the 1850s. In its early years, this movement encouraged southerners to invest in shipping lines, railroads, textile mills ("bring the spindles to the cotton"), and other enterprises. "Give us factories, machine shops, work shops," declared southern proponents of King Commerce, "and we shall be able ere long to assert our rights."

Economic diversification in the South did make headway during the 1850s. The slave states quadrupled their railroad mileage, increased the amount of capital invested in manufacturing by 77 percent, and boosted their output of cotton textiles by 44 percent. But like Alice in Wonderland, the faster the South ran, the farther behind it seemed to fall—for northern industry was growing even faster. The slave states' share of the nation's manufacturing capacity actually dropped from 18 to 16 percent during the decade. In 1860, the North had five times more industrial output per capita than the South, and it had three times the railroad capital and mileage per capita and per thousand square miles. Southerners had a larger percentage of their capital invested in land and slaves in 1860 than they had had 10 years earlier. Some 80 percent of the South's labor force worked in agriculture—the same as 60 years earlier. By contrast, while farming remained, at 40 percent, the largest single occupation in the North, the northern economy developed a strong manufacturing and commercial sector whose combined labor force almost equaled that of agriculture by 1860.

The Sovereignty of King Cotton

A good many southerners preferred to keep it that way. "That the North does our trading and manufacturing mostly is true," wrote an Alabama planter in 1858. "We are willing that they should. Ours is an agricultural people, and God grant that we may continue so. It is the freest, happiest, most independent, and with us, the most powerful condition on earth." In the later 1850s, the drive for economic diversification in the South lost steam. King Cotton reasserted its primacy over King Commerce as cotton output *and* prices continued to rise, suffusing the South in a glow of prosperity. "Our Cotton is the most wonderful talisman on earth," declared a planter. "By its power we are transmuting whatever we choose into whatever we want." In a speech that became famous, James Hammond of

South Carolina told his fellow senators in 1858 that "the slaveholding South is now the controlling power of the world. . . . No power on earth dares to make war on cotton. Cotton *is* king."

Even the commercial conventions in the South seemed to have embraced this gospel. In 1854, they merged with a parallel series of planters' conventions, and thereafter the delegates heard as much about cotton as they did about commerce. By the later 1850s, one of the main goals of these conventions was to reopen the African slave trade, prohibited by law since 1808. Many southerners rejected that goal, however, partly on moral grounds and partly on economic grounds. Older slave states such as Virginia, which profited from the sale of slaves to the booming cotton frontier of the Deep South, objected to any goal that would lower the price of their largest export. The conventions also lobbied for the annexation of Cuba, which would bring a productive agricultural economy and 400,000 more slaves into the United States.

Nowhere in the South, said defenders of slavery, did one see such "scenes of beggary, squalid poverty, and wretchedness" as one could find in any northern city. Black slaves, they insisted, enjoyed a higher standard of living than white "wage slaves" in northern factories. Black slaves never suffered from unemployment or wage cuts, they received free medical care, and they were taken care of in old age.

This argument reached its fullest development in the writings of George Fitzhugh, a Virginia farmer-lawyer whose newspaper articles were gathered into two books published in 1854 and 1857, *Sociology for the South* and *Cannibals All*. Free-labor capitalism, said Fitzhugh, was a competition in which the strong exploited and starved the weak. Slavery, by contrast, was a paternal institution that guaranteed protection of the workers. "Capital exercises a more perfect compulsion over free laborers than human masters over slaves," wrote Fitzhugh, "for free laborers must at all times work or starve, and slaves are supported whether they work or not. . . . What a glorious thing is slavery, when want, misfortune, old age, debility, and sickness overtake [the slave]."

Labor Conditions in the North

How true was this portrait of poverty and starvation among northern workers? Some northern labor leaders did complain that the "slavery" of the wage system gave "bosses" control over the hours, conditions, and compensation of labor. Use of this wage-slavery theme in labor rhetoric declined during the prosperous years of the 1850s, and no evidence indicates that a northern working man ever offered to change places with a southern slave. Average per capita income was about 40 percent higher in the North than in the South. Although that average masked large disparities between rich and poor—even between the middle class and the poor—those disparities were no greater, and probably less, in the North than in the South.

To be sure, substantial numbers of recent immigrants, day laborers, and young single women in large northern cities lived on the edge of poverty—or slipped over the edge. Many women seamstresses, shoe binders, milliners, and the like, who worked

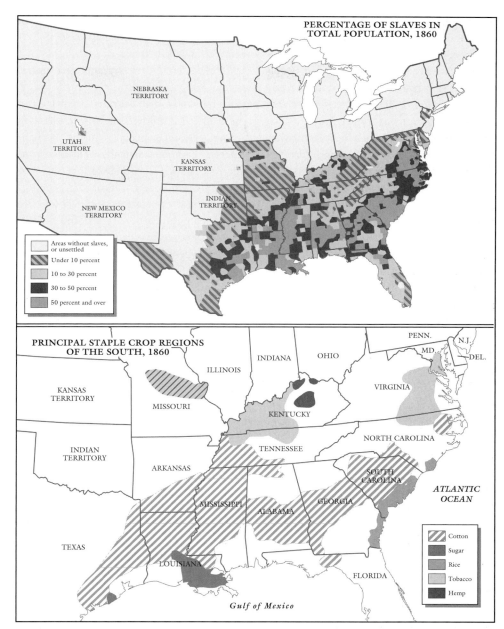

Map 14.2 Slavery and Staple Crops in the South, 1860 Note the close correlation between the concentration of the slave population and the leading cash crops of the South. Nothing better illustrates the economic importance of slavery. View an animated version of this map or related maps at http://www.thomsonedu.com/history/murrin.

60 or 70 hours per week in the outwork system, earned less than a living wage. Some of them resorted to prostitution in order to survive. The widespread adoption of the newly invented sewing machine in the 1850s did nothing to make life easier for seamstresses; it only lowered their per-unit piecework wages and forced them to turn out more shirts and trousers than before. Many urban working-class families could not survive on the wages of an unskilled or semi-skilled father. The mother had to take in laundry, boarders, or outwork, and one or more children had to work. Much employment was seasonal or intermittent, leaving workers without wages for long periods, especially during the winter. The poverty, overcrowding, and disease in the tenement districts of a few large cities—especially New York City—seemed to lend substance to pro-slavery claims that slaves were better off.

But they were not—even apart from the psychological contrast between being free and being a slave. New York City's poverty, although highly concentrated and visible, was exceptional. In the North, only one-fourth of the people lived in cities or towns of more than 2,500 people. Wages and opportunities for workers were greater in the North than anywhere else in the world, including the South. That was why 4 million immigrants came to the United States from 1845 to 1860 and why seven-eighths of them settled in free states. It was also why twice as many white residents of slave states migrated to free states than vice versa. And it was one reason why northern farmers and workers wanted to keep slaves *and* free blacks out of the territories, where their cheaper labor would lower wages.

The Panic of 1857

In fall 1857, the relative prosperity of the North was interrupted by a financial panic that caused a short-lived but intense depression. When the Crimean War in Europe (1854–56) cut off Russian grain from the European market, U.S. exports had mushroomed to meet the deficiency. After the Crimean War ended, U.S. grain exports slumped. The sharp rise in interest rates in Britain and France, caused by the war, spread to U.S. financial markets in 1857 and dried up sources of credit. Meanwhile, the economic boom of the preceding years had caused the American economy to overheat: Land prices had soared, railroads had built beyond the capacity of earnings to service their debts, and banks had made too many risky loans.

This speculative house of cards came crashing down in September 1857. The failure of one banking house sent a wave of panic through the financial community. Banks suspended specie payments, businesses failed, railroads went bankrupt, construction halted, and factories shut down. Hundreds of thousands of workers were laid off, and others went on part-time schedules or took wage cuts, just as the cold winter months were arriving. The specter of class conflict such as had occurred during the European revolutions of 1848 haunted the public. Unemployed workers in several northern cities marched in parades carrying banners demanding work or bread. A mob broke into the shops of flour merchants in New York City. On November 10, a crowd gathered on Wall Street and threatened to break into the U.S. customs house and subtreasury vaults, where $20 million was stored. Soldiers and marines had to be called out to disperse the mob.

But the country got through the winter with little violence. No one was killed in the demonstrations—in contrast to the dozens who had been killed in ethnic riots a few years earlier and the hundreds killed in the guerrilla war in Kansas. Class conflict turned out to be the least threatening of the various discords that endangered society in the 1850s. Charity and public works helped tide the poor over the winter, and the panic inspired a vigorous religious revival. Spontaneous prayer meetings arose in many northern cities, bringing together bankers and seamstresses, brokers and streetsweepers. They asked God's forgiveness for the greed and materialism that, in a self-flagellating mood, they believed had caused the panic.

Perhaps God heeded their prayers. In any event, the depression was short-lived. By early 1858, banks had resumed specie payments; the stock market rebounded in the spring; factories reopened; railroad construction resumed; and by spring 1859, recovery was complete. The modest labor union activities of the 1850s revived after the depression, as workers in some industries went on strike to bring wages back to prepanic levels. In

The Panic on Wall Street This cartoon satirizes the consternation among New York investors and financiers when banks and businesses crashed in autumn 1857. Notice the smirk on the faces of two men in the foreground, who undoubtedly stood to benefit from foreclosures on defaulted property. The panic was no laughing matter, though, because it led to a short but sharp recession in 1857 and 1858.

February 1860, the shoemakers of Lynn, Massachusetts, began the largest strike in U.S. history up to that time, eventually involving 20,000 workers in the New England shoe industry. Despite the organization of several national unions of skilled workers during the 1850s, however, less than 1 percent of the labor force was unionized in 1860.

Sectionalism and the Panic

The Panic of 1857 probably intensified sectional hostility more than it did class conflict. The South largely escaped the depression. Its export-driven economy seemed insulated from domestic downturns. After a brief dip, cotton and tobacco prices returned to high levels and production continued to increase: The cotton crop set new records in 1858 and 1859. Southern boasts about the superiority of the region's economic and labor systems took on added bravado. "Who can doubt, that has looked at recent events, that cotton is supreme?" asked Senator James Hammond in March 1858. "When thousands of the strongest commercial houses in the world were coming down," he told Yankees, "what brought you up? . . . We have poured in upon you one million six hundred thousand bales of cotton. . . . We have sold it for $65,000,000, and saved you."

Northerners were not grateful for their rescue. In fact, many of them actually blamed the South for causing the depression or for blocking measures to ease its effects in the North. Southern congressmen had provided most of the votes for a new tariff in 1857 that brought duties to their lowest levels in 40 years. Some northern Republicans blamed the tariff for causing the panic and wanted to revise certain duties upward to help hard-hit industries, especially Pennsylvania iron, which were being undercut by cheaper imports. They directed their arguments to workers as much as to manufacturers. "We demand that American labor-ers shall be protected against the pauper labor of Europe," they declared. Tariff revision would "give employment to thousands of mechanics, artisans, laborers, who have languished for months in unwilling idleness." In each session of Congress from 1858 through 1860, however, a combination of southerners and about half of the northern Democrats blocked Republican efforts to raise tariffs. In the words of one bitter Pennsylvania Republican, this was proof that Congress remained "shamelessly prostituted, in a base subserviency to the Slave Power." Republicans made important gains in the Pennsylvania congressional elec-tions of 1858, setting the stage for a strong bid in a state that they had to carry if they were to win the presidency in 1860.

Three other measures acquired additional significance after the Panic of 1857. Repub-licans supported each of them as a means to promote economic health and to aid farmers and workers, but southerners perceived all of them as aimed at helping *northern* farmers and workers and used their power to defeat them. One was a homestead act to grant 160 acres of public land to each farmer who settled and worked the land. Believing that this bill "would prove a most efficient ally for Abolition by encouraging and stimulating the set-tlement of free farms with Yankees," southern senators defeated it after the House had passed it in 1859. The following year both houses passed the homestead act, but Buchanan vetoed it and southern senators blocked an effort to pass it over his veto. A similar fate befell bills for land grants to a transcontinental railroad and for building agricultural and mechanical colleges to educate farmers and workers. In the Old Northwest, where these measures were popular, Republican prospects for 1860 were enhanced by southern and Democratic opposition to them.

The Free-Labor Ideology

Focus Question

What were the "free-labor ideology" and "herrenvolk democracy"? How did these concepts relate to the politics of the 1850s?

By the later 1850s, the Republican antislavery argument had become a finely honed philosophy that historians have labeled a **"free-labor ideology."** It held that all work in a free society was honorable, but that slavery degraded the calling of manual labor by equating it with bondage. Slaves worked inefficiently, by compulsion; free men were stimulated to work hard and efficiently by the desire to get ahead. Social mobility was central to the free-labor ideology. Free workers who practiced the virtues of industry, thrift, self-discipline, and sobriety could move up the ladder of success. "I am not ashamed to confess," Abraham Lincoln told a working-class audience in 1860, "that twenty-five years ago I was a hired laborer, mauling rails, at work on a flat-boat—just what might happen to any poor man's son!" But in the free states, said Lincoln, a man knows that

> he can better his condition. . . . There is no such thing as a freeman being fatally fixed for life, in the condition of a hired laborer. . . . The man who labored for another last year, this year labors for himself, and next year will hire others to labor for him. . . . The free labor system opens the way for all—gives hope to all, and energy, and progress, and improvement of condition to all.

Lincoln drew too rosy a picture of northern reality, for large numbers of wage laborers in the North had little hope of advancing beyond that status. Still, he expressed a belief that was widely shared in the antebellum North. "There is not a working boy of average ability in the New England states, at least," observed a visiting British industrialist in 1854, "who has not an idea of some mechanical invention or improvement in manufactures, by which, in good time, he hopes to better his condition, or rise to fortune and social distinction." Americans could point to numerous examples of men who had achieved dramatic upward mobility. Belief in this "American dream" was most strongly held by Protestant farmers, skilled workers, and white-collar workers who had some real hope of getting ahead. These men tended to support the Republican Party and its goal of excluding slavery from the territories.

Slavery was the antithesis of upward mobility. Bondsmen were "fatally fixed in that condition for life," as Lincoln noted. Slaves could not hope to move up the ladder of success, nor could free men who lived in a society where they had to compete with slave labor. "Slavery withers and blights all it touches," declared an Iowa Republican. "It is a curse upon the poor, free, laboring white men." In the United States, social mobility often depended on geographic mobility. The main reason so many families moved into new territories was to make a new start, to get ahead. But, declared a Republican editor, if slavery goes into the territories, "the free labor of all the states will not. If the free labor of the states goes there, the slave labor of the southern states will not, and in a few years the country will teem with an active and energetic population."

Southerners contended that free labor was prone to unrest and strikes. Of course it was, said Lincoln in a speech to a New England audience during the shoemakers' strike of 1860. "I am glad to see that a system prevails in New England under which laborers *can* strike when they want to (*Cheers*). . . . I like the system which lets a man quit when he wants to, and wish it might prevail everywhere (*Tremendous applause*)." Strikes were one of the ways in which free workers could try to improve their prospects. "I want every man," said Lincoln, "to have the chance—and I believe a black man is entitled to it—in which he can better his condition." That was why Republicans were determined to contain the expansion of slavery, because if the South got its way in the territories, "free labor that can strike will give way to slave labor that cannot!"

The Impending Crisis

From the South came a maverick voice that echoed the Republicans. Hinton Rowan Helper considered himself a spokesman for the nonslaveholding whites of the South. Living in upcountry North Carolina, a region of small farms and few slaves, he had brooded for years over slavery's retarding influence on southern development. In 1857, he poured out his bitterness in a book entitled *The Impending Crisis of the South*. Using selective statistics from the 1850 census, he pictured a South mired in economic backwardness, widespread illiteracy, poverty for the masses, and great wealth for the elite. He contrasted this dismal situation with the bustling, prosperous northern economy and its near-universal literacy, neat farms, and progressive institutions. What caused this startling contrast? "Slavery lies at the root of all the shame, poverty, ignorance, tyranny, and imbecility of the South," he wrote. Slavery monopolized the best land, degraded all labor to the level of bond labor, denied schools to the poor, and impoverished all but "the lords of the lash [who] are not only absolute masters of the blacks [but] of all nonslaveholding whites, whose freedom is merely nominal, and whose unparalleled illiteracy and degradation is purposely and fiendishly perpetrated." The remedy? Nonslaveholding whites must organize and use their votes to overthrow "this entire system of oligarchical despotism."

No southern publisher dared touch this book. Helper lugged his bulky manuscript to New York City, where a printer brought it out in summer 1857. *The Impending Crisis* was virtually banned in the South, and few southern whites read it, but it made a huge impact in the North. Republicans welcomed it as confirmation of all they had been saying about the evils of slavery and the virtues of free labor. The Republican Party subsidized an abridged edition and distributed thousands of copies as campaign documents. During the late 1850s, a war of books (Helper's *Impending Crisis* versus Fitzhugh's *Cannibals All*) exacerbated sectional tensions. Fitzhugh's book circulated freely in the North, whereas the sale or possession of Helper's book was a criminal offense in many parts of the South. The New England Antislavery Society even invited Fitzhugh to New Haven to debate the abolitionist Wendell Phillips. Fitzhugh expressed surprise at his courteous reception in the North, aware that Phillips and other abolitionists could not set foot in the South without peril to their life. Northern spokesmen did not hesitate to point out the moral: A free society could tolerate free speech and a free press, but a slave society could not.

Southern Nonslaveholders

How accurate was Helper's portrayal of southern poor whites degraded by slavery and ready to revolt against it? The touchy response of many southern leaders suggested that

North Wind Picture Archives

A Southern Yeoman Farmer's Home   This modest log cabin on the edge of a small clearing, with the farmer's wife drawing water from a well in the foreground, was typical of nonslaveholders' farms in the backcountry of the South. Often stigmatized as poor whites, many of these families were in fact comfortable by the standards of the day. They did not feel the sense of oppression by the planter class that Hinton Rowan Helper believed they should feel.

the planters felt uneasy about that question. After all, slaveholding families constituted less than one-third of the white population in slave states, and the proportion was declining as the price of slaves continued to rise. Open hostility to the planters' domination of society and politics was evident in the mountainous and upcountry regions of the South. These would become areas of Unionist sentiment during the Civil War and of Republican strength after it.

But Helper surely exaggerated the disaffection of most nonslaveholders in the South. Three bonds held them to the system: kinship, economic interest, and race. In the Piedmont and the low-country regions of the South, nearly half of the whites lived in slaveholding families. Many of the rest were cousins or nephews or in-laws of slaveholders in the South's extensive and tightly knit kinship network. Moreover, many young, ambitious nonslaveholders hoped to buy slaves eventually. Some of them *rented* slaves. And because slaves could be made to do the menial, unskilled labor in the South—the "mudsill" tasks, in Senator Hammond's language—white workers monopolized the more skilled, higher-paying jobs.

Even if they did not own slaves, white people owned the most important asset of all—white skin. White supremacy was an article of faith in the South (and in most of the North, for that matter). Race was a more important social distinction than class. The southern legal system, politics, and social ideology were based on the concept of **"herrenvolk democracy"** (the equality of all who belonged to the "master race"). Subordination was the Negro's fate, and slavery was the best means of subordination. Emancipation would loose a flood of free blacks on society and would undermine the foundations of white supremacy. Thus many of the poor whites in the South and immigrant workers or poorer farmers in the North supported slavery.

The *herrenvolk* theme permeated pro-slavery rhetoric. "With us," said John C. Calhoun in 1848, "the two great divisions of society are not the rich and the poor, but white and black; and all the former, the poor as well as the rich, belong to the upper class, and are respected and treated as equals." True freedom as Americans understood it required equality of rights and status (although not of wealth or income). Slavery ensured such freedom for all whites by putting a floor under them, a mudsill of black slaves that kept whites from falling into the mud of inequality. "Break down slavery," said a Virginia congressman, "and you would with the same blow destroy the great Democratic principle of equality among men."

The Lincoln-Douglas Debates

Abraham Lincoln believed the opposite. For him, slavery and freedom were incompatible; the one must die that the other might live. This became the central theme of a memorable series of **debates between Lincoln and Douglas** in 1858, which turned out to be a dress rehearsal for the presidential election of 1860.

The debates were arranged after Lincoln was nominated to oppose Douglas's reelection to the Senate. State legislatures elected U.S. senators at that time, so the campaign was technically for the election of the Illinois legislature. The real issue, however, was the senatorship, and Douglas's prominence gave the contest national significance. Lincoln launched his bid with one of his most notable speeches. "'A house divided against itself cannot stand,'" he said, quoting the words of Jesus recorded in the Gospel of Mark (3:25). "I believe this government cannot endure, permanently half slave and half free. . . . It will become all one thing, or all the other." Under the Dred Scott decision, which Douglas had endorsed, slavery was legal in all of the territories. And what, asked Lincoln, would prevent the Supreme Court, using the same reasoning that had led it to interpret the Constitution as protecting property in slaves, from legalizing slavery in free states? (A case based on this question was then before the New York courts.) The advocates of slavery, charged Lincoln, were trying to "push it forward, till it shall become lawful in all the States." But Republicans intended to keep slavery out of the territories, thus stopping its growth and placing it "where the public mind shall rest in the belief that it is in the course of ultimate extinction."

The seven open-air debates between Douglas and Lincoln focused almost entirely on the issue of slavery. Douglas asked: Why could the country not continue to exist half slave and half free as it had for 70 years? Lincoln's talk about the "ultimate extinction" of slavery would provoke the South to secession. Douglas professed himself no friend of slavery, but if people in the southern states or in the territories wanted it, they had the right to have it. Douglas did not want black people—either slave or free—in Illinois. Lincoln's policy would not only free the slaves but would also grant them equality. "Are you in favor of conferring upon the negro the rights and privileges of citizenship?" Douglas called out to supporters in the crowd. "No, no!" they shouted back. He continued:

> Do you desire to strike out of our State Constitution that clause which keeps slaves and free negroes out of the State . . . in order that when Missouri abolishes slavery she can send one hundred thousand emancipated slaves into Illinois, to become citizens and voters on an equality with yourselves? ("Never," "no.") . . . If you desire to allow them to come into the State and settle with the white man, if you desire them to vote . . . then support Mr. Lincoln and the Black Republican party, who are in favor of the citizenship of the negro. ("Never, never.")

Douglas's demagoguery put Lincoln on the defensive. He responded with cautious denials that he favored "social and political equality" of the races. The "ultimate extinction" of slavery might take a century. It would require the voluntary cooperation of the South and would perhaps be contingent on the emigration of some freed slaves from the country. But come what may, freedom must prevail. Americans must reaffirm the principles of the founding fathers. In Lincoln's words, a black person was entitled to all the natural rights enumerated in the Declaration of Independence, the right to life, liberty and the pursuit of happiness. *(Loud cheers.)* I hold that he is as much entitled to these as the white man. I agree with Judge Douglas he is not my equal in many respects. . . . But in the right to eat the bread, without leave of anybody else, which his own hand earns, *he is my equal and the equal of Judge Douglas, and the equal of every living man. (Great applause.)*

Lincoln deplored Douglas's "care not" attitude whether slavery was voted up or down. He "looks to no end of the institution of slavery," said Lincoln. By endorsing the Dred Scott decision, Lincoln claimed, Douglas looks to its "perpetuity and nationalization." Douglas was thus "eradicating the light of reason and liberty in this American people." That was the real issue in the election, insisted Lincoln:

That is the issue that will continue in this country when these poor tongues of Judge Douglas and myself shall be silent. It is the eternal struggle between these two principles—right and wrong—throughout the world. . . . The one is the common right of humanity and the other the divine right of kings. . . . No matter in what shape it comes, whether from a king who seeks to bestride the people of his own nation and live by the fruit of their labor, or from one race of men as an apology for enslaving another race, it is the same tyrannical principle.

The Freeport Doctrine

The popular vote for Republican and Democratic state legislators in Illinois was virtually even in 1858, but because apportionment favored the Democrats, they won a majority of seats and reelected Douglas. Lincoln, however, was the ultimate victor; his performance in the debates lifted him from political obscurity, while Douglas further alienated southern Democrats. In the Freeport debate, Lincoln had asked Douglas how he reconciled his support for the Dred Scott decision with his policy of popular sovereignty, which supposedly gave residents of a territory the power to vote slavery down. Douglas replied that even though the Court had legalized slavery in the territories, the enforcement of that right would depend on the people who lived there. This was a popular answer in the North, but it gave added impetus to southern demands for congressional passage of a federal slave code in territories such as Kansas, where the Free Soil majority had by 1859 made slavery virtually null. In the next two sessions of Congress after the 1858 elections, southern Democrats, led by Jefferson Davis, tried to pass a federal slave code for all territories. Douglas and northern Democrats joined with Republicans to defeat it. Consequently, southern hostility toward Douglas mounted as the presidential election of 1860 approached.

The 1859–60 session of Congress was particularly contentious. Once again a fight over the speakership of the House set the tone. Republicans had won a plurality of House seats, but lacking a majority, they could not elect a Speaker without the support of a few border-state representatives from the American (Know-Nothing) Party. The problem was that the Republican candidate for Speaker was John Sherman, who, along with 67 other congressmen, had signed an endorsement of Hinton Rowan Helper's *The Impending Crisis of the South* (without, Sherman later admitted, having read it). This was a red flag to southerners, even to ex-Whigs from the border states, who refused to vote for Sherman. Through 43 ballots and two months, the House remained deadlocked. Tensions escalated, and members came armed to the floor. One observer commented that "the only persons who do not have a revolver and knife are those who have two revolvers."

As usual, southerners threatened to secede if a Black Republican became Speaker. Several of them wanted a shootout on the floor of Congress. We "are willing to fight the question out," wrote one, "and to settle it right there." The governor of South Carolina told one of his state's congressmen: "If . . . you upon consultation decide to make the issue of force in Washington, write or telegraph me, and I will have a regiment in or near Washington in the shortest possible time." To avert a crisis, Sherman withdrew his candidacy and the House finally elected a conservative ex-Whig as Speaker on the 44th ballot.

John Brown at Harpers Ferry

Southern tempers were frayed even at the start of this session of Congress because of what had happened at Harpers Ferry, Virginia, in the previous October. After his exploits in Kansas, John Brown had disappeared from public view but had not been idle. Like the Old Testament warriors he admired and resembled, Brown intended to carry his war against slavery into Babylon—the South. His favorite New Testament passage was Hebrews 9:22: "Without shedding of blood there is no remission of sin." Brown worked up a plan to capture the federal arsenal at Harpers Ferry, arm slaves with the muskets he seized there, and move southward along the Appalachian Mountains attracting more slaves to his army along the way until the "whole accursed system of bondage" collapsed.

Brown recruited five black men and seventeen whites, including three of his sons, for this reckless scheme. He also had the secret support of a half-dozen Massachusetts and New York abolitionists, who had helped him raise funds. On the night of October 16, 1859, Brown led his men across the Potomac River and occupied the sleeping town of Harpers Ferry without resistance. Few slaves flocked to his banner, but the next day, state militia units poured into town and drove Brown's band into the fire-engine house. At dawn on October 18, a company of U.S. marines commanded by Colonel Robert E. Lee and Lieutenant J. E. B. Stuart stormed the engine house and captured the surviving members of Brown's party. Four townsmen, one marine, and ten of Brown's men (including two of his sons) were killed; not a single slave was liberated.

John Brown's raid lasted 36 hours, but its repercussions resounded for years. Brown and six of his followers were promptly tried by the state of Virginia, convicted, and hanged. This scarcely ended matters. The raid sent a wave of revulsion and alarm through the South. Although no slaves had risen in revolt, it revived fears of slave insurrection that were never far beneath the surface of southern consciousness. Exaggerated reports of Brown's network of abolitionist supporters confirmed southern suspicions that a widespread northern conspiracy was afoot, determined to destroy their society. Although Republican leaders denied any connection with Brown and disavowed his actions, few southerners believed them. Had not Lincoln talked of the extinction of slavery? And had not William H. Seward, who was expected to be the next Republican presidential nominee, given a campaign speech in 1858 in which he predicted an irrepressible conflict between the free and slave societies?

Many northerners, impressed by Brown's dignified bearing and eloquence during his trial, considered him a martyr to freedom. In his final statement to the court, Brown said:

> I see a book kissed, which I suppose to be the Bible, which teaches me that all things whatsoever I would that men should do to me, I should do even so to them. It teaches me, further, to remember them that are in bonds as bound with them. I endeavored to act up to that instruction. . . . Now, if it is deemed necessary that I should forfeit my life for the furtherance of the ends of justice, and mingle my blood further with the blood of my children and with the blood of millions in this slave country whose rights are disregarded by wicked, cruel, and unjust enactments, I say, let it be done.

On the day of Brown's execution, bells tolled in hundreds of northern towns, guns fired salutes, and ministers preached sermons of commemoration. "The death of no man in America has ever produced so profound a sensation," commented one northerner. Ralph Waldo Emerson declared that Brown had made "the gallows as glorious as the cross."

This outpouring of northern sympathy for Brown shocked and enraged southerners and weakened the already frayed threads of the Union. "The Harper's Ferry invasion has advanced the cause of disunion more than any event that has happened since the formation of the government," observed a Richmond, Virginia, newspaper. "I have always been a fervid Union man," wrote a North Carolinian, but "the endorsement of the Harper's Ferry outrage . . . has shaken my fidelity. . . . I am willing to take the chances of every possible evil that may arise from disunion, sooner than submit any longer to Northern insolence."

Something approaching a reign of terror now descended on the South. Every Yankee seemed to be another John Brown; every slave who acted suspiciously seemed to be an insurrectionist. Hundreds of northerners were run out of the South in 1860, some wearing a coat of tar and feathers. Several "incendiaries," both white and black, were lynched. "Defend yourselves!" Senator Robert Toombs cried out to the southern people. "The enemy is at your door . . . meet him at the doorsill, and drive him from the temple of liberty, or pull down its pillars and involve him in a common ruin."

Conclusion

Few decades in American history witnessed a greater disjunction between economic well-being and political upheaval than the 1850s. Despite the recession following the Panic of 1857, the total output of the American economy grew by 62 percent during the decade.

Railroad mileage more than tripled, value added by manufacturing nearly doubled, and gross farm product grew by 40 percent. Americans were more prosperous than ever before.

Yet a profound malaise gripped the country. Riots between immigrants and nativists in the mid-1850s left more than 50 people dead. Fighting in Kansas between pro-slavery and antislavery forces killed at least 200. Fistfights broke out on the floor of Congress. A South Carolina congressman bludgeoned a Massachusetts senator to unconsciousness with a heavy cane. Representatives and senators came to congressional sessions armed with weapons as well as with violent words.

The nation proved capable of absorbing the large influx of immigrants despite the tensions and turmoil of the mid-1850s. It might also have been able to absorb the huge territorial expansion of the late 1840s had not the slavery issue been reopened in an earlier territorial acquisition, the Louisiana Purchase, by the Kansas-Nebraska Act of 1854. This legislation, followed by the Dred Scott decision in 1857, seemed to authorize the unlimited expansion of slavery. Within two years of its founding in 1854, however, the Republican Party emerged as the largest party in the North on a platform of preventing all future expansion of slavery. By 1860, the United States had reached a fateful crossroads. As Lincoln had said, it could not endure permanently half-slave and half-free. The presidential election of 1860 would decide which road America would take into the future.

SUGGESTED READINGS

For a detailed and readable treatment of the mounting sectional conflict in the 1850s, see **Allan Nevins**, *Ordeal of the Union*, 2 vols. (1947), and *The Emergence of Lincoln*, 2 vols. (1950). The Kansas-Nebraska Act and its political consequences are treated in **Gerald W. Wolff**, *The Kansas-Nebraska Bill: Party, Section, and the Coming of the Civil War* (1977). The conflict in Kansas is treated in **Nicole Etcheson**, *Bleeding Kansas: Contested Liberty in the Civil War Era* (2004). For the cross-cutting issue of nativism and the Know-Nothings, see **William E. Gienapp**, *The Origins of the Republican Party, 1852–1856* (1987), and **Tyler Anbinder**, *Nativism and Politics: The Know Nothing Party in the Northern United States* (1992). Two excellent studies of the role of Abraham Lincoln in the rise of the Republican Party are **Don E. Fehrenbacher**, *Prelude to Greatness: Lincoln in the 1850s* (1962), and **Kenneth Winkle**, *The Young Eagle: The Rise of Abraham Lincoln* (2003). The southern response to the growth of antislavery political sentiment in the North is the theme of **William J. Cooper, Jr.**, *The South and the Politics of Slavery 1828–1856* (1978).

The year 1857 witnessed a convergence of many crucial events; for a stimulating book that pulls together the threads of that year of crisis, see **Kenneth M. Stampp**, *America in 1857: A Nation on the Brink* (1990). For economic developments during the era, an older classic is still the best introduction: **George Rogers Taylor**, *The Transportation Revolution, 1815–1860* (1951). An important dimension of the southern economy is elucidated in **Fred Bateman and Thomas Weiss**, *A Deplorable Scarcity: The Failure of Industrialization in the Slave Economy* (1981). The political impact of the Panic of 1857 is the subject of **James L. Huston**, *The Panic of 1857 and the Coming of the Civil War* (1987). Still the best study of the Republican free-labor ideology is **Eric Foner**, *Free Soil, Free Labor, Free Men: The Ideology of the Republican Party before the Civil War*

(2nd ed., 1995). For southern yeoman farmers, a good study is **Stephanie McCurry**, *Masters of Small Worlds: Yeoman Households, Gender Relations, and the Political Culture of the Antebellum South Carolina Low Country* (1995). The best single study of the Dred Scott case is **Don E. Fehrenbacher**, *The Dred Scott Case: Its Significance in American Law and Politics* (1978), which was published in an abridged version with the title *Slavery, Law, and Politics: The Dred Scott Case in Historical Perspective* (1981). A thought-provoking biography of John Brown is **David S. Reynolds**, *John Brown: Abolitionist* (2005).

Visit the Liberty Equality Power Companion Web site for resources specific to this textbook: http://www.thomsonedu.com/history/murrin

Also find self-tests and additional resources at ThomsonNOW. ThomsonNOW is an integrated online suite of services and resources with proven ease of use and efficient paths to success, delivering the results you want—NOW!

www.thomsonedu.com/login/

Secession and Civil War, 1860–1862

As the year 1860 began, the Democratic Party was one of the few national institutions left in the country. The Methodists and Baptists had split into Northern and Southern churches in the 1840s over the issue of slavery; several voluntary associations had done the same; the Whig Party and the nativist American Party had been shattered by sectional antagonism in the mid-1850s. Finally, in April 1860, even the Democratic Party, at its national convention in Charleston, South Carolina, split into Northern and Southern camps. This virtually ensured the election of a Republican president. Such a prospect aroused deep fears among Southern whites that a Republican administration might use its power to bring liberty and perhaps even equality to the slaves.

When Abraham Lincoln was elected president exclusively by Northern votes, the lower-South states seceded from the Union. When Lincoln refused to remove U.S. troops from **Fort Sumter,** South Carolina, the new Confederate States army opened fire on the fort. Lincoln called out the militia to suppress the insurrection. Four more slave states seceded. In 1861, the country drifted into a civil war whose immense consequences no one could foresee.

The Election of 1860

A hotbed of Southern-rights radicalism, Charleston, South Carolina, turned out to be the worst possible place for the Democrats to hold their national convention. Sectional confrontations took place inside the convention hall and on the streets. Since 1836, the Democratic Party had required a two-thirds majority of delegates for a presidential nomination, a rule that in effect gave Southerners veto power if they voted together. Although Stephen A. Douglas had the backing of a simple majority of the delegates, southern Democrats were determined to deny him the nomination. His opposition to the Lecompton constitution in Kansas and to a federal slave code for the territories had convinced pro-slavery Southerners that they would be unable to control a Douglas administration.

The first test came in the debate on the platform. Southern delegates insisted on a plank favoring a federal slave code for the territories. Douglas could not run on a platform that contained such a plank, and if the party adopted it, Democrats were sure to lose every state in the North. By a slim majority, the convention rejected the plank and reaffirmed the 1856 platform endorsing popular sovereignty. Fifty Southern delegates thereupon walked out of the convention. Even after they left, Douglas could not muster a two-thirds majority, nor

CHRONOLOGY

1860	Lincoln elected president (November 6) • South Carolina secedes (December 20) • Federal troops transfer from Fort Moultrie to Fort Sumter (December 26)
1861	Rest of lower South secedes (January–February) • Crittenden Compromise rejected (February) • Jefferson Davis inaugurated as provisional president of new Confederate States of America (February 18) • Abraham Lincoln inaugurated as president of the United States (March 4) • Fort Sumter falls; Lincoln calls out troops, proclaims blockade (April) • Four more states secede to join Confederacy (April–May) • Battle of Bull Run (Manassas) (July 21) • Battle of Wilson's Creek (August 10) • The *Trent* affair (November–December)
1862	Union captures Forts Henry and Donelson (February 6 and 16) • Congress passes Legal Tender Act (February 25) • Battle of Pea Ridge (March 7–8) • Battle of the *Monitor* and *Merrimac (Virginia)* (March 9) • Battle of Glorieta Pass (March 26–28) • Battle of Shiloh (April 6–7) • Union Navy captures New Orleans (April 25) • Stonewall Jackson's Shenandoah Valley campaign (May–June) • Seven Days' battles (June 25–July 1) • Second Battle of Manassas (Bull Run) (August 29–30) • Lee invades Maryland (September) • Battle of Corinth (October 3–4) • Battle of Perryville (October 8)
1863	Congress passes National Banking Act (February 25)

could any other candidate. After 57 futile ballots, the convention adjourned to meet in Baltimore six weeks later to try again.

By then the party was too badly shattered to be put back together. That pleased some pro-slavery radicals, who were convinced that the South would never be secure in a nation dominated by a Northern majority. The election of a Black Republican president, they believed, would provide the shock necessary to mobilize a Southern majority for secession. Two of the most prominent **secessionists** were William L. Yancey and Edmund Ruffin. In 1858, they founded the League of United Southerners to "fire the Southern heart . . . and at the proper moment, by one organized, concerted action, we can precipitate the Cotton States into a revolution." After walking out of the Democratic convention, the eloquent Yancey inspired a huge crowd in Charleston's moonlit courthouse square to give three cheers "for an Independent Southern Republic" with his concluding words: "Perhaps even now, the pen of the historian is nibbed to write the story of a new revolution."

The second convention in Baltimore reprised the first at Charleston. This time, an even larger number of delegates from Southern states walked out. They formed their own Southern Rights Democratic Party and nominated John C. Breckinridge of Kentucky (the incumbent vice president) for president on a slave-code platform. When regular Democrats nominated Douglas, the stage was set for what would become a four-party election. A coalition of former southern Whigs, who could not bring themselves to vote Democratic, and northern Whigs, who considered the Republican Party too radical, formed the Constitutional Union Party, which nominated John Bell of Tennessee for president. Bell had no chance of winning; the party's purpose was to exercise a conservative influence on a campaign that threatened to polarize the country.

The Republicans Nominate Lincoln

From the moment the Democratic Party broke apart, it became clear that 1860 could be the year when the dynamic young Republican Party elected its first president. The Republicans could expect no electoral votes from the 15 slave states. In 1856, however, they had won all but five northern states, and with only two or three of those five they could win the presidency. The crucial states were Pennsylvania, Illinois, and Indiana. Douglas might still carry them and throw the presidential election into the House, where anything could happen. Thus the Republicans had to carry at least two of the swing states to win.

THE POLITICAL QUADRILLE
Music by Dred Scott

Library of Congress, Prints and Photographs Division

The Political Quadrille This cartoon depicts the four presidential candidates in 1860. Clockwise from the upper left are John C. Breckinridge, Southern Rights Democrat; Abraham Lincoln, Republican; John Bell, Constitutional Union; and Stephen A. Douglas, Democrat. All are dancing to the tune played by Dred Scott, symbolizing the importance of the slavery issue in this campaign. Each candidate's partner represents a political liability: for example, Breckinridge's partner is the disunionist William L. Yancey wearing a devil's horns, while Lincoln's partner is a black woman who supposedly gives color to Democratic accusations that Republicans believed in miscegenation.

As the Republican delegates poured into Chicago for their convention—held in a huge building nicknamed the Wigwam because of its shape—their leading presidential prospect was William H. Seward of New York. An experienced politician who had served as governor and senator, Seward was by all odds the most prominent Republican, but in his long career he had made many enemies. His antinativist policies had alienated some former members of the American Party, whose support he would need to carry Pennsylvania. His "Higher Law" speech against the Compromise of 1850 and his "Irrepressible Conflict" speech in 1858, predicting the ultimate overthrow of slavery, had given him a reputation for radicalism that might drive away voters in the vital swing states of the lower North.

Several of the delegates, uneasy about that reputation, staged a stop-Seward movement. The next candidate to the fore was Abraham Lincoln. Although he too had opposed nativism, he had done so less prominently than Seward. His "House Divided" speech had made essentially the same point as Seward's "Irrepressible Conflict" speech, but his reputation was still that of a more moderate man. He was from one of the lower-North states where the election would be close, and his rise from a poor farm boy and rail-splitter to successful lawyer and political leader perfectly reflected the free-labor theme of social mobility extolled by the Republican Party. By picking up second-choice votes from states that switched from their favorite sons, Lincoln overtook Seward and won the nomination on the third ballot. Seward accepted the outcome gracefully, and the Republicans headed into the campaign as a united, confident party.

Their confidence stemmed in part from their platform, which appealed to many groups in the North. Its main plank pledged exclusion of slavery from the territories. Other planks called for a higher tariff (especially popular in Pennsylvania), a homestead act (popular in the Northwest), and federal aid for construction of a transcontinental railroad and for improvement of river navigation. This program was designed for a future in which the "house divided" would become a free-labor society modeled on Northern capitalism. Its blend of idealism and materialism proved especially attractive to young people; a large majority of first-time voters in the North voted Republican in 1860. Thousands of them joined Wide-Awake clubs and marched in huge torchlight parades through the cities of the North.

Southern Fears

Militant enthusiasm in the North was matched by fear and rage in the South. Few people there could see any difference between Lincoln and Seward—or for that matter between Lincoln and William Lloyd Garrison. They were all Black Republicans and abolitionists. Had not Lincoln branded slavery a moral, social, and political evil? Had he not said that the Declaration of Independence applied to blacks as well as whites? Had he not expressed a hope that excluding slavery from the territories would put it on the road to ultimate extinction? To Southerners, the Republican pledge not to interfere with slavery in the states was meaningless.

A Republican victory in the presidential election would put an end to the South's political control of its destiny. Two-thirds of the time from 1789 to 1860, Southerners (all slaveholders) had been president of the United States. No northern president had ever won reelection. Two-thirds of the Speakers of the House and presidents pro tem of the Senate had been Southerners. Southern justices had been a majority on the Supreme Court since 1791. Lincoln's election would mark an irreversible turning away from this Southern ascendancy. Even Southern moderates warned that the South could not remain in the Union if Lincoln won. "This Government and Black Republicanism cannot live together," said one of them. "At no period of the world's history have four thousand millions of property [that is, the slave owners] debated whether it ought to submit to the rule of an enemy." And what about the three-quarters of Southern whites who did not

From the Ralph E. Becker Collection of Political Americana, The Smithsonian Institution Neg #49814

Wide-Awake Parade in New York, October 5, 1860 The Wide-Awakes were an organization of young Republicans who roused political enthusiasm by marching in huge torchlight parades during the political campaign of 1860. A year later, many of these same men would march down the same streets in army uniforms carrying rifles instead of torches on their way to the front.

Voting in the 1860 Election

Candidate	All States		Free States (18)		Slave States (15)	
	Popular	Electoral	Popular	Electoral	Popular	Electoral
Lincoln	1,864,735	180	1,838,347	180	26,388	0
Opposition to Lincoln	2,821,157	123	1,572,637	3	1,248,520	120
"Fusion" Tickets*	595,846	—	580,426	—	15,420	—
Douglas	979,425	12	815,857	3	163,568	9
Breckinridge	669,472	72	99,381	0	570,091	72
Bell	576,414	39	76,973	0	499,441	39

* In several states, the two Democratic parties and the Constitutional Union Party arranged a single anti-Lincoln ballot. These "fusion" tickets carried several counties but failed to win any state.

belong to slaveholding families? Lincoln's election, warned an Alabama secessionist, would show that "the North [means] to free the negroes and force amalgamation between them and the children of the poor men of the South." If Georgia remained in a Union "ruled by Lincoln and his crew," a secessionist in that state told nonslaveholders, "in TEN years or less our CHILDREN will be the *slaves* of negroes."

Most whites in the South voted for Breckinridge, who carried 11 slave states. Bell won the upper-South states of Virginia, Kentucky, and Tennessee. Missouri went to Douglas—the only state he carried, although he came in second in the popular vote. Although Lincoln received less than 40 percent of the popular vote, he won every free state and swept the presidency by a substantial margin in the electoral college (three of New Jersey's seven electoral votes went to Douglas). **(See Map 15.1, Election of 1860 and Southern Secession, in the color insert following page 624.)**

The Lower South Secedes

Focus Question
Why did political leaders in the lower South think that Lincoln's election made secession imperative?

Lincoln's victory provided the shock that Southern fire-eaters had craved. The tension that had been building up for years suddenly exploded like a string of firecrackers, as seven states seceded one after another. According to the theory of secession, when each state ratified the Constitution and joined the Union, it authorized the national government to act as its agent in the exercise of certain functions of sovereignty, but the states had never given away their fundamental underlying sovereignty. Any state, then, by the act of its own convention, could withdraw from its "compact" with the other states and reassert its individual sovereignty. Therefore, the South Carolina legislature called for such a convention and ordered an election of delegates to consider withdrawing from the United States. On December 20, 1860, the South Carolina convention did withdraw, by a vote of 169 to 0.

The outcome was closer in other lower-South states. Unconditional unionism was rare, but many conservatives and former Whigs, including Alexander H. Stephens of Georgia, shrank from the drastic step of secession. At the conventions in each of the next six states to secede, some delegates tried to delay matters with vague proposals for "cooperation" among all Southern states, or even with proposals to wait until after Lincoln's inauguration on March 4, 1861, to see what course he would pursue. Those minority factions were overridden by proponents of immediate secession. The conventions followed the example of South Carolina and voted to take their states out of the Union: Mississippi on January 9, 1861, Florida on the 10th, Alabama on the 11th, Georgia on the 19th, Louisiana on the 26th, and Texas on February 1. In those six states as a whole, 20 percent of the delegates voted against secession, but most of these, including Stephens, "went with their states" after the final votes had been tallied. Delegates from the seven seceding states met in Montgomery, Alabama, in February to create a new nation to be called the Confederate States of America.

Northerners Affirm the Union

Most people in the North considered secession unconstitutional and treasonable. In his final annual message to Congress, on December 3, 1860, President Buchanan insisted that the Union was not "a mere voluntary association of States, to be dissolved at pleasure by any one of the contracting parties." If secession was consummated, Buchanan warned, it would create a disastrous precedent that would make the United States government "a rope of sand." He continued:

> Our thirty-three States may resolve themselves into as many petty, jarring, and hostile republics. . . . By such a dread catastrophe the hopes of the friends of freedom throughout the world would be destroyed. . . . Our example for more than eighty years would not only be lost, but it would be quoted as proof that man is unfit for self-government.

European monarchists and conservatives were already expressing smug satisfaction at "the great smashup" of the republic in North America. They predicted that other disaffected minorities would also secede and that the United States would ultimately collapse into anarchy and revolution. That was precisely what Northerners and even some upper-South **Unionists** feared. "The doctrine of secession is anarchy," declared a Cincinnati newspaper. "If any minority have the right to break up the Government at pleasure, because they have not had their way, there is an end of all government." Lincoln denied that the states had ever possessed independent sovereignty before becoming part of the United States. Rather, they had been colonies or territories that never would have become part of the United States had they not accepted unconditional sovereignty of the national government. No government, said Lincoln, "ever had provision in its organic law for its own termination. . . . No State, upon its own mere motion, can lawfully get out of the Union. . . . They can only do so against law, and by revolution."

In that case, answered many Southerners, we invoke the right of revolution to justify secession. After all, the United States was born of revolution. The secessionists maintained that they were merely following the example of their forefathers in declaring independence from a government that threatened their rights and liberties. An Alabaman asked rhetorically: "[Were not] the men of 1776, who withdrew their allegiance from George III and set up for themselves . . . Secessionists?"

Northerners could scarcely deny the right of revolution: They too were heirs of 1776. But "the right of revolution, is never a legal right," said Lincoln. "At most, it is but a moral right, when exercised for a morally justifiable cause. When exercised without such a cause revolution is no right, but simply a wicked exercise of physical power." The South, in Lincoln's view, had no morally justifiable cause. In fact, the event that had precipitated secession was his own election by a constitutional majority. For Southerners to cast themselves in the mold of 1776 was "a libel upon the whole character and conduct" of the Founding Fathers, said the antislavery poet and journalist William Cullen Bryant. They rebelled "to establish the rights of man . . . and principles of universal liberty," whereas Southerners in 1861 were rebelling to protect "a domestic despotism. . . . Their motto is not liberty, but slavery."

Compromise Proposals

Bryant conveniently overlooked the fact that slavery had existed in most parts of the republic founded by the revolutionaries of 1776. In any event, most people in the North agreed with Lincoln that secession was a "wicked exercise of physical power." The question was what to do about it. All kinds of compromise proposals came before Congress when it met in December 1860. To sort them out, the Senate and the House each set up a special committee. The Senate committee came up with a package of compromises sponsored by Senator John J. Crittenden of Kentucky. The Crittenden Compromise consisted of a series of proposed constitutional amendments: to guarantee slavery in the states perpetually against federal interference; to prohibit Congress from abolishing slavery in the District of Columbia or on any federal property (forts, arsenals, naval bases, and so on); to deny Congress the power to interfere with the interstate slave trade; to compensate slaveholders who were prevented from recovering fugitive slaves who had escaped to the North; and, most important, to protect slavery south of latitude 36°30' in all territories "now held *or hereafter acquired.*"

Given the appetite of the South for more slave territory in the Caribbean and Central America, that italicized phrase, in the view of most Republicans, might turn the United States into "a great slavebreeding and slavetrading empire." But even though endorsement of the territorial clause in the Crittenden Compromise would require Republicans to repudiate the platform on which they had just won the election, some conservatives in the party were willing to accept it in the interest of peace and conciliation. Their votes, together with those of Democrats and upper-South Unionists whose states had not seceded, might have gotten the compromise through Congress. It is doubtful, however, that the approval of three-quarters of the states required for ratification would have been forthcoming. In any case, word came from Springfield, Illinois, where President-elect Lincoln was preparing for his inaugural trip to Washington, telling key Republican senators and congressmen to stand firm against compromise on the territorial issue. "Entertain no proposition for a compromise in regard to the *extension* of slavery," wrote Lincoln.

> Filibustering for all South of us, and making slave states would follow . . . to put us again on the high-road to a slave empire. . . . We have just carried an election on principles fairly stated to the people. Now we are told in advance, the government shall be broken up, unless we surrender to those we have beaten. . . . If we surrender, it is the end of us. They will repeat the experiment upon us *ad libitum*. A year will not pass, till we shall have to take Cuba as a condition upon which they will stay in the Union.

Lincoln's advice was decisive. The Republicans voted against the Crittenden Compromise, which therefore failed in Congress. Most Republicans, though, went along with a proposal by Virginia for a "peace convention" of all the states to be held in Washington in February 1861. Although the seven seceded states sent no delegates, hopes that the convention might accomplish something encouraged Unionists in the eight other slave states either to reject secession or to adopt a wait-and-see attitude. In the end, the peace convention produced nothing better than a modified version of the Crittenden Compromise, which suffered the same fate as the original.

Nothing that happened in Washington would have made any difference to the seven states that had seceded. No compromise could bring them back. "We spit upon every plan to compromise," said one secessionist. No power could "stem the wild torrent of passion that is carrying everything before it," wrote former U.S. Senator Judah P. Benjamin of Louisiana. Secession "is a revolution [that] can no more be checked by human effort . . . than a prairie fire by a gardener's watering pot."

Establishment of the Confederacy

While the peace convention deliberated in Washington, the seceded states focused on a convention in Montgomery, Alabama, that drew up a constitution and established a government for the new Confederate States of America. The Confederate constitution contained clauses that guaranteed slavery in both the states and the territories, strengthened the principle of state sovereignty, and prohibited its Congress from enacting a protective (as distinguished from a revenue) tariff and from granting government aid to internal improvements. It limited the president to a single six-year term. The convention delegates constituted themselves a provisional Congress for the new nation until regular elections could be held in November 1861. For provisional president and vice president, the convention turned away from radical secessionists, such as Yancey, and elected Jefferson Davis, a moderate secessionist, and Alexander Stephens, who had originally opposed Georgia's secession but ultimately had supported it.

Davis and Stephens were two of the most able men in the South, with 25 years of service in the U.S. Congress between them. A West Point graduate, Davis had commanded a regiment in the Mexican War and had been secretary of war in the Pierce administration—a useful fund of experience if civil war became a reality. But perhaps the main reason they were elected was to present an image of moderation and respectability to the eight upper-South states that remained in the Union. The Confederacy needed those states—at least some of them—if it was to be a viable nation, especially if war came. Without the upper South, the Confederate states would have less than one-fifth of the population (and barely one-tenth of the free population) and only one-twentieth of the industrial capacity of the Union states.

Confederate leaders appealed to the upper South to join them because of the "common origin, pursuits, tastes, manners and customs [that] bind together in one brotherhood the . . . slaveholding states." Residents of the upper South were indeed concerned about preserving slavery, but the issue was less salient there. A strong heritage of Unionism competed with the commitment to slavery. Virginia had contributed more men to the pantheon of Founding Fathers than any other state. Tennessee took pride in being the state of Andrew Jackson, who was famous for his stern warning to John C. Calhoun: "Our Federal Union— It must be preserved." Kentucky was the home of Henry Clay, the Great Pacificator, who had put together compromises to save the Union on three occasions. These states would not leave the Union without greater cause.

The Fort Sumter Issue

Focus Question
Why did compromise efforts to forestall secession fail, and why did war break out at Fort Sumter?

As each state seceded, it seized the forts, arsenals, customs houses, and other federal property within its borders. Still in federal hands, however, were two remote forts in the Florida keys, another on an island off Pensacola, and Fort Moultrie in the Charleston harbor. Moultrie quickly became a bone of contention. In December 1860, the self-proclaimed republic of South Carolina demanded its evacuation by the 84-man garrison of the U.S. Army. An obsolete fortification, Moultrie was vulnerable to attack by the South Carolina militia that swarmed into the area. On the day after Christmas 1860, Major Robert Anderson, commander at Moultrie, moved his men to Fort Sumter, an uncompleted but immensely strong bastion on an artificial island in the channel leading into Charleston Bay. A Kentuckian married to a Georgian, Anderson sympathized with the South but remained loyal to the United States. He deplored the possibility of war and hoped that moving the garrison to Sumter would ease tensions by reducing the possibility of an attack. Instead, it lit a fuse that eventually set off the war.

South Carolina sent a delegation to President Buchanan to negotiate the withdrawal of the federal troops. Buchanan, previously pliable, surprised them by saying no. He even tried to reinforce the garrison. On January 9, the unarmed merchant ship *Star of the West,* carrying 200 soldiers for Sumter, tried to enter the bay but was driven away by South Carolina artillery. Loath to start a war, Major Anderson refused to return fire with Sumter's guns. Matters then settled into an uneasy truce. The Confederate government sent General Pierre G. T. Beauregard to take command of the troops ringing Charleston Bay with their cannons pointed at Fort Sumter, and waited to see what the incoming Lincoln administration would do.

When Abraham Lincoln took the oath of office as the 16th—and, some speculated, the last—president of the *United* States, he knew that his inaugural address would be the most important in American history. On his words would hang the issues of union or disunion, peace or war. His goal was to keep the upper South in the Union while cooling passions in the lower South, hoping that, in time, Southern loyalty to the Union would reassert itself. In his address, he demonstrated both firmness and forbearance: firmness in purpose to preserve the Union, forbearance in the means of doing so. He repeated his pledge not "to interfere with the institution of slavery where it exists." He assured the Confederate states that "the government will not assail *you*." His first draft had also included the phrase "unless you *first* assail it," but William H. Seward, whom Lincoln had appointed secretary of state, persuaded him to drop those words as too provocative. Lincoln's first draft had also stated his intention to use "all the powers at my disposal [to] reclaim the public property and places which have fallen." He deleted that statement as too warlike and said only that he would "hold, occupy, and possess the property, and places belonging to the government," without defining exactly what he meant or how he would do it. In his eloquent peroration, Lincoln appealed to Southerners as Americans who shared with other Americans four score and five years of national history. "We are not enemies, but friends," he said.

> Though passion may have strained, it must not break, our bonds of affection. The mystic chords of memory, stretching from every battlefield and patriot grave to every living heart and hearthstone all over this broad land, will yet swell the chorus of the Union when again touched, as surely they will be, by the better angels of our nature.

Lincoln hoped to buy time with his inaugural address—time to demonstrate his peaceful intentions and to enable southern Unionists (whose numbers Republicans overestimated) to regain the upper hand. But the day after his inauguration, Lincoln learned that time was running out. A dispatch from Major Anderson informed him that provisions for the soldiers at Fort Sumter would soon be exhausted. The garrison must either be resupplied or evacuated. Any attempt to send in supplies by force would undoubtedly provoke a response from Confederate guns at Charleston. And by putting the onus of starting a war on Lincoln's shoulders, such an action would undoubtedly divide the North and unite the South, driving at least four more states into the Confederacy. Thus, most members of Lincoln's cabinet, along with the army's General-in-Chief Winfield Scott, advised Lincoln to withdraw the troops from Sumter. That, however, would bestow a great moral victory on the Confederacy. It would confer legitimacy on the Confederate government and would probably lead to diplomatic recognition by foreign powers. Having pledged to "hold, occupy, and possess" national property, could Lincoln afford to abandon that policy during his first month in office? If he did, he would go down in history as the president who consented to the dissolution of the United States.

The pressures from all sides caused Lincoln many sleepless nights; one morning he rose from bed and keeled over in a dead faint. Finally, he hit upon a solution that evidenced the mastery that would mark his presidency. He decided to send in unarmed ships with supplies but to hold troops and warships outside the harbor with authorization to go into action only if the Confederates used force to stop the supply ships. And he would give South Carolina officials advance notice of his intention. This stroke of genius shifted the decision for war or peace to Jefferson Davis. In effect, Lincoln flipped a coin and said to Davis, "Heads I win; tails you lose." If Confederate troops fired on the supply ships, the South would stand convicted of starting a war by attacking "a mission of humanity" bringing "food for hungry men." If Davis allowed the supplies to go in peacefully, the U.S. flag would continue to fly over Fort Sumter. The Confederacy would lose face at home and abroad, and southern Unionists would take courage.

Davis did not hesitate. He ordered General Beauregard to compel Sumter's surrender before the supply ships got there. At 4:30 A.M. on April 12, 1861, Confederate guns set off the Civil War by firing on Fort Sumter. After a 33-hour bombardment in which the rebels fired 4,000 rounds and the skeleton gun crews in the garrison replied with 1,000—with no one killed on either side—the burning fort lowered the U.S. flag in surrender.

Choosing Sides

News of the attack triggered an outburst of anger and war fever in the North. "The town is in a wild state of excitement," wrote a Philadelphia diarist. "The American flag is to be seen everywhere. . . . Men are enlisting as fast as possible." A Harvard professor born during George Washington's presidency was astounded by the public response. "The heather is on fire," he wrote. "I never knew what a popular excitement can be." A New York woman wrote that the "time before Sumter" seemed like another century. "It seems as if we were never alive till now; never had a country till now."

Because the tiny U.S. Army—most of whose 16,000 soldiers were stationed at remote frontier posts—was inadequate to quell the "insurrection," Lincoln called on the states for 75,000 militia. The free states filled their quotas immediately. More than twice as many men volunteered as Lincoln had requested. Recognizing that the 90 days' service to which the militia were limited by law would be too short a time, on May 3, Lincoln issued a call for three-year volunteers. Before the war was over, more than 2 million men would serve in the Union army and navy.

The eight slave states still in the Union rejected Lincoln's call for troops. Four of them— Virginia, Arkansas, Tennessee, and North Carolina—soon seceded and joined the Confederacy. Forced by the outbreak of actual war to choose between the Union and the Confederacy, most residents of those four states chose the Confederacy. As a former Unionist in North Carolina remarked, "The division must be made on the line of slavery. The South must go with the South. . . . Blood is thicker than Water."

Few found the choice harder to make than **Robert E. Lee** of Virginia. One of the most promising officers in the U.S. Army, Lee believed that Southern states had no legal right to secede. General-in-Chief Winfield Scott wanted Lee to become field commander of the Union army. Instead, Lee sadly resigned from the army after the Virginia convention passed an ordinance of secession on April 17. "I must side either with or against my section," Lee

Slavery and Secession   The higher the proportion of slaves and slaveholders in the population of a southern state, the greater the intensity of secessionist sentiment.

	Population Who Were Slaves	White Population in Slaveholding Families
Seven states that seceded December 1860–February 1861 (South Carolina, Mississippi, Florida, Alabama, Georgia, Louisiana, Texas)	47%	38%
Four states that seceded after the firing on Fort Sumter (Virginia, Arkansas, Tennessee, North Carolina)	32	24
Four border slave states remaining in Union (Maryland, Delaware, Kentucky, Missouri)	14	15

told a Northern friend. "I cannot raise my hand against my birthplace, my home, my children." Along with three sons and a nephew, Lee joined the Confederate army. "I foresee that the country will have to pass through a terrible ordeal," he wrote, "a necessary expiation perhaps for our national sins."

Most Southern whites embraced war against the Yankees with less foreboding and more enthusiasm. When news of Sumter's surrender reached Richmond, a huge crowd poured into the state capitol square and ran up the Confederate flag. "Everyone is in favor of secession [and] perfectly frantic with delight," wrote a participant. "I never in all my life witnessed such excitement." The London *Times* correspondent described crowds in North Carolina with "flushed faces, wild eyes, screaming mouths, hurrahing for 'Jeff Davis' and 'the Southern Confederacy.'" No one in those cheering crowds could know that before the war ended, at least 260,000 Confederate soldiers would lose their lives (along with 365,000 Union soldiers) and that the slave South they fought to defend would be utterly destroyed.

The Border States

Except for Delaware, which remained firmly in the Union, the slave states that bordered free states were sharply divided by the outbreak of war. Leaders in these states talked vaguely of neutrality, but they were to be denied that luxury—Maryland and Missouri immediately, and Kentucky in September 1861 when first Confederate and then Union troops crossed their borders. **(See Map 15.2, Principal Military Campaigns of the Civil War, in the color insert following page 624.)**

The first blood was shed in Maryland on April 19, 1861, when a mob attacked Massachusetts troops traveling through Baltimore to Washington. The soldiers fired back, and, in the end, 12 Baltimoreans and 4 soldiers were dead. Confederate partisans burned bridges and tore down telegraph wires, cutting Washington off from the North for nearly a week until additional troops from Massachusetts and New York reopened communications and seized key points in Maryland. The troops also arrested many Confederate sympathizers, including the mayor and police chief of Baltimore, a judge, and two dozen state legislators. To prevent Washington from becoming surrounded by enemy territory, federal forces turned Maryland into an occupied state. Although thousands of Marylanders slipped into Virginia to join the Confederate army, a substantial majority of Maryland residents remained loyal to the Union.

The same was true of Missouri. Aggressive action by Union commander Nathaniel Lyon provoked a showdown between Unionist and pro-Confederate militia that turned into a riot in St. Louis on May 10 and 11, 1861, in which 36 people died. Lyon then led his troops in a summer campaign that drove the Confederate militia, along with the governor and pro-Southern legislators, into Arkansas, where they formed a Missouri Confederate government in exile. Reinforced by Arkansas regiments, these rebel Missourians invaded their home state, and on August 10 defeated Lyon (who was killed) in the bloody battle of Wilson's Creek in the southwest corner of Missouri. The victorious Confederates marched northward all the way to the Missouri River, capturing a Union garrison at Lexington 40 miles east of Kansas City on September 20. By then, Union forces made up of regiments from Iowa, Illinois, and Kansas as well as Missouri had regrouped and drove the ragged Missouri Confederates back into Arkansas.

From then until the war's end, Unionists maintained political control of Missouri through military power. Even so, continued guerrilla attacks by Confederate **"bushwhackers"** and counterinsurgency tactics by Unionist "jay-hawkers" turned large areas of the state into a no-man's-land of hit-and-run raids, arson, ambush, and murder. During these years, the famous postwar outlaws Jesse and Frank James and Cole and Jim Younger rode with the notorious rebel guerrilla chieftains William Quantrill and "Bloody Bill" Anderson. More than any other state, Missouri suffered from a civil war within the Civil War, and its bitter legacy persisted for generations.

In elections held during summer and fall 1861, Unionists gained firm control of the Kentucky and Maryland legislatures. Kentucky Confederates, like those of Missouri, formed a state government in exile. When the Confederate Congress admitted both Kentucky and Missouri to full representation, the Confederate flag acquired its 13 stars. Nevertheless, two-thirds of the white population in the four border slave states favored the Union, although some of that support was undoubtedly induced by the presence of Union troops.

The Creation of West Virginia

The war produced a fifth Union border state: West Virginia. Most of the delegates from the portion of Virginia west of the Shenandoah Valley had voted against secession. A region of mountains, small farms, and few slaves, western Virginia's economy was linked more closely to nearby Ohio and Pennsylvania than to the South. Its largest city, Wheeling, was 330 miles from Richmond but only 60 miles from Pittsburgh. Delegates who had opposed Virginia's secession from the Union returned home determined to secede from Virginia. With the help of Union troops, who crossed the Ohio River and won a few small battles against Confederate forces in the area during summer 1861, they accomplished their goal. Through a complicated process of conventions and referendums—carried out in the midst of raids and skirmishes—they created the new state of West Virginia, which entered the Union in 1863.

Indian Territory and the Southwest

To the south and west of Missouri, civil war raged along a different border—between Southern states and territories—for control of the resources of that vast region. In the Indian Territory (present-day Oklahoma), the Native Americans, who had been resettled there from Eastern states in the generation before the war, chose sides and carried on bloody guerrilla warfare against each other as ferocious as the bushwhacking in Missouri. The more prosperous Indians of the five "civilized tribes" (Cherokees, Creeks, Seminoles, Chickasaws, and Choctaws), many of them of mixed blood and some of them slaveholders, tended to side with the Confederacy. Some tribes signed treaties of alliance with the Confederate government. Aided by white and black Union regiments operating out of Kansas and Missouri, the pro-Union Indians gradually gained control of most of the Indian Territory.

In the meantime, Confederates had made their boldest bid to fulfill antebellum Southern ambitions to win the Southwest. A small army composed mostly of Texans pushed up the Rio Grande valley into New Mexico in 1861. The following February, they launched a deeper strike to capture Santa Fe. With luck, they hoped to push even farther westward and northward to gain the mineral wealth of California and Colorado gold mines, whose millions were already helping to finance the Union war effort and could do wonders for Confederate finances. A good many Southerners lived in these Western territories and in California.

At first, the Confederate drive up the Rio Grande went well. The Texans won a victory over the Unionist New Mexico militia and a handful of regulars at the battle of Valverde, 100 miles south of Albuquerque, on February 21, 1862. They continued up the valley, occupied Albuquerque and Santa Fe, and pushed on toward Fort Union near Santa Fe. But Colorado miners who had organized themselves into Union regiments and had carried out the greatest march of the war, over the rugged Rockies in winter, met the Texans in the battle of Glorieta Pass on March 26–28. The battle was a tactical draw, but a unit of Coloradans destroyed the Confederate wagon train, forcing the Southerners into a disastrous retreat back to Texas. Of the 3,700 who had started out to win the West for the Confederacy, only 2,000 made it back. The Confederates had shot their bolt in this region; the West and Southwest remained safe for the Union.

The Balance Sheet of War

Focus Question
What were Northern advantages in the Civil War? What were Southern advantages?

If one counts three-quarters of the border state population (including free blacks) as pro-Union, the total number of people in Union states in 1861 was 22.5 million, compared with 9 million in the Confederate states. The North's military manpower advantage was even greater because the Confederate population total included 3.7 million slaves compared with 300,000 slaves in Union areas. At first, neither side expected to recruit blacks as soldiers. Eventually, the Union did enlist 180,000 black soldiers and 16,000 black sailors; the Confederacy held out against that drastic step until the war was virtually over. Altogether, about 2.1 million men fought for the Union and 850,000 for the Confederacy. That was close to half of the North's male population of military age (18 to 40) and three-quarters of the comparable Confederate white population. Because the labor force of the South consisted mainly of slaves, the Confederacy was able to enlist a larger proportion of its white population. The North's economic superiority was even greater. The Union states possessed nine-tenths of the country's industrial capacity and registered shipping, four-fifths of its bank capital, three-fourths of its railroad mileage and rolling stock, and three-fourths of its taxable wealth.

These statistics gave pause to some Southerners. In a long war that mobilized the total resources of both sides, the North's advantages might prove decisive. But in 1861, few anticipated how long and intense the war would be. Both sides expected a short and victorious conflict. Confederates seemed especially confident, partly because of their vaunted sense of martial superiority over the "bluebellied" Yankee nation of shopkeepers. Many Southerners really did believe that one of their own could lick three Yankees. "Let brave men advance with flintlocks and old-fashioned bayonets, on the popinjays of Northern cities," said ex-Governor Henry Wise of Virginia, now a Confederate general, and "the Yankees would break and run."

Although this turned out to be a grievous miscalculation, the South did have some reason to believe that its martial qualities were superior. A higher proportion of Southerners than Northerners had attended West Point and other military schools, had fought in the Mexican War, or had served as officers in the regular army. Volunteer military companies were more prevalent in the antebellum South than in the North. As a rural people, Southerners were proficient in hunting, riding, and other outdoor skills useful in military operations. Moreover, the South had begun to prepare for war earlier than the North. As each state seceded, it mobilized militia and volunteer military companies. On March 6, 1861, the Confederate Congress had authorized an army of 100,000 men. By the time Lincoln called for 75,000 militia after the fall of Fort Sumter, the Confederacy already had 60,000 men under arms. Not until summer 1861 would the North's greater manpower manifest itself in the form of a larger army.

Strategy and Morale

Even when fully mobilized, the North's superior resources did not guarantee success. Its military task was much more difficult than that of the South. The Confederacy had come into being in firm control of 750,000 square miles—a vast territory larger than all of Western Europe and twice as large as the 13 colonies in 1776. To win the war, Union forces would have to invade, conquer, and occupy much of that territory, cripple its people's ability to sustain a war of independence, and destroy its armies. Britain had been unable to accomplish a similar task in the war for independence, even though it enjoyed a far greater superiority of resources over the United States in 1776 than the Union enjoyed over the Confederacy in 1861. Victory does not always ride with the heaviest battalions.

The Red Badge of Courage (1951)

Directed by John Huston. Starring Audie Murphy (The Youth) and Bill Mauldin (The Loud Soldier).

Stephen Crane's short novel *The Red Badge of Courage* became an instant classic when it was published in 1895. Civil War veterans praised its realistic descriptions of the confusion, terror, chaos, courage, despair, and adrenaline-driven rage of men in battle. A story of young Henry Fleming (The Youth) and his buddy Wilson (The Loud Soldier) in their first battle (Chancellorsville), the novel traces Henry's transition from boyhood to manhood, from raw recruit to veteran, over two days of violent combat. Intended by Crane as a portrait of soldiers facing the ultimate moment of truth in combat, the novel strives for universality rather than specificity as a Civil War story. Thus the battle is not actually named (although circumstances make clear that it is Chancellorsville, despite the film misleadingly dating it in 1862). The 304th New York regiment is fictional, and even the fact that it is a Civil War battle is scarcely mentioned. Crane did achieve a sort of universality; the novel is a story of men at war, not simply a story of the Civil War.

The film remains more faithful to the book than most movies based on novels. Most of the dialogue is taken directly from Crane. Henry Fleming's self-doubts, fears, and eventual heroism after he first runs away are brilliantly portrayed on the screen by action and dialogue against a background of a narrator's words. Fleming is played by Audie Murphy, America's most decorated soldier in the Second World War, and Wilson by Bill Mauldin, whose Willie and Joe cartoons provided the most enduring images of the American infantryman in that war. They make the characters come alive with moving performances.

Much of the credit for this success belongs to director John Huston, who brought out the best in his inexperienced actors. One of Hollywood's most prominent directors, Huston had lobbied Louis Mayer of MGM to produce the film. Believing that "Nobody wants to see a Civil War movie," Mayer finally gave in but provided Huston with a skimpy budget. When Huston flew to Africa immediately after the filming was completed to begin directing *The African Queen,* studio executives cut several of Huston's scenes and reduced the movie's length to 69 minutes. The studio also did little to promote the film, and because audiences failed to identify with its grim realism and mostly unknown cast, *The Red Badge of Courage* was a box-office failure. Like the novel, however, it has become a classic that is still, more than a half-century after it was filmed, one of the best cinematic portrayals of the psychology of men in combat.

Audie Murphy (Henry Fleming) and Bill Mauldin (The Loud Soldier), in *The Red Badge of Courage.*

The Everett Collection

To "win" the war, the Confederacy did not need to invade or conquer the Union or even to destroy its armies; it needed only to stand on the defensive and prevent the North from destroying Southern armies—to hold out long enough to convince Northerners that the cost of victory was too high. Most Confederates were confident in 1861 that they were more than equal to the task. Most European military experts agreed. The military analyst of the London *Times* wrote:

> It is one thing to drive the rebels from the south bank of the Potomac, or even to occupy Richmond, but another to reduce and hold in permanent subjection a tract of country nearly as large as Russia in Europe. . . . No war of independence ever terminated unsuccessfully except where the disparity of force was far greater than it is in this case. . . . Just as England during the revolution had to give up conquering the colonies so the North will have to give up conquering the South.

The important factor of **morale** also seemed to favor the Confederacy. To be sure, Union soldiers fought for powerful symbols: nation, flag, constitution. "We are fighting to maintain the best government on earth" was a common phrase in their letters and diaries. It is a "grate [sic] struggle for Union, Constitution, and law," wrote a New Jersey soldier. A Chicago newspaper declared that the South had "outraged the Constitution, set at defiance all law, and trampled under foot that flag which has been the glorious and consecrated symbol of American Liberty."

But Confederates, too, fought for nation, flag, constitution, and liberty—of whites. In addition, they fought to defend their land, homes, and families against invading "Yankee vandals," who many Southern whites quite literally believed were coming to "free the negroes and force amalgamation between them and the children of the poor men of the South." An army fighting in defense of its homeland generally has the edge in morale. "We shall have the enormous advantage of fighting on our own territory and for our very existence," wrote a Confederate leader. "All the world over, are not one million of men defending themselves at home against invasion stronger in a mere military point of view, than five millions [invading] a foreign country?"

The Richmond Grays   This photograph depicts a typical volunteer military unit that joined the Confederate army in 1861. Note the determined and confident appearance of these young men. By 1865, one-third of them would be dead and several others maimed for life.

Cook Collection, Valentine Museum, Richmond, Virginia

Mobilizing for War

More than four-fifths of the soldiers on both sides were volunteers; in the first two years of the war, nearly all of them were. The Confederacy passed a conscription law in April 1862, and the Union followed suit in March 1863, but even afterward, most recruits were volunteers. In both North and South, patriotic rallies with martial music and speeches motivated local men to enlist in a company (100 men) organized by the area's leading citizens. The recruits elected their own company officers (a captain and two lieutenants), who received their commissions from the state governor. A regiment consisted of 10 infantry companies, and each regiment was commanded by a colonel, with a lieutenant colonel and a major as second and third in command—all of them appointed by the governor. Cavalry regiments were organized in a similar manner. Field artillery units were known as batteries, a grouping of four or six cannon with their caissons and limber chests (two-wheeled, horse-drawn vehicles) to carry ammunition; the full complement of a six-gun battery was 155 men and 72 horses.

Volunteer units received a state designation and number in the order of their completion—the 2nd Massachusetts Volunteer Infantry, the 5th Virginia Cavalry, and so on. In most regiments, the men in each company generally came from the same town or locality. Some Union regiments were composed of men of a particular ethnic group. By the end of the war, the Union army had raised about 2,000 infantry and cavalry regiments and 700 batteries; the Confederates had organized just under half as many. As the war went on, the original thousand-man complement of a regiment was usually whittled down to half or less by disease, casualties, desertions, and detachments. The states generally preferred to organize new regiments rather than keep the old ones up to full strength.

These were citizen-soldiers, not professionals. They carried their peacetime notions of democracy and discipline into the army. That is why, in the tradition of the citizen militia, the men elected their company officers and sometimes their field officers (colonel, lieutenant colonel, and major) as well. Professional military men deplored the egalitarianism and slack discipline that resulted. Political influence often counted for more than military training in the election and appointment of officers. These civilians in uniform were extremely awkward and unmilitary at first, and some regiments suffered battlefield disasters because of inadequate training, discipline, and leadership. Yet this was the price that a democratic society with a tiny professional army had to pay to mobilize large armies almost overnight to meet a crisis. In time, these raw recruits became battle-hardened veterans commanded by experienced officers who had survived the weeding-out process of combat or of examination boards or who had been promoted from the ranks.

As the two sides organized their field armies, both grouped four or more regiments into brigades and three or more brigades into divisions. By 1862, they began grouping two or more divisions into corps and two or more corps into armies. Each of these larger units was commanded by a general appointed by the president. Most of the higher-ranking generals on both sides were West Point graduates, but others were appointed because they represented an important political, regional, or (in the North) ethnic constituency whose support Lincoln or Davis wished to solidify. Some of these "political" generals, like elected regimental officers, were incompetent, but as the war went on, they too either learned their trade or were weeded out. Some outstanding generals emerged from civilian life and were promoted up the ranks during the war. In both the Union and the Confederate armies, the best officers (including generals) *led* their men by example as much as by precept; they commanded from the front, not the rear. Combat casualties were higher among officers than among privates, and highest of all among generals, who died in action at a rate 50 percent higher than enlisted men.

Weapons and Tactics

In Civil War battles, the infantry rifle was the most lethal weapon. Muskets and rifles caused 80 to 90 percent of the combat casualties. From 1862 on, most of these weapons were "rifled"—that is, they had spiral grooves cut in the barrel to impart a spin to the bullet. This innovation was only a decade old, dating to the perfection in the 1850s of the "minié ball" (named after French army Captain Claude Minié, its principal inventor), a cone-shaped lead bullet with a base that expanded on firing to "take" the **rifling** of the barrel. This made it possible to load and fire a muzzle-loading rifle as rapidly (two or three times per minute) as the old smoothbore musket. Moreover, the rifle had greater accuracy and at least four times the effective range (400 yards or more) of the smoothbore.

Civil War infantry tactics adjusted only gradually to the greater lethal range and accuracy of the new rifle, however, for the prescribed massed formations had emerged from experience with the smoothbore musket. Close-order assaults against defenders equipped with rifles resulted in enormous casualties. The defensive power of the rifle became even greater when troops began digging into trenches. Massed frontal assaults became almost suicidal. Soldiers and their officers learned the hard way to adopt skirmishing tactics, taking advantage of cover and working around the enemy flank.

Logistics

Wars are fought not only by men and weapons but also by the logistical apparatus that supports and supplies them. The Civil War is often called the world's first modern war because of the role played by railroads, steam-powered ships, and the telegraph, which did not exist in earlier wars fought on a similar scale (those of the French Revolution and Napoleon). Railroads and steamboats transported supplies and soldiers with unprecedented speed and efficiency; the telegraph provided instantaneous communication between army headquarters and field commanders.

Yet these modern forms of transport and communications were extremely vulnerable. Cavalry raiders and guerrillas could cut telegraph wires, burn railroad bridges, and tear up the tracks. Confederate cavalry became particularly skillful at sundering the supply lines of invading Union armies and thereby neutralizing forces several times larger than their own. The more deeply the Union armies penetrated into the South, the more men they had to detach to guard bridges, depots, and supply bases.

Once the campaigning armies had moved away from their railhead or wharfside supply base, they returned to dependence on animal-powered transport. Depending on terrain, road conditions, length of supply line, and proportion of artillery and cavalry, Union armies required one horse or mule for every two or three men. Thus a large invading Union army of 100,000 men (the approximate number in Virginia from 1862 to 1865 and in Georgia in 1864) would need about 40,000 draft animals. Confederate armies, operating mostly in friendly territory closer to their bases, needed fewer. The poorly drained dirt roads typical of much of the South turned into a morass of mud in the frequently wet weather. These logistical problems did much to offset the industrial supremacy of the North, particularly during the first year of the war when bottlenecks, shortages, and inefficiency marked the logistical effort on both sides. By 1862, though, the North's economy had fully geared up for war, making the Union army the best-supplied army in history up to that time.

Confederate officials accomplished impressive feats of improvisation in creating war industries, especially munitions and gunpowder, but the Southern industrial base was too slender to sustain adequate production. Particularly troublesome for the Confederacy was its inability to replace rails and rolling stock for its railroads. Although the South produced plenty of food, the railroads deteriorated to the point that food could not reach soldiers or civilians. As the war went into its third and fourth years, the Northern economy grew stronger and the Southern economy grew weaker.

Financing the War

One of the greatest defects of the Confederate economy was finance. Of the three methods of paying for a war—taxation, loans, and **treasury notes** (paper money)—treasury notes are the most inflationary because they pump new money into the economy. By contrast, taxation and loans (war bonds) soak up money and thus counteract inflation. Although Confederate treasury officials were quite aware of this difference, the Confederate Congress, wary of dampening patriotic ardor, was slow to raise taxes. And because most capital in the South was tied up in land and slaves, little was available for buying war bonds.

So, expecting a short war, the Confederate Congress authorized a limited issue of treasury notes in 1861, to be redeemable in **specie** (gold or silver) within two years after the end of the war. The first modest issue was followed by many more because the notes declined in value from the outset. The rate of decline increased during periods of Confederate military reverses, when people wondered whether the government would survive. At the end of 1861, the Confederate inflation rate was 12 percent every *month;* by early 1863, it took eight dollars to buy what one dollar had bought two years earlier; just before the war's end, the Confederate dollar was worth one U.S. cent.

In 1863, the Confederate Congress tried to stem runaway inflation by passing a comprehensive law that taxed income, consumer purchases, and business transactions and included a "tax in kind" on agricultural products, allowing tax officials to seize 10 percent of a farmer's crops. This tax was extremely unpopular among farmers, many of whom hid their crops and livestock or refused to plant, thereby worsening the Confederacy's food shortages. The tax legislation was too little and too late to remedy the South's fiscal chaos. The Confederate government raised less than 5 percent of its revenue by taxes and less than 40 percent by loans, leaving 60 percent to be created by the printing press. That turned out to be a recipe for disaster.

In contrast, the Union government raised 66 percent of its revenue by selling war bonds, 21 percent by taxes, and only 13 percent by printing treasury notes. The **Legal Tender** Act authorizing these notes—the famous "greenbacks," the origin of modern paper money in the United States—passed in February 1862. Congress had enacted new taxes in 1861, including the first income tax in American history, and had authorized the sale of war bonds. By early 1862, however, these measures had not yet raised enough revenue to pay for the rapid military buildup. To avert a crisis, Congress created the greenbacks. Instead of promising to redeem them in specie at some future date, as the South had done, Congress made them "legal tender"—that is, it required everyone to accept them as real money at face value. The North's economy suffered inflation during the war— about 80 percent over four years—but that was mild compared with the 9,000 percent inflation in the Confederacy. The greater strength and diversity of the North's economy, together with wiser fiscal legislation, accounted for the contrast.

The Union Congress also passed the National Banking Act of 1863. Before the war, the principal form of money had been notes issued by state-chartered banks. After Andrew Jackson's destruction of the Second Bank of the United States (chapter 12), the number and variety of **banknotes** had skyrocketed until 7,000 different kinds of state bank notes were circulating in 1860. Some were virtually worthless; others circulated at a discount from face value. The National Banking Act of 1863 resulted from the desire of Whiggish Republicans to resurrect the centralized banking system and create a more stable banknote currency, as well as to finance the war. Under the act, chartered national banks could issue banknotes up to 90 percent of the value of the U.S. bonds they held. This provision created a market for the bonds and, in combination with the greenbacks, replaced the glut of state banknotes with a more uniform national currency. To further the cause, in 1865, Congress imposed a tax of 10 percent on state banknotes, thereby taxing them out of existence.

National banknotes would be an important form of money for the next half-century. They had two defects, however: First, because the number of notes that could be issued was tied to each bank's holdings of U.S. bonds, the volume of currency available depended on the amount of federal debt rather than on the economic needs of the country. Second, the banknotes tended to concentrate in the Northeast, where most of the large national banks were located, leaving the South and West short. The creation of the Federal Reserve System in 1913 (chapter 21) largely remedied these defects, but Civil War legislation established the principle of a uniform national currency issued and regulated by the federal government.

Navies, the Blockade, and Foreign Relations

To sustain its war effort, the Confederacy needed to import large quantities of material from abroad. To shut off these imports and the exports of cotton that paid for them, on April 19, 1861, Lincoln proclaimed a **blockade** of Confederate ports. At first, the blockade was more a policy than a reality because the navy had only a few ships on hand to enforce it. The task was formidable; the Confederate coastline stretched for 3,500 miles, with two dozen major ports and another 150 bays and coves where cargo could be landed. The U.S. Navy, which since the 1840s had been converting from sail to steam, recalled its ships from distant seas, took old sailing vessels out of mothballs, and bought or chartered merchant ships and armed them. Eventually, the navy placed several hundred warships on blockade duty. But in 1861, the blockade was so thin that 9 of every 10 vessels slipped through it on their way to or from Confederate ports.

King Cotton Diplomacy

The Confederacy, however, inadvertently contributed to the blockade's success when it adopted King Cotton diplomacy. Cotton was vital to the British economy because textiles were at the heart of British industry, and three-fourths of Britain's supply of raw cotton came from the South. If that supply was cut off, Southerners reasoned, British factories would shut down, unemployed workers would starve, and Britain would face the prospect of revolution. Rather than risk such a consequence, people in the South believed that Britain (and other powers) would recognize the Confederacy's independence and then use the powerful British navy to break the blockade.

Southerners were so firmly convinced of cotton's importance to the British economy that they kept the 1861 cotton crop at home rather than try to export it through the blockade, hoping thereby to compel the British to intervene. But the strategy backfired. Bumper crops in 1859 and 1860 had piled up a surplus of cotton in British warehouses and delayed the anticipated "cotton famine" until 1862. In the end, the South's voluntary embargo of cotton cost them dearly. The Confederacy missed its chance to ship out its cotton and store it abroad, where it could be used as collateral for loans to purchase war matériel.

Moreover, the Confederacy's King Cotton diplomacy contradicted its own foreign policy objective: to persuade the British and French governments to refuse to recognize the legality of the blockade. Under international law, a blockade must be "physically effective" to be respected by neutral nations. Confederate diplomats claimed that the Union effort was a mere "paper blockade," yet the dearth of cotton reaching European ports as a result of the South's embargo suggested to British and French diplomats that the blockade was at least partly effective, and by 1862 it was. Slow-sailing ships with large cargo capacity rarely tried to run the blockade, and the sleek, fast, steam-powered **blockade runners** that became increasingly prominent had a smaller cargo capacity and charged high rates because of the growing risk of capture or sinking by the Union navy. Although most blockade runners got through, by 1862 the blockade had reduced the Confederacy's seaborne commerce enough to convince the British government to recognize it as legitimate. The blockade was also squeezing the South's economy. After lifting its cotton embargo in 1862, the Confederacy had increasing difficulty exporting enough cotton through the blockade to pay for needed imports.

Confederate foreign policy also failed to win diplomatic recognition by other nations. That recognition would have conferred international legitimacy on the Confederacy and might even have led to treaties of alliance or of foreign aid. The French Emperor Napoleon III expressed sympathy for the Confederacy, as did influential groups in the British Parliament, but Prime Minister Lord Palmerston and Foreign Minister John Russell refused to recognize the Confederacy while it was engaged in a war it might lose, especially if recognition might jeopardize relations with the United States. The Union foreign policy team of Secretary of State Seward and Minister to England Charles Francis Adams did a superb job. Seward issued blunt warnings against recognizing the Confederacy; Adams softened them with the velvet glove of diplomacy. Other nations followed Britain's lead; by 1862, it had become clear that Britain would withhold recognition until the Confederacy had virtually won its independence, but such recognition would have come too late to help the Confederacy win.

The Trent *Affair*

If anything illustrated the frustrations of Confederate diplomacy, it was the *Trent* Affair, which came tantalizingly close to rupturing British–American relations to Confederate advantage, but did not. In October 1861, Southern envoys James Mason and John Slidell slipped through the blockade. Mason hoped to represent the Confederacy in London and Slidell in Paris. On November 8, Captain Charles Wilkes of the U.S.S. *San Jacinto* stopped the British mail steamer *Trent,* with Mason and Slidell on board, near Cuba. Wilkes arrested the two Southerners, took them to Boston, and became an instant hero in the North. When the news reached England, the British government and public were outraged by Wilkes's "high-handed" action. Although the Royal Navy had acted in similar fashion during the centuries when Britannia ruled the waves, John Bull (England) would not take this behavior from his brash American cousin Jonathan (the United States). Britain demanded an apology and the release of Mason and Slidell. The popular press on both sides of the Atlantic stirred up war fever. Soon, however, good sense prevailed and Britain softened its demands. With a philosophy of "one war at a time," the Lincoln administration released Mason and Slidell the day after Christmas 1861, declaring that Captain Wilkes had acted "without instructions." The British accepted this statement in lieu of an apology, and the crisis ended.

The Confederate Navy

Lacking the capacity to build a naval force at home, the Confederacy hoped to use British shipyards for the purpose. Through a loophole in the British neutrality law, two fast commerce raiders built in Liverpool made their way into Confederate hands in 1862. Named the *Florida* and the *Alabama,* they roamed the seas for the next two years, capturing or sinking Union merchant ships and whalers. The *Alabama* was the most feared raider. Commanded by the leading Confederate sea dog, Raphael Semmes, she sank 62 merchant vessels plus a Union warship before another warship, the U.S.S. *Kearsarge* (whose captain, John A. Winslow, had once been Semmes's messmate in the old navy), sank the *Alabama* off Cherbourg, France, on June 19, 1864. Altogether, Confederate privateers and commerce raiders destroyed or captured 257 Union merchant vessels and drove at least 700 others to foreign registry. This Confederate achievement, although spectacular, made only a tiny dent in the Union war effort, especially when compared with the 1,500 blockade runners captured or destroyed by the Union navy, not to mention the thousands of others that decided not to even try to beat the blockade.

The Monitor *and the* Virginia

Its inadequate shipbuilding facilities prevented the Confederate navy from challenging Union seapower where it counted most—along the coasts and rivers of the South.

Still, though plagued by shortages on every hand, the Confederate navy department demonstrated great skill at innovation. Southern engineers developed "torpedoes" (mines) that sank or damaged 43 Union warships in southern bays and rivers. The South also constructed the world's first combat submarine, the *H. L. Hunley,* which sank a blockade ship off Charleston in 1864 but then went down herself before she could return to shore. Another important innovation was the building of ironclad "rams" to sink the blockade ships. The idea of iron armor for warships was not new— the British and French navies had prototype ironclads in 1861—but the Confederacy built the first one to see action. It was the C.S.S. *Virginia,* commonly called (even in the South) the *Merrimac* because it was rebuilt from the steam frigate U.S.S. *Merrimack,* which had been burned to the waterline by the Union navy at Norfolk when the Confederates seized the naval base there in April 1861. Ready for its trial-by-combat on March 8, 1862, the *Virginia* steamed out to attack the blockade squadron at Hampton Roads. She sank one warship with her iron ram and another with her 10 guns. Other Union ships ran aground trying to escape, to be finished off (Confederates expected) the next day. Union shot and shells bounced off the *Virginia*'s armor plate. It was the worst day the U.S. Navy would have until December 7, 1941.

Panic seized Washington and the whole northeastern seaboard. In almost Hollywood fashion, however, the Union's own ironclad sailed into Hampton Roads in the nick of time and saved the rest of the fleet. This was the U.S.S. *Monitor,* completed just days earlier at the Brooklyn navy yard. Much smaller than the *Virginia,* with two 11-inch guns in a **revolving turret** (an innovation) set on a deck almost flush with the water, the *Monitor* looked like a "tin can on a shingle." It presented a small target and was capable of concentrating considerable firepower in a given direction with its revolving turret. The next day, the *Monitor* fought the *Virginia* in history's first battle between ironclads. It was a draw, but the *Virginia* limped home to Norfolk never again to menace the Union fleet. Although the Confederacy built other ironclad rams, some never saw action and none achieved the initial success of the *Virginia.* By the war's end, the Union navy had built or started 58 ships of the *Monitor* class (some of them double-turreted), launching a new age in naval history that ended the classic "heart of oak" era of warships.

Campaigns and Battles, 1861–1862

Focus Question
How did the Union's and Confederacy's respective military advantages manifest themselves in the campaigns and battles of 1861–62?

Wars can be won only by hard fighting. Some leaders on both sides overlooked this truth. One of them was Winfield Scott, General-in-Chief of the U.S. Army. Scott, a Virginian who had remained loyal to the Union, evolved a military strategy based on his conviction that a great many Southerners were eager to be won back to the Union. The main elements of his strategy

The *Monitor* and *Merrimac* The above black-and-white photograph shows the crew of the Union ironclad *Monitor* standing in front of its revolving two-gun turret. In action, the sun canopy above the turret would be taken down, and all sailors would be at their stations inside the turret or the hull, as shown in the color painting of the famed battle, on March 9, 1862, between the *Monitor* and the Confederate *Virginia* (informally called the *Merrimac* because it had been converted from the captured U.S. frigate *Merrimack*). There is no photograph of the *Virginia*, which was blown up by its crew two months later when the Confederates retreated toward Richmond because its draft was too deep to go up the James River.

were a naval blockade and a combined army-navy expedition to take control of the Mississippi, thus sealing off the Confederacy on all sides and enabling the Union to "bring them to terms with less bloodshed than by any other plan." The Northern press ridiculed Scott's strategy as the Anaconda Plan, after the South American snake that squeezes its prey to death.

The Battle of Bull Run

Most Northerners believed that the South could be overcome only by victory in battle. Virginia emerged as the most likely battleground, especially after the Confederate government moved its capital to Richmond in May 1861. "Forward to Richmond," clamored Northern newspapers, and forward toward Richmond moved a Union army of 35,000 men in July, despite Scott's misgivings and those of the army's field commander, Irvin McDowell. McDowell believed his raw, 90-day Union militia were not ready to fight a real battle. They got no farther than Bull Run, a sluggish stream 25 miles southwest of Washington, where a Confederate army commanded by Beauregard had been deployed to defend a key rail junction at Manassas.

Another small Confederate army in the Shenandoah Valley under General Joseph E. Johnston had given a Union force the slip and had traveled to Manassas by rail to reinforce Beauregard. On July 21, the attacking Federals forded Bull Run and hit the rebels on the left flank, driving them back. By early afternoon, the Federals seemed to be on the verge of victory, but a Virginia brigade commanded by **Thomas J. Jackson** stood "like a stone wall," earning Jackson the nickname he carried ever after. By midafternoon, Confederate reinforcements, including one brigade just off the train from the Shenandoah Valley, had grouped for a screaming counterattack (the famed "rebel yell" was first heard here). They drove the exhausted and disorganized Yankees back across Bull Run in a retreat that turned into a rout.

Although the Battle of Manassas (or Bull Run, as Northerners called it) was small by later Civil War standards, it made a profound impression on both sides. Of the 18,000 soldiers actually engaged on each side, Union casualties (killed, wounded, and captured) were about 2,800 and Confederate casualties 2,000. The victory exhilarated Confederates and confirmed their belief in their martial superiority. It also gave them a morale advantage in the Virginia theater that persisted for two years. And yet, Manassas also bred overconfidence. Some in the South thought the war was won. Northerners, by contrast, were jolted out of their expectations of a short war. A new mood of reality and grim determination gripped the North. Congress authorized the enlistment of up to 1 million three-year volunteers. Hundreds of thousands flocked to recruiting offices in the next few months. Lincoln called General **George B. McClellan** to Washington to organize the new troops into the Army of the Potomac.

An energetic, talented officer who was only 34 years old and small of stature but great with an aura of destiny, McClellan soon won the nickname "The Young Napoleon." He had commanded the Union forces that gained control of West Virginia, and he took firm control in Washington during summer and fall 1861. He organized and trained the Army of the Potomac into a large, well-disciplined, and well-equipped fighting force. He was just what the North needed after its dispiriting defeat at Bull Run. When Scott stepped down as General-in-Chief on November 1, McClellan took his place.

As winter approached, however, and McClellan did nothing to advance against the smaller Confederate army whose outposts stood only a few miles from Washington, his failings as a commander began to show. He was a perfectionist in a profession where nothing could ever be perfect. His army was perpetually *almost* ready to move. McClellan was afraid to take risks; he never learned the military lesson that no victory can be won without risking defeat. He consistently overestimated the strength of enemy forces facing him and used these faulty estimates as a reason for inaction until he could increase his own force. When newspapers began to publish criticism of McClellan from within the administration and among Republicans in Congress (he was a Democrat), he accused his critics of political motives. Having built a fine fighting machine, he was afraid to start it up for fear it might break. The caution that McClellan instilled in the Army of the Potomac's officer corps persisted for more than a year after Lincoln removed him from command in November 1862.

Naval Operations

Because of McClellan, no significant action occurred in the Virginia theater after the Battle of Bull Run until spring 1862. Meanwhile, the Union navy won a series of victories over Confederate coastal forts at Hatteras Inlet on the North Carolina coast, Port Royal Sound in South Carolina, and other points along the Atlantic and Gulf coasts. These successes provided new bases from which to expand and tighten the blockade. They also provided small Union armies with take-off points for operations along the southern coast. In February and March 1862, an expeditionary force under General Ambrose Burnside won a string of victories and occupied several crucial ports on the North Carolina sounds. Another Union force captured Fort Pulaski at the mouth of the Savannah River, cutting off that important Confederate port from the sea.

One of the Union navy's most impressive achievements was the capture in April 1862 of New Orleans, the Confederacy's largest city and principal port. Most Confederate troops in the area had been called up the Mississippi to confront a Union invasion of Tennessee, leaving only some militia, an assortment of steamboats converted into gunboats, and two strong forts flanking the river 70 miles below New Orleans. That was not enough to stop Union naval commander David G. Farragut, a native of Tennessee who was still loyal to the U.S. Navy in which he had served for a half century. In a daring action on April 24, 1862, Farragut led his fleet upriver past the forts, scattering the Confederate fleet and fending off fire rafts. He lost four ships, but the rest won through and compelled the surrender of New Orleans with nine-inch naval guns trained on its streets. Fifteen thousand Union soldiers marched in and occupied the city and its hinterland.

Fort Henry and Fort Donelson

These victories demonstrated the importance of seapower even in a civil war. Even more important were Union victories won by the combined efforts of the army and fleets of river gunboats on the Tennessee and Cumberland rivers, which flow through Tennessee and Kentucky and empty into the Ohio River just before it joins the Mississippi. The unlikely hero of these victories was Ulysses S. Grant, who had failed in several civilian occupations after resigning from the peacetime military in 1854. Grant rejoined when war broke out. His quiet efficiency and determined will won him promotion from Illinois colonel to brigadier general and the command of a small but growing force based at Cairo, Illinois, in fall 1861. When Confederate units entered Kentucky in September,

Grant moved quickly to occupy the mouths of the Cumberland and Tennessee rivers. Unlike McClellan, who had known nothing but success in his career and was afraid to jeopardize that record, Grant's experience of failure made him willing to take risks. Having little to lose, he demonstrated that willingness dramatically in the early months of 1862.

Military strategists on both sides understood the importance of these navigable rivers as highways of invasion into the South's heartland. The Confederacy had built forts at strategic points along the rivers and had begun to convert a few steamboats into gunboats and rams to back up the forts. The Union also converted steamboats into "timberclad" gunboats—so called because they were armored just enough to protect the engine and the paddle wheels but not enough to impair speed and shallow draft for river operations. The Union also built a new class of ironclad gunboats designed for river warfare. Carrying 13 guns, these flat-bottomed, wide-beamed vessels drew only six feet of water. Their hulls and paddle wheels were protected by a sloping casemate sheathed in iron armor up to 2 1/2 inches thick.

When the first of these strange-looking but formidable craft were ready in February 1862, Grant struck. His objectives were Forts Henry and Donelson on the Tennessee and Cumberland rivers just south of the Kentucky–Tennessee border. The gunboats knocked out Fort Henry on February 6. Fort Donelson proved a tougher nut to crack. Its guns repulsed a gunboat attack on February 14. The next day, the 17,000-man Confederate army attacked Grant's besieging army, which had been reinforced to 27,000 men. With the calm decisiveness that became his trademark, Grant directed a counterattack that penned the defenders back up in their fort. Cut off from support by either land or river, the Confederate commander asked for surrender terms on February 16. Grant's reply made him instantly famous when it was published in the North: "No terms except an immediate and unconditional surrender can be accepted. I propose to move immediately upon your works." With no choice, the 13,000 surviving Confederates surrendered (some had escaped), giving Grant the most striking victory in the war thus far.

These victories had far-reaching strategic consequences. Union gunboats now ranged all the way up the Tennessee River to northern Alabama, enabling a Union division to occupy the region, and up the Cumberland to Nashville, which became the first Confederate state capital to surrender to Union forces on February 25. Confederate military units pulled out of Kentucky and most of Tennessee and reassembled at Corinth in northern Mississippi. Jubilation spread through the North and despair through the South. By the end of March 1862, however, the Confederate commander in the western theater, Albert Sidney Johnston (not to be confused with Joseph E. Johnston in Virginia), had built up an army of 40,000 men at Corinth. His plan was to attack Grant's force of 35,000, which had established a base 20 miles away at Pittsburg Landing on the Tennessee River just north of the Mississippi–Tennessee border.

The Battle of Shiloh

On April 6, the Confederates attacked at dawn near a church called Shiloh, which gave its name to the battle. They caught Grant by surprise and drove his army toward the river. After a day's fighting of unprecedented intensity, with total casualties of 15,000, Grant's men brought the Confederate onslaught to a halt at dusk. One of the Confederate casualties was Johnston, who bled to death when a bullet severed an artery in his leg—the highest-ranking general on either side to be killed in the war. Beauregard, who had been transferred from Virginia to the West, took command after Johnston's death.

Some of Grant's subordinates advised retreat during the dismal night of April 6–7, but Grant would have none of it. Reinforced by fresh troops from a Union army commanded by General Don Carlos Buell, the Union counterattacked the next morning (April 7) and, after 9,000 more casualties to the two sides, drove the Confederates back to Corinth. Although Grant had snatched victory from the jaws of defeat, his reputation suffered a decline for a time because of the heavy Union casualties (13,000) and the suspicion that he had been caught napping the first day.

Union triumphs in the western theater continued. The combined armies of Grant and Buell, under the overall command of the top-ranking Union general in the West, Henry W. Halleck, drove the Confederates out of Corinth at the end of May. Meanwhile, the Union gunboat fleet fought its way down the Mississippi to Vicksburg, virtually wiping out the Confederate fleet in a spectacular battle at Memphis on June 6. At Vicksburg, the Union

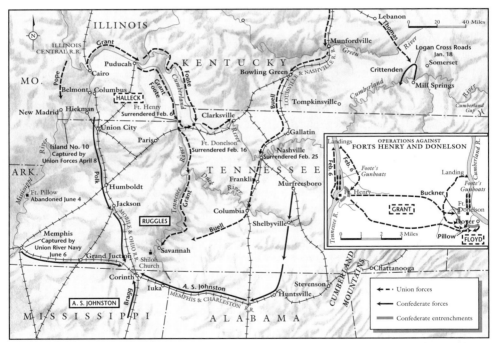

Map 15.3   Kentucky–Tennessee Theater, Winter–Spring 1862   This map illustrates the importance of rivers and railroads as lines of military operations and supply. Grant and Foote advanced up (southward) the Tennessee and Cumberland rivers, while Buell moved along the Louisville and Nashville Railroad. Confederate divisions under the overall command of General Albert Sidney Johnston used railroads to concentrate at the key junction of Corinth.

gunboats from the north connected with part of Farragut's fleet that had come up from New Orleans, taking Baton Rouge and Natchez along the way. The heavily fortified Confederate bastion at Vicksburg, however, proved too strong for Union naval firepower to subdue. Nevertheless, the dramatic succession of Union triumphs in the West from February to June, including a decisive victory at the battle of Pea Ridge in northwest Arkansas on March 7 and 8, convinced the North that the war was nearly won. "Every blow tells fearfully against the rebellion," boasted the leading Northern newspaper, the New York *Tribune*. "The rebels themselves are panic-stricken, or despondent. It now requires no very far reaching prophet to predict the end of this struggle."

The Virginia Theater

But affairs in Virginia were about to take a sharp turn in favor of the Confederacy. Within three months, the Union, which had been so near a knockout victory that spring, was back on the defensive. In the western theater, the broad rivers had facilitated the Union's invasion of the South, but in Virginia a half-dozen small rivers flowing west to east lay athwart the line of operations between Washington and Richmond and provided the Confederates with natural lines of defense. McClellan persuaded a reluctant Lincoln to approve a plan to transport his army down Chesapeake Bay to the tip of the Virginia peninsula, formed by the tidal portions of the York and James rivers. That would shorten the route to Richmond and give the Union army a seaborne supply line secure from harassment by Confederate cavalry and guerrillas.

This was a good plan—in theory—and the logistical achievement of transporting 110,000 men and all their equipment, animals, and supplies by sea to the jump-off point near Yorktown was impressive. But once again, McClellan's failings began to surface. A small Confederate blocking force at Yorktown held him for the entire month of April, as he cautiously dragged up siege guns to blast through defenses that his large army could have punched through in days on foot. McClellan slowly followed the retreating Confederate force up the peninsula to a new defensive line only a few miles east of Richmond, all the while bickering with Lincoln and Secretary of War Edwin M. Stanton over the reinforcements they were withholding to protect Washington against a possible strike by Stonewall Jackson's small Confederate army in the Shenandoah Valley.

Jackson's month-long campaign in the Shenandoah (May 8–June 9), one of the most brilliant of the war, demonstrated what could be accomplished through deception, daring, and mobility. With only 17,000 men, Jackson moved by forced marches so swift that his infantry earned the nickname "Jackson's foot cavalry." Darting here and there through the valley, they marched 350 miles in the course of one month; won four battles against three separate Union armies, whose combined numbers surpassed Jackson's by more than 2 to 1 (but which Jackson's force always outnumbered at the point of contact); and compelled Lincoln to divert to the valley some of the reinforcements McClellan demanded.

Even without those reinforcements, McClellan's army substantially outnumbered the Confederate force defending Richmond, commanded by Joseph E. Johnston. As usual, though, McClellan overestimated Johnston's strength at double what it was and acted accordingly. Even so, by the last week of May, McClellan's army was within six miles of Richmond. A botched

Confederate counterattack on May 31 and June 1 (the Battle of Seven Pines) produced no result except 6,000 Confederate and 5,000 Union casualties. One of those casualties was Johnston, who was wounded in the shoulder. Jefferson Davis named Robert E. Lee to replace him.

The Seven Days' Battles

That appointment marked a major turning point in the campaign. Lee had done little so far to earn a wartime reputation, having failed in his only field command to dislodge Union forces from control of West Virginia. His qualities as a commander began to manifest themselves when he took over what he renamed the Army of Northern Virginia. Those qualities were boldness, a willingness to take great risks, an almost uncanny ability to read the enemy commander's mind, and a charisma that won the devotion of his men. While McClellan continued to dawdle, Lee sent his dashing cavalry commander, J. E. B. "Jeb" Stuart, to lead a reconnaissance around the Union army to discover its weak points. Lee also brought Jackson's army in from the Shenandoah Valley and launched a June 26 attack on McClellan's right flank in what became known as the Seven Days' battles. Constantly attacking, Lee's army of 88,000

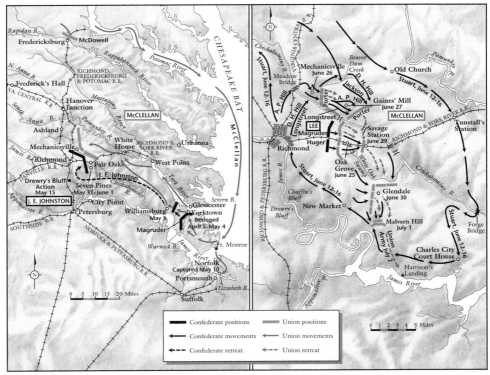

Map 15.4　Peninsula Campaign, April–May 1862 [and] Seven Days' Battles, June 25–July 1, 1862　General McClellan used Union naval control of the York and James rivers to protect his flanks in his advance up the peninsula formed by these rivers (left map). When Robert E. Lee's Army of Northern Virginia counterattacked in the Seven Days' Battles (right map), McClellan was forced back to the James River at Harrison's Landing.

drove McClellan's 100,000 away from Richmond to a new fortified base on the James River. The offensive cost the Confederates 20,000 casualties (compared with 16,000 for the Union) and turned Richmond into one vast hospital, but it reversed the momentum of the war.

Confederate Counteroffensives

Northern sentiments plunged from the height of euphoria in May to the depths of despair in July. "The feeling of despondency here is very great," wrote a New Yorker, while a Southerner exulted that "Lee has turned the tide, and I shall not be surprised if we have a long career of successes." The tide turned in the western theater as well, where Union conquests in the spring had brought 50,000 square miles of Confederate territory under Union control. To occupy and administer this vast area, however, drew many thousands of soldiers from combat forces, which were left depleted and deep in enemy territory and vulnerable to cavalry raids. During summer and fall 1862, the cavalry commands of Tennesseean Nathan Bedford Forrest and Kentuckian John Hunt Morgan staged repeated raids in which they burned bridges, blew up tunnels, tore up tracks, and captured supply depots and the Union garrisons trying to defend them. By August the once-formidable Union war machine in the West seemed to have broken down.

These raids paved the way for infantry counteroffensives. After recapturing some territory, Earl Van Dorn's Army of West Tennessee got a bloody nose when it failed to retake Corinth on October 3 and 4. At the end of August, Braxton Bragg's Army of Tennessee launched a drive northward from Chattanooga through east Tennessee and Kentucky. It had almost reached the Ohio River in September but was turned back at the Battle of Perryville on October 8. Even after these defeats, the Confederate forces in the western theater were in better shape than they had been four months earlier.

The Second Battle of Bull Run

Most attention, though, focused on Virginia. Lincoln reorganized the Union corps near Washington into the Army of Virginia under General John Pope, who had won minor successes as commander of a small army in Missouri and Tennessee. In August, Lincoln ordered the withdrawal of the Army of the Potomac from the peninsula to reinforce Pope for a drive southward from Washington. Lee quickly seized the opportunity provided by the separation of the two Union armies confronting him, by the ill will between McClellan and Pope and their subordinates, and by the bickering among various factions in Washington. To attack Pope before McClellan could reinforce him, Lee shifted most of his army to northern Virginia, sent Jackson's foot cavalry on a deep raid to destroy its supply base at Manassas Junction, and then brought his army back together to defeat Pope's army near Bull Run on August 29 and 30. The demoralized Union forces retreated into the Washington defenses, where Lincoln reluctantly gave McClellan command of the two armies and told him to reorganize them into one.

Lee decided to keep up the pressure by invading Maryland. On September 4, his weary troops began splashing across the Potomac 40 miles upriver from Washington. This move, which took place at the same time Braxton Bragg was invading Kentucky, presented several

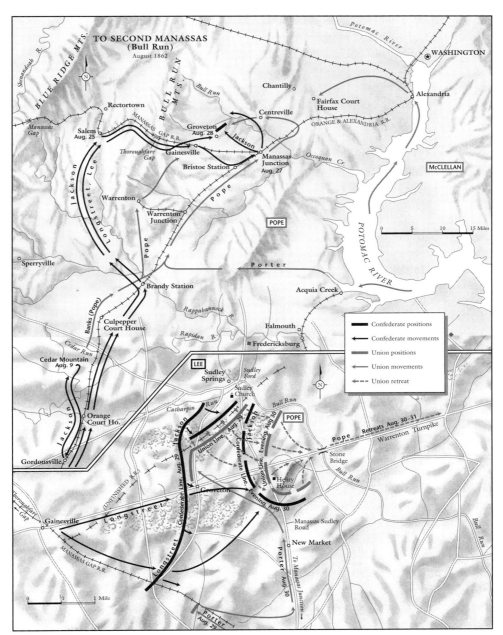

Map 15.5 Second Battle of Manassas (Bull Run), August 29–30, 1862 Note that some of the heaviest fighting took place around the house owned by Judith Henry, which was destroyed and the elderly widow killed in her house in the first battle.

momentous possibilities: Maryland might be won for the Confederacy. Another victory by Lee might influence the U.S. congressional elections that fall and help Democrats gain control of Congress, and might even force the Lincoln administration to negotiate peace with the Confederacy. Successful invasion of Maryland, coming on top of other Confederate successes, might even persuade Britain and France to recognize the Confederacy and offer mediation to end the war, especially since the long-expected cotton famine had finally materialized. In fact, in September 1862, the British and French governments were considering recognition and awaiting the outcome of Lee's invasion to decide whether to proceed. Great issues rode with the armies as Lee crossed the Potomac and McClellan cautiously moved north to meet him.

Conclusion

The election of 1860 had accomplished a national power shift of historic proportions. Through their domination of the Jeffersonian Republican coalition during the first quarter of the 19th century and of the Jacksonian Democrats thereafter, Southern political leaders had maintained effective control of the national government for most of the time before 1860. South Carolina's secession governor, Francis Pickens, described this leverage of power in a private letter to a fellow South Carolinian in 1857:

> We have the Executive [Buchanan] with us, and the Senate & in all probability the H[ouse of] R[epresentatives] too. Besides we have repealed the Missouri line & the Supreme Court in a decision of great power, has declared it . . . unconstitutional null and void. So, that before our enemies can reach us, they must first break down the Supreme Court—change the Senate & seize the Executive & . . . restore the Missouri line, repeal the Fugitive slave law & change the whole govern[men]t. As long as the Govt. is on our side I am for sustaining it, & using its power for our benefit, & placing the screws upon the throats of our opponents.

In 1860, Pickens's worst-case scenario started to come true. With Lincoln's election, the South lost control of the executive branch—and perhaps also of the House. They feared that the Senate and Supreme Court would soon follow. The Republicans, Southerners feared, would launch a "revolution" to cripple slavery and, as Lincoln had said in his "House Divided" speech two years earlier, place it "in course of ultimate extinction." The "revolutionary dogmas" of the Republicans, declared a South Carolina newspaper in 1860, were "active and bristling with terrible designs." Worst of all, the Northern Black Republicans would force racial equality on the South: "Abolition preachers will be on hand to consummate the marriage of your daughters to black husbands."

Thus the South launched a preemptive counterrevolution of secession to forestall a revolution of liberty and equality they feared would be their fate if they remained in the Union. As the Confederate secretary of state put it in 1861, the Southern states had formed a new nation "to preserve their old institutions [from] a revolution [that] threatened to destroy their social system."

Seldom has a preemptive counterrevolution so quickly brought on the very revolution it tried to prevent. If the Confederacy had lost the war in spring 1862, as appeared likely after

Union victories from February to May of that year, the South might have returned to the Union with slavery intact. Instead, successful Confederate counteroffensives in summer 1862 convinced Lincoln that the North could not win the war without striking against slavery. Another issue that rode with Lee's troops as they crossed the Potomac into Maryland in September 1862 was the fate of an emancipation proclamation Lincoln had drafted two months earlier and then put aside to await a Union victory.

SUGGESTED READINGS

The most comprehensive one-volume study of the Civil War years is **James M. McPherson, *Battle Cry of Freedom: The Civil War Era*** (1988). The fullest and most readable narrative of the military campaigns and battles is **Shelby Foote, *The Civil War: A Narrative*,** 3 vols. (1958–1974). For the naval war, see **Ivan Musicant, *Divided Waters: The Naval History of the Civil War*** (1995). For the perspective of the soldiers and sailors who fought the battles, see **Bell I. Wiley's** two books: ***The Life of Johnny Reb*** (1943) and ***The Life of Billy Yank*** (1952). The motives of soldiers for enlisting and fighting are treated in **James M. McPherson, *For Cause and Comrades: Why Men Fought in the Civil War*** (1997).

For the home front in North and South, see **Phillip Shaw Paludan, *"A People's Contest": The Union and Civil War, 1861–1865*** (1988), and **Emory Thomas, *The Confederate Nation, 1861–1865*** (1979). For women and children, see **Nina Silber, *Daughters of the Union: Northern Women Fight the Civil War*** (2005); **George C. Rable, *Civil Wars: Women and the Crisis of Southern Nationalism*** (1989); and **James Marten, *The Children's Civil War*** (1998).

For biographical studies of leaders on both sides, consult the following: **Phillip S. Paludan, *The Presidency of Abraham Lincoln*** (1994); **William C. Cooper, *Jefferson Davis, American*** (2000); **Stephen W. Sears, *George B. McClellan: The Young Napoleon*** (1988); **Brooks D. Simpson, *Ulysses S. Grant*** (2000); and **Emory M. Thomas, *Robert E. Lee*** (1995). For a study of the Fort Sumter crisis and the outbreak of the war that sets these events in their long-term context, see **Maury Klein, *Days of Defiance: Sumter, Secession, and The Coming of the Civil War*** (1997). A superb study of Lincoln and his Cabinet is **Doris Kearns Goodwin, *Team of Rivals: The Political Genius of Abraham Lincoln*** (2005). For the guerrilla war in Missouri, the most useful of several books is **Michael Fellman, *Inside War: The Guerrilla Conflict in Missouri during the Civil War*** (1989). Of the many studies of diplomacy during the war, the most useful is **David P. Crook, *The North, The South, and the Powers 1861–1865*** (1974), an abridged version of which was published with the title *Diplomacy during the Civil War* (1975).

Visit the Liberty Equality Power Companion Web site for resources specific to this textbook: http://www.thomsonedu.com/history/murrin

Also find self-tests and additional resources at ThomsonNOW. ThomsonNOW is an integrated online suite of services and resources with proven ease of use and efficient paths to success, delivering the results you want—NOW!

www.thomsonedu.com/login/

A New Birth of Freedom, 1862–1865

One of the great issues awaiting resolution as the armies moved into Maryland in September 1862 was emancipation of the slaves. The war had moved beyond the effort to restore the old Union. It now required the North to mobilize every resource that might bring victory or to destroy any enemy resource that might inflict defeat. To abolish slavery would strike at a vital Confederate resource (slave labor) and mobilize that resource for the Union along with the moral power of fighting for freedom. Slaves had already made clear their choice by escaping to Union lines by the tens of thousands. Lincoln had made up his mind to issue an emancipation proclamation and was waiting for a Union victory to give it credibility and potency.

This momentous decision would radically enlarge the scope and purpose of the Union war effort. It would also polarize Northern public opinion and political parties. So long as the North fought simply for restoration of the Union, Northern unity was impressive, but the events of 1862 and 1863 raised the divisive question of what kind of Union was to be restored. Would it be a Union without slavery, as abolitionists and radical Republicans hoped? Or "the Union as it was, the Constitution as it is," as Democrats desired? The answer to this question would determine not only the course of the war but also the future of the United States.

Slavery and the War

Focus Question
What factors led Lincoln to his decision to issue the Emancipation Proclamation?

At first, the leaders of both the Union and the Confederacy tried to keep the issue of slavery out of the war. For Southern leaders to proclaim that the defense of slavery was the aim of the war might prompt nonslaveholders to ask why they were risking their lives to protect their rich neighbors' property. Even more important, it might jeopardize Confederate efforts to win recognition and support from Britain. So the Confederates proclaimed liberty rather than slavery as their war aim—the same liberty their ancestors had fought for in 1776. The unspoken corollary of that aim was the liberty of whites to own blacks.

CHRONOLOGY

1862	Confederacy enacts conscription (April 16) • Lincoln informs the cabinet of intention to issue Emancipation Proclamation (July 22) • Battle of Antietam (September 17) • Lincoln issues preliminary Emancipation Proclamation (September 22) • Battle of Fredericksburg (December 13) • Battle of Stones River (December 31–January 2)
1863	Lincoln issues final Emancipation Proclamation (January 1) • Union enacts conscription (March 3) • Richmond bread riot (April 2) • Battle of Chancellorsville (May 1–5) • Battle of Gettysburg (July 1–3) • Vicksburg surrenders (July 4) • Port Hudson surrenders (July 9) • New York draft riot (July 13–16) • Assault on Fort Wagner (July 18) • Battle of Chickamauga (September 19–20) • Battles of Chattanooga (November 24–25)
1864	Battle of the Wilderness (May 5–6) • Battle of Spotsylvania (May 8–19) • Fighting at Petersburg leads to nine-month siege (June 15–18) • Fall of Atlanta (September 1) • Reelection of Lincoln (November 8) • Battle of Nashville (December 15–16)
1865	Capture of Fort Fisher (January 15) • Confederates evacuate Richmond (April 2) • Lee surrenders at Appomattox (April 9) • Booth assassinates Lincoln (April 14) • Last Confederate army surrenders (June 23) • 13th Amendment abolishing slavery ratified (December 6)

In the North, the issue of emancipation was deeply divisive. Lincoln had been elected on a platform pledged to contain the expansion of slavery, but that pledge had provoked most of the Southern states to quit the Union. For the administration to take action against slavery in 1861 would be to risk the breakup of the fragile coalition Lincoln had stitched together to fight the war: Republicans, Democrats, and border-state Unionists. Spokesmen for the latter two groups served notice that, although they supported a war for the Union, they would not support a war against slavery. In July 1861, with Lincoln's endorsement, Congress passed a resolution affirming that Northern war aims included no intention "of overthrowing or interfering with the rights or established institutions of the States"—in plain words, slavery—but intended only "to defend and maintain the supremacy of the Constitution and to preserve the Union."

Many Northerners saw matters differently. They insisted that a rebellion sustained *by* slavery in defense *of* slavery could be suppressed only by striking *against* slavery. As the black leader Frederick Douglass stated, "To fight against slaveholders, without fighting against slavery, is but a halfhearted business, and paralyzes the hands engaged in it. . . . War for the destruction of liberty must be met with war for the destruction of slavery." A good many Union soldiers began to grumble about protecting the property of traitors in arms against the United States.

Wars tend to develop a logic and momentum that go beyond their original purposes. When Northerners discovered at Bull Run in July 1861 that they were not going to win an easy victory, many of them began to take a harder look at slavery. Slaves constituted the principal labor force in the South. They raised most of the food and fiber, built most of the military fortifications, worked on the railroads and in mines and munitions factories.

Southern newspapers boasted that slavery was "a tower of strength to the Confederacy" because it enabled the South "to place in the field a force so much larger in proportion to her white population than the North." Precisely, responded abolitionists. So why not convert this Confederate asset to a Union advantage by confiscating slaves as enemy property and using them to help the Northern war effort? As the war ground on into 1862 and casualties mounted, this argument began to make sense to many Yankees.

The "Contrabands"

The slaves entered this debate in a dramatic fashion. As Union armies penetrated the South, a growing number of slaves voted for freedom with their feet. By twos and threes, by families, and eventually by scores, they escaped from their masters and came over to the Union lines. By obliging Union officers either to return them to slavery or accept them, these escaped slaves began to make the conflict a war for freedom.

Although some commanders returned escaped slaves to their masters or prevented them from entering Union camps, most increasingly did not. Their rationale was first expressed by General Benjamin Butler. In May 1861, three slaves who had been working for the Confederate army escaped to Butler's lines near Fortress Monroe at the mouth of the James River in Virginia. Butler refused to return them, on the grounds that they were **"contraband of war."** The phrase caught on. For the rest of the war, slaves who came within Union lines were known as contrabands. On August 6, 1861, Congress passed a confiscation act that authorized the seizure of all property, including slaves, that was being used for Confederate military purposes. The following March, Congress forbade the return of slaves who entered Union lines—even those belonging to owners loyal to the Union.

The Border States

This problem of slavery in the loyal border states preoccupied Lincoln. On August 30, 1861, John C. Frémont, whose political influence had won him a commission as major general and command of Union forces in Missouri, issued an order freeing the slaves of all Confederate sympathizers in Missouri. This caused such a backlash among border-state Unionists, who feared it was a prelude to a general abolition edict, that Lincoln revoked the order, lest it "alarm our Southern Union friends, and turn them against us."

In spring 1862, Lincoln tried persuasion instead of force in the border states. At his urging, Congress passed a resolution offering federal compensation to states that voluntarily abolished slavery. Three times, from March to July 1862, Lincoln urged border-state congressmen to accept the offer. He told them

Library of Congress, Prints and Photographs Division

Contrabands Coming into Union Lines This photograph taken in 1862 or 1863 shows "contrabands" fording the Rappahannock River in Virginia to reach freedom. They have "liberated" several draft animals as well as themselves.

that the Confederate hope that their states might join the rebellion was helping to keep the war alive. Adopt the proposal for **compensated emancipation,** he pleaded, and that hope would die. The pressure for a bold antislavery policy was growing stronger, he warned them in May. Another Union general had issued an emancipation order; Lincoln had suspended it, but "you cannot," Lincoln told the border-state congressmen, "be blind to the signs of the times."

They did seem to be blind. They complained that they were being coerced, bickered about the amount of compensation, and wrung their hands over the prospects of economic ruin and race war, even if emancipation were to take place gradually over a 30-year period, as Lincoln had suggested. At a final meeting, on July 12, Lincoln, in effect, gave them an ultimatum: Accept compensated emancipation or face the consequences. In fact, thousands of slaves had already run away to Union camps in the border states. "The incidents of the war cannot be avoided," he said. "If the war continue long . . . the institution in your states will be extinguished by mere friction and abrasion . . . and you will have nothing valuable in lieu of it." Again they failed to see the light, and by a vote of 20 to 9, they rejected the proposal for compensated emancipation.

The Decision for Emancipation

That very evening, Lincoln decided to issue an emancipation proclamation in his capacity as commander-in-chief with power to order the seizure of enemy property. Several factors, in addition to the recalcitrance of the border states, impelled Lincoln to this fateful decision. One was a growing demand from his own party for bolder action: Congress had just passed a second confiscation act calling for seizure of the property of active Confederates. Another was rising sentiment in the Army to "take off the kid gloves" when dealing with "traitors." From General Henry W. Halleck, who had been summoned to Washington as general-in-chief, went orders to General Grant in northern Mississippi instructing him on the treatment of rebel sympathizers inside Union lines: "Handle that class without gloves, and take their property for public use." Grant himself had written several months earlier that if the Confederacy "cannot be whipped in any other way than through a war against slavery, let it come to that." Finally, Lincoln's decision reflected his sentiments about the "unqualified evil" and "monstrous injustice" of slavery.

The military situation, however, rather than his moral convictions, determined the timing and scope of Lincoln's emancipation policy. Northern hopes that the war would soon end had risen after the victories of early 1862 but had then plummeted amid the reverses of that summer.

Three courses of action seemed possible. One, favored by the so-called Peace Democrats, urged an armistice and peace negotiations to patch together some kind of Union, but that would have been tantamount to conceding Confederate victory. Republicans therefore reviled the Peace Democrats as traitorous **Copperheads,** after the poisonous snake. A second alternative was to keep on fighting—in the hope that with a few more Union victories, the rebels would lay down their arms and the Union could be restored. Such a policy would leave slavery intact, a course of action that General McClellan strongly advocated. He wrote

Lincoln an unsolicited letter of advice on July 7, 1862, warning him that "neither confiscation of property . . . [n]or forcible abolition of slavery should be contemplated for a moment." Yet that was precisely what Lincoln was contemplating. This was the third alternative: an effort to mobilize all the resources of the North and to destroy all the resources of the South, including slavery—a war not to restore the old Union but to build a new one.

After his meeting with the border-state representatives convinced him that attempts at compromise were futile, Lincoln made his decision. On July 22, he formally notified the cabinet of his intention to issue an emancipation proclamation. It was "a military necessity, absolutely essential to the preservation of the Union," said Lincoln. "We must free the slaves or be ourselves subdued. The slaves [are] undeniably an element of strength to those who [have] their service, and we must decide whether that element should be with us or against us. . . . The Administration must set an example, and strike at the heart of the rebellion."

The cabinet agreed, except for Postmaster General Montgomery Blair, a resident of Maryland and a former Democrat, who warned that the border states and the Democrats would rebel against the proclamation and perhaps cost the administration the fall congressional elections as well as vital support for the war. Lincoln might have agreed two months earlier. Now he believed that the strength gained from an emancipation policy—from the slaves themselves, from the dynamic Republican segment of Northern opinion, and in the eyes of foreign nations—would more than compensate for the hostility of Democrats and border-state Unionists. Lincoln did, however, accept the advice of Secretary of State Seward to delay the proclamation "until you can give it to the country supported by military success." Otherwise, Seward argued, it might be viewed "as the last measure of an exhausted government, a cry for help . . . our last shriek, on the retreat." Lincoln slipped his proclamation into a desk drawer and waited for a military victory.

New Calls for Troops

Meanwhile, Lincoln issued a call for 300,000 new three-year volunteers for the army. In July, Congress passed a militia act giving the president greater powers to mobilize the state militias into federal service and to draft men into the militia if the states failed to do so. Although not a national draft law, this was a step in that direction. In August, Lincoln called up 300,000 militia for nine months of service, in addition to the 300,000 three-year volunteers. (These calls eventually yielded 421,000 three-year volunteers and 88,000 nine-month militia.) The Peace Democrats railed against these measures and provoked antidraft riots in some localities. The government responded by arresting rioters and antiwar activists under the president's suspension of the writ of habeas corpus.[1]

Democrats denounced these "arbitrary arrests" as unconstitutional violations of civil liberties, and added this issue to others on which they hoped to gain control of the next

---

[1] A writ of habeas corpus is an order issued by a judge to law enforcement officers requiring them to bring an arrested person before the court to be charged with a crime so that the accused can have a fair trial. The U.S. Constitution, however, permits the suspension of this writ "in cases of rebellion or invasion," so that the government can arrest enemy agents, saboteurs, or any individual who might hinder the defense of the country, and hold such individuals without trial. Lincoln had suspended the writ, but political opponents charged him with usurping a power possessed only by Congress in order to curb freedom of speech of antiwar opponents and political critics guilty of nothing more than speaking out against the war. This issue of "arbitrary arrests" became a controversial matter in both the Union and Confederacy (where the writ was similarly suspended during part of the war).

House of Representatives in the fall elections. With the decline in Northern morale following the defeat at Second Bull Run and the early success of the Confederate invasion of Kentucky, prospects for a Democratic triumph seemed bright. One more military victory by Lee's Army of Northern Virginia might crack the North's will to continue the fight. It would certainly bring diplomatic recognition of the Confederacy by Britain and France. Lee's legions began crossing the Potomac into Maryland on September 4, 1862.

The Battle of Antietam

The Confederate invasion ran into difficulties from the start. Western Marylanders responded impassively to Lee's proclamation that he had come "to aid you in throwing off this foreign yoke" of Yankee rule. Lee split his army into five parts. Three of them, under the overall command of Stonewall Jackson, occupied the heights surrounding the Union garrison at Harpers Ferry, which lay athwart the Confederate supply route from the Shenandoah Valley. The other two remained on watch in the South Mountain passes west of Frederick. Then, on September 13, Union commander George B. McClellan had an

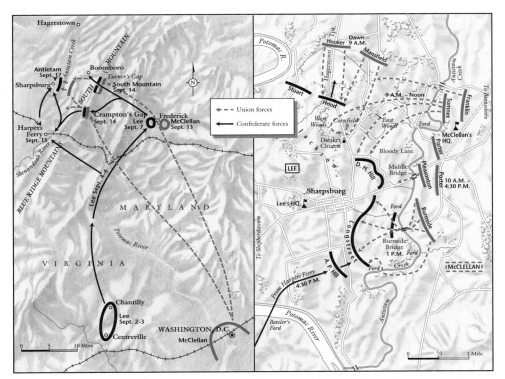

Map 16.1   Lee's Invasion of Maryland, 1862 and the Battle of Antietam, September 17, 1862   Both the advantages and disadvantages of Lee's defensive position in this battle are illustrated by the right-hand map. The Confederate flanks were protected by water barriers (the Potomac River on the left and Antietam Creek on the right), but the Confederates fought with their back to the Potomac and only Boteler's Ford as the single line of retreat across the river. If Burnside's attack on the Confederate right had succeeded before A. P. Hill's division arrived, Lee's forces could have been trapped north of the river.

extraordinary stroke of luck. In a field near Frederick, two of his soldiers found a copy of Lee's orders for these deployments. Wrapped around three cigars, they had apparently been dropped by a careless Southern officer when the Confederate army passed through Frederick four days earlier. With this new information, McClellan planned to pounce on the separated segments of Lee's army before they could reunite. "Here is a paper," he exulted, "with which if I cannot whip 'Bobbie Lee,' I will be willing to go home."

But McClellan moved so cautiously that he lost much of his advantage. Although Union troops overwhelmed the Confederate defenders of the South Mountain passes on September 14, they advanced too slowly to save the garrison at Harpers Ferry, which surrendered 12,000 men to Jackson on September 15. Lee then managed to reunite most of his army near the village of Sharpsburg by September 17, when McClellan finally crossed Antietam Creek to attack. Even so, the Union forces outnumbered the Confederates by 2 to 1 (80,000 to 40,000 men), but McClellan, as usual, believed that the enemy outnumbered *him*. Thus he missed several opportunities to inflict a truly crippling defeat on the Confederacy. The battle of Antietam (called Sharpsburg by the Confederates) nevertheless proved to be the single bloodiest day in American history, with more than 23,000 casualties (killed, wounded, and captured) in the two armies.

Attacking from right to left on a four-mile front, McClellan's Army of the Potomac achieved potential breakthroughs at a sunken road northeast of Sharpsburg (known ever after as Bloody Lane) and in the rolling fields southeast of town. But fearing counterattacks from phantom reserves that he was sure Lee possessed, McClellan held back 20,000 of his troops and failed to follow through. Thus the battle ended in a draw. The battered Confederates still clung to their precarious line, with the Potomac at their back, at the end of a day in which more than 6,000 men on both sides were killed or mortally wounded—almost as many Americans as were killed or mortally wounded in combat during the entire seven years of the Revolutionary War.

Even though he received reinforcements the next day, McClellan did not renew the attack. Nor did he follow up vigorously when the Confederates finally retreated across the Potomac on the night of September 18.

The Emancipation Proclamation

Lincoln was not happy with this equivocal Union victory, despite its important consequences. Britain and France decided to withhold diplomatic recognition of the Confederacy. Northern Democrats failed to gain control of the House in the fall elections. And most significant of all, on September 22, Lincoln seized the occasion to issue his preliminary emancipation proclamation. This was less than a total surprise to the public because the president had already hinted that something of the sort might be in the offing. A month earlier, after Horace Greeley had written a strong editorial in the New York *Tribune* calling for action against slavery, Lincoln had responded with a public letter to Greeley (much as a president today might use a televised news conference). "My paramount object in this struggle," wrote Lincoln, "is to save the Union. . . . If I could save the Union without freeing *any* slave I would do it, and if I could save it by freeing *all* the slaves I would do it; and if I could save it by freeing some and leaving others alone I would also do that." Knowing that the issue of Union united Northerners, while the prospect of emancipation still divided them, Lincoln had crafted these phrases carefully to maximize public support for his anticipated proclamation. He portrayed emancipation not as an end in itself—despite his personal convictions to that effect— but only as an instrument, a *means* toward saving the Union.

Lincoln's proclamation of September 22 did not go into effect immediately. Rather, it stipulated that if any state, or part of a state, was still in rebellion on January 1, 1863, the president would proclaim the slaves therein "forever free." Confederate leaders scorned this warning, and by January 1 no Southern state had returned to the Union. After hosting a New Year's Day reception at the White House, Lincoln signed the final proclamation as an "act of justice" as well as "a fit and necessary war measure for suppressing said rebellion."

The Emancipation Proclamation exempted the border states, plus Tennessee and those portions of Louisiana and Virginia already under Union occupation because these areas were deemed not to be in rebellion, and Lincoln's constitutional authority for the proclamation derived from his power as commander-in-chief to confiscate enemy property. Although the proclamation could do nothing to liberate slaves in areas under Confederate control, it essentially made the Northern soldiers an army of liberation, however reluctant many of them were to risk their lives for that purpose. The North was now fighting for freedom as well as for Union. If the North won the war, slavery would die. But in the winter and spring of 1862–63, victory was far from assured.

A Winter of Discontent

Focus Question
What were the sources of internal dissent and dissension in the Confederacy? In the Union?

Although Lee's retreat from Maryland and Braxton Bragg's retreat from Kentucky suggested that the Confederate tide might be ebbing, the tide soon turned. The Union could never win the war simply by turning back Confederate invasions. Northern armies would have to invade the South, defeat its armies, and destroy its ability to fight.

Displeased by McClellan's "slows" after Antietam, Lincoln replaced him on November 7 with General Ambrose E. Burnside. An imposing man whose muttonchop whiskers gave the anagram "sideburns" to the language, Burnside proposed to cross the Rappahannock River at Fredericksburg for a move on Richmond before bad weather forced both sides into winter quarters. Although Lee put his men into a strong defensive position on the heights behind Fredericksburg, Burnside nevertheless attacked on December 13. He was repulsed with heavy casualties that shook the morale of both the army and the public. When Lincoln heard the news, he said: "If there is a worse place than hell, I am in it."

News from the western theater did little to dispel the gloom in Washington. The Confederates had fortified Vicksburg on bluffs commanding the Mississippi River. This precaution gave them control of an important stretch of the river and preserved transportation links between the states to the east and west. Grant proposed to sever those links, and in November 1862, he launched a two-pronged drive against Vicksburg. With 40,000 men, he marched 50 miles southward from Memphis by land, while his principal subordinate William T. Sherman came down the river with 32,000 men accompanied by a gunboat fleet. Confederate cavalry raids destroyed the railroads and supply depots in Grant's rear, however, forcing him to retreat to Memphis. Meanwhile, Sherman attacked the Confederates at Chickasaw Bluffs on December 29 with no more success than Burnside had enjoyed at Fredericksburg.

The only bit of cheer for the North came in central Tennessee at the turn of the year. There, Lincoln had removed General Don Carlos Buell from command of the Army of the Cumberland for the same reason he had removed McClellan—lack of vigor and aggressiveness. Buell's successor, William S. Rosecrans, had proved a fighter in subordinate commands. On the Confederate side, Davis stuck with Braxton Bragg as commander of the Army of Tennessee, despite dissension from some subordinate officers within his ranks.

On the day after Christmas 1862, Rosecrans moved from his base at Nashville to attack Bragg's force 30 miles to the south at Murfreesboro. The ensuing three-day battle (called Stones River by the Union and Murfreesboro by the Confederacy) resulted in Confederate success on the first day (December 31) but defeat on the last. Both armies suffered devastating casualties. The Confederate retreat to a new base 40 miles farther south enabled the North to call Stones River a victory. Lincoln expressed his gratitude to Rosecrans: "I can never forget . . . that you gave us a hard-earned victory which, had there been a defeat instead, the nation could scarcely have lived over."

As it was, the nation scarcely lived over the winter of 1862–63. Morale declined, and desertions rose so sharply in the Army of the Potomac that Lincoln replaced Burnside with Joseph Hooker, a controversial general whose nickname "Fighting Joe" seemed to promise a vigorous offensive. Hooker did lift morale in the Army of the Potomac, but elsewhere matters went from bad to worse.

Renewing the campaign against Vicksburg, Grant bogged down in the swamps and rivers that protected that Confederate bastion on three sides. Only on the east, away from the river, did he find high ground suitable for an assault on Vicksburg's defenses. Grant's problem was to get his army across the Mississippi to that high ground, along with supplies and transportation to support an assault. For three months, he floundered in the Mississippi-Yazoo bottomlands, while disease and exposure depleted his troops. False rumors of excessive drinking that had dogged Grant for years broke out anew, but Lincoln resisted pressures to remove him from command. "What I want," Lincoln said, "is generals who will fight battles and win victories. Grant has done this, and I propose to stand by him." Lincoln reportedly added that he would like to know Grant's brand of whiskey so that he could send some to his other generals.

The Rise of the Copperheads

Lincoln's reputation reached a low point during this Northern winter of discontent. A visitor to Washington in February 1863 found that "the lack of respect for the President in all parties is unconcealed. . . . If a Republican convention were to be held tomorrow, he would not get the vote of a State." In this climate, the Copperhead faction of the Democratic Party found a ready audience for its message that the war was a failure and should be abandoned. Having won control of the Illinois and Indiana legislatures the preceding fall, Democrats there called for an armistice and a peace conference. They also demanded retraction of the "wicked, inhuman, and unholy" Emancipation Proclamation.

In Ohio, the foremost Peace Democrat, Congressman Clement L. Vallandigham, was planning to run for governor. What had this wicked war accomplished? Vallandigham asked Northern audiences: "Let the dead at Fredericksburg and Vicksburg answer." The Confederacy could never be conquered; the only trophies of the war were "debt, defeat, sepulchres." The solution was to "stop the fighting. Make an armistice. Withdraw your army from the seceded states." Above all, give up the unconstitutional effort to abolish slavery.

Vallandigham and other Copperhead spokesmen had a powerful effect on Northern morale. Alarmed by a wave of desertions, the army commander in Ohio had Vallandigham arrested in May 1863. A military court convicted him of treason for aiding and abetting the enemy. The court's action raised serious questions of civil liberties. Was the conviction a violation of Vallandigham's First Amendment right of free speech? Could a military court try a civilian under **martial law** in a state such as Ohio where civil courts were functioning?

Lincoln was embarrassed by the swift arrest and trial of Vallandigham, which he learned about from the newspapers. To keep Vallandigham from becoming a martyr, Lincoln commuted his sentence from imprisonment to banishment—to the Confederacy! On May 15, Union cavalry escorted Vallandigham under a flag of truce to Confederate lines in Tennessee, where the Southerners reluctantly accepted their uninvited guest. He soon escaped to Canada on a blockade runner. There, from exile, Vallandigham conducted his campaign for governor of Ohio—an election he lost in October 1863, after the military fortunes of the Union had improved.

Economic Problems in the South

Low morale in the North followed military defeat. By contrast, Southerners were buoyed by their military success but were suffering from food shortages and hyperinflation. The tightening Union blockade, the weaknesses and imbalances of the Confederate economy, the escape of slaves to Union lines, and enemy occupation of some of the South's prime agricultural areas made it increasingly difficult to produce both guns and butter. Despite the conversion of hundreds of thousands of acres from cotton to food production, the deterioration of Southern railroads and the priority given to army shipments made food scarce in some areas. A drought in summer 1862 made matters worse. Prices rose much faster than wages. The price of salt, which was necessary to preserve meat in those days before refrigeration,

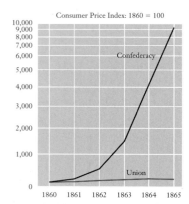

Wartime Inflation in the Confederacy and the Union

shot out of sight. Even the middle class suffered, especially in Richmond, whose population had more than doubled since 1861. "The shadow of the gaunt form of famine is upon us," wrote a war department clerk in March 1863. "I have lost twenty pounds, and my wife and children are emaciated." The rats in his kitchen were so hungry that they nibbled bread crumbs from his daughter's hand "as tame as kittens. Perhaps we shall have to eat them!"

Poor people were worse off, especially the wives and children of nonslaveholders away in the army. By spring 1863, food supplies were virtually gone. Wrote a North Carolina farm woman to the governor in April 1863:

A crowd of we Poor women went to Greenesborogh yesterday for something to eat as we had not a mouthful of meet nor bread in my house. What did they do but put us in gail in plase of giveing us aney thing to eat. . . . I have 6 little children and my husband in the armey and what am I to do?

Some women took matters into their own hands. Denouncing "speculators" who allegedly hoarded goods to drive up prices, they marched to stores, asked the price of bacon or corn-meal or salt, denounced such "extortion," and took what they wanted without paying. On April 2, 1863, a mob of more than 1,000 women and boys looted several shops in Richmond before the militia, under the personal command of Davis, forced them to disperse. The Confederate government subsequently released some emergency food stocks to civilians, and state and county governments aided the families of soldiers. Better crops in 1863 helped alleviate the worst shortages, but serious problems persisted.

The Wartime Draft and Class Tensions

In both South and North, the draft intensified social unrest and turned it in the direction of class conflict. The burst of patriotic enthusiasm that had prompted a million men to join the colors in North and South during 1861 had waned by spring 1862. That April, the Confederacy enacted a draft that made all white men (with certain occupational exemptions) ages 18 to 35 liable to conscription. A drafted man could hire a substitute, but the price of substitutes soon rose beyond the means of the average Southern farmer or worker, giving rise to the bitter cry that it was "a rich man's war and a poor man's fight."

The cry grew louder in October 1862 when the Confederate Congress raised the draft age to 45 and added a clause exempting one white man from the draft on every plantation with 20 or more slaves. The purpose of this "overseer exemption" was to keep up production and prevent slave uprisings. It had been prompted by the complaints of planters' wives, who had been left alone to manage the slaves after the departure of husbands, sons, and overseers for the army. The so-called **Twenty Negro Law** was regarded as blatant discrimination by nonslaveholding farm families whose men were also at the front. In addition, raising the age limit to 45 took away many fathers of children too young to work the farm. The law provoked widespread draft-dodging and desertions.

Similar discontent greeted the enactment of a conscription law in the North. In summer 1863, some 30,000 Union soldiers—who had enlisted in 1861 for two years rather than the normal three—would be leaving military service, along with 80,000 of the nine-month militia called into service the preceding autumn. To meet the looming shortfall of men, Congress decreed in March that all male citizens ages 20 to 45 must enroll for the draft. Not all of them would necessarily be called (administrative policy exempted married men over 35), but all would be liable.

The law was intended more to encourage volunteers to come forward than to draft men directly into the army. In three of the president's four calls for troops under this law, the War Department set a quota for every congressional district and allowed 50 days for the quota to be met with volunteers before resorting to a draft lottery. Some districts avoided drafting anyone by offering large bounties to volunteers. The bounty system produced glaring abuses, including **"bounty jumpers"** who enlisted and then deserted as soon as they got their money—often to enlist again under another name somewhere else.

The drafting process was also open to abuse. Like the Confederate law, the Union law permitted hiring substitutes. To keep the price from skyrocketing as it had in the Confederacy, the law allowed a drafted man the alternative of paying a **"commutation fee"** of $300 that exempted him from the current draft call (but not necessarily from the next one). That provision raised the cry of "rich man's war, poor man's fight" in the North as well. The Democratic Party nurtured this sense of class resentment and racism intensified it. Democrats in Congress opposed conscription, just as they opposed emancipation. Democratic newspapers told white workers, especially the large Irish American population, that the draft would force them to fight a war to free the slaves, who would then come north to take their jobs. This volatile issue sparked widespread violence when the Northern draft got

Collection of the New-York Historical Society

The New York City Draft Riot   The worst urban violence in all of American history occurred in New York City, on July 13–16, 1863, when thousands of men and women, mostly poor Irish Americans, attacked draft offices, homes, businesses, and individuals. Black residents of the city were among the mob's victims because they symbolized labor competition to Irish Americans, who did not want to be drafted to fight a war to free the slaves. This illustration shows the burning of the Colored Orphan Asylum, a home for black orphans. More than 100 people were killed in the disturbance, most of them rioters shot down by police and soldiers.

underway in summer 1863. The worst riot occurred in New York City on July 13–16, where huge mobs consisting mostly of Irish Americans demolished draft offices, lynched several blacks, and destroyed huge areas of the city in four days of looting and burning.

Draft riots in the North and bread riots in the South exposed alarming class fissures that deepened with the strains of full-scale war. Although inflation was much less serious in the North than in the South, Northern wages lagged behind price increases. Labor unions sprang up in several industries and struck for higher wages. In some areas, such as the anthracite coal fields of eastern Pennsylvania, labor organizations dominated by Irish Americans combined resistance to the draft and opposition to emancipation with violent strikes against industries owned by Protestant Republicans. Troops sent in to enforce the draft sometimes suppressed the strikes as well. These class, ethnic, and racial hostilities provided a volatile mixture in several Northern communities.

A Poor Man's Fight?

The grievance that it was a rich man's war and a poor man's fight was more apparent than real. Property, excise, and income taxes to sustain the war bore proportionately more heavily on the wealthy than on the poor. In the South, wealthy property owners suffered greater damage and confiscation losses than did nonslaveholders. The war liberated 4 million slaves, the poorest class in America. Both the Union and Confederate armies fielded men from all strata of society in proportion to their percentage of the population. If anything, among those who volunteered in 1861 and 1862, the planter class was overrepresented in the Confederate army and the middle class in the Union forces because those privileged groups believed they had more at stake in the war and joined up in larger numbers during the early months of enthusiasm. Those volunteers—especially the officers—suffered the highest percentage of combat casualties.

Nor did conscription fall much more heavily on the poor than on the rich. Those who escaped the draft by decamping to the woods, the territories, or Canada were mostly poor. The Confederacy abolished substitution in December 1863 and made men who had previously sent substitutes liable to the draft. In the North, several city councils, political machines, and businesses contributed funds to pay the commutation fees of drafted men who were too poor to pay out of their own pockets. In the end, it was neither a rich man's war nor a poor man's fight. It was an American war.

Blueprint for Modern America

The 37th Congress (1861–63)—the Congress that enacted conscription, passed measures for confiscation and emancipation, and created the greenbacks and the national banking system (see chapter 15)—also enacted three laws that, together with the war legislation, provided what one historian has called "a blueprint for modern America": the Homestead Act, the Morrill Land-Grant College Act, and the Pacific Railroad Act. For several years before the war, Republicans and some northern Democrats had tried to pass these laws to provide social benefits and to promote economic growth, only to see them defeated by Southern opposition or by President Buchanan's veto. The secession of Southern states, ironically, enabled Congress to pass all three laws in 1862.

The Homestead Act granted a farmer 160 acres of land virtually free after he had lived on the land for five years and had made improvements on it. The Morrill Land-Grant College Act gave each state thousands of acres to fund the establishment of colleges to teach "agricultural and mechanical arts." The Pacific Railroad Act granted land and loans to railroad companies to spur building a transcontinental railroad from Omaha to Sacramento. Under these laws, the U.S. government ultimately granted 80 million acres to homesteaders, 25 million acres to states for land-grant colleges, and 120 million acres to several transcontinental railroads. Despite waste, corruption, and exploitation of the original Indian owners of this land, these laws helped farmers settle some of the most fertile land in the world, studded the land with state colleges, and spanned it with steel rails in a manner that altered the landscape of the western half of the country.

Women and the War

The war advanced many other social changes, particularly with respect to women. In factories and on farms, women replaced men who had gone off to war. Explosions in ordnance plants and arsenals killed at least 100 women, who were as surely war casualties as men killed in battle. The war accelerated the entry of women into the teaching profession, a trend that had already begun in the Northeast and now spread to other parts of the country. It also brought significant numbers of women into the civil service. During the 1850s, a few women had worked briefly in the U.S. Patent Office (including Clara Barton, who became a famous wartime nurse and founded the American Red Cross). The huge expansion of government bureaucracies after 1861 and the departure of male clerks to the army provided openings that were filled partly by women. After the war, the private sector began hiring women as clerks, bookkeepers, "typewriters" (the machine was invented in the 1870s), and telephone operators (the telephone was another postwar invention).

Women's most visible impact was in the field of medicine. The outbreak of war prompted the organization of soldiers' aid societies, hospital societies, and other voluntary associations to provide home-front support for the soldiers, and women played a leading role. Their most important function was to help—and sometimes to prod—the medical branches of the Union and Confederate armies to provide more efficient, humane care for sick and wounded soldiers. Dr. Elizabeth Blackwell, the first American woman to earn an M.D. (1849), organized a meeting of 3,000 women in New York City on April 29, 1861. They put together the Women's Central Association for Relief, which became the nucleus for the most powerful voluntary association of the war, the U.S. Sanitary Commission.

Eventually embracing 7,000 local auxiliaries, the Sanitary Commission was an essential adjunct of the Union army's medical bureau. Most of its local volunteers were women, as were most of the nurses it provided to army hospitals. Nursing was not a new profession for women, but it lacked respect as a wartime profession, being classed only slightly above prostitution. The fame won by Florence Nightingale of Britain during the Crimean War a half-dozen years earlier had begun to change that perception. As thousands of middle and even upper-class women volunteers flocked to army hospitals, nursing began its transformation from a menial occupation to a respected profession.

The nurses had to overcome the deep-grained suspicions of army surgeons and the opposition of husbands and fathers who shared the cultural sentiment that the shocking, embarrassingly physical atmosphere of an army hospital was no place for a respectable woman. Many thousands of women went to work, winning grudging and then enthusiastic admiration. One Confederate surgeon praised women nurses as far superior to the convalescent soldiers who had formerly done that job, "rough country crackers" who did not "know castor oil from a gun rod nor laudanum from a hole in the ground." In the North, the treasurer of the Sanitary Commission, who at first had disliked the idea of his wife working as a nurse, was converted by her performance as a volunteer for the Sanitary Commission during summer 1862. "The little woman has come out amazingly strong during these past two months," he wrote. "Have never given her credit for a tithe of the enterprise, pluck, discretion, and force of character that she has shown."

The war also bolstered the fledgling women's rights movement. It was no coincidence that Elizabeth Cady Stanton and Susan B. Anthony founded the National Woman Suffrage Association in 1869, only four years after the war. Although a half century passed before women won the vote, this movement could not have achieved the momentum that made it a force in American life without the work of women in the Civil War.

The Confederate Tide Crests and Recedes

The Army of Northern Virginia and the Army of the Potomac spent the winter of 1862–63 on opposite banks of the Rappahannock River. With the coming of spring, Union commander Joe Hooker resumed the offensive with hopes of redeeming the December disaster at Fredericksburg. On April 30, instead of charging straight across the river, Hooker crossed his men several miles upriver and came in on Lee's rear. Lee quickly faced most of his troops about and confronted the enemy in dense woods, known locally as the Wilderness, near the crossroads hostelry of Chancellorsville. Nonplussed, Hooker lost the initiative.

The Battle of Chancellorsville

Even though the Union forces outnumbered the Confederates by almost two to one, Lee boldly went over to the offensive. On May 2, Stonewall Jackson led 28,000 men on a stealthy march through the woods to attack the Union right flank late in the afternoon. As a result of the negligence of the Union commanders, the surprise was complete. Jackson's assault crumpled the Union flank as the sun dipped below the horizon. Jackson then rode out to scout the terrain for a moonlight attack but was wounded on his return by jittery Confederates who mistook him and his staff for Union cavalry. Nevertheless, Lee resumed the attack the next day. In three more days of fighting that caused 12,800 Confederate and 16,800 Union casualties (the largest number for a single battle in the war so far), Lee drove the Union troops back across the Rappahannock. It was a brilliant victory.

In the North, the gloom grew deeper. "My God!" exclaimed Lincoln when he heard the news of Chancellorsville. "What will the country say?" Copperhead opposition intensified.

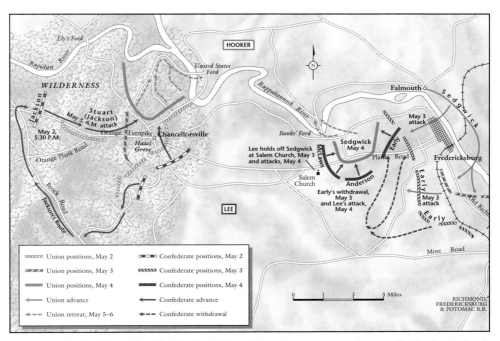

Map 16.2 Battle of Chancellorsville, May 2–6, 1863 This map demonstrates the advantage of holding "interior lines," which enabled General Lee to shift troops back and forth to and from the Chancellorsville and Fredericksburg fronts over the course of three days while the two parts of the Union army remained separated.

Southern sympathizers in Britain renewed efforts for diplomatic recognition of the Confederacy. Southern elation, however, was tempered by grief at the death on May 10 of Jackson, who had contracted pneumonia after amputation of his arm. Nevertheless, Lee decided to parlay his tactical victory at Chancellorsville into a strategic offensive by again invading the North. A victory on Union soil would convince Northerners and foreigners alike that the Confederacy was invincible. As his army moved north in June 1863, Lee was confident of success. "There never were such men in an army before," he wrote of his troops. "They will go anywhere and do anything if properly led."

The Gettysburg Campaign

At first, all went well. The Confederates brushed aside or captured Union forces in the northern Shenandoah Valley and in Pennsylvania. Stuart's cavalry threw a scare into Washington by raiding behind Union lines into Maryland and Pennsylvania. That very success led to trouble. With Stuart's cavalry separated from the rest of the army, Lee lost the vital intelligence that the cavalry garnered as the army's eyes. By June 28, several detachments of Lee's forces were scattered about Pennsylvania, far from their base and vulnerable.

At this point, Lee learned that the Army of the Potomac was moving toward him, now under the command of George Gordon Meade. Lee immediately ordered his own army to reassemble in the vicinity of Gettysburg, an agricultural and college town at the hub of a dozen roads leading in from all directions. There, on the morning of July 1, the vanguard of the two armies met in a clash that grew into the greatest battle in American history. (**See Map 16.3, Battle of Gettysburg, July 1–3, 1863, in the color insert following p. 624.**)

As the fighting spread west and north of town, couriers pounded up the roads on lathered horses to summon reinforcements to both sides. The Confederates fielded more men and broke the Union lines late that afternoon, driving the survivors to a defensive position on Cemetery Hill south of town. General Richard Ewell, Jackson's successor as commander of the Confederate Second Corps, judging this position too strong to take with his own troops, chose not to press the attack as the sun went down on what he presumed would be another Confederate victory.

When the sun rose the next morning, however, the reinforced Union army was holding a superb defensive position from Culp's Hill and Cemetery Hill south to Little Round Top. Lee's principal subordinate, First Corps commander James Longstreet, advised against attack, urging instead a maneuver to the south, toward Washington, to force the Federals to attack Lee in a strong defensive position. But Lee believed his army invincible. After its victory on July 1, a move to the south might look like a retreat. Pointing to the Union lines, he said: "The enemy is there, and I am going to attack him there." Longstreet reluctantly led the attack on the Union left. Once committed, his men fought with fury. The Union troops fought back with equal fury. As the afternoon passed, peaceful areas with names like Peach Orchard, Wheat Field, Devil's Den, and Little Round Top were turned into killing fields. By the end of the day, Confederate forces had made small gains at great cost, but the main Union line had held firm.

Lee was not yet ready to yield the offensive. Having attacked both Union flanks, he thought the center might be weak. On July 3, he ordered a frontal attack on Cemetery Ridge, led by a fresh division under George Pickett. After a two-hour artillery barrage, Pickett's 5,000 men and 8,000 additional troops moved forward on that sultry afternoon in a picture-book assault that forms our most enduring image of the Civil War. "Pickett's Charge" was shot to pieces; scarcely half of the men returned unwounded to their own lines. It was the final act in an awesome three-day drama that left some 50,000 men killed, wounded, or captured: 23,000 Federals and 25,000 to 28,000 Confederates.

Lee limped back to Virginia pursued by the Union troops. Lincoln was unhappy with Meade for not cutting off the Confederate retreat. Nevertheless, Gettysburg was a great Northern victory, and it came at the same time as other important Union successes in Mississippi, Louisiana, and Tennessee.

The Vicksburg Campaign

In mid-April, Grant had begun a move that would put Vicksburg in a vise. The Union ironclad fleet ran downriver past the big guns at Vicksburg with little damage. Grant's troops marched down the Mississippi's west bank and were ferried across the river 40 miles south of Vicksburg.

There they kept the Confederate defenders off balance by striking east toward Jackson instead of marching north to Vicksburg. Grant's purpose was to scatter the Confederate

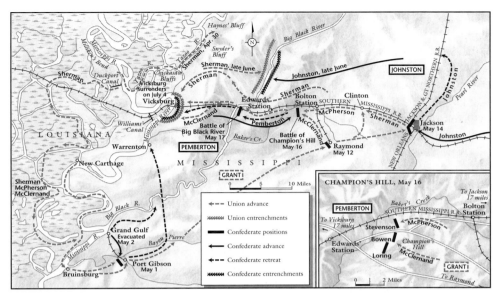

Map 16.4 Vicksburg Campaign, April–July 1863 This map illustrates Grant's brilliant orchestration of the campaign that involved Sherman's feint at Haynes' Bluff (top of map) on April 30 while the rest of the Union forces crossed at Bruinsburg (bottom of map) and then cleared Confederate resistance out of the way eastward to Jackson before turning west to invest Vicksburg.

forces in central Mississippi and to destroy the rail network so that his rear would be secure when he turned toward Vicksburg. It was a brilliant strategy, flawlessly executed. During the first three weeks of May, Grant's troops marched 180 miles, won five battles, and trapped 32,000 Confederate troops and 3,000 civilians in Vicksburg between the Union army on land and the Union gunboats on the river.

But the Confederate army was still full of fight. Confederate soldiers threw back Union assaults against the Vicksburg trenches on May 19 and 22. Grant then settled down for a siege. By late June, he had built up his army to 70,000 men to ward off a Confederate army of 30,000 scraped together by Joseph Johnston to try to rescue Vicksburg. Running out of supplies, the Vicksburg garrison surrendered on July 4. Grant then turned east and drove off Johnston's force. On July 9, the Confederate garrison at Port Hudson, 200 river miles south of Vicksburg, surrendered to a besieging Union army. Northern forces now controlled the entire length of the Mississippi River. "The Father of Waters again goes unvexed to the sea," said Lincoln. The Confederacy had been torn in two, and Lincoln knew who deserved the credit. "Grant is my man," he said, "and I am his the rest of the war."

Chickamauga and Chattanooga

Northerners had scarcely finished celebrating the twin victories of Gettysburg and Vicksburg when they learned of an important—and almost bloodless—triumph in Tennessee. After the traumatic Battle of Stones River at the end of 1862, the Union Army of the Cumberland and the Confederate Army of Tennessee had shadowboxed for nearly six months. On June 24,

Union commander Rosecrans finally assaulted the Confederate defenses in the Cumberland foothills of east-central Tennessee. He used his cavalry and a mounted infantry brigade armed with new repeating rifles to get around the Confederate flanks while his infantry threatened the Confederate front. In the first week of July, the Confederates retreated all the way to Chattanooga.

After a pause for resupply, Rosecrans's army advanced again in August, this time in tandem with a smaller Union army in eastern Tennessee commanded by Burnside, who had come to this theater after being removed from command in Virginia. Again the outnumbered Confederates fell back, evacuating Knoxville on September 2 and Chattanooga on September 9. This action severed the South's only direct east-west rail link. Having sliced the Confederacy in half with the capture of Vicksburg and Port Hudson, Union forces now stood poised for a campaign into Georgia that threatened to slice it into three parts. For the Confederacy, it was a stunning reversal of the situation only four months earlier, after Chancellorsville, when the Union cause had appeared hopeless.

Confederate General Braxton Bragg reached into his bag of tricks and sent fake deserters into Union lines with tales of a Confederate retreat toward Atlanta. He then laid a trap for Rosecrans's troops as they advanced through the mountain passes south of Chattanooga. To help him spring it, Davis approved the detachment of Longstreet with two divisions from Lee's army to reinforce Bragg. On September 19, the Confederates turned and counterattacked Rosecrans's now outnumbered army in the valley of Chickamauga Creek.

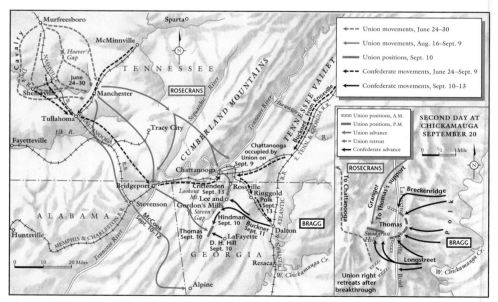

Map 16.5 Road to Chickamauga, June–September 1863 From Murfreesboro to Chattanooga, Rosecrans's campaign of maneuver on multiple fronts, as shown on this map, forced Bragg's Army of Tennessee all the way south into Georgia in a campaign with minimal casualties before Bragg counterattacked at Chickamauga.

On that day and the next, in ferocious fighting that produced more casualties (35,000) than any other single battle save Gettysburg, the Confederates finally scored a victory. On September 20, after a confusion of orders left a division-size gap in the Union line, Longstreet's men broke through, sending part of the Union army reeling back to Chattanooga. Only a firm stand by corps commander George H. Thomas—a Virginian who had remained loyal to the Union—prevented a Union rout. For this feat, Thomas earned the nickname "Rock of Chickamauga." Lincoln subsequently appointed Thomas commander of the Army of the Cumberland to replace Rosecrans, who was, in Lincoln's words, "confused and stunned like a duck hit on the head" after Chickamauga.

Lincoln also sent two army corps from Virginia under Hooker and two from Vicksburg under Sherman to reinforce Thomas, whose troops in Chattanooga were under virtual siege by Bragg's forces, which held most of the surrounding heights. More important, Lincoln put Grant in overall command of the beefed-up Union forces there. When Grant arrived in late October, he welded the various Northern units into a new army and opened a new supply line into Chattanooga. On November 24, Hooker's troops drove Confederate besiegers off massive Lookout Mountain.

The next day, an assault on Bragg's main line at Missionary Ridge east of Chattanooga won a smashing success against seemingly greater odds than Pickett had faced at Gettysburg. The Union troops that had been routed at Chickamauga two months earlier redeemed themselves by driving the Confederates off Missionary Ridge and 20 miles south into Georgia.

These battles climaxed a string of Union victories in the second half of 1863, which made that year one of "calamity . . . defeat . . . utter ruin," in the words of a Confederate official. The Southern diarist Mary Boykin Chesnut found "gloom and unspoken despondency hang[ing] like a pall everywhere." Jefferson Davis removed the discredited Bragg from command of the Army of Tennessee and reluctantly replaced him with Joseph E. Johnston, in whom Davis had little confidence. Lincoln summoned Grant to Washington and appointed him general-in-chief of all Union armies in March 1864, signifying a relentless fight to the finish.

Black Men in Blue

Focus Question
What contribution did women and African Americans make to the war efforts in both the North and South?

The events of the second half of 1863 also confirmed emancipation as a Union war aim. Northerners had not greeted the Emancipation Proclamation with great enthusiasm. Democrats and border-state Unionists continued to denounce it, and many Union soldiers resented the idea that they would now be risking their lives for black freedom. The Democratic Party had hoped to capitalize on this opposition, and on Union military failures, to

Library of Congress, Prints and Photographs Division

Part of Company E, 4th U.S. Colored Infantry Organized in July 1863, most of the men were former slaves from North Carolina. The 4th fought in several actions on the Petersburg and Richmond fronts in 1864, helping to capture part of the Petersburg defenses on June 15. Of the 166 black regiments in the Union Army, the 4th suffered the fourth-largest number of combat deaths.

win important off-year elections. Northern military victories knocked one prop out from under the Democratic platform, and the performance of black soldiers fighting for the Union knocked out another.

The enlistment of black soldiers was a logical corollary of emancipation. Free Negroes in the North had tried to enlist in 1861, but they were rejected. Proposals to recruit black soldiers, Democrats said, were part of a Republican plot to establish "the equality of the black and white races." In a way, that charge was correct. One consequence of black men fighting for the Union would be to advance the black race a long way toward equal rights. "Once let the black man get upon his person the brass letters, U.S.," said Frederick Douglass, "and a musket on his shoulder and bullets in his pocket, and there is no power on earth which can deny that he has earned the right to citizenship."

But it was pragmatism more than principle that pushed the North toward black recruitment. One purpose of emancipation was to deprive the Confederacy of black laborers and to use them for the Union. Putting some of those former laborers in uniform was a compelling idea, especially as white enlistments lagged and the North had to enact conscription in 1863. Some Union commanders in occupied portions of Louisiana, South Carolina, and Missouri began to organize black regiments in 1862. The Emancipation Proclamation legitimized this policy with its proposal to enroll able-bodied male contrabands in new black regiments, although these units would serve as labor battalions, supply troops, and garrison forces rather than as combat troops. They would be paid less than white soldiers, and their officers would be white. In other words, black men in blue would be second-class soldiers, just as free blacks in the North were second-class citizens.

Black Soldiers in Combat

Continuing pressure from abolitionists, as well as military necessity, partly eroded discrimination. Congress enacted equal pay in 1864. Officers worked for better treatment of their men. Above all, the regiments lobbied for the right to fight as combat soldiers. Even some previously hostile white soldiers came around to the notion that black men might just as well stop enemy bullets as white men. In May and June 1863, black regiments in

Louisiana fought well in an assault on Port Hudson and in defense of a Union outpost at Milliken's Bend, near Vicksburg. "The bravery of the blacks in the battle of Milliken's Bend completely revolutionized the sentiment of the army with regard to the employment of negro troops," wrote the assistant secretary of war, who had been on the spot with Grant's army. "I heard prominent officers who formerly in private had sneered at the idea of the negroes fighting express themselves after that as heartily in favor of it."

Even more significant was the action of the 54th Massachusetts Infantry, the first black regiment raised mainly in the North. Its officers, headed by Colonel Robert Gould Shaw, came from prominent New England antislavery families. Two sons of Frederick Douglass were in the regiment—one of them as sergeant major. Shaw worked hard to win the right for the regiment to fight. On July 18, 1863, he succeeded: The 54th was assigned to lead an assault on Fort Wagner, part of the network of Confederate defenses protecting Charleston. Although the attack failed, the 54th fought courageously, suffering 50 percent casualties, including Colonel Shaw, who was killed. This battle "made Fort Wagner such a name to the colored race as Bunker Hill had been for ninety years to the white Yankees," declared the New York *Tribune*.

The battle took place just after white mobs of draft rioters in New York had lynched blacks. Abolitionist and Republican commentators drew the moral: Black men who fought for the Union deserved more respect than white men who rioted against it. Lincoln made this point eloquently in a widely published letter to a political meeting in August 1863. When final victory was achieved, he wrote, "there will be some black men who can remember that, with silent tongue, and clenched teeth, and steady eye, and well-poised bayonet, they have helped mankind on to this great consummation; while, I fear, there will be some white ones, unable to forget that, with malignant heart, and deceitful speech, they have strove to hinder it."

Emancipation Confirmed

Lincoln's letter set the tone for Republican campaigns in state elections that fall. The party swept them all, including Ohio, where they buried Vallandigham under a 100,000-vote margin swelled by the soldier vote, which went 94 percent for his opponent. In effect, the elections were a powerful endorsement of the administration's emancipation policy. If the Emancipation Proclamation had been submitted to a referendum a year earlier, observed a newspaper editor in November 1863, "the voice of a majority would have been against it. And yet not a year has passed before it is approved by an overwhelming majority."

Emancipation would not be assured of survival until it had been christened by the Constitution. On April 8, 1864, the Senate passed the 13th Amendment to abolish slavery, but Democrats in the House blocked the required two-thirds majority there. Not until after Lincoln's reelection in 1864 would the House pass the amendment, which became part of the Constitution on December 6, 1865. In the end, though, the fate of slavery depended on the outcome of the war. And despite Confederate defeats in 1863, that outcome was by no means certain. Some of the heaviest fighting lay ahead. Many Southerners succumbed to defeatism in the winter of 1863–64. "I have never actually despaired of the cause," wrote a Confederate War Department official in November, but "steadfastness is yielding to a sense of hopelessness." Desertions from Confederate armies increased. Inflation galloped out of control. According to a Richmond diarist, a merchant told a poor woman in October 1863 that the price of a barrel of flour was $70: "'My God!' exclaimed she, 'how can I pay such prices? I have seven children; what shall I do?' 'I don't know, madam,' said he, coolly, 'unless you eat your children.'"

The Davis administration, like the Lincoln administration a year earlier, had to face congressional elections during a time of public discontent, for the Confederate constitution mandated such elections in odd-numbered years. Political parties had ceased to exist in the Confederacy after Democrats and former Whigs had tacitly declared a truce in 1861 to form a united front for the war effort. Many congressmen had been elected without opposition in 1861. By 1863, however, significant hostility to Davis had emerged. Although it was not channeled through any organized party, it took on partisan trappings, as an inchoate anti-Davis faction surfaced in the Confederate Congress and in the election campaign of 1863.

The Year of Decision

Some antiadministration candidates ran on a quasi-peace platform (analogous to that of the Copperheads in the North) that called for an armistice and peace negotiations. The movement left unresolved the terms of such negotiations—reunion or independence—but any peace overture from a position of weakness was tantamount to conceding defeat. The peace movement was especially strong in North Carolina, where for a time it appeared that the next governor would be elected on a peace platform (in the end, the "peace candidate" was defeated). Still, antiadministration candidates made significant gains in the 1863 Confederate elections, although they fell about 15 seats short of a majority in the House and two seats short in the Senate.

Out of the Wilderness

Shortages, inflation, political discontent, military defeat, high casualties, and the loss of thousands of slaves bent but did not break the Southern spirit. As spring 1864 came on, a renewed determination infused both home front and battlefront. The Confederate armies no longer had the strength to invade the North or to win the war with a knockout blow, but they could still fight a war of attrition, as the patriots had done in the War of 1775–83 against Britain (chapter 6). If they could hold out long enough and inflict enough casualties on the Union armies, they might weaken the Northern will to continue fighting. And if they could just hold out until the Union presidential election in November, Northern voters might reject Lincoln and elect a Peace Democrat.

Northerners were vulnerable to this strategy of psychological attrition. Military success in 1863 had created a mood of confidence, and people expected a quick, decisive victory in 1864. The mood grew with Grant's appointment as general-in-chief. When Grant decided to remain in Virginia with the Army of the Potomac and to leave Sherman in command of the Union forces in northern Georgia, Northerners expected these two heavyweights to floor the Confederacy with a one-two punch. Lincoln was alarmed by this euphoria. "The people are too sanguine," he told a reporter. "They expect too much at once." Disappointment might trigger despair.

Lincoln was nearly proved right. Grant's strategic plan was elegant in its simplicity. While smaller Union armies in peripheral theaters carried out auxiliary campaigns, the two principal armies in Virginia and Georgia would attack the main Confederate forces under Lee and Johnston. Convinced that in years past Union armies in various theaters had "acted independently and without concert, like a balky team, no two ever pulling together," Grant ordered simultaneous offensives on all fronts, to prevent the Confederates from shifting reinforcements from one theater to another.

Grant's offensives began the first week of May. The heaviest fighting occurred in Virginia. When the Army of the Potomac crossed the Rapidan River, Lee attacked its flank in the thick scrub forest of the Wilderness, where Union superiority in numbers and artillery would count for little (and where Lee had defeated Hooker a year earlier at Chancellorsville). Lee's action brought on two days (May 5–6) of the most confused, frenzied fighting the war had yet seen. Hundreds of wounded men burned to death in brush fires set off by exploding shells or muzzle flashes. The battle surged back and forth, with the Confederates inflicting 18,000 casualties and suffering 12,000. Having apparently halted Grant's offensive, they claimed a victory.

Spotsylvania and Cold Harbor

Grant did not admit defeat, nor did he retreat, as other Union commanders in Virginia had done. Instead, he moved toward Spotsylvania Courthouse, a key crossroads 10 miles

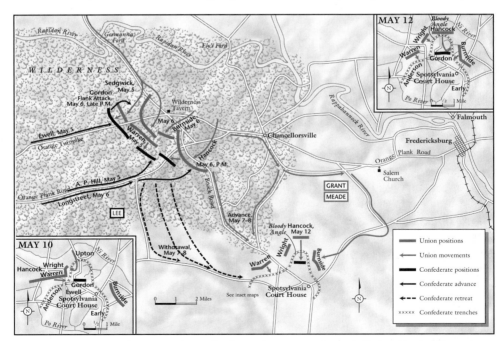

Map 16.6   Battle of the Wilderness and Spotsylvania, May 5–12, 1864   Four major battles with a total of more than 100,000 casualties to both sides were fought within a few miles of Fredericksburg between December 1862 and May 1864. Compare this map with the Chancellorsville map on p. 605. The first battle of Fredericksburg on December 13, 1862 (described p. 597) was fought in the same vicinity as the Fredericksburg fighting on May 3, 1863, shown on the Chancellorsville map.

closer to Richmond. Skillfully, Lee pulled back to cover the road junction. Repeated Union assaults during the next 12 days (May 8–19) left another 18,000 Northerners and 12,000 Southerners killed, wounded, or captured. The Confederates fought from an elaborate network of trenches and log breastworks they had constructed virtually overnight. Civil War soldiers had learned the advantages of trenches, which gave the defense an enormous advantage and made frontal assaults almost suicidal.

Having achieved no better than stalemate around Spotsylvania, Grant again moved south around Lee's right flank in an effort to force the outnumbered Confederates into an open fight. Lee, however, anticipated Grant's moves and confronted him from behind formidable defenses at the North Anna River, Totopotomoy Creek, and near the crossroads inn of Cold Harbor, only 10 miles northeast of Richmond. Believing the Confederates must be exhausted and demoralized by their repeated retreats, Grant decided to attack at Cold Harbor on June 3—a costly mistake. Lee's troops were ragged and hungry but far from demoralized. Their withering fire inflicted 7,000 casualties in less than an hour. (By coincidence, this was the same number of casualties suffered during the same length of time by the men in Pickett's Charge at Gettysburg exactly 11 months before.) "I regret this assault more than any other one I have ordered," said Grant.

Stalemate in Virginia

Now Grant moved all the way across the James River to strike at Petersburg, an industrial city and rail center 20 miles south of Richmond. If Petersburg fell, the Confederates could not hold Richmond. Once more Lee's troops raced southward on the inside track and blocked Grant's troops. Four days of Union assaults (June 15–18) produced another 11,000 Northern casualties but no breakthrough. Such high Union losses in just six weeks—some 65,000 killed, wounded, and captured, compared with 37,000 Confederate casualties—cost the Army of the Potomac its offensive power. Grant reluctantly settled down for a siege along the Petersburg–Richmond front that would last more than nine grueling months.

Meanwhile, other Union operations in Virginia had achieved little success. Benjamin Butler bungled an attack up the James River against Richmond and was stopped by a scraped-together army under Beauregard. A Union thrust up the Shenandoah Valley was blocked at Lynchburg in June by

Union Supply Base at City Point, Virginia During the Union army's siege of Petersburg from June 1864 to April 1865 the army built up a huge complex of wharfs and warehouses at City Point on the James River (today's Hopewell, Virginia) where ships unloaded supplies and trains carried them to the front. Note the boxcars of the U.S. Military Rail Road shown in the photograph.

Library of Congress, Prints and Photographs Division

Jubal Early, commanding Stonewall Jackson's old corps. Early then led a raid all the way to the outskirts of Washington on July 11 and 12 before being driven back to Virginia. Union cavalry under Philip Sheridan inflicted considerable damage on Confederate resources in Virginia—including the mortal wounding of Jeb Stuart in the battle of Yellow Tavern on May 11—but again failed to strike a crippling blow. In the North, frustration set in over failure to win the quick, decisive victory the public had expected in April.

The Atlanta Campaign

In Georgia, Sherman's army seemed to have accomplished more at less cost than Grant had in Virginia, but there too Union efforts had bogged down in apparent stalemate by August. The strategy and tactics of both Sherman and Johnston in Georgia contrasted with those of Grant and Lee in Virginia. Sherman forced Johnston south toward Atlanta by constantly flanking him to the Union right, generally without bloody battles. Grant constantly forced Lee back by flanking moves to the Union left, but only after bloody battles. By the end of June, Sherman had advanced 80 miles at the cost of 17,000 casualties to Johnston's 14,000—only one-third of the combined losses of Grant and Lee.

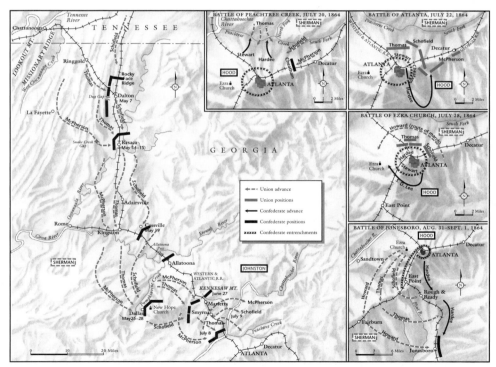

Map 16.7 Campaign for Atlanta, May–September 1864   The main map illustrates Sherman's campaign of maneuver that forced Johnston back to Atlanta with relatively few battles. The first three inset maps show the Confederate counterattacks launched by Hood and the fourth shows how the Union army got astride the last two railroads entering Atlanta from the south and forced Hood to evacuate the city.

Davis grew alarmed by Johnston's apparent willingness to yield territory without a fight. Sherman again flanked the Confederate defenses (after a failed attack) at Kennesaw Mountain in early July. He crossed the Chattahoochee River and drove Johnston back to Peachtree Creek less than five miles from Atlanta. Fearing that Johnston would abandon the city, on July 17, Davis replaced him with John Bell Hood.

A fighting general from Lee's army who had lost a leg at Chickamauga, Hood immediately prepared to counterattack against the Yankees. He did so three times, in late July. Each time, the Confederates reeled back in defeat, suffering a total of 15,000 casualties to Sherman's 6,000. At last, Hood retreated into the formidable earthworks ringing Atlanta and launched no more attacks, although his army did manage to keep Sherman's cavalry and infantry from taking the two railroads leading into Atlanta from the south. Like Grant at Petersburg, Sherman seemed to settle down for a siege.

Peace Overtures

By August, the Confederate strategy of attrition seemed to be working. Union casualties on all fronts during the preceding three months totaled a staggering 110,000—double the number for any comparable period of the war. "Who shall revive the withered hopes that bloomed at the opening of Grant's campaign?" asked the leading Democratic newspaper, the *New York World.* "STOP THE WAR!" shouted Democratic headlines. "All are tired of this damnable tragedy."

Even Republicans joined the chorus of despair. "Our bleeding, bankrupt, almost dying country longs for peace," wrote Horace Greeley of the New York *Tribune.* Greeley became involved in abortive "peace negotiations" spawned by Confederate agents in Canada. Those agents convinced Greeley that they carried peace overtures from Davis, but Lincoln, aware that Davis's condition for peace was Confederate independence, was skeptical. Still, given the mood of the North in midsummer 1864, Lincoln could not reject any opportunity to stop the bloodshed. He deputized Greeley to meet with the Confederate agents in Niagara Falls on the Canadian side of the border. At almost the same time (mid-July), two other Northerners met under a flag of truce with Davis in Richmond. Lincoln had carefully instructed them—and Greeley—that his conditions for peace were "restoration of the Union and abandonment of slavery."

Davis would no more accept those terms than Lincoln would accept his. Although neither of the peace contacts came to anything, the Confederates gained a propaganda victory by claiming that Lincoln's terms had been the only obstacle to peace. Northern Democrats ignored the Southern refusal to accept reunion as a condition of peace and focused on the slavery issue as the sole stumbling block. "Tens of thousands of white men must yet bite the dust to allay the negro mania of the President," ran a typical Democratic editorial. By August, even staunch Republicans such as national party chairman Henry Raymond and his associate Thurlow Weed were convinced that "the desire for peace" and the impression that Lincoln "is fighting not for the Union but for the abolition of slavery" made his reelection "an impossibility." Lincoln thought so, too. "I am going to be beaten," he told a friend in August, "and unless some great change takes place, *badly* beaten."

Lincoln faced enormous pressure to drop emancipation as a condition of peace so the onus could be shifted to Jefferson Davis's insistence on Confederate independence. Lincoln refused to yield. He would rather lose the election than go back on the promise he had made in the Emancipation Proclamation. "No human power can subdue this rebellion without using the Emancipation lever as I have done," he told weak-kneed Republicans. Some 130,000 black soldiers and sailors were fighting for the Union. They would not do so if they thought the North intended to forsake them:

> If they stake their lives for us they must be prompted by the strongest motive . . . the promise of freedom. And the promise being made, must be kept. . . . There have been men who proposed to me to return to slavery the[se] black warriors. . . . I should be damned in time & eternity for so doing. The world shall know that I will keep my faith to friends and enemies, come what will.

At the end of August, the Democrats nominated McClellan for president. The platform on which he ran declared that "after four years of failure to restore the Union by the experiment of war . . . [we] demand that immediate efforts be made for a cessation of hostilities." Southerners were jubilant. Democratic victory on that platform, said the *Charleston Mercury*, "must lead to peace and our independence [if] for the next two months *we hold our own and prevent military success by our foes.*"

The Prisoner-Exchange Controversy

The Democratic platform also condemned the Lincoln administration's "shameful disregard" of prisoners of war in Confederate prison camps. This raised another contentious matter. By midsummer 1864, the plight of Union and Confederate captives had become one of the most bitter issues of the war. The upcoming presidential election and the generally worse conditions in Southern prisons made it mainly a Northern political issue.

In 1862, the Union and Confederate armed forces had signed a cartel for the exchange of prisoners captured in battle. The arrangement had worked reasonably well for a year, making large prison camps unnecessary. When the Union army began to organize regiments of former slaves, however, the Confederate government announced that if they were captured, they and their white officers would be put to death for the crime of fomenting slave insurrections. In practice, the Confederate government did not enforce this policy because Lincoln threatened retaliation on Confederate prisoners of war if it did so, but Confederate troops sometimes murdered black soldiers and their officers as they tried to surrender—most notably at Fort Pillow, a Union garrison on the Mississippi north of Memphis, where cavalry commanded by Nathan Bedford Forrest slaughtered scores of black (and some white) prisoners on April 12, 1864.

In most cases, Confederate officers returned captured black soldiers to slavery or put them to hard labor on Southern fortifications. Expressing outrage at this treatment of soldiers wearing the United States uniform, the Lincoln administration in 1863 suspended the exchange of prisoners until the Confederacy agreed to treat white and black prisoners alike. The Confederacy refused. The South would "die in the last ditch," said the Confederate exchange agent, before "giving up the right to send slaves back to slavery as property recaptured."

There matters stood as the heavy fighting of 1864 poured many thousands of captured soldiers into hastily contrived prison compounds that quickly became death camps. Prisoners were subjected to overcrowding, poor sanitation, contaminated water, scanty rations, inadequate medical facilities, and exposure to deep-South summer heat and northern winter cold. The suffering of Northern prisoners was especially acute, because the deterioration of the Southern economy made it hard to feed and clothe even Confederate soldiers and civilians, let alone Yankee prisoners. Nearly 16 percent of all Union soldiers held in Southern prison camps died, compared with 12 percent of Confederate soldiers in Northern camps. Andersonville was the most notorious hellhole. A stockade camp of 26 acres with neither huts nor tents, designed to accommodate 15,000 prisoners, it held 33,000 in August 1864. They died at the rate of more than 100 per day. Altogether, 13,000 Union soldiers died at Andersonville.

The suffering of Union prisoners brought heavy pressure on the Lincoln administration to renew exchanges, but the Confederates would not budge on the question of exchanging black soldiers. After a series of battles on the Richmond–Petersburg front in September 1864, Lee proposed an informal exchange of prisoners. Grant agreed, on condition that black soldiers captured in the fighting be included "the same as white soldiers." Lee replied that "negroes belonging to our citizens are not considered subjects of exchange and were not included in my proposition." No exchange, then, responded Grant. The Union government was "bound to secure to all persons received into her armies the rights due to soldiers." Lincoln backed this policy. He would not sacrifice the principle of equal treatment of black prisoners, even though local Republican leaders warned that many in the North "will work and vote against the President, because they think sympathy with a few negroes, also captured, is the cause of a refusal" to exchange prisoners.

The Issue of Black Soldiers in the Confederate Army

During the winter of 1864–65, the Confederate government quietly abandoned its refusal to exchange black prisoners, and exchanges resumed. One reason for this reversal was a Confederate decision to recruit slaves to fight for the South. Two years earlier, Davis had denounced the North's arming of freed slaves as "the most execrable measure recorded in the history of guilty man." Ironically, a few black laborers and body servants with Southern armies had taken up arms in the heat of battle and had unofficially fought alongside their masters against the Yankees. By February 1865, Southern armies were desperate for manpower, and slaves constituted the only remaining reserve. Supported by Lee's powerful influence, Davis pressed the Confederate Congress to enact a bill for recruitment of black soldiers. The assumption that any slaves who fought for the South would have to be granted freedom generated bitter opposition to the measure. "What did we go to war for, if not to protect our property?" asked a Virginia senator. By three votes in the House and one in the Senate, the Confederate Congress finally passed the bill on March 13, 1865. Before any Southern black regiments could be organized, however, the war ended.

Lincoln's Reelection and the End of the Confederacy

Focus Question
Why did Lincoln expect in August 1864 to be defeated for reelection? What changed to enable him to win reelection by a substantial margin?

Despite Republican fears, battlefield events, rather than political controversies, had the strongest impact on U.S. voters in 1864. In effect, the election became a referendum on whether to continue fighting for unconditional victory. Within days after the Democratic national convention had declared the war a failure, the military situation changed dramatically.

The Capture of Atlanta

After a month of apparent stalemate on the Atlanta front, Sherman's army again made a large movement by the right flank to attack the last rail link into Atlanta from the south. At the battle of Jonesboro on August 31 and September 1, Sherman's men captured the railroad. Hood abandoned Atlanta to save his army. On September 3, Sherman sent a jaunty telegram to Washington: "Atlanta is ours, and fairly won."

This news had an enormous impact on the election. "VICTORY!" blazoned Republican headlines. "IS THE WAR A FAILURE? OLD ABE'S REPLY TO THE DEMOCRATIC CONVENTION." A New York Republican wrote that the capture of Atlanta, "coming at this political crisis, is the greatest event of the war." The *Richmond Examiner* glumly concurred. The fall of Atlanta, it declared, "came in the very nick of time [to] save the party of Lincoln from irretrievable ruin."

The Shenandoah Valley

If Atlanta was not enough to brighten the prospects for Lincoln's reelection, events in Virginia's Shenandoah Valley were. After Early's raid through the valley all the way to Washington in July, Grant put Philip Sheridan in charge of a reinforced Army of the Shenandoah and told him to "go after Early and follow him to the death." Sheridan infused the same spirit into the three infantry corps of the Army of the Shenandoah that he had previously imbued in his cavalry. On September 19, they attacked Early's force near Winchester, and after a day-long battle sent the Confederates flying to the south. Sheridan pursued them, attacking again on September 22 at Fisher's Hill 20 miles south of Winchester. Early's line collapsed, and his routed army fled 60 more miles southward.

Early's retreat enabled Sheridan to carry out the second part of his assignment in the Shenandoah Valley, which had twice served as a Confederate route of invasion and whose farms helped feed Confederate armies. Sheridan now set about destroying the valley's crops and mills so thoroughly that "crows flying over it for the balance of the season will have to carry their provender with them." Sheridan boasted that by the time he was through, "the Valley, from Winchester up to Staunton, ninety-two miles, will have little in it for man or beast."

But Jubal Early was not yet willing to give up. Reinforced by a division from Lee, on October 19 he launched a dawn attack across Cedar Creek, 15 miles south of Winchester.

He caught the Yankees by surprise and drove them back in disorder. At the time of the attack, Sheridan was at Winchester, returning to his army from Washington, where he had gone to confer on future strategy. He jumped onto his horse and sped to the battlefield in a ride that became celebrated in poetry and legend. By sundown, Sheridan's charisma and tactical leadership had turned the battle from a Union defeat into another Confederate rout. The battle of Cedar Creek ended Confederate power in the valley.

Sherman's and Sheridan's victories ensured Lincoln's reelection on November 8 by a majority of 212 to 21 in the electoral college. Soldiers played a notable role in the balloting. Every Northern state except three whose legislatures were controlled by Democrats had passed laws allowing absentee voting by soldiers. Seventy-eight percent of the military vote went to Lincoln—compared with 54 percent of the civilian vote. The men who were doing the fighting had sent a clear message that they meant to finish the job.

From Atlanta to the Sea

Many Southerners got the message, but not Davis. The Confederacy remained "as erect and defiant as ever," he told his Congress in November 1864. "Nothing has changed in the purpose of its Government, in the indomitable valor of its troops, or in the unquenchable spirit of its people." It was this last-ditch resistance that Sherman set out to break in his famous march from Atlanta to the sea.

Sherman had concluded that "We are not only fighting hostile armies, but a hostile people." Defeat of the Confederate armies was not enough to win the war; the railroads, factories, and farms that supported those armies must also be destroyed. The will of the civilians who sustained the war must be crushed. Sherman expressed more bluntly than anyone else the meaning of total war and was ahead of his time in his understanding of psychological warfare. "We cannot change the hearts of those people of the South," he said, "but we can make war so terrible and make them so sick of war that generations would pass away before they would again appeal to it."

In Tennessee and Mississippi, Sherman's troops had burned everything of military value within their reach. Now Sherman proposed to do the same in Georgia. He urged Grant to let him march through the heart of Georgia, living off the land and destroying all resources not needed by his army—the same policy Sheridan was carrying out in the Shenandoah Valley. Grant and Lincoln were reluctant to authorize such a risky move, especially with Hood's army of 40,000 men still intact in northern Alabama. Sherman assured them that he would send George Thomas to take command of a force of 60,000 men in Tennessee, who would be more than a match for Hood. With another 60,000, Sherman could "move through Georgia, smashing things to the sea. . . . I can make the march, and make Georgia howl!"

Lincoln and Grant finally consented. On November 16, Sherman's avengers marched out of Atlanta after burning a third of the city, including some nonmilitary property. Southward they marched 280 miles to Savannah, wrecking everything in their path that could by any stretch of the imagination be considered of military value.

The Battles of Franklin and Nashville

They encountered little resistance. Instead of chasing Sherman, Hood invaded Tennessee with the hope of recovering that state for the Confederacy, a disastrous campaign that virtually destroyed his army. On November 30, the Confederates attacked part of the Union force at Franklin, a town 20 miles south of Nashville. The slaughter claimed no fewer than 12 Confederate generals and 54 regimental commanders as casualties. Instead of retreating, Hood moved on to Nashville, where on December 15 and 16, Thomas launched an attack that almost wiped out the Army of Tennessee. Its remnants retreated to Mississippi, where Hood resigned in January 1865.

Fort Fisher and Sherman's March through the Carolinas

News of Hood's defeat produced, in the words of a Southern diarist, "the darkest and most dismal day" of the Confederacy's short history, but worse was yet to come. Lee's army in Virginia drew its dwindling supplies overland from the Carolinas and through the port of Wilmington, North Carolina, the only city still accessible to blockade runners. Massive Fort Fisher guarded the mouth of the Cape Fear River below Wilmington, its big guns keeping blockade ships at bay and protecting the runners. The Union navy had long wanted to attack Fort Fisher, but the diversion of ships and troops to the long, futile campaign against Charleston had delayed the effort. In January 1865, though, the largest armada of the war—58 ships with 627 guns—pounded Fort Fisher for two days, disabling most of its big guns. Army troops and marines landed and stormed the fort, capturing it on January 15. That ended the blockade running, and Sherman soon put an end to supplies from the Carolinas as well.

At the end of January, Sherman's soldiers headed north from Savannah, eager to take revenge on South Carolina, which to their mind had started the war. Here, they made even less distinction between civilian and military property than they had in Georgia and left even less of Columbia standing than they had of Atlanta. Seemingly invincible, Sherman's army pushed into North Carolina and brushed aside the force that Joseph E. Johnston had assembled to stop them. The devastation left in their wake appalled Confederates. "All is gloom, despondency, and inactivity," wrote a South Carolinian. "Our army is demoralized and the people panic stricken. To fight longer seems to be madness."

But the war would not end until the Confederate armies surrendered, as Lincoln made clear in his second inaugural address on March 4, 1865. In the best-known words from that address, he urged a binding up of the nation's wounds "with malice toward none [and] charity for all." Even more significant, given that the conflict still raged, were these words:

> American Slavery is one of those offences which, in the providence of God . . . He now wills to remove [through] this terrible war, as the woe due to those by whom the offence came. . . . Fondly do we hope—fervently do we pray—that this mighty scourge of war may speedily pass away. Yet if God wills that it continue, until all the wealth piled by the bondman's two hundred and fifty years of unrequited toil shall be sunk, and until every drop of blood drawn with the lash, shall be paid by another drawn with the sword, as was said three thousand years ago, so still it must be said "the judgments of the Lord, are true and righteous altogether."

Casualties in Civil War Armies and Navies   Confederate records are incomplete; the Confederate data listed here are therefore estimates. The actual Confederate totals were probably higher.

	Killed and Mortally Wounded in Combat	Died of Disease	Died in Prison	Miscellaneous Deaths*	Total Deaths	Wounded, Not Mortally	Total Casualties
Union	111,904	197,388	30,192	24,881	364,345	277,401	641,766
Confederate (estimated)	94,000	140,000	26,000	No Estimates	260,000	195,000	455,000
Both Armies (estimated)	205,904	337,388	56,192	24,881	624,365	472,401	1,096,766

*Accidents, drownings, causes not stated, etc.

The Road to Appomattox

The Army of Northern Virginia was now the only entity that kept the Confederacy alive, and it was on the verge of disintegration. Scores of its soldiers were deserting every day. On April 1, Sheridan's cavalry and an infantry corps smashed the right flank of Lee's line at Five Forks and cut off the last railroad into Petersburg. The next day, Grant attacked all along the line and forced Lee to abandon both Petersburg and Richmond. As the Confederate government fled its capital, its army set fire to all the military stores it could not carry. The fires spread and destroyed more of Richmond than the Northern troops had destroyed of Atlanta or Columbia.

Lee's starving men limped westward, hoping to turn south and join the remnants of Johnston's army in North Carolina. Sheridan's cavalry raced ahead and cut them off at Appomattox, 90 miles from Petersburg, on April 8. When the weary Confederates tried a breakout attack the next morning, their first probe revealed solid ranks of Union infantry arrayed behind the cavalry. It was the end. "There is nothing left for me to do," said Lee, "but to go and see General Grant, and I would rather die a thousand deaths." Lee met with Grant at the house of Wilmer McLean, who in 1861 had lived near Manassas, where a shell had crashed through his kitchen roof during the first battle of Bull Run. McLean had moved to the remote village of Appomattox to escape the war, only to have its final drama played out in his parlor. There, the son of an Ohio tanner dictated surrender terms to a scion of one of Virginia's First Families.

The terms were generous. Thirty thousand captured Confederates were allowed to go home on condition that they promise never again to take up arms against the United States. After completing the surrender formalities on April 9, Grant introduced Lee to his staff, which

Library of Congress, Prints and Photographs Division

Abraham Lincoln in 1865   This is the last photograph of Lincoln, taken on April 10, 1865, four days before his assassination. Four years of war had left their mark on the 56-year-old president; note the lines of strain, fatigue, and sadness in his face.

included Colonel Ely Parker, a Seneca Indian. As Lee shook hands with Parker, he stared for a moment at Parker's dark features and said: "I am glad to see one real American here." Parker replied solemnly: "We are all Americans." And indeed they now were.

The Assassination of Lincoln

Wild celebrations broke out in the North at news of the fall of Richmond, followed soon by news of Appomattox. Almost overnight, the celebrations turned to mourning. On the evening of April 14, the care-worn Abraham Lincoln sought to relax by attending a comedy at Ford's Theatre. In the middle of the play, John Wilkes Booth broke into Lincoln's box and shot the president fatally in the head. A prominent actor, Booth was a native of Maryland and a frustrated, unstable egotist who hated Lincoln for what he had done to Booth's beloved South. As he jumped from Lincoln's box to the stage and escaped out a back door, he shouted Virginia's state motto at the stunned audience: "Sic semper tyrannis" ("Thus always to tyrants").

Lincoln's death in the early morning of April 15 produced an outpouring of grief throughout the North and among newly freed slaves in the South. The martyred president did not live to see the culmination of his great achievement in leading the nation to a victory that preserved its existence and abolished slavery. Within 11 days after Lincoln's death, his assassin was trapped and killed in a burning barn in Virginia (April 26). The remaining Confederate armies surrendered one after another (April 26, May 4, May 26, June 23), and Union cavalry captured the fleeing Jefferson Davis in Georgia (May 10). The trauma of civil war was over, but the problems of peace and reconstruction had just begun.

Conclusion

Northern victory in the Civil War resolved two fundamental questions of liberty and power left unresolved by the Revolution of 1776 and the Constitution of 1789: (1) whether this fragile republican experiment in federalism called the United States would survive as one nation; and (2) whether that nation, founded on a charter of liberty, would continue to exist as the largest slaveholding country in the world. Before 1861, the question of whether a state could secede from the Union had remained open. Eleven states did secede, but their defeat in a war that cost 625,000 lives resolved the issue: Since 1865, no state has seriously threatened secession. And in 1865, the adoption of the 13th Amendment to the Constitution confirmed the supreme power of the national government to abolish slavery and ensure the liberty of all Americans.

The Civil War also accomplished a regional transfer of power from South to North. From 1800 to 1860, the slave states had used their leverage in the Jeffersonian Republican and Jacksonian Democratic parties to control national politics most of the time. A Southern slaveholder was president of the United States during two-thirds of the years from 1789 to 1861. Most congressional leaders and Supreme Court justices during that period were Southerners.

In the 50 years after 1861, no native of a Southern state was elected president, only one served as Speaker of the House and none as president pro tem of the Senate, and only 5 of the 26 Supreme Court justices appointed during that half-century were from the South. In 1860, the South's share of the national wealth was 30 percent; in 1870, it was 12 percent.

The institutions and ideology of a plantation society and a caste system that had dominated half the country before 1861 went down with a great crash in 1865—to be replaced by the institutions and ideology of free-labor capitalism. Once feared as the gravest threat to liberty, the power of the national government sustained by a large army had achieved the greatest triumph of liberty in American history. With victory and peace in 1865, the reunited nation turned its attention to the issue of equality.

SUGGESTED READINGS

Several studies offer important information and insights about questions of strategy and command in military operations: **Joseph G. Glatthaar**, *Partners in Command: The Relationships between Leaders in the Civil War* (1993); **Richard M. McMurry**, *Two Great Rebel Armies* (1989); **Michael C. Adams**, *Our Masters the Rebels: A Speculation on Union Military Defeat in the East, 1861–1865* (1978), reissued under the title *Fighting for Defeat* (1992); **Mark Grimsley**, *The Hard Hand of War: Union Military Policy toward Southern Civilians, 1861–1865* (1995); and **Gary W. Gallagher**, *The Confederate War* (1997). Excellent studies of the Emancipation Proclamation and the 13th Amendment are **Allen C. Guelzo**, *Lincoln's Emancipation Proclamation* (2004) and **Michael Vorenberg**, *Final Freedom: The Civil War, the Abolition of Slavery, and the Thirteenth Amendment* (2001).

Of the many books about black soldiers in the Union army, the most useful is **Joseph T. Glatthaar**, *Forged in Battle: The Civil War Alliance of Black Soldiers and White Officers* (1990). The Confederate debate about enlisting and freeing slave soldiers is chronicled in **Robert Durden**, *The Gray and the Black: The Confederate Debate on Emancipation* (1972) and **Bruce Levine**, *Confederate Emancipation: Southern Plans to Free and Arm Slaves During the Civil War* (2006). Conscription in the Confederacy and Union is treated in **Albert B. Moore**, *Conscription and Conflict in the Confederacy* (1924), and **James W. Geary**, *We Need Men: The Union Draft in the Civil War* (1991).

For the draft riots in New York, see **Adrian Cook**, *The Armies of the Streets: The New York Draft Riots of 1863* (1974). The best study of the civil liberties issue in the North is **Mark E. Neely, Jr.**, *The Fate of Liberty: Abraham Lincoln and Civil Liberties* (1990), and the same author has covered the same issue in the Confederacy in *Southern Rights: Political Prisoners and the Myth of Confederate Constitutionalism* (1999). For Civil War medicine, **Alfred Jay Bollet**, *Civil War Medicine: Challenges and Triumphs* (2002) is indispensable. A succinct account of the emancipation issue is **Ira Berlin, et al.**, *Slaves No More: Three Essays on Emancipation and the Civil War* (1992).

The activities of women in the U.S. Sanitary Commission, as spies, and even as soldiers, are covered in **Jeanie Attie**, *Patriotic Toil: Northern Women and the Civil War* (1998); and **Elizabeth D. Leonard**, *All the Daring of a Soldier: Women of the Civil War Armies* (1999).

Visit the Liberty Equality Power Companion Web site for resources specific to this textbook: http://www.thomsonedu.com/history/murrin

Also find self-tests and additional resources at ThomsonNOW. ThomsonNOW is an integrated online suite of services and resources with proven ease of use and efficient paths to success, delivering the results you want—NOW!

www.thomsonedu.com/login/

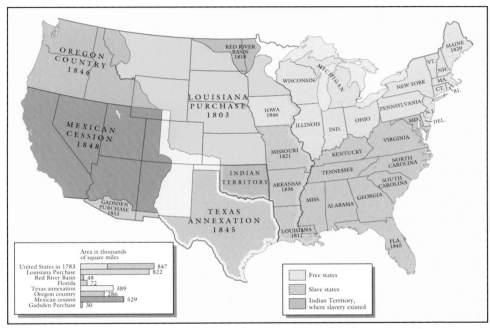

Map 13.1   Free and Slave States and Territories, 1848   Two developments of critical importance to the controversy over the expansion of slavery in the 1840s and 1850s are illustrated by this map: the larger number of slave than free states entering the Union from the territories acquired from France (Louisiana Purchase) and Spain (Florida) and the huge amount of new territory added by the acquisition of Texas and the Southwest from Mexico and the settlement of the Oregon boundary in the 1840s. View an animated version of this map or related maps at http://www.thomsonedu.com/history/murrin.

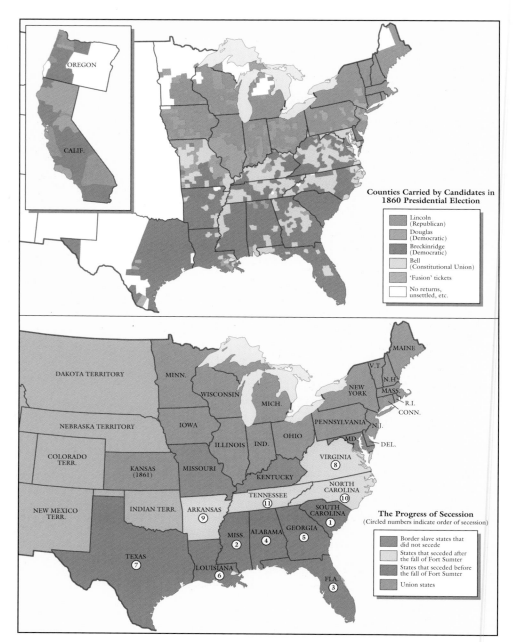

Map 15.1 Election of 1860 and Southern Secession Note the similarity of the geographical voting patterns in the upper map to the map on p. 532. Another striking pattern shows the correlation between the vote for Breckinridge (upper map) and the first seven states to secede (lower map).

View an animated version of this map or related maps at http://www.thomsonedu.com/history/murrin.

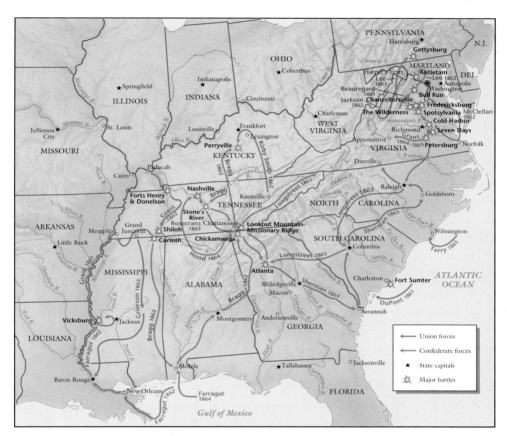

Map 15.2   Principal Military Campaigns of the Civil War   This map vividly illustrates the contrast between the vast distances over which the armies fought in the western theater of the war and the concentrated campaigns of the Army of the Potomac and the Army of Northern Virginia in the East.

View an animated version of this map or related maps at http://www.thomsonedu.com/history/murrin.

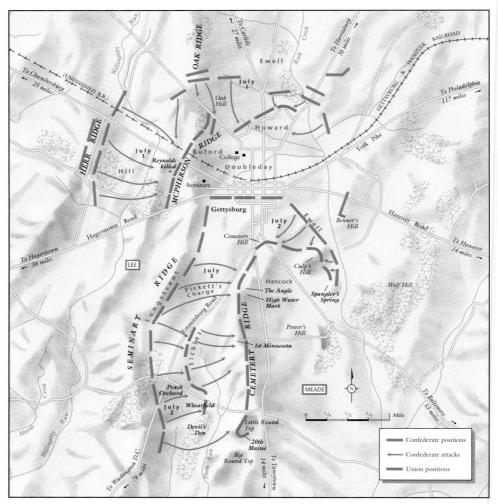

Map 16.3   Battle of Gettysburg, July 1–3, 1863   On July 2 and 3, the Union army had the advantage of interior lines at Gettysburg, which enabled General Meade to shift reinforcements from his right on Culp's Hill to his left near Little Round Top over a much shorter distance than Confederate reinforcements from one flank to the other would have to travel.

Reconstruction, 1863–1877

From the beginning of the Civil War, the North fought to "reconstruct" the Union. Lincoln first attempted to restore the Union as it had existed before 1861, but once the abolition of slavery became a Northern war aim, the Union could never be reconstructed on its old foundations. Instead, it must experience a "new birth of freedom," as Lincoln had said at the dedication of the military cemetery at Gettysburg.

But precisely what did "a new birth of freedom" mean? At the very least, it meant the end of slavery. The slave states would be reconstructed on a free-labor basis. But what would liberty look like for the 4 million freed slaves? Would they become citizens equal to their former masters in the eyes of the law? Would they have the right to vote? Should Confederate leaders and soldiers be punished for treason? On what terms should the Confederate states return to the Union? What would be the powers of the states and of the national government in a reconstructed Union?

Wartime Reconstruction

Lincoln pondered the problems of Reconstruction long and hard. At first he feared that whites in the South would never extend equal rights to the freed slaves. After all, even most Northern states denied full civil equality to the few black people within their borders. In 1862, Lincoln encouraged freedpeople to emigrate to all-black countries such as Haiti, where they would have a chance to get ahead without having to face the racism of whites. Black leaders, abolitionists, and many Republicans objected to that policy. Black people were Americans, they asserted. Why should they not have the rights of American citizens instead of being urged to leave the country?

Lincoln eventually acknowledged the logic and justice of that view, but in beginning the process of reconstruction, he first reached out to Southern *whites* whose allegiance to the Confederacy was lukewarm. On December 8, 1863, Lincoln issued his Proclamation of Amnesty and Reconstruction, which offered presidential pardon to Southern whites (with the exception of Confederate government officials and high-ranking military officers) who took an oath of allegiance to the United States and accepted the abolition of slavery. In any state where the number of white males aged 21 or older who took this oath equaled 10 percent of the number of voters in 1860, that nucleus could reestablish a state government to which Lincoln promised presidential recognition.

CHRONOLOGY

1863	Lincoln issues Proclamation of Amnesty and Reconstruction
1864	Congress passes Wade-Davis bill; Lincoln kills it by pocket veto
1865	Congress establishes Freedmen's Bureau • Andrew Johnson becomes president, announces his reconstruction plan • Southern states enact Black Codes • Congress refuses to seat Southern congressmen elected under Johnson's plan
1866	Congress passes civil rights bill and expands Freedmen's Bureau over Johnson's vetoes • Race riots in Memphis and New Orleans • Congress approves 14th Amendment • Republicans increase congressional majority in fall elections
1867	Congress passes Reconstruction acts over Johnson's vetoes • Congress passes Tenure of Office Act over Johnson's veto
1868	Most Southern senators and representatives readmitted to Congress under congressional plan of Reconstruction • Andrew Johnson impeached but not convicted • Ulysses S. Grant elected president • 14th Amendment is ratified
1870	15th Amendment is ratified
1871	Congress passes Ku Klux Klan Act
1872	Liberal Republicans defect from party • Grant wins reelection
1873	Economic depression begins with the Panic
1874	Democrats win control of House of Representatives
1875	Democrats implement Mississippi Plan • Congress passes civil rights act
1876	Centennial celebration in Philadelphia • Disputed presidential election causes constitutional crisis
1877	Compromise of 1877 installs Rutherford B. Hayes as president • Hayes withdraws troops from South
1883	Supreme Court declares civil rights act of 1875 unconstitutional

Because the war was still raging, this policy could be carried out only where Union troops controlled substantial portions of a Confederate state: Louisiana, Arkansas, and Tennessee in early 1864. Nevertheless, Lincoln hoped that once the process had begun in those areas, it might snowball as Union military victories convinced more and more Confederates that their cause was hopeless. In the end, those military victories were long delayed, and in most parts of the South, reconstruction did not begin until 1865.

Another problem that slowed the process was growing opposition within Lincoln's own party. Many Republicans believed that white men who had fought *against* the Union should not be rewarded with restoration of their political rights while black men who had fought *for* the Union were denied those rights. The Proclamation of Reconstruction had stated that any provision which may be adopted by [a reconstructed] State government in relation to the freed people of such State, which shall recognize and declare their permanent freedom, provide for their education, and which may yet be consistent, as a temporary arrangement, with their present condition as a laboring, landless, and homeless class, will not be objected to by the national Executive.

This seemed to mean that white landowners and former slaveholders could adopt labor regulations and other measures to control former slaves, so long as they recognized their freedom and made minimal provision for their education.

Radical Republicans and Reconstruction

These changes were radical advances over slavery, but for many Republicans they were not radical enough. Led by Thaddeus Stevens in the House and Charles Sumner in the Senate, the radical Republicans wanted to go much further. If the freedpeople were landless, they said, provide them with land by confiscating the plantations of leading Confederates as punishment for treason. Radical Republicans also distrusted oaths of allegiance sworn by ex-Confederates. Rather than simply restoring the old ruling class to power, asked Charles Sumner, why not give freed slaves the vote, to provide a genuinely loyal nucleus of supporters in the South?

These radical positions did not command a majority of Congress in 1864. Yet the experience of Louisiana, the first state to reorganize under Lincoln's more moderate policy, convinced even nonradical Republicans to block Lincoln's program. With the protection of Union soldiers in the occupied portion of Louisiana (New Orleans and several parishes in the southern half of the state), enough white men took the oath of allegiance to satisfy Lincoln's conditions. They adopted a new state constitution and formed a government that abolished slavery and provided a school system for blacks. But despite Lincoln's private appeal to the new government to grant literate blacks and black Union soldiers the right to vote, the reconstructed Louisiana legislature chose not to do so. It also authorized planters to enforce restrictive labor policies on black plantation workers. Louisiana's actions alienated a majority of congressional Republicans, who refused to admit representatives and senators from the "reconstructed" state.

At the same time, though, Congress failed to enact a reconstruction policy of its own. This was not for lack of trying. In fact, both houses passed the Wade-Davis reconstruction bill (named for Senator Benjamin Wade of Ohio and Representative Henry Winter Davis of Maryland) in July 1864. That bill did not **enfranchise** blacks, but it did impose such stringent loyalty requirements on Southern whites that few of them could take the required oath. Lincoln therefore vetoed it.

Lincoln's action infuriated many Republicans. Wade and Davis published a blistering "manifesto" denouncing the president. This bitter squabble threatened for a time to destroy Lincoln's chances of being reelected. Union military success in fall 1864, however, combined with sober second thoughts about the consequences of a Democratic electoral victory, reunited the Republicans behind Lincoln. The collapse of Confederate military resistance the following spring set the stage for compromise between the president and Congress on a policy for the postwar South. Two days after Appomattox, Lincoln promised that he would soon announce such a policy, which probably would have included voting rights for some blacks and stronger measures to protect their civil rights. But three days later, Lincoln was assassinated.

Andrew Johnson and Reconstruction

Focus Question
What were the positions of Presidents Abraham Lincoln and Andrew Johnson and of the moderate and radical Republicans in Congress on the issues of restoring the South to the Union and protecting the rights of freed slaves?

In 1864, Republicans had adopted the name Union Party to attract the votes of War Democrats and border-state Unionists who could not bring themselves to vote Republican. For the same reason, they also nominated Andrew Johnson of Tennessee as Lincoln's running mate.

Of "poor white" heritage, Johnson had clawed his way up in the rough-and-tumble politics of east Tennessee. This region of small farms and few slaves held little love for the planters who controlled the state. Andrew Johnson denounced the planters as "stuck-up aristocrats" who had no empathy with the Southern yeomen for whom Johnson became a self-appointed spokesman. Johnson, although a Democrat, was the only senator from a seceding state who refused to support the Confederacy. For this stance, the Republicans rewarded him with the vice presidential nomination, hoping to attract the votes of pro-war Democrats and upper-South Unionists.

Booth's bullet therefore elevated to the presidency a man who still thought of himself as primarily a Democrat and a Southerner. The trouble this might cause in a party that was mostly Republican and Northern was not immediately apparent, however. In fact, Johnson's enmity toward the "stuck-up aristocrats" whom he blamed for leading the South into secession prompted him to utter dire threats against "traitors." "Treason is a crime and must be made odious," he said, soon after becoming president. "Traitors must be impoverished. . . . They must not only be punished, but their social power must be destroyed."

Radical Republicans liked the sound of this pronouncement. It seemed to promise the type of reconstruction they favored—one that would deny political power to ex-Confederates and would enfranchise blacks. They envisioned a coalition between these new black voters and the small minority of Southern whites who had never supported the Confederacy. These men could be expected to vote Republican. Republican governments in Southern states would guarantee freedom and would pass laws to provide civil rights and economic opportunity for freed slaves. Not incidentally, they would also strengthen the Republican Party nationally.

Johnson's Policy

From a combination of pragmatic, partisan, and idealistic motives, therefore, Radical Republicans prepared to implement a progressive reconstruction policy. But Johnson unexpectedly refused to cooperate. Instead of calling Congress into special session, he moved ahead on his own. On May 29, 1865, Johnson issued two proclamations. The first provided a blanket **amnesty** for all but the highest-ranking Confederate officials and military officers, and those ex-Confederates with taxable property worth $20,000 or more—the "stuck-up aristocrats." The second named a provisional governor for North Carolina and directed him to call an election of delegates to frame a new state constitution. Only white men who had received amnesty and taken an oath of allegiance could vote. Similar proclamations soon followed for other former Confederate states. Johnson's policy was clear: He would exclude both blacks and upper-class whites from the reconstruction process. The backbone of the new South would be yeomen whites who, like himself, had remained steadfastly loyal to the Union, along with those who now proclaimed themselves loyal.

Although at first many Republicans supported Johnson's policy, the radicals were dismayed. They feared that restricting the vote to whites would lead to oppression of the newly freed slaves and restoration of the old power structure in the South. They began to sense that Johnson (who had owned slaves) was as dedicated to white

Andrew Johnson and Frederick Douglass   By 1866, the president and the leading black spokesman for equal rights represented opposite poles in the debate about Reconstruction. Johnson wanted to bring the South back into the Union on the basis of white suffrage; Douglass wanted black men to be granted the right to vote. Johnson's resistance to this policy as Republicans tried to enact it was a factor in his impeachment two years later.

supremacy as any Confederate. "White men alone must govern the South," he told a Democratic senator. After a tense confrontation with a group of black men led by Frederick Douglass, who had visited the White House to urge black suffrage, Johnson told his private secretary: "Those damned sons of bitches thought they had me in a trap! I know that damned Douglass; he's just like any nigger, and he would sooner cut a white man's throat than not."

Moderate Republicans believed that black men should participate to some degree in the reconstruction process, but in 1865 they were not yet prepared to break with the president. They regarded his policy as an "experiment" that would be modified as time went on. "Loyal negroes must not be put down, while disloyal white men are put up," wrote a moderate Republican. "But I am quite willing to see what will come of Mr. Johnson's experiment." If the new Southern state constitutions failed to enfranchise at least literate blacks and those who had fought in the Union army, said another moderate, "the President then will be at liberty to pursue a sterner policy."

Southern Defiance

As it happened, none of the state conventions enfranchised a single black. Some of them even balked at ratifying the 13th Amendment (which abolished slavery). The rhetoric of some white Southerners began to take on a renewed anti-Yankee tone of defiance that sounded like 1861 all over again. Reports from Unionists and army officers in the South told of neo-Confederate violence against blacks and their white sympathizers. Johnson seemed to encourage such activities by his own rhetoric, which sounded increasingly like that of a Southern Democrat, and by allowing the organization of white militia units in the South. "What can be hatched from such an egg," asked a Republican newspaper, "but another rebellion?"

Then there was the matter of presidential pardons. After talking fiercely about punishing traitors, and after excluding several classes of them from his amnesty proclamation, Johnson began to issue special pardons to many ex-Confederates, restoring to them all property and political rights. Moreover, under the new state constitutions, Southern voters were electing hundreds of ex-Confederates to state offices. Even more alarming to Northerners, who thought they had won the war, was the election to Congress of no fewer than nine ex-Confederate congressmen, seven ex-Confederate state officials, four generals, four colonels, and even the former Confederate vice president, Alexander H. Stephens. To apprehensive Republicans, it appeared that the rebels, unable to capture Washington in war, were about to do so in peace.

Somehow the aristocrats and traitors Johnson had denounced in April had taken over the reconstruction process. Instead of weapons, they had resorted to flattering the presidential ego. Thousands of prominent ex-Confederates or their tearful female relatives applied for pardons, confessing the error of their ways and appealing for presidential mercy. Reveling in his power over these once-haughty aristocrats who had disdained him as a humble tailor, Johnson waxed eloquent on his "love, respect, and confidence" toward

Southern whites, for whom he now felt "forbearing and forgiving." More effective, perhaps, was the praise and support Johnson received from leading Northern Democrats. Although the Republicans had placed him on their presidential ticket in 1864, Johnson was after all a Democrat. That party's leaders enticed Johnson with visions of reelection as a Democrat in 1868 if he could manage to reconstruct the South in a manner that would preserve a Democratic majority there.

The Black Codes

That was just what the Republicans feared. Their concern that state governments devoted to white supremacy would reduce the freedpeople to a condition close to slavery was confirmed in fall 1865, when some of those governments enacted "**Black Codes.**"

One of the first tasks of the legislatures of the reconstructed states was to define the rights of 4 million former slaves. The option of treating them exactly like white citizens was scarcely considered. Instead, the states excluded black people from juries and the ballot box, did not permit them to testify against whites in court, banned interracial marriage, and punished blacks more severely than whites for certain crimes. Some states defined any unemployed black person as a vagrant and hired him out to a planter, forbade blacks to lease land, and provided for the apprenticing to whites of black youths who did not have adequate parental support.

These Black Codes aroused anger among Northern Republicans, who saw them as a brazen attempt to reinstate a **quasi-slavery.** "We tell the white men of Mississippi," declared the *Chicago Tribune,* "that the men of the North will convert the State of Mississippi into a frog pond before they will allow such laws to disgrace one foot of the soil in which the bones of our soldiers sleep and over which the flag of freedom waves." And, in fact, the Union army's occupation forces did suspend the implementation of Black Codes that discriminated on racial grounds.

Land and Labor in the Postwar South

The Black Codes, although discriminatory, were designed to address a genuine problem. The end of the war had left black-white relations in the South in a state of limbo. The South's economy was in a shambles. Burned-out plantations, fields growing up in weeds, and railroads without tracks, bridges, or **rolling stock** marked the trail of war. Nearly half of the livestock in the former Confederacy and most other tangible assets except the land had been destroyed. Many people, white as well as black, lived from meal to meal. Law and order broke down in many areas. The war had ended early enough in the spring to allow the planting of at least some food crops, but who would plant and cultivate them? One-quarter of the South's white farmers had been killed in the war; the slaves were slaves no more. "We have nothing left to begin anew with," lamented a South Carolina planter. "I never did a day's work in my life, and I don't know how to begin."

Despite all of this trouble, life went on. Soldiers' widows and their children plowed and planted. Slaveless planters and their wives calloused their hands for the first time. Confederate veterans drifted home and went to work. Former slave owners asked their former slaves to work the land for wages or shares of the crop, and many did so. Others refused, because for them to leave the old place was an essential part of freedom. In slavery times, the only way to become free was to run away, and the impulse to leave the scene of bondage persisted. "You ain't, none o' you, gwinter feel rale free," said a black preacher to his congregation, "till you shakes de dus' ob de Ole Plantashun offen yore feet" (dialect in original source).

Thus the roads were alive with freedpeople who were on the move in summer 1865. Many of them signed on to work at farms just a few miles from their old homes. Others moved into town. Some looked for relatives who had been sold away during slavery or from whom they had been separated during the war. Some wandered aimlessly. Crime increased as people, both blacks and whites, stole food to survive, and as whites organized vigilante groups to discipline blacks and force them to work.

The Freedmen's Bureau

Into this vacuum stepped the U.S. Army and the **Freedmen's Bureau.** Tens of thousands of troops remained in the South as an occupation force until civil government could be restored. The Freedmen's Bureau (its official title was Bureau of Refugees, Freedmen, and Abandoned Lands), created by Congress in March 1865, became the principal agency for overseeing relations between former slaves and owners. Staffed by army officers, the bureau established posts throughout the South to supervise free-labor wage contracts between landowners and freedpeople. The Freedmen's Bureau also issued food rations to 150,000 people daily during 1865, one-third of them to whites. Southern whites viewed the Freedmen's Bureau with hostility. Without it, however, the postwar chaos and devastation in the South would have been much greater—as some whites privately admitted. Bureau agents used their influence with black people to encourage them to sign free-labor contracts and return to work.

In negotiating labor contracts, the bureau tried to establish minimum wages. Lack of money in the South, however, caused many contracts to call for **share wages**—that is, paying workers with shares of the crop. At first, landowners worked their laborers in large groups (called gangs) under direct supervision, but many black workers resented this arrangement as reminiscent of slavery. Thus, a new system evolved, called **sharecropping,** whereby a black family worked a specific piece of land in return for a share of the crop produced on it.

Land for the Landless

Freedpeople, of course, would have preferred to farm their own land. "What's de use of being free if you don't own land enough to be buried in?" asked one black sharecropper. "Might juss as well stay slave all yo' days" (dialect in original). Some black farmers did manage to save up enough money to buy small plots of land. Demobilized black soldiers purchased land with their bounty payments, sometimes pooling their money to buy an

Sharecroppers Working in the Fields   This photograph shows two families of sharecroppers picking cotton. Freed slaves resisted landowners' efforts to work them in gangs as they had in slavery, so the owners rented land to black families in return for a share of the crop. These croppers do not appear to be overjoyed with the new system.

entire plantation on which several black families settled. Northern philanthropists helped some freedmen buy land. Most ex-slaves found the purchase of land impossible. Few of them had money, and even if they did, whites often refused to sell their land because it would mean losing a source of cheap labor and encouraging notions of black independence.

Several Northern radicals proposed legislation to confiscate ex-Confederate land and redistribute it to freedpeople, but those proposals went nowhere. The most promising effort to put thousands of slaves on land of their own also failed. In January 1865, after his march through Georgia, General William T. Sherman had issued a military order setting aside thousands of acres of abandoned plantation land in the Georgia and South Carolina low country for settlement by freed slaves. The army even turned over some of its surplus mules to black farmers. The expectation of **"40 acres and a mule"** excited freedpeople in 1865, but President Johnson's Amnesty Proclamation and his wholesale issuance of pardons restored most of this property to pardoned ex-Confederates. The same thing happened to white-owned land elsewhere in the South. Placed under the temporary care of the Freedmen's Bureau for subsequent possible distribution to freedpeople, by 1866 nearly all of this land had been restored to its former owners by order of President Johnson.

Education

Abolitionists were more successful in helping freedpeople obtain an education. During the war, freedmen's aid societies and missionary societies founded by abolitionists had sent teachers to Union-occupied areas of the South to set up schools for freed slaves. After the war, this effort was expanded with the aid of the Freedmen's Bureau. Two thousand Northern teachers, three-quarters of them women, fanned out into every part of the South. There they trained black teachers to staff first the mission schools and later the public schools established by Reconstruction state governments. After 1870, the missionary societies concentrated more heavily on making higher education available to African Americans. Many of the traditionally black colleges in the South today were founded and supported by their efforts. This education crusade, which the black leader W. E. B. Du Bois described as "the most wonderful peace-battle of the nineteenth century," reduced the Southern black illiteracy rate to 70 percent by 1880 and to 48 percent by 1900.

The Advent of Congressional Reconstruction

Political reconstruction shaped the civil and political rights of freedpeople. By the time Congress met in December 1865, the Republican majority was determined to control the process by which former Confederate states would regain full representation. Congress refused to admit the representatives and senators elected by the former Confederate states under Johnson's reconstruction policy and set up a special committee to formulate new terms. The committee held hearings at which Southern Unionists, freedpeople, and U.S. Army officers testified to abuse and terrorism in the South. Their testimony convinced Republicans of the need for stronger federal intervention to define and protect the civil rights of freedpeople. Many radicals wanted to go further and grant the ballot to black men, who would join with white Unionists and Northern settlers in the South to form a Southern Republican Party.

Most Republicans realized that Northern voters would not support such a radical policy, however. Racism was still strong in the North, where most states denied the right to vote to the few blacks living within their borders. Moderate Republicans feared that Democrats would exploit Northern racism in the congressional elections of 1866 if Congress made black suffrage a cornerstone of Reconstruction. Instead, the special committee decided to draft a constitutional amendment that would encourage Southern states to enfranchise blacks but would not require them to do so.

Schism between President and Congress

Meanwhile, Congress passed two laws to protect the economic and civil rights of freedpeople. The first extended the life of the Freedmen's Bureau and expanded its powers. The second defined freedpeople as citizens with equal legal rights and gave federal courts appellate jurisdiction to enforce those rights. To the dismay of moderates who were trying to heal the widening breach between the president and Congress, Johnson vetoed both measures. He followed this action with an intemperate speech to Democratic supporters in which he denounced Republican leaders as traitors who did not want to restore the Union except on terms that would degrade white Southerners. Democratic newspapers applauded the president for vetoing bills that would "compound our race with niggers, gypsies, and baboons."

The 14th Amendment

Johnson had thrown down the gauntlet to congressional Republicans, and they did not hesitate to take it up. With more than a two-thirds majority in both houses, they passed the Freedmen's Bureau and Civil Rights bills over the president's vetoes. Then, on April 30, 1866, the special committee submitted to Congress its proposed 14th Amendment to the Constitution. After lengthy debate, the amendment received the required two-thirds majority in Congress on June 13 and went to the states for ratification. Section 1 defined all native-born or naturalized persons, including blacks, as American citizens and prohibited the states from abridging the "privileges and immunities" of citizens, from depriving "any person of life, liberty, or property without due process of law," and from denying to any person "the equal protection of the laws." Section 2 gave states the option of either enfranchising black males or losing a proportionate number of congressional seats and electoral votes. Section 3 disqualified a significant number of ex-Confederates from holding federal or state office. Section 4 guaranteed the national debt and repudiated the Confederate debt. Section 5 empowered Congress to enforce the 14th Amendment by "appropriate legislation." The 14th Amendment had far-reaching consequences. Section 1 has become the most important provision in the Constitution for defining and enforcing civil rights.

The 1866 Elections

Republicans entered the 1866 congressional elections campaign with the 14th Amendment as their platform. They made clear that any ex-Confederate state that ratified the amendment would be declared "reconstructed" and that its representatives and senators would be seated in Congress. Tennessee ratified the amendment, but Johnson counseled other Southern legislatures to reject the amendment, which they did. Johnson then prepared for an all-out campaign to gain a friendly Northern majority in the congressional elections.

Johnson began his campaign by creating a National Union Party made up of a few conservative Republicans who disagreed with their party, some border-state Unionists who supported the president, and Democrats. The inclusion of Democrats doomed the effort from the start. Many Northern Democrats still carried the taint of having opposed the war effort, and many Northern voters did not trust them. The National Union Party was further damaged by race riots in Memphis and New Orleans, where white mobs including former Confederate soldiers killed 80 blacks, among them several former Union soldiers. The riots bolstered Republican arguments that national power was necessary to protect "the fruits of victory" in the South. Perhaps the biggest liability of the National Union Party was Johnson. In a whistle-stop tour through the North, he traded insults with hecklers and embarrassed his supporters by comparing himself to Christ and his Republican adversaries to Judas.

Republicans swept the election: They gained a three-to-one majority in the next Congress. Having rejected the Reconstruction terms embodied in the 14th Amendment, Southern Democrats now faced far more stringent terms. "They would not cooperate in rebuilding what they destroyed," wrote an exasperated moderate Republican, so "we must remove the rubbish and rebuild from the bottom. Whether they are willing or not, we must compel obedience to the Union and demand protection for its humblest citizen."

The Reconstruction Acts of 1867

In March 1867, the new Congress enacted over Johnson's vetoes two laws prescribing new procedures for the full restoration of the former Confederate states (except Tennessee, which had already been readmitted) to the Union. These laws represented a complex compromise between radicals and moderates that had been hammered out in a confusing sequence of committee drafts, caucus decisions, all-night debates on the floor, and frayed tempers. The Reconstruction acts of 1867 divided the 10 Southern states into five military districts, directed army officers to register voters for the election of delegates to new constitutional conventions, and enfranchised males aged 21 and older (including blacks) to vote in those elections. The acts also disenfranchised (for these elections only) those ex-Confederates who were disqualified from holding office under the not-yet-ratified 14th Amendment—fewer than 10 percent of all white voters. When a state had adopted a new constitution that granted equal civil and political rights regardless of race and had ratified

NEW YORK, SATURDAY, MAY 26, 1866.

The Burning of a Freedmen's School   Because freedpeople's education symbolized black progress, whites who resented and resisted this progress sometimes attacked and burned freedmen's schools, as in this dramatic illustration of a white mob burning a school during antiblack riots in Memphis in May 1866.

the 14th Amendment, it would be declared reconstructed, and its newly elected congressmen would be seated.

These measures embodied a true revolution. Just a few years earlier, Southern whites had been masters of 4 million slaves and part of an independent Confederate nation. Now they were shorn of political power, with their former slaves not only freed but also politically empowered. To be sure, radical Republicans who warned that the revolution was incomplete as long as the old master class retained economic and social power turned out to be right in the end. In 1867, however, the emancipation and enfranchisement of black Americans seemed, as a sympathetic French journalist described it, "one of the most radical revolutions known in history."

Like most revolutions, the reconstruction process did not go smoothly. Many Southern Democrats breathed defiance and refused to cooperate. The presence of the army minimized anti-black violence, but thousands of white Southerners who were eligible to vote refused to do so, hoping that their nonparticipation would delay the process long enough for Northern voters to come to their senses and elect Democrats to Congress.

Blacks and their white allies organized **Union leagues** to inform and mobilize the new black voters into the Republican Party. Democrats branded Southern white Republicans as **"scalawags"** and Northern settlers as **"carpetbaggers."** By September 1867, the 10 states had 735,000 black voters and only 635,000 white voters registered. At least one-third of the registered white voters were Republicans.

President Johnson did everything he could to block Reconstruction. He replaced several Republican generals in command of Southern military districts with Democrats. He had his attorney general issue a ruling that interpreted the Reconstruction acts narrowly, thereby forcing a special session of Congress to pass a supplementary act in July 1867. He encouraged Southern whites to obstruct the registration of voters and the election of convention delegates.

Johnson's purpose was to slow the process until 1868 in the hope that Northern voters would repudiate Reconstruction in the presidential election of that year, when Johnson planned to run as the Democratic candidate. Off-year state elections in fall 1867 encouraged that hope. Republicans suffered setbacks in several Northern states, especially where they endorsed referendum measures to enfranchise black men. "I almost pity the radicals," chortled one of President Johnson's aides after the 1867 elections. "After giving ten states to the negroes, to keep the Democrats from getting them, they will have lost the rest."

The Impeachment of Andrew Johnson

Focus Question
Why was Andrew Johnson impeached? Why was he acquitted?

Johnson struck even more boldly against Reconstruction after the 1867 elections, despite warnings that he was risking **impeachment.** "What does Johnson mean to do?" an exasperated Republican asked another. "I am afraid his doings will make us all favor impeachment." In February 1868, Johnson took a fateful step. He removed from office Secretary of War Edwin M. Stanton, who had administered the War Department in support of the congressional Reconstruction policy. This appeared to violate the Tenure of Office Act, passed the year before over Johnson's veto, which required Senate consent for such removals. By a vote of 126 to 47 along party lines, the House impeached Johnson on February 24. The official reason for impeachment was that he had violated the Tenure of Office Act (which Johnson considered unconstitutional). The real reason was Johnson's stubborn defiance of Congress on Reconstruction.

Under the U.S. Constitution, impeachment by the House does not remove an official from office. It is more like a grand jury indictment that must be tried by a petit jury—in this case, the Senate, which sat as a court to try Johnson on the impeachment charges brought by the House. If convicted by a two-thirds majority of the Senate, he would be removed from office.

The impeachment trial proved long and complicated, which worked in Johnson's favor by allowing passions to cool. The Constitution specifies the grounds on which a president can be impeached and removed: "Treason, Bribery, or other high Crimes and Misdemeanors." The issue was whether Johnson was guilty of any of these acts. His able defense counsel exposed technical ambiguities in the Tenure of Office Act that raised doubts about whether Johnson had actually violated it. Several moderate Republicans feared that the precedent of impeachment might upset the delicate balance of powers between the executive branch, Congress, and the judiciary that was an essential element of the Constitution. Behind the scenes, Johnson strengthened his case by promising to appoint the respected General John M. Schofield as secretary of war and to stop obstructing the Reconstruction acts. In the end, seven Republican senators voted for acquittal on May 16, and the final tally fell one vote short of the necessary two-thirds majority.

The Completion of Formal Reconstruction

The impeachment trial's end cleared the poisonous air in Washington, and Johnson quietly served out his term. Constitutional conventions met in the South during winter and spring 1867–68. Hostile whites described them as "Bones and Banjoes Conventions" and the Republican delegates as "ragamuffins and jailbirds." In sober fact, however, the delegates were earnest advocates of a new order, and the constitutions they wrote were among the most progressive in the nation. Three-quarters of the delegates to the 10 conventions were Republicans. About 25 percent of those Republicans were Northern whites who had relocated to the South after the war; 45 percent were native Southern whites who braved the social ostracism of the white majority to cast their lot with the despised Republicans; and 30 percent were blacks. Only in the South Carolina convention were blacks in the majority.

The new state constitutions enacted **universal male suffrage**, putting them ahead of most Northern states on that score. Some of the constitutions disenfranchised certain classes of ex-Confederates for several years, but by 1872, all such disqualifications had been removed. The constitutions mandated statewide public schools for both races for the first time in the South. Most states permitted segregated schools, but schools of any kind for blacks represented a great step forward. Most of the constitutions increased the state's responsibility for social welfare beyond anything previously known in the South.

Violence in some parts of the South marred the voting on ratification of these state constitutions. The **Ku Klux Klan,** a night-riding white terrorist organization, made its first appearance during the elections. Nevertheless, voters in seven states ratified their constitutions and elected new legislatures that ratified the 14th Amendment in spring 1868. That amendment became part of the U.S. Constitution the following summer, and the newly elected representatives and senators from those seven states, nearly all Republicans, took their seats in the House and Senate.

The 15th Amendment

The remaining three Southern states completed the reconstruction process in 1869 and 1870. Congress required them to ratify the 15th as well as the 14th Amendments. The 15th Amendment prohibited states from denying the right to vote on grounds of race, color, or previous condition of servitude. Its purpose was not only to prevent the reconstructed states from any future revocation of black suffrage, but also to extend equal suffrage to the border states and to the North. With final ratification of the 15th Amendment in 1870, the Constitution became truly color blind for the first time in U.S. history.

But the 15th Amendment still left half of the population disenfranchised. Many supporters of woman suffrage were embittered by its failure to ban discrimination on the grounds of gender as well as race. The radical wing of the suffragists, led by Elizabeth Cady Stanton and Susan B. Anthony, therefore opposed the 15th Amendment, causing a split in the woman suffrage movement.

This movement had shared the ideological egalitarianism of abolitionism since the Seneca Falls Convention of 1848. In 1866, male and female abolitionists formed the American Equal Rights Association (AERA) to work for both black and woman suffrage. Although some Republicans sympathized with the suffragists, they knew that no strong constituency among male voters favored granting the vote to women. A woman suffrage amendment to the state constitution of Kansas in 1867 suffered a lopsided defeat in a referendum. Most members of the AERA recognized that although Reconstruction politics made black enfranchisement possible, woman suffrage would have to wait until public opinion could be educated up to the standard of gender equality.

Stanton and Anthony refused to accept this reasoning. Why should illiterate Southern blacks have the right to vote, they asked, when educated Northern women remained shut out from the polls? It was "infinitely more important to secure the rights of 10 million women than to bring a million more men to the polls," declared Stanton. The 15th Amendment would establish "the most odious form of aristocracy the world has ever seen: an aristocracy of sex." When a majority of delegates at the 1869 convention of the AERA voted to endorse the 15th Amendment, several women led by Stanton and Anthony walked out and founded the National Woman Suffrage Association. The remainder reorganized themselves as the American Woman Suffrage Association. For the next two decades, these rival organizations, working for the same cause, remained at odds with each other.

The Election of 1868

Just as the presidential election of 1864 was a referendum on Lincoln's war policies, so the election of 1868 was a referendum on the Reconstruction policy of the Republicans. The Republican nominee was General **Ulysses S. Grant**. Although he had no political experience, Grant commanded greater authority and prestige than anyone else in the country. As general-in-chief of the army, he had opposed Johnson's Reconstruction policy in 1866 and had broken openly with the president in January 1868. That spring, Grant agreed to run for the presidency in order to preserve in peace the victory for Union and liberty he had won in war.

The Democrats turned away from Andrew Johnson, who carried too many political liabilities. They nominated Horatio Seymour, the wartime governor of New York, bestowing on him the dubious privilege of running against Grant. Hoping to put together a majority consisting of the South plus New York and two or three other Northern states, the Democrats adopted a militant platform denouncing the Reconstruction acts as "a flagrant usurpation of power . . . unconstitutional, revolutionary, and void." The platform also demanded "the abolition of the Freedmen's Bureau, and all political instrumentalities designed to secure negro supremacy."

The vice presidential candidate, Frank Blair of Missouri, became the point man for the Democrats. In a public letter, he proclaimed, "There is but one way to restore the Government and the Constitution, and that is for the President-elect to declare these [Reconstruction] acts null and void, compel the army to undo its usurpations at the South, disperse the carpet-bag State Governments, [and] allow the white people to reorganize their own governments."

The only way to achieve this bold counterrevolutionary goal was to suppress Republican voters in the South. This the Ku Klux Klan tried its best to do. Federal troops failed to prevent much of the violence because martial law had been lifted in the states where civilian governments had been restored. In Louisiana, Georgia, Arkansas, and Tennessee, the Klan or Klan-like groups committed dozens of murders and intimidated thousands of black voters. The violence helped the Democratic cause in the South, but probably hurt it in the North, where many voters perceived the Klan as an organization of neo-Confederate paramilitary guerrillas. In fact, many Klansmen were former soldiers, and such famous Confederate generals as Nathan Bedford Forrest and John B. Gordon held high positions in the Klan.

Seymour did well in the South, carrying five former slave states and coming close in others despite the solid Republican vote of the newly enfranchised blacks. Grant, however, swept the electoral vote 214 to 80. Seymour actually won a slight majority of the white voters nationally; without black enfranchisement, Grant would have had a minority of the popular vote.

The Grant Administration

A great military commander, Grant is usually branded a failure as president. That indictment is only partly correct. Grant's inexperience and poor judgment betrayed him into several unwise appointments of officials who were later convicted of corruption, and his back-to-back administrations (1869–77) were plagued by scandals. His secretary of war was impeached for selling appointments to army posts and Indian reservations, and his attorney general and secretary of the interior resigned under suspicion of malfeasance in 1875.

Although he was an honest man, Grant was too trusting of subordinates. He appointed many former members of his military family, as well as several of his wife's relatives, to offices for which they were scarcely qualified. In an era notorious for corruption at all levels of government, many of the scandals were not Grant's fault. The Tammany Hall "Ring" of "Boss" William Marcy Tweed in New York City may have stolen more money from taxpayers than all of the federal agencies combined. It was said that the only thing the Standard Oil Company could not do with the Ohio legislature was to refine it. In Washington, one of the most widely publicized scandals, the **Credit Mobilier** affair, concerned Congress rather than the Grant administration. Several congressmen had accepted stock in the Credit Mobilier, a construction company for the Union Pacific Railroad, which received loans and land grants from the government. In return, the company expected lax congressional supervision, thereby permitting financial manipulations by the company.

What accounted for this explosion of corruption in the postwar decade, which one historian has called "The Era of Good Stealings"? During the war, expansion of government contracts and the bureaucracy had created new opportunities for the unscrupulous. Following the intense sacrifices of the war years came a relaxation of tensions and standards. Rapid postwar economic growth, led by an extraordinary rush of railroad construction, further encouraged greed and get-rich-quick schemes of the kind satirized by Mark Twain and Charles Dudley Warner in their 1873 novel *The Gilded Age,* which gave its name to the era.

Civil Service Reform

Some of the apparent increase in corruption during the Gilded Age was more a matter of perception. During a civil service reform movement to purify the government bureaucracy and make it more efficient, reformers focused a harsh light into the dark corners of corruption hitherto unilluminated because of the nation's preoccupation with war and reconstruction. Thus reformers' publicity may have exaggerated the actual extent of corruption. In reality, during the Grant administration, several government agencies made real progress in eliminating abuses that had flourished in earlier administrations.

The chief target of civil service reform was the **"spoils system."** With the slogan "To the victor belongs the spoils," the victorious party in an election rewarded party workers with appointments as postmasters, customs collectors, and the like. The hope of getting appointed to a government post was the glue that kept the faithful together when a party was out of power. An assessment of 2 or 3 percent on the beneficiaries' government salaries kept party coffers filled when the party was in power. The spoils system politicized the bureaucracy and staffed it with unqualified personnel who spent more time working for their party than for the government. It also plagued every incoming president (and other elected officials) with the "swarm of office seekers" that loom so large in contemporary accounts (including those of the humorist Orpheus C. Kerr, whose nom de plume was pronounced "Office Seeker").

Civil service reformers wanted to separate the bureaucracy from politics by requiring competitive examinations for the appointment of civil servants. This movement gathered steam during the 1870s and finally achieved success in 1883 with the passage of the

Pendleton Act, which established the modern structure of the civil service. When Grant took office, he seemed to share the sentiments of civil service reformers; several of his cabinet officers inaugurated examinations for certain appointments and promotions in their departments. Grant also named a civil service commission headed by George William Curtis, a leading reformer and editor of *Harper's Weekly*. But many congressmen, senators, and other politicians resisted civil service reform. **Patronage** greased the political machines that kept them in office and all too often enriched them and their political chums. They managed to subvert reform, sometimes using Grant as an unwitting ally and thus turning many reformers against the president.

Foreign Policy Issues

A foreign policy controversy added to Grant's woes. The irregular procedures by which his private secretary had negotiated a treaty to annex Santo Domingo (now the Dominican Republic) alienated leading Republican senators, who defeated ratification of the treaty. Politically inexperienced, Grant acted like a general who needed only to give orders rather than as a president who must cultivate supporters. The fallout from the Santo Domingo affair widened the fissure in the Republican Party between "spoilsmen" and "reformers."

The Grant administration had some solid foreign policy achievements to its credit, however. Hamilton Fish, the able secretary of state, negotiated the Treaty of Washington in 1871 to settle the vexing Alabama Claims. These were damage claims against Britain for the destruction of American shipping by the C.S.S. *Alabama* and other Confederate commerce raiders built in British shipyards. The treaty established an international tribunal to arbitrate the U.S. claims, thus creating a precedent for the peaceful settlement of disputes. It resulted in the award of $15.5 million in damages to U.S. shipowners and a British expression of regret.

The events leading to the Treaty of Washington also resolved another long-festering issue between Britain and the United States: the status of Canada. The seven separate British North American colonies were especially vulnerable to U.S. desires for annexation. In fact, many bitter Northerners demanded British cession of Canadian colonies to the United States as fair payment for the wartime depredations of the *Alabama* and other commerce raiders. Such demands tended to strengthen the loyalty of many Canadians to Britain as a counterweight to the aggressive Americans. In 1867, Parliament passed the British North America Act, which united most of the Canadian colonies into a new and largely self-governing Dominion of Canada.

Canadian nationalism was further strengthened by the actions of the Irish American Fenian Brotherhood. A secret society organized during the Civil War, the Fenians believed that an invasion of Canada would strike a blow for the independence of Ireland. Three times from 1866 to 1871, small "armies" of Fenians, composed mainly of Irish American veterans of the Union Army, crossed the border into Canada, only to be driven back after comic-opera skirmishes. The Fenian raids intensified Canadian anti-Americanism and complicated the negotiations leading to the Washington Treaty, but after its signing, Canadian-American tensions cooled. The treaty also helped resolve disputes over American commercial fishing in Canadian waters. U.S. troops prevented further Fenian raids, and American demands for annexation of Canada faded away. These events gave birth to the modern nation of Canada.

Reconstruction in the South

During Grant's two administrations, the "Southern Question" was the most intractable issue. A phrase in Grant's acceptance of the presidential nomination in 1868 had struck a responsive chord in the North: "Let us have peace." With the ratification of the 15th Amendment, many people breathed a sigh of relief at this apparent resolution of "the last great point that remained to be settled of the issues of the war." It was time to deal with other matters that had been long neglected. Ever since the annexation of Texas a quarter-century earlier, the nation had known scarcely a moment's respite from sectional strife. "Let us have done with Reconstruction," pleaded the New York *Tribune* in 1870. "LET US HAVE PEACE." But there was no peace. Reconstruction was not over; it had hardly begun. State governments elected by black and white voters were in place in the South, but Democratic violence against Reconstruction and the instability of the Republican coalition that sustained it portended trouble.

Blacks in Office

Because the Republican Party had no antebellum roots in the South, most Southern whites perceived it as a symbol of conquest and humiliation. In the North, the Republican Party represented the most prosperous, educated, and influential elements of the population, but in the South, most of its adherents were poor, illiterate, and landless.

About 80 percent of Southern Republican voters were black. Although most black leaders were educated and many had been free before the war, most black voters were illiterate ex-slaves. Neither the leaders nor their constituents, however, were as ignorant or as venal as stereotypes have portrayed them. Of 14 black representatives and two black senators elected in the South between 1868 and 1876, all but three had attended secondary school and four had attended college. Several of the blacks elected to state offices were among the best-educated men of their day. Jonathan Gibbs, secretary of state in Florida from 1868 to 1872 and state superintendent of education from 1872 to 1874, was a graduate of Dartmouth College and Princeton Theological Seminary. Francis L. Cardozo, secretary of state in South Carolina for four years and treasurer for another four, was educated at the University of Glasgow and at theological schools in Edinburgh and London.

It is true that some lower-level black officeholders, as well as their constituents, could not read or write, but the fault for that situation lay not with them but with the slave regime that had denied them an education. Illiteracy did not preclude an understanding of political issues for them any more than it did for Irish American voters in the North, some of whom were also illiterate. Southern blacks thirsted for education. Participation in the Union League and the experience of voting were forms of education. Black churches and fraternal organizations proliferated during Reconstruction and tutored African Americans in their rights and responsibilities.

Linked to the myth of black incompetence was the legend of the "Africanization" of Southern governments during Reconstruction. The theme of "Negro rule"—by which the "barbarous African" exercised "unbridled power" in the 10 Southern states—was a staple of Democratic propaganda. It was enshrined in folk memory and in generations of textbooks. In fact, blacks held only 15 to 20 percent of public offices, even at the height of Reconstruction in the early 1870s. No states had black governors (although the black lieutenant governor of Louisiana acted as governor for a month), and only one black man became a state supreme court justice. Nowhere except in South Carolina did blacks hold office

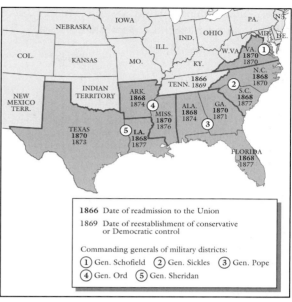

Map 17.1 Reconstruction in the South The dates for each state listed on this map show how short-lived "Radical Reconstruction" was in most Southern states.

in numbers anywhere near their proportion of the population; in that state, they constituted 52 percent of all state and federal elected officials from 1868 to 1876.

"Carpetbaggers"

Next to "Negro rule," carpetbagger corruption and scalawag rascality have been the prevailing myths of Reconstruction. Carpetbaggers did hold a disproportionate number of high political offices in Southern state governments during Reconstruction. More than half of the Republican governors and nearly half of the congressmen and senators were Northerners. A few did resemble the proverbial adventurer who came south with nothing but a carpetbag in which to stow the loot plundered from a helpless people. Most of the Northerners were Union army officers who stayed on after the war as Freedmen's Bureau agents, teachers in black schools, business investors, pioneers of a new political order—or simply because they liked the climate.

Like others who migrated to the West as a frontier of opportunity, those who settled in the postwar South hoped to rebuild its society in the image of the free-labor North. Many were college graduates at a time when fewer than 2 percent of Americans had attended college. Most brought not empty carpetbags but considerable capital, which they invested in what they hoped would become a new South. They also invested human capital—themselves—in a drive to modernize the region's social structure and democratize its politics. But they underestimated the hostility of Southern whites, most of whom regarded them as agents of an alien culture and leaders of an enemy army—as indeed they had been—in a war that for many Southerners was not yet over.

"Scalawags"

Most of the native-born whites who joined the Southern Republican Party came from the upcountry Unionist areas of western North Carolina and Virginia, eastern Tennessee, and elsewhere. Others were former Whigs who saw an opportunity to rebuild the South's economy in partnership with equally Whiggish Northern Republicans. Republicans, said a North Carolina scalawag, were the "party of progress, of education, of development. . . . Yankees and Yankee notions are just what we want in this country. We want their capital to build factories and work shops, and railroads."

But Yankees and Yankee notions were just what most Southern whites did not want. Democrats saw that the Southern Republican Party they abhorred was a fragile coalition of blacks and whites, Yankees and Southerners, hill-country yeomen and low-country entrepreneurs, illiterates and college graduates. The party was weakest along the seams where these disparate elements joined, especially the racial seam. Democrats attacked that weakness with every weapon at their command, from social ostracism of white Republicans to economic intimidation of black employees and sharecroppers. The most potent Democratic weapon was violence.

The Ku Klux Klan

The generic name for the secret groups that terrorized the Southern countryside was the Ku Klux Klan, but some went by other names (the Knights of the White Camelia in Louisiana, for example). Part of the Klan's purpose was social control of the black population. Sharecroppers who tried to extract better terms from landowners, or black people who were considered too "uppity," were likely to receive a midnight whipping—or worse—from white-sheeted Klansmen. Scores of black schools, perceived as a particular threat to white supremacy, went up in flames.

The Klan's main purpose was political: to destroy the Republican Party by terrorizing its voters and, if necessary, by murdering its leaders. No one knows how many politically motivated killings took place—certainly hundreds, probably thousands. Nearly all of the victims were Republicans; most of them were black. In one notorious incident, the Colfax Massacre in Louisiana (April 18, 1873), a clash between black militia and armed whites left three whites and nearly 100 blacks dead. Half of the blacks were killed in cold blood after they had surrendered. In some places, notably Tennessee and Arkansas, Republican militias formed to suppress and disarm the Klan, but in most areas the militias were outgunned and outmaneuvered by ex-Confederate veteran Klansmen. Some Republican governors were reluctant to use black militia against white guerrillas for fear of sparking a racial bloodbath—as happened at Colfax.

© CORBIS

Two Members of the Ku Klux Klan   Founded in Pulaski, Tennessee, in 1866 as a
social organization similar to a college fraternity, the Klan evolved into a terrorist
group whose purpose was intimidation of Southern Republicans. The Klan, in which
former Confederate soldiers played a prominent part, was responsible for the
beating and murder of hundreds of blacks and whites alike from 1868 to 1871.

The answer seemed to be federal troops. In 1870 and 1871, Congress enacted three
laws intended to enforce the 14th and 15th Amendments. Interference with voting rights
became a federal offense, and any attempt to deprive another person of civil or political
rights became a felony. The third law, passed on April 20, 1871, and popularly called the
Ku Klux Klan Act, gave the president power to suspend the writ of **habeas corpus** and
send in federal troops to suppress armed resistance to federal law.

Armed with these laws, the Grant administration moved against the Klan. Because Grant
was sensitive to charges of "military despotism," he used his powers with restraint. He suspended the writ of habeas corpus in only nine South Carolina counties. Nevertheless, there

The Birth of a Nation (1915)

Directed by D. W. Griffith. Starring Lillian Gish (Elsie Stoneman), Henry B. Walthall (Ben Cameron), Ralph Lewis (Austin Stoneman), George Siegmann (Silas Lynch).

Few if any films have had such a pernicious impact on historical understanding and race relations as *Birth of a Nation*. This movie popularized a version of Reconstruction that portrayed predatory carpetbaggers and stupid, brutish blacks plundering a prostrate South and lusting after white women. It perpetuated vicious stereotypes of rapacious black males. It glorified the Ku Klux Klan of the Reconstruction era, inspiring the founding of the "second Klan" in 1915, which became a powerful force in the 1920s (see chapter 24).

The first half of the film offers a conventional Victorian romance of the Civil War. The two sons and daughter of Austin Stoneman (a malevolent radical Republican who is a thinly disguised Thaddeus Stevens) become friends with the three sons and two daughters of the Cameron family of "Piedmont," South Carolina, through the friendship of Ben Cameron and Phil Stoneman at college. The Civil War tragically separates the families. The Stoneman and Cameron boys enlist in the Union and Confederate armies and—predictably—

face each other on the battlefield. Two Camerons and one Stoneman are killed in the war, and Ben Cameron is badly wounded and captured, to be nursed back to health by—you guessed it—Elsie Stoneman. After the war, the younger Camerons and Stonemans renew their friendship. During the Stonemans' visit to South Carolina, Ben Cameron and Elsie Stoneman, and Phil Stoneman and Flora Cameron, fall in love. If the story had stopped there, *Birth of a Nation* would have been just another Hollywood romance. But Austin Stoneman brings south with him Silas Lynch, an ambitious, leering mulatto demagogue who stirs up the animal passions of the ignorant black majority to demand "Equal Rights, Equal Politics, Equal Marriage." A "renegade Negro," Gus, stalks the youngest Cameron daughter, who saves herself from rape by jumping from a cliff to her death. Silas Lynch tries to force Elsie to marry him. "I will build a Black Empire," he tells the beautiful, virginal Elsie (Lillian Gish was the Hollywood beauty queen of silent films),"and you as my queen shall rule by my side."

and elsewhere federal marshals backed by troops arrested thousands of suspected Klansmen. Federal grand juries indicted more than 3,000 members, and several hundred defendants pleaded guilty in return for suspended sentences. To clear clogged court dockets so that the worst offenders could be tried quickly, the Justice Department dropped charges against nearly 2,000 others. About 600 Klansmen were convicted; most of them received fines or light jail sentences, but 65 went to a federal penitentiary for terms of up to five years.

The Election of 1872

These measures broke the back of the Klan in time for the 1872 presidential election. A group of dissident Republicans had emerged to challenge Grant's reelection. They believed

Finally, provoked beyond endurance, white South Carolinians led by Ben Cameron organize the Ku Klux Klan to save "the Aryan race." Riding to the rescue of embattled whites in stirring scenes that anticipated the heroic actions of the cavalry against Indians in later Hollywood Westerns, the Klan executes Gus, saves Elsie, disperses black soldiers and mobs, and carries the next election for white rule by intimidating black voters. The film ends with a double marriage that unites the Camerons and Stonemans in a symbolic rebirth of a nation that joins whites of the North and South in a new union rightfully based on the supremacy of "the Aryan race."

The son of a Confederate lieutenant colonel, David Wark (D. W.) Griffith was the foremost director of the silent movie era. He pioneered many precedent-setting cinematic techniques and profoundly influenced filmmaking throughout the world. *Birth of a Nation* was the first real full-length feature film, technically and artistically superior to anything before it. Apart from its place in the history of cinema, though, why should anyone today watch a movie that perpetuates such wrongheaded history and noxious racist stereotypes? Precisely *because* it reflects and amplifies an interpretation of Reconstruction that prevailed from the 1890s to the 1950s, and thereby shaped not only historical understanding but also contemporary behavior (as in its inspiration for the Klan of the 1920s). Although Birth of a Nation aroused controversy in parts of the North and was picketed by the NAACP, some 200 million people saw the film in the United States and abroad from 1915 to 1946. The story, and director Griffith, demonstrated in dramatic fashion how the South, having lost the Civil War, won the battle for how the war and especially Reconstruction would be remembered for more than half a century.

© Bettmann/CORBIS

Henry B. Walthall (Ben Cameron) kissing the hand of Elsie Stoneman (Lillian Gish) in Birth of a Nation.

that conciliation of Southern whites rather than continued military intervention was the only way to achieve peace in the South. Calling themselves Liberal Republicans, these dissidents nominated Horace Greeley, the famous editor of the New York *Tribune*. Under the slogan "Anything to beat Grant," the Democratic Party also endorsed Greeley's nomination, although he had long been their antagonist. On a platform denouncing "bayonet rule" in the South, Greeley urged his fellow Northerners to put the issues of the Civil War behind them and to "clasp hands across the bloody chasm which has too long divided" North and South.

This phrase would come back to haunt Greeley. Most voters in the North were still not prepared to trust Democrats or Southern whites. Powerful anti-Greeley cartoons by political cartoonist Thomas Nast showed Greeley shaking the hand of a Klansman dripping with the blood of a murdered black Republican. Nast's most famous cartoon portrayed Greeley as a pirate captain bringing his craft alongside the ship of state, while Confederate leaders, armed to the teeth, hid below waiting to board it.

Grant swamped Greeley on election day. Republicans carried every Northern state and 10 of the 16 Southern and border states. Blacks in the South enjoyed more freedom in voting than they would again for a century. This apparent triumph of Republicanism and Reconstruction would soon unravel.

The Panic of 1873

The U.S. economy had grown at an unprecedented pace since recovering from a mild postwar recession. In eight years, 35,000 miles of new railroad track were laid down, equal to all the track laid in the preceding 35 years. The first **transcontinental railroad** had been completed on May 10, 1869, when a golden spike was driven at Promontory Summit, Utah Territory, linking the Union Pacific and the Central Pacific. But the building of a second transcontinental line, the Northern Pacific, precipitated a Wall Street panic in 1873 and plunged the economy into a five-year depression.

Jay Cooke's banking firm, fresh from its triumphant marketing of Union war bonds, took over the Northern Pacific in 1869. Cooke pyramided every conceivable kind of equity and loan financing to raise the money to begin laying rails west from Duluth, Minnesota. Other investment firms did the same as a fever of speculative financing gripped the country. In September 1873, the pyramid of paper collapsed. Cooke's firm was the first to go bankrupt. Like dominoes, thousands of banks and businesses also collapsed. Unemployment rose to 14 percent, and hard times set in.

The Retreat from Reconstruction

Focus Question
Why did a majority of the Northern people and their political leaders turn against continued federal involvement in Southern Reconstruction in the 1870s?

It is an axiom of American politics that the voters will punish the party in power in times of economic depression. That axiom held true in the 1870s. Democrats made large gains in the congressional elections of 1874, winning a majority in the House for the first time in 18 years.

Public opinion also began to turn against Republican policies in the South. The campaign by Liberal Republicans and Democrats against "bayonet rule" and "carpetbag corruption" that left most Northern voters unmoved in 1872 found a growing audience in subsequent years. Intraparty battles among Republicans in Southern states enabled Democrats to regain control of several state governments. Well-publicized corruption scandals also discredited

Republican leaders. Although corruption was probably no worse in Southern states than in many parts of the North, Southern postwar poverty made waste and extravagance seem worse. White Democrats scored propaganda points by claiming that corruption proved the incompetence of "Negro-carpetbag" regimes.

Northerners grew increasingly weary of what seemed to be the endless turmoil of Southern politics. Most of them had never had a strong commitment to racial equality, and they were growing more and more willing to let white supremacy regain sway in the South. "The truth is," confessed a Northern Republican, "our people are tired out with this worn out cry of 'Southern outrages'!!! Hard times & heavy taxes make them wish the 'nigger,' 'everlasting nigger,' were in hell or Africa."

By 1875, only four Southern states remained under Republican control: South Carolina, Florida, Mississippi, and Louisiana. In those states, white Democrats had revived paramilitary organizations under various names: White Leagues (Louisiana), Rifle Clubs (Mississippi), and Red Shirts (South Carolina). Unlike the Klan, these groups operated openly. In Louisiana, they fought pitched battles with Republican militias in which scores were killed. When the Grant

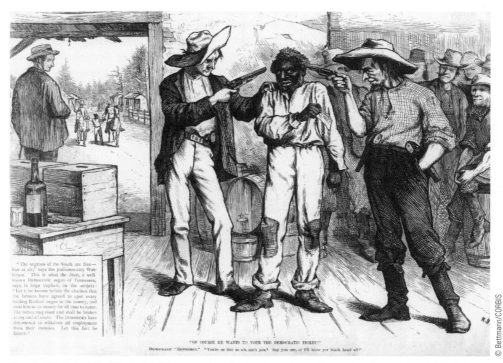

How the Mississippi Plan Worked This cartoon shows how black counties could report large Democratic majorities in the Mississippi state election of 1875. The black voter holds a Democratic ticket while one of the men, described in the caption as a "Democratic reformer," holds a revolver to his head and says: "You're as free as air, ain't you? Say you are, or I'll blow your black head off!"

administration sent large numbers of federal troops to Louisiana, people in both North and South cried out against military rule. The protests grew even louder when soldiers marched onto the floor of the Louisiana legislature in January 1875 and expelled several Democratic legislators after a contested election. Was this America? asked Republican Senator Carl Schurz in a widely publicized speech: "If this can be done in Louisiana, how long will it be before it can be done in Massachusetts and Ohio? How long before a soldier may stalk into the national House of Representatives, and, pointing to the Speaker's mace, say 'Take away that bauble!'"

The Mississippi Election of 1875

The backlash against the Grant administration affected the Mississippi state election of 1875. Democrats there devised a strategy called the Mississippi Plan. The first step was to "persuade" the 10 to 15 percent of white voters still calling themselves Republicans to switch to the Democrats. Only a handful of carpetbaggers could resist the economic pressures, social ostracism, and threats that made it "too damned hot for [us] to stay out," wrote one white Republican who changed parties. "No white man can live in the South in the future and act with any other than the Democratic Party unless he is willing and prepared to live a life of social isolation and remain in political oblivion."

The second step in the Mississippi Plan was to intimidate black voters because even with all whites voting Democratic, the party could still be defeated by the 55 percent black majority. Economic coercion against black sharecroppers and workers kept some of them away from the polls, but violence was the most effective method. Democratic "rifle clubs" showed up at Republican rallies, provoked riots, and shot down dozens of blacks in the ensuing melees. Governor Adelbert Ames—a native of Maine, a Union general who had won a medal of honor in the war, and one of the ablest of Southern Republicans—called for federal troops to control the violence. Grant intended to comply, but Ohio Republicans warned him that if he sent troops to Mississippi, the Democrats would exploit the issue of "bayonet rule" to carry Ohio in that year's state elections. Grant yielded—in effect giving up Mississippi for Ohio. The U.S. attorney general replied to Ames's request for troops:

> The whole public are tired out with these annual autumnal outbreaks in the South, and the great majority are now ready to condemn any interference on the part of the government. . . . Preserve the peace by the forces in your own state, and let the country see that the citizens of Mississippi, who are . . . largely Republican, have the courage to fight for their rights.

Governor Ames did try to organize a loyal state militia, but that proved difficult—and in any case, he was reluctant to use a black militia for fear of provoking a race war. "No matter if they are going to carry the State," said Ames with weary resignation, "let them carry it, and let us be at peace and have no more killing." The Mississippi Plan worked like a charm. In five of the state's counties with large black majorities, the Republicans polled 12, 7, 4, 2, and 0 votes, respectively. What had been a Republican majority of 30,000 in 1874 became a Democratic majority of 30,000 in 1875.

The Supreme Court and Reconstruction

Even if Grant had been willing to continue intervening in Southern state elections, Congress and the courts would have constricted such efforts. The new Democratic majority in the House threatened to cut any appropriations for the Justice Department and the army intended for use in the South. In 1876, the Supreme Court handed down two decisions that declared parts of the 1870 and 1871 laws for enforcement of the 14th and 15th Amendments unconstitutional. In *U.S.* v. *Cruikshank* and *U.S.* v. *Reese,* the Court ruled on cases from Louisiana and Kentucky. Both cases grew out of provisions in these laws authorizing federal officials to prosecute *individuals* (not states) for violations of the civil and voting rights of blacks. But, the Court pointed out, the 14th and 15th Amendments apply to actions by *states:* "No State shall . . . deprive any person of life, liberty, or property . . . nor deny to any person . . . equal protection of the laws": the right to vote "shall not be denied . . . by any State." Therefore, the portions of these laws that empowered the federal government to prosecute individuals were declared unconstitutional.

The Court did not say what could be done when states were controlled by white-supremacy Democrats who had no intention of enforcing equal rights. (In the mid-20th century, the Supreme Court would reverse itself and interpret the 14th and 15th Amendments much more broadly.) Meanwhile, in another ruling, *Civil Rights Case* (1883), the Court declared unconstitutional a civil rights law passed by Congress in 1875. That law, enacted on the eve of the Democratic takeover of the House elected in 1874, was a crowning achievement of Reconstruction. It banned racial discrimination in all forms of public transportation and public accommodations. If enforced, it would have effected a sweeping transformation of race relations—in the North as well as in the South. Even some of the congressmen who voted for the bill doubted its constitutionality, however, and the Justice Department had made little effort to enforce it. Several cases made their way to the Supreme Court, which in 1883 ruled the law unconstitutional—again on grounds that the 14th Amendment applied only to states, not to individuals. Several states—all in the North—passed their own civil rights laws in the 1870s and 1880s, but less than 10 percent of the black population resided in those states. The mass of African Americans lived a segregated existence.

The Election of 1876

In 1876, the remaining Southern Republican state governments fell victim to the passion for reform. The mounting revelations of corruption at all levels of government ensured that reform would be the leading issue in the presidential election. In this centennial year of the birth of the United States, marked by a great exposition in Philadelphia, Americans wanted to put their best foot forward. Both major parties gave their presidential nominations to governors who had earned reform reputations in their states: Democrat Samuel J. Tilden of New York and Republican Rutherford B. Hayes of Ohio.

Democrats entered the campaign as favorites for the first time in two decades. It seemed likely that they would be able to put together an electoral majority from a "solid South" plus New York and two or three other Northern states. To ensure a solid South, they looked to the lessons of the Mississippi Plan. In 1876, a new word came into use to describe Democratic techniques of intimidation: *bulldozing*. To bulldoze black voters meant to trample them down or keep them away from the polls. In South Carolina and Louisiana, the Red Shirts and the White Leagues mobilized for an all-out bulldozing effort.

The most notorious incident, the Hamburg Massacre, occurred in the village of Hamburg, South Carolina, where a battle between a black militia unit and 200 Red Shirts resulted in the capture of several militiamen, five of whom were shot "while attempting to escape." This time Grant did send in federal troops. He pronounced the Hamburg Massacre "cruel, blood-thirsty, wanton, unprovoked . . . a repetition of the course that has been pursued in other Southern States."

The federal government also put several thousand deputy marshals and election supervisors on duty in the South. Although they kept an uneasy peace at the polls, they could do little to prevent assaults, threats, and economic coercion in backcountry districts, which reduced the potential Republican tally in the former Confederate states by at least 250,000 votes.

Disputed Results

When the results were in, Tilden had carried four Northern states, including New York with its 35 electoral votes. Tilden also carried all of the former slave states except—apparently—Louisiana, South Carolina, and Florida, which produced disputed returns. Because Tilden needed only one of them to win the presidency, while Hayes needed all three, and because Tilden seemed to have carried Louisiana and Florida, it appeared initially that he had won the presidency. But frauds and irregularities reported from several bulldozed districts in the three states clouded the issue. For example, a Louisiana parish that had recorded 1,688 Republican votes in 1874 reported only 1 in 1876. Many other similar discrepancies appeared. The official returns ultimately sent to Washington gave all three states—and therefore the presidency—to Hayes, but the Democrats refused to recognize the results, and they controlled the House.

The country now faced a serious constitutional crisis. Armed Democrats threatened to march on Washington. Many people feared another civil war. The Constitution offered no clear guidance on how to deal with the matter. A count of the state electoral votes required the concurrence of both houses of Congress, but with a Democratic House and a Republican Senate, such concurrence was not forthcoming. To break the deadlock, Congress created a special electoral commission consisting of five representatives, five senators, and five Supreme Court justices split evenly between the two parties, with one member, a Supreme Court justice, supposedly an independent—but in fact a Republican.

Tilden had won a national majority of 252,000 popular votes, and the raw returns gave him a majority in the three disputed states. But an estimated 250,000 Southern Republicans

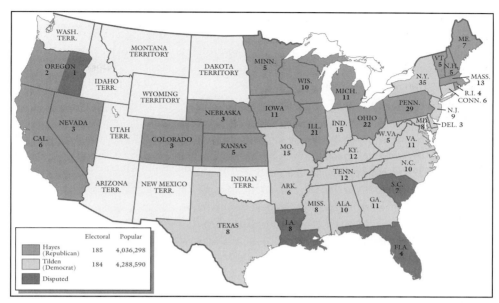

Map 17.2   Hayes-Tilden Disputed Election of 1876   A comparison of this map with those on pp. 523 and 527 shows the persistence of geographical voting patterns once Southern Democrats had overthrown most Republican state governments and effectively disenfranchised many black voters.

had been bulldozed away from the polls. In a genuinely fair and free election, the Republicans might have carried Mississippi and North Carolina as well as the three disputed states. While the commission agonized, Democrats and Republicans in Louisiana and South Carolina each inaugurated their own separate governors and legislatures (Republicans in Florida gave up the fight at the state level). Only federal troops in the capitals at New Orleans and Columbia protected the Republican governments in those states.

The Compromise of 1877

In February 1877, three months after voters had gone to the polls, the electoral commission issued its ruling. By a partisan vote of 8 to 7—with the "independent" justice voting with the Republicans—the commission awarded all of the disputed states to Hayes. The Democrats cried foul and began a **filibuster** in the House to delay the final electoral count beyond the inauguration date of March 4, so as to throw the election to the House of Representatives, an eventuality that threatened to bring total anarchy. But, behind the scenes, a compromise began to take shape. Both Northern Republicans and Southern Democrats of Whig heritage had similar interests in liquidating the sectional rancor and in getting on with the business of economic recovery and development. Among these neo-Whigs were Hayes and his advisers. To wean Southern Whiggish Democrats away from a House filibuster, Hayes promised his support as president for federal appropriations to rebuild war-destroyed **levees** on the lower Mississippi and federal aid for a southern transcontinental railroad. Hayes's lieutenants also hinted at the appointment of a Southerner as postmaster general, who would have a considerable amount of patronage at his disposal—the appointment of thousands of local postmasters.

Most important, Southerners wanted to know what Hayes would do about Louisiana and South Carolina. Would he withdraw the troops and allow the Democrats who already governed those states in fact to do so in law as well? Hayes signaled his intention to end "bayonet rule," which he had for some time considered a bankrupt policy. He believed that the goodwill and influence of Southern moderates would offer better protection for black rights than federal troops could provide. In return for his commitment to withdraw the troops, Hayes asked for—and received—promises of fair treatment of freedpeople and respect for their constitutional rights.

The End of Reconstruction

Such promises were easier to make than to keep, as future years would reveal. In any case, the Democratic filibuster collapsed, and Hayes was inaugurated on March 4. He soon fulfilled his part of the Compromise of 1877: ex-Confederate Democrat David Key of Tennessee became postmaster general; in 1878, the South received more federal money for internal improvements than ever before; and federal troops left the capitals of Louisiana and South Carolina. The last two Republican state governments collapsed. The old abolitionist and radical Republican warhorses denounced Hayes's actions as a sellout of Southern blacks. His was a policy "of weakness, of subserviency, of surrender," in the words of the venerable crusader William Lloyd Garrison, a policy that sustained "might against right . . . the rich and powerful against the poor and unprotected."

Voices of protest could scarcely be heard above the sighs of relief that the crisis was over. Most Americans, including even most Republicans, wanted no more military intervention in state affairs. "I have no sort of faith in a local government which can only be propped up by foreign bayonets," wrote the editor of the New York *Tribune* in April 1877. "If negro suffrage means that as a permanency then negro suffrage is a failure."

Conclusion

Before the Civil War, most Americans had viewed a powerful government as a threat to individual liberties. That is why the first 10 amendments to the Constitution (the Bill of Rights) imposed strict limits on the powers of the federal government. During the Civil War and especially during Reconstruction, however, the national government had to exert an unprecedented amount of power to free the slaves and guarantee their equal rights as free citizens. That is why the 13th, 14th, and 15th Amendments to the Constitution contained clauses stating that "Congress shall have power" to enforce these provisions for liberty and equal rights.

During the post–Civil War decade, Congress passed civil rights laws and enforcement legislation to accomplish this purpose. Federal marshals and troops patrolled the polls to protect black voters, arrested thousands of Klansmen and other violators of black civil rights, and even occupied state capitals to prevent Democratic paramilitary groups from overthrowing legitimately elected Republican state governments.

By 1875, many Northerners had grown tired of or alarmed by this continued use of military power to intervene in the internal affairs of states. The Supreme Court stripped the federal government of much of its authority to enforce certain provisions of the 14th and 15th Amendments. Traditional fears of military power as a threat to individual liberties came to the fore again.

The withdrawal of federal troops from the South in 1877 constituted both a symbolic and a substantive end of the 12-year postwar era known as Reconstruction. Reconstruction had achieved the two great objectives inherited from the Civil War: (1) to reincorporate the former Confederate states into the Union, and (2) to accomplish a transition from slavery to freedom in the South. That transition was marred by the economic inequity of sharecropping and the social injustice of white supremacy. A third goal of Reconstruction, enforcement of the equal civil and political rights promised in the 14th and 15th Amendments, was betrayed by the Compromise of 1877. In subsequent decades, the freed slaves and their descendants suffered repression into segregated, second-class citizenship. Not until another war hero-turned-president sent troops into Little Rock (chapter 28), 80 years after they had been withdrawn from New Orleans and Columbia, did the federal government launch a second Reconstruction to fulfill the promises of the first.

SUGGESTED READINGS

The most comprehensive and incisive history of Reconstruction is **Eric Foner, *Reconstruction: America's Unfinished Revolution 1863–1872*** (1988). For a skillful abridgement of this book, see Foner, *A Short History of Reconstruction* (1990). Also valuable is **Kenneth M. Stampp, *The Era of Reconstruction, 1865–1877*** (1965). Important for their insights on Lincoln and the reconstruction question are **Peyton McCrary, *Abraham Lincoln and Reconstruction: The Louisiana Experiment*** (1978) and **LaWanda Cox, *Lincoln and Black Freedom: A Study in Presidential Leadership*** (1981). A superb study of the South Carolina Sea Islands as a laboratory of Reconstruction is **Willie Lee Rose, *Rehearsal for Reconstruction: The Port Royal Experiment*** (1964).

Three important studies of Andrew Johnson and his conflict with Congress over Reconstruction are **Eric L. McKitrick, *Andrew Johnson and Reconstruction*** (1960); **Hans L. Trefousse, *The Radical Republicans: Lincoln's Vanguard for Racial Justice*** (1969); and **Michael Les Benedict, *The Impeachment and Trial of Andrew Johnson*** (1973). Two books by **Michael Perman** connect events in the South and in Washington during Reconstruction: *Reunion without Compromise: The South and Reconstruction, 1865–1868* (1973) and *The Road to Redemption: Southern Politics 1868–1879* (1984). For counter-Reconstruction violence in the South, see **George C. Rable, *But There Was No Peace: The Role of Violence in the Politics of Reconstruction*** (1984) and **Nicholas Lemann, *Redemption: The Last Battle of the Civil War*** (2006). The evolution of sharecropping and other aspects of the transition from slavery to freedom are treated in **Roger L. Ransom and Richard Sutch**, *One Kind of Freedom: The Economic Consequences of Emancipation* (1977).

Of the many books on African Americans in Reconstruction, the following are perhaps the most valuable: **Thomas Holt**, *Black over White: Negro Political Leadership in South Carolina during Reconstruction* (1977) and **Laura F. Edwards**, *Gendered Strife and Confusion: The Political Culture of Reconstruction* (1997). An excellent collection of essays on the Freedmen's Bureau is **Paul A. Cimbala and Randall Miller, eds.**, *The Freedmen's Bureau and Reconstruction* (1999). Both black and white churches are the subject of **Daniel Stowell**, *Rebuilding Zion: The Religious Reconstruction of the South, 1863–1877* (1998).

Visit the Liberty Equality Power Companion Web site for resources specific to this textbook: http://www.thomsonedu.com/history/murrin

Also find self-tests and additional resources at ThomsonNOW. ThomsonNOW is an integrated online suite of services and resources with proven ease of use and efficient paths to success, delivering the results you want—NOW!

www.thomsonedu.com/login/

A Transformed Nation: The West and the New South, 1865–1900

"How I do wish you could all come out here," the new Kansas homesteader Mary Abell wrote to her family back east in 1871. "It is such a beautiful country—I did not know there was any thing so beautiful in the whole world as the country we passed over in coming here." Just arrived from New York with her husband, Abell was clearly excited about the prospect of a new life in the West: "Robert has got a piece of land that suits him," she told her sister. "It seems so fortunate." She knew there was much to do in the days ahead—"There is a house to be built fences to make—a well to be dug and a cow to be got." But Abell didn't seem to mind: "I should never be content to live East now," she said. "Things there would look very little."

Abell was part of a great wave of settlement in the post–Civil War era that would transform the West. From 1865 to 1890, the white population in the trans-Mississippi west increased some 400 percent to 8,628,000—a figure that includes both native-born and white immigrants. The dream of western lands also inspired many African Americans, whose cherished hopes for liberty led hundreds of thousands to leave the South for points west from 1880 to 1910. At the same time, immigrants from China, Mexico, and other countries were drawn to the economic opportunities of the West as part of a global movement of peoples in this period.

All of these men and women were driven by desires for a better life, but their desires often conflicted with the rights and desires of the diverse peoples who already inhabited the West, including a variety of Indian cultures and societies; borderlands villages of Spanish-speaking peoples; settlements of Chinese miners and laborers; and Mexicans in California, among others. Settlement set in motion conflict and resistance in numerous places. Who would gain power over Western lands? Whose liberty would be respected? What efforts would be made to achieve equality—or deny equality—to all of these peoples? This chapter explores the transformation of the West and the South during the late 19th century, part of a larger process of industrialization in this period.

The Homestead Act

Mary Abell and her husband were able to become homesteaders because of a remarkable piece of legislation that took effect on January 1, 1863—the same day that the Emancipation Proclamation became law. Meant to provide free land for western settlers, the **Homestead Act** was

CHRONOLOGY

1862	Sioux uprising in Minnesota; 38 Sioux executed
1864	Colorado militia massacres Cheyenne in village at Sand Creek, Colorado
1866	Cowboys conduct first cattle drive north from Texas
1869	President Grant announces his "peace policy" toward Indians
1876	Sioux and Cheyenne defeat Custer at Little Big Horn
1880	James A. Garfield elected president
1881	Garfield assassinated; Chester A. Arthur becomes president
1883	Pendleton Act begins reform of civil service
1884	Grover Cleveland elected president
1887	Dawes Severalty Act dissolves Indian tribal units and implements individual ownership of tribal lands
1888	Benjamin Harrison elected president
1889	Government opens Indian Territory (Oklahoma) to white settlement
1890	Wounded Knee massacre • New Mississippi constitution pioneers black disenfranchisement in South • Republicans try but fail to enact federal elections bill to protect black voting rights • Congress enacts McKinley Tariff
1892	Grover Cleveland again elected president
1895	Booker T. Washington makes his Atlanta Compromise address
1896	*Plessy* v. *Ferguson* legalizes "separate but equal" state racial segregation laws
1898	*Williams* v. *Mississippi* condones use of literacy tests and similar measures to restrict voting rights

the result of a dream that stretched back decades. "Go West, young man!" had been a famous saying during the 1850s, associated with an extended campaign for a homestead law by newspaper editor Horace Greeley. The saying embodied a cherished American ideal: the belief that individual ownership of land by farmers was at the heart of a virtuous citizenry and a sound democratic republic. That ideal had fueled Jeffersonian agrarianism, too.

In the 1850s, many people believed that a western "safety valve" was necessary to ward off the potential evils of industrialization, urbanization, and capitalist expansion. Free land in the West would help prevent a system of perpetual wage labor, or "wage slavery," by allowing individual farmers to support themselves. Thus free land would ultimately help preserve American values of democratic individualism.

In fact, the provisions of the Homestead Act were remarkably egalitarian for their day—at least up to a point. Both men and unmarried women were eligible to file for up to 160 acres of surveyed land in the public domain, as long as they were over the age of 21. (Married women were assumed to be dependents of their homesteading husbands.) Immigrants who affirmed their intention to become citizens were also eligible. As long as homesteaders lived on the land for five years, not only cultivating it but also "improving" it by building a house or barn, they could receive full title for a fee of only $10. Utilizing these provisions, white homesteaders ultimately claimed some 285 million acres of land, a remarkable redistribution of public acreage by the government.

But we need to consider the Act's costs as well. Despite a surface egalitarianism, the Homestead Act privileged white farmers over African Americans and Hispanics, who rarely had the resources necessary to homestead. After all, even free land required tools, seed, plus often costly transportation to a far-away place: experts in the Agriculture Department estimated such needs at $1,000, an unimaginably large amount for most Americans at the time. The act denied access to Chinese laborers, who could not become U.S. citizens and had few property rights. It made no provisions for the truly poor in eastern cities.

But the Act's most obvious cost was its severe impact on such groups as New Mexico sheepherders or Native Americans for whom such settlement did not open up land but instead took it away. The Homestead Act was in fact part of a larger process of conquest, driven by the twin pressures of industrialization and white settlement, through which Indians were irrevocably stripped of their lands.

A final problem with the Act was extensive corruption in its implementation. Those who agitated for a Homestead Act in the antebellum period had been fueled by a sense of idealism. Ironically, however, through chicanery, outright fraud, and government giveaways, more public land actually fell into the hands of railroads and other corporations, as well as speculators, than into the hands of individual farmers during this period. Clearly, this result was not the intention of the Homestead Act's framers, but it did reflect the new power of an emerging corporate order (see chapter 19).

Was the Homestead Act a success or failure in American life? To younger sons in Norwegian or German farm families who could expect to inherit no land at home, the opportunity to obtain 160 acres in Minnesota or Nebraska seemed miraculous. But that perspective was not shared by Native Americans. This chapter explores the complex answers to that seemingly simple question as part of a broader examination of the industrialization of the West, a process that went into high gear after the Civil War.

An Industrializing West

Focus Question
How did the industrialization of the West affect Americans in different ways?

Traditionally, historians have associated industrialization with the East in the post–Civil War era, but in fact the West also industrialized in this period. That industrialization had many linked components: settlement of the West, including the creation of farms, communities, and western cities; production of commodities such as cattle and timber that could be shipped east; the creation of western consumers and thus the demand for manufactured goods; the extensive extraction of resources through mining and logging; and the ability to ship commodities efficiently using a nationally linked transportation network. These western processes of resource extraction may have looked different from the factory-centered industrialization that developed in the East and Midwest at this time (see chapter 19), but they still involved the transformation of an agrarian economy to an industrial society. Like eastern industrialization, western industrialization also had global reach, pulling immigrants from China, Peru, Chile, Hawaii, European countries, and Mexico to the already diverse West.

Railroads

Nothing was more important to the industrialization of the West than the railroad. Just as free land for homesteaders was a long-held dream for many Americans, so, too, was the creation of a transcontinental railroad that would link East and West and allow the transportation of people and commodities over long distances. The two dreams were connected: the settlement of the West would be greatly facilitated by the extension of the railroad into far-flung territory. Thus it was no accident that in 1862, the year the government passed the Homestead Act, it also passed the **Pacific Railroad Bill,** which provided large loans and extremely generous subsidies of land to two railroad companies, the **Union Pacific** (working west) and the **Central Pacific** (working east), in order to enable them to build a transcontinental line stretching from Omaha, Nebraska, to Sacramento, California. (Railroad lines already existed from Omaha to the East.) Two years later, the government also provided a substantial monetary subsidy for each mile of track laid in the West. Ultimately, the government would give away 131 million acres of land to support transcontinental railroads, including huge land subsidies to three additional railroads: the Atchison, Topeka, and Santa Fe (following the Santa Fe Trail between Missouri and the Southwest); the Southern Pacific (from Southern California to New Orleans); and the Northern Pacific (from the Great Lakes to the Columbia River).

These lavish subsidies set off a frenzy of railroad building; they also made a few individuals very rich, including **the "Big Four" of the Central Pacific:** Leland Stanford, Collis P. Huntington, Mark Hopkins, and Charles Crocker. Big in every way (they collectively weighed 860 pounds), the four men had come to California during the Gold Rush and had shrewdly sized up its entrepreneurial opportunities. They now avidly seized the historic opportunity at hand and formed a partnership that effectively split up the work necessary in such a giant task, including the work of influencing lawmakers. Like so many others involved in the notoriously corrupt postwar railway boom, they were not shy about using bribery or graft to achieve their aims. The leader of the Union Pacific, Thomas C. Durant, was not shy either, having been the chief architect of the scandalous Crédit Mobilier scheme (see chapter 17).

Having provided generous subsidies, the government expected the railroads to obtain their own financing, and so various railroads sold millions of dollars of stocks or bonds, many selling as much stock as the market would bear without much relationship to the actual value of the railroads. This "watered" stock was part of the runaway corruption that surrounded financing railroads. The Big Four participated wholeheartedly in this corruption, creating construction contracts, for instance, that paid them $90 million for work that only cost them $32.2 million.

Once financing had been arranged for this complex venture, the Union Pacific and Central Pacific embarked on a daunting task that would engage some 20,000 workers at a time. From 1865 on, the two railroads raced against one another, as whoever laid the most track stood to gain in government subsidies as well as later commerce. The Union Pacific employed primarily Irish laborers, while the Central Pacific employed a workforce that was by 1867 almost 90 percent Chinese. All worked almost constantly.

Chinese Laborers and the Railroads

A global economy had drawn thousands of **Chinese laborers** to California during the Gold Rush, beginning in 1849. Mostly peasants emigrating from the Pearl River delta of Guangdong Province in southeast China, they were pushed from home by poverty and unstable political conditions related to China's defeat in the British Opium Wars; they were pulled to America by their hope to make a better living in "Gold Mountain." While only a few hundred men emigrated in 1849 and 1850, by the mid-1850s, thousands of Chinese immigrants arrived annually. By 1870, there were some 63,000 Chinese in the United States, with over three-quarters settled in California.

Almost entirely men, Chinese immigrants intended to be sojourners, not permanent settlers: they planned to take their hard-earned savings home to the wives and families they had left behind. At first they worked as independent prospectors panning for gold, but as gold profits dwindled, they moved into other areas of work. In the 1860s, labor contractors in China actively recruited young men to come to America to build the transcontinental railroad, as well as to work as agricultural laborers, to develop fisheries and vineyards, and to help reclaim California swamplands. Some 12,000 Chinese laborers ultimately built the Central Pacific Railroad, often under exceptionally harsh conditions, and with substantially less pay than white laborers.

Even before they began working on the railroads, Chinese miners and laborers faced extremes of prejudice from white nativists. In 1850, the California State legislature responded to anti-foreigner agitation with a Foreign Miners' Tax aimed at all foreigners; two years later, the legislature specifically targeted Chinese immigrants. Western labor leaders, particularly Dennis Kearney of the Workingman's Party of California, inflamed nativist crowds of white workers with anti-Chinese rhetoric: in 1877, during the national Great Railway Strike (see chapter 19), mobs of white workers rioted against Chinese workers in San Francisco's Chinatown. Violence against Chinese workers occurred in numerous places in the West during the 1870s and 1880s, including a massacre in Rock Springs, Colorado, after the Union Pacific Railroad decided to hire Chinese workers. Twenty-eight Chinese died in an attack that included burning down Chinese homes; similar attacks soon occurred throughout the West.

At the local level, Chinese immigrants faced a host of discriminatory ordinances specifically targeting them, from queue ordinances regulating the length of men's hair (and thus targeting the distinctive braid worn by Chinese men); to sidewalk ordinances preventing the carrying of baskets on shoulders. At the state level, California laws denied Chinese the right to own land, to testify in court, to intermarry with whites, and to immigrate. Under these conditions, Chinese workers created communities of their own against stiff odds. Yet by 1850, a thriving Chinatown had emerged in San Francisco, and Chinese sections emerged in numerous communities throughout the West.

In 1882, the federal government weighed in with its first discriminatory law targeting a specific immigrant group. The **Chinese Exclusion Act** suspended Chinese immigration for 10 years with the exception of a few job categories such as merchants. Interest in trade with China dictated against preventing immigration by wealthy businessmen, but the virulent white **nativism** that had taken hold throughout the West encouraged Congress to outlaw Chinese laborers, who supposedly endangered "the good order of certain localities." The Chinese Exclusion Act was renewed in 1892. That the Exclusion Act achieved its aim can be seen in the declining population of Chinese in this period: from 105,465 in 1880 to 89,863 in 1900, during a period in which immigration swelled for other groups (for more on Chinese immigrants, see chapter 20).

The Golden Spike

By the early spring of 1869, what one commentator called the "irrepressible railroad" was almost an accomplished fact. The only question was where East and West would meet. In the final stages of track-laying, the two railroads—which would receive money, after all, based on miles of track built—actually built some track parallel to one another before finally being instructed by no less than President Grant to determine a meeting point.

The result, on May 10, 1869, was the historic driving of a **"golden spike"** in Promontory, Utah, to mark the merging of the two lines. Present that day, we know from the historical record, were "men of every color, creed, and nationality," including the Chinese laborers who had built the railroad and laid the very last track. But official photographs of the event leave them out—a silence that speaks volumes about racial prejudice at the time.

This first transcontinental railroad was soon followed by others, although there were numerous difficulties and abortive attempts. The Northern Pacific ran out of capital in 1873 and went into receivership; the Santa Fe fell short of its goal. Still, by 1893, a total of five trans-continental railroads would be in service, and track mileage west of the Mississippi would increase from 3,272 miles at the end of the Civil War to 72,473 miles. No single factor was as important to the industrialization of the West as the building of railroads, which provided an internal infrastructure for the western economy as well as connection to eastern markets.

© Bettmann/CORBIS

The Golden Spike   This carefully posed scene records the merging of the Central Pacific and Union Pacific Railroads at Promontory Point, Utah, on May 10, 1869, to create the nation's first transcontinental railroad. A celebration of the industrialization of the American West, the photograph includes hundreds of white laborers, but reflects the racial prejudice of the time in excluding Chinese railroad workers who also played a central role in building the railroad.

Railroads and Borderlands Communities

Railroads also changed ordinary people's lives across the West. The arrival of the railroads, as well as the Anglo settlers who followed swiftly in their wake, dramatically changed established patterns of life in the borderlands communities of northern New Mexico and southern Colorado. In the 1870s, Hispanic villagers living communally in this area maintained an economy that included grazing sheep and cattle on the open range, as well as freighting—the transportation of goods by wagons. That way of life had not changed much even in the wake of the conquest and annexation of the northern provinces of Mexico by the United States in 1848.

But the coming of the railroads in the 1880s put new pressure on Hispanic village life. In places like Rio Arriba County, New Mexico, Hispanic villagers who had done a thriving trade hauling goods found their livelihood replaced by the railroads. As a result, communities that had combined trade with grazing and farming were now forced to go back only to farming and grazing, even though this combination had never produced quite enough for their needs. Even worse, in a pattern repeated throughout the West, Hispanic villagers found that Anglo settlement and fencing of once-open lands reduced the available range for grazing.

As Anglo-owned livestock companies moved in, bringing in better breeds and buying up grazing land, they began to squeeze out the Hispanic farmers. With fewer sources of income, by the 1890s, villagers were starting to depend on credit for the first time, borrowing money from an Anglo merchant to fund their grazing, and in the turbulent economy of that decade, many of them were unable to pay their debts. The end result was the loss of their sheep—and livelihood—to Anglo businessmen who had extended credit to them. Many ended up working for livestock companies, sometimes caring for herds they had once owned themselves. Eventually others ended up as miners, forced to become wage laborers.

Resentment became active resistance in the 1880s, when a secret organization, **las Gorras Blancas (White caps),** rode mostly at night to cut fences, tear up railroad track, and burn bridges. "Our purpose is to protect the rights of the people in general and especially those of the helpless classes," the group declared in its platform. But the group had only limited success in achieving these goals. There was no question that industrialization had transformed lives in the borderlands, making many formerly independent producers newly dependent on corporations.

Mining

A similar process held true in mining. The California Gold Rush of 1849 and the early 1850s had drawn miners from across the United States—and from Mexico, Europe, China, Chile, and other countries, as well—to pan for gold. After the Civil War, mining continued to be part of a global industrial economy, but the image of the individual prospector striking it rich on his own claim became increasingly quaint. By the 1870s, the majority of miners were wage laborers who worked for corporations, not for themselves. Mining was big business, with groups of investors consolidating holdings in some of the richest mines. **George Hearst,** for instance, began by investing in 1859 in the legendary Comstock Lode in Nevada—the richest vein of silver in America. "If you're ever inclined to think that there's no such thing as luck," Hearst remarked, "just think of me." In 1877, Hearst and business partners bought the Homestake Mine in the Black Hills, and then enriched their holdings still further by buying up the claims of surrounding miners. Other financiers invested in the industries related to mining, including railroads, lumber companies, and smelters.

Gold Rush miners had worked the surface of the earth with picks, shovels, and tin pans, but as this placer mining gave out, miners and mining companies developed new technologies to extract ore, whether on the surface of the earth or underground. **Hydraulic mining,** used as early as the 1850s, employed high-pressure jets of water to wash away banks of earth and even mountains in order to extract gold. By the 1880s, hydraulic mining produced 90 percent of California's gold, but it also ravaged the environment, tearing away indiscriminately at earth, boulders, and trees, and leaving desolate landscapes in its wake. The debris (tailings) from hydraulic mining clogged rivers and caused floods, ruining farms with muddy waste. Other types of mining destroyed landscapes as well, with copper mining in particular creating strip-mining moonscapes.

Railroads played a central role in the development of industrial mining. It wasn't just that they allowed access to mines; they also made it possible to perform a new kind of mining late in the century. Gold discoveries had propelled the first waves of western settlement, but by the 1870s, silver eclipsed gold in volume and some years even in value. Mining of copper became profitable with the arrival of the railroads, as they for the first time allowed transportation of huge quantities of ore. In the mining town of Butte, Montana, mining had centered around diminishing supplies of silver up until 1881, but the arrival of railroads that year made it possible to extract Butte's rich lode of copper, known as the "richest hill on earth." The same held true for large-scale copper mining in southern Arizona, which was also catalyzed by the arrival of the railroads in the 1880s. Such large-scale resource extraction was at the heart of western industrialization. **(See Map 18.1, Mining and Cattle Frontiers, 1870s, in the color insert following page 816.)**

Miners' working conditions grew steadily worse by the end of the century in the heavily mechanized hard-rock mines. Mining on the Comstock Lode involved work in mines with temperatures of well over 100 degrees—sometimes as much as 150 degrees deep underground. Miners died of the heat, of poor ventilation, of the release of toxic gases, and of accidents with mining equipment. Accidents disabled one out of every 30 miners in the 1870s. By the end of the 19th century, mining was the most dangerous industry in the country.

Unions struggled with varying degrees of success to gain a foothold in the 1870s and 1880s, but with wage cuts in the early 1890s, there was a new burst of labor radicalism and resistance. A violent confrontation between miners and the National Guard occurred at Coeur d'Alene, Idaho, in 1892; the next year, individual mining unions met at Butte, Montana, to form the **Western Federation of Miners (WFM),** whose radical politics included a call to transform the American economic system. In 1893, a violent strike at Cripple Creek, Colorado, centered around mine owners' attempts to move from an eight-hour to a ten-hour day. These strikes were part of nationwide labor activism and resistance in the 1890s (see chapter 19). The WFM would ultimately be important in helping to found the 20th-century Industrial Workers of the World (IWW) (see chapter 20). The IWW's leader, William "Big Bill" Haywood, remembered being approached by a WFM organizer as a young man in Idaho. "I had never heard of the need of workingmen organizing for mutual protection," Haywood said, but he soon became a leader of the WFM himself. The industrialization of the West became a radicalizing political experience for many.

Ranching

It wasn't just miners who went on strike: by the 1880s, even some cowboys attempted strikes for better pay and better working conditions. The idea of a striking cowboy initially goes against the grain: this mythic figure in American life symbolizes solitary, rugged individualism, after all. But cowboys were also employees; and increasingly in the late 19th century,

Oklahoma! (1955)

Directed by Fred Zinnemann. Starring Gordon MacRae (Curly); Shirley Jones (Laurey); and Rod Steiger (Jud).

Only a history textbook would ask you to connect the great Rodgers & Hammerstein musical *Oklahoma!* to the range wars of the late-19th-century West. But think about it: when the cast sings "The Farmer and the Cowman" during a square dance, right before launching into a colorful fistfight, they express the different worldviews of farmers and cattle ranchers. "Whyn't those dirtscratchers stay in Missouri where they belong?" asks a cowman, and another protests, the farmer "come out west and built a lot of fences! And built 'em right acrost our cattle ranges!" It's up to the song's refrain to tell us how to resolve this dispute:

> The farmer and the cowman should be friends,
> Oh, the farmer and the cowman should be friends.
> One man likes to push a plow,
> The other likes to chase a cow,
> But that's no reason why they cain't be friends.

The song is every bit as campy as these lyrics indicate, and if you never got a chance to see (or be in) a school production in high school, then you could do worse than to rush out and rent a copy of the 1955 movie *Oklahoma!*, based on the extraordinarily popular Broadway musical of 1943. The dancing cowboys alone are worth the price of admission.

But don't be fooled: *Oklahoma!* isn't really about Oklahoma, even if it is set in 1907 right before the territory became a state. It's really about a mythic Western space in Americans' imagination, where Americans come together in harmony at square dances and box suppers and where a cowboy like the masculine hero Curly is no wage laborer for life, but instead is about to become a prosperous farmer. *Oklahoma!* may be set in Indian Territory, but there are no Native Americans here. It is an entirely white, native-born world except for the peddler Ali Hakim, and he is clearly just passing through. There's certainly no indication of Oklahoma's arid climate and the devastating drought of the Great Depression, which would have been in recent memory when the musical was written in 1943. In fact, some of the people associated with the musical were uneasy about the title "Oklahoma," precisely because they were afraid it would remind audiences of the "Okies," the poverty-stricken

they were employees of large industrial corporations. Contrary to most Hollywood images, they were also a diverse group: among trail cowboys, approximately one-third were African American, Mexican, or Indian.

Cattle Drives and the Open Range

A postwar boom in the range cattle industry had its beginnings in southern Texas. The Spaniards had introduced longhorn cattle there in the 18th century. This hardy breed multiplied rapidly; by the 1850s, millions of them roamed freely on the Texas plains. The market for them was limited in this sparsely settled region; the nearest railhead was usually too far distant to make shipping them north and east economically feasible.

farmers forced to flee the arid plains during the Depression. Instead, this is a world of green abundance where "the corn is as high as an elephant's eye." The only shadow in this sunlit world with its "bright golden haze on the meadow" is Jud, the hired hand.

And perhaps that's why Jud is the most interesting character in this movie musical. Played with a heavy, menacing scowl by no less than Rod Steiger, Jud is the dark side of the Western dream, a man with a deep violent streak (unlike the boys-will-be-boys scuffling of the cowboys) and an unhealthy liking for "girly pictures." All of these negative qualities are loaded onto his status as the "hired hand"; he provides an uneasy reminder that class did exist in the West and that not everyone was on the brink of becoming prosperous. Jud is the only real problem in the mythic world of *Oklahoma!*, and the musical blithely dispatches him by having him fall on his own knife in a fight with Curly.

A huge hit right in the midst of World War II, the show's determined American exuberance and confidence struck deep chords. The show's brilliant choreographer Agnes DeMille remembered that soldiers and sailors would stand weeping at the back of the theater, so deeply did *Oklahoma!* evoke what they considered the essence of America. "Oh, what a beautiful mornin'," sings Curly at the beginning, and it reassured Americans that having grown up on that mythic frontier, they were at the dawn of a new era.

Vibrant movie posters for the 1955 movie musical *Oklahoma!* emphasized the fresh-faced, homespun appeal of romantic leads Gordon MacRae (Curly) and Shirley Jones (Laurey), who began her movie career with this role.

The Civil War changed all that. Beef supplies in the older states dropped drastically, and prices rose to the unheard-of sum of $40 per head. The postwar explosion of population and railroads westward brought markets and railheads ever closer to western cattle that were free to anyone who rounded them up and branded them.

Astute Texans quickly saw that the longhorns represented a fortune on the hoof—if they could be driven northward the 800 miles to the railhead at Sedalia, Missouri. In spring 1866, cowboys hit the trail with 260,000 cattle in the first of the great drives. Disease, stampedes, bad weather, Indians, and irate farmers in Missouri (who were afraid that the Texas fever carried by some of the longhorns would infect their own stock) killed or ran off most of the cattle.

Only a few thousand head made it to Sedalia, but the prices they fetched convinced ranchers that the system would work, if only they could find a better route. By 1867, the rails of the Kansas Pacific had reached Abilene, Kansas, 150 miles closer to Texas, making it possible to drive the herds through a sparsely occupied portion of Indian Territory. About 35,000 longhorns reached Abilene that summer, where they were loaded onto cattle cars for the trip to Kansas City or Chicago. This success resulted in the interlocking institutions of the cattle drive and the Chicago stockyards. The development of refrigerated rail cars in the 1870s enabled Chicago to ship dressed beef all over the country. Abilene mushroomed overnight from a sleepy village whose one bartender spent his spare time catching prairie dogs into a boomtown where 25 saloons stayed open all night, and the railroad made almost as much money shipping liquor into town as it did shipping cattle out.

More than a million longhorns bellowed their way north on the **Chisholm Trail** to Abilene over the next four years, while the railhead crept westward to other Kansas towns, chiefly Dodge City, which became the most wide-open and famous of the cow towns. As **buffalo** and Indians disappeared from the grasslands north of Texas, ranches moved northward to take their place. Cattle drives grew shorter as railroads inched forward. Ranchers grazed their cattle for free on millions of acres of open, unfenced government land. But clashes with **"grangers"** (the ranchers' contemptuous term for farmers), on the one hand, and with a growing army of sheep ranchers on the other—not to mention rustlers—led to several "range wars." Most notable was the Johnson County War in Wyoming in 1892. Grangers and small ranchers there (who had sometimes gotten their start by rustling) defeated the hired guns of the Stock Growers' Association, which represented larger ranchers.

By that time, however, the classic form of **open-range grazing** was already in decline. The boom years of the early 1880s had overstocked the range and driven down prices. Then came record cold and blizzards on the southern range in winter 1884–85, followed by even worse weather on the northern plains two years later. Hundreds of thousands of cattle froze or starved to death. These catastrophes spurred reforms that ended open-range grazing. The ranchers who survived turned to growing hay and supplemental feed for the winter. They reduced the size of their herds, started buying or leasing land and fencing in their cattle, and invested in scientific breeding that crossed longhorns with higher-quality stock to produce a better grade of beef.

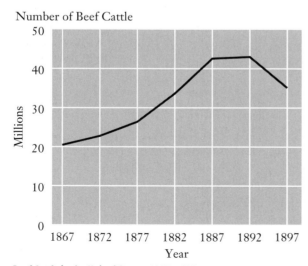

Number of Beef Cattle

Beef Cattle in the United States, 1867–1897

The Industrialization of Ranching

As open-range grazing declined, more industrialized ranching expanded. We don't usually think of ranching as an industrial process—industrialization tends to conjure up images of eastern factories belching smoke—but in fact major ranching companies operated as big businesses by the end of the century. As historian David Igler has shown, by 1900, the California corporation **Miller & Lux** was one of the largest industrial enterprises in the country, having integrated raising cattle on vast landholdings together with meatpacking in San Francisco. Its two founding partners were both ambitious German immigrants who had started out working as butchers in San Francisco but quickly moved into ownership of their own shops: despite their remarkably similar backgrounds—or perhaps because of them—they never liked each other much. Still, they were enormously successful business partners, building a corporation that shared many similarities with other large companies in the late 19th century. Mobilizing large amounts of capital, they employed over a thousand laborers in extensive operations that tightly connected ranchlands with the city.

Industrial Cowboys

Cowboys did not just ride the open range in the Texan cattle drives that have became the stuff of legend; they also rode the extensive Miller & Lux landholdings. Before the 1870s, the most valuable of the firm's cowboys were *vaqueros,* Mexican cowboys who rounded up cattle, branded them, and drove them to San Francisco. The tradition of *vaqueros* had arrived in the New World with the Spanish, who introduced herding by men on horseback. By the late 19th century, the raising of cattle herds by *vaqueros* had been practiced for centuries in California.

Not surprisingly, the head *vaquero* at Miller & Lux was a Mexican American, **Rafael Cuen.** His was a position of skill, and he was given a great deal of respect. Yet his salary was not as high as that of the white workers in the corporation who occupied parallel positions of authority, reflecting prevalent discrimination against Mexicans; it's possible this carried an especially sharp sting given the fact that his father had once owned (and lost) a piece of the Miller & Lux land. After the 1870s, the arrival of railroads took a toll on the positions of *vaqueros* like Cuen: cattle were shipped to market by rail.

Mexican Americans

Throughout the late 19th century, Mexican Americans, many of whom had owned their land for generations, lost both property and political influence to the incoming Anglo-American settlers. Many elite *Californios* who were ranchers in southern California, for instance, had to sell their lands to pay outstanding debts after devastating droughts in the 1860s virtually destroyed the ranching industry. But even as early as 1849 in the northern California goldfields, resentment of "foreigners" provoked violence against Mexican American miners—and the Foreign Miners' Tax of 1850 effectively forced Mexican Americans out of the goldfields (even though they were not "foreigners"). As the 19th century progressed, hordes of

Anglo-American "squatters" invaded the expansive holdings of the Mexican American elite, *Californios* who were forced to seek relief in the courts. Although their claims were generally upheld, these legal proceedings often stretched on for years. After exorbitant legal fees and other expenses were taken into account, a legal triumph was often a Pyrrhic victory. In the end, most Mexican American landholders in northern California, like those in southern California, had to sell the very lands they had fought to keep in order to pay their mounting debts.

Elsewhere, the migration of Anglos into eastern Texas had played a role in fomenting the war for Texas independence and in bringing about the war with Mexico (see chapter 13). By the latter half of the 19th century, eastern Texas was overwhelmingly Anglo; most *Tejanos* (people of Mexican origin or descent) were concentrated in the Rio Grande Valley of southern Texas. As in California, Anglos in Texas used force and intimidation, coupled with exploitative legal maneuvering, to disenfranchise the *Tejanos*. The **Texas Rangers** often acted as an Anglo vigilante force that exacted retribution for the real or imagined crimes of Mexican Americans. Eventually, Mexican Americans in Texas were reduced to a state of peonage, dependent on their Anglo protectors for political and economic security.

Similar patterns prevailed in New Mexico, but the effects were mitigated somewhat because New Mexicans continued to outnumber Anglo-American settlers. Earlier in the 19th century, international trade along the Santa Fe Trail had strengthened the political and economic status of the New Mexican elites. Now these same elites consolidated their position by acting as power brokers between poorer New Mexicans and wealthy Anglos. Despite such difficult conditions, Spanish-speaking peoples maintained their cultural traditions in the face of Anglo settlement, with the Roman Catholic Church serving as an important center of community life. An influx of immigrants from Mexico toward the end of the century created a new basis for community as well.

Itinerant Laborers

The *vaquero* Rafael Cuen was a highly skilled worker of great value to his employer; he was one of the lucky employees who had long-term employment. But for many workers in the West, itineracy was the norm; a virtual army of workers and wanderers traveled the western countryside. Most low-level jobs in ranching were seasonal, meaning that workers were forced to move from place to place periodically in search of work. And as western industrialization uprooted many workers from their traditional lives, more and more people took to the road. As Henry George said in his bestselling 1879 book *Progress and Poverty,* a scathing indictment of the current economic system, "the 'tramp' comes with the locomotive." For George, who had been a prospector before becoming a newspaper editor in California, the fault lay in a system of "land monopoly" that allowed control of land and resources by the few at the expense of the many.

At Miller & Lux, **itinerant laborers** were Chinese, Portuguese, Italian, Mexican, and Mexican American, in addition to white, native-born Americans. One of the itinerant laborers who hired on to an irrigation crew was a man named Joseph Warren Matthews, a farmer who had heavy debts. To pay these debts, he had taken on a series of grueling temporary jobs, including wage labor for a lumber company in the Pacific Northwest, work in the Alaskan goldfields, pipe laying for a water company, ore smelting, and digging ditches. His situation underlined the precariousness of many lives in the industrializing West.

Homesteading and Farming

Many homesteaders and farmers shared that precariousness: not only were 49 percent of all homesteaders unable to "prove up" their claims, but many were ultimately forced off their homesteads by the unforgiving climate of the Great Plains.

For much of the antebellum period, the Great Plains were known as the Great American Desert and assumed to be uninhabitable. By the 1850s, however, many boosters of western expansion promoted the idea that the Great Plains were a potentially lush American garden perfect for settlement. In this view, aridity was not a problem; the folk belief that "rainfall follows the plow"—that settlement would somehow prevent droughts—even gained credence among some geologists and other experts.

A great wave of settlement of the Great Plains occurred during the late 1870s to the mid-1880s, when rainfall was in fact relatively abundant. But the truth was that the average normal rainfall on the plains west of the 98th meridian (a line running roughly from the center of the Dakotas through the center of Texas) was scarcely enough to support farming except in certain river valleys. Years of drought inevitably followed, beginning in 1886 and lasting through the mid-1890s—and fueling farmers' discontent and protests (see chapter 19). Homesteaders and farmers in Minnesota, Iowa, and parts of Kansas and Nebraska were relatively lucky because those areas offered rich soil and adequate rainfall. In Iowa, for instance, farmers had great success with a "corn and hog" farm economy. But other land was arid and unproductive, producing heartbreak for homesteaders and farmers. Between 1888 and 1892, half the population of Kansas and Nebraska was forced to give up and move back east to Illinois or Iowa.

The Experience of Homesteading

Homesteading families on the Great Plains literally built their houses from the ground up: in an environment without trees, they cut the dense prairie sod into blocks and stacked them up to form walls, providing a small window and a door in a "soddy" of around 18 by 24 feet. **Soddies** were a practical solution to a difficult problem on the plains, but they were also dark, dank, and claustrophobic.

As Kansas homesteader Mary Abell (an excerpt from one of her letters opens this chapter) explained to her sister: "Imagine living in a place dug out of the side of a hill (one side to the weather with door and window—top covered with dirt and you have our place of abode). No one east would think of putting pigs in such a place." Abell's letters from 1871 to 1875 made clear the hard labor involved in homesteading: in addition to caring for five

Library of Congress, Prints and Photographs Division

A Nebraska Soddy   This appealing young family stands proudly in front of their Nebraska soddy in 1884 or 1885, during a time when rainfall was abundant on the Great Plains. A long-term drought began in 1886, however, making us wonder whether this family was able to hang on to its homestead through the coming difficult times.

children, in the fall of 1873, she had been her husband's "sole help in getting up and stacking at least 25 tons of hay and oats." Less than a week later, "one of those dreadful prairie fires" swept through the Abells' land, and they lost not only their hay and oats but also chickens and farm equipment. In 1874, she faced both drought and grasshoppers, and wrote her family that "none of you have the least conception" of "actual want, destitution." In 1875, Abell died at the age of 29.

Of course, not all homesteaders faced the same dire straits. Many of the 4 million immigrants who came from Germany, the Czech region of the Austro-Hungarian empire, and the Scandinavian countries from 1865 to 1890 settled in the upper Midwest and northern plains and became successful farmers. The northern plains region had the highest proportion of foreign-born residents in the nation during the last quarter of the century. These European immigrants formed homogenous ethnic enclaves that maintained the distinctive culture and traditions of their homelands. Swedish immigrants in Minnesota, for instance, spoke Swedish with one another and centered their lives around the Swedish Lutheran church; their children attended Swedish schools and learned to read the Swedish bible, sing Swedish songs, and recite Swedish history; and both men and women wore traditional Swedish dress on holidays. By the end of the century, there were also homogenous ethnic communities of Germans, Czechs, Poles, Hungarians, and Norwegians dotting the northern landscape.

Gender and Western Settlement

The Homestead Act was unusual in allowing unmarried women to make claims; between 5 percent and 15 percent of homestead entries in different locales went to women in the late 19th century. Many of these women probably "proved up" only to immediately sell their land, rather than farm it themselves: but still, the existence of women homesteaders reminds us that in some ways, gender arrangements were different in the West than in other regions of the country.

The most pronounced difference was a gender-divided society in mining camps and towns, which were overwhelmingly masculine. During the Gold Rush, California was up to 93 percent male, and many ranches, including Miller & Lux holdings, were exclusively male as well. Mining towns were known as violent places, and many observers were anxious to establish a more respectable family life there.

Prostitutes from all over the world were drawn to mining towns throughout the late 19th century, but nowhere except in San Francisco were women systematically forced into sexual slavery. There, the situation of Chinese laborers encouraged an exploitative world trade in women. While by the last decades of the century, Chinese merchants were allowed to bring their wives and daughters to America, laborers had no such rights. By custom, as well, respectable Chinese women were expected to stay home. The numbers of Chinese women in America remained extremely low in the 19th century, never rising above 5,000.

The difficulty in bringing Chinese women to America encouraged a brutal international trade in prostitution. Chinese women who were kidnapped or purchased from poor parents were sold into indentured servitude or slavery and unknowingly shipped to America to become prostitutes. In San Francisco, an estimated 85 percent to 97 percent of Chinese women were prostitutes in 1860; around 72 percent in 1870; and between 21 percent to 50 percent in 1880. They faced a singularly harsh existence. However, some women managed to escape prostitution. Some women married men who had saved up enough money to purchase the contracts that bound them; Protestant missionaries worked to rescue prostitutes, as well.

As these few examples show, settlement patterns of the West produced—at least for a short period of time—societies with unequal numbers of men and women, with different results in different places. The impact of these disparities continues to intrigue historians, who still puzzle, for instance, over the reasons why several western states were the first to grant woman suffrage (see chapter 21). In the realm of Western myth, one obvious legacy of the West's early gender arrangements is the enduring place in American culture of the white cowboy as an icon of rugged masculinity.

Conquest and Resistance: American Indians in the Trans-Mississippi West

Focus Question
How did the Indian peoples of the trans-Mississippi West respond to white settlement and U.S. government policies?

The westward expansion of ranching and farming after 1865 doomed the free range of the Plains Indians and the buffalo. In the 1830s, eastern tribes had been forcibly moved to preserves west of the Mississippi so as permanently to separate whites and Indians. In scarcely a decade, white settlers had penetrated these lands via the overland trails to the Pacific Coast. In the 1850s, when the Kansas and Nebraska territories opened to white settlement, the government forced a dozen tribes living there to cede 15 million acres, leaving them on reservations totaling less than 1.5 million acres. Thus began what historian Philip Weeks has called the "policy of concentration": No longer were Indians to be pushed west onto the arid plains that early white explorers had christened The Great American Desert. Rather, as white settlers moved onto and through the plains and mountains, they began to covet these large spaces, which earlier treaties had assigned to the Indians for "as long as waters shall run and the grass shall grow."

Even before the Civil War, the nomadic Plains Indians, whose culture and economy were based on the buffalo, faced pressure not only from the advancing tide of white settlement but also from the forced migration of eastern tribes into their domain. In the aftermath of the Civil War, the process of concentrating Indian tribes on reservations accelerated. Chiefs of the five **"civilized tribes"**—Cherokees, Creeks, Choctaws, Chickasaws, and Seminoles—had signed treaties of alliance with the Confederacy. At that time, they were living in Indian Territory (most of present-day Oklahoma), where their economy was linked to the South. Many of them, especially members of the mixed-blood upper class, were slaveholders. Bitter toward the United States, the tribal leaders cast their lot with the Confederacy on the principle that "the enemy of my enemy is my friend." The Cherokee leader Stand Watie rose to brigadier general in the Confederate army and was the last Confederate commander to surrender, on June 23, 1865. **(See Map 18.2, Indian Reservations, 1875 and 1900, in the color insert following page 816.)**

Siding with the Confederacy proved to be a costly mistake for these tribes. The U.S. government "reconstructed" Indian Territory more quickly and with less contention than it reconstructed the former Confederate states. Treaties with the five tribes in 1866 required them to grant tribal citizenship to their freed slaves and reduced tribal lands by half. The government then settled Indians who had been dispossessed from other areas on the land it had taken from these tribes.

Conflict with the Sioux

The Civil War had set in motion a generation of Indian warfare that was more violent and widespread than anything since the 17th century. During the war, the Union army was forced to pull many units out of frontier posts to fight the Confederacy. Moreover, the drain on the Union treasury to finance the war compounded the usual corruption of Indian agents and delayed annuity payments to tribes that had sold their land to the government. These events had dire consequences on the northern plains.

Herded onto reservations along the Minnesota River by the **Treaty of Traverse des Sioux** in 1851, the Santee Sioux were angry when late annuity payments in summer

1862 threatened starvation. Warriors began to speak openly of reclaiming ancestral hunting grounds. Then on August 17, a robbery in which five white settlers were murdered seemed to open the floodgates. The warriors persuaded Chief Little Crow to take them on the warpath, and over the next few weeks, at least 500 white Minnesotans were massacred.

Hastily mobilized militia and army units finally suppressed the uprising. A military court convicted 319 Indians of murder and atrocities and sentenced 303 of them to death. Appalled by this ferocious retaliation, Lincoln personally reviewed the trial transcripts and reduced the number of executions to 38—the largest act of executive clemency in American history. Even so, the hanging of 38 Sioux on December 26, 1862, was the largest mass execution the country has ever witnessed. The government evicted the remaining Sioux from Minnesota to Dakota Territory.

In the meantime, the army's pursuit of fleeing Santee Sioux provoked other Sioux tribes farther west. By 1864, and for a decade afterward, fighting flared between the army and the Sioux across the northern plains. It reached a climax in 1874 and 1875 after gold-seekers poured into the Black Hills of western Dakota, a sacred place to the Sioux. At the **battle of Little Bighorn** in Montana Territory on June 25, 1876, Sioux warriors led by **Sitting Bull** and **Crazy Horse,** along with their Cheyenne allies, wiped out **George A. Custer** and the 225 men with him in the Seventh Cavalry. In retaliation, General Philip Sheridan carried out a winter campaign in which the Sioux and Cheyenne were crushed.

Largest and most warlike of the Plains tribes, the Sioux were confined to a reservation in Dakota Territory where poverty, disease, apathy, and alcoholism reduced this once-proud people to desperation.

Suppression of Other Plains Indians

Just as the Sioux uprising in Minnesota had triggered war on the northern plains in 1862, a massacre of Cheyennes in Colorado in 1864 sparked a decade of conflict on the southern plains. The discovery of gold near Pike's Peak set off a rush to Colorado in 1858–59. The government responded by calling several Cheyenne and Arapaho chiefs to a council, and with a combination of threats and promises, the agents persuaded the chiefs to sign a treaty giving up all claims to land in this region (guaranteed by an earlier treaty of 1851) in exchange for a reservation at Sand Creek in southeast Colorado.

In 1864, hunger and resentment on the reservation prompted many warriors to return to their old hunting grounds and to raid white settlements. Skirmishes soon erupted into open warfare. In the fall, Cheyenne Chief Black Kettle, believing that he had concluded peace with the Colorado settlers, returned to the reservation. There, at dawn on November 29, militia commanded by Colonel John Chivington surrounded and attacked Black Kettle's unsuspecting camp, killing 200 Indians, half of them women and children.

The notorious **Sand Creek massacre** set a pattern for several similar attacks on Indian villages in subsequent years. Ever since the earliest battles between colonists and Indians in the

17th century, whites had followed the strategy of burning Indian crops and villages as a means of destroying or driving off the Indians. Sherman and Sheridan had adopted a similar strategy against the Confederates and followed it again as military commanders responsible for subduing the Plains Indians. Their purpose was to corral all of the Indians onto the reservations that were being created throughout the West. In addition to trying to defeat the Indians in battle, which proved to be difficult against the mounted Plains Indians, the army encouraged the extermination of the buffalo herds. Professional hunters slaughtered the large, clumsy animals by the millions for their hides, thus depriving Plains Indians of both physical and spiritual sustenance. When the buffalo became nearly extinct in 1883, the Plains Indians understood that their old way of life was gone forever. "Nothing happened after that," recalled one Crow warrior. "We just lived. There were no more war parties, no capturing horses from the Piegan and the Sioux, no buffalo to hunt. There is nothing more to tell."

The Indians were left with no alternative but to come into the reservations, and by the 1880s, nearly all of them had done so. Chief Joseph of the Nez Percé pronounced the epitaph for their way of life when federal troops blocked the escape of his band from Montana to Canada in 1877:

> I am tired of fighting. Our chiefs are killed. The old men are all dead. It is cold and we have no blankets . . . no food. . . . The little children are freezing to death. . . . Hear me, my chiefs; I am tired; my heart is sick and sad. From where the sun now stands, I will fight no more forever.

The "Peace Policy"

Many Eastern reformers condemned America's violent repression of the Indians. The most prominent was **Helen Hunt Jackson,** whose 1881 book *A Century of Dishonor* was an outraged indictment of anti-Indian violence, exploitation, and broken treaties. Yet as sympathetic as Jackson was to the Indians' plight, she was not sympathetic to Indian culture; like other white Protestant reformers of her day, she believed that Indians must be stripped of their culture in order to assimilate productively to American society.

In this view she was in alignment with the government: in 1869, President Grant had announced a new **"peace policy"** toward Indians, urging "their civilization and ultimate citizenship." "Civilization" meant acceptance of white culture, including the English language, Christianity, and individual ownership of property. It also meant allegiance to the United States rather than to a tribe. In 1869, Grant established a Board of Indian Commissioners and staffed it with humanitarian reformers. In 1871, the century-long policy of negotiating treaties with Indian "nations" came to an end. From then on, Indians became "wards of the nation," to be civilized and prepared for citizenship, first on reservations and eventually on individually owned parcels of land that were carved out of the reservations. Most Indians acquiesced in the "reconstruction" that offered them citizenship by the 1880s; they had little choice.

The Dawes Severalty Act and Indian Boarding Schools

In order to further the goal of Indian ownership of private property, Protestant reformers in the 1880s found themselves in a strange alliance with land-hungry westerners, who greedily eyed the 155 million acres of land tied up in reservations. If part of that land could be allotted directly to individual ownership by Indian families, the remainder would become available for purchase by whites. The 1887 **Dawes Severalty Act** combined these impulses toward greed and reform. This landmark legislation called for the dissolution of Indian tribes as legal entities, offered Indians the opportunity to become citizens, and allotted each head of family 160 acres of farmland or 320 acres of grazing land as long as they were "severed" from their tribe.

For whites who were eager to seize reservation land, the Dawes Act brought a bonanza. At noon on April 22, 1889, the government threw open specified parts of the Indian Territory to "Boomers," who descended on the region like locusts and by nightfall had staked claim to nearly 2 million acres. Indians did not just lose the lands legally opened for white settlement: many Indians who received individual land titles through the Dawes Act also lost these lands to unscrupulous whites through fraud and misrepresentation. Eventually, whites gained title to 108 million acres of former reservation land.

For Indians, the Dawes Severalty Act was a disaster. Private ownership of land was an alien concept to most tribes, yet Indians received little training for a transition to farming, much less appropriate tools or supplies. Moreover, the poor quality of their land allotments made farming difficult, if not impossible. In addition the Dawes Act directly attacked Indian culture by forbidding Indian religions, the telling of Indian myths and legends, and the practices of medicine men.

Indian boarding schools established beginning in the late 1870s were another attempt to strip Indians of their culture. Children were taken from their families to the Hampton Institute in Virginia and the Carlisle Institute in Pennsylvania, among other schools. There they were forbidden to speak Indian languages or wear Indian clothing: as one 1890 set of instructions from the U.S. Bureau of Indian Affairs put it, "Pupils must be compelled to converse with each other in English, and should be properly rebuked or punished for persistent violation of this rule." The writer Zitkala-Sa, a Yankton Sioux, later remembered her life in an Indian school: "the melancholy of those black days has left so long a shadow that it darkens the path of years that have since gone by."

Indian schools may have had assimilation to white culture as a goal, but they also had a very narrow vision of the place Indians would hold in a white world. Girls were taught domestic science but little more and were educated for menial jobs as servants; many spent long hours working in school laundries as virtual servants of the schools that were supposed to teach them. Students resisted as best they could by running away, often only to be caught and returned to school again; many adults later resisted the training they had received by returning to Indian traditions. This was the case with Zitkala-Sa: after graduation from an Indian boarding school, Zitkala-Sa taught at the Carlisle School and became a much-praised writer in New York. But later she would undergo a spiritual crisis: she compared herself to a "slender tree" that had been "uprooted from my mother, nature, and God," and lamented that she had "forgotten the healing in trees and brooks." Eventually she left New York, married a Sioux, and became an activist for Native American rights.

The Ghost Dance

At a time of despair for many Indians, a new visionary religious movement swept through Indian peoples in 1890, offering a different kind of resistance to white domination. The **Ghost Dance** began with the visions of the Paiute shaman Wovoka, who counseled Indians that if they gave up alcohol, lived a simple life, and devoted themselves to prayer, white men would disappear from the earth, Indian lands would be restored, and dead Indians would rejoin the living. This message of hope was embodied in the Ghost Dance ritual, involving days of worship expressed in part through dance.

When the Ghost Dance religion spread to those Sioux led by Sitting Bull and they began days of ecstatic dancing, Indian agents grew alarmed: as one agent telegraphed authorities, "Indians are dancing in the snow and are wild and crazy. *We need protection and we need it now.*" The results of the ensuing confrontations between Indians and authorities were tragic: first Sitting Bull and his grandson were killed in a skirmish with reservation authorities; then a few days later, a trigger-happy military—members of the Seventh Cavalry, Custer's old regiment—opened fire on Sioux men, women, and children at **Wounded Knee** in the Pine Ridge Reservation, killing 146 Indians, including 44 women and 18 children, as well as 25 soldiers. For many, the massacre at Wounded Knee symbolized the death of 19th-century Plains Indian culture. While Indians throughout the West would adapt to a new world with great resilience, working to preserve their cultural practices, there was no question that their old world had been demolished.

Sitting Bull and Buffalo Bill: Popular Myths of the West

Only a few years before he was killed, Sitting Bull had been one of the chief attractions in the entertainment extravaganza known as **Buffalo Bill Cody's Wild West Show.** No mere victim of white exploitation, Sitting Bull had been a canny negotiator of fees for his appearances in 1885; he required an interpreter, several attendants, and a salary that came to half the annual salary of the typical Indian agent. He also used press interviews while on the Wild West tour to ask the U.S. government to live up to its promises to Indians. If Sitting Bull was being used by Cody, he was certainly using Cody right back.

Having "real" Indians in his show was of vital importance to Cody, who capitalized on the public's hunger for "authentic" spectacular entertainments in his popular Wild West shows. Cody was an extraordinary mix of the new industrializing West, the frontier West, and an emerging culture of mass entertainment. Having begun his career as a soldier in the Civil War, Cody then worked for one of the transcontinental railroad lines (where he gained the nickname "Buffalo Bill" for slaughtering buffalo) before becoming a scout for the Fifth Cavalry. When Cody became the subject of a popular dime Western novel, the

Sitting Bull and Buffalo Bill   Before he was killed in 1890 during the Ghost Dance movement, the renowned Sioux leader Sitting Bull became an important part of Buffalo Bill's Wild West Show, negotiating shrewdly for his salary. In this remarkable 1885 staged image, the elaborately costumed Buffalo Bill and Sitting Bull appear as virtual equals, both resting a hand on the same rifle.

most improbable turn in Cody's career occurred: he decided to dramatize his own life in a series of theatrical entertainments. By the year Sitting Bull joined Buffalo Bill's Wild West Show with its band of trick riders and sharpshooters, it required 18 railroad cars to transport performers (including a number of Indians), work crews, animals, and equipment.

The Wild West Show celebrated the white conquest of the West in a series of acts called "The Drama of Civilization," which showed scenes of an emigrant train crossing the prairie, Buffalo Bill rescuing a pioneer family from Indians, and a mining camp. Billed as

"America's National Entertainment," these shows revealed just how tightly linked industrialization and conquest were in Americans' thinking—and even in their entertainment.

Industrialization and the New South

Focus Question
How did industrialization shape African American experience in the post-Reconstruction South?

Like the West, the South underwent a surge of industrialization in the last decades of the 19th century. Boosters like the energetic and influential Henry Grady, editor of the Atlanta *Constitution,* proclaimed that a **New South** had emerged, one hospitable to industry and to Northern investment.

Some people scoffed at such promotional talk in a world that was still decidedly rural, but in fact the pace of industrialization quickened in the last decades of the century, with textiles leading the way. In 1880, the South had only 5 percent of the country's textile-producing capacity; by 1900, it had 23 percent and was well on its way to surpassing New England a generation later. Tobacco also industrialized, with James B. Duke of North Carolina transforming the industry with his installation of cigarette-making machines at Durham in 1885. In 1890, he created the American Tobacco Company, which controlled 90 percent of the market.

Railroads and iron also saw a surge in growth. Between 1877 and 1900, the South built railroads faster than any other region in the country. In 1880, the former slave states produced only 9 percent of the nation's pig iron; by 1890, after a decade of extraordinary expansion for the industry nationwide, that proportion had doubled. Most of the growth was concentrated in northern Alabama, where the proximity of coal, limestone, and ore made the new city of Birmingham the "Pittsburgh of the South."

But there were limits to Southern industrialization. It was difficult to catch up with well-established Northern industries. Thus Southerners competed in the few areas in which they could find markets for local crops and resources: textiles produced from their own cotton; cigarettes manufactured from Southern tobacco; as well as lumber, sugar, and iron.

Not all of the wealth from the new industries went into the pockets of Southerners, though. Over the late 19th century, Southern industry attracted more and more Northern capital in a pattern that held true across industries. At first, for instance, Southerners supplied most of the capital in the expansion of the textile industry. But after 1893, an increasing amount came from the North, as New England mill owners began to recognize the benefits of relocating to the low-wage, nonunion South. In the tobacco industry, too, initial Southern capital gave way to Northern financing, especially after James Duke moved to New York in the 1880s. But most dependent on Northern capital were the railroads and iron industries. When in 1886 Southern railroads switched their tracks from the regional gauge to the national standard, the symbolic domination of the North seemed complete.

Heavy Northern investment in Southern industry meant that the South had less control over economic decisions that affected its welfare. Some historians have referred to the South's "colonial" relationship to the North in the late 19th century. One result was that the low wages prevailing in the South made for inequitable distribution of the economic benefits of industrial growth. Average Southern per capita income remained only two-fifths of the average in the rest of the country well into the 20th century.

Race and Industrialization

Even those low wages were unequally distributed, as the politics of race influenced the structuring of industrial jobs. Along the piedmont from Virginia to Alabama, new cotton mills sprang up for a white labor force drawn from farm families on the worn-out red clay soil of this region. About 40 percent of the workers were women, and 25 percent were children aged 16 and younger. Living in company towns, they labored long hours for wages about half the level prevailing in New England's mills, with their cheap labor giving mill owners a competitive advantage.

At first many African Americans confidently assumed that there would be jobs for them in this new textile industry. And why not? Blacks had worked before the Civil War in mills, and they continued to work in tobacco factories in the postwar era, albeit in the lowest-paid jobs and performing the dirtiest work. There seemed no reason why such a large and inexpensive workforce might not become a mainstay of the mills.

But industrialization did not mean progress for blacks in most places. Instead, it went hand in hand with segregation in the increasingly white supremacist world of the 1880s and 1890s. To attract white workers, mill owners promised them segregated environments. The bargain offered was this: mill workers might not earn very much, but they would gain what one historian has called the **"wages of whiteness,"** a sense of racial superiority that could serve as compensation for their low economic status. Thus the New South was built around the politics of race, and many African Americans lost ground in the emerging industrial economy. For most African Americans, agricultural work was thus the only option.

Southern Agriculture

A major success story, however, was increasing black ownership of land in the post-Reconstruction period, with almost 200,000 farmers achieving that cherished goal. Most black landowners in the South were in the Upper South or coastal areas; others were in the trans-Mississippi West.

Still, most blacks were tenants rather than landowners, and many blacks and whites faced lives of grinding rural poverty. Those who owned land risked sliding into tenantry; those who did not own land found it impossible to make the leap to land ownership. One-crop specialization, overproduction, declining prices, and an exploitative credit system all contributed to the problem. The basic institution of the Southern rural economy was the crop lien system, which came into being because of the shortage of money and credit in the war-ravaged South. Few banks had survived the war, and land values had plummeted, which left farmers unable to secure a bank loan with their land as collateral. Instead, merchants in the crossroads country stores that sprang up across the South provided farmers with supplies and groceries in return for a lien on their next crop.

This system might have worked well if the merchants had charged reasonable interest rates and if cotton and tobacco prices had remained high enough for the farmer to pay off his debts after harvest with a little left over. But the country storekeeper charged a credit price 50 or 60 percent above the cash price, partly because he had no competition and partly because of the high risk of loss on his loans. And crop prices, especially for cotton, were dropping steadily. Cotton prices declined from an average of 12 cents per pound in the 1870s to 6 cents in the 1890s. As prices fell, many farmers went deeper and deeper into debt to the merchants. **Sharecroppers** and tenants incurred a double indebtedness: to the landowner whose land they sharecropped or rented, and to the merchant who furnished them supplies on credit. Because many landowners became merchants, and vice versa, that indebtedness was often to the same man.

One reason cotton prices fell was overproduction. Britain had encouraged the expansion of cotton growing in Egypt and India during the Civil War to make up for the loss of American cotton. After the war, Southern growers had to face international competition. By 1878, the Southern crop had reached the output of the best antebellum year, and during the next 20 years, output doubled. This overproduction drove prices ever lower. To obtain credit, farmers had to plant every acre with the most marketable cash crop—cotton. This practice exhausted the soil and required ever-increasing amounts of expensive fertilizer, which fed the cycle of overproduction and declining prices.

It also reduced the amount of land that could be used to grow food crops. Farmers who might otherwise have produced their own cornmeal and raised their own hogs for bacon became dependent on merchants for these supplies. Before the Civil War, the cotton states had been nearly self-sufficient in food; by the 1890s, they had to import nearly half their food at a price 50 percent higher than it would have cost to grow their own. Many Southerners recognized that only diversification could break this dependency, but the crop lien system locked them into it. "We ought to plant less [cotton and tobacco] and more of grain and grasses," said a North Carolina farmer in 1887, "but how are we to do it; the man who furnishes us rations at 50 percent interest won't let us; he wants money crop planted. . . . It is cotton! cotton! cotton! Buy everything and make cotton pay for it." Many sharecroppers, particularly blacks, fell into virtual peonage.

Exodusters and Emigrationists

Given the multiple difficulties rural African Americans faced—from persistent poverty to dependence on white owners to racial discrimination and violence—it is not surprising that many dreamed of leaving the South entirely. In the late 1870s, a movement called Exodus gained momentum among African Americans who believed that they might have to "repeat the history of the Israelites" and "seek new homes beyond the reign and rule of Pharaoh." Most pinned their hopes on internal emigration to the West, although some explored the possibility of emigration to Liberia as well. In 1875, Benjamin Singleton, a former Tennessee slave, helped a group of African Americans establish new lives in an agrarian colony in western Kansas; three years later, he circulated an alluring advertisement picturing prairie abundance in the hopes of enticing a few hundred more settlers. Instead, in the spring of 1879, some 20,000 African Americans began an exodus to Kansas from all over the Southwest—drawn not just by the advertisement but also by rumors that there was free land available for settlers as well as free supplies from the government. The rumors were false, but many of these **Exodusters** stayed on in Kansas anyway, although not as homesteaders amidst the prairie abundance but as domestics and laborers in Kansan towns, including towns they founded such as Nicodemus.

Race Relations in the New South

The desire to emigrate for better jobs, autonomy, and a place where African Americans could be truly free did not end with the Exodusters. "The disposition among the colored people to migrate now is strong, and is increasing," commented a white Southerner in 1889. There was a net loss of 537,000 African Americans in the South between 1880 and 1910. Economic reasons were important, but so too was the worsening world of white supremacy that arose in that period.

Adherence to the industrial ideology behind the New South, with its emphasis on racial cooperation, was shallow at best among broad classes of whites. Instead, many refused to let go of the legacy of the defeated plantation South. They celebrated the Lost Cause by organizing fraternal and sororal organizations such as the **United Daughters of the Confederacy (UDC).** The UDC, like the Daughters of the American Revolution (DAR) on which it was modeled, was open only to whites who could prove their relation to the "first families" of the South. Its members decorated the graves of Confederate soldiers, funded public statues of Confederate heroes, and sought to preserve a romanticized history of the slavery era. Several white Southern authors became famous writing stories about this fabled South. Thomas Nelson Page's racist sentimental story "Marse Chan" created a national craze for Southern literature in the 1880s. Published in a Northern magazine, the story was written in what Page claimed to be authentic black dialect, with an aging freedman telling of the glorious days before the war when slaves supposedly had little work to do. Such stories romanticized the Southern plantation, cleansing it of the horrors of slavery.

The national appeal of such stories made it clear that anti-black racism was not just a Southern phenomenon. Certainly, there was shockingly little Northern reaction to the wave of **lynchings** of black men in the South in the 1890s. Lynchings rose to an all-time high, averaging 188 per year, while the viciousness of racist propaganda reached an all-time low. At a time when many professional middle-class African American men and women were steadily gaining economically, even as a downward spiral in the rural economy frustrated whites, lynchings of black men were not just extraordinarily violent acts. They were also clear symbolic messages to entire black communities to keep their "place" in a white-dominated society. Ritualized expressions of white power, lynchings were not secret or furtive events, but often well-orchestrated community affairs advertised in advance and sometimes even including men, women, and children as spectators.

In 1892, three respected African American businessmen who owned a grocery store in Memphis, Tennessee, were taken from the jail where they awaited trial and lynched by a white mob. Their ostensible crime was attempted murder—firing on three white intruders who had burst into their store—but their real offense was successfully challenging the dominance of a white grocery store in their area.

In response to the lynching, the African American journalist **Ida B. Wells** embarked on an extensive anti-lynching campaign involving an economic boycott as well as a series of fiery editorials in her newspaper, *Free Speech,* that called into question the usual white rationale for lynching: the supposed rape or molestation of a white woman. Correctly exposing this common trumped-up charge as "the old racket," Wells ignited the wrath of white Memphis residents and was forced to flee for her life to the North. But there her anti-lynching campaign met with indifference from Northerners until Wells traveled to England on a speaking tour. She received widespread publicity as she called into question how civilized America could be if it tolerated a barbaric practice like lynching; she also touched a nerve back home. Upperclass white Northerners indifferent to the murder of blacks but sensitive to English opinion finally sat up and began to notice her campaign. Her English travels were a brilliant strategy to shake up Northern complacency and challenge Northern complicity in lynching.

The Emergence of an African American Middle Class

Wells was part of an extensive African American middle class that came of age in the 1880s and 1890s. These men and women, educated in the emerging black colleges, became teachers, doctors, lawyers, ministers, and business owners. They formed numerous civic organizations, such as the 1896 **National Association of Colored Women,** which was part of the women's club movement of the late 19th century (see chapter 19). Echoing the moral reform activities of white middle-class women, its president, Mary Church Terrell, called on middle-class black women to work with "the masses of our women" and to "uplift and claim them."

Such institution building, combined with increasing prosperity, gave middle-class blacks great optimism that "racial uplift" might reduce or even eliminate racism in American society. "We as a race are enjoying the brightest rays of Christian civilization," wrote one bishop in the African Methodist Episcopal (AME) Church. Middle-class blacks believed that through education and self-improvement, they could become "best men" and "best women," seen as equals by middle-class whites. These were not naïve hopes, as black entry into the middle class surged in the 1880s and early 1890s.

The Rise of Jim Crow

But these visible successes of middle-class African Americans enraged white supremacists, who denied any possibility of class solidarity across racial lines. Serious anti-black riots broke out in Wilmington, North Carolina, in 1898 and in Atlanta in 1906. Several states adopted new constitutions that disenfranchised most black voters by means of literacy or property

© The Granger Collection, New York

Ida B. Wells   A passionate crusader for justice, the renowned journalist Ida B. Wells received death threats after she began a campaign against lynching in her Memphis, Tennessee newspaper, *Free Speech*, in 1892. Forced to leave Memphis, Wells moved to Chicago and continued her anti-lynching crusade in pamphlets, newspaper columns, and public lectures delivered both in the U.S. and in England. Together with Booker T. Washington, Wells was one of the most prominent African American leaders of the 1890s.

qualifications (or both), poll taxes, and other clauses implicitly aimed at black voters. The new constitutions contained "understanding clauses" or "grandfather clauses" that enabled registrars to register white voters who were unable to meet the new requirements. In *Williams* v. *Mississippi* (1898), the U.S. Supreme Court upheld these disenfranchisement clauses on the grounds that they did not discriminate "on their face" against blacks. Most blacks lost the right to vote, and the Republican Party almost disappeared from most southern states. State Democratic parties then established primary elections in which only whites could vote. For the next 60 years, the primary was the only meaningful election in the South.

During these same years, most southern states passed **Jim Crow laws** (the name came from blackface minstrelsy; see chapter 10) mandating racial segregation in public facilities of all kinds. Many African Americans resisted: in 1884, Ida B. Wells, at the time a young schoolteacher, refused to give up her seat in a railway "ladies' car." The conductor "tried to drag me out of the seat," she remembered, "but the moment he caught hold of my arm I fastened my teeth in the back of his hand. I had braced my feet against the seat in front and was holding to the back, and as he had already been badly bitten he didn't try it again by himself. He went forward and got the baggageman and another man to help him and of course they succeeded in dragging me out." Wells sued the railroad, winning her case in a lower court before losing it on appeal.

In 1896 came a tremendous setback for American equality. In the landmark case of **Plessy v. Ferguson** (1896), the Supreme Court sanctioned Jim Crow laws so long as the separate facilities for blacks were equal to those for whites—which, in practice, they never were. At this "nadir" of the black experience in freedom, as one historian has called the 1890s, a new black leader emerged as successor of the abolitionists and Reconstruction politicians who were fading from the scene. **Booker T. Washington,** a 39-year-old educator who had founded Tuskegee Institute in Alabama, gave a speech at the 1895 Atlanta Exposition that made him famous—and has been controversial ever since.

Speaking to a white audience at this celebration of Southern industry and progress, Washington was introduced as "a representative of Negro enterprise and civilization." Assuring his audience that he wanted to "cement the friendship of the races," Washington talked of the "new era of industrial progress" and told the industrialists before him that they should hire African Americans rather than immigrants. "Cast down your bucket where you are," he told them, "among the eight million of Negroes whose habits you know." If they did so, Washington said, they would not only find people to "run your factories," but could also be assured that they would be surrounded by a "faithful, law-abiding, and unresentful" people. In the most famous sentence of the speech, Washington then promised that "in all things that are purely social we can be as separate as the fingers, yet one as the hand in all things essential to mutual progress." In effect, Washington accepted segregation as a temporary accommodation between the races in return for white support of black efforts for education, social uplift, and economic progress.

It was a complex, canny speech, much like the man himself, and Washington's listeners came away with very different impressions. Many African Americans applauded his appeal for black inclusion in the new industrial order; many white audience members simply took away the idea that Washington approved of segregation, vocational training for blacks, and a permanent, second-class status. An eloquent response to Washington came from the emerging African American leader **W. E. B. Du Bois** in his 1903 masterpiece, *The Souls of Black Folk,* a set of essays written between 1897 and 1903. Criticizing Washington for a policy of conciliation and submission, Du Bois reminded his audience that "only a firm adherence to their higher ideals and aspirations will ever keep those ideals within the realm of possibility."

The Politics of Stalemate

Focus Question
Why did politicians fail to address many of the most serious economic and social issues facing the nation in the post-Reconstruction world?

During the 20 years between the Panic of 1873 and the Panic of 1893, serious economic and social issues beset the American polity. As described in the next chapter, the strains of rapid industrialization, an inadequate monetary system, agricultural distress, and labor protest built up to potentially explosive force. The two mainstream political parties, however, seemed indifferent to these problems. Paralysis gripped the national government as the Civil War continued to cast its shadow, preventing political leaders from grappling with new issues facing the country because they remained mired in the passionate partisanship of the past.

The Republican Party did not disappear from the South after 1877. Nor was the black vote immediately and totally suppressed. Republican presidential candidates won about 40 percent of the votes in former slave states throughout the 1880s, and some blacks continued to win elections to state legislatures until the 1890s. Until 1901, every U.S. Congress but one had at least one black representative from the South. Independent parties occasionally formed coalitions with Republicans to win local or state elections, especially in Virginia.

Even so, "bulldozing" of black voters (chapter 17) continued to keep the southern states solid for the Democrats. In 1880, the Democratic Party hoped to build on this foundation to win the presidency for the first time in a generation. Taking their cue from the Republicans, the Democrats nominated a Civil War hero, General Winfield Scott Hancock. His opponent was another Civil War general, **James A. Garfield,** who had served in Congress since the war. In an election with the closest popular vote in American history (Garfield had a plurality of only 10,000 votes out of 9 million cast), Hancock carried every southern state, while Garfield won all but three northern states—and the election.

Knife-Edge Electoral Balance

The five presidential elections from 1876 through 1892, taken together, were the most closely contested elections in American history. No more than 1 percent separated the popular vote of the two major candidates in any of these contests except 1892, when the margin was 3 percent. The Democratic candidate won twice (**Grover Cleveland** in 1884 and 1892), and in two other elections carried a tiny plurality of popular votes (Tilden in 1876 and Cleveland in 1888) but lost narrowly in the Electoral College. During the 20 years covered by these five administrations, the Democrats controlled the House of Representatives in seven Congresses to the Republicans' three, while the Republicans controlled the Senate in eight Congresses to the Democrats' two. During only 6 of those 20 years did the same party control the presidency and both houses, and then by razor-thin margins.

The few pieces of major legislation during these years—the Pendleton Civil Service Act of 1883, the Interstate Commerce Act of 1887, and the Sherman Antitrust Act of 1890—could be enacted only by bipartisan majorities, and only after they had been watered down by numerous compromises. Politicians often debated the tariff, but the tariff laws they passed had little real impact on the economy. Tariffs were still the principal source of federal tax revenue, but because the federal budget amounted to less than 3 percent of the gross national product (compared with 20 percent today), federal fiscal policies played only a marginal role in the economy.

Divided government and the even balance between the two major parties accounted for the political stalemate. Neither party had the power to enact a bold legislative program; both parties avoided taking firm stands on controversial issues. Both parties practiced the politics of the past rather than the politics of the present. Individuals voted Republican or Democratic in the 1880s because they or their fathers had done so during the passionate years of the 1860s. Every Republican president from 1869 to 1901 had fought in the Union army; the one Democratic president, Grover Cleveland, had not. At election time, Republican candidates "waved the bloody shirt" to keep alive the memory of the Civil War. They castigated Democrats as former rebels or Copperheads who could not be trusted with the nation's destiny. Democrats, in turn, especially in the South, denounced racial equality and branded Republicans as the party of "Negro rule"—a charge that took on added intensity in 1890 when Republicans tried (and failed by one vote in the Senate) to enact a federal elections law to protect the voting rights of African Americans. From 1876 almost into the 20th century, scarcely anyone but a Confederate veteran could be elected governor or senator in the South.

Availability rather than ability or a strong stand on issues became the prime requisite for presidential and vice presidential nominees. Geographical availability was particularly important. The solid Democratic South and the rather less solid Republican North gave each party a firm bloc of electoral votes in every election. But in three large northern states—New York, Ohio, and Indiana—the two parties were so closely balanced that the shift of a few thousand votes would determine the margin of victory for one or the other party in the state's electoral votes. These three states alone represented 74 electoral votes, fully one-third of the total necessary for victory. The party that carried New York (36 electoral votes) and either of the other two won the presidency.

It is not surprising that of 20 nominees for president and vice president by the two parties in five elections, 16 were from these three states. Only once did each party nominate a presidential candidate from outside these three states: Democrat Winfield Scott Hancock of Pennsylvania in 1880 and Republican James G. Blaine of Maine in 1884—both lost.

Civil Service Reform

The most salient issue of national politics in the early 1880s was civil service reform. Old-guard factions in both parties opposed it. Republicans split into three factions known in the colorful parlance of the time as **Mugwumps** (the reformers), **Stalwarts** (who opposed reform), and

Half-Breeds (who supported halfway reforms). Mugwumps and Half-Breeds combined to nominate James A. Garfield for president in 1880. Stalwarts received a consolation prize with the nomination of **Chester A. Arthur** for vice president. Four months after Garfield took office, a man named Charles Guiteau approached the president at the railroad station in Washington and shot him. Garfield lingered for two months before dying on September 19, 1881.

Described by psychiatrists as a paranoid schizophrenic, Guiteau was viewed by the public as a symbol of the spoils system at its worst. He had been a government clerk and a supporter of the Stalwart faction of the Republican Party but had lost his job under the new administration. As he shot Garfield, he shouted, "I am a Stalwart and Arthur is president now!" This tragedy gave a final impetus to civil service reform. If the spoils system could cause the assassination of a president, it was time to get rid of it.

Although a Stalwart, President Arthur supported reform. In 1883, Congress passed the Pendleton Act, which established a category of civil service jobs that were to be filled by competitive examinations. At first, only one-tenth of government positions fell within that category, but a succession of presidential orders gradually expanded the list to about half by 1897. State and local governments began to emulate federal civil service reform in the 1880s and 1890s.

Like the other vice presidents who had succeeded presidents who died in office (John Tyler, Millard Fillmore, and Andrew Johnson), Arthur failed to achieve nomination for president in his own right. The Republicans turned in 1884 instead to their most charismatic figure, James G. Blaine of Maine. His 18 years in the House and Senate had included six years (1869–75) as Speaker of the House. He had made enemies over the years, however, especially among Mugwumps, who believed that his cozy relationship with railroad lobbyists while Speaker and rumors of other shady dealings disqualified him for the presidency.

The Mugwumps, heirs of the old Conscience Whig element of the Republican Party, had a tendency toward elitism and self-righteousness in their self-appointed role as spokesmen for political probity. They were small in number but large in influence. Many were editors, authors, lawyers, college professors, or clergymen. Concentrated in the Northeast, particularly in New York, they admired the Democratic governor of that state, Grover Cleveland, who had gained a reputation as an advocate of reform and "good government." When Blaine won the Republican nomination, the Mugwumps defected to Cleveland.

In such a closely balanced state as New York, that shift could make a decisive difference, but Blaine hoped to neutralize it by shaving a few percentage points from the normal Democratic majority of the Irish vote. He made the most of his Irish ancestry on the maternal side, but that effort was rendered futile late in the campaign when a Protestant clergyman characterized the Democrats as the party of "Rum, Romanism, and Rebellion." Although Blaine was present when the Reverend Samuel Burchard made this remark, he failed to repudiate it. When the incident hit the newspapers, Blaine's hope for Irish support went glimmering. Cleveland carried New York State by 1,149 votes (a margin of one-tenth of 1 percent) and thus became the first Democrat to be elected president in 28 years.

The Tariff Issue

Ignoring a rising tide of farmer and labor discontent, Cleveland decided to make or break his presidency on the tariff issue. He devoted his annual State of the Union message in December 1887 entirely to the tariff, maintaining that lower duties would help all Americans by reducing the cost of consumer goods and by expanding American exports through reciprocal agreements with other nations. Republicans responded that low tariffs would flood the country with products from low-wage industries abroad, forcing American factories to close and throwing American workers out on the streets. The following year, the Republican nominee for president, Benjamin Harrison, pledged to retain the protective tariff. To reduce the budget surplus that had built up during the 1880s, the Republicans also promised more generous pensions for Union veterans.

The voters' response was ambiguous. Cleveland's popular-vote plurality actually increased from 29,000 in 1884 to 90,000 in 1888 (out of more than 10 million votes cast). Even so, a shift of six-tenths of 1 percent put New York in the Republican column and Harrison in the White House. Republicans also gained control of both houses of Congress. They promptly made good on their campaign pledges by passing legislation that almost doubled Union pensions and by enacting the **McKinley Tariff of 1890.** Named for Congressman William McKinley of Ohio, this law raised duties on a large range of products to an average of almost 50 percent, the highest since the infamous Tariff of Abominations in 1828.

The voters reacted convincingly—and negatively. They handed the Republicans a decisive defeat in midterm congressional elections, converting a House Republican majority of 6 to a Democratic majority of 147, and a Senate Republican majority of eight to a Democratic majority of six. Nominated for a third time in 1892, Cleveland built on this momentum to win the presidency by the largest margin in 20 years, but this outcome was deceptive. On March 4, 1893, when Cleveland took the oath of office for the second time, he stood atop a social and economic volcano that would soon erupt. When the ashes settled and the lava cooled, the political landscape would be forever altered.

Conclusion

In 1890, the superintendent of the U.S. Census made a sober announcement of dramatic import: "Up to and including 1880 the country had a frontier of settlement, but at present the unsettled area has been so broken into by isolated bodies of settlement that there can hardly be said to be a frontier line . . . any longer."

This statement prompted a young historian at the University of Wisconsin, Frederick Jackson Turner, to deliver a paper in 1893 that became the single most influential essay ever published by an American historian. For nearly 300 years, said Turner, the existence of a frontier of European-American settlement advancing relentlessly westward had shaped American character. To the frontier Americans owed their upward mobility, their high standard of living, and the rough equality of opportunity that made liberty and democracy possible. "American social development has been continually beginning over again on the frontier," declared Turner. He continued:

> This perennial rebirth, this fluidity of American life, this expansion westward with its new opportunities . . . furnish the forces dominating American character. . . . Frontier individualism has from the beginning promoted democracy [and] that restless, nervous energy, that dominant individualism . . . and withal that buoyancy and exuberance which comes with freedom—these are traits of the frontier, or traits called out elsewhere because of the existence of the frontier.

For many decades, Turner's insight dominated Americans' perceptions of themselves and their history. Today, however, the Turner thesis is largely discredited as failing to explain the experiences of the great majority of people throughout most of American history who lived and worked in older cities and towns or on farms or plantations hundreds of miles from any frontier, and whose culture and institutions were molded more by their place of origin than by a frontier. The whole concept of a frontier as a line of white settlement beyond which lay empty land has been discredited because other peoples had lived on that land for millennia.

The Turner thesis also ignored the environmental consequences of the westward movement. The virtual destruction of the bison, the hunting almost to extinction of other forms of wildlife, the ravaging of virgin forests by indiscriminate logging, and the plowing of semi-arid grasslands on the plains drastically changed the ecological balance in the West. These ecological changes stored up trouble for the future in the form of soil erosion, dust bowls, and diminished biodiversity. Thoughtful Americans began to express concern about these problems in the 1890s, foreshadowing the launching of a conservation movement in the following decade.

The significance of the Turner thesis, however, is not whether he got everything right; in the 1890s, he expressed a widely shared belief among white Americans. They believed that liberty and equality were at least partly the product of the frontier, of the chance to go west and start a new life. And now that opportunity seemed to be ending. In fact, to many Americans it seemed that a new and worrisome power had overtaken American life, threatening American liberty: the power of the corporation.

SUGGESTED READINGS

For general histories of the West, see **Robert V. Hine and John Mack Faragher, *The American West: A New Interpretive History*** (2000); **Richard White, *"It's Your Misfortune and None of My Own": A New History of the American West*** (1991); **William Deverell, ed., *A Companion to the American West*** (2004); and **Patricia Nelson Limerick, *The Legacy of Conquest: The Unbroken Past of the American West*** (1987). For one of the "classics" of Western history, see **Henry Nash Smith, *Virgin Land: The American West as Symbol and Myth*** (1950).

On industrial ranching, see especially **David Igler, *Industrial Cowboys: Miller & Lux and the Transformation of the Far West, 1850–1920*** (2001). Influential and useful treatments of the industrial transformation of the West are **William Cronon, *Nature's Metropolis: Chicago and the Great West*** (1991), and **William G. Robbins, *Colony and Empire: The Capitalist Transformation of the American West*** (1994).

Histories that explore the Chinese in America include **Ronald Takaki,** *Strangers from a Different Shore: A History of Asian Americans* (1989, rev. 1998); **Yong Chen,** *Chinese San Francisco, 1850–1943: A Trans-Pacific Community* (2000); **Judy Yung,** *Unbound Feet: A Social History of Chinese Women in San Francisco* (1995); **Erika Lee,** *At America's Gates: Chinese Immigration during the Exclusion Era, 1882–1943* (2003); and **Sucheng Chan,** *This Bittersweet Soil: The Chinese in California Agriculture, 1860–1910* (1986). For a discussion of Southwest borderlands, see **Sarah Deutsch,** *No Separate Refuge: Culture, Class, and Gender on an Anglo-Hispanic Frontier in the American Southwest, 1880–1940* (1987). On mining, see **Elizabeth Jameson,** *All That Glitters: Class, Conflict, and Community in Cripple Creek* (1998). On women, see **Rebecca J. Mead,** *How the Vote Was Won: Woman Suffrage in the Western United States, 1868–1914* (2004); **Peggy Pascoe,** *Relations of Rescue: The Search for Female Moral Authority in the American West, 1974–1939* (1990); and **Sandra Myres,** *Western Women and the Frontier Experience, 1880–1915* (1982).

On the 19th- and 20th-century myths of the frontier, see **Richard White and Patricia Nelson Limerick,** *The Frontier in American Culture* (1994). The Indians' response to the reservation system after the 1860s is discussed in **Frederick Hoxie, Peter C. Mancall, and James H. Merrill, eds.,** *American Nations: Encounters in Indian Country, 1850 to the Present* (2001) and **Robert M. Utley,** *The Indian Frontier of the American West, 1846–1890* (1984). For a fascinating discussion of Buffalo Bill, see **Joy S. Kasson,** *Buffalo Bill's West: Celebrity, Memory, and Popular History* (2000).

On the New South, see especially **Edward I. Ayers,** *The Promise of the New South: Life after Reconstruction* (1992) and the classic **C. Vann Woodward,** *Origins of the New South, 1877–1913* (1951). The Lost Cause ideology is examined in **Gaines M. Foster,** *Ghosts of the Confederacy: Defeat, the Lost Cause, and the Emergence of the New South* (1987). The rising tide of white racism is chronicled by **Joel Williamson,** *The Crucible of Race: Black-White Relations in the American South Since Emancipation* (1984), which was also published in an abridged edition with the title *A Rage for Order: Black-White Relations in the American South Since Emancipation* (1986).

On African American political action after the war, the best book is **Steven Hahn,** *A Nation under Our Feet: Black Political Struggles in the Rural South from Slavery to the Great Migration* (2003). On black experience after Reconstruction, see **Glenda Elizabeth Gilmore,** *Gender and Jim Crow: Women and the Politics of White Supremacy in North Carolina, 1896–1920* (1996); **Leon Litwack,** *Trouble in Mind: Black Southerners in the Age of Jim Crow* (1998); and **Michele Mitchell,** *Righteous Propagation: African Americans and the Politics of Racial Destiny after Reconstruction* (2004). On Ida B. Wells' anti-lynching campaign, a good place to start is **Gail Bederman,** *Manliness and Civilization: A Cultural History of Gender and Race in the United States, 1880–1917* (1995).

Visit the Liberty Equality Power Companion Web site for resources specific to this textbook: http://www.thomsonedu.com/history/murrin

Also find self-tests and additional resources at ThomsonNOW. ThomsonNOW is an integrated online suite of services and resources with proven ease of use and efficient paths to success, delivering the results you want—NOW!

www.thomsonedu.com/login/

The Emergence of Corporate America, 1865–1900

In the summer of 1877, the same year that President Rutherford B. Hayes withdrew federal troops from the South and effectively ended Reconstruction, he called out the military to suppress the most serious labor uprising in the nation's history. The Great Railroad Strike was no local, isolated disturbance: it was a national event that ultimately involved hundreds of thousands of people across America; claimed at least 100 lives; resulted in injuries to hundreds more; and caused the destruction of millions of dollars of property. It also caught many onlookers by surprise: "Sudden as a thunderburst from a clear sky," one journalist wrote, "the crisis came upon the country. It seemed as if the whole social and political structure was on the very brink of ruin."

But the strike was not so sudden as it seemed to shocked middle-class observers: the truth was that tensions between capital and labor had been building for years. The end of the Civil War had inaugurated an era of economic expansion such as America had never seen before, but it also fueled a process of industrialization that left many workers as permanent wage-earners, with little hope of the independence that had been a cherished part of antebellum free-labor ideology. As a roller-coaster economy also subjected employers to boom-and-bust cycles, many resorted to periodic price-cutting and wage-cutting, even while demanding longer hours. As a result, capital and labor had never been more at odds with one another.

A wage cut triggered the Great Railway Strike. In July, the Baltimore and Ohio Railroad cut wages by 10 percent—its third recent wage reduction. B & O workers had seen their wages drop steadily ever since 1873, a depression year. A brakeman earning $70 per month in 1873 earned only $30 by 1877; conductors' earnings slipped from $90 to $50. A small decline in the price of goods during this period was not enough to make up for such punitive cuts, and so when workers in Martinsburg, West Virginia, received news of the wage cuts, they walked out in protest. Soon workers up and down the B & O line joined them. "At the present state of wages," one group of railroad workers said, "we cannot live and provide our wives and children with the necessities of life."

The strike touched a nerve nationally and spread rapidly; within a few days, what had begun as a local protest had traveled to Baltimore, Philadelphia, Pittsburgh, New York, Louisville, Chicago, St. Louis, Kansas City, and San Francisco. Women as well as men

CHRONOLOGY

1869	Knights of Labor founded
1873	"Crime of 1873" demonetizes silver • Financial panic begins economic depression
1877	Railroad strikes cost 100 lives and millions of dollars in damage
1878	Bland-Allison Act to remonetize silver passed over Hayes's vetos
1883	Railroads establish four standard time zones
1886	Knights of Labor membership crests at 700,000 • Haymarket riot causes antilabor backlash • American Federation of Labor founded
1887	Interstate Commerce Act creates the first federal regulatory agency
1888	Edward Bellamy publishes *Looking Backward*
1890	Congress passes Sherman Antitrust Act • Congress passes Sherman Silver Purchase Act
1892	Homestead strike fails • Populists organize the People's Party
1893	Financial panic begins economic depression • Congress repeals Sherman Silver Purchase Act
1894	"Coxey's army" of the unemployed marches on Washington • Pullman strike paralyzes the railroads and provokes federal intervention
1896	William McKinley defeats William Jennings Bryan for the presidency

joined angry crowds in the streets; workers from a variety of industries walked out in sympathy; and in some places the strike crossed both gender and racial lines—as in Galveston, Texas, where black laundresses struck for higher wages. Strikers and militia in a number of cities fired on each other, and workers set fire to railroad cars and depots. Alarmed at the possibility of a "national insurrection," President Hayes called in the army.

The strike finally ended in early August— "The strikers have been put down by *force*," Hayes noted in his diary—but it left troubling questions in its wake: Had America become a permanently unequal society? Who held power in the emerging corporate order? How was liberty now defined, and whose liberty would the government uphold?

This chapter examines the emergence of a new corporate order in American life in the last decades of the 19th century. It explores the expansive, boom-and-bust economy of post–Civil War America, the rise of "robber barons," and the consolidation of middle-class culture within an emerging national culture of consumption. It explores working-class culture in cities and looks closely at the rise of national labor organizations, as well as a series of violent altercations between labor and capital. Finally, it examines farmers' protests and the political crisis of the 1890s.

America's preoccupation with sectional issues before the Civil War and the gnawing problems of Reconstruction after the war had diverted attention from the economic and social problems associated with industrialization. But in 1877, those problems burst spectacularly into view. For a time, economic growth promised to deflect class conflict. By the 1890s, however, a new corporate society had created opportunity but also inequality for many Americans.

An Expansive and Volatile Economy

The decades following the Civil War saw an unprecedented surge of growth in the economy. Statistics give us a snapshot of this extraordinary rise in American production: the **gross national product** was $9 billion for the five-year period from 1869–73; it was $37 billion for the period from 1897–1901. What's more, in the 1880s, manufacturing began to outstrip agriculture as a source of new value added to the economy, underlining America's ongoing transformation to an industrial society. In the period from 1878 to 1893, for instance, manufacturing increased by 180 percent, compared to a 26 percent increase for agriculture. America moved from fourth in the world in production in 1865

Library of Congress, Prints and Photographs Division

The Great Railway Strike   On August 11, 1877, the national magazine *Harper's Weekly* printed this illustration with the caption, "The Great Strike—the Sixth Maryland Regiment Fighting Its Way Through Baltimore." At first glance the illustration seems sympathetic to the strikers being fired upon in the foreground. The article accompanying this illustration, however, talked of the "reign of terror inaugurated by the railroad strikers" and "scenes of riot and bloodshed" such as "we have never before witnessed in the uprising of labor against capital."

to first in 1900; its industrial production now outstripped the combined output of France, Germany, and Great Britain. It was a stunning economic coming of age.

But this tremendous economic growth was also accompanied by spectacular volatility. The two, in fact, were closely connected in an unregulated economy. Cycles of overexpansion and overproduction were followed by inevitable cycles of contraction. The boom years right after the Civil War were followed by a crash in 1873 and a depression lasting through 1878, and there were additional depressions from 1882–85 and from 1893–97.

Not surprisingly, significant labor uprisings correlated with economic downturns, as employers and businesses sought to cut their losses by cutting wages or laying workers off. **The Great Railroad Strike of 1877** occurred during an extended depression; 1886, another depression year, saw 1,400 strikes involving half a million workers. The great Homestead Strike of 1892 followed the announcement of a wage cut of 18 percent.

Just as workers struggled to eke out a living, many business owners also periodically faced the threat of failure. The American economy may have grown enormously in this period, but expansion often meant saturation of markets followed by price-cutting of products, lower profits, and the inevitable layoffs. As the president of the stovemaker's association lamented in 1888, "It is a chronic case of too many stoves and not enough people to buy them." Around 10 percent of businesses failed each year, many of these small enterprises. During the depression years of the 1870s, bankruptcies rose from 5,000 in 1873 to more than 10,000 in 1878. The rate of collapse was even greater during the depression years of the 1890s.

Still, the enormous growth of the economy in this period meant great opportunity and increased prosperity for many Americans. Titans of industry piled up previously unimaginable fortunes. A flourishing middle class achieved new power, establishing a variety of public institutions such as libraries, symphonies, and museums. The working class, however, shared unequally in this rising prosperity.

Engines of Economic Growth

Focus Question

What were the main engines of American economic growth in the last third of the 19th century?

What fueled the dynamic economy of the post–Civil War era? We can start with railroads, the largest single employer of labor in this period. An important spur to economic growth, railroads increased greatly in miles of track—from 30,000 in 1860 to some 200,000 in 1900. Railroad expansion meant a greater need for coal and iron, then steel, to build railroad cars and lay track: steel production soared from 732,000 tons in 1878 to 10,188,000 tons by 1900. The steel industry in turn was a catalyst for a host of other industries, in a pattern repeated across the American industrial landscape.

As a result, manufacturing expanded dramatically in this period. Again, statistics help tell the story: In 1859, the value of American manufactured goods was $1.9 billion, but by 1899, it had risen to $13 billion. Likewise, just before the Civil War, there were 140,000 factories and manufacturing shops across the country; this figure had risen to 512,000 in 1899, and included the rise of industrial giants such as Carnegie Steel.

Technological Innovation and Celebrations of the Machine

Technological innovation and increased manufacturing fed one another. Growth in manufacturing spurred invention, and invention in turn spurred increased and more efficient manufacturing. Railroads, for instance, ran on a promise of reliability and efficiency, but poorly constructed tracks and rails were a significant hindrance to delivering on that promise. Technological advances like automatic signals, air brakes, and knuckle couplers all improved the efficiency and thus potentially contributed to the profitability of railroads; similarly, the switch from iron to steel tracks, combined with the use of the Bessemer and then the open-hearth process in steel mills, not only aided efficient production of railroad tracks but also promoted the tremendous growth of the new steel industry.

Technological innovations were related to market needs. No one understood this better than **Thomas Alva Edison,** who invented an astonishing array of devices in this period, from a patented vote-recording machine before he was 21 to the phonograph, the incandescent light bulb, and the kinetoscope (or movie camera). "The Wizard of Menlo Park" is often assumed to have been a solitary genius working in a quiet lab far from the hustle and bustle of business. Nothing could be further from the truth. While Edison was certainly a genius, he was also a savvy businessman and self-promoter who kept a sharp

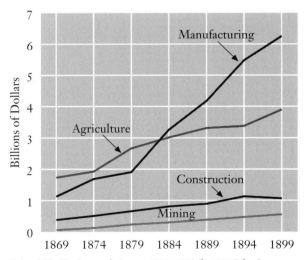

Value Added by Economic Sector, 1869–1899 (in 1879 Prices)

eye on the market. "I have always kept," he once told a reporter, "strictly within the lines of commercially useful inventions." In 1876, Edison moved a group of workers to Menlo Park, New Jersey, to set up an "invention factory" that deliberately mimicked the world of manufacturing. Incorporating the Edison Electric Light Company in 1878, he worked closely with financiers, and when he decided to produce a spectacular display of his new Edison lamps in 1882, he carefully chose Wall Street as the site of his demonstration.

Technological innovation was central to the creation of corporate America. In addition to Edison's wizardry, there were numerous other inventions in this period, from Kodak cameras to the Otis elevator to the gasoline engine to Alexander Graham Bell's telephone, which he demonstrated at the 1876 Philadelphia Centennial Exhibtion to astonished onlookers (characteristically, Edison would greatly improve upon Bell's telephone transmitter the next year). An international fair trumpeting American industrial progress to the world, the Centennial Exhibition displayed inventions and innovations ranging from the Westinghouse air brake to the typewriter to Fleischmanns' yeast. Underlining America's romance with technology, its most prominent exhibition was the colossal Corliss steam engine, the world's largest power generator. Visitors were agreeably awed by its size; the poet Walt Whitman, one of the 10 million visitors to the fair, insisted on sitting in silent contemplation of this mechanical marvel. The antebellum Market Revolution had become a full-fledged Industrial Revolution, and many Americans embraced the new technological order with a sense of pride and wonder.

Changes in Business Organization and Practice

Before the Civil War, most American businesses were local, family-run affairs that received little or no aid from the government and did not sell stock to raise capital. But railroad companies inaugurated a new era of big business that had profound effects on business practice. Many businesses now organized as corporations rather than single proprietorships: this mode of organization provided a flexible means of raising capital by allowing shares in a company to be sold directly to the public. New, expanded corporations used boards of directors as a management tool, allowing for shared responsibility and promoting a new scale and complexity of enterprise.

Railroads were big business in every way, requiring huge tracts of land as well as enormous amounts of capital. In order to encourage railroad building, between 1862 and 1871 the government stepped in with extremely generous land subsidies—over 100 million acres of federal lands—as well as monetary subsidies based on miles of track built. This largesse signaled the beginning of a close relationship between government and business in the postwar period—so much so that throughout the late 19th century, government supported the rights of corporations rather than the rights of workers in a series of legal cases as well as major strikes.

Even with government support, railroad companies still faced something of a catch-22: they stood to gain greatly if they managed to build enough miles of track, but in order to build, they first needed often staggering sums of money. The answer to this dilemma came in the form of financiers, bankers, and a wealthy elite—many of whom seized a golden opportunity to obtain power in the new industrial order. The savvy young banker **J. P. Morgan,** for instance, not only helped finance the Albany & Susquehanna Railroad in upstate New York but joined its board in 1870. Morgan would become the most celebrated and powerful banker of the late 19th century, in large part through his shrewd investing in a variety of industries, including Edison's first electric power plant in 1882. By the turn of the century, Morgan's banking firm had built an empire of leveraged financing and corporate directorates. Numerous other bankers would also gain new power through providing the finance capital needed by industry.

But there were financial losers as well as winners in the railroad-building frenzy of the post–Civil War era. More than 300 companies, most of them railroads, were listed on a greatly expanded New York Stock Exchange right after the war. But not all of these companies were sound; in fact, shaky financing characterized much of the railway boom, which was accompanied by a speculative fever reminiscent of the Gold Rush. The most notorious speculator was the secretive Jay Gould, who built a railroad empire using bribery, trickery, and manipulation. Ordinary investors who hoped to make their fortunes by investing in the railroads often lost their shirts instead when rickety financial scaffoldings collapsed.

The most spectacular and far-reaching downfall of the postwar years was that of **Jay Cooke,** the legendary financial genius behind the sale of Union bonds during the Civil War. Cooke was undone by his attempts to finance the Northern Pacific Railroad: he ran out of capital in 1873 after selling risky bonds and mortgaging government property. When the Northern Pacific went into receivership, Cooke was forced to close his powerful Philadelphia banking house. Within hours, his closure triggered the crash of the New York Stock Exchange, which in turn began the Panic of 1873. In the severe depression that followed, 18,000 businesses went under.

But it wasn't only Jay Cooke or Jay Gould who participated in the late 19th-century culture of speculation. A wider culture of speculation prevailed in the new corporate society. During periods when the economy was hot, many ordinary people also engaged in speculation—only to lose everything when the economy suddenly cooled off again. The reporter Elizabeth Garver Jordan remembered that after the panic of 1893, her meager earnings suddenly became vital to her middle-class Milwaukee family. Her father, a real estate dealer, had bought up "huge tracts of land in and around Milwaukee" on speculation. But when "every bank in the city failed," her father "went down in the debacle with most of Milwaukee's other business men." The "shock and strain" were "too much for him," she recalled, and "his health broke." Speculation clearly meant turmoil in many individuals' lives.

One prominent industrialist who announced his disdain for speculation was **Andrew Carnegie,** the industrial titan who built giant Carnegie Steel after the Civil War. "I have never bought or sold a share of stock speculatively in my life," Carnegie somewhat self-righteously asserted in his autobiography. "I have adhered to the rule never to purchase what I did not pay for, and never to sell what I did not own." An immigrant from Scotland in 1848 at the age of 12, Carnegie began his career—like so many in this period—with the railroads. Cutting his teeth in industry by working as an errand boy on the Pennsylvania

Railroad, Carnegie spent 12 years in positions of increasing authority before striking out on his own—as he said, "determined to make a fortune." First forming a rail-making concern in 1862 and then a locomotive factory in 1866, Carnegie turned to steel in 1872, employing the new Bessemer process that allowed efficient production of steel from pig iron.

"Watch the pennies, and the pounds will take care of themselves," Carnegie was famous for saying, and he kept close track of expenses, paying punitively low wages to workers and forcing them to work long hours. He also developed a system of cost analysis that allowed him to undercut competitors. One of Carnegie's major strengths was an important innovation in 19th-century business organization: vertical integration. Carnegie steadily took control of all parts of the steel-making process, starting with the mining of the raw material of iron ore and ending with the transportation and marketing of the final product. Vertical integration was a powerful new form of business organization that allowed for unprecedented consolidation and the building of business on a previously unimagined scale.

Another titan, **John D. Rockefeller** of Standard Oil, also innovated with business structure. A legendarily ruthless competitor who led a private life of quiet, prim rectitude, Rockefeller either bought out or ruined his rivals through practices such as "predatory pricing" (selling below cost until he bankrupted a competitor) and demanding secret **rebates** from railroads that wanted his business. Having invested in oil during the Civil War, Rockefeller incorporated in 1870, and then in the 1880s pioneered a new form of corporate structure, the **trust,** as a way of making a determined assault on competitors in the oil refinery business. As a congressional investigating committee commented in 1886, it was well known that "the Standard Oil Company brooks no competition; that its settled policy and firm determination is to crush out all who may be rash enough to enter the field against it; that it hesitates at nothing in the accomplishment of this purpose."

A vehicle for the creation of a monopoly (a term Rockefeller avoided later in life, preferring to talk of "cooperation" among businesses), a trust was initially used by Rockefeller to gain control over the oil refining industry and create the horizontal integration of one aspect of his business. Soon, like Carnegie, he engaged in vertical integration as well in order to gain control over every aspect of the oil industry, from extraction of crude oil to marketing. By the 1890s, Rockefeller controlled an astonishing 90 percent of the oil business, with Standard Oil a major force on the world stage.

It might seem obvious that monopolies were a violation of fair trade, but a weak federal government and a conservative Supreme Court set few limits on corporations in this period, despite significant antitrust agitation in the 1880s and 1890s. By then, many Americans feared the power wielded by tycoons who had established monopolies or monopoly market shares not only in oil and steel, but also in sugar, tobacco, and transportation, among other industries. The Sherman Antitrust Act of 1890 was an attempt to declare any form of **"restraint of trade"** illegal, but it was so vague as to be almost useless in the actual prosecution of corporations. Several states passed antitrust legislation, but other states virtually negated this legislation by passing laws favorable to trusts. Numerous corporations, for instance, rushed to set up headquarters in New Jersey after it passed an 1889 law allowing holding companies. In 1895, the Supreme Court dealt a crippling blow to the already weak Sherman Antitrust Act when it ruled in *U.S.* v. *E.C. Knight Company* that the federal government did not have authority over manufacturing because it was not commerce—a form of semantic hair-splitting that revealed the conservative Court's unwillingness to curtail the power of big business. As a result, the American Sugar Refining Company, which had driven out competitors, including the plaintiff, E.C. Knight, retained its 98 percent share of the national market. Only in the 20th century would the Supreme Court begin seriously to tackle the questions raised by the consolidation of giant businesses and the concentration of power in the hands of a wealthy few.

Wealth and Society

Both Rockefeller and Carnegie justified their business practices, as well as their right to wealth, with an emerging post–Civil War vocabulary of **social Darwinism.** "The growth of a large business," Rockefeller wrote, "is merely a survival of the fittest, the working out of a law of nature and a law of God." In assuming that market forces were in fact laws of nature, both Rockefeller and Carnegie drew upon the influential work of the English author Herbert Spencer, who had coined the phrase "survival of the fittest" in applying the evolutionary theories of Charles Darwin to human society. Social Darwinism was popular among both white intellectuals and a wider middle-class reading public to explain existing racial and class hierarchies in society: according to its tenets, human history could be understood in terms of an ongoing struggle among races, with the strongest and the fittest invariably triumphing. The wealth and power of the Anglo-Saxon race were ample testimony, in this view, to its superior fitness.

Social Darwinism reflected a widely shared belief that human society operated according to principles that were every bit as scientific as those governing the natural world. The ability of 19th-century biologists, chemists, and physicists to penetrate the mysteries of the natural world generated confidence in science, in people's ability to know and control their physical environment. That confidence, in turn, prompted intellectuals to apply the scientific method to the human world. The social sciences—economics, political science, anthropology, sociology, psychology—took shape in the late 19th century, each trying to discover the scientific laws governing individual and group behavior. Awed by the accomplishments of natural scientists, social scientists were prone to exaggerate the degree to which social life mimicked natural life; hence the appeal of Social Darwinism, a philosophy that allegedly showed how closely the history of human beings resembled the history of animal evolution.

At first popular mostly among intellectuals, Social Darwinism was quickly adopted as a way of explaining social and racial hierarchy by a broader public, with "survival of the fittest" becoming a popular catchphrase. There was no question that such theory provided a comfortable way of understanding the glaring social inequality of the post–Civil War era: workers were doomed to be permanent wage laborers not because of some fault in the emerging corporate system, but because they were not "fit." The rich, meanwhile, were entitled to every dollar that came their way.

The estimated number of *millionaires* (a word that came into use during this era) in 1860 was 300; by 1892, the number was 4,000. While this was not a large proportion of the population, it was nevertheless a highly visible group. Many practiced what the economist Thorstein Veblen described in *The Theory of the Leisure Class* (1899) as "conspicuous consumption." They sent agents to Europe to buy paintings and tapestries from impoverished aristocrats. In their mansions on Fifth Avenue and their summer homes at Newport, Rhode Island, they entertained lavishly, sometimes spending on a single party an amount that would have supported a tenement full of immigrant families for a year. At one famous costume ball in New York in 1897, guests in satin gowns sewn with jewels impersonated aristocrats: 50 women came dressed as Marie Antoinette, one wearing $250,000 worth of jewels. Such aristocratic pretensions extended to marriage: between 1874 and 1911, 72 American heiresses married British peers. The extravagant habits of a wealthy elite gave substance to Mark Twain's labeling of this era as the Gilded Age.

Class Distinction and Cultural Hierarchy

The well-publicized activities of the wealthy sharpened a growing sense of class distinction in this era. "No observing person can help being aware of an increasing tendency toward a strong *demarcation of classes* in this country," the antebellum abolitionist Lydia Maria Child wrote to a friend in 1877. Different classes "are as much strangers to each other, as if they live in different countries." Throughout the late 19th century, many Americans worried over the class distinctions they saw emerging around them as part of the corporate reordering of American life. The existence of classes was not new in American society, of course—the middle class itself had emerged in the antebellum era with its own distinctive culture—but now class distinctions seemed sharper, class divides more difficult to cross. Was this acceptable in a republican society that promised equality for all? A source of uneasiness at first, class distinctions became a source of alarm among numerous observers in the 1880s and especially the 1890s, when widespread labor activism challenged the existing social order.

But members of different classes would emerge with strikingly different proposed solutions to the problems of corporate America. By the 1890s, many members of the middle class sought not so much to reduce class distinction as to create additional barriers between classes. Fearing working-class violence in the 1880s and 1890s, the middle class erected fortress-like armories in numerous cities. No better symbol existed of the great gulf that had grown up between the classes in the post–Civil War era.

The Consolidation of Middle-class Culture

Focus Question
How did American middle-class culture change in response to the rise of corporations?

A broad middle class consolidated and extended its social and cultural power during the late 19th century. The corporate reordering of American society catalyzed the creation of new institutions of middle-class life, as well as changes in individuals' lives. But race and class went hand in hand: while a thriving African American middle class emerged in African American communities in the post–Civil War era (see chapter 18), its existence was barely acknowledged by the dominant white middle class. Immersed in a world of goods produced by the new corporate economy, the new white middle class also engaged in distinctive styles of consumption that marked a significant change from antebellum middle-class life.

White-Collar Workers

The new corporate order produced a need for salaried managers, professionals, office workers, and retail clerks. The expansion of this "white-collar" work—a term that entered

Urban Fortresses   In the 1880s and 1890s, numerous armories were built in cities across the country to protect against a perceived threat from the "dangerous classes"—workers and the poor. This immense, castle-like 1894 armory in Brooklyn, New York, was meant to inspire awe.

common usage during the late 19th century and referred to detachable, starched white collars for shirts—marked a change from the antebellum period. Agricultural labor dropped from 53 percent of the gainfully employed in 1870, to 35 percent in 1900, and to 21 percent in 1930; clerical work in the same period rose from less than 1 percent to over 8 percent. By 1900, there were 235,000 bank tellers nationwide, 232,000 salesmen and clerks, and 34,000 real estate agents. The profession of engineer, directly related to the expansion of manufacturing, leapt by an astonishing 586 percent, between 1870 and 1900. In other words, men entered white-collar professions, including management, in large numbers in the post–Civil War decades. By the 1880s, the term "business man" had replaced the antebellum term "merchant."

The Middle-class Home

As was true in the antebellum period, the center of middle-class life was the home and family. But domesticity took on a more consumer-oriented tinge, as the Victorian parlor grew ever more cluttered with doilies, cushions, statuary, clocks, paintings, pianos, and bric-a-brac. Styles of decorating grew more elaborate, reflecting the impact of an expanded world of manufactured consumer goods. When novelist Harriet Beecher Stowe and her sister Catharine Beecher published a revised edition of their antebellum guide *The American Woman's Home* in 1869, they offered humble advice that reflected the prewar reverence for the natural: bring some ivy indoors, they counseled their readers, offering suggestions for making an inexpensive indoor garden that would "gladden the heart." But such advice was already a throwback in the consumption-oriented postwar world. By the 1880s, many women of means not only filled their homes with expensive objects from domestic manufacturers, but also drew upon an international marketplace and vocabulary of decorating, as well. The 1882 Chicago mansion of Bertha Palmer, for instance, featured a Spanish music room, an English dining room, a Moorish ballroom, a Flemish library, and French and Chinese drawing rooms. This "cosmopolitan domesticity" not only shored up status but also marked an imperialist relationship to a wider world of consumption. By the turn of the 20th century, the profession of interior decorator was well-established among a wealthy elite, part of the larger trend of professionalization and the emergence of experts in this period.

Department Stores as Middle-class Communities of Taste

At the center of the new consuming culture, these glittering new "palaces of consumption" dramatically changed the experience of buying goods in cities. Stores such as Marshall Field & Co. in Chicago (1865) and R.H. Macy's in New York (1866) sold a wide variety of items—from perfume to shoes to hats to clothing to household goods—all under one roof. Organizing such an extensive variety of items in different departments rather than different stores was a major retailing innovation. But department stores also changed the experience of shopping in other ways. Customers strolled down carpeted aisles—arranged to mimic city streets—and gazed at a dazzling array of goods arrayed in glass cases. Ornate interiors with mirrors and lights added to a sensory experience of profusion, color, and excitement. Theodore Dreiser captured the desire that experience created in his novel *Sister Carrie*, as his main character Carrie "passed along the busy aisles, much affected by the remarkable displays of trinkets, dress goods, stationery, and jewelry. Each separate counter was a show place of dazzling interest and attraction." As Carrie left the store, she "longed for dress and beauty with a whole heart."

The stores sought to appeal to middle-class women with an elaborate variety of services and amenities, including restaurants, ladies' parlors, check rooms, "retiring rooms," libraries, information bureaus, free wrapping, and free delivery. The new Otis elevator took customers from floor to floor in what were some of the earliest "skyscrapers" of up to 10 stories. Store tearooms quickly became popular places for middle-class women to meet in an urban public space—a novelty at the time.

Domesticity vs. Work

Many middle-class women continued to adhere to the ideology of domesticity, assuming that their place was in the home. Yet an increasing number of women began to explore the world of work—whether out of necessity in the turbulent economy of the late 19th century, or because they chose to enter a wider sphere of life. Historians are not sure how many middle-class women went to work: statistics of the period do not separate out working-class and middle-class women. By 1900, however, 21 percent of all women were in the workforce, as opposed to 9.7 percent of women in 1860. After the Civil War, women moved into nursing and office work in large numbers, while continuing to be a mainstay in teaching. By the end of the 19th century, middle-class women were also becoming editors, literary agents, and journalists in larger numbers, while also entering the professions of medicine and law in small numbers. College women moved to cities to take up work in increasing numbers by the turn of the 20th century, living in apartments on their own as "bachelor girls" and as the subject of numerous newspaper articles.

The increased interest in work was reflected in literature of the period. Louisa May Alcott's 1873 novel *Work*, for instance, imagined an ideal cross-class, cross-race world of supportive female workers, while Elizabeth Stuart Phelps spoke for many discontented middle-class women in her 1877 novel *The Story of Avis*, in which the despairing heroine ultimately gave up being an artist for her marriage. But it was writer and economist Charlotte Perkins Gilman's 1892 biting novella *The Yellow Wallpaper* that spoke most powerfully of a new domestic claustrophobia. In that brief work, the unnamed heroine desires to write after the birth of a child but is told by her husband and doctor that she must rest instead. As a result she becomes virtually imprisoned in her home. Drawing upon Gilman's own experiences, the novel is a bitter indictment of an unequal society.

Few middle-class observers—men or women—were able to imagine women combining work with family. And yet many women had to do so: the nationally known journalist Jane Croly, for instance, who wrote columns under the name "Jenny June," supported her sick husband and four children as an editor and author during the 1880s before becoming the first female professor of journalism at Rutgers University.

The Women's Club Movement and Public Lives

Jane Croly began one of the most important movements among middle-class women in the late 19th century: the women's club movement. In 1868, the New York Press Club decided to bar women journalists from a celebratory dinner for the great novelist Charles Dickens, who was touring the United States. Croly was insulted and furious, but turned that fury toward a positive purpose: forming the women's club Sorosis (the name was chosen to suggest sisterhood). Composed primarily of professional women writers, Sorosis met regularly to discuss topics of the day and to exchange professional advice.

Sorosis inaugurated a movement of women's clubs among working and nonworking middle-class women in communities across the nation. Distinct from antebellum moral reform societies, the new women's clubs were secular and had a variety of different purposes, from intellectual discussion to civic reform. Providing sociability for women without male involvement or supervision, women's clubs also offered leadership opportunities and provided a bridge to middle-class women's activism during the Progressive era. While many clubs in the 1860s and 1870s did not support woman suffrage, by the turn of the 20th century, the women's club movement was an important source of support for the revived suffrage movement. What's more, by 1900, women had used the women's club movement to move into and even take over a variety of civic organizations—a way of practicing politics by other means in an era before women had the vote.

This was especially important in the Jim Crow South, where black men were disfranchised in the 1890s (see chapter 21). Middle-class black women drew on their extensive experiences in church organizations and Republican aid societies to create effective new networks of public civic organizations. African American women also joined the largest women's social organization of the late 19th century, the Woman's Christian Temperance Union (WCTU). Under the leadership of Frances Willard beginning in 1879, the WCTU engaged in a variety of social reform activities nationally and endorsed woman suffrage in 1884.

The New Woman

A clear indication that white middle-class women's positions in society were changing by the turn of the 20th century was the ubiquitous discussion of the "New Woman" in the 1890s. A cultural icon of cartoons, illustrations, paintings, short stories, and essays, the New Woman was depicted as a public figure who was athletic, self-confident, young, and independent: she wore the new, less confining fashion of shirtwaists and skirts; rode a bicycle; and even smoked in some images. The painter John Singer Sargent captured this dawning moment of confidence for women in several compelling portraits of strong women.

But to some observers, the New Woman was a fearsome thing, threatening the sanctity of the home and traditional gender roles. A backlash against middle-class women's new roles took different shapes but was often rooted in new "scientific" expertise. Arguing against women's higher education, for instance, the Harvard Medical School professor Edward H. Clarke asserted in 1873 that intellectual work damaged women's reproductive organs. "A girl could study and learn," he warned, "but she could not do all this and retain uninjured health, and a future secure from neuralgia, uterine disease, hysteria, and other derangements of the nervous system."

The Comstock Law (1872) made it illegal to send reproductive literature or devices through the mails on the grounds that they were "obscene," eroding women's already-limited control of reproduction. As women took to bicycles during the bicycle craze of the 1890s, experts warned that it would be unhealthy for women to expend so much strength in physical activity. Women actively resisted these attacks in articles, lectures, and through their own actions, both large and small. Frances Willard of the WCTU, for instance, took up bicycling at age 53 in part, she said, because she knew her example would "help women to a wider world."

Higher Education and Professional Organizations

That wider world included education. Women moved into higher education in large numbers in the late 19th century. In the Midwest and the West, public universities as well as land-grant universities (a result of the 1862 Morrill Act) expanded and began to admit women in the 1860s. In the East there were fewer coeducational institutions, but the founding of women's colleges—with Vassar leading the way in 1865—meant that by 1890, women were approximately 40 percent of all college graduates nationally.

Oddly enough, this move into higher education did not translate into greater ease of access to professional education. Women had broken into medical training in 1849 with the admission of Elizabeth Blackwell to Geneva Medical College in upstate New York. But as separate medical colleges gave way to medical schools within universities in the late 19th century, women began to lose ground in medical education. Professional organizations often excluded women as well; at the turn of the 20th century, the American Medical Association, a gatekeeper to the profession, was an all-white, all-male organization. As other national professional organizations were founded in the 1870s and 1880s—including the American Bar Association, the American Historical Association, and the American Economic Association—they too erected barriers to the entry of women and blacks. Professionalization was thus a double-edged sword: while new professional organizations established much-needed uniform standards and training in a variety of professions and disciplines, they also closed ranks against women and minorities.

Middle-class Cultural Institutions

A politics of exclusion and distinction often characterized new middle-class cultural institutions. In the decades after the Civil War, a significant achievement of the middle class was the creation of new and imposing cultural institutions in American cities. Symphonies, opera companies, museums, and public libraries were housed in imposing buildings that transformed the city landscape. The American museum evolved from a warehouse of curiosities to an ornate space for the display of fine art and scientific artifacts. Newly rich art patrons donated collections to establish museums such as the Metropolitan and Natural History museums in New York, the Field Museum and the Art Institute in Chicago, and the Fine Arts Museum in Boston.

Museums served as markers of class identity as well as repositories of art. In New York, founders of the Metropolitan Museum of Art made the paternalistic claim in 1880 that they sought to "diffuse knowledge of art in its higher forms of beauty" so as to "educate and refine a practical and laborious people." Yet the museum was remarkably ambivalent about those same "laborious people," closing its doors to the public on Sundays—the one day when many workers might have visited—and articulating a fastidious set of rules for behavior within the museum. At one point the museum even evicted a patron because he was wearing overalls, which caused a brief newspaper scandal. The museum spent far more energy courting wealthy art collectors with private receptions. For the newly wealthy in the emerging corporate order, the museum offered a form of alchemy: as one museum leader said, it would "convert pork into porcelain, grain and produce into priceless pottery, the rude ores of commerce into sculptured marble, and railroad shares and mining stocks . . . into the glorified canvas of the world's masters." Donations to museums by the newly wealthy could magically transform social status upward.

The attempt to create cultural hierarchy—and physical distance from the working class—was everywhere an aspect of middle-class institution building. In the antebellum period, for instance, performances of Shakespeare had often been rowdy, participatory, cross-class events. Shakespeare was a beloved part of popular culture. By the end of the century, however, the middle class had not only claimed Shakespeare as an icon of high culture, but had succeeded in imposing a new set of standards for audience behavior at the theater. Vocal audience participation gave way to an expectation of total silence during performances as a marker of gentility.

That gentility could also be found in a new art movement: American Impressionism. Influenced by French Impressionism, artists such as William Merrit Chase and Childe Hassam painted light-flecked landscapes or flower-filled urban parks, recording middle-class pleasures in cities strikingly devoid of workers. Yet some painters, such as Thomas Eakins or Thomas Anshutz, were already pioneering a style that would develop into the "realism" of the early 20th century, with its grittier view of city life and less idealized vision of the human form.

Within literary magazines and books, critics sought to create permanent genteel standards and decried the vulgarity of an extensive popular "low" literature of dime novels and westerns. *Century* and *Harper's New Monthly* published serial novels by great authors and a variety of articles and "tasteful" fiction, including an emerging literature of nostalgia for slavery with virulently racist portrayals of blacks. This white nostalgia for black subordination paralleled growing middle-class alarm over the "insubordination" of the working class in late 19th-century labor strife.

Yet increasingly over the late 19th century, mere gentility began to seem arid to some middle-class writers. The dean of American letters, William Dean Howells, called for a new "realism" based on close observation of and engagement with life. His novels explored issues that had rarely been touched by American authors, including divorce, the moral bankruptcy of capitalism, and interracial marriage. Discouraged by the widening gulf between the classes, in 1886 Howells even broke with most of his class in his plea for clemency for the defendants in the **Haymarket** affair (see later section).

The gulf between the classes also alarmed Edward Bellamy, whose 1888 utopian novel, *Looking Backward,* imagined a world in the year 2000 in which "labor troubles" and social inequities had been eradicated through a form of socialism called Nationalism. Bellamy's powerful fictional indictment of Gilded Age society resonated with half a million readers, making his novel one of the most popular of the 19th century. More than 160 Nationalist clubs sprang up in which members of the middle class mulled over the possibilities of government ownership of industry. For some authors and artists in the 1880s and 1890s, a pull away from genteel standards was inspired by a broader understanding of the considerable social costs of the new corporate order.

Yet the drive for class differentiation continued unabated for most in the middle class. One important spatial realization of this drive was the post–Civil War suburbanization movement. As early as 1873, *Scribner's* magazine noted that "the middle class, who cannot live among the rich, and will not live among the poor . . . go out of the city to find their houses." By the end of the 19th century, suburban communities of detached houses, surrounded by lawns, were markers of the middle-class status of businessmen and professionals who worked by day in cities and traveled back and forth by train or streetcar to their homes. Embracing a rural aesthetic, these suburbanites nevertheless needed the transportation powered by the new industrial order. Ironically, many children of those who fled cities by the end of the century would return in the early 20th century, finding vitality in the very parts of the city—immigrant and working-class communities—their parents had left behind.

Racial Hierarchy and the City: The 1893 Columbian Exhibition

A pernicious assumption of racial superiority was threaded throughout white middle-class institutions in the late 19th century. We can see this clearly in the 1893 Columbian Exposition in Chicago, a world's fair displaying American achievements to the nation and to the world. At the heart of this enormously successful fair was a monumental set of gleaming buildings called the "White City," meant to evoke the classical grandeur of Greece and Rome and to trumpet the maturation of American civilization. With its broad, open courts studded with statuary and interspersed with lagoons, canals, fountains, and parks, the White City was an exemplar of the new City Beautiful movement, whose advocates hoped to impose a new and more refined cultural order on what they saw as a chaotic urban environment.

With paid admissions at 21,480,141 in a nation with a population of 63 million, this was by far the most successful fair in American history, and Americans from all over the country flocked to see its astonishing array of exhibitions, from an Agricultural Hall displaying American farm machinery to the Woman's Building to the many state buildings to international exhibitions. The fair celebrated both technological innovations and high cultural achievements, and many fairgoers dutifully recorded their impressions in special printed books that thoughtfully guided them through the fair, beginning with the category "My first day in the 'White City.'"

The World's Columbian Exposition   The opening day of this Chicago World's Fair on May 1, 1893, drew well over 100,000 visitors.

Library of Congress, Prints and Photographs Division

But by far the most popular part of the Fair was an amusement strip called the Midway Plaisance, located at some distance from the White City, which included "ethnographic" displays of life in "primitive" villages in Africa, Morocco, China, and other locations. It was hard to miss the implication that civilization occurred in America and Europe, while primitivism belonged to people of color from Africa, the Middle East, and Asia.

The very structure of the fair thus embodied and reinforced a racial hierarchy that posited the superiority of white, middle-class civilization. Moreover, the fair denied African Americans a voice, refusing their repeated requests to display black achievements. Outraged, the anti-lynching crusader Ida B. Wells (see chapter 18) published a pamphlet, with contributions from several black leaders, titled "The Reason Why the Colored American Is Not in the World's Columbian Exposition." Exploring the intertwined histories of American slavery and racism, this pamphlet offered a detailed accounting of the refusal by the fair to include African Americans. "Theoretically open to all Americans, the Exposition practically is, literally and figuratively, a 'White City',," the pamphlet asserted. Wells boycotted the Fair on "Colored American Day," but former abolitionist Frederick Douglass attended in order to give a stirring speech. "Men talk of the Negro problem," he said. "There is no Negro problem. The problem is whether the American people have honesty enough, loyalty enough, honor enough, patriotism enough to live up to their own Constitution."

The City and Working-class Culture

As much as the white middle class attempted to impose a genteel order on city life, the city's vitality escaped such bounds. Cities grew rapidly after the Civil War. From 1870 to 1880, for instance, New York grew to over 1 million in population, a 25 percent rate of increase in just one decade. Chicago's growth was even more startling: from 30,000 residents in 1850 to 500,000 in 1880 to 1,700,000 by 1900. While San Francisco was a much smaller city, with fewer than 250,000 inhabitants, it, too, grew at a dramatic rate of 163 percent in the 1870s. In 1860, about one in five Americans lived in cities; by 1900, this number had doubled to two in five.

A fast-growing industrial economy created new jobs at an astonishing rate: between 1870 and 1910, jobs in iron and steel grew by 1,200 percent; in the oil, rubber, and chemical industries, by 1,900 percent. This tremendous job growth drew workers from a number of countries, with 85 percent of immigrants before 1880 from Germany, Ireland, England, and the Scandinavian countries; and with 80 percent from eastern and southern Europe after 1880. By 1900, more than one-third of the U.S. population worked as industrial workers, and most lived in cities.

Working-class Women and Men

For men, large as well as smaller cities often offered a variety of job possibilities—at least in flush times. Cincinnati, for instance, boasted firms that manufactured or processed beer, tobacco, lumber, meat, liquor, clothing, books, carriages, clothes, tools, and baked goods. Women had many fewer opportunities for work; in 1900, only 18.3 percent of the workforce was female. Most working-class families were in agreement with the middle class that married women's place was in the home. But young, single working-class women often worked outside the home before marriage: both young men and women were expected to supplement the family's earnings. In 1900, around one-third of all single women living in cities worked for wages in the garment trade and other industries. Young, single workers helped fuel a lively culture of urban entertainments at the turn of the 20th century.

Commercial Amusements

While the poorest workers could not afford commercial amusements, most workers shared in a new culture of leisure that included dance halls, music halls, vaudeville houses, nickelodeons (early storefront movie theaters), and amusement parks. Storefront vaudeville theaters, for instance, began to advertise "cheap amusements" to a broad working public in the 1880s. With roots in such antebellum entertainments as minstrelsy, circuses, and dime museums, vaudeville shows offered a variety of miscellaneous short acts for only a dime: a typical show might include sentimental ballads, acrobats, soft-shoe dances, magicians, mind readers, one-act plays, blackface minstrelsy, sports stars from baseball or boxing, puppeteers, jugglers, and dancing bears. Not considered respectable middle-class fare at first, vaudeville became increasingly popular, and eventually became a cross-class, national phenomenon.

Amusement parks such as Steeplechase Park at Coney Island, built in 1895, attracted a large working-class audience of men and women while soon also appealing to middle-class youth. Older middle-class commentators found the unchaperoned mingling of young men and women in an urban public space troubling, even shocking, but that loosening of restraint was what made Coney Island so pleasurable and exciting. A new kind of institution in American life, Coney Island was a structured world promoting gaiety and play, with dozens of rides and titillating attractions such as the "Blowhole Theater," whose jets of air blew women's skirts up. "Will she throw her arms around your neck and yell?" asked a sign for the "Cannon Coaster," providing its own answer: "Well, I guess, yes!"

The rides at Coney Island offered young men and women a temporary escape from their industrial working lives, yet ironically enough many of the rides themselves imitated the industrial workplace. The 1884 Switchback Railroad, for instance, an early precursor to the roller coaster, was directly inspired by the operation of gravity-powered coal cars in the shafts of coal mines. New innovations in technology and transportation found a pleasurable mirror at Coney Island and at the other amusement parks around the country that quickly sprang up in imitation.

While vaudeville theaters and amusement parks at first attracted a primarily working-class crowd of pleasure-seekers, they eventually crossed class lines by appealing to large middle-class audiences, as well. Both the working class and the middle class sometimes pushed at the boundaries between them. In the 1880s, for instance, labor unions in New York City resisted middle-class control by demanding that trustees open the Metropolitan and Natural History museums on their free day, Sunday. More than 100 labor organizations, representing some 50,000 workers, petitioned the museums. After a lengthy campaign, both museums capitulated in 1892.

Popular Literature

Just as in the antebellum period, urban workers read a wide variety of dime novels (cheap paperbacks that sold for a dime; see chapter 10) and newspapers. Beginning in the 1860s and 1870s, a flourishing cheap literature reflected the presence of working women in the new industrial order: the popular 1871 story "Bertha the Sewing Machine Girl; or, Death at the Wheel," inspired many imitators and was staged as a popular play in New York City. Its author, Laura Jane Libbey, published more than 60 novels in the 1880s appealing to a working-class audience. Working women read a variety of romances as well, purchasing dime novels from newsstands and pushcarts in large cities. Featuring wealthy heroines or working women who discovered that by birth they were actually aristocrats, these romantic tales offered fantasies that—in imagination, at least—closed the gulf between the classes.

Dime novels appealing to working-class men often told heroic stories of working-class manhood in which men overcame numerous obstacles to become the foremen or owners of factories. Such stories allowed a form of imagined compensation for the loss of independence men actually experienced as permanent wage earners.

Emergence of a National Culture

The rise of a corporate society may have created a gulf between classes in post–Civil War America, but paradoxically it also created a shared national culture. New technological innovations as well as an emerging consumer culture reshaped almost all Americans' lives. Electricity, streetcars, and elevators were just a few of the industrial innovations that changed urban dwellers' everyday relationship to physical space. Even people's relationship to time changed. Before the post–Civil War boom in railroads, there was no such thing as "standard" time: instead, many localities and cities kept their own time, derived from the sun's meridian in each locality. If the clock read noon in Chicago, for instance, it read 11:50 in St. Louis, 11:38 in St. Paul, and 11:27 in Omaha, with many other local times in between. This situation played havoc with railroad timetables.

In a sign of corporations' power over American life, in 1883 a consortium of railroad companies agreed to standardize North American time with the creation of four different time zones—much as they exist today—in which all clocks would be set to exactly the same time. This was a corporate act, not an official government act, and some grumbling followed about the arrogance of railroad presidents changing "God's time." The U.S. attorney general even ruled that government agencies need not change their clocks until authorized to do so by Congress; the next day, he missed a train by eight minutes because he had not reset his watch to the new Eastern Standard Time. "Railroad time" was quickly adopted by people everywhere, although Congress did not officially sanction standard time zones until 1918.

Advertising

A plethora of consumer goods also standardized experience as manufacturers produced national brands such as Ivory soap, Quaker oats, and Jell-O. Advertising firms such as J. Walter Thompson (founded in 1878) and N.W. Ayer & Son (founded in 1869) became an important part of corporate culture, working hand in hand with manufacturers to create national marketing campaigns. In 1899, for instance, N.W. Ayer & Son worked closely with the National Biscuit Company to create a national campaign for a new biscuit (what we would call a cracker today). First the name "Uneeda Biscuit" was carefully chosen, beating out such alternatives as "Taka Cracker," "Hava Cracker," and "Wanta Cracker." Next a distinctive shape was chosen for the cracker and special packaging was created. A national advertising campaign was devised with trademarks and popular catch phrases ("Do You Know Uneeda Biscuit?" and "Lest you forget, we say it yet, Uneeda Biscuit"). Finally, ads were placed in numerous newspapers and magazines, as well as on outdoor signs and streetcars. The results were spectacular: within one year, the National Biscuit Company was selling 10 million packages of Uneeda Biscuits per month, with an annual profit of $3 million. N.W. Ayer crowed that it had produced the "advertising success of the century."

Not surprisingly, expenditures on advertising increased enormously: from some $50 million in 1867 to $500 million by 1900. But national advertising did not just affect what people chose to buy; it sometimes reflected and spread dominant racial stereotypes. Several national brands—including Aunt Jemima mixes and Cream of Wheat, with its portrayal of the character Rastus—created trademark images that hearkened back to blackface minstrelsy (a racist entertainment popular in the antebellum period; see chapter 10) and to mythic images of supposedly happy slaves. At the 1893 Columbian Exposition, the manufacturer of Aunt Jemima mixes even hired an African American woman to play the part of Aunt Jemima, asking her to tell nostalgic tales of plantation life in her new corporate role as a plantation "mammy." Thus a nostalgia for slavery could be found in corporate advertising culture as well as in literature of the period.

A Shared Visual Culture

With their bright, colorful images, advertisements changed daily visual experience. Advertising featured little visual imagery before the 1880s, but with multicolor advertising trade cards (including baseball cards from cigarette companies) a fad in the 1880s, followed by increased visual imagery in ads in the 1890s, advertising helped create a shared national visual culture.

Technological improvements in lithography and the half-tone process in the 1880s and 1890s lay behind this shared visual culture. Picture postcards became popular in the 1890s, as did stereographs that allowed people to become vicarious travelers by viewing the wonders of the world through stereoscopes. The Kodak camera allowed people to take snapshots for the first time, creating a visual record of ordinary life. The most popular magazines and newspapers of the 1890s also created a new shared visual culture. *Ladies' Home Journal*, for instance, a socially conservative magazine founded in 1893 that argued women's place was in the home, achieved enormous success with its profusion of illustrations, photographs, and advertisements. It reached an impressive circulation of 500,000 within only a few years. Cheap new popular magazines such as *Munsey's* reached audiences of hundreds of thousands of national readers with a steady diet of racy stories and photographs of celebrities and chorus girls. Such magazines dwarfed the circulation figures of their more staid literary cousins like the *Atlantic Monthly*.

Urban newspapers also created a shared visual culture. The new sensational or "yellow" newspapers (so-called because of the popularity of the *New York World*'s first color comic, "The Yellow Kid") of the late 1880s and early 1890s responded to the demands of an expanded culture of consumption by adding illustrated women's pages, Sunday sections, society pages, and sports pages. On those sports pages, readers could follow the standings of the first national teams in baseball.

Mail-order Catalogues

How did people outside of cities participate nationally in the new culture of consumption? It was the brilliant idea of A. Montgomery Ward, who had worked at Marshall Field's firm in Chicago, to create a mail-order business reaching out to rural consumers. Starting with a single price sheet of items in 1872, Ward expanded to an 8-page-booket within two years, then a 72-page catalogue, and by 1884 was producing a thick, 240-page catalogue that listed close to 1,000 items for sale—everything from women's underclothing to entire houses.

Ward attempted to reproduce the face-to-face experience of going to a country store as much as possible within the imaginative realm of the catalogue, and customers responded as though Ward was an old friend. "As you advertise everything for sale that a person wants," one man wrote, "I thought I would write you, as I am in need of a wife, and see what you could do for me." Montgomery Ward and Sears, Roebuck used the nation's rapidly expanding rail system to speed goods across the country. Similarly, chain stores such as the Great Atlantic and Pacific Tea Company (A&P) and Woolworth's developed extensive national systems of food and dry goods stores, bringing a national consumer culture to localities across the nation.

The department stores, mail-order houses, and chain stores would not have been possible without the standardization of the goods they sold. Standardization had long been central to the American system of manufactures. Already in the 1850s, the American system had allowed for the mass production of many items built with interchangeable parts. Numerous entrepreneurs after the Civil War adapted these basic techniques to the production of additional consumer goods. Fashionable items of clothing and housewares, once obtainable only by the wealthy, could now be made relatively cheaply and quickly. After 1885, the ready-made clothing industry grew two to three times faster than any other industry. By 1915, it was the nation's third largest industry, ranking just behind steel and oil.

A national culture of consumption had grown up in the last decades of the 19th century, but not everyone had equal access to it. Wages that did not keep pace with the booming economy meant less money to spend, not to mention a struggle to put food on the table. "Eight hours for work, eight hours for rest, eight hours for what we will" was a famous slogan of the labor movement in the post–Civil War era. In the demand for "eight hours for what we will," workers voiced their belief that they had a right to leisure time under their own control. As one worker told a Senate committee in 1883, "a workingman wants something besides food and clothes in this country. . . . He wants recreation. Why should not a workingman have it as well as other people?"

Why not indeed? While some alarmed middle-class observers believed that all workers were revolutionaries who wanted to overturn the American government, only a small percentage were political radicals, much less revolutionaries. The truth was more prosaic: workers wanted fair wages and fair conditions in the workplace. They wanted equality in a system in which power had been systematically stripped from them, and liberty legally defined as the right of corporations. Broad-based workers' movements throughout the late 19th century attempted to rectify a situation in which equal opportunities no longer seemed to be available to all.

Workers' Resistance to the New Corporate Order

Focus Question
How did post–Civil War economic changes affect working people? How did they respond?

Although the average per capita income of all Americans increased by 35 percent from 1878 to 1893, **real wages** advanced only 20 percent. That advance masked sharp inequalities of wages by skill, region, race, and gender. Many unskilled and semiskilled workers made barely enough to support themselves, much less a family; many families, especially recent immigrants (who formed a large part of the blue-collar workforce), needed two or three wage earners to survive.

Conditions in the industrial workplace were often dangerous. The drive for even greater speed and productivity on railroads and in factories gave the United States the unhappy distinction of having the world's highest rate of industrial accidents. The railroads were particularly hazardous, with over 72,000 deaths of employees on the tracks between 1890 and 1917. What one historian has called "mechanized violence" characterized other industries as well: coal mines threatened underground collapses, explosions, and the release of toxic gases; iron mills and steel mills required work with molten metals at open hearths; textile mills threatened mutilation and dismemberment.

Yet there was little government regulation of industrial safety, and workmen's compensation did not appear until the 1930s. As a result, many families were impoverished by workplace accidents that killed or maimed their chief breadwinner. This was one source of a rising tide of labor discontent. Another was the erosion of worker autonomy in factories, where new machinery took over tasks once performed by skilled workers and where managers made decisions about the procedures and pace of operations once made by workers. Many crafts that had once been a source of pride to those who practiced them became just a job that could be performed by anyone. Labor increasingly became a commodity bartered for wages rather than a craft whereby the worker sold the product of his labor rather than the labor itself. For the first time in American history, the census of 1870 reported that a majority of employed persons worked for wages paid by others rather than working for themselves.

Skilled artisans considered this an alarming trend. Their efforts to preserve or recapture independence from bosses and robber barons fueled much of the labor unrest in the 1870s and 1880s. In 1866, the leaders of several craft unions had formed the National Labor Union, which advocated for an eight-hour day at a time when many industries required workers to work for 10 or even 12 hours daily. Labor parties sprang up in several states; the Labor Reform candidate for governor of Massachusetts in 1870 won 13 percent of the vote. While the advocacy of an eight-hour day would remain a central demand of the postwar labor movement, the National Labor Union would fade in the 1870s. During the depression that followed the Panic of 1873, workers were virtually powerless to push their agenda.

The National Labor Union withered away in the depression of the 1870s, but industrial violence escalated. In the anthracite coal fields of eastern Pennsylvania, the Molly Maguires (an amalgam of a labor union and a secret order of Irish Americans) carried out guerrilla warfare against mine owners. In the later 1870s, the Greenbackers (a group that urged currency expansion to end **deflation**) and labor reformers formed a coalition that elected several local and state officials plus 14 congressmen in 1878. In 1880, the Greenback-Labor candidate for president won 3 percent of the popular vote.

The Great Railroad Strike of 1877

The Great Railroad Strike of 1877 (see previous discussion), the worst labor violence in U.S. history up to that time, underscored the deep discontent of workers nationwide. But this spontaneous, unorganized labor upheaval did not produce solutions to workers' dilemmas. On the contrary, fears of a workers' "insurrection" led to a new cohesion in the middle class, which began to talk of a "war" between capital and labor. Not only did the middle class strongly support military intervention in the wake of 1877, but it supported the construction of armories in the nation's largest cities.

The Knights of Labor

Many workers in the wake of 1877 looked to a new labor organization for inspiration. **The Knights of Labor** had been founded in 1869 in Philadelphia as a secret fraternal organization, one of many such artisan societies in eastern cities. Under the leadership of Terence Powderly, a machinist by trade, it became public in 1879 and then expanded rapidly in the wake of the Great Railroad Strike, finally achieving hundreds of thousands of members nationally in the 1880s.

The Knights of Labor offered workers an inspiring vision of an alternative to competitive corporate society. Rooted in the artisan republicanism of the antebellum era (see chapter 7), with even its name suggesting a nostalgic look backward, the Knights opposed the wage labor system, declaring "an inevitable and irresistible conflict between the wage-system of labor and republican system of government." Instead it offered an inclusive vision of a "cooperative commonwealth" that would include both men and women and would not discriminate by race. In its platform it called for an eight-hour day, equal pay for women, public ownership of railroads, abolition of child labor, and a **graduated income tax.**

By the late 1870s, the Knights were a potent national federation of unions—or "assemblies," as they were officially known—and departed in several respects from the norm of labor organization at that time. Most of its assemblies were organized by industry rather than by craft, giving many unskilled and semiskilled workers union representation for the first time. It was also a more inclusive labor organization than most, although in local practice the Knights did not live up to its lofty ideals. Only some assemblies admitted women or blacks. Tendencies toward exclusivity of craft, gender, and race divided and weakened many assemblies.

A paradox of purpose also plagued the Knights. Most members wanted to improve their lot within the existing system through higher wages, shorter hours, better working conditions—the bread-and-butter goals of working people. This meant **collective bargaining** with employers; it also meant strikes. The assemblies won some strikes and lost some. Powderly and the Knights' national leadership discouraged strikes, however, partly out of practicality: a losing strike often destroyed an assembly, as employers replaced strikes with strikebreakers, or **"scabs."**

Another reason for Powderly's antistrike stance was philosophical. Strikes constituted a tacit recognition of the legitimacy of the wage system. In Powderly's view, wages siphoned off to capital a part of the wealth created by labor. The Knights, he said, intended "to secure to the workers the full enjoyment of the wealth they create." This was a goal grounded both in the past independence of skilled workers and in a radical vision of the future, in which workers' **cooperatives** would own the means of production. "There is no reason," said Powderly, "why labor cannot, through cooperation, own and operate mines, factories, and railroads."

The Knights did sponsor several modest workers' cooperatives. Their success was limited, though, partly from lack of capital and of management experience and partly because even the most skilled craftsmen found it difficult to compete with machines in a mass-production economy. Ironically, the Knights gained their greatest triumphs through strikes. In 1884 and 1885, successful strikes against the Union Pacific and Missouri Pacific railroads won prestige and a rush of new members, which by 1886 totaled 700,000. Expectations ran high, but defeat in a second strike against the Missouri Pacific in spring 1886 was a serious blow. Then came the Haymarket bombing in Chicago.

Haymarket

Chicago was a hotbed of labor radicalism. In 1878, the newly formed Socialist Labor Party won 14 percent of the vote in the city, electing five aldermen and four members of the Illinois legislature. With recovery from the depression after 1878, the Socialist Labor Party fell onto lean times. Four-fifths of its members were foreign-born, mostly Germans. Internal squabbles generated several offshoots of the party in the 1880s. One of these embraced anarchism and called for the violent destruction of the capitalist system so that a new socialist order could be built on its ashes. **Anarchists** infiltrated some trade unions in Chicago and leaped aboard the bandwagon of a national movement centered in that city for a general strike on May 1, 1886, to achieve the eight-hour workday. Chicago police were notoriously hostile to labor organizers and strikers, so the scene was set for a violent confrontation.

The May 1 showdown coincided with a strike at the McCormick farm machinery plant in Chicago. A fight outside the gates on May 3 brought a police attack on the strikers in which four people were killed. Anarchists then organized a protest meeting at Haymarket

Square on May 4. Toward the end of the meeting, when the rain-soaked crowd was already dispersing, the police suddenly arrived in force. When someone threw a bomb into their midst, the police opened fire. When the wild melee was over, 50 people lay wounded and 10 dead, 6 of them policemen.

This affair set off a wave of hysteria against labor radicals. Police in Chicago rounded up hundreds of labor leaders. Eight anarchists (seven of them German-born) went on trial for conspiracy to commit murder, although no evidence turned up to prove that any of them had thrown the bomb. All eight were convicted; seven were sentenced to hang. One of the men committed suicide; the governor commuted the sentences of two others to life imprisonment; the remaining four were hanged on November 11, 1887. The case became a cause célèbre that bitterly divided the country. Many workers, civil libertarians, and middle-class citizens who were troubled by the events branded the verdicts judicial murder, but most Americans applauded the summary repression of un-American radicalism.

The Knights of Labor were caught in this anti-labor backlash. Although the Knights had nothing to do with the Haymarket affair and Powderly had repeatedly denounced anarchism, his opposition to the wage system sounded suspiciously like socialism, perhaps even anarchism, to many Americans. Membership in the Knights plummeted from 700,000 in spring 1886 to fewer than 100,000 by 1890.

As the Knights of Labor waned, a new national labor organization waxed. Founded in 1886, the American Federation of Labor (AFL) was a loosely affiliated association of unions organized by trade or craft: cigar-makers, machinists, carpenters, and so on. Under the leadership of Samuel Gompers, an immigrant cigar-maker, the AFL accepted capitalism and the wage system, and worked for better conditions, higher wages, shorter hours, and occupational safety within the system— "pure and simple unionism," as Gompers called it. Most AFL members were skilled workers, and few were women or blacks—a strategy that enabled the AFL to survive and even to prosper in a difficult climate (see chapter 20).

The Homestead Strike

During the 1890s, strikes occurred with a frequency and a fierceness that made 1877 and 1886 look like mere preludes to the main event. The most dramatic confrontation took place in 1892 at the **Homestead** plant (near Pittsburgh) of the Carnegie Steel Company. Carnegie and his plant manager, Henry Clay Frick, were determined to break the power of the country's strongest union, the Amalgamated Association of Iron, Steel, and Tin Workers. Frick used a dispute over wages and work rules as an opportunity to close the plant (a **"lockout"**), preparatory to reopening it with nonunion workers. When the union called a strike and refused to leave the plant, Frick called in 300 Pinkerton guards to oust them. (The Pinkerton detective agency had evolved since the Civil War era into a private security force that specialized in antiunion activities.) A full-scale gun battle between strikers and Pinkertons erupted on July 6, leaving nine strikers and seven Pinkertons dead and scores wounded. Frick persuaded the governor to send in 8,000 militia to protect the

Pennsylvania Militia at Carnegie's Homestead Steel Mill, 1892 After the shoot-out between striking workers and Pinkerton guards, the Pennsylvania militia reopened the mills and protected strikebreakers from striking workers. This photograph shows the militia using steel beams manufactured by the mill as a makeshift barricade.

strikebreakers, and the plant reopened. Public sympathy, much of it pro-union at first, shifted when an anarchist tried to murder Frick on July 23. The failed Homestead strike crippled the Amalgamated Association; another strike against U.S. Steel (successor of Carnegie Steel) in 1901 destroyed it.

The Depression of 1893–1897

By the 1890s, the use of state militias to protect strikebreakers had become common. Events after 1893 brought an escalation of conflict. The most serious economic crisis since the 1873–78 depression was triggered by the Panic of 1893, a collapse of the stock market that plunged the economy into a severe four-year depression. Its complex origins included an economic slowdown abroad, which caused British banks to call some of their American loans, thereby draining gold from the United States at a time of political controversy about the American monetary system and nervousness in financial circles. Other causes included declining farm prices and attendant rural unrest and the overly rapid expansion of railroad construction and manufacturing capacity after 1885. The bankruptcy of the Reading Railroad and the National Cordage Company in early 1893 set off a process that by the end of the year had caused 491 banks and 15,000 other businesses to fail. By mid-1894, the unemployment rate had risen to more than 15 percent.

An Ohio reformer named Jacob Coxey conceived the idea of sending Congress a "living petition" of unemployed workers to press for appropriations to put them to work on road building and other public works. "Coxey's army," as the press dubbed it, inspired other groups to hit the road and ride the rails to Washington during 1894. This descent of the unemployed on the capital provoked arrests by federal marshals and troops, and ended in anticlimax when Coxey and others were arrested for trespassing on the Capitol grounds. Coxey's idea for using public works to relieve unemployment turned out to be 40 years ahead of its time.

The Pullman Strike

The explosive tensions between capital and labor fueled the Pullman strike of 1894. George M. Pullman had made a fortune in the manufacture of sleeping cars and other rolling stock for railroads. Workers in his large factory complex lived in the company town of Pullman just south of Chicago, with paved streets, clean parks, and decent houses rented from the company. But Pullman controlled many aspects of their lives, including banning liquor from the town and punishing workers whose behavior did not suit his ideas of decorum. When the Panic of 1893 caused a sharp drop in orders for Pullman cars, the company laid off one-third of its workforce and cut wages for the rest by 30 percent, but did not reduce company house rents or company store prices. Pullman refused to negotiate with a workers' committee, which called a strike and appealed to the American Railway Union (ARU) for help.

The ARU had been founded the year before by Eugene V. Debs. A native of Indiana, Debs had been elected secretary of the Brotherhood of Locomotive Firemen in 1875 at the age of 20. By 1893, he had become convinced that the conservative stance of the various craft unions in railroading (firemen, engineers, brakemen, and so forth) was divisive and contrary to the best interests of labor. He formed the ARU to include all railroad workers in one union. With 150,000 members, the union won a strike against the Great Northern Railroad in spring 1894. When George Pullman refused the ARU's offer to arbitrate the strike of Pullman workers, Debs launched a boycott by which ARU members would refuse to run any trains that included Pullman cars. When the railroads attempted to fire the ARU sympathizers, whole train crews went on strike and quickly paralyzed rail traffic.

Over the protests of Illinois Governor John P. Altgeld, who sympathized with the strikers, President Grover Cleveland sent in federal troops. That action inflamed violence instead of containing it. The U.S. attorney general (a former railroad lawyer) obtained a federal injunction against Debs under the Sherman Antitrust Act on grounds that the boycott and the strike were a conspiracy in restraint of trade. This creative use of the Sherman Act, whose purpose had been to curb corporations, was upheld by the Supreme Court in 1895 and became a powerful weapon against labor unions in the hands of conservative judges.

For a week in July 1894, the Chicago railroad yards resembled a war zone. Millions of dollars of equipment went up in smoke. Thirty-four people, mostly workers, were killed. Finally, 14,000 state militia and federal troops restored order and broke the strike. Debs went to jail (for violation of the federal injunction) for six months. He emerged from prison a socialist.

To many Americans, 1894 was the worst year of crisis since the Civil War. The Pullman strike was only the most dramatic event of a year in which 750,000 workers went on strike and another 3 million were unemployed. But it was a surge of discontent from farmers that wrenched American politics off its foundations in the 1890s.

Farmers' Movements

Focus Question
What provoked the farmer protest movements in the last third of the 19th century?

Between 1870 and 1890, America's soaring grain production increased three times as fast as the American population. Only rising exports could sustain such expansion in farm production. But by the 1880s, the improved efficiency of large farms in Eastern Europe brought intensifying competition and consequent price declines, especially for wheat, just as competition from Egypt and India had eroded prices for American cotton. Prices on the world market for these two staples of American agriculture—wheat and cotton—fell about 60 percent from 1870 to 1895, while the wholesale price index for all commodities (including other farm products) declined by 45 percent during the same period. Not surprisingly, distress was greatest and protest loudest in the wheat-producing West and the cotton-producing South.

Victims of a world market largely beyond their control, farmers lashed out at targets nearer home: railroads, banks, commission merchants, and the monetary system. In truth, these institutions did victimize farmers, although not always intentionally.

Resistance to Railroads

The power wielded by the railroad companies inevitably aroused hostility. Companies often charged less for long hauls than for short hauls in areas with little or no competition. The rapid proliferation of tracks produced overcapacity in some areas, which led to rate-cutting wars that benefited some shippers at the expense of others—usually large shippers at the expense of small ones. To avoid "ruinous competition" (as the railroads viewed it), companies formed "**pools**" by which they divided traffic and fixed their rates. Some of these practices made sound economic sense, but others appeared discriminatory and exploitative. Railroads gave credence to farmers' charges of monopoly exploitation by keeping rates higher in areas with no competition (most farmers lived in areas served by only one line) than in regions with competition. Grain elevators, many of which were owned by railroad companies, came under attack for cheating farmers by rigging the classification of their grain.

Farmers responded by organizing cooperatives to sell crops and buy supplies. The umbrella organization for many of these cooperatives was the Patrons of Husbandry, known as the Grange, founded in 1867. But because farmers could not build their own railroads, they organized "antimonopoly" parties and elected state legislators who enacted "Granger laws" in several states. These laws established railroad commissions that fixed maximum freight rates and warehouse charges. Railroads challenged the laws in court. Eight challenges made their way to the U.S. Supreme Court, which in *Munn* v. *Illinois* (1877) ruled that states could regulate businesses clothed with a "public interest"— railroads and other common carriers, millers, innkeepers, and the like. It was a landmark decision.

The welter of different and sometimes conflicting state laws, plus rulings by the U.S. Supreme Court in the 1880s that states could not regulate interstate railroad traffic, brought a drive for federal regulation. After years of discussion, Congress passed the Interstate Commerce Act in 1887. This law, like most such laws, reflected compromise between the varying viewpoints of shippers, railroads, and other pressure groups. It outlawed pools, discriminatory rates, long-haul versus short-haul differentials, and rebates to favored shippers. It required that freight and passenger rates must be "reasonable and just." What that meant was not entirely clear, but the law created the Interstate Commerce

The Kansas State Historical Society Topeka, Kansas

Returning to Illinois, 1894   This photograph shows one of the thousands of farm families who had moved into Kansas, Nebraska, and other plains states in the wet years of the 1870s and 1880s, only to give up during the dry years of the 1890s. Their plight added fuel to the fire of rural unrest and protest during those years.

Commission (ICC) to define the requirement on a case-by-case basis. Because the ICC had minimal enforcement powers, however, federal courts frequently refused to issue the orders the ICC requested. Staffed by men who were knowledgeable about railroading, the ICC often sympathized with the viewpoint of the industry it was supposed to regulate. Nevertheless, its powers of publicity had some effect on railroad practices, and freight rates continued to decline during this period as railroad operating efficiency improved.

Credit and Money

Focus Question
What issues were at stake in the contest between "free silver" and the "gold bugs"?

The long period of price deflation from 1865 to 1897, unique in American history, made credit even more costly for farmers. When the price of wheat or cotton declined, farmers had even less money to pay back loans from country-store merchants. Thus it was not surprising that angry farmers who denounced banks or country-store merchants for gouging them also attacked a monetary system that brought deflation.

The federal government's monetary policies worsened deflation problems. The 1862 emergency wartime issuance of treasury **"greenback"** notes (see chapter 15) had created a dual currency—gold and greenbacks—with the greenback dollar's value relative to gold rising and falling according to Union military fortunes. After the war, the Treasury moved to bring the greenback dollar to par with gold by reducing the amount of greenbacks in circulation. This limitation of the money supply produced deflationary pressures. To complicate matters further, national banknotes backed by the banks' holding of government bonds continued to circulate as money. Because national banks were concentrated in the Northeast, the South and West suffered from downward pressures on prices they received for their crops because of money scarcity. Western farmers were particularly vociferous in their protests against this situation, which introduced a new sectional conflict into politics— not North against South, but East against West.

Because parity between greenbacks and gold would not be reached until 1879, a controversy arose in the postwar years over whether Union war bonds should be paid off in greenbacks or in gold. Congress resolved this issue in 1869 by passing the Public Credit Act, which required payment in gold. Because little silver had been coined into money for years, Congress enacted a law in 1873 that ended the coinage of silver dollars, thus putting the United States on the road to joining the international gold standard. In 1874, President Grant vetoed a bill sponsored by anti-deflation western congressmen to increase the number of greenbacks in circulation, setting the stage for enactment of the important Specie Resumption Act in 1875. When the provisions of this act went fully into effect on January 1, 1879, the U.S. dollar reached par with the gold dollar on the international market.

Grant's role in bringing about these steps toward "sound money" is more important than is generally recognized, but the benefits of his achievement were sharply debated then and remain controversial today. On the one hand, they strengthened the dollar, placed government credit on a firm footing, and helped create a financial structure for the remarkable economic growth that tripled the GNP during the last quarter of the 19th century. On the other hand, the restraints on money supply hurt the rural economy in the South and West; they hurt debtors who found that deflation enlarged their debts by increasing the value of greenbacks; and they probably worsened the two major depressions of the era (1873–78 and 1893–97) by constraining credit.

The Greenback and Silver Movements

Many farmers in 1876 and 1880 supported the Greenback Party, whose platform called for the issuance of more U.S. Treasury notes (greenbacks). Even more popular was the movement for **"free silver."** Until 1873, government mints had coined both silver and gold dollars at a ratio of 16 to 1—that is, 16 ounces of silver were equal in value to one ounce of gold. However, when new discoveries of gold in the West after 1848 placed more gold in circulation relative to silver, that ratio undervalued silver, so that little was being sold for coinage. This was the principal reason for the law of 1873 demonetizing silver, except for small coins. Anti-deflationists later branded this law as "the Crime of 1873"—a conspiracy to destroy silver, the people's money, in favor of gold, the bankers' money.

Ironically, just when the law of 1873 was enacted, the production of new silver mines began to increase dramatically, which soon brought the price of silver below the old ratio of 16 to 1. Silver miners joined with farmers to demand a return to silver dollars. In 1878, Congress responded by passing, over President Hayes's veto, the Bland-Allison Act requiring the Treasury to purchase and coin not less than $2 million nor more than $4 million of silver monthly. Once again, silver dollars flowed from the mint, but those amounts failed to absorb the increasing production of silver and did little, if anything, to slow deflation. The market price of silver dropped to a ratio of 20 to 1.

Pressure for "free silver"—that is, for government purchase of all silver offered for sale at a price of 16 to 1 and its coinage into silver dollars—continued through the 1880s. The admission of five new western states in 1889 and 1890 contributed to the passage of the Sherman Silver Purchase Act in 1890. That act increased the amount of silver coinage, but not at the 16-to-1 ratio. Even so, it went too far to suit **"gold bugs,"** who wanted to keep the United States on the international gold standard.

President Cleveland blamed the Panic of 1893 on the Sherman Silver Purchase Act, which caused a run on the Treasury's gold reserves triggered by uncertainty over the future of the gold standard. Cleveland called a special session of Congress in 1893 and persuaded it to repeal the Sherman Silver Purchase Act, setting the stage for the most bitter political contest in a generation.

Grangers and the Farmers' Alliance

Agrarian reformers supported the free silver movement, but many had additional griev-ances concerning problems of credit, railroad rates, and the exploitation of workers and farmers by the "money power." Both the Grange and the Farmers' Alliance, a new farmers' organization that expanded rapidly in the 1880s, addressed these political concerns. Both also addressed farm families' social and cultural needs, providing them with a sense of community that helped reduce rural isolation. The Grange sponsored picnics and cultural events, actively encouraging the participation of women. Local chapters were required to have female members, and women took up positions of leadership at the local level and also attended national meetings. The Grangers were not anti-consumption, but they desired to avoid middlemen: this made them a good audience for the new mail-order cat-alogues. Indeed, the innovative retailer Montgomery Ward first gained a foothold in the mail-order business by styling himself the official supply house for the Grange and includ-ing signed testimonials from Grange members in his early catalogues.

The Farmers' Alliance also provided a sense of community for farmers. Starting in Texas as the Southern Farmers' Alliance, it expanded into other southern states and the North. By 1890, the movement had evolved into the National Farmers' Alliance and Industrial Union, which was affiliated with the Knights of Labor. It was also affiliated with a separate Colored Farmers' Alliance, formed by African Americans who recognized the utility of the Farmers' Alliance but were not welcome in the larger whites-only organization. Reaching out to 2 mil-lion farm families, the Farmers' Alliance set up marketing cooperatives to eliminate the mid-dlemen who profited as "parasites" on the backs of farmers. Like the Grange, the Alliance served the social needs of farm families as well as their economic needs, organizing picnics and educational institutes in addition to camp meetings. Appealing to women as well as men, the Alliance created what one historian has called a "movement culture" that helped farmers to overcome their isolation, especially in the sparsely settled regions of the West. The Alliance also gave farmers a sense of pride and solidarity to counter the image of "hick" and "hayseed" being purveyed by an increasingly urban American culture.

The Farmers' Alliance developed a comprehensive political agenda. At a national con-vention in Ocala, Florida, in December 1890, it set forth these objectives: (1) a graduated income tax; (2) direct election of U.S. senators (instead of election by state legislatures); (3) free and unlimited coinage of silver at a ratio of 16 to 1; (4) effective government con-trol and, if necessary, ownership of railroad, telegraph, and telephone companies; and (5) the establishment of **"subtreasuries"** (federal warehouses) for the storage of crops, with government loans at 2 percent interest on those crops. The most important of these goals, especially for southern farmers, was the subtreasuries. Government storage would allow farmers to hold their crops until market prices were more favorable. Low-interest government loans on the value of these crops would enable farmers to pay their annual debts and thus escape the ruinous interest rates of the crop lien system in the South and bank mortgages in the West.

These were radical demands for the time. Nevertheless, most of them eventually became law: the income tax and the **direct election of senators** by constitutional amendments in 1913; government control of transportation and communications by various laws in the 20th century; and the subtreasuries in the form of the Commodity Credit Corporation in the 1930s.

Anticipating that the Republicans and the Democrats would resist these demands, many Alliancemen were eager to form a third party. In Kansas they had already done so, launching the People's Party, whose members were known as Populists, in summer 1890. White Southerners, mostly Democrats, opposed the idea of a third party for fear that it might open the way for the return of the Republican Party, and African Americans, to power.

In 1890, farmers helped elect numerous state legislators and congressmen who pledged to support their cause, but the legislative results were thin. By 1892, many Alliance members were ready to take the third-party plunge. The two-party system seemed fossilized and unable to respond to the explosive problems of the 1890s.

The Rise and Fall of the People's Party

Enthusiasm for a third party was particularly strong in the plains and mountain states, five of which had been admitted since the last presidential election: North and South Dakota, Montana, Wyoming, and Idaho. The most prominent leader of the Farmers' Alliance was Leonidas L. Polk of North Carolina. A Confederate veteran, Polk commanded support in the West as well as in the South. He undoubtedly would have been nominated for president by the newly organized People's Party had not death cut short his career at the age of 55 in June 1892.

The first nominating convention of the People's Party met at Omaha a month later. The preamble of their platform expressed the grim mood of delegates. "We meet in the midst of a nation brought to the verge of moral, political, and material ruin," it declared. "The fruits of the toil of millions are boldly stolen to build up colossal fortunes for a few. . . . From the same prolific womb of governmental injustice we breed the two great classes—tramps and millionaires." The platform called for unlimited coinage of silver at 16 to 1; creation of the subtreasury program for crop storage and farm loans; government ownership of railroad, telegraph, and telephone companies; a graduated income tax; direct election of senators; and laws to protect labor unions against prosecution for strikes and boycotts. To ease the lingering tension between southern and western farmers, the party nominated Union veteran James B. Weaver of Iowa for president and Confederate veteran James G. Field of Virginia for vice president.

Despite winning 9 percent of the popular vote and 22 electoral votes, Populist leaders were shaken by the outcome. In the South, most of the black farmers who were allowed to vote stayed with the Republicans. Democratic bosses in several southern states dusted off the racial demagoguery and intimidation machinery of Reconstruction days to keep white farmers in line for the party of white supremacy. Only in Alabama and Texas, among southern states, did the Populists get more than 20 percent of the vote. They did even worse in the older agricultural states of the Midwest, where their share of the vote ranged from 11 percent in Minnesota down to 2 percent in Ohio. Only in distressed wheat states such as Kansas, Nebraska, and the Dakotas and in the silver states of the West did the Populists do well, carrying Kansas, Colorado, Idaho, and Nevada.

The party remained alive, however, and the anguish caused by the Panic of 1893 seemed to boost its prospects. In several western states, Populists or a Populist-Democratic coalition controlled state governments for a time, and a Populist-Republican coalition won the state elections of 1894 in North Carolina. Women as well as men campaigned for the Populists: Mary Lease, a former homesteader and one of the few women practicing law in Kansas, became famous for her impassioned speeches against corporate power. "We endured hardships, dangers and privations, hours of loneliness, fear and sorrow," she said of the homesteading years. "Yet after all our years of toil and privations, dangers and hardship on the Western frontier, monopoly is taking our homes from us."

In 1893, President Cleveland's success in getting the Sherman Silver Purchase Act repealed drove a wedge into the Democratic Party. Southern and western Democrats turned against Cleveland. In what was surely the most abusive attack on a president ever delivered by a member of his own party, Senator Benjamin Tillman of South Carolina told his constituents in 1894: "When Judas betrayed Christ, his heart was not blacker than this scoundrel, Cleveland, in deceiving the Democracy. He is an old bag of beef and I am going to Washington with a pitchfork and prod him in his fat ribs."

The Silver Issue

Clearly the silver issue stirred deep emotions. For many people silver meant far more than a mere change in monetary policy: it also represented a widespread yearning for a more equitable society in which corporations and banks held less power. Thus when Democratic dissidents stood poised to take over the party in 1896, they adopted free silver as the centerpiece of their program. This stand raised possibilities for a fusion with the Populists, who hoped the Democrats would adopt other features of their platform as well. Meanwhile, out of the West came a new and charismatic figure, a silver-tongued orator named **William Jennings Bryan**, whose shadow would loom large across the political landscape for the next generation. A one-term congressman from Nebraska, Bryan had taken up the cause of free silver. He came to the Democratic convention in 1896 as a young delegate— only 36 years old. Given the opportunity to make the closing speech in the debate on the silver plank in the party's platform, Bryan brought the house to its feet in a frenzy of cheering with his peroration: "You shall not press down upon the brow of labor this crown of thorns, you shall not crucify mankind upon a cross of gold."

This speech catapulted Bryan into the presidential nomination. He ran on a platform that not only endorsed free silver but also embraced the idea of an income tax, condemned trusts, and opposed the use of injunctions against labor. Bryan's nomination created turmoil in the People's Party. Although some Populists wanted to continue as a third party, most of them saw fusion with silver Democrats as the road to victory. At the Populist convention, the fusionists got their way and endorsed Bryan's nomination. In effect, the Democratic whale swallowed the Populist fish in 1896.

The Election of 1896

The Republicans nominated **William McKinley,** who would have preferred to campaign on his specialty, the tariff. Bryan made that impossible. Crisscrossing the country in an unprecedented whistle-stop campaign covering 18,000 miles, Bryan gave as many as 30 speeches a day, focusing almost exclusively on the free silver issue. Republicans responded by denouncing the Democrats as irresponsible inflationists. Free silver, they said, would mean a 57-cent dollar and would demolish the workingman's gains in real wages achieved over the preceding 30 years.

Under the skillful leadership of Ohio businessman Mark Hanna, chairman of the Republican National Committee, McKinley waged a "front-porch campaign" in which various delegations visited his home in Canton, Ohio, to hear carefully crafted speeches that were widely publicized in the mostly Republican press. Hanna sent out an army of speakers and printed pamphlets in more than a dozen languages to reach immigrant voters. His propaganda portrayed Bryan as a wild man from the prairie whose monetary schemes

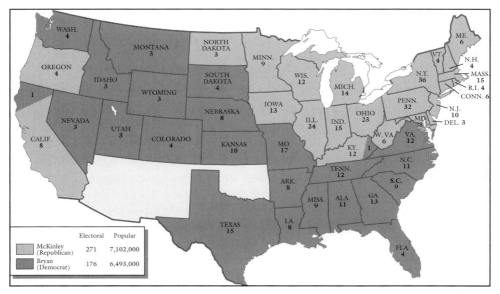

Map 19.1 Presidential Election of 1896 Once again, note the continuity of voting patterns over the two generations from the 1850s to the 1890s by comparing this map with Map 14.1 on page 532 and Map 15.1, Election of 1860, Southern Secession, in the color insert following page 624.

would further wreck an economy that had been plunged into depression during a Democratic administration. McKinley's election, by contrast, would maintain the gold standard, revive business confidence, and end the depression.

The 1896 election was the most impassioned and exciting in a generation. Many Americans believed that the fate of the nation hinged on the outcome. The number of voters jumped by 15 percent over the 1892 election. The sectional pattern of South and West versus Northeast and North Central was almost as pronounced as the North–South split of 1860. Republicans won a substantial share of the urban, immigrant, and labor vote by arousing fear about the Democratic 57-cent dollar and by inspiring hope with the slogan of McKinley as "the advance agent of prosperity." McKinley rode to a convincing victory by carrying every state in the northeast quadrant of the country. Bryan carried most of the rest. Republicans won decisive control of Congress as well as the presidency. They would maintain control for the next 14 years. The election of 1896 marked a crucial turning point in American political history away from the stalemate of the preceding two decades.

Whether by luck or by design, McKinley did prove to be the advance agent of prosperity. The economy pulled out of the depression during his first year in office and entered into a long period of growth—not because of anything the new administration did (except perhaps to encourage a revival of confidence) but because of the mysterious workings of the business cycle. With the discovery of rich new goldfields in the Yukon, in Alaska, and in South Africa, the silver issue lost potency, and a cascade of gold poured into the world economy. The long deflationary trend since 1865 reversed itself in 1897. Farmers entered a new—and unfamiliar—era of prosperity. Bryan ran against McKinley again in 1900 but lost even more emphatically. The nation seemed embarked on a placid sea of plenty. But below the surface, the currents of protest and reform that had boiled up in the 1890s still ran strong. They would soon surface again.

Conclusion

The 1890s were a major watershed in American history. In the past lay a largely rural society and agricultural economy; in the future lay cities and a commercial-industrial economy. Before the 1890s, most immigrants had come from northern and western Europe, and many became farmers. Later immigrants largely came from eastern and southern Europe, and nearly all settled in cities. Before the 1890s, the old sectional issues associated with slavery, the Civil War, and Reconstruction remained important forces in American politics; after 1900, racial issues would not play an important part in national politics for another 60 years. The election of 1896 ended 20 years of even balance between the two major parties and led to more than a generation of Republican dominance.

Most important, the social and political upheavals of the 1890s shocked many people into recognition that the liberty and equality they had taken for granted as part of the American dream was in danger of disappearing before the onslaught of wrenching economic changes that had widened and deepened the gulf between classes. The strikes and violence and third-party protests of the decade were a wake-up call. As the forces of urbanization and industrialism increased during the ensuing two decades, many middle-class Americans supported greater government power to carry out progressive reforms to cure the ills of an industrializing society.

SUGGESTED READINGS

General histories of the Gilded Age include Rebecca Edwards, *New Spirits: Americans in the Gilded Age, 1865–1905* (2006) and **Alan Trachtenberg,** *The Incorporation of America: Culture and Society in the Gilded Age* (1982). For the impact of the railroad on the Gilded Age economy and culture, see **George R. Taylor and Irene D. Neu,** *The American Railroad Network, 1861–1890* (2003). For the rise of industry and "big business," the following are useful: **Walter Licht,** *Industrializing America* (1995); **Glenn Porter,** *The Rise of Big Business, 1860–1910,* rev. ed. (1992); and **Harold G. Vatter,** *The Drive to Industrial Maturity: The U.S. Economy, 1865–1914* (1975). The best biography of Rockefeller is **Ron Chernow,** *Titan* (1998).

On the middle class and class hierarchy see **Sven Beckert,** *The Monied Metropolis: New York City and the Consolidation of the American Bourgeoisie, 1850–1896* (2001); **Stuart Blumin,** *The Emergence of the Middle Class: Social Experience in the American City, 1760–1900* (1989); and **Lawrence W. Levine,** *Highbrow/Lowbrow: the Emergence of Cultural Hierarchy in America* (1988). Several interesting essays on late 19th-century middle-class culture appear in **Burton J. Bledstein and Robert D. Johnston, eds.,** *The Middling Sorts: Explorations in the History of the American Middle Class* (2001).

For discussions of the relation of class hierarchy to race, see **Gail Bederman,** *Manliness and Civilization: A Cultural History of Gender and Race in the United States, 1880–1917* (1995) and **Matthew Frye Jacobson,** *Barbarian Virtues: The United States Encounters Foreign Peoples at Home and Abroad, 1876–1917* (2000). The effects of white-collar work on men and women are detailed in **Olivier Zunz,** *Making America Corporate, 1870–1920* (1990) and **Susan Porter Benson,** *Counter Cultures: Saleswomen, Managers, and Customers in American Department Stores, 1890–1940* (1986).

The rise of the department store is examined in **William Leach,** *Land of Desire: Merchants, Power, and the Rise of a New American Culture* (1993) and **Elaine S. Abelson,** *When Ladies Go A-Thieving: Middle-Class Shoplifters in the Victorian Department Store* (1989). Middle-class consumer culture is also discussed in **Ellen Gruber Garvey,** *The Adman in the Parlor: Magazines and the Gendering of Consumer Culture, 1880s to 1910s* (1996), while the cultural development of American museums is the subject of **Steven Conn,** *Museums and American Intellectual Life, 1876–1926* (1998).

Conflicting visions of the Chicago World's Fair can be found in **Robert W. Rydell,** *All the World's a Fair: Visions of Empire at the American International Expositions, 1876–1916* (1984); **James Gilbert,** *Perfect Cities: Chicago's Utopias of 1893* (1991); and **Christopher Robert Reed,** *"All the World Is Here": The Black Presence at the White City* (2000).

On working-class and popular culture in cities, see **Nan Enstad,** *Ladies of Labor, Girls of Adventure: Working Women, Popular Culture, and Labor Politics at the Turn of the Century* (1999); **John F. Kasson,** *Amusing the Million: Coney Island at the Turn of the Century* (1978); **David Nasaw,** *Going Out: The Rise and Fall of Public Amusements* (1993); **Kathy Peiss,** *Cheap Amusements: Working Women and Leisure in Turn-of-the-Century New York* (1986); and **Roy Rosenzweig and Elizabeth Blackmar,** *The Park and the People: A History of Central Park* (1992).

The labor movement is treated in **David Montgomery**, *The Fall of the House of Labor: The Workplace, the State, and American Labor Activism* (1987) and **Melvin Dubofsky**, *Industrialism and The American Worker, 1865–1920*, rev. ed. (1985). For the Knights of Labor, see **Leon Fink**, *Workingman's Democracy: The Knights of Labor and American Politics* (1983) and **Robert E. Weir**, *Beyond Labor's Veil: The Culture of the Knights of Labor* (1996). Two of the spectacular labor conflicts of the era are described in **Philip S. Foner**, *The Great Labor Uprising of 1877* (1977) and **Paul Krause**, *The Battle for Homestead, 1880–1892* (1992). For Haymarket and Pullman, see **Carl Smith**, *Urban Disorder and the Shape of Belief: The Great Chicago Fire, the Haymarket Bomb, and the Model Town of Pullman* (1995).

On the legacies of Populism, see **Elizabeth Sanders**, *Roots of Reform: Farmers, Workers and the American State, 1877–1917* (1999). A fresh interpretation of several populist movements in American history is **Michael Kazin**, *The Populist Persuasion: An American History* (1995). The best survey of the Populist movement is **Lawrence Goodwyn**, *Democratic Promise: The Populist Moment in America* (1976), which was published in an abridged edition with the title *The Populist Moment* (1978). The politics of the 1890s culminating in the climactic election of 1896 are treated in **J. Rogers Hollingsworth**, *The Whirligig of Politics: The Democracy of Cleveland and Bryan* (1963) and **Paul W. Glad**, *McKinley, Bryan, and the People* (1964). For the beginnings of Progressive reform during this era, see the early chapters of **Michael McGerr**, *A Fierce Discontent: Rise and Fall of the Progressive Movement in America, 1870–1920* (2003).

An Industrial Society, 1900–1920

With the collapse of populism in 1896 and the end of the depression in 1897, the American economy embarked on a remarkable stretch of growth. By 1910, the United States had secured its status as the world's greatest industrial power.

Corporations were changing the face of America. Their railroad and telegraph lines crisscrossed the country. Their factories employed millions. Their production and management techniques became the envy of the industrialized world. A new kind of building—the skyscraper—came to symbolize America's corporate power. These modern towers were made possible by the use of steel rather than stone framework and by the invention of electrically powered elevators.

Impelled upward by rising real estate values, they were intended to evoke the same sense of grandeur as Europe's medieval cathedrals. But these monuments celebrated man, not God; material wealth, not spiritual riches; science, not faith; corporations, not the commonweal. Reaching into the sky, dwarfing Europe's cathedrals, they were convincing embodiments of America's worldly might.

This chapter continues the story begun in the last chapter about how the newly powerful corporations transformed America: how they intensified their search for new forms of production and management; how the jobs they generated attracted millions of immigrants, southern blacks, and young single women to northern cities; and how they triggered an urban cultural revolution that made amusement parks, dance halls, vaudeville theater, and movies integral features of American life.

The power of the corporations dwarfed that of individual wage earners, but wage earners sought to limit the power of corporations through labor unions and strikes and by organizing institutions of collective self-help within their own ethnic or racial communities. Many found opportunities and liberties they had not known before. Immigrant entrepreneurs invented ways to make money through legal and illegal enterprise; young, single, working-class women pioneered a sexual revolution; and radicals dared to imagine building a new society where no one suffered from poverty, inequality, and powerlessness. The power of the new corporations, in other words, did not go unchallenged. Even so, a more egalitarian society would prove difficult to attain.

CHRONOLOGY

1897	Depression ends; prosperity returns
1899	Theodore Roosevelt urges Americans to live the "strenuous life"
1900–14	Immigration averages more than 1 million per year
1901	U.S. Steel is formed from 200 separate companies • Andrew Carnegie devotes himself to philanthropic pursuits • 1 of every 400 railroad workers dies on the job
1904	20 percent of the North's urban population lives below poverty line
1905	*Lochner* v. *New York:* Supreme Court declares unconstitutional a New York state law limiting the workday of bakery employees • Industrial Workers of the World (IWW) founded
1907–11	An average of 73 of every 100 Italian immigrants return to Italy
1909	Henry Ford unveils his Model T • Immigrants and their children constitute more than 96 percent of labor force building and maintaining railroads
1910	Black skilled tradesmen in northern cities reduced to 10 percent of total skilled trades workforce • 20,000 nickelodeons dot northern cities
1911	Triangle Shirtwaist Company fire kills 146 workers • Frederick Winslow Taylor publishes *The Principles of Scientific Management*
1913	Henry Ford introduces the first moving assembly line • 66 men, women, and children killed in "Ludlow massacre" • John D. Rockefeller establishes Rockefeller Foundation
1914	Henry Ford introduces the $5-per-day wage • Theda Bara, movies' first sex symbol, debuts • *The Masses,* a radical journal, begins publication
1919	Japanese farmers in California sell $67 million in agricultural goods, 10 percent of state's total
1920	Nation's urban population outstrips rural population for first time
1921	1,250,000 Model Ts sold, a 16-fold increase over 1912

Sources of Economic Growth

Focus Question
How did corporations respond to the economic opportunities and turmoil of the late 19th century?

A series of technological innovations in the late 19th century fired up the nation's economic engine, but technological breakthroughs alone do not fully explain the nation's spectacular economic boom. New corporate structures and new management techniques—in combination with the new technology—created the conditions that powered economic growth.

Technology

Two of the most important new technologies were the harnessing of electric power and the invention of the gasoline-powered internal combustion engine. Scientists had long been fascinated by electricity, but only in the late 19th century did they find ways to make it practically useful. The work of Thomas Edison, George Westinghouse, and Nikola Tesla produced the incandescent bulb that brought electric lighting into homes and offices and the alternating current (AC) that made electric transmission possible over long distances. From 1890 to 1920, the proportion of American industry powered by electricity rose from virtually nil to almost one-third. Older industries switched from expensive and cumbersome steam power to more efficient and cleaner electrical power. New sectors of the metalworking and machine-tool industries arose in response to the demand for electric generators and related equipment. Between 1900 and 1920, virtually every major city built electric-powered transit systems to replace horse-drawn trolleys and carriages. By 1912, some 40,000 miles of electric railway and trolley track had been laid. In New York City, electricity made possible the construction of the first subways. Electric lighting—on city streets, in department store windows, in brilliantly lit amusement parks such as New York's Coney Island—gave cities a new allure. The public also fell in love with the movies, which depended on electricity to project images onto a screen. Electric power, in short, stimulated capital investment and accelerated economic growth.

Surf Avenue and Luna Park, Coney Island, 1913 With its 1 million lights, Surf Avenue in Brooklyn, New York, advertised itself as the most brilliantly lit thoroughfare in the world. The avenue included the entrance to Luna Park, one of Coney Island's most popular attractions.

The first gasoline engine was patented in the United States in 1878, and the first "horse-less carriages" began appearing on European and American roads in the 1890s, but few thought of them as serious rivals to trains and horses. Rather, they were seen as playthings for the wealthy, who liked to race them along country roads.

In 1900, Henry Ford was an eccentric 37-year-old mechanic who built race cars in Michigan. In 1909, Ford unveiled his Model T: an unadorned, even homely car, but reliable enough to travel hundreds of miles without servicing and cheap enough to be affordable to most working Americans. Ford had dreamed of creating an automobile civilization with his Model T, and Americans began buying his car by the millions. The stimulus this insatiable demand gave to the economy can scarcely be exaggerated. Millions of cars required millions of pounds of steel alloys, glass, rubber, petroleum, and other material. Millions of jobs in coal and iron-ore mining, oil refining and rubber manufacturing, steel-making and machine tooling, road construction, and service stations came to depend on automobile manufacturing.

Corporate Growth

Successful inventions such as the automobile required more than the mechanical ingenuity and social vision of inventors such as Henry Ford. They relied on corporations with sophisticated organizational and technical know-how to mass-produce and mass-distribute the newly invented products. Corporations had played an important role in the nation's economic life since the 1840s, but in the late 19th and early 20th centuries, they underwent significant changes. The most obvious change was in their size. Employment in Chicago's International Harvester factory, where agricultural implements were built, nearly quadrupled from 4,000 in 1900 to 15,000 in 1916. Delaware's DuPont Corporation, a munitions and chemical manufacturer, employed 1,500 workers in 1902 and 31,000 workers in 1920. Founded with a few hundred employees in 1903, the Ford Motor Company employed 33,000 at its Detroit Highland Park plant by 1916 and 42,000 by 1924. That same year, the 68,000 workers employed at Ford's River Rouge plant (just outside Detroit) made it the largest factory in the world.

This growth in scale was in part a response to the enormous domestic market. By 1900, railroads provided the country with an efficient transportation system that allowed corporations to ship goods virtually anywhere in the United States. A national network of telegraph lines allowed constant communication between buyers and sellers separated by thousands of miles. And the population, which was expanding rapidly, demonstrated an ever-growing appetite for goods and services.

Mass Production and Distribution

Manufacturers responded to this burgeoning domestic market by developing **mass-production** techniques that increased production speed and lowered unit costs. Mass production often meant replacing skilled workers with machines that were coordinated to permit high-speed, uninterrupted production at every stage of the manufacturing process. Mass-production techniques had become widespread in basic steel manufacturing and sugar refining by the 1890s, and they spread to the machine-tool industry and automobile manufacturing in the first two decades of the 20th century.

Such production techniques were profitable only if large quantities of output could be sold. Although the domestic market offered a vast potential for sales, manufacturers often found distribution systems inadequate. This was the case with North Carolina smoking tobacco manufacturer James Buchanan Duke, who almost single-handedly transformed the cigarette into one of the best-selling commodities in American history. In 1885, at a time when relatively few Americans smoked, Duke invested in several Bonsack cigarette machines, each of which manufactured 120,000 cigarettes per day. To create a market for the millions of cigarettes he was producing, Duke advertised his product aggressively throughout the country. He also established regional sales offices so that his sales representatives could keep in touch with local jobbers and retailers. As cigarette sales skyrocketed, more corporations sought to emulate Duke's techniques. Over the course of the next 20 years, those corporations that integrated mass production and mass distribution, as Duke did in the 1880s and 1890s, came to define American "big business." **(See Map 20.1, Industrial America, 1900–1920, in the color insert following p. 816.)**

Corporate Consolidation

Corporate expansion also reflected a desire to avoid market instability. The rapid industrial growth of the late 19th century had unsettled industrialists. As promising economic opportunities arose, more industrialists sought to take advantage of them, but overexpansion and increasingly furious competition often turned rosy prospects into less-than-rosy results. Bankrupting busts quickly followed buoyant booms. Soon, corporations began looking for ways to insulate themselves from harrowing downturns in the business cycle.

The railroads led the way in tackling this problem. Rather than engaging in ruinous rate wars, railroads began cooperating. They shared information on costs and profits, established standardized rates, and allocated discrete portions of the freight business among themselves. These cooperative arrangements were variously called "pools," "cartels," or "trusts." The 1890 Sherman Antitrust Act declared such cartel-like practices illegal, but the law's enforcement proved to be short-lived (see chapter 19). Still, the railroads' efforts rarely succeeded for long because they depended heavily on voluntary compliance. During difficult economic times, the temptation to lower freight rates and exceed one's market share could become too strong to resist.

Corporations' efforts to restrain competition and inject order into the economic environment continued unabated, however. Mergers now emerged as the favored instrument of control. By the 1890s, investment bankers, such as J. P. Morgan, possessed both the capital and the financial skills to engineer the complicated stock transfers and ownership renegotiations that mergers required. James Duke again led the way in 1890 when he and four competitors merged to form the American Tobacco Company. Over the next eight years, the quantity of cigarettes produced by Duke-controlled companies quadrupled, from 1 billion to almost 4 billion per year. Moreover, American Tobacco used its powerful position in cigarette manufacture to achieve dominance in pipe tobacco, chewing tobacco, and snuff manufacture as well.

The **merger movement** intensified as the depression of the 1890s lifted. In the years from 1898 to 1904, many of the corporations that would dominate American business throughout most of the 20th century acquired their modern form: Armour and Swift in meatpacking, Standard Oil in petroleum, General Electric and Westinghouse in electrical manufacture, American Telephone and Telegraph (AT&T) in communications, International Harvester in the manufacture of agricultural implements, and DuPont in munitions and chemical processing. The largest merger occurred in steel in 1901, when Andrew Carnegie and J. P. Morgan together fashioned the U.S. Steel Corporation from 200 separate iron and steel companies. U.S. Steel, with its 112 blast furnaces and 170,000 steelworkers, controlled 60 percent of the country's steelmaking capacity. Moreover, its 78 iron-ore boats and 1,000 miles of railroad gave it substantial control over procuring raw materials and distributing finished steel products.

Revolution in Management

The growth in the number and size of corporations revolutionized corporate management. The ranks of managers mushroomed, as elaborate corporate hierarchies defined both the status and the duties of individual managers. Increasingly, senior managers took over from owners the responsibility for long-term planning. Day-to-day operations fell to middle managers who oversaw particular departments (e.g., purchasing, research, production, labor) in corporate headquarters or who supervised regional sales offices or directed particular factories. Middle managers also managed the people—accountants, clerks, foremen, engineers, salesmen—in these departments, offices, or factories. The rapid expansion within corporate managerial ranks created a new middle class, whose members were intensely loyal to their employers but at odds both with blue-collar workers and with the older middle class of shopkeepers, small businessmen, and independent craftsmen.

As management techniques grew in importance, companies tried to make them more scientific. Firms introduced cost-accounting methods into purchasing and other departments charged with controlling the inflow of materials and the outflow of goods. Many corporations began requiring college or university training in science, engineering, or accounting for entry into middle management. Corporations that had built their success on a profitable invention or discovery sought to maintain their competitive edge by creating research departments and hiring professional scientists—those with doctorates from American or European universities—to come up with new technological and scientific breakthroughs. Such departments were modeled on the industrial research laboratory set up by the inventor-entrepreneur Thomas Edison in Menlo Park, New Jersey, in 1876 (see chapter 19).

Scientific Management on the Factory Floor

The most controversial and, in some respects, the most ambitious effort to introduce scientific practices into management occurred in production. Managers understood that improvements in factory organization as well as technological innovation could enhance the speed and efficiency of mass production. So, in league with engineers, they sought optimal arrangements of machines and deployments of workers that would achieve the highest speed in production with the fewest human or mechanical interruptions. Some of these managers, such as Frederick Winslow Taylor, the chief engineer at Philadelphia's Midvale Steel Company in the 1880s, styled themselves as the architects of **scientific management.** They examined every human task and mechanical movement involved in each production process. In "time-and-motion studies," they recorded every distinct movement a worker made in performing his or her job, how long it took, and how often it was performed. They hoped thereby to identify and eliminate wasted human energy. Eliminating waste might mean reorganizing a floor of machinery so as to reduce "down time" between production steps; it might mean instructing workers to perform their tasks differently; or it might mean replacing uncooperative skilled workers with machines tended by unskilled, low-wage laborers. Regardless of the method chosen, the goal was the same: to make human labor emulate the smooth and apparently effortless operation of an automatic, perfectly calibrated piece of machinery.

Taylor publicized his vision, first through speeches to fellow engineers and managers, and then through his writings. By the time he published *The Principles of Scientific Management* (1911), his ideas had already captivated countless corporate managers and engineers, many of whom sought to introduce "Taylorism" into their own production systems.

Introducing scientific management practices rarely proceeded easily. Time-and-motion studies were costly, and Taylor's formulas for increasing efficiency and reducing waste often were less scientific than he claimed. Taylor also overestimated workers' willingness to play the mechanical role he assigned them. Skilled workers and general foremen whom Taylor sought to eliminate often resisted his schemes. In the end, managers and engineers who persisted in their efforts to apply scientific management usually modified Taylor's principles.

Henry Ford's engineers initially adopted Taylorism and with apparent success. By 1910, they had broken down automobile manufacturing into a series of simple, sequential tasks. Each worker performed only one task: adding a carburetor to an engine, inserting a windshield, mounting tires onto wheels. Then, in 1913, Ford's engineers introduced the first moving assembly line, a continuously moving conveyor belt that carried cars in production through each workstation. This innovation eliminated precious time previously wasted in transporting car parts (or partially built cars) by crane or truck from one work area to another. It also limited the time available to workers to perform their assigned tasks. Only the foreman, not the workers, could stop the line or change its speed.

© Hulton Archive/Getty Images

The World's First Automobile Assembly Line   Introduced at his Highland Park plant in 1913, this innovation cut production time on Model Ts by 90 percent, allowing Ford to reduce the price of his cars by more than half and to double the hourly wages of his employees.

By 1913, the continuous assembly line made Ford Motor Company's new Highland Park plant the most tightly integrated and continuously moving production system in American industry. The pace of production exceeded all expectations. Between 1910 and 1914, production time on Ford Model Ts dropped by 90 percent, from an average of more than 12 hours per car to 1.5 hours. A thousand Model Ts began rolling off the assembly line each day. This striking increase in the rate of production enabled Ford to slash the price of a Model T from $950 in 1909 to only $295 in 1923, a reduction of 70 percent. The number of Model Ts purchased by Americans increased 16-fold between 1912 and 1921, from 79,000 to 1,250,000. The assembly line quickly became the most admired—and most feared—symbol of American mass production.

Problems immediately beset the system, however. Repeating a single motion all day long induced mental stupor, and managerial efforts to speed up the line produced physical exhaustion—both of which increased the incidence of error and injury. Some workers tried to organize a union to gain a voice in production matters, but most Ford workers expressed their dissatisfaction simply by quitting. By 1913, employee turnover at Highland Park had reached the astounding rate of 370 percent per year. At that rate, Ford had to hire 51,800 workers every year just to keep his factory fully staffed at 14,000.

A problem of that magnitude demanded a dramatic solution. Ford provided it in 1914 by raising the wage he paid his assembly-line workers to $5 per day, double the average manufacturing wage then prevalent in American industry. The result: Workers, especially young and single men, flocked to Detroit. Highland Park's high productivity rate permitted Ford to absorb the wage increase without cutting substantially into profits.

Taylor had believed that improved efficiency would lead to dramatic wage gains. With his decision to raise wages, Ford was being true to Taylor's principles. Ford went even further, however, in his innovations. He set up a sociology department, forerunner of the personnel department, to collect job, family, and other information about his employees. He sent social workers into workers' homes to inquire into (and "improve") their personal lives. For the foreign-born, he instituted Americanization classes. He offered his employees housing subsidies, medical care, and other benefits. In short, Ford recognized that workers were more complex than Taylor had allowed and that high wages alone would not transform them into the perfectly functioning parts of the mass-production system Taylor had envisioned.

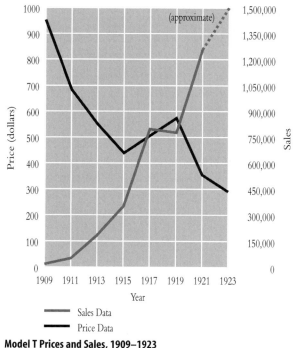

Model T Prices and Sales, 1909–1923

Source: From Alfred D. Chandler, Jr., ed., *Giant Enterprise: Ford, General Motors, and the Automobile Industry* (New York: Harcourt, Brace and World, 1964), pp. 32–33.

Although Ford's success impelled others to move in his direction, it would take time for modern management to come of age. Not until the 1920s did a substantial number of corporations establish personnel departments, institute welfare and recreational programs for employees, and hire psychologists to improve human relations in the workplace.

"Robber Barons" No More

Focus Question
How and why did American elites seek to alter their robber baron image in the late 19th and early 20th centuries?

Innovations in corporate management were part of a broader effort among elite industrialists to shed their "robber baron" image. The swashbuckling entrepreneurs of the 19th century—men such as Cornelius Vanderbilt, Jay Gould, Jay Cooke, and Leland Stanford—had wielded their economic power brashly and ruthlessly, while lavishing money on European-style palaces, private yachts, personal art collections, and extravagant entertainments. But the depression of the 1890s—along with the populist political movement and labor protests such as the Homestead and Pullman strikes—shook the confidence of members of this elite. Industrialists were terrified when in 1892 anarchist Alexander Berkman marched into the office of Henry Clay Frick, **Andrew Carnegie's** right-hand man, and shot him at point-blank range (Frick survived). Although such physical assaults were rare, anger over ill-gotten and ill-spent wealth was widespread. In the 1890s, popular rage forced Mrs. Bradley Martin and her husband to flee to England after she spent $370,000 (roughly $3.5 million in 2007 dollars) on one evening of entertainment for her friends in New York's high society.

Seeking a more favorable image, some industrialists began to restrain their displays of wealth and use their private fortunes to advance the public welfare. As early as 1889, Andrew Carnegie had advocated a "gospel of wealth." The wealthy, he believed, should consider all income in excess of their needs as a "trust fund" for their communities. In 1901, the year in which he formed U.S. Steel, Carnegie withdrew from industry and devoted himself to philanthropic pursuits, especially in art and education. By the time he died in 1919, he had given away or entrusted to several Carnegie foundations 90 percent of his fortune. Among the projects he funded were New York's Carnegie Hall, Pittsburgh's Carnegie Institute (now Carnegie-Mellon University), and 2,500 public libraries throughout the country.

Other industrialists, including John D. Rockefeller, soon followed Carnegie's lead. A devout Baptist with an ascetic bent, Rockefeller had never flaunted his wealth (unlike the Vanderbilts and others), but his ruthless business methods in assembling the Standard Oil Company and in crushing his competition made him one of the most reviled of the robber barons. In the wake of journalist Ida Tarbell's stinging 1904 exposé of Standard Oil's business practices, and of the federal government's subsequent prosecution of Standard Oil for monopolistic practices in 1906, Rockefeller transformed himself into a public-spirited philanthropist. Between 1913 and 1919, his Rockefeller Foundation dispersed an estimated $500 million. His most significant gifts included money to establish the University of Chicago and the Rockefeller Institute for Medical Research (later renamed Rockefeller University). His charitable efforts did not escape criticism, however; many Americans interpreted them as an attempt to establish control over American universities, scientific research, and public policy. Still, Rockefeller's largesse helped build for the Rockefeller family a reputation for public-spiritedness and good works, one that grew even stronger in the 1920s and 1930s. Many other business leaders, such as Julius Rosenwald of Sears Roebuck and Daniel and Simon Guggenheim of the American Smelting and Refining Company, also dedicated themselves to philanthropy during this time.

Obsession with Physical and Racial Fitness

The fractious events of the 1890s also induced many wealthy Americans to engage in what Theodore Roosevelt dubbed "the strenuous life." In an 1899 essay with that title, Roosevelt exhorted Americans to live vigorously, to test their physical strength and endurance in competitive athletics, and to experience nature through hiking, hunting, and mountain climbing. He articulated a way of life that influenced countless Americans from a variety of classes and cultures.

The 1890s were a time of heightened enthusiasm for competitive sports, physical fitness, and outdoor recreation. Millions of Americans began riding bicycles and eating healthier foods. A passion for athletic competition gripped American universities. The power and violence of football helped make it the sport of choice at the nation's elite campuses, and, for 20 years, Ivy League schools were the nation's football powerhouses. In athletic competition, as in nature, one could discover and recapture one's manhood, one's virility. The words "sissy" and "pussyfoot" entered common usage in the 1890s as insults hurled at men whose masculinity was found wanting.

In the vigorous new climate of the 1890s, young women began to engage in sports and other activities. They put away their corsets and long dresses and began wearing simple skirts, shirtwaists, and other clothing that gave them more comfort and freedom of movement. By the standards of the 1920s, these changes would seem mild, but in the 1890s, they were radical.

In the country at large, the new enthusiasm for athletics and the outdoor life reflected a widespread dissatisfaction with the growing regimentation of industrial society. Among wealthy Americans, the quest for physical superiority reflected a deeper and more ambiguous anxiety: their *racial* fitness. Most of them were native-born Americans whose families had lived in the United States for several generations and whose ancestors had come from the British Isles, the Netherlands, or some other region of northwestern Europe. Having embraced the principles of Social Darwinism (see chapter 19), they liked to attribute their success and good fortune to their "racial superiority." They saw themselves as "natural" leaders, members of a noble Anglo-Saxon race endowed with uncommon intelligence, imagination, and discipline. But events of the 1890s had challenged the legitimacy of the elite's wealth and authority, and the ensuing depression mocked their ability to exert economic leadership. The immigrant masses laboring in factories, despite their poverty and alleged racial inferiority, seemed to possess a vitality that the "superior" Anglo-Saxons lacked. Immigrant families were overflowing with children. The city neighborhoods where these families lived exhibited social and cultural energy (especially apparent in popular entertainments—vaudeville, amusement parks, nickelodeons, and dance halls) that were missing in the sedate environs of the wealthy.

Some rich Americans, such as Henry Adams, Henry Cabot Lodge, and other members of Boston's declining political elite, reacted to the immigrants' vigor and industry by calling for a halt to further immigration, but not the ebullient Roosevelt; he argued instead for American men to live the strenuous life and to test themselves unceasingly at work and at play. Through such struggles, the dominance of the "English-speaking peoples" would reassert itself and allow them to enjoy the rewards that racial superiority and racial fitness had put within their grasp: power, prosperity, civilization, and liberty. Roosevelt called on each married American woman, meanwhile, to have at least four children—an absolute necessity, he declared, in order to reproduce the "race" in numbers sufficient to maintain its vigor and dominance.

Immigration

Focus Question
What hardships and successes did immigrants experience in the United States?

A key factor causing this racial consternation among American elites was the extraordinarily large numbers of immigrants in America. The United States had always been a nation of immigrants, but never had so many come in so short a time. Between 1880 and 1920, some 23 million immigrants came to a country that numbered only 76 million in 1900. From 1900 to 1914, an average of 1 million immigrants arrived each year. In many cities of the Northeast and Midwest, immigrants and their children constituted a majority of the population. In 1920s Boston, New York City, Chicago, and Milwaukee, immigrants accounted for more than 70 percent of the total population; in Buffalo, Detroit, and Minneapolis, more than 60 percent; and in Philadelphia, Pittsburgh, and Seattle, more than 50 percent. Everywhere in the country, except in the South, the working class was overwhelmingly ethnic.

European immigration accounted for approximately three-fourths of the total. Some states received significant numbers of non-European immigrants—Chinese, Japanese, and Filipinos in California; Mexicans in California and the Southwest; and French Canadians in New England. Although their presence profoundly affected regional economies, politics, and culture, their numbers, relative to the number of European immigrants, were small. Immigrants from Latin America were free to enter the United States throughout this period, but few did until 1910, when the social disorder caused by the Mexican Revolution propelled a stream of refugees to southwestern parts of the United States. One-half million French Canadians had migrated to New England and the upper Midwest between 1867 and 1901. After that, the rate slowed as the pace of industrialization in their Quebec homeland quickened.

European Immigration

Most of the European immigrants who arrived between 1880 and 1914 came from Eastern and Southern Europe. Among them were 3 to 4 million Italians, 2 million Russian and Polish Jews, 2 million Hungarians, and an estimated 5 million Slavs and other peoples from eastern and southeastern Europe (Poles, Bohemians, Slovaks, Russians, Ukrainians, Lithuanians, Serbians, Croatians, Slovenians, Montenegrins, Bulgarians, Macedonians, and Greeks). Hundreds of thousands came as well from Turkey, Armenia, Lebanon, Syria, and other Near Eastern lands abutting the European continent.

These post-1880 arrivals were called "new immigrants" to underscore the cultural gap separating them from the "old immigrants," who had come from northwestern Europe—Great Britain, Scandinavia, and Germany. Old immigrants were regarded as racially fit,

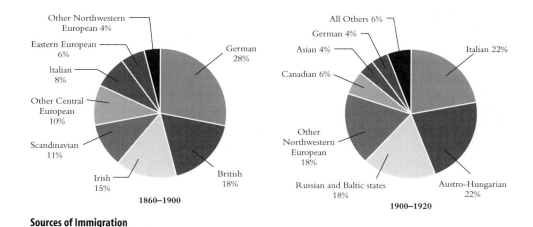

Sources of Immigration

Source: Data from *Historical Statistics of the United States, Colonial Times to 1970* (White Plains, NY: Kraus International, 1989), pp. 105–109.

culturally sophisticated, and politically mature. The new immigrants, by contrast, were often regarded as racially inferior, culturally impoverished, and incapable of assimilating American values and traditions. This negative view of the new immigrants reflected in part a fear of their alien languages, religions, and economic backgrounds. Few spoke English, and most adhered to Catholicism, Orthodoxy, or Judaism rather than Protestantism. Most, with the exception of Jewish immigrants, were peasants, unaccustomed to urban industrial life, but they were not as different from the old immigrants as the label implied. For example, many of the earlier-arriving Catholic peasants from Ireland and Germany had had no more familiarity with American values and traditions than did the Italians and Slavs who arrived later.

In fact, the old and new European immigrants were more similar than different. Both came to America for the same reasons: either to flee religious or political persecution or to escape economic hardship. The United States attracted a small but steady stream of political refugees throughout the 19th century: labor militants from England; nationalists from Ireland; socialists and anarchists from Germany, Russia, Finland, and Italy. Many of these people possessed talents as skilled workers, labor organizers, political agitators, and newspaper editors and thus exercised influence in their ethnic communities. However, only the anti-Semitic policies of Russia in the late 19th and early 20th centuries triggered a mass emigration (in this case Jewish) of political refugees.

Most mass immigration was propelled instead by economic hardship. Europe's rural population was growing faster than the land could support. European factories absorbed some, but not all, of the rural surplus. Industrialization and urbanization were affecting the European countryside in ways that disrupted rural ways of life. As railroads penetrated rural areas, village artisans found themselves unable to compete with the cheap manufactured goods that arrived from city factories. These handicraftsmen were among the first to emigrate. Meanwhile, rising demand for food in the cities accelerated the growth of commercial agriculture in the hinterland. Some peasant families lost their land. Others turned to producing crops for the market, only to discover that they could not compete with larger, more efficient producers. In addition, by the last third of the 19th century, peasants faced competition from North American farmers. Prices for agricultural commodities plummeted everywhere. The economic squeeze that spread distress among American farmers in the 1880s and 1890s caused even more hardship among Europe's peasantry, and many of them decided to try their luck in the New World.

An individual's or family's decision to emigrate often depended on having a contact—a family member, relative, or fellow villager—already established in an American city. These people provided immigrants with a destination, inspiration (they were examples of success in America), advice about jobs, and financial aid. Sometimes whole villages in southern Italy or western Russia—or at least all of the young men—seemed to disappear, only to reappear in a certain section of Chicago, Pittsburgh, or New York. Villages without contacts in the United States were relatively unaffected by the emigration mania.

Most immigrants viewed their trip to the United States as a temporary sojourn. They came not in search of permanent settlement but in search of high wages that would enable them to improve their economic standing in their homeland. For them, America was a land of economic opportunity, not a land to call home. This attitude explains why men vastly outnumbered women and children in the migration stream. From 1899 to 1910, three-fourths of the immigrants from Southern and Eastern Europe were adult men. Some had left wives and children behind; more were single. Most wanted merely to make enough money to buy a farm in their native land. True to their dream, many did return home. For every 100 Italian immigrants who arrived in the United States between 1907 and 1911, for example, 73 returned to Italy. Before the First World War, an estimated 60 percent to 80 percent of all Slavic immigrants eventually returned to the land of their birth.

The rate of return was negligible among certain groups, however. Jews had little desire to return to the religious persecution they had fled, and only 5 percent returned to Europe. The rate of return was also low among the Irish, who saw few opportunities in their long-suffering (although much-loved) Emerald Isle. In the early 20th century, however, such groups were exceptional. Most immigrants looked forward to returning to Europe. Not until the First World War shut down transatlantic travel did most immigrants begin to regard their presence in the United States as permanent.

Immigration tended to move in rhythm with the U.S. business cycle. It rose in boom years and fell off during depressions. It remained high during the first 14 years of the new century when the U.S. economy experienced sustained growth, broken only briefly by the Panic of 1907–08.

Chinese and Japanese Immigration

The relatively small numbers of Chinese and Japanese immigrants who came to the United States in the late 19th and early 20th centuries reflected the efforts of native-born Americans and their allies to keep them out. As many as 300,000 Chinese immigrants arrived in the United States between 1851 and 1882, and more than 200,000 Japanese immigrants journeyed to Hawaii and the western continental United States between 1891 and 1907. They contributed in major ways to the development of two of the West's major industries: railroad building and commercial agriculture. These two immigrant groups might have formed two of America's largest, each numbering in the millions, but the U.S. government began to exclude Chinese immigrant laborers in 1882 (The Chinese Exclusion Act) and Japanese immigrant laborers in 1907 (see chapter 22). The government also interpreted a 1790 law to mean that Chinese, Japanese, and other East Asian immigrants were ineligible for citizenship. These exclusions remained in force until the 1940s and 1950s. They expressed the racial prejudice felt by most native-born white Americans toward nonwhite Asian immigrants, and they also revealed how determined America was to remain a nation of European immigrants and their descendants.

The factors propelling Chinese and Japanese immigrants were similar to those motivating their European counterparts. The rural population in those countries was increasing at a rate faster than the rural economies could support. Chinese and Japanese rural peasants were being integrated into an international market for agriculture, contributing to the global oversupply of agricultural goods and depressing prices. Many Chinese and Japanese immigrants, like their European counterparts, conceived of their movement beyond their countries' borders as temporary. They intended to move abroad just long enough to make enough money to establish themselves economically in their homelands. Thus the early streams of Chinese and Japanese migration to the United States were overwhelmingly composed of men looking for work. Similar to the European immigrants, the Chinese and Japanese sojourners tended to follow precise migratory paths—from one region or village in China or Japan to one city or region in the United States.

Conditions in China were more desperate than those in Japan, where industrialization had begun to generate new wealth and absorb some of the rural population. Chinese immigrants, as a result, often suffered greater hardship than did their Japanese counterparts. In the 19th century, many were forced to sign contracts with suppliers of overseas laborers that subjected them to slave-like conditions: They were herded onto boats for the transpacific voyage, bound to particular employers for years on end, thrust into dangerous working conditions, and paid paltry wages. The conditions of their labor in the western states where they tended to settle inflamed the sentiments of white working men, who saw the Asian migration as a threat to their own wages and livelihoods. These white workers might have made common cause with Asian immigrant workers, but the racial prejudice they harbored toward the "yellow hordes" was simply too great. White workers became leaders of the movements in the western states to keep these immigrants out.

Significant numbers of Chinese and Japanese immigrants continued to try to enter the United States during the period of Asian immigrant exclusion—after 1882 in the case of the Chinese and 1907 in the case of the Japanese. Some were desperate to reunite themselves with family members already living in the United States, while others were driven by deteriorating economic circumstances in their homeland. Many attempted to enter the United States with forged papers declaring them to be merchants (a permitted class of Chinese and Japanese immigrants) when they were not, or to have been resident in the United States before the exclusion laws had gone into effect (and thus entitled to return). San Francisco was their principal port of entry, and Angel Island, in San Francisco harbor, became the counterpart of Ellis Island in New York harbor: the place where inspectors for the U.S. Bureau of Immigration interrogated them and scrutinized their documents and, more often than not, sent them back to Asia.

Other East Asian immigrants attempted to enter the United States through Canada or Mexico, hoping to find an unpatrolled part of the land border and to cross into the United States undetected. They became, in effect, America's first illegal aliens. That a certain percentage of East Asian immigrants were illegals subject to deportation generated considerable fear among the Asian immigrant populations resident in the United States, deepening tendencies within these communities to secrecy and to separation from mainstream American culture and society. Despite these considerable hardships, Asian immigrants would prove to be resourceful and to find ways to build homes and livelihoods in America.

Immigrant Labor

In the first decade of the 20th century, immigrant men and their male children constituted 70 percent of the workforce in 15 of the 19 leading U.S. industries. They concentrated in industries where work was the most backbreaking. Immigrants built the nation's railroads and tunnels; mined its coal, iron ore, and other minerals; stoked its hot and sometimes deadly steel furnaces; and slaughtered and packed its meat in Chicago's putrid packing-houses. In 1909, first- and second-generation immigrants—especially Greeks, Italians, Japanese, and Mexicans—constituted more than 96 percent of the labor force that built and

© Bettmann/CORBIS

Immigrant Japanese Children Arrive at Angel Island, San Francisco Harbor, 1905   Beginning in 1907, as a result of the "gentlemen's agreement" between the United States and Japanese governments, it would no longer be possible for Japanese immigrants such as these children to come to the United States.

maintained the nation's railroads. Of the 750,000 Slovaks who arrived in America before 1913, at least 600,000 headed for the coal mines and steel mills of western Pennsylvania. The steel mills of Pittsburgh, Buffalo, Cleveland, and Chicago also attracted disproportionately large numbers of Poles and other Slavs.

Immigrants also performed "lighter" but no less arduous work. Jews and Italians predominated in the garment manufacturing shops of New York City, Chicago, Philadelphia, Baltimore, and Boston. In 1900, French-Canadian immigrants and their children held one of every two jobs in New England's cotton textile industry. By 1920, the prosperity of California's rapidly growing agricultural industry depended primarily on Mexican and Filipino labor. In these industries, immigrant women and children, who worked for lower wages than men, formed a large part of the labor force. Few states restricted child labor. More than 25 percent of boys and 10 percent of girls aged 10 to 15 were "gainfully employed."

Immigrants were as essential as fossil fuels to the smooth operation of the American economic machine. Sometimes, however, the machine consumed workers as well as coal and oil. Those who worked in heavy industry, mining, or railroading were especially vulnerable to accident and injury. In 1901, for instance, 1 in every 400 railroad workers died on the job and 1 in every 26 suffered injury. Between the years 1906 and 1911, almost one-quarter of the recent immigrants employed at the U.S. Steel Corporation's South Works (Pittsburgh) were injured or killed on the job. Lax attention to safety rendered even light industry hazardous and sometimes fatal. In 1911, a fire broke out on an upper floor of the **Triangle Shirtwaist Company,** a New York City garment factory. The building had no fire escapes. The owners of the factory, moreover, had locked the entrances to each floor as a way of keeping their employees at work. A total of 146 workers, mostly young Jewish and Italian women, perished in the fire or from desperate nine-story leaps to the pavement below.

Chronic fatigue and inadequate nourishment increased the risk of accident and injury. Workweeks averaged 60 hours—10 hours every day except Sunday. Workers who were granted Saturday afternoons off, thus reducing their workweek to a mere 55 hours, considered themselves fortunate. Steelworkers were not so lucky. They labored from 72 to 89 hours per week and were required to work one 24-hour shift every two weeks.

Most workers had to labor long hours simply to eke out a meager living. In 1900, the annual earnings of American manufacturing workers averaged only $400 to $500 per year. Skilled jobs offered immigrants far more (as much as $1,500 to $2,000 per year), but most of them were held by Yankees and by the Germans, Irish, Welsh, and other Europeans who had come as part of the old immigration. Through their unions, workers of Northern European extraction also controlled access to new jobs that opened up and usually managed to fill them with a son, relative, or fellow countryman. Consequently, relatively few of the new immigrants rose into the prosperous ranks of skilled labor. In any case, employers were replacing many skilled workers with machines operated by cheaply paid operatives.

From the 1870s to 1910, real wages paid to factory workers and common laborers did rise, but not steadily. Wages fell sharply during depressions, and the hope for increases during periods of recovery often collapsed under the weight of renewed mass immigration, which brought hundreds of thousands of new job seekers into the labor market. One of every five industrial workers was unemployed, even during the boom years of the early 20th century.

Most working families required two or three wage earners to survive. If a mother could not go out to work because she had small children at home, she might rent rooms to some of the many single men who had recently immigrated. But economic security was difficult to attain. In his 1904 book, *Poverty,* social investigator Robert Hunter conservatively estimated that 20 percent of the industrial population of the North lived in poverty.

Living Conditions

Strained economic circumstances confined many working-class families to cramped and dilapidated living quarters. Many of them lived in two- or three-room apartments, with several people sleeping in each room. To make ends meet, one immigrant New York City family of eight living in a two-room apartment took in six boarders. Some boarders considered themselves lucky to have their own bed. That luxury was denied the 14 Slovaks who shared eight beds in a small Pittsburgh apartment and the New York City printer who slept on a door he unhinged every night and balanced across two chairs. The lack of windows in city tenements allowed little light or air into these apartments, and few had their own toilets or running water. Crowding was endemic. The population density of New York City's Lower East Side—where most of the city's Jewish immigrants settled—reached 700 per acre in 1900, a density greater than that of the poorest sections of Mumbai (formerly Bombay), India. Overcrowding and poor sanitation resulted in high rates of infectious diseases, especially diphtheria, typhoid fever, and pneumonia.

By 1900, this crisis in urban living had begun to yield to the insistence of urban reformers that cities adopt housing codes and improve sanitation. Between 1880 and 1900, housing inspectors condemned the worst of the tenements and ordered landlords to make improvements. City governments built reservoirs, pipes, and sewers to carry clean water to the tenements and to carry away human waste. Newly paved roads lessened the dirt, mud, and stagnant pools of water and thus further curtailed the spread of disease. As a result, urban mortality rates fell in the 1880s and 1890s.

Nevertheless, improvements came far more slowly to the urban poor than they did to the middle and upper classes. Cities such as Pittsburgh built extensive systems of paved roads in wealthy districts but not in working-class areas. Water supplies and pressures were far better in prosperous than in poor neighborhoods. At the outbreak of the First World War, many working-class families still lacked running water in their homes.

Building Ethnic Communities

The immigrants may have been poor, but they were not helpless. Migration had required a good deal of resourcefulness, self-help, and mutual aid—assets that survived in the new surroundings of American cities.

A Network of Institutions

Each ethnic group quickly established a network of institutions that supplied a sense of community and multiplied sources of communal assistance. Some immigrants simply reproduced those institutions that had been important to them in the Old Country. The devout established churches and synagogues. Lithuanian, Jewish, and Italian radicals reestablished Old World socialist and anarchist organizations. Irish nationalists set up clandestine chapters of the Clan Na Gael to keep alive the struggle to free Ireland from the English. Germans felt at home in their traditional *Turnevereins* (athletic clubs) and musical societies.

Immigrants developed new institutions as well. In the larger cities, foreign-language newspapers disseminated news, advice, and culture. Each ethnic group created fraternal societies to bring together immigrants who had known each other in the Old Country, or who shared the same craft, or who had come from the same town or region. Most of these societies provided members with a death benefit (ranging from a few hundred to a thousand dollars) that guaranteed the deceased a decent burial and the family a bit of cash. Some fraternal societies made small loans as well. Among those ethnic groups that prized home ownership, especially the Slavic groups, the fraternal societies also provided mortgage money. And all of them served as centers of sociability—places to have a drink, play cards, or simply relax with fellow countrymen. The joy, solace, and solidarity these groups generated helped countless immigrants adjust to American life.

The Emergence of an Ethnic Middle Class

Within each ethnic group, a sizable minority directed their talents and ambitions toward economic gain. Some of these entrepreneurs first addressed their communities' needs for basic goods and services. Immigrants preferred to buy from fellow countrymen with whom they shared a language, a history, and presumably a bond of trust. Enterprising individuals responded by opening dry-goods stores, food shops, butcher shops, and saloons in their ethnic neighborhoods. Those who could not afford to rent a store hawked their fruit, clothing, or dry goods from portable stands, wagons, or sacks carried on their backs. The work was endless and the competition tough. Men often enlisted the entire family—wife, older children, younger children—in their undertakings. Few family members were ever paid for their labor, no matter how long or hard they worked. Although many of these small businesses failed, enough survived to give some immigrants and their children a toehold in the middle class.

Other immigrants turned to small industry, particularly garment manufacture, truck farming, and construction. A clothing manufacturer needed only a few sewing machines to become competitive. Many Jewish immigrants, having been tailors in Russia and Poland, opened such facilities. If a rented space proved beyond their means, they set up shop in their own apartments. Competition among these small manufacturers was fierce, and work environments were condemned by critics as "sweatshops." Workers suffered from inadequate lighting, heat, and ventilation; 12-hour workdays and 70-hour work-weeks during peak seasons, with every hour spent bent over a sewing machine; and poor pay and no employment security, especially for the women and children who made up a large part of this labor force. Even at this level of exploitation, many small manufacturers failed, but over time, significant numbers of them managed to firm up their position as manufacturers and to evolve into stable, responsible employers. Their success contributed to the emergence of a Jewish middle class.

The story was much the same in urban construction, where Italians who had established themselves as labor contractors, or *padroni,* went into business for themselves to take advantage of the rapid expansion of American cities. Although few became general contractors on major downtown projects, many of them did well building family residences or serving as subcontractors on larger buildings.

One who did make the leap from small to big business was Amadeo P. Giannini, the son of Italian immigrants, who used his savings from a San Francisco fruit and vegetable stand to launch a career in banking. Determined to make bank loans available and affordable to people of ordinary means, Giannini generated a huge business in small loans. Expanding on his ethnic base of small depositors, he eventually made his bank—the Bank of America—into the country's largest financial institution.

In southern California, Japanese immigrants chose agriculture as their route to the middle class. Working as agricultural laborers in the 1890s, they began to acquire their own land in the early years of the 20th century. Altogether, they owned only 1 percent of California's total farm acreage. Their specialization in fresh vegetables and fruits (particularly strawberries), combined with their family-labor-intensive agricultural methods, was yielding $67 million in annual revenues by 1919—one-tenth of the total California agriculture revenue that year. Japanese farmers sold their produce to Japanese fruit and vegetable wholesalers in Los Angeles, who had chosen a mercantile route to middle-class status. The success of Japanese farmers was all the more impressive given that the state of California had passed the Alien Land Law in 1913, prohibiting Japanese and other Asian aliens from owning property in the state. Japanese immigrant farmers thus depended on their native-born children or friendly whites to acquire land for them, arrangements that made them more vulnerable to losing the land—or control of it—than if they had been able to own it outright themselves.

Each ethnic group created its own history of economic success and social mobility. From the emerging middle classes came leaders who would provide their ethnic groups with identity, legitimacy, and power and would lead the way toward Americanization and assimilation. Their children tended to do better in school than the children of working-class ethnics, and academic success served as a ticket to upward social mobility in a society that increasingly depended on university-trained engineers, managers, lawyers, doctors, and other professionals.

Political Machines and Organized Crime

The underside of this success story was the rise of government corruption and organized crime. Many ethnic entrepreneurs operated on the margins of economic failure and bankruptcy, and some accepted the help of those who promised financial assistance. Sometimes the help came from honest unions and upright government officials, but other times it did not. Unions were generally weak, and some government officials, lacking experience and economic security, were susceptible to bribery. Economic necessity became a breeding ground for government corruption and greed. A contractor who was eager to win a city contract—to build a trolley system, a sewer line, or a new city hall, for example—would find it necessary to pay off government officials who could throw the contract his way. By 1900, such payments, referred to as "graft," had become essential to the day-to-day operation of government in most large cities. Graft, in turn, made local officeholding a source of economic gain. Politicians began building political organizations called machines to guarantee their success in municipal elections. The machine "bosses" used a variety of legal and illegal means to bring victory on election day. They won the loyalty of urban voters—especially immigrants—by providing poor neighborhoods with paved roads and sewer systems. They helped newly arrived immigrants find jobs (often on city payrolls) and occasionally provided food, fuel, or clothing to families in dire need. Many of their clients were grateful for these services in an age when government provided little public assistance.

The bosses who ran the political machines—including "King Richard" Croker in New York, James Michael Curley in Boston, Tom Pendergast in Kansas City, Martin Behrman in New Orleans, and Abe Ruef in San Francisco—served their own needs first. They saw to it that construction contracts went to those who offered the most graft, not to those who were likely to do the best job. They protected gamblers, pimps, and other purveyors of urban vice who contributed large amounts to their machine coffers. They often required city employees to contribute to their campaign chests, to solicit political contributions, and to get out the vote on election day. And they engaged in widespread election fraud by rounding up truckloads of newly arrived immigrants and paying them to vote a certain way; having their supporters vote two or three times; and stuffing ballot boxes with the votes of phantom citizens who had died, moved away, or never been born.

Big-city machines, then, were both positive and negative forces in urban life. Reformers despised them for disregarding election laws and encouraging vice, but many immigrants valued them for providing social welfare services and for creating opportunities for upward mobility.

The history of President John F. Kennedy's family offers one example of the economic and political opportunities opened up by machine politics. Both of Kennedy's grandfathers, John Francis Fitzgerald ("Honey Fitz") and Patrick Joseph Kennedy, were the children of penniless Irish immigrants who arrived in Boston in the 1840s. Fitzgerald excelled at academics and won a coveted place in Harvard's Medical School, but left Harvard that same year, choosing a career in politics instead. Between 1891 and 1905, Fitzgerald served as a Boston city councilor, Massachusetts state congressman and senator, U.S. congressman, and mayor of Boston. For much of this period, he derived considerable income and power from his position as the North End ward boss, where he supervised the trading of jobs for votes and favors for cash in his section of Boston's Democratic and Irish-dominated political machine.

Patrick Kennedy, an East Boston tavern owner and liquor merchant, became an equally important figure in Boston city politics. In addition to running the Democratic Party's affairs in Ward Two, he served on the Strategy Board, a secret council of Boston's machine politicians that met regularly to devise policies, settle disputes, and divide up graft. Both Fitzgerald and Kennedy derived a substantial income from their political work and used it to lift their families into middle-class prosperity. Kennedy's son (and the future president's father), Joseph P. Kennedy, would go on to make a fortune as a Wall Street speculator and liquor distributor and to groom his sons for Harvard and the highest political offices in the land. But his rapid economic and social ascent had been made possible by his father's and father-in-law's earlier success in Boston machine politics.

Underworld figures, too, influenced urban life. In the early years of the 20th century, gangsterism was a scourge of Italian neighborhoods, where Sicilian immigrants had established outposts of the notorious Mafia, and in Irish, Jewish, Chinese, and other ethnic communities as well. Favorite targets of these gangsters were small-scale manufacturers and contractors, who were threatened with violence and economic ruin if they did not pay a gang for "protection." Gangsters enforced their demands with physical force, beating up or killing those who failed to abide by the "rules." In Chinese communities, secret societies originating in China, or *tongs,* and initially set up in America to strengthen communal life among the immigrants, occasionally crossed the line into crime. Sometimes this transition resulted from good intentions—for example, tong members might smuggle into the United States the wife and children of an immigrant Chinese man who had no legal way of reuniting his family—but other times, tongs enmeshed themselves in far more damaging criminal activities such as the opium trade, prostitution, and gambling.

Greedy for money, power, and fame, and willing to use any means necessary, many immigrant and ethnic criminals considered themselves authentic entrepreneurs cut from the American mold. By the 1920s, petty extortion had escalated in urban areas, and underworld crime had become big business. Al Capone, the ruthless Chicago mobster who made a fortune from gambling, prostitution, and bootleg liquor during Prohibition, once claimed: "Prohibition is a business. All I do is to supply a public demand. I do it in the best and least harmful way I can." New York City's Arnold Rothstein, whose financial sophistication won him a gambling empire and the power to fix the 1919 World Series, nurtured his reputation as "the J. P. Morgan of the underworld." Mobsters like Rothstein and Capone were charismatic figures, both in their ethnic communities and in the nation at large. Few immigrants, however, followed their criminal path to economic success.

African American Labor and Community

Focus Question
What were the similarities and differences between the immigrant and African American experiences in the early 20th century?

Unlike immigrants, African Americans remained a predominantly rural and southern people in the early 20th century. Most blacks were sharecroppers and tenant farmers. The markets for cotton and other southern crops had stabilized in the early 20th century, but black farmers remained vulnerable to exploitation. Landowners, most of whom were white, often forced sharecroppers to accept artificially low prices for their crops. At the same time, they charged high prices for seed, tools, and groceries at the local stores they controlled. Few rural areas generated enough business to support more than one store or to create a competitive climate that might force prices down. Those sharecroppers who traveled elsewhere to sell their crops or purchase their necessities risked retaliation— either physical assaults by white vigilantes or eviction from their land. Thus most remained beholden to their landowners, mired in poverty and debt.

Some African Americans sought a better life by migrating to industrial areas of the South and the North. In the South, they worked in iron and coal mines, in furniture and cigarette manufacture, as railroad track layers and longshoremen, and as laborers in the steel mills of Birmingham, Alabama. By the early 20th century, their presence was growing in the urban North as well, where they worked on the fringes of industry as janitors, elevator operators, teamsters, longshoremen, and servants of various kinds. Altogether, about 200,000 blacks left the South for the North and West between 1890 and 1910.

In southern industries, blacks were subjected to hardships and indignities that even the newest immigrants were not expected to endure. Railroad contractors in the South, for example, treated their black track layers like prisoners. Armed guards marched them to work in the morning and back at night. Track layers were paid only once a month and forced to purchase food at the company commissary, where the high prices claimed most of what they earned. Their belongings were locked up to discourage them from running away. Although other southern employers of black workers did not engage in labor practices as harsh as those of the railroad contractors, they still confined blacks to the dirtiest and most grueling jobs. The "Jim Crow" laws passed by every southern state legislature in the 1890s legalized this rigid separation of the black and white races (see chapter 18).

The nation's worsening racial climate adversely affected southern blacks who came north, even though these migrants had moved to states that generally did not have Jim Crow laws. Northern industrialists generally refused to hire black migrants for manufacturing jobs, preferring the labor of European immigrants. Only when those immigrants went on strike did employers turn to African Americans. Black workers first gained a foothold in the Chicago meatpacking industry in 1904, when 28,000 immigrant packinghouse workers walked off their jobs. Employers hoped that the use of black strike-breakers would inflame racial tensions between white and black workers and thus undermine labor unity and strength.

African Americans who had long resided in northern urban areas also experienced intensifying discrimination in the late 19th and early 20th centuries. In 1870, about one-third of the black men in many northern cities had been skilled tradesmen: blacksmiths, painters, shoemakers, and carpenters. Serving both black and white clients, these men enjoyed steady work and good pay, but by 1910 only 10 percent of black men made a living in this way. In many cities, the number of barber shops and food catering businesses owned by blacks also went into sharp decline, as did black representation in the ranks of restaurant and hotel waiters. These barbers, food caterers, and waiters had formed a black middle class whose livelihood depended on the patronage of white clients. By the early 20th century, this middle class was in decline, the victim of growing racism. Whites were no longer willing to engage the services of blacks, preferring to have their hair cut, beards shaved, and food prepared and served by European immigrants. The residential segregation of northern blacks also rose in these years, as whites excluded them from growing numbers of urban neighborhoods.

African Americans did not lack for resourcefulness. In urban areas of settlement, they laced their communities with the same array of institutions—churches, fraternal insurance societies, political organizations—that solidified ethnic neighborhoods. A new black middle class arose, consisting of ministers, professionals, and businesspeople who serviced the needs of their racial group. Black-owned real estate agencies, funeral homes, doctors' offices, newspapers, groceries, restaurants, and bars opened for business on the commercial thoroughfares of African American neighborhoods. Many businessmen had been inspired by the words of black educator Booker T. Washington, and specifically by his argument that blacks should devote themselves to self-help and self-sufficiency. **Madame C. J. Walker** offers one example of a black woman who built a lucrative business from the hair and skin lotions she devised and sold to black customers throughout the country. In many cities, African American real estate agents achieved significant wealth and power.

THE JAZZ SINGER (1927)

Directed by Alan Crosland. Starring Al Jolson (Jake Rabinowitz/Jack Robin), May McAvoy (Mary Dale), and Warner Oland (Cantor Rabinowitz).

The *Jazz Singer* was a sensation when it opened because it was the first movie to use sound (although relatively few words of dialogue were actually spoken). It also starred Al Jolson, the era's most popular Broadway entertainer, and bravely explored an issue that the film industry usually avoided—the religious culture and generational dynamics of a "new immigrant" family.

The movie focuses on Jake Rabinowitz and his immigrant parents, who are Jewish and devout. Jake's father is a fifth-generation cantor whose job it is to fill his New York City synagogue with ancient and uplifting melodies on the Sabbath and Jewish holidays. Cantor Rabinowitz looks upon his work as sacred, and he expects Jake to take his place one day. But Jake has other ideas. He loves music but is drawn to the new rhythmic ragtime and sensual jazz melodies emerging from his American surroundings. In an early scene, we encounter Jake at a dance hall, absorbed in playing and singing ragtime tunes and forgetting that he should be at home preparing for Yom Kippur, the holiest day in the Jewish calendar. His distraught father finds him and whips him, and Jake, in anger and pain, runs away. These early scenes allow us to glimpse important themes in the immigrant experience of the early 20th century: the deep attraction among the children of immigrants to the energy and vitality of American popular culture and the strains that this attraction often caused between these children and parents desperate to maintain the traditions they had brought with them from Europe.

Jake's estrangement from his family and community gives him the space to reinvent himself as Jack Robin, the jazz singer. His love relationship with a prominent (and non-Jewish) stage actress, Mary Dale, brings him the big break he needs, a starring role in a Broadway show. Jack hopes to use his return to New York to reconcile with his father. This eventually happens when Jake, on the eve of Yom Kippur once again, agrees to skip his show's premiere in order to take his ailing father's place as cantor in the synagogue. Jake's melodies soar and reach his bedridden father who, thinking that his son has succeeded him as cantor and thus fulfilled his (the father's) deepest wish, peacefully dies.

His father is deceived, for Jake returns to his Broadway show as soon as Yom Kippur ends to deliver an outstanding performance as the "Jazz Singer." His

Nevertheless, entrepreneurial success remained a tougher task among African Americans than among immigrants. Black communities were often smaller and poorer than their white ethnic ones; economic opportunities were fewer, and black businessmen found it more difficult than their white ethnic counterparts to cultivate customers outside of their core community. Racial prejudice stood as an obstacle to black business future lies with Broadway rather than with a synagogue, and with the gentile Mary. The movie, however, makes it seem as though everything will work out: Jake's mother is in the audience for the Broadway show, enjoying her son's success and, in effect, blessing him for the career and woman he has chosen. That this resolution requires misleading the father reminds us, however, that the strains between immigrant parents and their American-born children could be deep and sometimes not resolvable.

The movie also allows us to ask questions about the relationship between immigrants and African Americans. As part of his Broadway performance, Jake does a blackface routine, using burnt cork to turn his face and neck black and thus to appear to audiences as a "black" entertainer. From the early 19th to the early 20th centuries, "blacking up" was a performance style popular among white entertainers who wanted both to appropriate and ridicule expressive aspects of black culture. What did it mean for a child of Jewish immigrants, himself vulnerable to being stigmatized as an outsider in America, to "black up"? Jake may have been expressing in part his desire to draw closer to rich elements in black musical culture. But Jake may also have been signaling his desire to distance himself from African

A billboard in New York City advertising *The Jazz Singer*. Al Jolson is shown in blackface.

Americans by participating in tradition popular among white American entertainers. Ironically, "blacking up" may have been a way for an entertainer to embrace not black but white America, and for someone like Jake to be accepted by non-Jewish white Americans as one of their own.

success. Meanwhile, blacks were so marginalized in politics that they had little opportunity to gain power or wealth through holding political office or controlling a political machine. Thus the African American middle class remained smaller and more precarious than did its counterpart in ethnic communities, less able to lead the way toward affluence and assimilation.

A'Lelia Bundles/Walker Family Collection/www.madamcjwalker.com

Madame C. J. Walker   This prominent African American entrepreneur, pictured here behind the wheel of her car, built a successful business selling hair and skin lotions to black customers throughout the country.

Workers and Unions

Middle-class success eluded most immigrants and blacks in the years before the First World War. Even among Jews, whose rate of social mobility was rapid, most immigrants were working class. For most workers, the path toward a better life lay in improving their working conditions, not in escape from the working class. Henry Ford's $5-per-day wage, double the average manufacturing wage, raised the hopes of many. Young immigrant men, in particular, flocked to Detroit to work for Ford. But in the early decades of the 20th century, few other manufacturers were prepared to follow Ford's lead, and most factory workers remained in a fragile economic state.

Samuel F. Gompers and the AFL

For those workers, the only hope for economic improvement lay in organizing unions powerful enough to wrest wage concessions from reluctant employers. This was not an easy task. The charged, often violent, labor protests of the Gilded Age had been put down. Labor organizations, such as the Knights of Labor, that had unified workers had been defeated. Federal and state governments had shown themselves ready to use military force to break strikes. The courts, following the lead of the U.S. Supreme Court, repeatedly found unions in violation of the Sherman Antitrust Act, even though that act had been intended to control corporations, not unions. Judges in most states usually granted employer requests for injunctions—court orders that barred striking workers from picketing their place of employment (and thus from obstructing employer efforts to hire replacement workers). Before 1916, no federal laws protected workers' right to organize or required employers to bargain with the unions to which their workers belonged.

This hostile legal environment retarded the growth of unions from the 1890s through the 1920s. It also made the major labor organization of those years, the American Federation of Labor (AFL), more timid and conservative than it had been before the depression of the 1890s. In the aftermath of that depression, the AFL focused on organizing craft, or skilled, workers such as carpenters, typographers, plumbers, painters, and machinists. Because of their skills, these workers commanded more respect from employers than did the unskilled laborers. Employers negotiated contracts, or trade agreements, with craft unions that stipulated the wages workers were to be paid, the hours they were to work, and the rules under which new workers would be accepted into the trade. These agreements were accorded the same legal protection that American law bestowed on other commercial contracts.

As the AFL emphasized these bread-and-butter issues, it withdrew from the political activism that had once occupied its attention. It no longer agitated for governmental regulation of the economy and the workplace. The AFL had concluded that labor's powerful opponents in the legislatures and the courts would find ways to undermine whatever governmental gains organized labor managed to achieve. That conclusion was reinforced by a 1905 ruling, *Lochner* v. *New York,* in which the U.S. Supreme Court declared unconstitutional a seemingly innocent New York state law limiting bakery employees to a 10-hour day.

The AFL's "business" unionism took its most forceful expression from its president, **Samuel F. Gompers.** A onetime Marxist and cigarmaker who had helped found the AFL in 1886, Gompers was reelected to the AFL presidency every year from 1896 until his death in 1924. The AFL showed considerable vitality under his leadership, especially in the early years when its membership quadrupled from less than a half million in 1897 to more than 2 million in 1904. Aware of the AFL's growing significance and conservatism, the National Civic Federation, a newly formed council of corporate executives, agreed to meet periodically with the organization's leaders to discuss the nation's industrial and labor problems.

Nevertheless, the AFL had limited success. Its 2 million members represented only a small portion of the industrial workforce. Its concentration among craft workers, moreover, distanced it from most workers, who were not skilled. Unskilled and semiskilled workers could only be organized into an industrial union that offered membership to all workers in a particular industry. Gompers understood the importance of such unions and allowed several of them, including the United Mine Workers (UMW) and the International Ladies Garment Workers Union (ILGWU), to participate in the AFL. But AFL ranks remained dominated by skilled workers who looked down upon the unskilled. Ethnic background intensified these craftsmen's sense of superiority over the unskilled. Most skilled workers were from old immigrant stock—particularly English, Scottish, German, and Irish—and they shared the common prejudice against immigrants from Southern and Eastern Europe.

AFL members demonstrated even worse prejudice toward black workers. In the early 20th century, more than 10 AFL unions excluded African Americans from membership. The AFL's racist policies partially account for the shrinking numbers of black tradesmen between 1870 and 1910. White and black workers sometimes managed to set aside their suspicions of each other and cooperate. The UMW allowed black workers to join and to rise to positions of leadership. In New Orleans, black and white dockworkers constructed a remarkable experiment in biracial unionism that flourished from the 1890s through the early 1920s. But these moments of cooperation were rare.

Although blacks made up too small a percentage of the working class to build alternative labor organizations that would counteract the influence of the AFL, the new immigrants from Eastern and Southern Europe were too numerous to be ignored. Their participation in the UMW enabled that union to grow from only 14,000 in 1897 to more than 300,000 in 1914. In 1909, a strike of 20,000 women workers against the owners of New York City's garment factories inspired tens of thousands of workers, male and female, to join the ILGWU.

"Big Bill" Haywood and the IWW

When the AFL failed to help them organize, immigrants turned to other unions. The most important was the Industrial Workers of the World (IWW), founded by western miners in 1905 and led by William "Big Bill" Haywood. The IWW rejected the AFL principle of craft organization, hoping instead to organize all workers into "one big union." It scorned the notion that only a conservative union could survive in American society, declaring its commitment to revolution instead.

The IWW refused to sign collective bargaining agreements with employers, arguing that such agreements only trapped workers in capitalist property relations. Capitalism had to be overthrown through struggles between workers and their employers at the point of production. Although hundreds of thousands of workers passed through its ranks or participated in its strikes, the IWW's membership rarely exceeded 20,000. Nevertheless, few labor organizations inspired as much fear. The IWW organized the poorest and most isolated workers—lumbermen, miners, and trackmen in the West, textile workers and longshoremen in the East. Emboldened by IWW leaders, these workers waged strikes against employers who were unaccustomed to having their authority challenged. Violence lurked beneath the surface of these strikes and occasionally erupted in bloody skirmishes between strikers and police, National Guardsmen, or the private security forces hired by employers. Some blamed the IWW for the violence, seeing it as a direct outgrowth of calls for a "class war." Others understood that the IWW was not solely responsible. Employers had shown themselves quite willing to resort to violence to

Underwood Photo Archives

Men at Work   This photo of male workers stoking a boiler conveys some of the grime and heat associated with much early-1900s blue-collar work as well as the strength and concentration required of workmen.

enforce their will on employees. In 1913, for example, at Ludlow, Colorado, the Colorado Fuel and Iron Company, a subsidiary of Rockefeller's Standard Oil Company, brought in a private security force and the local militia (which it controlled) to break up a UMW strike. When the company evicted strikers and their families from their homes, the union set up 13 tent colonies to obstruct the entrances to the mines. The standoff came to a bloody conclusion in April 1914 when company police, firing into one colony of tents, killed 66 men, women, and children.

The **"Ludlow massacre"** outraged the nation. At hearings held by the U.S. Commission on Industrial Relations, John D. Rockefeller, Jr., was humiliated by Commissioner Frank Walsh's disclosure that the industrialist had been complicit in the events leading up to the violence. The massacre revealed yet again what the IWW strikes had already demonstrated: that many American workers resented their low wages and poor working conditions; that neither the government nor employers offered workers a mechanism for airing and peacefully resolving their grievances; and that workers, as a result, felt compelled to protest through joining unions and waging strikes, even if it meant risking their lives. On the eve of the First World War, almost 40 years after the Great Railroad Strike of 1877 (chapter 19), industrial conflict still plagued the nation.

Nickelodeons in Major American Cities, 1910

Cities	Population	Nickelodeons (estimate)	Seating Capacity	Population per Seat
New York	4,338,322	450	150,000	29
Chicago	2,000,000	310	93,000	22
Philadelphia	1,491,082	160	57,000	26
St. Louis	824,000	142	50,410	16
Cleveland	600,000	75	22,500	27
Baltimore	600,000	83	24,900	24
San Francisco	400,000	68	32,400	12
Cincinnati	350,000	75	22,500	16
New Orleans	325,000	28	5,600	58

Source: Garth Jowett, *Film: The Democratic Art* (Boston: Little, Brown, 1976), p. 46.

The Joys of the City

Industrial workers might be missing their fair share of the nation's prosperity, but they were crowding the dance halls, vaudeville theaters, amusement parks, and ballparks offered by the new world of commercial entertainment. Above all, they were embracing a new technological marvel, the movies.

Movies were well suited to poor city dwellers with little money, little free time, and little command of the English language. Initially, the movies cost only a nickel. The **"nickelodeons"** where they were shown were usually converted storefronts in working-class neighborhoods. Movies required little leisure time because at first they lasted only 15 minutes on average. Viewers with more time on their hands could stay for a cycle of two or three films (or for several cycles). And even non-English-speakers could understand what was happening on the "silent screen." By 1910, at least 20,000 nickelodeons dotted northern cities.

These early "moving pictures" were primitive by today's standards, but they were thrilling just the same. The figures appearing on the screen were "larger than life." Moviegoers could transport themselves to parts of the world they would otherwise never see, encounter people they would otherwise never meet, and watch boxing matches they could otherwise not afford to attend. The darkened theater provided a setting in which secret desires, especially sexual ones, could be explored. As one newspaper innocently commented in 1899: "For the first time in the history of the world it is possible to see what a kiss looks like."

No easy generalizations are possible about the content of these early films, more than half of which came from France, Germany, and Italy. American-made films tended toward slapstick comedies, adventure stories, and romances. Producers did not yet shy away, as they soon would, from the lustier or seedier sides of American life. The Hollywood formula of happy endings had yet to be worked out. In fact, the industry, centered in New

York City and Fort Lee, New Jersey, had yet to locate itself in cheery southern California. In 1914, the movies' first sex symbol, Theda Bara, debuted in a movie that showed her tempting an upstanding American ambassador into infidelity and ruin. She would be the first of the big screen's vamps, so-called because the characters they portrayed, like vampires, thrived on the blood (and death) of men.

The New Sexuality and the Rise of Feminism

The appearance of the vamp was one sign that popular culture had become an arena in which Americans were beginning to experiment with more open expressions of sexuality. Another sign was the growing numbers of women who began insisting that they be accorded the same sexual freedom long enjoyed by men. This impulse was strongest among young, single, working-class women who were entering the workforce in large numbers and mixing at workplaces, in loosely supervised ways, with men their own age. The associations between young men and women that sprang up at work carried over into their leisure. Young people of both sexes flocked to the dance halls that were opening in every major city. They rejected the stiff formality of earlier ballroom dances such as the cotillion or the waltz for the freedom and intimacy of newer forms, such as the fox trot, tango, and bunny-hug. They went to movies and to amusement parks together, and they engaged, far more than their parents had, in premarital sex. It is estimated that the proportion of women having sex before marriage rose from 10 percent to 25 percent in the generation that was coming of age between 1910 and 1920.

Feminism

This movement toward sexual freedom was one expression of women's dissatisfaction with the restrictions that had been imposed on them by earlier generations. By the second decade of the 20th century, eloquent spokeswomen had emerged to make the case for full female freedom and equality. The author Charlotte Perkins Gilman called for the release of women from domestic chores through the collectivization of housekeeping. Social activist Margaret Sanger insisted, in her lectures on birth control, that women should be free to enjoy sexual relations without having to worry about unwanted motherhood. The anarchist Emma Goldman denounced marriage as a kind of prostitution and embraced the ideal of "free love"— love unburdened by contractual commitment. Alice Paul, founder of the National Women's Party, brought a new militancy to the campaign for woman suffrage (see chapter 21).

These women were among the first to use the term *feminism* to describe their desire for complete equality with men. Some of them came together in Greenwich Village, a community of radical artists and writers in lower Manhattan, where they found a supportive environment in which to express and live by their feminist ideals. Crystal Eastman, a leader of the feminist **Greenwich Village** group called Heterodoxy, defined the feminist challenge as "how to arrange the world so that women can be human beings, with a chance to exercise their infinitely varied gifts in infinitely varied ways, instead of being destined by the accident of their sex to one field of activity."

Margaret Sanger on Trial, 1916   Feminist Margaret Sanger, left, was put on trial for using the U.S. mail service to circulate her book *The Woman Rebel,* which advocated birth control. A federal law barred the use of the mails to spread birth control advice or techniques.

The movement for sexual and gender equality aroused considerable anxiety. Parents worried about the promiscuity of their children. Conservatives were certain that sexual assertiveness among women would transform American cities into dens of iniquity. Vice commissions sprang up in every major city to clamp down on prostitution, drunkenness, and pornography. The campaign for prohibition—a ban on the sale of alcoholic beverages—gathered steam. Movie theater owners were pressured into excluding "indecent" films from their screens. Many believed the lurid tales of international vice lords scouring foreign lands for innocent girls who could be delivered to American brothel owners. This "white slave trade" inspired passage of the 1910 Mann Act, which made the transportation of women across state lines for immoral purposes a federal crime.

Nor did it escape the attention of conservatives that Greenwich Village was home not only to the dangerous exponents of "free love" but also to equally dangerous advocates of class warfare. Prominent IWW organizer Elizabeth Gurley Flynn was a member of Heterodoxy; her lover, Carlo Tresca, was an IWW theoretician. "Big Bill" Haywood also frequented Greenwich Village, where he was lionized as a working-class hero. When Greenwich Village radicals began publishing an avant-garde artistic journal in 1914, they called it *The Masses;* its editor was Max Eastman, the brother of Crystal. This convergence of labor and feminist militancy intensified conservative feeling that the nation had strayed too far from its roots.

Cultural conservatism was strongest in those areas of the country that were least involved in the ongoing industrial and sexual revolutions: in farming communities and small towns; in the South, where industrialization and urbanization were proceeding at a slower rate than elsewhere; and among old social elites, who felt pushed aside by the new corporate men of power.

Conservatives and radicals alike shared a conviction that the country could not afford to ignore its social problems—the power of the corporations; the poverty and powerlessness of wage earners; the role of women and African Americans. Conservatives were as determined to restore 19th-century moral standards as radicals were determined to achieve working-class emancipation and women's equality. But in politics, neither would become the dominant force. That role would fall to the so-called progressives, a diverse group of reformers who confidently and optimistically believed they could bring order and justice to the new society.

Conclusion

Between 1900 and 1920, corporate power, innovation, and demands had stimulated the growth of cities, attracted millions of immigrants, enhanced commercial opportunities, and created the conditions for a vibrant urban culture. Many Americans thrived in this new environment, taking advantage of business opportunities or, as in the case of women, discovering liberties in dress, employment, dating, and sex that they had not known. Millions of Americans, however, remained impoverished, unable to rise in the social order or to earn enough in wages to support their families. African Americans who had migrated to the North in search of economic opportunity suffered more than any other single group, as they found themselves shut out of most industrial and commercial employment.

Henry Ford, whose generous $5-per-day wage drew tens of thousands to his Detroit factories, was an exceptional employer. Although other employers had learned to restrain their crass displays of wealth and had turned toward philanthropy in search of a better public image, they remained reluctant to follow Ford's lead in improving the conditions in which their employees labored.

Working-class Americans proved resourceful in creating self-help institutions to serve their own and each other's needs. In some cities, they gained a measure of power through the establishment of **political machines.** Labor unions arose and fought for a variety of reforms, but their success was limited. How to inject greater equality and opportunity into an industrial society in which the gap between rich and poor had reached alarming proportions remained a daunting challenge.

SUGGESTED READINGS

For a general overview of the period, see **Alan Dawley,** *Struggles for Justice: Social Responsibility and the Liberal State* (1991) and **Nell Irvin Painter,** *Standing at Armageddon: The United States, 1877–1919* (1987). On economic growth and corporate development, see **Harold G. Vatter,**

The Drive to Industrial Maturity: The United States Economy, 1860–1914 (1975); **Glenn Porter,** *The Rise of Big Business, 1860–1910* (1973); and **Robert Kanigel,** *The One Best Way: Frederick Winslow Taylor and the Enigma of Efficiency* (1997). For a discussion of Ford's labor policies and their impact on immigrant workers, see **Stephen Meyer III,** *The Five Dollar Day: Labor Management and Social Control in the Ford Motor Company, 1908–1921* (1981).

On the changing character of American elites, see **Steve Fraser and Gary Gerstle, eds.,** *Ruling America: Wealth and Power in a Democracy* (2005). For an excellent overview concerning immigration, consult **Roger Daniels,** *Coming to America: A History of Immigration and Ethnicity in American Life* (2002). The best single-volume history of eastern and southern European immigrants during this period is **John Bodnar,** *The Transplanted: A History of Immigration* (1985). For an innovative account of European immigrants' encounters with racial patterns in the United States, see **Matthew Frye Jacobson,** *Whiteness of a Different Color: European Americans and the Alchemy of Race* (1998).

The experience of Chinese immigrants during the period of American exclusion is discussed in **Erika Lee,** *At America's Gates: Chinese Immigration During the Exclusion Era, 1882–1943* (2003), while **Steven P. Erie,** *Rainbow's End: Irish Americans and the Dilemmas of Urban Machine Politics, 1840–1945* (1988), insightfully examines the benefits and costs of big-city machines. **David Montgomery,** *The Fall of the House of Labor, 1865–1925* (1987) and **Herbert Gutman,** *Work, Culture, and Society in Industrializing America* (1976) are essential sources on both immigrant and nonimmigrant labor during this period.

John Hope Franklin and Alfred A. Moss Jr., *From Slavery to Freedom: A History of Negro Americans,* 8th ed. (2000) offers a comprehensive account of African American life, while an important account of black female workers can be found in **Jacqueline Jones,** *Labor of Love, Labor of Sorrow: Black Women, Work and the Family from Slavery to the Present* (1985). On the rise of mass culture, see **David Nasaw,** *Going Out: The Rise and Fall of Public Amusements* (1993) and **Warren I. Susman,** *Culture as History: The Transformation of American Society in the Twentieth Century* (1984). On the new woman and feminism, consult **Nancy F. Cott,** *The Grounding of Modern Feminism* (1987) and **Christine Stansell,** *American Moderns: Bohemian New York and the Creation of a New Century* (2000).

Visit the Liberty Equality Power Companion Web site for resources specific to this textbook: http://www.thomsonedu.com/history/murrin

Also find self-tests and additional resources at ThomsonNOW. ThomsonNOW is an integrated online suite of services and resources with proven ease of use and efficient paths to success, delivering the results you want—NOW!

www.thomsonedu.com/login/

21

Progressivism

Progressivism was a reform movement that took its name from individuals who left the Republican Party in 1912 to join Theodore Roosevelt's new party, the Progressive Party. The term *progressive,* however, refers to a much larger and more varied group of reformers than those who gathered around Roosevelt in 1912.

As early as 1900, these reformers had set out to cleanse and reinvigorate an America whose politics and society they considered in decline. Progressives wanted to rid politics of corruption, tame the power of the "trusts," and, in the process, inject more liberty into American life. They fought against prostitution, gambling, drinking, and other forms of vice. They first appeared in municipal politics, organizing movements to oust crooked mayors and to break up local gas or streetcar monopolies. They carried their fights to the states and finally to the nation. Two presidents, Theodore Roosevelt and Woodrow Wilson, placed themselves at the head of this movement.

Progressivism was popular among a variety of groups who brought to the movement distinct, and often conflicting, aims. On one issue, however, most progressives agreed: the need for an activist government to right political, economic, and social wrongs. Some progressives wanted government to become active only long enough to clean up the political process, root out vice, upgrade the electorate, and break up trusts. These problems were so difficult to solve that many other progressives endorsed the notion of a permanently active government—with the power to tax income, regulate industry, protect consumers from fraud, empower workers, safeguard the environment, and provide social welfare. Many progressives, in other words, came to see the federal government as the institution best equipped to solve social problems.

Such positive attitudes toward government power marked an important change in American politics. Americans had long been suspicious of centralized government, viewing it as the enemy of liberty. The Populists had broken with that view (see chapter 19), but they had been defeated. The progressives had to build a new case for strong government as the protector of liberty and equality.

Progressivism and the Protestant Spirit

Focus Question
Which groups of Americans spearheaded the progressive movement?

CHRONOLOGY

1889	Hull House established
1890–1904	All ex-Confederate states pass laws designed to disenfranchise black voters • Virtually all states adopt the Australian (secret) ballot
1900	La Follette elected governor of Wisconsin • City commission plan introduced in Galveston, Texas
1901–14	More than 1,000 African Americans lynched
1901	Johnson elected reform mayor of Cleveland • McKinley assassinated; Roosevelt becomes president
1902	Direct primary introduced in Mississippi • Initiative and referendum introduced in Oregon • Roosevelt sides with workers in coal strike
1903	*McClure's Magazine* publishes Standard Oil exposé • Federal court dissolves Northern Security Company
1904	Roosevelt defeats Alton B. Parker for presidency
1905	National Forest Service established
1906	La Follette elected to U.S. Senate • Congress passes Hepburn Act • Upton Sinclair publishes *The Jungle* • Congress passes Pure Food and Drug Act and Meat Inspection Act
1907	Reformer Hughes elected New York governor • Financial panic shakes economy
1908	Taft defeats Bryan for presidency
1909	Congress passes Payne-Aldrich tariff bill
1910	Ballinger-Pinchot controversy • NAACP founded • Wilson elected governor of New Jersey
1911	National Urban League founded • City manager plan introduced in Sumter, South Carolina • Wisconsin Industrial Commission established
1912	Roosevelt forms Progressive Party • Wilson defeats Roosevelt, Taft, and Debs for presidency
1913	16th and 17th Amendments ratified • Congress passes Underwood-Simmons Tariff • Congress establishes Federal Reserve
1914	Congress establishes Federal Trade Commission • Congress passes Clayton Antitrust Act
1916	Louis Brandeis appointed to Supreme Court • Kern-McGillicuddy Act, Keating-Owen Act, and Adamson Act passed • National Park Service formed • National Women's Party founded
1919	18th Amendment ratified
1920	19th Amendment ratified

Progressivism emerged first and most strongly among young, mainly Protestant, middle-class Americans who felt alienated from their society. Many had been raised in devout Protestant homes in which religious conviction had often been a spur to social action. They were expected to become ministers or missionaries or to serve their church in some other way. They had abandoned this path, but they never lost their zeal for righting moral wrongs and for uplifting the human spirit. They were distressed by the immorality and corruption in American politics and by the gap that separated rich from poor. They became, in the words of one historian, "ministers of reform."

Other Protestant reformers retained their faith. This was true of William Jennings Bryan, the former Populist leader who became an ardent progressive and evangelical. Throughout his political career, Bryan always insisted that Christian piety and American democracy were integrally related. Billy Sunday, a former major league baseball player who became the most theatrical evangelical preacher of his day, elevated opposition to saloons and the "liquor trust" into a righteous crusade. And Walter Rauschenbusch led a movement known as the Social Gospel, which emphasized the duty of Christians to work for the social good.

Protestants formed a large and diverse population, sizable sections of which showed little interest in reform. Thus it is important to identify smaller and more cohesive groups of reformers. Of the many that arose, three were of particular importance, especially in the early years: investigative journalists, who were called **"muckrakers"**; the founders and supporters of settlement houses; and socialists.

Muckrakers, Magazines, and the Turn toward "Realism"

The term *muckraker* was coined by Theodore Roosevelt, who had intended it as a criticism of newspaper and magazine reporters who, for no purpose other than monetary reward, wrote stories about scandalous situations. But the label became a badge of honor among journalists who were committed to exposing repugnant aspects of American life. During the first decade of the 20th century, they presented the public with one startling revelation after another. Ida Tarbell revealed the shady practices by which John D. Rockefeller had transformed his Standard Oil Company into a monopoly. Lincoln Steffens unraveled the webs of bribery and corruption that were strangling local governments in the nation's cities. George Kibbe Turner documented the extent of prostitution and family disintegration in the ethnic ghettos of those cities. These muckrakers wanted to shock the public into recognizing the shameful state of political, economic, and social affairs and to prompt "the people" to take action.

The tradition of investigative journalism reached back at least to the 1870s, when newspaper and magazine writers exposed the corrupt practices of New York City's Boss Tweed and his Tammany Hall machine. The 20th-century rise of the muckrakers reflected two factors, one economic—expanded newspaper and magazine circulation—and the other intellectual—increased interest in **"realism."** Together they transformed investigative reporting into something of national importance.

From 1870 to 1909, daily newspapers rose in number from 574 to 2,600, and their circulation increased from less than 3 million to more than 24 million. During the first decade of the 20th century, the magazine revolution of the 1880s and 1890s (see chapter 19) accelerated. Cheap, 10-cent periodicals such as *McClure's Magazine* and *Ladies' Home Journal,* with circulations of 400,000 to 1 million, began to displace genteel and relatively

M^cCLURE'S MAGAZINE

Christmas 1903

NINE SHORT STORIES
Pictures in Color

The Story of
Rockefeller

OPENING OF
THE SECOND PART OF
THE HISTORY
OF STANDARD OIL
By
Ida M. Tarbell

John La Farge on the Hundred
Greatest Pictures, and
Other Features

S. S. McCLURE CO., NEW YORK AND LONDON

Culver Pictures

Pioneering Investigative Journalism   This Christmas 1903 issue of
McClure's Magazine featured the second part of Ida Tarbell's exposé of John
D. Rockefeller's business practices. Tarbell's revelations were regarded as
sensational, and they convinced many middle-class Americans of the need
for economic and political reform.

expensive 35-cent publications such as *Harper's* and *The Atlantic Monthly*. The expanded
readership brought journalists considerably more money and prestige and attracted many
talented and ambitious men and women to the profession. Wider circulation also made
magazine publishers more receptive to stories—particularly sensational ones about ill-gotten
economic power, government corruption, and urban vice—that might appeal to their
expanded readership.

The American middle class's growing intellectual interest in "realism" also favored the
muckrakers. "Realism" was a way of thinking that prized detachment, objectivity, and
skepticism. Those who embraced it pointed out that constitutional theory, with its
emphasis on citizenship, elections, and democratic procedures, had little to do with the

way government in the United States actually worked. What could one learn about bosses, machines, and graft from studying the Constitution? There was also a sense that the nation's glorification of the "self-made man" and of "individualism" was preventing Americans from coping effectively with large-scale organizations—corporations, banks, labor unions—and their sudden centrality to the nation's economy and to society. The realists, finally, criticized the tendency, which was prevalent among American writers and artists, to emulate European styles, and they called on them to pioneer new styles that would be better able to capture American life and thought.

By the first decade of the 20th century, intellectuals and artists of all sorts—philosophers John Dewey and William James; social scientists Thorstein Veblen and Charles Beard; novelists Frank Norris, Theodore Dreiser, and Upton Sinclair; painters John Sloan, George Bellows, and other members of the "Ashcan School"; photographers Jacob Riis and Lewis Hine; architects Louis Sullivan and Frank Lloyd Wright; jurists Oliver Wendell Holmes and Louis Brandeis—were attempting to create truer, more realistic ways of representing and analyzing American society. Many of them were inspired by the work of investigative journalists, and some had been newspapermen. Years of firsthand observation enabled them to describe American society as it "truly was." They brought shadowy figures vividly to life. They pictured for Americans the captain of industry who ruthlessly destroyed his competitors; the con artist who tricked young people new to city life; the innocent immigrant girl who fell prey to the white slave traders; the corrupt policeman under whose protection urban vice flourished.

A large middle class, uneasy about the state of American society, applauded the muckrakers for telling these stories and became interested in reform. Members of this class pressured city and state governments to send crooked government officials to jail and to stamp out the sources of corruption and vice. Between 1902 and 1916, more than 100 cities launched investigations of the prostitution trade. At the federal level, all three branches of government felt compelled to address the question of "the trusts"—the concentration of power in the hands of a few industrialists and financiers. Progressivism began to crystallize into a political movement centered on the abuses the muckrakers had exposed.

Settlement Houses and Women's Activism

Established by middle-class reformers, settlement houses were intended to help the largely immigrant urban poor cope with the harsh conditions of city life. Much of the inspiration for settlement houses came from young, college-educated, Protestant women who were from comfortable but not particularly wealthy backgrounds. Some had imbibed a commitment to social justice from parents and grandparents who had fought to abolish slavery. Highly educated, talented, and sensitive to social injustice, they rebelled against being relegated solely to the roles of wife and mother and sought to assert their independence in socially useful ways.

Women Enrolled in Institutions of Higher Education, 1870–1930

Year	Women's Colleges (thousands of students)	Coed Institutions (thousands of students)	Total (thousands of students)	Percentage of All Students Enrolled
1870	6.5	4.6	11.1	21.0%
1880	15.7	23.9	39.6	33.4
1890	16.8	39.5	56.3	35.9
1900	24.4	61.0	85.4	36.8
1910	34.1	106.5	140.6	39.6
1920	52.9	230.0	282.9	47.3
1930	82.1	398.7	480.8	43.7

Source: From Mabel Newcomer, *A Century of Higher Education for American Women* (New York: Harper and Row, 1959), p. 46.

Hull House

Jane Addams and Ellen Gates Starr established the nation's first settlement house, in Chicago, in 1889. The two women had been inspired by a visit the year before to London's Toynbee Hall, where a small group of middle-class men had been living and working with that city's poor since 1884. Addams and Starr bought a decaying mansion that had once been the country home of a prominent Chicagoan, Charles J. Hull. By 1889, **"Hull House"** stood amidst factories, churches, saloons, and tenements inhabited by poor, largely foreign-born working-class families.

Addams quickly emerged as the guiding spirit of Hull House. She moved into the building and demanded that all who worked there do the same. She and Starr enlisted extraordinary women such as Florence Kelley, Alice Hamilton, and Julia Lathrop. They set up a nursery for the children of working mothers, a penny savings bank, and an employment bureau, soon followed by a baby clinic, a neighborhood playground, and social clubs. Determined to minister to cultural as well as economic needs, Hull House sponsored an orchestra, reading groups, and a lecture series. Members of Chicago's widening circle of reform-minded intellectuals, artists, and politicians contributed their energies to the enterprise. John Dewey taught philosophy and Frank Lloyd Wright lectured on architecture. Clarence Darrow, the workingman's lawyer, and Henry Demarest Lloyd, Chicago's radical muckraker, spent considerable time at Hull House. In 1893, Illinois Governor John P. Altgeld named Hull House worker Florence Kelley as the state's chief factory inspector. Her investigations led to Illinois's first factory law, which prohibited child labor, limited the employment of women to eight hours a day, and authorized the state to hire inspectors to enforce the law.

The Hull House activists seemed to have unlimited energy, imagination, and commitment. Julia Lathrop used her appointment to the State Board of Charities to agitate for

Brown Brothers

Jane Addams The founder of the settlement house movement, Addams was the most famous woman reformer of the progressive era. This photograph dates from the 1890s or 1900s, Hull House's formative period.

improvements in the care of the poor, the handicapped, and the delinquent. With Edith Abbott and Sophonisba Breckinridge, she established the Department of Social Research at the University of Chicago (which would evolve into the nation's first school of social work). Alice Hamilton, who had overcome gender discrimination to become a doctor, pioneered in the field of public health.

The Hull House leaders did not command the instant fame accorded the muckrakers. Nevertheless, they were steadily drawn into the public arena. Thousands of women across the country were inspired to build their own settlement houses on the Hull House model (eventually more than 400 settlement houses would open nationwide). By 1910, Jane Addams had become one of the nation's most famous women. She and other settlement house workers played a critical role in fashioning the progressive agenda and in drafting pieces of progressive legislation.

The Cultural Conservatism of Progressive Reformers

In general, settlement house workers were more sympathetic toward the poor, the illiterate, and the downtrodden than the muckrakers were. Although she disapproved of machine politics, Jane Addams saw firsthand the benefits that machine politicians delivered to their constituents. She respected the cultural inheritance of the immigrants and admired their resourcefulness. Although she wanted them to become Americans, she encouraged them to integrate their "immigrant gifts" into their new identities. Those attitudes were more liberal than those of other reformers, who considered many immigrants to be culturally, even racially, inferior.

But there were limits even to Addams's sympathy for the immigrants. In particular, she disapproved of the new working-class entertainments that gave adolescents extensive and unregulated opportunities for intimate association. She was also troubled by the emerging sexual revolution (see chapter 20). Addams tended to equate female sexuality with prostitution, and she joined many other women reformers in a campaign to suppress both. Addams and others had identified a serious problem in American cities, where significant numbers of immigrant and rural women new to urban life were lured into prostitution or chose it as a job preferable to 65 poorly paid hours per week in a sweatshop.

The reformers' zeal on this matter, however, exaggerated the dimensions of the problem and led to some questionable legislation, such as the Mann Act (1910), which made it illegal to transport a woman across state lines "for immoral purposes." If this law permitted the prosecution of true traffickers in women, it also allowed the government to interfere in the private sexual relations of consenting adults. This is what happened in the case of Jack Johnson, the African American heavyweight boxing champion, who was arrested and convicted for "transporting" his white secretary, Lucy Cameron, across state lines. That Johnson's and Cameron's relationship was consensual and would culminate in marriage did not deter the authorities, who wanted to punish Johnson for his dominance of white boxers and his relationship with a white woman.

The cultural conservatism evident in the attitudes of Jane Addams and others on female sexuality also emerged in their attitudes toward alcohol. Drinking rivaled prostitution as a problem in poor, working-class areas. Many men wasted their hard-earned money on drinks at the local saloon, a drain on meager family resources that created tension between these men and their wives. Domestic fights and family violence sometimes ensued. Settlement house workers were well aware of the ill effects of alcoholism (250 saloons did business in Chicago's 19th Ward alone) and sought to combat it. They called on working people to

© CORBIS

Jack Johnson, Heavyweight Boxing Champion   Johnson angered whites in America both for defeating white boxers in the ring and for dating and marrying white women. The identity of Johnson's female companion in this photograph is not known.

refrain from drink and pushed legislation that would shut down the saloons. The progressives joined forces with the Women's Christian Temperance Union (245,000 members strong by 1911) and the Anti-Saloon League. By 1916, through their collective efforts, these groups had won prohibition of the sale and manufacture of alcoholic beverages in 16 states. In 1919, their crowning achievement was the 18th Amendment to the U.S. Constitution, making prohibition the law of the land (see chapter 23).

In depicting alcohol and saloons as unmitigated evils, however, the prohibition movement ignored the role saloons played in ethnic, working-class communities. On Chicago's South Side, for example, saloons provided thousands of workers with the only decent place to eat lunch. The meatpacking plants where they labored had no cafeterias, and few workers could stomach eating their lunch where animals were slaughtered, dressed, and packed. Some saloons catered to particular ethnic groups: They served traditional foods and drinks, provided meeting space for fraternal organizations, and offered camaraderie to men longing to speak in their native tongue. Saloonkeepers sometimes functioned as informal bankers, cashing checks and making small loans. Not surprisingly, many immigrants shunned the prohibition movement. They had no interest in being "uplifted" and "reformed" in this way. Here was a gulf separating the immigrant masses from the Protestant middle class that even compassionate reformers such as Jane Addams could not bridge.

A Nation of Clubwomen

Settlement house workers comprised only one part of a vast network of female reformers. Hundreds of thousands of women belonged to local women's clubs. Conceived in the 1860s and 1870s as self-help organizations in which women would be encouraged to sharpen their minds, refine their domestic skills, and strengthen their moral faculties (see chapter 19), these clubs, by 1900, began taking on tasks of social reform. Clubwomen typically focused their energies on improving schools, building libraries and playgrounds, expanding educational and vocational opportunities for girls, and securing fire and sanitation codes for tenement houses. In so doing, they made traditional female concerns— the nurturing and education of children, the care of the home—questions of public policy.

Clubwomen rose to prominence in black communities, too, and addressed similar sorts of issues; on matters of sexuality and alcohol, they often shared the conservative sentiments of their white counterparts. Some groups of black clubwomen ventured into community affairs more boldly than their white counterparts, however, especially in southern states, where black men were being stripped of the right to vote, to serve on juries, and to hold political office. Whites were prepared to punish any African American, male or female, who showed too much initiative or was thought to be challenging the principles of white supremacy. Even so, many black female activists persevered in the face of such threats, determined to provide leadership in their communities and voice their people's concerns.

Socialism and Progressivism

Issues such as women's sexuality and men's alcoholism drew progressives in a conservative direction, but other issues drew them to socialism. In the early 20th century, socialism stood for the transfer of control over big businesses from the capitalists who owned them to the laboring masses who worked in them. Socialists believed that such a transfer, usually defined in terms of government ownership and operation of corporations, would make it impossible for wealthy elites to control society.

The Socialist Party of America, founded in 1901, became a political force during the first 16 years of the century, and socialist ideas influenced progressivism. In 1912, at the peak of its influence, the Socialist Party enrolled more than 115,000 members. Its presidential candidate, the charismatic **Eugene Victor Debs** of Terre Haute, Indiana, attracted almost a million votes—6 percent of the total votes cast that year. In that same year, 1,200 Socialists held elective office in 340 different municipalities. Of these, 79 were mayors of cities as geographically and demographically diverse as Schenectady, New York; Milwaukee, Wisconsin; Butte, Montana; and Berkeley, California. More than 300 newspapers and periodicals, with a combined circulation exceeding 2 million, spread the socialist gospel. The most important socialist publication was *Appeal to Reason,* published by Julius Wayland from Kansas and sent out each week to 750,000 subscribers. In 1905, Wayland published, in serial form, a novel by an obscure muckraker named Upton Sinclair, which depicted the scandalous working conditions in Chicago's meatpacking industry. When it was later published in book form in 1906, *The Jungle* created such an outcry that the federal government was forced to regulate the meat industry.

The Many Faces of Socialism

Socialists came in many varieties. In Milwaukee, they consisted of predominantly German working-class immigrants and their descendants; in New York City, their numbers were strongest among Jewish immigrants from Eastern Europe. In the Southwest, tens of thousands of disgruntled native-born farmers who had been Populists in the 1890s now flocked to the socialist banner. In Oklahoma alone, these erstwhile Populists were numerous enough by 1912 to support 11 socialist weeklies. In that same year, Oklahoma voters gave a higher percentage of their votes, more than 16 percent, to the Socialist candidate Debs than did the voters of any other state. In the West, socialism was popular among miners, timber cutters, and others who labored in isolated areas where industrialists possessed extraordinary power over work, politics, and community life. These radicals gravitated to the militant labor union, the Industrial Workers of the World (IWW) (see chapter 20), which found a home in the Socialist Party from 1905 to 1913.

Socialists differed from each other not only in their occupations and ethnic origins but also in their politics. The IWW was the most radical socialist group, with its incessant calls for revolution. By contrast, mainstream socialism, as articulated by Debs, was more respectful of American political, cultural, and religious traditions. Mainstream socialists saw themselves as the saviors rather than the destroyers of the American republic—as the true heirs of Thomas Jefferson. Their confidence that the nation could be redeemed through conventional politics—through the election of Debs as president—is evidence of their affection for American democracy. And their faith in redemption reveals the degree to which Protestant religious beliefs underlay their quest for social justice and what they called a "cooperative commonwealth." Evolutionary socialists, led by Victor Berger of Milwaukee, abandoned talk of revolution altogether and chose instead an aggressive brand of reform politics. They were dubbed **"gas and water socialists"** because of their interest in improving city services.

These differences would, after 1912, fragment the socialist movement. For a decade or so, however, these divergent groups managed to coexist in a single political party, thanks, largely, to the leadership of Debs. When he was released from a Chicago jail in 1895 after serving time for his role in the strike against the Pullman Company (see chapter 19), Debs declared to a gathering of 100,000 admirers: "Manifestly the spirit of '76 still survives. The fires of liberty and noble aspirations are not yet extinguished. . . . The vindication and glorification of American principles of government, as proclaimed to the world in the Declaration of Independence, is the high purpose of this convocation."

Socialists and Progressives

Debs's speeches both attracted and disturbed progressives. On the one hand, he spoke compellingly about the dangers of unregulated capitalism and excessively concentrated wealth, both progressive concerns. His confidence that a strong state could bring the economic system under control mirrored the progressives' own faith in the positive uses of government. Progressives often worked hand-in-hand with socialists to win economic and political reforms, especially at the municipal and state levels, and many intellectuals and reformers easily moved back and forth between socialism and progressivism. Florence Kelley, Hull House reformer and Illinois factory inspector, was one such person; Clarence Darrow, a Chicago trial lawyer who successfully defended the IWW's William Haywood in 1907 against charges that he had murdered a former Idaho governor, was another. Walter Lippmann, who would become a close adviser to President Wilson during the First World War, began his political career in 1912 as an assistant to the Socialist mayor of Schenectady. Several of the era's most prominent intellectuals, including John Dewey, Richard Ely, and Thorstein Veblen, also traveled back and forth between the socialist and progressive camps. So did Helen Keller, the country's leading spokesperson for the disabled.

On the other hand, Debs's talk of revolution scared progressives, as did his efforts to organize a working-class political movement independent of middle-class involvement or control. Although progressives wanted to tame capitalism, they stopped short of wanting to eliminate it. They wanted to improve working and living conditions for the masses but not cede political control to them. The progressives hoped to offer a political program with enough socialist elements to counter the appeal of Debs's more radical movement. In this, they were successful.

Municipal Reform

Progressive-era reform battles first erupted over control of municipal transportation networks and utilities. Private corporations typically owned and operated street railways and electrical and gas systems. Many of the corporations used their monopoly power to charge exorbitant fares and rates, and they often won that power by bribing city officials who belonged to one of the political machines. Corporations achieved generous reductions in real estate taxes in the same way.

The attack on private utilities and their protectors in city government gained momentum in the mid-1890s. In Detroit, reform-minded Mayor Hazen S. Pingree led successful fights to control the city's gas, telephone, and trolley companies. In Chicago in 1896 and 1897, a group of middle-class reformers ousted a corrupt city council and elected a mayor, Carter Harrison, Jr., who promised to protect Chicago's streetcar riders from exploitation. In Cleveland, the crusading reformer Tom Johnson won election as mayor in 1901, curbed the power of the streetcar interests, and brought honest and efficient government to the city.

Occasionally, a reform politician of Johnson's caliber would rise to power through one of the regular political parties. But this path to power was a difficult one, especially in cities where the political parties were controlled by machines. Consequently, progressives worked for reforms that would strip the parties of their power. Two of their favorite reforms were the city commission and the city manager forms of government.

The City Commission Plan

First introduced in Galveston, Texas, in 1900, in the wake of a devastating tidal wave, the city commission shifted municipal power from the mayor and his aldermen to five city commissioners, each responsible for a different department of city government. In Galveston and elsewhere, the impetus for this reform came from civic-minded businessmen who were determined to rebuild government on the same principles of efficient and scientific management that had energized the private sector. The results were often impressive. The Galveston commissioners restored the city's credit after a brush with bankruptcy, improved the city's harbor, and built a massive seawall to protect the city from future floods. They accomplished all of this on budgets that had been cut by one-third. In Houston, Texas; Des Moines, Iowa; Dayton, Ohio; Oakland, California; and elsewhere, city commissioners similarly improved urban infrastructures, expanded city services, and strengthened the financial health of the cities. Many commissions established publicly owned utilities. By 1913, more than 300 cities, most of them small to middling in size, had adopted the city commission plan.

The City Manager Plan

The city commission system did not always work to perfection, however. Sometimes the commissioners used their position to reward electoral supporters with jobs and contracts; other times, they pursued power and prestige for their respective departments. The city manager plan was meant to overcome such problems. Under this plan, the commissioners continued to set policy, but policy implementation now rested with a "chief executive." This official, who was not elected but appointed by the commissioners, would curtail rivalries among commissioners and ensure that no outside influences interfered with the impartial, businesslike management of the city. The job of city manager was explicitly modeled after that of a corporation executive. First introduced in Sumter, South Carolina, in 1911 and then in Dayton, Ohio, in 1913, by 1919 the city manager plan had spread to 130 cities.

The Costs of Reform

Although these reforms limited corruption and improved services, they were not universally popular. Poor and minority voters, in particular, found that their influence in local affairs was weakened by the shift to city commissioners and city managers. Previously, candidates for municipal office (other than the mayor) competed in ward elections rather than in citywide elections. Voters in working-class wards commonly elected workingmen to represent them, and voters in immigrant wards made sure that fellow ethnics represented their interests on city councils. Citywide elections diluted the strength of these constituencies. Candidates from poor districts often lacked the money needed to mount a citywide campaign, and they were further hampered by the nonpartisan nature of such elections. Denied the support of a political party or platform, they had to make themselves personally known to voters throughout the city. That was a much easier task for the city's "leading citizens"—manufacturers, merchants, and lawyers—than it was for workingmen. In Dayton, the percentage of citizens voting Socialist rose from 25 percent to 44 percent in the years following the introduction of the commission manager system, but the number of Socialists elected to office declined from five to zero. Progressive political reforms thus frequently reduced the influence of radicals, minorities, and the poor in elections.

Political Reform in the States

Focus Question
How did progressive reformers hope to create a "responsible" and "virtuous" electorate? What were the consequences of their reforms?

As at the local level, political parties at the state level were often dominated by corrupt politicians who did the bidding of powerful private lobbies. In New Jersey in 1903, for example, industrial and financial interests, working through the Republican Party machine, controlled numerous appointments to state government, including the chief justice of the state supreme court, the attorney general, and the commissioner of banking and insurance. Such webs of influence ensured that New Jersey would provide large corporations such as the railroads with favorable political and economic legislation.

Restoring Sovereignty to "the People"

Progressives introduced reforms designed to undermine the power of party bosses, restore sovereignty to "the people," and encourage honest, talented individuals to enter politics. One such reform was the direct primary, a mechanism that enabled voters, rather than party bosses, to choose party candidates. Mississippi introduced this reform in 1902 and Wisconsin in 1903. By 1916, all but three states had adopted the direct primary. Closely related was a movement to strip state legislatures of their power to choose U.S. senators. State after state enacted legislation that permitted voters to choose Senate candidates in primary elections. In 1912, a reluctant U.S. Senate was obliged to approve the 17th Amendment to the Constitution, mandating the direct election of senators. The state legislatures ratified this amendment in 1913.

Populists had first proposed direct election of U.S. senators in the 1890s; they also proposed the **initiative** and the **referendum,** both of which were adopted first by Oregon in 1902 and then by 18 other states between 1902 and 1915. The initiative allowed reformers to put legislative proposals before voters in general elections without having to wait for state legislatures to act. The referendum gave voters the right in general elections to repeal an unpopular act that a state legislature had passed. Less widely adopted but important nevertheless was the **recall**, a device that allowed voters to remove from office any public servant who had betrayed his trust. As a further control over the behavior of elected officials, numerous states enacted laws that regulated corporate campaign contributions and restricted lobbying activities in state legislatures. These laws neither eliminated corporate privilege nor destroyed the power of machine politicians. Nevertheless, they made politics more honest and strengthened the influence of ordinary voters.

Creating a Virtuous Electorate

Progressive reformers focused as well on creating a responsible electorate that understood the importance of the vote and that resisted efforts to manipulate elections. To create this ideal electorate, reformers had to see to it that all of those citizens who were deemed virtuous could cast their votes free of coercion and intimidation. At the same time, reformers sought to disenfranchise citizens who were considered irresponsible and corruptible. In pursuing these goals, progressives substantially altered the composition of the electorate and strengthened government regulation of voting. The results were contradictory. On the one hand, progressives enlarged the electorate by extending the right to vote to women; on the other hand, they either initiated or tolerated laws that barred large numbers of minority and poor voters from the polls.

The Australian Ballot

Government regulation of voting had begun in the 1890s, when virtually every state adopted the **Australian,** or secret, **ballot.** This reform required voters to vote in private rather than in public. It also required the government, rather than political parties, to print the ballots and supervise the voting. Before this time, each political party had printed its own ballot with only its candidates listed. At election time, each party mobilized its loyal supporters. Party workers offered liquor, free meals, and other bribes to entice voters to the polls and to "persuade" them to cast the party ballot. Because the ballots were cast in public, few voters who had accepted gifts of liquor and food dared to cross watchful party officials. Critics argued that the system corrupted the electoral process. They also pointed out that it made "ticketsplitting"—dividing one's vote between candidates of two or more parties—virtually impossible.

The Australian ballot solved these problems. Although it predated progressivism, it embodied the progressives' determination to use government power to encourage citizens to cast their votes responsibly and wisely.

Personal Registration Laws

That same determination was apparent in the progressives' support for the personal registration laws that virtually every state passed between 1890 and 1920. These laws allowed prospective voters to register to vote only if they appeared at a designated government office with proper identification. Frequently, these laws also mandated a certain period of residence in the state before registration and a certain interval between registration and actual voting.

Personal registration laws were meant to disenfranchise citizens who showed no interest in voting until election day, when a party worker arrived with a few dollars and offered a free ride to the polls. However, they also excluded many hardworking, responsible, poor people who wanted to vote but had failed to register, either because their work schedules made it impossible or because they were intimidated by the complex regulations. The laws were particularly frustrating for immigrants with limited knowledge of American government and of the English language.

Disenfranchisement

Progressives also promoted election laws expressly designed to keep noncitizen immigrants from voting. In the 1880s, 18 states had passed laws allowing immigrants to vote without first becoming citizens. Progressives reversed this trend. At the same time, the newly formed Bureau of Immigration and Naturalization (1906) made it more difficult to become a citizen. Applicants for citizenship now had to appear before a judge, who interrogated them, in the English language, on American history and civics. In addition, immigrants were required to provide two witnesses to vouch for their "moral character" and their "attachment to the principles of the Constitution." Finally, immigrants had to swear (and, if necessary, prove) that they were not anarchists or polygamists and that they had resided continuously in the United States for five years.

Most progressives defended the new rigor of the process. U.S. citizenship, they believed, carried responsibilities; it was not to be bestowed lightly. This position was understandable, given the electoral abuses progressives had exposed. Nevertheless, the reforms also denied the vote to a large proportion of the population. In cities and towns where immigrants dominated the workforce, the numbers of registered voters fell steeply. Nowhere was exclusion more startling than in the South, where between 1890 and 1904, every ex-Confederate state passed laws designed to strip blacks of their right to vote. Because laws explicitly barring blacks from voting would have violated the 15th Amendment, this exclusion had to be accomplished indirectly—through literacy tests, property qualifications, and poll taxes mandated by the legislatures of the ex-Confederate states. Any citizen who failed a reading test, or who could not sign his name, or who did not own a minimum amount of property, or who could not pay a poll tax, lost his right to vote. The citizens who failed these tests most frequently were blacks—who formed the poorest and least educated segment of the southern population—but a large portion of the region's poor whites also failed the tests. The effects of **disenfranchisement** were stark. In 1900, only 1,300 blacks voted in Mississippi elections, down from 130,000 in the 1870s. Virginia's voter turnout dropped from 60 percent of adult men (white and black) in 1900 to 28 percent in 1904.

Many progressives in the North, such as Governor Robert La Follette of Wisconsin, criticized southern disenfranchisement. Some, including Jane Addams and John Dewey, joined in 1910 with W. E. B. Du Bois and other black reformers to found the National Association for the Advancement of Colored People (NAACP), an interracial political organization that made black equality its primary goal. In the South, however, white progressives rarely challenged disenfranchisement, and most had little difficulty

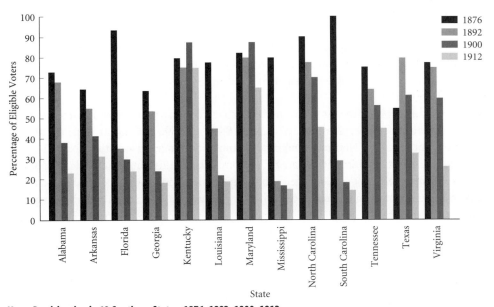

Voter Participation in 13 Southern States, 1876, 1892, 1900, 1912

Source: Data from *Historical Statistics of the United States, Colonial Times to 1970* (White Plains, N.Y.: Kraus International, 1989).

justifying it with progressive ideology. Because progressives everywhere considered the right to vote a precious gift granted only to those who could handle its responsibilities, they equally believed that it must be withheld from people who were deemed racially or culturally unfit. Progressives in the North excluded many immigrants on just those grounds. Progressives in the South saw the disenfranchisement of African Americans in the same light.

Disillusionment with the Electorate

In the process of identifying those groups "unfit" to hold the franchise, some progressives soured on the electoral process altogether. The more they looked for rational and virtuous voters, the fewer they found. In *Drift and Mastery* (1914), Walter Lippmann argued that ordinary people had been overwhelmed by industrial and social changes. Because these changes seemed beyond their comprehension or control, they "drifted," unable to "master" the circumstances of modern life or take charge of their own destiny. Lippmann did not suggest that such ordinary people should be barred from voting, but he did argue that more political responsibility should rest with appointed officials who possessed the training and knowledge necessary to make government effective and just. The growing disillusionment with the electorate, in combination with intensifying restrictions on the franchise, created an environment in which fewer and fewer Americans actually went to the polls. Voting participation rates fell from 79 percent in 1896 to only 49 percent in 1920.

Woman Suffrage

The major exception to this trend was the enfranchisement of women. This momentous reform was adopted by several states during the 1890s and the first two decades of the 20th century and became federal law with the ratification of the 19th Amendment to the Constitution in 1920.

Launched in 1848 at the famous Seneca Falls convention (see chapter 12), the women's rights movement floundered in the 1870s and 1880s. In 1890, suffragists came together in a new organization, the **National American Woman Suffrage Association** (NAWSA), led by Elizabeth Cady Stanton and Susan B. Anthony. Thousands of young, college-educated women campaigned door-to-door, held impromptu rallies, and pressured state legislators.

Wyoming, which attained statehood in 1890, became the first state to grant women the right to vote, followed in 1893 by Colorado and in 1896 by Idaho and Utah. The main reason for success in these sparsely populated western states was not egalitarianism but rather the conviction that women's supposedly gentler and more nurturing nature would tame and civilize the men who had populated the frontier.

This notion reflected a subtle but important change in the suffrage movement. Earlier generations had insisted that women were fundamentally equal to men, but the new suffragists argued that women were different from men. Women, they stressed, possessed a moral sense and a nurturing quality that men lacked. Consequently, they understood the civic obligations implied by the franchise and could be trusted to vote virtuously. Their votes would hasten to completion the progressive task of cleansing the political process of corruption. Their experience as mothers and household managers, moreover, would enable them to guide local and state governments in efforts to improve education, sanitation, family wholesomeness, and the condition of women and children in the workforce. In other words, the enfranchisement of women would enhance the quality of both public and private life without insisting they were the equals of men in all respects.

Suffragists were slow to ally themselves with blacks, Asians, and other disenfranchised groups. In fact, many suffragists, especially those in the South and West, opposed the franchise for Americans of color. They, like their male counterparts, believed that members of these groups lacked moral strength and thus did not deserve the right to vote. Unlike the suffrage pioneers of the 1840s and 1850s, many progressive-era suffragists were little troubled by racial discrimination and injustice. (**See Map 21.1, Woman Suffrage Before 1920, in the color insert following page 816.**)

Washington, California, Kansas, Oregon, and Arizona followed the lead of the other western states by enfranchising women in the years from 1910 to 1912. After a series of setbacks in eastern and midwestern states, the movement regained momentum under the leadership of the strategically astute Carrie Chapman Catt, who became president of NAWSA in 1915 and successfully coordinated myriad grassroots campaigns. Equally important was Alice Paul, a radical who founded the Congressional Union in 1913 and later renamed it the National Woman's Party. Paul and her supporters focused their attention on the White House, picketing President Wilson's home 24 hours a day, brandishing large posters that chastised him for abandoning his democratic principles, and daring the police to arrest them. Several suffrage demonstrators were jailed, where they continued their protests by going on hunger strikes (refusing to eat). Aided by a heightened enthusiasm for democracy generated by America's participation in the First World War (see chapter 23), which generated a more positive popular response to Paul's tactics than might otherwise have been the case, the suffragists achieved their goal of universal woman suffrage in 1920.

Predictions that suffrage for women would radically alter politics turned out to be false. The political system was neither cleansed of corruption, nor did the government rush headlong to address the private needs of women and their families. Although the numbers of voters increased after 1920, voter participation rates continued to decline. Still, the extension of the vote to women, 144 years after the founding of the nation, was a major political achievement.

Economic and Social Reform in the States

In some states, progressive reform extended well beyond political parties and the electorate. Progressives also wanted to limit corporate power, strengthen organized labor, and offer social welfare protection to the weak. State governments were pressured into passing such legislation by progressive alliances of middle-class and working-class reformers and by dynamic state governors.

Robert La Follette and Wisconsin Progressivism

Nowhere did the progressives' campaign for social reform flourish as it did in Wisconsin. The movement arose first in the 1890s, in hundreds of Wisconsin cities and towns, as citizens began to mobilize against the state's corrupt Republican Party and the special privileges the party had granted to private utilities and railroads. These reform-minded citizens came from varied backgrounds. They were middle class and working class, urban and rural, male and female, intellectual and evangelical, Scandinavian Protestant and German Catholic. Wisconsin progressivism had already gained considerable momentum by 1897, when Robert La Follette assumed its leadership.

La Follette was born into a prosperous farming family in 1855. He entered politics as a Republican in the 1880s and embraced reform in the late 1890s. Elected governor in 1900, he secured for Wisconsin both a direct primary and a tax law that stripped the railroad corporations of tax exemptions they had long enjoyed. In 1905, he pushed through a civil service law mandating that every state employee meet a certain level of competence.

Wisconsin Historical Society

Robert La Follette, Wisconsin Progressive   This photograph of La Follette campaigning in Wisconsin in 1897 captures the intensity and combativeness that "Fighting Bob" brought to progressivism.

A tireless campaigner and a spellbinding speaker, "Fighting Bob" won election to the U.S. Senate in 1906. Meanwhile, Wisconsin's advancing labor and socialist movements impelled progressive reformers to focus their legislative efforts on issues of corporate greed and social welfare. By 1910, reformers had passed state laws that regulated railroad and utility rates, instituted the nation's first state income tax, and provided workers with compensation for injuries, limitations on work hours, restrictions on child labor, and minimum wages for women.

Many of these laws were written by social scientists at the University of Wisconsin, with whom reformers had close ties. In the first decade of the 20th century, John R. Commons, University of Wisconsin economist, drafted Wisconsin's civil service and public utilities laws. In 1911, Commons designed and won legislative approval for the Wisconsin Industrial Commission, which brought together employers, trade unionists, and professionals and gave them broad powers to investigate and regulate relations between industry and labor throughout the state. Never before had a state government so plainly committed itself to the cause of industrial justice. For the first time, the rights of labor would be treated with the same respect as the rights of industry. Equally important was the responsibility the commission delegated to nonelected professionals: social scientists, lawyers, engineers, and others. These professionals, Wisconsin reformers believed, would succeed where political parties had failed—namely, in providing the public with expert and honest government.

The "Wisconsin idea" found quick adoption in Ohio, Indiana, New York, and Colorado; and in 1913, the federal government established its own Industrial Relations Commission and hired Commons to direct its investigative staff. In other areas, too, reformers began urging state and federal governments to shift the policy-making initiative away from political parties and toward administrative agencies staffed by professionals.

Progressive Reform in New York

New York was second only to Wisconsin in the vigor and breadth of its progressive movement. As in Wisconsin, New York progressives focused first on fighting political corruption. Revelations of close ties between leading Republican politicians and life insurance companies vaulted reform lawyer Charles Evans Hughes into the governor's mansion in 1907. Hughes immediately established several public service commissions to regulate railroads and utility companies. Also, as in Wisconsin, the labor movement exercised its influence. New York City garment workers struck and forced state legislators to regulate working conditions. With the establishment of the Factory Investigating Committee, New York, like Wisconsin, became a pioneer in labor and social welfare policy.

New York state legislators also faced pressure from middle-class reformers—settlement house workers such as Lillian Wald of the Henry Street Settlement and lawyers such as Louis Brandeis—who had become convinced of the need for new laws to protect the disadvantaged. This combined pressure from working-class and middle-class constituencies persuaded some state Democrats, including Assemblyman Alfred E. Smith and Senator Robert F. Wagner, to convert from machine to reform politics. Their appearance in the progressive ranks represented the arrival of a new reform sensibility. Wagner and Smith were both ethnic Catholics (Wagner was born in Germany, and Smith was the grandchild of Irish immigrants). They opposed prohibition, city commissions, voter registration laws, and other reforms whose intent seemed anti-immigrant or anti-Catholic. Meanwhile, they supported reforms meant to improve the working and living conditions of New York's urban poor. They agitated for a minimum wage, factory safety, workmen's compensation, the right of workers to join unions, and the regulation of excessively powerful corporations. Their participation in progressivism accelerated the movement's shift, first in New York and then elsewhere, away from a preoccupation with political parties and electorates and toward questions of economic justice and social welfare.

A Renewed Campaign for Civil Rights

Focus Question
How did W. E. B. Du Bois's approach to African American reform differ from that of Booker T. Washington?

At the same time that politicians such as Smith and Wagner introduced an ethnic sensibility into progressivism, a new generation of African American activists began insisting that the issue of racial equality also be placed on the reform agenda.

The Failure of Accommodationism

Booker T. Washington's message—that blacks should accept segregation and disenfranchisement as unavoidable and focus their energies instead on self-help and self-improvement—faced increasing criticism from black activists such as **W. E. B. Du Bois**, Ida B. Wells, Monroe Trotter, and others. Washington's accommodationist leadership (see chapter 18), in their eyes, brought southern blacks no reprieve from racism. More than 100 blacks had been lynched in 1900 alone; between 1901 and 1914, at least 1,000 others would be hanged.

Increasingly, unsubstantiated rumors of black assaults on whites became occasions for white mobs to rampage through black neighborhoods and indiscriminately destroy life and property. In 1908, a mob in Springfield, Illinois, attacked black businesses and individuals; a force of 5,000 state militia was required to restore order. The troops were too late, however, to stop the lynching of two innocent black men, one a successful barber and the other an 84-year-old man who had been married to a white woman for more than 30 years. There was a sad irony in the deaths of these African Americans. Murdered in Abraham Lincoln's hometown and within walking distance of his grave, they died just as black and white Americans everywhere were preparing to celebrate the centennial of the Great Emancipator's birth.

Booker T. Washington had long believed that blacks who educated themselves or who succeeded in business would be accepted as equals by whites. As Du Bois and other black militants observed, however, white rioters made no distinction between rich blacks and

Antiblack Violence   In 1913, a white mob destroyed a large part of the black section of Omaha, Nebraska. Race riots of this scale and devastation in early 20th-century America convinced many blacks that Booker T. Washington's message of accommodation was not working

poor, or between solid citizens and petty criminals. All that had seemed to matter was the color of one's skin. Similarly, many black militants knew from personal experience that individual accomplishment was not enough to overcome racial prejudice. Du Bois was a brilliant scholar who became, in 1899, the first African American to receive a doctorate from Harvard University. Had he been white, Du Bois would have been asked to teach at Harvard or another elite academic institution, but no prestigious white university, in the South or North, made him an offer.

From the Niagara Movement to the NAACP

Seeing no future in accommodation, Du Bois and other young black activists came together at Niagara Falls in 1905 to fashion a new political agenda. They demanded that African Americans regain the right to vote in states that had taken it away, that segregation be abolished, and that the many discriminatory barriers to black advancement be removed. They declared their commitment to freedom of speech, the brotherhood of all men, and respect for the working man. Although their numbers were small, the members of the so-called Niagara movement were inspired by the example of the antebellum abolitionists. Meeting in Boston, Oberlin, and Harpers Ferry—all places of special significance to the abolitionist cause—they hoped to rekindle the militant, uncompromising spirit of that earlier crusade (see chapters 12 and 14).

The 1908 Springfield riot had shaken many whites. Some, especially those already working for social and economic reform, now joined in common cause with the Niagara movement. Together, black and white activists planned a conference for Lincoln's birthday in 1909 to revive, in the words of author William English Walling, "the spirit of the abolitionists" and to "treat the Negro on a plane of absolute political and social equality." Oswald Garrison Villard, the grandson of William Lloyd Garrison, called on "all believers in democracy to join in a National conference for the discussion of present evils, the voicing of protests, and the renewal of the struggle for civil and political liberty." The conference brought together distinguished progressives, white and black, including Mary White Ovington, Jane Addams, John Dewey, William Dean Howells, Ida B. Wells, and Du Bois. They drew up plans to establish an organization dedicated to fighting racial discrimination and prejudice. In May 1910, the **National Association for the Advancement of Colored People** (NAACP) was officially launched, with Moorfield Storey of Boston as president, Walling as chairman of the executive committee, and Du Bois as the director of publicity and research.

The formation of the NAACP marked the beginning of the modern civil-rights movement. The organization launched a magazine, *The Crisis,* edited by Du Bois, to publicize and protest the lynchings, riots, and other abuses directed against black citizens. Equally important was the Legal Redress Committee, which initiated lawsuits against city and state governments for violating the constitutional rights of African Americans. The committee scored its first major success in 1915, when the U.S. Supreme Court ruled that the so-called grandfather clauses of the Oklahoma and Maryland constitutions violated the 15th Amendment. (These clauses allowed poor, uneducated whites—but not poor, uneducated blacks—to vote, even if they failed to pay their state's poll tax or to pass its literacy test, by exempting the descendants of men who had voted before 1867.) NAACP lawyers won again in 1917 when the Supreme Court declared unconstitutional a Louisville, Kentucky, law that required all blacks to reside in predetermined parts of the city.

By 1914, the NAACP had enrolled thousands of members in scores of branches throughout the United States. The organization's success generated other civil-rights groups. The National Urban League, founded in 1911, worked to improve the economic and social conditions of blacks in cities. It pressured employers to hire blacks, distributed lists of available jobs and housing in African American communities, and developed social programs to ease the adjustment of rural black migrants to city life.

Progress toward racial equality was sluggish. Attacking segregation and discrimination through lawsuits was, by its nature, a slow strategy that would take decades to complete. The growing membership of the NAACP, although impressive, was not large enough to qualify it as a mass movement, and its interracial character made the organization seem dangerously radical to millions of whites. White NAACP leaders responded to this hostility by limiting the number and power of African Americans who worked for the organization.

This policy, in turn, outraged black militants who argued that no civil-rights organization should be in the business of appeasing white racists.

Despite its limitations, the NAACP made significant strides. It gave Du Bois the security and visibility he needed to carry on his fight against Booker T. Washington's accommodationist philosophy. Even before his death in 1915, Washington's influence in black and white communities had receded. The NAACP, more than any other organization, helped resurrect the issue of racial equality at a time when many white Americans had accepted as normal the practices of racial segregation and discrimination.

National Reform

Focus Question

What were the key similarities and differences in the progressive politics of Theodore Roosevelt and Woodrow Wilson?

The more progressives focused on economic and social matters, the more they sought to increase their influence in national politics. Certain problems demanded national solutions. No patchwork of state regulations, for example, could adequately curtail the power of the trusts, protect workers, or monitor the quality of consumer goods. Moreover, state and federal courts often were hostile toward progressive goals: They repeatedly struck down as unconstitutional reform laws regulating working hours or setting minimum wages, on the grounds that they impinged on the freedom of contract and trade. A national progressive movement could force passage of laws that were less vulnerable to judicial veto or elect a president who could overhaul the federal judiciary with progressive-minded judges.

National leadership would not emerge from Congress. The Democratic Party had been scarred by the Populist challenge of the 1890s. Divided between the radical Bryanites and the conservative followers of Grover Cleveland, and consequently unable to speak with one voice on questions of social and economic policy, after 1896 the Democrats seemed incapable of winning a national election. The Republican Party was more unified and popular, but it was controlled by a conservative Old Guard. Led by Senator Nelson Aldrich of Rhode Island and House Speaker Joseph G. Cannon of Illinois, the Republican Old Guard was pro-business and devoted to a 19th-century style of backroom patronage. When Robert La Follette arrived in the Senate from Wisconsin in 1907, the Old Guard ostracized him as a dangerous radical.

National progressive leadership came from the executive rather than the legislative branch, and from two presidents in particular, Republican Theodore Roosevelt and Democrat Woodrow Wilson. These two presidents sponsored reforms that profoundly affected the lives of Americans and altered the nature of the American presidency.

The Roosevelt Presidency

When the Republican bosses chose Theodore Roosevelt as William McKinley's running mate in 1900, their purpose was more to remove this headstrong, unpredictable character from New York state politics than to groom him for national leadership. As governor of New York, Roosevelt had been a moderate reformer, but even his modest efforts to rid the state's Republican Party of corruption and to institute civil service reform were too much for the state party machine, led by Thomas C. Platt. Consigning Roosevelt to the vice presidency seemed a safe solution. McKinley was a young, vigorous politician, fully in control of his party and his presidency. Less than a year into his second term, in September 1901, McKinley was shot by an anarchist assassin. The president clung to life for nine days, and then died. Upon succeeding McKinley, Theodore Roosevelt, age 42, became the youngest chief executive in the nation's history.

Born to an aristocratic New York City family, Roosevelt nevertheless developed an uncommon affection for "the people." Asthmatic, sickly, and nearsighted as a boy, he remade himself into a vigorous adult. With an insatiable appetite for high-risk adventure—everything from "dude ranching" in the Dakota Territory, to big-game hunting in Africa, to wartime combat—he was also a voracious reader and an accomplished writer. Aggressive and swaggering in his public rhetoric, he was in private a skilled, patient negotiator. A believer in the superiority of the English-speaking peoples, he nevertheless appointed members of "inferior" races to important posts in his administration. Rarely has a president's personality so enthralled the American public. He is the only 20th-century president immortalized on Mount Rushmore.

Regulating the Trusts

Roosevelt quickly revealed his flair for the dramatic. In 1902, he ordered the Justice Department to prosecute the Northern Securities Company, a $400 million monopoly that controlled all railroad lines and traffic in the Northwest from Chicago to Washington state. Never before had an American president sought to use the Sherman Antitrust Act to break up a business monopoly. The news shocked J. P. Morgan, the banker who had brokered the deal that had created Northern Securities. Morgan rushed to the White House, where he is said to have told Roosevelt, "If we have done anything wrong, send your man to my man and they can fix it up." Roosevelt would have none of this "fixing." In 1903, a federal court ordered Northern Securities dissolved, and the U.S. Supreme Court upheld the decision the next year. Roosevelt was hailed as the nation's "trust-buster."

Roosevelt, however, did not believe in breaking up all, or even most, large corporations. Industrial concentration, he believed, brought the United States wealth, productivity, and a rising standard of living. Rather than bust them up, Roosevelt argued, government should regulate the industrial giants and punish those that used their power improperly. This new role would require the federal government to expand its powers. A newly fortified government—the centerpiece of a political program that Roosevelt would later call the **New Nationalism**—was to be led by a forceful president, who was willing to use all of the powers at his disposal to achieve prosperity and justice.

Toward a "Square Deal"

Roosevelt displayed his willingness to use government power to protect the economically weak in a 1902 coal miners' strike. Miners in the anthracite fields of eastern Pennsylvania wanted recognition for their union, the United Mine Workers (UMW). They also wanted a 10 percent to 20 percent increase in wages and an eight-hour day. When their employers, led by George F. Baer of the Reading Railroad, refused to negotiate, they went on strike. In October, the fifth month of the strike, Roosevelt summoned the mine owners and John Mitchell, the UMW president, to the White House. Baer expected Roosevelt to threaten the striking workers with arrest by federal troops if they failed to return to work. Instead, Roosevelt supported Mitchell's request for arbitration and warned the mine owners that if they refused to go along, 10,000 federal troops would seize their property. Stunned, the mine owners agreed to submit the dispute to arbitrators, who awarded the unionists a 10 percent wage increase and a nine-hour day.

The mere fact that the federal government had ordered employers to compromise with their workers carried great symbolic weight. Roosevelt enjoyed a surge of support from Americans convinced that he shared their dislike for ill-gotten wealth and privilege. He also raised the hopes of African Americans when, only a month into his presidency, he dined with Booker T. Washington at the White House and then shrugged off the protests of white southerners, who accused him of undermining segregation.

In his 1904 election campaign, Roosevelt promised that, if reelected, he would offer every American a "square deal." The slogan resonated with voters and helped carry Roosevelt to a victory (57 percent of the popular vote) over the conservative Democrat Alton B. Parker. To the surprise of many observers, Roosevelt had aligned the Republican Party with the cause of reform.

Expanding Government Power: The Economy

Emboldened by his victory, the president intensified his efforts to extend government regulation of economic affairs. His most important proposal was to give the government power to set railroad shipping rates and thereby to eliminate the industry's discriminatory marketing practices. The government, in theory, already possessed this power through the Interstate Commerce Commission (ICC), a regulatory body established by Congress in 1887, but the courts had so weakened the ICC's oversight and regulatory functions as to render it virtually powerless. Roosevelt achieved his goal in 1906, when Congress passed the Hepburn Act, which significantly increased the ICC's powers of rate review and enforcement. Roosevelt supported the Pure Food and Drug Act, passed by Congress that same year, which protected the public from fraudulently marketed and dangerous foods and medications. He also campaigned for the Meat Inspection Act (1906), which committed the government to monitoring the quality and safety of meat being sold to American consumers.

Expanding Government Power: The Environment

Roosevelt also did more than any previous president to extend federal control over the nation's physical environment. Roosevelt was not a "preservationist" in the manner of John Muir, founder of the Sierra Club, who insisted that the beauty of the land and the well-being of its wildlife should be protected from all human interference. Instead, Roosevelt viewed the wilderness as a place to live strenuously, to test oneself against the rough outdoors, and to match wits against strong and clever game. Roosevelt further believed that in the West— that land of ancient forests, lofty mountain peaks, and magnificent canyons—Americans could learn something important about their nation's roots and destiny. To preserve this West, Roosevelt oversaw the creation of 5 new national parks, 16 national monuments, and 53 wildlife reserves. The work of his administration led directly to the formation of the National Park Service in 1916.

Roosevelt also emerged a strong supporter of the **"conservationist"** movement. Conservationists cared little for national parks or grand canyons. They wanted to manage the environment, so as to ensure that the nation's resources were put to the most efficient economic use. Roosevelt shared the conservationists' belief that the plundering of western timberlands, grazing areas, water resources, and minerals had reached crisis proportions. Only broad regulatory controls would restore the West's economic potential.

To that end, Roosevelt appointed a Public Lands Commission in 1903 to survey public lands, inventory them, and establish permit systems to regulate the kinds and numbers of users. Soon after, the Departments of Interior and Agriculture placed certain western lands rich in natural resources and waterpower off-limits to agricultural users. Government officials also limited waterpower development by requiring companies to acquire permits and pay fees for the right to generate electricity on public land. When political favoritism and corruption within the Departments of the Interior and Agriculture threatened these efforts at regulation, Roosevelt authorized the hiring of university-trained experts to replace state and local politicians. Scientific expertise, rather than political connections, would now determine the distribution and use of western territory.

Gifford Pinchot, a specialist in forestry management and Roosevelt's close friend, led the drive for scientific management of natural resources. In 1905, he persuaded Roosevelt to relocate jurisdiction for the national forests from the Department of the Interior to the Department of Agriculture, which, Pinchot argued, was the most appropriate department to oversee the efficient "harvest" of the nation's forest crop. The newly created National Forest Service, under Pinchot's control, quickly instituted a system of competitive bidding for the right to harvest timber on national forest lands. Pinchot and his expanding staff of college-educated foresters also implemented a new policy that exacted user fees from livestock ranchers who had previously used national forest grazing lands for free. Armed with new legislation and authority, Pinchot and fellow conservationists in the Roosevelt administration declared vast stretches of federal land in the West off-limits to mining and dam construction.

The Republican Old Guard disliked these initiatives. When Roosevelt recommended prosecution of cattlemen and lumbermen who were illegally using federal land for private gain, congressional conservatives struck back with legislation (in 1907) that curtailed the president's power to create new government land reserves. Roosevelt responded by seizing another 17 million acres for national forest reserves before the new law went into effect. To his conservative opponents, excluding commercial activity from public land—a program they regarded as socialistic—was bad enough, but flouting the will of Congress with a 17-million-acre land grab violated constitutional principles governing the separation of powers. Yet, to millions of American voters, Roosevelt's willingness to defy western cattle barons, mining tycoons, and other "malefactors of great wealth" increased his popularity.

Progressivism: A Movement for the People?

Historians have long debated how much Roosevelt's economic and environmental reforms altered the balance of power between the "interests" and the people. Some have demonstrated that many corporations were eager for federal government regulation—that railroad corporations wanted relief from the rate wars that were driving them into bankruptcy, for example, and that the larger meatpackers believed that the costs of government food inspections would drive smaller meatpackers out of business. So, too, historians have shown that agribusinesses, timber companies, and mining corporations in the West believed that government regulation would aid them and hurt smaller competitors. According to this view, government regulation benefited the corporations more than it benefited workers, consumers, and small businessmen.

This view has some validity. These early reforms often curtailed corporate power only to a limited extent. Corporations fought with some success to turn the final versions of the reform laws to their advantage. But in 1907, the progressive program was still evolving. Popular anger over corporate power and political corruption remained a driving force of progressivism. The presence in the Senate of La Follette, Albert Beveridge of Indiana, and other anticorporate Republicans gave that anger an influential national voice. Whether the corporations or the people would benefit most from progressive reforms had yet to be determined.

The Republicans: A Divided Party

The financial panic of 1907 further strained relations between Roosevelt reformers and Old Guard conservatives in the Republican Party. When several New York banks failed in a speculative effort to corner the copper market, they triggered a run on banks, a short but severe dip in industrial production, and widespread layoffs. Everywhere, people worried that a major depression, like that of the 1890s, was in the offing. Only the timely decision of J. P. Morgan and his fellow bankers to pour private cash into the collapsing banks saved the nation from an economic crisis. Prosperity quickly returned, but the panic jitters lingered. Conservatives blamed Roosevelt's "radical" economic policies for the fiasco. To Roosevelt and his fellow progressives, however, the panic merely pointed out how little impact their reforms had actually made on the reign of "speculation, corruption, and fraud."

Roosevelt, as a result, began calling for an overhaul of the banking system and regulation of the stock market. The Republican Old Guard, meanwhile, was more determined than ever to run the "radical" Roosevelt out of the White House. Sensing that he might fail to win his party's nomination, and mindful of a rash promise he had made in 1904 not to run again in 1908, Roosevelt decided not to seek reelection. It was a decision he would soon regret. Barely 50 years old, he was too young and energetic to end his political career, and much of his reform program had yet to win Congressional approval.

The Taft Presidency

Roosevelt thought he had found in **William Howard Taft,** his secretary of war, an ideal successor. Taft had worked closely with Roosevelt on foreign and domestic policies. He had supported Roosevelt's progressive reforms and offered him shrewd advice. Roosevelt believed Taft possessed both the ideas and the skills to complete the reform Republican program.

To reach that conclusion, however, Roosevelt had to ignore some obvious differences between Taft and himself. Taft neither liked nor was particularly adept at politics. With the exception of a judgeship in an Ohio superior court, he had never held elective office. He was by nature a cautious and conservative man. As Roosevelt's handpicked successor, Taft easily won the election of 1908, defeating Democrat William Jennings Bryan with 52 percent of the vote. His conservatism soon revealed itself in his choice of corporation lawyers, rather than reformers, for cabinet positions.

Battling Congress

Taft's troubles began when he appeared to side against progressives in an acrimonious congressional battle over tariff legislation. Progressives had long desired tariff reduction, believing that competition from foreign manufacturers would benefit American consumers and check the economic power of American manufacturers. Taft had raised expectations for tariff reduction when he called Congress into special session to consider a reform bill that called for a modest reduction of tariffs and an inheritance tax. The bill passed the House but was gutted in the Senate. When congressional progressives pleaded with Taft to use his power to whip conservative senators into line, he pressured the Old Guard into including a 2 percent corporate income tax in their version of the bill, but he did not insist on tariff reductions. As a result, the Payne-Aldrich Tariff he signed into law on August 5, 1909, did nothing to encourage imports. Progressive Republicans, bitterly disappointed, held Taft responsible.

They were further angered when Taft withdrew his support of their efforts to strip Speaker Joe Cannon of his legislative powers. By 1910, Republican insurgents had entered into an alliance with reform-minded congressional Democrats. Then a bruising fight over Taft's conservation policies brought relations between Taft and the insurgent Republicans to the breaking point.

The Ballinger-Pinchot Controversy

Richard A. Ballinger, secretary of the interior, had aroused progressives' suspicions by reopening for private commercial use 1 million acres of land that the Roosevelt administration had previously brought under federal protection. Gifford Pinchot, still head of the National Forest Service, obtained information implicating Ballinger in the sale of Alaskan coal deposits to a private syndicate. Pinchot showed the information, including an allegation that Ballinger had personally profited from the sale, to Taft. Taft defended Ballinger, Pinchot went public with his charges, and a contentious congressional investigation ensued. Whatever hope Taft may have had of escaping political damage disappeared when Roosevelt, returning from an African hunting trip by way of Europe in spring 1910, staged a publicized rendezvous with Pinchot in England. In so doing, Roosevelt signaled his continuing support for his old friend Pinchot and his displeasure with Taft.

Roosevelt's Return

When Roosevelt arrived in the United States later that summer, he quickly returned to politics. In September, Roosevelt embarked on a speaking tour, the high point of which was his elaboration at Osawatomie, Kansas, of his New Nationalism, an ambitious reform program that called for the federal government to stabilize the economy, protect the weak, and restore social harmony.

The 1910 congressional elections confirmed the popularity of Roosevelt's positions. Insurgent Republicans trounced conservative Republicans in primary after primary, and the Democrats' embrace of reform brought them a majority in the House of Representatives for

Theodore Roosevelt Launches His New Nationalism Campaign, 1910   This photograph of Roosevelt at Osawatomie, Kansas, captures some of the strength and exuberance of Roosevelt's public style. Roosevelt's appearance at Osawatomie marked his formal return to politics. For the occasion, he unveiled his New Nationalism, a far-reaching program of reform that called on the government to control the powerful corporations in the interests of the commonweal.

the first time since 1894. When Robert La Follette, who was challenging Taft for the Republican presidential nomination, seemed to suffer a nervous breakdown in February 1912, Roosevelt announced his own candidacy. In the 13 states sponsoring preferential primaries, Roosevelt won nearly 75 percent of the delegates, but the party's national leadership remained in the hands of the Old Guard, and they were determined to deny Roosevelt the Republican nomination. At the Republican convention in Chicago, Taft won renomination on the first ballot.

The Bull Moose Campaign

Roosevelt had expected this outcome. The night before the convention opened, he had told an assembly of 5,000 supporters that the party leaders would not succeed in derailing their movement. "We stand at Armageddon," he declared, and "we battle for the Lord." The next day, Roosevelt and his supporters withdrew from the convention and from the Republican Party. In August, the reformers reassembled as the new **Progressive Party**, nominated Roosevelt for president and California governor Hiram W. Johnson for vice president, and hammered out the reform platform they had long envisioned: sweeping regulation of the corporations, extensive protections for workers, a sharply graduated income tax, and woman suffrage. "I am as strong as a bull moose," Roosevelt roared as he readied for combat; his proud followers took to calling themselves **"Bull Moosers."**

Some of them, however, probably including Roosevelt, knew that their mission was futile. They had failed to enroll many Republican insurgents who had supported Roosevelt in the primaries but who now refused to abandon the GOP. Consequently, the Republican vote would be split between Roosevelt and Taft, making them both vulnerable to the Democrats' candidate, Woodrow Wilson.

The Rise of Woodrow Wilson

Few would have predicted in 1908 that the distinguished president of Princeton University, Woodrow Wilson, would be the 1912 Democratic nominee for president of the United States. Before 1910, Wilson had never run for elective office, nor had he ever held an appointed post in a local, state, or federal administration. The son of a Presbyterian minister from Virginia, Wilson had practiced law for a short time after graduating from Princeton (then still the College of New Jersey) in 1879 before settling on an academic career. Earning his doctorate in political science from Johns Hopkins in 1886, he taught history and political science at Bryn Mawr and Wesleyan (Connecticut) before returning to Princeton in 1890. He became president of Princeton in 1902, a post he held until he successfully ran for the governorship of New Jersey in 1910.

Identifying himself with the anti-Bryan wing of the Democratic Party, Wilson attracted the attention of wealthy conservatives, who saw him as a potential presidential candidate. They convinced the bosses of the New Jersey Democratic machine to nominate Wilson for governor in 1910. Wilson accepted the nomination and won the governorship handily. He then shocked his conservative backers by declaring his independence from the state's

Democratic machine and moving New Jersey into the forefront of reform. Wilson's Presbyterian upbringing had instilled in him a strong sense that society should be governed by God's moral law. As a young man in the 1880s, he had come to believe that the social consequences of unregulated industrialization were repugnant to Christian ethical principles. Although these beliefs had receded from view somewhat during his tenure as Princeton University president, they had not disappeared. Their presence in his consciousness helps to explain his emergence in 1911 and 1912 as one of the nation's leading progressives.

The Election of 1912

At the Democratic convention of 1912, Wilson was something of a dark horse, running a distant second to House Speaker Champ Clark of Missouri. When the New York delegation gave Clark a simple majority of delegates, virtually everyone assumed that Clark would soon command the two-thirds majority needed to win the nomination. But Wilson's managers held onto Wilson's delegates and began chipping away at Clark's lead. On the fourth day, on the 46th ballot, Wilson won the nomination. The exhausted Democrats closed ranks behind their candidate.

Given the split in Republican ranks, Democrats had their best chance in 20 years of regaining the White House. A Wilson victory, moreover, would give the country its first southern-born president in almost 50 years. Finally, whatever its outcome, the election promised to deliver a hefty vote for reform. Both Roosevelt and Wilson were running on reform platforms, and the Socialist Party candidate, Eugene V. Debs, was attracting larger crowds and generating greater enthusiasm than had been expected. Taft was so certain of defeat that he barely campaigned.

Debate among the candidates focused on the trusts. All three reform candidates—Roosevelt, Wilson, and Debs—agreed that corporations had acquired too much economic power. Debs argued that the only way to ensure popular control of that power was for the federal government to assume ownership of the trusts. Roosevelt called for the establishment of a powerful government that

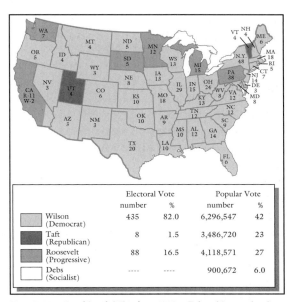

	Electoral Vote		Popular Vote	
	number	%	number	%
Wilson (Democrat)	435	82.0	6,296,547	42
Taft (Republican)	8	1.5	3,486,720	23
Roosevelt (Progressive)	88	16.5	4,118,571	27
Debs (Socialist)	----	----	900,672	6.0

Map 21.2   Presidential Election, 1912   Taft and Roosevelt split the Republican vote, allowing Wilson to win with a plurality of the popular vote (42 percent) and a big majority (82 percent) of the electoral vote.

would regulate and, if necessary, curb the power of the trusts. This was the essence of his New Nationalism, the program he had been advocating since 1910.

Rather than regulate the trusts, Wilson declared his intention to break them up. He wanted to reverse the tendency toward economic concentration and thus restore opportunity to the people. This philosophy, which Wilson labeled the **New Freedom,** called for a temporary concentration of governmental power in order to dismantle the trusts. But once that was accomplished, Wilson promised, the government would relinquish its power.

Wilson won the November election with 42 percent of the popular vote to Roosevelt's 27 percent and Taft's 23 percent; Debs made a strong showing with 6 percent, the largest in his party's history. The three candidates who had pledged themselves to reform programs—Wilson, Roosevelt, and Debs—together won a remarkable 75 percent of the vote.

The Wilson Presidency

Wilson quickly assembled a cabinet of talented men who could be counted on for wise counsel, loyalty, and influence over vital Democratic constituencies. He cultivated a public image of himself as a president firmly in charge of his party and as a faithful tribune of the people.

Tariff Reform and a Progressive Income Tax

Like his predecessor, Wilson first turned his attention to tariff reform. The House passed a tariff-reduction bill within a month, and Wilson used his leadership skills to push the bill through a reluctant Senate. The resulting Underwood-Simmons Tariff of 1913 reduced tariff barriers from approximately 40 percent to 25 percent. To make up for revenue lost to tariff reductions, Congress then passed an income tax law. The 16th Amendment to the Constitution, ratified by the states in 1913, had already given the government the right to impose an income tax. The law passed by Congress made good on the progressive pledge to reduce the power and privileges of wealthy Americans by requiring them to pay taxes on a greater *percentage* of their income than the poor.

The Federal Reserve Act

Wilson then asked Congress to overhaul the nation's financial system. Virtually everyone in both parties agreed on the need for greater regulation of banks and currency, but they differed sharply over how to proceed. The banking interests and their congressional supporters wanted the government to give the authority to regulate credit and currency flows either to a single bank or to several regional banks. Progressives opposed the vesting of so much financial power in private hands and insisted that any reformed financial system must be publicly controlled. Wilson worked out a compromise plan that included both private and public controls, and he marshaled the votes to push it through both the House and the Senate. By the end of 1913, Wilson had signed the **Federal Reserve Act,** the most important law passed in his first administration.

The Federal Reserve Act established 12 regional banks, each controlled by the private banks in its region. Every private bank in the country was required to deposit an average of 6 percent of its assets in its regional Federal Reserve bank. The reserve would be used to make loans to member banks and to issue paper currency (Federal Reserve notes) to facilitate financial transactions. The regional banks were also instructed to use their funds to shore up member banks in distress and to respond to sudden changes in credit demands by easing or tightening the flow of credit. A Federal Reserve Board appointed by the president and responsible to the public rather than to private bankers would set policy and oversee activities within the 12 reserve banks.

The Federal Reserve system strengthened the nation's financial structure and was in most respects an impressive political achievement for Wilson. In its final form, however, it revealed that Wilson was retreating from his New Freedom pledge. The Federal Reserve Board was a less powerful and less centralized federal authority than a national bank would have been, but it nevertheless represented a substantial increase in government control of banking. Moreover, the bill authorizing the system made no attempt to break up private financial institutions that had grown too powerful or to prohibit the interlocking directorates that large banks used to augment their power. Because it sought to work with large banks rather than to break them up, the Federal Reserve system seemed more consonant with the principles of Roosevelt's New Nationalism than with those of Wilson's New Freedom.

From the New Freedom to the New Nationalism

Wilson's failure to mount a vigorous antitrust campaign confirmed his drift toward the New Nationalism. For example, in 1914, Wilson supported the Federal Trade Commission Act, which created a government agency by that name to regulate business practices. The Federal Trade Commission (FTC) had wide powers to collect information on corporate pricing policies and on cooperation and competition among businesses. The FTC might have attacked trusts for "unfair trade practices," but the Senate stripped the FTC Act's companion legislation, the Clayton Antitrust Act, of virtually all provisions that would have allowed the government to prosecute the trusts. Wilson supported this weakening of the Clayton Act, having decided that the breakup of large-scale industry was no longer practical or preferable. The FTC, in Wilson's eyes, would help businesses, large and small, to regulate themselves in ways that contributed to national well-being. In accepting giant industry as an inescapable feature of modern life and in seeking to regulate industrial behavior by means of government agencies such as the FTC, Wilson had become, in effect, a New Nationalist.

At first, Wilson's drift to New Nationalist policies led him to support business interests. His nominations to the Federal Reserve Board, for example, were generally men who had worked for Wall Street firms and large industrial corporations. At the same time, he usually refused to use government powers to aid organized groups of workers and farmers. Court rulings had made worker and farmer organizations vulnerable to prosecution under the terms of the Sherman Antitrust Act of 1890. AFL president Samuel Gompers and other labor leaders tried but failed to convince Wilson to insert into the Clayton Antitrust Act a clause that would unambiguously grant labor and farmer organizations immunity from further antitrust prosecutions.

Nor did Wilson, at this time, view with any greater sympathy the campaign for African American political equality. He supported efforts by white southerners in his cabinet, such as Postmaster General Albert Burleson and Treasury Secretary William McAdoo, to segregate their government departments, and he largely ignored pleas from the NAACP to involve the federal government in a campaign against lynching.

In late 1915, however, Wilson moved to the left, in part because he feared losing his reelection in 1916. The Bull Moosers of 1912 were retreating back to the Republican Party. Wilson remembered how much his 1912 victory, based on only 42 percent of the popular vote, had depended on the Republican split. To halt the progressives' rapprochement with the GOP, he made a bid for their support. In January 1916, he nominated Louis Brandeis to the Supreme Court. Not only was Brandeis one of the country's most respected progressives, but he was also the first Jew nominated to serve on the country's highest court. Congressional conservatives did everything they could to block the confirmation of a man they regarded as dangerously radical, but Wilson, as usual, was better organized, and by June his forces in the Senate had emerged victorious.

Wilson followed up this victory by pushing through Congress the first federal workmen's compensation law (the Kern-McGillicuddy Act, which covered federal employees), the first federal law outlawing child labor (the Keating-Owen Act), and the first federal law guaranteeing workers an eight-hour day (the Adamson Act, which covered the nation's 400,000 railway workers). The number of Americans affected by these acts was rather small. Nevertheless, Wilson had reoriented the Democratic Party to a New Nationalism that cared as much about the interests of the powerless as the interests of the powerful.

Trade unionists flocked to Wilson, as did most of the prominent progressives who had followed the Bull Moose in 1912. Meanwhile, Wilson had appealed to the supporters of William Jennings Bryan by supporting legislation that made federal credit available to farmers in need. He had put together a reform coalition capable of winning a majority at the polls. In the process, he had transformed the Democratic Party. From 1916 on, the Democrats, rather than the Republicans, became the chief guardians of the American reform tradition.

That Wilson did so is a sign of the strength of the reform and radical forces in American society. By 1916, the ranks of middle-class progressives had grown broad and deep. Working-class protest had also accelerated in scope and intensity. In Lawrence, Massachusetts, in 1912, and in Paterson, New Jersey, in 1913, for example, the IWW organized strikes of textile workers that drew national attention, as did the 1914 strike by Colorado mine workers that ended with the infamous Ludlow massacre (see chapter 20). These protests reflected the mobilization of those working-class constituencies—immigrants, women, the unskilled—long considered inconsequential both by mainstream labor leaders and party politicians. Assisted by radicals, these groups had begun to fashion a more inclusive and politically ambitious labor movement. Wilson and other Democrats understood the potential strength of this new labor movement, and the president's pro-labor legislative agenda in 1916 can be understood, in part, as an effort to channel labor's new constituents into the Democratic Party. It was a successful strategy that contributed to Wilson's reelection in 1916.

Conclusion

By 1916, the progressives had accomplished a great deal. They demonstrated that traditional American concerns with democracy and liberty could be adapted to an industrial age. They exposed and curbed some of the worst abuses of the American political system. They enfranchised women and took steps to protect the environment. They broke the hold of laissez-faire economic policies on national politics and replaced it with the idea of a strong federal government committed to economic regulation and social justice. They transformed the presidency into a post of legislative and popular leadership. They enlarged the executive branch by establishing new commissions and agencies charged with administering government policies.

The progressives, in short, had presided over the emergence of a new national government, one in which power increasingly flowed away from municipalities and states and toward Washington. This reorientation followed a compelling logic: A national government stood a better chance of solving the problems of growing economic inequality, mismanagement of natural resources, and consumer fraud than did local and state governments. This emphasis on involving the federal government in economic and social affairs became progressivism's most enduring legacy. It made the movement a forerunner of the liberalism and "New Deal" that emerged under Franklin Roosevelt's leadership in the 1930s (see chapter 25).

The promise of effective federal government intervention, however, also brought a new danger: the possibility that government administrators might use their power to fashion themselves into a new bureaucratic elite impervious to popular control. Some progressives, such as Walter Lippmann, were already arguing that their knowledge, objectivity, and dedication equipped them to make critical decisions on behalf of the people without consulting them. Other progressives in government claimed to be responsive to the people while they cultivated close ties with corporations that they were expected to regulate on the people's behalf. In some instances, in other words, progressive reformers were doing as much to advance their own bureaucratic interests or those of their corporate allies as they were helping to improve the welfare of ordinary Americans.

These elitist tendencies did not go unchallenged. The democratic movements of the progressive era—those involving workers, women, minorities, consumers, and environmentalists—were determined to hold both elected and appointed government officials accountable to the popular will. Their success in moving Wilson to the left in 1916 demonstrated that the forces of democracy could win. But the struggle between the contrasting progressive impulses toward democracy and elitism would go on, manifesting itself not simply in domestic politics but also in foreign affairs, where the United States was seeking to balance its interest in spreading liberty with the protection of its international economic interests.

SUGGESTED READINGS

No topic in 20th-century American history has generated as large and rapidly changing a scholarship as has progressivism. Today, few scholars treat this political movement in the terms set forth by the progressives themselves: as a movement of "the people" against the "special interests." In

The Age of Reform: From Bryan to FDR (1955), **Richard Hofstadter** argues that progressivism was the expression of a declining Protestant middle class at odds with the new industrial order. In *The Search for Order, 1877–1920* (1967), **Robert Wiebe** finds the movement's core in a rising middle class, closely allied to the corporations and bureaucratic imperatives that were defining this new order. **Gabriel Kolko,** *The Triumph of Conservatism: A Reinterpretation of American History* (1963), and **James Weinstein,** *The Corporate Ideal in the Liberal State, 1900–1918* (1969), both argue that progressivism was the work of businessmen, who were eager to ensure corporate stability and profitability in a dangerously unstable capitalist economy.

Without denying the importance of this corporate search for order, **Nell Irvin Painter,** *Standing at Armageddon: The United States, 1877–1919* (1987), and **Alan Dawley,** *Struggles for Justice: Social Responsibility and the Liberal State* (1991), insist on the role of the working class, men and women, whites and blacks, in shaping the progressive agenda. **James T. Kloppenberg,** *Uncertain Victory: Social Democracy and Progressivism in European and American Thought, 1870–1920* (1986), and **Thomas J. Knock,** *To End All Wars: Woodrow Wilson and the Quest for a New World Order* (1992), emphasize the influence of socialism on progressive thought, while **Martin J. Sklar,** *The Corporate Reconstruction of American Capitalism, 1900–1916: The Market, the Law and Politics* (1988), stresses the role of progressivism in "containing" or taming socialism.

Daniel T. Rodgers reconstructs the international networks of reform that nourished progressivism in *Atlantic Crossings: Social Politics in a Progressive Age* (1998). **Nick Salvatore** superbly captures the charisma and enigma of Debs in his *Eugene V. Debs: Citizen and Socialist* (1982). **Paul Boyer,** *Urban Masses and Moral Order in America, 1820–1920* (1978), treats progressivism as a cultural movement to enforce middle-class norms on unruly urban and immigrant populations. **Theda Skocpol,** *Protecting Soldiers and Mothers: The Political Origins of Social Policy in the United States* (1992), and **Robyn Muncy,** *Creating a Female Dominion in American Reform, 1890–1935* (1991), reconstruct the central role of middle-class Protestant women in shaping progressive social policy, while **Robert M. Crunden,** *Ministers of Reform: The Progressives' Achievement in American Civilization, 1889–1920* (1982), stresses the religious roots of progressive reform. **Michael Kazin,** *A Godly Hero: the Life of William Jennings Bryan* (2006), is indispensable not just on Bryan but also on the religious dimensions of progressivism, while **Alexander Keyssar,** *The Right to Vote: The Contested History of Democracy in the United States* (2000) is an essential guide to political reform during this period. An impressive recent attempt to synthesize the literature on progressivism is **Michael McGerr,** *A Fierce Discontent: The Rise and Fall of the Progressive Movement in America, 1870–1920* (2003).

22

Becoming a World Power, 1898–1917

For much of the 19th century, most Americans were preoccupied by continental expansion. They treasured their distance from European societies, monarchs, and wars. Elections rarely turned on international events, and presidents rarely made their reputations as statesmen in the world arena. The diplomatic corps, like most agencies of the federal government, was small and inexperienced. The government projected its limited military power westward and possessed virtually no capacity or desire for involvement overseas.

The nation's rapid industrial growth in the late 19th century forced a turn away from such continentalism. Technological advances, especially the laying of transoceanic cables and the introduction of steamship travel, diminished America's physical isolation. The babel of languages one could hear in American cities testified to how much the Old World had penetrated the New. Then, too, Americans watched anxiously as England, Germany, Russia, Japan, and other industrial powers intensified their competition for overseas markets and colonies, and some believed America too needed to enter this contest. The voices making this argument grew more insistent and persuasive as the economic depression of the 1890s stripped the United States of its prosperity and pride.

A war with Spain in 1898 gave the United States an opportunity to upgrade its military and acquire colonies and influence in the Western Hemisphere and Asia. Under Presidents William McKinley and Theodore Roosevelt, the United States pursued these initiatives and established a small but strategically important empire. Not all Americans supported this imperial project, and many protested the subjugation of the peoples of Cuba, Puerto Rico, and the Philippines that imperial expansion seemed to entail. In the eyes of anti-imperialists, the United States seemed to be becoming the kind of nation that many Americans had long despised—one that valued power more than liberty.

Roosevelt brushed aside these objections and set about creating an international system in which a handful of industrial nations pursued their global economic interests, dominated world trade, and kept the world at peace. Woodrow Wilson, however, was more troubled by America's imperial turn. His doubts became apparent in his efforts to devise a policy toward postrevolutionary Mexico that restrained American might and respected Mexican desires for liberty. It was a worthy ambition but one that proved exceedingly difficult to achieve.

CHRONOLOGY

1893	Frederick Jackson Turner publishes an essay announcing the end of the frontier
1898	Spanish-American War (April 14–August 12) • Treaty of Paris signed (December 10), giving U.S. control of Philippines, Guam, and Puerto Rico • U.S. annexes Hawaii
1899–1902	American-Filipino War
1899–1900	U.S. pursues Open Door policy toward China
1900	U.S. annexes Puerto Rico • U.S. and other imperial powers put down Chinese Boxer Rebellion
1901	U.S. forces Cuba to adopt constitution favorable to U.S. interests
1903	Hay–Bunau-Varilla Treaty signed, giving U.S. control of Panama Canal Zone
1904	"Roosevelt corollary" to Monroe Doctrine proclaimed
1905	Roosevelt negotiates end to Russo-Japanese War
1906–17	U.S. intervenes in Cuba, Nicaragua, Haiti, Dominican Republic, and Mexico
1907	Roosevelt and Japanese government reach a "gentlemen's agreement" restricting Japanese immigration to U.S. and ending the segregation of Japanese schoolchildren in California
1907–09	Great White Fleet circles the world
1909–13	William Howard Taft conducts "dollar diplomacy"
1910	Mexican Revolution
1914	Panama Canal opens
1914–17	Wilson struggles to develop a policy toward Mexico
1917	U.S. purchases Virgin Islands from Denmark

The United States Looks Abroad

By the late 19th century, sizable numbers of Americans had become interested in extending their country's influence abroad. The most important groups were Protestant missionaries, businessmen, and imperialists.

Protestant Missionaries

Protestant missionaries were among the most active promoters of American interests abroad. Overseas missionary activity grew quickly between 1870 and 1900, most of it directed toward China. Between 1880 and 1900, the number of women's missionary societies doubled, from 20 to 40; by 1915, these societies enrolled 3 million women. Convinced of the superiority of the Anglo-Saxon race, Protestant missionaries considered it their Christian duty to teach the Gospel to the "ignorant" Asian masses and save their souls. Missionaries also believed that their efforts would free those masses from their racial destiny, enabling them to become "civilized." In this "civilizing" effort, missionaries resembled progressive reformers who sought to uplift America's immigrant masses at home.

Businessmen

For different reasons, industrialists, traders, and investors also began to look overseas, sensing that they could make fortunes in foreign lands. Exports of American manufactured goods rose substantially after 1880. By 1914, American foreign investment already equaled a sizable 7 percent of the nation's gross national product. Companies such as Eastman Kodak (film and cameras), Singer Sewing Machine Company, Standard Oil, American Tobacco, and International Harvester had become multinational corporations with overseas branch offices.

Some industrialists became entranced by the prospect of clothing, feeding, housing, and transporting the 400 million people of China. James B. Duke, who headed American Tobacco, was selling 1 billion cigarettes per year in East Asian markets. Looking for ways to fill empty boxcars heading west from Minnesota to Tacoma, Washington, the railroad tycoon James J. Hill imagined stuffing them with wheat and steel destined for China and Japan. He actually published and distributed wheat cookbooks throughout East Asia to convince Asians to shift from a rice-based to a bread-based diet (so that there would be a market there for U.S. flour exports). Although export trade with East Asia during this period never fulfilled the expectations of Hill and other industrialists, their talk about the "wealth of the Orient" impressed on politicians its importance to American economic health.

Events of the 1890s only intensified the appeal of foreign markets. First, the 1890 U.S. census announced that the frontier had disappeared and that America had completed the task of westward expansion. Then, in 1893, a young historian named Frederick Jackson Turner published an essay, "The Significance of the Frontier in American History," that articulated what many Americans feared: that the frontier had been essential to the growth of the economy and to the cultivation of democracy.

Living in the wilderness, Turner argued, had transformed the Europeans who settled the New World into Americans. They shed their European clothing styles, social customs, and political beliefs, and acquired distinctively American characteristics—rugged individualism, egalitarianism, and a democratic faith. How, Turner wondered, could the nation continue to prosper now that the frontier had gone?

In recent years, historians of the American West have criticized **Turner's "frontier thesis."** They have argued that the very idea of the frontier as uninhabited wilderness overlooked the tens of thousands of Indians who occupied the region and that much else of what Americans believed about the West was based more on myth than on reality. They have also pointed out that it makes little sense to view the 1890s as a decade in which opportunities for economic gain disappeared in the West.

Even though these points are valid, they would have meant little to Americans living in Turner's time. For them, as for Turner, concern about the disappearing frontier expressed a fear that the increasingly urbanized and industrialized nation had lost its way. Turner's essay appeared just as the country was entering the deepest, longest, and most conflict-ridden depression in its history (see chapter 19). What could the republic do to regain its economic prosperity and political stability? Where would it find its new frontiers? One answer to these questions focused on the pursuit of overseas expansion. As Senator Albert J. Beveridge of Indiana declared in 1899: "We are raising more than we can consume. . . . We are making more than we can use. Therefore, we must find new markets for our produce, new occupation for our capital, new work for our labor."

Imperialists

Eager to assist in the drive for overseas expansion was a group of politicians, intellectuals, and military strategists who viewed such expansion as a key ingredient in the pursuit of world power. They wanted the United States to take its place alongside Britain, France, Germany, and Russia as a great imperial nation. They believed that the United States should build a strong navy, solidify a sphere of influence in the Caribbean, and extend markets into Asia. Their desire to control ports and territories beyond the continental borders of their own country made them **imperialists.** Many of them were also Social Darwinists (see chapter 19) who believed that America's destiny required that it prove itself the military equal of the strongest European nations and the master of the "lesser" peoples of the world.

One of the best-known imperialists of the period was Admiral **Alfred Thayer Mahan.** In an influential book, *The Influence of Sea Power upon History, 1660–1783* (1890), Mahan argued that past empires, beginning with Rome, had relied on their capacity to control the seas. Mahan called for the construction of a U.S. navy with enough ships and firepower to make its presence felt everywhere in the world. To be effective, that global fleet would require a canal across Central America through which U.S. warships could pass swiftly from the Atlantic to the Pacific oceans. It would also require a string of far-flung service bases from the Caribbean to the southwestern Pacific. Mahan recommended that the U.S. government take possession of Hawaii and other strategically located Pacific islands with superior harbor facilities.

Presidents William McKinley and Theodore Roosevelt would eventually make almost the whole of Mahan's vision a reality, but in the early 1890s, Mahan doubted that Americans would accept the responsibility and costs of empire. Although the imperialists counted in their ranks such prominent figures as Theodore Roosevelt and Senator Henry Cabot Lodge of Massachusetts, many Americans still insisted that the United States should not aspire to world power by acquiring overseas bases and colonizing foreign peoples.

Mahan underestimated, however, the government's alarm over the scramble of Europeans to extend their imperial control. Every U.S. administration from the 1880s on committed itself to a "big navy" policy. By 1898, the U.S. Navy ranked fifth in the world, and by 1900, it ranked third. Already in 1878, the United States had secured rights to Pago Pago, a superb deep-water harbor in Samoa (a collection of islands in the southwest Pacific inhabited by Polynesians), and in 1885, it had leased Pearl Harbor from the Hawaiians. Both harbors were expected to serve as fueling stations for the growing U.S. fleet.

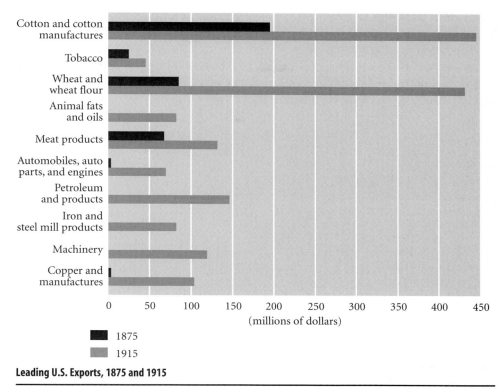

Leading U.S. Exports, 1875 and 1915

Source: Data from *Historical Statistics of the United States, Colonial Times to 1970* (White Plains, N.Y.: Kraus International, 1989).

These attempts to project U.S. power overseas had already deepened the government's involvement in the affairs of distant lands. In 1889, the United States established a protectorate over part of Samoa, a move meant to forestall German and British efforts to weaken American influence on the islands. In the early 1890s, President Grover Cleveland's administration was increasingly drawn into Hawaiian affairs, as tensions between American sugar plantation owners and native Hawaiians upset the islands' economic and political stability. In 1891, U.S. plantation owners succeeded in deposing the Hawaiian king and putting into power Queen Liliuokalani. But when Liliuokalani strove to establish her independence from American interests, the planters, assisted by U.S. sailors, overthrew her regime, too. Cleveland declared Hawaii a protectorate in 1893, but he resisted the imperialists in Congress who wanted to annex the islands.

Still, imperialist sentiment in Congress and across the nation continued to gain strength, fueled by "jingoism." Jingoists were nationalists who thought that a swaggering foreign policy and a willingness to go to war would enhance their nation's glory. They were constantly on the alert for insults to their country's honor and swift to call for military

The U.S. Navy, 1890–1914: Expenditures and Battleship Size

Fiscal year	Total Federal Expenditures	Naval Expenditures	Naval Expenditures as Percentage of Total Federal Expenditures	Size of Battleships (average tons displaced)
1890	$318,040,711	$ 22,006,206	6.9%	11,000
1900	520,860,847	55,953,078	10.7	12,000
1901	524,616,925	60,506,978	11.5	16,000
1905	657,278,914	117,550,308	20.7	16,000
1909	693,743,885	115,546,011	16.7	27,000 (1910)
1914	735,081,431	139,682,186	19.0	32,000

Sources: (for expenditures) E. B. Potter, *Sea Power: A Naval History* (Annapolis: Naval Institute Press, 1982), p. 187; (for size of ships) Harold Sprout, *Toward a New Order of Sea Power* (New York: Greenwood Press, 1976), p. 52.

retaliation. This predatory brand of nationalism emerged in each of the world's big powers in the late 19th century. In the United States, it manifested itself in terms of an eagerness for war. The anti-imperialist editor of the *Nation*, E. L. Godkin, exclaimed in 1894: "The number of men and officials of this country who are now mad to fight somebody is appalling." Recent feminist scholarship has emphasized the degree to which men of the 1890s saw war as an opportunity to revive frontier-like notions of masculinity—of men as warriors and conquerors—that were proving difficult to sustain in industrializing and bureaucratizing America. Spain's behavior in Cuba in the 1890s gave those men the war they sought.

The Spanish-American War

Focus Question
In going to war against Spain in 1898, was the United States impelled more by imperialist or anti-imperialist motives?

By the 1890s, the islands of Cuba and Puerto Rico were virtually all that remained of the vast Spanish empire in the Americas. Relations between the Cubans and their Spanish rulers had long been deteriorating. The Spanish had taken 10 years to subdue a revolt begun in 1868. In 1895, the Cubans staged another revolt, sparked by their continuing resentment of Spanish control and by a depressed economy caused in part by an 1894 U.S. tariff law that made Cuban sugar too expensive for the U.S. market. The fighting was brutal. Cuban forces destroyed large areas of the island to make it uninhabitable by the Spanish. The Spanish army, led by General Valeriano Weyler, responded in kind, forcing large numbers of Cubans into concentration camps. Denied adequate food, shelter, and sanitation, an estimated 200,000 Cubans—one-eighth of the island's population—died of starvation and disease.

Uncle Sam Gives Spain More Than It Can Handle By going to war in 1898, this poster suggests, the United States had toppled "brutal Spain" and the remnants of its empire.

Such tactics, especially those ascribed to "Butcher" Weyler (as he was known in much of the U.S. press), inflamed American opinion. Many Americans sympathized with the Cubans, who seemed to be fighting the kind of anticolonial war Americans had waged more than 100 years earlier. Americans stayed well informed about the atrocities by reading the *New York Journal,* owned by William Randolph Hearst, and the *New York World,* owned by Joseph Pulitzer. Hearst and Pulitzer were transforming newspaper publishing in much the same way Sam McClure and others had revolutionized the magazine business (see chapter 21). To boost circulation, they sought out sensational and shocking stories and described them in lurid detail. They were accused of engaging in **"yellow journalism"**—embellishing stories with titillating details when the true reports did not seem dramatic enough.

The sensationalism of the yellow press and its frequently jingoistic accounts failed to bring about American intervention in Cuba, however. In the final days of his administration, President Cleveland resisted mounting pressure to intervene. William McKinley, who succeeded him in 1897, denounced the Spanish even more harshly, with the aim of forcing Spain into concessions that would satisfy the Cuban rebels and end the conflict. Initially, this strategy seemed to be working: Spain relieved "Butcher" Weyler of his command, began releasing incarcerated Cubans from concentration camps, and granted Cuba limited autonomy. Still, Spaniards living on the island refused to be ruled by a Cuban government, and the Cuban rebels continued to demand full independence. Late in 1897, when riots broke out in Havana, McKinley ordered the battleship *Maine* into Havana harbor to protect U.S. citizens and their property. Two unexpected events then set off a war.

The first was the February 9, 1898, publication in Hearst's *New York Journal* of a letter stolen from Depuy de Lôme, the Spanish minister to Washington, in which he described McKinley as "a cheap politician" and a "bidder for the admiration of the crowd." The de Lôme letter also implied that the Spanish cared little about resolving the Cuban crisis through negotiation and reform. The news embarrassed Spanish officials and outraged U.S. public opinion. Then, only six days later, the *Maine* exploded in Havana harbor, killing 260 American sailors. Although subsequent investigations revealed that the most probable cause of the explosion was a malfunctioning boiler, Americans were certain that it had been the work of Spanish agents. "Remember the Maine!" screamed the headlines in the yellow press. On March 8, Congress responded to the clamor for war by authorizing $50 million to mobilize U.S. forces. In the meantime, McKinley notified Spain of his conditions for avoiding war: Spain would pay an indemnity for the *Maine,* abandon its concentration camps, end the fighting with the rebels, and commit itself to Cuban independence. On April 9, Spain accepted all the demands but the last. Nevertheless, on April 11, McKinley asked Congress for authority to go to war. Three days later, Congress approved a war resolution, which included a declaration (spelled out in the Teller Amendment) that the United States would not use the war as an opportunity to acquire territory in Cuba. On April 24, Spain responded with a formal declaration of war against the United States.

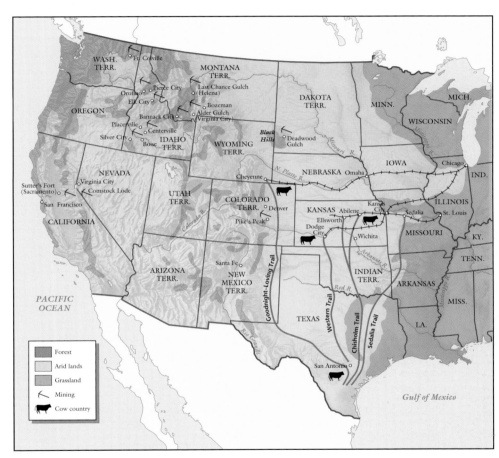

Map 18.1 Mining and Cattle Frontiers, 1870s   Most of the mines shown on this map produced gold and silver. The next generation would begin to exploit the copper to be found in Montana and Arizona, and later generations would extract oil from Texas and Oklahoma and coal and oil from Wyoming.

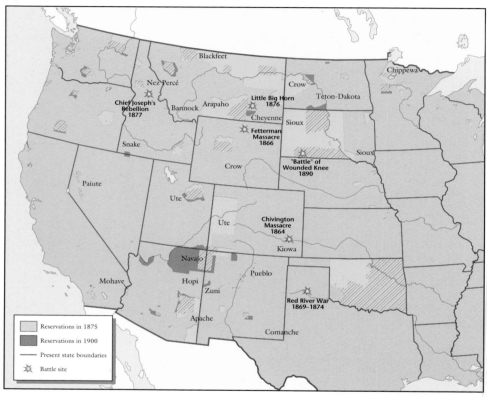

Map 18.2   Indian Reservations, 1875 and 1900   Before the Civil War, Indians had hunted and trapped over most of this vast region. The shrinking areas on which they were confined by the reservation policy vividly illustrates that for the first Americans, the story was not "the expansion of America" but "the contraction of America."

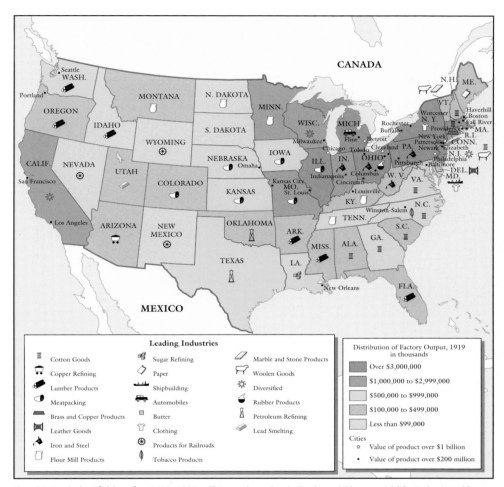

Map 20.1   Industrial America, 1900–1920   This map shows that the Northeast, Midwest, and California dominated factory production in the United States from 1900 to 1920. It also reveals the state-by-state distribution of various industries—clothing in New York, automobiles in Michigan, petroleum refining in Texas and Oklahoma, and lumber in Oregon, Washington, and Idaho. View an animated version of this map or related maps at http://www.thomsonedu.com/history/murrin.

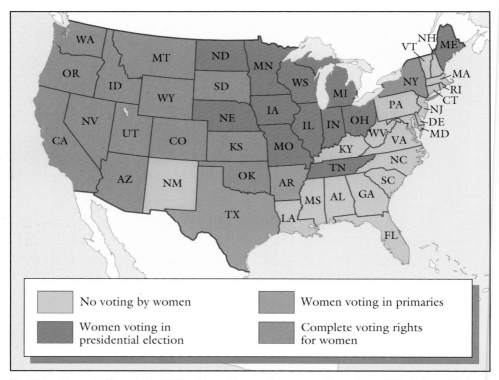

Map 21.1 Woman Suffrage Before 1920 This map illustrates how woman suffrage prior to 1920 had advanced furthest in the West.

"A Splendid Little War"

Secretary of State John Hay called the fight with Spain "a splendid little war." Begun in April, it ended in August. More than 1 million men volunteered to fight, and fewer than 500 were killed or wounded in combat. The American victory over Spain was complete, not just in Cuba but in the neighboring island of Puerto Rico and in the Philippines, Spain's strategic possession in the Pacific.

Actually, the war was more complicated than it seemed. The main reason for the easy victory was U.S. naval superiority. In the war's first major battle, a naval engagement in Manila harbor in the Philippines on May 1, a U.S. fleet commanded by Commodore George Dewey destroyed an entire Spanish fleet and lost only one sailor (to heat stroke). On land, the story was different. On the eve of war, the U.S. Army consisted of only 26,000 troops. These soldiers were skilled at skirmishing with Indians but ill-prepared and ill-equipped for all-out war. A force of 80,000 Spanish regulars awaited them in Cuba, with another 50,000 in reserve in Spain. Congress immediately increased the army to 62,000 and called for an additional 125,000 volunteers. The response to this call was astounding, but outfitting, training, and transporting the new recruits overwhelmed the army's capacities. Its standard-issue, blue flannel uniforms proved too heavy for fighting in tropical Cuba. Rations were so poor that soldiers referred to one common item as "embalmed beef." Most of the volunteers had to make do with ancient Civil War rifles that still used black, rather than smokeless, powder. The initial invasion force of 16,000 men took more than five days to sail the short distance from Tampa, Florida, to Daiquiri, Cuba. Moreover, the army was unprepared for the effects of malaria and other tropical diseases.

That the Cuban revolutionaries were predominantly black also came as a shock to the U.S. forces. In their attempts to arouse support for the Cuban cause, U.S. newspapers had portrayed Cuban rebels as fundamentally similar to white Americans. They were described as intelligent, civilized, and democratic, possessing an "Anglo-Saxon tenacity of purpose." And, they were "fully nine-tenths" white, according to one report. The Spanish oppressors, by contrast, were depicted as dark-complexioned— "dark cruel eyes, dark swaggering men" wrote author Sherwood Anderson—and as possessing the characteristics of their "dark race": barbarism, cruelty, and indolence. The U.S. troops' first encounters with Cuban and Spanish forces challenged these stereotypes. Their Cuban allies appeared poorly outfitted, rough in their manners, and primarily black-skinned. The Spanish soldiers appeared well disciplined, tough in battle, and light complexioned.

The Cuban rebels were actually skilled guerrilla fighters, but racial prejudice prevented most U.S. soldiers and reporters from crediting their military expertise. Instead, they judged the Cubans harshly—as primitive, savage, and incapable of self-control or self-government. White U.S. troops preferred not to fight alongside the Cubans; increasingly, they refused to coordinate strategy with them.

At first, the U.S. Army's logistical unpreparedness and its racial misconceptions did little to diminish the soldiers' hunger for a good fight. No one was more eager for battle than Theodore Roosevelt, who, along with Colonel Leonard Wood, led a volunteer cavalry unit

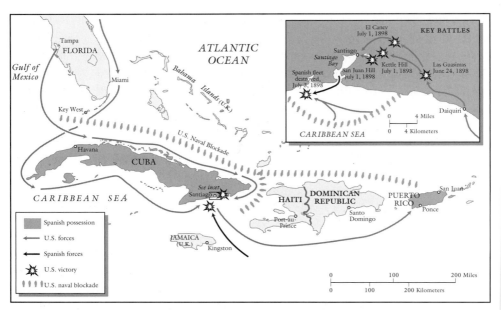

Map 22.1   Spanish-American War in Cuba, 1898   This map shows the following: the routes taken by U.S. ships transporting troops from Florida to Cuba; the concentration of troop landings and battles around Santiago, Cuba; and a U.S. naval blockade, stretching hundreds of miles from Puerto Rico to Cuba, that attempted to keep the Spanish troops in Cuba and Puerto Rico from being reinforced.
View an animated version of this map or related maps at http://www.thomsonedu.com/history/murrin.

composed of Ivy League gentlemen, western cowboys, sheriffs, prospectors, Indians, and small numbers of Hispanics and ethnic European Americans. Roosevelt's **Rough Riders,** as the unit came to be known, landed with the invasion force and played an active role in the three battles fought in the hills surrounding Santiago. Their most famous action, the one on which Roosevelt would build his lifelong reputation as a military hero, was a furious charge up Kettle Hill into the teeth of Spanish defenses. Roosevelt's bravery was stunning, although his judgment was faulty. Nearly 100 men were killed or wounded in the charge. Reports of Roosevelt's bravery overshadowed the equally brave performance of other troops, notably the **9th and 10th Negro Cavalries,** which played a pivotal role in clearing away Spanish fortifications on Kettle Hill and allowing Roosevelt's Rough Riders to make their charge. One Rough Rider commented: "If it had not been for the Negro cavalry, the Rough Riders would have been exterminated." Another added: "I am a Southerner by birth, and I never thought much of the colored man. But . . . I never saw such fighting as those Tenth Cavalry men did. They didn't seem to know what fear was, and their battle hymn was 'There'll be a hot time in the old town tonight.'" The 24th and 25th Negro Infantry Regiments performed equally vital tasks in the U.S. Army's conquest of the adjacent San Juan Hill.

Theodore Roosevelt saw the Rough Rider regiment that he commanded in the Spanish-American War as a melting pot of different groups of white Americans. Combat, he further believed, would forge these many groups into one, as war had always done in the American past. African Americans were the group most conspicuously absent from the Rough Rider mix. Yet the fury of the fighting on Kettle Hill and San Juan Hill so scrambled the white and black regiments that by the time the troops reached the San Juan summit, they were racially intermixed. Combat had brought blacks into the great American melting pot, a phenomenon that Roosevelt celebrated at the time. The black troops, he declared, were "an excellent breed of Yankee," and no "Rough Rider will ever forget," he added, "the tie that binds us to the Ninth and Tenth Cavalry."

But Roosevelt did not truly believe that blacks were the equals of whites or that they could be absorbed into the American nation. So, a few months after returning home, he began downplaying the role of black troops and questioned their ability to fight. The heroic role of black soldiers disappeared not only from Roosevelt's own memory but also from accounts and illustrations of the great charge. The attack on black fighting abilities would become so widespread that by the start of the First World War, the U.S. military had largely excluded black troops from combat roles. Thus, an episode that had demonstrated the possibility of interracial cooperation in America ended in the hardening of racial boundaries.

The taking of Kettle Hill, San Juan Hill, and other high ground surrounding Santiago gave the U.S. forces a substantial advantage over the Spanish defenders in Santiago. Nevertheless, logistical and medical problems nearly did them in. The troops were short of food, ammunition, and medical facilities. Their ranks were devastated by malaria, typhoid, and dysentery, and more than 5,000 soldiers died from disease. Even the normally ebullient Roosevelt was close to despair: "We are within measurable distance of a terrible military disaster," he wrote his friend Henry Cabot Lodge on July 3.

Fortunately, the Spanish had lost the will to fight. On the very day Roosevelt wrote to Lodge, Spain's Atlantic fleet tried to retreat from Santiago harbor and was promptly destroyed by a U.S. fleet. The Spanish army in Santiago surrendered on July 16; on July 18, the Spanish government asked for peace. While negotiations for an armistice proceeded, U.S. forces overran the neighboring island of Puerto Rico. On August 12, the U.S. and Spanish governments agreed to an armistice, but before the news could reach the Philippines, the United States had captured Manila and had taken prisoner 13,000 Spanish soldiers.

The armistice required Spain to relinquish its claim to Cuba, cede Puerto Rico and the Pacific island of Guam to the United States, and tolerate the American occupation of Manila until a peace conference could be convened in Paris on October 1, 1898. At that conference, American diplomats startled their Spanish counterparts by demanding that Spain also cede the Philippines to the United States. After two months of stalling, the Spanish government agreed to relinquish their coveted Pacific colony for $20 million. The transaction was sealed by the Treaty of Paris on December 10, 1898.

© Bettmann/CORBIS

Rough Riders and 10th Cavalry   Roosevelt poses with his Rough Riders (above) while members of the 10th Cavalry appear below. Both groups played pivotal roles in the battles of San Juan and Kettle Hills, but America would celebrate only the Rough Riders, not the black cavalrymen.

© The Granger Collection, New York

The United States Becomes a World Power

Focus Question
What different mechanisms of control did the United States use to achieve its aims in Hawaii, Cuba, the Philippines, Puerto Rico, and China?

America's initial war aim had been to oust the Spanish from Cuba—an aim that both imperialists and anti-imperialists supported, but for different reasons. Imperialists hoped to incorporate Cuba into a new American empire; anti-imperialists hoped to see the Cubans gain their independence. But only the imperialists condoned the U.S. acquisition of Puerto Rico, Guam, and particularly the Philippines, which they viewed as integral to the extension of U.S. interests into Asia. Soon after the war began, President McKinley had cast his lot with the imperialists. First, he annexed Hawaii, giving the United States permanent control of Pearl Harbor. Next, he set his sights on setting up a U.S. naval base at Manila. Never before had the United States sought such a large military presence outside the Western Hemisphere.

In a departure of equal importance, McKinley announced his intent to administer much of this newly acquired territory as U.S. colonies. Virtually all territory the United States had obtained in the 19th century had been part of the North American continent. These lands had been settled by Americans, who had eventually petitioned for statehood. By 1900, most of these territories had been admitted to the Union with the same rights as existing states; others, such as New Mexico, Arizona, and Oklahoma, would soon acquire statehood status. In the case of the new overseas territories, however, only Hawaii would be allowed to follow this traditional path toward statehood. There, the powerful U.S. sugar plantation owners prevailed on Congress to pass an act in 1900 extending U.S. citizenship to all Hawaiian citizens and putting Hawaii on the road to statehood. No such influential group of Americans resided in the Philippines. The country was made a U.S. colony and placed under a U.S. administration that took its orders from Washington rather than from the Filipino people. Such colonization was necessary, in the eyes of American imperialists, to prevent other powers, such as Japan and Germany, from gaining a foothold somewhere in the 400-island archipelago and launching attacks on the U.S. naval base in Manila.

The McKinley administration might have taken a different course. The United States might have negotiated an arrangement with **Emilio Aguinaldo,** the leader of an anticolonial movement in the Philippines, that would have given the Philippines independence in exchange for a U.S. naval base at Manila. An American fleet stationed there would have been able to protect both American interests and the fledgling Philippine nation from predatory assaults by Japan, Germany, or Britain. Alternatively, the United States might have annexed the Philippines outright and offered Filipinos U.S. citizenship as the first step toward statehood. McKinley and his supporters, however, believed that the "inferior" Filipino people lacked the capacity for self-government. The United States would undertake a solemn mission to "civilize" the Filipinos and thereby prepare them for independence,

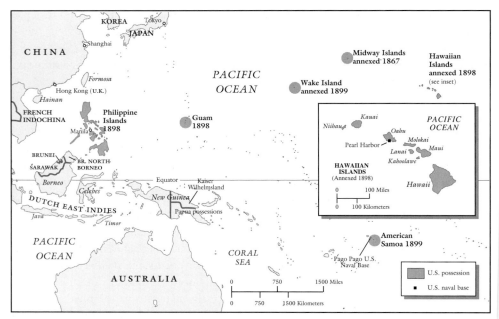

Map 22.2 American South Pacific Empire, 1900 By 1900, the American South Pacific empire consisted of a series of strategically located islands with superior harbor facilities, stretching from the Hawaiian Islands and Samoa in the middle of the Pacific to the Philippines on the ocean's western edge.

but until that mission was complete, the Philippines would submit to rule by presidentially appointed U.S. governors.

The Debate over the Treaty of Paris

The proposed acquisition of the Philippines aroused opposition both in the United States and in the Philippines. The Anti-Imperialist League, strong in the Northeast, enlisted the support of several elder statesmen in McKinley's own party, as well as the former Democratic President Grover Cleveland, the industrialist Andrew Carnegie, and the labor leader Samuel Gompers. William Jennings Bryan, meanwhile, marshaled a vigorous anti-imperialist protest among Democrats in the South and West, while Mark Twain, William James, William Dean Howells, and other men of letters lent the cause their prestige. Some anti-imperialists believed that subjugating the Filipinos would violate the nation's most precious principle: the right of all people to independence and self-government. Moreover, they feared that the military and diplomatic establishment needed to administer the colony would threaten political liberties at home.

Other anti-imperialists were motivated more by self-interest than by democratic ideals. U.S. sugar producers, for example, feared competition from Filipino producers. Trade unionists worried that poor Filipino workers would flood the U.S. labor market and depress wage rates. Some businessmen warned that the costs of maintaining an imperial outpost would exceed any economic benefits that the colony might produce. Many Democrats, meanwhile, simply wanted to gain partisan advantage by opposing the Republican administration's foreign policy. Still other anti-imperialists feared the contaminating effects of contact with "inferior" Asian races.

The contrasting motivations of the anti-imperialists weakened their opposition. Even so, they almost dealt McKinley and his fellow imperialists a defeat in the U.S. Senate. On February 6, 1899, the Senate voted 57 to 27 in favor of the Treaty of Paris, only one vote beyond the minimum two-thirds majority required for ratification. Two last-minute developments may have brought victory. First, William Jennings Bryan, in the days before the vote, abandoned his opposition and announced his support for the treaty. (He would later explain that he had decided for ratification in order to end the war with Spain, intending to continue his work for Filipino independence through diplomatic means.) Second, on the eve of the vote, Filipinos rose in revolt against the U.S. army of occupation. With another war looming and the lives of American soldiers imperiled, a few senators who had been reluctant to vote for the treaty may have felt obligated to support the president.

The American-Filipino War

The acquisition of the Philippines immediately embroiled the United States in a long, brutal war to subdue the Filipino rebels. In four years of fighting, more than 120,000 American soldiers served in the Philippines and more than 4,200 of them died. The war cost $160 million, or eight times what the United States had paid Spain to acquire the archipelago. The war brought Americans face-to-face with an unpleasant truth: that American actions in the Philippines were virtually indistinguishable from Spain's actions in Cuba. Like Spain, the United States refused to acknowledge a people's aspiration for self-rule. Like "Butcher" Weyler, American generals permitted their soldiers to use savage tactics. Whole communities suspected of harboring guerrillas were driven into concentration camps, and their houses, farms, and livestock were destroyed. American soldiers killed so many Filipino rebels (whom they called "goo-goos") that the ratio of Filipino dead to wounded reached 15 to 1, a statistic that made the American Civil War, in which one soldier had died for every five wounded, seem relatively humane. One New York infantryman wrote home that his unit had killed 1,000 Filipinos—men, women, and children—in retaliation for the murder of a single American soldier: "I am in my glory when I can sight my gun on some dark skin and pull the trigger," he exclaimed. A total of 15,000 Filipino soldiers died in the fighting. Estimates of total Filipino deaths from gunfire, starvation, and disease range from 50,000 to 200,000.

The United States finally gained the upper hand in the war after General Arthur MacArthur (father of Douglas) was appointed commander of the islands in 1900. MacArthur did not lessen the war's ferocity, but he understood that it could not be won by guns alone. He offered amnesty to Filipino guerrillas who agreed to surrender, and he cultivated close relations with the islands' economic elites. McKinley supported this effort to build a Filipino constituency sympathetic to the U.S. presence. To that end, he sent

William Howard Taft to the islands in 1900 to establish a civilian government. In 1901, Taft became the colony's first "governor-general" and declared that he intended to prepare the Filipinos for independence. He transferred many governmental functions to Filipino control and launched a program of public works (roads, bridges, schools) that would give the Philippines the infrastructure necessary for economic development and political independence. By 1902, this dual strategy of ruthless war against those who had taken up arms and concessions to those who were willing to live under benevolent American rule had crushed the revolt. Though sporadic fighting continued until 1913, Americans had secured control of the Philippines. The explicit commitment of the United States to Philippine independence (a promise that was deferred until 1946), together with an extensive program of internal improvements, eased the nation's conscience.

Controlling Cuba and Puerto Rico

Helping the Cubans achieve independence had been a major rationalization for the war against Spain. Even so, in 1900, when General Leonard Wood, now commander of U.S. forces in Cuba, authorized a constitutional convention to write the laws for a Cuban republic, the McKinley administration made clear it would not easily relinquish control of the island. At McKinley's urging, the U.S. Congress attached to a 1901 army appropriations bill the **Platt Amendment** (Orville Platt was the Republican senator from Connecticut), delineating three conditions for Cuban independence: (1) Cuba would not be permitted to make treaties with foreign powers; (2) the United States would have broad authority to intervene in Cuban political and economic affairs; and (3) Cuba would sell or lease land to the United States for naval stations. The delegates to Cuba's constitutional convention were so outraged by these conditions that they refused even to vote on them. But the dependence of Cuba's vital sugar industry on the U.S. market and the continuing presence of a U.S. army on Cuban soil rendered resistance futile. In 1901, by a vote of 15 to 11, the delegates reluctantly wrote the Platt conditions into their constitution. "There is, of course, little or no independence left Cuba under the Platt Amendment," Wood candidly admitted to his friend Theodore Roosevelt, who had recently succeeded the assassinated McKinley as president.

Cuba's status, in truth, differed little from that of the Philippines. Both were colonies of the United States. In the case of Cuba, economic dependence closely followed political subjugation. Between 1898 and 1914, U.S. trade with Cuba increased more than tenfold (from $27 million to $300 million), while investments more than quadrupled (from $50 million to $220 million). In 1903, the United States compelled Cuba to lease it 45 square miles of land and water on the island nation's southeast coast. There the United States built the U.S. Naval Station at Guantanamo Bay, a facility that it maintains to this day. The United States also intervened in Cuban political affairs five times between 1906 and 1921 to protect its economic interests and those of the indigenous ruling class with whom it had become closely allied. The economic, political, and military control that the United States imposed on Cuba would fuel anti-American sentiment there for years to come.

Puerto Rico received somewhat different treatment. The United States did not think independence appropriate, even though under Spanish rule the island had enjoyed a large measure of political autonomy and a parliamentary form of government. Nor did the United States follow its Cuban strategy by granting Puerto Rico nominal independence under informal economic and political controls. Instead, it annexed the island outright with the Foraker Act (1900). Unlike every previous annexation authorized by Congress since 1788, this act contained no provision for making the inhabitants of Puerto Rico citizens of the United States. Instead, Puerto Rico was designated an "unincorporated" territory, which meant that Congress would dictate the island's government and specify the rights of its inhabitants. Puerto Ricans were allowed no role in designing their government, nor was their consent to its establishment sought. With the Foraker Act, Congress had, in effect, invented a new, imperial mechanism for ensuring sovereignty over lands deemed vital to U.S. economic and military security. The U.S. Supreme Court upheld the constitutionality of this mechanism in a series of historic decisions, known as the Insular Cases, in the years from 1901 to 1904.

In some respects, Puerto Rico fared better than "independent" Cuba. Puerto Ricans were granted U.S. citizenship in 1917 and won the right to elect their own governor in 1947. Still, Puerto Ricans enjoyed fewer political rights than Americans in the 48 states. Moreover, throughout the 20th century, they endured a poverty rate far exceeding that of

"A Philippine Album: American Era Photographs" by Jonathan Best. (Bookmark, Manila 1998)

The "Water Cure" in the Philippines   This extraordinary photograph shows U.S. soldiers forcing water into the mouth of a Filipino guerrilla to the point where it would overflow his esophagus and pour into his breathing channels, creating the sensation of drowning. It reveals U.S. forces using brutal tactics to break down the resistance of their Filipino opponents.

the mainland. As late as 1948, for example, three-fourths of Puerto Rican households subsisted on $1,000 or less annually, a figure below the U.S. poverty line. In its skewed distribution of wealth and its lack of industrial development, Puerto Rico resembled the poorly developed nations of Central and South America more than it did the affluent country that took over its government in 1900.

The subjugation of Cuba and the annexation of Puerto Rico troubled Americans far less than the U.S. takeover in the Philippines. Since the first articulation of the Monroe Doctrine in 1823, the United States had, in effect, claimed the Western Hemisphere as its sphere of influence. Within that sphere, many Americans believed, the United States possessed the right to act unilaterally to protect its interests. Before 1900, most of its actions (with the exception of the Mexican War) had been designed to limit the influence of European powers—Britain, France, Russia, and Spain—on the countries of the hemisphere. After 1900, however, the United States assumed a more aggressive role, seizing land, overturning governments it did not like, and forcing its economic and political policies on weaker neighbors in order to turn the Caribbean Sea into what policy makers called (with the example of ancient Rome in mind) an American Mediterranean.

China and the "Open Door"

Except for the Philippines and Guam, the United States made no effort to take control of Asian lands. Such a policy might well have triggered war with other world powers that were already well established in the area. Nor were Americans prepared to tolerate the financial and political costs Asian conquest would have entailed. The United States opted for a diplomatic rather than a military strategy to achieve its foreign policy objectives. For China, in 1899 and 1900, it proposed the policy of the "open door."

The United States was concerned that the actions of the other world powers in China would block its own efforts to open up China's markets to American goods. Britain, Germany, Japan, Russia, and France each coveted their own chunk of China, where they could monopolize trade, exploit cheap labor, and establish military bases. By the 1890s, each of these powers was building a sphere of influence, either by wringing economic and territorial concessions from the weak Chinese government or by seizing outright the land and trading privileges they desired.

To prevent China's breakup and to preserve U.S. economic access to the whole of China, McKinley's secretary of state, John Hay, sent **"open door" notes** to the major world powers. The notes asked each power to open its Chinese sphere of influence to the merchants of other nations and to grant them reasonable harbor fees and railroad rates. Hay also asked each power to respect China's sovereignty by enforcing Chinese tariff duties in the territory it controlled.

None of the world powers embraced either of Hay's requests, although Britain and Japan gave provisional assent. France, Germany, Russia, and Italy responded evasively, indicating their support for the Open Door policy in theory but insisting that they could not implement it until all of the other powers had done so. Hay put the best face on their

Challenges to America's Open Door China Policy   Although imperial powers had defeated the Chinese Boxers, here depicted as a slain Chinese dragon, this cartoon suggests that they would soon be fighting each other for the spoils of victory. Appearing in the British magazine, *Puck,* the cartoon presents Russia (the bear) and Britain (the lion) as the two principal antagonists, with menacing France (the fox) and Japan (mountain cat) snarling in the foreground, and various birds of prey (the United States, Germany, Austria, and Italy) hovering over the kill.

responses by declaring that all of the powers had agreed to observe his Open Door principles and that he regarded their assent as "final and definitive." Americans took Hay's bluff as evidence that the United States had triumphed diplomatically over its rivals. The rivals may have been impressed by Hay's diplomacy, but whether they intended to uphold the United States' Open Door policy was not at all clear.

The first challenge to Hay's policy came from the Chinese. In May 1900, a Chinese organization, colloquially known as the **"Boxers,"** sparked an uprising to rid China of all "foreign devils" and foreign influences. Hundreds of Europeans were killed, as were many Chinese men and women who had converted to Christianity. When the Boxers laid siege to the foreign legations in Beijing and cut off communication between that city and the outside world, the imperial powers raised an expeditionary force to rescue the diplomats and punish the Chinese rebels. The force, which included 5,000 U.S. soldiers, rushed over from the Philippines, broke the Beijing siege in August, and ended the Boxer Rebellion soon thereafter.

Hay feared that other major powers would use the rebellion as a reason to demand greater control over Chinese territory. He sent out a second round of Open Door notes, now asking each power to respect China's political independence and territorial integrity, in addition to guaranteeing unrestricted access to its markets. Impressed by America's show of military strength and worried that the Chinese rebels might strike again, the imperialist rivals responded more favorably to this second round of notes. Britain, France, and Germany endorsed Hay's policy outright. With that support, Hay was able to check Russian and Japanese designs on Chinese territory. Significantly, when the powers decided that the Chinese government should pay them reparations for their property and personnel losses during the Boxer Rebellion, Hay convinced them to accept payment in cash rather than in territory. By keeping China intact and open to free trade, the United States had achieved a major foreign policy victory. Americans began to see themselves as China's savior as well.

Theodore Roosevelt, Geopolitician

Focus Question
What were the similarities and differences in the foreign policies of Theodore Roosevelt, William Howard Taft, and Woodrow Wilson?

Roosevelt had been a driving force in the transformation of U.S. foreign policy during the McKinley Administration. As assistant secretary of the navy, as a military hero, as a speaker and writer, and then as vice president, Roosevelt worked tirelessly to remake the country into one of the world's great powers. He believed that the Americans were a racially superior people destined for supremacy in economic and political affairs. He did not assume, however, that international supremacy would automatically accrue to the United States. A nation, like an individual, had to strive for greatness and cultivate physical and mental fitness; it had to build a military force that could convincingly project power overseas; and it had to be prepared to fight. All great nations, Roosevelt declared, ultimately depended on the skill and dedication of their warriors.

Roosevelt's appetite for a good fight caused many people to rue the ascension of this "cowboy" to the White House after McKinley's assassination in 1901. But behind his blustery exterior lay a shrewd analyst of international relations. As much as he craved power for himself and the nation, he understood that the United States could not rule every portion of the globe through military or economic means. Consequently, he sought a balance of power among the industrial nations through negotiation rather than war. Such a balance would enable each imperial power to safeguard its key interests and contribute to world peace and progress. **(See Map 22.3, Colonial Possessions, 1900, in the color insert following page 912.)**

Absent from Roosevelt's geopolitical thinking was concern for the interests of less powerful nations. Roosevelt had little patience with the claims to sovereignty of small countries or the human rights of weak peoples. In his eyes, the peoples of Latin America, Asia (with the exception of Japan), and Africa were racially inferior and thus incapable of self-government or industrial progress. They were better suited to subservience and subsistence than to independence and affluence.

The Roosevelt Corollary

Ensuring U.S. dominance in the Western Hemisphere ranked high on Roosevelt's list of foreign policy objectives. In 1904, he issued a "corollary" to the Monroe Doctrine, which had asserted the right of the United States to keep European powers from meddling in hemispheric affairs. In his corollary, Roosevelt declared that the United States possessed a further right: the right to intervene in the domestic affairs of nations in the Western Hemisphere to quell disorder and forestall European intervention. The **Roosevelt corollary** formalized a policy that the United States had already deployed against Cuba and Puerto Rico in 1900 and 1901. Subsequent events in Venezuela and the Dominican Republic had further convinced Roosevelt of the need to expand the scope of U.S. intervention in hemispheric affairs.

Both Venezuela and the Dominican Republic were controlled by dictators who had defaulted on debts owed to European banks. Their delinquency prompted a German-led European naval blockade and bombardment of Venezuela in 1902 and a threatened invasion of the Dominican Republic by Italy and France in 1903. The United States forced the German navy to retreat from the Venezuelan coast in 1903. In the Dominican Republic, after a revolution had chased the dictator from power, the United States assumed control of the nation's customs collections in 1905 and refinanced the Dominican national debt through U.S. bankers.

The willingness of European bankers to loan money to Latin America's corrupt regimes had created the possibility that the countries ruled by these regimes would suffer bankruptcy, social turmoil, and foreign intervention. The United States, under Roosevelt, did not hesitate to intervene to make sure that loans were repaid and social stability was restored. But rarely in Roosevelt's tenure did the United States show a willingness to help the people who had suffered under these regimes establish democratic institutions or achieve social justice. When Cubans seeking true national independence rebelled against their puppet government in 1906, the United States sent in the Marines to silence them. (**See Map 22.4, United States Presence in Latin America, 1895–1934, in the color insert following page 912.**)

The Panama Canal

Roosevelt's varied interests in Latin America embraced the building of a canal across Central America. The president had long believed, along with Admiral Mahan, that the nation needed a way of moving its ships swiftly from the Pacific Ocean to the Atlantic Ocean, and back again. Central America's narrow width, especially in its southern half, made it the logical place to build a canal. In fact, a French company had obtained land rights and had begun construction of a canal across the Colombian province of Panama in the 1880s. But even though a "mere" 40 miles of land separated the two oceans, the French were stymied by technological difficulties and by the financial costs of literally moving mountains. Moreover, French doctors found they were unable to check the spread of malaria and yellow fever among their workers. By the time Roosevelt entered the White House in 1901, the French Panama Company had gone bankrupt.

Roosevelt was not deterred by the French failure. He first presided over the signing of the Hay-Pauncefote Treaty with Great Britain in 1901, releasing the United States from an

1850 agreement that prohibited either country from building a Central American canal without the other's participation. He then instructed his advisers to develop plans for a canal across Nicaragua. The Panamanian route chosen by the French was shorter than the proposed Nicaraguan route, and the canal begun by the French was 40 percent complete, but the French company wanted $109 million for it, more than the United States was willing to pay. In 1902, however, the company reduced the price to $40 million, a sum that Congress deemed appropriate. Secretary of State Hay quickly negotiated an agreement with Tomas Herran, the Colombian chargé d'affaires in Washington. The agreement, formalized in the Hay-Herran Treaty, accorded the United States a six-mile-wide strip across **Panama** on which to build the **canal.** Colombia was to receive a onetime $10 million payment and annual rent of $250,000.

The Colombian legislature, however, rejected the proposed payment as insufficient and sent a new ambassador to the United States with instructions to ask for a onetime payment of $20 million and a share of the $40 million being paid to the French company. Actually, the Colombians (not unreasonably) were hoping to stall negotiations until 1904, when they would regain the rights to the canal zone and consequently to the $40 million sale price promised to the French company.

As negotiations failed to deliver the result he desired, Roosevelt encouraged the Panamanians to revolt against Colombian rule. Panamanians had staged several rebellions in the previous 25 years, all of which had failed, but the 1903 rebellion succeeded, mainly because a U.S. naval force prevented the Colombian government from landing troops in its Panama province. Meanwhile, the U.S.S. *Nashville* put U.S. troops ashore to help the new nation secure its independence. The United States formally recognized Panama as a sovereign state only two days after the rebellion against Colombia began.

Philippe Bunau-Varilla, a director of the French company from which the United States had bought the rights to the canal, declared himself Panama's diplomatic representative, even though he was a French citizen operating out of a Wall Street law firm and hadn't set foot in Panama in 15 years. Before the true Panamanian delegation (appointed by the new Panamanian government) even reached the United States for negotiations over the canal, Bunau-Varilla had gone to Washington, where he and Secretary of State Hay signed the Hay–Bunau-Varilla Treaty (1903). The treaty granted the United States a 10-mile-wide canal zone in Panama in return for the package Colombia had rejected—$10 million down and $250,000 annually. Thus the United States secured its canal, not by dealing with the newly installed Panamanian government, but with Bunau-Varilla's French company. When the Panamanian delegation arrived in Washington and read the treaty, one of them became so enraged that he knocked Bunau-Varilla cold. Under the circumstances, however, the Panamanian delegation's hands were tied. If it objected to the counterfeit treaty, the United States might withdraw its troops from Panama, leaving the new country at the mercy of Colombia. The instrument through which the United States secured the Canal Zone is known in Panamanian history as "the treaty which no Panamanian signed," and it bedeviled relations between the two countries for much of the 20th century.

Roosevelt's severing of Panama from Colombia prompted angry protests in Congress. The Hearst newspapers decried the Panama foray as "nefarious" and "a quite unexampled instance of foul play in American politics." Roosevelt was not perturbed. Elihu Root (secretary of state in Roosevelt's second administration), after hearing Roosevelt defend his action before a meeting of his cabinet, jokingly told the president, "You have shown that you were accused of seduction and you have conclusively proved that you were guilty of rape." Roosevelt later gloated, "I took the Canal Zone and let Congress debate!"

Roosevelt turned the building of the canal into a test of American ingenuity and willpower. Engineers overcame every obstacle; doctors developed drugs to combat malaria and yellow fever; armies of construction workers "made the dirt fly." The canal remains a testament to the labor of some 30,000 workers, imported mainly from the West Indies, who, over a 10-year period, labored 10 hours a day, 6 days a week, for 10 cents an hour. Roosevelt visited the canal site in 1906, the first American president to travel overseas while in office. When the canal was triumphantly opened to shipping in 1914, the British ambassador James Bryce described it as "the greatest liberty Man has ever taken with Nature." The canal shortened the voyage from San Francisco to New York by more than 8,000 miles and significantly enhanced the international prestige of the United States. The

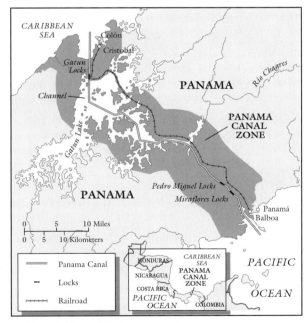

Map 22.5 Panama Canal Zone, 1914 This map shows the route of the completed canal through Panama and the 10-mile-wide zone surrounding it that the United States controlled. The inset map locates the Canal Zone in the context of Central and South America.

strategic importance of the canal, in turn, made the United States even more determined to preserve political order in Central America and the Caribbean.

In 1921, the United States paid the Colombian government $25 million as compensation for its loss of Panama. Panama waited more than 70 years, however, to regain control of the 10-mile-wide strip of land that Bunau-Varilla, in connivance with the U.S. government, had bargained away in 1903. President Jimmy Carter signed a treaty in 1977 providing for the reintegration of the Canal Zone into Panama, and the canal was transferred to Panama in 2000.

Keeping the Peace in East Asia

In East Asia, Roosevelt strove to preserve the Open Door policy in China and the balance of power throughout the region. The chief threats came from Russia and Japan, both of whom wanted to seize large chunks of China. At first, Russian expansion into Manchuria and Korea prompted Roosevelt to support Japan's 1904 attack on the Russian Pacific fleet anchored at Port Arthur, China. Once the ruinous effects of the war on Russia became clear, however, Roosevelt entered into secret negotiations to arrange a peace. He invited representatives of Japan and Russia to Portsmouth, New Hampshire, and prevailed on them to negotiate a compromise. The settlement favored Japan by perpetuating its control over most of the territories it had won during the brief **Russo-Japanese War.** Its chief prize was Korea, which became a protectorate of Japan, but Japan also acquired the southern part of Sakhalin Island, Port Arthur, and the South Manchurian Railroad. Russia avoided paying Japan a huge indemnity and it retained Siberia, thus preserving its role as an East Asian power. Finally, Roosevelt protected China's territorial integrity by inducing the armies of both Russia and Japan to leave Manchuria. Roosevelt's success in ending the Russo-Japanese War won him the Nobel Prize for Peace in 1906; he was the first American to earn that award.

Although Roosevelt succeeded in negotiating a peace between these two world powers, he subsequently ignored, and sometimes encouraged, challenges to the sovereignty of weaker Asian nations. In a secret agreement with Japan (the Taft-Katsura Agreement of 1905), for example, the United States agreed that Japan could dominate Korea in return for a Japanese promise not to attack the Philippines. And in the Root-Takahira Agreement of 1908, the United States tacitly reversed its earlier stand on the inviolability of Chinese borders by recognizing Japanese expansion into southern Manchuria.

In Roosevelt's eyes, the overriding need to maintain peace with Japan justified ignoring the claims of Korea and, increasingly, of China. Roosevelt admired Japan's industrial and military might and regarded Japanese expansion into East Asia as a natural expression of its imperial ambition. The task of American diplomacy, he believed, was first to allow the Japanese to build a secure sphere of influence in East Asia (much as the United States had done in Central America and the Caribbean), and second to encourage them to join the United States in pursuing peace rather than war. This was a delicate diplomatic task that required both sensitivity and strength, especially when anti-Japanese agitation broke out in California in 1906.

North Wind Picture Archive

Anti-Asian Hysteria in San Francisco   In 1906, in the midst of a wave of anti-Asian prejudice in California, the San Francisco school board ordered the segregation of all Asian schoolchildren. Here, a nine-year-old Japanese student submits an application for admission to a public primary school and is refused by the principal, Miss M. E. Dean.

White Californians had long feared the presence of East Asian immigrants (see chapter 20). They had pressured Congress into passing the Chinese Exclusion Act of 1882, which ended most Chinese immigration to the United States. They next turned their racism on Japanese immigrants, whose numbers in California had reached 24,000. In 1906, the San Francisco school board ordered the segregation of Asian schoolchildren, so that they would not "contaminate" white children. In 1907, the California legislature debated a law to end Japanese immigration to the state. Anti-Asian riots erupted in San Francisco and Los Angeles, encouraged in part by hysterical stories in the press about the "Yellow Peril."

Outraged militarists in Japan began talking of a possible war with the United States. Roosevelt assured the Japanese government that he too was appalled by the Californians' behavior. In 1907, he reached a **"gentlemen's agreement"** with the Japanese, by which the Tokyo government promised to halt the immigration of Japanese adult male laborers to the United States in return for Roosevelt's pledge to end anti-Japanese discrimination in California. Roosevelt did his part by persuading the San Francisco school board to rescind its segregation ordinance.

At the same time, Roosevelt worried that the Tokyo government would interpret his sensitivity to Japanese honor as weakness. So he ordered the main part of the U.S. fleet, consisting of 16 battleships, to embark on a 45,000-mile world tour, including a splashy stop in Tokyo Bay. Many Americans deplored the cost of the tour and feared that the appearance of the U.S. Navy in a Japanese port would provoke military retaliation. Roosevelt brushed his critics aside, and, true to his prediction, the Japanese were impressed by the **Great White Fleet's** show of strength. Their response seemed to lend validity to the African proverb Roosevelt often invoked: "Speak softly and carry a big stick."

In fact, Roosevelt's handling of Japan was arguably the most impressive aspect of his foreign policy. Unlike many other Americans, he refused to let racist attitudes cloud his thinking. He knew when to make concessions and when to stand firm. His policies lessened the prospect of a war with Japan while preserving a strong U.S. presence in East Asia.

William Howard Taft, Dollar Diplomat

William Howard Taft brought impressive foreign policy credentials to the job of president. He had gained valuable experience in colonial administration as the first governor-general of the Philippines. As Roosevelt's secretary of war and chief negotiator for the Taft-Katsura agreement of 1905, he had learned a great deal about conducting diplomacy with imperialist rivals. Yet Taft lacked Roosevelt's grasp of balance-of-power politics and capacity for leadership in foreign affairs. Furthermore, Taft's secretary of state, Philander C. Knox, a corporation lawyer from Pittsburgh, lacked diplomatic expertise. Knox's conduct of foreign policy seemed directed almost entirely toward expanding opportunities for corporate investment overseas, a disposition that prompted critics to deride his policies as **"dollar diplomacy."**

Taft and Knox believed that U.S. investments would effectively substitute "dollars for bullets," and thus offer a more peaceful and less coercive way of maintaining stability and order. Taking a swipe at Roosevelt's "big stick" policy, Taft announced that "modern diplomacy is commercial."

The inability of Taft and Knox to grasp the complexities of power politics, however, led to a diplomatic reversal in East Asia. Prodded by banker associates, Knox sought to expand American economic activities in China—even in Manchuria, where they encroached on the Japanese sphere of influence. In 1911, Knox proposed that a syndicate of European and American bankers buy the Japanese-controlled South Manchurian Railroad to open up North China to international trade. Japan reacted by signing a friendship treaty with Russia, its former enemy, which signaled their joint determination to exclude American, British, and French goods from Manchurian markets. Knox's plan to purchase the railroad collapsed, and the United States' Open Door policy suffered a serious blow. Knox's further efforts to increase American trade with Central and South China triggered further hostile responses from the Japanese and the Russians and contributed to the collapse of the Chinese government and the onset of the Chinese Revolution in 1911.

Dollar diplomacy worked better in the Caribbean, where no major power contested U.S. policy. Knox encouraged U.S. investment. Companies such as United Fruit of Boston, which established extensive banana plantations in Costa Rica and Honduras, grew powerful enough to influence both the economies and the governments of Central

American countries. When political turmoil threatened their investments, the United States simply sent in its troops. Thus, when Nicaraguan dictator José Santos Zelaya reportedly began negotiating with a European country to build a second trans-Isthmian canal in 1910, a force of U.S. Marines toppled his regime. Marines landed again in 1912 when Zelaya's successor, Adolfo Diaz, angered Nicaraguans with his pro-American policies. This time the Marines were instructed to keep the Diaz regime in power. Except for a brief period in 1925, U.S. troops would remain in Nicaragua continuously from 1912 until 1933. Under Taft, the United States continued to do whatever American policy makers deemed necessary to bolster friendly governments and maintain order in Latin America.

Woodrow Wilson, Struggling Idealist

Woodrow Wilson's foreign policy in the Caribbean initially appeared no different from that of his Republican predecessors. In 1915, the United States sent troops to Haiti to put down a revolution; they remained as an army of occupation for 21 years. In 1916, when the people of the Dominican Republic (who shared the island of Hispaniola with the Haitians) refused to accept a treaty making them more or less a protectorate of the United States, Wilson forced them to accept the rule of a U.S. military government. When German influence in the Danish West Indies began to expand, Wilson purchased the islands from Denmark, renamed them the Virgin Islands, and added them to the U.S. Caribbean empire. By the time Wilson left office in 1921, he had intervened militarily in the Caribbean more often than any American president before him.

Wilson's relationship with Mexico in the wake of its revolution, however, reveals that he was troubled by a foreign policy that ignored a less powerful nation's right to determine its own future. He deemed the Mexicans capable of making democracy work and, in general, showed a concern for morality and justice in foreign affairs—matters to which Roosevelt and Taft had paid scant attention. Wilson wanted U.S. foreign policy to advance democratic ideals and institutions in Mexico.

Wilson's Mexican dealings were motivated by more than his fondness for democracy. He also feared that political unrest in Mexico could lead to violence, social disorder, and a revolutionary government hostile to U.S. economic interests. With a U.S.-style democratic government in Mexico, Wilson believed, property rights would be respected and U.S. investments would remain secure. Wilson's desire both to encourage democracy and to limit the extent of social change made it difficult to devise a consistent foreign policy toward Mexico.

The Mexican Revolution broke out in 1910 when dictator Porfirio Diaz, who had ruled for 34 years, was overthrown by democratic forces led by Francisco Madero. Madero's talk of democratic reform frightened many foreign investors, especially those in the United States and Great Britain, who owned more than half of all Mexican real estate, 90 percent of its oil reserves, and practically all of its railroads. Thus, when Madero was overthrown early in 1913 by Victoriano Huerta, a conservative general who promised to protect foreign investments, the dollar diplomatists in the Taft administration and in Great Britain breathed a sigh of relief. Henry Lane Wilson, the U.S. ambassador to Mexico, had helped engineer Huerta's coup. Before close relations between the United States and Huerta could be worked out, however, Huerta's men murdered Madero.

Woodrow Wilson, who became president shortly after Madero's assassination in 1913, might have overlooked it (as did the European powers) and entered into close ties with Huerta on condition that he protect U.S. property. Instead, Wilson refused to recognize Huerta's "government of butchers" and demanded that Mexico hold democratic elections. Wilson favored Venustiano Carranza and **Francisco ("Pancho") Villa,** two enemies of Huerta who commanded rebel armies and who claimed to be democrats. In April 1914, Wilson used the arrest of several U.S. sailors by Huerta's troops as a reason to send a fleet into Mexican waters. He ordered the U.S. Marines to occupy the Mexican port city of Veracruz and to prevent a German ship there from unloading munitions meant for Huerta's army. In the resulting battle between U.S. and Mexican forces, 19 Americans and 126 Mexicans were killed. The battle brought the two countries dangerously close to war. Eventually, however, American control over Veracruz weakened and embarrassed Huerta's regime to the point where Carranza was able to take power.

Carranza did not behave as Wilson had expected. Rejecting Wilson's efforts to shape a new Mexican government, he announced a bold land reform program. That program called for the distribution of some of Mexico's agricultural land to impoverished peasants and the transfer of developmental rights on oil lands from foreign corporations to the Mexican government. If the program went into effect, U.S. petroleum companies would lose control of their Mexican properties, a loss that Wilson deemed unacceptable. Wilson now threw his support to Pancho Villa, who seemed more willing than Carranza to protect U.S. oil interests. When Carranza's forces defeated Villa's forces in 1915, Wilson reluctantly withdrew his support of Villa and prepared to recognize the Carranza government.

Furious that Wilson had abandoned him, Villa and his soldiers pulled 18 U.S. citizens from a train in northern Mexico and murdered them, along with another 17 in an attack on Columbus, New Mexico. Determined to punish Villa, Wilson received permission from Carranza to send a U.S. expeditionary force under General John J. Pershing into Mexico to hunt down Villa's "bandits." Pershing's troops pursued Villa's forces 300 miles into Mexico but failed to catch them. The U.S. troops did, however, clash twice with Mexican troops under Carranza's command, once again bringing the countries to the brink of war. The United States, about to enter the First World War, could not afford a fight with Mexico; in 1917, Wilson quietly ordered Pershing's troops home and grudgingly recognized the Carranza government.

Wilson's policies toward Mexico in 1913–17 seemed to have produced few concrete results, except to reinforce an already deep antagonism among Mexicans toward the United States. His repeated changes in strategy, moreover, seemed to indicate a lack of skill and decisiveness in foreign affairs. Actually, however, Wilson recognized something that Roosevelt and Taft had not: that more and more peoples of the world were determined to control their own destinies. The United States, under Wilson, was looking for a way to support these peoples' democratic aspirations while also safeguarding its own economic interests. The First World War would make this quest for a balance between democratic principles and national self-interest all the more urgent.

Conclusion

We can assess the dramatic turn in U.S. foreign policy after 1898 either in relation to the foreign policies of rival world powers or against America's own democratic ideals. By the first standard, U.S. foreign policy looks impressive. The United States achieved its major objectives in world affairs: It tightened its control over the Western Hemisphere and projected its military and economic power into Asia. It did so while sacrificing relatively few American lives and while constraining the jingoistic appetite for truly extensive military adventure and conquest. The United States added only 125,000 square miles to its empire in the years from 1870 to 1900, while Great Britain, France, and Germany enlarged their empires by 4.7, 3.5, and 1.0 million square miles, respectively. Relatively few foreigners were subjected to U.S. colonial rule. By contrast, in 1900, the British Empire extended more than 12 million square miles and embraced one-fourth of the world's population. At times, American rule could be brutal, as it was to Filipino soldiers and civilians alike, but on the whole it was no more severe than British or French rule and significantly less severe than that of German, Belgian, or Japanese imperialists. McKinley, Roosevelt, Taft, and Wilson all placed limits on American expansion and avoided, until 1917, extensive foreign entanglements and wars.

If measured against the standard of America's own democratic ideals, however, U.S. foreign policy after 1898 must be judged more harshly. It demeaned the peoples of the Philippines, Puerto Rico, Guam, Cuba, and Colombia as inferior and primitive and denied them the right to govern themselves. In choosing to behave like the imperialist powers of Europe, the United States abandoned its longstanding claim to being a different kind of nation—one that valued liberty more than power.

Many Americans of the time judged their nation by both standards and thus faced a dilemma that would extend throughout the 20th century. On the one hand, they believed with Roosevelt that the size, economic strength, and honor of the United States required it to accept the role of world power and policeman. On the other hand, they continued to believe with Wilson that they had a mission to spread the democratic values of 1776 to the farthest reaches of the earth. The Mexico example demonstrates how hard it was for the United States to reconcile these two very different approaches to world affairs.

SUGGESTED READINGS

General works on America's imperialist turn in the 1890s and early years of the 20th century include **John Dobson,** *America's Ascent: The United States Becomes a Great Power, 1880–1914* (1978); **Walter LaFeber,** *The Cambridge History of Foreign Relations: The Search for Opportunity, 1865–1913* (1993); and **Emily Rosenberg,** *Spreading the American Dream: American Economic* *and Cultural Expansion, 1890–1945* (1982). **David F. Trask**, *The War with Spain in 1898* (1981) is a comprehensive study of the Spanish-American War, but it should be supplemented with **Philip S. Foner**, *The Spanish-Cuban-American War and the Birth of American Imperialism*, 2 vols. (1972). **Gerald F. Linderman**, *The Mirror of War: American Society and the Spanish-American War* (1974) brilliantly recaptures the shock that overtook Americans who discovered that their Cuban allies were black and the Spanish enemies were white. The role of gender in the Spanish-American War is explored in **Kristin L. Hoganson**, *Fighting for American Manhood: How Gender Politics Provoked the Spanish-American and Philippine-American Wars* (1998).

Stuart Creighton Miller, *"Benevolent Assimilation": The American Conquest of the Philippines, 1899–1903* (1982) examines the Filipino-American war, while **Paul A. Kramer**, *The Blood of Government: Race, Empire, the United States, and the Philippines* (2006) analyzes the effects of U.S. colonialism on the Philippines and America. **Louis A. Perez**, *Cuba under the Platt Amendment, 1902–1934* (1986), explores the extension of U.S. control over Cuba, while **Marilyn B. Young**, *The Rhetoric of Empire: American China Policy, 1895–1901* (1968) examines the unfolding Open Door policy. The acquisition of Guam and Samoa is the subject of **Paul M. Kennedy**, *The Samoan Tangle* (1974), and the history of Puerto Rico following its annexation by the United States is explored in **Raymond Carr**, *Puerto Rico: A Colonial Experiment* (1984). The anti-imperialist movement is analyzed in E. **Berkeley Tompkins**, *Anti-Imperialism in the United States, 1890–1920: The Great Debate* (1970).

Howard K. Beale, *Theodore Roosevelt and the Rise of America to World Power* (1956), is still a crucial work on Roosevelt's foreign policy, but it should be supplemented with **Richard H. Collin**, *Theodore Roosevelt's Caribbean: The Panama Canal, the Monroe Doctrine and the Latin American Context* (1990). Consult **Emily Rosenberg**, *Financial Missionaries to the World: The Politics and Culture of Dollar Diplomacy, 1900–1930* (1999), on the "dollar diplomacy" that emerged during the Taft Administration. On Wilson's foreign policy, see **Thomas J. Knock**, *To End All Wars: Woodrow Wilson and the Quest for a New World Order* (1992); **Lloyd C. Gardner**, *Safe for Democracy: The Anglo-American Response to Revolution, 1913–1923* (1984); **John S. D. Eisenhower**, *Intervention: The United States and the Mexican Revolution, 1913–1917* (1993); and **Mary A. Renda**, *Taking Haiti: Military Occupation and the Culture of U.S. Imperialism, 1915–1940* (2001).

Visit the Liberty Equality Power Companion Web site for resources specific to this textbook: http://www.thomsonedu.com/history/murrin

Also find self-tests and additional resources at ThomsonNOW. ThomsonNOW is an integrated online suite of services and resources with proven ease of use and efficient paths to success, delivering the results you want-NOW!

www.thomsonedu.com/login/

23

War and Society,
1914–1920

The First World War broke out in Europe in August 1914. The **Triple Alliance** of Germany, Austria-Hungary, and the Ottoman Empire squared off against the **Triple Entente** of Great Britain, France, and Russia. The United States entered the war on the side of the Entente (the Allies, or Allied Powers, as they came to be called) in 1917. Over the next year and a half, the United States converted its large, sprawling economy into a disciplined war production machine, raised a 5-million-man army, and provided both the war matériel and troops that helped propel the Allies to victory. The United States emerged from the war as the world's mightiest country. In these and other respects, the war was a great triumph.

But the war also convulsed American society more deeply than any event since the Civil War. This was the first **"total" war,** meaning that combatants devoted virtually all of their resources to the fight. Thus the U.S. government had no choice but to pursue a degree of industrial control and social regimentation that was unprecedented in American history. Needless to say, this degree of government control was a controversial measure in a society that had long distrusted state power. Moreover, significant numbers of Americans from a variety of constituencies opposed the war. To overcome this opposition, Wilson couched American war aims in disinterested and idealistic terms: The United States, he claimed, wanted a "peace without victory," a "war for democracy," and liberty for the world's oppressed peoples. Because these words drew deeply on American political traditions, Wilson believed that Americans would find them inspiring, put aside their suspicions, and support him.

Although many people in the United States and abroad responded enthusiastically to Wilson's ideals, Wilson needed England and France's support to deliver peace without victory, and this support never came. At home, disadvantaged groups stirred up trouble by declaring that American society had failed to live up to its democratic and egalitarian ideals. Wilson supported repressive policies to silence these rebels and to enforce unity and conformity on the American people. In the process, he tarnished the ideals for which America had been fighting. Only a year after the war ended, Wilson's hopes for peace without victory abroad had been destroyed, and America was being torn apart by violent labor disputes and race riots at home.

CHRONOLOGY

1914	First World War breaks out (July–August)
1915	German submarine sinks the *Lusitania* (May 7)
1916	Woodrow Wilson unveils peace initiative • Wilson reelected as "peace president"
1917	Germany resumes unrestricted submarine warfare (February) • Tsar Nicholas II overthrown in Russia (March) • U.S. enters the war (April 6) • Committee on Public Information established • Congress passes Selective Service Act, Espionage Act, Immigration Restriction Act • War Industries Board established • Lenin's Bolsheviks come to power in Russia (November)
1918	Lenin signs treaty with Germany, pulls Russia out of war (March) • Germany launches offensive on western front (March–April) • Congress passes Sabotage Act and Sedition Act • French, British, and U.S. troops repel Germans, advance toward Germany (April–October) • Eugene V. Debs jailed for making antiwar speech • Germany signs armistice (November 11)
1919	Treaty of Versailles signed (June 28) • Chicago race riot (July) • Wilson suffers stroke (October 2) • Police strike in Boston • 18th Amendment (Prohibition) ratified
1919–20	Steelworkers strike in Midwest • Red Scare prompts "Palmer raids" • Senate refuses to ratify Treaty of Versailles • Universal Negro Improvement Association grows under Marcus Garvey's leadership
1920	Anarchists Sacco and Vanzetti convicted of murder
1923	Marcus Garvey convicted of mail fraud
1924	Woodrow Wilson dies
1927	Sacco and Vanzetti executed

Europe's Descent into War

Europe began its descent into war on June 28, 1914, in Sarajevo, Bosnia, when a Bosnian nationalist assassinated Archduke Franz Ferdinand, heir to the Austro-Hungarian throne. This act was meant to protest the Austro-Hungarian imperial presence in the Balkans and to encourage the Bosnians, Croatians, and other Balkan peoples to join the Serbs in establishing independent nations. Austria-Hungary responded to this provocation on July 28 by declaring war on Serbia, holding it responsible for the archduke's murder.

The conflict might have remained local if an intricate series of treaties had not divided Europe into two hostile camps. Germany, Austria-Hungary, and Italy, the so-called Triple Alliance, had promised to come to each other's aid if attacked. Italy would soon opt out of this alliance, to be replaced by the Ottoman Empire. Arrayed against the nations of the Triple Alliance were Britain, France, and Russia in the Triple Entente. Russia was obligated by another treaty to defend Serbia against Austria-Hungary, and consequently on July 30, it mobilized its armed forces to go to Serbia's aid. That brought

Germany into the conflict to protect Austria-Hungary from Russian attack. On August 3, German troops struck not at Russia but at France, Russia's western ally. To reach France, German troops had marched through neutral Belgium. On August 4, Britain reacted by declaring war on Germany. Within the space of only a few weeks, Europe was engulfed in war.

Complicated alliances and defense treaties of the European nations undoubtedly hastened the rush toward war. But equally important was the competition among the European powers to build the strongest economies, the largest armies and navies, and the grandest colonial empires. Britain and Germany, in particular, were engaged in a bitter struggle for European and world supremacy. Few Europeans had any idea that these military buildups might lead to a terrible war that would kill nearly an entire generation of young men and expose the barbarity lurking in their civilization. Historians now believe that several advisers close to the German emperor, Kaiser Wilhelm II, were actually eager to engage Russia and France in a fight for supremacy on the European continent. They expected that a European war would be swift and decisive—in Germany's favor. England and France also believed in their own superiority. Millions of young men, rich and poor, rushed to join the armies on both sides and share in the expected glory.

Victory was not swift. The two camps were evenly matched. Moreover, the first wartime use of machine guns and barbed wire made defense against attack easier than staging an offensive. (Both tanks and airplanes had been invented by this time, but military strategists on both sides were slow to put them to offensive use.) On the western front, after the initial German attack narrowly failed to take Paris in 1914, the two opposing armies confronted each other along a battle line stretching from Belgium in the north to the Swiss border in the south. Troops dug trenches to protect themselves from artillery bombardment and poison gas attacks. Commanders on both sides mounted suicidal ground assaults on the enemy by sending tens of thousands of infantry, armed only with rifles, bayonets, and grenades, out of the trenches and directly into enemy fire. Barbed wire further retarded forward progress, enabling enemy artillery and machine guns to cut down appalling numbers of men. In 1916, during one 10-month German offensive at Verdun (France), 600,000 German troops died; 20,000 British troops were killed during only the first day of an Entente assault on the Somme River (also in France). Many of those who were not killed in combat succumbed to disease that spread rapidly in the cold, wet, and rat-infested trenches. In Eastern Europe, the armies of Germany and Austria-Hungary squared off against those of Russia and Serbia. Although that front did not employ trench warfare, the combat was no less lethal. By the time the First World War ended, an estimated 8.5 million soldiers had died and more than twice that number had been wounded. Total casualties, both military and civilian, had reached 37 million. Europe had lost a generation of young men, as well as its confidence, stability, and global supremacy.

The Road to War, Summer 1914

1. June 28 — Assassination at Sarajevo
2. July 28 — Austria-Hungary declares war on Serbia
3. July 30 — Russia begins mobilization
4. August 1 — Germany declares war on Russia
5. August 3 — Germany declares war on France
6. August 4 — Great Britain declares war on Germany
7. August 6 — Russia and Austria-Hungary at war
8. August 12 — Great Britain declares war on Austria-Hungary

Legend:
- Allied powers and possessions, 1916
- Central powers, 1916
- Neutral countries
- ✦ ✦ ✦ ✦ British naval blockade
- ——— Trench line, Western front, 1915
- – – – Eastern front, 1915

Map 23.1   Europe Goes to War   In the First World War, Great Britain, France, and Russia squared off against Germany, Austria-Hungary, and the Ottoman Empire. Most of the fighting occurred in Europe along the western front in France (solid line) or the eastern front in Russia (dashed line). This map also shows Britain's blockade of German ports. British armies based in Egypt (then a British colony) clashed with Ottoman armies in Arabia and other parts of the Ottoman Empire. View an animated version of this map or related maps at http://www.thomsonedu.com/history/murrin.

American Neutrality

Focus Question
Why did the U.S. policy of neutrality fail, and why did the United States get drawn into war?

Soon after the fighting began, Woodrow Wilson told Americans that this was a European war; neither side was threatening a vital American interest. The United States would therefore proclaim its **neutrality** and maintain normal relations with both sides while seeking to secure peace. Normal relations meant that the United States would continue trading with both camps. Wilson's neutrality policy met with lively opposition, especially from Theodore Roosevelt, who was convinced that the United States should join the Entente to check German power and expansionism. Most Americans, however, applauded Wilson's determination to keep the country out of war.

Neutrality was easier to proclaim than to achieve, however. Many Americans, especially those with economic and political power, identified culturally more with Britain than with Germany. They shared with the English a language, a common ancestry, and a commitment to liberty. Wilson revered the British parliamentary system of government. His closest foreign policy adviser, Colonel Edward M. House, was pro-British, as was Robert Lansing, a trusted counselor in the State Department. William Jennings Bryan, Wilson's secretary of state, objected to this pro-British tilt, but he was a lone voice in Wilson's Cabinet. Germany had no such attraction for U.S. policy makers. On the contrary, Germany's acceptance of monarchical rule, the prominence of militarists in German politics, and its lack of democratic traditions inclined U.S. officials to judge Germany harshly.

The United States had strong economic ties to Great Britain as well. In 1914, the United States exported more than $800 million in goods to Britain and its allies, compared with $170 million to Germany and Austria-Hungary (which came to be known as the Central Powers). As soon as the war began, the British and then the French turned to the United States for food, clothing, munitions, and other war supplies. The U.S. economy, which had been languishing in 1914, enjoyed a boom as a result. Bankers began to issue loans to the Allied Powers, further knitting together the American and British economies and giving American investors a direct stake in an Allied victory. Moreover, the British navy had blockaded German ports, which damaged the United States' already limited trade with Germany. By 1916, U.S. exports to the Central Powers had plummeted to barely $1 million, a fall of more than 99 percent in two years.

The British blockade of German ports clearly violated American neutrality. The Wilson administration protested the British navy's search and occasional seizure of American merchant ships, but it never retaliated by suspending loans or exports to Great Britain. To do so would have plunged the U.S. economy into a recession. In failing to protect its right to trade with Germany, however, the United States compromised its neutrality and allowed itself to be drawn into war.

Submarine Warfare

To combat British control of the seas and to check the flow of U.S. goods to the Allies, Germany unveiled a terrifying new weapon, the *Unterseeboot,* or U-boat, the first militarily effective submarine. Early in 1915, Germany announced its intent to use its U-boats to sink on sight enemy ships en route to the British Isles. On May 7, 1915, without warning, a German U-boat torpedoed the British passenger liner **Lusitania,** en route from New York to London. The ship sank in 22 minutes, killing 1,198 men, women, and children, 128 of them U.S. citizens. Americans were shocked by the sinking. Innocent civilians who had been given no warning of attack and no chance to surrender had been murdered in cold blood. The attack appeared to confirm what anti-German agitators were saying: that the Germans were by nature barbaric and uncivilized. The circumstances surrounding the sinking of the *Lusitania,* however, were more complicated than most Americans realized.

Before its sailing, the Germans had alleged that the *Lusitania* was secretly carrying a large store of munitions to Great Britain (a charge later proved true), and that it therefore was subject to U-boat attack. Germany had warned American passengers not to travel on British passenger ships that carried munitions. Moreover, Germany claimed, with some justification, that the purpose of the U-boat attacks—the disruption of Allied supply lines—was no different from Britain's purpose in blockading German ports. Because its surface ships were outnumbered by the British navy, Germany claimed it had no alternative but to choose the underwater strategy. If a submarine attack seemed more reprehensible than a conventional sea battle, the Germans argued, it was no more so than the British attempt to starve the German people into submission with a blockade.

American political leaders might have used the *Lusitania* incident to denounce both Germany's U-boat strategy and Britain's blockade as actions that violated the rights of citizens of neutral nations. Only Secretary of State Bryan had the courage to say so, however, and his stand proved so unpopular in Washington that he resigned from office; Wilson chose the pro-British Lansing to take his place. Wilson denounced the sinking of the *Lusitania* and demanded that Germany pledge never to launch another attack on the citizens of neutral nations, even when they were traveling in British or French ships. Germany acquiesced to Wilson's demand.

The resulting lull in submarine warfare was short-lived, however. In early 1916, the Allies began to arm their merchant vessels with guns and depth charges capable of destroying German U-boats. Considering this a provocation, Germany renewed its campaign of surprise submarine attacks. In March 1916, a German submarine torpedoed the French passenger liner *Sussex,* causing a heavy loss of life and injuring several Americans. Again Wilson demanded that Germany spare civilians from attack. In the so-called *Sussex* pledge, Germany once again relented but warned that it might resume unrestricted submarine warfare if the United States did not prevail on Great Britain to permit neutral ships to pass through the naval blockade.

The German submarine attacks strengthened the hand of Theodore Roosevelt and others who had been arguing that war with Germany was inevitable and that the United States must prepare to fight. By 1916, Wilson could no longer ignore these critics. Between January and September of that year, he sought and won congressional approval for bills to increase the size of the army and navy, tighten federal control over National Guard forces, and authorize the building of a merchant fleet. Although Wilson had conceded ground to the pro-war agitators, he did not share their belief that war with Germany was either inevitable or desirable. To the contrary, he accelerated his diplomatic initiatives to secure peace, and he dispatched Colonel House to London in January 1916 to draw up a peace plan with the British foreign secretary, Lord Grey. This initiative resulted in the House-Grey memorandum of February 22, 1916, in which Britain agreed to ask the United States to negotiate a settlement between the Allies and the Central Powers. The British believed that the terms of such a peace settlement would favor the Allies. They were furious when Wilson revealed that he wanted an impartial, honestly negotiated peace in which the claims of the Allies and Central Powers would be treated with equal respect and consideration. Britain now rejected U.S. peace overtures, and relations between the two countries grew unexpectedly tense.

The Peace Movement

Underlying Wilson's 1916 peace initiative was a vision of a new world order in which relations between nations would be governed by negotiation rather than war and in which justice would replace power as the fundamental principle of diplomacy. In a major foreign policy address on May 27, 1916, Wilson formally declared his support for what he would later call the League of Nations, an international parliament dedicated to the pursuit of peace, security, and justice for all the world's peoples.

Many Americans supported Wilson's efforts to commit national prestige to the cause of international peace rather than conquest and to keep the United States out of war. Carrie Chapman Catt, president of the National American Woman Suffrage Association, and Jane Addams, founder of the Women's Peace Party, actively opposed the war. In 1915, an international women's peace conference at The Hague (in the Netherlands) had drawn many participants from the United States. A substantial pacifist group emerged among the nation's Protestant clergy. Midwestern progressives such as Robert La Follette, William Jennings Bryan, and George Norris urged that the United States steer clear of this European conflict, as did leading socialists such as Eugene V. Debs. In April 1916, many of the country's most prominent progressives and socialists joined hands in the American Union Against Militarism and pressured Wilson to continue pursuing the path of peace.

Wilson's peace campaign also attracted support from the country's sizable Irish and German ethnic populations, who wanted to block a formal military alliance with Great Britain. That many German ethnics, who continued to feel affection for their native land and culture, would oppose U.S. entry into the war is hardly surprising. And the Irish viewed England as an arrogant imperial power that kept Ireland subjugated. That view was confirmed when England crushed the Easter Rebellion that Irish nationalists had launched on Easter Monday 1916 to win their country's independence. The Irish in America, like those in Ireland, wanted to see Britain's strength sapped (and Ireland's prospects for freedom enhanced) by a long war.

Wilson's Vision: "Peace without Victory"

The 1916 presidential election revealed the breadth of peace sentiment. At the Democratic convention, Governor Martin Glynn of New York, the Irish American speaker who renominated Wilson for a second term, praised the president for keeping the United States out

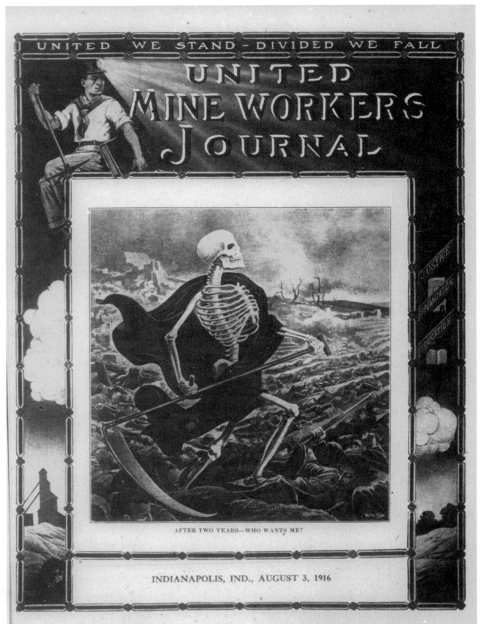

The Horror of War   This cover of the *United Mine Workers Journal* (1916) presents the Great War in the bleakest possible terms: as giving the Grim Reaper license to claim the bodies and souls of Europe's young men. Progressive labor unions were part of the broad coalition in the United States opposed to America's entry into war.

of war. His portrayal of Wilson as the "peace president" electrified the convention and made "He kept us out of war" a campaign slogan. The slogan proved particularly effective against Wilson's Republican opponent, Charles Evans Hughes, whose close ties to Theodore Roosevelt seemed to place him in the pro-war camp. Combining the promise of peace with a pledge to push ahead with progressive reform, Wilson won a narrow victory.

Emboldened by his electoral triumph, Wilson intensified his quest for peace. On December 16, 1916, he sent a peace note to the belligerent governments, entreating them to consider ending the conflict and, to that end, to state their terms for peace. Although Germany refused to specify its terms and Britain and France announced a set of conditions too extreme for Germany ever to accept, Wilson pressed ahead, initiating secret peace negotiations with both sides. To prepare the American people for what he hoped would be a new era of international relations, Wilson appeared before the Senate on January 22, 1917, to outline his plans for peace. In his speech, he reaffirmed his commitment to the League of Nations, but for such a league to succeed, Wilson argued, it would have to be handed a sturdy peace settlement. This entailed a **"peace without victory."** Only a peace settlement that refused to crown a victor or humiliate a loser would ensure the equality of the combatants, and "only a peace between equals can last."

Wilson listed the crucial principles of a lasting peace: freedom of the seas; disarmament; and the right of every people to self-determination, democratic self-government, and security against aggression. He was proposing a revolutionary change in world order, one that would allow all of the world's peoples, regardless of their size or strength, to achieve political independence and to participate as equals in world affairs. These views, rarely expressed by the leader of a world power, stirred the despairing masses of Europe and elsewhere caught in deadly conflict.

German Escalation

Wilson's oratory came too late to serve the cause of peace. Sensing the imminent collapse of Russian forces on the eastern front, Germany had decided, in early 1917, to throw its full military might at France and Britain. On land it planned to launch a massive assault on the trenches, and at sea it prepared to unleash its submarines to attack all vessels heading for British ports. Germany knew that this last action would compel the United States to enter the war, but it was gambling on being able to strangle the British economy and leave France isolated before significant numbers of American troops could reach European shores.

On February 1, the United States broke off diplomatic relations with Germany. Wilson continued to hope for a negotiated settlement, however, until February 25, when the British intercepted and passed on to the president a telegram from Germany's foreign secretary, Arthur Zimmermann, to the German minister in Mexico. The infamous **"Zimmermann telegram"** instructed the minister to ask the Mexican government to attack the United States in the event of war between Germany and the United States. In return, Germany would pay the Mexicans a large fee and regain for them the "lost provinces" of Texas, New Mexico, and Arizona. Wilson, Congress, and the American public were outraged by the story.

In March, news arrived that Tsar Nicholas II's autocratic regime in Russia had collapsed and had been replaced by a liberal-democratic government under the leadership of Alexander Kerensky. As long as the tsar ruled Russia and stood to benefit from the Central Powers' defeat, Wilson could not honestly claim that America's going to war against Germany would bring democracy to Europe. The fall of the tsar and the need of Russia's fledgling democratic government for support gave Wilson the rationale he needed to justify American intervention.

Appearing before a joint session of Congress on April 2, Wilson declared that the United States must enter the war because "the world must be made safe for democracy." He continued:

> We shall fight for the things which we have always carried nearest our hearts—for democracy, for the right of those who submit to authority to have a voice in their own Governments, for the rights and liberties of small nations, for a universal dominion of right by such a concert of free peoples as shall bring peace and safety to all nations and make the world itself at last free. To such a task we dedicate our lives and our fortunes.

Inspired by his words, Congress broke into thunderous applause. On April 6, Congress voted to declare war by a vote of 373 to 50 in the House and 82 to 6 in the Senate.

The United States thus embarked on a grand experiment to reshape the world. Wilson had given millions of people around the world reason to hope, both that the terrible war would end soon and that their strivings for freedom and social justice would be realized. Although he was taking America to war on the side of the Allies, he stressed that America would fight as an "associated power," a phrase meant to underscore America's determination to keep its war aims separate from and more idealistic than those of the Allies.

Still, Wilson understood all too well the risks of his undertaking. A few days before his speech to Congress, he had confided to a journalist his worry that the American people, once at war, will "forget there ever was such a thing as tolerance. To fight you must be brutal and ruthless, and the spirit of ruthless brutality will enter into the very fibre of our national life, infecting Congress, the courts, the policeman on the beat, the man in the street."

American Intervention

The entry of the United States into the war gave the Allies the muscle they needed to defeat the Central Powers, but it almost came too late. Germany's resumption of unrestricted submarine warfare took a frightful toll on Allied shipping. From February through July 1917, German subs sank almost 4 million tons of shipping, more than one-third of Britain's entire merchant fleet. One of every four large freighters departing Britain in those months never returned; at one point, the British Isles were down to a mere four weeks of provisions. American intervention ended Britain's vulnerability in dramatic fashion. U.S. and British naval commanders now grouped merchant ships into convoys and provided them with warship escorts through the most dangerous stretches of the North Atlantic. Destroyers armed with depth charges were particularly effective as escorts. Their shallow draft made them invulnerable to torpedoes, and their great acceleration and speed allowed them to pursue slow-moving U-boats. The U.S. and British navies had begun to use sound waves (later called "sonar") to pinpoint the location of underwater craft, and this new technology increased the effectiveness of destroyer attacks. By the end of 1917, the tonnage of Allied shipping lost each month to U-boat attacks had declined by two-thirds, from almost 1 million tons in April to 350,000 tons in December. The increased flow of supplies stiffened the resolve of the exhausted British and French troops.

The French and British armies had bled themselves white by taking the offensive in 1916 and 1917 and had scarcely budged the trench lines. The Germans had been content in those years simply to hold their trench position in the West because they were engaged in a huge offensive against the Russians in the East. The Germans intended first to defeat Russia and then to shift their eastern armies to the West for a final assault on the weakened British and French lines. Their opportunity came in the winter and spring of 1918.

A second Russian revolution in November 1917 had overthrown Kerensky's liberal-democratic government and had brought to power a revolutionary socialist government under Vladimir Lenin and his Bolshevik Party. Lenin pulled Russia out of the war on the grounds that the war did not serve the best interests of the working classes, that it was a conflict between rival capitalist elites interested only in wealth and power (and indifferent to the slaughter of soldiers in the trenches). In March 1918, Lenin signed a treaty at Brest-Litovsk that added to Germany's territory and resources and enabled Germany to shift its eastern forces to the western front.

Russia's exit from the war hurt the Allies. Not only did it expose French and British troops to a much larger German force, but it also challenged the Allied claim that they were fighting a just war against German aggression. Lenin had published the texts of secret Allied treaties showing that Britain and France, like Germany, had plotted to enlarge their nations and empires through war. The revelation that the Allies were fighting for land and riches rather than democratic principles outraged large numbers of people in France and Great Britain, demoralized Allied troops, and threw the French and British governments into disarray.

The treaties also embarrassed Wilson, who had brought America into the war to fight for democracy, not territory. Wilson quickly moved to restore the Allies' credibility by unveiling, in January 1918, a concrete program for peace. His **Fourteen Points** reaffirmed America's commitment to an international system governed by laws rather than by might and renounced territorial aggrandizement as a legitimate war aim. This document provided the ideological cement that held the Allies together at a critical moment. (The Fourteen Points are discussed more fully in the section "The Failure of the International Peace.")

In March and April 1918, Germany launched its huge offensive against British and French positions, sending Allied troops reeling. A ferocious assault against French lines on May 27 met with little resistance; German troops advanced 10 miles a day—a faster pace than any on the western front since the earliest days of the war—until they reached the Marne River, within striking distance of Paris. The French government prepared to evacuate the city. At this perilous moment, a large American army—fresh, well-equipped, and oblivious to the horrors of trench warfare—arrived to reinforce what remained of the French lines.

In fact, these American troops, part of the American Expeditionary Force (AEF) commanded by General **John J. Pershing,** had begun landing in France almost a year earlier. During the intervening months, the United States had had to create a modern army from scratch, because its existing force was so small, ranking only 17th in the world. Men had to be drafted, trained, and supplied with food and equipment; ships for transporting them to Europe had to be found or built. In France, Pershing put his troops through additional training before committing them to battle. He was determined that the American soldiers— or "doughboys," as they were called—should acquit themselves well on the battlefield. The army he ordered into battle to counter the German spring offensive of 1918 fought well. Many American soldiers fell, but the German offensive ground to a halt. Paris was saved, and Germany's best chance for victory slipped from its grasp.

Buttressed by this show of AEF strength, the Allied troops staged a major offensive of their own in late September. Millions of Allied troops (including more than a million from the AEF) advanced across the 200-mile-wide Argonne forest in France, cutting German supply lines. By late October, they had reached the German border. Faced with an invasion of their homeland and with rapidly mounting popular dissatisfaction with the war, German leaders asked for an armistice, to be followed by peace negotiations based on Wilson's Fourteen Points. Having forced the Germans to agree to numerous concessions, the Allies ended the war on November 11, 1918. The carnage was finally over.

Mobilizing for "Total" War

> ### Focus Question
> What problems did the United States encounter in mobilizing for total war, and how successfully were those problems overcome?

Compared to Europe, the United States suffered little from the war. The deaths of 112,000 American soldiers paled in comparison to European losses: 900,000 by Great Britain, 1.2 million by Austria-Hungary, 1.4 million by France, 1.7 million by Russia, and 2 million by Germany. The U.S. civilian population was spared most of the war's ravages— the destruction of homes and industries, the shortages of food and medicine, the spread of disease—that afflicted millions of Europeans. Only with the flu epidemic that swept across the Atlantic from Europe in 1919 to claim approximately 500,000 lives did Americans briefly experience wholesale suffering and death.

Still, the war had a profound effect on American society. Every military engagement the United States had fought since the Civil War—the Indian wars, the Spanish-American War, the American-Filipino War, the Boxer Rebellion, the Latin American interventions—had been limited in scope. Even the troop mobilizations that seemed large at the time—the more than 100,000 needed to fight the Spanish and then the Filipinos—failed to tax severely American resources.

The First World War was different. It was a "total" war to which every combatant had committed virtually all of its resources. The scale of the effort in the United States became apparent early in 1917 when Wilson asked Congress for a conscription law that would permit the federal government to raise a multimillion-man army. The United States would also have to devote much of its agricultural, transportation, industrial, and population resources to the war effort if it wished to end the European stalemate. Who would organize this massive effort? Who would pay for it? Would Americans accept the sacrifice and regimentation it would demand? These were vexing questions for a nation long committed to individual liberty, small government, and a weak military.

Organizing Industry

At first, Wilson pursued a decentralized approach to mobilization, delegating tasks to local defense councils throughout the country. When that effort failed, however, Wilson created several centralized federal agencies, each charged with supervising nationwide activity in its assigned economic sector.

The success of these agencies varied. The Food Administration, headed by mining engineer and executive Herbert Hoover, substantially increased production of basic foodstuffs and put in place an efficient distribution system that delivered food to millions of troops and European civilians. Treasury Secretary William McAdoo, as head of the U.S. Railroad Administration, also performed well in shifting the rail system from private to public control, coordinating dense train traffic, and making capital improvements that allowed goods to move rapidly to eastern ports, where they were loaded onto ships and sent to Europe. At the other extreme, the Aircraft Production Board and Emergency Fleet Corporation did a poor job of supplying the Allies with combat aircraft and merchant vessels. On balance, the U.S. economy performed wonders in supplying troops with uniforms, food, rifles, munitions, and other basic items; it failed badly, however, in producing more sophisticated weapons and machines such as artillery, aircraft, and ships.

At the time, many believed that the new government war agencies possessed awesome power over the nation's economy and thus represented a near revolution in government. Most such agencies, however, were more powerful on paper than in fact. Consider, for example, the **War Industries Board** (WIB), an administrative body established by Wilson in July 1917 to harness manufacturing might to military needs. The WIB floundered for its first nine months, lacking the statutory authority to force manufacturers and the military to adopt its plans. Only the appointment of Wall Street investment banker Bernard

Baruch as WIB chairman in March 1918 turned the agency around. Rather than attempting to force manufacturers to do the government's bidding, Baruch permitted industrialists to charge high prices for their products. He won exemptions from antitrust laws for corporations that complied with his requests. In general, he made war production too lucrative an activity to resist; however, he did not hesitate to unleash his wrath on corporations that resisted WIB enticements.

Baruch's forceful leadership worked reasonably well throughout his nine months in office. War production increased, and manufacturers discovered the financial benefits of cooperation between the public and private sectors. But Baruch's approach created problems, too. His favoritism toward large corporations hurt smaller competitors. Moreover, the cozy relationship between government and corporation that he encouraged violated the progressive pledge to protect the people against the "interests." Achieving cooperation by boosting corporate profits, finally, was a costly way for the government to do business. The costs of the war soared to $33 billion, a figure more than three times expectations.

Securing Workers, Keeping Labor Peace

The government worried as much about labor's cooperation as about industry's compliance, for the best-laid production plans could be disrupted by a labor shortage or an extended strike. War increased the demand for industrial labor while cutting the supply. European immigrants had long been the most important source of new labor for American industry, and during the war they stopped coming. Meanwhile, millions of workers already in America were conscripted into the military and thus lost to industry.

Manufacturers responded to the labor shortage by recruiting new sources of labor from the rural South; a half million African Americans migrated to northern cities between 1916 and 1920. Another half million white southerners followed the same path during that period. Hundreds of thousands of Mexicans fled their revolution-ridden homeland for jobs in the Southwest and Midwest. Approximately 40,000 northern women found work as streetcar conductors, railroad workers, metalworkers, munitions makers, and in other jobs customarily reserved for men. The number of female clerical workers doubled between 1910 and 1920, with many of these women finding work in the government war bureaucracies. Altogether, a million women toiled in war-related industries.

These workers alleviated but did not eliminate the nation's labor shortage. Unemployment, which had hovered around 8.5 percent in 1915, plunged to 1.2 percent in 1918. Workers were quick to recognize the benefits of the tight labor market. They quit jobs they did not like and took part in strikes and other collective actions in unprecedented numbers. From 1916 to 1920, more than 1 million workers went on strike every year. Union membership almost doubled, from 2.6 million in 1915 to 5.1 million in 1920. Workers commonly sought higher wages and shorter hours through strikes and unionization. Wages rose an average of 137 percent from 1915 to 1920, although inflation largely negated these gains. The average workweek declined in that same period from 55 to 51 hours. Workers also struck in response to managerial attempts to speed up production and tighten discipline. As time passed, increasing numbers of workers began to wonder why the war for democracy in Europe had no counterpart in their factories at home. "Industrial democracy" became the battle cry of an awakened labor movement.

Wilson's willingness to include labor in his 1916 progressive coalition reflected his awareness of labor's potential power (see chapter 21). In 1918, he bestowed prestige on the newly formed **National War Labor Board** (NWLB) by appointing former president William Howard Taft to be co-chair alongside Samuel Gompers, president of the American Federation of Labor. The NWLB brought together representatives of labor, industry, and the public to resolve labor disputes.

Raising an Army

To raise an army, the Wilson administration committed itself to conscription—the drafting of most men of a certain age, irrespective of their family's wealth, ethnic background, or social standing. The Selective Service Act of May 1917 empowered the administration to do just that. By war's end, local Selective Service boards had registered 24 million young men age 18 and older and had drafted nearly 3 million of them into the military; another 2 million volunteered for service.

Relatively few men resisted the draft, even among recently arrived immigrants. Foreign-born men constituted 18 percent of the armed forces—a percentage greater than their share of the total population. Almost 400,000 African Americans served, representing

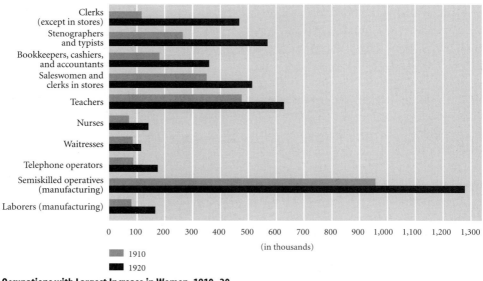

Occupations with Largest Increase in Women, 1910–20

Source: Joseph A. Hill, *Women in Gainful Occupations, 1870–1920*, U.S. Bureau of the Census, Monograph no. 9 (Washington, DC: Government Printing Office, 1929), p. 33.

National Archives

Women Doing "Men's Work"   Labor shortages during the war allowed thousands of women to take industrial jobs customarily reserved for men. Here women operate pneumatic hammers at the Midvale Steel and Ordnance Company, Nicetown, Pennsylvania, 1918.

approximately 10 percent of armed forces, the same as the percentage of African Americans in the total population.

The U.S. Army, under the command of Chief of Staff Peyton March and General John J. Pershing, faced the difficult task of fashioning these ethnically and racially diverse millions into a professional fighting force. Teaching raw recruits to fight was hard enough, Pershing and March observed; the generals refused the task of teaching them to put aside their prejudices. Rather than integrate the armed forces, they segregated black soldiers from white. Virtually all African Americans were assigned to all-black units and barred from combat. Being stripped of a combat role was particularly galling to blacks, who, in previous wars, had proven themselves to be among the best American fighters. Pershing was fully aware of the African American contribution. He had commanded African American troops in the 10th Cavalry, the all-black regiment that had distinguished itself in the Spanish-American War (chapter 22). Pershing's military reputation had depended so heavily on the black troops who fought for him that he had acquired the nickname Black Jack.

For a time, the military justified its intensified discrimination against blacks by referring to the results of rudimentary IQ (intelligence quotient) tests administered by psychologists to 2 million AEF soldiers. These tests allegedly "proved" that native-born Americans and immigrants from the British Isles, Germany, and Scandinavia were well endowed with intelligence, whereas African Americans and immigrants from Southern and Eastern

Europe were poorly endowed. The tests were scientifically so ill-conceived, however, that their findings revealed nothing about the true distribution of intelligence in the soldier population. Their most sensational revelation was that more than half of the soldiers in the AEF—white and black—were "morons," men who had failed to reach the mental age of 13. After trying to absorb the apparent news that most U.S. soldiers were feeble-minded, the military sensibly rejected the pseudo-science on which these intelligence findings were based. In 1919, it discontinued the IQ testing program.

Given the racial and ethnic differences among American troops and the short time Pershing and his staff had to train recruits, the AEF's performance was impressive. The United States increased the army from a mere 100,000 to 5 million in little more than a year. The Germans sank no troop ships, nor were any soldiers killed during the dangerous Atlantic crossing. In combat, U.S. troops became known for their sharpshooting skills. The most decorated soldier in the AEF was Sergeant Alvin C. York of Tennessee, who captured 35 machine guns, took 132 prisoners, and killed 17 German soldiers with 17 bullets. York had learned his marksmanship hunting wild turkeys in the Tennessee hills. "Of course, it weren't no trouble no how for me to hit them big [German] army targets," he later commented. "They were so much bigger than turkeys' heads." One of the most decorated AEF units was **New York's 369th Regiment,** a black unit recruited in Harlem. Bowing to pressure from civil

National Archives

The 369th Returns to New York   Denied the opportunity to fight in the U.S. Army, this unit fought for the French. For the length and distinction of its service in the front lines, this entire unit was awarded the *Croix de Guerre* (War Cross) by the French government.

rights groups to allow some black troops to fight, Pershing had offered the 369th to the French army. The 369th entered the French front line, served in the forward Allied trenches for 191 days (longer than any other U.S. regiment), and scored several major successes. In gratitude for its service, the French government decorated the entire unit with one of its highest honors—the *Croix de Guerre* (War Cross).

Paying the Bills

The government incurred huge debts buying food, uniforms, munitions, weapons, vehicles, and sundry other items for the U.S. military. To help pay its bills, it sharply increased tax rates. The new taxes hit the wealthiest Americans the hardest: The richest were slapped with a 67 percent income tax and a 25 percent inheritance tax. Corporations were ordered to pay an "excess profits" tax. Proposed by the Wilson administration and backed by Robert La Follette and other congressional progressives who feared that the "interests" would use the war to enrich themselves, these taxes were meant to ensure that all Americans would sacrifice something for the war.

Tax revenues, however, provided only about one-third of the $33 billion that the government ultimately spent on the war. The rest came from the sale of **Liberty Bonds.** These 30-year government bonds offered individual purchasers a return of 3.5 percent in annual interest. The government offered five bond issues between 1917 and 1920, and all quickly sold out, thanks, in no small measure, to a high-powered sales pitch, orchestrated by Treasury Secretary William G. McAdoo, that equated bond purchases with patriotic duty. McAdoo's agents blanketed the country with posters, sent bond "salesmen" into virtually every American community, enlisted Boy Scouts to go door-to-door, and staged rallies at which movie stars such as Mary Pickford, Douglas Fairbanks, and Charlie Chaplin stumped for the war.

Arousing Patriotic Ardor

The Treasury's bond campaign was only one aspect of an extraordinary government effort to arouse public support for the war. In 1917, Wilson set up a new agency, the **Committee on Public Information** (CPI), to popularize the war. Under the chairmanship of George Creel, a midwestern progressive and a muckraker, the CPI distributed 75 million copies of pamphlets explaining U.S. war aims in several languages. It trained a force of 75,000 "Four-Minute Men" to deliver succinct, uplifting war speeches to numerous groups in their home cities and towns. It papered the walls of virtually every public institution (and many private ones) with posters, placed advertisements in mass-circulation magazines, sponsored exhibitions, and peppered newspaper editors with thousands of press releases on the progress of the war.

Faithful to his muckraking past (see chapter 21), Creel wanted to give the people the facts of the war, believing that well-informed citizens would see the wisdom of Wilson's policies. He also saw his work as an opportunity to achieve the progressive goal of uniting all Americans into a single moral community. Americans everywhere learned that the United States had entered the war "to make the world safe for democracy," to help the world's weaker peoples achieve self-determination, and to bring a measure of justice into the conduct of international affairs. Americans were asked to affirm those ideals by doing everything they could to support the war.

This uplifting message affected the American people, although not necessarily in ways anticipated by CPI propagandists. It imparted to many a deep love of country and a sense of participation in a grand democratic experiment. Among others, particularly those experiencing poverty and discrimination, it sparked a new spirit of protest. Workers, women, European ethnics, and African Americans began demanding that America live up to its democratic ideals at home as well as abroad. Workers rallied to the cry of "industrial democracy." Women seized on the democratic fervor to bring their fight for suffrage to a successful conclusion (see chapter 21). African Americans began to dream that the war might deliver them from second-class citizenship. European ethnics believed that Wilson's support of their countrymen's rights abroad would improve their own chances for success in the United States.

Although the CPI had helped to unleash it, this new democratic enthusiasm troubled Creel and others in the Wilson administration. The United States, after all, was still deeply divided along class, ethnic, and racial lines. Workers and industrialists regarded each other with suspicion. Cultural differences compounded this class division, for the working class was overwhelmingly ethnic in composition, and the industrial and political elites consisted mainly of the native-born whose families had been Americans for generations. Progressives had fought hard to overcome these divisions. They had tamed the power of capitalists, improved the condition of workers, encouraged the Americanization of immigrants, and articulated a new, more inclusive idea of who could belong to the American nation.

But their work was far from complete when the war broke out, and the war opened up new social and cultural divisions. German immigrants still formed the largest foreign-born population group at 2.3 million. Another 2.3 million immigrants came from some part of the Austro-Hungarian Empire, and more than 1 million Americans—native-born and immigrants—supported the Socialist Party and the Industrial Workers of the World, both of which had opposed the war. The decision to authorize the CPI's massive unity campaign indicates that the progressives understood how widespread the discord was. Still, they had not anticipated that the promotion of democratic ideals at home would exacerbate, rather than lessen, the nation's social and cultural divisions.

Wartime Repression

By early 1918, the CPI's campaign had developed a darker, more coercive side. Inflammatory advertisements called on patriots to report on neighbors, coworkers, and ethnics whom they suspected of subverting the war effort. Propagandists called on all immigrants, especially those from Central, Southern, and Eastern Europe, to pledge themselves to "100 percent Americanism" and to repudiate all ties to their homeland, native language, and ethnic customs. The CPI aroused hostility toward Germans by spreading lurid tales of German atrocities and encouraging the public to see movies such as *The Prussian Cur* and

Renamed German American Words

Original German Name	Renamed "Patriotic" Name
hamburger	salisbury steak, liberty steak, liberty sandwich
sauerkraut	liberty cabbage
Hamburg Avenue, Brooklyn, New York	Wilson Avenue, Brooklyn, New York
Germantown, Nebraska	Garland, Nebraska
East Germantown, Indiana	Pershing, Indiana
Berlin, Iowa	Lincoln, Iowa
pinochle	liberty
German shepherd	Alsatian shepherd
Deutsches Hans of Indianapolis	Athenaeum of Indiana
Germania Maennerchor of Chicago	Lincoln Club
Kaiser Street	Maine Way

Sources: From La Vern J. Rippley, *The German Americans* (Boston: Twayne Publishers, 1976), p. 186; and Robert H. Ferrell, *Woodrow Wilson and World War I, 1917–1921* (New York: Harper and Row, 1985), pp. 205–206.

The Beast of Berlin. The Justice Department arrested thousands of German and Austrian immigrants whom it suspected of subversive activities. Congress passed the Trading with the Enemy Act, which required foreign-language publications to submit all war-related stories to post office censors for approval.

German Americans became the objects of popular hatred. American patriots sought to expunge every trace of German influence from American culture. In Boston, performances of Beethoven's symphonies were banned, and the German-born conductor of the Boston Symphony Orchestra was forced to resign. Although Americans would not give up the German foods they had grown to love, they would no longer call them by their German names. Sauerkraut was rechristened "liberty cabbage," and hamburgers became "liberty sandwiches." Libraries removed works of German literature from their shelves, and Theodore Roosevelt and others urged school districts to prohibit the teaching of the German language. Patriotic school boards in Lima, Ohio, and elsewhere burned the German books in their districts.

German Americans risked being fired from work, losing their businesses, and being assaulted on the street. A St. Louis mob lynched an innocent German immigrant whom they suspected of subversion. After only 25 minutes of deliberation, a St. Louis jury acquitted the mob leaders, who had brazenly defended their crime as an act of patriotism. German Americans began hiding their ethnic identity, changing their names, speaking German only in the privacy of their homes, and celebrating their holidays only with trusted friends. This experience devastated the once-proud German American community; many would never recover from the shame and vulnerability they experienced in those years.

The anti-German campaign escalated into a general anti-immigrant crusade. Congress passed the **Immigration Restriction Act of 1917,** over Wilson's veto, which declared that all adult immigrants who failed a reading test would be denied admission to the United States. The act also banned the immigration of laborers from India, Indochina, Afghanistan, Arabia, the East Indies, and several other countries within an Asiatic Barred Zone. This legislation marked the beginning of a movement in Congress that, four years later, would close the immigration door to virtually all transoceanic peoples.

Congress also passed the 18th Amendment to the Constitution, which prohibited the manufacture and distribution of alcoholic beverages (see chapter 21). The crusade for prohibition was not new, but anti-immigrant feelings generated by the war gave it added impetus. Prohibitionists pictured the nation's urban ethnic ghettos as scenes of drunkenness, immorality, and disloyalty.

Imperial War Museum, London

The Campaign of Fear   By 1918, the government's appeal to Americans' best aspirations—to spread liberty and democracy—had been replaced by a determination to arouse fear of subversion and conquest. Here the German enemy is depicted as a terrifying brute who violates Lady Liberty and uses his *kultur* club to destroy civilization.

They also accused German American brewers of operating a "liquor trust" to sap people's will to fight. The states quickly ratified the 18th Amendment, and in 1919, Prohibition became the law of the land.

More and more, the Wilson administration relied on repression to achieve domestic unity. In the **Espionage, Sabotage, and Sedition Acts** passed in 1917 and 1918, Congress gave the administration sweeping powers to silence and imprison dissenters. These acts went far beyond outlawing behavior that no nation at war could be expected to tolerate, such as spying for the enemy, sabotaging war production, and calling for the enemy's victory. Now citizens could be prosecuted for writing or uttering any statement that could be construed as profaning the flag, the Constitution, or the military. These acts constituted the most drastic restrictions of free speech at the national level since the Alien and Sedition Acts of 1798 (see chapter 8).

Government repression fell most heavily on the IWW and the Socialist Party. Both groups had opposed intervention before 1917. Although they subsequently muted their opposition, they continued to insist that the true enemies of American workers were to be found in the ranks of American employers, not in Germany or Austria-Hungary. The government responded by banning many socialist materials from the mails and by disrupting socialist and IWW meetings. By spring 1918, government agents had raided countless IWW offices and had arrested 2,000 IWW members, including its entire executive board. Many of those arrested would be sentenced to long jail terms. William Haywood, the IWW president, fled to Europe and then to the Soviet Union rather than go to jail. Eugene V. Debs, the head of the Socialist Party, received a 10-year jail term for making an antiwar speech in Canton, Ohio, in summer 1918.

This federal repression, carried out in an atmosphere of supercharged patriotism, encouraged local governments and private citizens to initiate their own antiradical crusades. In the mining town of Bisbee, Arizona, a sheriff with an eager force of 2,000 deputized citizens kidnapped 1,200 IWW members, herded them into cattle cars, and dumped them onto the New Mexico desert with little food or water. Vigilantes in Butte, Montana, chained an IWW organizer to a car and let his body scrape the pavement as they drove the vehicle through city streets. Next, they strung him up to a railroad trestle, castrated him, and left him to die. The 250,000 members of the American Protective League, most of them businessmen and professionals, routinely spied on fellow workers and neighbors. They opened mail and tapped phones and otherwise harassed those suspected of disloyalty. Attorney General Thomas Gregory publicly endorsed the group and sought federal funds to support its "police" work.

The spirit of coercion even infected institutions that had long prided themselves on tolerance. In July 1917, Columbia University fired two professors for speaking out against U.S. intervention in the war. The National Americanization Committee, which before 1917 had pioneered a humane approach to the problem of integrating immigrants into American life, now supported surveillance, internment, and deportation of aliens suspected of anti-American sentiments.

Wilson bore responsibility for this climate of repression. He did attempt to block certain pieces of repressive legislation; for example, he vetoed both the Immigration Restriction Act and the Volstead Act (the act passed to enforce Prohibition), only to be overridden by Congress. But Wilson did little to halt Attorney General Gregory's prosecution of radicals or Postmaster General Burleson's campaign to exclude Socialist Party publications from the mail. He ignored pleas from progressives that he intervene in the Debs case to prevent the ailing 62-year-old from going to jail. His acquiescence in these matters cost him dearly among progressives and socialists. Wilson believed, however, that once the Allies, with U.S. support, won the war and arranged a just peace in accordance with the Fourteen Points, his administration's wartime actions would be forgiven and the progressive coalition would be restored.

The Failure of the International Peace

Focus Question
What were Woodrow Wilson's peace proposals, and how did they fare?

In the month following Germany's surrender on November 11, 1918, Wilson was confident about the prospects of achieving a just peace. Both Germany and the Allies had publicly accepted the Fourteen Points as the basis for negotiations. Wilson's international prestige was enormous. People throughout the world were inspired by his dream of a democratic, just, and harmonious world order free of poverty, ignorance, and war. Poles, Lithuanians, and other Eastern Europeans whose pursuit of nationhood had been frustrated for 100 years or more now believed that independence might be within their reach. Zionist Jews in Europe and the United States dared to dream of a Jewish homeland within their lifetimes. Countless African and Asian peoples imagined achieving their freedom from colonial domination.

To capitalize on his fame and to maximize the chances for a peace settlement based on his Fourteen Points, Wilson broke with diplomatic precedent and decided to head the American delegation to the Paris Peace Conference in January 1919. Enormous crowds of enthusiastic Europeans turned out to hail Wilson's arrival on the Continent in December. Some 2 million French citizens—the largest throng ever assembled on French soil—lined the parade route in Paris to catch a glimpse of "Wilson, *le juste* [the just]." In Rome, Milan, and La Scala, Italians acclaimed him "The Savior of Humanity" and "The Moses from Across the Atlantic."

In the Fourteen Points, Wilson had translated his principles for a new world order into specific proposals for international peace and justice. The first group of points called for all nations to abide by a code of conduct that embraced free trade, freedom of the seas, open diplomacy, disarmament, and the resolution of disputes through mediation. A second group, based on the principle of self-determination, proposed redrawing the map of Europe to give the subjugated peoples of the Austro-Hungarian, Ottoman, and Russian empires national sovereignty. The last point called for establishing the League of Nations, an assembly in which all nations would be represented and in which all international disputes would be given a fair hearing and an opportunity for peaceful solutions.

The Paris Peace Conference and the Treaty of Versailles
Although representatives of 27 nations began meeting in Paris on January 12, 1919, to discuss Wilson's Fourteen Points, negotiations were controlled by the "Big Four": Wilson, Prime Minister David Lloyd George of Great Britain, Premier Georges Clemenceau of France, and Prime Minister Vittorio Orlando of Italy. When Orlando quit the conference after a dispute with Wilson, the Big Four became the Big Three. Wilson quickly learned

that his negotiating partners' support for the Fourteen Points was much weaker than he had believed. The cagey Clemenceau mused: "God gave us the Ten Commandments, and we broke them. Wilson gives us Fourteen Points. We shall see." Clemenceau and Lloyd George refused to include most of Wilson's points in the peace treaty. The points having to do with freedom of the seas and free trade were omitted, as were the proposals for open diplomacy and Allied disarmament. Wilson won partial endorsement of the principle of self-determination: Belgian sovereignty was restored, Poland's status as a nation was affirmed, and the new nations of Czechoslovakia, Yugoslavia, Finland, Lithuania, Latvia, and Estonia were created. In addition, some lands of the former Ottoman Empire—Armenia, Palestine, Mesopotamia, and Syria—were to be placed under League of Nations' trustee-ships with the understanding that they would someday gain their independence. Wilson failed in his efforts to block a British plan to transfer former German colonies in Asia to Japanese control, an Italian plan to annex territory inhabited by 200,000 Austrians, and a French plan to take from Germany its valuable Saar coal mines. **(See Map 23.2, Europe and the Near East After the First World War, in the color insert following page 912.)**

Nor could Wilson blunt the drive to punish Germany for its wartime aggression. In addi-tion to awarding the Saar basin to France, the Allies gave portions of northern Germany to Denmark and portions of eastern Germany to Poland and Czechoslovakia. Germany was stripped of virtually its entire navy and air force, and forbidden to place soldiers or forti-fications in western Germany along the Rhine. It was allowed to keep an army of only 100,000 men. In addition, Germany was forced to admit its responsibility for the war. In accepting this "war guilt," Germany was, in effect, agreeing to compensate the victors in cash (reparations) for the pain and suffering it had inflicted on them.

Lloyd George and Clemenceau brushed off the protests of those who viewed this desire to prostrate Germany as a cruel and vengeful act. That the German people, after their nation's 1918 defeat, had overthrown the monarch (Kaiser Wilhelm II) who had taken them to war, and had reconstituted their nation as a democratic republic—the first in their country's history—won them no leniency. On June 28, 1919, Great Britain, France, the United States, Germany, and other European nations signed the Treaty of Versailles. In 1921, an Allied commission notified the Germans that they were to pay the victors $33 billion, a sum well beyond the resources of a defeated and economically ruined Germany.

The League of Nations

The Allies' single-minded pursuit of self-interest disillusioned many liberals and socialists in the United States, but Wilson seemed undismayed. He had won approval of the most important of his Fourteen Points—that which called for the creation of the League of Nations. The League, whose structure and responsibilities were set forth in the Covenant attached to the peace treaty, would usher in Wilson's new world order. Drawing its mem-bership from the signatories to the Treaty of Versailles (except, for the time being, Germany), the League would function as an international parliament and judiciary, establishing rules of international behavior and resolving disputes between nations through rational and

© Bettmann/CORBIS

Wilson in Paris, 1919 This photograph shows President Wilson (on right), recently arrived in Paris to negotiate the Treaty of Versailles, striding confidently and comfortably alongside his two allies, British Prime Minister Lloyd George (on left) and French Premier Clemenceau (in center). In the negotiations themselves, Lloyd George and Clemenceau would prove to be as much adversaries as allies to Wilson.

peaceful means. A nine-member executive council—the United States, Britain, France, Italy, and Japan would have permanent seats on the council, while the other four seats would rotate among the smaller powers—was charged with administering decisions.

Wilson believed that the League would redeem the failures of the Paris Peace Conference. Under its auspices, free trade and freedom of the seas would be achieved, reparations against Germany would be reduced or eliminated, disarmament of the Allies would proceed, and the principle of self-determination would be extended to peoples outside Europe. Moreover, the **Covenant (Article X)** would endow the League with the power to punish aggressor nations through economic isolation and military retaliation.

Wilson versus Lodge: The Fight over Ratification

The League's success, however, depended on Wilson's ability to convince the U.S. Senate to ratify the Treaty of Versailles. Wilson knew that this would not be easy. The Republicans had gained a majority in the Senate in 1918, and two groups within their ranks were determined to frustrate Wilson's ambitions. One group was a caucus of 14 midwesterners and westerners known as the **"irreconcilables."** Most of them were conservative isolationists who wanted the United States to preserve its separation from Europe, but a few were prominent progressives—Robert La Follette, William Borah, and Hiram Johnson—who had voted against the declaration of war in 1917. The self-interest displayed by England and France at the peace conference convinced this group that the Europeans were incapable of decent behavior in international matters.

Senator **Henry Cabot Lodge** of Massachusetts led the second opposition group. Its members rejected Wilson's belief that every group of people on earth had a right to form their own nation; that every state, regardless of its size, its economic condition, and the vigor and intelligence of its people, should have a voice in world affairs; and that disputes between nations could be settled in open, democratic forums. They subscribed instead to Theodore Roosevelt's vision of a world controlled by a few great nations, each militarily strong, secure in its own sphere of influence, and determined to avoid war through a carefully negotiated balance of power. These Republicans preferred to let Europe return to the power politics that had prevailed before the war rather than experiment with a new world order that might constrain and compromise U.S. power and autonomy.

This Republican critique was a cogent one that merited extended discussion. Particularly important were questions that Republicans raised about Article X, which gave the League the right to undertake military actions against aggressor nations. Did Americans want to authorize an international organization to decide when the United States would go to war? Was this not a violation of the Constitution, which vested war-making power solely in the Congress? Even if the constitutional problem could be solved, how could the United States ensure that it would not be forced into a military action that might damage its national interest?

It soon became clear, however, that several Republicans, including Lodge, were as interested in humiliating Wilson as in developing an alternative approach to foreign policy. They accused Wilson of promoting socialism through his wartime expansion of government power. They were angry that he had failed to include any distinguished Republicans, such as Lodge, Elihu Root, or William Howard Taft, in the Paris peace delegation. And they were still bitter about the 1918 congressional elections, when Wilson had argued that a Republican victory would embarrass the nation abroad. Although Wilson's electioneering had failed to sway the voters (the Republicans won a majority in both Houses), his suggestion that a Republican victory would injure national honor had infuriated Theodore Roosevelt and his supporters. Roosevelt died in 1919, but his close friend Lodge kept his rage alive: "I never thought I could hate a man as much as I hate Wilson," Lodge conceded in a moment of candor.

As chairman of the Senate Foreign Relations Committee, charged with considering the treaty before reporting it to the Senate floor, Lodge did everything possible to obstruct ratification. He packed the committee with senators who were likely to oppose the treaty. He delayed action by reading every one of the treaty's 300 pages aloud and by subjecting it to endless criticism in six long weeks of public hearings. When his committee finally reported the treaty to the full Senate, it came encumbered with nearly 50 amendments whose adoption Lodge made a precondition of his support. Some of the amendments expressed reasonable concerns—namely, that participation in the League not diminish the role of Congress in determining foreign policy, compromise American sovereignty, or involve the United States in an unjust or ill-advised war—but many were meant only to complicate the task of ratification.

Despite Lodge's obstructionism, the treaty's chances for ratification by the required two-thirds majority of the Senate remained good. Many Republicans were prepared to vote for ratification if Wilson indicated his willingness to accept some of the proposed amendments. Wilson could have salvaged the treaty and, along with it, U.S. participation in the League of Nations, but he refused to compromise with the Republicans and announced that he would carry his case directly to the American people instead. In September 1919, Wilson undertook a whirlwind cross-country tour that covered more than 8,000 miles with 37 stops. He addressed as many crowds as he could reach, sometimes speaking for an hour at a time, four times a day.

On September 25, after giving a speech at Pueblo, Colorado, Wilson suffered excruciating headaches throughout the night. His physician ordered him back to Washington, where on October 2 he suffered a near-fatal stroke. Wilson hovered near death for two weeks and remained seriously disabled for another six. His condition improved somewhat in November, but his left side remained paralyzed, his speech was slurred, his energy level low, and his emotions unstable. Wilson's wife, Edith Bolling Wilson, and his doctor isolated him from Congress and the press, withholding news they thought might upset him and preventing the public from learning how much his body and mind had deteriorated.

Many historians believe that the stroke impaired Wilson's political judgment. He refused to consider any of the Republican amendments to the treaty, even after it had become clear that compromise offered the only chance of winning U.S. participation in the League of Nations. When Lodge presented an amended treaty for a ratification vote on November 19, Wilson ordered Senate Democrats to vote against it; 42 (of 47) Democratic senators complied, and with the aid of 13 Republican irreconcilables, the Lodge version was defeated. Only moments later, the unamended version of the treaty—Wilson's version—received only 38 votes.

The Treaty's Final Defeat

As the magnitude of the calamity became apparent, supporters of the League in Congress, the nation, and the world urged the Senate and the president to reconsider. Wilson would not budge. A bipartisan group of senators desperately tried to work out a compromise without consulting him. When that effort failed, the Senate put to a vote, one more time, the Lodge version of the treaty. Because 23 Democrats, most of them southerners, still refused to break with Wilson, this last-ditch effort at ratification failed on March 8, 1920, by a margin of seven votes. Wilson's dream of a new world order died that day. The crumpled figure in the White House seemed to bear little resemblance to the hero who, barely 15 months before, had been greeted in Europe as the world's savior. Wilson filled out his remaining 12 months in office as an invalid, presiding over the interment of progressivism. He died in 1924.

The judgment of history lies heavily on these events, for many believe that the flawed treaty and the failure of the League contributed to Adolf Hitler's rise in Germany and the outbreak of a second world war more devastating than the first. It is necessary to ask, then,

Woodrow Wilson's Fourteen Points, 1918: Record of Implementation

1. Open covenants of peace openly arrived at	Not fulfilled
2. Absolute freedom of navigation upon the seas in peace and war	Not fulfilled
3. Removal of all economic barriers to the equality of trade among nations	Not fulfilled
4. Reduction of armaments to the level needed only for domestic safety	Not fulfilled
5. Impartial adjustments of colonial claims	Not fulfilled
6. Evacuation of all Russian territory; Russia to be welcomed into the society of free nations	Not fulfilled
7. Evacuation and restoration of Belgium	Fulfilled
8. Evacuation and restoration of all French lands; return of Alsace-Lorraine to France	Fulfilled
9. Readjustment of Italy's frontiers along lines of Italian nationality	Compromised
10. Self-determination for the former subjects of the Austro-Hungarian Empire	Compromised
11. Evacuation of Romania, Serbia, and Montenegro; free access to the sea for Serbia	Compromised
12. Self-determination for the former subjects of the Ottoman Empire; secure sovereignty for Turkish portion	Compromised
13. Establishment of an independent Poland with free and secure access to the sea	Fulfilled
14. Establishment of a League of Nations affording mutual guarantees of independence and territorial integrity	Compromised

Sources: From G. M. Gathorne-Hardy, *The Fourteen Points and the Treaty of Versailles,* Oxford Pamphlets on World Affairs, no. 6 (1939), pp. 8–34; and Thomas G. Paterson et al., *American Foreign Policy: A History,* 2nd ed. (Lexington, MA: Heath, 1983), vol. 2, pp. 282–93.

whether American participation in the League would have significantly altered the course of world history.

The mere fact of U.S. membership in the League would not have magically solved Europe's postwar problems. The U.S. government was inexperienced in diplomacy and prone to mistakes. Its freedom to negotiate solutions to international disputes would have been limited by the large number of American voters who remained strongly opposed to U.S. entanglement in European affairs. Even if such opposition could have been overcome, the United States would still have confronted European countries determined to go their own way.

Nevertheless, one thing is clear: No stable international order could have arisen after the First World War without the full involvement of the United States. The League of Nations required American authority and prestige in order to operate effectively as an international parliament. We cannot know whether the League, with American involvement, would have offered the Germans a less humiliating peace, allowing them to rehabilitate their economy and salvage their national pride; nor whether an American-led League would have stopped Hitler's expansionism before it escalated into full-scale war in 1939. Still, it seems fair to suggest that American participation would have strengthened the League and improved its ability to bring a lasting peace to Europe.

The Postwar Period: A Society in Convulsion

Focus Question
What issues convulsed American society in the immediate aftermath of war, and how were they resolved?

The end of the war brought no respite from the forces convulsing American society. Workers were determined to regain the purchasing power they had lost to inflation. Employers were determined to halt or reverse the wartime gains labor had made. Radicals saw in this conflict between capital and labor the possibility of a socialist revolution. Conservatives were certain that the revolution had already begun. Returning white servicemen were nervous about regaining their civilian jobs and looked with hostility on the black, Hispanic, and female workers who had been recruited to take their places. Black veterans were in no mood to return to segregation and subordination. The federal government, meanwhile, uneasy over the centralization of power during the war, quickly dismantled such agencies as the War Industries Board and the National War Labor Board. By so doing, it deprived itself of mechanisms that might have enabled it to intervene in social conflicts and keep them from erupting into rage and violence.

Labor-Capital Conflict

Nowhere was the escalation of conflict more evident than in the workplace. In 1919, 4 million workers—one-fifth of the nation's manufacturing workforce—went on strike. In January 1919, a general strike paralyzed the city of Seattle when 60,000 workers walked off their jobs. By August, walkouts had been staged by 400,000 eastern and midwestern coal miners, 120,000 New England textile workers, and 50,000 New York City garment workers. Then came two strikes that turned public opinion sharply against labor. In September, Boston policemen walked off their jobs after the police commissioner refused to negotiate with their newly formed union. Rioting and looting soon broke out. Massachusetts Governor Calvin Coolidge, outraged by the policemen's betrayal of their sworn public duty, refused to negotiate with them, called out the National Guard to restore order, and fired the entire police force. His tough stand would bring him national fame and the Republican vice presidential nomination in 1920.

Hard on the heels of the policemen's strike came a strike by more than 300,000 steelworkers in the Midwest. No union had established a footing in the steel industry since the 1890s, when Andrew Carnegie had ousted the ironworkers' union from his Homestead, Pennsylvania, mills. Most steelworkers labored long hours (the 12-hour shift was still standard) for low wages in dangerous workplaces. The organizers of the **1919 steel strike** had somehow managed to persuade steelworkers with varied skill levels and ethnic backgrounds to put aside their differences and demand an eight-hour day and union recognition. When the employers rejected those demands, the workers walked off their jobs. The employers responded by procuring armed guards to beat up the strikers and by hiring nonunion labor to keep the plants running. In many areas, local and state police prohibited union meetings, ran strikers out of town, and opened fire on those who disobeyed orders. In Gary, Indiana, a confrontation between unionists and armed guards left 18 strikers dead. To arouse public support for their antiunion campaign, industry leaders portrayed the strike leaders as dangerous and violent radicals bent on the destruction of political liberty and economic freedom. They succeeded in arousing public opinion against the steelworkers, and the strike collapsed in January 1920.

Radicals and the Red Scare

The steel companies succeeded in putting down the strike by fanning the public's fear that revolutionary sentiment was spreading among workers. Radical sentiment was indeed on the rise. Mine workers and railroad workers had begun calling for the permanent nationalization of coal mines and railroads. Longshoremen in San Francisco and Seattle refused to load ships carrying supplies to the White Russians who had taken up arms against Lenin's Bolshevik government. Socialist trade unionists mounted the most serious challenge to Gompers's control of the AFL in 25 years. In 1920, nearly a million Americans voted for the Socialist presidential candidate Debs, who ran his campaign from the Atlanta Federal Penitentiary. Small groups of anarchists contemplated, and occasionally carried out, bomb attacks on businessmen and public officials.

This radical surge did not mean, however, that leftists had fashioned themselves into a single movement or political party. On the contrary, the Russian Revolution had split the American Socialist Party. One faction, which would keep the name Socialist and would continue under Debs's leadership, insisted that radicals follow a democratic path to socialism.

The other group, which would take the name Communist, wanted to establish a Lenin-style "dictatorship of the proletariat." Small groups of anarchists, some of whom advocated campaigns of terror to speed the revolution, represented yet a third radical tendency.

Few Americans noticed the disarray in the radical camp. Most assumed that radicalism was a single, coordinated movement bent on establishing a communist government on American soil. They saw the nation's immigrant communities as breeding grounds for Bolshevism. Beginning in 1919, this perceived **"red scare"** prompted government officials and private citizens to embark on yet another campaign of repression.

The postwar repression of radicalism closely resembled the wartime repression of dissent. Thirty states passed sedition laws to punish those who advocated revolution. Numerous public and private groups intensified Americanization campaigns designed to strip foreigners of their subversive ways and remake them into loyal citizens. Universities fired radical professors, and vigilante groups wrecked the offices of socialists and assaulted IWW agitators. A newly formed veterans' organization, the American Legion, took on the American Protective League's role of identifying seditious individuals and organizations and ensuring the public's devotion to "100 percent Americanism."

The Red Scare reached its climax on New Year's Day 1920, when federal agents broke into the homes and meeting places of thousands of suspected revolutionaries in 33 cities. Directed by Attorney General A. Mitchell Palmer, these widely publicized "Palmer raids" were meant to expose the extent of revolutionary activity. Palmer's agents uncovered three pistols, no rifles, and no explosives. Nevertheless, they arrested more than 4,000 people and kept many of them in jail for weeks without formally charging them with a crime. Finally, those who were not citizens (approximately 600) were deported and the rest were released.

Palmer's failure to expose a revolutionary plot blunted support for him in official circles, but, undeterred, Palmer now alleged that revolutionaries were planning a series of assaults on government officials and government buildings for May 1, 1920. When nothing happened on that date, his credibility suffered another blow.

As Palmer's exaggerations of the Red threat became known, many Americans began to reconsider their near-hysterical fear of dissent and subversion. Even so, the political atmosphere remained hostile to radicals, as the **Sacco and Vanzetti case** revealed. In May 1920, two Italian-born anarchists, Nicola Sacco and Bartolomeo Vanzetti, were arrested in Brockton, Massachusetts, and charged with armed robbery and murder. Both men proclaimed their innocence and insisted that they were being punished for their political beliefs. Their foreign accents and their defiant espousal of anarchist doctrines in the courtroom inclined many Americans, including the judge who presided at their trial, to view them harshly. Despite the weak case against them, they were convicted of first-degree murder and sentenced to death. Their lawyers attempted numerous appeals, all of which failed. Anger over the verdicts began to build among Italian Americans, radicals, and liberal intellectuals. Protests compelled the governor of Massachusetts to appoint a commission to review the case, but no new trial was ordered. On August 23, 1927, Sacco and Vanzetti were executed, still insisting they were innocent.

Reds (1981)

Directed by Warren Beatty. Starring Warren Beatty (John Reed), Diane Keaton (Louise Bryant), Edward Herrmann (Max Eastman), Jerzy Kosinski (Grigory Zinoviev), Jack Nicholson (Eugene O'Neill), and Maureen Stapleton (Emma Goldman).

In this epic film, Warren Beatty, producer, director, and screenplay cowriter, attempts to integrate the history of the American Left in the early 20th century with a love story about two radicals of that era, John "Jack" Reed and Louise Bryant. Reed was a well-known radical journalist whose dispatches from Russia during its 1917 revolution were published as a book, *Ten Days That Shook the World,* that brought him fame and notoriety. Bryant never developed the public reputation that Reed enjoyed, but she was an integral member of the radical circles that gathered in apartments and cafés in New York's Bohemian Greenwich Village before and during the First World War.

At times, the love principals in this movie seem to resemble Warren Beatty and Diane Keaton more than they do the historical figures they are meant to represent. In general, however, the movie keeps love and politics in balance and thus successfully conveys an important and historically accurate message about the American Left, especially before the First World War: namely, that its participants wanted to revolutionize the personal as well as the political. Thus equality between men and women, women's right to enjoy the same

sexual freedom as men, and marriage's impact on personal growth and adventure were issues debated with the same fervor as building a radical political party and accelerating the transition to socialism. (See the section entitled, The New Sexuality and the Rise of Feminism," in chapter 20.)

Reds is also an exceptionally serious film about political parties and ideologies. The film follows the arc of John Reed's and Louise Bryant's lives from their prewar days as discontented members of the Portland, Oregon, social elite, through their flight to the freedom and radicalism of Greenwich Village, to the hardening of their radicalism as a result of repression during the First World War at home and the Bolshevik triumph in November 1917. In this movie, Beatty has recreated detailed and complex stories about internal fights within the Left both in the United States and Russia, through which he seeks to show how hopes for social transformation went awry. To give this film added historical weight, Beatty introduces "witnesses," individuals who actually knew the real Reed and Bryant and who appear on screen periodically to share their memories, both serious and whimsical, about the storied couple and the times in which they lived.

© Paramount Pictures/Courtesy: Everett Collection.

Diane Keaton as Louise Bryant and Warren Beatty as John Reed, together in Russia in the midst of that country's socialist revolution.

Racial Conflict and the Rise of Black Nationalism

The more than 400,000 blacks who served in the armed forces believed that a victory for democracy abroad would help them achieve democracy for their people at home. At first, despite the discrimination they encountered in the military, they maintained their conviction that they would be treated as full-fledged citizens upon their return. Many began to talk about the birth of a New Negro—independent and proud. Thousands joined the National Association for the Advancement of Colored People (NAACP), an organization at the forefront of the fight for racial equality. By 1918, 100,000 African Americans subscribed to the NAACP's magazine, *The Crisis,* whose editor, W. E. B. Du Bois, had urged them to support the war.

This wartime optimism made the postwar discrimination and hatred African Americans encountered difficult to endure. Many black workers who had found jobs in the North were fired to make way for returning white veterans. Returning black servicemen, meanwhile, had to scrounge for poorly paid jobs as unskilled laborers. In the South, lynch mobs targeted black veterans who refused to tolerate the usual insults and indignities; 10 of the 70 blacks lynched in the South in 1919 were veterans.

The worst anti-black violence that year occurred in the North, however. Crowded conditions during the war had forced black and white ethnic city dwellers into uncomfortably close proximity. Many white ethnics regarded blacks with a mixture of fear and prejudice. They resented having to share neighborhoods, trolleys, parks, streets, and workplaces with blacks. Many also wanted African Americans barred from unions, seeing them as threats to their job security.

Racial tensions escalated into race riots. The deadliest explosion occurred in Chicago in July 1919, when a black teenager who had been swimming in Lake Michigan was killed by whites after coming too close to a whites-only beach. Rioting soon broke out, with white mobs invading black neighborhoods, torching homes and stores, and attacking innocent residents. Led by war veterans, some of whom were armed, blacks fought back, turning the border areas between white and black neighborhoods into battle zones. Fighting raged for five days, leaving 38 dead (23 black, 15 white) and more than 500 injured. Race rioting in other cities pushed the death toll to 120 before summer's end.

The riots made it clear to blacks that the North was not the Promised Land. Confined to unskilled jobs and to segregated neighborhoods with substandard housing and exorbitant rents, black migrants in Chicago, New York, and other northern cities suffered economic hardship throughout the 1920s. The NAACP carried on its campaign for civil rights and racial equality, but many blacks no longer shared its belief that they would one day be accepted as first-class citizens. They turned instead to a leader from Jamaica, **Marcus Garvey,** who gave voice to their bitterness: "The first dying that is to be done by the black man in the future," Garvey declared in 1918, "will be done to make himself free. And then when we are finished, if we have any charity to bestow, we may die for the white man. But as for me, I think I have stopped dying for him."

Garvey called on blacks to give up their hopes for integration and to set about forging a separate black nation. He reminded blacks that they possessed a rich culture stretching

Marcus Garvey, Black Nationalist   This portrait was taken in 1924, after Garvey's conviction on mail fraud charges.

back over the centuries that would enable them to achieve greatness as a nation. Garvey's ambition was to build a black nation in Africa that would bring together all of the world's people of African descent. In the short term, he wanted to help American and Caribbean blacks to achieve economic and cultural independence.

Garvey's call for black separatism and self-sufficiency—or black nationalism, as it came to be known—elicited a favorable response among African Americans. In the early 1920s, the Universal Negro Improvement Association (UNIA), which Garvey had founded, enrolled millions of members in 700 branches in 38 states. His newspaper, the *Negro World,* reached a circulation of 200,000. The New York chapter of UNIA undertook an economic development program that included the establishment of grocery stores, restaurants, and factories. Garvey's most visible economic venture was the Black Star Line, a shipping company with three ships flying the UNIA flag from their masts.

This black nationalist movement did not endure for long. Garvey entered into bitter disputes with other black leaders, including W. E. B. Du Bois, who regarded him as a flamboyant, self-serving demagogue. Garvey sometimes showed poor judgment, as when he expressed support for the Ku Klux Klan on the grounds that it shared his pessimism about the possibility of racial integration. Inexperienced in economic matters, Garvey squandered

UNIA money on abortive business ventures. The U.S. government regarded his rhetoric as inflammatory and sought to silence him. In 1923, he was convicted of mail fraud involving the sale of Black Star stocks and was sentenced to five years in jail. In 1927, he was deported to Jamaica, and the UNIA folded. Nevertheless, Garvey's philosophy of black nationalism endured.

Conclusion

The resurgence of racism in 1919 and the consequent turn to black nationalism among African Americans were signs that the high hopes of the war years had been dashed. Industrial workers, immigrants, and radicals also found their pursuit of liberty and equality interrupted by the fear, intolerance, and repression unleashed by the war. They came to understand as well that Wilson's commitment to these ideals counted for less than did his administration's and Congress's determination to discipline a people whom they regarded as dangerously heterogeneous and unstable. Of the reform groups, only woman suffragists made enduring gains—especially the right to vote—but, for the feminists in their ranks, these steps forward failed to compensate for the collapse of the progressive movement and, with it, their program of achieving equal rights for women across the board.

A similar disappointment engulfed those who had embraced and fought for Wilson's dream of creating a new and democratic world order. The world in 1919 appeared as volatile as it had been in 1914. More and more Americans—perhaps even a majority—were coming to believe that U.S. intervention had been a mistake.

In other ways, the United States benefited a great deal from the war. By 1919, the American economy was by far the world's strongest. Many of the nation's leading corporations had improved productivity and management during the war. U.S. banks were poised to supplant those of London as the most influential in international finance. The nation's economic strength triggered an extraordinary burst of growth in the 1920s, and millions of Americans rushed to take advantage of the prosperity that this "people's capitalism" had put within their grasp. But even affluence failed to dissolve the class, ethnic, and racial tensions that the war had exposed. And the failure of the peace process added to Europe's problems, delayed the emergence of the United States as a leader in world affairs, and created the preconditions for another world war.

SUGGESTED READINGS

On America's neutrality and road to war, consult **Arthur S. Link**, *Woodrow Wilson: Revolution, War and Peace* (1979), and **John Milton Cooper Jr.**, *The Vanity of Power: American Isolationism and the First World War, 1914–1917* (1969). **Roland C. Marchand**, *The American Peace Movement and Social Reform, 1898–1918* (1972), reconstructs the large and influential antiwar movement, while **John W. Chambers**, *To Raise an Army: The Draft Comes to Modern America* (1987), analyzes American efforts to prepare for war by raising a multimillion-man fighting machine. **David Kennedy**, *Over Here: The First World War and American Society* (1980), is a superb account of the effects of war on American society. For details on industrial mobilization, consult **Robert D. Cuff,** *The War Industries Board: Business-Government Relations during World War I* (1973). **David Montgomery,** *The Fall of the House of Labor: The Workplace, the State, and American Labor Activism, 1865–1925* (1987), expertly reconstructs the escalation of labor-management tensions during the war, but it should be read alongside **Joseph A. McCartin,** *Labor's Great War: The Struggle for Industrial Democracy and the Origins of Modern Labor Relations, 1912–1921* (1997).

For a pioneering effort to situate U.S. domestic politics during the war in an international context, see **Alan Dawley,** *Changing the World: American Progressives in War and Revolution* (2003). On the migration of African Americans to northern industrial centers and the movement of women into war production, see **Joe William Trotter Jr., ed.,** *The Great Migration in Historical Perspective: New Dimensions of Race, Class, and Gender* (1991), and **Maurine W. Greenwald,** *Women, War and Work* (1980). **Stephen Vaughn,** *Holding Fast the Inner Lines: Democracy, Nationalism, and the Committee on Public Information* (1980), is an important account of the CPI, the government's central propaganda agency. **Harry N. Scheiber,** *The Wilson Administration and Civil Liberties, 1917–1921* (1960) and **Geoffrey R. Stone,** *Perilous Times: Free Speech in War Time from the Sedition Act of 1798 to the War on Terrorism* (2004), analyze the repression of dissent.

On Wilson, Versailles, and the League of Nations, consult **Thomas J. Knock,** *To End All Wars: Woodrow Wilson and the Quest for a New World Order* (1992); **Arno Mayer,** *The Politics and Diplomacy of Peacemaking: Containment and Counterrevolution at Versailles, 1918–1919* (1967); **Lloyd C. Gardner,** *Safe for Democracy: The Anglo-American Response to Revolution, 1913–1923* (1984); **John Milton Cooper, Jr.,** *Breaking the Heart of the World: Woodrow Wilson and the Fight for the League of Nations* (2001); and **Katherine A. S. Siegel,** *Loans and Legitimacy: The Evolution of Soviet-American Relations, 1919–1933* (1996). On Republican opposition to the League of Nations, see **William C. Widenor,** *Henry Cabot Lodge and the Search for an American Foreign Policy* (1980).

Nell Irvin Painter, *Standing at Armageddon: The United States, 1877–1919* (1987), offers a good overview of the class and racial divisions that convulsed American society in 1919. On the Red Scare, consult **Robert K. Murray,** *Red Scare: A Study in National Hysteria* (1955). **William Tuttle, Jr.,** *Race Riot: Chicago in the Red Summer of 1919* (1970), examines race conflict after the First World War, while **Judith Stein,** *The World of Marcus Garvey: Race and Class in Modern Society* (1986), explores the emergence of Marcus Garvey and the Universal Negro Improvement Association.

Visit the Liberty Equality Power Companion Web site for resources specific to this textbook: http://www.thomsonedu.com/history/murrin

Also find self-tests and additional resources at ThomsonNOW. ThomsonNOW is an integrated online suite of services and resources with proven ease of use and efficient paths to success, delivering the results you want—NOW!

www.thomsonedu.com/login/

The 1920s

In 1920, Americans elected as president, Warren G. Harding, a man who could not have been more different from his predecessor Woodrow Wilson. A Republican, Harding presented himself as a common man with common desires. In his 1920 campaign, he called for a "return to normalcy." Although he died in office in 1923, his carefree spirit is thought to characterize the 1920s.

To many Americans, the decade was one of fun rather than reform, of good times rather than high ideals. It was, in the words of novelist F. Scott Fitzgerald, the "Jazz Age," a time when the search for personal gratification seemed to replace the quest for public welfare.

Despite Harding's call for a return to a familiar past, America seemed to be rushing headlong into the future. The word *modern* began appearing everywhere: modern times, modern women, modern technology, the modern home, modern marriage. Although the word was rarely defined, it connoted certain beliefs: that science was a better guide to life than religion; that people should be free to choose their own lifestyles; that sex should be a source of pleasure for women as well as men; that women and minorities should be equal to white men and enjoy the same rights.

Many other Americans, however, reaffirmed their belief that God's word transcended science; that people should obey the moral code set forth in the Bible; that women were not equal to men; and that blacks, Mexicans, and Eastern European immigrants were inferior to Anglo-Saxon whites. They made their voices heard in a resurgent **Ku Klux Klan** and the fundamentalist movement, and on issues such as evolution and immigration. In seeking to restore an older America, some in their ranks were prepared to deny individual Americans the liberty to choose their own ways of living and to insist that all people were not fundamentally equal.

Modernists and traditionalists confronted each other in party politics, in legislatures, in courtrooms, and in the press. Their battles belie the vision of the 1920s merely as a time for the pursuit of leisure.

Prosperity

Focus Question
What were the achievements and limitations of "people's capitalism" in the 1920s?

CHRONOLOGY

1920	Prohibition goes into effect • Warren G. Harding defeats James M. Cox for presidency • Census reveals that a majority of Americans live in urban areas • 8 million cars on road
1921	Sheppard-Towner Act passed
1922	United States, Britain, Japan, France, and Italy sign Five-Power Treaty, agreeing to reduce size of their navies
1923	Teapot Dome scandal lands Secretary of the Interior Albert Fall in jail • Harding dies in office; Calvin Coolidge becomes president
1924	Dawes Plan to restructure Germany's war debt put in effect • Coolidge defeats John W. Davis for presidency • Ku Klux Klan membership approaches 4 million • Johnson-Reed Act cuts immigration by 80 percent and discriminates against East and South Asians and Southern and Eastern Europeans
1925	Scopes trial upholds right of Tennessee to bar teaching of evolution in public schools • *Survey Graphic* publishes a special issue announcing the Harlem Renaissance • F. Scott Fitzgerald publishes *The Great Gatsby* • U.S. withdraws Marines from Nicaragua
1926	Revenue Act cuts income and estate taxes • U.S. sends Marines back to Nicaragua to end civil war and protect U.S. property
1927	Coolidge vetoes McNary-Haugen bill, legislation meant to relieve agricultural distress • Babe Ruth hits 60 home runs • Charles Lindbergh flies across the Atlantic
1928	15 nations sign Kellogg-Briand pact, pledging to avoid war • Coolidge vetoes McNary-Haugen bill again • Herbert Hoover defeats Alfred E. Smith for presidency
1929	Union membership drops to 3 million • 27 million cars on roads • William Faulkner publishes *The Sound and the Fury* • Josh Gibson joins the National Negro League
1930	Los Angeles's Mexican population reaches 100,000

On balance, the First World War had been good for the American economy. American industries had emerged intact, even strengthened, from the war. The war needs of the Allies had created an insatiable demand for American goods and capital. Manufacturers and bankers had exported so many goods and extended so many loans to the Allies that by war's end, the United States was the world's leading creditor nation. New York City challenged London as the hub of world finance. At home, the government had helped large corporations and banks to consolidate their power. Corporate America had responded by raising productivity and efficiency to new heights through advances in technology and management.

Postwar economic turmoil and depression hampered these advances for a time. From 1919 to 1921, the country struggled to redirect industry from wartime to civilian production, a process slowed by the government's hasty withdrawal from its wartime role as economic regulator and stabilizer. Workers went on strike to protest wage reductions or increases in the workweek. Farmers were hit by a depression as the overseas demand for American foodstuffs fell from its 1918–19 peak. Disgruntled workers and farmers even joined forces to form statewide farmer-labor parties, which for a time threatened to disrupt the country's two-party system in the upper Midwest. In 1924, the two groups formed a national Farmer-Labor Party. Robert La Follette, their presidential candidate, received an impressive 16 percent of the vote that year, but then the third-party movement fell apart.

Its collapse reflected a rising public awareness of how vigorous and productive the economy had become. Beginning in 1922, the nation embarked on a period of remarkable growth. From 1922 to 1929, the gross national product grew at an annual rate of 5.5 percent, rising from $149 billion to $227 billion. The unemployment rate never exceeded 5 percent, and real wages rose about 15 percent.

A Consumer Society

The variety of products being produced matched the rate of economic growth. In the 19th century, economic growth had rested primarily on the production of capital goods, such as factory machinery and railroad tracks. In the 1920s, however, growth rested more on consumer goods. Some products, such as cars and telephones, had been available since the early 1900s, but in the 1920s their sales reached new levels. In 1920, just 12 years after Ford introduced the Model T, 8 million cars were on the road. By 1929, there were 27 million— one for every five Americans. Other consumer goods became available for the first time: tractors, washing machines, refrigerators, electric irons, radios, and vacuum cleaners. The term **"consumer durable"** was coined to describe such goods, which, unlike food, clothing, and other perishables, were meant to last. Even perishables took on new allure. Scientists had discovered the importance of vitamins in the diet and began urging Americans to consume more fresh fruits and vegetables. The agricultural economy of southern California grew rapidly as urban demand for the region's fresh fruits and vegetables skyrocketed. Improvements in refrigeration and in packaging, meanwhile, allowed fresh produce to travel long distances and extended its shelf life in grocery stores. And more stores were being operated by large grocery chains that could afford the latest refrigeration and packaging technology.

The public responded to these innovations with excitement. American industry had made fresh food and stylish clothes available to the masses. Refrigerators, vacuum cleaners, and washing machines would spare women the drudgery of housework. Radios would expand the public's cultural horizons. Cars, asphalt roads, service stations, hot dog stands, "tourist cabins" (the forerunners of motels), and traffic lights seemed to herald a wholly new automobile civilization. By the middle of the decade, the country possessed a network of paved roads. City dwellers now had easy access to rural areas and made a ritual of day-long excursions. Camping trips and long-distance vacations became routine. Farmers and their families could now hop into their cars and head for the nearest town with its stores, movies, amusement parks, and sporting events. Suburbs proliferated, billed as the perfect mix of urban and rural life. Young men and women everywhere discovered that cars were a place where they could "make out," and even make love, without fear of reproach by prudish parents or prying neighbors.

In the 1920s, some Americans also discovered the benefits of owning stocks. The number of stockholders in AT&T, the nation's largest corporation, rose from 140,000 to 568,000. U.S. Steel stockholder numbers increased from 96,000 to 146,000. By 1929, as many as 7 million Americans owned stock, most of them people of middle-class or upper-class means. This spread of stock ownership reflected the need for working capital among the nation's corporations. Because privately held wealth could not satisfy that need, corporations sought to sell their stocks and bonds to the general public. The New York Stock Exchange, first organized in 1792, assisted in processing complicated transactions.

A People's Capitalism

Capitalists boasted that they had created a **"people's capitalism"** in which virtually all Americans could participate. Now, everyone could own a piece of corporate America. Now, everyone could have a share of luxuries and amenities. Poverty, capitalists claimed, was banished, and the gap between rich and poor all but closed. If every American could own a car and house, buy quality clothes, own stock, take vacations, and go to the movies, then economic inequality would cease to matter as a political issue.

Actually, although wages were rising, millions of Americans still earned too little to partake fully of the marketplace. The percentage of Americans owning stocks remained small. Social scientists Robert and Helen Lynd discovered, in their celebrated 1929 study of Muncie, Indiana, that working-class families who bought a car often lacked money for other goods. One housewife admitted, "We don't have no fancy clothes when we have the car to pay for. . . . The car is the only pleasure we have." Another declared, "I'll go without food before I'll see us give up the car." Many industrialists resisted pressure to increase wages, and workers lacked the organizational strength to force them to pay more.

One solution came with the introduction of consumer credit. Car dealers, home appliance salesmen, and other merchants began to offer installment plans that enabled consumers to purchase a product by making a down payment and promising to pay the rest in installments. By 1930, 15 percent of all purchases—including 60 percent of all cars and 75 percent of all radios—were made on the installment plan.

Even so, many poor Americans benefited little from the consumer revolution. Middle-class Americans acquired a disproportionate share of consumer durables. They also could afford to purchase far more fresh fruits and vegetables and stocks than most working-class Americans.

The Rise of Advertising and Mass Marketing

But even middle-class consumers had to be wooed. How could they be persuaded to buy another car only a few years after they had bought their first one? General Motors had the answer. In 1926, it introduced the concept of the annual model change. GM cars took on a different look every year as GM engineers changed headlights and chassis colors, stream-lined bodies, and added new features. The strategy worked. GM leaped past Ford and became the world's largest car manufacturer.

Henry Ford reluctantly introduced his Model A in 1927 to provide customers with a colorful alternative to the drab Model T. Having spent his lifetime selling a product renowned for its utility and reliability, Ford rejected the idea that sales could be increased by appealing to the intangible hopes and fears of consumers. He was wrong. The desire to be beautiful, handsome, or sexually attractive; to exercise power and control; to demon-strate competence and success; to escape anonymity, loneliness, and boredom; to experi-ence pleasure—all such desires, once activated, could motivate a consumer to buy a new car even when the old one was still serviceable, or to spend money on goods that might have once seemed frivolous.

Arousing such desires required more than bright colors, sleek lines, and attractive pack-aging. It called for advertising campaigns intended to make a product seem to be the answer to the consumer's desires. To create those campaigns, corporations turned to a new kind of company: professional advertising firms. The new advertising entrepreneurs, people such as Edward Bernays, Doris Fleischmann, and Bruce Barton, tended to be well-educated, sen-sitive to public taste, and knowledgeable about human psychology. In their campaigns, these advertisers played on the emotions and vulnerabilities of their target audiences. One cosmetics ad decreed: "Unless you are one woman in a thousand, you must use powder and rouge. Modern living has robbed women of much of their natural color." A perfume manufacturer's ad pronounced: "The first duty of woman is to attract. . . . It does not mat-ter how clever or independent you may be, if you fail to influence the men you meet, con-sciously or unconsciously, you are not fulfilling your fundamental duty as a woman." A mouthwash ad warned about one unsuspecting gentleman's bad breath—"the truth that his friends had been too delicate to mention," while a tobacco ad matter-of-factly declared: "Men at the top are apt to be pipe-smokers. . . . It's no coincidence—pipe-smoking is a calm and deliberate habit—restful, stimulating. His pipe helps a man think straight. A pipe is back of most big ideas."

Advertising professionals believed they were helping people to manage their lives in ways that would increase their satisfaction and pleasure. American consumers responded enthusiastically. Their interest in fashion, their eagerness to fill their homes with the lat-est products, their alacrity to take up the craze of the moment (the mah-jongg card game, crossword puzzles, miniature golf)—all evidenced Americans' preoccupation with self-improvement and personal pleasure. The most enthusiastic of all were middle-class Americans, who could afford to buy what the advertisers were selling. Many of them were newcomers to middle-class ranks, searching for ways to affirm—or even create—their new identity. The aforementioned ad for pipe tobacco, for example, was targeted at the new middle-class man, imagined by advertisers to be someone holding a salaried position in a corporate office or bank, or working as a commission salesman, or owning a small business.

Selling Beauty and Health   This advertisement hints at the negative health effects of smoking, but touts "Luckies" as a healthful cigarette more appropriate for the delicate bodies of beautiful women.

As male wage earners moved into the new middle class, their wives were freed from the necessity of working outside the home. Advertisers appealed to the new middle-class woman, too, as she refocused her attention toward dressing in the latest fashion, managing the household, and raising children. Vacuum cleaners and other consumer durables would make her more efficient, and books on child-rearing, many imbued with a popularized Freudianism, would enable her to mold her children for future success in work and marriage. Cosmetics would aid women in their "first duty"—to be beautiful and sexual for their husbands and boyfriends.

Changing Attitudes toward Marriage and Sexuality

That husbands and wives were encouraged to pursue sexual satisfaction together was one sign of how prescriptions for married life had changed since the 19th century, when women were thought to lack sexual passion and men were tacitly expected to satisfy their drives through extramarital liaisons. Modern husbands and wives were expected to share other leisure activities as well—dining out, playing cards with friends, going to the movies, attending concerts, and discussing the latest selection from the newly formed Book-of-the-Month Club. Husbands and wives now aspired to a new ideal—to be best friends, full partners in the pursuit of happiness.

The public pursuit of pleasure was also noticeable among young and single middle-class women. The so-called **flappers** of the 1920s set out to break the informal rules governing young women's lives: they donned short dresses, rolled their stockings down, wore red lipstick, and smoked in public. They took their inspiration from depictions of saucy, working-class women of the previous decade that moviemakers had popularized and refined. Flappers were signaling their desire for independence and equality, but they had little thought of achieving those goals through politics, as had their middle-class predecessors in the woman suffrage movement. Rather, they aimed to create a new female personality endowed with self-reliance, outspokenness, and a new appreciation for the pleasures of life.

An Age of Celebrity

> **Focus Question**
> What was the age of celebrity and what caused it to arise?

The pursuit of pleasure became both an individual and a group endeavor. Mass marketers began to understand that big sums of money could be made by staging mega-events, mostly connected to sports, that tens of thousands would attend and that radio announcers would broadcast to a virtual audience of millions. Newspapers and word-of-mouth would ensure that enthusiasts would discuss these events for days, even weeks and months. Baseball and boxing became the two sports where mass marketing had advanced the furthest. When Yankee Stadium opened in 1923, it set a new standard for the scale and magnificence of sports amphitheaters. Boxing matches began drawing audiences that would have been unimaginable 20 years earlier. To succeed on this scale, these sports required not just stirring athletic competitions but also individual athletes who seemed larger than life and whose exploits and character could be endlessly promoted.

No sports figure achieved greater fame than did George Herman "Babe" Ruth, who overcame the hardships of a poor and orphaned youth in Baltimore to become the slugging star, the "Sultan of Swat," of the New York Yankees. In the 1920s, Ruth hit more home runs than baseball experts had thought humanly possible, culminating in 1927, when he hit a magical 60, a record that would last for 34 years and that would be surpassed only three times in the 20th century. A close second in popularity to Ruth was heavyweight prizefighter Jack Dempsey, whose combination of ruthlessness and efficiency in the ring with gentleness outside it enthralled millions.

Americans also drew their celebrities from the movies, where stars such as comedian Charles Chaplin and the exotically handsome Rudolph Valentino stirred laughter and sexual longings, respectively, in audiences. These and other figures became so familiar on the silver screen that they created an insatiable appetite among movie fans for news about their private lives as well, an interest that the movie industry was only too eager to exploit.

The popular figures of the 1920s did not earn their status through their accomplishments in politics or war, but through their prowess at a game or their skill at acting in front of a camera. Historians have tended to criticize such celebrity worship, especially when the lionized individual seemed to possess no quality greater than the ability to hit a ball 400 feet or to smash an opponent's face. But such scholarly criticism perhaps has been too quick to overlook the human longing to experience the intensity of emotions associated with competition and triumph or to draw close to someone who demonstrates that the impossible— whether in the form of a physical feat, or a love relationship, or an escape from a confining life—could be accomplished.

Some of these sentiments can be discerned in the adulation bestowed on **Charles A. Lindbergh,** the young pilot who, in 1927, became the first individual to cross the Atlantic in a solo flight. Piloting his single-engine white monoplane, *The Spirit of St. Louis,* Lindbergh flew nonstop (and without sleep) for 34 hours from the time he took off from Long Island until he landed at Le Bourget Airport in Paris. Thousands of Parisians were waiting for him at the airfield and began charging his plane as soon as it landed. When he returned to New York, an estimated 4 million fans lined the parade route. This shy young man from Minnesota instantly became the most famous and adored man in America, mobbed by crowds everywhere he went. None of this fame could have happened without the new machinery of celebrity culture—aggressive journalists and radio commentators, promoters, and others who understood how fame could yield a profit. It mattered, too, that Lindbergh performed his feat in an airplane, one of the era's newest and most exciting innovations. But Lindbergh's celebrity involved more than hype and technology: He accomplished what others said could not be done, and he did it on his own in a time when corporations and other private institutions of power seemed to be shrinking the realm for individual initiative. Some of Lindbergh's popularity no doubt rested on his ability to demonstrate that an individual of conviction and skill could still make a difference in an increasingly industrialized and bureaucratized world.

Celebrating Business Civilization

Industrialists, advertisers, and merchandisers in the 1920s began to claim that their accomplishments lay at the heart of American civilization. Business, they argued, made America great, and businessmen provided the nation with its wisest, most vigorous leadership. In

1924, President Calvin Coolidge declared that "the business of America is business." Even religion became a business. Bruce Barton, in his best seller *The Man Nobody Knows* (1925), depicted Jesus as a business executive "who picked up twelve men from the bottom ranks of business and forged them into an organization that conquered the world." Elsewhere, Barton hailed Jesus as an early "national advertiser," and proclaimed that Peter and Paul were really not so different from Americans who sold vacuum cleaners.

Some corporate leaders adopted benevolent attitudes toward their employees. They set up workplace cafeterias, hired doctors and nurses to staff on-site medical clinics, and engaged psychologists to counsel troubled workers. They built ball fields and encouraged employees to join industry-sponsored leagues. They published employee newsletters and gave awards to employees who did their jobs well and with good spirit. Some employers set up profit-sharing plans and offered stock options to reward employees for their efforts, and some even gave employees a voice in determining working conditions.

The real purpose of these measures—collectively known as welfare capitalism—was to encourage employees to be loyal to their firm and to convince them (contrary to what labor union critics had been arguing) that industry did have the best interests of its employees at heart. Management had an understandable fear of union power, arising from the paralyzing strikes of 1919. As the decade proceeded and as prosperity rolled on, welfare capitalism reflected the confidence that capitalism had become more responsive to employee concerns and thus more humane.

Industrial Workers

Many industrial workers benefited from the nation's prosperity. Most of them enjoyed rising wages and a reasonably steady income. Skilled craftsmen in the older industries of construction, railroad transportation, and printing fared especially well. Their real wages rose by 30 percent to 50 percent over the decade. The several million workers employed in the large mass-production industries (such as automobile and electrical equipment manufacture) also did well. Their wages were relatively high, and some of them enjoyed good benefits—paid sick leave, paid vacations, life insurance, stock options, and retirement pensions. Although all workers in companies with these programs were eligible for such benefits, skilled workers were in the best position to claim them.

Semiskilled and unskilled industrial workers had to contend with a labor surplus throughout the decade. As employers replaced workers with machines, the aggregate demand for industrial labor increased at a lower rate than it had in the preceding 20 years. Despite a weakening demand for labor, rural whites, rural blacks, and Mexicans continued their migration to the cities, stiffening the competition for factory jobs. Employers could hire and fire as they saw fit and could therefore keep wage increases lagging behind increases in productivity.

This softening demand for labor helps explain why many working-class families benefited little from the decade's prosperity or from its consumer revolution. An estimated 40 percent of workers remained mired in poverty, unable to afford a healthy diet or adequate housing, much less any of the more costly consumer goods. In 1930, for instance, only 25 percent to 40 percent of American households owned a washing machine, a vacuum cleaner, and a radio, and only 50 percent had a car.

The million or more workers who labored in the nation's two largest industries, coal and textiles, suffered the most during the 1920s. Throughout the decade, both industries experienced severe overcapacity. By 1926, only half of the coal mined each year was being sold. Many New England textile cities experienced levels of unemployment that sometimes approached 50 percent. One reason was that many textile industrialists had shifted their operations to the South, where taxes and wages were lower. But the southern textile industry also suffered from excess capacity, exerting a downward pressure on prices and wages there as well. Plant managers pressured their workers to speed up production. Workers loathed the frequent "speed-ups" of machines and the "stretch-outs" in the number of spinning or weaving machines each worker was expected to tend. By the late 1920s, labor strife and calls for unionization were rising among disgruntled workers in both the South and the North.

Unionization of textiles and coal, and of more prosperous industries as well, would have brought workers a larger share of the decade's prosperity. Some labor leaders, such as Sidney Hillman of the Amalgamated Clothing Workers, argued that unionization would actually increase corporate profits by compelling employers to observe uniform wage and hour schedules that would restrain ruinous competition. Hillman pointed out—as Henry Ford had in the preceding decade—that rising wages would enable workers to purchase

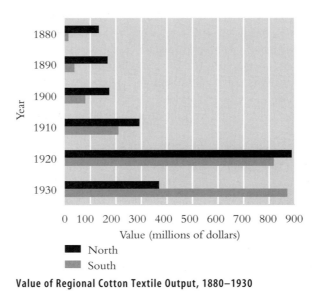

Value of Regional Cotton Textile Output, 1880–1930

Source: Data from Nancy F. Kane, *Textiles in Transition: Technology, Wages, and Industry Relocation in the U.S. Textile Industry, 1880–1939* (New York: Greenwood Press, 1988), p. 29.

more consumer goods and thus increase corporate sales and revenues, but Hillman's views were ignored outside the garment industry.

Elsewhere, unions lost ground as business and government, backed by middle-class opinion, remained hostile to labor organization. Employers attacked unions as un-American. A conservative Supreme Court whittled away at labor's legal protections. In 1921, it ruled that lower courts could issue injunctions against union members, prohibiting them from striking or picketing an employer. State courts also enforced what union members called **"yellow dog" contracts,** written pledges by which employees promised not to join a union while they were employed. Any employee who violated that pledge was subject to immediate dismissal.

These measures crippled efforts to organize trade unions. Membership fell from a high of 5 million in 1920 to less than 3 million in 1929, a mere 10 percent of the nation's industrial workforce. Other forces contributed to the decline, too. Many workers, especially those benefiting from welfare capitalist programs, decided they no longer needed trade unions. And the labor movement hurt itself by moving too slowly to open its ranks to semiskilled and unskilled factory workers.

Women and Work

Women workers experienced the same hardships as men in the industrial workforce and fewer of the benefits. They were largely excluded from the ranks of the skilled craftsmen and thus missed out on the substantial wage increases that the men in those positions enjoyed. Women also had trouble finding work in the automobile industry, the highest paying of the mass-production industries. They had better access to the electrical equipment and meat-packing industries, although they were often segregated in departments given over to "women's work." Where women were allowed to compete for the same jobs as men, they usually earned less. Thus, a female trimmer in a meat-packing plant typically made 37 cents per hour, only two-thirds of what a male trimmer earned. The textile industry had long been a major source of employment for women, but, in the 1920s, women and men alike in this ailing manufacturing sector suffered high rates of unemployment and declining wages.

White-collar work established itself, in the 1920s, as a magnet for women. This sector grew rapidly in a decade in which corporations expanded and refined their managerial and accounting practices. Discrimination prevented women from becoming managers, accountants, or supervisors, but they did dominate the lower-level ranks of secretaries, typists, filing clerks, bank tellers, and department store clerks. By the 1930s, 2 million women, or 20 percent of the female workforce, labored in these and related occupations. Initially, these positions had a glamour that factory work lacked. Work environments were cleaner and brighter, and women had the opportunity—indeed were expected—to dress well and fashionably. But wages were low and managerial authority was absolute. Unions had virtually no presence in white-collar places of employment, and workers had difficulty finding alternative ways of protesting unfair managers or difficult working conditiosns.

© Hulton-Deutsch Collection/CORBIS

Amelia Earhart, Aviation Pioneer   Earhart strikes a flapper pose in front of the biplane that she was preparing to fly across the Atlantic.

Women with ambitious work aspirations most often pursued the "female" professions, such as teaching, nursing, social work, and librarianship. Opportunities in several of these fields, especially teaching and social work, were growing, and women responded by enrolling in college in large numbers. The number of female college students increased by 50 percent during the 1920s. Some of these college graduates used their new skills in new fields, such as writing for women's magazines. A few, drawing strength from their feminist forebears during the progressive era, managed to crack such male bastions of work as mainstream journalism and university research and teaching. In every field of endeavor, even such new and exotic ones as airplane flying, at least one woman arose to demonstrate that her sex had the necessary talent and drive to match or exceed what men had done.

Thus in 1932, Amelia Earhart became the first woman to fly the Atlantic solo, matching Lindbergh's feat and inspiring women everywhere. Even so, Earhart's feat failed to improve substantially opportunities for women who wanted to work as pilots in the airline industry. In this industry, as in most lines of work, gender prejudices remained too entrenched, and the women who had broken the gender line remained, by and large, solitary figures.

The Women's Movement Adrift

Many supporters of the 19th Amendment to the Constitution, which, in 1920, gave women the right to vote, expected it to transform American politics. Women voters would reverse the decline in voter participation, cleanse politics of corruption, and launch a variety of reform initiatives that would improve the quality of life for women and men alike. This female-inspired transformation, however, failed to materialize. Voter participation rates did not increase, nor did American politics become imbued with female-inspired virtue and honesty. The women's movement, instead, seemed to succumb to the same exhaustion and frustration as had the more general progressive movement from which it had emerged 20 years earlier. Younger women searching for independence and equality (such as the flappers discussed earlier in this chapter) often turned away from reform altogether, preferring a lifestyle that emphasized private achievement and personal freedom to a political career devoted to improving the collective status of America's women. Those who continued to agitate for reform found progress more difficult to achieve once the conservative Republican administrations of Harding and Coolidge took office.

Despite the difficult political environment in which they had to work, some female reformers made significant strides in the 1920s. In 1921, one group succeeded in getting Congress to pass the **Sheppard-Towner Act,** a major social welfare program that provided federal funds for prenatal and child health care centers throughout the United States. It remained in effect until 1929. In 1923, Alice Paul, still head of the National Woman's Party (NWP, see chapter 20), and her allies prevailed on Congress to consider an Equal Rights Amendment (ERA) to the Constitution, phrased as follows: "Men and women shall have equal rights throughout the United States and every place subject to its jurisdiction." And the National American Woman Suffrage Association, the major force behind the struggle for suffrage, transformed itself in 1920 into the **League of Women Voters** (LWV). During the next decade, the LWV launched numerous initiatives to encourage women to run for elective office, to educate voters about the issues before them, and to improve the condition of those Americans—the poor, female and child laborers, the mentally ill—who needed assistance.

Sometimes the women's movement was stymied not just by external opposition but also by internal division— as it was over the ERA. The NWP and other supporters of the ERA insisted that there could be no compromise with the proposition that women were the equals of men in every respect. But, the LWV countered, child-rearing and mothering duties did render women different from men in key respects and thus, in some instances, in need of special treatment by Congress and other lawmaking bodies.

The question of female difference crystallized around the issue of protective labor legislation for women. Over the years, a series of state and federal laws had given women protections at the workplace—limitations on the hours of labor, prohibitions on overnight work, and other such measures—that men did not have. Many women reformers supported these measures, believing they were vital to protecting the masses of women workers from the worst forms of exploitation and thus enabling them to have enough time and energy to perform their vital roles as mothers and wives. Fearing that a successful ERA would render this protective legislation unconstitutional, the LWV and its allies opposed the ERA. Alice Paul and her allies countered by arguing that female protective laws did not really benefit women. Instead, employers used these laws as an excuse to segregate women in stereotyped jobs that were mostly low status and low paying and thus to deny women the opportunities for advancement and fulfillment open to men.

This issue of whether women should be treated like men in all respects or offered some protections that no men enjoyed was a genuinely complicated one, and women activists would continue to argue about it with each other for decades. In the 1920s, however, their inability to speak with a single voice on this matter weakened their cause in the eyes of their adversaries.

The Politics of Business

Focus Question
What were the similarities and differences in the politics of Harding, Coolidge, and Hoover?

Republican presidents governed the country from 1921 to 1933. In the beginning, this transition engulfed national politics in scandal, as Warren Harding, the first of the decade's three Republican presidents, allowed high-ranking members of his administration to indulge in spectacular forms of corruption. But his successor, Calvin Coolidge, restored virtue and honor to the presidency while carrying out his 1924 campaign pledge to overturn the legacy of progressivism and reduce the role of the government in economic affairs. The most significant challenge to Coolidge's small government program came from his own secretary of commerce and then his successor as president, Herbert Hoover, who sought to sustain the spirit of activist government that Theodore Roosevelt had introduced to Republican politics, albeit in somewhat altered form.

Harding and the Politics of Personal Gain
Warren Gamaliel Harding defeated Democrat James M. Cox for the presidency in 1920. From modest origins as a newspaper editor in the small town of Marion, Ohio, Harding had risen to the U.S. Senate chiefly because the powerful Ohio Republican machine knew it could count on him to do its bidding. He gained the presidency for the same reason. The Republican Party bosses believed that almost anyone they nominated in 1920 could defeat the Democratic opponent. They chose Harding because they could control him. Harding's good looks and geniality made him a favorite with voters, and he swept into office with 61 percent of the popular vote, the greatest landslide since 1820.

To his credit, Harding released the aging Socialist Party leader Eugene V. Debs from jail and took other measures to cool the passions unleashed by the Red Scare. He also included

Warren G. Harding with Friends and Attendants   This photograph was shot in St. Augustine, Florida. Harding is third from the right. Attorney General Harry M. Daugherty, boss of the Ohio Republican machine, stands to the left of the President, dressed in black and supporting himself with a cane.

talented men in his cabinet. His choices of Herbert Hoover as secretary of commerce, Charles Evans Hughes as secretary of state, and Andrew Mellon as secretary of the treasury were particularly impressive appointments. Still, Harding lacked the will to alter his ingrained political habits. He had built his political career on a willingness to please the lobbyists who came to his Senate office asking for favors and deals. He had long followed Ohio boss Harry M. Daugherty's advice and would continue to do so with Daugherty as his attorney general. Harding apparently did not consider men such as Daugherty self-serving or corrupt. They were his friends; they had been with him since the beginning of his political career. He made sure the "boys" had jobs in his administration, and he continued to socialize with them. Many a night he could be found drinking (despite **Prohibition**), gambling, and womanizing with the "Ohio Gang" at its K Street hangout. Sometimes the gang even convened in the White House. Alice Roosevelt Longworth, Theodore Roosevelt's daughter, once came into the White House study and found the air "heavy with tobacco smoke," its tables cluttered with "bottles containing every imaginable brand of whiskey, . . . [and] cards and poker chips at hand."

The K Street house was more than a place to carouse. It was a place of business where the Ohio Gang became rich selling government appointments, judicial pardons, and police protection to bootleggers. By 1923, the corruption could no longer be concealed. Journalists and senators began to focus public attention on the actions of Secretary of the Interior Albert Fall, who had persuaded Harding to transfer control of large government oil reserves at **Teapot Dome,** Wyoming, and Elk Hills, California, from the navy to the Department of the Interior. Fall had immediately leased the deposits to two oil tycoons, Harry F. Sinclair and Edward L. Doheny, who pumped oil from the wells in exchange for providing the navy with a system of fuel tank reserves. Fall had issued the leases secretly, without allowing other oil corporations to compete for them, and he had accepted almost $400,000 from Sinclair and Doheny.

Fall would pay for this shady deal with a year in jail. He was not the only Harding appointee to do so. Charles R. Forbes, head of the Veterans' Bureau, would go to Leavenworth Prison for swindling the government out of $200 million in hospital supplies. The exposure of Forbes's theft prompted his lawyer, Charles Cramer, to commit suicide; Jesse Smith, Attorney General Daugherty's close friend and housemate, also killed himself, apparently to avoid being indicted and brought to trial. Daugherty managed to escape conviction and incarceration for bribery by burning incriminating documents held by his brother's Ohio bank. Still, Daugherty left government service in disgrace.

Harding initially kept himself blind to this widespread use of public office for private gain but grew depressed when he finally realized what had been going on. In summer 1923, in poor spirits, he left Washington for a West Coast tour. He fell ill in Seattle and died from a heart attack in San Francisco. The train returning his body to Washington attracted crowds of grief-stricken mourners who little suspected the web of corruption and bribery in which Harding had been caught. Even as the revelations poured forth in 1924 and 1925, few Americans seemed bothered. Some of this insouciance reflected the carefree atmosphere of the 1920s, but much of it had to do with the character of the man who succeeded Harding.

Coolidge and Laissez-Faire Politics

Calvin Coolidge rarely smiled. At the many dinners he attended as vice president, he said hardly a word. Silence was his public creed, much to the chagrin of Washington's socialites. He was never enticed into carousing with the "boys," nor did he ever stand by as liquor was being served. He believed that the best government was the government that governed least, and that the welfare of the country hinged not on politicians but on the people—their willingness to work hard, to be honest, and to live within their means.

Born in Vermont and raised in Massachusetts, Calvin Coolidge gained national visibility in September 1919, when as governor of Massachusetts he took a firm stand against Boston's striking policemen (see chapter 23). His reputation as a man who battled labor radicals earned him a place on the 1920 national Republican ticket. His image as an ordinary man helped convince voters in 1920 that the Republican Party would return the country to its commonsensical ways after eight years of reckless reforms. Coolidge won his party's presidential nomination handily in 1924 and easily defeated his Democratic opponent, John W. Davis. Coolidge's popularity remained strong throughout his first full term, and he probably would have been re-nominated and reelected in 1928, but he chose not to run.

Coolidge took greatest pride in those measures that reduced the government's control over the economy. The Revenue Act of 1926 slashed the high income and estate taxes that progressives had pushed through Congress during the First World War. Coolidge curtailed the power of the Federal Trade Commission to regulate business affairs and endorsed Supreme Court decisions invalidating progressive era laws that had strengthened organized labor and protected children and women from employer exploitation.

Hoover and the Politics of Associationalism

Republicans in the 1920s did more than simply remove government restraints and regulations from the economy. Some, led by Secretary of Commerce Herbert Hoover, conceived of government as a dynamic, even progressive, economic force. Hoover did not want government to control industry, but he did want government to persuade private corporations to abandon their wasteful, selfish ways and turn to cooperation and public service. Hoover envisioned an economy built on the principle of association. Industrialists, wholesalers, retailers, operators of railroad and shipping lines, small businessmen, farmers, workers, doctors—each of these groups would form a trade association whose members would share economic information, discuss problems of production and distribution, and seek ways of achieving greater efficiency and profit. Hoover believed that the very act of associating in this way—an approach that historian Ellis Hawley has called **"associationalism"**—would convince participants of the superiority of cooperation over competition, of negotiation over conflict, of public service over selfishness.

A graduate of Stanford University, Hoover had worked first as a mining engineer and then as an executive in multinational mining corporations. During the war, he had directed the government's Food Administration (see chapter 23). From that experience, he had come to appreciate the role that government could play in coordinating the activities of thousands of producers and distributors scattered across the country.

Hoover's ambition as secretary of commerce was to make the department the grand orchestrator of economic cooperation. During his eight years in that post (1921–29), he organized more than 250 conferences and repeatedly brought together government officials, representatives of business, policy makers, and others who had a stake in strengthening the economy.

Hoover achieved some notable successes. He persuaded farmers to join together in marketing cooperatives, steel executives to abandon the 12-hour day for their employees, and some groups of bankers in the South to organize their institutions into regional associations with adequate resources and expertise. Hoover's dynamic conception of government did not endear him to Coolidge, who declared in 1927: "That man has offered me unsolicited advice for six years, all of it bad."

The Politics of Business Abroad

Republican domestic policy disagreements over whether to pursue laissez-faire or associationalism spilled over into foreign policy as well. As secretary of commerce, Hoover intended to apply associationalism to international relations. He wanted the world's leading nations to meet regularly in conferences, to limit military buildups, and to foster an international environment in which capitalism could flourish. Aware that the United States must help create such an environment, Hoover hoped to persuade American bankers to adopt investment and loan policies that would aid European recovery. If they refused to do so, he was prepared to urge the government to take an activist, supervisory role in foreign investment.

In 1921 and 1922, Hoover helped design the Washington Conference on the Limitation of Armaments. Although he did not serve as a negotiator at the conference—Secretary of State Charles Evans Hughes reserved that role for himself and his subordinates—Hoover did supply Hughes's team with a wealth of economic information, and he helped Hughes to use that information to design forceful, detailed proposals for disarmament. Those proposals gave U.S. negotiators a decided advantage over their European and Asian counterparts and helped them win a stunning accord, the **Five-Power Treaty,** by which the United States, Britain, Japan, France, and Italy agreed to scrap more than 2 million tons of warships. Hughes also obtained pledges from all of the signatories that they would respect the "Open Door" in China, long a U.S. foreign policy objective (see chapter 22).

These triumphs redounded to Hughes's credit but not to Hoover's, and Hughes used it to consolidate his control over foreign policy. He rebuffed Hoover's efforts to put international economic affairs under the direction of the Commerce Department and rejected Hoover's suggestion to intervene in the international activities of U.S. banks.

Hughes was not entirely laissez faire in approach, as he demonstrated in his 1923 reaction to a crisis in Franco-German relations. The victorious Allies had imposed on Germany an obligation to pay $33 billion in war reparations (see chapter 23). In 1923, when the impoverished German government suspended its payments, France sent troops to occupy the Ruhr valley, whose industry was vital to the German economy. German workers retaliated by going on strike, and the crisis threatened to undermine Europe's precarious economic recovery. Hughes did not stand on the sidelines. He intensified American financial pressure on the French and compelled them to attend a U.S.-sponsored conference in 1924 to restructure Germany's debt obligation.

The conference produced the **Dawes Plan** (after the Chicago banker and chief negotiator, Charles G. Dawes), which reduced German reparations from $542 million to $250 million annually and called on U.S. and foreign banks to stimulate the German economy with a quick infusion of $200 million in loans. Within a matter of days, banker J. P. Morgan, Jr., raised more than $1 billion from American investors. Money poured into German financial markets, and the German economy appeared to stabilize.

The Dawes Plan won applause on both sides of the Atlantic, but soon the U.S. money flooding into Germany created its own problems. American investors were so eager to lend to Germany that their investments became speculative and unsound. At this point, a stronger U.S. government effort to direct loans to sound investments, a strategy that Hoover supported, might have helped. But neither Hughes nor his successor as secretary of state, Frank Kellogg, was interested in such initiatives, and neither was Secretary of the Treasury Mellon. The laissez-faire approach had reasserted itself, and Hoover's plan to involve the U.S. government directly in international economic matters had been rebuffed.

The Republicans' continued pursuit of disarmament and world peace seemed to diverge from their general reluctance to involve the U.S. government in foreign affairs. To follow up the success of the 1922 Five-Power treaty, Secretary of State Kellogg drew up a treaty with Aristide Briand, the French foreign minister, outlawing war as a tool of national policy. In 1928, representatives of the United States, France, and 13 other nations met in Paris to sign the Kellogg-Briand pact, an agreement that soon attracted the support of 48 other nations. Coolidge viewed Kellogg-Briand, however, not as a way of extending U.S. government power abroad but as a way of reducing further the size of the U.S. government at home. With the threat of war removed, the United States could scale back its military forces and eliminate much of the bureaucracy needed to support a large standing army and navy. Unfortunately, the pact contained no enforcement mechanism, thus rendering itself ineffective as a foreign policy tool.

The Republican administrations flexed U.S. power more effectively in Latin American affairs. U.S. investments in the region more than doubled from 1917 to 1929, and the U.S. government continued its policy of intervening in the internal affairs of Latin America to protect U.S. interests. Republican administrations did attempt initially to curtail American military involvement in the Caribbean. The Coolidge administration pulled American troops out of the Dominican Republic in 1924 and Nicaragua in 1925. In the case of Nicaragua, however, U.S. Marines returned in 1926 to end a war between liberal and conservative Nicaraguans and to protect American property; this time they stayed until 1934. U.S. troops, meanwhile, occupied Haiti continuously between 1919 and 1934, keeping in power governments friendly to U.S. interests. Opposition to such heavy-handed tactics continued to build in the United States, but it would not yield a significant change in U.S. policy until the 1930s (see chapter 25).

Farmers, Small-Town Protestants, and Moral Traditionalists

Focus Question
What did farmers and conservative Protestants fear in the 1920s, and what policies did they support?

Although many Americans benefited from the prosperity of the 1920s, others did not. Overproduction was impoverishing substantial numbers of farmers. Beyond these economic hardships, many moral-traditionalist white Protestants, especially those in rural areas and small towns, believed that the country was being overrun by racially inferior and morally suspect foreigners.

Agricultural Depression

The 1920s brought hard times to the nation's farmers after the boom period of the war years. During the war, domestic demand for farm products had risen steadily and foreign demand had exploded as the war disrupted agricultural production in France, Ukraine,

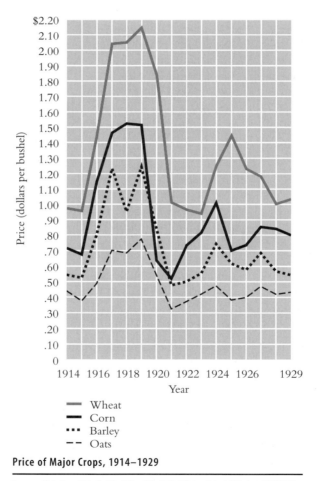

Price of Major Crops, 1914–1929

Source: Data from *Historical Statistics of the United States, Colonial Times to 1970* (White Plains, N.Y.: Kraus International, 1989), pp. 511–12.

and other European food-producing regions. Soon after the war, however, Europe's farmers quickly resumed their customary levels of production. Foreign demand for American foodstuffs fell precipitously, leaving U.S. farmers with an oversupply and depressed prices.

A rise in agricultural productivity made possible by the tractor also worsened the plight of many farmers. The number of tractors in use almost quadrupled in the 1920s, and 35 million new acres came under cultivation. Produce flooded the market. Prices fell even further, as did farm incomes. By 1929, the annual per capita income of rural Americans was only $223, one-quarter that of the non-farm population. Hundreds of thousands had to sell their farms and either scrape together a living as tenants or abandon farming altogether. Many chose to abandon farm life, packed their belongings into jalopies or loaded them onto trains, and headed for the city.

Those who stayed on the land grew increasingly assertive in their demands. Early in the decade, radical farmers working through such organizations as the Nonpartisan League of North Dakota and farmer-labor parties in Minnesota, Wisconsin, and other midwestern states led the movement. By the second half of the decade, however, leadership had passed from farming radicals to farming moderates, and from small farmers in danger of dispossession to larger farmers and agribusinesses seeking to extend their holdings. By lobbying through such organizations as the Farm Bureau Federation, the more powerful agricultural interests pressured Congress to set up economic controls that would protect them from failure. Their proposals, embodied in the McNary-Haugen Bill, called on the government to erect high tariffs on foreign produce and to purchase surplus U.S. crops. The government would then sell the surplus crops on the world market for whatever prices they fetched. Any money lost in international sales would be absorbed by the government rather than by the farmers. The McNary-Haugen Bill passed Congress in 1927 and in 1928, only to be vetoed by President Coolidge both times.

Cultural Dislocation

Added to the economic plight of the farmers was a sense of cultural dislocation among the majority who were white, Protestant, and of northwest European descent. These farmers had long perceived themselves as the backbone of the nation—hardworking, honest, God-fearing yeomen, guardians of independence and liberty.

The 1920 census challenged the validity of that view. For the first time, a slight majority of Americans now lived in urban areas. That finding in itself signified little because the census classified as "urban" those towns with a population as small as 2,500. But the census figures did reinforce the widespread perception that both the economic and cultural vitality of the nation had shifted from the countryside to the metropolis. Industry, the chief engine of prosperity, was an urban phenomenon. Commercialized leisure—the world of amusement parks, department stores, professional sports, movies, cabarets, and theaters—was to be enjoyed in cities; so too were flashy fashions and open sexuality. Catholics, Jews, and African Americans, who together outnumbered white Protestants in many cities, seemed to be the principal creators of this new world. They were also thought to be the

Brown Brothers

Consumer Culture Penetrates the Countryside   By the 1920s, cars, Coca-Cola, radios, and other commodities had found their way to the country's smallest towns. Here a farmer tunes his radio as he milks his cow.

purveyors of Bolshevism and other modes of radicalism. Cities, finally, were the home of secular intellectuals who had scrapped their belief in Scripture and in God and had embraced science as their new, unimpeachable authority.

Throughout the progressive era, rural white Americans had believed that the cities could be redeemed, that city dwellers could be reformed, that the Protestant values of rural America would triumph. War had crushed that confidence and had replaced it with the fear that urban culture and urban people would undermine all that "true" Americans held dear.

These fears grew even more intense with the changes brought by prosperity. Urban-industrial America increased in power and affluence and spread its consumer culture and its commodities to the countryside as never before. Even small towns now sported movie theaters and automobile dealerships. Radio waves carried news of city life into isolated farmhouses. The growth in the circulation of national magazines also broke down the wall separating country from city. Mail-order catalogs—Sears, Roebuck, and Company and others—invited farmers to fantasize that they too could fill their homes with refrigerators, RCA Victrolas, and Hoover vacuum cleaners. **(See Map 24.1, Urbanization, 1920, in the color insert following page 912.)**

Rural white Americans showed ambivalence toward this cultural invasion. On the one hand, most country dwellers were eager to participate in the consumer marketplace. On the other hand, many worried that doing so would expose the countryside to atheism, immorality, and radicalism. They expressed their determination to protect their imperiled way of life in their support for Prohibition, the Ku Klux Klan, immigration restriction, and religious fundamentalism.

Prohibition

The 18th Amendment to the Constitution, which prohibited the manufacture and sale of alcohol, went into effect in January 1920. Initially it drew support from a large and varied constituency that included farmers, middle-class city dwellers, feminists, and progressive reformers who loathed the powerful "liquor trust" and who saw firsthand the deleterious effects of drink on the urban poor. It soon became apparent, however, that Prohibition was doing as much to encourage law-breaking as abstinence. With only 1,500 federal agents to enforce the law, the government could not possibly police the drinking habits of 110 million people. With little fear of punishment, those who wanted to drink did so, either brewing liquor at home or buying it from speakeasies and bootleggers.

Because the law prevented legitimate businesses from manufacturing liquor, organized crime added alcohol to its portfolio. Mobsters procured much of their liquor from Canadian manufacturers, smuggled it across the border, protected it in warehouses, and distributed it to speakeasies. Al Capone's Chicago-based mob alone employed 1,000 men to protect its liquor trafficking, which was so lucrative that Capone became the richest (and most feared) gangster in America. Blood flowed in the streets of Chicago and other northern cities as rival mobs fought one another to enlarge their share of the market.

These unexpected consequences caused many early advocates of Prohibition, especially in the cities, to withdraw their support. Not so for Prohibition's rural, white Protestant supporters, however. The violence spawned by liquor trafficking confirmed their view of alcohol as evil. The high-profile participation of Italian, Irish, and Jewish gangsters in the bootleg trade reinforced their belief that Catholics and Jews were threats to law and morality. Many rural white Protestants became more, not less, determined to rid the country of liquor once and for all; some among them resolved to rid the country of Jews and Catholics as well.

The Ku Klux Klan

The original Ku Klux Klan, formed in the South in the late 1860s, had died out with the defeat of Reconstruction and the reestablishment of white supremacy (see chapter 17). The new Klan was created in 1915 by William Simmons, a white southerner who had been inspired by D. W. Griffith's racist film, *Birth of a Nation,* in which the early Klan was depicted as having saved the nation from predatory blacks. By the 1920s, control of the Klan had passed from Simmons to a Texas dentist, Hiram Evans, and its ideological focus had expanded from a loathing of blacks to a hatred of Jews and Catholics as well. Evans's Klan propagated a nativist message that the country should contain—or better yet, eliminate—the influence of Jews and Catholics and restore "Anglo-Saxon" racial purity, Protestant supremacy, and traditional morality to national life. This message swelled Klan ranks and expanded its visibility and influence in the North and South alike.

By 1924, as many as 4 million Americans are thought to have belonged to the Klan, including the half-million members of its female auxiliary, Women of the Ku Klux Klan. Not only was the Klan strong in states of the Old Confederacy such as Louisiana and Texas and in border states such as Oklahoma and Kansas, but it thrived, too, in such northern states as Indiana, Pennsylvania, Washington, and Oregon. It even drew significant membership from the cities of those states. Indiana, for example, was home to 500,000 Klansmen and women, many of them in the Indianapolis area. In 1924, Indiana voters elected a Klansman to the governorship and sent several other Klan members to the statehouse.

In some respects, the Klan resembled other fraternal organizations. It offered its members friendship networks, social services, and conviviality. Its rituals, regalia, and mock-medieval language (the Imperial Wizard, Exalted Cyclops, Grand Dragons, and such) gave initiates a sense of superiority, valor, and mystery similar to what other fraternal societies, from the Masons to the Knights of Columbus, imparted to their members.

But the Klan also thrived on hate. It spread lurid tales of financial extortion by Jewish bankers and sexual exploitation by Catholic priests. The accusations were sometimes general, as in the claim that an international conspiracy of Jewish bankers had caused the agricultural depression, or allegations that the pope had sent agents to the United States with instructions to destroy liberty and democracy. More common, and more incendiary, however, were the seemingly plausible, yet totally manufactured, tales of Jewish or Catholic depravity. Stories circulated of Jewish businessmen who had opened amusement parks and dance halls to which they lured innocent adolescents, tempting them with sexual transgression and profiting handsomely from their moral debasement. Likewise, Catholic priests and nuns were said to prey on Protestant girls and boys who had been forced into convents and Catholic orphanages. These outrageous stories sometimes provoked attacks on individual Jews and Catholics. More commonly, they prompted campaigns to boycott Jewish businesses and Catholic institutions, and to ruin reputations.

The emphasis on sexual exploitation in these stories reveals the anxiety Klan members felt about society's growing acceptance of sexual openness and sexual gratification. Many Klan supporters lived in towns suffused with these modern attitudes. That such attitudes might reflect the yearnings of Protestant children rather than the manipulation of deceitful Jews and Catholics was a truth some Protestant parents found difficult to accept.

Immigration Restriction

Although most white Protestants never joined the Klan, many of them did respond to the Klan's nativist argument that the country and its values would best be served by limiting the entry of outsiders. That was the purpose of the Johnson-Reed **Immigration Restriction Act of 1924.**

By the early 1920s, most Americans believed that the country could no longer accommodate the million immigrants who had been arriving each year before the war and the more than 800,000 who arrived in 1921. Industrialists no longer needed unskilled European laborers to operate their factories, their places having been taken either by machines or by

African American and Mexican workers. Most labor movement leaders were convinced that the influx of workers unfamiliar with English and with trade unions had weakened labor solidarity. Progressive reformers no longer believed that immigrants could be easily Americanized or that harmony between the native-born and the foreign-born could be readily achieved. Congress responded to constituents' concerns by passing an immigration restriction act in 1921. In 1924, the more comprehensive Johnson-Reed Act imposed a yearly quota of 165,000 immigrants from countries outside the Western Hemisphere, effectively reducing total immigration to only 20 percent of the prewar annual average.

The sponsors of the 1924 act believed that certain groups—British, Germans, and Scandinavians, in particular—were racially superior and that, consequently, these groups should be allowed to enter the United States in greater numbers; however, because the Constitution prohibited the enactment of explicitly racist laws, Congress had to achieve this racist aim through subterfuge. Lawmakers established a formula to determine the annual immigrant quota for each foreign country, which was to be computed at 2 percent of the total number of immigrants from that country already resident in the United States in the year 1890. In 1890, immigrant ranks had been dominated by the British, Germans, and Scandinavians, so the new quotas would thus allow for a relatively larger cohort of immigrants from those countries. Immigrant groups that were poorly represented in the 1890 population—Italians, Greeks, Poles, Slavs, and Eastern European Jews—were effectively locked out.

The Johnson-Reed Act also reaffirmed the long-standing policy of excluding Chinese immigrants, and it added Japanese and other groups of East and South Asians to the list of groups that were altogether barred from entry. The act did not officially limit immigration from nations in the Western Hemisphere, chiefly because agribusiness interests in Texas and California had convinced Congress that cheap Mexican labor was indispensable to their industry's prosperity. Still, the establishment of a Border Patrol along the U.S.–Mexican border and the imposition of a $10 head tax on all prospective Mexican immigrants made entry into the United States more difficult than it had been.

The Johnson-Reed Act accomplished Congress's underlying goal. Annual immigration from transoceanic nations fell by 80 percent. The large number of available slots for English and German immigrants regularly went unfilled, while the smaller number of available slots for Italians, Poles, Russian Jews, and others prevented hundreds of thousands of them from entering the country. A "national origins" system put in place in 1927 further reduced the total annual quota to 150,000 and reserved more than 120,000 of these slots for immigrants from northwestern Europe. Except for minor modifications in 1952, the Johnson-Reed Act would govern U.S. immigration policy until 1965.

Remarkably few Americans, outside of the ethnic groups being discriminated against, objected to these laws at the time they were passed—an indication of how broadly acceptable racism and nativism had become. In fact, racism and religious bigotry enjoyed a resurgence during the Jazz Age. The pseudoscience of eugenics, based on the idea that nations could improve the racial quality of their population by expanding its stronger racial strains

Annual Immigrant Quotas under the Johnson-Reed Act, 1925–1927

Northwest Europe and Scandinavia		Eastern and Southern Europe		Other Countries	
Country	Quota	Country	Quota	Country	Quota
Germany	51,227	Poland	5,982	Africa (other than Egypt)	1,100
Great Britain and Northern Ireland	34,007	Italy	3,845	Armenia	124
		Czechoslovakia	3,073	Australia	121
Irish Free State (Ireland)	28,567	Russia	2,248	Palestine	100
		Yugoslavia	671		
Sweden	9,561	Romania	603	Syria	100
Norway	6,453	Portugal	503	Turkey	100
France	3,954	Hungary	473	New Zealand and Pacific Islands	100
Denmark	2,789	Lithuania	344	All others	1,900
Switzerland	2,081	Latvia	142		
Netherlands	1,648	Spain	131		
Austria	785	Estonia	124		
Belgium	512	Albania	100		
Finland	471	Bulgaria	100		
Free City of Danzig	228	Greece	100		
Iceland	100				
Luxembourg	100				
Total (number)	142,483	Total (number)	18,439	Total (number)	3,745
Total (%)	86.5%	Total (%)	11.2%	Total (%)	2.3%

Note: Total annual immigrant quota was 164,667.
Source: From *Statistical Abstract of the United States* (Washington, D.C.: Government Printing Office, 1929), p. 100.

and shrinking its weaker ones, found supporters not only in Congress but among the ranks of prestigious scientists as well. Universities such as Harvard and Columbia set quotas similar to those of the Johnson-Reed Act to reduce the proportion of Jews among their undergraduates.

Fundamentalism versus Liberal Protestantism

Of all the movements protesting against the modern elements of urban life in the 1920s, Protestant fundamentalism was perhaps the most enduring. **Fundamentalists** regarded the Bible as God's word and thus the source of all "fundamental" truth. They believed that every event depicted in the Bible, from the creation of the world in six days to the resurrection of

Christ, happened exactly as the Bible described it. For fundamentalists, God was a deity who intervened directly in the lives of individuals and communities and who made known both his pleasure and his wrath to those who acknowledged his divinity. Sin had to be actively purged, and salvation actively sought.

The rise of the fundamentalist movement from the 1870s through the 1920s roughly paralleled the rise of urban-industrial society. Fundamentalists recoiled from the "evils" of the city—from what they perceived as its poverty, its moral degeneracy, its irreligion, and its crass materialism. Fundamentalism took shape in reaction against two additional aspects of urban society: the growth of liberal Protestantism and the revelations of science.

Liberal Protestants believed that religion had to be adapted to the skeptical and scientific temper of the modern age. No biblical story in which a sea opens up, the sun stands still, or a woman springs forth from a man's rib could possibly be true. The Bible was to be mined for its ethical values rather than for its literal truth. Liberal Protestants removed God from his active role in history and refashioned him into a distant and benign deity who watched over the world but did not intervene to punish or to redeem. They turned religion away from the quest for salvation and toward the pursuit of good deeds, social conscience, and love for one's neighbor. Although those with a liberal bent constituted only a minority of Protestants, they were articulate, visible, and influential in social reform movements. Fundamentalism arose in part to counter the "heretical" claims of the liberal Protestants.

Liberal Protestants and fundamentalists both understood that science was the source of most challenges to Christianity. Scientists believed that rational inquiry was a better guide to the past and to the future than prayer and revelation. Scientists even challenged the ideas that God had created the world and had fashioned humankind in his own image. These were assertions that many religious peoples, particularly fundamentalists, simply could not accept. Conflict was inevitable. It came in 1925, in Dayton, Tennessee.

The Scopes Trial

No aspect of science aroused more anger among fundamentalists than Charles Darwin's theory of evolution. There was no greater blasphemy than to suggest that man emerged from lower forms of life instead of being created by God. In Tennessee in 1925, fundamentalists succeeded in passing a law that forbade teaching "any theory that denies the story of the divine creation of man as taught in the Bible."

For Americans who accepted the authority of science, denying the truth of evolution was as ludicrous as insisting that the sun revolved around the earth. They ridiculed the fundamentalists, but they worried that the passage of the Tennessee law might signal the onset of a campaign to undermine First Amendment guarantees of free speech. The American Civil Liberties Union (ACLU), founded by liberals during the Red Scare of 1919 and 1920, began searching for a teacher who would be willing to challenge the constitutionality of the Tennessee law. They found their man in John T. Scopes, a 24-year-old biology teacher in Dayton, Tennessee. After confessing that he had taught evolution to his students, Scopes was

INHERIT THE WIND (1960)

Directed by Stanley Kramer.
Starring Fredric March (Matthew Harrison Brady), Spencer Tracy (Henry Drummond), Gene Kelly
(E. K. Hornbeck), Dick York (Bertram T. Cates), Claude Akins (Rev. Jeremiah Brown), and Donna Anderson
(Rachel Brown).

Inherit the Wind is a fictionalized drama about the 1925 Scopes Trial in Dayton, Tennessee (see p. 891 for a discussion of the actual trial). It begins with the arrest of Bertram T. Cates (the name given by the moviemakers to the John T. Scopes character) and ends with Cates's conviction on the charge of breaking a state law prohibiting the teaching of evolution in Tennessee schools. The climactic moment in the movie, as in the real Scopes story, is the courtroom clash between Matthew Harrison Brady (a thinly fictionalized version of William Jennings Bryan) and Henry Drummond (the Clarence Darrow character) over the Bible, truth, and scientific inquiry. That the two actors who played Brady and Drummond, Fredric March and Spencer Tracy, were as prominent in American cinema as Bryan and Darrow had been in American politics enhanced the movie's appeal. A popular film, *Inherit the Wind* shaped how a generation that came of age in the 1960s interpreted the meaning of the Scopes trial. The film's broad influence makes it a particularly important and interesting historical document to explore.

The director of *Inherit the Wind*, Stanley Kramer, liked to engage important political issues in his movies: *Home of the Brave* (1949) explored racism in the U.S. army; *On the Beach* (1959) examined the social consequences of nuclear war; and *Judgment at Nuremberg* (1961) investigated the nature of Nazi criminality. Some movie critics have expressed frustration with these "message movies," charging that Kramer often sacrificed historical and personal nuance in order to drive his political point home. He does this in *Inherit the Wind* by portraying the Scopes camp in the most positive possible light. To help us identify with E. K. Hornbeck (meant to represent the irascible Baltimore-based journalist, H. L. Mencken), for example, he casts the amiable Gene Kelly in the role. Kramer cele-

brates Drummond (representing Darrow) not just for his commitment to defending science and reason but for having more integrity than anyone else in the courtroom. Kramer does try to endow Brady with some positive qualities and to honor him for his past achievements in politics. Ultimately, however, Kramer cannot resist depicting Brady as pompous, calculating, and, by the trial's end, dangerously out of control.

This caricature of Brady/Bryan reveals the roots of *Inherit the Wind* in a 1955 play by the same name. The creators of that play were not especially concerned about making their Brady character resemble Bryan. Instead, they wanted Brady to represent an entirely different figure in American politics, Senator Joseph McCarthy, who led a campaign in the 1950s to oust communists and their supporters from their jobs in the U.S. government. McCarthy's anticommunist operation was terrifying not just to the radicals he sought to expose but also to liberals and others who believed that McCarthy's unscrupulous methods were threatening the core political values of the American republic (see chapter 27). In identifying Brady with McCarthy, the playwrights sought to discredit both men.

The play and movie also criticize McCarthyism by introducing to the 1920s evolution battle an entirely fictitious fire and brimstone preacher, Reverend Jeremiah Brown, who, in the manner of a 1950s McCarthyite anticommunist, viciously and publicly condemns those, including his own daughter, Rachel, who dare to challenge the authority of those in power. Both Brown and Brady are portrayed in the play and movie as successful manipulators of public opinion, much as McCarthy was thought to have distorted the minds of Americans everywhere with his messages of fear and hate.

Spencer Tracy playing Henry Drummond (the fictional Clarence Darrow) on left and Fredric March playing Matthew Harrison Brady (the fictional William Jennings Bryant) on right.

That Kramer allowed his movie about a trial in the 1920s to be influenced by events that he lived through in the 1950s is itself an interesting subject to discuss. It causes us to ask how much historians' views of the past are themselves shaped by the times in which these historians lived. But however much we come to see *Inherit the Wind* as a commentary on politics in 1950s America, we still need to acknowledge the power of the final courtroom scene in the movie, in which Drummond and Brady battle each other about the meaning of science and religion. Their confrontation allows us to glimpse what was at stake in 1925 when a trial in the small town of Dayton, Tennessee, transfixed the nation.

arrested. The case quickly attracted national attention. William Jennings Bryan, the former Populist, progressive, and secretary of state, announced that he would help prosecute Scopes, and the famous liberal trial lawyer Clarence Darrow rushed to Dayton to lead Scopes's defense. That Bryan and Darrow had once been allies in the progressive movement only heightened the drama. A small army of journalists descended on Dayton, led by H. L. Mencken, a Baltimore-based journalist famous for his savage critiques of the alleged stupidity and prudishness of small-town Americans.

The trial dragged on, and most of the observers expected Scopes to be convicted. He was, but the hearing took an unexpected turn when Darrow persuaded the judge to let Bryan testify as an "expert on the Bible." Darrow knew that Bryan's testimony would have no bearing on the question of Scopes's innocence or guilt. The jury was not even allowed to hear it. His aim was to expose Bryan as a fool for believing that the Bible was a source of literal truth and thus to embarrass the fundamentalists. In a riveting confrontation, Darrow made Bryan's defense of the Bible look problematic and led Bryan to admit that the "truth" of the Bible was not always easy to determine. But Darrow could not shake Bryan's belief that the Bible was God's word and thus the source of all truth.

In his account of the trial, Mencken portrayed Bryan as a pathetic figure devastated by his humiliating experience on the witness stand, a view popularized in the 1960 movie *Inherit the Wind*. When Bryan died only a week after the trial ended, Mencken claimed that the trial had broken Bryan's heart. Bryan deserved a better epitaph than the one Mencken had given him. Diabetes caused his death, not a broken heart. Nor was Bryan the innocent fool that Mencken made him out to be. He remembered when social conservatives had used Darwin's phrase "survival of the fittest" to prove that the wealthy and politically powerful were racially superior to the poor and powerless. His rejection of Darwinism evidenced his democratic faith that all human beings were creatures of God and thus capable of striving for perfection and equality.

The public ridicule attendant on the Scopes trial took its toll on fundamentalists. Many of them retreated from politics and refocused their attention on purging sin from their own hearts rather than from the hearts of others. In the end, the fundamentalists prevailed on three more states to prohibit the teaching of evolution, but the controversy had even more far-reaching effects. Worried about losing sales, publishers quietly removed references to Darwin from their science textbooks, a policy that would remain in force until the 1960s. In this respect, the fundamentalists had scored a significant victory.

Ethnic and Racial Communities

Focus Question

How were the experiences of ethnic and racial groups in 1920s America similar and how were they different?

The 1920s were a decade of change for ethnic and racial minorities. Government policy simultaneously discouraged the continued immigration of "new immigrants" from Southern and Eastern Europe and encouraged the migration of African Americans from the South to the North and of Mexicans across the Rio Grande and into the American Southwest. Some minorities benefited from the prosperity of the decade; others created and sustained vibrant subcultures. All, however, experienced a surge in religious and racial discrimination that made them uneasy in Jazz Age America.

European American Ethnics

European American ethnics—and especially the Southern and Eastern European majority among them—were concentrated in the cities of the Northeast and Midwest. Many were semiskilled and unskilled industrial laborers who suffered economic insecurity. In addition, they faced cultural discrimination. Catholics and Jews were targets of the Klan and its politics of hate. Catholics generally opposed Prohibition, viewing it as a crude attempt by Protestants to control their behavior. Southern and Eastern Europeans, particularly Jews and Italians, resented immigration restriction and the implication that they were inferior to Anglo-Saxon whites. Many Italians were outraged by the execution of Nicola Sacco and Bartolomeo Vanzetti in 1927 (chapter 23). If the two men had been native-born white Protestants, Italians argued, their lives would have been spared.

Southern and Eastern Europeans everywhere endured intensive Americanization campaigns. State after state passed laws requiring public schools to instruct children in the essentials of citizenship. Several states, including Rhode Island, extended these laws to private schools as well, convinced that the children of immigrants who were attending Catholic parochial schools were spending too much time learning about their native religion, language, and country. An Oregon law tried to eliminate Catholic schools altogether by ordering all children aged 8 to 16 to enroll in public schools. But attending a public school was no guarantee of acceptance, either—a lesson learned by Jewish children who had excelled in their studies only to be barred from Harvard, Columbia, and other elite universities.

Southern and Eastern Europeans responded to these insults and attacks by strengthening the very institutions and customs Americanizers sought to undermine. Ethnic associations flourished in the 1920s—Catholic churches and Jewish synagogues, fraternal and mutual benefit societies, banks and charitable organizations, athletic leagues and youth groups. Children learned their native languages and customs at home and at church if not at school, and they joined with their parents to celebrate their ethnic heritage. Among Italians and French Canadians, saints' days were occasions for parades, speeches, band concerts, games, and feasts, all serving to solidify ethnic bonds and affirm ethnic identity.

Many of these immigrants and their children, however, also embraced the new consumer culture. They flocked to movies and amusement parks, to baseball games and boxing matches. Children usually entered more enthusiastically into the world of American mass culture than did their immigrant parents, a behavior that often set off family conflicts.

**Democratic Presidential Voting in Chicago
by Ethnic Groups, 1924 and 1928**

	Percent Democratic	
	1924	1928
Czechoslovaks	40%	73%
Poles	35	71
Lithuanians	48	77
Yugoslavs	20	54
Italians	31	63
Germans	14	58
Jews	19	60

Source: From John M. Allswang, *A House for All Peoples: Ethnic Politics in Chicago, 1890–1936* (Lexington: University Press of Kentucky), p. 42.

The famed New York Yankee, Lou Gehrig, had to fight to convince his German-born mother that playing baseball was honorable work. But many ethnics found it possible to reconcile their own culture with American culture. Youngsters who went to the movies did so with friends from within their community. Ethnics also played baseball in leagues organized around churches or ethnic associations. In these early days of radio, ethnics living in large cities could always find programs in their native language and music from their native lands.

European American ethnics also resolved to develop sufficient political muscle to defeat the forces of nativism and to turn government policy in a more favorable direction. One sign of this determination was a sharp rise in the number of immigrants who became U.S. citizens. The percentage of immigrant Poles, Slavs, Italians, Lithuanians, and Hungarians who became naturalized citizens nearly doubled during the decade; the percentage of naturalized Greeks almost tripled. Armed with the vote, ethnics turned out on election day to defeat unsympathetic city councilmen, mayors, state representatives, and even an occasional governor. Their growing national strength first became apparent at the Democratic national convention of 1924, when urban-ethnic delegates almost won approval of planks calling for the repeal of Prohibition and condemnation of the Klan. After denying the presidential nomination to William G. McAdoo—Woodrow Wilson's treasury secretary, son-in-law, and heir apparent—they nearly secured it for their candidate, **Alfred E. Smith,** the Irish American governor of New York. McAdoo represented the rural and southern constituencies of the Democratic Party. His forces ended up battling Smith's urban-ethnic forces for 103 ballots, until both men gave up and supporters from each camp switched their votes to a compromise candidate, the corporate lawyer John W. Davis.

The nomination fight damaged the Democratic Party in the short term, and popular Calvin Coolidge easily defeated the little-known Davis. This split between the party's rural

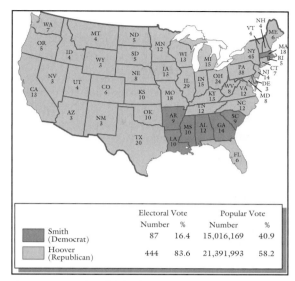

		Electoral Vote		Popular Vote	
		Number	%	Number	%
▮	Smith (Democrat)	87	16.4	15,016,169	40.9
▮	Hoover (Republican)	444	83.6	21,391,993	58.2

Map 24.2   Presidential Election, 1928   This map shows Hoover's landslide victory in 1928, as he carried all but eight states and won almost 84 percent of the electoral vote.

Protestant and urban-ethnic constituencies would keep the Democrats from the White House for nearly a decade, but the convention upheaval of 1924 also marked an important milestone in the bid by European American ethnics for political power. They would achieve a second milestone at the Democratic national convention of 1928 when, after another bitter nomination struggle, they secured the presidential nomination for Al Smith. Never before had a major political party nominated a Catholic for president. Herbert Hoover crushed Smith in the general election, as nativists stirred up anti-Catholic prejudice yet again and as large numbers of southern Democrats either stayed home or voted Republican. Even so, the campaign offered encouraging signs, none more so than Smith's beating Hoover in the nation's 12 largest cities. European American ethnics would yet have their day.

African Americans

Despite the urban race riots of 1919 (see chapter 23), African Americans continued to leave their rural homes for the industrial centers of the South and the North. In the 1920s alone, nearly a million blacks traveled North. In New York City and Chicago, their numbers grew so large—300,000 in New York and 234,000 in Chicago—that they formed cities unto themselves. When word of New York City's urban black enclave reached the Caribbean, thousands of West Indian blacks set off for Harlem. Within these black metropolises emerged complex societies consisting of workers, businessmen, professionals,

Death Rates from Selected Causes for New York City Residents, 1925

Cause of Death	Total Population	African American Population
General death rate (per 1,000 population)	11.4	16.5
Pneumonia	132.8	282.4
Pulmonary tuberculosis	75.5	258.4
Infant mortality (per 1,000 live births)	64.6	118.4
Maternal mortality (per 1,000 total births)	5.3	10.2
Stillbirths (per 1,000 births)	47.6	82.7
Homicide	5.3	19.5
Suicide	14.8	9.7

Note: Rate is per 100,000 population, unless noted.
Source: Cheryl Lynn Greenberg, *"Or Does It Explode?" Black Harlem in the Great Depression* (New York: Oxford University Press, 1991), p. 32.

intellectuals, artists, and entertainers. Social differentiation intensified as various groups—long-resident northerners and newly arrived southerners, religious conservatives and cultural radicals, African Americans and African Caribbeans—found reason to disapprove of one another's ways. Still, the diversity and complexity of urban black America were thrilling, nowhere more so than in Harlem, the "Negro capital." Black writer James Weldon Johnson described Harlem in the 1920s:

> Throughout colored America Harlem is the recognized Negro capital. Indeed, it is Mecca for the sightseer, the pleasure-seeker, the curious, the adventurous, the enterprising, the ambitious, and the talented of the entire Negro world. . . . Not merely a colony or a community or a settlement—not at all a "quarter" or a slum or a fringe—[Harlem is] . . . a black city, located in the heart of white Manhattan, and containing more Negroes to the square mile than any other spot on earth. It strikes the uninformed observer as a phenomenon, a miracle straight out of the skies.

Not even the glamour of Harlem could erase the reality of racial discrimination, however. Most African Americans could find work only in New York City's least-desired and lowest-paying jobs. Because they could rent apartments only in areas that real estate agents and banks had designated as "colored," African Americans suffered the highest rate of residential segregation of any minority group. Although Harlem had its fashionable districts where affluent blacks lived, much of the area's housing stock was poor and rents were high. Harlem became a black ghetto, an area set apart from the rest of the city by the skin color of its inhabitants, by its higher population density and poverty rate, by its higher incidence of infectious diseases, and by the lower life expectancy of its people.

Blacks did enjoy some important economic breakthroughs in the 1920s. Henry Ford, for example, hired large numbers of African Americans to work in his Detroit auto factories. Even here, however, a racist logic was operating, for Ford believed that black and white workers, divided along racial lines, would not challenge his authority. Until the 1940s, in fact, unions made less headway at Ford plants than at the plants of other major automobile manufacturers.

Racial divisions carried over from work to play. African Americans loved baseball as much as white Americans did, and Babe Ruth enjoyed a large black following, but black baseball players were barred from playing in the lily-white major leagues. In response, they formed their own Negro Leagues in the United States and also played professional ball in Mexico and the Caribbean, where they earned extra income and escaped some of the prejudice that met them everywhere in the United States. Cuba, Puerto Rico, Mexico, and other countries in which African Americans played did not organize baseball along racial lines.

The greatest black baseball player was probably Josh Gibson, who joined the Homestead Grays of the National Negro League in 1929 at the age of 18. In his 17-year career, he compiled statistics that surpassed those of any professional ballplayer of his era, white or black, including those of the legendary Babe Ruth. Gibson slugged 962 career home runs, hit 84 home runs in a single season, and compiled a .373 lifetime batting average. Because he died in 1947, at the age of 35, just months before the integration of major league baseball, Gibson never got the opportunity to test his skills against the best white ballplayers, and they never got a chance to play against him.

African Americans grew pessimistic about achieving racial equality. After Marcus Garvey's black nationalist movement collapsed in the mid-1920s (see chapter 23), no comparable organization arose to take its place. The NAACP continued to fight racial discrimination, and the Urban League carried on quiet negotiations with industrial elites to secure jobs for African Americans. Black socialists led by A. Philip Randolph built a strong all-black union, the Brotherhood of Sleeping Car Porters, but the victories were small and white allies were scarce. The political initiatives emerging among European American ethnics had few counterparts in the African American community.

In terms of black culture, however, the 1920s were vigorous and productive. Black musicians coming north to Chicago and New York brought with them their distinctive musical styles, most notably the blues and ragtime. Influenced by the harmonies and techniques of European classical music, which black musicians learned from their European American ethnic counterparts, these southern styles metamorphosed into jazz. Urban audiences, first black and then white, found this new music alluring. They responded to its melodies, its sensuality, its creativity, its savvy. In Chicago, Detroit, New York, New Orleans, and elsewhere, jazz musicians came together in cramped apartments, cabarets, and nightclubs to jam, compete, and entertain. Willie Smith, Charles P. Johnson, Count Basie, Fats Waller, Duke Ellington, and Louis Armstrong were among the most famous musicians of the day. By the late 1920s, they were being hailed in Europe as well.

Jazz seemed to express something quintessentially modern. Jazz musicians broke free of convention, improvised, and produced new sounds that created new sensations. Both blacks and whites found in jazz an escape from the routine, the predictability, and the conventions of their everyday lives.

© Bettmann/CORBIS

Josh Gibson, Negro Leagues Star   This photograph captures Gibson in 1944, near the end of his career, being tagged out at home plate by Ted Radcliffe in the 10th annual East-West All Star Game at Comiskey Park, Chicago.

The Harlem Renaissance

Paralleling the emergence of jazz was a black literary and artistic awakening known as the **Harlem Renaissance.** Black novelists, poets, painters, sculptors, and playwrights set about creating works rooted in their own culture instead of imitating the styles of white Europeans and Americans. The movement had begun during the war, when blacks sensed that they might at last be advancing to full equality. It was symbolized by the image of the "New Negro," a black man or woman who would no longer be deferential to whites but who would display his or her independence through talent and determination. The "New Negro" would be assertive in every field—at work, in politics, in the military, and in arts and letters. As racial discrimination intensified after the war, cultural activities took on special significance. The world of culture was one place where blacks could express their racial pride and demonstrate their talent.

Langston Hughes, a young black poet, said of the Harlem Renaissance: "We younger Negro artists who create now intend to express our individual dark-skinned selves without fear or shame. If white people are pleased, we are glad. If they are not, it doesn't matter. We know we are beautiful. And ugly, too." Writers Claude McKay, Jean Toomer, and Zora Neale Hurston; poet Countee Cullen; and painter Aaron Douglas were other prominent Renaissance participants. In 1925, *Survey Graphic,* a white liberal magazine, devoted an entire issue to "Harlem—the Mecca of the New Negro." Alain Locke, an art and literary critic and professor of philosophy at Howard University in Washington, D.C., edited both the issue and the book *The New Negro,* published later that year. Locke became the movement's leading visionary and philosopher.

But even these cultural advances failed to escape white prejudice. The most popular jazz nightclubs in Harlem, most of which were owned and operated by whites, often refused to admit black customers. The only African Americans permitted inside were the jazz musicians, singers and dancers, prostitutes, and kitchen help. Moreover, the musicians often had to perform what the white patrons wanted to hear. Duke Ellington, for example, was called on to play "jungle music," which for whites revealed the "true" African soul—sensual, innocent, primitive. Such pressures curtailed the artistic freedom of black musicians and reinforced racist stereotypes of African Americans as inferior people who were closer to nature than the "more civilized" white audiences who came to hear their music.

Black artists and writers experienced similar pressures. Many of them depended for their sustenance on the support of wealthy white patrons. Those patrons were generous, but they wanted a return on their investment. Charlotte Mason, the New York City matron who supported Hughes and Hurston, for example, expected them to entertain her friends by demonstrating "authentic Negritude" in their work. Hurston accepted this role, but for Hughes it became intolerable. Both Hughes and Hurston paid a price for their patron's support, including the collapse of their once-close friendship with each other.

Mexican Americans

After the Johnson-Reed Act of 1924, Mexicans became the country's chief source of immigrant labor. A total of 500,000 Mexicans came to the United States in the 1920s. Some headed for the steel, auto, and meatpacking plants of the Midwest, but most settled in the Southwest, where they worked on the railroads and in construction, agriculture, and manufacturing. In Texas, three of every four construction workers and eight of every ten migrant farm workers were Mexicans. An official of the San Antonio Chamber of Commerce declared: "Mexican farm labor is rapidly proving the making of this State." In California, Mexican immigrants made up 75 percent of the state's agricultural workforce.

Mexican farm laborers in Texas worked long hours for little money. As a rule, they earned 50 cents to a dollar less per day than Anglo workers. They were usually barred from becoming machine operators or assuming other skilled positions. Forced to follow the crops, they had little opportunity to develop settled homes and communities. Mexican farm workers depended for shelter on whatever facilities farm owners offered. Because farm owners rarely required the services of Mexican workers for more than several days or weeks, few were willing to spend the money required to provide decent homes and schools. Houses typically lacked even wooden floors or indoor plumbing. Mexican laborers found it difficult to protest these conditions because their knowledge of English was limited. Few owned cars or trucks that would have allowed them to escape a bad employer

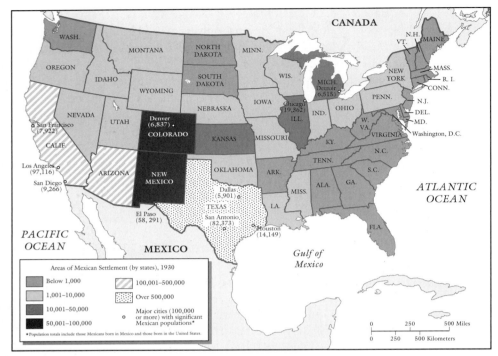

Map 24.3   Mexican Population in the United States, 1930   By 1930, Mexican immigrants had established their pattern of settling primarily in the U.S. Southwest. Texas had the largest concentration of Mexican immigrants, followed by California and Arizona, and then by New Mexico and Colorado. Though Texas had a larger overall population, Los Angeles had surpassed San Antonio as the city with the largest single Mexican community in the United States.

and search for a good one. Many were in debt to employers who had advanced them money and who threatened them with jail if they failed to fulfill the terms of their contract. Others feared deportation; they lacked visas, having slipped into the United States illegally rather than pay the immigrant tax or endure harassment from the Border Patrol.

Increasing numbers of Mexican immigrants, however, found their way to California, where, on the whole, wages exceeded those in Texas. Some escaped agricultural labor altogether for construction and manufacturing jobs. Many Mexican men in Los Angeles, for example, worked in the city's large railroad yards, at the city's numerous construction sites, and as unskilled workers in local factories. Mexican women labored in the city's garment shops, fish canneries, and food processing plants. By 1930, Los Angeles had become the largest area of settlement for Mexicans in the United States.

The Los Angeles Mexican American community increased in complexity as it grew in size. By the mid-1920s, it included a growing professional class, a proud group of *californios* (Spanish-speakers who had been resident in California for generations), many musicians and entertainers, a small but energetic band of entrepreneurs and businessmen,

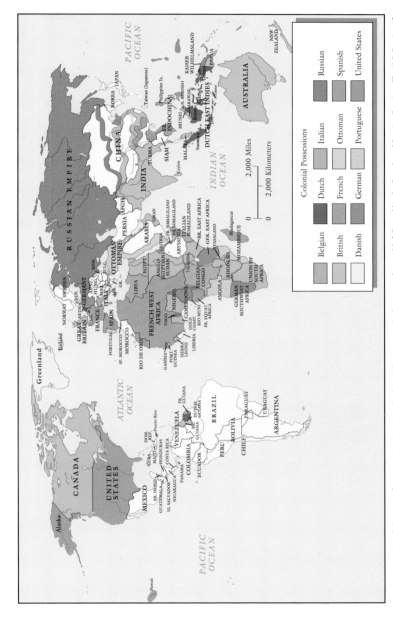

Map 22.3   Colonial Possessions, 1900   In 1900, the British Empire was the largest in the world, followed by the French and Russian Empires. The U.S. Empire, if measured by the square miles of land held as colonial possessions, was small by comparison.

Map 22.4 United States Presence in Latin America, 1895–1934   The United States possessed few colonies in Latin America but intervened (often repeatedly) in Mexico, Cuba, Nicaragua, Panama, Haiti, the Dominican Republic, and Venezuela to secure its economic and political interests.

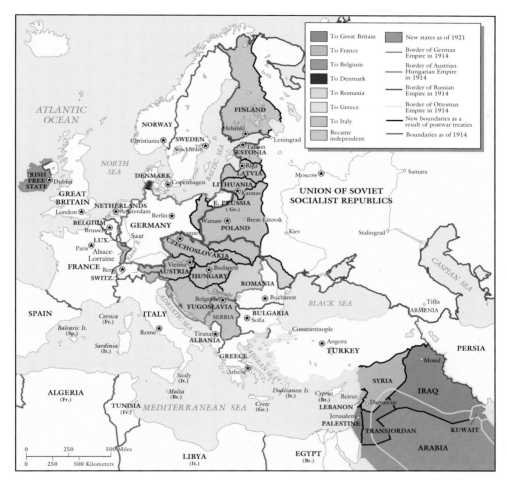

Map 23.2 Europe and the Near East After the First World War The First World War and the Treaty of Versailles changed the geography of Europe and the Near East. Nine nations in Europe, stretching from Yugoslavia in the south to Finland in the north, were created (or reformed) out of the defeated Austro-Hungarian and Ottoman Empires. In the Near East, meanwhile, Syria, Lebanon, Palestine, Transjordan, and Iraq were carved out of the Ottoman Empire, placed under British or French control, and promised eventual independence.

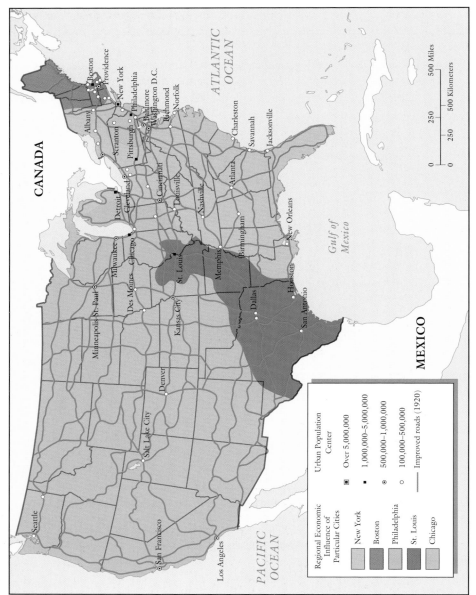

Map 24.1 Urbanization, 1920 By 1920, New York City had surpassed 5 million people, and Boston, Philadelphia, Pittsburgh, Detroit, Chicago, and St. Louis had surpassed 1 million. Another 10 cities, from Los Angeles, California, to Buffalo, New York, had surpassed 500,000. This map, through its color coding, also shows the regions in which the country's five largest cities exercised economic influence.

conservative clerics and intellectuals who had fled or been expelled from revolutionary Mexico, and Mexican government officials who had been sent to counter the influence of the conservative exiles and to strengthen the ties of the immigrants to their homeland. This diverse mix created much internal conflict, but it also generated considerable cultural vitality. Los Angeles became the same kind of magnet for Mexican Americans that Harlem had become for African Americans.

Mexican musicians flocked to Los Angeles, as did Mexican playwrights. The city supported a vigorous Spanish-language theater. Mexican musicians performed on street corners, at ethnic festivals and weddings, at cabarets, and on the radio. Especially popular were folk ballads, called *corridos,* that spoke to the experiences of Mexican immigrants. Although different in form and melody from the African American blues, *corridos* resembled the blues in their emphasis on the suffering, hope, and frustrations of ordinary people.

This flowering of Mexican American culture in Los Angeles could not erase the low wages, high rates of infant mortality, racial discrimination, and other hardships Mexicans faced; nor did it encourage Mexicans, in Los Angeles or elsewhere, to mobilize themselves

Security Pacific Collection/Los Angeles Public Library

Mexican American Women Workers, 1920s   These women were employed at a tortilla factory in Los Angeles.

as a political force. Unlike European immigrants, Mexican immigrants showed little interest in becoming American citizens and acquiring the vote. Yet the cultural vibrancy of the Mexican immigrant community did sustain many individuals who were struggling to survive in a strange, and often hostile, environment.

The "Lost Generation" and Disillusioned Intellectuals

Focus Question
To whom did the phrase "Lost Generation" refer and what caused these individuals to become disillusioned?

Many native-born white artists and intellectuals also felt uneasy in America in the 1920s. Their unease arose not from poverty or discrimination but from alienation. They despaired of American culture and regarded the average American as anti-intellectual, small-minded, materialistic, and puritanical. The novelist Sinclair Lewis, for example, ridiculed small-town Americans in *Main Street* (1920), "sophisticated" city dwellers in *Babbitt* (1922), physicians in *Arrowsmith* (1925), and evangelicals in *Elmer Gantry* (1927).

Before the First World War, intellectuals and artists had been deeply engaged with "the people." Although they were critical of many aspects of American society, they believed they could help bring about a new politics and improve social conditions. Some of them joined the war effort on the side of the Allies before the United States had officially intervened. Ernest Hemingway, John Dos Passos, and e. e. cummings, among others, sailed to Europe and volunteered their services, usually as ambulance drivers carrying wounded Allied soldiers from the front.

America's intellectuals were shaken by the war's effect on American society. The wartime push for consensus created intolerance of radicals, immigrants, and blacks. Intellectuals had been further dismayed by Prohibition, the rebirth of the Ku Klux Klan, the rise of fundamentalism, and the execution of Sacco and Vanzetti. Not only had many Americans embraced conformity for themselves, but they seemed determined to force conformity on others. The young critic Harold Stearns wrote in 1921 that "the most moving and pathetic fact in the social life of America today is emotional and aesthetic starvation." Before these words were published, Stearns had sailed for France. So many alienated young men like Stearns showed up in Paris that Gertrude Stein, an American writer whose Paris apartment became a gathering place for them, took to calling them the **"Lost Generation."**

Their indictment of America was often too harsh. Most of these writers possessed little knowledge of how most Americans lived. Few expressed sympathy for the plight of farmers or the working-class poor. Few knew much about the rich cultural heritage of immigrant communities. Still, they managed to convert their disillusionment into a rich literary sensibility. The finest works of the decade focused on the psychological toll of living in what the poet T. S. Eliot referred to as *The Waste Land* (1922).

F. Scott Fitzgerald's novel *The Great Gatsby* (1925) told of a man destroyed by his desire to be accepted into a world of wealth, fancy cars, and fast women. In the novel *A Farewell to Arms* (1929), Ernest Hemingway wrote of an American soldier overwhelmed by the senselessness and brutality of war who deserts the army for the company of a woman he loves. Playwright Eugene O'Neill created characters haunted by despair, loneliness, and unfulfilled longing. Writers created innovations in style as well as in content. Sherwood Anderson, in his novel *Winesburg, Ohio* (1919), blended fiction and autobiography. John Dos Passos, in *Manhattan Transfer* (1925), mixed journalism with more traditional literary methods. Hemingway wrote in an understated, laconic prose that somehow drew attention to his characters' rage and vulnerability.

White Southern writers found a tragic sensibility surviving from the South's defeat in the Civil War that spoke to their own loss of hope. One group of such writers, calling themselves the Agrarians, argued that the enduring agricultural character of their region offered a more hopeful path to the future than did the mass-production and mass-consumption regime that had overtaken the North. In 1929, William Faulkner published *The Sound and the Fury,* the first in a series of novels set in northern Mississippi's fictional Yoknapatawpha County. Faulkner explored the violence and terror that marked relationships among family members and townspeople, while maintaining compassion and understanding. Faulkner, Lewis, Hemingway, O'Neill, and Eliot would each receive the Nobel Prize for Literature.

Democracy on the Defensive

Disdain for the masses led many intellectuals to question democracy. If ordinary people were as stupid, prejudiced, and easily manipulated as they seemed, how could they be entrusted with the fate of the nation? Although few intellectuals were as frank as Mencken, who dismissed democracy as "the worship of jackals by jackasses," their distrust of democracy ran deep. Walter Lippmann, a former radical and progressive, declared that modern society had rendered democracy obsolete. In his view, average citizens, buffeted by propaganda emanating from powerful opinion makers, could no longer make the kind of informed, rational judgments needed to make democracy work. They were vulnerable to demagogues who played on their emotions and fears. Lippmann's solution, and that of many other political commentators, was to shift government power from the people to educated elites. Those elites, who would be appointed rather than elected, would conduct foreign and domestic policy in an informed, intelligent way. Only then, in Lippmann's view, could government be effective and just.

Mencken and Lippmann enjoyed especially strong influence and prestige among university students, whose ranks and political significance were growing. But their antidemocratic views did not go uncontested. The philosopher **John Dewey,** who taught at Columbia University but whose reputation and influence extended well beyond academia, was the most articulate spokesman for the "pro-democracy" position. He acknowledged that the concentration of power in giant organizations had eroded the authority of Congress, the presidency, and other democratic institutions, but democracy, he insisted, was not doomed. The people could reclaim their freedom by making big business subject to government control. Government could use its power to democratize corporations and to regulate the communications industry to ensure that every citizen had access to the facts needed to make reasonable, informed political decisions.

Dewey's views attracted the support of a wide range of liberal intellectuals and reformers, including Robert and Helen Lynd; Rexford Tugwell, professor of economics at Columbia; and Felix Frankfurter, a rising star at Harvard's law school. Some of these activists had ties to labor leaders and to New York Governor Franklin D. Roosevelt. They formed the vanguard of a new liberal movement committed to taking up the work the progressives had left unfinished.

But these reformers were utterly without power, except in a few states. The Republican Party had driven reformers from its ranks. The Democratic Party was a fallen giant, crippled by a split between its principal constituencies—rural Protestants and urban ethnics—over Prohibition, immigration restriction, and the Ku Klux Klan. The labor movement was moribund. The Socialist Party had never recovered from the trauma of war and Bolshevism. La Follette's Farmer-Labor Party had stalled after a promising debut. John Dewey and his friends tried to launch yet another third party, but they failed to raise money or arouse mass support.

Reformers took little comfort in the presidential election of 1928. Hoover's smashing victory suggested that the trends of the 1920s—the dominance of the Republicans, the centrality of Prohibition to political debate, the paralysis of the Democrats, the growing economic might of capitalism, and the pervasive influence of the consumer culture—would continue unabated.

Conclusion

Signs abounded in the 1920s that Americans were creating a new and bountiful society. The increased accessibility of cars, radios, vacuum cleaners, and other consumer durables; rising real wages, low unemployment, and installment buying; the widening circle of stock owners; the spread of welfare capitalism—all these pointed to an economy that had become more prosperous, more consumer-oriented, even somewhat more egalitarian. Moves to greater equality within marriage and to enhanced liberty for single women suggested that economic change was propelling social change as well.

Even so, many working-class and rural Americans benefited little from the decade's prosperity. Moreover, the decade's social changes aroused resistance, especially from white farmers and small-town Americans, who feared that the rapid growth of cities and the large urban settlements of European and Mexican Catholics, Jews, and African Americans were rendering their white Protestant America unrecognizable.

In the Democratic Party, farmers, small-town Americans, and moral traditionalists fought bitterly against the growing power of urban, ethnic constituencies. Elsewhere, the traditionalists battled hard to protect religion's authority against the inroads of science and to purge the nation of "inferior" population streams. In the process they arrayed themselves against American traditions of liberty and equality, even as they posed as the defenders of the best that America had to offer.

Their resistance to change caused many of the nation's most talented artists and writers to turn away from their fellow Americans in disgust. Meanwhile, although ethnic and racial minorities experienced high levels of discrimination, they nevertheless found enough freedom to create vibrant ethnic and racial communities and to launch projects—as in the case of African Americans in Harlem and Mexican Americans in Los Angeles—of cultural renaissance.

The Republican Party, having largely shed its reputation for reform, took credit for engineering the new economy of consumer plenty. It looked forward to years of political dominance. A steep and unexpected economic depression, however, would soon dash that expectation, revive the Democratic Party, and destroy Republican political power for a generation.

SUGGESTED READINGS

William Leuchtenberg, *The Perils of Prosperity, 1914–1932* (1958), and Ellis Hawley, *The Great War and the Search for a Modern Order: A History of the American People and Their Institutions, 1917–1933* (1979), offer useful overviews of the 1920s. Important works on the consumer revolution include Warren I. Susman, *Culture as History: The Transformation of American Society in the Twentieth Century* (1984); Roland Marchand, *Advertising the American Dream: Making Way for Modernity, 1920–1940* (1985); and Kathy Lee Peiss, *Hope in a Jar: The Making of America's Beauty Culture* (1998). John D. Hicks, *Republican Ascendancy, 1921–1933* (1960) still serves as a good introduction to national politics, but consult, too, Thomas B. Silver, *Coolidge and the Historians* (1982); Ellis Hawley, ed., *Herbert Hoover as Secretary of Commerce: Studies in New Era Thought and Practice* (1974); and John W. Dean, *Warren G. Harding* (2004). For a penetrating look at U.S. imperialism in the Caribbean in the 1920s, see Mary A. Renda, *Taking Haiti: Military Occupation and the Culture of U.S. Imperialism* (2001).

On agricultural distress and protest, see Theodore Saloutos and John D. Hicks, *Twentieth Century Populism: Agricultural Discontent in the Middle West, 1900–1939* (1951). For an examination of the economic and social effects of Prohibition, see Norman Clark, *Deliver Us From Evil: An Interpretation of American Prohibition* (1976). The best treatment of the Scopes trial can be found in Michael Kazin, *A Godly Hero: The Life of William Jennings Bryan* (2006). On the 1920s resurgence of the Ku Klux Klan, consult Nancy MacLean, *Behind the Mask of Chivalry: The Making of the Second Ku Klux Klan* (1994). Frederic Morton Szasz, *The Divided Mind of Protestant America, 1880–1930* (1982), expertly analyzes the split in Protestant ranks between liberals and fundamentalists. John Higham, *Strangers in the Land: Patterns of American Nativism, 1865–1925* (1955), remains an excellent work on the spirit of intolerance that gripped America in the 1920s. On hostility toward immigrants and ethnics, see, also, Mae Ngai, *Impossible Subjects: Illegal Aliens and the Making of Modern America* (2004) and Jerome Karabel, *The Chosen: The Hidden History of Admission and Exclusion at Harvard, Yale, and Princeton* (2005). Irving Bernstein, *The Lean Years: A History of the American Worker, 1920–1933* (1960), remains the most thorough examination of 1920s workers.

On ethnic communities, Americanization, and political mobilization in the 1920s, see **Gary Gerstle**, *Working-Class Americanism: The Politics of Labor in a Textile City, 1914–1960* (1989); **George J. Sánchez**, *Becoming Mexican American: Ethnicity, Culture and Identity in Chicano Los Angeles, 1900–1945* (1993); and **Kristi Andersen**, *The Creation of a Democratic Majority, 1928–1936* (1979). On the Harlem Renaissance, see **Nathan Huggins**, *Harlem Renaissance* (1971). **Malcolm Cowley**, *Exiles Return* (1934), is a marvelous account of the writers and artists who comprised the "Lost Generation." For a provocative interpretation of the intertwined character of white and black literary cultures in 1920s New York, see **Ann Douglas**, *Terrible Honesty: Mongrel Manhattan in the 1920s* (1995).

Visit the Liberty Equality Power Companion Web site for resources specific to this textbook: http://www.thomsonedu.com/history/murrin

Also find self-tests and additional resources at ThomsonNOW. ThomsonNOW is an integrated online suite of services and resources with proven ease of use and efficient paths to success, delivering the results you want—NOW!

www.thomsonedu.com/login/

The Great Depression and the New Deal, 1929–1939

The **Great Depression** began on October 29, 1929 (Black Tuesday) with a spectacular stock market crash. On that one day, stock values plummeted $14 billion. By the end of that year, stock prices had fallen 50 percent from their September highs. By 1932, the worst year of the depression, they had fallen another 30 percent. In three years, $74 billion of wealth had simply vanished. Meanwhile, the unemployment rate had soared to 25 percent.

Many Americans who lived through the Great Depression could never forget the scenes of misery they saw everywhere. In cities, the poor meekly awaited their turn for a piece of stale bread and thin gruel at ill-funded soup kitchens. Scavengers poked through garbage cans for food, scoured railroad tracks for coal that had fallen from trains, and sometimes ripped up railroad ties for fuel. Hundreds of thousands of Americans built makeshift shelters out of cardboard, scrap metal, and whatever else they could find in the city dump. They called their towns "Hoovervilles," after the president whom they despised for his apparent refusal to help them.

The Great Depression brought cultural crisis as well as economic crisis. In the 1920s, American business leaders had successfully redefined the national culture in business terms, as Americans' values became synonymous with the values of business: economic growth, freedom of enterprise, and acquisitiveness. But the swagger and bluster of American businessmen during the 1920s made them vulnerable to attack in the 1930s, as jobs, incomes, and growth all disappeared. With the prestige of business and business values in decline, how could Americans regain their hope and recover their confidence in the future? The first years of the 1930s held no convincing answers.

The gloom broke in early 1933 when Franklin Delano Roosevelt became president and unleashed the power of government to regulate capitalist enterprises, to restore the economy to health, and to guarantee the social welfare of Americans who were unable to help themselves. Roosevelt called his pro-government program a "new deal for the American people," and it would dominate national politics for the next 40 years. Hailed as a hero, Roosevelt became (and remains) the only president to serve more than two terms. In the short term, the New Deal failed to restore prosperity to America, but the "liberalism" it championed found acceptance among millions, who agreed with Roosevelt that only a large and powerful government could guarantee Americans their liberty.

CHRONOLOGY

1929	Herbert Hoover assumes the presidency • Stock market crashes on "Black Tuesday"
1930	Tariff Act (Hawley-Smoot) raises tariffs
1931	More than 2,000 U.S. banks fail
1932	Unemployment rate reaches 25 percent • Reconstruction Finance Corporation established • Bonus Army marches on Washington • Roosevelt defeats Hoover for presidency
1933	Roosevelt assumes presidency • Hundred Days legislation defines First New Deal (March–June) • Roosevelt administration recognizes the Soviet Union • Good Neighbor Policy toward Latin America launched
1934	Father Charles Coughlin and Huey Long challenge conservatism of First New Deal • 2,000 strikes staged across country • Democrats overwhelm Republicans in off-year election • Radical political movements emerge in Wisconsin, Minnesota, Washington, and California • Indian Reorganization Act restores tribal land, provides funds, and grants limited right of self-government to American Indians • Reciprocal Trade Agreement lowers tariffs
1935	Committee for Industrial Organization (CIO) formed • Supreme Court declares NRA unconstitutional • Roosevelt unveils his Second New Deal • Congress passes Social Security Act • National Labor Relations Act (Wagner Act) guarantees workers' right to join unions • Holding Company Act breaks up utilities' near-monopoly • Congress passes Wealth Tax Act • Emergency Relief Administration Act passed; funds Works Progress Administration and other projects • Rural Electrification Administration established • Number of Mexican immigrants returning to Mexico reaches 500,000
1936	Roosevelt defeats Alf Landon for second term • Supreme Court declares AAA unconstitutional • Congress passes Soil Conservation and Domestic Allotment Act to replace AAA • Farm Security Administration established
1937	United Auto Workers defeat General Motors in sit-down strike • Roosevelt attempts to "pack" the Supreme Court • Supreme Court upholds constitutionality of Social Security and National Labor Relations acts • Severe recession hits
1938	Conservative opposition to New Deal does well in off-year election • *Superman* comic debuts
1939	75,000 gather to hear Marian Anderson sing at Lincoln Memorial.

Causes of the Great Depression

Focus Question
What caused the crash of 1929, and why did the ensuing Depression last so long?

America had experienced other depressions, or "panics," and no one would have been surprised if the boom of the 1920s had been followed by a one- or two-year economic downturn. No one was prepared, however, for the economic catastrophe of the 1930s.

Stock Market Speculation

In 1928 and 1929, the New York Stock Exchange had undergone a remarkable run-up in prices. In less than two years, the Dow Jones Industrial Average had doubled. Money had poured into the market, but many investors were buying on 10 percent "margin," putting up only 10 percent of the price of a stock and borrowing the rest from brokers or banks. Few thought they would ever have to repay these loans with money out of their own pockets. Instead, investors expected to resell their shares within a few months at dramatically higher prices, pay back their loans from the proceeds, and still clear a handsome profit. And, for a while, that is exactly what they did. In 1928 alone, for example, RCA stock value increased 400 percent.

The possibility of making a fortune by investing a mere a few thousand dollars only intensified investors' greed. As speculation became rampant, money flowed indiscriminately into all kinds of risky enterprises. The stock market spiraled upward, out of control. When, in October 1929, confidence in future earnings finally faltered, creditors began demanding that investors who had bought stocks on margin repay their loans. The market crashed from its dizzying heights.

Still, the crash, by itself, fails to explain why the Great Depression lasted as long as it did. Poor decision making by the Federal Reserve Board, an ill-advised tariff that took effect soon after the depression hit, and a lopsided concentration of wealth in the hands of the rich deepened the economic collapse and made recovery more difficult.

Mistakes by the Federal Reserve Board

In 1930 and 1931, the Federal Reserve curtailed the amount of money in circulation and raised interest rates, thereby making credit more difficult for the public to secure. Although employing a tight money policy during the boom years of 1928 or 1929 might have restrained the stock market and strengthened the economy, it was disastrous once the market had crashed. What the economy needed in 1930 and 1931 was an expanded money supply, lower interest rates, and easier credit. Such a course would have made it easier for debtors to pay their creditors. Instead, by choosing the opposite course, the Federal Reserve plunged an economy starved for credit deeper into depression. Higher interest rates also triggered an international crisis, as the banks of Germany and Austria, heavily dependent on U.S. loans, went bankrupt. The German-Austrian collapse, in turn, spread financial panic through Europe and ruined U.S. manufacturers and banks specializing in European trade and investment.

An Ill-Advised Tariff

The Tariff Act of 1930, also known as the Hawley-Smoot Tariff Act, accelerated economic decline abroad and at home. Throughout the 1920s, agricultural interests had sought higher tariffs to protect American farmers against foreign competition. But Hawley-Smoot not only raised tariffs on 75 agricultural goods from 32 percent to 40 percent (the highest

Unemployed Men in New York City, 1931   The thousands of men waiting to register at the Emergency Unemployment Relief office became so frustrated that they rioted. Police reserves arrived to restore order.

rate in American history), it also raised tariffs by a similar percentage on 925 manufactured products. Industrialists had convinced their supporters in the Republican-controlled Congress that such protection would give American industry much-needed assistance. The legislation was a disaster. Angry foreign governments retaliated by raising their own tariff rates to keep out American goods. International trade, already weakened by the tight credit policies of the Federal Reserve, took another blow at the very moment when it desperately needed a boost.

A Maldistribution of Wealth

A maldistribution in the nation's wealth that had developed in the 1920s also stymied economic recovery. Although average income rose in the 1920s, the incomes of the wealthiest families rose higher than the rest. Between 1918 and 1929, the share of the national income that went to the wealthiest 20 percent of the population rose by more than 10 percent, while the share that went to the poorest 60 percent fell by almost 13 percent. The Coolidge administration contributed to this maldistribution by lowering taxes on the wealthy, thereby increasing the proportion of the national wealth concentrated in their hands. The deepening inequality of income distribution slowed consumption and held back the growth of consumer-oriented industries (cars, household appliances, processed and packaged foods, recreation), the most dynamic elements of the U.S. economy. Even when the rich spent their money lavishly—building huge mansions, buying expensive cars, vacationing on the French Riviera—they still spent a smaller proportion of their total incomes on consumption than wage earners did. The average 1920s wage earner, for example, might spend one-quarter to one-half of his annual earnings to buy a car.

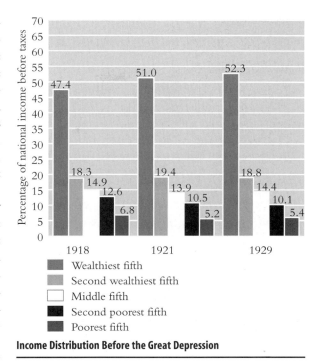

Income Distribution Before the Great Depression

Source: From Gabriel Kolko, *Wealth and Power in America: An Analysis of Social Class and Income Distribution* (New York: Praeger, 1962), p. 14.

Putting more of the total increase in national income into the pockets of average Americans during the 1920s would have steadied the demand for consumer goods and kept the newer consumer industries correspondingly stronger. Such an economy might have recovered relatively quickly from the stock market crash of 1929. Instead, recovery from the Great Depression lagged until 1941, more than a decade later.

Hoover: The Fall of a Self-Made Man

In 1928, Herbert Hoover seemed to embody the American dream. From modest beginnings, Hoover had parlayed his intelligence and drive into gaining admission to Stanford University, becoming a mining engineer, and then rising rapidly to top management positions in the corporate world. A talented and tireless administrator, Hoover won an international reputation in the First World War for his success, as head of the U.S. Food Administration, in feeding millions of European soldiers and civilians. Then, in the 1920s, he became an active and influential secretary of commerce (see chapters 23 and 24). As the decade wound down, no American seemed better qualified to become president of the United States, an office that Hoover assumed in March 1929. Hoover was certain he could make prosperity a permanent feature of American life. "We in America today are nearer to the final triumph over poverty than ever before in the history of any land," he declared in August 1928. A little more than a year later, the Great Depression struck.

Hoover's Program

To cope with the crisis, Hoover first turned to the associational principles he had followed as secretary of commerce (see chapter 24). He encouraged organizations of farmers, industrialists, and bankers to share information, bolster one another's spirits, and devise policies to aid economic recovery. He urged farmers to restrict output, industrialists to hold wages at pre-depression levels, and bankers to help each other remain solvent. The federal government would provide them with information, strategies of mutual aid, occasional loans, and morale-boosting speeches.

Hoover turned to other aggressive policies once he realized that associationalism was failing. To ease the European crisis, Hoover secured a one-year moratorium on loan payments that European governments owed American banks. He steered through Congress the Glass-Steagall Act of 1932, which was intended to help American banks meet the demands of European depositors who wished to convert their dollars to gold. And to ease the crisis at home, he began to expand the government's economic role. The Reconstruction Finance Corporation (RFC), created in 1932, made $2 billion available in loans to ailing banks and to corporations willing to build low-cost housing, bridges, and other public works. The RFC was the biggest federal peacetime intervention in the economy up to that point in American history. The Home Loan Bank Board, set up that same year, offered funds to savings and loans, mortgage companies, and other financial institutions that lent money for home construction and mortgages.

Despite this new government activism, Hoover was uncomfortable with the idea that the government should be responsible for restoring the nation's economic welfare. When RFC expenditures, in 1932, created the largest peacetime deficit in U.S. history, Hoover tried to balance the federal budget. He supported the Revenue Act of 1932, which aimed to erase the deficit by raising taxes. He also insisted that the RFC issue loans only to relatively healthy institutions that were capable of repaying them and that it favor public works, such as toll bridges, that were likely to become self-financing. As a result of these constraints, the RFC spent considerably less than Congress had authorized. Hoover was especially reluctant to engage the government in providing relief to unemployed and homeless Americans. To give money to the poor, he insisted, would destroy their desire to work, undermine their sense of self-worth, and erode their capacity for citizenship.

Hoover saw no similar peril in extending government assistance to ailing banks and businesses. Critics pointed to the seeming hypocrisy of Hoover's policies. For example, in 1930, Hoover refused a request of $25 million to help feed Arkansas farmers and their families but approved $45 million to feed the same farmers' livestock. In 1932, shortly after rejecting an urgent request from the city of Chicago for aid to help pay its teachers and municipal workers, Hoover approved a $90 million loan to rescue that city's Central Republic Bank.

The Bonus Army

In spring 1932, a group of army veterans mounted a particularly emotional challenge to Hoover's policies. In 1924, Congress had authorized a $1,000 bonus for First World War veterans in the form of compensation certificates that would mature in 1945. Now the veterans were demanding that the government pay the bonus immediately. A group of Portland, Oregon, veterans, calling themselves the Bonus Expeditionary Force, hopped onto empty boxcars of freight trains heading east, determined to stage a march on Washington. As the impoverished "army" moved eastward, its ranks multiplied, so that by the time it reached Washington its numbers had swelled to 20,000, including wives and children. The so-called **Bonus Army** set up camp in the Anacostia Flats, southeast of the Capitol, and petitioned Congress for early payment of the promised bonus. The House of Representatives agreed, but the Senate turned them down. Hoover refused to meet with the veterans. In July, federal troops led by Army Chief of Staff Douglas MacArthur and 3rd Cavalry Commander George Patton entered the veterans' Anacostia encampment, set the tents and shacks ablaze, and dispersed the protestors. In the process, more than 100 veterans were wounded and one infant died.

News that veterans and their families had been attacked in the nation's capital served only to harden anti-Hoover opinion. In the 1932 elections, the discredited Republicans were voted out of office after having dominated national politics (excepting Woodrow Wilson's two terms) for 36 years. Hoover received only 39.6 percent of the popular vote

© Bettmann/CORBIS

The Bonus Army's Encampment Set Ablaze   U.S. troops under the command of General Douglas MacArthur torched the tents and shacks that housed thousands of First World War veterans who had come to Washington to demand financial assistance from the government.

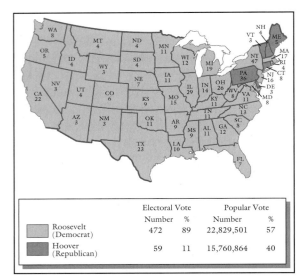

	Electoral Vote		Popular Vote	
	Number	%	Number	%
Roosevelt (Democrat)	472	89	22,829,501	57
Hoover (Republican)	59	11	15,760,864	40

Map 25.1 Presidential Election, 1932 The trauma of the Great Depression can be gauged by the shifting fortunes of President Herbert Hoover. In 1928, he had won 444 electoral votes and carried all but eight states (see Map 24.2, p. 897). In 1932, by contrast, he won only 59 electoral votes and carried only seven states. His Democratic opponent, Franklin D. Roosevelt, was the big winner.

and just 59 (of 531) electoral votes. Hoover left the presidency in 1933 a bewildered man, reviled by Americans for his seeming indifference to suffering and his ineptitude in dealing with the economy's collapse.

A Culture in Crisis

The economic crisis of the early 1930s expressed itself not just in politics but also in culture, especially in the literature and cinema of the time. Many writers who, in the 1920s, had castigated ordinary Americas for their small-mindedness and crass materialism now felt compelled to travel among them, learn about their condition, and seek signs of social renewal. But writers found mostly economic misery and a deep spiritual depression. Edmund Wilson, a literary critic, traveled the country in 1930 and 1931 and wrote numerous essays about how Americans had lost their way and knew not where to turn. When he reached San Diego, he got hold of the city's coroner reports on the numerous individuals who, in desperation, had taken their own lives. Wilson had believed that San Diego, that lovely outpost of the American frontier sitting astride the great and beckoning Pacific, would be a place where the American dream still thrived. But here, too, Wilson claimed, failure and death suffused life and snuffed out hope. He reported on the city's suicides in this fashion:

> They drive their cars into dark alleys, get into the back seat and shoot themselves; they hang themselves in hotel bedrooms, take overdoses of suphonal or barbital; they slip off to the municipal golf-links and there stab themselves with carving-knives; or they throw themselves into the bay, blue and placid, where gray battleships and cruisers guard the limits of their broad-belting nation.

A sense of aimlessness and hopelessness characterized one of the major literary works of the early 1930s, the Studs Lonigan trilogy (1932–35) written by the Chicago-born writer James T. Farrell. In another decade, one easily imagines that Farrell might have cast his scrappy Irish-American protagonist, Studs, as an American hero whose pluck and guile enable him to achieve wealth, success, and influence. But Studs lacks the necessary focus and is too easily overcome by the harshness of his environment. He dies poor and alone, not even having reached the age of 30. The popular writer Nathaniel West, meanwhile, was publishing *Miss Lonelyhearts* (1933) and *A Cool Million* (1934), novels similarly organized around central characters succumbing to failure, drift, and even insanity.

One can detect parallel themes of despair in the period's cinema, especially in such movies as *Fugitive from a Chain Gang* (1932), in which an industrious and honorable man, James Allen, returns from Europe a war hero, only to sink into vagabondage. Caught by the police when he becomes an innocent accessory to a crime, Allen is sentenced to 10 years on a Georgia chain gang. Unable to tolerate the hardship and injustice of his punishment, Allen escapes from jail and uses his intelligence and character to start a new life for himself under an alias. He finds himself a woman and satisfying work as an engineer, but must abandon both once his true identity is revealed. His desire to stay out of prison condemns him to being a man always on the run, unable to prove his innocence or to earn a decent living or build enduring relationships. It is a powerful and bleak film that was, nevertheless, popular with moviegoers and given an Academy Award for Best Picture.

Less grim but still sobering were the gangster movies of the early 1930s, especially *Little Caesar* (1930) and *The Public Enemy* (1931), which told stories of hard-nosed, crooked, and violent men who made themselves into figures of wealth and influence by living outside the law and bending the social environment in which they lived to their will. These gangsters usually had to pay for their sins by dying or going to jail, but, before that happened, they were often portrayed sympathetically, as individuals who, against all odds, found a way to succeed. Moviegoers liked the intensity, suspense, and violence of gangster–police confrontations offered in these films but they were drawn, too, to the gangsters, modern-day outlaws who demonstrated how tough it was to succeed in America and how necessary it might be to break the rules.

The lawlessness that was so integral to the gangster movies also surfaced in the wild comedy of Groucho, Chico, Harpo, and Zeppo Marx, entertainers who, in the 1920s and 1930s, made the transition from vaudeville stage to silver screen. In their films, the Marx Brothers ridiculed figures of authority, broke every rule of etiquette, smacked around their antagonists (and each other), and deliberately and delightfully mangled the English language. Anarchy ruled their world. Many of the moviegoers who went to see the Marx Brothers on the big screen simply wanted to enjoy 90 minutes of side-splitting laughter, if only to escape the harshness of their daily lives.

But some of the Marx Brothers movies carried a more serious political message, perhaps none more so than *Duck Soup* (1933), a withering political satire set in the fictional nation of Fredonia. Fredonia's dictatorial leaders are pompous and small-minded, its legal system is a fraud, and its citizens are clueless and easily misled; by the movie's end, the latter are called to arms through spectacularly ludicrous song and dance scenes, and then led off to fight a meaningless but deadly war. In one of the film's most famous and controversial lines, Rufus T. Firefly, leader of Fredonia (played by Groucho Marx), declares to his troops: "And remember while you're out there risking life and limb through shot and shell, we'll be in here thinking what a sucker you are."

Duck Soup contains some of the funniest scenes the Marx Brothers ever filmed, but it also delivers the dispiriting message that people could not hope to better themselves through politics, which had been emptied of meaning and honesty. This cinematic sentiment paralleled the conviction held by many Americans in 1932 and early 1933 that their own politicians, especially Hoover and the Republicans, had failed them in a time of need. In such ways did the political pessimism of the early 1930s seep into the era's culture.

The Democratic Roosevelt

Between 1933 and 1935, the mood of the country shifted sharply, and politics would, once again, generate hope rather than despair. This change was largely attributable to the personality and policies of Hoover's successor, **Franklin D. Roosevelt,** and to the social movements that emerged during his presidency.

An Early Life of Privilege

Roosevelt was born in 1882 into a patrician family descended, on his father's side, from Dutch gentry who in the 17th century had built large estates on the fertile land along the Hudson River. By the 1880s, the Hyde Park manor where Roosevelt grew up had been in the family for more than 200 years. His mother's family—the Delanos—traced its ancestry back to the *Mayflower*. Roosevelt's education at Groton, Harvard College, and Columbia Law School was typical of the path followed by the sons of America's elite.

The Roosevelt family was wealthy, although not spectacularly so by the standards of the late 19th century. His parents' net worth of more than $1 million was relatively small in comparison to the fortunes being amassed by industrialists and railroad tycoons, many of whom commanded fortunes of $50 million to $100 million or more. This widening gap in wealth concerned families like the Roosevelts, who worried that the new industrial elite would dislodge them from their social position. Moreover, they took offense at the newcomers' allegedly vulgar displays of wealth, lack of taste and etiquette, indifference to the natural environment, and hostility toward those less fortunate than themselves. Theodore Roosevelt, an older cousin of Franklin Roosevelt, had called on the men of his gentry class to set a better example by devoting themselves to public service and the public good.

Though young Franklin wanted to follow in his famous cousin's footsteps, it took a long time for him to show Teddy's seriousness of purpose. He distinguished himself neither at school nor at law. Prior to the 1920s, he could point to few significant political achievements, and he owed much of his political ascent in the Democratic Party to his famous name. He was charming, gregarious, and fun-loving, always eager to sail, party, and enjoy the company of women other than his wife, Eleanor. Then, in 1921, at the age of 39, Roosevelt was both stricken and transformed by a devastating illness, polio, which paralyzed him from the waist down for the rest of his life.

During the two years that Roosevelt spent bedridden, he seemed to acquire a new determination and focus. He developed a compassion for those suffering misfortune that would later enable him to reach out to the millions caught in the Great Depression. Roosevelt's physical debilitation also transformed his relationship with Eleanor, with whom he had shared a testy and increasingly loveless marriage. Eleanor's dedication to nursing Franklin back to health forged a new bond between them. More conscious of his dependence on others, he now welcomed her as a partner in his career. Eleanor soon displayed a talent for political organization and public speaking that surprised those who knew her only as a shy, awkward woman. She was an indispensable player in the revival of Franklin's political fortunes, which began in 1928 with his election to the governorship of New York state. Eleanor would also become an active, eloquent First Lady, her husband's trusted ally, and an architect of American liberalism.

Roosevelt Liberalism

As governor of New York for four years (1929–33), Roosevelt had initiated various reform programs, and his success made him the front-runner for the 1932 Democratic presidential nomination. Even so, he had little assurance that he would be the party's choice. Since 1924, the Democrats had been divided between southern and midwestern agrarians on the one hand and northeastern ethnics on the other. The agrarians favored government regulation—both of the nation's economy and of the private affairs of its citizens. Their support of government intervention in the pursuit of social justice marked them as economic progressives, while their advocacy of Prohibition revealed a cultural conservatism as well as a nativistic strain. By contrast, urban ethnics opposed Prohibition and other forms of government interference in the private lives of its citizens. Urban ethnics were divided over whether the government should regulate the economy, with former New York governor Al Smith increasingly committed to a laissez-faire policy, and Senator Robert Wagner of New York and others supporting more federal control.

Roosevelt understood the need to carve out a middle ground. As governor of New York, and then as a presidential candidate in 1932, he surrounded himself with men and women who embraced the new reform movement called liberalism. **Frances Perkins,** Harry Hopkins, Raymond Moley, Rexford Tugwell, Adolph Berle, Samuel Rosenman—all were interventionist in economic matters and libertarian on questions of personal behavior. They shared with the agrarians and Wagner's supporters a desire to regulate capitalism, but they agreed with Al Smith that the government had no business telling people how to live their lives. Although it seemed unlikely at first, Roosevelt did manage to unite the party behind him at the 1932 Democratic Party convention. In his convention acceptance speech, he declared: "Ours must be the party of liberal thought, of planned action, of enlightened international outlook, and of the greatest good for the greatest number of citizens." He promised "a new deal for the American people."

The First New Deal, 1933–1935

Focus Question
What do you consider to be the three or four most important pieces of legislation in the First New Deal? Why?

© The Granger Collection, New York

From Herbert Hoover to Franklin D. Roosevelt   This 1933 photograph shows the outgoing and incoming presidents on the way to FDR's inauguration. By this time, the two men detested each other, a sentiment that, in this photograph, FDR concealed better than his predecessor.

By the time Roosevelt assumed office in March 1933, the economy lay in shambles. From 1929 to 1932, industrial production had fallen by 50 percent, while new investment had declined from $16 billion to less than $1 billion. In those same years, more than 100,000 businesses went bankrupt. In early 1933, with the nation's banking system on the verge of collapse, 34 states had ordered all the banks in their jurisdictions to close their doors. No one seemed to be able to bring the unemployment rate under control. Some Americans feared that the opportunity for reform had already passed.

Not Roosevelt. "This nation asks for action, and action now," Roosevelt declared in his inaugural address. Roosevelt was true to his word. In his first Hundred Days, from early March through early June 1933, Roosevelt persuaded Congress to pass 15 major pieces of legislation to help bankers, farmers, industrialists, workers, homeowners, the unemployed, and the hungry. He also prevailed on Congress to repeal Prohibition. Not all of the new laws helped relieve distress and promote recovery, but, in the short term, that seemed to matter little. Roosevelt had brought excitement and hope to the nation. He was confident, decisive, and defiantly cheery. "The only thing we have to fear is fear itself," he declared.

Legislation Enacted During the "Hundred Days," March 9–June 16, 1933

Date	Legislation	Purpose
March 9	Emergency Banking Act	Provide federal loans to private bankers
March 20	Economy Act	Balance the federal budget
March 22	Beer-Wine Revenue Act	Repeal Prohibition
March 31	Unemployment Relief Act	Create the Civilian Conservation Corps
May 12	Agricultural Adjustment Act	Establish a national agricultural policy
May 12	Emergency Farm Mortgage Act	Provide refinancing of farm mortgages
May 12	Federal Emergency Relief Act	Establish a national relief system, including the Civil Works Administration
May 18	Tennessee Valley Authority Act	Promote economic development of the Tennessee Valley
May 27	Securities Act	Regulate the purchase and sale of new securities
June 5	Gold Repeal Joint Resolution	Cancel the gold clause in public and private contracts
June 13	Home Owners Loan Act	Provide refinancing of home mortgages
June 16	National Industrial Recovery Act	Set up a national system of industrial self-government and establish the Public Works Administration
June 16	Glass-Steagall Banking Act	Create Federal Deposit Insurance Corporation; separate commercial and investment banking
June 16	Farm Credit Act	Reorganize agricultural credit programs
June 16	Railroad Coordination Act	Appoint federal coordinator of transportation

Source: Arthur M. Schlesinger Jr., *The Coming of the New Deal* (Boston: Houghton Mifflin, 1959), pp. 20–21.

Roosevelt used the radio to reach out to ordinary Americans. On the second Sunday after his inauguration, he launched a series of radio addresses known as "fireside chats," speaking in a plain, friendly, and direct voice to the forlorn and discouraged. In his first chat, he explained the banking crisis in simple terms but without condescension. "I want to take a few minutes to talk with the people of the United States about banking," he began. An estimated 20 million Americans listened.

To hear the president speaking warmly and conversationally—as though he were actually there in the room—was riveting. An estimated 500,000 Americans wrote letters to Roosevelt within days of his inaugural address. Millions more would write to him and to **Eleanor Roosevelt** over the next few years. Many of the letters were simply addressed to "Mr. or Mrs. Roosevelt, Washington, D.C." Democrats began to hang portraits of Franklin Roosevelt in their homes, often next to a picture of Jesus or the Madonna.

Roosevelt was never the benign father figure he made himself out to be. He skillfully crafted his public image. Compliant news photographers agreed not to show him in a wheelchair or struggling with the leg braces and cane he used to take even small steps.

His political rhetoric sometimes promised more than he was prepared to deliver in actual legislation. This was not simply a strategy meant to confuse his opponents and to sustain his own appeal. Roosevelt was struggling to keep together a party that was divided over a variety of issues. At the same time, he was attempting to establish a strong federal government in a polity that had long been hostile to that idea. Not only did Roosevelt have to overcome ideological opposition to a centralized state, but he had to find individuals able to run federal agencies in a nation in which that kind of administrative experience was in short supply.

Saving the Banks

Roosevelt's first order of business was to save the nation's financial system. With so many of the nation's banks already closed by inauguration day, Roosevelt's first act was to order the rest of the country's banks to cease all business—a bold move he brazenly called a "bank holiday." At his request, Congress rushed through the Emergency Banking Act (EBA), which made federal loans available to private bankers, and followed that with the Economy Act (EA), which committed the government to balancing the budget.

Both the EBA and the EA were fiscally conservative programs that Hoover had proposed. The EBA made it possible for private bankers to retain financial control of their institutions, and the EA announced the government's intention of pursuing a fiscally prudent course. Only after the financial crisis had eased did Roosevelt turn to the structural reform of banking. A second Glass-Steagall Act (1933) separated commercial banking from investment banking. It also created the Federal Deposit Insurance Corporation (FDIC), which assured depositors that the government would protect up to $5,000 of their savings. The Securities Act (1933) and the Securities Exchange Act (1934) imposed long-overdue regulation on the New York Stock Exchange, both by reining in buying on the margin and by establishing the Securities and Exchange Commission (SEC) to enforce federal law.

Economic Relief

Roosevelt understood the need to temper financial prudence with compassion. Congress responded swiftly in 1933 to Roosevelt's request to establish the Federal Emergency Relief Administration (FERA), granting it $500 million for relief to the poor. To head FERA, Roosevelt appointed a brash young reformer, Harry Hopkins, who disbursed $2 million during his first two hours on the job. Roosevelt next won congressional approval for the Civilian Conservation Corps (CCC), which put more than 2 million single young men to work planting trees, halting erosion, and otherwise improving the environment. The following winter, Roosevelt launched the Civil Works Administration (CWA), an ambitious work-relief program, also under Harry Hopkins's direction, which hired 4 million unemployed people at $15 per week and put them to work on 400,000 small-scale government projects. For middle-class Americans threatened with the loss of their homes, Roosevelt won Congressional approval for the Homeowners' Loan Corporation (1933) to refinance mortgages. These direct subsidies to millions of jobless and home-owning Americans lent credibility to Roosevelt's claim that the New Deal would set the country on a new course.

Agricultural Reform

In 1933, Roosevelt expected economic recovery to come not from relief, but through agricultural and industrial cooperation. He regarded the Agricultural Adjustment Act, passed in May, and the National Industrial Recovery Act (NIRA), passed in June, as the most important legislation of his Hundred Days. Both were based on the idea that curtailing production would trigger economic recovery. By shrinking the supply of agricultural and manufactured goods, Roosevelt's economists reasoned, they could restore the balance of normal market forces. As demand for scarce goods exceeded supply, prices would rise and revenues would climb. Farmers and industrialists, earning a profit once again, would increase their investment in new technology and hire more workers, and prosperity and full employment would be the final result.

To curtail farm production, the **Agricultural Adjustment Administration (AAA),** which was set up by the Agricultural Adjustment Act, began paying farmers to keep a portion of their land out of cultivation and to reduce the size of their herds. The program was controversial. Many farmers were skeptical of a government offer to pay more money for working less land and husbanding fewer livestock, but few refused to accept payments. As one young Kansas farmer reported:

> There were mouthy individuals who seized every opportunity to run down the entire program . . . condemning it as useless, crooked, revolutionary, or dictatorial; but . . . when the first AAA payments were made available, shortly before Christmas, these same wordy critics made a beeline for the courthouse. They jostled and fell over each other in their mad scramble to be the first in line to receive allotment money.

The AAA had made no provision, however, for the countless tenant farmers and farm laborers who would be thrown out of work by the reduction in acreage. In the South, the victims were disproportionately black. A Georgia sharecropper wrote Harry Hopkins of his misery: "I have Bin farming all my life But the man I live with Has Turned me loose taking my mule [and] all my feed. . . . I can't get a Job so Some one said Rite you." New Dealers within the Department of Agriculture, such as Rexford Tugwell and Jerome Frank, were sympathetic to the plight of sharecroppers, but they failed during the First New Deal to extend to them the government's helping hand.

The programs of the AAA also proved inadequate to Great Plains farmers, whose economic problems had been compounded by ecological crisis. Just as the depression rolled in, the rain stopped falling on the plains. The land, stripped of its native grasses by decades of excessive plowing, dried up and turned to dust. And then the dust began to blow, sometimes traveling 1,000 miles across open prairie. Dust became a fixed feature of daily life on the plains (which soon became known as the Dust Bowl), covering furniture, floors, and stoves, and penetrating people's hair and lungs. The worst dust storm occurred on April 14, 1935,

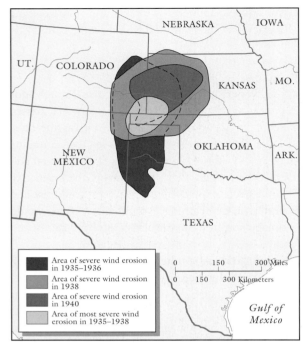

Map 25.2 Dust Bowl, 1935–1940 This map shows the areas in six states—Texas, New Mexico, Oklahoma, Colorado, Kansas, and a bit of Nebraska—claimed by the Dust Bowl between 1935 and 1940. The light shading in the center shows the area where the winds caused the worst damage.

when a great mass of dust, moving at speeds of 45 to 70 miles per hour, roared through Colorado, Kansas, and Oklahoma, blackening the sky, suffocating cattle, and dumping thousands of tons of topsoil and red clay on homes and streets.

The government responded to this calamity by establishing the Soil Conservation Service (SCS) in 1935. Recognizing that the soil problems of the Great Plains could not be solved simply by taking land out of production, SCS experts urged plains farmers to plant soil-conserving grasses and legumes in place of wheat. They taught farmers how to plow along contour lines and how to build terraces—techniques that had been proven effective in slowing the runoff of rainwater and improving its absorption into the soil. Plains farmers were open to these suggestions, especially when the government offered to subsidize those willing to implement them. Bolstered by the new assistance, plains agriculture began to recover.

Still, the government offered little assistance to the rural poor—the tenant farmers and sharecroppers. Nearly 1 million had left their homes by 1935, and another 2.5 million would leave after 1935. Most headed west, piling their belongings onto their jalopies, snaking along Route 66 until they reached California. They became known as Okies, because many, although not all, had come from Oklahoma. Their dispossession and forced migration disturbed many Americans, for whom the plight of these once-sturdy yeomen became a symbol of how much had gone wrong with the American dream.

In 1936, the Supreme Court ruled that AAA-mandated limits on farm production constituted an illegal restraint of trade. Congress responded by passing the Soil Conservation and Domestic Allotment Act, which justified the removal of land from cultivation for reasons of conservation rather than economics. This new act also called on landowners to share their government subsidies with sharecroppers and tenant farmers, although many landowners managed to evade this and subsequent laws that required them to share federal funds.

FDR Library

Searching for a Better Life   Scenes like this one were common in the 1930s as farm families in Oklahoma and Texas who had lost their land began heading to California. Here a family's entire belongings are packed onto a truck, and the mother tends to her baby on an isolated road. The woman's fur collar suggests that this family had once known better times.

The use of subsidies, begun by the AAA, did eventually bring stability and prosperity to agriculture, but at high cost. Agriculture became the most heavily subsidized sector of the U.S. economy, and the Department of Agriculture grew into one of the government's largest bureaucracies. The rural poor, black and white, never received a fair share of federal benefits. Beginning in the 1930s, and continuing in the 1940s and 1950s, they would be forced off the land and into the cities of the North and West.

Industrial Reform

American industry was so vast that Roosevelt's administration never contemplated paying individual manufacturers direct subsidies to reduce, or even halt, production. Instead, the government decided to limit production through persuasion and association—techniques that Hoover had also favored. To head the **National Recovery Administration (NRA)**, authorized under the National Industrial Recovery Act, Roosevelt chose General Hugh Johnson, a participant in industrial planning experiments during the First World War. Johnson's first task was to persuade industrialists and businessmen to agree to raise employee wages to a minimum of 30 to 40 cents per hour and to limit employee hours to a maximum of 30 to 40 hours per week. The limitation on hours was meant to reduce the quantity of goods that any factory or business could produce.

Johnson launched a high-powered publicity campaign. He distributed NRA pamphlets and pins throughout the country. He used the radio to exhort all Americans to do their part. He staged an NRA celebration in Yankee Stadium and a parade down New York City's Fifth Avenue. He sent letters to millions of employers asking them to place a "blue eagle"—the logo of the NRA—on storefronts, at factory entrances, and on company stationery to signal their participation in the campaign to limit production and restore prosperity. Blue eagles soon sprouted everywhere, usually accompanied by the slogan "We Do Our Part."

Johnson understood, however, that his propaganda campaign could not by itself guarantee recovery. So he brought together the largest producers in every sector of manufacturing and asked each group (or conference) to work out a code of fair competition that would specify prices, wages, and hours throughout the sector. He also asked each conference to restrict production.

In summer and fall 1933, the NRA codes drawn up for steel, textiles, coal mining, rubber, garment manufacture, and other industries seemed to be working. The economy

© Bettmann/CORBIS

Selling the NRA Through Sex and Sunburn   Americans were asked to display their support for the NRA by pasting eagles onto their factory entrances, storefronts, and even clothes. The young women in this photo dispensed with pasting, choosing instead to allow the sun to burn their bare backs around a stenciled blue eagle and NRA lettering, which were being applied by the woman in the white gown.

improved, and hard times seemed to be easing. But in winter and spring 1934, economic indicators plunged downward once again, and manufacturers began to evade the code provisions. Government committees set up to enforce the codes were powerless to punish violators. By fall 1934, it was clear that the NRA had failed. When the Supreme Court declared the NRA codes unconstitutional in May 1935, the Roosevelt administration allowed the agency to die.

Rebuilding the Nation's Infrastructure

In addition to establishing the NRA, the National Industrial Recovery Act launched the Public Works Administration (PWA). The PWA had a $3.3 billion budget to sponsor internal improvements that would strengthen the nation's infrastructure of roads, bridges, sewage systems, hospitals, airports, and schools. The labor needed for these construction projects would shrink relief rolls and reduce unemployment, but the projects could be justified in terms that conservatives approved: economic investment rather than short-term relief.

The PWA authorized the building of three major dams in the West—Boulder, Grand Coulee, and Bonneville—that opened up large stretches of Arizona, California, and Washington to industrial and agricultural development. It funded the construction of the Triborough Bridge in New York City and the 100-mile causeway linking Florida to Key West. It also appropriated money for the construction of thousands of new schools.

The TVA Alternative

One piece of legislation passed during Roosevelt's First New Deal specified a strategy for economic recovery significantly different from the one promoted by the NIRA. The Tennessee Valley Authority Act (1933) called for the government—rather than private corporations—to promote economic development throughout the Tennessee Valley, a vast river basin winding through parts of Kentucky, Tennessee, Mississippi, Alabama, Georgia, and North Carolina. The act created the **Tennessee Valley Authority (TVA)** to control flooding on the Tennessee River, harness its water power to generate electricity, develop local industry (such as fertilizer production), improve river navigability, and ease the poverty and isolation of the area's inhabitants. In some respects, the TVA's mandate resembled that of the PWA, but the TVA enjoyed even greater authority. The extent of its control over economic development reflected the influence of Rexford Tugwell and other New Dealers who were committed to a government-planned and government-operated economy. Although they rarely said so, these reformers were drawn to socialism.

The accomplishments of the TVA were many. It built, completed, or improved more than 20 dams, including the huge Wheeler Dam near Muscle Shoals in Alabama. At several of the dam sites, the TVA built hydroelectric generators and soon became the nation's largest producer of electricity. Its low electric rates compelled private utility companies to reduce their rates as well. The TVA also constructed waterways to bypass non-navigable stretches of the river, reduced the danger of flooding, and taught farmers how to prevent soil erosion and use fertilizers. **(See Map 25.3, Tennessee Valley Authority, in the color insert following page 1056.)**

Although the TVA was one of the New Deal's most celebrated successes, it generated little support for more ambitious experiments in national planning. For the government to have assumed control of established industries and banks would have been quite a different matter from bringing prosperity to an impoverished region. Like Roosevelt, few members of Congress or the public favored the radical growth of governmental power that such programs would have entailed. Thus, the thought of replacing the NRA with a nationwide TVA, for instance, made little headway. The New Deal never embraced the idea of the federal government as a substitute for private enterprise.

The New Deal and Western Development

As the TVA showed, New Deal programs could make an enormous difference to a particular region's welfare. Other regional beneficiaries of the New Deal included the New York City area, which prospered from the close links of local politicians to the Roosevelt administration. The region that benefited most from the New Deal, however, was the West. Between 1933 and 1939, per capita payments for public works projects, welfare, and federal loans in the Rocky Mountain and Pacific Coast states outstripped those of any other region.

Dam building was central to this western focus. Western real estate and agricultural interests wanted to dam the West's major rivers to provide water and electricity for urban and agricultural development, but the costs were prohibitive, even to the largest capitalists, until the New Deal offered to defray the expenses with federal dollars. Western interests found a government ally in the Bureau of Reclamation, a hitherto small federal agency (in existence since 1902) that became, under the New Deal, a prime dispenser of funds for dam construction, reservoir creation, and the provision of water to western cities and farms. Drawing on PWA monies, the bureau oversaw the building of the Boulder Dam (later renamed Hoover Dam), which provided drinking water for southern California, irrigation water for California's Imperial Valley, and electricity for Los Angeles and southern Arizona. It also authorized the Central Valley Project and the All-American Canal, vast water-harnessing projects in central and southern California meant to provide irrigation, drinking water, and electricity to California farmers and towns. The greatest construction project of all was the Grand Coulee Dam on the Columbia River in Washington, which created a lake 150 miles long. Together with the Bonneville Dam (also on the Columbia), the Grand Coulee gave the Pacific Northwest the cheapest electricity in the country and created a new potential for economic and population growth. Not surprisingly, these two dams also made Washington state the largest per capita recipient of New Deal aid.

These developments attracted less attention in the 1930s than the TVA because their benefits did not fully materialize until after the Second World War. Also, dam building in

Improving the Nation's Infrastructure   The federal government built several major dams in the West to boost agricultural and industrial development. This is a photograph of the mammoth Boulder Dam (later renamed the Hoover Dam) on the Colorado River.

the West was not seen as a radical experiment in government planning and management. Unlike the TVA, the Bureau of Reclamation hired private contractors to do the work. Moreover, the benefits of these dams were intended to flow first to large agricultural and real estate interests, not to the poor; they were intended to aid private enterprise, rather than bypass it. In political terms, dam building in the West was more conservative than it was in the Tennessee Valley. Even so, this activity made the federal government a key architect of the modern American West.

Map 25.4   Federal Water Projects in California Built or Funded by the New Deal   This map demonstrates how much California cities and agriculture benefited from water projects—dams, canals, aqueducts, pumping stations, and power plants—begun under the New Deal. The projects extended from the Shasta Dam in the northern part of the state to the All-American Canal that traversed the Imperial Valley south of San Diego, and included the Colorado River Aqueduct that would bring vital drinking water to Los Angeles.

Political Mobilization, Political Unrest, 1934–1935

Although Roosevelt and the New Dealers quickly dismantled the NRA in 1935, they could not stop the political forces it had set in motion. Ordinary Americans now believed they could make a difference. If the New Dealers could not achieve economic recovery, then the people would find others who could.

Populist Critics of the New Deal

Some critics were disturbed by what they perceived as the conservative character of New Deal programs. Banking reforms, the AAA, and the NRA, they alleged, all seemed to favor large economic interests. Ordinary people had been ignored.

In the South and Midwest, millions listened regularly to the radio addresses of Louisiana Senator **Huey Long,** a former governor of that state and an accomplished orator. In attacks on New Deal programs, he alleged that "not a single thin dime of concentrated, bloated, pompous wealth, massed in the hands of a few people has been raked down to relieve the masses." Long offered a simple alternative: "Break up the swollen fortunes of America and . . . spread the wealth among all our people." He called for a redistribution of wealth that would guarantee each American family a $5,000 estate.

Long's rhetoric inspired hundreds of thousands of Americans to join the Share the Wealth clubs his supporters organized. Most came from middle-class ranks or from the ranks of skilled workers. Long's supporters worried that the big business orientation of New Deal programs would undermine their economic and social status. By 1935, Roosevelt regarded Long as the man most likely to unseat him in the presidential election of 1936. Before that campaign began, however, Long was assassinated.

Meanwhile, in the Midwest, **Father Charles Coughlin,** the "radio priest," delivered his stinging critique of the New Deal to a weekly radio audience of between 30 and 40 million listeners. Like Long, Coughlin appealed to anxious middle-class Americans and to privileged groups of workers who believed that middle-class status was slipping from their grasp. A devoted Roosevelt supporter at first—he had once called the New Deal "Christ's Deal"—Coughlin had become, by 1934, a harsh critic. He charged that the New Deal was run by bankers and the NRA aimed to resuscitate corporate profits without concern for the average working man. Coughlin called for a strong government to compel capital, labor, agriculture, professionals, and other interest groups to do its bidding. He founded the National Union of Social Justice (NUSJ) in 1934 as a precursor to a political party that would challenge the Democrats in 1936. Coughlin increasingly admired dictators such as Italy's Benito Mussolini, who built their power and programs through decree rather than through democratic consent. If necessary, he admitted in 1936, he would "'dictate' to preserve democracy."

As Coughlin's disillusionment with the New Deal deepened, a strain of anti-Semitism became apparent in his radio talks, as in his accusation that Jewish bankers were masterminding a world conspiracy to dispossess the toiling masses. Although Coughlin was a compelling speaker, he failed to build the NUSJ into an effective political force. Its successor, the Union Party, attracted only a tiny percentage of voters in 1936. Embittered, Coughlin moved further to the political right. By 1939, his denunciations of democracy and Jews had become so extreme that some radio stations refused to carry his addresses. Still, millions of Americans continued to put their faith in the "radio priest."

Another popular figure was Francis E. Townsend, a California doctor who claimed that the way to end the depression was to give every senior citizen $200 per month with the stipulation that seniors would spend those dollars, thus putting more money in circulation and reviving economic demand. Townsend also pushed hard for a pension program to ease the plight of the nation's elderly. While the Townsend movement did not last long, it did prod a nervous Roosevelt administration to make relief for the elderly—a program that Roosevelt would label Social Security—an important component of the New Deal.

Labor Protests

The attacks by Long, Coughlin, and Townsend on the New Deal deepened popular discontent and inspired other insurgent movements. The most important of them was the labor movement. Workers began joining unions in response to the National Industrial Recovery Act, and especially its Clause 7 (a), which granted workers the right to join labor unions of their own choosing, and obligated employers to recognize unions and bargain with them in good faith. Union members made quite modest demands at first: (1) they wanted employers to observe the provisions of the NRA codes; (2) they wanted to be treated fairly by their foremen; and (3) they wanted employers to recognize and negotiate with their unions.

Few employers, however, were willing to grant their employees any say in working conditions. Many ignored the NRA's wage and hour guidelines altogether and used their influence over NRA code authorities to thwart worker requests for wage increases and union recognition. Workers flooded Washington with letters addressed to President Roosevelt, Labor Secretary Frances Perkins, and General Hugh Johnson, asking them to force employers to comply with the law. A Rhode Island textile worker who had been fired for joining a union asked why the NRA had neither responded to his complaint nor punished the company that had fired him. "If people can be arrested for violating certain laws," he wondered, "why can't this company?"

When their pleas went unanswered, workers began to take matters into their own hands. In 1934, they staged 2,000 strikes, some of which escalated into armed confrontations between workers and police. In Toledo, Ohio, in May, 10,000 workers surrounded the Electric Auto-Lite plant, declaring that they would block all exits and entrances until the company agreed to shut down operations and negotiate a union contract. Two strikers were killed in an exchange of gunfire. In Minneapolis, unionized truck drivers and warehousemen fought police, private security forces, and the National Guard in a series of street battles from May through July that left four dead and hundreds wounded. In San Francisco in July, skirmishes between longshoremen and employers killed two and wounded scores of strikers. This violence provoked a general strike in San Francisco that shut down the city's transportation, construction, and service industries for two weeks. In September, 400,000 textile workers at mills from Maine to Alabama walked off their jobs. Attempts by employers to bring in replacement workers triggered violent confrontations that caused several deaths, hundreds of injuries, and millions of dollars in property damages.

Anger at the Polls

By late September, textile union leaders had lost their nerve and called off the strike, but workers took their anger to the polls. In Rhode Island, they broke the Republican Party's 30-year domination of state politics. In the South Carolina gubernatorial race, working-class voters rejected a conservative Democrat, Coleman Blease, and chose instead Olin T. Johnston, a former mill worker and an ardent New Dealer. In the country as a whole, Democrats won 70 percent of the contested seats in the Senate and House. The Democrats increased their majority, from 310 to 319 (out of 432) in the House, and from 60 to 69 (out of 96) in the Senate. No sitting president's party had ever done so well in an off-year election.

The victory was not an unqualified one for Roosevelt and the First New Deal, however. The 74th Congress would include the largest contingent of radicals ever sent to Washington: Tom Amlie of Wisconsin, Ernest Lundeen of Minnesota, Maury Maverick of Texas, Vito Marcantonio of New York, and some 30 others. Their support for the New Deal depended on whether Roosevelt delivered more relief, more income security, and more political power to farmers, workers, the unemployed, and the poor.

Radical Third Parties

Radical critics of the New Deal also made an impressive showing in state politics in 1934 and 1936. They were particularly strong in states gripped by labor unrest. In Wisconsin, for example, Philip La Follette, the son of Robert La Follette (see chapter 21), was elected governor in 1934 and 1936 as the candidate of the radical Wisconsin Progressive Party. In Minnesota, discontented agrarians and urban workers organized the Minnesota Farmer-Labor (MFL) Party and elected their candidate to the governorship in 1930, 1932, 1934, and 1936. In Washington, yet another radical third party, the Commonwealth Builders, elected both senators and almost half the state legislators in 1932 and 1934. And in California, the socialist and novelist Upton Sinclair and his organization, End Poverty in California (EPIC), came closer to winning the governorship than anyone had expected.

A widespread movement to form local labor parties offered further evidence of voter volatility, as did the growing appeal of the **Communist Party.** The American Communist Party (CP) had emerged in the early 1920s with the support of radicals who wanted to adopt the Soviet Union's path to socialism (see chapter 23). The CP began to attract attention in the early 1930s, as its organizers spread out among the poorest and most vulnerable populations in America—homeless urban blacks in the North, black and white sharecroppers in the South, Chicano and Filipino agricultural workers in the West—and mobilized them into unions and unemployment leagues. CP members also played significant roles in strikes described earlier, and they were influential in the Minnesota Farmer-Labor Party and in Washington's Commonwealth Builders. Once they stopped preaching world revolution in 1935 and began calling instead for a "popular front" of democratic forces against fascism (a term used to describe the new kinds of dictatorships appearing in Hitler's Germany and Mussolini's Italy), their ranks grew even more. By 1938, approximately 80,000 Americans were thought to have been members of the Communist Party.

Although the Communist Party proclaimed its allegiance to democratic principles beginning in 1935, it nevertheless remained a dictatorial organization that took its orders from the Soviet Union. Many Americans feared the growing strength of the CP and began to call for its suppression. The CP, however, was never strong enough to gain power for itself. Its chief role in 1930s politics was to channel popular discontent into unions and political parties that would, in turn, force New Dealers to respond to the demands of the nation's poor.

The Second New Deal, 1935–1937

Focus Question
What was "underconsumptionism," and how did it inform the legislation of the Second New Deal? How was the Second New Deal different from the first?

The labor unrest of 1934 had taken Roosevelt by surprise. For a time, he kept his distance from the masses mobilizing in his name, but in spring 1935, with the 1936 presidential election looming, he decided to place himself at their head. He called for the "abolition of evil holding companies," attacked the wealthy for their profligate ways, and called for new programs to aid the poor and downtrodden. Rather than becoming a socialist, as his critics charged, Roosevelt sought to reinvigorate his appeal among poorer Americans and turn them away from radical solutions.

Philosophical Underpinnings

To point the New Deal in a more populist direction, Roosevelt turned increasingly to a relatively new economic theory, **underconsumptionism.** Advocates of this theory held that a chronic weakness in consumer demand had caused the Great Depression. The path to recovery lay, therefore, not in restricting production, as the architects of the First New Deal had tried to do, but in boosting consumer expenditures through government support for strong labor unions (to force up wages), higher social welfare expenditures (to put more money in the hands of the poor), and ambitious public works projects (to create hundreds of thousands of new jobs).

Underconsumptionists did not worry that new welfare and public works programs might strain the federal budget. If the government found itself short of revenue, it could always borrow additional funds from private sources. These reformers, in fact, viewed government borrowing as a useful antidepression tool. Those who lent the government money would receive a return on their investment; those who received government assistance would have additional income to spend on consumer goods; and manufacturers would profit from increases in consumer spending. Government borrowing, in short, would stimulate the circulation of money through the economy, increase consumer demand, and end the depression. This fiscal policy, a reversal of the conventional wisdom that government should always balance its budget, would in the 1940s come to be known as Keynesianism, after John Maynard Keynes, the British economist who had been its most forceful advocate.

Many politicians and economists rejected the notion that increased government spending and the deliberate buildup of federal deficits would lead to prosperity. Roosevelt was not easily convinced that he should put aside his concern for fiscal restraint and balanced budgets, but in 1935, as the nation entered its sixth year of the depression, he was willing to give the new ideas a try. Reform-minded members of the 1934 Congress were eager for a new round of legislation directed more to the needs of ordinary Americans than to the needs of big business.

Legislation

Congress passed much of that legislation in January to June 1935—a period that came to be known as the Second New Deal. Two of the acts were of historic importance: the **Social Security Act** and the National Labor Relations Act. The Social Security Act, passed in May, required the states to set up welfare funds from which money would be disbursed to the elderly poor, the unemployed, unmarried mothers with dependent children, and the disabled. It also enrolled a majority of working Americans in a pension program that guaranteed them

Selected WPA Projects in New York City, 1938

Construction and Renovation	Education, Health, and Art	Research and Records
East River Drive	Adult education: homemaking, trade and technical skills, and art and culture	Sewage treatment, community health, labor relations, and employment trends surveys
Henrik Hudson Parkway		
Bronx sewers	Children's education: remedial reading, lip reading, and field trips	
Glendale and Queens public libraries		Museum and library catalogs and exhibits
King's County Hospital	Prisoners' vocational training, recreation, and nutrition	
Williamsburg housing project	Dental clinics	Municipal office clerical support
School buildings, prisons, and firehouses	Tuberculosis examination clinics	Government forms standardization
Coney Island and Brighton Beach boardwalks	Syphilis and gonorrhea treatment clinics	
Orchard Beach	City hospital kitchen help, orderlies, laboratory technicians, nurses, doctors	
Swimming pools, playgrounds, parks, drinking fountains	Subsistence gardens	
	Sewing rooms	
	Central Park sculpture shop	

Source: John David Millet, *The Works Progress Administration in New York City* (Chicago: Public Administration Service, 1938), pp. 95–126.

a steady income upon retirement. A federal system of employer and employee taxation was set up to fund the pensions. Despite limitations on coverage and inadequate pension levels, the Social Security Act of 1935 provided a sturdy foundation on which future presidents and congresses would erect the American welfare state.

Equally historic was the passage, in June, of the National Labor Relations Act (NLRA). This act delivered what the NRA had only promised: the right of every worker to join a union of his or her own choosing and the obligation of employers to bargain with that union in good faith. The **NLRA**, also called the **Wagner Act** after its Senate sponsor, Robert Wagner of New York, set up a National Labor Relations Board (NLRB) to supervise union elections and to investigate claims of unfair labor practices. The NLRB was to be staffed by federal appointees with power to impose fines on employers who violated the law. Union leaders hailed the act as their Magna Carta.

Congress also passed the Holding Company Act to break up the 13 utility companies that controlled 75 percent of the nation's electric power. It passed the Wealth Tax Act, which increased tax rates on the wealthy from 59 percent to 75 percent, and on corporations from 13.75 percent to 15 percent; and it passed the Banking Act, which strengthened the power of the Federal Reserve Board over its member banks. It created the Rural Electrification Administration (REA) to bring electric power to rural households. Finally, it passed the huge $5 billion Emergency Relief Appropriation Act. Roosevelt funneled part of this sum to the PWA and the CCC and used another part to create the National Youth Administration (NYA), which provided work and guidance to the nation's youth.

Roosevelt directed most of the new relief money, however, to the **Works Progress Administration** (WPA) under the direction of Harry Hopkins, now known as the New Deal's "minister of relief." The WPA built or improved thousands of schools, playgrounds, airports, and hospitals. WPA crews raked leaves, cleaned streets, and landscaped cities. In the process, the WPA provided jobs to approximately 30 percent of the nation's jobless.

By the time the decade ended, the WPA, in association with an expanded Reconstruction Finance Corporation, the PWA, and other agencies, had built 500,000 miles of roads, 100,000 bridges, 100,000 public buildings, and 600 airports. The New Deal had transformed America's urban and rural landscapes. The awe generated by these public works projects helped Roosevelt retain popular support at a time when the success of the New Deal's economic policies was uncertain. The WPA also funded a vast program of public art, supporting the work of thousands of painters, architects, writers, playwrights, actors, and intellectuals. Beyond extending relief to struggling artists, it fostered the creation of art that spoke to the concerns of ordinary Americans, adorned public buildings with colorful murals, and boosted public morale.

Victory in 1936: The New Democratic Coalition

Roosevelt described his Second New Deal as a program to limit the power and privilege of the wealthy few and to increase the security and welfare of ordinary citizens. In his 1936 reelection campaign, he excoriated the corporations as "economic royalists" who had "concentrated into their own hands an almost complete control over other people's property, other people's money, other people's labor—other people's lives." He called on voters to strip the corporations of their power and "save a great and precious form of government for ourselves and the world." American voters responded by handing Roosevelt the greatest victory in the history of American presidential politics. He received 61 percent of the popular vote; Alf Landon of Kansas, his Republican opponent, received only 37 percent. Only two states, Maine and Vermont, representing a mere eight electoral votes, went for Landon.

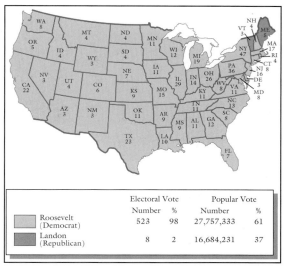

	Electoral Vote		Popular Vote	
	Number	%	Number	%
Roosevelt (Democrat)	523	98	27,757,333	61
Landon (Republican)	8	2	16,684,231	37

Map 25.5   Presidential Election, 1936   In 1936, Franklin D. Roosevelt's reelection numbers were overwhelming: 98 percent of the electoral vote, and more than 60 percent of the popular vote. No previous election in American history had been so one-sided.

The 1936 election won the Democratic Party its reputation as the party of reform and the party of the "forgotten American." Of the 6 million Americans who went to the polls for the first time, many of them European ethnics, 5 million voted for Roosevelt. Among the poorest Americans, Roosevelt received 80 percent of the vote. Black voters in the North deserted the Republican Party—the "Party of Lincoln"—calculating that their interests would best be served by the "Party of the Common Man." Roosevelt also did well among white middle-class voters, many of whom stood to benefit from the Social Security Act. These constituencies would constitute the "Roosevelt coalition" for most of the next 40 years, helping to solidify the Democratic Party as the new majority party in American politics.

Rhetoric Versus Reality

Roosevelt's 1935–36 anti-corporate rhetoric was more radical than the laws he supported. The Wealth Tax Act took considerably less out of wealthy incomes and estates than was advertised, and the utility companies that the Holding Company Act should have broken up remained largely intact. Moreover, Roosevelt promised more than he delivered to the nation's poor. Farm workers, for example, were not covered by the Social Security Act or by the National Labor Relations Act. Consequently, thousands of African American sharecroppers in the South, along with substantial numbers of Mexican American farm workers in the Southwest, missed out on protections and benefits brought by these laws. The sharecroppers were shut out because southern Democrats would not have voted for an act

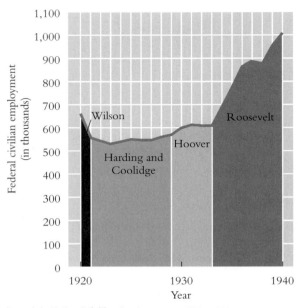

Growth in Federal Civilian Employment, 1920–1940

Source: Data from *Historical Statistics of the United States, Colonial Times to 1970* (White Plains, N.Y.: Kraus International, 1989), p. 1102.

that was seen as improving the economic or social condition of southern blacks. For the same reason, the New Deal made little effort to restore voting rights to southern blacks or to protect their basic civil rights. White supremacy lived on in New Deal democracy.

Roosevelt's 1935–36 populist stance also obscured the support that some capitalists were giving the Second New Deal. In the West, Henry J. Kaiser headed a consortium of six companies that built the Hoover, Bonneville, and Grand Coulee dams; and in Texas, building contractors Herman and George Brown were bankrolling a group of elected officials that included a young Democratic congressman named Lyndon Johnson. In the Midwest and the East, Roosevelt's corporate supporters included real estate developers, mass merchandisers (such as Bambergers and Sears, Roebuck), clothing manufacturers, and the like. These firms, in turn, had financial connections with recently established investment banks such as Lehman Brothers and Goldman Sachs, competitors of the House of Morgan and its allies in the Republican banking establishment, and with consumer-oriented banks such as the Bank of America and the Bowery Savings Bank. They tolerated strong labor unions, welfare programs, and high levels of government spending in the belief that these developments would strengthen consumer spending, but they had no intention of surrendering their own wealth or power. The Democratic Party had become, in effect, the party of the masses and one section of big business. The conflicting interests of these two constituencies would create tensions within the Democratic Party throughout the years of its political domination.

Men, Women, and Reform

The years 1936 and 1937 were exciting ones for academics, policy makers, and bureaucrats who designed and administered the rapidly growing roster of New Deal programs and agencies. Fueled by idealism and dedication, they were confident they could make the New Deal work. They planned and won congressional approval for the Farm Security Administration (FSA), an agency designed to improve the economic lot of tenant farmers,

Rates of Unemployment in Selected Male and Female Occupations, 1930

Male Occupations	Percentage Male	Percentage Unemployed
Iron and steel	96%	13%
Forestry and fishing	99	10
Mining	99	18
Heavy manufacturing	86	13
Carpentry	100	19
Laborers (road and street)	100	13
Female Occupations	**Percentage Female**	**Percentage Unemployed**
Stenographers and typists	96%	5%
Laundresses	99	3
Trained nurses	98	4
Housekeepers	92	3
Telephone operators	95	3
Dressmakers	100	4

Source: U.S. Department of Commerce, Bureau of the Census, *Fifteenth Census of the United States, 1930, Population* (Washington, D.C.: Government Printing Office, 1931).

sharecroppers, and farm laborers. They drafted and passed laws that outlawed child labor, set minimum wages and maximum hours for adult workers, and committed the federal government to building low-cost housing. They investigated and tried to regulate concentrations of corporate power.

Although they worked on behalf of "the people," the New Dealers constituted a new class of technocrats. The prospect of building a strong state committed to prosperity and justice fired their imaginations. They delighted in the intellectual challenge and the technical complexity of social policy. They did not welcome interference from those they regarded as less intelligent or motivated by obsolete ideologies.

This was particularly true of the men. Many had earned advanced degrees in law and economics at elite universities such as Harvard, Columbia, and Wisconsin. Not all had been raised among wealth and privilege, however, as was generally the case with earlier generations of reformers. To his credit, Franklin Roosevelt was the first president since his cousin Theodore Roosevelt to welcome Jews and Catholics into his administration. Some became members of Roosevelt's inner circle of advisers—men such as Thomas "Tommy the Cork" Corcoran, Jim Farley, Ben Cohen, and Samuel Rosenman. These men had struggled to make their way, first on the streets and then in school and at work. They brought to the New Deal intellectual aggressiveness, quick minds, and mental toughness.

The profile of New Deal women was different. Although a few, notably Eleanor Roosevelt and Secretary of Labor Frances Perkins, were more visible than women in previous administrations had been, many of the female New Dealers worked in relative obscurity, in agencies such as the Women's Bureau or the Children's Bureau (both in the Department of Labor). Women who worked on major legislation, as did Mary Van Kleeck on the Social Security Act, or who directed major programs, as did Jane Hoey, chief of the Social Security's Bureau of Public Assistance, received less credit than men in comparable positions. Moreover, female New Dealers tended to be a generation older than their male colleagues and were more likely to be Protestant than Catholic or Jewish. Many of them had known each other since the days of progressive-era reform and woman suffrage (see chapter 21).

The New Deal offered these female reformers little opportunity to advance the cause of women's equality. Demands for greater economic opportunity, sexual freedom, and full equality for women and men were put forward less often in the 1930s than they had been in the preceding two decades. One reason was that the women's movement had lost momentum after achieving the vote in 1920 (see chapter 24). Another was that prominent New Deal women, rather than vigorously pursuing a campaign for equal rights, chose to concentrate instead on "protective legislation"—laws that safeguarded female workers, whom they considered more fragile than men. Those who insisted that women needed special protections could not easily argue that women were the equal of men in all respects.

Even so, feminism was hemmed in on all sides by a male hostility that the depression had only intensified. Many American men had built their male identities on the value of hard work and the ability to provide economic security for their families. For them, the loss of work unleashed feelings of inadequacy. Male vulnerability increased as unemployment rates of men—most of whom labored in blue-collar industries—rose higher than those of women, many of whom worked in white-collar occupations less affected by job cutbacks. Many fathers and husbands resented wives and daughters who had taken over their breadwinning roles.

This male anxiety had political and social consequences. Several states passed laws outlawing the hiring of married women. New Deal relief agencies were reluctant to authorize aid for unemployed women. The labor movement made protection of the male wage earner one of its principal goals. The Social Security pension system left out waitresses, domestic servants, and other largely female occupations. Some commentators even proposed ludicrous gender remedies to the problem of unemployment. Norman Cousins of the *Saturday Evening Post,* for example, suggested that the depression could be ended simply by firing 10 million working women and giving their jobs to men. "Presto!" he declared. "No unemployment, no relief rolls. No Depression."

Many artists introduced a strident masculinism into their painting and sculpture. Mighty *Superman,* the new comic-strip hero of 1938, reflected the spirit of the times. Superman was depicted as a working-class hero who, on several occasions, saved workers from coal mine explosions and other disasters caused by the greed and negligence of villainous employers.

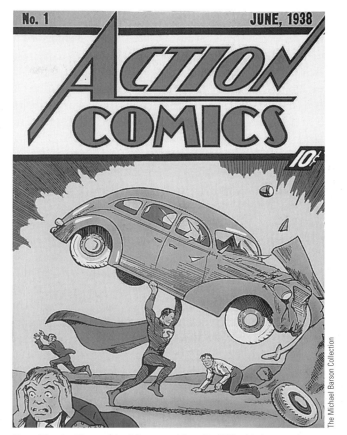

The Michael Barson Collection

Man of Steel The comic book *Superman* debuted in 1938, with the cover that appears in this reproduction. The character Superman partook of the New Deal's commitment to help ordinary Americans in need while offering men a fantasy about unconquerable male power.

Superman's greatest vulnerability, however, other than kryptonite, was his attraction to the sexy and aggressive *working* woman, Lois Lane. He could never resolve his dilemma by marrying Lois and tucking her away in a safe domestic sphere, because the continuation of the comic strip demanded that Superman be repeatedly exposed to kryptonite and female danger. But the producers of male and female images in other mass media, such as the movies, faced no such technical obstacles. Anxious men could take comfort from the conclusion of the movie *Woman of the Year,* in which Spencer Tracy persuades the ambitious Katharine Hepburn to exchange her successful newspaper career for the bliss of motherhood and homemaking. From a thousand different points, 1930s politics and culture made it clear that a woman's proper place was in the home. Faced with such obstacles, it is not surprising that women activists failed to make feminism a major part of New Deal reform.

Labor in Politics and Culture

In 1935, John L. Lewis of the United Mine Workers, Sidney Hillman of the Amalgamated Clothing Workers, and the leaders of six other unions that had seceded from the American Federation of Labor (AFL) cobbled together a new labor organization. The Committee for Industrial Organization (**CIO**—later renamed the Congress of Industrial Organizations) aspired to organize millions of unskilled and semiskilled workers whom the AFL had largely ignored. In 1936, Lewis and Hillman created a second organization, Labor's Non-Partisan League (LNPL), to develop a labor strategy for the 1936 elections. Although professing the league's nonpartisanship, Lewis intended from the start that the LNPL's role would be to channel labor's money, energy, and talent into Roosevelt's reelection campaign. Roosevelt welcomed the league's help, and labor would become a key constituency of the new Democratic coalition. The passage of the Wagner Act and the creation of the NLRB in 1935 enhanced the labor movement's status and credibility. Membership in labor unions climbed steadily, and, in short order, union members began flexing their new muscles.

In late 1936, the United Auto Workers (UAW) took on General Motors, widely regarded as the most powerful corporation in the world. Workers occupied key GM factories in Flint, Michigan, declaring that their **sit-down strike** would continue until GM agreed to recognize the UAW and negotiate a collective bargaining agreement. Frank Murphy, the pro-labor governor of Michigan, refused to use National Guard troops to evict the strikers, and Roosevelt declined to send federal troops. A 50-year-old practice of using soldiers to break strikes ended, and General Motors capitulated after a month of resistance. Soon, the U.S. Steel Corporation, which had defeated unionists in the bloody strike of 1919 (see chapter 23), announced that it was ready to negotiate a contract with the newly formed CIO steelworkers union.

The labor movement's public stature grew along with its size. Many writers and artists, funded through the WPA, depicted the labor movement as the voice of the people and the embodiment of the nation's values. Murals sprang up in post offices and other public buildings featuring portraits of blue-collar Americans at work. Broadway's most celebrated play in 1935 was Clifford Odets's *Waiting for Lefty,* a raw drama about taxi drivers who confront their bosses and organize an honest union. Audiences were so moved by the play that they often spontaneously joined in the final chorus of "Strike, Strike, Strike," the words that ended the play. *Pins and Needles,* a 1937 musical about the hopes and dreams of garment workers, performed by actual members of the International Ladies Garment Workers Union, became the longest-running play in Broadway history (until *Oklahoma!* broke its record of 1,108 performances in 1943).

Similarly, many of the most popular novels and movies of the 1930s celebrated the decency, honesty, and patriotism of ordinary Americans. In *Mr. Deeds Goes to Town* (1936) and *Mr. Smith Goes to Washington* (1939), **Frank Capra** delighted movie audiences with fables of simple, small-town heroes vanquishing the evil forces of wealth and decadence. Likewise, in *The Grapes of Wrath,* the best-selling novel of 1939, John

Steinbeck told an epic tale of an Oklahoma family's fortitude in surviving eviction from their land, migrating westward, and suffering exploitation in the "promised land" of California. In 1940, John Ford turned Steinbeck's novel into one of that year's highest-grossing and most acclaimed movies. Moviegoers found special meaning in the declaration of one of the story's main characters, Ma Joad: "We'll go on forever . . . 'cause we're the people." In themselves and in one another, Americans seemed to discover the resolve they needed to rebuild a culture that had surrendered its identity to corporations and business.

John Steinbeck wrote about the Okie migrants to California as an outsider. But the Okies produced a writer and musician of their own who became, in the late 1930s, a popular folk singer. Born in 1913 in Okemah, Oklahoma, Woody Guthrie grew up in nearby Pampa, Texas. He wasn't born poor—his father was a small businessman and a local politician—but by the time he reached his twenties, Guthrie had known a great deal of hardship: his father's business failed, three family homes burned down, one sister died from burns, and then the drought and dust storms struck. In the 1930s, Guthrie joined the large migration of Okies to California. There, his musical gifts were discovered, chiefly because radio stations, in particular, were keen to put "singing cowboys" on the air. Guthrie had emerged from a country music tradition in Texas and Oklahoma and found an audience among the many people from those states who had gone to California.

But Guthrie quickly developed a broader appeal as he cast himself as the bard of ordinary Americans everywhere. He loved America for the beauty of its landscape and its people, sentiments he expressed in one of his most popular songs, "This Land Is Your Land," which he wrote in 1940 in response to Irving Berlin's "God Bless America" (a song Guthrie did not like because of the false sense of complacency he thought it induced). Guthrie did not possess a refined singing voice, but his "hillbilly" lyrics, melodies, and humor were inventive and often inspiring. He would become a powerful influence on subsequent generations of musicians, including such major figures as Bob Dylan and Bruce Springsteen.

Guthrie traveled ceaselessly in the 1930s, from Los Angeles to New York and from Texas to Washington state. The more he learned about the hardships of individual Americans, the angrier and more politically active he became. He drew close to the labor movement and to the Communist Party, and increasingly, in his writings and songs, he criticized the industrialists, financiers, and their political agents who, he believed, had brought the calamity of the Depression on America. But Guthrie always associated his criticism with the hope that the working people of America, if united, could take back their land—which is the message he meant to convey when he sang "This Land Is Your Land"—and restore its greatness. The optimism of his message underscored how much the cultural mood had changed since the early 1930s. In his focus on ordinary working Americans, in his hope for the future, and in his fusion of dissent and patriotism, Guthrie was emblematic of the dominant stream of culture and politics in the late 1930s.

America's Minorities and the New Deal

Focus Question
Which minority groups in American society benefited the most from the New Deal and which benefited the least?

Reformers in the 1930s generally believed that issues of capitalism's viability, economic recovery, and the inequality of wealth and power outweighed problems of racial and ethnic discrimination; only in the case of American Indians did New Dealers pass legislation specifically designed to improve a minority's social and economic position. Because they were disproportionately poor, most minority groups did profit from the populist and pro-labor character of New Deal reforms, but the gains were distributed unevenly. Eastern and Southern European ethnics benefited the most, and African Americans and Mexican Americans advanced the least.

Eastern and Southern European Ethnics

Eastern and Southern European immigrants and their children had begun mobilizing politically in the 1920s in response to religious and racial discrimination (see chapter 24). Roosevelt understood their political importance well, for he was a product of New York Democratic politics, where men such as Robert Wagner and Al Smith had begun to organize the ethnic vote even before 1920 (see chapter 21). He made sure that a significant portion of New Deal monies for welfare, building and road construction, and unemployment relief reached the urban areas where most European ethnics lived. As a result, Jewish and Catholic Americans, especially those descended from Eastern and Southern European immigrants, voted for Roosevelt in overwhelming numbers. The New Deal did not eliminate anti-Semitism and anti-Catholicism from American society, but it did allow millions of European ethnics to believe, for the first time, that they would overcome the second-class status they had long endured.

Eastern and Southern European ethnics also benefited from their strong working-class presence. Forming one of the largest groups in the mass-production industries of the Northeast, Midwest, and West Coast, they formed a large part of the labor movement's new membership. Roosevelt accommodated himself to their wishes because he understood and feared the power they wielded through their labor organizations.

African Americans

The New Deal did more to reproduce patterns of racial discrimination than to advance the cause of racial equality. African Americans who belonged to CIO unions or who lived in northern cities benefited from New Deal programs, but most blacks lived in the rural South, where they were barred from voting, largely excluded from AAA programs, and denied federal protection in their efforts to form agricultural unions. The CCC ran separate camps for black and white youth. The TVA hired few blacks. Those enrolled in the

CWA and other work-relief programs frequently received less pay than whites for doing the same jobs. Roosevelt consistently refused to support legislation to make lynching a federal crime.

This failure to push a strong civil-rights agenda did not mean that New Dealers were racist. Eleanor Roosevelt spoke out frequently against racial injustice. In 1939, she resigned from the Daughters of the American Revolution when the organization refused to allow black opera singer **Marian Anderson** to perform in its concert hall. She then pressured the federal government into granting Anderson permission to sing from the steps of the Lincoln Memorial. On Easter Sunday, 75,000 people gathered to hear Anderson and to demonstrate their support for racial equality. The president did not attend.

Roosevelt did eliminate segregationist practices in the federal government that had been in place since Woodrow Wilson's presidency. He appointed Mary McLeod Bethune, Robert Weaver, William Hastie, and other African Americans to important second-level posts in his administration. Working closely with each other in what came to be known as the Black Cabinet, these officials fought hard to end discrimination in New Deal programs.

Roosevelt, however, refused to support the Black Cabinet if it meant alienating white southern senators who controlled key congressional committees. He believed that pushing for civil rights would cost him the support of the white South. Meanwhile, African Americans and their supporters were not yet strong enough as an electoral constituency or as a reform movement to force Roosevelt to accede to their wishes.

Mexican Americans

The Mexican American experience in the Great Depression was particularly harsh. In 1931, Hoover's secretary of labor, William N. Doak, announced a plan for repatriating illegal aliens (returning them to their land of origin) and giving their jobs to American citizens. The federal campaign quickly focused on Mexican immigrants in California and the Southwest. The U.S. Immigration Service staged a series of highly publicized raids, rounded up large numbers of Mexicans and Mexican Americans, and demanded that each detainee prove his or her legal status. Those who failed to produce the necessary documentation were deported. Local and state governments pressured many more Mexicans into leaving. The combined efforts of federal, state, and local governments created a climate of fear in Mexican communities that prompted 500,000 to return to Mexico by 1935. This total equaled the number of Mexicans who had come to the United States in the 1920s. Los Angeles lost one-third of its Mexican population. Included in repatriate ranks were a significant number of legal immigrants who were unable to produce their immigration papers, the American-born children of illegals, and some Mexican Americans who had lived in the Southwest for generations.

The advent of the New Deal in 1933 eased but did not eliminate pressure on Chicano communities. New Deal agencies made more money available for relief, thereby lightening the burden on state and local governments. But federal laws, more often than not, failed to dissuade local officials from continuing their campaign against Mexican immigrants. Where Mexicans gained access to relief rolls, they received payments lower than those given to "Anglos" (whites) or were compelled to accept tough agricultural jobs that paid less than living wages.

Life grew harder for immigrant Mexicans who stayed behind. The Mexican cultural renaissance that had emerged in 1920s Los Angeles (see chapter 24) stalled. Hounded by government officials, Mexicans everywhere sought to escape public attention and scrutiny. In Los Angeles, where their influence had been felt throughout the city in the 1920s, they retreated into the separate community of East Los Angeles. To many, they became the "invisible minority."

Mexicans and Mexican Americans who lived in urban areas and worked in blue-collar industries, however, did benefit from New Deal programs. In Los Angeles, for example, Chicanos employed in canneries, in garment and furniture shops, and on the docks responded to the New Deal's pro-labor legislation by joining unions in large numbers and winning concessions from their employers. Most Chicanos, however, lived in rural areas and labored in agricultural jobs, and the New Deal offered them little help. The National Labor Relations Act did not protect their right to organize unions, and the Social Security Act excluded them from the new federal welfare system.

American Indians

From the 1880s until the early 1930s, federal policy had contributed to the elimination of American Indians as a distinctive population. The Dawes Act of 1887 (see chapter 18) had called for tribal lands to be broken up and allotted to individual owners in the hope that Indians would adopt the work habits of white farmers. But American Indians had proved stubbornly loyal to their languages, religions, and cultures. Few of them succeeded as farmers, and many lost land to white speculators. By 1933, nearly half the American Indians living on reservations whose land had been allotted were landless, and many who retained allotments held land that was largely desert or semidesert.

The shrinking land base in combination with a growing population deepened American Indian poverty. The assimilationist pressures on American Indians, meanwhile, reached a climax in the intolerant 1920s, when the Bureau of Indian Affairs (BIA) outlawed Indian religious ceremonies, forced children from tribal communities into federal boarding schools, banned polygamy, and imposed limits on the length of men's hair.

Government officials working in the Hoover administration began to question this draconian policy, but its reversal had to await the New Deal and Roosevelt's appointment of **John Collier** as the commissioner of the BIA. Collier pressured the CCC, AAA, and other New Deal agencies to employ Indians on projects that improved reservation land and trained Indians in land conservation methods. He prevailed on Congress to pass the Pueblo Relief Act of 1933, which compensated Pueblos for land taken from them in the 1920s, and the Johnson-O'Malley Act of 1934, which provided funds to the states for Indian health care, welfare, and education. As part of his campaign to make the BIA more responsive to American Indian needs, Collier increased the number of Indian BIA employees from a paltry few hundred in 1933 to a respectable 4,600 in 1940.

Collier also took steps to abolish federal boarding schools, encourage enrollment in local public schools, and establish community day schools. He insisted that American Indians be allowed to practice their traditional religions, and he created the Indian Arts and Crafts Board in 1935 to nurture traditional Indian artists and to help them market their works.

The centerpiece of Collier's reform strategy was the Indian Reorganization Act (also known as the Wheeler-Howard Act) of 1934, which revoked the allotment provisions of the Dawes Act. The IRA restored land to tribes, granted Indians the right to establish constitutions and bylaws for self-government, and provided support for new tribal corporations that would regulate the use of communal lands. This landmark act signaled the government's recognition that American Indian tribes possessed the right to chart their own political, cultural, and economic futures. It reflected Collier's commitment to "cultural pluralism," a doctrine that celebrated the diversity of peoples and cultures in American society and sought to protect that diversity against the pressures of assimilation. Collier hoped that the IRA would invigorate traditional Indian cultures and tribal societies and sustain both for generations. Cultural pluralism was not a popular creed in America during the depression years, which makes its acceptance as the rationale for the IRA all the more remarkable.

Collier encountered opposition everywhere: from Protestant missionaries and cultural conservatives who wanted to continue an assimilationist policy; from white farmers and businessmen who feared that the new legislation would restrict their access to Native American land; and even from a sizable number of Indian groups, some of which had embraced assimilation and others that viewed the IRA cynically, as one more attempt by the federal government to impose "the white man's will" on the Indian peoples. This opposition made the IRA a more modest bill than the one Collier had originally championed.

A vocal minority of Indians continued to oppose the act even after its passage. The Navajo, the nation's largest tribe, voted to reject its terms along with 76 other tribes. Still, 181 tribes, nearly 70 percent of the total, supported Collier's reform and began organizing new governments under the IRA. Although their quest for independence would suffer setbacks, these tribes gained significant measures of freedom and autonomy during the New Deal.

The New Deal Abroad

When he first entered office, Roosevelt seemed to favor a nationalist approach to international relations. The United States, he believed, should pursue foreign policies to benefit its domestic affairs, without regard for the effects of those policies on world trade and international stability. Thus, in June 1933, Roosevelt pulled the United States out of the World Economic Conference in London, a meeting called by leading nations to strengthen the gold standard and thereby stabilize the value of their currencies. Roosevelt feared that the United States would be forced into an agreement designed to keep the gold content of the dollar high and U.S. commodity prices low, which would frustrate New Deal efforts to inflate the prices of agricultural and industrial goods.

Soon after his withdrawal from the London conference, however, Roosevelt put the United States on a more internationalist course. In November 1933, he became the first president to recognize the Soviet Union and to establish diplomatic ties with its Communist rulers. In December 1933, he inaugurated a **Good Neighbor Policy** toward Latin America by formally renouncing U.S. rights to intervene in the affairs of Latin American nations. To back up his pledge, Roosevelt ordered home the Marines stationed in Haiti and Nicaragua, scuttled the Platt Amendment that had given the United States control over the Cuban government since 1901, and granted Panama more political autonomy and a greater administrative role in operating the Panama Canal (see chapter 22).

None of this, however, meant that the United States had given up its influence over Latin America. When a 1934 revolution brought a radical government to power in Cuba, the U.S. ambassador there worked with conservative Cubans to replace the government with a regime more favorable to U.S. interests. The United States did refrain from sending troops to Cuba. It also kept its troops at home in 1936 when a radical government in Mexico nationalized several U.S.-owned and British-owned petroleum companies. The United States merely demanded that the new Mexican government compensate the oil companies for their lost property, which Mexico eventually did. Although the United States was still the dominant power in hemispheric affairs, its newfound restraint inspired Latin American hopes that a new era had dawned.

The Roosevelt administration's recognition of the Soviet Union and embrace of the Good Neighbor Policy can be seen as an international expression of the liberal principles that guided its domestic policies. These diplomatic initiatives, however, also reflected Roosevelt's interest in stimulating international trade. American businessmen wanted access to the Soviet Union's domestic market. Latin America was already a major market for the United States, but one in need of greater stability. To win the support of American traders and investors, Roosevelt stressed how the Good Neighbor Policy would improve the region's business climate.

Roosevelt further expressed his interest in building international trade through his support for the Reciprocal Trade Agreement, passed by Congress in 1934. This act allowed his administration to lower U.S. tariffs by as much as 50 percent in exchange for similar reductions by other nations. By the end of 1935, the United States had negotiated reciprocal trade agreements with 14 countries. Roosevelt's emphasis on international trade—a move consonant with the Second New Deal's program of increasing the circulation of goods and money through the economy—further solidified support for the New Deal in parts of the business community, especially among those firms, such as United Fruit and Coca-Cola, with large overseas investments.

Actually increasing the volume of international trade was more difficult than passing legislation to encourage it. In Germany and Italy, belligerent nationalists Adolf Hitler

Unemployment, 1920–1945

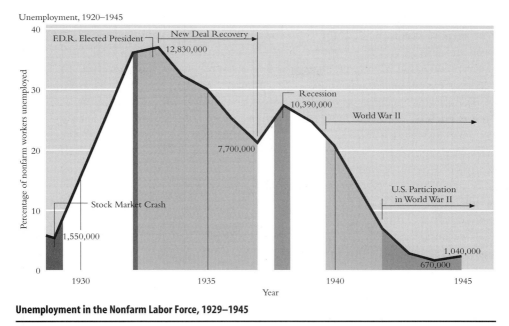

Unemployment in the Nonfarm Labor Force, 1929–1945

Source: Data from *Historical Statistics of the United States, Colonial Times to 1970* (White Plains, N.Y.: Kraus International, 1989), p. 126.

and Benito Mussolini told their people that the solution to their ills lay not in foreign trade but in military strength and conquest. Throughout the world, similar appeals to national pride proved more popular than calls for tariff reductions and international trade. In the face of this historical current, the New Deal's internationalist economic policies made little headway.

Stalemate, 1937–1940

By 1937 and 1938, the New Deal had begun to lose momentum. One reason was an emerging split between working-class and middle-class Democrats. After the UAW's victory over General Motors in 1937, other workers began to imitate the successful tactics of the Flint, Michigan, militants. Sit-down strikes spread to many industries and regions, a development that many middle-class Americans found disturbing.

The Court-Packing Fiasco

The president's proposal on February 5, 1937, to alter the makeup of the Supreme Court exacerbated middle-class fears. Roosevelt asked Congress to give him the power to appoint one new Supreme Court justice for every member of the court who was older than age 70 and who had served for at least 10 years. His stated reason was that the current justices were too old and feeble to handle the large volume of cases coming before them, but his real purpose was to prevent the conservative justices on the court—most of whom had been appointed by Republican presidents—from dismantling his New Deal. His proposal, if accepted, would have given him the authority to appoint six additional justices, thereby securing a pro–New Deal majority.

The president seemed genuinely surprised by the storm of indignation that greeted his "**court-packing**" proposal. Roosevelt's political acumen had apparently been dulled by his 1936 victory. His inflated sense of power infuriated many who had previously been New Deal enthusiasts. Although working-class support for Roosevelt remained strong, many middle-class voters turned away from the New Deal. In 1937 and 1938, a conservative opposition took shape, uniting Republicans, conservative Democrats (many of them southerners), and civil libertarians who were determined to protect private property and government integrity.

Ironically, Roosevelt's court-packing scheme may have been unnecessary. In March 1937, just one month after he proposed his plan, Supreme Court Justice Owen J. Roberts, a former opponent of New Deal programs, decided to support them. In April and May, the Court upheld the constitutionality of the Wagner Act and Social Security Act, both by a 5-to-4 margin. The principal reforms of the New Deal would endure. Roosevelt allowed his court-reform proposal to die in Congress that summer. Within three years, five of the aging justices had retired, giving Roosevelt the opportunity to fashion a court more to his liking. Nonetheless, Roosevelt's reputation had suffered.

The Recession of 1937–1938

Whatever hope Roosevelt may have had for a quick recovery from the court-packing fiasco was dashed by a sharp recession that struck the country in late 1937 and 1938. The New Deal programs of 1935 had stimulated the economy, prompting Roosevelt to scale back relief programs. Meanwhile, new payroll taxes took $2 billion from wage earners' salaries to finance the Social Security pension fund even though the government did not intend to begin paying benefits until 1941. Thus, the government substantially shrunk the volume of dollars it was putting into circulation. Starved for money, the economy and stock market crashed once again. Unemployment, which had fallen to 14 percent, shot back up to 20 percent. In the 1938 elections, voters vented their frustration by electing many conservative Democrats and Republicans who were opposed to the New Deal. These conservatives could not dismantle the New Deal reforms already in place, but they did block the passage of new programs.

Conclusion

Roosevelt first assumed the presidency in the same week that Adolf Hitler established a Nazi dictatorship in Germany. Some feared that Roosevelt, by accumulating more power into the hands of the federal government than had ever been held in peacetime, aspired to autocratic rule. Nothing of the sort happened. Roosevelt and the New Dealers not only strengthened democracy, they also inspired millions of Americans who had never before voted to go to the polls. Groups that had been marginalized— Eastern and Southern European ethnics, unskilled workers, American Indians—now believed that their political activism could make a difference.

Not everyone benefited to the same degree from the broadening of American democracy. Northern factory workers, farm owners, European American ethnics, and middle-class consumers (especially homeowners) were among the groups who benefited most. In contrast, the socialist and communist elements of the labor movement failed to achieve their radical aims. Southern industrial workers, black and white, benefited little from New Deal reforms; so did farm laborers. Feminists made no headway. African Americans and Mexican Americans gained meager influence over public policy.

New Deal reforms might not have mattered to any group if the Second World War had not rescued the New Deal economic program. With government war orders flooding factories from 1941 on, the economy grew vigorously, unemployment vanished, and prosperity finally returned. The architects of the Second New Deal, who had argued that large government expenditures would stimulate consumer demand and trigger economic recovery, were vindicated.

The war also solidified the political reforms of the 1930s: an increased role for the government in regulating the economy and in ensuring the social welfare of those unable to help themselves; strong state support of unionization, agricultural subsidies, and progressive tax policies; and the use of government power and money to develop the West and Southwest. In sharp contrast to progressivism, the reforms of the New Deal endured. Voters returned Roosevelt to office for unprecedented third and fourth terms, and these same voters remained wedded for the next 40 years to Roosevelt's central idea: that a powerful state would enhance the pursuit of liberty and equality.

SUGGESTED READINGS

T. H. Watkins, *The Great Depression: America in the 1930s* (1993), provides a broad overview of society and politics during the 1930s. No work better conveys the tumult and drama of that era than **Arthur M. Schlesinger Jr.'s** three-volume *The Age of Roosevelt: The Crisis of the Old Order* (1957), *The Coming of the New Deal* (1958), and *The Politics of Upheaval* (1960), but Schlesinger's work must now be supplemented with **David M. Kennedy,** *Freedom from Fear: The American People in Depression and War, 1929–1945* (1999). On Hoover's failure to restore prosperity and popular morale, see **David Burner,** *Herbert Hoover: A Public Life* (1979).

The most complete biography of FDR, and one that is remarkably good at balancing Roosevelt's life and times, is **Kenneth S. Davis,** *FDR* (1972–1993), in four volumes. For a vivid description of the political dangers confronting Roosevelt as he assumed office in 1933, see Jonathan Alter, *The Defining Moment: FDR's Hundred Days and the Triumph of Hope* (2006). On Eleanor Roosevelt, see **Blanche Wiesen Cook,** *Eleanor Roosevelt,* vol. 1 (1992). On the New Deal, see **William E. Leuchtenberg,** *Franklin D. Roosevelt and the New Deal, 1932–1940* (1963); **Anthony J. Badger,** *The New Deal: The Depression Years, 1933–1940* (1989); and **Steve Fraser and Gary Gerstle, eds.,**

The Rise and Fall of the New Deal Order, 1930–1980 (1989). **Ellis Hawley,** *The New Deal and the Problem of Monopoly* (1966), is essential to understand the First New Deal's industrial policy, while **Steven Fraser,** *Labor Will Rule: Sidney Hillman and the Rise of American Labor* (1991), examines the role of the labor movement in national politics.

Michael Denning, *The Cultural Front: The Laboring of American Culture in the Twentieth Century* (1996), is essential reading on the centrality of labor and the "common man" to literary and popular culture in the 1930s, as is **Lary May,** *The Big Tomorrow: Hollywood and the Politics of the American Way* (2000). For the economic and cultural ties between the New Deal and the rebirth of the labor movement, see **Lizabeth Cohen,** *Making a New Deal: Industrial Workers in Chicago, 1919–1939* (1990). **Irving Howe and Lewis Coser,** *The American Communist Party: A Critical History, 1919–1957* (1957), is still the best single-volume history of the Communist Party during the 1930s.

Harvard Sitkoff, *A New Deal for Blacks* (1978), is a wide-ranging examination of the place of African Americans in New Deal reform. **Abraham Hoffman,** *Unwanted Mexican Americans in the Great Depression: Repatriation Pressures, 1929–1939* (1974), analyzes the repatriation campaign, while the problems of illegal alienage created by that campaign are expertly analyzed in **Mae Ngai,** *Impossible Subjects: Illegal Aliens and the Making of Modern America* (2004). The importance of John Collier and the Indian Reorganization Act are treated well in **Lawrence C. Kelly,** *The Assault on Assimilation: John Collier and the Origins of Indian Policy Reform* (1983). **James T. Patterson,** *Congressional Conservatism and the New Deal* (1967), expertly analyzes the growing opposition to the New Deal in the late 1930s, while **Alan Brinkley,** *The End of Reform: New Deal Liberalism in Recession and War* (1995), provocatively examines the efforts of New Dealers to adjust their beliefs and programs as they lost support, momentum, and confidence in the late 1930s.

Visit the Liberty Equality Power Companion Web site for resources specific to this textbook: http://www.thomsonedu.com/history/murrin

Also find self-tests and additional resources at ThomsonNOW. ThomsonNOW is an integrated online suite of services and resources with proven ease of use and efficient paths to success, delivering the results you want—NOW!

www.thomsonedu.com/login/

America during the Second World War

The Second World War brought unprecedented destruction to much of the globe. The United States—whose own towns, farms, and cities would escape the impact of combat operations—lurched toward direct engagement in this conflict. Mobilization for war, already underway before formal U.S. entry in 1941, first lifted the nation out of the Great Depression and, then, transformed its economy. At war's end, the military might and productive capacity of the victorious United States—spurred by innovative technologies and new working relationships among government, business, labor, and scientific researchers—dwarfed that of all other nations. Franklin Roosevelt's wartime presidency, invoking military necessity as the justification, significantly expanded the power of the national government.

As the war proceeded, Americans came to reconsider how to understand liberty and equality. Although a government-directed publicity campaign initially stressed how wartime sacrifices would protect and preserve an "American way of life," the ongoing fight against fascist dictatorships overseas soon raised questions about what might—and should—change in the United States itself. Might the nation, while striving for military victory, also reorder its economy, rework its politics, and refashion the cultural and social patterns that had shaped racial, ethnic, and gender relationships during the 1930s? Could the interrelated tasks of reconstructing a war-ravaged world and strengthening forces for peace require the creation of new institutions, both at home and abroad?

The Road to War: Aggression and Response

Focus Question
How did events in Asia and in Europe affect debate within the United States over whether or not to embrace more interventionist policies overseas?

Tensions growing out of the First World War, heightened by a worldwide economic depression, fostered international instability during the 1930s. In Japan, Italy, and Germany, economic stagnation nurtured ultranationalist political movements that championed aggressive foreign policies. Elsewhere in Europe and in the United States, economic problems inclined governing majorities to turn inward, concentrating on promoting recovery and avoiding foreign entanglements.

CHRONOLOGY

1931	Japanese forces seize Manchuria
1933	Hitler takes power in Germany
1936	Spanish Civil War begins • Germany and Italy agree to cooperate as the Axis Powers
1937	Neutrality Act broadens provisions of Neutrality Acts of 1935 and 1936 • Roosevelt makes "Quarantine" speech • Japan invades China
1938	France and Britain appease Hitler at Munich
1939	Hitler and Stalin sign Soviet–German nonaggression pact • Hitler invades Poland; war breaks out in Europe • Congress amends Neutrality Act to assist Allies
1940	Paris falls after German *blitzkreig* (June) • Battle of Britain carried to U.S. by radio broadcasts • Roosevelt makes "destroyers-for-bases" deal with Britain • Selective Service Act passed • Roosevelt wins third term
1941	Lend-Lease established • Roosevelt creates Fair Employment Practices Commission • Roosevelt and Churchill proclaim the Atlantic Charter • U.S. engages in undeclared naval war in North Atlantic • Congress narrowly repeals Neutrality Act • Japanese forces attack Pearl Harbor (December 7)
1942	Rio de Janeiro Conference (January) • President signs Executive Order 9066 for internment of Japanese Americans (February) • General MacArthur driven from Philippines (May) • U.S. victorious in Battle of Midway (June) • German army defeated at Battle of Stalingrad (August) • Operation TORCH begins (November)
1943	Axis armies in North Africa surrender (May) • Allies invade Sicily (July) and Italy (September) • "Zoot suit" incidents in Los Angeles; racial violence in Detroit • Allies begin drive toward Japan through South Pacific islands
1944	Allies land at Normandy (D-day, June 6) • Allied armies reach Paris (August) • Allies turn back Germans at Battle of the Bulge (September) • Roosevelt reelected to fourth term • Bretton Woods Conference creates IMF and World Bank • Dumbarton Oaks Conference establishes plan for UN
1945	U.S. firebombs Japan • Yalta Conference (February) • Roosevelt dies; Truman becomes president (April) • Germany surrenders (May) • Hiroshima and Nagasaki hit with atomic bombs (August) • Japan surrenders (September) • United Nations established (December)

The Rise of Aggressor States

The first signs of another world war appeared in Asia. On September 18, 1931, Japanese military forces seized Manchuria, and Japan renamed the puppet state it created Manchukuo. This aggression by Japan violated the charter of the League of Nations, the Washington naval treaties, and the Kellogg-Briand Pact (see chapter 24). Focused on domestic matters, nations such as the United States hesitated to oppose Japan's move with military force. Instead, the Hoover-Stimson Doctrine (1931) announced a U.S. policy of "nonrecognition" toward Manchukuo, and the League of Nations merely condemned Japan's move. Japan simply ignored these rhetorical rebukes.

Two ultranationalist states in Europe also soon embarked on military aggression. **Adolf Hitler's** National Socialist (Nazi) Party, which came to power in Germany during 1933, announced a bold approach to addressing economic ills and political instability. Hitler created a one-party dictatorial state; denounced the Versailles peace settlement of 1919 as unfair to Germany; further blamed its problems on a Jewish conspiracy; claimed a genetic superiority for the "Aryan race" of German-speaking peoples; and promised a new Germanic empire, the **Third Reich.** His fascist regime also withdrew from the League of Nations in 1933 and, in a blatant violation of the Versailles treaty, dramatically boosted Germany's military budget.

Another, less powerful fascist government, headed by Benito Mussolini, had come to power in Italy during the 1920s. As Mussolini introduced authoritarian controls over Italy's domestic life, he launched his own military buildup and prepared for territorial expansion. Mussolini talked of making the Mediterranean an Italian-dominated sea. Building on earlier moves against Albania and Libya, Mussolini sent his armies, in 1935, into Ethiopia. After a brief and bloody conflict, Mussolini converted this previously independent African kingdom into an Italian colony and, then, began forging close ties with Hitler's regime in Germany.

U.S. Neutrality

In the United States, memories of involvement in the First World War helped justify efforts to isolate the nation from the foreign troubles of the 1930s. Antiwar books and movies, such as *All Quiet on the Western Front* (1931), implicitly portrayed President Woodrow Wilson's earlier call for making "the world safe for democracy" (see chapter 23) as part of a cynical power game directed by business and governmental elites. Appeals to noble ideals merely allowed corrupt power brokers to turn young soldiers into cannon fodder. During the mid-1930s, a U.S. Senate committee headed by Republican Gerald P. Nye of North Dakota elaborated on this view of recent history. After well-publicized hearings, the Nye Committee charged that bankers and munitions makers, in search of profits, had conspired with their counterparts in Britain and France to maneuver the United States into the First World War. An influential group of historians, endorsing different variations of this critique, charged Wilson with having ignored the U.S. national interest when plunging his nation into the war in 1915. Twenty years later, popular opinion polls suggested overwhelming opposition to a similar U.S. involvement in the foreign conflicts of the 1930s.

The U.S. Congress backed this stance with a series of **Neutrality Acts.** These measures aimed at keeping the United States free from the kind of entangling financial relationships that had supposedly pulled it into the First World War. Neutrality laws passed in 1935 and 1936 established an embargo on arms sales to **belligerent** nations, prohibited U.S. loans to any country at war, and curtailed travel by U.S. citizens on vessels belonging to any warring power. The **"cash-and-carry"** provision in the Neutrality Act of 1937 extended the earlier arms embargo to include any foreign trade with belligerents. It did allow nations at war to continue buying products in the United States if they paid in hard cash and transported goods away in their own ships, rather than on U.S. ships.

Critics of this neutrality legislation charged that foreswearing U.S. intervention actively aided expansionist powers such as Nazi Germany. In March 1936, Hitler's forces entered the Rhineland, an area of Germany from which the 1919 peace settlement had barred military installations. A few months later, Hitler and Mussolini began assisting General Francisco Franco, a fellow fascist seeking the overthrow of Spain's fragile Republic and the restoration of a monarchy closely tied to the Catholic Church and the Spanish military. Franco's opponents, including that nation's communist movement, appealed to nonfascist nations for assistance. Only the communist Soviet Union responded.

Fearing conflict in Spain could flare into a wider war, the governments of Britain, France, and the United States refused to become involved. The U.S. Congress extended its arms embargo to include civil wars, a move that blocked the Spanish Republic from obtaining weaponry in the United States and implicitly benefited General Franco's already well-armed fascist forces. As with the other pieces of neutrality legislation, President Roosevelt, who was personally sympathetic to more interventionist policies, signed this measure.

The Spanish Civil War, however, helped sharpen foreign policy debate in the United States. Conservative groups generally hailed General Franco as a staunch anticommunist who would promote social stability and religious values in Spain. In contrast, the political left saw the Spanish Republic being sacrificed to a fascist movement that threatened to spread repression all across Europe. Cadres of Americans, including members of an "Abraham Lincoln Brigade," crossed the Atlantic to fight alongside the anti-Franco forces in Spain. U.S. peace groups, which had generally presented a united front during the 1920s, differed over how best to avoid a wider war. Some advocated neutrality and isolation, but others argued that the threat of **fascism** now demanded a turn toward interventionism, beginning in Spain.

Roosevelt's administration did tilt in an interventionist direction, more overtly than before. Seeking to influence domestic debate, Roosevelt called for international cooperation against expansionist nations. In his controversial "Quarantine the Aggressors" Speech of October 1937, the president suggested the possibility of Congress modifying earlier neutrality measures. Still suspicious of foreign entanglements, a majority of legislators refused to budge, even if this meant a victory by Franco in Spain's civil war.

The Mounting Crisis

As Americans were weighing policies of maintaining strict neutrality against ones of opposing aggression overseas, expansionist forces in Japan seized the initiative. During the summer of 1937, after an exchange of gunfire between Japanese and Chinese troops at the Marco Polo Bridge near Beijing, Japanese armies mounted a full scale invasion of China. Japan's forces captured Shanghai, Nanjing, Shandong, and Beijing. Japan demanded that China accept economic and political direction from Tokyo. As the Nationalist Chinese government of Jiang Jieshi (formally spelled Chiang Kai-sheck) struggled to survive, Japan unveiled ambitious plans for an East Asian Co-Prosperity Sphere, a self-sufficient economic zone under Japanese leadership.

This expansionist vision, which Japan promised would liberate Asian nations from Western colonialism, worried the Roosevelt administration and heightened tensions between the United States and Japan. In late 1937, Japanese planes sank the *Panay,* a U.S. gunboat, as it was evacuating Americans from Nanjing. Japan's quick apology and promise to pay for damages defused a potential crisis. Still, the *Panay* incident and Japan's brutality in Nanjing, which took the lives of perhaps 300,000 Chinese civilians, further fueled interventionist efforts in the United States. President Roosevelt began consulting, secretly, with British leaders about how to respond to the threat of war in Asia, where Britain still held valuable colonies. In May 1938, FDR publicly announced a program of naval rearmament that went beyond treaty limits that Japan had already violated.

Meanwhile, in Europe, Germany continued on the march. In March 1938, Hitler used the threat of military action to engineer the annexation of Austria, a neighboring nation, into the Third Reich, and he soon suggested a similar plan for the Sudetenland, a portion of Czechoslovakia inhabited by 3.5 million people of German descent. French and British leaders, still hoping to avoid war, met with Hitler in Munich in September 1938. Without consulting the leaders of Czechoslovakia or those of the neighboring Soviet Union, they acquiesced to Germany's power play in the Sudetenland. In return, Hitler pledged to seek no more territory. Hailed by Britain's prime minister as a guarantee of "peace in our time," the arrangement soon became a symbol of what interventionists called the "appeasement" of aggression.

Any hope that the Munich Conference would guarantee peace faded quickly. In March 1939, German troops marched into the Czechoslovakian capital of Prague; within a few months, Hitler announced the annexation of the rest of Czechoslovakia. Then, in an August 1939 surprise, he protected his eastern flank by signing a nonaggression pact with the Soviet Union, supposedly his sworn enemy. In a secret protocol, Hitler and Soviet leader **Joseph Stalin** agreed on a plan to divide up Poland, Hitler's next target, and the Baltic States (Latvia, Lithuania, and Estonia), which were long coveted by the Soviet Union.

The Outbreak of War in Europe

When Hitler's armies stormed onto Polish soil on September 1, 1939, the Second World War officially began. Britain and France, the Allies, already pledged to defend the Polish government, declared war against Germany but could not mobilize in time to help Poland. Within weeks, Germany's war machine overran that nation. Then, as a brutal campaign of Nazi repression wracked Poland, an eerie calm—which observers called a *sitzkrieg,* or "sitting war"—settled over the rest of Europe during the winter of 1939–40.

Suddenly, in April 1940, a full-scale German **blitzkrieg,** or "lightning war," began. Employing massed tank formations, motorized infantry and artillery, and massive air support, German military forces moved swiftly. They raced through Denmark, Norway, the Netherlands, Belgium, Luxembourg, and into France. The speed of the Nazi advance shocked Allied strategists in Paris and London. Britain dramatically evacuated its troops, but not their valuable equipment, from the French coastal town of Dunkirk, just before it fell to a German onslaught. Early in June, Italy joined Germany and declared war on the Allies. Later in June, German troops marched into Paris.

Hitler declared France's western and northern regions to be occupied German territory and installed a pro-Nazi French government at Vichy in southern France. In an act of powerful symbolism, he staged France's formal surrender in the same railway car in which Germany had capitulated to France at the end of the First World War. General Charles DeGaulle, seeking safety in London, countered by proclaiming *France Libre* (Free France), an anti-Nazi government pledged to end the German occupation and topple the Vichy regime.

After only six weeks of combat, Hitler's military juggernaut gave Nazi Germany control of Europe's Atlantic coastline. Germany's sway extended from the North Sea south to Spain, where Franco's fascist government remained officially neutral but effectively in the camp of Germany and Italy, which after announcing their own formal alliance, became the Axis Powers. The Axis gained another member, in September 1940, when Japan joined them in signing the Tripartite Pact. Britain now loomed directly in Hitler's gun sights.

The U.S. Response to War in Europe

Meanwhile, alarmed at the Nazi surge, President Roosevelt pressured Congress to modify its neutrality legislation and called for other "measures short of war" to help Britain and France. Late in 1939, Congress lifted the ban on selling military armaments to belligerents and authorized arms sales to all buyers who could pay cash and use their own ships for transport. Because its naval forces dominated the Atlantic sea lanes, Britain primarily benefited from this revised cash-and-carry policy.

The United States took other steps toward intervention. Congress granted the White House's request for new military funding and for enactment of the Selective Training and Service Act of 1940, the first peacetime draft in U.S. history. Worried about Britain's precarious military and financial position, Roosevelt facilitated the shipment of military supplies, sometimes claimed to be "surplus," to Great Britain. He also added two distinguished, pro-interventionist Republicans to what now seemed a war cabinet. Henry Stimson became secretary of war and Frank Knox secretary of the navy. These appointments gave Roosevelt's foreign policy a bipartisan image, if not fully bipartisan support.

Hitler focused his attention on the British Isles. From August through October 1940, Germany's air force, the **Luftwaffe,** conducted daily raids on Britain's air bases and nearly knocked out its Royal Air Force (RAF). On the verge of a kayo, however, Hitler suddenly changed strategy and ordered, instead, the bombing of London and other British cities—first by day and, then, by night. In addition to allowing the RAF time to recover, Hitler's move steeled Britain's resolve and bolstered the interventionist argument in the United States. Use of German airpower against British civilians, in what became known as "the Battle of Britain," aroused sympathy in the United States for their plight. U.S. radio correspondents began reporting, nightly, during Nazi bombing raids. The dramatic radio broadcasts of CBS's Edward R. Murrow, observed the writer Archibald MacLeish, "skillfully burned the city of London in our homes, and we felt the flames."

Map 26.1   German Expansion at Its Height   This map shows the expansion of German power from 1938 through 1942. Which countries fell to German control? Why might Americans have differed over whether these moves by Germany represented a strategic threat to the United States?

The Roosevelt administration, in turn, inched closer to intervention. In September 1940, it announced the transfer of 50 naval destroyers, from the era of World War I, to the British navy. In exchange, Britain granted the United States the right to build eight naval bases in its colonial territories in the Western Hemisphere. This "Destroyers-for-Bases" deal infuriated Roosevelt's opponents. Senator Burton K. Wheeler of Montana mailed out, at governmental expense, more than a million anti-interventionist postcards, a move that Secretary of War Stimson condemned as approaching "very near the line of subversion . . . if not treason."

After deciding to seek an unprecedented third term as president in 1940, however, Roosevelt seemed to shift course. He certainly began to speak more circumspectly, dishonestly according to his critics, about intervention. With his New Deal domestic programs fading from view and his foreign policy controversial, he appeared likely to face a strong Republican challenge. The GOP, turning away from candidates opposed to interventionism, nominated Wendell Willkie, a lawyer and business executive with solidly pro-Allied and internationalist leanings, to oppose FDR. While generally supporting Roosevelt's policy toward the Allies, this former Democrat also charged that the president would soon carry the United States directly into battle. In response, Roosevelt courted anti-interventionist votes by assuring "American mothers" that "your boys are not going to be sent into any foreign wars." Although the Republicans did better than they had done in 1936, Roosevelt rather easily defeated Willkie, gaining nearly 55 percent of the popular vote, and FDR's Democratic Party retained control of Congress. Once safely reelected, Roosevelt unveiled an ambitious plan to support Britain's war effort.

The president's moves continued to generate significant opposition. The America First Committee, organized by the head of Sears, Roebuck, and Company, intensified its crusade against intervention. The aviator-hero Charles A. Lindbergh, its most famous member, flew to mass rallies, all across the country, and joined anti-Roosevelt politicians, such as Senators Wheeler and Nye, in denouncing aid to the Allies.

Interventionists came to label all of their opponents as "isolationists," a single, derogatory term that obscures the diversity within the uneasy coalition opposed to U.S. engagement in the Second World War. Pacifists within this broad constituency opposed all wars, even those against fascist regimes, as immoral and mutually destructive. Some political progressives such as Senator Wheeler condemned fascism but feared that U.S. entry into war would lead to centralization of governmental power at home. Other anti-interventionists, such as Lindbergh, praised the fascist states as bulwarks against communism, and some even covertly shared Hitler's anti-Semitism. Avowedly anti-Semitic and pro-fascist organizations, such as the German-American Bund, openly defended Hitler's racial policies and denounced the "Jew Deal," a reference to the presence of Jewish advisers in President Roosevelt's inner circle. During the fall of 1941, a special subcommittee of the U.S. Senate began "Propaganda Hearings" into whether or not the Hollywood film industry, with its many Jewish producers, calculatedly made movies, such as *Confessions of a Nazi Spy* (1939), which promoted interventionism.

The opposition to aiding the Allies, then, did tap anti-Semitic sentiment in the United States. In 1939, congressional leaders had quashed the Wagner-Rogers bill, which would have boosted immigration quotas to admit 20,000 Jewish children into the United States. Seemingly bowing to anti-Semitic prejudices, the United States adopted a restrictive refugee policy. The consequences of the U.S. stance became especially grave after June 1941, when Hitler established the death camps that would systematically exterminate millions of Jews, gypsies, homosexuals, and anyone else whom the Nazis deemed unfit for life in the Third Reich and its occupied territories.

The Fight Against Interventionism   The movement to keep the United States out of the Second World War mobilized powerful personalities, impassioned rhetoric, and colorful imagery. This emblem, for example, invokes nationalistic and patriotic imagery in the cause of avoiding, rather than engaging in, war.

Meanwhile, those who favored assisting the Allied cause mounted a popular campaign of their own. The most prominent group, the Committee to Defend America by Aiding the Allies, headed by William Allen White, a well-known Republican journalist, organized more than 300 local chapters in just a few weeks during the spring of 1940. These organizations, much like their opponents, gathered a diverse constituency. Interventionists agreed, however, that a fascist-dominated Europe would soon threaten the security and safety of the United States. Isolationists claimed to stand for "America First," according to a pro-interventionist folk song, but ignored the likelihood that the fascists already saw "America next."

An "Arsenal of Democracy"

Franklin Roosevelt now vigorously pressed the case for stronger anti-Axis measures. Recognizing the sorry state of Britain's finances, the president proposed that the United States would now "lend-lease," or loan rather than sell, munitions to the Allies. Making the United States a "great arsenal of democracy," FDR claimed, would "keep war away from our country and our people." Debate over a **Lend-Lease Act** became bitter, and a divided Congress narrowly passed this controversial measure, which carried the patriotic-sounding title of "House Resolution 1776," on March 11, 1941. Several months later, when Germany turned its attention away from Britain and suddenly attacked the Soviet Union, its recent ally, in violation of the 1939 nonaggression pact, Roosevelt extended lend-lease assistance to Joseph Stalin's communist government.

While proclaiming an official U.S. policy of nonbelligerence, Roosevelt next began coordinating his military strategy with that of Britain. He secretly pledged to follow a Europe-first approach if the United States ever found itself fighting a two-front war against Germany and Japan, its Axis partner in Asia. Publicly, Roosevelt deployed U.S. Marines to Greenland and Iceland, a move that freed up the British forces that had been protecting these strategic Danish possessions following Germany's 1940 conquest of Denmark.

In August 1941, Roosevelt and Winston Churchill, Britain's Prime Minister, met on a ship off the coast of Canada. They worked toward formalizing a wartime alliance and concluded their meeting by issuing an "Atlantic Charter," which disavowed territorial expansion, endorsed protection of human rights and self-determination, and pledged the postwar creation of a new world organization that would ensure "general security." Roosevelt also agreed to Churchill's request that the U.S. Navy provide convoys, as far as Iceland, to the ships that were carrying lend-lease supplies to Britain. Soon, in an undeclared war in the North Atlantic, the U.S. Navy engaged Germany's formidable **"wolf packs,"** groups of submarines that preyed on Allied shipping.

The White House now firmly believed that defeating Hitler would require formal U.S. entry into the war, but it lacked domestic support for making this move. Privately, the president likely hoped Germany would commit some provocative act in the North Atlantic that would swing U.S. popular opinion decisively behind intervention. The October 1941 sinking of a U.S. destroyer, the *Reuben James,* did convince a majority in Congress to back Roosevelt's calls for repealing the neutrality legislation of the 1930s. Still, the tone of debate became so bitter and the margin favoring repeal so slim that the White House acknowledged Congress would still not pass a formal declaration of war.

Hitler's military strategy in Europe only complicated Roosevelt's course. While avoiding a repetition of the *Reuben James* episode in the North Atlantic, Germany focused its military energies on the Soviet Union, the communist-led nation for which most Americans felt far less empathy than they did for Great Britain. As it turned out, however, conflict with Japan, rather than with Germany, would bring the United States formally into the Second World War.

Pearl Harbor

Relations between Japan and the United States had steadily worsened during the late 1930s and early 1940s. In response to Japan's 1937 invasion of China, the United States extended economic credits to the beleaguered Nationalist Chinese government and curtailed sales of equipment to Japan. In 1939, the United States abrogated its Treaty of Commerce and Navigation with Japan, an action that meant further restrictions on U.S. exports to that island nation. A 1940 ban on the sale of aviation fuel and high-grade scrap iron aimed at slowing military advances by Japan throughout much of Southeast Asia.

Measures of this kind failed to halt Japanese expansion, now aided by the conflict then engulfing Europe. The European war prevented France, the Netherlands, and Great Britain from supporting their colonies in Asia, and militarists in Japan saw an opportunity to enlarge their own East Asian Co-Prosperity Sphere. Japanese forces thus pushed deep into French Indochina, seeking the raw materials Japan could no longer buy from the United States. Military planners in Tokyo also secretly prepared plans for attacks against Singapore, the Netherlands East Indies (later Indonesia), and the Philippines, a U.S. colonial possession.

Roosevelt continued to maneuver. He expanded the trade embargo against Japan, promised further assistance to Nationalist China, and accelerated an ongoing U.S. military buildup in the Pacific. In mid-1941, the president played his most potent diplomatic card: He froze all Japanese financial assets held in the United States. This move effectively gave the Roosevelt administration control over all commerce between the two countries, including trade in petroleum, the vital commodity that fueled Japan's economy and its dreams for expansionism.

Japanese expansionists now squarely faced a fateful decision. Despite diminishing economic and military prospects, they refused to abandon their goal of creating an East Asian empire. Instead, they began planning a preemptive attack against the United States. In light of their nation's limited supplies of raw materials, especially oil, Japanese strategists saw little hope for winning a prolonged war but imagined that a crippling, surprise blow might limit U.S. military capabilities and even bring economic concessions from Washington. General Hideki Tojo, who became his nation's wartime prime minister, viewed Japanese strategy as something of a rash gamble: "Sometimes a man has to jump with his eyes closed," Tojo remarked.

On December 7, 1941, Japanese bombers swooped down on U.S. naval facilities at **Pearl Harbor,** in Hawaii. Specially modified to operate from aircraft carriers, the planes destroyed much of the U.S. Pacific Fleet. Altogether, Japan sank or severely damaged 19 ships; destroyed or disabled nearly 200 aircraft; and killed more than 2,200 Americans. The damage might have been worse. U.S. aircraft carriers, which were out to sea at the time of the attack, avoided the Japanese bombers, which also failed to take out Pearl Harbor's fuel storage tanks and repair facilities.

Japan's assault against Pearl Harbor brought the United States into war rather than bringing it to terms. In a dramatic message to Congress, broadcast over radio, on December 8,

Roosevelt decried the attack. Coining the phrase that would serve as a U.S. battle cry throughout the war, he called December 7 "a date which will live in infamy."

Pearl Harbor would also live on in historical debates. Roosevelt's most implacable critics quickly began asking, for example, why much of the U.S. Pacific Fleet at Pearl Harbor lay vulnerable and unprepared, rather than on a state of full alert. Could Roosevelt and his advisers really have been unaware of an impending attack? U.S. intelligence, it would later be revealed, had broken Japan's secret diplomatic code—calling the decrypted messages "MAGIC"—and enjoyed some insight into Japanese intentions. Other critics came to charge FDR with adopting a series of calculated policies that were designed to provoke Japan. Deliberately inciting a Japanese attack, in this view, provided Roosevelt with a way of opening a "back door" through which the United States could enter the Second World War.

Most historians, however, view the Roosevelt administration as more unlucky and confused than duplicitous and devious. Its plan for deterring Japanese expansion by increasing U.S. naval forces in the Pacific and stationing bombers in the Philippines, within striking distance of Japan, simply failed to work. U.S. intelligence, based on intercepted messages and visual sightings, did expect a major military move from Japan in late 1941, but one toward Singapore or other British or Dutch possessions in Asia rather than at Pearl Harbor. Moreover, strategists in Washington, including the president, doubted that Japan's military planners had the skill or daring that an attack on Pearl Harbor entailed.

Pearl Harbor disarmed the noninterventionist movement and brought the United States, officially, into the Second World War. On December 8, 1941, Congress declared war against Japan. Representative Jeanette Rankin, a longtime peace activist from Montana who had voted against entry into the First World War, now stood as a lone dissenter. Nothing in the Tripartite Pact specifically required Hitler, unaware of Japan's plans for Pearl Harbor, to support his Axis ally. Roosevelt's "date of infamy" speech never even mentioned Germany, but a presidential radio address, delivered a day later, bluntly accused all three Axis Powers of hatching a coordinated plan to attack the United States. Two days later, on December 11, Germany (soon joined by Italy) did declare war on the United States. Hitler mistakenly assumed that fighting Japan would keep the United States preoccupied in the Pacific and, therefore, out of any major combat operations across the Atlantic Ocean. Axis strategists drastically underestimated the United States's ability to mobilize swiftly and effectively.

Fighting the War in Europe

Focus Question

What military strategies did the United States and the Allies ultimately adopt when fighting in both the European and Asian theaters of the Second World War?

Initially, the war went badly for the Allies. Even as Hitler tried to consolidate his grip over Western Europe, his forces were rolling across North Africa, and his submarines were slashing away at Allied supply lines in the Atlantic Ocean. During the months that followed Pearl Harbor, German U-boats, according to U.S. General George Marshall, came to "threaten our entire war effort." U.S. officials concealed the actual toll, but German subs operating in Atlantic waters, sometimes within sight of the U.S. shoreline, sank nearly 400 ships in less than six months. In the Pacific, Japan seemed unstoppable. Its forces overran Malaya, the Dutch East Indies, and the Philippines; then, Japan moved against the British in Burma and the Australians in New Guinea.

New governmental bureaucracies quickly guided a crash program for U.S. mobilization. Establishing military priorities—acquiring naval bases, securing landing rights for aircraft, ensuring points for radio transmission, and gaining access to raw materials for military production—became the immediate order of business. Soon thereafter, a series of governmental agencies, often staffed by people from the business world, began to direct economic decision making.

At the same time, a newly formed Joint Chiefs of Staff, consisting of representatives from each of the armed services, oversaw military matters. In January 1943, after 16 months of around-the-clock work, builders completed the War Department's Pentagon complex, a giant five-story, five-sided building that symbolized the nation's new military might—and the new place of the military in American life. Technological breakthroughs assisted the U.S. military effort. In 1942, aircraft equipped with radar, a critical new technology developed in collaboration with Britain, proved effective against submarines. During 1943, Germany's U-boat threat faded "from menace to problem," in the words of one U.S. naval strategist.

A highly sophisticated Allied code-breaking operation also played a crucial role in changing the course of battle. Realizing the importance of radio communication to his war plans, Hitler's scientists had integrated the complex ENIGMA encryption machine, first introduced during the 1920s, into Germany's war effort. Experts initially considered Germany's ENIGMA messages immune to code-breaking efforts. The cipher keys changed daily and offered 150 million million million ways of encoding any message. Then a group of Polish mathematicians, who had escaped just before German armies subdued their country, brought key ideas for decoding ENIGMA's secrets to Britain. Their insights contributed to a successful and super-secret Allied code-breaking program headquartered at Bletchley Park in England. At its height, the Bletchley Park endeavor, not officially acknowledged until 1974, employed 4,000 people, including many from the United States.

The Allied code-breakers gradually perfected their operation. Decrypted German messages, called "ULTRA" for "ultra-secret," gave the Allies a crucial military advantage, beginning with the Battle of Britain and Germany's campaigns in North Africa. Amazingly, German commanders never discovered how many of their intercepted and decoded radio communications reached Allied commanders—sometimes even before making their way to their intended German recipients. In the postwar world, the code-breaking operation at Bletchley Park would contribute to the development of computer technology.

Campaigns in North Africa and Italy

The Allied Powers continually clashed over military strategy. Although other nations, such as China, joined the Allied ranks, the United States, Great Britain, and the Soviet Union dominated. These three nations agreed on making Europe the primary focus of their efforts, and Roosevelt and his military strategists established a unified command with their British counterparts. The Soviet Union's Stalin, his armies facing the bulk of Germany's forces in Eastern Europe, called for a second front in Western Europe, created by an invasion across the English Channel into France, to relieve pressure on the USSR. Many of Roosevelt's advisers agreed: If German troops succeeded in knocking the Soviet Union out of the war, Hitler could turn his full attention toward Britain. Churchill, however, urged instead the invasion of North Africa, garrisoned by German forces and officially under the colonial control of Vichy France, as a way of first nibbling away at the edges of Nazi power—and at areas he considered vital to maintaining Britain's colonial interests in the Mediterranean.

A North African campaign against German forces, code-named TORCH, began with Anglo-American landings in Morocco and Algeria in November 1942. Under the command of U.S. General **Dwight D. Eisenhower,** the initial invasion force included 400 ships, 1,000 planes, and more than 100,000 troops. To ease his way, Eisenhower signed an armistice agreement with Admiral Jean Darlan, a Nazi sympathizer and the person officially in charge of Vichy France's colonies in North Africa. This arrangement, which allowed Darlan and his colleagues to retain their political positions, outraged Eisenhower's Free-French allies, notably General Charles De Gaulle, and many people in the United States. When Darlan's opponents assassinated him, shortly after the beginning of TORCH, one of Eisenhower's aides called it an "act of providence." Even as TORCH, aided by the ULTRA intercepts, moved forward, Free French leaders, particularly De Gaulle, continued to nurture their resentments against their U.S. Allies.

At a meeting in Casablanca, Morocco, in January 1943, Roosevelt sided with Churchill. Arguing that a cross-Channel invasion of France still seemed too risky, they succeeded in postponing it to some indefinite future. Roosevelt hoped clear-cut Allied victories, in advance of any Channel crossing, could bolster his own sagging political popularity in the United States. To assuage Stalin's fear that Britain and the United States might sign a separate peace with Hitler, Roosevelt and Churchill promised to remain at war until Germany agreed to an "unconditional surrender." Continuing disagreement over the timing for opening the Second Front in France, however, still strained relations among the Allies.

Meanwhile, in Eastern Europe, Joseph Stalin's Red Army slowly turned the tide of battle with a decisive victory after more than five months of bloody warfare in and around the Soviet city of Stalingrad. Abandoning a largely defensive response to Hitler's offensive during the late summer of 1942, Stalin's forces finally counterattacked in early 1943. They cut off and, then, ground down an entire German army, more than 1 million soldiers, at Stalingrad, and sent other German forces reeling backward for the first time during the war.

Stalin's Allies could soon claim victories of their own. Although Hitler poured reinforcements into North Africa, he failed to stop either TORCH or a drive westward from

Egypt by British forces. Caught in between, nearly 200,000 Axis troops in North Africa surrendered to the Allies during the spring of 1943. Later that summer, the Allies followed up the North African campaign by overrunning the island of Sicily and then fighting their way, slowly, northward through Italy's rugged mountains. Allied successes did boost civilian morale in the United States and Britain, but the Italian campaign also diverted badly needed resources away from the upcoming cross-Channel invasion, without loosening the Nazi stranglehold over Western Europe.

Some U.S. officials increasingly worried about the postwar implications of the Roosevelt-Churchill strategy. Secretary of War Henry Stimson, for example, warned that the Allied campaigns through Africa and Italy might leave the Soviet Union as the dominant power in most of Europe. Unless the United States soon directly confronted German might, he colorfully argued, Germany could be left holding "the leg for Stalin to skin the deer," making "dangerous business for us at the end of the war." Finally heeding such advice, Roosevelt agreed to establish a firm date for the cross-Channel invasion the Allies had so long promised Stalin.

Operation OVERLORD

Named Operation OVERLORD and directed by General Dwight Eisenhower, the invasion began on June 6, 1944, D-day. During the preceding months, Allied commanders assembled, in England, one of the largest invasion forces in world history. German officials obviously knew about these preparations, but a disinformation campaign and diversionary tactics fooled them into expecting the Allied landing would come at the narrowest part of the English Channel rather than in the Normandy region of France. A new code-breaking machine, which dramatically increased the number of ULTRA intercepts, allowed Allied intelligence officers to confirm that their deceptions had worked.

After several delays, because of inhospitable weather, Allied commanders executed their daring plan. As naval gunner crews pounded the Normandy shore, three divisions of paratroopers dropped behind enemy lines and disrupted German communications. Finally, at dawn on June 6, more than 4,000 Allied ships began landing troops and supplies. The first U.S. forces to come ashore at Omaha Beach met especially heavy German fire and took enormous casualties, but waves of invading troops continued to land. Only three weeks after D-day, more than a million Allied personnel controlled the French coast, clearing the way for the long-awaited second front. **(See Map 26.2, Allied Advances and Collapse of German Power, in the color insert following page 1056.)**

Just as the 1943 Battle of Stalingrad had reversed the course of the war in the East, OVERLORD changed the momentum in the West. Within three months, U.S., British, and Free French troops entered Paris. After repulsing a desperate German counteroffensive in Belgium, at the Battle of the Bulge in December 1944 and January 1945, forces under Eisenhower's command swept eastward, crossed the Rhine River, and prepared to head toward Berlin to meet up with westward-advancing Soviet troops.

The Allies, not surprisingly, disagreed on how to orchestrate Germany's final defeat. British strategists urged a rapid advance, in hopes of meeting up with Stalin's troops in

Berlin or even farther to the east of that city. General Eisenhower dissented. He favored a strategy that would produce fewer casualties among his troops and might assuage the suspicious Soviets about the postwar intentions of their western Allies. Doubtful that his troops could beat the Soviets into Berlin anyway, Eisenhower decided that any attempt to race to Berlin would undermine chances for postwar cooperation between the United States and the Soviet Union.

Eisenhower's view prevailed. He moved his troops cautiously along a broad front and, then, halted them at the Elbe River, west of Berlin. This guaranteed that Soviet troops, who took staggering casualties while approaching Berlin, would enter the German capital first. Although Hitler took his own life in order to avoid capture, the majority of Germany's Nazi elite and its wartime leadership did fall into Allied hands.

As the war in Europe drew to a close, the horrors perpetrated by the leaders of the Third Reich became fully visible. Hitler's murderous campaign of extermination, now called the Holocaust, took the lives of more than 5 million Jews, roughly half of Europe's prewar population of 10 million. The Nazis also murdered hundreds of thousands of other people, including gypsies, homosexuals, intellectuals, communists, the physically and mentally challenged, and people from various other identity groups. Only Germany's defeat closed down Hitler's death camps, but the Allies might have saved at least some people if they had helped them escape and emigrate. Allied leaders, however, worried about how to deal with large numbers of refugees and claimed they could not spare scarce ships to transport people to sanctuary. In 1943, after officials in Romania proposed the evacuation of 70,000 endangered Jews from its territory, for instance, the Allies never seriously considered accepting the offer. With few places to go, people who might have been spared went off to Nazi death camps.

The attempt to respond to Nazi atrocities continued for years. In 1945 and 1946, the Allies first brought 24 of Germany's top officials to trial at Nuremberg for "crimes against humanity." After a series of subsequent trials, more than 10,000 former German officials stood convicted of war crimes. Large quantities of money, gold, and jewelry that Nazi leaders had stolen from victims of the Holocaust and deposited in Swiss banks, however, remained concealed for more than 50 years. Not until 1997 did groups representing Holocaust survivors and the U.S. government force an investigation of the Swiss banking industry's holdings of stolen "Nazi gold," an inquiry that finally prompted some restitution for the families who had been victimized.

Meanwhile, following Hitler's suicide in April and Germany's final surrender on May 8, 1945, the military foundations for a postwar European settlement fell into place. Soviet armies controlled Eastern Europe; British and U.S. forces predominated in Italy and the rest of the Mediterranean; the four European Allies divided up zones of occupation in Germany and Austria. Allied leaders also turned to the task of transforming these military-produced arrangements into a comprehensive postwar political settlement in Europe, even as the war in the Pacific, which had officially begun at Pearl Harbor, remained far from over.

The Pacific Theater

For six months after Pearl Harbor, Japan's forces steadily advanced. Singapore fell easily. Japan overwhelmed U.S. naval garrisons in the Philippines and on Guam and Wake islands. After taking heavy casualties, Filipino and U.S ground troops surrendered at Bataan and Corregidor in the Philippines. After a much larger Japanese fleet ravaged a U.S naval contingent in the Java Sea, Japan's naval forces headed southward to menace Australia and New Zealand and eastward to threaten Hawaii.

Seizing the Offensive in the Pacific

As the United States rapidly built up its combat capabilities, military strategists adopted, of necessity, a largely defensive strategy. Then, in May 1942, the first U.S. naval victory, at the Battle of the Coral Sea, relieved some of the Japanese pressure on Australia. In response, Japanese naval commanders decided to hit back hard. They amassed 200 ships and 600 planes to destroy what remained of the U.S. Pacific fleet and to take Midway Island, perhaps in preparation for an assault against Hawaii. U.S. Naval Intelligence, however, broke enough of the Japanese code to warn Admiral Chester W. Nimitz. Surprising the Japanese armada, U.S. planes sank four Japanese carriers and destroyed a total of 322 planes. The Battle of Midway, in early June 1942, preserved the presence of the U.S. Navy in the mid-Pacific. Nimitz's forces did suffer substantial losses at Midway, but the far greater ones that they inflicted prevented Japanese commanders from continuing their offensive in the Pacific.

Two months later, U.S. amphibious forces splashed ashore at Guadalcanal in the Solomon Islands and finally ended Japan's threat to Australia. Although bloody engagements in the Solomons continued for months, on both land and sea, they ultimately achieved their major objective: permanently seizing the military initiative in the Pacific. According to prewar plans, Europe was to have received the highest priority, but by 1943, the United States, now massively rearmed, could devote roughly equal resources to both theaters of the war.

Combat in the Pacific Theater became, in the historian John Dower's phrase, a "war without mercy." Battlefield conditions reinforced racial prejudices, and the brutality already evident during Japan's initial assault against China continued. Japanese militarists expected the war would confirm the superiority of the divine Yamato race. Japanese captors, particularly on the Asian mainland, mistreated prisoners in almost unimaginable ways. The Japanese army's infamous "Unit 731" tested bacteriological weapons in China and conducted horrifying medical experiments on live subjects. Following the surrender of U.S. and Filipino troops in 1942, Japanese commanders, in what became known as the "Bataan Death March," forced their captives to walk, on meager rations of food and water, more than 60 miles.

The United States exhibited its own signs of racially based behavior. Wartime imagery, in both the U.S. government publications and in popular culture, often portrayed all Japanese people as animalistic subhumans. On the battlefield, U.S. troops could, on occasion, rival their Japanese adversaries in disrespecting enemy dead and in killing opposing forces rather than taking prisoners. The longer the war in the Pacific lasted, the more brutal it became.

China Policy

U.S. policy makers continued to hope that China's Nationalist government might eventually mount an effective military opposition against Japan and emerge, after the war, to lead a strong and united nation. Neither hope seemed realistic.

The United States tried to bolster China's armed forces. General Joseph W. Stillwell, who had been advising Chinese commanders on military matters since the Japanese invasion of the late 1930s, continually clashed with Jiang Jieshi. Friction between the prickly "Vinegar Joe" and Jiang eventually prompted Roosevelt, who hoped the Nationalist leader could become an important U.S. ally, to withdraw Stillwell from China. Stillwell's departure, however, brought no improvement in the performance of Jiang's military forces.

China's political instability complicated matters. The U.S. officials most attuned to Chinese politics agreed with Stillwell: Incompetence and corruption riddled Jiang Jieshi's Nationalist government. It could avoid engaging the Japanese invaders but still make extravagant demands for U.S. military assistance. China's ongoing civil war, which Jiang's forces seemed to be losing, further worried U.S. officials. A powerful communist movement, led by Mao Zedong, clearly fought more effectively than the Nationalist government against China's Japanese invaders, but the White House continued to envision Jiang as the future leader of a noncommunist China. On this crucial matter, the Nationalist leader's powerful backers in the United States, members of the "China Lobby," successfully pressured FDR and other political leaders, particularly those in the Republican Party, to support the Nationalist cause. Roosevelt thus insisted that Nationalist China retain its status as a full member of the Allied Powers, and he convinced Stalin to support Jiang, rather than his fellow communist Mao. All the while, Japan's advance into Chinese territory continued.

U.S. Strategy in the Pacific

In contrast to the European Theater, no unified command guided the war in the Pacific. Consequently, makeshift, compromise military decisions actions often emerged. General Douglas MacArthur, who commanded U.S. Army forces, insisted on an offensive launched from his headquarters in Australia through New Guinea and the Philippines and on to Japan. In May 1942, Japan had humbled the haughty and imperious MacArthur by forcing him out of the Philippines, and he had pledged he would, one day, return in victory. He now claimed that controlling the Philippines at war's end would advance U.S. strategic interests in the postwar world. Admiral Nimitz, the hero of Midway, saw strategic calculations somewhat differently. He favored a direct advance toward Japan, across the smaller islands of the central Pacific. Taking this route meant that the drive against Japan would bypass MacArthur's beloved Philippines.

Unable to decide between the two strategies, the Joint Chiefs of Staff authorized both, which moved forward, amidst fierce fighting and heavy casualties. MacArthur's forces took

New Guinea, and those commanded by Nimitz liberated the Marshall Islands and the Marianas in 1943 and 1944. Supporting these efforts, a Marine platoon of Navajo Indians established a unique, highly effective radio communication system. Employing their own language in imaginative coded variations, which Japanese intelligence officers never cracked, the members of this **Navajo Signal Corps** ensured that U.S. troops could securely exchange messages.

By late 1944, U.S. military forces finally came within range of Japan. The fall of Saipan meant that U.S. bombers could easily reach Japanese targets. The capture of the islands of Iwo Jima and of Okinawa during spring 1945 further shortened the distance between U.S. bases and Japan's major population centers. The battle for Okinawa, however, also confirmed the human costs of the island-hopping strategy: 120,000 Japanese and 48,000 American soldiers died. After contemplating these numbers, U.S. military planners dreaded the prospect of invading Japan's home islands.

Increasingly, reliance on airpower looked more and more enticing. Key members of the U.S. military had long attributed almost magical qualities to aerial bombardment. Some had even insisted that the mere threat of bombing could provide a means of deterring war as well as a way of conducting it. Careful analyses of strategic bombing during the Second World War, though, suggested less sanguine assessments. The Nazi bombardment during the Battle of Britain, for example, had inflicted heavy damage but only appeared to strengthen civilian morale, while never giving Hitler the quick victory he had expected. Subsequent Allied bombing against Germany, including controversial campaigns against

National Archives #127-N-69559-A

Navajo Signal Corps   Sending messages in their native language, which neither the Japanese nor the Germans could decipher, Navajo Indians in the Signal Corps made a unique contribution to preserving the secrecy of U.S. intelligence.

the civilian populations of Hamburg and Dresden, produced equally mixed results. Even as the Allies wreaked havoc on German cities, they endured losses in planes and pilots that seemed almost impossible to sustain over any length of time.

Nonetheless, U.S. strategists continued to see strategic bombing providing the crucial U.S. advantage in the Pacific. In February 1944, General Henry Harley ("Hap") Arnold devised a plan for firebombing major Japanese cities "not only because they are greatly congested but because they contain numerous war industries." Bombers added to the horror of war, Arnold conceded, but when used "with the proper degree of understanding" could become "the most humane of all weapons." President Roosevelt endorsed Arnold's air campaign, but it proved difficult to execute from bases in China.

In time, U.S. military victories opened the way for a more effective and lethal operation, run by General Curtis LeMay from Saipan in the Marianas. The blunt-talking LeMay, whom Arnold dubbed "the Babe Ruth of bombers," once summarized his strategy as "bomb and burn them until they quit." According to the official U.S. position, incendiary raids against Japanese cities constituted "precision" rather than "area" bombing. In actuality, as LeMay admitted, the United States measured the success of a mission by square miles of Japanese territory left scorched. According to a later estimate, the number of Japan's civilians who perished as a result of these raids exceeded the total of its troops killed in battle. Air attacks on Tokyo during the night of March 9–10, 1945, inaugurated the new policy. They leveled nearly one-quarter of the city and incinerated more than 100,000 people. **(See Map 26.3, Pacific Theater Offensive Strategy and Final Assault Against Japan, in the color insert following page 1056.)**

Meanwhile, as the war in the Pacific neared its end, a combined sea and air strategy emerged. The United States, under the agreement reached at the 1943 Casablanca Conference, still sought Japan's "unconditional surrender" by blockading its seaports, bombarding its cities from the air, and, perhaps, invading its home islands with U.S. combat units. Critics of the policy of unconditional surrender, which most Japanese assumed meant the death of their emperor, later suggested that it may have encouraged Japan's government to continue fighting, even when defeat seemed inevitable. This same stance also possibly prevented U.S. negotiators from more vigorously pursuing the peace feelers sent by some Japanese leaders. Anything less than unconditional surrender, its proponents counterclaimed, would have encouraged continued Japanese resistance. Whatever the case, the United States adopted a strategy of achieving total victory through massive destruction.

A New President, the Atomic Bomb, and Japan's Surrender

On April 13, 1945, newspaper headlines across the country announced: "PRESIDENT ROOSEVELT DEAD." After more than 13 years in office, an already frail FDR succumbed to a massive cerebral hemorrhage. Sorrow and shock spread through the armed forces, where many young servicemen and women could effectively remember no other president; through diplomatic conference halls, where Roosevelt's personal magnetism had often brought unity, if not always clarity; and among his many supporters, for whom Roosevelt had symbolized optimism during both economic depression and war.

Over the years, Roosevelt also accumulated a host of critics and enemies. His victory over Republican Thomas E. Dewey in 1944 rested on the smallest popular-vote margin in a presidential race since 1912. The GOP, extending gains it had made during the 1942 congressional elections, cut further into the once-overwhelming Democratic majorities in the Senate and House. Politically and physically weakened, Roosevelt fought to retain his dominant place in the political spotlight. Unaware of Roosevelt's precarious health, both Republican and Democrats assumed FDR would lead the United States into the postwar world.

Emerging from Roosevelt's shadow, the new president, **Harry S Truman,** initially seemed an unimposing presence. Born on a farm near Independence, Missouri, Truman had served in France during the First World War; become a U.S. Senator in 1934; and suddenly surfaced as Roosevelt's vice-presidential running mate in 1944. Roosevelt offered an upper-class image of well-practiced and worldly charm. The blunt-spoken Truman proudly presented himself as a "little man from Missouri." He also knew little about international affairs or about any informal understandings that Roosevelt may have made with Churchill and Stalin. During the period between Roosevelt's Fourth Inauguration in March 1945 and his death in mid-April, Truman met with FDR only three times.

Only after succeeding Roosevelt did Truman learn about events at Los Alamos, New Mexico. There, since the late 1930s, scientists from all across the world had been secretly working on a new weapon. Advances in theoretical physics suggested that the process of splitting atoms (fission) would release a tremendous amount of energy that could be packaged as a nuclear bomb. Fearful of Germany's outpacing the United States in this research, Albert Einstein, a Jewish refugee from Germany, had successfully implored Roosevelt to launch, on the basis of recent atomic knowledge, a crash bomb-building program. The government subsequently enlisted top researchers in the Manhattan Project, a huge, secret, military-directed operation. On July 16, 1945, the Project tested a workable atomic device at Trinity Site, near Alamogordo, New Mexico.

Truman and his top policy makers, eager to end the war quickly, decided to put the new weapon to immediate use. Planners agreed that any ground invasion of Japan's home islands would cost far too much in U.S. casualties. In addition, the Soviet Union, in a joint decision confirmed at a meeting of the Allies at the Potsdam Conference during the summer of 1945, would soon enter the Pacific Theater. Truman hoped to limit any advances that Soviet troops might make in the Far East as a way of curtailing Stalin's postwar influence there. Winston Churchill called the atomic bomb a "miracle of deliverance and a peace giver," and Truman, who always insisted it had been dropped on primarily military targets in Japan, later publicly claimed that he had never lost a night's sleep over its use.

Privately, he and other U.S. officials admitted to having greater qualms. Certainly, disagreement marked discussions over where and how to employ the new device. A commission of atomic scientists recommended a "demonstration" that would impress Japan with the bomb's destructive power without producing civilian casualties. General George C. Marshall suggested using it on purely military installations or only on manufacturing sites, after first warning away Japanese workers.

Total War: Dresden and Hiroshima The effects of "total war" are graphically illustrated in these photographs—of the devastation of Dresden, Germany (top), by the British Bomber Command and the U.S. 8th Air Force on February 13 and 14, 1945, and that of Hiroshima, Japan (bottom), by the U.S. 509th Composite Group on August 6, 1945. In the initial attack on Dresden, 786 aircraft dropped 5,824,000 pounds (2,600 long tons) of bombs on the city, killing an estimated 60,000 people and injuring another 30,000. An area of more than 2.5 square miles in the city center was demolished, and some 37,000 buildings were destroyed. To critics, the bombing of Dresden, a target that many argued was of little strategic value, exemplified the excessive use of airpower.

In sobering comparison, Hiroshima was devastated by one bomb weighing only 10,000 pounds (4.4 long tons)—an atomic bomb—dropped from one aircraft. The single U-235 bomb killed 68,000 people outright, injured another 30,000, and left 10,000 missing. (These figures do not include those who later developed diseases from deadly gamma rays.) The bomb obliterated almost five square miles of the city's center and destroyed 40,653 buildings. Truman reported the strike as "an overwhelming success." Many hailed the atomic bomb as a necessary step toward military victory; others worried about the dawn of the "nuclear age."

Ultimately, the Truman administration discarded these options. The United States needed, according to Secretary of War Henry Stimson, to make "a profound psychological impression on as many inhabitants as possible." In addition, LeMay's aerial bombardment of Japanese cities provided a powerful prologue to a nuclear attack. Many U.S. officials came to see the targeting of **Hiroshima** and Nagasaki, Japanese cities previously untouched by U.S. fire bombing, as a small departure from existing policy. "Fat Man" and "Little Boy," as the two atomic bombs dropped on August 6 and 9, 1945 were nicknamed, could seem merely larger and more lethal incendiary devices.

Stimson and most other observers soon acknowledged, however, that atomic weaponry introduced a new level of violence to world affairs. Colonel Paul Tibbets, who piloted the U.S. plane that dropped the first bomb on Hiroshima, reported that "the shimmering city became an ugly smudge . . . a pot of bubbling hot tar." Teams of U.S. observers who entered Hiroshima and Nagasaki in the aftermath of their bombing were stunned at the instantaneous incineration of both human beings and manmade structures, and shocked to contemplate the longer-lasting horror of radiation disease. Shortly after the atomic bombs fell on Japan, Stimson reconsidered his earlier view. He wrote Truman that atomic weaponry meant "a first step in a new control by man over the forces of nature too revolutionary and dangerous to fit into old concepts." The destruction of Hiroshima and Nagasaki inaugurated the "atomic age," one in which dreams of peace mingled with nightmares of destruction, potentially on a global scale.

During the late summer days of 1945, however, Americans who knew someone involved in the worldwide military effort invariably sighed with relief. News reports of August 15 heralded Japan's defeat. Those of September 2 reported its formal surrender, on **"VJ Day,"** aboard the battleship *Missouri* in Tokyo Bay. Spontaneously, all across the nation, people flooded into the streets to celebrate the end of the Second World War.

The War at Home: The Economy

Focus Question
How did mobilizing for war produce political, economic, and social changes in the United States?

Securing military victory overseas depended on reviving, and then rapidly expanding, the domestic economy of the United States. Prewar production brought the Great Depression of the 1930s closer to an end, and wartime conditions quickly completed the recovery process. Moreover, innovations in wartime production processes promised to transform the nation's economic structure, its corporate and financial institutions, its labor force, and, perhaps, even the relationship between the economy and the national government.

Government's Role in the Economy

The federal bureaucracy grew, by one calculation, nearly 400 percent during the war. New governmental planning and regulatory agencies proliferated. The powerful War Production Board oversaw the conversion of factories to wartime production and, later, their expansion. It also planned resource usage and enforced production priorities and schedules. The War Labor Board adjudicated labor–management disputes, and the War Manpower Commission allocated workers to various industries. The Office of Price Administration regulated prices to control inflation and rationed scarce commodities such as gasoline, rubber, steel, shoes, coffee, sugar, and meat. Some observers who wished to expand on the New Deal of the 1930s imagined how the wartime system of economic controls might be adapted to peacetime conditions, while most of the Republicans and conservative Democrats in Congress looked forward to its postwar dismantlement.

From 1940 to 1945, the U.S. economy expanded rapidly, and the gross national product (GNP) rose, year-by-year, by 15 percent or more! When Roosevelt called for the production of 60,000 planes shortly after Pearl Harbor, skeptics sneered. Within a few years, though, the nation produced nearly 300,000 planes in a number of different designs. The Maritime Commission oversaw the construction of millions of tons of new ships. A once stagnant economy spewed out prodigious quantities of other supplies, including 2.5 million trucks and 50 million pairs of shoes. A worldwide war became one of "massed machines," the military journalist Hanson Baldwin observed.

In the cause of increasing production, most industries forged close relationships with governmental bureaucracies. Washington promoted, under the acronym of R&D, a coordinated plan for scientific and technological research and development. Greatly increased federal funding helped spawn new industries, such as electronics, and transform others, such as rubber and chemicals. Eventually, an Office of Scientific Research and Development contracted with universities and scientists for a variety of projects. Support from this governmental agency helped adapt radar and penicillin (initially British discoveries), rocket engines, and other new products for wartime use. The Manhattan Project provided the most dramatic example of the emergence of powerful new links between military-oriented R&D and the national government. In addition, this massive effort, which employed a number of people who had fled Nazi tyranny during the 1930s, demonstrated how much European-trained refuges might contribute to scientific and technological innovation.

Business and Finance

Washington pumped billions of dollars into the wartime economy. To finance the military effort, government spending rose from $9 billion in 1940 to $98 billion in 1944. In 1941, the national debt stood at $48 billion; at the end of the war, it would reach $280 billion. As production shifted from autos to tanks, from refrigerators to guns, the array of new consumer goods coming into the marketplace drastically shrank. In order to ensure that U.S. troops were adequately clothed, fed, and supplied, the government also set up an elaborate

National Archives

Rita Hayworth Scraps Her Bumpers Movie stars aided the war effort by promoting the sale of war bonds and urging sacrifice. Here Hayworth urges Americans to scrap their unessential car parts.

system for rationing the amount of certain products—including foods, fabrics, and fuel—people could purchase. With fewer consumer products available, people invested in war bonds, turning their savings into tanks and planes. Sales of war bonds to ordinary people provided a relatively insignificant contribution to overall wartime spending, but bond drives helped raise personal saving to record levels and gave bondholders a direct stake, psychologically as well as economically, in the Allied cause.

Wartime conditions encouraged steps toward achieving greater economic equality. The rationing of items needed for the war effort overseas meant more equitable distribution of scarce goods at home. Increased taxes on wealthier Americans also helped redistribute income and narrow the gap in wealth between the very well-to-do and other people. Observers sympathetic to economic planning saw war bonds, rationing, and progressive taxation encouraging a sense of shared sacrifice and helping ease at least some of the domestic tensions evident during the 1930s.

At the same time, however, the war's emphasis on harmony helped Republicans and conservative Democrats make the case for sidetracking some of the earlier New Deal efforts, including controversial ones aimed at directly assisting the less affluent. The remarkable Republican surge in the off-year elections of 1942—the GOP gained 44 seats in the House and seven in the Senate—strengthened the anti–New Deal coalition in Congress. In 1943, legislators abolished the job-creation programs of the Works Progress Administration (WPA), the Civilian Conservation Corps (CCC), and the National Youth Administration (NYA) (see chapter 25). They also shut down the Rural Electrification Administration (REA) and Farm Security Administration (FSA), agencies most active in economically depressed rural areas. Moreover, as business executives flocked into government, to run the new wartime agencies, administrators in Washington began adopting a relatively cooperative stance toward large corporations.

Large businesses whose products seemed essential to wartime victory invariably flourished, often with governmental assistance. What seemed essential, of course, could become a matter of definition. Coca-Cola and the Wrigley chewing gum empire gained precious sugar allotments by arguing that GIs overseas needed to enjoy their products. The Kaiser Corporation, whose spectacular growth during the 1930s had been spurred by contracts for federal dam projects, now turned to building ships, aircraft, and military vehicles, including the famous "Jeep." By 1943, Kaiser controlled nearly one-third of the nation's military construction business, much of it taking place in Southern California, along the coastal corridor that stretched from San Francisco to San Diego. Elsewhere, federal subsidies and tax breaks enabled factories to expand and retool and corporations to prosper. The "cost-plus" provision, built into military contracts, guaranteed that manufacturers doing business with wartime Washington would gain a profit.

The Second World War also helped boost the economic power wielded by the largest corporations. After Roosevelt ordered his justice department to postpone enforcement of antitrust laws, government lawyers tucked away long-planned legal cases, such as one against America's great oil cartel. Congressional efforts to investigate possible collusion in the awarding of large government contracts and to increase assistance to small businesses made little headway. The top 100 companies, which had provided 30 percent of the nation's total manufacturing output in 1940, contributed 70 percent by 1943. Many smaller businesses, left to dealing in smaller niche markets only indirectly connected to war-related production, complained that Washington-based agencies short-changed them when allocating scare resources.

The Workforce

During the early years of the military buildup, people who had scrounged for jobs during the Great Depression began to find regular work. The primary job of governmental agencies, according to their leaders, involved obtaining employment for the people employers seemed most likely to hire. Thus, positions in heavy industry invariably went to men, and most of the skilled jobs to men of European descent. Initially, government-financed training centers also concentrated on white males and did much less for women and, particularly in the South, workers of color. As military service depleted the ranks of white males, however, other people became candidates for well-paid production jobs. In time, both private employers and public officials encouraged women to seek wartime work outside of their homes; African Americans from the rural South to move to industrial cities, including ones in the North and Far West; and Mexicans to enter the United States under the *Bracero* Agreement of 1942. In response to wartime necessities, then, the composition of the U.S. workforce changed significantly during the early 1940s.

Filling positions never before open to them, women became welders, shipbuilders, lumberjacks, and miners. Women won places in prestigious symphony orchestras, and one Major League Baseball owner financed creation of a separate women's league to give new life to the national pastime. Many employers hired married women who, before the war, would have been lucky to obtain a position even in traditionally "female occupations," such as teaching. Women of color moved into clerical and sales jobs, positions in which they had not previously been welcomed. Although wartime workplaces did generally remain segregated by sex—women usually working with other women and men alongside other men—the range of jobs open to women expanded.

The scope of unpaid labor, primarily provided by women, also expanded. Volunteer activities outside the home—such as Red Cross projects, civil defense work, and recycling drives—claimed more of the time of women, children, and older people. Government publications exhorted women to expand their homemaker routines: "Work in a garden this summer." "Save waste fats for explosives." "Wear it out, use it up, make it do, or do without." Both in the home and in the workplace, women's responsibilities and workloads increased.

The new labor market improved economic prospects for workers of color, especially African Americans. Many moved to labor-scarce cities in the North and West and into jobs previously closed to them. Despite the beginning of the northward migration earlier in the twentieth century, the prewar African American population had remained largely southern, rural, and agricultural; by the late 1940s, a substantial percentage of African Americans lived and worked outside of the South, in urban-industrial areas of the country. Although the war hardly eliminated discriminatory employment practices, twice as many African Americans held skilled jobs at the end of the conflict as at its beginning.

Washington did take some steps to address workplace discrimination. In June 1942, under pressure from African American union leaders led by A. Philip Randolph of the Brotherhood of Railway Porters, President Roosevelt issued an executive order creating the Fair Employment Practices Commission (FEPC). FDR charged this new governmental agency with attacking racial discrimination in hiring decisions. In 1943, the national government announced that it would not recognize as a collective bargaining agent any labor union that discriminated on the basis of race. In addition, the War Labor Board moved to outlaw the practice of paying different wages to whites and nonwhites for doing the same job.

For most of the people who found jobs, the war brought significantly higher wages and longer work hours. Although the government tried to limit wage increases during the war, the need to ensure rising production totals and the availability of overtime invariably meant larger paychecks. During the war, average weekly earnings for industrial workers rose nearly 70 percent. Farmers, who had suffered through many years of low prices and overproduction, doubled their incomes and then doubled them again.

The Labor Front

The labor union movement seemingly stood to benefit from the scarcity of home front workers during the war years. Membership rolls rose by 50 percent. Although women and workers of color joined unions in unprecedented numbers, white males, who still comprised the bulk of unionized workers, became the main beneficiaries of organized labor's new clout.

The commitment of most labor unions to their new female workers remained suspect. Not a single woman served on the executive boards of either the American Federation of Labor (AFL) or the Congress of Industrial Organizations (CIO). The International Brotherhood of Teamsters required its female members to accept revocation of their membership when the war ended. Unions did seek contracts stipulating equal pay for men and women who worked in the same position, but these helped only those women who could find a "male job." In addition, unions typically justified their stance on women employees as a way of ensuring employers would pay a "family wage," one on which a single male breadwinner could support a spouse and children. Union leaders seemed most interested in pressing for equal-pay provisions in order to maintain wage levels in jobs that they expected men to reclaim at war's end. It was also generally expected, when peace returned and employers trimmed workforces, that returning veterans, primarily men of European descent, would enjoy special preferences for the available job slots.

Some union leaders even resisted efforts to hire women and workers of color. Incorporating job-seekers from these groups, who were traditionally paid less than white males, into the wartime workforce might, they feared, jeopardize the gains unions had won during the hard-fought struggles of the 1930s. Early in the war, then, many union locals in the well-paying aircraft and shipbuilding industries flatly refused to enroll African Americans as members. After creation of the FEPC, some union leaders condemned governmental efforts to address racial discrimination as communist inspired. After greater numbers of African Americans managed to find jobs, racial tensions in the workplace sometimes led to direct confrontations. In various parts of the country—at a defense plant in Lockland, Ohio, at a transit company in Philadelphia, at a shipbuilding company in Mobile, for instance—white workers walked off the job to protest the hiring of African Americans. Management intended to use the war, protestors generally charged, as an excuse to erode union power by changing the composition of the workforce.

Other forms of grassroots labor militancy, although muted by a wartime no-strike pledge, persisted into the 1940s. Wildcat strikes erupted among bus drivers in St. Louis, assembly-line workers in Detroit, and streetcar conductors in Philadelphia. In the Motor City, a disgruntled group of aircraft workers, angry at increasing regimentation of the production process, fanned out across a factory floor and cut off the neck ties worn by supervisory personnel. Despite the no-strike assurance, the United Mine Workers called a walk-out in the bituminous coal fields in 1943. A hard line by the War Labor Board against the union's demands only appeared to prolong the strike. Roosevelt's secretary of interior blasted both sides in the dispute and called the walkout "a black and stupid chapter in the history of the home front." A Congress increasingly hostile to union interests weighed in as well. In 1943, it passed the Smith-Connally Act, which empowered the president to seize plants or mines if strikes interrupted war production. The Second World War, then, may have quieted but never halted labor–management conflict.

Assessing Economic Change

Overall, the war had a substantial effect on the nation's political economy. During the conflict, most workplaces became more inclusive, in terms of gender and race, than ever before. So did labor unions. More people entered the paid labor force, and many earned more than rationing restrictions on consumer goods allowed them to spend. In a remarkable reversal of conditions during the Great Depression, savings piled up. Wartime production demands helped strengthen organized labor's place in the U.S. economy. By the end of the Second World War, union membership stood at an all-time high.

Perhaps most significantly, the Second World War helped accelerate long-term changes in the institutional scale of economic life. Big government, big business, and big labor all grew even larger. Scientific and technological innovations forged new links of mutual interest between governmental agencies and large corporations, particularly those directly involved in military-related production. An older United States—one marked by family farms, family-run businesses, and small towns—did not disappear, but urban-based, bureaucratized institutions were increasingly coming to dominate daily life, especially in most areas of the nation's burgeoning economy.

A New Role for Government?

The growth of governmental power during war years prompted new debate over the role of government in a postwar world. During the heyday of the New Deal during the 1930s, a relatively broad view of governmentally guaranteed "security" had enabled creation of programs such as the Social Security System and of federal agencies to secure home mortgages and personal savings accounts. At the same time, grassroots community-based groups, often working with labor unions, had begun building a set of cooperative social welfare and health institutions they hoped would create a vast, nonprofit security-safety net.

Although the New Deal had begun running out of political cards even before U.S. entry into the war, President Roosevelt and some of his advisers began to suggest new initiatives as military victory seemed increasingly likely. They talked of reharnessing the national government's power behind expanded efforts to enhance security in everyday life. Some dreamed, for example, of extending the government's wartime health care and day care programs into a more comprehensive social welfare system.

In 1944, FDR introduced his most ambitious domestic agenda in years: a "Second Bill of Rights." He called for measures to ensure that Americans could enjoy the right to a wide range of substantive liberties. These were to include regular employment, adequate food and shelter, appropriate educational opportunities, and guaranteed health care. Whenever people could not otherwise obtain these material conditions, the national government should use its power to ensure their availability. Translating this vision into reality, its proponents generally assumed, would require the national government to continue the kind of economic and social planning it was doing in wartime. The Second Bill of Rights, then, proposed that postwar politics and governance focus on guaranteeing individuals and families security in their everyday lives.

The vision of providing greater security appealed to more than hardcore New Dealers. Large insurance companies and some private businesses, recognizing the popularity of security-focused proposals, came forward with new private alternatives to governmental programs. Insurers expanded earlier efforts to market their own array of programs, directed toward individual policy holders, for providing security against sickness, disability, and unexpected death. At the same time, insurance companies worked with some large corporations to develop group insurance plans as substitutes and also as supplements to the kind of governmental programs already provided by the New Deal and imagined in the Second Bill of Rights.

The War at Home: Social Issues and Social Movements

The wartime years, along with the search for military victory overseas, highlighted a wide range of domestic social issues. Many people, ordered by their military superiors or attracted by new employment possibilities, moved away from the communities in which they had grown up. Mobilizing for military victory seemed to demand a willingness to change. At the same time, the wartime emphasis on preserving traditional ideals, including liberty and equality, helped spotlight how often social conditions in everyday life departed from idealized depictions.

Selling the War

The effort to sell a war overseas brought new attention to social issues at home. During the First World War, government propagandists had portrayed a struggle to end war and bring about a more democratic and peaceful world. Fighting for such idealistic goals, however, carried far less appeal during the 1940s. Only 20 years after Woodrow Wilson's "war to end all wars," after all, the United States found itself fighting a Second, and far wider, World War. Attuned to popular attitudes, the Roosevelt administration called on citizens to fight more for the preservation of a vague concept called the "American Way of Life" at home than for the transformation to a more democratic, peaceful world.

The work of the illustrator Norman Rockwell and of the movie director Frank Capra, masters of nostalgia, exemplified wartime image-making. Rockwell produced a set of iconic paintings that visualized President Roosevelt's "Four Freedoms": Freedom of Speech, Freedom of Worship, Freedom from Want, and Freedom from Fear. Using his neighbors in Arlington, Vermont, as models, Rockwell depicted these values as already comfortably rooted in small-town America. Originally published in the *Saturday Evening Post* magazine, Rockwell's "Four Freedoms" eventually adorned millions of posters distributed by the government.

Hollywood studios and directors eagerly answered the wartime call. "The American film is our most important weapon," proclaimed one Hollywood executive. The film factory produced both commercial movies with military themes, such as *Destination Tokyo* (1943), and documentaries, such as the *Why We Fight* series, directed by Frank Capra. During the 1930s, Capra's films had championed the decency and good sense of ordinary people (portrayed by stars such as Gary Cooper and Barbara Stanwyck) in movies such as *Mr. Deeds Comes to Town* (1936). Commissioned by Washington to dramatize why citizens should fight against the Axis, Capra put Rockwell-like characters in motion and contrasted the freedom of their daily routines with the tightly regimented lifestyles in the military-dominated dictatorships of Germany, Italy, and Japan.

Much of Hollywood followed Capra to war. Many of its shining stars and lesser players served in combat units, while most other Hollywood personalities sold war bonds, entertained the troops, and worked on documentaries for the Army's Pictorial Division. Darryl F. Zanuck of Twentieth Century Fox filmed Allied troops in North Africa and the Aleutian Islands, and the director-producer John Ford crafted powerful documentaries about Pearl Harbor and the Battle of Midway. Walt Disney's studio devoted most of its animation resources to the production of war-related cartoons and short features.

The advertising industry also contributed. The Roosevelt administration encouraged it to sell his "Four Freedoms," and most advertising professionals obliged. In their vision, freedom generally appeared in the form of new washing machines, improved kitchen appliances, streamlined automobiles, a wider range of lipstick hues, and other consumer products. Although wartime rationing prevented people from immediately acquiring these kinds of products, wartime ads promised that, once the fighting ended, technological know-how would transform the United States into a consumer's paradise. People could soon enjoy living in a bigger and better version of the prosperity-soaked world still associated, in popular memory and culture, with the 1920s (see chapter 24).

After initially resisting the idea of establishing a specific propaganda agency, Roosevelt finally did authorize, during the spring of 1942, creation of the Office of War Information (OWI). The OWI replaced an earlier, less aggressive effort, located in an Office of Facts and Figures. The President charged the OWI with coordinating a full range of informational initiatives. Many New Deal Democrats saw the OWI catering to advertisers who preferred

CASABLANCA (1942)

Directed by Michael Curtiz. Starring Humphrey Bogart (Rick Blaine), Ingrid Bergman (Ilsa Lund), Paul Henreid (Victor Lazlo), Conrad Veidt (Major Strasser), Claude Rains (Captain Renault), Dooley Wilson (Sam)

Casablanca, perhaps the most popular movie ever produced by the old Hollywood studio system, began as a rather modest wartime collaboration between Warner Brothers and the OWI. The studio provided the stars, the script, and the crew. The OWI offered guidance on how best to portray the Allied cause. It successfully urged, for example, that the role of "Sam," an African American piano player and singer, be related, more specifically than in earlier drafts of the script, to contemporary civil-rights issues.

Released in New York City at the same time, November 1942, that Allied forces were pursuing their TORCH campaign in North Africa, *Casablanca* contains numerous references to wartime themes and events. Most powerfully and pointedly, the film's own placement in cinematic time, December 1941, creates numerous opportunities to disparage isolationism. On several occasions, dialogue in the movie cleverly alludes to a real-life incident, the Japanese attack on Pearl Harbor, which will not happen until after *Casablanca*'s own narrative time frame ends. This technique, used in virtually every Hollywood film about familiar historical events, encourages viewers to take pride in their ability to spot historical references. Most important to *Casablanca*'s political agenda, these allusions to past events underscore its support for the necessity of U.S. involvement in the Second World War.

More often than not, though, *Casablanca* works to conceal its political messages by entangling them in a set of personal dilemmas faced by its male lead, "Rick Blaine," memorably played by Humphrey Bogart. Once an antifascist activist, who had "run guns to Ethiopia" and had fought fascism in Spain during the 1930s, Rick now only wants to isolate himself from larger causes and to preside over his gambling saloon in Casablanca. Remaining aloof from global politics, he watches refugees from fascism stream through this North African city on their way, hopefully, to freedom in the United States. For mysterious reasons, however, Blaine cannot or will not return home but, instead, runs "Rick's American Café," located at the edge of the North African frontier.

There seems little mystery, however, about the root cause of Rick's personal isolationism: a beautiful woman named "Ilsa Lund," portrayed by Ingrid Bergman. Before the Nazis stormed into Paris in 1939, Rick and Ilsa had planned to flee the city together, but she had left him waiting at the train station. Only when Ilsa unexpectedly resurfaces, two years later in Casablanca, does Rick learn why she had abandoned him. As she was preparing to leave Paris, news arrived that her husband, an antifascist crusader named "Victor Lazlo," had not perished, as she had thought, at the hands of the Nazis. Respecting her marriage vows, Ilsa had rushed to the injured Victor and nursed him back to health.

Trapped in Casablanca with a now-recovered Lazlo, Ilsa presents Rick with a series of personal and political dilemmas. She pleads with him, after her own husband's entreaties go unheeded, to help Victor escape to the United States, from where he can resume his antifascist activism. As long as Lazlo stays in Casablanca—nominally under the legal control of Vichy France but effectively under the thumb of a murderous Nazi officer, "Major Strasser"—his political reputation presumably protects him from immediate danger. At the same time, though, Lazlo's continued presence in North Africa makes him of little immediate value to the Allied cause, the one that the brooding Rick refuses to assist. Although Rick claims his noninterventionist policy stems from a commitment to political neutrality, the movie makes clear that personal considerations dominate his politics. Lazlo will only leave Casablanca with Ilsa, whom Rick suspects remains as romantically attracted to him as he still is to her.

Casablanca's script conveniently provides Rick with the means to help Ilsa and Lazlo—or Ilsa and himself—flee together: two blank "letters of transit," which have been hidden in Rick's Café. These documents, according to the movie's shaky legal logic, permit anyone, even Lazlo, to depart from Casablanca on the next plane flight. If Rick were to give the letters to Lazlo, he stands, once again, to lose Ilsa and to compromise his noninterventionist political principles. If he uses the documents to flee Casablanca with Ilsa, he will harm the Allied cause by preventing Lazlo from actively rejoining it. Will Rick, once a heroic activist, continue to remain uninvolved? Is there any way he can reconcile the conflicting demands he now confronts?

As *Casablanca* constructs Rick Blaine, Bogart's character can cut through all of these problems simply by embracing the role of a lone outlaw-hero, the iconic protagonist of so many of Hollywood's western movies. Blaine thus abandons his earlier reluctance to take a stance—along with the married woman he still loves—and takes the kind of decisive, if technically illegal, action that marks him as both manly and principled.

Symbolically structured as what film scholars call a "disguised western," *Casablanca* ends with Rick becoming a modern, North African version of an Old West gunfighter. At the point of a pistol, Blaine forces a duplicitous Vichy police officer, "Captain Renault," to sign the letters of transit over to Victor and Ilsa. Then, Rick turns his persuasive charms on Ilsa, who has mistakenly come to believe he will allow her to abandon Lazlo and leave Casablanca with him. These two lovers must set aside personal feelings, Rick implores her, and help her husband return to his antifascist work. When Major Strasser makes a last-ditch effort to stop Victor and Ilsa from boarding an outbound plane, Blaine simply guns him down. As the movie ends, Rick plans to light out, with Captain Renault rather than Ilsa as his traveling companion, for the North African frontier and join a Free French brigade—and the Allied cause.

Casablanca thus frames the fictional Rick Blaine's personal and political problems as symbolically parallel to those that the United States and its like-minded citizens faced before their own real-life entry into the Second World War. Seeing Humphrey Bogart make all the "correct" decisions, presumably, will help convince *Casablanca*'s wartime viewers that their political leaders, and they, are now working through the consequences of having made similarly appropriate ones. Watching *Casablanca* today, perhaps, helps convince viewers that people such as the fictional Rick Blaine really did make up America's "greatest generation."

Everett Collection

One of Classical Hollywood's most powerful motion pictures, *Casablanca* (1943) highlighted the personal and political dilemmas raised by U.S. entry into the Second World War. Here, Rick (Humphrey Bogart), Ilsa (Ingrid Bergman), and Sam (Dooley Wilson) uneasily recall their past in pre-war Paris and ponder their wartime futures.

imagery extolling the future joys of consumerism rather than those promoting broader visions of liberty and equality. Interpreting OWI-sponsored images very differently, Republicans blasted the agency for cranking out crass political appeals for causes favored by Roosevelt's New Dealers. While fending off its critics, the OWI set up branch offices throughout the world, published a widely distributed magazine called *Victory,* and produced hundreds of films, posters, and radio broadcasts.

Gender Issues

Popular portrayals of why the nation was fighting the Second World War increasingly clashed with how wartime mobilization was changing everyday life. The gap between Rockwell-type imagery and daily demands became readily apparent in the range of social issues affecting women.

The wartime United States called on women to serve their country as more than wives and mothers. Some 350,000 women volunteered for military duty during the war, and more than a thousand became pilots for the Women's Air force Service Pilots (WASPs). Not everyone approved of the changes. One member of Congress asked, "What has become of the manhood of America?" Most of his colleagues, however, supported creation of a woman's corps in each branch of the military, an innovation proposed but never adopted during the First World War.

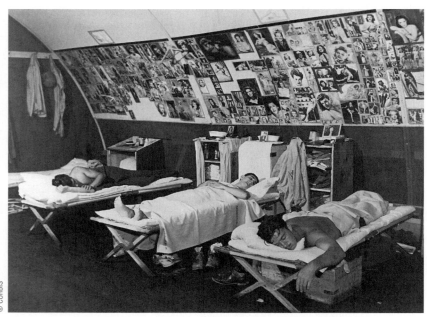

© CORBIS

Pin-up Girls   Male GIs often surrounded themselves with pin-up girls, images very different from that of the home front Rosie-the-Riveter.

Military service by women, together with their expanding roles in the wartime labor market, prompted debate over the possibility of enacting new legal-constitutional measures. Congress debated, without ever passing, a national equal-pay law and an Equal Rights Amendment (ERA) to the U.S. Constitution. Women's organizations disagreed among themselves over how to proceed. Groups claiming to speak for middle-class women, for example, strongly backed the ERA, but ones representing women who worked outside their homes, often for low wages, opposed its passage. They saw the ERA as a potential threat to the constitutionality of the array of special protective legislation, regulating hours and hazardous conditions, which reformers of the Progressive Era had struggled to obtain for women workers. Wartime conditions, then, helped refocus an earlier debate: Should working women continue to be accorded a protected status, in view of their vulnerability to exploitation in male-directed work environments, or would they ultimately benefit from gaining completely equal legal and constitutional status with men?

Even as wartime necessity helped alter older gender patterns in employment, widespread imagery frequently worked to frame the changes as temporary. Works of popular culture, for example, often portrayed the wartime participation of women in the workplace as a short-term anomaly and as a temporary sacrifice intended, ultimately, to preserve and protect their "natural" sphere in the home. Moreover, most wartime imagery tended to reinforce familiar ideals of femininity. A typical ad suggesting that women take on farm work declared: "A woman can do anything if she knows she looks beautiful doing it."

In some ways, the war may have even widened the symbolic gap between notions of femininity and masculinity. Male-dominated military culture seemed to foster the glamour-girl ideal. Service publications regularly featured pin-up sections and encouraged servicemen to decorate their wartime world—their sleeping quarters, their airplanes, even their tanks—with overt images of female sexuality. The home front entertainment industry, led by Hollywood, promoted its glamorous female stars as anxious to "please their boys" in the military. Some of the wartime popular culture came to associate masculinity with misogyny. Coming out of the war, the tough-guy genre, on prominent display in Hollywood's thrillers and in the author Mickey Spillane's series of "Mike Hammer" detective novels, portrayed female sexuality as both alluring and threatening to men.

Public policy making sometimes worked to reinforce gender divisions. The military assigned most of the women who joined the armed services to clerical and supply jobs, usually within the United States. The government and some private employers did provide, with differing degrees of enthusiasm and financial support, day care programs for mothers working outside of their homes. Although the thousands of centers set up during the conflict provided a precedent for future policy makers, the actual number of facilities met only a fraction of the child care need. Many centers, moreover, quickly shut their doors after the war's end. Meanwhile, social scientists often blamed mothers who worked outside of their homes during the war years for an apparent spike in rates of juvenile delinquency and divorce, and they pondered how new public policies might reverse these trends.

Racial Issues

The Second World War affected issues related to race as well as gender. The United States entered the global conflict as a nation in which many areas of daily life, particularly in the South and Southwest, featured highly visible signposts of racial and ethnic separatism. Citizens of African descent constantly negotiated an elaborate system of legalized segregation throughout southern states. Effectively disenfranchised politically in the South, African Americans in the rest of the country continued to experiment with how best to use the political power they had gained during the 1930s. In California and throughout the Southwest, residents who traced their ancestry back to Mexico, including many who had long resided in the United States, continued to work on addressing a wide range of issues involving employment, education, and housing.

After the United States formally entered the war, President Roosevelt refused to abandon the settled policy of racial segregation in the U.S. armed forces. Although the Army integrated Latino and American Indian soldiers, along with those from various European ethnic groups, into its combat units, military leaders refused to do the same for people of African and Japanese ancestry. Groups such as the NAACP pressed for integration, but Roosevelt's top advisers claimed that eliminating Jim Crow in the military could interfere with the nation's combat capabilities. The Red Cross and the U.S. Army even adopted the scientifically absurd practice of segregating donated blood into separate stores of "white" and "black" plasma.

Military officials often placed African Americans in inferior or highly dangerous support positions and initially excluded most of the segregated fighting units from combat duty. The White House deferred to these decisions, supported by white Democrats from the South who feared that permitting African Americans to join the fight for freedom abroad on an equal basis with other Americans might encourage attempts at desegregation at home. Toward the end of the war, when troop shortages forced the government to put segregated African American units into combat, these units invariably performed with distinction.

Wartime social tensions sometimes flared into open conflict. Within the military, for example, a 1944 explosion at an ammunition depot at Port Chicago, near San Francisco, killed 300 U.S. Navy dockworkers, all of them inadequately trained and most of African descent. When naval officers ordered other black sailors to similar duty, some refused, citing dangerous working conditions. The resulting court martial of 50 African Americans became the largest mass trial in naval history. A military court found all of them guilty of disobeying orders and imposed lengthy prison terms. After the war, the navy reduced the sentences and released the prisoners but refused requests to overturn their convictions. The Port Chicago incident remained a vivid memory among African Americans, and civil-rights groups continually pressed for redress. Finally, in 1999, one of the convicted sailors, Freddie Meeks, received a presidential pardon.

Meanwhile, on the wartime home front, a variety of volatile racial issues continued to simmer. As the wartime production system created more jobs, vast numbers of people from the rural South, including several hundred thousand African Americans, continued to move northward to cities such as Los Angeles and Detroit. The people already living in these areas often chafed at the influx of newcomers, who competed with them for jobs and housing and who placed greater demands on public services such as transportation, education, and recreational facilities.

Urban housing projects sometimes became sites of conflict. White residents of these facilities generally charged governmental agencies, when they attempted to challenge racial discrimination, with acting heavy-handedly, while persons of color criticized public officials for failing to move aggressively enough. In Buffalo, New York, threats of violence caused officials to cancel the construction of one housing project. In Detroit, in early 1942, that city's mayor deployed police officers in order to prevent clashes at the racially integrated Sojourner Truth site from escalating into something more serious.

The type of social strains evident early on in Detroit began to flare into violence. This escalation most often occurred in overcrowded urban spaces, where diverse populations and cultures already competed and clashed with one another. In Detroit, in June 1943, conflict between white and black youth at an amusement park rapidly spiraled into a multiple-day riot. Nearly 40 people, most of them African American, lost their lives before federal troops, dispatched by FDR at the request of the mayor of Detroit and the governor of Michigan, arrived in the Motor City. Critics of Detroit's police force charged it with not responding forcefully enough to the first disturbances, while the NAACP charged it with overreacting and with targeting black people, 17 of whom died as a result of deadly force used by officers. The violence in Detroit left hundreds injured and inflicted millions of dollars worth of damage to property. Federal troops remained in the city for six months after their initial deployment in June. The following month, Roosevelt sent another military force into New York City's Harlem to quell disturbances there.

Clashes extended beyond those between people of European and African descent. In Los Angeles, the "Zoot Suit Riots" of 1943 grew out of a complex set of social issues that had been roiling that fast-growing metropolis over the past several years. These included competition for control over contested public spaces, such as dance halls and jazz clubs; cultural-ethnic differences in dress and entertainment styles; and ethnic bitterness, especially growing out of the contentious 1942 "Sleepy Lagoon" murder case, which had produced controversial guilty verdicts (later reversed) against a group of Mexican American defendants. When social tensions finally produced violence, in late May and early June of 1943, the worst incidents initially pitted servicemen of European descent against young Mexican American men who were sporting **zoot suits.** This flamboyant outfit, which featured oversized coats and trousers, had come to exemplify ethnic pride and protest against wartime restrictions that seemed to fall hardest on communities of color.

For several days, increasingly larger groups of soldiers and sailors from nearby military bases entered the fray and stormed through parts of Los Angeles. Critics claimed that the city's police force did little to stop roving bands of servicemen, sometimes augmented by white residents of LA, who broadened their targets to include both African and Mexican Americans, whether zoot-suited or not. Police, the same critics charged, seldom hesitated to crack the heads of the young men who fought back. Largely ignoring the greater dimensions of what was going on in their city, members of the LA city council passed a resolution that made wearing a zoot suit a criminal offense. Finally, military authorities barred servicemen from coming into LA, a move that helped restore order.

Even when wartime tensions did not produce the kind of violence seen in Detroit and Los Angeles, the Second World War highlighted long-standing social issues. For many American Indians, for instance, the wartime years increased the pressures associated with longer-term patterns of migration and assimilation. Approximately 25,000 Indian men and several hundred Indian women served in the armed forces. Tens of thousands of other Indian men and women, many leaving their reservations for the first time, found wartime

© Universal Pictures/ Courtesy: Everett Collection

Zoot Suit Directed by Luis Valdez and based on his earlier stage play, the motion picture *Zoot Suit* (1981) recalled ethnic tensions in Los Angles during the Second World War. Starring Edward J. Olmos and Daniel Valdez, this innovative musical drama highlighted the struggles waged by Mexican Americans over space, identity, and legally protected rights. *Zoot Suit* explores, for example, how styles of masculine dress could become matters over which people would fight.

work in urban areas. Rapid City, South Dakota, near the Pine Ridge Reservation, attracted more than 2,000 Indians, most of whom settled in informal camps around city. Other cities with nearby reservations—such as Gallup, New Mexico; Flagstaff, Arizona; and Billings, Montana—became magnets for those seeking wartime work. Many people moved back and forth between city and reservation, where economic opportunities remained limited, and tried to juggle the problems produced by living in two significantly different worlds.

People of Japanese descent faced a unique set of social issues during the war. Shortly after the attack on Pearl Harbor, a powerful anti-Japanese political movement claimed to see signs of an impending sabotage campaign along the nation's West Coast, where most people of Japanese descent then lived. One military report claimed that a "large, unassimilated, tightly knit racial group, bound to an enemy nation by strong ties of race, culture, custom, and religion . . . constituted a menace" that justified extraordinary action.

Lacking evidence of any significant pockets of disloyalty, President Roosevelt nonetheless overrode objections from within his own administration and caved into political pressures. In February 1942, he issued Executive Order 9066, which directed the forced relocation of first- and second-generation Japanese Americans (called Issei and Nisei, respectively) and their internment in hastily constructed detainment camps located far away from West Coast areas. Significantly, in Hawaii, where the presumed danger of subversion should have been much greater, no similar mass internment took place. There, people of Japanese ancestry constituted nearly 40 percent of the population, and U.S. officials conceded their centrality to the local wartime economy.

The Roosevelt administration ultimately uprooted nearly 130,000 people of Japanese descent from their West Coast homes. Native-born U.S. citizens, including many young children, comprised two-thirds of the detainees. The relocation forced Japanese Americans to abandon their possessions and businesses or to sell them for a pittance before being transported to flimsy barracks surrounded by barbed wire and under armed guard. Many left behind thriving agricultural enterprises that were vital to wartime production. Civil libertarians generally condemned the internment program as militarily unnecessary and as unconstitutional, but a divided U.S. Supreme Court upheld its validity in *Korematsu* v. *U.S.* (1944). The Roosevelt administration closed the camps even before Japan's surrender, and in 1988, the U.S. Congress finally officially apologized for the internment. It also authorized payment of a cash indemnity to anyone who had been confined in the internment facilities.

Social Movements

The global fight against fascism proved helpful to the movements that were working for social change in America. German Nazism, with its doctrines of Aryan supremacy and racial inequality, helped expose the ugly underpinnings of older social science research. "The Huns have wrecked the theory of the master race with which we were so contented so long," lamented one pro-segregationist politician from Alabama. At the same time, the antifascist climate of the war years gave greater visibility to an expanding body of alternative research that saw racial difference as embedded in culture, rather than biology, and buttressed a growing conviction that a democracy could eliminate discrimination and bridge racial and ethnic gulfs.

The northward migration of African Americans contributed to efforts for social change. The nearly 750,000 African Americans who relocated to northern cities began to taste, for the first time in their lives, the real possibility of exerting political power. They found an outspoken advocate of civil rights within the White House. First Lady Eleanor Roosevelt repeatedly antagonized southern Democrats and members of her husband's administration by her advocacy of civil rights and her well-publicized participation in integrated social and political functions.

The *Amsterdam News,* a newspaper aimed at African Americans, called for a "Double V" campaign—victory at home as well as abroad. The labor leader A. Philip Randolph promised to lead tens of thousands of black workers in a march on Washington to demand more defense jobs and integration of the military forces. President Roosevelt feared the event would embarrass his administration and urged that it be canceled. Randolph's persistence ultimately forced Roosevelt to create the Fair Employment Practices Commission (FEPC). If this new agency gained little effective power over day-to-day events, its existence helped advance the ideal of nondiscrimination.

Particularly in urban areas such as Detroit and New York City, civil-rights groups, old and new, used the wartime years to construct a wider base from which to fight for jobs and political power. Founded in 1942, the inter-racial Committee (later, Congress) on Racial Equality (CORE) promised to find new, nonviolent ways of opposing discrimination. Testing a variety of strategies during the war, activists from CORE, led by Bayard Rustin, staged well-organized, well-publicized sit-ins. They called for integrating restaurants, theaters, and other public facilities, especially in wartime Washington, D.C.

The global dimension of the war effort proved of particular help to social movements addressing issues of importance to Mexican American communities. In California and throughout the Southwest during the war years, Latino organizations highlighted the irony of fighting overseas on behalf of a nation that denied equality at home and challenged the United States to live up to its democratic rhetoric. Approximately 500,000 Mexican Americans served, often with great distinction, in the military. Not wishing to anger this constituency, the Roosevelt administration, which also feared harm to its Good Neighbor Policy in Latin America, saw the 1943 zoot-suit incidents in LA as requiring a response from Washington. Consequently, the president's coordinator of Inter-American affairs, Nelson Rockefeller, allocated federal money to train Spanish-speaking workers for wartime employment, to improve education for Mexican Americans, and to provide high school graduates with new opportunities to enter college.

Organizations such as the League of United Latin American Citizens (LULAC) continually pressed for change. Although legal precedents in California and in Southwestern states formally classified Latinos as "white," actual practices usually discriminated against citizens and immigrants of Mexican descent. In Texas, Mexican American activists, working closely with the Mexican government, mounted several drives against discrimination. In

California, as the war was about to end in 1945, attorneys for LULAC backed an ambitious effort by several families to mount a legal challenge, grounded in the latest social science research, against cities in Orange County that segregated Mexican American children into separate and obviously unequal schools.

People of Japanese descent, despite the internment, also laid the basis for postwar campaigns to achieve greater equality for Asian Americans. The courage and sacrifice of Japanese American combat units, composed of volunteers from the stateside internment camps and from Hawaii, became legendary. Members of the 100th Battalion and the 442nd Regimental Combat Team, segregated units, suffered stunning causalities, often while undertaking extremely dangerous combat missions in Europe. In the Pacific Theater, 6,000 members of the Military Intelligence Service provided invaluable service against the same enemy their detractors once claimed they covertly supported.

Leaders of many social movements, then, came to see fighting for the American Way of Life as representing a commitment not to the past but to the future, one to be marked by new struggles on behalf of liberty and equality. After researching his influential study of racial relations, *An American Dilemma* (1944), the Swedish sociologist Gunnar Myrdal declared the need for "fundamental change." The African American novelist Richard Wright expressed a similar sentiment more tersely: The United States needed to address its "white problem."

In the face of divisive issues and new social movements, the OWI mounted informational campaigns that stressed national unity and contrasted America's "melting pot" ethos with the obsession in Germany and Japan about racial "purity." Many wartime motion pictures, plays, radio dramas, and musical pieces tried to foster a sense of national community by expressing pride in cultural diversity. As members of each of the nation's racial and ethnic groups distinguished themselves in the military, the claim to greater equality of condition— "Americans All," in the words of a wartime slogan—took on greater force. Governmental imagery extolling social solidarity and freedom provided another way in which the wartime years assisted the work of social activists.

Shaping the Peace

Focus Question
What major institutions and policies did the United States and the Allies adopt in their effort to shape the reconstruction of the postwar world?

Even before the war ended, U.S. policy makers began considering postwar peace arrangements. The Truman administration claimed to be building on Roosevelt's wartime conferences and agreements as it tried to shape a postwar framework for international relations.

Under Truman's leadership, the United States worked to establish the United Nations (UN), new international economic institutions, and other dispute-settling arrangements.

International Organizations

In the Atlantic Charter of 1941 and at a conference in Moscow in October 1943, the Allied powers pledged to create a replacement for the defunct League of Nations. Internationalist-minded Americans saw the new UN offering a more realistic version of Woodrow Wilson's earlier vision, one in which the United States would lead a world body that could deter aggressor nations and promote peaceful political change.

At the Dumbarton Oaks Conference in Washington in August 1944 and at a subsequent meeting in San Francisco in April 1945, the Allies worked out the UN's organizational structure. It included a General Assembly, in which each member nation would be represented and cast one vote. A smaller body, the Security Council, would include five permanent members from the Allied Coalition—the United States, Great Britain, the Soviet Union, France, and Nationalist China—and six rotating members. The Security Council would assume primary responsibility for taking action to maintain peace, but each of the permanent members could veto any council decision. A UN Secretariat, headed by a Secretary General, would handle day-to-day business, and an Economic and Social Council would sponsor measures to improve living conditions throughout the world.

The U.S. Senate, with only two dissenting votes, approved joining the UN in July 1945. This victory for internationalism contrasted sharply with the Senate's 1919 rejection of U.S. membership in the League of Nations. Opponents of Wilson's dream had then worried that the League would press internationalist policies that might limit the ability of the United States to pursue its own national interest. Following the Second World War, however, a newly powerful United States appeared able to dominate international organizations such as the UN. It seemed unlikely that decisions by it or other international bodies could seriously hamstring U.S. foreign policy. In addition, most U.S. leaders now saw the lack of a coordinated, international response to aggression during the 1930s as a major factor in the outbreak of the Second World War and wished to avoid reliving the "appeasement" policies of that era.

Eleanor Roosevelt, the former first lady and still a committed social activist, played a prominent role in promoting an internationalist agenda in the postwar period. A delegate to the first meeting of the UN's General Assembly, she chaired its Commission on Human Rights and guided the drafting of a Universal Declaration of Human Rights, adopted by the UN in 1948. The document set forth "inalienable" human rights and freedoms as cornerstones of international law.

A series of postwar economic agreements also illustrated a growing acceptance by U.S. leaders of the value of international organizations. At the Bretton Woods (New Hampshire) Conference of 1944, representatives from 45 nations created the International Monetary Fund (IMF), which they hoped could maintain a stable system of international exchange by ensuring the conversion of each nation's currency into that of every other at fixed and stable rates. The U.S. dollar, pegged at a value of $32 dollars for an ounce of gold, would provide the linchpin. Exchange rates could be altered only with the agreement of the IMF. This financial system, according to its architects, would facilitate smoothly flowing trade relationships and create the economic basis for preventing the kind of political instability that had paved the road to war during the 1930s.

Postwar U.S. planners participated in setting up other international economic organizations. At the Bretton Woods conference, they established the International Bank for Reconstruction and Development, later renamed the World Bank. Its creators envisioned it providing loans to war-battered countries and facilitating the resumption of world trade. In 1948, the United States also spearheaded implementation of the General Agreement on Tariffs and Trade (GATT). GATT established the institutional groundwork for subsequent meetings at which nations could come together and negotiate nondiscriminatory trade arrangements that would, in theory, operate freely and fairly throughout the world. Rather than confronting one another by raising protective tariffs or threatening military action over economic disputes, GATT would supposedly encourage nations to resolve their differences through cooperation, by engaging in a good-faith, internationally supervised bargaining process.

Spheres of Interest and Postwar Settlements

During their wartime negotiations, Stalin, Churchill, and Roosevelt had apparently assumed that the most powerful nations—their own—would enjoy special "spheres of influence" in the postwar world. As early as January 1942, the Soviet ambassador to the United States reported to Stalin that Roosevelt had tacitly assented to the Soviets exercising effective postwar control over the Baltic states of Lithuania, Latvia, and Estonia. In 1944, Stalin and Churchill agreed, informally and secretly, that Britain would continue to dominate Greece and that the Soviets could oversee Romania and Bulgaria. U.S. leaders, meanwhile, assumed that Latin America would remain within their sphere of influence. Roosevelt sometimes seemed to imply that he accepted Stalin's goal of having states friendly to the USSR on its vulnerable western border. At the Tehran Conference of November 1943, however, FDR also told Stalin that U.S. voters of Eastern European descent expected their homelands to be independent of Soviet control after the war.

Historians continue to differ on precisely how Roosevelt might have intended to reconcile his contradictory hints about the postwar Soviet sphere of influence. As long as the Soviet military remained essential to Germany's defeat—and Roosevelt also wanted the USSR to join the war against Japan—the ailing U.S. president struck a conciliatory tone with Stalin. After Roosevelt's death, however, the powerful position gained by the Soviets in Eastern Europe quickly became a focus of tensions between the United States and the USSR.

Early in the war, both nations did favor some plan for the dismemberment and deindustrialization of a defeated Nazi Germany. At a conference held at Yalta, Ukraine, in February 1945, the three major Allied powers agreed to divide Germany into four zones of occupation (with France's postwar government as the other occupying force). Later, as relations among the victors worsened, this temporary division of Germany hardened into a Soviet-dominated zone in the East and the other three zones to its west. The victors also divided Berlin, the German capital, into separate zones, even though the city lay uneasily within the Soviet-controlled portion of Germany.

Postwar differences also involved Poland. At the Yalta Conference, the Soviets agreed to hold elections in postwar Poland and to oversee creation of a government "responsible to the will of the people." Stalin also claimed, apart from these formalities, that the other Allied leaders tacitly acknowledged that the USSR would effectively dominate postwar Poland. Stalin apparently left Yalta expecting Poland would be in the USSR's sphere of influence, but many in the United States soon charged him with bad faith for failing to hold free elections and for not relinquishing Soviet control over Poland. Other critics, particularly powerful within Republican ranks, blamed Roosevelt and some of his key advisers for not bargaining harder or, even, for selling out to Stalin at Yalta. Observers more sympathetic to Roosevelt's problems with his allies, however, viewed the agreements reached at Yalta as inevitably ambiguous. With tough battles against Germany and Japan still looming on the horizon, British and U.S. leaders seemingly chose to sacrifice clarity in hopes of gaining further cooperation, especially on military matters, from Stalin.

In Asia, military projections likewise influenced postwar settlements. At a November 1943 conference in Tehran, and again at Yalta, Stalin pledged to send Soviet troops to Asia as soon as Germany surrendered. The first U.S. atomic bomb fell on Hiroshima, however, just one day before the Soviets were to enter the Pacific Theater of the war, and the United States assumed total charge of the occupation and postwar reorganization of Japan. After Soviet armies drove into the Korean Peninsula, the United States and the USSR divided Korea, which had been controlled by Japan, into separate zones of occupation. Here, as in Germany, these zones would later emerge as two antagonistic states, one beholden to the United States and the other to the Soviet Union (see chapter 27).

The fate of the European colonies seized by Japan in Southeast Asia provided another contentious issue. Most U.S. officials preferred to see the former British and French colonies become independent nations, but they also worried about the left-leaning politics of many anticolonial nationalist movements. As the Truman administration became more suspicious of the expansionist intentions of Stalin's Soviet regime, it became increasingly tempting to support British and French efforts to reassemble their colonial empires.

The United States maintained its own sphere of influence in the Pacific. In the Philippines, the Truman administration honored a long-standing pledge to grant independence. A government friendly to the United States, which agreed to respect American economic interests and accept U.S. military bases, took power in 1946. U.S. advisers from these bases soon began assisting the Philippine government in its campaign against leftist rebels, the Hukbalahaps, or Huks. In 1947, the United Nations designated the Mariana, Caroline, and Marshall Islands as the "Trust Territories of the Pacific" and authorized the United States to administer their affairs.

Although the nations of Latin America had been only indirectly involved in military conflict and peace negotiations, the Second World War encouraged Roosevelt to build on his Good Neighbor Policy of the 1930s (see chapter 25). Following the German invasion of Poland in 1939, Latin American leaders stood nearly united behind the Allies. After formal U.S. entry into the war, at a conference in Rio de Janeiro in January 1942, every Latin American country except Chile and Argentina broke diplomatic ties with the Axis governments. When naval warfare in the Atlantic severed commercial connections between Latin America and Europe, Latin American countries became critical suppliers of raw materials to the United States.

Wartime conferences avoided making many clear-cut decisions about the Middle East, especially about the founding of a Jewish state. The Second World War prompted survivors of the Holocaust and Jews from around the world to take direct action. **Zionism,** the international movement to found a Jewish state in Palestine, the ancient homeland of Jewish people, attracted thousands of Jews to the Middle East. They began efforts to carve out, against the wishes of Palestinians and other Arab people, a new Jewish state, Israel.

Conclusion

The world landscape changed dramatically during the Second World War. For the United States, wartime mobilization finally ended the Great Depression and focused most of the national government's attention on international concerns. The war brought not only victory over dictatorial, expansionist regimes but also left the United States as the world's preeminent economic and military power.

At home, the administration of President Franklin Roosevelt—concerned with successfully prosecuting a global war against fascism—embraced economic planning and assigned broad executive powers to governmental bureaucracies. Cooperative ties among government, business, and scientific researchers gradually took shape. These sectors worked together to provide the seemingly miraculous growth in the economic productivity that ultimately propelled the U.S. military effort.

Even as the war overseas went on, domestic debates over liberty and equality continued at home. Many Americans saw the Second World War as a struggle to protect and preserve the liberties they already enjoyed. Others, inspired by a struggle against racism and injustice abroad, insisted that a war for freedom should include efforts to advance social justice at home.

News of Japan's 1945 surrender prompted joyous celebrations throughout the United States. Still, most people seemed uncertain about postwar prospects. Internationally, could the United States maintain a cooperate relationship with its wartime Allies, especially the Soviet Union? Domestically, how would the wrenching dislocations of war affect both individuals and institutions? The nation, moreover, now faced the future without the charismatic leadership of Franklin D. Roosevelt.

SUGGESTED READINGS

On the United States and the coming of World War II, see **Robert Dallek, *Franklin D. Roosevelt and American Foreign Policy, 1932–1945*** (1979), and **Waldo H. Heinrichs, *Threshold of War: Franklin D. Roosevelt and American Entry into World War II*** (1988). On the isolationist coalition, see **Justus Doenecke, *Storm on the Horizon: The Challenge to American Intervention, 1939–1941*** (2003). For the war's military aspects, consult **John Keegan, *The Second World War*** (2005); **Gerhard L. Weinberg, *A World at Arms: A Global History of World War II*** (1994); and **Gerald F. Linderman, *The World within War: America's Combat Experience in World War II*** (1997). Few narrative histories can match the dramatic sweep of **Stephen Ambrose's** many works, such as ***D-Day: June 6, 1944: The Climactic Battle of World War II*** (1994). **Michael Beschloss, *The Conquerors: Roosevelt, Truman and the Destruction of Hitler's Germany, 1941–1945*** (2002) is also highly readable. The decision to drop atomic bombs on Japan is adroitly analyzed in **J. Samuel Walker, *Prompt and Utter Destruction: Truman and the Use of the Atomic Bombs against Japan*** (2005).

David Kennedy's *The American People in World War II: Freedom from Fear, Part II* (2003) is a recent overview of the wartime years. See also, **William L. O'Neill, *A Democracy at War: American's Fight at Home and Abroad in World War II*** (1993), and **Michael C. C. Adams, *The Best War Ever: America and World War II*** (1994). The superb synthesis by **John Morton Blum, *V Was for Victory: Politics and American Culture during World War II*** (1976) may be supplemented by the essays in **Lewis A. Erenberg and Susan E. Hirsch, eds., *The War in American Culture: Society and Consciousness during World War II*** (1996), and **Thomas Patrick Doherty, *Projections of War: Hollywood, American Culture, and World War II*** (1993). **Richard W. Steele, *Free Speech and the Good War*** (1999) examines governmental efforts to regulate dissent. **Karen Anderson, *Wartime Women: Sex Roles, Family Relations, and the Status of Women during World War II*** (1981) surveys women's roles during the war. **Ronald Takaki, *Double Victory: A Multicultural History of America in World War II*** (2000) is a good synthesis of issues related to race and ethnicity.

Visit the Liberty Equality Power Companion Web site for resources specific to this textbook: http://www.thomsonedu.com/history/murrin

Also find self-tests and additional resources at ThomsonNOW. ThomsonNOW is an integrated online suite of services and resources with proven ease of use and efficient paths to success, delivering the results you want—NOW!

www.thomsonedu.com/login/

The Age of Containment, 1946–1953

The Second World War, popularly portrayed as a struggle to preserve the "American Way of Life," ended up transforming much of it. The fight against fascism had propelled foreign-policy issues to the center of domestic politics, and postwar international tensions kept them there. As combat operations against the Axis powers gave way to conflict between the United States and the Soviet Union, U.S. leaders overhauled military strategy. They claimed a broad authority for the nation's commander in chief—and, hence, the office of the president—and the need for a global stand against communism. An aggressive campaign to shore up "national security," in addition, came to affect many areas of domestic life.

The early postwar years, between 1946 and 1953, raised questions about the reach of governmental power. What role should Washington, whose bureaucracies had undertaken extensive economic planning during the Second World War, play in the postwar economy? Could a more powerful national government help people enjoy greater security in their own daily lives? How might such a government affect liberty and equality? Debate over issues such as these marked the presidency of Democrat Harry Truman (1945–53), who struggled to implement his anticommunist agenda and to build upon social welfare measures from the New Deal era of the 1930s.

Creating a National Security State, 1945–1949

Focus Question
What major conflicts between the United States and the Soviet Union shaped the Cold War, and what were the principal elements of the foreign policy called containment?

The wartime alliance between the United States and the Soviet Union proved little more than a marriage of convenience. The shared goal of defeating the Axis had forced these two nations, capitalist and communist, to cooperate, but collaboration scarcely lasted beyond victory. Relations between the United States and the Soviet Union produced a **Cold War** marked by mutual suspicion and growing tension.

CHRONOLOGY

1946	Baruch plan for atomic energy proposed • Employment Act passed • Republicans gain control of Congress in November elections
1947	Truman Doctrine announced • HUAC begins hearings on communist infiltration of Hollywood • George Kennan's "Mr. X" article published • National Security Act passed (CIA and NSC established) • Marshall Plan adopted • Truman's loyalty order announced • Taft-Hartley Act passed over Truman's veto • Jackie Robinson and Larry Doby break major league baseball's color line
1948	Berlin Airlift begins • Truman wins reelection • The *Kinsey Report* and Dr. Benjamin Spock's *Baby and Child Care* published
1949	NATO established • China "falls" to communism • NSC-68 drafted • Soviet Union explodes atomic device • Truman unveils his Fair Deal
1950	Korean War begins • Senator Joseph McCarthy charges communist infiltration of State Department • McCarran Internal Security Act passed
1951	Truman removes General MacArthur as commander in Korea
1952	GI Bill of Rights passed • Dwight Eisenhower elected president

Onset of the Cold War

Historians have dissected the beginning of the Cold War from many different perspectives. The traditional interpretation focuses on Soviet expansionism. It sees a historical Russian appetite for new territory, an ideological zeal to spread international communism, or some interplay between these two desires. According to this view, the United States needed to check the expansionist designs of a malevolent USSR. Other historians—generally called revisionists—argue that the Soviet Union's obsession with securing its borders, an understandable response to the invasion of its territory during both world wars, dominated its foreign policy. The United States, in this view, might have tried harder to reassure the USSR, pursuing conciliatory policies instead of ones that intensified Soviet fears. Still other scholars maintain that assigning blame to one side or the other obscures how clashing interests and differing political cultures produced potentially dangerous confrontations, but never direct military conflict, between the two superpowers.

In every account, Harry Truman's administration plays a central role. The new U.S. president initially hoped that he could somehow deal with the Soviets but quickly came to distrust Soviet Premier Joseph Stalin. As differences between the former allies emerged, Truman turned to a group of hard-line, anti-Soviet advisers.

The atomic bomb provided an immediate source of U.S.-Soviet friction. At the Potsdam Conference of July 1945, Truman had casually told Stalin, without mentioning the atomic bomb, about a new U.S. weapon of "unusual destructive force." Well-informed by Soviet intelligence operations about the Manhattan Project, Stalin casually replied that Truman should make "good use" of this weapon. Less calmly, Stalin ordered his scientists to intensify the Soviet Union's own nuclear weapons program. Truman likely hoped that the bomb would scare the Soviets, and it did. Historians still debate whether it frightened the Soviets into more cautious behavior or made them more fearful and aggressive.

As atomic warfare against Japan gave way to atomic diplomacy with the Soviet Union, U.S. leaders clashed among themselves over how to proceed. A group that included Secretary of War Henry Stimson, predicting the Soviets would soon possess their own atomic weapons, urged Truman to share nuclear technology with the USSR, in hopes of forestalling a nuclear arms race. The president's more hard-line confidants, fearing Soviet intentions and doubting their nuclear knowledge, rejected this approach.

In 1946, Truman authorized Bernard Baruch, a special presidential representative at the United Nations, to explore ways of controlling the spread of atomic weapons. The Baruch Plan proposed that the United States would abandon its nuclear weapons, but only after the Soviets met certain conditions. Soviet leaders would have to agree to a process for outside monitoring and verification of their atomic energy program and would have to

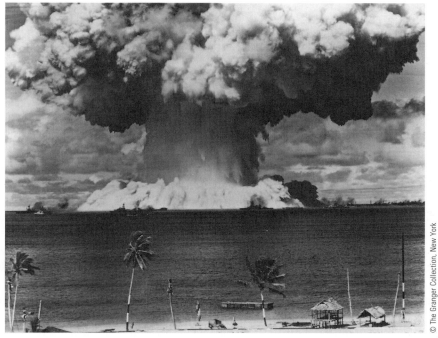

Testing the Atomic Bomb at Bikini Atoll   This atomic test, one of 23 detonations at Bikini Atoll in the Marshall Islands during the late 1940s, raised a column of water 5,000 feet high. Although Bikini islanders were evacuated from the blast sites, the radiation still affected nearby people, including U.S. service personnel, and the area's ecology for years to come. As nuclear-related imagery spread through Cold War culture, new "bikini" swimsuits for "bombshell" women became a fashion rage.

surrender veto power in the UN in cases regarding nuclear issues. Unwilling to submit to these conditions, Soviet leaders rejected the Baruch Plan. They counterproposed that the United States unilaterally destroy its atomic weapons as the initial step toward any final agreement. The United States opposed this idea, and both nations used the deadlock to justify seeking to outpace the other in developing nuclear weapons.

Additional sources of friction involved U.S. loan policies and Soviet domination of Eastern Europe. Under pressure from Republicans in Congress, Truman ended lend-lease assistance to the Soviet Union at the end of the war and, on advice from his own camp, linked extension of future reconstruction loans to signs of Soviet cooperation with the United States over the future of Europe. This linkage strategy never worked. The Soviet Union's need for capital and its suspicions about Western intentions provided excuses for an aggressive, hard-line stance. A repressive sphere of Soviet influence over Eastern Europe, which the USSR called defensive and the United States labeled expansionist, fell into place. By 1946, the two nations, once uneasy allies, seemed ready to become bitter adversaries.

Harry Truman increasingly placed his personal stamp on the presidency by pledging to stop the campaign of communist expansionism he claimed Moscow directed. Truman's anticommunist initiatives, in both foreign and domestic affairs, relied on new measures for extending the reach and power of the executive branch of the national government.

Containment Abroad: The Truman Doctrine

In March 1947, the president announced what became known as the Truman Doctrine. This pronouncement came during a speech to Congress about the civil war in Greece, a conflict in which communist-led insurgents appeared ready to topple a corrupt but pro-Western government. A war-weakened Britain had long considered Greece within its sphere of influence, but it could no longer maintain its formerly strong presence there or in other parts of the Middle East. Truman's advisers claimed that a leftist victory in Greece would expose nearby Turkey, a nation considered critical to the U.S. strategic position in the Mediterranean, to Soviet expansionism.

Seeking to justify U.S. aid to Greece and Turkey, Truman made his case to Congress in especially dramatic terms. Both the threat of communism and U.S. security interests, he said, now spanned the globe. The future of "free peoples" everywhere hung in the balance. Unless the United States aided those who were "resisting attempted subversion by armed minorities or by outside pressures," totalitarian communism would spread and, ultimately, threaten the United States.

The global vision of U.S. national security outlined in the Truman Doctrine encountered some skepticism. Henry Wallace, who had become Truman's most visible Democratic critic, chided the president for exaggerating the Soviet threat and urged a more concilia-tory approach toward Moscow. Conservative Republicans, though firmly anti-Soviet, looked suspiciously at the increase of executive power and the vast expenditures the Truman Doctrine seemed to imply. If the president wanted to win support for his position, Republican Senator Arthur Vandenberg had already advised, Truman should "scare hell" out of people.

The rhetoric the president used when announcing the Truman Doctrine seemed to have followed this advice. Gaining backing from both Republicans and Democrats, Congress did approve Truman's request for $400 million in assistance to Greece and Turkey, most of it for military aid, in the spring of 1947. This vote signaled broad, if not unanimous, bipartisan support for a national security policy that came to be called **containment.**

The term *containment* first appeared in a 1947 article in the influential journal *Foreign Affairs* by **George Kennan,** the U.S. State Department's premier Soviet expert. Writing under the pseudonym "X," Kennan argued that the "main element" in any U.S. policy "must be that of a long-term, patient but firm and vigilant containment of Russian expansive tendencies." This article and the word containment quickly became associated, to Kennan's subsequent displeasure, with the urgent tone of the Truman Doctrine and with a military-dominated approach to world affairs.

Containment eventually came to provide a convenient catchphrase for the Truman administration's global, anticommunist national security policy. Although Kennan had envisioned containment primarily as a careful political strategy that tried to limit Soviet gains in Europe, the White House's rearticulation lacked Kennan's nuances and, instead, turned containment in militarized and globalized directions. Truman's version came to link all leftist insurgencies, wherever they occurred, to a **totalitarian movement** directed from Moscow. Soviet communism threatened the security of the United States by dangerous ideas as well as by military might. Even a relatively small gain by the Soviets in one part of the globe would, in this view, encourage them to extend, perhaps even accelerate, their aggressive initiatives. Although postwar debates over foreign policy did include sharp disagreements over precisely how and where to pursue containment, few U.S. leaders questioned the need for a global and activist foreign policy aimed against the spread of communism.

Truman's Loyalty Program

Only nine days after proclaiming the Truman Doctrine, the president issued Executive Order 9835. It declared there should be "a loyalty investigation" of every civilian employee "of any department or agency of the executive branch of the Federal Government." Newly established loyalty boards would determine whether or not there were "reasonable grounds" for concluding that a person working for the U.S. government belonged to an organization or held political ideas that might pose a "security risk." Any employees found to pose such a danger would lose their government jobs. The Truman loyalty program also authorized the attorney general's office to identify organizations it deemed **subversive,** and to place them on a special Attorney General's List.

The Truman Loyalty Program rested on a controversial assessment of Soviet espionage activity in the United States. Although knowledgeable observers consistently recognized that the Soviets had conducted spy operations inside the U.S. government during the 1940s, there has been sharp disagreement over their scope and success. Were the Soviets operating only at the fringes of government or had they penetrated its top levels? Were they simply collecting readily obtainable information or stealing vital national secrets?

Debate over questions such as these now takes place in light of evidence unavailable before the 1989 collapse of the Soviet Union. Previously closed Soviet archives and declassified files of U.S. surveillance agencies suggest both nations engaged in a wide range of spying activities. The wartime alliance had made it easier than ever before for the Soviet Union to obtain intelligence in the United States. By 1943, for instance, a super-secret U.S. Army counterintelligence unit had begun intercepting transmissions between Moscow and the United States. Called the "VENONA files" and not publicly revealed until 1995, these intercepted messages showed that the USSR helped finance America's Communist Party; placed informants in important U.S. governmental agencies; and began obtaining secret information about U.S. atomic work as early as 1944. U.S. officials, in short, justifiably saw Soviet espionage as a legitimate concern. Historians still differ, however, over the significance and reliability of specific pieces of evidence in the VENONA files and even over how much members of the Truman administration actually knew about information in these intercepts.

There can be little doubt, though, that the case Truman made on behalf of his loyalty policy failed to satisfy a diverse group of critics. The president claimed, in effect, that the United States faced relatively few security risks but that their potential for doing grave harm demanded a response unprecedented in peacetime. Many Republicans charged the Truman administration with underestimating the threat and warned that hundreds, perhaps thousands, of communists now worked in the federal bureaucracy. The Democrats, these Republicans argued, lacked the will to create the kind of aggressive loyalty program that could root them out. From a very different perspective, civil liberties groups saw a more limited threat and argued for a carefully calibrated response. Truman's approach, they insisted, failed to distinguish between, for example, an atomic scientist with ties to the Soviet Union and a politically outspoken clerical worker in the Interior Department. Truman's loyalty plan, therefore, angered both fervent anticommunists, who accused the president of doing too little to fight subversion at home, and civil libertarians, who charged him with whipping up fears that far exaggerated the menace and exceeded constitutional limitations on governmental power.

The National Security Act, the Marshall Plan, and the Berlin Crisis

Shaking off criticism from all sides, the Truman administration continued to pursue its anticommunist initiatives. It secured congressional passage of the National Security Act of 1947, which created several new governmental bureaucracies. The law began the process that transformed the old Navy and War Departments into a unified Department of Defense, finally established in 1949. It instituted another new arm of the executive branch, the National Security Council (NSC), and gave it broad authority over the planning and execution of foreign policy. It established the Air Force as a separate service alongside the Army and Navy, and it created, as a successor to the wartime Office of Strategic Services (OSS), a new Central Intelligence Agency (CIA).

The CIA, charged with gathering sensitive political information and conducting covert activities, proved to be the most flexible of the new national security bureaucracies.

Shrouded from public scrutiny and even close oversight by Congress, its secretly funded operations crisscrossed the globe. The CIA reached out, for example, to anti-Stalinist groups in Eastern Europe and even to some within the Soviet Union. It helped finance, in hopes of preventing the rise of communist-led organizations, pro-U.S. labor unions in Western Europe. It covertly intervened in overseas political campaigns, bolstering anti-communist parties in France and Japan. The CIA secretly claimed credit for preventing the Italian Communist Party from winning a nationwide electoral victory in 1948. The Truman administration came to see CIA operations as integral to its anticommunist foreign policy.

Truman's White House also considered its economic policies in Western Europe an important part of the containment effort. Concerned that Western Europe's severe economic problems might benefit communist-dominated movements, Secretary of State George C. Marshall hoped U.S. aid would quickly rejuvenate the region's economy. Under his 1947 Marshall Plan, the United States would extend funds designed to allow postwar Western European governments to coordinate a broad program of economic reconstruction. Between 1946 and 1951, the United States provided nearly $13 billion in assistance to 17 Western European nations.

The Truman administration consistently hailed the Marshall Plan, which Congress approved in early 1948, for complementing other national security initiatives. It credited aid from the United States for helping brighten the economic scene in Western Europe, where industrial production quickly rebounded. Improving standards of living, the White House claimed, enhanced political stability in Western Europe and undermined the appeal of communist-led movements. In response to conservative critics who complained of a "giveaway" program, supporters of the Marshall Plan insisted that U.S. economic aid expanded both markets and investment opportunities for U.S. firms wanting to do business in Western Europe.

The Truman administration also moved to beef up U.S. military resources, depleted as a result of an earlier postwar demobilization effort. After the USSR facilitated the installation of a pro-Soviet government in Czechoslovakia, during the spring of 1948, the president's key military advisers claimed Stalin likely intended a military strike against Western Europe. A brief war scare gripped Washington. Planners urged an immediate increase in across-the-board military spending and reinstitution of the military draft. Truman, addressing a joint session of Congress, declared that "moral God-fearing peoples . . . must save the world from Atheism" and from Soviet "totalitarianism."

U.S. policy makers viewed the future of postwar Germany, initially divided into four zones of occupation (see chapter 26), as crucial to the security of Western Europe. In June 1948, the United States, Great Britain, and France announced a currency-reform program as the first step toward integrating their separate sectors into the Federal Republic of Germany, popularly known as West Germany. Soviet leaders expressed alarm. Having twice been invaded by German armies during the preceding 35 years, they wanted, as a hedge against a third attack, any post-occupation Germany to remain economically enfeebled. Hoping to sidetrack

Western plans, in June 1948, the Soviets cut off all highways, railroads, and water routes linking Berlin, which was located within their own domain, to the western zones of occupation.

This Soviet attempt to seal off Berlin provided an opportunity for the newly created U.S. Air Force to display its capabilities. Under the direction of General Curtis LeMay, U.S. and British pilots began "Operation Vittles" or "the Berlin Airlift." Specially outfitted planes, flying around the clock, soared over the Soviet blockade and delivered virtually all of the items Berliners needed to continue their daily routines. The United States, hinting at a military response, also began negotiating for U.S. air bases in Western Europe and immediately stationed in Britain two squadrons of B-29s, reputably able to deliver atomic bombs to Soviet targets. Although these planes actually lacked nuclear capability, officials in the Pentagon began planning for an atomic attack, during some future confrontation, against the USSR. Once Stalin recognized the Berlin Airlift would continue, he abandoned his blockade, in May 1949, and moved to convert the Soviet-occupied sector of East Germany into the German Democratic Republic. The western portion of a divided Berlin, an anti-communist enclave inside East Germany, quickly became a prominent focus of Cold War tensions.

The Election of 1948

National security issues helped Harry Truman win the 1948 election. His victory capped a remarkable political story, one that featured a feisty incumbent president and a trio of challengers.

Truman faced significant political opposition that had been building since 1946. Dissident Democrats, who thought his containment policies too militant and his domestic ones too tame, began looking to an old Truman rival, former Vice-President (1941–45) Henry A. Wallace. After Wallace, whom Truman inherited from Roosevelt as his secretary of commerce, criticized U.S. policy toward the Soviet Union, the president ousted him from the cabinet in September 1946. This move angered those Democrats who saw Wallace, not Truman, as FDR's rightful successor. Later, the off-year national elections of November 1946 gave the Republicans control of Congress for the first time since 1928. GOP leaders saw this victory portending an end to their 20-year losing streak in presidential races. Although Truman's political fortunes did seem somewhat improved by late 1947, few political handicappers liked his chances in 1948.

Truman faced three prominent opponents. To his political left, a new Progressive Party, which nominated Henry Wallace for president, hoped to attract the disaffected Democrats who charged Truman with abandoning FDR's legacy. In addition, South Carolina's J. Strom Thurmond became the pro-segregationist candidate of a new States' Rights (or "Dixiecrat") party, and Thomas E. Dewey, the Republican who had run well during a losing race against Franklin Roosevelt in 1944, returned as the GOP nominee. Targeting Dewey, his most serious challenger, Truman called the GOP-controlled Congress into a special session and presented it with a list of domestic policy proposals that were abhorrent to most

Republicans. After GOP legislators predictably ignored Truman's wish list, the president targeted "that do-nothing, good-for-nothing, worst Congress."

Dewey helped Truman's cause by running an exceedingly cautious campaign. A pro-Democratic newspaper caricatured Dewey's standard speech as four "historic sentences: Agriculture is important. Our rivers are full of fish. You cannot have freedom without liberty. The future lies ahead." Ignoring critics, he remained confident of a November victory. When his campaign train, the "Victory Special," arrived in Truman's old political base of Kansas City, Dewey pointedly booked the same hotel suite the president used whenever he came to town.

Meanwhile, Truman mounted an energetic, tub-thumping effort. It featured blunt and caustic attacks on his opponents, most famously delivered from the back of his own campaign train. Dewey was plotting "a real hatchet job on the New Deal," the president charged, and the GOP, controlled by a cabal of "cunning men," was preparing for "a return of the Wall Street economic dictatorship." "Give 'em hell, Harry!" shouted his Democratic supporters. In November, Truman won slightly less than 50 percent of the popular vote but secured a solid majority in the Electoral College. The Democratic Party also regained control of Congress.

Truman's victory now seems less surprising to historians than it did to political analysts in 1948. Despite Republican victories in the 1946 congressional elections, the Democratic Party retained the core of its old New Deal base. In fact, Democratic congressional candidates who identified with Franklin Roosevelt rather than with his successor generally polled a higher percentage of the November vote in their districts than did Truman. Voter loyalty to the memory of Roosevelt and his New Deal coalition helped bring the Democrats their victory.

After accepting his party's call for new civil-rights measures, Truman survived the revolt of the Dixiecrats, disaffected white Southern Democrats, in 1948. Strom Thurmond had denounced Truman for backing a "civil wrongs" program and charged that "radicals, subversives, and reds" now controlled the national Democratic Party. He claimed that Dixiecrats did not oppose all civil-rights legislation but insisted that the U.S. Constitution required that state governments, not the federal government, possessed

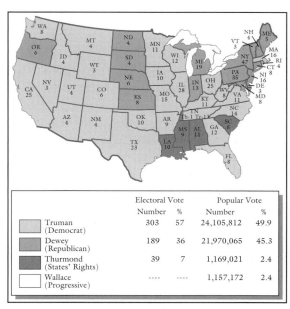

	Electoral Vote		Popular Vote	
	Number	%	Number	%
Truman (Democrat)	303	57	24,105,812	49.9
Dewey (Republican)	189	36	21,970,065	45.3
Thurmond (States' Rights)	39	7	1,169,021	2.4
Wallace (Progressive)	----	----	1,157,172	2.4

Map 27.1   Presidential Election, 1948   This electoral map helps show how, in this close election, Truman won the presidency with less than 50 percent of the popular vote.

the power to enact antidiscrimination measures. The Dixiecrat movement did portend longer-term political changes among southern whites, people who had loyally voted Democratic since Reconstruction. As a presidential candidate in 1948, however, Thurmond secured only the electoral votes of four Deep South states, while Truman carried all of the other states of the old Confederacy.

Truman's hard-line anticommunist rhetoric proved crucial to sidetracking Henry Wallace's once-promising campaign. Wallace and his supporters had never expected to win the presidency but hoped to do well enough to rekindle support for their vision of the New Deal and to build pressure for a less militantly anti-Soviet foreign policy. Eventually, though, many Democrats abandoned the Progressives because of their refusal to reject support from the U.S. Communist Party—a point that Truman contrasted with his own anticommunist stance. Henry Wallace received less than 3 percent of the popular tally and no electoral votes. The 1948 election left the Progressive Party in shambles and suggested a lesson for elections to come: Successful presidential candidates could never appear "soft" on national security issues if they hoped to gain the White House.

The Era of the Korean War, 1949–1952

Meanwhile, to carry out his containment policy, Truman continued to marshal the nation's economic and military resources. After a series of Cold War crises during 1949 and the outbreak of war on the Korean peninsula in 1950, he reaffirmed his administration's anticommunist stance.

NATO, China, and the Bomb

In April 1949, the United States, Canada, and 10 European nations formed the **North Atlantic Treaty Organization (NATO).** Under this "mutual defense" pact, each nation pledged that an attack against one would automatically be treated as a strike against all. Prominent critics, such as Republican Senator Robert Taft, called NATO a provocation to the Soviet Union, an "entangling alliance" that violated the traditional U.S. foreign policy, and a threat to the constitutionally guaranteed power of Congress to declare war. Because of NATO's mutual defense feature, Taft argued, the policies of other countries, rather than those of the United States, could bring the nation into a foreign conflict. The NATO concept prevailed, however, and the idea of pursuing containment through similar arrangements would expand during the 1950s. **(See Map 27.2, Divided Germany and the NATO Alliance, in the color insert following page 1056.)**

Meanwhile, events in China heightened Cold War tensions. Although the United States had extended billions of dollars in military aid and economic assistance to Jiang Jieshi's struggling Nationalist government, Jiang had steadily lost ground to the forces of Mao Zedong, who promised that a communist China would soon gain an important role in world affairs and that Chinese peasants would enjoy the fruits of a sweeping program of land reform. Experienced U.S. diplomats privately predicted Jiang's inevitable downfall.

Publicly, however, the Truman administration continued to portray Jiang as the capable and respected leader of a "free China." Then, in 1949, Mao's armies finally forced Jiang and his supporters to retreat from the Chinese mainland to the nearby island of Formosa (Taiwan). Mao's communist movement established the People's Republic of China, while Jiang's National Chinese government took root on Formosa. The two Chinas, like the two Germanys, became evocative symbols of a global Cold War.

Many people in the United States wondered how Mao's communist forces could have triumphed. Financed by conservative business leaders, the powerful "China lobby" excoriated Truman and his new secretary of state, Dean Acheson, for having "lost" China to the communists. Critics of Acheson's state department forced the removal of several analysts who had warned of Jiang's impending collapse or had merely emphasized his shortcomings. Although Acheson had once made some tentative, highly secret moves toward negotiating with the People's Republic, new international tensions and domestic political pressures ultimately convinced the Truman administration to embrace Jiang's regime on Taiwan and refuse to recognize or officially deal with Mao's "Red China." Nonrecognition remained U.S. policy for more than 20 years, even after the friction between communist China and the Soviet Union, which experienced "China hands" in the U.S. State Department had predicted, became evident.

In September 1949, Truman announced another event that reinforced his administration's anticommunist resolve. The Soviet Union, years earlier than many of the president's aides had expected, had conducted a successful "nuclear explosion." The USSR's crude atomic device, which ended the U.S. nuclear monopoly, increased concern about the threat posed by Soviet communism. Already besieged by domestic critics who saw recent history filled with Soviet gains and U.S. losses, Truman secretly pondered whether U.S. scientists should take the next step in nuclear weaponry: development of a hydrogen bomb. Acheson, who had once shared Henry Stimson's fears about a nuclear arms race, now threw the State Department's influence behind the H-bomb project.

NSC-68

In responding to events of 1949, the Truman administration began formally reviewing its foreign-policy assumptions. George Kennan, increasingly concerned about the emergence of a global, largely militarized redesign of his containment concept, resigned from the State Department's policy staff. As a result, the task of overseeing this review fell to Paul Nitze, a hard-liner who insisted on confronting the USSR throughout the world, lest small gains in one corner encourage more aggressive Soviet moves elsewhere. Nitze effectively dominated production of a policy paper identified as **NSC-68** (National Security Council Document 68), which provided a blueprint for both the rhetoric and the substance of future Cold War foreign policy. In the words of one of NSC-68's architects, the United States should "find every weak spot in the enemy's armor . . . and hit him with anything that comes to hand. Anything we do short of an all-out effort is inexcusable."

NSC-68 opened with an alarming account of a global ideological clash between "freedom," spread by U.S. power, and "slavery," promoted by the Soviet Union, the center of an international communist movement. Despairing of fruitful negotiations with the Soviets, NSC-68 urged a full-scale effort to expand U.S. influence. It endorsed covert action, economic pressure, propaganda campaigns, and a massive military buildup. Because some Americans might oppose larger military spending and budget deficits, the report cautioned, U.S. leaders should portray their actions as defensive and present greater military spending as a stimulus to the economy rather than as a potential drain on national resources. Although the details of NSC-68 remained classified for more than two decades, people in the United States certainly learned about its major assumptions. Led by Secretary of State Acheson, officials from the Truman administration stumped the country, preaching the key tenets of NSC-68 and popularizing its view of the Cold War as a global showdown between good and evil.

The Korean War

Supporters of NSC-68 could claim vindication in June 1950, when communist North Korea invaded South Korea. Truman characterized the attack as a simple case of Soviet-inspired aggression. According to a spokesperson for the State Department, the relationship between the USSR and North Korea resembled "that between Walt Disney and Donald Duck." President Truman invoked the rhetoric of containment and the domino-like vision of NSC-68: "If aggression is successful in Korea, we can expect it to spread through Asia and Europe to this hemisphere."

The situation on the Korean Peninsula, however, was more complicated. Japanese military forces had occupied all of Korea between 1905 and 1945, and Japan's defeat in the Second World War had encouraged most Koreans to hope they might reestablish their own independent nation. Instead, separate zones of occupation, resulting from separate wartime military operations by the United States and the Soviet Union, became two distinct states, with the 38th parallel providing the boundary between them. The Soviet Union supported North Korea's communist government, headed by the dictatorial Kim Il-sung. The United States backed the aging, American-educated Syngman Rhee to head up an unsteady, sometimes autocratic, government in South Korea. Separated by an arbitrary and militarized border, many Koreans saw themselves divided as much by internal political and religious differences as by Cold War considerations. Nonetheless, both Kim and Rhee recognized that patronage from the rival superpowers could help bolster their regimes and advance their conflicting plans for Korea.

As Rhee's policies, especially those favoring large landholders, generated internal opposition, Kim decided on unifying Korea under his control. He gambled that the United States would not, or could not, effectively intervene in Korea. At one point, after all, even the militantly anticommunist Dean Acheson had suggested the Korean peninsula fell outside the U.S. "defense perimeter." On June 25, 1950, Kim's communist troops moved across the 38th parallel into South Korea. Earlier, he had consulted Soviet and Chinese leaders and, after arguing for the likelihood of a quick North Korean victory, received their approval. His South Korean nation under attack, Syngman Rhee appealed to the Truman administration for military assistance. Over the strong opposition of General Omar Bradley, Head of the Joint Chiefs of Staff, supporters of U.S. intervention, led by Nitze and Acheson, prevailed.

The situation quickly escalated into a wider Cold War conflict, the **Korean War.** The Soviets, unaware of the details of Kim's plans, were boycotting the UN on the day North Korea launched its invasion and could not veto a U.S. proposal to send a UN military force, under U.S. command, to Korea. Under UN auspices, the United States rushed assistance to Rhee, who moved to quell dissent in the South as well as to repel the armies of the North.

U.S. leaders soon began debating their goal in Korea. Should they seek only to contain communism by driving North Korea's forces back over the 38th parallel? Or should they try to "roll back" communist power and reunify Korea under Rhee's leadership? Rollback initially seemed fanciful, as North Korean forces pushed rapidly southward. Within three months of their incursion, they took Seoul, the capital of South Korea, and probed into the southern tip of the Korean Peninsula. UN troops, most of them from the United States and under the command of General **Douglas MacArthur,** initially seemed unprepared. Soon, however, U.S.-supplied firepower took its toll on North Korea's elite troops and, later, on the untrained recruits Kim sent to replace them.

MacArthur then devised a plan that most other military commanders considered crazy: an amphibious landing behind enemy lines. Those stunned by his audacious proposal became even more astounded by its results. On September 15, 1950, a sizeable contingent of U.S. Marines landed at Inchon, suffered minimal casualties, and recaptured nearby Seoul in less than two weeks.

The shifting tide of battle devastated Korea. Many observers would call the Korean conflict a "limited" war, largely because it never spread off the Korean Peninsula or involved nuclear weapons. Intense bombing, however, preceded every U.S military move, and neither side seemed concerned about civilian casualties. Estimates of Koreans left dead and wounded reached perhaps one-tenth of the total population of both Koreas. While battling for control of Seoul, for example, rival forces reduced the city to rubble, with only the capitol building and a train station left standing.

As MacArthur's troops drove northward, Truman faced a crucial decision. Emboldened by success, the general urged moving beyond containment to an all-out war of "liberation" and the reunification of Korea. MacArthur's supporters in Washington saw an opportunity to demonstrate the feasibility of junking the policy of merely containing communism in favor of rolling it back. Other advisers warned, however, that Mao's China would likely retaliate if U.S. forces approached its border. After a joint meeting on Wake Island, far closer to MacArthur's home turf than to Truman's, the president did allow MacArthur to carry the war into North Korea but cautioned against provoking China.

Unimpressed by the threat of Chinese intervention, MacArthur advanced his forces to near the Yalu River on the Chinese-Korean border. China responded by sending at least 400,000 troops into North Korea, which forced retreating UN forces back across the 38th parallel. "We face an entirely new war," MacArthur admitted. Alarmists in Washington considered several possibilities: evacuating UN forces from Korea; employing atomic weaponry against China; or, perhaps, even mounting a preemptive nuclear strike against the USSR.

Truman pondered his options. After apparently wavering briefly, he made a crucial decision: It was not the time to employ atomic weapons, in Korea or anywhere else. Then, after MacArthur's troops stopped the Chinese advance and even regained the initiative, Truman also rejected any idea of further escalating the war in favor of settling for a military stalemate at the point where the 38th parallel bisected the Korean Peninsula. General MacArthur, directly challenging the president, argued publicly for an all-out offensive into North Korea—and, possibly, even into China as well. Invoking the principle that the U.S. Constitution made military officers subordinant to the president, the nation's commander-in-chief, a now-angry Harry Truman, summarily relieved MacArthur from his post in April 1951.

MacArthur returned home as a war hero and as a potential Republican presidential candidate. Opinion polls reported overwhelming opposition to Truman's decision to dump the popular general, now a hero of both the Korean and the Second World War. During U.S. Senate hearings on MacArthur's dismissal, however, equally distinguished military strategists dismissed his scenario for Korea as the "wrong war in the wrong place." MacArthur's once luminous image, along with his political ambitions, soon faded away.

Truman mobilized his remaining political resources behind an unsuccessful search for translating a temporary truce into a more permanent peace settlement for Korea. As negotiations stalled, another military hero, Dwight Eisenhower, whom Republicans tapped as their 1952 candidate for president, promised he would personally go to Korea, if elected, and accelerate the peace process. Harry Truman would leave office, in 1953, without securing a formal end to the Korean War.

Korea and Containment

Meanwhile, this conflict brought NSC-68's recommendations to life and spurred the Truman administration to expand its containment initiatives. It announced plans to rearm West Germany, scarcely five years after Nazi Germany's defeat, and to increase NATO's military forces. A proposal for direct U.S. military aid to Latin American governments, which legislators had voted down in the past, slid through Congress. In the Philippines, the United States stepped up military assistance to suppress the leftist Huk rebels. In 1951, the United States finally signed a formal peace treaty with Japan and inked a security pact that gave the United States the power to establish military bases on the Japanese island of Okinawa. The Truman administration acquired similar bases in the Middle East, bolstering the U.S. strategic position in that oil-rich area. The ANZUS mutual defense pact of 1952 linked the United States

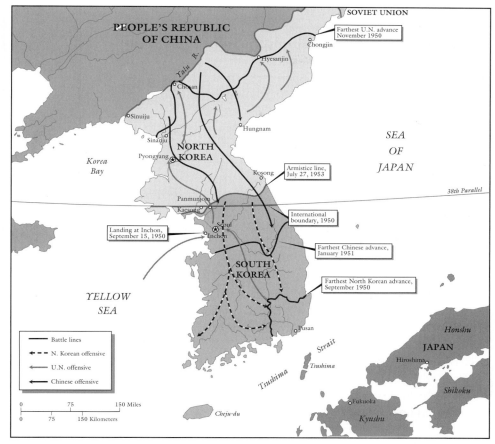

Map 27.3   Korean War   This map shows the lines of battle and the armistice line that still divides the two Koreas. Note the advances made first by North Korea and then by UN (United States-led) troops.
View an animated version of this map or related maps at http://www.thomsonedu.com/history/murrin

strategically to Australia and New Zealand. And in French Indochina, Truman began assisting France's effort to prevent a communist-led independence movement from ousting its colonial regime.

Throughout the world, U.S. policy makers continued to oppose any movement whose political orientation seemed left-leaning and to give support to pro-United States parties and people. The U.S. occupation government in Japan, for example, increasingly restricted the activities of labor unions, suspended an antitrust program that American officials had earlier implemented, and barred communists from posts in the government and in the universities. As in Germany, the United States tried to convert a formerly fascist foe into an anticommunist ally by strengthening pro-U.S. elites and by promoting a U.S. model of economic growth.

In Africa, anticommunism prompted the United States to ally with South Africa. In 1949, that nation's all-white (and militantly anticommunist) Nationalist Party had instituted a legal-social system, called **apartheid,** based on elaborate rules of racial separation and subordination of blacks. Some officials in the State Department warned that any pact with South Africa, by implying support for apartheid, hardly presented the United States as an apostle of freedom, but the Truman administration nonetheless concluded an alliance with South Africa's white supremacist regime.

The Truman administration's anticommunism, again in line with NSC-68, included more than military moves. Truman's global "Campaign of Truth," an intensive informational and psychological offensive, used mass-media imagery and cultural exchanges to counter the Soviet's anticapitalist propaganda. A rhetoric that framed U.S. policy in terms of defending fundamental values took hold. As the Defense Department replaced the old War Department, U.S. policy makers increasingly talked about defending "national security" rather than advancing the "national interest."

Beginning with the Truman Doctrine of 1947, in short, the United States reinvented itself as a superpower with a global reach. In response to the specter of Soviet-led communism, the United States solidified its position within Iran, Greece, and Turkey, all once inside Britain's sphere of influence; initiated the Marshall Plan and NATO; transformed former enemies—Italy, Germany, and Japan—into anti-Soviet bulwarks; assumed control of hundreds of islands in the Pacific Ocean; launched research to develop an H-bomb; winked at apartheid to win an anticommunist ally in South Africa; solidified its sphere of influence in Latin America; acquired military bases around the world; and devised a master plan, NSC-68, for using military, economic, and covert action to advance far-flung national security goals.

As the Truman administration moved to fortify the U.S. strategic position overseas, its policies also produced what the historian Michael Sherry has called "the militarization of American life." With strong bipartisan support in Congress, the White House accelerated what would become a massive military buildup and, as a result, an increasing merger between military and economic policy making. The fight against communism and for greater security, at home and abroad, continually justified the expansion of the power of the governmental bureaucracies charged with protecting national security. Congress granted a new Atomic Energy Commission, for example, broad powers to oversee development of a U.S. nuclear power industry. To develop both the weaponry and the policies implied by a global security strategy, Congress created a think tank— **RAND,** an acronym for Research and Development. The Pentagon joined with aircraft manufacturers in an ultimately successful effort to develop surface-to-surface missiles. The Pentagon's soaring budget and its expensive contracts did worry cost-conscious members of Congress, but the prospect of governmental spending creating new jobs in their home districts helped mute opposition to a foreign policy that emphasized military initiatives.

Pursuing National Security at Home

Focus Question
How did the foreign policy of containment affect domestic policy and American life?

Although bipartisan support for Truman's national security measures overseas generally prevailed, the president's programs for containing subversive influences at home encountered bitter, sustained opposition. Militant anticommunists, sometimes taking their cue from Truman's own rhetoric, leveled increasingly alarming allegations about internal communist subversion and about his administration's unwillingness to respond appropriately. Civil libertarians, on the other hand, continued to complain about "witch-hunts" against people whose only apparent sin seemed dissent from prevailing policy choices. As the political climate became increasingly volatile, even some dedicated anticommunists began to worry that wild goose chases after unlikely subversives could discredit the government's effort to identify authentic Soviet agents. The widespread search for signs of subversion, which took place outside the control of the Truman White House, eventually touched many areas of postwar life.

Anticommunism and the U.S. Labor Movement

The issue of anticommunism, for example, helped unsettle the U.S. labor movement. After the end of the Second World War, militant workers had struck for increased wages and for a greater voice in workplace routines and production decisions. Labor strikes had brought both the auto and the electronics industries to a standstill. In Stamford, Connecticut, and Lancaster, Pennsylvania, general strikes had led to massive work stoppages that later spread to other U.S. large cities. After the president threatened to seize mines and railroads shut down by work stoppages and to order strikers back to work, labor militancy slowly began to subside.

Unimpressed, the Republican-controlled Congress effectively tapped anticommunist sentiment to pass the Labor-Management Relations Act of 1947. Opponents of the law, popularly known as the Taft-Hartley Act, charged that it seemed to have more to do with countering gains made by organized labor during the 1930s than with combating communism. It limited a union's power to conduct boycotts, to compel employers to accept "closed shops" in which only union members could be hired, and to conduct any strike that the president judged harmful to national security. In addition, the measure required that union officials sign affidavits stating that they did not belong to the Communist Party or to any other "subversive" organization. If a union refused to comply, it could lose some of the legal protections otherwise available under national labor laws. Truman vetoed Taft-Hartley, but Congress swiftly overrode him. By the end of the Truman era, some type of loyalty-security check had been conducted on about 20 percent of the U.S. workforce, more than 13 million people.

Instructors on Strike   Employees of an Arthur Murray Dance Studio in New York City demonstrate both the conga, a popular Latin American dance style in 1947, and their determination to form a union affiliated with Local 16 of the United Office and Professional Workers of America. During the immediate postwar period, workers in a wide range of occupations mounted strikes to secure higher wages, better conditions, and greater job security through unionization campaigns.

Anticommunism also affected both internal union politics and labor-management relations. Some workers had long charged communist organizers with displaying greater loyalty to the Communist Party than to their own unions or to the nation. Differences over whether to support the Democratic Party or Henry Wallace's Progressive effort in 1948 had embittered relations within the organized labor movement. During the years following Truman's victory, the Congress of Industrial Organizations (CIO) expelled 13 unions—a full third of its membership—for their political ties. In addition, outspoken labor activists discovered that their ideas about politics and economics, if they seemed to resemble communist tenets, could put their own jobs at risk. The anticommunist issue, forcefully invoked by businesspeople and conservative labor leaders, increasingly found its way into labor-management relations during the 1940s.

HUAC and the Search for Subversives

The entertainment industry attracted special attention. In 1947, only three days after Truman unveiled his famous Doctrine, the **House Un-American Activities Committee (HUAC)** opened hearings into subversive influences in Hollywood. Basking in the gaze of newsreel cameras, committee members seized on the refusal of a group of screenwriters, producers, and directors—all current or former members of the American Communist Party—to testify about their own politics and that of others in the film community. Known as "the Hollywood Ten," this group claimed that the First Amendment barred HUAC from scrutinizing political convictions. The federal courts upheld HUAC's investigative powers, however, and the Hollywood Ten eventually went to prison for contempt of Congress.

Studio heads also drew up a secret **blacklist,** a directory of alleged subversives whom they agreed not to hire. Movie moguls denied the existence of such a list, but their disavowals sounded unconvincing. As the staunchly anticommunist actor and producer John Wayne later conceded, "The only thing our side did that was anywhere near blacklisting was just running a lot of people out of the business." Leaders in other sectors of the entertainment industry, particularly television, adopted a similar policy. Although prominent celebrities such as the Hollywood Ten dominated media accounts of blacklisting activities, many anonymous labor union members, who worked behind the scenes in technical and support positions, also lost their source of livelihood in the entertainment business.

In time, hundreds of people charged with being subversives found their employment prospects resting on their willingness to appear as "friendly witnesses" before HUAC or some similar investigative committee. There, investigators would require witnesses to provide the names of other people who supposedly had attended a pro-communist meeting or event, usually at some point during an increasingly distant past. Some of those called to testify, such as the writer Lillian Hellman, refused to answer any questions. Others, such as the director Elia Kazan, cooperated and agreed to "name names." Individual decisions over whether to participate in the ritualistic process of naming names created personal anguish and political rancor that would divide members of the entertainment business and labor union movement for decades.

The search for subversives also created new political celebrities. Ronald Reagan, who served as president of the Screen Actors Guild and as a secret informant for the FBI (identified as "T-10"), eagerly testified before HUAC about communist influences within the movie industry. Richard Nixon, once an obscure member of Congress from California, began his rapid political ascent when he backed Whittaker Chambers, a journalist formally active in communist circles. Chambers, newly repentant and staunchly anticommunist, came before HUAC in 1948. He charged **Alger Hiss,** a prominent Democrat with a lengthy career in public service, with having been a party member who had slipped classified information to Soviet agents during the late 1930s.

The Hiss-Chambers-Nixon affair instantly sparked controversy. Hiss charged anticommunist zealots, expecially in the FBI, with framing him with bogus evidence, including documents Chambers had retrieved from a pumpkin patch on his farm. The federal government, legally barred from indicting Hiss on espionage charges, successfully prosecuted him for committing perjury while testifying before Congress. To Nixon and his supporters, the case of Alger Hiss, who had advised FDR during the Yalta Conference (see chapter 26), demonstrated the

It's Okay—We're Hunting Communists This 1947 "Herblock" (Herbert Block)
cartoon presents a critical view of the impact of HUAC's communist-hunting.

need for greater vigor in hunting down subversively inclined Democrats in Washington. Hiss
and his supporters, however, would continue to stick to their frame-up story.

During the mid-1990s, the availability of long-classified documents prompted an
extensive, extra-legal review of the Hiss controversy. A small group of scholars contended
that the evidentiary trail left unsettled the key questions of what precise information Hiss
might have revealed—and under what circumstances. Most observers, however, concluded that substantial evidence suggested that Hiss and several other high-ranking governmental officials had likely passed some information to the Soviets during the 1930s and
1940s and subsequently lied about their actions. Armed with an enhanced documentary
record, then, historians continue to debate the details of individual causes, including that
of Alger Hiss, into a new century.

Elaborating its own anti-subversive efforts, the Truman administration implemented its
loyalty program and dismissed hundreds of federal employees. In addition, Truman's

attorney general, Tom Clark (whom the president later appointed to the U.S. Supreme Court), authorized J. Edgar Hoover, head of the FBI, to compile a secret FBI file of alleged subversives whom the government could then detain, without any legal hearing, during a time of national emergency.

Fears that subversives from overseas might immigrate to the United States prompted Congress to pass the McCarran-Walter Act of 1952. It empowered U.S. immigration officials to deny entry to persons they determined could endanger national security by bringing dangerous ideas into the country. The law also authorized the deportation of immigrants, even those who had gained U.S. citizenship, if they belonged to organizations on the Attorney General's List.

At the same time, Hoover's FBI compiled its own confidential dossiers on a wide range of people. It often targeted artists and intellectuals, including some, such as Ernest Hemingway and John Steinbeck, with no ties to the Communist Party. The FBI and other federal agencies paid special attention to prominent African Americans. The FBI kept close tabs, for instance, on a wide range of civil-rights activists, including Bayard Rustin, a founder of CORE (see chapter 26). The U.S. State Department and immigration officials singled out Richard Wright (author of the acclaimed novel *Native Son*), W. E. B. Du Bois (the nation's most celebrated African American historian), and Paul Robeson (a well-known entertainer-activist) because of their links to the U.S. Communist Party and their identification with anti-imperialist and antiracist organizations throughout the world. In addition, suspicions of homosexuality could make people, including the only nominally closeted Rustin, into targets for governmental surveillance and discriminatory treatment.

Targeting Difference

Public signs of homosexual behavior, as the stance adopted by Bayard Rustin suggested, increased during the postwar era. Continuing a trend begun during the Second World War, more visible and assertive gay and lesbian subcultures emerged, particularly in larger cities such as New York and San Francisco. Dr. Alfred Kinsey's controversial research on sexual behavior—his first volume, on male sexuality, appeared in 1948—suggested that U.S. life included far more same-sex relationships than previous studies had ever imagined. Kinsey's volumes, which attracted considerable popular attention, claimed to find people pursuing a wide range of sexual behaviors, ranging from exclusively heterosexual to exclusively homosexual. In late 1952, the issue of transsexuality hit the headlines when the press revealed that, after a series of "sex-change" operations in Europe, George W. Jorgensen, Jr. had become a "blonde beauty," Christine Jorgensen.

By this time, in response to aggressive policing practices and to laws that criminalized homosexual behavior, a small "homophile" movement, aimed at combating legal discrimination, had emerged. Gays formed the Mattachine Society (in 1950), and lesbians later founded the Daughters of Bilitis, organizations that advocated equal rights for homosexuals. Why should the law of the land only protect sexual acts and social relationships generally viewed as "normal," these activists cautiously asked?

Meanwhile, an aggressive effort to contain these signs of homosexuality gained ground. *The Kinsey Report*'s implicit claim that homosexuality might be seen as simply another form of sexuality, alongside the discreet militancy of the Mattachine Society and the Daughters of Bilitis, helped fuel this campaign. The fact that several founders of the Mattachine Society had also been members of the Communist Party, coupled with the claim that Soviet agents could more easily blackmail homosexuals than heterosexuals, helped identify homosexuality as a threat to national security. "One homosexual can pollute a Government office," in much the same way as could a person with communist ideas, claimed a report from the U.S. Senate.

Now, historians of sexuality see a "Lavender Scare" about homosexuality accompanying the "Red Scare" about communism. Popular imagery, for example, portrayed both homosexuality and communism as subversive "diseases" that inwardly "sick" people, who seemed outwardly little different than other Americans, could spread throughout the body politic. It would take, according to this logic, sustained inquiries by knowledgeable experts to uncover all of the subversive communists and homosexuals working in sensitive positions in the U.S. government. Suspicion of "sexual deviance" became an acceptable basis for subjecting government employees to loyalty board hearings and, ultimately, denying them the same legal-constitutional protections enjoyed by heterosexuals.

The "Great Fear"

Some cultural historians view the search for subversives during the late 1940s and early 1950s unfolding against a backdrop of a widespread anxiety they call the "Great Fear." The very real events that energized the Truman administration, such as atomic tests by the Soviets, also heightened the emotional impact of stories about communist agents having stolen U.S. nuclear secrets or about gay subversives shaping U.S. foreign policy. A growing sense of insecurity, in turn, spurred even greater efforts to safeguard national security.

As this feeling of anxiety began to settle over U.S. politics, the U.S. Justice Department arrested, in 1950, several members of an alleged spy ring. Julius and Ethel Rosenberg, both members of the American Communist Party, became the central characters in this controversial episode.

The Rosenberg case, as with that of Hiss, became a Cold War melodrama. Their trial, the verdicts of guilty, the sentences of death, the numerous legal appeals, the worldwide protests, and their 1953 executions at Sing Sing Prison all provoked intense controversy. Could the Rosenbergs, the parents of two young children, have been involved in the theft of nuclear secrets? And if so, were their death sentences, on the charge of espionage, the constitutionally appropriate punishment? To their supporters, the Rosenbergs (who died maintaining their innocence) became symbols of how easily anticommunist hysteria could override rational analysis and legal-constitutional safeguards. Federal officials seemed primarily interested in calming the Great Fear by locating—and then sacrificing—convenient scapegoats. To others, however, the evidence presented at the couple's trial clearly showed that they had channeled nuclear information to the Soviets.

New cartloads of documents, including those that became available in the 1990s, have helped to focus, without quite ending, controversy over the Rosenberg case. The evidentiary record, as most historians now view it, demonstrates Julius Rosenberg's involvement in some kind of spying and Ethel Rosenberg's knowledge about his activities. Studies of other Cold War spy cases, however, also suggest that the U.S. government declined even to indict people who almost certainly had passed on important atomic-related information to the Soviets. In some instances, officials apparently feared a court trial would have revealed ongoing counter-espionage operations by the United States. Among all the people actually prosecuted for involvement with the Soviets, moreover, only Julius and Ethel Rosenberg faced a charge that carried the death penalty. Questions about precisely what information Julius Rosenberg helped convey to the USSR and how useful it actually proved to Soviet nuclear scientists also remain at issue.

The performance of the U.S. justice system during the Great Fear became another matter for sustained debate. How well did U.S. courts balance legitimate concerns about safeguarding national security with the protection of civil liberties? During the 1949 prosecution of leaders of the American Communist Party, for instance, the trial judge accepted Truman's Justice Department's claim that merely holding a leadership position in this political party helped further an international conspiracy against the United States and the larger "free world." The Marxist ideology of the American Communist Party and its theoretical publications, even in the absence of any proof of subversive *acts* by individual defendants, justified convicting the party's leaders of having committed the crime of sedition against the U.S. government.

This case eventually went to the U.S. Supreme Court and produced the landmark decision of *Dennis* v. *U.S.* (1951). Civil libertarians insisted that the government failed to present any evidence that Communist Party publications and speeches, by themselves, posed a "clear and present danger" to national security. In this view, the beliefs of the members of any political group, even an avowedly communist one, enjoyed the protection of the First Amendment. The government, in short, could only put actions, not ideas or political preferences, on trial. Although two dissenting Supreme Court justices adopted versions of this position, the majority modified the High Court's own "clear and present danger" doctrine and upheld the broader view of sedition-by-expression earlier advanced by the Truman administration and lower federal courts.

Even before the *Dennis* case reached the Supreme Court, however, the anticommunist credentials of Truman administration were drawing increased scrutiny from more zealous red-hunters. In Congress, most Republicans and many Democrats, denouncing Truman's initiatives as too limited, joined to pass the McCarran Internal Security Act of 1950. It authorized the detention, during any national emergency, of alleged subversives in special camps. It also created the Subversive Activities Control Board (SACB) to investigate organizations suspected of links to the Communist Party and to oversee registration of groups allegedly controlled by communists.

The Truman administration responded ambiguously. Although the president vetoed the McCarran Internal Security Act—a symbolic response that Congress quickly overrode—his administration authorized the FBI's J. Edgar Hoover to devise a secret detention program, which contained even fewer procedural safeguards than the one created by Congress, and continued to enforce its own loyalty program. Still, Truman could never defuse doubts about his anticommunist credentials and those of key members of his administration.

McCarthyism

Republican Senator Joseph McCarthy of Wisconsin eventually emerged as the Truman administration's primary accuser. An intelligence officer during the Second World War, McCarthy had entered national politics in the guise of a battle-hardened combat vet, "Tailgunner Joe." Enjoying a meteoric rise, which took him to the U.S. Senate in 1946, the rough-hewn McCarthy apparently preferred to be known as a brawler and boozer than as a legislator. The Great Fear, however, helped McCarthy refashion himself as a hard-driving, two-fisted anticommunist investigator, one who seemingly leaped out from the pages of a hard-boiled detective thriller.

In a famous 1950 speech at Wheeling, West Virginia, McCarthy charged Truman's State Department with employing hundreds of known communists. People rightly feared the future, according to McCarthy, "not because our only powerful potential enemy has sent men to invade our shores, but rather because of the traitorous actions of those who have been treated so well by this Nation." The people in this camp, according to McCarthy, included Secretary of State Acheson and his predecessor, General George C. Marshall.

A master of political imagery and sexual innuendo, McCarthy subtly linked together the Lavender and Red Scares. He portrayed anticommunists in Truman's administration as both overly privileged and insufficiently manly. Dean Acheson and his aides might pose as hard-headed realists who understood the dangers of communism, but McCarthy dismissed their claims. Lacking the all-around toughness of authentic anticommunists (such as the Wisconsin senator himself), people such as Acheson, who had been "born with silver spoons in their mouths," had degenerated into effete "enemies from within." To accentuate the secretary of state's supposed lack of manliness, McCarthy derided Acheson as the "Red Dean of fashion" and as the leader of the "lace handkerchief crowd."

By the final years of Truman's presidency, McCarthy seemed an unstoppable political force. Although McCarthy failed to substantiate most of his charges or to identify specific violations of the law, he lacked neither imagination nor potential targets. During the summer of 1950, a subcommittee of the U.S. Senate, after examining government files, concluded that McCarthy's charges against the State Department amounted to "the most nefarious campaign of half-truths and untruths in the history of this republic." McCarthy simply charged that the files had been "raped," and he went after Millard Tydings, the courtly Democratic senator who had chaired the subcommittee. The defeat of Tydings, whose opponents circulated a fabricated photograph linking him to pro-communist activities, in the November 1950 election seemed to confirm McCarthy's political clout and lack of scruples.

McCarthy's tactics produced considerable controversy. Despite his apparent recklessness, some influential people tolerated and even encouraged him. Conservative, staunchly anticommunist leaders within the Roman Catholic Church, for instance, embraced McCarthy, who was a Catholic. Leading Republicans welcomed McCarthy's assaults on their Democratic rivals. In contrast, the historically minded among the senator's opponents saw him as the latest personification of a form of populist-style demagoguery, which became labelled **"McCarthyism."**

The National Security Constitution

Too much attention to the theatrics of McCarthyism, however, can obscure long-term political-constitutional shifts during the era of the Great Fear. Widespread concern about national security helped U.S. leaders refashion the nation's structure of governance. The sovereign people ratified only one addition to the formal, written Constitution during this era: The 22nd Amendment, adopted in 1951, responded to Roosevelt's election to third and fourth terms in the White House by limiting future presidents to two terms. But congressional legislation, especially the National Security Act of 1947 and the assumption of new powers by executive branch agencies—particularly the CIA, FBI, and the Pentagon—effectively changed the nation's constitutional structure and its approach to governance. The view that the presidency possessed only limited powers gave way to an opposing vision, which had been voiced during earlier times of perceived crisis such as the Second World War. Cold War conditions provided renewed justification for greatly extending the power of the national government, especially of the executive branch.

When Truman took the United States into a congressionally undeclared war in Korea, he encountered few constitutional obstacles. The idea of constitutional limitations only came into play after he asserted his presidential authority in 1952 and ordered his commerce secretary to seize control of the domestic steel industry in order to prevent a threatened strike. Truman could have invoked the Taft-Hartley Act to obtain a 60-day "cooling off" period, but he resisted using a measure he had earlier (and unsuccessfully) vetoed. Truman claimed, in effect, that the Cold War had dramatically changed constitutional practice. The president, the nation's commander-in-chief, possessed virtually unlimited power whenever safeguarding national security required emergency action.

The "steel seizure case" (officially known as *Youngstown Sheet & Tube Company* v. *Sawyer*) quickly reached the U.S. Supreme Court. There, three justices, all Truman appointees, agreed with the president's claims of emergency executive powers. Six other justices, for differing reasons, rejected Truman's position as too broadly framed, but all expressed significant support, whenever national security issues came into play, for somewhat less expansive views of presidential authority. Most constitutional scholars would come to see this 1952 case as a short-term defeat for Truman but hardly a long-term setback for national-security powers.

Truman's Fair Deal

Focus Question

What were the guiding assumptions of the Fair Deal, and which of its major initiatives seemed likely to pass through Congress? Which proposals seemed likely to stall there, and why?

Meanwhile, Harry Truman needed to operate within relatively narrow political boundaries when his administration left the national security arena and entered that of social welfare policy making. Truman's policy initiatives, which culminated in what the White House would call the Fair Deal, grew out of the Democratic Party's effort to frame a domestic agenda for the post-New Deal era.

Truman claimed to share much of Franklin Roosevelt's earlier vision. Many Democrats thus pressed him to embrace an expansive view, such as that set forth in FDR's Second Bill of Rights (1944) (see chapter 26), of how the national government might enhance the everyday security of ordinary citizens. Following the Second World War, after all, most Western European nations were creating or expanding their own "welfare states." These systems of governance, based on the principle and practice of using economic and social planning to guarantee all citizens certain substantive rights, such as access to adequate housing and medical care, featured an aggressive use of state power.

In the United States, however, proposals for governmental planning and new social welfare measures generally stalled. Critics had already assailed wartime Washington's extensive use of governmental power to regulate economic relationships as unnecessary and in conflict with the U.S. Constitution. During Truman's presidency, opposition to the kind of expansive social agenda suggested in FDR's Second Bill of Rights grew stronger. Any attempt to update the New Deal agenda for a postwar world, insisted most Republicans and some Democrats, could provide dangerous precedents for unconstitutionally trampling on private rights and erode traditional ideas about individual initiative and responsibility. Dixiecrat Democrats, for example, often joined with conservative Republicans to block any congressional legislation that might give Washington additional economic powers on the theory that such a move might imply analogous authority to begin dismantling white supremacy in the South. Weighing in on behalf of powerful business interests, the National Association of Manufacturers (NAM) consistently denounced the Truman administration as a menace to the nation's private, free-enterprise economic system.

The Employment Act of 1946 and the Promise of Economic Growth

The Truman administration, faced with this kind of opposition to economic planning and European-style welfare policies, sought an alternative vision of domestic social policy making. The 1946 debate over a "Full Employment Bill" provided it. This measure, as initially conceived, would have empowered Washington to ensure employment for all citizens seeking work. To the bill's opponents, the phrase "full employment" implied a step toward the European model of a welfare state, perhaps even toward socialism.

As the Democratic effort to enact this measure lost momentum, a scaled-back version moved forward. The law that Congress finally passed, renamed the Employment Act of 1946, called for "maximum" (rather than full) employment and specifically declared that private enterprise, not government, bore primary responsibility for economic decision making. The act nonetheless created a new executive branch body, the Council of Economic Advisers, to formulate long-range policy recommendations, and it thus signaled that the national government would assume some still undefined responsibility for the health and performance of the U.S. economy.

Moreover, the Employment Act of 1946 suggested that economic expertise now provided a vital national resource. The idea that *advice* from economic experts, as an alternative to government *planning,* could guarantee a constantly expanding economy helped muster crucial support for creating the Council of Economic Advisers. An influential group of economists, many of them disciples of Britain's John Maynard Keynes, pressed for this move. Their economic know-how, they claimed, could help government eliminate the boom-and-bust cycles that had long afflicted the nation's economy. Instead of abandoning the economy to the largely uncoordinated decisions of private individuals and corporations, economic expertise could help governmental and business leaders identify the policies most likely to produce growth.

The promise of economic expansion quickly came to dazzle postwar leaders. Using the relatively new measure of gross national product (GNP), economists claimed they could objectively calculate the nation's growing economic bounty. Developed in 1939, GNP—defined as the total dollar value of all goods and services produced in the nation during a given year—became the standard gauge of economic health. Corporate executives, who had generally feared that the end of the war would bring long-term labor unrest and trigger a deep recession, came to view a rising GNP as an important predictor of social stability. The Truman administration's domestic policy makers also welcomed the prospect of an expanding economy, which would automatically increase federal tax revenues and, thus, help remove some of the political obstacles blocking the financial path for the administration's domestic agenda. "With economic expansion, every problem is capable of solution," insisted one celebrant of economic growth. Another likened the promise of ongoing growth to finding the proverbial rainbow *and* the pot of gold at its end.

Truman and his advisers enthusiastically spread the gospel of governmentally stimulated economic growth. This new faith nicely dovetailed with the spending levels their national security plans required. The Cold War could serve as "an automatic pump primer" for the U.S. economy. At the same time, security-related assistance programs such as the Marshall Plan could create overseas markets and investment opportunities for U.S. businesses. The goal of sustained economic growth at home, in short, became linked to development in the world at large—and to the all-pervasive concern about protecting U.S. national security. Sharp increases in governmental spending for the Pentagon thus signaled a general economic policy that critical observers eventually began to call "military Keynesianism"—the practice of stimulating and regulating the economy through governmental spending in the military sector. *U.S. News and World Report*, a conservative weekly, suggested that government officials seemed to "have found the magic formula for almost endless good times."

Shaping the Fair Deal

In 1949, Truman unveiled a set of social welfare proposals he called the Fair Deal. He proposed extending popular New Deal programs, particularly Social Security and minimum wage laws; enacting legislation dealing with civil rights, national health care, and federal aid for education; and repealing the Taft-Hartley Act of 1947. The president also urged substantial spending on public housing projects, and his secretary of agriculture called for new governmental subsidies to support farm prices. The core assumption on which Truman built his entire Fair Deal—that sustained economic growth could finance enlarged government programs for specifically targeted groups—came to dominate policy planning. Changes to two prominent programs, both of which predated Truman's administration, illustrate the approach to domestic social policy that became standard procedure during the Fair Deal years.

The first, the so-called **GI Bill** (officially titled the Serviceman's Readjustment Act of 1944), provided a comprehensive social benefit package but only for those people who had served in the armed forces. Far more inclusive and clearly defined than programs for veterans of previous wars, the GI Bill gained crucial support from the conservative leadership of the American Legion. The law provided vets with financial assistance for college and job-training programs. Slightly more than 50 percent of veterans sought such funds, and during 1947, the year of peak enrollment, roughly half of the nation's entire college and university population received aid under the GI Bill. In addition, it gave veterans preferential treatment when applying for government jobs; favorable financial terms when borrowing money to purchase homes or businesses; and, eventually, comprehensive medical care in hospitals run by the Veterans Administration (VA). The Veterans Readjustment Assistance Act of 1952, popularly known as the GI Bill of Rights, extended these benefits to those who had served in the Korean War. The Truman administration never revived FDR's proposal for a Second Bill of Rights, but the Fair Deal did ensure that veterans would enjoy some of its key provisions.

The Social Security program also expanded during Truman's Fair Deal. Rebutting attacks against this New Deal measure by conservatives who denounced it as a poorly designed and unwarranted extension of federal power, advocates of Social Security stressed its carefully targeted provisions. Certainly, people who were disabled and blind deserved assistance, and older people had surely earned the "income security" provided by Social Security through their years of work and the monetary contributions withheld from their own paychecks. Under the Social Security Act of 1950, the level of benefits increased significantly; the retirement-related portions of the program became more flexible; and

The Postwar College Scene   This picture by the famed photojournalist Margaret Bourke-White shows veterans of the Second World War dominating available space in a classroom at the University of Iowa. Tapping financial support offered under the GI Bill (1944), more than 600 vets enrolled in 1946 at Iowa. Returning servicemen, who comprised more than 60 percent of this University's total enrollment, often taxed existing facilities here and at other universities throughout the country.

more than 10 million additional people, including agricultural workers, came into the Social Security system.

The Fair Deal's more expansive (and more expensive) proposals, however, either failed to gain congressional approval or passed in scaled-back form. Truman's plan for a comprehensive national health insurance program faced opposition from several different quarters. Consumer groups and labor unions, intent on creating nonprofit, community-run health plans, generally saw Truman's proposal for a centralized health system as a blueprint for unnecessarily bureaucratizing medical care. From a different perspective, the American Medical Association (AMA) and the American Hospital Association (AHA) opposed any direct governmental intervention in the traditional fee-for-service medical system and steered Congress toward a less intrusive alternative—expanding the federal financing of new hospitals under the previously enacted Hill-Burton Act (1946). In addition, large insurance companies, which were continuing to push their own private plans in cooperation with businesses (see chapter 26), also weighed in against the Truman plan. Opinion polls suggested that many voters, especially those who could enroll in affordable private health insurance plans such as the popular Blue Cross and Blue Shield systems, found themselves confused by or simply uninterested in Truman's initiative.

The Fair Deal's housing proposals met a similarly mixed reception. The severe postwar shortage of affordable housing in urban areas did stir some support for Washington's participation in home-building programs. Even some conservative Republicans, notably Senator Robert Taft of Ohio, supported the Housing Act of 1949 as a necessary response to a postwar housing pinch. Part of Truman's Fair Deal package, this measure authorized construction of 810,000 public housing units and provided federal funds for "urban renewal" zones, areas to be cleared of rundown dwellings and then rebuilt with new construction. The Housing Act of 1949 proclaimed ambitious goals but provided relatively modest funding, especially for its public-housing component. Private construction firms and realtors welcomed funding for urban renewal and for federal home loan guarantee programs such as those established under the GI Bill and those directed by the Federal Housing Administration (FHA). At the same time, they continually lobbied effectively against a more extensive program of publicly financed housing projects.

The Fair Deal, in short, proved most successful in advancing narrowly targeted social welfare measures. This meant the Truman administration provided significant assistance to veterans and to older Americans but failed to achieve its more ambitious goals of national health care and public housing construction. With opponents of the broader Fair Deal proposals dismissing them as "welfare schemes," the White House found it easier to advance the narrower initiatives that it could defend as fiscally sound "security" measures for specifically delineated groups of deserving recipients.

Civil Rights

The Truman administration also struggled to place at least some of the national government's power behind a growing civil-rights movement. A global struggle against the fascism of the Axis Powers had earlier assisted domestic campaigns against discrimination (see chapter 26), and subsequent efforts benefited from the postwar battle against communism. After returning to the home front, few service personnel of African, Latino, and Native American descent wished to remain passive bystanders when public laws and policing practices sometimes reduced them to second-class citizens. Moreover, people of color who had moved to larger cities, seeking to escape discrimination and find wartime employment, not only wanted to secure but to build on the social and economic gains they and their families had made during the earlier 1940s. Drives to translate the vision of liberty and equality on prominent display in FDR's Second Bill of Rights into reality also continued to animate some lawyers and grassroots activists during the immediate postwar period. The national government, from their perspectives, needed to mobilize its powerful resources to fight discrimination and injustice in the Cold War United States.

During his 1948 presidential campaign, Truman strongly endorsed the proposals of a civil-rights committee he had established in 1946. Its controversial report, entitled "To Secure These Rights," called for federal legislation against lynching; creation of a special civil-rights division within the Department of Justice; adoption of new initiatives against discrimination in employment, housing, and public facilities; and a plan for desegregating the U.S. military. These proposals had helped prompt the Dixiecrat revolt of 1948, but they also gained Truman significant support from African Americans and Latinos.

Truman continued to support the civil-rights cause. When successive congresses failed to enact legislation against lynching and poll taxes, which prevented most southern blacks from voting, leaders of the civil-rights movement turned to the White House and to the federal courts. The threat by A. Philip Randolph, head of the Brotherhood of Sleeping Car Porters, to work with activists such as Bayard Rustin in organizing a protest campaign, pushed Truman to issue an executive order, in 1948, which set in motion a gradual phasing out of the military's system of racial segregation.

Much as the antifascist environment of the Second World War had forced the Roosevelt administration to address some civil-rights issues, the Cold War climate helped energize Truman's Fair Dealers. Truman spoke candidly about how much legalized segregation tarnished the image of the United States in a Cold War world "which is 90 percent colored." Although the Cold War could help justify action against African American leaders whom governmental officials considered linked to subversive causes, it also made the federal government's tacit support of Jim Crow a foreign policy liability. Continuing efforts to preserve racialized segregation, spearheaded by Dixiecrats from the South, seemed in direct conflict with Washington's claim to represent liberty and equality in a world threatened by Soviet totalitarianism. The symbol of U.S. constitutional law still upholding racial separatism worked to the advantage of attorneys for the NAACP and for Latino groups such as LULAC, when they mounted court challenges against discriminatory measures, especially in the field of public education.

Lawyers from Truman's Justice Department appeared in court to support suits brought by civil-rights organizations. Working in concert, attorneys made the case against government-backed public school segregation and against "restrictive covenants" (legal agreements that prevented racial or religious minorities from acquiring real estate). In 1946, the Supreme Court declared restrictive covenants unconstitutional and began chipping away at the "separate-but-equal" principle, used since *Plessy* v. *Ferguson* (1896) to justify the legality of racially segregated public schools. A federal court in California, ruling on the case brought the previous year in Orange County by LULAC and the NAACP, held that segregating students of Mexican descent in separate, and unequal, schools violated their constitutional rights. According to one of the federal courts that heard this case—as *Mendez* v. *Westminster School District* in 1946—a separate school system could never pass constitutional muster, especially in a nation that had only recently emerged victorious over Nazi racism. The practice of "co-mingling" a diverse student body within the same educational institution "instills and develops a common cultural attitude," which would be "imperative for the perpetuation of American institutions and ideals," the court argued.

Subsequent court rulings cast further doubt on the future of the *Plessy* precedent. In 1948, a second federal court—with the case now entitled *Westminster School District* v. *Mendez*—agreed with the first: segregating Mexican-descended students violated their constitutional rights. Two years later, in cases involving students of African descent, the U.S. Supreme Court ruled unconstitutional, under the 14th Amendment, racial segregation in state-financed graduate and law schools. The familiar arguments used to legitimate racial segregation in other areas of public education now seemed ripe for successful constitutional challenges.

The years immediately after the Second World War, in sum, marked a turning point in domestic policy making. The New Deal's vision of comprehensive socioeconomic planning gave way to the Fair Deal's view: The nation could expect that uninterrupted economic growth would enable Washington to finance, through rising tax revenues, programs designed to assist specific groups. As one supporter of this approach argued, postwar policy makers were sophisticated enough to embrace "partial remedies," such as the GI Bill, rather than to wait for fanciful "cure-alls," such as FDR's Second Bill of Rights. Partisans of the Fair Deal hoped that at least some of these limited programs could be expanded in the years to come.

Signs of a Changing Culture

> ### Focus Question
> How did a resurgent civil-rights movement and a new suburban culture help signal changes in American life during the immediate postwar era?

The postwar years also accelerated the pace of cultural change. Encouraged by the advertising industry, most people seemed, at one level, to view most things new and novel as signs of progress. Yet, at another level, the speed and scope of cultural change generated widespread feelings of uneasiness and anxiety, which likely contributed to the Great Fear about subversion.

The Baseball "Color Line"

The complex interplay between celebrating and fearing change can be seen in the effort, during the 1940s and early 1950s, to desegregate the sport-entertainment business known as Organized Baseball. In 1947, the national pastime finally abandoned its policy of racial segregation when Jack Roosevelt (**Jackie**) **Robinson**, a multi-sport star at UCLA who had later played baseball in the Negro National League, took over first base for the Brooklyn Dodgers. Some ballplayers of European descent, including several in Robinson's own club, considered a boycott. Baseball's leadership, seeking new sources of on-field talent and seeing a steady stream of African American fans coming through the turnstiles, quickly displayed the power it could wield over its labor force. It squelched dissent by threatening to suspend any player who refused to play with or against Robinson.

Officially, Organized Baseball desegregated. Shortly after Robinson's debut, the Cleveland Indians acquired center fielder Larry Doby and, somewhat later, the already legendary hurler, Leroy (Satchel) Paige. Other top-flight players abandoned the Negro leagues for clubs in the American and National circuits. The skills of Robinson, named Rookie of the Year in 1947 and the National League's Most Valuable Player in 1949, and other players of African descent quickly carried the day. Although talented light-skinned Latinos had long passed through the racial barrier, Orestes ("Minnie") Minoso, a Cuban-born veteran of the Negro Leagues, became the first Afro-Latino to break into the Big Leagues in 1949. Close students of the game soon credited players such as Robinson and Minoso, fleet-footed and daring base runners, with reintroducing an aggressive style of play to a sport that had come to emphasize home runs and a base-to-base approach to scoring runs.

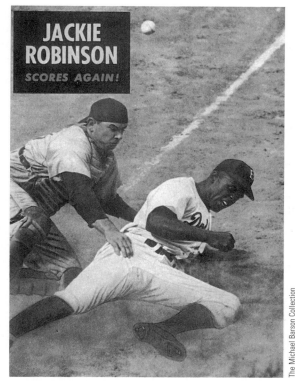

The Michael Barson Collection

Jackie Robinson   In 1947, Jackie Robinson joined the Brooklyn Dodgers and became the first African American since the 19th century to play major league baseball. He had served as a lieutenant in the Army during the Second World War. Racial integration of the national pastime of baseball became a powerful symbol of progress in race relations.

Major League teams began fielding greater numbers of African American and Latino players, and some mounted extensive recruiting operations in Mexico and throughout the Caribbean. Years later, during the 50th anniversary of Robinson's debut, Major League Baseball would stage elaborate memorial ceremonies for Robinson, who had died in 1972, and would congratulate itself for having been at the forefront of the fight against racial prejudice during the Cold War years.

As historians generally note, however, baseball's Cold War leadership had unofficially limited its own desegregation effort. It allowed several teams—which claimed, improbably, that they could find no talented African American or Latino prospects—to wait years before integrating their rosters. More commonly, clubs restricted the number of African American and Latino players they would take on and adopted a Jim Crow policy for hiring managers, coaches, and front-office personnel. When age forced Jackie Robinson's retirement as a player, for instance, he found himself effectively shut out of the game he had earlier helped integrate.

Even many of the players who followed in Robinson's on-field footsteps confronted continuing obstacles. African American and Latino players, who faced subtle barriers while competing for a spot on a Major League roster, often encountered overt, off-the-field discrimination during the annual spring training period in the South and Southwest. Young prospects endured similar problems while playing for minor league teams, generally located in relatively small towns with few services or businesses that catered to people of color. Spanish-speaking players faced special difficulties that extended beyond language. Even stars such as Minoso, accustomed to playing top-quality baseball in the Negro Leagues and Caribbean winter leagues, struggled to convince managers, sportswriters, and teammates (African Americans as well as Caucasians) that they could "understand" the subtleties of either the "national pastime" or of the larger North American culture.

New Suburban Developments

The culture of postwar suburbia also showed how the celebration of cultural change and a resistance to its impact could coexist in an uneasy tension. Suburbs had long been part of the national landscape. During the late 1940s, however, suburban living came within the means of millions of families. The new Long Island town of Levittown, New York, which welcomed its first residents in October 1947, quickly became the preeminent symbol of postwar suburban culture.

Nearly everything about Levittown seemed unprecedented. Levitt & Sons, a construction company that had mass-produced military barracks during the Second World War, claimed to be completing a five-room bungalow every 15 minutes. Architectural critics might sneer at these "little boxes," but potential buyers would brave long lines for a chance to purchase one. By 1950, New York's Levittown contained more than 10,000 homes and 40,000 residents, and bulldozers and construction crews were sweeping through similarly planned developments across the country.

To assist potential buyers, the national government continued to offer an extensive set of programs. The FHA, established during the New Deal, helped underwrite an elaborate lending system. Typically, people who bought FHA-financed homes needed only 5 percent of the purchase price as a down payment; they could borrow the rest and guarantee their loan with a long-term, government-insured mortgage. Military veterans enjoyed even more favorable terms under the GI loan program. This kind of public assistance to middle-income families made it cheaper for them to purchase a suburban house than to rent a significantly smaller apartment in most cities. Moreover, homeowners enjoyed another valuable governmental subsidy. They could deduct the interest payments on their mortgages from their federal income tax.

The postwar suburb gained a reputation for being an ideal place in which to raise children, which U.S. families were having in unprecedented numbers. Toward the end of the Second World War, a number of demographic forces, including earlier marriages and rising incomes, had begun to fuel a **"baby boom"** that would last until the end of the 1950s. The baby boom generation, a key segment of the U.S. population for decades to come, made an immediate imprint on suburban culture. With houses generally occupying only about 15 percent of suburban lots, baby boomers could, with the help of their parents, convert the large lawns into lush, green private playgrounds. In addition, suburban children could claim credit for generating and consuming growing segments of the nation's GNP, especially those connected to entertainment, leisure, and public education. Suburban schools were as new as the homes, and school boards used their well-appointed facilities to attract both skilled, enthusiastic teachers and the children of other middle-income families.

In many respects, postwar suburban culture exuded a sense of optimism. Suburbia often symbolized new possibilities, confidence in the future, and acceptance of change. It also encouraged the vision of continued economic growth. Because the output of developers never caught up with the demand of buyers during the early Cold War era, suburbanites discovered they could often sell their existing home at a substantial profit and move up to a more spacious, more expensive dwelling in an even newer suburb. A suburban home, in short, became both a symbol of success and an important, highly liquid financial asset.

At the same time, some of the most noticeable markers of postwar suburban culture seemed to symbolize resistance to certain kinds of changes. As many contemporary observers noted, the new suburbs appeared to offer many of its residents a material and psychological refuge. Most obviously, buying a suburban home could provide many families of European descent a way of cushioning the impact of social and demographic change. As African American families continued to migrate to northern and western cities in search of jobs and greater opportunity,

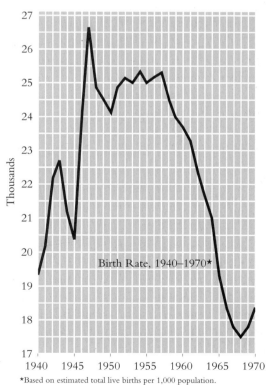

*Based on estimated total live births per 1,000 population.

The Baby Boom

white families began to see moving to the new suburbs as a way to avoid living in racially integrated communities. Governmental policies generally contributed to this trend through the financial incentives provided to homebuyers. Moreover, after the U.S. Supreme Court declared restrictive covenants unconstitutional, local officials rarely enforced the decision. Various informal and extralegal arrangements prevented, until well into the 1960s, any African American from buying a home in Long Island's Levittown.

Other policies and practices also helped segregate the new postwar suburbs. Although land and building costs would have been cheaper in these areas than in urban locales, most suburbanites jealously guarded their community's legal power to veto the building of public housing projects, whose units were likely to become racially and ethnically integrated. As a result, the federal government clustered housing projects on relatively expensive, high-density urban sites, a practice that helped make suburban living seem all that more desirable. At the same time, the lending industry generally channeled government-guaranteed loans for single-family homes toward the new suburbs, and private lenders routinely denied African Americans and Latinos the credit they needed to buy a newly built home. Their individual decisions, bankers insisted, rested purely on economic calculations. African American and Latino buyers invariably lacked the financial resources, lenders claimed, to qualify for a loan on a new suburban home. They needed to readjust their sights and seek housing within urban areas or in older suburbs. Any discrimination produced by this system, the housing-lending industry contended, flowed from the unintentional consequences of entirely race-blind, marketplace calculations.

The people who dominated the new suburban housing industry thus denied they were intentionally contributing to the spatial patterning of racial discrimination. William Levitt could proudly identify his private housing projects with the public crusade against communism. "No man who owns his house and lot can be a Communist," he remarked in 1948. "He has too much to do." Even as Levitt was claiming he could help solve the problem of housing—and perhaps even that of communist subversion—he was also resisting any suggestion that his firm's business-related choices bore any direct relationship to racial discrimination.

Similarly, developers saw the new suburbia's gender politics as the "natural" byproduct of larger marketplace forces. The financial industry, adopting a policy that resembled its approach to racial matters, extended the vast majority of its loan guarantees to men of European descent. Only rarely could single women, from any ethnic background, obtain loans. The FHA, a governmental agency, justified the gender tilt in its policies by insisting that men were the primary family breadwinners and that single women seldom made enough money to qualify as good credit risks.

Postwar Hollywood

Postwar Hollywood turned out powerful symbols of the Cold War era's fascination with—and fear of—cultural change. When the postwar era began, Hollywood still dominated the entertainment business. Enjoying the reopening of overseas markets and welcoming the return of their male stars from military service, the major studios expected to prosper during the postwar era. According to marketing studies, most people simply "went to the movies," giving little thought to what picture they might see. In 1946, Hollywood's attendance figures and profits reached all-time highs. As one historian later estimated, the average number of moviegoers in a single week, 90 million, amounted to nearly three-quarters of the people realistically able to reach a motion picture theater!

Hollywood, still congratulating itself for having cheered the nation through the Depression and the Second World War, expected to perform much the same service during the onset of the Cold War. Perhaps no movie genre seemed better designed to cheerlead than the Hollywood musical. Filled with lively stars, upbeat tunes, and flashy dance sequences, musicals invariably expressed optimism about the future. MGM's *On the Town* (1949), based on a 1944 Broadway smash and updated to the Cold War period, epitomized the early postwar musical. It saturated movie screens with hopeful imagery. During 24 hours of shore leave, three U.S. sailors sing and dance their way through New York City, sample the fruits of both elite and popular culture, and fall in love with three equally vibrant young women. Moving at a breakneck pace, *On the Town* suggested just how much three virile servicemen might accomplish in one day. Ending with a title card proudly proclaiming it had been filmed in "Hollywood, USA," this musical also seemed to herald the U.S. film industry's own bright future.

Even as *On the Town* arrived in movie theaters, however, Hollywood's fortunes were starting to change. By 1949, attendance figures—along with profits—began to plummet. During the next decade, Hollywood would lose fully half of its 1946 audience, and many studios would face bankruptcy.

Cultural historians once blamed television for keeping potential moviegoers at home, but Hollywood's difficulties set in even before TV became a serious rival. The same year MGM shot *On the Town*, for instance, the U.S. Supreme Court ruled that antitrust laws required the major studios to give up their highly profitable ownership of local movie theaters. This decision, the *Paramount Case* (1948), rocked Hollywood just as it faced labor strife, internal conflict over blacklisting, and soaring production costs. TV simply delivered another, albeit substantial, blow to an industry already reeling backward.

Meanwhile, as Hollywood struggled to adapt to changing times, images of fear and hopelessness began to pervade some of its own productions. An important cycle of 1940s motion pictures, first noticed by critics in France, came to be called *films noirs* or "dark cinema." The images of crime and of social behavior in many of these movies challenged established censorship limits, which the Hollywood studios had been enforcing under their Production Code since the mid-1930s. The industry, in fact, had refused to allow production of earlier versions of some of the noirish film scripts brought to the screen during the Cold War era. Nearly always filmed in black and white and often set at night in large cities, *films noirs* purported to peek into the dark corners of the American Way of Life. Noir characters continued to pursue dreams and hopes but with little chance of ever succeeding. Failure and loss, in *films noirs*, seemed to be the rule rather than the exception.

Most of Hollywood's *films noirs* conspicuously featured alluring *femmes fatales*, beautiful and dangerous women who challenge the prevailing order, particularly its gender hierarchies. Portrayed as in revolt against the popular injunction to support her man, the *femme fatale* character represented an image very different from that of the always faithful, and eternally nurturing, wife and mother. Usually unmarried or childless, amoral *femmes fatales* threaten both men, who were generally portrayed as weak and ineffectual, and other, less assertive women. Ultimately, however, Hollywood's *femmes fatales* fail to overcome the male-dominated forces they seek to challenge.

In *The File on Thelma Jordan* (1949), an archetypal *noir*, Barbara Stanwyck's title character cynically infiltrates the marriage of a weak-willed district attorney. Neither love nor even lust drives her illicit affair with him. Instead, she calculatedly seduces him as part of a cleverly ambitious, but ultimately unsuccessful, scheme to manipulate the criminal justice system. The postwar era's most prominent female stars—including Stanwyck, Joan Crawford, Rita Hayworth, and Lana Turner—achieved both popular and critical acclaim playing *femmes fatales*, women whose desire for radical change ultimately ends in failure.

In sum, developments in the national pastime of baseball, in the new suburbia, and in the Hollywood film industry provide three vivid examples of a more general cultural pattern: an ambivalent response to changes ushered in during the Cold War era. Alterations in supposedly settled cultural patterns could signal both the promise of living in the postwar United States and the potentially disastrous consequences of confronting changes that threatened to overwhelm both the daily lives of individuals and the cultural cohesion of the nation.

By the early 1950s, according to many contemporary observers, Cold War U.S. culture seemed in need, at the very least, of new symbols of stability. Particularly in the realms of politics and governance, there appeared a deeply felt desire for signs of reassurance. With a positive approval rating hovering under 30 percent, Harry Truman seemed to symbolize disarray, even despair. The "Little Man from Missouri" now seemed far too small a figure to lead the United States out of a time marked by ambiguous, even dire, signposts. Most people, including Truman, appeared to look forward to the end of his tenure in the White House.

From Truman to Eisenhower

Harry Truman refused even to consider running for another term in 1952. Still, his tumultuous years in the public spotlight put his Democratic Party on the defensive, and denunciations of communism and of Truman fueled an energetic Republican campaign.

The Election of 1952

Adlai Stevenson of Illinois, the Democratic presidential candidate in 1952, tried to take a hard line on national security. He warned that "Soviet secret agents and their dupes" had "burrowed like moles" into governments throughout the world. "We cannot let our guard drop for even a moment," he claimed. Stevenson approved of the conviction of the American Communist Party's leaders and the dismissal of schoolteachers who were party members. A solidly anticommunist stance, however, could not save Stevenson or the Democratic Party. The GOP's formula for electoral victory could be reduced to a simple equation, "K_1C_2": "Korea, corruption, and communism."

The Republicans first linked Stevenson's candidacy to the unpopular Truman presidency. They criticized Truman for mishandling the Korean War and highlighted revelations about some members of Truman's administration having solicited kickbacks in exchange for the granting of governmental contracts. The GOP's staunchly anticommunist vice-presidential candidate, Senator Richard Nixon of California, called Stevenson "Adlai the appeaser" and charged him with holding a Ph.D. from "Dean Acheson's Cowardly College of Communist Containment." Some Republicans even questioned the manliness of the Democratic contender, a soft-spoken lawyer-politician who remained unmarried following his 1949 divorce.

A Soldier-Politician

For their presidential candidate, Republicans looked to a hero of the Second World War, General Dwight David Eisenhower, popularly known as "Ike." Eisenhower had grown up in Kansas, graduated from West Point, ascended through Army ranks, and directed the Normandy invasion of 1944 as Supreme Allied Commander. He had served as Army Chief of Staff from 1945 to 1948 and, after an interim period as president of Columbia University, had become the commander of NATO, a post he held until May 1952. Eisenhower had never sought elective office, but a half-century of public service, most of it in the military, had taught him skills he found useful during his sudden plunge into partisan politics. Initially uncomfortable in the spotlight, Eisenhower fought through early difficulties and, with help from a bevy of consultants, developed an appealing media persona.

Eisenhower's personal appeal generally dazzled political insiders and commentators. Although Ike's partisan affiliations had long remained vague—hazy enough for some Democrats to have courted him as their own presidential nominee in 1948—he eventually emerged as the GOP's savior. Key Republicans, in turn, convinced Eisenhower that Senator Robert Taft, the likely GOP nominee if Ike declined to run, leaned too far to the right on domestic issues and lacked a firm commitment to containment policies overseas. Eisenhower, claiming to take a middle-of-the-road stance on controversial issues, appeared ready to direct the nation through the Cold War as skillfully as he had led it through a hot one. A generally adoring Washington press corps, grumbled Adlai Stevenson, embraced

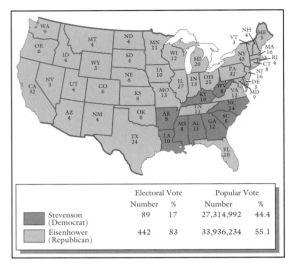

	Electoral Vote		Popular Vote	
	Number	%	Number	%
Stevenson (Democrat)	89	17	27,314,992	44.4
Eisenhower (Republican)	442	83	33,936,234	55.1

Map 27.4   Presidential Election, 1952   In this overwhelming victory for Eisenhower, Stevenson carried only a few states. Note that the so-called solid South remained largely Democratic. This trend would shift substantially over the next two decades.

the former war hero before learning "what his party platform would be" or "what would be the issues of the campaign." The Republican effort in 1952, the first to experiment with the possibilities of televised appeals, effectively tapped its presidential candidate's charisma. A popular GOP campaign simply announced: "I Like IKE!"

The first military leader to gain the presidency since Ulysses S. Grant (1869–77), Eisenhower achieved a great personal victory in 1952. The Eisenhower-Nixon ticket rolled up almost 7 million more popular votes than its Democratic opponents and dominated the Electoral College tally by a margin of 442 to 89. Despite Ike's trouncing of Stevenson, however, the Republican Party made relatively modest gains. It managed a single-vote majority in the U.S. Senate and an eight-vote edge over the Democrats in the House of Representatives. The Democratic coalition Franklin Roosevelt had forged during the 1930s thus survived. It did, however, show some signs of fraying, especially in the South. There, the votes of white southerners, many of which had gone to the Dixiecrats in 1948, began moving toward the Republicans. Eisenhower carried four states in the Democratic Party's once solid South.

Conclusion

An emphasis on aggressively safeguarding national security helped reshape national life during the years immediately following the Second World War. As worsening relations between the United States and the Soviet Union developed into a Cold War, the Truman administration pursued policies that expanded the power of the national government, particularly those of the executive branch. The militarization of foreign policy, presaged in the Truman Doctrine and solidified in NSC-68, intensified after the United States went to war in Korea in 1950.

The Cold War climate also affected the home front. People debated how best to protect national security, combat subversion, and calm cultural anxieties. The New Deal's vision, outlined in FDR's Economic Bill of Rights, faded, but Truman's Fair Deal offered a new view of social policy making. Fair Dealers promised that the wisdom of economic experts could guarantee economic growth and thereby provide the tax revenues to finance a set of effectively targeted social welfare programs. The Truman administration also pressed for national measures against racial discrimination.

The 1952 election of Dwight D. Eisenhower gave the Republicans the presidency for the first time in 20 years. Eisenhower's personal appeal, however, did not signal an imminent end to the power of the Democratic coalition that had held electoral sway since the 1930s. How would its vision of liberty and equality, as modified during the Fair Deal years, fare during the rest of the 1950s?

SUGGESTED READINGS

David Reynolds, *One World Divisible: A Global History since 1945* (2001) provides an international context for the emerging Cold War; **Walter LaFeber, *America, Russia, and the Cold War, 1945–2002*** (9th rev. ed., 2002) offers an expert interpretive synthesis of U.S. policies; and **Melvyn P. Leffler and David Painter, eds.,** *The Origins of the Cold War: Rewriting Histories* (2005) presents accessible essays on Cold War controversies. **Melvyn P. Leffler,** *The Specter of Communism* (1994) is a brief, critical account of the onset of the Cold War. Leffler's *A Preponderance of Power: National Security, the Truman Administration, and the Cold War* (1992) offers more detail, as do **Michael J. Hogan,** *A Cross of Iron: Harry S. Truman and the Origins of the National Security State, 1945–1954* (1998), and **Arnold A. Offner,** *Another Such Victory: President Truman and the Cold War, 1945-1953* (2002). **John Lewis Gaddis,** *The Cold War: A New History* (2005) and his many other books present a less critical view. **Alonso L. Hamby,** *Man of the People: A Life of Harry S. Truman* (1995) provides an overview of Truman and his presidency.

On the Korean War, **William Stueck,** *Rethinking the Korean War: A New Diplomatic and Strategic History* (2004) and *The Korean War: An International History* (1995) provide overviews, while **Bruce Cumings's** many books, including *Korea: The Unknown War* (coauthored with Jon Halliday) (1988), provide a more critical view. Postwar reconstruction of former enemies is expertly treated in **John Dower,** *Embracing Defeat: Japan in the Wake of World War II* (2000), and **Marc Trachtenberg,** *A Constructed Peace: The Making of the European Settlement, 1945–1963* (1999).

On communism and anticommunism in America during this period, **Allen Weinstein and Alexander Vassiliev,** *The Haunted Wood: Soviet Espionage in America, the Stalin Era* (1999) examines Soviet espionage. **Stanley I. Kutler,** *American Inquisition: Justice and Injustice in the Cold War* (1982) and **Ellen Schrecker,** *The Age of McCarthyism* (2001) stress the excesses of anticommunist crusading.

The effect of the Cold War and containment on American culture is the subject of many excellent studies. **Michael S. Sherry,** *In the Shadow of War: The United States Since the 1930s* (1995), a broad synthesis, and **Stephen Whitfield,** *The Culture of the Cold War* (rev. ed., 1996) are good places to begin. **Tom Englehardt,** *The End of Victory Culture and the Disillusioning of a Generation* (1995) provides an influential interpretation. **Paul Boyer,** *By the Bomb's Early Light* (1985) and **Alan Nadel,** *Containment Culture: American Narrative, Postmodernism, and the Nuclear Age* (1995) examine diverse cultural effects of the atomic age. **Lary May,** *The Big Tomorrow: Hollywood and the Politics of the American Way* (2000) examines Hollywood film culture. **Jessica Wang,** *American Science in an Age of Anxiety: Scientists, Anticommunism, and the Cold War* (1999) stresses FBI pressure on scientists to support the

Cold War. Lizabeth Cohen, *A Consumer's Republic: Mass Consumption in Postwar America* (2003) critically highlights the convergence of a number of important Cold War-era social and political forces.

Visit the Liberty Equality Power Companion Web site for resources specific to this textbook: http://www.thomsonedu.com/history/murrin

Also find self-tests and additional resources at ThomsonNOW. Thomson-NOW is an integrated online suite of services and resources with proven ease of use and efficient paths to success, delivering the results you want—NOW!

www.thomsonedu.com/login/

Affluence and Its Discontents, 1953–1963

With the end of the fighting in Korea in 1953, Cold War tensions somewhat abated. A new U.S. president, Dwight David Eisenhower (1953–61), modulated the pitch of the anticommunist rhetoric coming from the White House. Yet he and his successor, John F. Kennedy (1961–63), pledged not only to continue a global anticommunist foreign policy but to take it in new directions.

At home, Ike and JFK supported, with differing degrees of enthusiasm, efforts to extend some of the domestic programs initiated during the 1930s and 1940s. Sustained economic growth during the late 1950s and early 1960s encouraged talk about an age of "affluence." It also generated concern about the spread of social conformity, the behavior and cultural tastes of young people, and the impact of commercial mass culture. At the same time, discussions about the distribution of the nation's economic bounty and movements to end racial discrimination triggered new debates over the ways in which the use of governmental power might affect how people understood—and enjoyed—liberty and equality.

Foreign Policy, 1953–1960

Focus Question
In what ways did the "New Look" reorient the foreign policy of containment?

The U.S. strategy for containing communism began shifting focus and direction during the 1950s. Bipolar confrontations between the United States and the Soviet Union over European issues continued alongside greater attention to building up nuclear arsenals and directing often-subtle power plays in the **Third World**: the Middle East, Asia, Latin America, and Africa.

Eisenhower Takes Command
Eisenhower honored a campaign pledge by personally traveling to Korea, in hope of speeding the end of U.S. military involvement there. Negotiations to conclude the Korean War temporarily broke down, however, over whether or not North Korean and Chinese prisoners of war (POWs) could choose to remain in South Korea. Anxious to conclude

CHRONOLOGY

1953	Korean War ends • Julius and Ethel Rosenberg executed • *Playboy* magazine debuts
1954	Joseph McCarthy censured by U.S. Senate • Communist Control Act passed • *Brown* v. *Board of Education of Topeka* decision issued • SEATO formed • Arbenz government overthrown in Guatemala • Elvis Presley releases first record on Sun label • Geneva Peace Accords in Southeast Asia signed
1955	Montgomery bus boycott begins • *National Review* founded • *Brown II* decision issued • U.S. deals with Suez Crisis • Anti-Soviet uprisings occur in Poland and Hungary • Federal Highway Act passed • Eisenhower reelected
1957	Eisenhower sends troops to Lebanon • Eisenhower sends troops to Little Rock, Arkansas • Congress passes Civil Rights Act, first civil-rights legislation in 80 years • Soviets launch *Sputnik* • Gaither Report urges more defense spending
1958	National Defense Education Act passed by Congress • *The Affluent Society* published
1959	Khrushchev visits United States
1960	Civil Rights Act passed • U-2 incident ends Paris summit • Kennedy elected president • Sit-in demonstrations begin
1961	Bay of Pigs invasion fails • Berlin Wall erected • Freedom rides begin in the South • Kennedy announces Alliance for Progress
1962	Cuban Missile Crisis brings superpowers to brink of war • Kennedy sends troops to University of Mississippi to enforce integration
1963	Civil-rights activists undertake march on Washington • Betty Friedan's The Feminine Mystique published • Kennedy assassinated (November 22); Lyndon Johnson becomes president

matters, Eisenhower began to hint about using nuclear weapons if diplomacy failed. Talks soon resumed, and on July 27, 1953, both sides signed a truce that established a commission of neutral nations to handle the POW issue. (The POWs were subsequently allowed to determine whether they wished to be repatriated to their own countries.) A conflict during which more than 2 million Asians, mostly noncombatants, and 53,000 Americans died finally ended. A formal peace treaty remained unsigned, however, and the 38th parallel, which divided North and South Korea, became one of the most heavily fortified borders in the world.

At home, Ike gradually wrested control of the national security issue from more militant anticommunists, including Senator Joseph McCarthy. A Republican-controlled Congress did exceed the wishes of the Eisenhower administration when it passed the Communist Control Act of 1954. This measure barred the American Communist Party from running candidates in elections and extended the registration provisions of the 1950 McCarran Act. With a GOP president and a former general in the White House, however, most Republicans began to inch away from aggressively confrontational styles of anticommunist politics.

Joe McCarthy finally careened out of control. While heading up a special Senate Subcommittee on Investigations, popularly known as the "McCarthy Committee," the senator enjoyed broad subpoena powers and legal immunity from libel suits. He could charge reluctant witnesses with selling out their country and lead sympathetic ones through stories about a vast Red Menace. After differences with military officials prompted McCarthy to speculate about subversives in the U.S. Army, a Senate committee conducted a televised investigation into his charges. Under the glare of TV lights, McCarthy allowed himself to play the role of a crude bully, who carelessly hurled wild slanders in every direction. In March 1954, the veteran journalist Edward R. Murrow devoted one of his "See It Now" TV programs to a dissection of McCarthy. Borrowing a tactic from McCarthy's own political playbook, other critics even hinted that the senator and his aides seemed lacking in "manliness." Finally, in late 1954, McCarthy's U.S. Senate colleagues approved, by a margin of 65 to 22, a resolution censuring him for "unbecoming" conduct. McCarthyism began receding to the fringes of domestic political culture, and McCarthy faded from the limelight. He would die, in 1957, while still a seldom-noticed member of the senate.

Meanwhile, the Eisenhower administration crafted its own national security agenda. Coming in the wake of the bombast of McCarthyism, its relatively low-key style of anticommunism could seem eminently reasonable and moderate. The apparent unreliability of legislators such as McCarthy strengthened the case for the White House when it asserted a constitutional privilege to withhold classified national security materials from Congress. Eisenhower generally refrained, however, from vigorously pressing claims about presidential power, as Truman had done in the "steel seizure case" of 1952, and avoided any serious legal-constitutional confrontations with the judiciary.

Relatively free from congressional and judicial oversight, the Eisenhower administration extended earlier programs of domestic surveillance and of covert action overseas. It also backed a secret program to develop new aerial surveillance capabilities; by 1956, intelligence photographs taken from the new **U-2 spy planes** provided U.S. strategists with a clear view of the Soviet arsenal.

Most historians have come to see Eisenhower, especially at the beginning of his presidency, as an adroit political strategist. He could aggressively press the power of his office while often seeming to be doing relatively little. In the words of one scholar, Eisenhower conducted a "hidden hand presidency." Mindful of how the pugnacious style of his predecessor had often dragged Harry Truman into partisan disputes and political scandals, Ike carefully guarded his personal popularity and reputation. To do this, he preferred to remain in the background of public controversies and project an air of calm steadiness, which sometimes bordered on the aloof. In foreign policy, he usually allowed John Foster Dulles, his secretary of state from 1953 to 1959, to take center stage. Ike also encouraged the idea that George Humphrey, his secretary of the treasury, and Sherman Adams, his chief of staff, looked after domestic matters.

The New Look, Global Alliances, and Summitry

Generally working behind the scenes, Eisenhower oversaw a refashioning of the nation's anticommunist foreign policy. To begin, he allowed Secretary of State Dulles to warn, repeatedly, that Washington would consider adopting measures to "rollback," rather than simply to contain, communism. This approach differed from one that international observers, such as Britain's Winston Churchill, suggested. In their view, the change of leadership in Moscow, following the 1953 death of Joseph Stalin, created opportunities for significantly reducing Cold War tensions. Nikita Khrushchev, who would eventually emerge as the new Soviet leader, did talk about "peaceful coexistence." Seeking to free up resources to produce more consumer goods, Khrushchev also inaugurated reductions in the USSR's armed forces.

Meanwhile, the Eisenhower administration undertook a review and a subsequent revision of U.S. military and strategic policies. The head of the Joint Chiefs of Staff urged cutting back the U.S. military budget and emphasizing nuclear weaponry and air power. Dubbed the "New Look," these changes dovetailed with Eisenhower's concern that spiraling military expenditures might eventually strangle economic growth. The president, despite his background in the Army, came to rely on advanced nuclear capabilities, to deemphasize costly ground forces, and to listen attentively to the Air Force's "bomber generals," such as Curtis LeMay, who headed the Strategic Air Command (SAC). In addition, advocates of the New Look stressed the value of covert action, cultural outreach, and economic pressure.

Under Eisenhower, the United States elevated psychological warfare and "informational" programs into major Cold War weapons. The government-run Voice of America extended the reach of its radio broadcasts and increased the number of languages in which it programmed. Washington also secretly funded Radio Free Europe, Radio Liberty (beamed to the Soviet Union), and Radio Asia, all ostensibly privately run ventures. In 1953, Eisenhower persuaded Congress to create the United States Information Agency (USIA), an executive-branch office that coordinated anticommunist informational and propaganda campaigns.

A key centerpiece of the New Look, the doctrine of **"massive retaliation,"** gambled that the threat of unleashing U.S. nuclear weaponry would check Soviet expansion. The administration publicly hinted that it would not hesitate, in any future confrontation involving communist military moves and U.S national security, to launch a nuclear attack against the USSR. Secretly, it drew up plans for such an eventuality. To extend the U.S. nuclear umbrella, the Eisenhower administration placed additional weapons under the direct control of military commanders, particularly those in SAC.

Eisenhower's administration also concluded a set of global military alliances. It expanded NATO to include West Germany in 1955 and added two other mutual defense pacts with noncommunist nations in Central and Southeast Asia. The Southeast Asia Treaty Organization (SEATO), formed in 1954, linked the United States to Australia, France, Great Britain, New Zealand, Pakistan, the Philippines, and Thailand. The Central

Treaty Organization (CENTO), created in 1959, aligned the United States with Pakistan, Iran, Turkey, Iraq, and Great Britain.

Simultaneously trying to soothe relations with the USSR, Eisenhower also stressed the importance of negotiations, including high-level "summit meetings," with the Soviets. In May 1955, U.S. and Soviet leaders decided finally to end the postwar occupation of Austria and to transform it into an independent and neutral nation. Two months later, the United States, the Soviet Union, Britain, and France met in Geneva, Switzerland, and agreed to inaugurate cultural exchanges as one way of reducing Cold War suspicions. Some optimistic observers even began to talk about the reconciliatory "spirit of Geneva." During the fall of 1959, as a way of healing recent rifts over the future of a still-divided Berlin, Khrushchev toured the United States. His most publicized stops included a farm in Iowa, a Hollywood studio, and Disneyland. Although a 1960 Paris summit meeting fell apart, amidst a bitter war of words, after the Soviets shot down a U-2 spy plane over their territory, the tone of Cold War rhetoric seemed to grow somewhat less strident during Eisenhower's eight years in office.

The two superpowers even began to consider how they might reduce their stockpiles of nuclear weaponry. Eisenhower's **"Open Skies"** initiative of 1955 proposed mutual reconnaissance flights over each other's territory to verify disarmament efforts. Always suspicious and hyper-secretive, the Soviet leadership balked at this idea, but the rival nations did make some progress toward limiting atomic testing. Responding to the health hazards of radioactive fallout, both slowed the pace of aboveground testing and even discussed a broader test-ban agreement.

For some Americans, however, these efforts came far too late. Government documents finally declassified in the 1980s confirmed suspicions that people who had lived "downwind" from nuclear test sites during the 1940s and 1950s had contracted a disproportionate number of atomic-related illnesses. Subsequent revelations also showed that the U.S. government had covertly conducted experiments with radioactive materials on unsuspecting citizens.

Meanwhile, events in Eastern Europe tested the likelihood of the United States and the USSR actually squaring off, militarily, there. By the mid-1950s, many of the Soviet-dominated "satellite" countries in that region resented their badly managed communist economies and detested their police-state regimes, ultimately supported by Moscow's military might. Seizing on hints of what appeared to be a post-Stalin relaxation of the USSR's heavy hand, insurgents in Poland staged a brief rebellion in June 1956. They forced the Soviets to accept Wladyslaw Gomulka, an old foe of Stalin, as Poland's head of state. Hungarians then rallied in support of Imre Nagy, another anti-Stalinist communist, who pledged to create a multiparty political system. After failed attempts at finding some accommodation, which would have preserved Moscow's power over Hungary, Soviet military forces moved against the new Hungarian government.

The Hungarian insurgents appealed to the United States for assistance. They apparently took seriously earlier U.S. calls, especially by Secretary of State Dulles, for "rolling back" Soviet power and "liberating" Eastern Europe. More cautious U.S. military strategists, however, recognized the danger of mounting a U.S. military operation in Eastern Europe, so close to Soviet territory. Soviet armies brutally crushed the Hungarian uprising, killing thousands of people, including Nagy. Anticommunist critics of rollback rhetoric suggested that the failed Hungarian Revolution showed how advocating a policy that moved beyond containment might secure political advantage at home but produce tragedy abroad.

Covert Action and Economic Leverage

Meanwhile, the U.S. campaign to contain communism shifted toward the Third World. As it did, covert action and economic pressure, less visible and less expensive than military deployments, became major policy tools. Using secretive operations and economic diplomacy in Africa, Asia, and Latin America, the Eisenhower administration reasoned, seemed less likely to provoke domestic political controversies or showdowns with the Soviets.

The CIA, headed by Allen Dulles, brother of the secretary of state, played a key role in U.S. policy in the Third World during the 1950s. In 1953, the CIA helped engineer the election of the strongly anticommunist Ramón Magsaysay as president of the Philippines. That same year, the CIA facilitated a coup in Iran, which overthrew Mohammed Mossadegh's constitutional government, after it threatened to nationalize Iran's oil industry, and restored Shah Reza Pahlavi to power. Increasingly dictatorial in his domestic policies, the Shah assured Eisenhower that Iran would remain a firm ally of Washington and a close friend to oil interests in the United States and Europe. (The Shah remained in power until ousted in 1979 in another coup, this time led by Islamic fundamentalists.)

The CIA continually expanded its global reach and its influence within the Eisenhower administration. In 1954, CIA operatives secretly helped topple President Jacobo Arbenz Guzmán's elected government in Guatemala. Officials in Washington and executives of the United Fruit Company desired the ouster of Arbenz, whose broad support included that of Guatemala's Communist Party. Using up-to-date informational strategies, including phony newscasts created by the U.S. advertising industry, the CIA undermined domestic support for Arbenz, who had promised a program to nationalize and redistribute large tracts of Guatemalan land owned by United Fruit.

Impressed by what the Iranian and Guatemalan operations appeared to suggest about the potential of covert action, the National Security Council secretly widened the CIA's mandate. By 1960, the CIA deployed approximately 15,000 agents around the world, compared to only 6,000 when Eisenhower took office.

Eisenhower also employed new economic strategies—trade and aid—to fight communism and win Third World converts to the U.S cause. Governmental economic initiatives sought to open new opportunities for U.S. enterprises overseas, discourage other countries from adopting state-directed economic systems, and encourage expanded trade ties. Those who supported these efforts credited U.S. policy with encouraging greater stability in

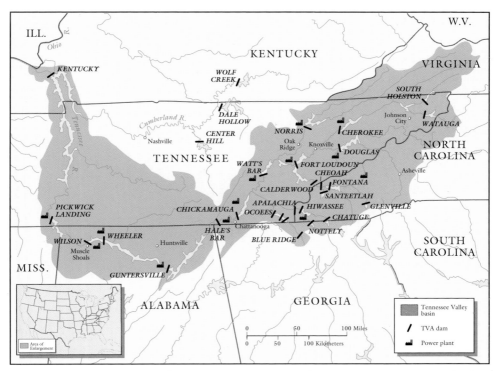

Map 25.3   Tennessee Valley Authority   This map shows the vast scale of the TVA, and pinpoints the locations of 29 dams and 13 power plants that emerged from this project.

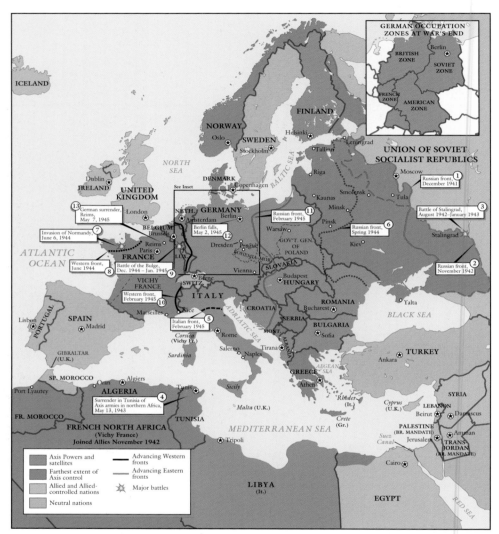

Map 26.2   Allied Advances and Collapse of German Power   This map depicts the final Allied advances and the end of the war in Germany. Through what countries did Soviet armies advance, and how might their advance have affected the postwar situation? How was Germany divided by occupying powers, and how might that division have affected postwar politics? View an animated version of this map or related maps at http://www.thomsonedu.com/history/murrin.

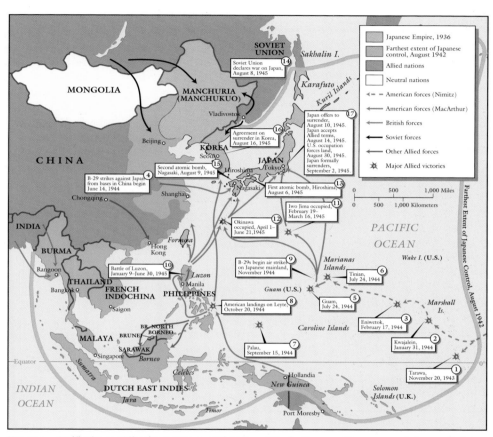

Map 26.3   Pacific Theater Offensive Strategy and Final Assault Against Japan   This map suggests the complicated nature of devising a war strategy in the vast Pacific region. What tactics did the United States use to advance upon and finally prevail over the island nation of Japan?

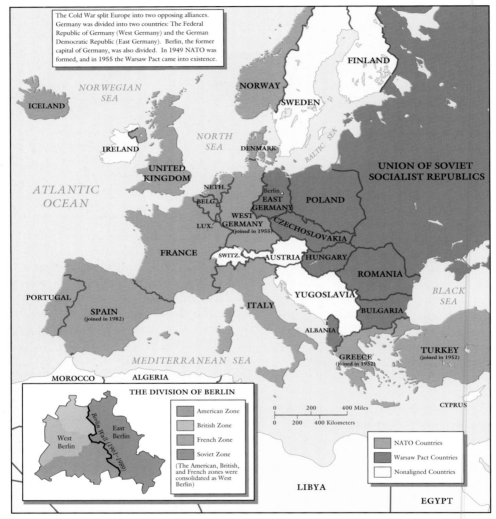

The Cold War split Europe into two opposing alliances. Germany was divided into two countries: The Federal Republic of Germany (West Germany) and the German Democratic Republic (East Germany). Berlin, the former capital of Germany, was also divided. In 1949 NATO was formed, and in 1955 the Warsaw Pact came into existence.

Map 27.2   Divided Germany and the NATO Alliance   This map shows the geopolitics of the Cold War. Which countries aligned with the United States through NATO? Which aligned with the Soviet Union through the Warsaw Pact? Note how Berlin became a divided city, although it was located within East Germany.

recipient countries. Critics at home and abroad noted, however, that U.S. aid programs could seem heavy-handed and often alienated Third World leaders by equating "freedom" only with free-market economic policies that U.S. investors favored.

U.S. military aid to the Third World rose even more sharply than economic assistance. Under a Mutual Security and Military Assistance Program, the United States spent $3 billion annually, instructed Third World governments in anticommunist policies, trained their military forces, and advised their domestic police forces. The buildup of armaments in Third World nations did provide the United States with stronger anticommunist allies but also contributed to the development of military dictatorships.

The United States and Third World Politics, 1953–1960

In pursuing its policies in Third World areas, the Eisenhower administration employed a broad definition of "communist." In many nations emerging from colonialism, groups advocating labor rights and land redistribution sometimes did ally with local communist movements. Their domestic political opponents could thus hope to win U.S. support by mentioning the word *communist*, especially to people in Washington, D.C.

Latin America

In Latin America, the Eisenhower White House favored autocratic regimes that welcomed U.S. economic investment and opposed leftist political movements. Eisenhower publicly honored unpopular dictators in Peru and Venezuela and privately confessed admiration for the anticommunist politics of Paraguay's General Alfredo Stroessner, who sheltered German-Nazi fugitives and ran his country much as if it were a private fiefdom. Eisenhower's administration continued to cultivate close ties with Cuban dictator Fulgencio Batista. Batista also enjoyed strong support from U.S. crime syndicates, which controlled the Cuba's gambling industry, and from the CIA, which secretly trained his repressive security forces.

The backlash against U.S. policy boosted the appeal of **"yankeephobia"** in much of Latin America. Two important events of the late 1950s dramatized the growing unpopularity that U.S. policy makers now faced throughout much of the southern part of the Western Hemisphere.

When Vice-President Richard Nixon visited this region on a 1958 goodwill tour, he generally encountered ill will. Constantly escalating protest demonstrations reached their climax during Nixon's last stop, in Caracas, Venezuela. At one point, protestors surrounded the vice-president's motorcade, laid siege to his Cadillac limousine, and forced Nixon, hustled to safety by armed Secret Service agents, to take refuge in the U.S. Embassy.

Events in Havana, Cuba, the following year, added substance to the symbolism of Caracas. A relatively broad-based Cuban opposition movement, headed by a charismatic revolutionary named Fidel Castro, toppled Batista's pro-U.S. regime in December 1959. Once in control, Castro promised to reduce Cuba's dependence on the United States and to create a state-directed economic system, one he claimed would improve living conditions for most Cubans. These policies, together with Castro's own increasingly autocratic rule, prompted many of Cuba's more affluent citizens to depart for Florida, and the Eisenhower administration to impose an economic boycott against Cuba. Castro turned to the Soviet Union, declared his allegiance to Marxist doctrine, moved against political dissent at home, and pledged support for Cuban-style insurgencies throughout Latin America.

The Eisenhower administration began laying down a two-track response. First, it reconsidered U.S. policies that seemed to have been generating animosity and sparking anti-U.S. political movements throughout Latin America. This review ultimately recommended that Washington start encouraging democratic political processes, protection for human rights, and policies of economic growth. At the same time, Allan Dulles and the CIA were working on their own initiatives toward Cuba and Castro. Looking back at earlier operations and surveying current assets, including its contacts in organized crime, the CIA began planning how best to depose the Cuban leader, who was becoming an increasingly visible symbol of opposition to U.S. policies on the world stage.

The Middle East, Asia, and Africa

Meanwhile, a growing distrust of nationalism and neutralism shaped U.S. policy toward the Middle East. In 1954, after Colonel Gamal Abdel Nasser led a successful military coup in Egypt, against a corrupt monarchy closely tied to Great Britain, he promised to help rescue other Arab nations from European domination and guide them toward policies of "positive neutralism" in the Cold War. Nasser denounced Israel, boosted Egypt's economic and military power, extended diplomatic recognition to the People's Republic of China, and purchased advanced weapons from communist Czechoslovakia.

The Eisenhower administration viewed these policies as neither positive nor neutral. It quickly cancelled the U.S. loans intended to finance construction of the Aswan Dam, which Egypt hoped to make the centerpiece of a project designed to improve agriculture along the Nile River and to provide power for new Egyptian industries. Nasser responded, in July 1956, by seizing the British-controlled Suez Canal, which connected the Red Sea to the Mediterranean, as a way of gaining new revenues and prestige for Egypt. The Suez also remained of both economic and symbolic importance to Britain, and its forces, joined by those of France and Israel, attacked Egypt in October and quickly seized back the canal. Observers of the international scene talked about "the Suez Crisis."

Eisenhower distrusted Nasser, but he opposed Britain's blatant attempt to retain its imperial position in the Middle East. Denouncing the Anglo-French-Israeli action, which coincided with the Soviet Union's brutal campaign to shore up its communist empire by crushing Hungary, the U.S. president threatened to destabilize Britain's currency unless the invasion ended. Eventually, a plan supported by the United States and the UN gave Egypt control over the Suez Canal, but U.S. influence in the area still suffered, particularly after the Soviet Union took over the financing for the Aswan Dam.

With Nasser-style nationalism now seeming to lean toward the USSR, the Eisenhower administration came to fear the spread of "Nasserism" throughout the energy-rich Middle East. In spring 1957, the president's **"Eisenhower Doctrine"** pledged that the United States would defend Middle Eastern countries "against overt armed aggression from any nation controlled by international communism." When ruling elites in Lebanon and Jordan faced potential revolts by domestic forces friendly to Nasser, Eisenhower dispatched U.S. Marines to Lebanon, and Britain helped Jordan's King Hussein retain his throne.

The Eisenhower administration moved with similar determination elsewhere in the Third World. It remained steadfast in its policy of trying to squelch political movements it considered too closely tied to communism. In 1958, for example, the CIA furnished planes and pilots to rebels trying to overthrow Achmed Sukarno, leader of Indonesia, who drew support from that nation's large Communist Party. The rebellion failed, and Sukarno tightened his grip on power. CIA operatives also became involved in a plan to eliminate Patrice Lumumba in the Congo. Lumumba's opponents killed the popular black nationalist leader in January 1961, but scholars still debate the CIA's precise role in precipitating his death.

Vietnam

Eisenhower's effort to thwart communism and neutralism in the Third World set the stage for a more through commitment in Indochina. There, communist-nationalist forces led by Ho Chi Minh (born Nguyen Tat Thanh) continued to seek independence from France. Ho Chi Minh had studied in the Soviet Union and in France before returning to Indochina in 1941 to fight against the Japanese armies that had overrun this French colony. When Japan withdrew at war's end, Ho had appealed to the United States to back independence for Indochina. Despite wartime criticism of European colonialism, U.S. leaders supported the return of French rule. In 1946, Ho Chi Minh and his Vietminh forces went to war against France and its ally, Bao Dai, the Paris-educated Vietnamese emperor who had reigned since the 1920s.

Despite U.S. willingness to finance its military operations, France could not retain its hold over Indochina. A stunning 1954 Vietminh victory, orchestrated by General Vo Nguyen Giap, at the battle of Dien Bien Phu, convinced France to begin pulling out of Indochina. The Geneva Peace Accords of 1954, which the United States ultimately refused to sign, ended France's colonial regime and divided the old Indochina into three sovereign nations: Laos, Cambodia, and Vietnam. The accords further split Vietnam into two jurisdictions—North Vietnam and South Vietnam—until a future, nationwide election could create a government that would unify it as a single country.

Eisenhower's advisers feared that events in Vietnam, where Ho Chi Minh stood poised to win any electoral contest, could set off a geopolitical chain reaction. Using now-familiar Cold War language, the White House insisted that "the loss of any of the countries of Southeast Asia to Communist aggression" would ultimately "endanger the stability and security" of Europe and Japan, a formulation becoming known as the "domino theory." As

Ho Chi Minh's communist government consolidated control over North Vietnam, Eisenhower supported creation of a noncommunist state in South Vietnam.

Ike additionally ordered, in advance of the planned reunification election, covert operations and economic programs throughout South Vietnam. In late 1954, Washington dispatched to South Vietnam Colonel Edward Lansdale, who had directed the CIA's campaign against the leftist insurgency in the Philippines from 1950 to 1953. Lansdale helped oversee creation in Saigon, South Vietnam's capital city, of the pro-U.S. government headed by Ngo Dinh Diem, an anticommunist Catholic who had been educated in the United States. Lansdale also took charge of covert activities against anti-Diem factions, especially those loyal to Ho Chi Minh.

At first, the U.S.-directed effort at nation-building seemed to make headway. With Washington's concurrence, Diem's regime renounced the Geneva Peace Accords and refused to participate in any national election intended to establish a unified Vietnamese government. Diem extended his own government's authority over South Vietnam, redistributed land formerly owned by the French, augmented his military forces, and even launched an industrialization program.

Diem's authoritarian policies, together with opposition from North Vietnam, soon undermined the stability of his government. Diem alienated much of South Vietnam's predominantly Buddhist population, and his narrowing circle of political allies became best known for their notorious corruption. With encouragement and material support from North Vietnam, Vietminh loyalists in the South spearheaded opposition to Diem. As time passed, Diem grew increasingly isolated from key constituencies in his struggling nation and progressively more dependent on U.S. support. Early on, French officials had warned their U.S. counterparts of Diem's liabilities, but the Eisenhower administration could see no alternative. It sent billions of U.S. dollars and military advisers to prop up his government.

Eisenhower struggled to frame a coherent U.S. policy toward Vietnam. Ike had once claimed that U.S. military involvement there would be a "tragedy" and had rebuffed, in 1954, advisers who urged direct U.S. military intervention, including even the possible use of atomic weapons, on behalf of France. Following French withdrawal from Indochina, however, Eisenhower committed economic and military aid, along with America's international prestige, to Diem's shaky political fortunes. The decision of how far the United States might actually go in order to fulfill Eisenhower's commitment to South Vietnam would fall to his successors in the White House.

Affluence: A "People of Plenty"

Focus Question
How could economic growth seem to be both an opportunity and a problem during the 1950s?

President Eisenhower's "farewell address" of 1961 famously criticized the increasingly cozy relationship between the groups that directed nation's foreign policy and its economic system. The former general warned that a "military-industrial complex" threatened to so accelerate the costs of Cold War containment that the burden of military expenditures would eventually harm the U.S. domestic economy.

Eisenhower's warning contained several ironies. Most obviously, his administration, while trying to contain costs, had watched ever-larger sums of money flow to the national security establishment. Eisenhower's selection of Charles Wilson of General Motors in 1953 and Neil McElroy of Procter & Gamble in 1957 to head the Department of Defense, moreover, seemingly dramatized the same linkage Ike decried in his final address. Government spending on national security—what critics called "military Keynesianism" (see chapter 27)—pumped money into the general economy and stimulated key industries.

In addition, Eisenhower's warnings about possible dangers came after eight years during which his White House had praised the nation's continued economic growth. In 1945, the United States had still teetered on the brink of economic depression. By 1960, it could claim a GNP more than five times that of Great Britain and at least ten times that of Japan. The output of major U.S. corporations, such as General Motors, surpassed the GNP of many sovereign nations.

Economic Growth

The 1950s marked the midpoint of a period of generally steady economic growth that began during the Second World War and continued until the early 1970s. Writing in the mid-1950s, the historian David Potter called Americans a "people of plenty." Corporations turned out vast quantities of consumer goods and enjoyed rising profits. Investments and business ventures overseas boosted corporate profits at home. The domestic economy intersected with an international marketplace dominated by U.S.-based firms. The label "Made in America" announced both the quality of particular products and the economic power of the nation at large. A global national-security policy, in addition to making the Pentagon one of the nation's largest consumers, helped keep raw materials and energy flowing from the Third World. Abundant supplies of inexpensive oil and natural gas, in particular, lowered production costs and allowed U.S. industries to substitute less costly, and less polluting, foreign energy sources for domestically mined coal.

Newer U.S. industries, such as chemicals and electronics, quickly came to dominate the world marketplace. The Corning Glass Company reported that most of its sales during the mid-1950s came from products that had not even been on the market in 1940. General Electric proudly proclaimed that "progress is our most important product."

The newest suburbs—and the products their residents consumed—remained prominent emblems of this particular view of progress. Because these outlying areas lacked, at best, adequate mass transit, life revolved around the automobile. Initially, if the male breadwinner required the family car to commute to work, his spouse needed to spend her day near home. As the opportunities for buying automobiles on credit expanded during

The "Mrs. America" Gas Kitchen   In 1959, the American National Exhibition in Moscow featured a "typical housewife" working in this RCA/Whirlpool "Mrs. America" gas kitchen, a symbol of the streamlined material progress of the postwar United States.

The Typical Housewife   This photograph depicts a different view of the "typical housewife" in her kitchen.

the mid-1950s, however, the two-car family and the new suburban shopping malls, surrounded by acres of free parking, became tangible symbols of economic growth. Widespread ownership of kitchen appliances, television sets, and automobiles marked those living in the United States, especially in the eyes of most of those in the rest of the world, as people of plenty.

Complaints about the limits of capitalism, widely expressed during the 1930s, all but disappeared from domestic political discourse. Capitalism seemed to work—and spectacularly well. Only a new vocabulary of superlatives, it seemed, could describe its wonders. In 1955, *Fortune* magazine hailed "The Changing American Market" and highlighted "The Rich Middle-Income Class" and "The Wonderful Ordinary Luxury Market." Harvard's celebrated economist John Kenneth Galbraith, who had simply entitled his 1952 study *American Capitalism,* gave his follow-up book a more grandiose-sounding title, *The Affluent Society* (1958). (This best seller actually took a far more critical look at the U.S. economy than Galbraith's first book; see following discussion.)

Words such as *plenty, abundance,* and ***affluence*** fit nicely with the dominant economic vision. The rate of growth and the burgeoning supply of consumer goods overshadowed all other economic indicators. Mainstream political discourse increasingly slid by what people *actually owned*—their accumulated wealth—to focus on their affluence—what they could, with the aid of generous credit terms, *consume.* From this perspective, observers could easily see the entire American Way of Life constantly improving. Some even predicted a leveling out of living standards between the top and the bottom levels of this growth-enabled consumer society. Any remaining gulf seemed not between people with cars and those without them, they announced, but between ones who drove Cadillacs and Lincolns and those who piloted Chevrolets and Fords. "Luxury has reached the masses," proclaimed *Fortune*.

Many economists claimed that greater government expenditures would generate even faster growth, but the Eisenhower administration demurred. Fearing that increased spending might fuel an inflationary spiral of rising prices and destabilize the economy, it kept expenditures for nonmilitary programs under tight control and remained committed, at least rhetorically, to restraining even the Pentagon's spending habits. As a result, by the late 1950s, the federal government began running balanced budgets.

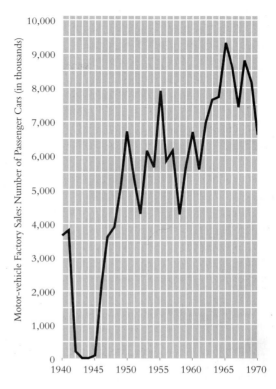

Auto Sales, 1940–1970

Highways and Waterways

The Eisenhower administration, after due deliberation, did endorse several costly new domestic programs. For one of these, the construction of an interstate highway system, it could invoke national-security considerations. Supposedly, during any military emergency, the government could rush supplies and personnel along federally financed superhighways. Creating a national tax on gasoline and other transportation-related products, the **Highway Act of 1956** authorized a national system of limited-access expressways. Touted as the largest public works project in world history, this program delighted the oil, concrete, and tire industries; provided steady work for construction firms and labor unions; and boosted the interstate trucking business. It also confirmed the victory of the automobile over competing modes of surface travel, including passenger trains, trolleys, and buses.

The White House also supported expensive water-diversion projects in the West. The Army Corps of Engineers and the Bureau of Reclamation—federal agencies with powerful supporters in business and Congress— spent billions of dollars on dams, irrigation canals, and reservoirs. Irrigation turned desert into crop land, and elaborate pumping systems even allowed rivers to flow uphill. No society in the history of the world had ever devoted

he Impala Convertible with Body by Fisher. Safety Plate Glass means better seeing in all new Chevies.

YOU'LL HAVE PLENTY TO SHOW OFF *in the high-spirited performance of your* **NEW CHEVROLET.** *With its radical new Turbo-Thrust V8* and new action in all engines, it's so quick, agile and eager that once you take the wheel, you'll never want to leave it. You've got your hands on something really special!*

Your pride can't help showing just a bit when you slide behind the wheel of this new Chevrolet. You couldn't be sitting prettier—and you know it.
    You're in charge of one of the year's most looked at, most longed for cars. Chevy's crisply sculptured contours and downright luxurious interiors are enough to make anybody feel like a celebrity.
    Move your foot a fraction on the gas pedal and you feel the instant, silken response of a unique new kind of V8. You ride smoothly and serenely—cushioned by deep coil springs at every wheel. You can even have a real air ride*, if you wish.
    See your Chevrolet dealer. . . . Chevrolet Division of General Motors, Detroit 2, Mich. **Optional at extra cost.*

CHEVROLET

Automobiles Symbolize a New Lifestyle   This ad for a 1958 pink convertible shows off not only the nation's new economic productivity and consumer lifestyle but also suggests the dominant ideal of family "togetherness."

a similar portion of its resources to water projects. By 1960, much of the arid West enjoyed reliable access to trillions of gallons of water. Governmental expenditures laid the basis for new economic growth in states such as Texas, California, and Arizona.

These water projects came at a price. Technologically complicated and costly, they apparently needed similarly complex and expensive bureaucracies to sustain them. As a consequence, local communities lost power to governmental agencies and to the large-scale private entrepreneurs who pushed aside smaller farmers and ranchers. In addition, several American Indian tribes found significant portions of their land being flooded for large water reservoirs or being purchased by agribusinesses or large ranching interests. Moreover, these vast projects—which diverted surface waters, tapped into ground-water tables, and dotted the West with dams and reservoirs—also produced ecological problems. They disrupted and degraded critical habitats and contributed to the buildup of salt by-products in the water and the soil. Some scientists also began to warn about the consequences to animal and plant life from the overuse, especially by larger farming operations, of pesticides such as DDT.

Labor–Management Accord

Most corporate leaders, supportive of the kind of government involvement required to build the Interstate Highway System highways and water projects, were learning to live with labor unions as well. The auto industry, where management and labor leaders had negotiated a mutually acceptable contract in 1950, showcased what some economic observers saw as a tacit accord between the two sides.

At the end of the Second World War, more than 14 million U.S. workers, roughly 35 percent of those who worked in nonagricultural jobs, held union cards. Hoping to consolidate this base and to move forward cautiously, most union leaders saw closer cooperation with corporate management, rather than aggressive new organizing drives, as the safest way to guarantee employment stability and secure political influence for their unions.

The United Auto Workers (UAW), which had been one of the most militant Congress of Industrial Organizations (CIO) unions during the 1930s, helped lead the way. Unions such as the UAW dropped demands for greater involvement in "management prerogatives." These included organization of the daily work routine, introduction of new technologies, investment priorities, and, most important, decisions on where to locate new facilities. Unions continued to bargain aggressively but on a relatively narrow range of issues that immediately affected worker paychecks and benefits. Union leaders also assured management that rank-and-file workers would abide by their union contracts and disavow the wildcat tactics that had been used during the 1930s and 1940s. In another sign of declining militancy within the labor movement, the American Federation of Labor (AFL) and the CIO, long at odds, merged in 1955. Finally, to police this new labor–management détente in an even-handed manner, both sides looked to the federal government's National Labor Relations Board (NLRB). The 1950s thus seemed to signal an end to the kind of fierce labor–capital conflicts that had marked the 1930s and had continued through the 1940s.

Some union activists, however, expressed concern about the new direction of the labor movement. Although membership rolls stood at record highs, nearly two-thirds of all unionized workers lived in only 10 states. Worse, there were already clear signs in some areas of union strength, such as the Northeastern United States, of companies beginning to move jobs elsewhere, beginning with states in the South. There, the union movement lacked strong roots, and the Taft-Hartley Act of 1947 allowed for state laws that frustrated new organizing drives, such as the ultimately underproductive effort known as "Operation Dixie."

Most business leaders, on the other hand, judged the new direction in labor–management relations as a substantial victory for their side. *Fortune* magazine noted that General Motors, while paying higher wages and shouldering costlier employee benefit packages, "got a bargain" on the larger issue of labor peace from its landmark 1950 contract with the UAW. To safeguard their control over decision making, corporations expanded their supervisory staffs, a practice that drove up consumer prices and curtailed worker participation in planning the work process. The labor–management accord also helped divide industrial workers from one another: Those employed in the most profitable sectors of the economy, such as the auto industry, could bargain far more effectively than those who worked in less lucrative sectors.

To further consolidate management's power, many businesses expanded benefits for their workers. Companies such as Sears and Eastman Kodak encouraged a cooperative corporate culture, which included health and pension plans, profit-sharing arrangements, and social programs. Some even created private recreational parks for the exclusive use of their employees. Reaching out to workers, executives decided, would reduce the appeal of both aggressive unions and more extensive governmental welfare measures.

Between the end of the Second World War and the early 1960s, a large percentage of U.S. wage-earners came to enjoy at least some of the fruits of affluence. Real wages (what workers make after adjusting their paychecks for inflation) rose steadily, while job openings remained plentiful. The frequency of industrial accidents dropped; fringe benefits (what workers receive in the form of health insurance, paid vacation time, and retirement plans) invariably improved; and job security was generally high.

Political Pluralism

Economic growth also appeared to help sustain a stable political system. Observers of the domestic scene during the 1950s could not help but see their own times in terms of memories of the past and visions of the future. In contrast to the conflicts of the 1930s, the disruptions during the Second World War, and the Great Fear of the early Cold War period, the 1950s seemed an era of relative tranquility. Moreover, domestic life in the United States seemed less troubled and chaotic than that in other parts of the Cold War world, as the increasingly prosperous nation worked, fairly effectively, to mute conflict and solve domestic problems.

According to the dominant viewpoint, which political scientists called "pluralism" (or "interest-group pluralism"), U.S. politics featured a roughly equal bargaining process among well-organized interest groups. John Kenneth Galbraith, for example, coined the term "countervailing power" to describe the ability of labor unions, consumer lobbies, farm organizations, and other groups to check the appetites of giant corporations. No single group could hope to dictate to the others, celebrants of pluralism claimed, because so many interests felt securely empowered. Pluralists shrugged off signs of an apparent decline in political participation, clearly evident in how few citizens went to the polls on election days, by arguing that relatively low voter turnouts simply showed widespread satisfaction with how well existing processes worked.

In addition to praising the process, pluralists invariably praised the results. Public leaders, it seemed, could find a realistic solution to virtually every political problem. Short-term conflicts over specific issues might never disappear, but supporters of the pluralist vision pointed out how affluence could moderate political passions and point warring interests toward a viable long-term agreement on fundamental arrangements. As a professor at Harvard Law School put it, constant economic growth meant that "in any conflict of interest," it was "always possible to work out a solution" because continuing affluence appeared to guarantee that any settlement would leave all interests "better off than before."

A Religious People

The celebration of political pluralism accompanied the exaltation of the stabilizing role of religion. Signs of religious commitment seemed part of most people's weekly, sometimes daily, routine. Formal church membership grew at more than double the rate of the U.S. population during the 1950s. Moreover, public life appeared solidly anchored in religious values. As part of the crusade against "atheistic communism," Congress emphasized the role of religion by constructing a nondenominational prayer room on Capitol Hill, adding the phrase "under God" to the Pledge of Allegiance, and declaring the phrase "In God We Trust," emblazoned on U.S. currency for nearly a century, to be the official national motto.

At the same time, observers claimed that intense religious allegiances no longer divided people as much as they had in the past. President Eisenhower urged people to practice their own religious creed, whatever it might be. "Our government makes no sense," he declared, "unless it is founded in a deeply felt religious faith—and I don't care what it is." Tommy Sands, a young pop singer, advised his teenage fans that "all religions are the greatest."

Prominent religious leaders noted how a widespread "faith in faith" could bring people together. Rabbi Morris Kretzer, head of the Jewish Chaplain's Organization, reassured Protestants and Catholics that they and their Jewish neighbors shared "the same rich heritage of the Old Testament . . . the sanctity of the Ten Commandments, the wisdom of the prophets, and the brotherhood of man." A 1954 survey claimed that more than 95 percent of the population identified with one of the three major faiths, and religious commentators talked about the unifying power of a "Judeo-Christian tradition." The era's leading study of religion, Will Herberg's *Protestant-Catholic-Jew* (1955), argued that these three major faiths were really "saying the same thing in affirming the 'spiritual ideals' and 'moral values' of the American Way of Life."

The media elevated several religious leaders to celebrity status. Norman Vincent Peale, a Protestant minister who linked an embrace of religiosity to the achievement of individual peace of mind, sold millions of books containing the message that belief in a Higher Power could bring "health, happiness, and goodness" to daily life. Some close students of religion, such as Herberg, found Peale's most famous book, *The Power of Positive Thinking* (1952) to be a lightweight version of religious theology, but it remained a best seller throughout the 1950s. The Catholic Bishop Fulton J. Sheen hosted an Emmy-winning, prime-time television program called *Life Is Worth Living,* which continues to play in reruns on cable TV. The Baptist evangelist Billy Graham, a friend of Sheen's and eventually a confidant of President Eisenhower, achieved super-star status during the 1950s. The best-selling *Peace with God* (1953) offered the same message Graham preached to large crowds and over television: Only a spiritual rebirth, through a direct commitment to Jesus Christ, would bring salvation to individuals who lived in a world filled with so many signs of sin and corruption.

Although observers generally identified Peale, Sheen, and Graham with relatively conservative, anticommunist political causes, their differing approaches to religion shared a broadly pluralist stance. Billy Graham, for instance, scrupulously avoided the kind of anti-Semitic and anti-Catholic rhetoric that sometimes accompanied the sermons of other protestant evangelists, and his own ministry abandoned all forms of racial segregation during the mid-1950s.

Moreover, appeals to religious faith could be found all across the political spectrum. Dorothy Day, who had been involved in religiously based community activism since the early 1930s, continued to work with an interdenominational coalition of communitarians. Especially through the pages of her *Catholic Worker* magazine, she promoted programs for redistributing income and wealth in more equitable ways and for securing a more peaceful world. Church leaders and laypeople from all three major denominations supported

Split-Level Living   This 1960 cartoon, by the *Washington Post's* "Herblock" (Herbert Block), illustrates the growing critique of Eisenhower-era social policy. While suburbanites enjoy new affluence in a split-level home, public services and distressed people remain underfunded.

efforts at addressing racial and religious discrimination, including the spiritually grounded efforts of Martin Luther King, Jr., and other civil rights leaders (see following discussion).

Discontents of Affluence

Celebrations of economic affluence, political pluralism, and religious commitment existed alongside a relatively vibrant body of social criticism. The widespread faith that the United States could deploy its abundant economic and political-social resources to solve virtually all of its remaining problems likely helped encourage this rich critical culture. The 1950s produced a sizeable and diverse body of literature that probed issues such as social conformity, unruly youth, mass culture, discrimination, and economic inequality.

Conformity in an Affluent Society

The sociologist William H. Whyte, Jr., gained a wide academic audience for *The Organization Man* (1956). This book indicted corporate culture for contributing to an unwanted by-product of affluence: social conformity. Criticizing the social, cultural, and psychological (although not the economic) role of large corporations, *The Organization Man* saw ordinary corporate employees deferring to the wishes and values of their bosses at the expense of their own individuality. Even among younger executives, Whyte's book claimed, the security of knowing what the corporate hierarchy desired—and when it wanted it— outweighed any concern about losing track of one's own sense of self.

The Lonely Crowd (1950) by another sociologist, David Riesman, offered an even broader critique of social conformity. This influential book claimed to see a shift from an "inner-directed" culture, in which people looked to themselves and to their immediate families for their sense of identity and self-worth, to an "other-directed" one, in which people constantly gazed at others for approval and measured their own worth against mass-mediated images. An other-directed society, in short, emphasized "adjustment" to the expectations of others rather than commitment to individual "autonomy."

Seeking to show how baby boomers would supposedly learn conformist values, *The Lonely Crowd* pointed to *Tootle, the Engine,* a popular children's book. After "Tootle" shows a preference for jumping the rails and frolicking in the nearby fields, people from his community use peer pressure to nudge him "back on the tracks." If he remains on the straight-and-narrow and follows lines laid down by others, Tootle learns, his future as a powerful and fast-moving streamliner will be assured. Riesman's book argued that this "modern cautionary tale," which stressed the importance of adjusting one's own path through life to the expectations of others, contrasted vividly with the self-reliant values served up in *Little Red Riding Hood* and other earlier conflict-filled fairy tales.

The critique of social conformity reached perhaps its widest audience through the best-selling books of journalist Vance Packard. *The Hidden Persuaders* (1957) argued that the advertising industry—especially through calculated appeals to the insecurities of consumers—encouraged conformist behavior, particularly in buying habits and cultural tastes. His book, Packard claimed, could help its readers "achieve a creative life in these conforming times," when so many people "are left only with the roles of being consumers or spectators."

If analysts looked hard enough, it seemed, evidence of conformity and loss of selfhood lurked nearly everywhere. Critics such as Whyte, Riesman, and Packard generally highlighted signs supposedly evident among middle-class men, but writers such as **Betty Friedan** warned about an analogous, although gendered, trend among many women, especially those with good educations and lively intellects who found themselves trapped in the new suburbia. Business corporations, for instance, expected that the wives of their male executives would help their husbands deal with the demands of corporate life, including the need for frequent dinner parties and occasional relocation moves. The organization man, it was said, should recognize that his ascent up the economic ladder could depend on how well an "organization woman," his spouse, conformed to her unpaid work for the greater good of the corporate world.

The affluent cultural climate of the 1950s, then, hardly discouraged social criticism, some of it occasionally quite pointed. Both the scholarly and more popular writings of the sociologist C. Wright Mills, for instance, denounced how corporate leaders and advertising executives operated as members of a "power elite." A relatively small coalition of the already powerful could set the agenda for public policy discussions, especially those involving national security and domestic spending priorities. This ruling elite, which also included military leaders and anticommunist politicians, shaped the crucial decisions on important policy issues. Moreover, its emphasis on generating sustained economic growth produced social problems that went far beyond the other-directedness analyzed in *The Lonely Crowd*. The much-vaunted American Way of Life, in Mills' view, featured increasingly regimented work routines and meaningless leisure-time activities that could never produce a true sense of satisfaction. Standing against the tide of pluralist accounts, Mills watched his claims undergo constant sifting and resifting. The numerous academics and journalists who espoused the pluralist faith during the 1950s invariably concluded that Mills, for all his passion and commitment, offered only simplistic "conspiracy theories." During the 1960s, however, his ideas about a "power elite" and a widespread sense of social "alienation" would circulate within a much more receptive cultural environment.

Restive Youth

Meanwhile, concern about young people, especially their cultural tastes and social behavior, intensified. At one point, in the mid-1950s, many criminologists linked a rise in the sale of comic books to a spike in reported rates of juvenile delinquency. *The Seduction of the Innocent* (1954), a popular study by the psychologist Frederick Wertham, blamed comics, especially those featuring images of sex and violence, for "mass-conditioning" children and for stimulating social unrest. Responding to regulatory legislation by some U.S. cities and to calls for additional measures by Congress, the comic book industry quickly embraced self-censorship. Publishers who adhered to new, industry-developed guidelines for portraying violence and deviant behavior began to display a seal of approval on their publications. The "great comic book scare" proved a relatively momentary fright.

Other worrisome signs, however, persisted. One of these, a former truck driver named **Elvis Presley,** rocked the pop music scene with several hits on the tiny Sun record label. Most of the major record distributors dismissed rock as a passing fad, but Sun's Sam Phillips detected something more substantial. As soon as Elvis began to make personal appearances, the overt sensuality that dominated his musical performance quickly validated Phillips' intuitions. Presley and other youthful (invariably male) rock stars—including Buddy Holly from West Texas, Richard Valenzuela (Richie Valens) from East Los Angeles, Frankie Lymon from Spanish Harlem, and "Little Richard" Penniman from Georgia—leaped over cultural and ethnic barriers. Rock derived new musical forms from older sources, especially African American rhythm and blues (R&B) and the "hillbilly" music of southern whites.

The first **rock 'n' rollers** seemingly spoke to the hopes and fears of millions of their youthful fans. They sang about the joy of "having a ball tonight," the pain of the "summertime blues," the torment of being "a teenager in love," and the promise of deliverance, through the power of rock, from "the days of old." Songs such as "Roll Over Beethoven" by Chuck Berry became powerful teen anthems.

Guardians of older, family-oriented forms of commercial culture found rock 'n' roll far more frightening than comic books. They denounced rock's sparse lyrics, pulsating guitars, and screeching saxophones as an assault on the very idea of music. Even the name of this music, it seemed obvious, played to raging teenage hormones. Religious groups thus denounced rock as the "Devil's music"; anticommunists detected a clever strategy by the Red Menace to corrupt youth; and segregationists saw its indebtedness to black musical forms as part of a sinister plot to encourage "race-mixing." Still a bellwether of conservative tastes, the FBI's J. Edgar Hoover saw rock music as "repulsive to right-thinking people" and as a social force that would soon have "serious effects on our young people." The danger of rock 'n' roll seemed abundantly evident in *The Blackboard Jungle* (1955), a hit movie (which featured "Rock Around the Clock" on its soundtrack) about a racially mixed group of sexually active students who, for good measure, terrorize teachers and mock any adult authority not "manly enough" to set limits on their excesses.

Eventually attentive to new turns in the product-centered culture of youth, the commercial entertainment industry soon recognized the potential breadth of rock 'n' roll's appeal. Its flexible cultural and musical vocabulary could attract its youthful audience with both critiques and celebrations of the consequences of material abundance. "Charlie Brown," for example, satirically contrasted pieties about staying in school with the bleak educational opportunities open to many students, especially those of African descent. Chuck Berry sang of a terminally bored teenager, riding around in his automobile, "with no particular place to go." The implied social criticism in songs such as these, which older listeners often failed to decode, anticipated the more overtly rebellious rock music of the 1960s.

At the same time, rock music and the larger youth culture of the 1950s could also merge seamlessly into that era's mass-consumption ethic. Sam Phillips, lacking the capital to distribute records to a rapidly expanding market, sold Presley's contract to RCA and watched the rest of his budding stars drift away from Sun to larger labels. The leading record companies and Top-40 radio stations saw middle-class teenagers, whose average weekly income/allowance reached $10 by 1958, as a market segment well worth targeting. In "Sweet Little Sixteen," Berry sang about an affluent teenager chasing after the latest fashions, the next rock 'n' roll show, and "about half-a million framed autographs." Record companies and disc jockeys began promoting a second generation of rock performers, such as the Beach Boys, and songs that exalted the pursuit of "fun, fun, fun," which apparently required the latest clothing fashions, late-model automobiles, and the top-selling rock 'n' roll records.

The Mass Culture Debate

Meanwhile, concern about social conformity and youth-oriented styles often joined a broader cultural debate over "mass culture." Much of the anxiety about the decline of individualism and the rise of disruptive young people encompassed deeper fears, especially among people who equated their own tastes with the future of civilization. From their perspective, the marketers who could apparently use standardized imagery to manipulate the cultural marketplace and sway the emotions of millions of people, those "hidden persuaders," also threatened to debase the fragile core of cultural life.

Cosmopolitan critics, connoisseurs of European-derived culture, decried the mass-marketed products flooding the newly affluent United States. They worried that the "bad"—such as comics and rock music—would soon purge anything "good" from the cultural marketplace and perhaps prevent future generations from even being able to distinguish between them. Moreover, they warned that a national mass media, by addressing millions of cultural consumers in the same manner, would obscure meaningful, and sometimes subtle, differences underneath a constant blur of pleasant, superficial imagery. After intensively studying a small town in upstate New York, for example, a team of sociologists claimed that mass-mediated images from outside this community seemed "so overwhelming that little scope is left for the expression of local cultural" forms.

Television, dominated by three large corporations (NBC, CBS, and ABC) and ultimately financed by revenues from national advertising accounts, provided a prominent target in the mass culture debate. Picturing millions of seemingly passive viewers gathered around "the boob tube," critics decried both the quality of television programming and its presumed impact on viewers. Network television, according to its critics, encouraged people to retreat into unreal, fabricated spaces, such as a mythical Old West or the fake competition on TV quiz shows. By the late 1950s, the television networks filled many of their prime-time hours with western-themed series (such as *Gunsmoke*) and quiz programs (such as the *$64,000 Question*), whose contestants had been supplied the answers they pretended to puzzle over. The head of the Federal Communications Commission (FCC) would later speak for the 1950s generation of TV critics when he denounced the entire medium as a "vast wasteland."

Social observers also noted how television even appeared to be recutting the fabric of everyday life. Architects rearranged living space within middle-class homes so that the TV set, serving as an electronic substitute for the traditional fireplace hearth, could become the focal point of family gatherings. New products—such as the frozen TV dinner, the TV tray, the recliner chair, and the influential magazine *TV Guide*—became extensions of a television-constructed culture.

The mass-produced cultural products that critics decried, however, also seemed inseparable from the pluralistic political system and the economic growth that these same observers generally celebrated. Was it possible to eliminate the curse of mass culture without sacrificing liberty and affluence? If, for example, Congress were to legislate against "dangerous" cultural products, might not such regulations shrink the boundaries for all legally protected expression? If local communities were to step in, as some had done with comics, the results might be even worse. The prospect of southern segregationists confiscating civil-rights literature or of local censorship boards rushing, unimpeded, to ban books by celebrated authors such as D. H. Lawrence hardly appealed to the cosmopolitan, well-educated critics of mass culture. Their critical diagnosis, in short, seemed short on viable remedies. Most important, the mass culture debate did nothing to halt the flood of products, especially TV programs, aimed at an ever-expanding audience.

Changing Gender Politics

Meanwhile, the 1950s saw the continuation of significant changes in how and where people lived and worked. This era particularly challenged ideas about the nature of gender relationships.

The New Suburbs and Gender Ideals

In middle-class homes, especially those located in the new suburbs, wives and mothers discovered just how "liberating" consumer technology might be. Colorful and chrome-plated appliances and "modern conveniences"—such as automatic clothes washers, more powerful vacuum cleaners, and home freezers—did ease old burdens but also created new ones. Clothes and floors now, according to advertisers, needed to be kept "spotlessly clean." Elaborate meals could be prepared in "a jiffy." Careful academic studies found that, contrary to what promoters of labor-saving devices promised, women could devote as much of their day to household tasks during the 1950s as had their grandmothers in the early 1900s. New household technologies did not so much reduce the time that women spent on domestic duties as shift it to different activities, ones requiring the household gadgets that accompanied the spread of affluence.

At first glance, the changing demands of housework fit into a broader pattern of "separate spheres." A set of clearly delineated and gendered barriers seemed to structure daily life, particularly in the newer suburbs. At its most rigid, the suburban lifestyle included a public sphere of work and politics dominated by men and a private sphere of housework and child care reserved for women. Because few businesses located in the suburbs, men began spending a good portion of their days commuting from home to work. Women who wanted to hold a job outside their homes initially found nearby employment opportunities about as scarce as child-care facilities. Consequently, mothers spent a great deal of time taking care of their baby-boomer children. In contrast to the urban neighborhoods or the rural communities in which many suburban housewives had grown up, the new suburbs of the 1950s contained few older relatives or younger single women who could assist with household and child-care duties.

Without mothers or grandmothers living close by, young suburban mothers turned elsewhere for child-rearing advice. Local Parents and Teachers Associations (PTAs), connected to neighborhood schools, offered the chance for women to exchange information with their neighbors, as did women's organizations such as the La Leche League. Increasingly, though, younger parents turned to an easily expandable shelf of child-care manuals. **Dr. Benjamin Spock's** *Baby and Child Care,* first published in 1946 with successive editions selling in the tens of millions, stood out from its competitors.

Following earlier advice books, Spock's book assigned virtually all child-care duties to women and underscored their nurturing role by stressing the need to constantly monitor a child's psychological growth. The future of the family—and the nation itself, Spock implied—depended on how well baby-boom-era mothers handled the daily responsibility of child-rearing. Other manuals picked up where Dr. Spock left off and counseled mothers on the care and feeding of teenagers.

The alarmist tone of many of these advice books reflected and helped generate a growing concern about teenage culture. A problem teen, according to one 1950s study, sprang from a "family atmosphere not conducive to development of emotionally well-integrated, happy youngsters, conditioned to obey legitimate authority." The ideal mother, from this perspective, did not work outside her home and devoted herself to rearing her own particular segment of the baby-boom generation. Women who desired careers outside of their home and marriage risked being labeled, in line with widespread psychological theories of the day, as maladjusted and deviant, real-life versions of the *femmes fatales* who populated *films noirs* (see chapter 27).

Slightly different versions of this message appeared nearly everywhere. Even the nation's most prestigious colleges for women assumed that their female students would pursue men and marriage instead of a career. In a 1955 commencement address at the prestigious, all-women Smith College, Adlai Stevenson, the Democratic Party's urbane presidential contender, reminded graduates that it was the duty of each to keep her husband "truly purposeful, to keep him whole." Popular magazines, psychology literature, and pop-culture imagery suggested that understanding, supportive wives and mothers held the keys to social stability. Conversely, women who desired alternative arrangements, either in their work or their sexual preferences, needed to be pressured, much as "Tootle, the Engine," to return to the straight and narrow path.

Competing portraits, however, painted different and more complicated pictures of gender arrangements. Most men told researchers that they preferred an active partner to a "submissive, stay-at-home" wife. Popular TV shows, such as "Father Knows Best" and "Leave It to Beaver," subtly suggested that middle-class fathers should become more engaged in family life than they normally seemed to be. Advice manuals still envisioned husbands earning their family's entire income but increasingly urged them to be "real fathers" at home. Parenting literature came to extol an ethic of "family togetherness," and institutions such as the Young Men's Christian Association (YMCA) began to offer courses on how to achieve this ideal.

The call for family togetherness seemed to be, in part at least, a response to what cultural historians have come to see as an incipient "male revolt" against "family values" and the "male breadwinner role." Hugh Hefner's *Playboy* magazine, which debuted in 1953, epitomized this rebellion. It ridiculed men who neglected their own happiness in order to support a wife and children as suckers rather than saints. *Playboy*'s first issue defiantly proclaimed: "We aren't a 'family magazine.'" Hefner advised women to pass *Playboy* "along to the man in your life and get back to your *Ladies Home Companion*." In this version of the good life, a man lived in his own "pad" rather than in the heavily mortgaged family home; drove a sports car rather than a four-door sedan or a station wagon; and courted the Playmate of the Month rather than the Mother of the Year.

Signs of Women's Changing Roles

Despite media images of homebound wives and mothers, greater numbers of women than ever before now worked outside of their homes. The rate of female employment, including that among married women, had begun to rise during the 1940s, and this trend continued throughout the 1950s. Women who were married often entered the labor force as part-time workers in the expanding clerical and service sectors. In 1948, about 25 percent of married mothers held jobs outside of the home; at the end of the 1950s, nearly 40 percent did. With the introduction of a new method of oral contraception in 1960, the birth control pill, women gained an additional measure of control over family planning and career decisions—and over decisions about their own sexual behavior. By 1964, one-quarter of the women who used contraception relied on "the pill." At the same time, women's groups began to press for an end to antiabortion laws that restricted the ability of women, particularly those without the means to travel overseas or to states that offered relatively liberal access to medical abortions, to find legal and relatively safe ways to terminate pregnancies.

Employment opportunities for women, especially when compared to those available to most men of European descent, still remained limited during the 1950s. Virtually all of the nation's nurses, telephone operators, secretaries, and elementary school teachers were women. Historically, pay scales in these areas lagged behind those for men in comparable fields; union jobs remained rare; and chances for rapid, or significant, advancement seemed elusive. As the number of low-paid jobs for women expanded during the 1950s, better-paid professional opportunities actually narrowed. Medical and law schools, along with most professional societies, admitted very few women. When Sandra Day (who would later become Justice Sandra Day O'Connor serving on the U.S. Supreme Court) graduated, with honors, from a prestigious law school during the 1950s, not a single private firm offered her a job, and she worked, without pay, in the public sector. The number of women on college and university faculties shrank during the 1950s, down from the already low levels of earlier decades.

The "family wage," as both ideal and practice, created a barrier to better-paying jobs for women. Employers still invoked the notion of a family wage to justify paying male workers higher wages and salaries than their female counterparts, even though significant numbers of women now needed to support not just themselves but also a family on their own paychecks. This was especially the case for women of color. By 1960, women headed slightly more than 20 percent of black families. Recognizing that idealized images of motherhood hardly characterized the lives of the many African American women who worked outside of their homes, *Ebony* magazine regularly celebrated black women who combined success in parenting and at work. It featured articles about educators and prominent entertainers, as well as about blue-collar workers, such as the only African American woman who worked as a mechanic at American Airlines.

Some of the mass-circulation magazines that targeted women of European descent also carried a relatively wide array of messages about gender roles. Although many social commentators continued to label a woman's desire to pursue activities outside of her home as "unnatural," popular publications increasingly featured stories about women successfully pursuing careers in public life and in business. The 1950s, in short, saw growing diversity in both the social roles that women were assuming and the ways in which commercial mass culture represented aspirations for further change.

The Fight against Discrimination, 1953–1960

Focus Question
How did the fight against discrimination raise new political issues and visions during the 1950s and early 1960s? How did the nation's political and social institutions respond to these issues?

When Dwight Eisenhower assumed the presidency in 1953, the U.S. Supreme Court was preparing to rehear a full-scale constitutional challenge to racially segregated educational systems. The NAACP and its chief legal strategist, Thurgood Marshall, spearheaded the attack on Jim Crow school arrangements. Before the rehearing took place, a vacancy in the Chief Justiceship allowed Ike to tap Earl Warren, a former Republican governor of California, to head the High Court. The Supreme Court, with Warren as its "Chief," entered the widening struggle against discrimination.

The Brown Cases, 1954–1955

The landmark Supreme Court case popularly known as "the *Brown* decision" actually included a series of constitutional challenges to school segregation. In 1954, Chief Justice Warren wrote a unanimous opinion (in **Brown v. Board of Education of Topeka**) striking down state-mandated segregation of public schools. This practice, according to Warren's relatively brief and broadly argued opinion, violated the constitutional right of African American students to equal protection of the law. A companion case, decided the same day (*Bolling* v. *Sharpe*), ruled against segregated schools in the District of Columbia. Although these decisions technically applied only to state-operated schools, they suggested that other segregated public facilities now lay open to constitutional challenge. In 1955, however, yet another Supreme

Court decision, known as *Brown II,* decreed that the process of public school desegregation should not go into effect immediately; it could, instead, move forward "with all deliberate speed."

Carrying out the broader implications of the *Brown* cases challenged the nation's political, social, and cultural institutions. A crucial part of the crusade against racial discrimination had long focused on the 16 states that the Census Bureau officially called "the South," but ongoing demographic changes ensured that the civil-rights struggle would not remain a regional matter.

During the 1950s, life in the South continued to become more like that in the rest of the country. New cultural forces, such as network television, penetrated this once relatively insular region, opening parts of it to ideas and practices that challenged the prevailing

© Bettmann/CORBIS

Segregation Dressed in his Air Force uniform, a young man from New York City is faced with a "colored waiting room" in an Atlanta bus terminal in 1956. Before the civil-rights revolution of the 1960s, southern states maintained legally enforced segregation in most public facilities, a practice popularly called Jim Crow (see chapter 18).

racial patterns. Machine technologies continued to displace the South's predominantly black field workers, and the absence of strong labor unions and the presence of favorable tax laws attracted more national chain stores and northern-based businesses. In addition, an improved generation of air-conditioning units, for businesses and homes, helped transform work, leisure, and demographic patterns throughout the southern United States.

At the same time, the racial and ethnic composition of cities in the West, Midwest, and Northeast changed to look more like that in areas of the South. In 1940, more than three-quarters of the nation's African Americans lived in the South. Following earlier trends, African Americans continued to leave the rural South and become important political constituencies in Los Angeles, Chicago, New York, Cleveland, and other urban areas. In these locales, most Democrats and many Republicans generally supported efforts to end racial discrimination. As more African Americans came to cast Democratic ballots, however, the GOP sought to refocus its appeal, reaching out to white voters in what had long been the Democratic Party's solid South and in the new suburban neighborhoods, especially in the Mid and Far West. At the same time, the nation's Spanish-speaking population continued to grow and to become an increasingly important political force, particularly in the West and Southwest. **(See Map 28.1, Shifts in African American Population Patterns, 1940–1960, in the color insert following page 1248.)**

The most familiar stories about the civil-rights crusade during the 1950s have long concentrated on the South, but recent histories help underscore its nationwide scope. By 1963, efforts to change the entire spectrum of racially based patterns and practices affected local, state, and national politics. Civil rights activists outside the South, where people of African and Latin American descent already exercised some measure of political leverage, worked for better jobs, improved housing, stronger neighborhood institutions, and greater influence within the larger political system. Cultivating ties to sympathetic politicians and labor unions, a relatively broad movement to end segregation and racial discrimination emerged, especially among African Americans, in virtually every northern and western city.

These urban-based movements employed a variety of tactics on behalf of several different goals. They pressed "shop where you can work" campaigns, which urged African American consumers to patronize only businesses that would employ them as workers. They tried to bring more blacks into the labor union movement and the fast-growing public service sector, so that they could find jobs in police and fire departments as well as in all of the various agencies of state and local government. Leading attorneys, while still supporting lawsuits such as *Brown*, joined with black lawyers to concentrate on the ordinary day-to-day legal problems of clients in their own communities. Increasingly, though, gaining additional political leverage seemed crucial to making gains in other areas, including economic ones.

The search for political power became particularly contested and inexorably connected to the struggle to dismantle systems of officially sanctioned segregation throughout the South. Here, white segregationists pledged "massive resistance" to the *Brown* decisions. When the Supreme Court's "all deliberate speed" approach in *Brown II* seemed to give them time to maneuver, their lawyers went to court in pursuit of traditional and newly invented delaying tactics. In 1956, 100 members of the U.S. Congress signed a "Southern Manifesto," which condemned the Supreme Court's desegregation rulings as a "clear abuse of judicial power" and pledged support for any state that intended "to resist forced integration by any lawful means."

Defiance did not always remain within legal bounds, especially in the South. There, white vigilantes unfurled the banners and donned the robes of the Ku Klux Klan, and new racist organizations, such as the White Citizens Council, appeared on the scene. As a result, people who joined the civil-rights cause constantly risked injury and death. Even those who were only indirectly connected to the struggle could fall victim to racist violence. In August 1955, two white Mississippians brutally murdered 14-year-old Emmett Till, because they decided this black visitor from Chicago had acted "disrespectful" toward a married white woman.

Mamie Till Bradley insisted that her son's death not remain a private incident. She demanded that his maimed corpse be displayed publicly for "the whole world to see" and insisted that his murderers be punished. To the surprise of many observers, Mississippi officials did indict two men for Till's murder. When they came to trial, though, an all-white Mississippi jury quickly found the pair—who would subsequently confess their crime to a magazine reporter—not guilty.

The Montgomery Bus Boycott and Martin Luther King, Jr.

In response to the uncertainty of judicial remedies, the southern civil-rights movement began supplementing legal maneuvering with ever-more ambitious and larger campaigns of direct action. Following an earlier 1953 campaign that secured partial desegregation of the public transportation system in Baton Rouge, Louisiana, activists in Montgomery, Alabama, raised their own sights. After police arrested **Rosa Parks** for defying a local segregation ordinance, Montgomery's black community quickly mobilized and demanded a complete end to segregated buses. They coupled their demand with an ambitious boycott of city buses, which required organizing a system of private carpools as an alternative mode of transit. Joining with Rosa Parks, a longtime bastion of the local NAACP chapter, many other black women in Montgomery helped coordinate the complicated, months-long boycott. Responding to events in Montgomery, the U.S. Supreme Court extended the premise of the *Brown* decisions on education and specifically declared segregation of public buses to be unconstitutional.

After a campaign lasting more than a year, the effort succeeded. City officials, saddled with continued financial losses and legal defeat in court, agreed to end Montgomery's separatist

© Don Cravens/Time Life Pictures/Getty Images

Montgomery Bus Boycott   The drive to desegregate municipal buses in Montgomery, Alabama, required an elaborately organized and skillfully coordinated effort. It primarily relied on the talents and commitment of volunteers, particularly women. African American residents of Montgomery shared automobile transportation, coordinated by the boycott movement, while avoiding city buses, such as the one standing vacant across the street.

transit policy. Events in Montgomery suggested that other local black activists, even in the legally segregated South, could effectively mobilize—and then organize—community resources to fight against racial discrimination.

The Montgomery boycott of 1955–56 also vaulted **Dr. Martin Luther King, Jr.,** one of its leaders and its primary spokesperson, into the national spotlight. Born, raised, and educated in Atlanta, Georgia, with a doctorate in theology from Boston University, King joined with other black ministers to follow up the victory in Montgomery by forming the Southern Christian Leadership Conference (SCLC). Increasingly able to mobilize against segregated public facilities and racial discrimination, the SCLC turned to the more difficult task of organizing an ongoing sociopolitical movement that could work for permanent change in other areas of race relations.

The relatively young male ministers in the SCLC tapped advice from across generational and gender divides. They turned, for example, to Bayard Rustin, who had been involved in civil-rights activism since the 1940s, and to Ella Baker, another veteran organizer with experience in CORE and the NAACP. Aided by Rustin's tactical advice and Baker's organizational skills, Dr. King thrived as the titular leader of the SCLC's ambitious effort to register African American voters throughout the South.

King and his associates relied on nonviolent direct action. Following in the footsteps of Rustin and CORE (see chapter 27), they espoused a moral, religiously grounded ethic. The civil-rights crusade, in this sense, intended to be more than just another pluralist interest group that sought a place at the bargaining table. According to Dr. King's well-publicized sermons and writings, nonviolent direct action would dramatize, through both word and deed, the evil of racial discrimination. The civil-rights crusade promised to bring "redemption and reconciliation" to the entire nation.

King's powerful presence and religiously rooted rhetoric, which attracted all national media, played especially well on television. The people who directed this commercial medium began to recognize how news coverage, especially when focused on easily dramatized examples of conflict, could swell their audience and boost their journalistic stature. Media accounts of events in the South emphasized the roles played by King and his followers, helping to elevate their specific activities in the broader, constantly volatile drama of civil rights. The southern-based activists who looked to Dr. King, however, comprised only one part of a much broader, highly diverse movement that reached throughout the nation and into the world.

The Politics of Civil Rights: From the Local to the Global

All across the country, civil-rights activists pressed forward. Shortly after the conclusion of the **Montgomery bus boycott,** for example, New York City passed the nation's first "open housing" ordinance, a model for other local and state measures intended to end racial discrimination in the sale and rental of homes and apartments. In other cities and states outside the South, civil-rights groups enjoyed considerable success in obtaining legislation to outlaw racial discrimination in hiring. The majority of people in a 1944 opinion poll had agreed that workers of European descent "should have the first chance" at any job opportunity, but subsequent surveys showed a steady erosion of this sentiment during the 1950s.

Efforts to obtain laws aimed at ending discrimination in housing, however, faced tougher going than those focused on the workplace. Typically, white homeowners in those urban and older suburban neighborhoods where African Americans or Latinos might hope to buy or rent tried to adopt the same exclusionary strategies used so effectively by their counterparts in the new suburbs.

In a number of instances, civil-rights groups continued to work, however, with sympathetic allies. In 1958, for example, a labor and civil-rights coalition in California, joining under slogans such as "Keep Mississippi Out of California" and "Fight Sharecropper Wages," defeated an anti-union "right-to-work" proposal. Such a measure, its opponents claimed, threatened to drive down pay for workers, of both European and non-European descent, to levels found in the antiunion, pro-segregationist states of the Deep South. Buoyed by this success, the same coalition began aggressively lobbying members of the California legislature to enact a statewide opening housing measure.

Political institutions in Washington, D.C., also felt pressure to act on civil-rights matters. The Supreme Court lent its support at crucial times, such as the Montgomery bus boycott, but the Constitution did not grant the federal judiciary the power to provide the on-the-ground policing required to translate its definitions of liberty and equality into everyday practices. Congress, with the ability to enact enforcement legislation, remained deeply divided on racial issues. With southern segregationists, all members of the Democratic Party's majority, holding key posts on Capitol Hill, antidiscrimination measures faced formidable congressional obstacles.

Even so, Congress did pass its first civil-rights measure in more than 80 years. **The Civil Rights Act of 1957** established new procedures for expediting lawsuits by African Americans claiming illegal abridgement of their right, under the 15th Amendment, to vote. Generally credited to the tactical wizardry of Lyndon Johnson of Texas, the Democratic leader in the Senate, this legislation also created a permanent Commission on Civil Rights, a largely advisory body empowered only to study alleged violations and recommend additional remedies. In 1960, again after crucial maneuvering by Johnson, a second civil-rights act expanded the legal remedies available to blacks who were being barred from voting in the South. These civil-rights measures, passed in the face of fierce opposition from southern Democrats, dramatized the difficulty of getting even relatively limited measures through Congress and clearing the obstacles segregationists could throw in the way of civil-rights legislation.

The office of the president, which theoretically possessed the constitutional power to enforce legislation and court orders, appeared reluctant, under Dwight Eisenhower, to take action. Lobbied by Republicans from the Northeast and West, Ike did support the Civil Rights Act of 1957 but held back when these same Republicans urged a dramatic presidential step, perhaps issuing an executive order barring racial discrimination on construction projects financed by federal funds. A confirmed gradualist, Eisenhower saw the fight against segregation as primarily a state and local matter, and he expressed doubts about political leaders in Washington being able to change the attitudes of people who were opposed to the integration of public facilities or job sites.

During the fall of 1957, however, events in Little Rock, Arkansas, finally forced Eisenhower's hand. In response to a federal court order, which demanded desegregation of the city's Central High, the state's governor, Orval Faubus, had promised fellow segregationists that black students would never enter the school building. Ike's initial temporizing allowed Faubus time to play to the white supremacist galleries of Arkansas, and the governor eventually deployed his state's National Guard to prevent any move toward desegregation. Confronting this direct challenge to national authority, Eisenhower took command of the Arkansas National Guard and sent members of the U.S. Army to Little Rock. Black students, escorted by armed troops, finally entered Central High. The primary issue at stake, Eisenhower insisted, involved the defiance of the law of the land rather than the specific politics of school desegregation.

The confrontation in Little Rock also underscored, as the Eisenhower administration conceded, the international dimension of civil-rights politics in the United States. Washington often found itself on the defensive when foreign critics pointed to the U.S. record on civil rights. The Soviet Union delighted in reminding people around the world, particularly those in the Third World, how racial discrimination showed "the façade of the so-called 'American democracy.'" Secretary of State Dulles warned that racial conflict at home was "not helpful to the influence of the United States abroad." Events in Arkansas seemed to reaffirm the image, carried throughout the world by the Eisenhower administration's informational campaign, of the United States as a powerful nation that supported liberty and equality. When the U.S. Supreme Court, in *Cooper* v. *Aaron* (1958), unanimously invalidated an Arkansas law intended to block further integrationist efforts, newspapers around the globe highlighted its action.

American Indian Policy

The Eisenhower administration also struggled with the politics of American Indian policy. It attempted to implement two programs, "termination" and "relocation," that were already underway before it took office. The first called for Washington to terminate the status of Indians as "wards of the United States" and grant them all the "rights and privileges pertaining to American citizenship." This policy, to be pursued on a tribe-by-tribe basis, aimed at abolishing Indian reservations, liquidating tribal assets, and curtailing the social services offered by the Bureau of Indian Affairs (BIA). In 1954, a year after Congress proposed this general approach, legislators enacted six specific bills of termination, which would change the legal status of more than 8,000 American Indians and affect the ownership of more than 1 million acres of tribal land.

Under the relocation program, which had begun in 1951, the government financed incentive packages intended to entice Indians to leave rural reservations and seek jobs in urban areas. In 1954, the BIA intensified its relocation efforts, with Minneapolis, St. Louis, Dallas, and several other cities joining Denver, Salt Lake City, and Los Angeles as relocation sites. Both relocation and termination rested on the assumption—widespread in the social-science literature of the day—that governmental planners could re-chart the lives of American Indians and that the nation's social and cultural systems could quickly assimilate all Indian people into the mainstream of U.S. life.

The initiatives, however, faced fierce criticism. After Congress enacted several more termination bills during the 1950s, almost 12,000 people lost their status as tribal members, and land formally held by tribes continued to fall into the hands of commercial, non-Indian developers. Indians from terminated tribes stood to forfeit both their exemption from state taxation and the social services provided by the BIA. In return, they gained relatively little, especially in economic benefits. Relocation went no better than termination. Even as this process weakened the links between migrants and communal life on the reservations they left, most relocated Indians complained of finding only low-paying, dead-end jobs and racial discrimination away from their tribal homes.

American Indian activists and their supporters mobilized against the **termination and relocation** policies. By 1957, their efforts forced the U.S. government to scale back the initial congressional timetable, which had called for liquidating every tribe within five years. Continued protests led both Republicans and Democrats to repudiate termination in their party platforms of 1960. Two years later, Congress finally ended the program. Despite the criticism it produced, the relocation program continued until 1967. By then, almost half of the nation's Indians lived in relocation cities. This policy, critics constantly noted, neither touched the deep-rooted problems that many Indians confronted, including a life expectancy only two-thirds that of whites, nor provided significantly better opportunities for employment or education.

The Growth of Spanish-Speaking Populations

Millions of Spanish-speaking people, many of whom had recently arrived in the United States, also began mobilizing in hopes of realizing the nation's commitments to liberty and equality. Despite the prospect of discriminatory practices in the U.S. job and housing markets, large numbers of Puerto Ricans began moving from their island commonwealth to the mainland during the 1950s. By 1960, New York City's Puerto Rican population was nearly 100 times greater than it had been before the Second World War. Large numbers of Puerto Ricans also settled in Chicago, Boston, and Hartford, Connecticut, during the 1950s. The commonwealth government of Puerto Rico promoted immigration as a way of easing population pressures, but it also encouraged migrants to maintain cultural ties with the island. Officially U.S. citizens, most of the newcomers spoke only Spanish, and the formation of social and cultural clubs helped connect them with the Puerto Rican communities they had left behind.

At the same time, Puerto Ricans also began to form organizations that could help address conditions in the United States. The Puerto Rican–Hispanic Leadership Forum, organized in 1957, presaged the emergence of groups that looked more to social and economic conditions—and, ultimately, greater political clout—in the United States than to cultural affinities with Puerto Rico.

Meanwhile, large numbers of Spanish-speaking people from Mexico continued moving to California and the Southwest. There they settled, sometimes uncomfortably, into already established Mexican American communities. In 1940, Mexican Americans had been the most rural of all the major ethnic groups; by 1950, in contrast, more than 65 percent of Mexican Americans were living in urban areas, a figure that would climb to 85 percent by 1970. As a result of this fundamental demographic shift, Mexican Americans began to become an important political force in many western and southwestern cities.

Controversy over continued immigration from Mexico intensified during the early 1950s. Beginning in 1942 and continuing until 1967, the U.S. government sponsored the *bracero* (or farmhand) program, which brought nearly 5 million Mexicans across the U.S.–Mexican border, theoretically on short-term contracts, to fill agricultural jobs. Many *braceros* and their families remained in the United States, however, after these agreements expired. Legal immigrants from Mexico, along with growing numbers of people who filtered across the border, joined them.

"Operation Wetback," an ongoing U.S. government dragnet of the early 1950s, targeted undocumented immigrants from Mexico. The choice of a term of ethnic derision, which implied that all people of Mexican ancestry had illegally swum across the Rio Grande River to reach the United States, hardly built support for this program in Mexican American communities. During a five-year period, the U.S. government claimed to have rounded up and deported to Mexico nearly 4 million people, allegedly all undocumented immigrants. This operation, its critics charged, not only swept up some people who lacked ready documentation but served to stigmatize longtime citizens of Mexican heritage and to justify discriminatory treatment by local and state governments and by employers.

Groups representing Mexican Americans gradually broadened older struggles, which traced back to the 1930s (see chapter 25), against discrimination. Labor organizers, often defying efforts by employers and FBI personnel to label their efforts as "communist inspired," sought higher wages and better working conditions in the factories and fields. Unions with left-leaning political reputations and large Mexican American memberships, such as the United Cannery, Agricultural, Packing and Allied Workers of America (UCAPAWA), faced ongoing harassment from the FBI, other governmental agencies, and private businesses. A lengthy strike in New Mexico by Mexican American zinc miners, who were affiliated with a union that had been expelled from the CIO in 1950, became the subject of the motion picture *Salt of the Earth* (1954). Pressure from Washington, the film industry, and anticommunist labor unions prevented, throughout the 1950s, popular distribution of this independent production, a collaboration among blacklisted filmmakers, striking miners, and their families.

At the same time, organizations representing Mexican American professionals, such as LULAC and the Unity League, parlayed their legal resources into lawsuits seeking the desegregation of schools and other public facilities in Southern California and throughout the Southwest. When preparing to go to court, however, lawyers for these groups immediately faced a strategic dilemma. Legal challenges brought on behalf of plaintiffs of African descent, as in the *Brown* cases, relied on the claim that state laws separating "whites" and "coloreds" violated guarantees of legal equality. Most states, though, classified persons whose ancestors came from Mexico—people who, theoretically, could be of "mixed" ancestry, including European, Indian, African, and even Asian—as legally "white." In the area of education, as earlier cases such as *Westminster* had shown (see chapter 27), school officials in states such as California and Texas segregated students of Mexican descent on the basis of real and alleged "language deficiencies," rather than on that of "race." The "other white" legal status of Mexican Americans, in other words, complicated the ability of organizations such as LULAC to frame court challenges. In practice, it also prevented lawyers from automatically relying on precedents involving "white-against-black" discrimination.

Urban-Suburban Issues

The ongoing expansion of suburbia during the 1950s focused increasing attention on public policies related to cities. A variety of measures, adopted by both governmental and private institutions and organizations, for example, continued to shift resources away from cities, especially from neighborhoods with significant numbers of Latinos and African Americans. Continuing the now-familiar policy of **red-lining**, many banks and loan institutions denied funds for home-buyers and businesses in areas they considered "decaying" or "marginal." Using the same supposedly neutral criteria employed for suburban loans, the lending industry saw these blighted areas as "bad risks." They contained aging buildings, densely clustered homes, and growing numbers of low-income people, many of whom were of non-European descent. The FHA and other governmental agencies thus concentrated their activities in the newer suburbs. In 1960, for example, the FHA failed to put up a single dollar for home loan guarantees in Camden or Paterson, New Jersey, cities in which minority populations were growing, while it focused on the recently built, largely all-white suburbs that surrounded them.

"Urban renewal" programs, authorized by the Housing Act of 1949 (see chapter 27), according to numerous social-science studies, too often seemed aimed at "urban removal." Although the law called for "a feasible method for the temporary relocation" of persons displaced by urban renewal projects, lax enforcement meant that developers could generally ignore the needs of these people. Throughout the 1950s, Robert Moses, who dominated the planning and execution of New York City's vast construction projects, effectively concealed the number of people dislocated by his urban renewal and highway building programs. Although this unelected planner-bureaucrat always had his defenders, who insisted his vision ultimately encompassed the greater good of all residents, maps of New York City's always changing landscape showed office buildings, freeways, and relatively expensive housing complexes inexorably replacing the older living units that people with low-income jobs could afford.

Roughly similar debates over goals and results—along with the same general patterns in building—marked the histories of other large cities during the 1950s. Plans for new, federally built public housing, for example, quickly faltered in most areas of the United States. Newer suburban areas with their middle-income homeowners used their political clout and local zoning laws to freeze out government-sponsored housing projects. In addition, private housing interests lobbied to limit the number of public units actually constructed, invariably on relatively expensive and already densely populated urban sites, and to deny them amenities, such as closets or closets with doors, that could be found in most private apartments. Publicly built facilities, originally conceived as short-term alternatives for families who would soon move to their own homes, became stigmatized as "the projects." They gained reputations for being housing of last resort, reserved for people with chronically low incomes and meager prospects for economic advancement. In addition to disrupting urban housing patterns, renewal-removal projects also helped disperse industries that had long provided entry-level jobs for semi- and unskilled workers.

The urban-suburban policies of the 1950s, in short, seemed to be in need of major repair. In 1960, both the Democratic and Republican parties pledged to create a new cabinet office for urban affairs and to reconsider Washington's role in addressing the cycle of continued suburban growth and onrushing urban decay.

Debating the Role of Government, 1955–1960

Discussion of urban-suburban issues during the late 1950s accompanied a broader debate over how the national government in Washington might deal with a wide range of socioeconomic matters. Although Eisenhower sometimes hinted that he favored rolling back domestic programs established during the 1930s and 1940s, he possessed neither the political support nor the personal will to do so. Actually, his administration presided over a modest expansion of earlier initiatives: a larger Social Security system, a higher minimum wage, better unemployment benefits, and a new Department of Health, Education, and Welfare (HEW). Eisenhower denied that this record suggested the White House favored "big government," and insisted his approach represented a "moderate Republicanism."

The New Conservatives

Eisenhower's self-professed moderation on domestic issues angered a growing group of people who soon became known as the "new conservatives." Conservatives within the GOP's ranks conceded Eisenhower's popularity—and the fact that he was the first Republican president since Herbert Hoover—but they also complained that his administration seldom represented the conservative principles for which the Republican Party supposedly stood. From their perspective, the Republicans who voted in support of domestic social programs looked as bad as the Northern Democrats with whom they often allied.

The most popular conservative Republican of the 1950s, Arizona's Barry Goldwater, often voiced his doubts about the programmatic and regional shape of the national GOP. Ruggedly handsome and militantly anticommunist, Goldwater won election to the U.S.

Senate in 1952. Once in Washington, he quickly emerged as the spokesperson for those Republicans who viewed Eisenhower's policies as insufficiently conservative and too indebted to GOP constituencies on the East Coast. Goldwater once quipped that his party—and the nation—might be better off if someone could magically saw off the northern part of the eastern seaboard and let it drift out into the Atlantic, presumably toward a socialist-minded Europe.

Still, Goldwater took care to distinguish his conservatism from that of the "radical right," whose attacks against Eisenhower sometimes veered into anti-Semitic diatribes and claims of Ike being a conscious agent of Moscow. Carefully framed and largely ghost-written, Goldwater's *The Conscience of a Conservative* (1960) helped popularize his conservative critique. By refusing to seriously consider stronger military measures against the Soviet Union and by not making "victory the goal of U.S. policy," he argued, Eisenhower had likely endangered national security with his version of containment. Goldwater also portrayed almost all domestic programs, including federal civil-rights legislation, as grave threats to individual liberty. The Eisenhower administration seemed largely content to follow the Democratic Party's "New Deal antics" in its own domestic policy making, the Arizona senator alleged.

While Goldwater was pressing the GOP to reject Eisenhower's moderate Republicanism, others, such as the publisher William F. Buckley, Jr., used the 1950s to frame a broadly conservative message for the 1960s. Buckley, who grew up in a wealthy, cosmopolitan, and fervently conservative family, first gained national attention while still in his twenties. In *God and Man at Yale* (1952), the devoutly Roman Catholic Buckley attacked what he saw as a "collectivist" and antireligious tilt in higher education. Most Ivy League educators, he claimed, would defend neither capitalism nor Christianity. Known for wrapping his brickbats in humor, Buckley once claimed that he would rather be governed by the first 2,000 names in the Boston phone book than by the faculty of Harvard.

Buckley helped found the *National Review* in 1955. This weekly magazine attracted a talented group of writers and avoided positions, particularly the anti-Semitism of some old-line conservatives and the hysterical anticommunism of groups such as the John Birch Society, which Democrats and members of the media could label as extremist. Buckley and his *National Review* colleagues, recognizing they could not refashion conservatism quickly, adopted strategies for the long run. To this end, they established Young Americans for Freedom (YAF) in 1960, several years before similar college-based political organizations emerged from the New Left (see chapter 29).

Adopting another long-term approach, called "fusionism," to building a conservative movement, Buckley's group avoided any strict litmus test. As a result, the *National Review* initially even provided a sounding board for Joe McCarthy's embattled followers and for some southern segregationists. Relatively quickly, however, the magazine—and the larger movement it hoped to create—came to feature creative tension coming from three broad, not-always-compatible constituencies. This threesome included "traditionalist" conservatives, who insisted that social stability depended on jettisoning all notions of equality and allowing the educated-talented few, people such as themselves, to dominate the nation's institutions. The magazine also published pieces by "libertarians," people who rejected the hierarchical, anti-egalitarian vision of more traditional conservatives but who favored reducing the power of government and enlarging the liberties of capitalist entrepreneurs. Finally, the *National Review* consistently featured staunch anticommunists, such as Barry Goldwater, who insisted that national power be used, far more aggressively than either Democratic or Republican administrations had done, to oppose Soviet-led communism.

Meanwhile, a different style of conservative activism emerged, at the grassroots, especially within many new suburban areas. Barry Goldwater's brand of conservatism proved especially appealing to suburbanites in the "Sunbelt states" that stretched from California, across the Southwest, eastward through Texas, and over to Florida. Fiercely anticommunist, the "suburban warriors" from these areas, beginning with California, also framed a militantly conservative domestic agenda. It focused on keeping both state and national officials from using their power to infringe on what these conservative suburbanites considered liberties constitutionally reserved to their own local communities. They called for maintaining grassroots control of local school curricula, tough zoning laws, and the lowest possible rates of taxation, especially on real estate.

Advocates of a More Active Government

While the new conservative movement mobilized and, then, organized, in hopes of scaling back domestic social policies, an even more eclectic group tried to make the case for expanding governmental programs. Many of these commentators began by calling for greater activism from the office of the president.

The initial indecision by the White House during the 1957 situation at Little Rock's Central High School suggested, at least to these critics, that Dwight Eisenhower held an unsteady grasp of domestic issues. The national election of 1956 had given him (and Vice President Nixon) another landslide victory over a Democratic ticket, headed again by Adlai Stevenson, but Eisenhower's continued personal popularity had done even less for the Republican Party, which had failed to regain control of Congress, than in the 1952 contest. (The GOP would shed additional congressional seats—as well as state legislatures and governors' mansions—in the mid-term races of 1958. After this election, Democrats outnumbered Republicans by nearly 2-to-1 margins in both the U.S. Senate and the House of Representatives.) Meanwhile, Eisenhower, who had rebounded from a mild heart attack before the 1956 election, seemed progressively enfeebled, physically as well as politically.

After the president suffered a second heart attack and a mild stroke during his second term, critics intensified calls for more vigorous leadership from the White House. Social activists criticized the reluctance to use Washington's power to attack racial discrimination, and many economists, pointing to an economic downturn in 1958–59 when unemployment figures rose precipitously, ridiculed the Eisenhower administration's commitment to a balanced budget. Even after economic conditions improved, economists such as John Kenneth Galbraith urged significant deficit spending by Washington as a spur to further growth. Eisenhower's advisers stoutly resisted this advice.

Many of these critics, while avoiding the rhetoric of conservatives such as Goldwater, also found the Eisenhower administration's national security moves to be insufficient. The 1957 Gaither Report, prepared by Paul Nitze and other people who had been associated with the NSC-68 document of 1950 (see chapter 27), savaged New Look policies. The Gaither Report claimed that the Soviet Union's GNP was growing even more quickly than that of the United States and that a rapidly expanding military sector accounted for much of this expansion. The Gaither Report urged an immediate increase of about 25 percent in the Pentagon's budget and a crash program for building fallout shelters. It also called for developing intercontinental ballistic missiles (ICBMs) and expanding conventional military forces. Another report, largely written by a young political scientist named Henry Kissinger and issued by the prestigious Rockefeller Foundation, argued that the New Look, by relying on massive nuclear retaliation and downplaying non-nuclear options, actually undermined national security. It joined the Gaither Report in seeking greater U.S. spending for a wide range of defense initiatives.

Eisenhower, who remained far more attentive to foreign policy than domestic issues, reacted cautiously. Although the White House agreed to accelerate the development of ICBMs, it opposed any significant effort to build fallout shelters or to expand existing capabilities for fighting limited, non-nuclear wars. In fact, the Eisenhower administration reduced the size of several army and air force units and kept its defense budget well below the levels critics had proposed. Eisenhower felt confident in pursuing this course because super-secret U-2 surveillance flights over the USSR revealed that the Soviets were lagging behind, rather than racing ahead of, the United States in military capability.

Concerns about national security and calls for greater government spending also affected U.S. educational policies. Throughout the 1950s, the more traditionalist educators had often complained about schools imparting "life adjustment" skills—getting along with others and adapting to social change—instead of teaching traditional academic subjects. Rudolf Flesch's best-selling *Why Johnny Can't Read* (1956) anticipated books that asked why Johnny and his classmates couldn't add or subtract very well either and why they lagged behind their counterparts in the Soviet Union in science. Washington's help in funding K–12 instruction seemed an obvious way to upgrade educational performance. Simultaneously, the nation's leading research universities sought greater federal aid. In summer 1957, a committee of prominent scientists implored the Defense Department to expand its support for basic scientific research. "Research is a requisite for survival" in the nuclear age, it declared.

The case for increased federal spending suddenly became more compelling. On October 4, 1957, the Soviet Union orbited the world's first artificial satellite, a 22-inch sphere called **Sputnik,** and seemingly soared far beyond the United States in both space exploration and military capabilities. The USSR could use the same missile technology needed to launch *Sputnik,* argued Eisenhower's critics, to rain down nuclear weapons on U.S. cities. Effectively safeguarding U.S. national security, therefore, appeared to demand rebuilding, as rapidly as possible, the nation's military arsenal, its educational institutions, and its research capabilities.

The specter of the original *Sputnik,* along with that of a second and much larger Soviet satellite, improved chances that a wide range of institutions, and not simply the Pentagon, would now obtain federal funding. Phrases such as "national security" and "national defense" seemed to clear the way for financial resources to flow more freely out of Washington. In 1958, Congress passed the National Defense Education Act, which funneled aid to college-level programs in science, engineering, foreign languages, and the social sciences. This law marked a milestone in the long battle to overcome congressional opposition to federal funding of public education, especially from southern representatives who feared that aid from Washington could increase pressure for racial integration. Legislators also created another R&D effort, to be overseen by a new National Aeronautics and Space Administration (NASA). This governmental agency pledged to harness U.S. educational and technological know-how so that the United States could counter the Soviet Union's successes with its *Sputniks* and preserve outer space for the benefit of "all mankind."

Many people also hoped that domestic social welfare programs would become the beneficiaries of increased federal spending. Galbraith's *The Affluent Society* (1958) saw a dangerous tilt in the "social balance," away from support for development of "public goods" and toward satisfaction of private desires. Already affluent families could afford to vacation in their own chrome-encrusted automobiles, but they would speed through shabby cities, motor along litter-filled roadsides, and gaze out at unsightly billboards. The researcher who developed a new carburetor is well rewarded, but anyone "who dreams up a new public service is [labeled] a wastrel," Galbraith's book sardonically noted.

Galbraith's critique seemed mild when compared to that of Michael Harrington. His passionate essays about the persistence of poverty recalled his apprenticeship at Dorothy Day's *Catholic Worker.* In 1959, *Commentary,* one of several influential national magazines featuring social criticism, published an article, which was immediately noticed in policy-making circles. In this essay, Harrington insisted that the need to address economic inequality remained as urgent as it had been during the 1930s. At least one-third of the nation's people—living in rural areas, small towns, and cities—barely subsisted in a land of supposed abundance and affluence. Avoiding the usual trappings of economic analysis, Harrington crafted dramatic stories about how economic deprivation ravaged the bodies and spirits of people whose lives had been largely untouched by the economic growth of the 1940s and 1950s.

During the 1960s, when addressing social and economic issues became a priority among policy makers drawn to Washington, pundits such as Galbraith and Harrington became political celebrities. These same people had honed their critiques, however, within the vibrant political culture of the late 1950s. The brief presidency of **John F. Kennedy** would, in fact, feature calls for more active foreign and domestic policies that had first emerged during the 1950s.

The Kennedy Years: Foreign Policy

Focus Question
What foreign and domestic policies did the Kennedy administration champion?

John Fitzgerald Kennedy's wealthy, politically ambitious father, Joseph P. Kennedy, claimed to have groomed his son for the White House. The young Kennedy graduated from Harvard in 1940, won military honors while serving in the Navy during the Second World War, won a 1946 election to represent his home district in Massachusetts in the lower house of Congress, and captured a Senate seat in 1952. Once in Washington, Kennedy became better known for his social life than for his command of legislative details, but he quickly parlayed his charm and youthful good lucks into political stardom. His 1953 marriage to Jacqueline Bouvier added yet another dash of glamour. A favorite of the media, Jackie won plaudits for her cultural tastes, choice in fashions, and fluency in several languages. After John Kennedy narrowly missed winning the Democratic vice presidential nomination in 1956, he immediately took aim at gaining the top spot on his party's 1960 ticket.

The Election of 1960

JFK, often accompanied by Jackie and by his brothers, Robert and Edward ("Ted") Kennedy, barnstormed across the country. This early presidential campaigning, along with a talented staff and his family's vast wealth, helped Kennedy overwhelm his Democratic challengers, including Senators Hubert Humphrey of Minnesota and Lyndon Johnson of Texas. By pledging to separate his Roman Catholic faith from his politics and by confronting those who appealed to anti-Catholic prejudice, Kennedy tried to defuse the religious issue that had doomed the candidacy of Al Smith in 1928 (see chapter 24).

Richard Nixon, running as the Republican standard bearer, spent much of the 1960 presidential campaign on the defensive. A widespread perception that the still-popular Eisenhower remained unenthusiastic about a Republican candidate who had served as his vice-president for eight years hardly cheered Nixon. Still, he tried to counter Kennedy's charisma with images of his own seasoned leadership, gained while at Ike's side. Nixon seemed notably off-balance during the first of several televised debates in which a cool, tanned Kennedy emerged, according to surveys of TV viewers, with a clear victory over a pale, nervous Nixon. (People who listened on radio assigned Nixon considerably higher marks.) Despite chronic and severe health problems, which Kennedy's entourage effectively concealed, JFK projected vigor and energy, if not experience.

Kennedy's 1960 campaign highlighted issues from the 1950s that, taken together, morphed into an agenda JFK would call the "New Frontier." Although Senator Kennedy's civil-rights record had been mixed, candidate Kennedy declared his support for new congressional legislation.

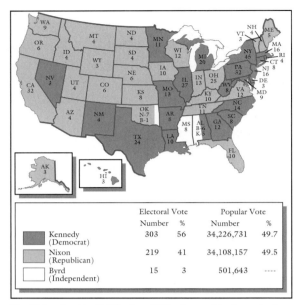

		Electoral Vote		Popular Vote	
		Number	%	Number	%
	Kennedy (Democrat)	303	56	34,226,731	49.7
	Nixon (Republican)	219	41	34,108,157	49.5
	Byrd (Independent)	15	3	501,643	----

Map 28.2   Presidential Election, 1960   In one of the closest elections in American history in terms of the popular vote, Kennedy only narrowly outpolled Nixon. Kennedy's more commanding victory in the electoral vote produced some discussion about the consequences if the electoral college one day produced a president who had failed to carry the popular vote, a situation that occurred in the election of 2000.

In an important symbolic act, he dispatched aides to Georgia to assist Martin Luther King, Jr., who was facing jail time for a minor traffic violation. Kennedy also promised to use the president's executive authority, which Eisenhower had refused to do, to fight against job discrimination and to press for new social welfare programs to rebuild rural communities, increase educational opportunities, and improve urban conditions.

Kennedy's New Frontier also recalled two other central issues of the late 1950s: promoting greater economic growth and conducting a more aggressive foreign policy. Dismissing Eisenhower's economic policies as overly timid and largely ineffectual, Kennedy proposed using tax cuts and deficit spending to juice the economy. On foreign policy, he criticized Eisenhower for failing to rid Latin America, and Cuba, of Fidel Castro and for allowing a "missile gap" to develop between the United States and the Soviet Union. By spending more on defense, Kennedy claimed, the United States could respond, more flexibly, against communism, especially in the Third World. The "American people are tired of the drift in our national course . . . and they are ready to move again," Kennedy proclaimed.

The closely contested 1960 presidential election defied easy analysis. Despite his early problems, Nixon ran a skilled campaign, and Kennedy outpolled him by only about 100,000 popular votes. Kennedy's victory in the Electoral College, moreover, rested on razor-thin margins in several states, including Illinois. Many Republicans urged Nixon to challenge Kennedy's suspicious vote total there, but the vice president chose to accept the disputed result. JFK's triumph owed a great debt to his vice presidential running mate, Lyndon Baines Johnson. A tireless campaigner, LBJ gained credit for the Democratic ticket carrying the Deep South and his home state of Texas. Democrats remained the majority party in Congress and across the country, but this did not translate into a groundswell of support for Kennedy or his New Frontier.

JFK and Jackie achieved their earliest success by riveting media attention on the White House. They hobnobbed with movie stars and hosted prominent intellectuals. Kennedy's debut as president featured designer clothing, a poignant appearance by the aged poet Robert Frost, and an oft-quoted inaugural speech in which JFK challenged people to "ask not what your country can do for you; ask what you can do for your country." The "best and the brightest," the name a journalist later bestowed (tongue in cheek) on the hard-driving people who joined Kennedy's administration, promised to launch exciting and difficult crusades, even one to the frontier of outer space. Implicitly recalling the Soviet's 1957 triumph with its *Sputniks,* JFK promised that the United States would beat the USSR in the ultimate event in the space race, landing a manned craft on the surface of the moon, before the end of the 1960s.

Kennedy's Foreign Policy Goals

Kennedy promised an aggressive national security stance, which would include new **flexible-response** capabilities. Although Secretary of Defense Robert McNamara quickly found that the alleged missile gap between the United States and the USSR had never existed, the Kennedy administration still boosted the defense budget. It strongly supported military assistance programs, informational initiatives, and covert-action planning. In one of his most popular innovations, the president created the Peace Corps, a volunteer program that would prepare Americans, especially young people, to assist struggling people in nations around the world. Once overseas, they would work on various projects aimed at improving living conditions and, additionally, undercutting the appeal of left-leaning, procommunist movements.

The Kennedy administration also repackaged Eisenhower's effort to reorient U.S. Latin American policy. Kennedy's "Alliance for Progress" elaborated on Ike's earlier desire to move away from reliance on dictators and to support broadly conceived socioeconomic programs. Unveiled in spring 1961, in hopes of checking the spread of anti-Americanism and Castro-like insurgencies, the Alliance for Progress promised $20 billion in loans over a 10-year period to Latin American countries that would undertake land reform and economic development measures. Most Latin Americans judged Kennedy's Alliance, which underestimated obstacles to social and economic innovation, as more of a symbolic gesture than a substantive blueprint for change in their region.

Cuba and Berlin

The first serious setback for the Kennedy presidency, an ill-conceived 1961 CIA mission against Cuba, also had its roots in the Eisenhower administration. The CIA, looking to earlier covert actions against anti-American governments in Iran and Guatemala as models, had worked out a secret, Eisenhower-endorsed invasion to oust Fidel Castro. Overriding dissent from some of his advisers, Kennedy reaffirmed White House support for this plan. On April 17, 1961, however, when U.S.-backed and-trained forces (mainly anticommunist Cuban exiles) landed at the Bahia de Cochinas (the **Bay of Pigs**) on the southern coast of Cuba, the popular uprising, which the CIA had predicted, failed to materialize.

Instead, forces loyal to Castro quickly surrounded and captured the invaders. Confronting a badly planned and poorly executed operation, Kennedy rejected any additional steps, including last-minute U.S. air strikes that CIA operatives had apparently misled their Cuban allies into believing were part of the plan. The White House initially tried to deny any U.S. involvement in the Bay of Pigs invasion, but the CIA's role quickly became public knowledge. A new wave of anti-Yankee sentiment swept across much of Latin America, and Castro used the invasion as justification for further tightening his grip over Cuban life and strengthening his ties to the Soviet Union.

Kennedy responded to the Bay of Pigs by admitting error and by devising new anti-Castro strategies. "I have made a tragic mistake," Kennedy told one adviser. "Not only were our facts in error, but our policy was wrong." Stung by the failed invasion, the White House continued to target Castro with a covert program, "Operation Mongoose." It included efforts to destabilize Cuba's economy and, in concert with organized crime figures, to assassinate the Cuban leader.

Meanwhile, two other dramatic confrontations began unfolding, more slowly, in Berlin and in Cuba. In June 1961, Nikita Khrushchev and Kennedy met in Vienna, Austria, where the Soviets proposed ending the Western presence in Berlin and reuniting the city as part of East Germany. Khrushchev's initiative responded to the steady flow of immigrants from East Germany into West Berlin, a migration that was both politically embarrassing and economically draining to the German communist regime. Kennedy refused to abandon West Berlin, and in August 1961, with Soviet approval, East Germany began to erect first a barbed-wire fence and then a concrete barrier to separate East from West Berlin. This "Berlin Wall" became a symbol of communist repression. Kennedy's assertion, *"Ich bin ein Berliner,"* delivered in front of the wall to a cheering crowd of West Berliners, provided a memorable moment in his presidency.

Superpower confrontation escalated to a potentially lethal, even catastrophic, level during the **Cuban Missile Crisis** of October 1962. Responding to pleas from Fidel Castro and seeing Kennedy, especially after their personal meeting in Vienna, as an inexperienced bungler, Khrushchev took a bold gamble: He began sending advanced Soviet armaments to Cuba. After a U-2 spy plane showed missile-launching sites in Cuba, the Kennedy administration announced it would not allow the Soviet Union to place nuclear warheads so close to U.S. soil. It demanded that the Soviets dismantle the missile silos and turn back its supply ships, presumably containing the warheads, then heading for Cuba.

The Cuban Missile Crisis began in earnest. After tense strategizing sessions with his top advisers, Kennedy rejected calls by some military leaders, notably General Curtis LeMay, for a strike against Cuba. JFK thus heeded warnings that any such rash action risked escalating into nuclear warfare between the United States and the Soviet Union. Instead, Kennedy ordered the U.S. Navy to "quarantine" Cuba. The president did authorize Strategic Air Command (SAC) to go on full alert, in preparation for a possible nuclear conflict. Secretary of Defense Robert McNamara later recalled leaving a presidential conference during the 13-day crisis, looking up at the sky, and wondering if the world would still be there 24 hours later. Reflections of this kind encouraged both the United States and the USSR to engage in secret diplomatic maneuvers to forestall a military showdown.

Delicate maneuvering by both governments (and several private go-betweens) finally ended the standoff. On October 28, 1962, Khrushchev ordered the Soviet missiles in Cuba to be dismantled and the supply ships to sail for home; Kennedy pledged not to invade Cuba and secretly promised to complete a previously ordered withdrawal of U.S. missiles from Turkey. When researchers finally gained access to Soviet archives during the mid-1990s, they discovered that the Missile Crisis had been even more dangerous than U.S. officials had ever imagined. Unknown to anyone in the Kennedy administration in 1962, the Soviets had already placed in Cuba tactical nuclear weapons, which could have been launched against U.S. targets in retaliation for any air strike.

The Missile Crisis underscored how easily the United States and the USSR could careen toward nuclear conflict, and the dangers of October 1962 encouraged the two nuclear superpowers to begin moving with greater caution. To prevent a similar confrontation or an accident involving nuclear weapons, they established a direct telephone hotline between Moscow and Washington, D.C. Later, during a spring 1963 commencement address at American University, Kennedy underscored the importance of the United States working to promote world peace. Some Kennedy watchers, then as well as now, have argued that this American University speech portended what a second JFK administration would have attempted to achieve in foreign policy.

Southeast Asia and "Flexible Response"

Meanwhile, though, in Southeast Asia, Kennedy continued earlier U.S. attempts to preserve a noncommunist state in South Vietnam. After the Bay of Pigs fiasco, in which the attempt to overthrow an already established communist government had failed, JFK seemed more determined than before to prevent any communist-led "war of national liberation" from ever succeeding.

Even so, the odds against preserving a pro-U.S. government in South Vietnam seemed to grow ever longer as Kennedy's own presidency lengthened. Opposition to the regime of Ngo Dinh Diem, who had been in power since 1954, had now coalesced in the National Liberation Front (NLF). Formed in December 1960, the NLF included nationalist factions that resented Diem's dependence on the United States, communists who demanded more extensive land reform, an array of political leaders who were fed up with Diem's corruption and cronyism, and groups beholden to Ho Chi Minh's communist government in the North. North Vietnam began sending additional supplies and, then, thousands of its own troops to the South to support the NLF.

The Kennedy administration saw Vietnam as a test case for its anticommunist strategy, especially the doctrine of flexible response. Although it accepted a 1962 deal that created a technically neutral but communist-influenced government in Laos, the White House appeared determined to hold the line in South Vietnam. Washington trained elite U.S. troops, the Green Berets, in counterinsurgency tactics; sent teams of social scientists, charged with nation building, to advise South Vietnam on socioeconomic policies; and dispatched other experts to train that nation's internal security forces. Finally, the Kennedy administration deployed, in ever larger increments, nearly 11,000 U.S. troops who would supposedly only advise, rather than actively fight alongside, South Vietnamese forces.

These U.S. moves seemed to create only new opportunities for corruption and greater distrust between South Vietnam's government and its citizens. When U.S. officials became aware that disgruntled South Vietnamese military officers were planning to topple Diem's already tottering regime, they gave them a green light to continue orchestrating their plan. In November 1963, the conspirators routed Diem—an act that could hardly have surprised the Kennedy administration—from his presidential palace and—in a genuine shock to U.S. officials—summarily murdered him. This coup d'état, which brought a military regime to power in Saigon, appeared to create even greater political instability in South Vietnam. The NLF and North Vietnam, in turn, ratcheted up their military pressure on the new government in Saigon.

The Southeast Asian policy of Kennedy's administration seemed no more coherent than that of Eisenhower's. The overall goal, to be sure, remained consistent: prevent communist forces from toppling any anticommunist government in Saigon. The United States could not afford to "lose" South Vietnam. Although some in JFK's inner circle urged sending U.S. combat forces into battle, the president continued to reject this option. On several occasions, the White House even talked about withdrawing some of its combat-ready advisers, perhaps as a substantive shift in policy or as a public relations move. As with his domestic agenda, Kennedy's presidency ended, unexpectedly, with its future direction in Vietnam in a state of flux or, perhaps, even disarray.

The Kennedy Years: Domestic Policy

Kennedy hesitated to follow up on his campaign proposal of increasing federal spending to speed economic growth. He feared that federal budget deficits might cost him support among fiscal conservatives and business leaders. Relations with corporate leaders, nevertheless, did turn temporarily ugly in 1962, when Kennedy clashed with the president of U.S. Steel over that company's decision to raise its prices beyond the guidelines suggested by the White House. Recoiling from this imbroglio, the Kennedy administration hoped to chart a steadier domestic course. Events did not always cooperate.

Policy Making During the Early 1960s

In 1962, the White House staff finally sat down with key members of Congress to discuss lowering tax rates as a means of promoting economic growth. The economy had nicely rebounded from its downturn of 1957–58, but proponents of a tax cut promised even more rapid growth. Lower tax rates for everyone and special deductions for businesses that invested in new plants and equipment, the tax-cutters argued, would spur investment in facilities and jobs. Despite opposition from those Democrats who thought these changes tilted toward corporations and the wealthy, the tax bill seemed headed for passage in the fall of 1963.

Most of Kennedy's ideas about social welfare policy recalled earlier proposals. There was talk of raising the federal minimum wage rate and of new urban rebuilding programs. Under the programs begun during the 1940s, Kennedy-era bulldozers continued to raze large parts of urban America, still at the expense, critics charged, of people who desperately needed affordable housing. One new departure, the Area Redevelopment Bill of 1961, called for directing federal grants and loans to areas, such as Appalachia, that the economic growth of the 1940s and 1950s had largely bypassed.

The Civil-Rights Movement, 1960–1963

Although JFK had talked about supporting new civil-rights legislation, he also tried to placate the segregationist wing of his Democratic Party. Initially, the Kennedy administration assigned greater priority to the fight against organized crime than the one against racial discrimination. The president and his brother, Robert, whom he had appointed attorney general, listened sympathetically when J. Edgar Hoover, director of the FBI, falsely warned of continuing links between Martin Luther King, Jr., and members of the American Communist Party. To monitor King's activities and gather information that Hoover would later use to smear the civil-rights leader, the FBI intensified surveillance, illegally tapped King's phone conversations, and placed "bugs" in his hotel rooms.

Meanwhile, in early 1960, African American students at North Carolina A&T, a historically black college in Greensboro, sat down at a drugstore lunch counter and politely asked to be served in the same manner as white customers. This "sit-in" marked an intensification of direct action. Young activists directly challenged local segregation laws by acting as if these measures simply did not exist. Targeting locations in both the South and the North, demonstrators staged nonviolent sit-ins at restaurants, bus and train stations, and other public facilities.

The courage and commitment of these demonstrators brought new energy—and media attention—to the antidiscrimination movement. Singing anthems such as "We Shall Overcome" and "Oh, Freedom" to promote solidarity, young people pledged their talents, their resources—indeed, their lives—to the civil-rights struggle. In 1961, an inter-racial group of activists from CORE and a new group that had emerged from the **sit-in movement, the Student Nonviolent Coordinating Committee (SNCC),** risked racist retaliation by conducting "freedom rides" across the South. The **freedom riders** were challenging the Kennedy administration to enforce the federal court decisions that had declared state laws requiring segregation on interstate buses (and in bus stations) to be unconstitutional.

This grassroots activism forced the Kennedy administration into action of its own. It first dispatched U.S. marshals to protect the freedom riders from racist violence. In 1962 (and again the following year), the White House called on National Guard troops and fed-eral marshals to prevent pro-segregationist mobs from halting court-ordered integration at several educational institutions in the Deep South, including the Universities of Mississippi and Alabama. In November 1962, Kennedy issued a long-promised executive order that banned racial discrimination in federally financed housing. The following February, he sent Congress a civil-rights bill that called for faster trials in lawsuits seeking to tear down barriers designed to prevent African Americans in the South from voting. Events of the early 1960s, especially in the South, however, always seemed to outpace the Kennedy administration's initiatives.

The racist violence that convulsed Birmingham, Alabama, in 1963 highlighted this dynamic. Birmingham's all-white police force unleashed dogs and high-pressure water hoses on African Americans, including young children, who were peacefully demonstrating on behalf of desegregating that city's public facilities. White supremacists later murdered four young girls and injured twenty other people when they bombed the Sixteenth Street Baptist Church, a center of the civil-rights campaign in Birmingham. After thousands of angry African Americans rallied in protest—and two more children were killed, this time by police officers—the Kennedy administration finally moved to staunch the bloodletting.

By this time, however, the determination and courage of civil-rights activists in defying the violence in Birmingham had produced another real-life, televised drama for the entire world to watch. Kennedy finally entered the picture. During an emotion-filled national television address, the president pleaded for a national commitment to the battle against discrimina-tion. Recent events in Alabama, he declared, had raised "a moral issue . . . as old as Scrip-tures and . . . as clear as the Constitution." The time for "patience" and "delay," Kennedy announced, had passed. Racial strife was already "retarding our Nation's economic and social progress and weakening the respect with which the rest of the world regards us." Against the backdrop of a televised battle line that seemed to stretch across the South, the issue of civil rights dominated national politics during the last six months of Kennedy's presidency.

The White House still hoped it might influence the direction and moderate the pace of change. It crafted additional legislation designed to dampen the enthusiasm for civil-rights demonstrations, without further inflaming white segregationists. Its proposed bill called for a ban against racial discrimination in public facilities and housing and for new measures to pro-tect the voting rights of African Americans in the South. When the administration recognized that its legislative proposals would not derail a "March on Washington for Jobs and Freedom," planned for the late summer of 1963, it belatedly endorsed the event, sponsored by a coalition of civil-rights and labor organizations.

On August 28, 1963, an integrated group of more than 200,000 people marched through the nation's capital to the Lincoln Memorial. There, Martin Luther King, Jr., delivered his famous "I Have a Dream" speech. Most other speakers generally applauded Kennedy's latest initiatives, but some urged a broader agenda. Demands included a higher minimum wage and a federal program to guarantee new jobs. Well-organized and smoothly run, this one-day demonstration received overwhelmingly favorable coverage from the national media, especially television, and put even greater political pressure on the White House and Congress to lend their assistance to the movement.

Women's Issues

The seeds of a resurgent women's movement were also being sown, although more quietly, during the early 1960s. All across the political spectrum, women began speaking out more forcefully and visibly than they had during the 1950s. The energy of suburban warriors on the political right nurtured the grassroots of their movement. Phyllis Schlafly, whose book *A Choice, Not an Echo* (1964) became one of the leading conservative manifestos, suggested how women could blend careers in politics with ones as wives and mothers. African American activists such as Bernice Johnson Reagon (whose work with the Freedom Singers combined music and social activism) and Fannie Lou Hamer (who spearheaded the organization of a racially integrated Freedom Democratic Party in Mississippi) fought discrimination based on both race and gender. Female union leaders pushed for greater employment opportunities and more equitable workplace environments. Chicana farm workers became key figures in union organizing efforts in California. Women also played an important role through organizations such as the Committee for a Sane Nuclear Policy (SANE) and the Women's Strike for Peace in orchestrating opposition to the U.S.–Soviet arms race.

During Kennedy's final year in office, 1963, Betty Friedan published *The Feminine Mystique,* which observers soon credited for helping to revive organized feminist activity in the United States. Friedan's book drew on her own social criticism from the late 1950s. Decrying the narrow confines of domestic life and the lack of public roles available to well-educated women, it resonated with the many middle-class women who became standard-bearers for "Second Wave Feminism."

Anxious to address women's concerns, Kennedy appointed a Presidential Commission on the Status of Women, chaired by Eleanor Roosevelt. Negotiating differences between moderate and more militant members, the commission issued a report that documented discrimination against women in employment opportunities and wages. Kennedy responded with a presidential order designed to eliminate gender discrimination within the federal civil service system. His administration also supported the Equal Pay Act of 1963, which made it a federal crime for employers to pay lower wages to women who were doing the same work as men.

The Assassination of John F. Kennedy

During fall 1963, the Kennedy White House, although still struggling to reframe both its domestic and foreign policies, expected JFK would rather easily win reelection in 1964. Then, around noontime, on November 22, 1963, the president was shot dead as his motorcade moved through Dealey Plaza in Dallas. Vice President Lyndon Johnson, who had accompanied Kennedy to Texas, hurriedly took the oath of office and then rushed back to Washington. Equally quickly, the Dallas police arrested Lee Harvey Oswald and pegged him as JFK's assassin. Oswald had loose ties to organized crime, had once lived in the Soviet Union, and had a bizarre set of political affiliations, including shadowy connections with groups interested in Cuba. Oswald, who declared his innocence, never faced trial. Jack Ruby, whose Dallas nightclub catered to powerful underworld figures, killed Oswald, on national television, while the alleged gunman was in police custody. A hastily conducted investigation by a special commission headed by Chief Justice Earl Warren concluded that both Oswald and Ruby had acted alone.

The Warren Commission's account of a lone gunman, Lee Harvey Oswald, came under intense scrutiny. Competing theories about the number of shots, the trajectory of the bullets, the nature of Kennedy's wounds, and the identity of his assassins began to proliferate. Over time, a myriad of conspiratorial scenarios—including ones pointing toward the CIA, high-ranking governmental officials, Castro's Cuba, anti-Castro Cubans, organized crime, and even Lyndon Johnson—took flight. Oliver Stone's *JFK* (1991) refocused attention on obvious shortcomings in the Warren Commission Report.

Kennedy's life and presidency remain topics of lively historical debate and tabloid-style speculation. Researchers have provided new details about his poor health, reliance on exotic medications, and dalliances with women, all of which his loyal aides and a compliant press had once kept from public view. As historians speculate about how such revelations might have affected Kennedy's ability to make crucial decisions, they continue to debate older questions, particularly what JFK might have done in Vietnam and on the domestic front had he won the 1964 presidential election. The passage of time, in short, has diminished neither scholarly nor popular interest in John F. Kennedy and his 1,000-day presidency.

Conclusion

After 1953, conflict between the United States and the Soviet Union increasingly migrated to the Third World, where conflict over Cuba, in 1962, brought the two superpowers to the brink of nuclear war. Even on those occasions, such as after the Missile Crisis, when signs of tension with the USSR seemed to subside, the United States continued to chart a determinedly anticommunist course. It pursued the buildup of nuclear weapons, new forms of economic pressure, and expanded abilities to conduct covert activities. Developments in the Third World, particularly in Cuba and Southeast Asia, became of growing concern to U.S. policy makers.

At home, the economy grew steadily between 1953 and 1963. A cornucopia of new consumer products encouraged talk about an age of affluence and abundance but also produced apprehension about conformity, unruly youth, and mass culture. At the same time, the millions of people sidelined by economic inequality and often disadvantaged by racial and ethnic discrimination moved to the center of public debate over liberty and equality. Some critics charged that the Eisenhower administration seemed overly cautious in using the power of government to spread affluence more widely or to fight discrimination. More quietly, particularly in the political and cultural arenas, a new conservative movement also began to take shape. These critics from the right claimed that Eisenhower and JFK used the power of government too much, not too little.

The policy initiatives of the Kennedy administration grew, in large part, from the political, social, and cultural criticism of the 1950s. Although Kennedy preferred to focus on matters of foreign policy, the press of events, particularly those associated with the civil-rights movement, forced the president to consider how the power of his office might be used to address the issues of liberty and equality at home.

The post-Kennedy era would continue to highlight questions about liberty, equality, and power. Was the United States encouraging freedom in the Third World, particularly in Vietnam? Was it sufficiently active in supporting equalitarian movements at home? The troubled era of "America's longest war," 1963–74, would turn on how different people attempted to respond to these questions.

SUGGESTED READINGS

James T. Patterson, *Grand Expectations: The United States, 1945–1974* (1996) provides a good overview of the years from 1953 to 1963. For accounts of Eisenhower's presidential leadership, begin with **Fred I. Greenstein,** *The Hidden-Hand Presidency: Eisenhower as Leader* (rev. ed., 1994). **Chester Pach, Jr. and Elmo Richardson,** *The Presidency of Dwight D. Eisenhower* (1991) presents a useful, brief history. On JFK, see **Robert Dallek,** *An Unfinished Life: John F. Kennedy, 1917–1963* (2003); **Richard Reeves,** *President Kennedy: Profile of Power* (1994); and **Seymour Hersh,** *The Dark Side of Camelot* (1997).

There are many studies of Eisenhower's foreign policy, but a good sense of the issues and scholarly debates can be gleaned from **Robert R. Bowie and Richard H. Immerman,** *Waging Peace: How Eisenhower Shaped an Enduring Cold War Strategy* (2000). **John Prados,** *Presidents' Secret Wars: CIA and Pentagon Covert Operations from World War II through the Persian Gulf* (1996), and **Zachary Karabell,** *Architects of Intervention: The United States, the Third World, and the Cold War, 1946–1962* (1999) put an important aspect of policy in a broad perspective. **Walter L. Hixson,** *Parting the Curtain: Propaganda, Culture, and the Cold War, 1945–1961* (1997) argues that cultural initiatives provided weapons in the Cold War. **Lawrence Freedman,** *Kennedy's Wars: Berlin, Cuba, Laos, and Vietnam* (2000) illuminates the major international crises of the Kennedy years.

For events on the home front, **James B. Gilbert,** *A Cycle of Outrage: America's Reaction to the Juvenile Delinquent in the 1950s* (1986) discusses cultural fears; **Karal Ann Marling,** *As Seen on TV: The Visual Culture of Everyday Life in the 1950s* (1994) stresses the importance of visual imagery; and **James B. Gilbert**, *Redeeming Culture: American Religion in an Age of Science* (1997) examines another aspect of America's changing culture. **W. T. Lhamon, Jr.,** *Deliberate Speed: The Origins of a Cultural Style in the American 1950s* (2002) advances a provocative interpretation. The highly readable examination of the struggle against racial discrimination by **Taylor Branch**, *Parting the Waters: America in the King Years, 1954–1963* (1988) may be augmented by **James Patterson**, *Brown v. Board of Education: A Civil Rights Milestone and Its Troubled Legacy* (2001); **Robert O. Self**, *American Babylon: Race and the Struggle for Postwar Oakland* (2003); **John D'Emilio**, *Lost Prophet: The Life and Times of Bayard Rustin* (2003); and **David L. Chappell**, *A Stone of Hope: Prophetic Religion and the Death of Jim Crow* (2004).

On women and families during the 1950s, **Elaine Tyler May**, *Homeward Bound: American Families in the Cold War Era* (rev. ed., 1999) stresses the new emphasis on domestic life and the family wage. Consult also, the relevant pages of **Ruth Rosen**, *The World Split Open: How the Modern Women's Movement Changed America* (2000). **Leila J. Rupp**, *Survival in the Doldrums: The American Women's Rights Movement, 1945 to the 1960s* (1987); **Joanne Meyerowitz, ed.,** *Not June Cleaver: Women and Gender in Postwar America, 1945–1960* (1994); **Stephanie Coontz**, *The Way We Never Were: American Families and the Nostalgia Trip* (1992); and **Martin Meeker**, *Contacts Desired: Gay and Lesbian Communications and Community, 1940s to 1970s* (2006) work against that grain.

29

America during Its Longest War, 1963–1974

T he years from 1963 to 1974 brought political, social, and cultural upheaval to most areas of the world, including the United States. Lyndon Baines Johnson promised to finish what John Kennedy had begun, but popular memory has come to recall LBJ's troubled presidency (1963–69) more negatively than Kennedy's. When looking at foreign policy, Johnson faced a critical question: Should the United States deploy its own combat forces to prop up South Vietnam, its beleaguered ally? When surveying the domestic scene, where Johnson hoped to focus his attention, he already knew what he would do: mobilize the federal government's power to promote greater liberty and equality. Very quickly, however, Johnson saw his domestic dreams begin to vanish in the face of the ongoing foreign nightmare in Vietnam and turmoil at home. By 1968, the United States was politically polarized and awash in both foreign and domestic crises.

The polarization so much in evidence during 1968 seemed to worsen during the years that followed. By 1974, when a series of political scandals, known as the "Watergate Crisis," forced Richard Nixon to leave the presidency under pressure of impeachment, the nation's political and social fabrics looked very different from those of 1963.

The Great Society

Focus Question
How did the Johnson administration define Great Society goals, and how did it approach problem solving? Why did the Great Society produce so much controversy?

Lyndon B. Johnson lacked Kennedy's media-friendly charisma, but he possessed other political assets. As a member of the House of Representatives during the late 1930s and early 1940s and as majority leader of the U.S. Senate during the 1950s Johnson mastered the art of interest-group horse trading. Few legislative issues, it appeared, defied an LBJ-forged consensus. Every significant interest group could be flattered, cajoled, or threatened into lending this towering Texan its support. During Johnson's time in Congress, his wealthy Texas benefactors gained valuable oil and gas concessions and lucrative construction contracts, while Johnson acquired his own personal fortune. Johnson's skill in gaining federal funding for

CHRONOLOGY

1963	Johnson assumes presidency and pledges to continue Kennedy's initiatives
1964	Congress passes Kennedy's tax bill, the Civil Rights Act of 1964, and the Economic Opportunity Act • Gulf of Tonkin Resolution gives Johnson authority to conduct undeclared war • Johnson defeats Barry Goldwater in presidential election
1965	Johnson announces plans for the Great Society • Malcolm X assassinated • U.S. intervenes in Dominican Republic • Johnson announces significant U.S. troop deployments in Vietnam • Congress passes Voting Rights Act • Violence rocks Los Angeles and other urban areas
1966	Black Power movement emerges • *Miranda* v. *Arizona* decision guarantees rights of criminal suspects • Ronald Reagan elected governor of California • U.S. begins massive air strikes in North Vietnam
1967	Large antiwar demonstrations begin • Beatles release *Sgt. Pepper's Lonely Hearts Club Band*
1968	Tet offensive accelerates debates over war (January) • Martin Luther King, Jr. assassinated (April) • Robert F. Kennedy assassinated (June) • Violence rocks Democratic national convention in Chicago • Civil Rights Act of 1968 passed • Vietnam peace talks begin in Paris • Richard Nixon elected president
1969	Nixon announces "Vietnamization" policy • Reports of My Lai massacre become public
1970	U.S. troops enter Cambodia • Student demonstrators killed at Kent State and Jackson State • First Earth Day observed • Environmental Protection Act passed • Clean Air Act passed
1971	*Pentagon Papers* published • White House "Plumbers" formed • Military court convicts Lieutenant Calley for My Lai incident
1972	Nixon crushes McGovern in presidential election
1973	Paris peace accords signed • *Roe* v. *Wade* upholds women's right to abortion • Nixon's Watergate troubles begin to escalate
1974	House votes impeachment, and Nixon resigns • Ford assumes presidency
1975	Saigon falls to North Vietnamese forces

ambitious building projects brought economic growth to cities such as Dallas and Houston and to much of the Southwest.

Kennedy's death gave Johnson, who had been frustrated by his limited job description while serving as JFK's vice president, the opportunity to display his political skills on the presidential stage. Confident of being able to forge a national consensus behind a bold program for social and economic change, Johnson began his presidency by asking Congress to honor JFK's memory. He urged passage of legislation that Kennedy's administration had proposed and bombarded legislators with much grander proposals of his own. Between January 8, when he delivered his first State of the Union address, until August 27, 1964, when he accepted the Democratic Party's presidential nomination, Johnson concentrated on three domestic issues: tax cutting, civil rights, and economic inequality.

Closing the New Frontier

Even as Johnson closed JFK's New Frontier, he staked out additional political territory. In May 1964, during an address at Michigan University, Johnson declared it was time to "move upward to the Great Society," which rested on "liberty and abundance for all." The Great Society, according to LBJ, would not provide Americans with "a safe harbor, a resting place, a final objective, a finished work," but rather "a challenge constantly renewed, beckoning us toward a destiny where the meaning of our lives matches the marvelous products of our labor."

To stimulate the economic growth needed to produce the Great Society's abundance, Johnson had first, several months earlier in his presidency, emphasized the importance of cutting taxes. Intensively lobbying members of Congress who opposed the budget deficits that tax reductions would produce, he secured passage of the $10 billion tax-cut package JFK had earlier proposed. Its supporters hailed the measure as the guarantor of continuing economic growth. Although economists continue to disagree as to how much this tax measure actually contributed to the economic boom of the mid-1960s, it *appeared* to work. GNP rose 7 percent in 1964 and 8 percent the following year, unemployment dropped, and inflation remained low.

Advocating greater liberty and equality, Johnson pushed a more extensive version of Kennedy's civil-rights proposal through Congress. In early February 1964, the House of Representatives passed its own civil-rights bill. It included an amendment, Title VII of the measure eventually signed into law, that barred discrimination based not simply on "race" but on "sex" as well. Some southern Democrats had hoped that such a provision might scuttle the entire bill, but other House members saw the addition as a welcome victory for women. This provision would soon assist an already resurgent women's movement.

Although Johnson was championing the civil-rights bill as another memorial to Kennedy, he fully recognized that southerners in the Democratic Party would continue trying to block it. Consequently, he and his allies in the U.S. Senate courted crucial Republican support for curtailing a southern-led filibuster, for hammering out compromises on key provisions, and for reconciling the differing bills passed by the two houses of Congress.

Johnson finally obtained the **Civil Rights Act of 1964,** a truly bipartisan measure, in July 1964. It strengthened existing federal remedies, to be monitored by a new Equal Employment Opportunity Commission (EEOC), against job discrimination. More controversially, the act's "public accommodations" provision, which resembled an 1875 civil-rights law that an earlier Supreme Court had invalidated, prohibited racial discrimination in all facilities—such as hotels, motels, and restaurants—in any way connected to the flow of interstate commerce. Opponents of this section saw it as an overextension of federal power and an attack on the personal liberties of property owners. Its proponents predicted, correctly as it turned out, that the current Supreme Court would reject these constitutional claims.

Finally, Congress responded favorably to Johnson's third domestic priority, legislation to deal with socioeconomic inequality. A month after passage of the Civil Rights Act of 1964, under constant prodding from the White House, legislators adopted another landmark measure, the Economic Opportunity Act (EOA). Coming only six months after Johnson had called for "an unconditional war on poverty in America," during his January 1964 State of the Union address, the EOA provided LBJ with the means to launch a multifront campaign.

A new executive agency, the Office of Economic Opportunity (OEO) would coordinate a variety of different initiatives. LBJ charged the OEO, first headed by R. Sargent Shriver, a member-by-marriage of the Kennedy family, with eliminating "the paradox of poverty in the midst of plenty." In addition to establishing the new agency, the EOA mandated federal-government loans for rural and small-business development; established a work-training program called the Jobs Corps; created Volunteers in Service to America (VISTA), a domestic version of the Peace Corps; provided low-wage, public service jobs for young people; and began the "work-study" program to assist college students. In addition, it authorized grassroots social initiatives, Community Action Programs (CAPs), to be planned by local community groups but funded by Washington.

Meanwhile, however, Lyndon Johnson and the rest of the nation could already see signs that conflict would surely accompany change, particularly on the issue of civil rights. During the same summer that Congress passed the Civil Rights Act of 1964 and created the OEO, violence connected to racial issues broke out in different parts of the country. In New York City, tensions between police officers and African American demonstrators, protesting policing practices that had led to the fatal shooting of a black youth, flared into confrontations during mid-July.

At almost the same time, a different kind of violence rolled through those parts of Mississippi where a coalition of civil-rights groups was sponsoring what it called **"Freedom Summer."** This campaign to register black voters, by an interracial group of young volunteers including white northern college students, produced a murderous backlash from some segregationists. At least six civil-rights workers met violent deaths during that blood-soaked Mississippi summer. In the most notorious incident, whose legal fallout would last into the 21st century, KKK members and law-enforcement officials from Neshoba County, Mississippi, conspired to kidnap and brutally murder three volunteers—James Chaney, Michael Schwerner, and Andrew Goodman.

Other activists pressed forward, only to see the grassroots organizing of that summer frustrated by Lyndon Johnson and a majority of the national Democratic Party. Pressured by LBJ, the 1964 Democratic convention voted to seat Mississippi's "regular" all-white delegates, people who clearly intended to desert LBJ and the national party during the fall election. Democratic leaders gave only token recognition to members of the alternative, racially diverse "Freedom Democratic Party" (FDP). This rebuff prompted people, such as Fannie Lou Hamer, who had risked their lives to create the FDP, to recall earlier suspicions about Lyndon Johnson. Although LBJ seemed more committed to civil rights than John Kennedy had been, where would Johnson—and Hubert Humphrey, his handpicked vice presidential running mate—stand after the 1964 election? During a bittersweet meeting with Humphrey, Fannie Lou Hamer pointedly wondered if a willingness to reject the FDP signaled that this longtime supporter might soon abandon the civil-rights cause altogether.

The Election of 1964

By the fall of 1964, changes occurring within GOP ranks made Democratic support seem especially important to civil-rights forces. After a series of bitterly contested primary contests, the Republicans nominated Senator Barry Goldwater of Arizona, the hero of conservatives from the South and Far West, to challenge Lyndon Johnson. Strategists for Goldwater predicted that an aggressive campaign, based on an unabashedly conservative platform, would stir the hearts of the millions of voters who presumably rejected both Democratic policies and Dwight Eisenhower's moderate Republican ones. Goldwater denounced Johnson's foreign policy for tolerating communist expansion and attacked his domestic agenda, including strong support for civil rights, for destroying individual liberties. One of only eight Republican senators who had opposed the 1964 Civil Rights Act, Goldwater denounced the measure as an unwarranted extension of national power to meet the kind of problem, discrimination, which only state and local governments could remedy.

As the presidential campaign heated up, Goldwater's well-documented tendency for making ill-considered pronouncements haunted his candidacy. Goldwater once suggested that people who feared nuclear war were "silly and sissified." He wondered, out loud, if Social Security should become a voluntary program. His proclamation, at the 1964 Republican convention, that "extremism in the pursuit of liberty is no vice" and "moderation in the pursuit of justice is no virtue," fed Democratic claims that Goldwater represented political "extremism" rather than Republican, or even principled conservative, values. In time, Democrats succeeded in denying Goldwater one of his primary assets, his refusal to temporize on most controversial issues. Instead, they successfully portrayed the blunt-speaking Goldwater as wildly mercurial, perhaps even fanatical or mentally unbalanced. Republicans, for their part, leveled equally outsized charges against LBJ. One anti-Johnson tract, *A Texan Looks at LBJ* (1964), accused him of everything from stuffing ballot boxes to plotting murderous violence against political opponents.

As fantastical name-calling of this kind marked the 1964 campaign trail, a significant bloc of normally Republican voters deserted Goldwater, whose candidacy seemed to have strayed too far from middle-of-the-road signposts. The senator from Arizona led the GOP to a spectacular defeat in November. Johnson carried 44 states and won more than 60 percent of the popular vote; the Democrats also gained 38 additional seats in Congress. On the surface the 1964 election seemed a triumph for Lyndon Johnson's vision for using governmental power to change domestic life.

In retrospect, however, the 1964 election signaled important political changes that would soon rebound against Johnson and, in time, the national Democratic Party. During the Democratic primaries, Alabama's segregationist governor, George Wallace, had run strongly as a "protest candidate" against the president in several states. Already well-positioned as an opponent of the civil-rights movement, Wallace began to broaden his message, denouncing

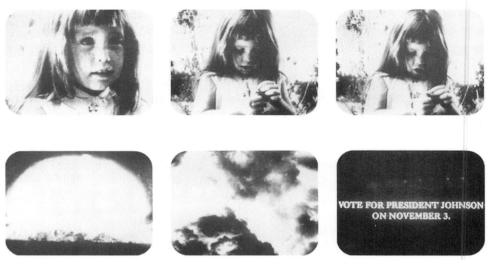

LBJ'S 1964 Campaign against Barry Goldwater   In this television ad from the 1964 campaign, Lyndon Johnson's supporters exploited Republican Barry Goldwater's image as a far-right extremist who might take the nation into a nuclear war.

any kind of "meddling" by Washington in local affairs. The 1964 election proved the last in which the Democratic Party would capture the White House by proposing to expand the domestic reach of the national government.

The GOP's 1964 effort, in contrast, merely provided a refueling stop for the conservative political machine that had propelled Goldwater's candidacy. His staff pioneered several innovative campaign tactics, such as direct-mail fundraising. While working to refine these techniques, conservative strategists insisted that 1964 would mark the beginning, not the end, of the Republican Party's movement to the right.

Goldwater's stand against national civil-rights legislation, his supporters noted, helped him carry five southern states. These victories—along with George Wallace's earlier appeal during the Democratic primaries—suggested just how much the GOP might gain by opposing additional civil-rights measures. After many years of tentative courtship, the Republican Party finally seemed ready to win over southern whites who had once been solidly Democratic. In an important sign of desertions to come, Senator J. Strom Thurmond of South Carolina announced during the 1964 campaign that he was permanently leaving the Democratic Party and joining the GOP.

Less-noticed voting trends in California provided conservatives with another sign of how racial issues were continuing to reshape political alignments. Although the Johnson-Humphrey ticket easily carried California, winning more than 60 percent of the popular vote, a coalition of real-estate interests and suburban activists sponsored a successful referendum, "Proposition 14." It repealed the state's recently enacted "Rumford Act," which prohibited racial discrimination in the sale or renting of housing. To overturn this statewide open housing measure, proponents of Proposition 14, which gained 65 percent of the vote throughout the state and much higher percentages in newer suburban areas, downplayed racial issues. Instead, they denounced the Rumford Act—because it regulated what property owners could do with their homes and apartment buildings—for trampling on personal liberties and constitutionally guaranteed freedoms.

The Goldwater campaign of 1964, especially in California and the Sunbelt states, also introduced an important group of conservative activists to national politics. Ronald Reagan— previously a radio personality, Hollywood actor, labor leader, corporate spokesperson, and Roosevelt Democrat—proved such an effective campaigner in 1964 that conservative Republicans in California began grooming him for electoral politics. Younger conservatives, such as William Rehnquist and Newt Gingrich, entered the national arena by working for Goldwater. Historians now generally credit Goldwater's 1964 candidacy for helping to refashion conservatism as a political force capable of dismantling the Democratic coalition that had dominated national politics since the 1930s.

Lyndon Johnson's Great Society

During the fall of 1964, however, the Democratic ranks seemed stronger than they had been in decades. Confident of his political support, Lyndon Johnson hoped to move quickly. Detailing plans he had hinted at during his 1964 campaign, Johnson fully unveiled a domestic vision designed, in his words, to "enrich and elevate our national life."

Some parts of LBJ's **Great Society** seemed constructed on top of the designs of his Democratic predecessors. Nationally funded medical coverage for the elderly (Medicare) and for low-income citizens (Medicaid) appeared to be capstones to efforts begun during the New Deal and Fair Deal eras. Similarly, an addition to the president's cabinet, the Department of Housing and Urban Development (HUD), built on earlier plans for improving coordination and execution of urban revitalization programs. This new cabinet post, LBJ promised, would prevent urban renewal from becoming urban removal (see chapter 28).

In 1965, Congress enacted two other milestone measures, both of which addressed matters long discussed—and long avoided. A new immigration law, the first measure ever directed through the Senate by newly elected Edward Kennedy, finally abolished the geographically discriminatory "national origins" quota system established in 1924. Henceforth, all nationalities of people wishing to immigrate to the United States faced roughly the same set of hurdles. This change, in practice, removed some of the previous barriers to people coming from regions outside of Europe (see chapter 31). **The Voting Rights Act of 1965,** which created a federal oversight system to monitor election procedures in the South, capped a long-term effort to end racial discrimination at the ballot box.

Other Great Society proposals rested on the economic growth that seemed, during the mid-1960s, destined to go on forever. Even an increasingly costly war in Southeast Asia could not dampen Johnson's optimism. Continuing prosperity would provide the tax dollars the president needed to underwrite his bold expansion of national power.

The array of Johnson-sponsored initiatives that rolled through Congress in 1965 and 1966 heartened LBJ's supporters and appalled his conservative critics. By one count, legislators passed nearly 200 new laws. The "Model Cities Program" offered smaller-scale alternatives to urban renewal efforts. Rent supplements and an expanded food stamp program went to help feed low-income families. Head Start provided educational opportunity for children who came from backgrounds social scientists labeled "disadvantaged." New educational programs targeted federal funds for upgrading classroom instruction, especially in low-income neighborhoods, and the Legal Services program promised government lawyers for clients who could not afford private attorneys. Planners of the Great Society stressed that measures such as these would provide social services that could help people fight their own way out of economic distress. This service-based approach to domestic social policy, Johnson insisted, would give people a "hand up" rather than a "handout."

The CAP initiative, part of the earlier EOA legislation, took a significantly different tack. Although drawing on social-science expertise, which had guided and informed other Great Society measures, this initiative ultimately sought to free ordinary citizens from the dictates and directions of social-service bureaucracies. CAP proposed to empower grassroots activists, working through neighborhood organizations rather than through political channels dominated by local city hall establishments, to design community-based projects. The most promising of these, EOA legislation promised, could gain funding from Washington.

Those who embraced CAP hailed its potential for redistributing power. It offered local communities the leverage that came from enjoying adequate financial resources while still allowing them, rather than outside bureaucracies, the political power to make crucial decisions about their own needs and priorities. By promoting "maximum feasible participation" by ordinary citizens rather than relying entirely on the expertise of social planners or on the political clout of party leaders, the architects of CAP hoped to grow new varieties of grassroots democracy that could change U.S. political culture from the bottom up.

Evaluating the Great Society

How did the Great Society—most of which initially enjoyed large, sometimes bipartisan majorities in Congress—become so controversial, so quickly? Most obviously, programs that further extended Washington's influence rekindled old debates about the use of the powers of the national government, as both an issue of constitutional law and a matter of pragmatic policy making. The Great Society, in this sense, gave an already well-positioned conservative movement another set of convenient targets. In addition, Johnson's extravagant rhetoric, such as promising to win an "unconditional" victory over poverty, raised expectations that no administration could possibly satisfy within the time frames voters normally use to judge the success or failure of governmental initiatives.

Perhaps most importantly, the expectation that continued economic growth would generate tax revenues sufficient to finance new social programs faded as the nation's economic engine began to sputter. Facing financial worries of their own, many people who had initially been willing to accept the Great Society became receptive to the argument, first popularized by George Wallace and the Goldwater campaign, that bureaucrats in Washington were taking their hard-earned dollars and wasting them on flawed social experiments. Worsening economic conditions, exacerbated by the escalating cost of the war in Vietnam, made federal expenditures on domestic social welfare measures more controversial than at any time since the 1930s.

Although historians agree about how Johnson's domestic programs lost support, there has been considerable disagreement about the Great Soiety's impact on daily life. Charles Murray's influential *Losing Ground* (1984) framed one powerful view. This study first charged that LBJ's social programs encouraged antisocial behavior. It argued that too many people, lured by what they could gain from Great Society measures, abandoned the goals of marrying, settling down, and seeking employment. Moreover, the money given over to Great Society programs created government deficits that slowed economic growth. Had ill-advised social spending not undermined personal initiative and disrupted the nation's economy, continued economic growth could have provided virtually all workers with a comfortable lifestyle. This conservative argument portrayed the Great Society as the cause of, not the solution for, economic distress and social disarray.

Most other close students of social policy treated the Great Society slightly more kindly. They found scant evidence, as opposed to colorful anecdotes, for the claim that most people preferred receiving welfare to seeking meaningful work. They generally blamed spending in the military sector because of the U.S. commitment in Vietnam, rather than outlays for domestic social programs, for generating the soaring budget deficits and a burgeoning national debt. Funds actually spent on Great Society programs, in this view, neither matched Johnson's promises nor reached the lavish levels claimed in conservative studies such as *Losing Ground.*

From a different perspective, many antipoverty activists faulted the Great Society for not seriously challenging the prevailing distribution of political and economic power in the United States. The Johnson administration, they argued, remained closely wedded to large-scale bureaucratic solutions, forged and then directed by people connected to Washington elites and entrenched interest groups. The White House jettisoned, for example, the CAP model for grassroots empowerment after local political officials complained about having to compete with activist groups for federal funds. In addition, by assuming that economic growth would continue to underwrite the financing of most federal initiatives, the people who planned the Great Society had also failed to consider revision of the tax code and other measures designed to redistribute income and wealth more equitably. Proponents of this critique concluded that the Johnson administration never seriously tried to fulfill its own domestic promises.

Most economists and historians have come to agree that the Great Society signaled a significant, though not revolutionary, break with the past. The national government, for the first time in several decades, devoted substantial new funding to social welfare programs. Washington's financial outlay on the domestic front increased more than 10 percent during every year of LBJ's presidency. According to one study, federal spending on social welfare in 1960 constituted 28 percent of total governmental outlays; by 1970, this figure had risen to more than 40 percent. Moreover, some Great Society programs produced significant change. Medicaid, the legal services program, and job training initiatives gave many low-income families access to things that more affluent families had long taken for granted. Civil-rights laws, even if they failed to eliminate all forms of discrimination, did use federal power to expand legally protected freedoms.

The Great Society, however, proved a political failure, unable to retain the popular support it had claimed in 1964–65. Variations on the severe evaluation framed in *Losing Ground* came to dominate popular memory and political culture. Continued allegiance to the Great Society agenda, as a matter of political pragmatism, could become a serious liability for nearly all Republican and most Democratic politicians during the late 1960s and early 1970s. Over time, as a highly critical view of the Great Society's flaws and failures helped energize the conservative wing of the GOP, fewer Democrats would risk stepping forward to defend Lyndon Johnson's vision. In short, Johnson's domestic policies helped inflame political passions, which soon turned against LBJ and his Great Society. A new generation of Democrats eventually came to dismiss "big government" as a relic of the past (see chapter 32).

Escalation in Vietnam

Focus Question

Through what incremental steps did the Johnson administration involve the United States ever more deeply in the war in Vietnam? What seemed to be the goal of its policies?

Meanwhile, Lyndon Johnson's ultimately divisive crusade to build a Great Society at home found its counterpart abroad. His pledge to preserve South Vietnam as a noncommunist, pro-U.S. enclave demanded ever more of his nation's resources. Even as Johnson's policies in Vietnam strained the U.S. economy, they polarized its politics and culture.

The Gulf of Tonkin Resolution

Immediately after John Kennedy's assassination, Johnson hesitated to widen the war in Southeast Asia. A committed Cold Warrior, however, LBJ hated the thought that his political associates—let alone the general electorate—might judge him "soft" on communism. He soon accepted the recommendation of his military advisers: Only the use of air strikes against targets in North Vietnam could save the South Vietnamese government from imminent collapse. He prepared a congressional resolution authorizing such an escalation of hostilities.

Events in the Gulf of Tonkin, off the coast of North Vietnam, provided the rationale for taking this resolution to Capitol Hill. On August 1, 1964, the U.S. destroyer *Maddox,* while on an intelligence-gathering mission in disputed waters that North Vietnam claimed as its own, exchanged gunfire with North Vietnamese ships. Three days later, the *Maddox* returned to the same area, accompanied by the *Turner Joy.* During severe weather, which distorted radar and sonar readings, U.S. naval commanders reported what possibly could have been signs of a failed North Vietnamese torpedo attack.

Although the *Maddox*'s commander later radioed that the episode needed further analysis, Johnson immediately denounced "unprovoked aggression" by North Vietnam against the United States and appealed to Congress for support. (A subsequent study concluded that the initial attack had likely occurred, but that reports of hostile fire on the second occasion lacked credible supporting evidence.) Congress quickly, and overwhelmingly, authorized the president to take "all necessary measures to repel armed attack." Johnson treated this **"Gulf of Tonkin Resolution"** as tantamount to a congressional declaration of war and cited it as legal justification for all subsequent U.S. military action in Vietnam.

Despite his vigorous response to events in the Gulf of Tonkin, Lyndon Johnson successfully positioned himself as a cautious moderate during the presidential campaign of 1964. When Barry Goldwater demanded stronger measures against North Vietnam and even hinted at possible use of tactical nuclear weapons, Johnson's campaign managers cited Goldwater's proposed strategies as further evidence of his extremist bent. One notorious TV ad even portrayed the Republican candidate as a threat to the survival of civilization. Johnson seemed to promise he would not commit U.S. combat troops to any land war in Southeast Asia.

Soon after the election, however, Johnson decisively deepened the U.S. involvement there. More than a year after the 1963 coup against Diem (see chapter 28), South Vietnam faced continued political chaos. The incompetence of successive governments in Saigon was still fueling popular discontent, and South Vietnamese troops were still deserting at an alarming rate. In January 1965, another Saigon regime collapsed, and factional discord stalled the emergence of any viable alternative.

Lacking an effective ally in South Vietnam, Johnson once more pondered his options. His close aides offered conflicting advice. National Security Adviser McGeorge Bundy predicted Saigon's defeat unless the United States greatly increased its own military role. Arguing for this same option, Walt W. Rostow assured Johnson that once North Vietnam recognized the United States would never abandon its commitment, this small nation could only conclude that it would never overrun South Vietnam. Undersecretary of State George Ball, by contrast, warned that the introduction of U.S. combat troops could not preserve South Vietnam. He wrote that "no one has demonstrated that a white ground force of whatever size can win a guerrilla war . . . in jungle terrain in the midst of a population that refuses cooperation to the white forces." Senate Majority Leader Mike Mansfield, who held an advanced degree in Asian history, urged Johnson to find some way of reuniting Vietnam as a neutral country. The Joint Chiefs of Staff, afflicted by interservice rivalries, provided conflicting readings of the current military situation and no clear guidance on how Johnson might proceed.

Although privately doubting U.S. chances of preserving an anticommunist South Vietnam, Johnson became obsessed about the political and diplomatic consequences of a U.S. pullout. He feared that the domestic reaction to anything resembling a communist victory—such as Washington's acceptance of a coalition government in Saigon that included the NLF—would enrage conservative activists in the United States and thereby endanger his

Great Society programs. Moreover, Johnson accepted the familiar Cold War proposition that a U.S. withdrawal would undoubtedly set off a "domino effect," toppling noncommunist governments in Asia. A pullback there would, then, encourage communist-leaning insurgencies in Latin America, increase Soviet pressure on West Berlin, and damage U.S. credibility around the world. Both Eisenhower and Kennedy, before him, had staked U.S. prestige on preserving a noncommunist South Vietnam. Johnson either had to abandon that commitment, by allowing South Vietnam's government to collapse, or chart an uncertain course by employing U.S. power to prop it up.

While remaining pessimistic about the results of his decision, Johnson chose the second option: dramatically expanding U.S. military involvement in Southeast Asia. He ordered a sustained campaign of bombing in North Vietnam, code-named "Rolling Thunder." He also deployed U.S. ground forces in order to help the government in Saigon regain lost territory, expanded U.S.-directed covert operations, and stepped up economic aid to the beleaguered South Vietnamese government. Only six months after the 1964 presidential election, with his advisers still divided, Johnson decided the United States had no choice but to wage a wider war.

The War Continues to Widen

The war grew more intense during 1965. Hoping to break the enemy's will, U.S. military commanders sought to inflict ever-increasing casualties. The Johnson administration authorized use of **napalm,** a toxic chemical that almost instantly charred both foliage and people, and allowed the Air Force to bomb new targets. Additional U.S. combat troops also arrived in South Vietnam, but every U.S. escalation seemed to require a further one. After North Vietnam rejected a Johnson-sponsored peace plan, which it viewed as little more than an offer for Hanoi to surrender, the United States once again stepped up its military effort. North Vietnam's leader, Ho Chi Minh, who was now pursuing a long-term strategy of attrition, became convinced that Johnson could not continue to find public or congressional support in the United States to fight such a costly war so far from U.S. shores.

In April 1965, Johnson applied his Cold War, anticommunist foreign policy closer to home. Responding to exaggerated reports about a communist threat to the government of the Dominican Republic, Johnson sent U.S. troops to unseat a left-leaning, but legally elected, president and to install a Dominican government eager to support U.S. interests. This U.S. incursion into the Dominican Republican violated a long-standing "good neighbor" pledge, by the United States, to avoid military intervention in Latin America. Although Johnson's action angered critics throughout the hemisphere, the overthrow of a leftist government in the Dominican Republic seemed to steel the White House's determination to hold the line against communism in Vietnam.

Later that same spring as yet another government, the fifth since Diem's 1963 murder, appeared in Saigon, U.S. strategists continued to wonder how they might stabilize South Vietnam. General William Westmoreland, who directed the U.S. military effort there, recommended moving even more aggressively and sending additional numbers of U.S. troops on "search and destroy" missions against communist forces. In July 1965, Johnson publicly announced he would send 50,000 additional military personnel to Vietnam. Privately, LBJ pledged that the Pentagon could have another 50,000, and he left open the possibility of sending even more. To supplement the search-and-destroy strategy, he also approved **"saturation bombing"** in the South Vietnamese countryside and an intensified air campaign against North Vietnam. **(See Map 29.1, Vietnam War, in the color insert following page 1248.)**

Some advisers urged Johnson to admit candidly the greatly expanded scope of the U.S. effort. They recommended seeking an outright declaration of war by Congress or at least legislation allowing the executive branch to wield the economic and informational controls that previous presidential administrations had used during wartime. But Johnson worried about arousing greater protests in Congress and from a growing antiwar movement. Rather than risk debates that could ramp up dissent against his policies, Johnson decided to stress the administration's willingness to negotiate and to act as if the war the United States was now fighting was not really a war. As the Johnson administration talked of seeing "light at the end of the tunnel" in Vietnam, it apparently hoped that most people in the United States would remain largely in the dark.

Over the remaining years of Lyndon Johnson's presidency, U.S. involvement steadily grew. By late 1965, the number of U.S. combat troops in Vietnam totaled more than 200,000; three years later, this figure had more than doubled, to about 535,000. The level of violence escalated as well. In pursuit of "Operation RANCHHAND," an effort to eliminate the natural cover for enemy troop movements, the United States dropped huge quantities of herbicides, scorching South Vietnam's croplands and defoliating roughly half of its forests. Approximately 1.5 million tons of bombs—more than all the tonnage dropped during the Second World War—pounded North Vietnamese cities and pummeled villages and hamlets in the South. Still, Johnson carefully avoided bombing close to the North Vietnamese–Chinese border or doing anything else that might provoke either China or the Soviet Union to go beyond supporting and supplying North Vietnam.

Despite all of the troops and violence, Vietnam remained a "limited" war. The U.S. strategy concentrated on straining the NLF and North Vietnam by continually escalating the cost they would pay, in lost lives and bombed-out infrastructure. Once the price of continuing to fight became too high, the Johnson administration reasoned, the other side would finally stop its effort to displace a pro-U.S., anticommunist government in South Vietnam.

The weekly "body count" of enemy purportedly killed became the primary measure for gauging U.S. progress in South Vietnam. Pentagon estimates that a kill ratio of 10 to 1 would force North Vietnam and the NLF to pull back not only encouraged the U.S. military to unleash more firepower but also to inflate enemy casualty figures. This same calculation provided an automatic justification for more U.S. troops: Whenever the number of enemy forces seemed to increase, the Pentagon required additional U.S. troops to maintain the desired kill ratio. Johnson, whose notorious temper flared at the first hint of bad news, welcomed improving kill statistics as a tangible sign that victory was around the corner. North Vietnam, assisted by the Soviet Union and China, however, managed to

An Image That Shocked This 1968 photo, widely reproduced because of the absence of formal governmental censorship during the Vietnam conflict, shows a South Vietnamese military officer summarily executing a suspected Viet Cong leader on the streets of Saigon. The prevalence of images such as this one complicated the U.S. government's attempt to portray its support of South Vietnam as a fight for freedom and the rule of law.

match every U.S. escalation. Conscripting younger fighters and employing more women in support positions, the North Vietnamese continued to funnel troops and supplies into the South, using a shifting network of roads and paths called the "Ho Chi Minh Trail." By the end of 1967, several of Johnson's key aides, most notably Secretary of Defense Robert McNamara, decided that the United States could not sustain, from any reasonable costs versus benefits perspective, its seemingly open-ended commitment to South Vietnam. The majority of Johnson's advisers, however, refused to accept such a gloomy assessment.

Meanwhile, the destruction wreaked by U.S. forces was giving NLF, North Vietnamese, Chinese, and Soviet leaders a decided advantage in what had become an international war of images. Critics of the U.S. effort, in the United States and around the world, highlighted pictures showing the results of Johnson's strategy. Demonstrations against the United States became especially prominent features of political life in Western Europe. Antiwar protestors hounded LBJ and members of his administration, everywhere they went, and the president began complaining of becoming a prisoner in his own White House.

In addition, the United States failed to find an attractive, or even very effective, ally in South Vietnam. The devastation of the countryside, the economic destabilization caused by the flood of U.S. dollars, and the corruption in Saigon took their toll. The "pacification" and "strategic hamlet" programs, which gathered Vietnamese farmers into tightly guarded villages, sounded viable in Washington but created greater chaos by uprooting at least one-quarter of the South Vietnamese citizenry from its villages and ancestral lands. Buddhist priests persistently demonstrated against foreign influence. When, in 1967, two generals, Nguyen Van Thieu and Nguyen Cao Ky, after having sustained a military regime longer than any of their predecessors, tried to legitimate their rule with a nationwide election, the effort fell short. A voting process marked by corruption only highlighted the precariousness of their political position and underscored their dependence on support from Washington.

The Media and the War

Johnson continually gave presidential lectures about the necessity for upholding the nation's honor and diplomatic commitments, but dissent slowly mounted. During the Second World War and the conflict in Korea, presidential administrations had restricted media coverage. Hoping to avoid the controversy that overt censorship would surely have caused, the Johnson administration employed informal ways of managing the flow of information about Vietnam. Many of the print reporters sent to Southeast Asia seemed content, at first, to accept the reassuring reports handed out by U.S. officials in Saigon. Only a relatively few, such as David Halberstam, ventured into the South Vietnamese countryside, where they saw a different conflict than the one being described back at U.S. headquarters. Even before media pundits started talking about television making Vietnam a **"living room war"**—one that people in the United States could watch in their own homes—Johnson kept three sets playing in his office in order to monitor what viewers might be seeing. Most of what he saw, early on, he liked.

Antiwar activists continually assailed what they viewed as the U.S. media's uncritical reporting about events and policies in Vietnam. According to a common complaint, too many media executives appeared willing to accept story frames constructed by the White House, and too many journalists seemed to base their stories on official handouts. During the early years of U.S. involvement, few print publications or TV reports contained stories that dissected either the U.S. military effort or the travails of Washington's South Vietnamese ally.

In time, however, the tone and substance of media coverage changed. Images of unrelenting destruction came across television screens. After gazing at his TV sets, LBJ began telephoning network executives, castigating them for critical broadcasts and urging them to root for the United States, not its communist enemies. Print journalists generally outpaced their TV counterparts in breaking away from the government line, and some followed Halberstam in forthrightly challenging U.S. officials in Saigon. Gloria Emerson's grim reports portrayed the U.S. effort as one in which poor and disproportionately nonwhite troops seemed to be fighting, and dying, so that wealthy families, many with "fortunate sons" who held draft exemptions, might reap war-related profits. In 1966 and 1967, Harrison Salisbury of the *New York Times* sent back stories from North Vietnam that highlighted the impact U.S. bombing missions exacted on civilian targets. Accounts by younger journalists, such as those published by Michael Herr in *Esquire,* represented the war as a violent, amoral, and drug-drenched venture into the surreal.

As the conflict dragged on, the media began to talk about a "war at home" that paralleled the one in Vietnam. TV and most print media adopted a stark, bipolar story frame: It pictured **"hawks"**—those who wanted to fight, as long and as hard as necessary, until the United States defeated the communist forces—fighting against **"doves"**—those who, whatever their earlier views, now desired to end U.S. involvement in Vietnam as quickly as possible. In response to those who called for an even greater use of military force, President Johnson insisted his administration was following time-tested containment policies. His secretary of state, Dean Rusk, warned doves·of the dangers of "appeasement." But an increasing number of influential U.S. politicians, led by J. William Fulbright of Arkansas, dissented. This influential head of the powerful Senate Foreign Relations Committee warned of misplaced priorities and of an "arrogance of power." Meanwhile, the antiwar movement merged into several other movements, many of which were coming to challenge the larger direction of U.S. politics and culture.

The War at Home

Focus Question

What domestic social movements emerged during America's longest war? How did they seek to change U.S. political culture and the direction of public policy? What role did commercial media play in the "movement of movements"?

Millions came to oppose the war in Southeast Asia, and support for the Great Society at home began to erode. By 1968, tensions escalated into confrontation, violence, and one of the most divisive presidential election campaigns in U.S. history.

The Movement of Movements

Popular memories generally will recall the 1960s as the time of a "youth revolt." Young people from a "New Left," most of them college students, protested against the war in Vietnam and in favor of social change, especially in race relations. Other imagery from the 1960s displays the colorful signs of a **"Counterculture,"** again viewed as a preoccupation of the college-aged population. Devotees of this Counterculture urged people to expand their minds, often with a little help from drugs and rock music, and to seek alternative ways of seeing, and then living out, their everyday world. Another set of iconic images from this time represents new forms of racial and ethnic consciousness, beginning with the **"Black Power"** movement. Now more easily accessible than ever before, all of this memorable imagery has etched pictures of life during America's longest war deeply into historical memory.

Increasingly, though, historians look beyond individual pictures of separate movements, each of which can claim its own background and trajectory, to a kaleidoscopic panorama composed of what one historian calls a "movement of movements." All across the political and cultural spectrum—not simply on some New Left or among the young or African Americans or cultural dissenters—people joined movements that aimed to challenge key parts of the established order. Activists from a wide variety of different backgrounds and circumstances placed their energies at the active service of one movement or another.

The combined energy produced by this movement of movements tended to tilt, albeit in different ways, against two dominant ideals of the 1950s and early 1960s: the faith in political (or interest group) pluralism and the parallel conviction that deeply held spiritual beliefs ultimately united, rather than divided, the nation and its diverse people (see chapter 28). As the war in Vietnam dragged on, people increasingly doubted that the

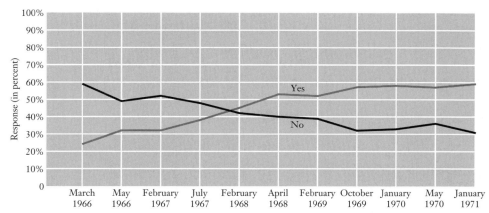

American Attitudes Toward the Vietnam War   Responses to the question: "Do you think that the United States made a mistake in sending troops to fight there?"

existing political system could actually solve problems. At the same time, disparate movements based on deeply held values—involving issues such as war and peace, race relationships, gender politics, the environment, and sexuality—appeared headed in different directions or on collision courses.

Ultimately, this movement of movements produced political, social, and cultural polarization. No one group, say a New Left or a youth culture, could lay exclusive claim to the historical era often called "the Long Sixties," the period from roughly 1963 to 1974, which coincided with America's longest war. Numerous social movements sought to redirect national life down different paths, often with no clear maps.

Most movements could not avoid dealing with commercial, particularly visual, media. Media imagery did not create or manufacture, for popular consumption, this movement of movements. Activists recognized, however, that even the briefest of time in the media spotlight could help them display their deep personal commitments and demonstrate their passionate disdain for policies they opposed. Often beginning with posters and pamphlets, movements such as the one pressing for a rapid U.S. withdrawal from Vietnam began to produce increasingly sophisticated imagery and to stage media-catching public demonstrations.

Television, in particular, offered these social movements a potentially vast audience. Some movement activists became media celebrities. In a 1965 internal memo, the then-head of SNCC referred to himself, tongue in cheek, as "Mr. Stokely Carmichael (star of stage, screen, and television)." Behind the scenes, less famous activists worked both to sustain their movements as viable organizations and to help script the kind of political performances that could attract media attention.

Four of the earliest and most prominent of the movements that accompanied America's longest war involved the New Left, the Counterculture, "Black Power," and antiwar protest.

Movements on College Campuses: A New Left

Colleges and universities became important sites for mobilizing students and organizing them as forces for social change. Only a relatively small number of college students ever became active in social movements, but their activities set the tone for campus politics, attracted extensive media interest, and eventually generated popular controversy.

In 1962, two years after conservatives had already formed the YAF (see chapter 28), students at the left end of the political spectrum established Students for a Democratic Society (SDS). Young men, mostly of European descent and eager to link their grand ideals to specific political activities, dominated the early SDS effort. Beginning with a call for mobilizing the power of government to expand liberty and promote equality, SDS endorsed measures, such as civil-rights laws, that seemed little different from those that Lyndon Johnson would soon champion.

SDS attracted far greater attention, however, for the more spiritual and personalized style of its politics. The "Port Huron Statement" of 1962, SDS's founding manifesto, pledged opposition to the "loneliness, estrangement, isolation" that supposedly afflicted so many people. It charged that arrogant political elites, immersed in the techniques of interest-group pluralism, ignored underlying moral values. These insiders allegedly prized the expertise of bureaucrats over active engagement by ordinary citizens and favored policies promoting economic growth over opportunities for meaningful work. SDS claimed to speak for alternative visions. In politics, it called for "participatory democracy"—grassroots political activities and small-scale institutions responsive to the needs of local communities.

Students from North Carolina A&T University had earlier sparked the sit-in movement of 1960 (see chapter 28), and college students continued to play important roles in many of the civil-rights dramas that followed. Localized struggles in communities throughout the South, such as those waged during Freedom Summer in Mississippi, seemed tangible examples of participatory democracy. They appeared to promise a regeneration of the nation's politics and a reorientation of its moral compass. Organizing efforts in the Deep South thus attracted idealistic white students from schools in the North. Only partially aware of the violence and social challenges they would face, these activists left their own campuses to work alongside those from historically black institutions, such as Tuskegee, who were trying to register African American voters and organize them for political action. Some of these students remained in the South; others turned their energies to neighborhood-based political projects in northern cities; and some brought their experiences in the South back to their own campuses.

New Left activists insisted on a constantly expanding view of what counted as "politics." Political practice should be broadly participatory, but active participation by large numbers of ordinary people only provided the starting point. Although voter registration drives in the South did seek greater access to the existing political process, New Left activists placed far greater emphasis on alternative, often disruptive political forms, such as sit-ins and demonstrations.

Their emerging vision of politics favored action over contemplation, improvisation over careful advance planning, and personal feelings over extended political analysis. As Mario Savio, a Berkeley graduate student who had participated in the Mississippi Freedom Summer, proclaimed in 1964, the dominant political machinery sometimes "becomes so odious" that "you can't even tacitly take part" in its operations. Instead, people needed to put their own "bodies upon the gears" and try "to make it stop." Later, a prominent Jewish rabbi, Abraham Herschel, offered a similar formulation of this basic political ideal: "Mere knowledge or belief" could sometimes be "too feeble a cure," and the "only remedy was the kind of personal sacrifice" exemplified by activists such as Martin Luther King, Jr.

Students attracted to an expansive concept of personalized politics saw their own campuses as centers for testing new political styles more than as places for ingesting the wisdom of the past. Seeing older academic-activists, such as C. Wright Mills, as attractive role models, these college students viewed their generation as uniquely situated to confront a political system dominated by powerful and entrenched interests. Although a worldview focused on personally expanding the range of political options seemed to appeal more to students in the humanities and social sciences than to those in the "hard" sciences, business, or engineering, plenty of potential recruits remained. The rapid expansion of higher education, along with the Baby-Boom population bulge, greatly swelled the number of young people who enrolled in colleges and universities during the early 1960s.

Students who embraced movement politics, following in the footsteps of academics such as Mills, saw activism and intellectualism as complementary pursuits. They denounced courses and research projects that appeared irrelevant to the pressing issues of the day. They confronted administrators who tried to impose lifestyle restrictions, such as sex-segregated living arrangements and dorm hours, on students that state laws otherwise treated as adults. Far worse, these politically active students argued, giant universities, accepting funding from the Pentagon and corporations, seemed oblivious to the social and moral implications of their war-related research. Although accounts of campus activism once highlighted only a few institutions, such as the University of California at Berkeley, recent histories have shown most schools, some even earlier than Berkeley, played host to social and political movements. Still, events at a few select schools, including Berkeley, dominated the media spotlight.

Initially working to mobilize around domestic issues such as civil rights, student-led movements at Berkeley became generational lightning rods. Protests on and around the Berkeley campus, which began in earnest in 1964, over restrictions against on-campus political activity, provided some of the most prominent, and lasting, symbols of what media pundits came to call "the war on campus." After organizing a "Free Speech Movement," in opposition to limits on political expression, students and sympathetic faculty mounted the "Berkeley Revolt." This effort included sit-ins, boycotts of classes, contention among faculty members, and intermittent clashes between dissenting students and law enforcement officials. Activists demanded an end to any cultural divide, let alone legal regulations, which tried to separate activism on campus from that in the wider world.

The Counterculture

Berkeley also came to symbolize the interrelationship, however uneasy, between political movements associated with a New Left and the vertiginous energies of a Counterculture. The Counterculture of the 1960s has always seemed a difficult "movement" to identify, especially since one of its self-defining slogans proclaimed "Do Your Own Thing." It elected no officers, held no formal meetings, and maintained no central office to issue manifestos. Bursting into view in low-income neighborhoods, such as San Francisco's Haight-Ashbury area, and along thoroughfares bordering college campuses, such as Berkeley's Telegraph Avenue, the Counterculture maintained a vague sense of unity through a loose infrastructure of small shops, restaurants, and overcrowded living units. People who claimed to speak for the Counterculture espoused values, styles, and institutions hailed as both "utopian" and as "realistic" alternatives to those of the prevailing or "straight" culture. Countercultural groups such as San Francisco's Diggers, a commune that mixed improvisational street-theater productions with social-service projects, distanced themselves from Great Society organizations.

Dissenting cultural ventures did not spring up spontaneously but drew on earlier models, such as the "Beat movement" of the 1950s. A loosely connected group of writers and poets, the Beats had denied that either the material abundance or conventional spiritual ideals of the 1950s fulfilled the promise of liberty. Rejecting the "people of plenty" credo, the Beats claimed that an overabundance of consumer goods, a commercialized culture industry, and oppressive technologies condemned most people to wander through alienated lives that seemed oppressive, emotionally crippling, or just plain boring.

Beat writers such as Jack Kerouac, author of *On the Road* (1957), praised the rebels of their generation. They saw nonconformists like themselves challenging settled social routines and seeking more instinctual, more sensual, and more authentic ways of living. The Beat poet Allen Ginsberg, in works such as *Howl* (1956), decried soulless materialism and puritanical moral codes for tempting a culture already awash in alienation to acts of madness and despair. In search of alternative visions and oppositional lifestyles, Ginsberg's poetry celebrated the kind of liberty that drugs, Eastern mysticism, and same-sex love affairs could supposedly provide. Beats such as Ginsberg, in contrast to critics who merely condemned conformity (see chapter 28), seemed commited to testing the possibilities of liberty by seeking to live their everyday lives beyond conventional boundaries.

Many of the Beats, especially Ginsberg, nonetheless had recognized how conventional commercial media might play to their advantage. Media exposure, respectful and (more often) disdainful, helped the Beats sustain bohemian-style communities in San Francisco's North Beach and New York City's Greenwich Village. In time, as influential cultural critics and college professors praised the Beats, young people began encountering their writings and poetry in humanities courses and literary-minded bookstores. Ginsberg's status as a dissenting celebrity continued to grow, especially on college campuses, and he eagerly promoted his iconic status as a link between the Beat movement of the 1950s and the Counterculture of the 1960s.

This Counterculture—perhaps best seen as a collection of alternative subcultures rather than a single impulse—left its imprint on a wide range of movements. These included nonprofit urban cooperatives, radical strains of feminism, **environmentalism,** and the fight against restrictions, especially involving sexuality, on lifestyle choices.

Mass media of the 1960s, however, initially treated the Counterculture as a source for titillating stories about longish and unkempt hair styles, flamboyant clothing, and uninhibited sexuality. The media also liked to portray countercultural lifestyles, among young people who came to be known as **"hippies,"** as being on the cutting edge of a supposedly massive, fun-filled youth rebellion. Observers of this Counterculture also highlighted its use of drugs, particularly marijuana and LSD, and its preference, often because of financial necessity, for communal living arrangements.

New musical stylings, such as the folk-rock of The Byrds and the acid-rock of The Grateful Dead, also helped identify the Counterculture. The singer-songwriter Bob Dylan, who had abandoned acoustic folk music and "gone electric" in 1965, gained unwanted recognition as the Counterculture's prophet-laureate. Fusing musical idioms used by African American blues artists such as Muddy Waters with poetic touches indebted to the Beats, Dylan's "Like a Rolling Stone" (1965) exploded onto both the Top-40 charts of AM radio and the freewheeling play lists of the alternative FM stations and college radio stations linked to the Counterculture. Publications primarily aimed at college students, including the magazine *Rolling Stone,* dispatched youthful journalists to report on—and also participate in—the countercultural scene.

The more traditional commercial marketplace also welcomed images and products from the Counterculture. The ad agency for Chrysler Motors, alert to the appeal of countercultural imagery, urged car buyers to break away from older patterns, purchase a youthful-looking 1965 model, and thereby join the "Dodge Rebellion." The clothing industry marketed colorful countercultural-looking styles as the latest in "hip" fashions. For women, this generally meant expensive versions of bohemian-style garb, which typically displayed a considerable amount of skin (as with the miniskirt) and avoided restrictive foundation garments (as in the braless look). Marketers urged men seeking a more youthful appearance to exchange white shirts and regimental neckties for more colorful and more casual clothing styles.

Recognizing the appeal of bands such as San Francisco's Jefferson Airplane, the popular music industry saw profits to be made from the sound, as well as the look, of the Counterculture. An early countercultural happening, "the Human Be-In," organized by community activists from San Francisco in early 1967, provided a model for subsequent, commercially dominated music festivals such as Monterrey Pop (later in 1967) and Woodstock (in 1969).

Back on college campuses, some of the students and faculty attracted to New Left political movements seemed baffled by the Counterculture. The novelist and LSD-guru Ken Kesey, for example, shocked a 1965 political demonstration at Berkeley with a style of politics indebted to the theatrics of the Counterculture. Accompanied by veterans from the Beat movement and youthful members of his communal group, "the Merry Pranksters," Kesey ridiculed other speakers. They were playing the same tired political game—parsing the details of alternative foreign policies—as Lyndon Johnson. Between singing choruses of "Home on the Range," Kesey advised pursuing pleasurable activities of genuine interest to oneself and, ultimately, of real help to others. Everyone should abandon conventional politics and pursue a more personalized political agenda, one focused on revolutionizing, especially through drugs such as LSD, how they lived their own lives.

African American Social Movements

Meanwhile, this movement of movements—and changing ideas about the nature of politics— also reshaped specific efforts to achieve freedom and equality for people of African descent. Initiatives that still looked to Dr. Martin Luther King, Jr., faced growing criticism for embracing too limited a vision of political action. Moreover, as with other areas of movement politics, the battle against discrimination involved differences over how to address the ever-present commercial mass media.

Early on, Dr. King tacitly acknowledged how much SCLC campaigns depended on commercial media, especially the weekly news magazines and television. Network TV images of the violence directed against his 1965 voter registration drive in Selma, Alabama, substantially aided his cause. In a moment that dramatically framed the politics at stake in Selma, ABC television interrupted the network premiere of *Judgment at Nuremberg,* an anti-Nazi movie, in favor of pictures showing all-white squads of Alabama state troopers beating peaceful voting-rights marchers. Lyndon Johnson also recognized the power of these images. Going on television several nights later, to urge Congress to speed passage of the landmark Voting Rights Act of 1965, he promised that "we shall overcome" the nation's "crippling legacy of bigotry and injustice," supposedly evident to people looking at TV images from Selma.

At the same time, however, other people interpreted such TV images differently. Growing numbers of people saw direct-action movements for liberty and equality as subversive agitation and demanded a renewed commitment to conventional forms of politics and to measures restoring law and order.

Less than a week after congressional passage of the Voting Rights Act, six days of violent conflict devastated parts of Los Angeles. The violence apparently began with an altercation, near the largely African American community of Watts, between a white California highway patrol officer and a black motorist. A growing crowd, additional law-enforcement officers, long-standing differences over policing practices in LA, and deep-seated grievances within Watts soon spiraled into what some called a "riot," others an "insurrection" or an "uprising." By whatever name, burning and looting swept over Watts and edged into other areas of south-central Los Angeles. Thirty-four people died; fires consumed hundreds of businesses and homes; heavily armed National Guard troops patrolled the city's streets; and platoons of television camera crews carried images from LA across the nation and around the world.

What should be the response to events in Watts, people immediately asked? Most local political leaders, including LA's mayor and police chief, denied any responsibility for the violence, blamed civil-rights "agitation" for the troubles, and sought additional resources for the LAPD. Dr. King rushed to the scene, preaching the politics of nonviolence, only to

HISTORY THROUGH FILM

Malcolm X (1992)

Directed by Spike Lee. Starring Denzel Washington (Malcolm X), Angela Bassett (Betty Shabbaz), Al Freeman, Jr. (Elijah Muhammad).

Spike Lee, the U.S. film industry's best-known African American director, campaigned aggressively to make a movie about Malcolm X. For nearly 25 years, Hollywood moguls had been trying to portray the Black Power leader who was gunned down in 1965 and whose *Autobiography* became a literary classic. Delays in obtaining financing, crafting a script, and finding a director always stymied production plans.

Lee, who had denounced the Hollywood establishment for passing over his celebrated (and controversial) *Do the Right Thing* (1989) for an Academy Award nomination, insisted that only he could do justice to the story of Malcolm X. Initially buoyed by a $34 million budget, Lee eventually encountered problems of his own, including his insistence on releasing a movie that ran for more than three hours. Lee called *Malcolm X* "my interpretation of the man. It is nobody else's."

Denzel Washington stars as Malcolm X.

Everett Collection

The finished film displays Lee's desire to show the presence of the past in the present. Produced by Lee's own independent production—whose name, "Forty Acres and a Mule," recalls the land-distribution program advanced by advocates of Radical Reconstruction after the Civil War—the movie argues for Malcolm X's continuing relevance to social and racial politics.

The segments that begin and end the movie employ collages of iconic images that underscore this aim. Against the backdrop of the Warner Brothers logo, the soundtrack introduces the actual voice of Malcolm X, decrying U.S. history as a story of racist actions. Malcolm's accusations continue as a giant American flag, perhaps a reference to the popular film *Patton* (1970), appears on screen. Then, the image of the flag is cut into pieces by jagged images from the homemade videotape of the 1991 incident in which Los Angeles police officers beat an African American man named Rodney King. Next, the flag begins to burn until, revealed behind it, a giant "X," adorned with remnants of the flag, dominates the film frame. The ending uses substantial archival footage of Malcolm, along with images of South African freedom fighter Nelson Mandela, while the soundtrack features the voice of Ossie Davis, the celebrated African American actor, giving a eulogy to Malcolm X.

Released near Thanksgiving, the film opened to packed houses and took in considerably more money than Oliver Stone's *JFK* had garnered when it had debuted only one year earlier. Despite a multimedia publicity blitz, *Malcolm X*'s box-office revenues steadily declined. Reviewers and industry spokespeople reported that the lengthy, episodic movie seemed to tax the patience and attention span of most filmgoers.

Watching *Malcolm X* on video or DVD, however, can allow a viewer to concentrate on its many stunning sequences, speeding by ones that seem to drag, and returning to ones that may seem unclear at first viewing. *Malcolm X* remains a fascinating cinematic history of the early Black Power movement and, more generally, of the social ferment that gripped the nation during its longest war.

encounter, as he had expected, anger from both LA's political establishment and local black organizations. Only aggressive, sometimes even violent, forms of political action, some black activists were insisting, could get the attention of Californians who ignored racial inequalities in jobs, housing, and law enforcement. Only the previous year, white suburbanites had voted overwhelmingly to scrap the Rumford Act, the hard-won open-housing law. Lyndon Johnson, stunned by what he saw on his trio of TV sets, quickly responded through the kind of politics he understood best. Even as fires continued to burn, LBJ ordered up new social-welfare resources for LA: "Let's move in—money, marbles, and chalk." Groups more attuned to participatory democracy began reorganizing local movements and creating new ones, such as the Watts Writers' Workshop, convinced that changing times dictated shifting forms of response.

Among African Americans, new movement initiatives had been appearing throughout the 1950s and 1960s (see chapter 28). Some of the most recent looked to Malcolm X, a charismatic African American minister whose February 1965 death amplified, rather than silenced, his powerful voice. While still calling himself Malcolm Little, he had engaged in petty criminal activities, served time in prison, and reoriented his life by joining the Nation of Islam during the 1950s. As Malcolm X, he soon became a leader of this North American–based group, popularly known as the "Black Muslims," which had emerged during the 1930s.

Malcolm X's fiery denunciations of the civil-rights movement, which gained him a lurid reputation in commercial media, found a receptive grassroots audience in many urban black neighborhoods in the North and West. Dr. King's gradualist, nonviolent campaign for new civil-rights laws, Malcolm X charged, simply ignored the everyday problems of most African Americans and the undesirability—indeed, the impossibility—of integration. "White America" would never accept persons of African descent as equals, and dark-skinned people should thus work, as the Nation of Islam and other "black nationalist" groups had long urged, to build and strengthen their own communities. Although he never advocated initiating confrontation, Malcolm X strongly endorsed self-defense, "by any means necessary."

Although mainstream media continued to portray Malcolm X as a dangerous subversive, he offered more than angry rhetoric. He called for pride in African American cultural practices and for economic reconstruction. He urged African Americans to "recapture our heritage and identity" and "launch a cultural revolution to unbrainwash an entire people." Seeking a broader movement, one that could forge multiracial coalitions, Malcolm X eventually broke from the Black Muslims and established his own Organization of Afro-American Unity. Murdered by enemies from the Nation of Islam, Malcolm X soon became, especially after the posthumous publication of his *Autobiography* (1965), a source for black-oriented political and cultural visions.

These visions, which reshaped many older movements and inspired new ones, diverged from the political perspectives that dominated Lyndon Johnson's administration. Officially committed to additional civil-rights legislation, particularly a national open-housing law and to new Great Society programs, the president was also coming to sense that many federal laws ignored the root causes of current conflicts. He began listening to members of his administration who suggested social programs, which would later be called "affirmative action" measures, specifically intended to assist African Americans. In a 1965 speech, he suggested that centuries of racial discrimination against people of African descent had produced "wounds" and "weaknesses" that had become "the special handicaps of those who are black in a Nation that happens to be mostly white."

Although Johnson intended his words to soothe, they tended to inflame. African Americans who now viewed empowering black communities as a major civil-rights goal, for example, wondered if the president's subliminal message might be that laws could not adequately advance liberty and equality because black culture and society seemed, from his perspective, "inadequate"? Could Johnson be hinting that differences in America arose because of "superior" and "inferior" societies and cultures?

Disparate answers from different movements to questions such as these—along with growing opposition to specific Johnson administration policies—became evident during the fall of 1965. When the president invited several hundred black leaders to the White House for a "racial summit," two veteran activists, A. Philip Randolph and Bayard Rustin, used the occasion to lobby for their "Freedom Budget," an implicit indictment of LBJ's funding priorities. They called for a 10-year plan for spending $100 billion on infrastructure projects in low-income neighborhoods. Other critics denounced a recent study written by Daniel Patrick Moynihan, a social scientist who had worked for both JFK and LBJ. The *Moynihan Report,* apparently intended as a prelude to new White House proposals but widely seen as a response to Watts, argued that social conditions within African American communities often made laws mandating equality largely irrelevant. It singled out the prevalence of families headed by single women. "The harsh fact is that . . . in terms of ability to win out in the competition of American life," this report concluded, African Americans were simply "not equal to most of the groups with which they will be competing."

People such as Rustin, who focused on pocketbook issues and on brick-and-mortar matters, dismissed this "black family debate" as a distraction. Most younger movement activists, however, argued that Moynihan's single report spoke volumes about the Johnson administration's paternalistic mindset. Accustomed to dealing with competing interests from which he could cobble a consensus, Lyndon Johnson privately denounced movement leaders for using, in reference to the Freedom Budget, *his* summit to start "raising unshirted hell and saying it's got to be a 100 billion."

Meanwhile, events in the South also highlighted the increasingly frenetic—and the also gradually more effective—movement-of-movements phenomenon. SNCC and Dr. King's SCLC continued to press forward, though often along separate paths. Their movements constantly faced the threat of violence and death and confronted state and local legal systems seemingly unable to restrain or punish vigilantes who attacked, or even killed, civil-rights workers. White southern legal officials, moreover, appeared no better at overseeing electoral contests. Charging that vote-counters had robbed of victory a SNCC-sponsored slate in a local election in Lowndes County, Alabama, Stokely Carmichael began to organize, against the advice of King's SCLC, an all-black political organization in that locale. To symbolize the militancy of this third-party movement, the "Lowndes County Freedom Organization," SNCC commissioned a special logo: a coiled black panther.

The following spring, SNCC joined other movements in a well publicized foray into Mississippi. In June 1966, a KKK gunman shot James Meredith, who was conducting a one-person "March against Fear" from Memphis, Tennessee, to Jackson, Mississippi. Convinced of the need to defy violence, representatives from most of the individual movements that comprised the wider antidiscrimination cause hastily gathered in Mississippi. Although state officials provided only minimal protection and armed KKK vigilantes assembled at almost every crossroad, most activists, including Stokely Carmichael and Dr. King, remained determined to stay on course.

An enlarged March against Fear became the first large-scale movement project—in contrast to the 1963 March on Washington or the 1965 voting-rights campaign in Alabama—that did not seek new civil-rights legislation. In this sense, it seemed an effort to demonstrate that movements for liberty and equality now also emphasized struggles for dignity, pride, and empowerment. Moreover, highly symbolic political activities of the kind coming into prominence obviously relied on media visibility, and Meredith's shooting had already focused national news coverage on Mississippi. Considerations such as these seemingly justified a difficult and dangerous group effort to complete the quixotic crusade one person had begun. Displaying a remarkable degree of solidarity—if not always unanimity—the March Against Fear ended with an interracial crowd of 15,000 people, most of whom had arrived in Mississippi just before the finale, marching into Jackson in late June.

This march also underscored differences, in rhetorical and programmatic emphases, among (and within) various movements. As Stokely Carmichael played to the omnipresent TV cameras, Dr. King, an old hand at this political art form, admiringly acknowledged the younger activist's shrewd grasp of media routines. After being hauled off to jail, during one of the local voter registration campaigns that accompanied the march, an enraged Carmichael claimed he would never again, passively and nonviolently, submit to arrest.

Carmichael now explicitly urged that the struggle not remain just one for "Freedom," the byword of the SCLC, but also for "Black Power." As different movements within this march's ranks chanted "Black Power," others called for "Freedom." During one lengthy debate among the marchers, Carmichael rejected a compromise slogan, "Black Equality," and insisted that Black Power best described the kind of politics that direct-action movements such as SNCC should now embrace.

Black Power did not magically spring forth from the March against Fear. Always a slippery concept to grasp, especially when applied to constantly shifting political values and strategies, Black Power provided an apparently inflammatory label for a sometimes commonsensical set of claims. At different times and places during the 1960s, African American activists determined that they should seek greater on-the-ground power both in—and for—their own communities. If black-led movements in cities such as LA and Oakland, for example, could not count on their state's hard-won open-housing law to remain in force or if local political establishments could block federal funding of CAP initiatives, seeking greater power for a grassroots black politics seemed a logical, if politically uncertain, move.

Operating from this perspective, in 1966, several college students from Oakland, who were already active in community-based projects, announced formation of a new Black Power organization. Taking its name, the "Black Panther Party," from SNCC's earlier effort in Lowndes County, this movement issued a platform that employed militant rhetoric on behalf of 10 objectives, many already familiar to local civil-rights groups. These included greater economic opportunities—for housing, education, and employment—and greater legal protections, especially against police misconduct and flawed legal proceedings. The group also created its own grassroots social programs, including ones to improve health and nutrition in low-income black neighborhoods.

The Panthers quickly became a media phenomenon. Adapting quasi-military symbols and organizational forms from Third World revolutionary movements, a trio of media-savvy young men—Huey Newton, Bobby Seale, and Eldridge Cleaver—quickly gained national attention for the Black Panthers. A 1967 rally on behalf of the Second Amendment right to use firearms for self-defense, against what armed demonstrators called "fascist pig" police officers, attracted the notice of J. Edgar Hoover. The FBI head eventually made destroying the Black Panther Party, by almost any available means, a key goal.

Far less flamboyantly than the Black Panthers, other groups and movements extended Black Power ideals to a wide range of issues. Fully embracing the word *black* and a cultural agenda that stressed racial identity, they asserted their power to pursue separate, African American–directed routes not just toward liberty and equality but, sometimes, "liberation" from the prevailing U.S. political culture. Receiving a more generous hearing from commercial media than Malcolm X had gained during his lifetime, many Black Power efforts, more importantly, forged political links and cultural networks within African American communities. "Black Is Beautiful" became a watchword. James Brown, the "Godfather" of soul music, captured this new spirit with his "Say It Loud, I'm Black and I'm Proud" (1968).

Against this rapidly changing backdrop, the U.S. Congress passed the **Civil Rights Act of 1968.** A central provision of this omnibus measure, the last *new* civil-rights legislation of the 20th century, sought to eliminate racial discrimination in the real estate market. This section of the law, popularly known as the "Fair Housing Act," provided a national version of open housing legislation. Its initial proponents, however, considered the final version shot through with exemptions and plagued by enfeebled enforcement mechanisms. Moreover, another section of the same Civil Rights Act declared it a crime to cross state lines in order to incite a "riot." Supporters hailed this provision as a law-and-order measure, while critics insisted it illegally targeted specific political activists, especially ones espousing Black Power. Whenever tested in federal court, though, this section passed constitutional scrutiny.

The Antiwar Movement

Meanwhile, one movement began to overshadow all others. Even as campus-centered ferment, countercultural activities, and African American empowerment efforts continued—and other movements, such as environmentalism and second-wave feminism, began to emerge—the one that sought to pressure Lyndon Johnson into abandoning his crusade in Vietnam dominated U.S. politics and culture.

The antiwar movement, as with the broader movement-of-movements impulse, never fell into neat categories. The dominant media frame of the day, hawks against doves, failed to account for the diverse coalition that came to oppose the Johnson administration. Some of the strongest "antiwar" sentiment, for example, blamed LBJ for not prosecuting the war *aggressively enough*. Convinced that he would never strive for a clear-cut victory, some people in this camp decided to oppose continued U.S. involvement, at least on Johnson's terms. At the other end of the antiwar spectrum, as the White House and its supporters constantly noted, were small movements that called for a North Vietnam–NLF victory. "Ho, Ho, Ho Chi-Minh/NLF's Gonna Win" went a chant that enraged Johnson and distressed many members of the antiwar coalition.

The broad middle ground of the anti-Johnson, antiwar alliance could never fully agree on many issues. A diverse constituency, in another concrete example of participatory democracy, continually debated how and why the United States had ever become committed to preserving a noncommunist South Vietnam. They also split over how and if the antiwar movement could change LBJ's course. In addition, the antiwar cause faced the same questions as all other movements of the 1960s: What kind of politics best expressed the ethical and spiritual values of its supporters? And how might mass-mediated images of this movement's activities represent its politics to a broader audience?

By 1967, the issue of Vietnam had become *the* controversy on most college campuses. At a series of "teach-ins," supporters and opponents of the war had already debated their positions. Later, these events had given way to street demonstrations, in both local communities and in Washington, D.C., against Johnson's Vietnam policies. Most male students possessed a direct stake in such activities. Their local draft boards normally granted them educational deferments, but these expired at graduation and could be revoked or denied, sometimes because of a young man's view of Johnson's policies. Many students, joining the less fortunate sons who did not attend college, complied with draft regulations, and a good number volunteered for service in Vietnam. A strong draft-resistance movement, often symbolized by the burning of draft cards and sometimes marked by the flight to foreign countries, especially Canada, also emerged. During October 1967, campus protests against war-related activities passed a crucial threshold when a pitched, bloody battle broke out between antiwar demonstrators and police at the University of Wisconsin in Madison.

That same year, 1967, saw two other important antiwar milestones. Long critical of the war, Dr. Martin Luther King, Jr. now faced intensive pressure, especially from activists among the clergy, to spell out his moral and spiritual position. At the same time, many of his civil-rights allies warned against doing anything that might break his already severely strained relationship with the Johnson White House and escalate attacks from enemies such as J. Edgar Hoover. Speaking in early April 1967, at New York's Riverside Church, Dr. King boldly laid out his views. In an analysis similar to that of Black Power spokespeople and of critical journalists such as Gloria Emerson, Dr. King noted a black-and-white truth. African American troops, mostly from low-income communities, served and died in numbers far greater than their proportion of the U.S. population "for a nation that has been unable to seat them together in the same schools" with the white soldiers now at their side in Vietnam. The immoral "madness" in Vietnam "must cease," Dr. King thundered, but he also wondered if "the world now demands a maturity of America that we may not be able to achieve."

This speech provided an important gauge of both the growing antiwar movement and the expanding polarization within the country. Although Dr. King had expected a backlash, he failed to anticipate that voices from all across the political-media spectrum would condemn his address. Although the editorial board of the *New York Times* did not, as some commentators did, call King a "traitor," it read his antiwar pronouncement through the familiar frame of narrowly imagined interest groups. The *Times* charged him with seeking media attention and with damaging the civil-rights cause by expounding on a matter about which he likely knew little and on which he might lack the political credentials to comment intelligently. Why should people give his foreign policy opinions more weight than those of the boxer Muhammad Ali, who had been widely condemned for his antiwar statements?

The same interrelated issues raised by King's speech—the nature of politics and the role of the media—also surrounded popular discussion of a massive 1967 antiwar demonstration in Washington, D.C. This event underscored how the politics of the New Left and the spirit of the Counterculture marched together, at least when in opposition to Lyndon Johnson's policies in Vietnam.

Noting the visual media's voracious appetite for pictures of political and cultural dissent, a small group of experienced activists decided to feed media outlets a uniquely prepared supply of imagery. To do this, they invented a kind of "nonmovement movement," which bypassed the hard work of mobilization and organization in favor of hoping media images would do the mobilizing and organizing for them. Two members of this group, Abbie Hoffman and Jerry Rubin, proclaimed themselves leaders of a (nonexistent) "Youth International Party"—or "YIPPIE!"—and simply waited for media coverage to surround their activities, as they knew it would.

Hoffman and Rubin raised the curtain on a neo-vaudevillian, countercultural style of politics. In one famous incident, they tossed fake money onto the floor of the New York Stock Exchange. Invoking the sit-in movement, they joked about staging department-store "loot-ins" to strike at "the property fetish that underlies genocidal war" in Vietnam. Even more audaciously, they announced their contribution to the 1967 antiwar march would be a separate trek to the Pentagon. There, they claimed, marchers chanting mystical incantations would levitate this five-sided head of the military-industrial complex several hundred feet into the air.

Although the Pentagon remained firmly planted, events around its perimeter generated eye-catching TV footage and gained novelist Norman Mailer a National Book Award for his first-person report. According to Mailer's admirers, his book *Armies of the Night* (1968), by interweaving Mailer's personal politics with a journalistic account of a public event, reinvented orthodox political reporting in a way that seemed to parallel how activists were reinventing what counted as politics.

1968

Other observers of events at the Pentagon and harsher critics of *Armies of the Night*'s journalistic style dissented. Might not media images of colorful quipsters such as Hoffman and Rubin be helping to fuel cultural polarization rather than to provide new models of useful political action? Might the media's taste for spectacular demonstrations be trivializing underlying issues, including moral ones? Questions such as these became even more pressing during the tumultuous 12 months of 1968, a year that saw violence and upheaval span most of the globe.

Turmoil in Vietnam

January of 1968 had not even concluded when Lyndon Johnson's crusade in Vietnam, though not the violence accompanying it, effectively ended. Late that month during a truce declared in observance of Tet, the Vietnamese lunar New Year celebration, NLF and North Vietnamese forces suddenly went on the attack throughout South Vietnam. One group even temporarily seized the grounds of the U.S. embassy in Saigon. U.S. strategists had fully expected some violation of the Tet truce, but they never anticipated the breadth and ferocity of the communist offensive.

The Johnson administration tried to assess the fallout. Militarily, U.S. forces emerged victorious from this **Tet offensive.** After regrouping, they inflicted heavy casualties on NLF and North Vietnamese troops, who gained relatively little territory at considerable cost. Supporters of the war in the United States soon blamed media imagery for exaggerating the effect of the early attacks, ignoring NLF and North Vietnamese losses, and thereby turning "victory" into "defeat." Critics of the war countered that the Tet offensive had initially caught U.S. military commanders ill-prepared and, later, highlighted their inability to effectively pursue the badly mauled enemy forces.

In any case, Tet proved a defeat for the Johnson administration. Events seemed to belie its constant assurances of improving fortunes and imminent victory. Walter Cronkite, the esteemed CBS-TV anchor, returned from a post-Tet tour of Vietnam and proclaimed, to a national television audience, that the United States would never prevail militarily on the battlefield and needed to consider negotiating its withdrawal. Reportedly, Lyndon Johnson mused that if he had lost the celebrity anchor then known as "the most trusted person in America," he had also lost much of the rest of the country.

LBJ received more bad news when he summoned his most trusted advisers and a distinguished group of elderly statespeople, the so-called wise men, to consider General Westmoreland's request for an additional 206,000 U.S. troops. To Johnson's surprise, a majority advised against another massive infusion of U.S. troops. If South Vietnam were to survive, its own forces needed to shoulder more of the military burden. Johnson capitulated to this argument, conceding that another large increase in U.S troops, even if forces could have been spared from other duties, would have further fanned opposition to his policies.

The Tet offensive threw Lyndon Johnson's own political future into question. Faced with open revolt by antiwar Democrats, who rallied behind a presidential bid by Senator

Eugene McCarthy of Minnesota, Johnson reconsidered, for the final time, his political options. Although LBJ controlled enough party-selected delegates to bury McCarthy's candidacy at the Democratic national convention, McCarthy's primary campaigns against Johnson, which attracted youthful volunteers and abundant media coverage, revealed how little political capital the president now possessed.

Eugene McCarthy, who was athletic enough to have considered a professional baseball career and sufficiently academic to have been a college professor, had always seemed uncomfortable with the path he did choose, electoral politics. After serving, capably but as if on autopilot, in both houses of Congress, McCarthy suddenly achieved instant political fame as an unorthodox presidential hopeful. LBJ technically defeated McCarthy in the 1968 New Hampshire primary, but the antiwar message of "Clean Gene" (as media pundits dubbed him) resonated both with voters who favored the United States bombing its way to victory and with those who favored a speedy withdrawal.

With McCarthy poised to defeat LBJ in the Wisconsin primary, Johnson surprised all but his closest aides and reconfigured the diplomatic and political landscapes. On March 31, 1968, he went on TV to declare a halt to the U.S. bombing of North Vietnam, to announce an offer to begin peace negotiations, and to proclaim he would not seek reelection. Deprived of his greatest asset, not being LBJ, Eugene McCarthy pledged to continue his fight for the Democratic nomination, He prepared to square off against his former senatorial colleague from Minnesota and Johnson's ever-loyal vice president, Hubert H. Humphrey.

Turmoil at Home

Among the many former LBJ supporters gladdened by the turn in political events, was Dr. Martin Luther King., Jr. He hoped that the Democratic Party would reject Humphrey and embrace an antiwar candidate, preferably Senator Robert Kennedy (RFK) of New York, JFK's younger brother, who had belatedly entered the presidential sweepstakes after Johnson's surprise announcement.

Less than a week after seeing glimmers of political hope, on April 4, 1968, King met the violent death he had long anticipated. While visiting Memphis, Tennessee, in support of a labor strike by African American sanitation workers, the civil-rights leader received an almost instantly fatal head wound, as he stood on the balcony of the Lorraine Motel. Law enforcement officials soon identified (and eventually apprehended) the alleged shooter: James Earl Ray, a drifter with a lengthy criminal record. Ray quickly pleaded guilty to having assassinated King, waived a jury trial, and received a 99-year sentence. Subsequently, though, Ray recanted and claimed to have been a pawn in some larger white supremacist conspiracy. Ray died in 1998, still insisting on his innocence, a claim that intrigued several members of the King family but convinced very few legal observers or historians.

As news of King's murder spread, violent protests swept through urban neighborhoods. More than 100 cities and towns witnessed outbreaks; 39 people died; 75,000 regular and National Guard troops were called to duty. When President Johnson proclaimed Sunday,

© UPI-Bettmann/Corbis.

Martin Luther King, Jr.'s Funeral Cortege   Martin Luther King, Jr.'s assassination in 1968 sparked both violent protests and solemn mourning for the slain civil rights leader. Thousands of his grieving supporters followed the cart, drawn by mules, which carried King's body through the streets of his native Atlanta.

April 7, as a day of national mourning for the slain civil-rights leader, parts of the nation's capital city, including neighborhoods near the White House, remained ablaze.

Claiming he would devise policies to end violence at home and in Vietnam, Robert Kennedy mounted a nonstop campaign for the Democratic presidential nomination. Unwilling to risk a test of his personal popularity, Humphrey stayed out of the Democratic primaries, inheriting most of the nonelected delegates previously pledged to LBJ and leaving RFK and McCarthy to fight over the rest. His celebrity-assisted campaign recalling memories of JFK's, Robert Kennedy sought to convince Democrats pledged to Humphrey or favoring McCarthy that only another Kennedy could win the presidency in November.

Then, on June 5, after besting Eugene McCarthy in California's primary, RFK fell victim to an assassin's bullets. Bystanders immediately grabbed Sirhan Sirhan, a Palestinian-born immigrant, who was later charged and convicted of killing Kennedy. Television coverage of Kennedy's body being returned to Washington, D.C., and of his funeral provided poignant, and disturbing, reminders of Dr. King's recent murder and of the assassination of JFK five years earlier. Was there, some people wondered, some "sickness" afflicting U.S. political culture? Did "government by gunplay" rather than political pluralism best describe the prevailing system of governance?

The violence of 1968 continued. During the Republican national convention in Miami, presidential candidate **Richard Nixon** promised to restore law and order. Inside the convention hall, he unveiled a surprise choice as his running mate, Governor Spiro Agnew of Maryland, an outspoken critic of movement activists. Outside, in a largely African American section of Miami, clashes broke out between police and citizens, during which four people lost their lives. Later that summer, in Chicago, thousands of people, drawn from a cross-section of the antiwar movement, converged on the Democratic Party's convention to protest the nomination of Hubert Humphrey, who was still loyally supporting Johnson's policy in Vietnam. Responding to acts of provocation by some demonstrators, including Abbie Hoffman and Jerry Rubin, police officers struck back. Some used indiscriminate force against antiwar activists and members of the media. Although an official report later talked about a "police riot," opinion polls showed that most people approved of how police officers had acted in Chicago. Humphrey easily captured the Democratic presidential nod, but differing views over Johnson's Vietnam policy and over the meaning of the violence in Chicago left his party bitterly divided.

The Election of 1968

Both Humphrey and Nixon worried about the candidacy of Alabama's George Wallace. After adroitly organizing a third-party run, Wallace stumbled badly by tabbing retired general Curtis LeMay, who immediately hinted at the possibility of using nuclear weaponry against North Vietnam, as a running mate. With his own views in favor of victory in Vietnam and against civil rights well established, Wallace could play to opinion polls that suggested growing sentiment against the Counterculture and the antiwar movement. If any "hippie" protestor ever blocked his motorcade, Wallace once announced, "it'll be the last car he'll ever lay down in front of." Declaring his independence from the interest groups that supposedly controlled the political process, Wallace also courted voters who saw themselves as captive to "tax-and-spend" bureaucracies in Washington.

George Wallace never expected to gain the presidency. He hoped, however, to secure enough electoral votes to deny Humphrey or Nixon a majority. Then, as the U.S. Constitution prescribed, the selection of a president would rest with the House of Representatives, where Wallace might act as a power broker on behalf of his favorite issues and his own political fortunes.

Nixon narrowly prevailed in November. Hinting at a secret plan to honorably end the war in Vietnam, Nixon also promised to restore tranquility at home. Although the former vice president won 56 percent of the electoral vote, he outpolled Humphrey in the popular vote by less than 1 percent. Humphrey had benefited when Johnson ordered a pause in the

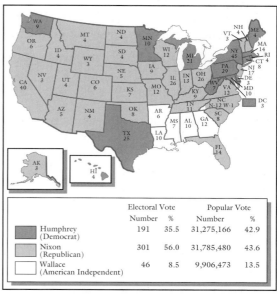

	Electoral Vote		Popular Vote	
	Number	%	Number	%
Humphrey (Democrat)	191	35.5	31,275,166	42.9
Nixon (Republican)	301	56.0	31,785,480	43.6
Wallace (American Independent)	46	8.5	9,906,473	13.5

Map 29.2 Presidential Election, 1968 George Wallace's independent, third-party candidacy influenced the election of 1968. Compare this map with ones of earlier and later election years to see how the southern states gradually left the Democratic column and, in time, became a base of Republican power.

bombing of North Vietnam and pledged to begin peace talks in Paris, an initiative that Nixon secretly worked to undermine through back-channel negotiations with the South Vietnamese government. In the end, Humphrey carried only Texas in the South. George Wallace picked up 46 electoral votes, all from states in the Deep South, and 13.5 percent of the popular vote nationwide. Nixon won five crucial southern states and claimed the support, from all across the country, of those whom he called "the forgotten Americans, the non-shouters, the non-demonstrators."

The Nixon Years, 1969–1974

Focus Question
What new domestic and foreign policies did the Nixon administration initiate?

Raised in a modest Quaker home in southern California, Richard Nixon campaigned for the presidency in 1968 as the kind of leader who could restore domestic tranquility. The beginning of Richard Nixon's presidency, however, coincided with more, rather than less, turmoil.

Lawbreaking and Violence

A handful of people on the political fringe, such as those in a tiny group known as the "Weather Underground," openly embraced violence. According to one assessment, authorities logged approximately 40,000 bomb threats, most unfounded, during the first 18 months of Nixon's first term. There were, though, nearly 200 actual and attempted bombings on college campuses during the 1969–70 academic year, with an explosion at the University of Wisconsin claiming the life of a late-working grad student. Nonlethal attacks rocked other targets, including the Bank of America, the Chase Manhattan Bank, and even the U.S. Congress. On one highly publicized occasion in 1970, three members of the Weather Underground blew themselves apart when their own bomb factory exploded.

At the same time, governmental officials stepped up their use of force. Several prominent Black Power figures, including Fred Hampton of the Black Panthers and the celebrated prison activist George Jackson, died under circumstances their supporters likened to political assassination but public officials considered normal law enforcement activities. J. Edgar Hoover's FBI went beyond shadowing members of entirely peaceful antiwar and women's organizations to harass activists, plant damaging rumors, and even operate as *agent provocateurs,* urging protestors to undertake actions that officials might later prosecute as criminal offenses. After a lengthy investigation of COINTELPRO—a once-secret FBI program aimed at disrupting a wide range of activist groups—a congressional committee concluded that the FBI had illegally ruined careers, severed friendships, besmirched reputations, bankrupted businesses, and even endangered lives. The Bureau terminated COINTELPRO in 1971, only after documents stolen by antiwar activists from an FBI office in Pennsylvania revealed its existence.

State and local officials stepped up their own efforts to restore order. During the fall of 1971, for instance, New York's Governor Nelson Rockefeller suddenly broke off negotiations with representatives for more than a thousand prison inmates, who had seized several cell blocks and taken a number of guards hostage while protesting what they considered to be intolerable living conditions at Attica State Prison. Rockefeller then ordered heavily armed state troopers and National Guard forces into the complex. When this "Attica Uprising" finally ended, 29 prisoners and 11 guards lay dead. At the same time, on college campuses, local officials and administrators seemed increasingly ready to employ force against demonstrators, a course praised by law-and-order advocates and decried by civil libertarians.

A New President

Richard Nixon continued to insist that his vast public experience made him the ideal president for such troubled times. After graduating from Whittier College, Nixon had studied law at Duke University and served in the Navy during the Second World War. He then enjoyed a meteoric political career that took him to the House of Representatives in 1946, the Senate in 1950, and the vice presidency in 1952. His 1960 presidential defeat, at the hands of John Kennedy, began an equally rapid descent. After his failure, in 1962, to win the California governorship, Nixon denounced media commentators and announced his retirement from politics.

Nixon, however, seemed to thrive on confronting a constant series of personal challenges. He entitled an early memoir of his political life *Six Crises*. The defeat of Goldwater, for whom Nixon had doggedly campaigned in 1964, and Johnson's problems resurrected the former vice president's political fortunes. He emerged from the 1968 election more confident than ever before, it seemed, of his leadership abilities.

Once in the White House, Nixon even expected to tame a media that had long bedeviled him. Although his staff remained suspicious of media figures, and eventually clashed with many of them, the president and his key aides felt they possessed more skill than Johnson's administration in the image-making arts. Media personalities might be considered "con artists," Nixon once mused, but politicians could expend "energy to try to rig the news . . . their way." Public officials and media reporters entered "the ring together, each trying to bamboozle the other." Nixon's close advisers, many with backgrounds in advertising and in Southern California's image-driven popular culture, threw themselves into the sport of shaping media portrayals of the Nixon White House.

The Economy

One area in which Nixon seemed less prepared to act almost immediately threatened to upset his political plans. Nixon's presidency coincided with economic problems that would have been unthinkable only a decade earlier. No single cause can account for these difficulties, but most economic analyses begin with the war in Vietnam. This expensive military commitment, along with increased domestic spending and a volatile international economy, began curtailing economic growth.

Lyndon Johnson, determined to stave off defeat in Indochina without cutting Great Society programs or raising taxes, had concealed the true costs of the war, even from his own economic advisers. Nixon inherited a deteriorating (although still favorable) balance of trade and rising rate of inflation. Between 1960 and 1965, consumer prices grew an average of only about 1 percent per year; by 1968, this figure exceeded 4 percent.

By 1971, just as the Nixon administration began planning for the 1972 election, economic conditions worsened, with the unemployment rate topping 6 percent. According to conventional wisdom, expressed in a technical economic concept called "the Phillips curve," when unemployment increases, prices should stay flat or even decline. Yet *both* unemployment and inflation remained on the rise. Economists coined the term **stagflation** to describe this puzzling convergence of economic stagnation and price inflation. Stagflation contributed to another disturbing trend: U.S. exports becoming less competitive in international markets. For the first time in the 20th century, the United States ran a trade deficit in 1971, importing more products than it exported.

With his plans for a two-term presidency perhaps in jeopardy, Richard Nixon faced yet another of his crises. Long opposed to governmental regulation of the economy but now fearful of the political consequences of stagflation and trade imbalances, he needed a quick cure for the nation's economic ills. Suddenly, in what one observer likened to a religious conversion, Nixon proclaimed his belief in governmentally imposed economic controls and announced, in August 1971, his "new economic policy." It included a 90-day freeze on any increases in both wages and prices, to be followed by government monitoring to detect "excessive" increases in either.

Seeking to address the trade deficit, Nixon radically revised the relationship between the United States and the world monetary structure. Dating from the 1944 Bretton Woods agreement (see chapter 26), the United States had tied the value of its dollar to that of gold, at the rate of $35 per ounce of the precious metal. To guarantee stability in currency markets, the United States stood ready to exchange, at this rate, its dollars for gold whenever any other nation's central bank requested it to do so. As dollars piled up in foreign banks because of trade deficits and military spending abroad, however, the fixed value of the U.S. dollar came under pressure from the threat that foreign banks might suddenly demand massive gold conversion. There had been a brief flurry of this kind of activity toward the end of LBJ's presidency, prompting Johnson to institute a "tax surcharge," but gold again steadily poured out of the United States under Nixon's watch.

The president had little choice but to abandon the fixed gold-to-dollar ratio in August 1971. Henceforth, the U.S. dollar would "float" in world currency markets. This meant its value, no longer pegged to a fixed price in gold, could fluctuate in relationship to that of all other currencies. The U.S. dollar, consequently, quickly devalued, and the Nixon administration expected U.S. goods would become cheaper, and thus more competitive, in global markets.

Social Policy

At the urging of Daniel Patrick Moynihan, the Democrat who had written the controversial 1965 report on black family structures, Nixon also proposed an equally dramatic overhaul of social welfare policy. A special presidential adviser on domestic issues, Moynihan suggested Nixon could sponsor truly "radical" changes because his popular political image as a "conservative" would help deflect criticism from within his own Republican party and from southern Democrats.

Following Moynihan's lead, Nixon advanced a "Family Assistance Plan" (FAP). Under FAP, every family would be guaranteed an annual income of $1,600. FAP also proposed scrapping most existing welfare measures, particularly the controversial and increasingly costly Aid to Families with Dependent Children (AFDC), which provided government payments to cover basic care for low-income children who had lost the support of a bread-winning parent. Moynihan touted FAP as advancing equality because it would replace existing arrangements, which assisted *only* those with special circumstances (such as mothers eligible for AFDC), with a system that aided *all* low-income families. The sheer simplicity of FAP, Nixon also promised, would allow for significantly trimming back federal bureaucracies

The FAP proposal debuted to tepid reviews. Conservatives decried the prospect of governmental income supplements for families with regularly employed, albeit low-paid, wage earners. From this perspective, FAP looked too costly—and too much like "socialism." People with a more favorable view of assistance programs, in contrast, argued that FAP's income guarantee seemed too miserly. The U.S. House of Representatives approved a modified version of FAP in 1970, but a curious alliance of senators who opposed Nixon's proposal for very different public policy reasons blocked its passage. In time, Nixon seemed to lose interest in pressing his own plan, and the nation's welfare system would not be overhauled until the 1990s.

Meanwhile, however, the Nixon White House and Congress agreed on several significant changes in domestic policy. In one important move, Congress passed the president's revenue-sharing plan, part of Nixon's "new federalism." It returned a portion of federal tax dollars to state and local governments in the form of **"block grants."** Instead of Washington specifying how these funds could be used, the block grant concept allowed state and local officials, within general guidelines, to spend the funds as they saw fit. In some areas, such as the construction of low-income housing, Nixon's new federalism provided state and local governments with significantly more federal money than they had earlier received under Great Society programs.

A Democratic-controlled Congress and a Republican White House also cooperated on other social-welfare matters. Although Nixon vetoed a congressional measure that would have established federally funded day-care centers for use by women who worked outside of their homes, he endorsed a less comprehensive bill that provided tax benefits for those who used existing facilities. The two branches of government also agreed to increase funding for many Great Society initiatives, including Medicare, Medicaid, rent subsidies for low-income people, and Supplementary Security Insurance (SSI) payments to those who were elderly, blind, or disabled. Moreover, in 1972, Social Security benefits were "indexed," which meant they would increase along with the inflation rate.

The reach of federal social-welfare programs actually *expanded* during Nixon's presidency. According to one estimate, the amount spent for nondefense programs grew nearly

50 percent during the years between Lyndon Johnson's last budget and Richard Nixon's 1971–72 one. In addition, the percentage of people living below the governmentally defined "poverty line" dropped during Nixon's first term as president. After reflecting on Nixon's domestic record, a prominent political scientist suggested, only partly in jest, that this Republican chief executive might well be called "the last Democratic president" of the 20th century.

Environmentalism

A new environmental movement became a significant political force during Nixon's presidency. Landmark legislation of the 1960s—such as the Wilderness Act of 1964, the National Wild and Scenic Rivers Act of 1968, and the National Trails Act of 1968—had already protected large areas of the country from commercial development. During the early 1970s, a broader environmental movement focused on people's health and on ecological balances. Accounts such as **Rachel Carson's** *Silent Spring* (1962) had raised concern that the pesticides used in agriculture, especially DDT, threatened bird populations. Air pollution in cities such as Los Angeles had become so toxic that simply breathing became equivalent to smoking several packs of cigarettes per day. Industrial processes, atomic weapons testing, and nuclear power plants had prompted fear of cancer-causing materials. The Environmental Defense Fund, a private organization formed in 1967, went to court in an effort to limit use of DDT and other dangerous toxins. "Earth Day," a festival-like event first held in 1970 and growing out of countercultural movements, aimed at raising popular awareness about the hazards of environmental degradation.

Although the Nixon administration did not sign up to help sponsor Earth Day, it did take environmental issues seriously. The White House supported creation of the **Environmental Protection Agency (EPA),** and Nixon signed several major pieces of congressional legislation. These included the Resources Recovery Act of 1970 (dealing with waste management), the Clean Air Act of 1970, the Water Pollution Control Act of 1972, the Pesticides Control Act of 1972, and the Endangered Species Act of 1973. National parks and wilderness areas were expanded, and a new law required that "environmental impact statements" be prepared in advance of any major government project.

The new environmental standards brought both unanticipated problems and significant improvements. The Clean Air Act's requirement for taller factory smokestacks, for example, moved pollutants higher into the atmosphere, where they produced a dangerous byproduct, "acid rain." Still, the act's restrictions on auto and smokestack emissions cleared smog out of city skies and helped people with respiratory ailments. This law would reduce six major airborne pollutants by one-third in a single decade. Lead emissions into the atmosphere would soon decline by 95 percent.

Controversies over Rights

New legislation on social and environmental concerns accompanied political struggles over constitutionally guaranteed rights. The struggle to define these rights embroiled the U.S. Supreme Court in controversy.

A majority of justices, supporters of the Great Society's political vision, had stood ready to announce an expanding list of constitutional rights. As this group had charted the Court's path during the 1960s, two Eisenhower appointees, Chief Justice Earl Warren and Associate Justice William Brennan, often led the way. Although nearly all of the Warren Court's decisions involving rights issues drew critical fire, perhaps the most emotional cases involved persons entangled in the criminal justice system.

Miranda v. *Arizona* (1966) had held that the Constitution required police officers to advise persons suspected of having committed a felony offense of their constitutional rights to remain silent and to consult an attorney, with the government providing a lawyer to people without money to hire their own. Defenders of this decision, which established the famous "Miranda warning," saw it as the logical extension of precedents involving liberty and equality. The Court's critics, in contrast, accused its majority of inventing liberties not found in the original Constitution or in any of its amendments. Amid rising public concern over crime, political conservatives made *Miranda* a symbol of the judicial coddling of criminals and the Warren Court's supposed disregard for constitutional limits on its own power.

Richard Nixon had campaigned for president as an opponent of the Warren Court and promised to appoint federal judges who would "apply" rather than "make" the law. Apparently worried about a Nixon victory, Earl Warren announced, prior to the 1968 election, his intention to retire as Chief Justice. A Republican–Southern Democratic alliance in the Senate, however, blindsided Lyndon Johnson and blocked his plan to anoint Associate Justice Abe Fortas, an LBJ confidante, as Warren's successor. Consequently, the victorious Nixon could appoint a Republican loyalist, Warren Burger, to replace Earl Warren. Subsequent vacancies, including one produced by the resignation of a scandal-plagued Fortas, allowed Nixon to bring three additional Republicans—Harry Blackmun, William Rehnquist, and Lewis Powell—onto the High Court.

This new "Burger Court" faced controversial rights-related cases of its own. Lawyers sympathetic to the Great Society vision advanced claims of a constitutionally protected right to receive federal economic assistance sufficient to provide an adequate living standard. The Supreme Court, however, rejected this claim when deciding *Dandridge* v. *Williams* (1970). It held that states could limit the amount they paid to welfare recipients and that payment schedules could vary from state to state without violating the constitutional requirement of equal protection of the law.

Rights-related claims involving health-and-safety legislation generally fared better. A vigorous consumer movement, drawing much of its inspiration from Ralph Nader's exposé about auto safety (*Unsafe at Any Speed,* 1965), joined with environmentalists to gain laws that recognized rights to workplace safety, consumer protection, and nontoxic environments. Overcoming opposition from many business groups, their efforts found congressional expression in such legislation as the Occupational Safety Act of 1973 and stronger consumer and environmental protection laws. The Burger Court invariably supported the constitutionality of these measures.

At the same time, a newly energized women's rights movement pressed another set of issues. It first sponsored an **"Equal Rights Amendment" (ERA)** to the Constitution. This measure, initially proposed during the 1920s and supported by both Republicans and Democrats, promised to explicitly guarantee that women possessed the same legal rights as men. Easily passed by Congress in 1972 and quickly ratified by more than half the states, the ERA suddenly stalled. Conservative women's groups, such as Phyllis Schlafly's "Stop ERA," charged that this constitutional change would undermine traditional "family

Women's Rights Demonstrators, August 16, 1970   Activists, who have gathered in Washington, D.C., to demonstrate on behalf of women's rights, take time to rest. Symbolically, they effectively "occupy" a statue erected in honor of a 19th-century military hero, Admiral David G. Farragut.

values" and expose women to new dangers, such as those they would encounter when serving in the U.S. military on a equal basis with men. The ERA failed to attain approval from the three-quarters of states needed to ratify any amendment to the Constitution. Ultimately, women's groups abandoned the ERA effort in favor of using the judicial system to adjudicate equal rights claims on a case-by-case, issue-by-issue basis.

One of these issues, whether a woman possessed a constitutional right to terminate a pregnancy, became far more controversial than the ERA. In **Roe v. Wade** (1973), the Burger Supreme Court narrowly ruled, with Republican Harry Blackmun writing the key opinion, that a state law making abortion a criminal offense violated a woman's "right to privacy." The *Roe* decision outraged antiabortion groups, which countered with their own rights-based arguments on behalf of unborn fetuses. This "Right-to-Life" movement soon provided important new sources of support, especially from religious groups, for the still expanding conservative wing of the Republican Party. On the other side, movements organizing on behalf of women's issues made the rights of privacy and individual liberty, especially as related to reproductive decisions, central rallying calls.

Outside of the Supreme Court spotlight, Richard Nixon's administration pressed forward, often relatively quietly, on several rights-related matters. With little controversy, the president signed a bipartisan congressional extension of the Voting Rights Act of 1965. Another Nixon-approved measure, popularly known as "Title IX," banned sexual discrimination in higher education. In time, it became the legal basis for pressing colleges to adopt "gender equity" in all areas of their programming, including intercollegiate athletics. In addition, Republican appointees of the Nixon administration, who assumed leadership positions in agencies such as the EEOC, successfully pressed for small policy changes that expanded the federal government's role in monitoring and enforcing laws barring both gender and racial discrimination in employment.

Perhaps most surprisingly, members of Nixon's administration refined the "affirmative action" concept, which had surfaced during Lyndon Johnson's presidency. Beginning with the limited "Philadelphia Plan" of 1969, which was applicable to a single city, the White House built on a campaign pledge to give African Americans tangible economic assistance. Ultimately, Nixon's Department of Labor required that all hiring and contracting that depended on federal funding take "affirmative" steps to enroll, without being held to any bright-line quota, greater numbers of African Americans as union apprentices. When Nixon's critics claimed to detect a clever plan to unsettle labor–union politics, other political observers noted how an important group in the Nixon administration hoped to chart a political course that could gain the GOP new support from African Americans.

Foreign Policy under Nixon and Kissinger

In 1968, while campaigning for the White House, Richard Nixon had promised an administration that would "bring us together." Instead, as it struggled with the issue that had brought down Lyndon Johnson, U.S. policy in Vietnam, Nixon's administration found itself making decisions that seemed to promote greater violence in Indochina and more divisiveness on the home front.

Even as it wrestled with domestic policy concerns, the Nixon White House appeared far more interested in international matters. Henry Kissinger, Nixon's national security adviser and then secretary of state, laid out a grand, three-part strategy: (1) **"détente"** with the Soviet Union, (2) normalization of relations with China, and (3) disengagement from direct military involvement in South Vietnam.

Détente and Normalization

Although Richard Nixon had built his early political career on a hard-line version of anti-communism, he and Kissinger considered themselves "realists" who favored flexibility when trying to advance the interests of the United States in the international arena. By seeking to ease tensions with the Soviet Union and China, the Nixon-Kissinger team expected that improving relations could lead these two major communist nations to reduce their support to North Vietnam, thus increasing chances for a successful U.S. pull-back from the war in Southeast Asia.

Arms-control talks took top priority in U.S.–Soviet relations. In 1969, the two super-powers opened the Strategic Arms Limitation Talks (SALT); after several years of high-level diplomacy, they signed an agreement (SALT I) that limited further development of both antiballistic missiles (ABMs) and offensive intercontinental ballistic missiles (ICBMs). SALT I's impact on the arms race proved relatively limited because it said nothing about the number of nuclear warheads that a single missile might carry. Still, the ability to conclude any arms-control pact signaled the possibility of improving relations between Washington and Moscow.

Nixon's overtures toward the People's Republic of China brought an even more dramatic break with the Cold War past. Secret negotiations, often conducted personally by Kissinger, led to a slight easing of U.S. trade restrictions and, then, to an invitation from China for U.S. table-tennis players to compete against Chinese teams. This much-celebrated "ping-pong diplomacy" presaged more significant exchanges. Most spectacularly, in 1972 Nixon visited China, with the U.S. media firmly in tow. TV crews pictured the president, once a bitter foe of "Red China," talking with communist leaders, including Mao Zedong, and strolling along China's Great Wall. A few months later, the UN admitted the People's Republic as the sole representative of China, and in 1973 the United States and China exchanged informal diplomatic missions.

Vietnamization

In Vietnam, the Nixon administration decided to speed withdrawal of U.S. ground forces, the policy called **"Vietnamization."** Putting this move, which had quietly begun under Johnson, in a grander frame, the president announced, in July 1969, a "Nixon Doctrine." It pledged that the United States would extend military assistance to anticommunist governments in Asia but would require them to supply their own combat forces. From the outset, Vietnamization imagined the removal of U.S. ground troops without accepting a coalition between the NLF and the government in Saigon or permitting North Vietnamese forces to defeat those of South Vietnam. While officially adhering to Johnson's 1968 bombing halt over the North, Nixon and Kissinger accelerated both the ground and air wars by launching new offensives inside South Vietnam. In 1970, they approved a controversial military invasion of Cambodia, an ostensibly neutral country, through which North Vietnam had been sending troops and military supplies into the South. A quick strike into Cambodia, the White House gambled, would buy further time for executing its Vietnamization strategy.

The 1970 Cambodian invasion, which gained the United States a scant military payoff, set off a new wave of protests around the world and in the United States. As the campus antiwar movement revived, many colleges and universities exploded in angry demonstrations. Bomb threats prompted some schools, which were besieged by student protestors, to begin the 1970 summer vacation earlier than originally planned. White police officers fatally shot two students at the all-black **Jackson State College** in Mississippi, and National Guard troops at **Kent** State University in Ohio opened fire on unarmed protestors, killing four students. As antiwar demonstrators descended on Washington, President Nixon seemed personally unnerved by the domestic furor surrounding his Vietnam policies.

© Bettmann/CORBIS

Jackson State   In 1970, the violence associated with America's longest war came home. In May, police gunfire killed two students and wounded 15 others at Jackson State University in Mississippi. This picture was taken through a bullet-riddled window in a women's dorm.

The continuing controversy over the "My Lai incident" further polarized sentiment over continuing the war. Shortly after the 1968 Tet episode, troops had entered the small Vietnamese hamlet of My Lai and murdered more than 200 civilians, most of them women and children. After a bungled cover-up, news of this massacre became public in 1969 and refocused debate over U.S policy. Military courts convicted only one officer, Lieutenant William Calley, of any offense. This controversial decision prompted charges that higher-ups had offered Calley up as a scapegoat for a failed strategy that emphasized body counts and lax rules of engagement. (Nearly forty years later, researchers found evidence of many other smaller-scale incidents resembling that at My Lai.) Injecting the White House into the Calley controversy, Nixon ordered that the young lieutenant, pending the results of his appeal, be confined to his officer's quarters rather than imprisoned. Ultimately, a higher military court ordered that Calley, because of procedural irregularities, be released from custody.

Meanwhile, the Nixon administration widened its operations to include Laos as well as Cambodia. Although the United States denied waging any such campaign, its bombing ravaged large areas of these largely agricultural countries. As the number of refugees in Cambodia swelled and food supplies dwindled, the communist guerrilla force there—the Khmer Rouge—became a well-disciplined army. The Khmer Rouge eventually came to power and, in a murderous attempt to eliminate dissent, turned Cambodia into a "killing field." It slaughtered more than a million Cambodians. While Nixon continued to talk about U.S. troop withdrawals and to conduct peace negotiations with North Vietnam and the NLF in Paris, the **Vietnam War** broadened into a conflict that seemed to be destabilizing all of Indochina.

Even greater violence was yet to come. In spring 1972, a North Vietnamese offensive approached within 30 miles of Saigon, and U.S. generals warned of imminent defeat. Nixon responded by resuming the bombing of North Vietnam and by mining its harbors. Just weeks before the November 1972 election, though, Kissinger again promised peace and announced a ceasefire. After Nixon's reelection, when peace negotiations again stalled, the United States unleashed even greater firepower. During the "Christmas bombing" of December 1972, the heaviest bombardment in history, B-52 planes pounded military and civilian targets in North Vietnam around the clock.

By this time, however, the Nixon administration found it increasingly difficult to carry out its war policies. Support, all across the political spectrum, seemed to grow ever thinner. Critics condemned the violence in Asia and the administration's effort to expand its domestic power when responding to dissent at home. Perhaps most importantly, sagging morale among troops in the field began to undermine the U.S. effort. An increasing number of soldiers questioned the purpose of their sacrifices; some refused to engage the enemy; and a few openly defied their own superiors. At home, Vietnam Veterans against the War (VVAW), a new organization, joined the antiwar coalition.

Running out of options, Nixon proceeded toward full-scale Vietnamization. In January 1973, the United States signed peace accords in Paris that provided a timetable for the withdrawal of U.S. troops. As U.S. ground forces departed, an increasingly demoralized and ineffectual South Vietnamese government, headed by Nguyen Van Thieu, continued to fight with U.S. support. In spring 1975, nearly two years after the Paris accords and with Nixon's successor in office, South Vietnam's army and Thieu's government would collapse as North Vietnamese armies entered the capital of Saigon. America's longest war ended in defeat.

The Aftermath of War

Between 1960 and 1973, approximately 3.5 million American men and women served in Vietnam: 58,000 died, 150,000 were wounded, and 2,000 were classified as missing. In the aftermath of this costly, divisive war, people struggled to understand why the United States failed to prevail over a small, barely industrialized nation. Those who supported the war to the end argued that it had been lost on the home front. They blamed an irresponsible media, a disloyal antiwar movement, and a Congress afflicted by a "failure of will." The war, they still insisted, had been for a laudable cause. Politicians, by setting unrealistic limits on the Pentagon, had prevented military strategists from attaining victory.

By contrast, others doubted the possibility of any U.S. "victory," short of devastating North Vietnam and risking a wider war with China. These analysts stressed the overextension of U.S. power, the misguided belief in national omnipotence, and the miscalculations of decision makers. Many concluded that the United States had waged a war in the wrong place for the wrong reasons. The conflict's human costs, to the United States and the people of Indochina, outweighed any possible gain from preserving a pro-U.S., noncommunist South Vietnam.

Regardless of their positions on the war, most Americans seemed to agree on a single proposition, which carried different meanings: There should be "no more Vietnams." For most national leaders, this meant the United States should not undertake another substantial military operation unless it involved clear and compelling political objectives, sustained public support, and realistic means to accomplish a goal that clearly advanced the national interest. Eventually, however, the people who wanted to aggressively reassert U.S. power in the world, worried that what they called "the Vietnam syndrome" might shape a timid and ineffective foreign policy.

Expanding the Nixon Doctrine

Meanwhile, Nixon and Kissinger extended the premise of the Nixon Doctrine to the entire world. The White House made it clear that the United States would not dispatch its own troops to quash insurgencies but would generously aid anticommunist governments or factions willing to fight their own battles.

During the early 1970s, U.S. Cold War strategy came to rely on supporting staunchly anticommunist regional powers. These included nations such as Iran under Shah Reza Pahlavi, South Africa with its apartheid regime, and Brazil with its repressive military dictatorship. All of these countries built large, U.S.-trained military establishments. U.S. military assistance, together with covert CIA operations, also incubated and protected anticommunist dictatorships in South Korea, the Philippines, and much of Latin America. U.S. arms sales to the rest of the world skyrocketed. In one of its most controversial foreign policies, moreover, the Nixon administration employed covert action against the elected socialist government of Salvador Allende Gossens in Chile in 1970. After Allende took office, Kissinger pressed for the destabilization of his government. On September 11, 1973, the Chilean military overthrew Allende, immediately suspended democratic rule, and announced that Allende had committed suicide.

Subsequent debates about U.S. foreign policy under Nixon and Kissinger often highlighted events in Chile in order to illustrate broader claims. Democratic Senator Frank Church, for example, directed Senate hearings during the mid-1970s that suggested policies toward Chile exemplified how the Nixon administration, in the name of anticommunism, often had wedded the United States to questionable covert activities and military dictators. Supporters of Nixon and Kissinger, in contrast, praised the pair for conducting a pragmatic foreign policy that combined détente directed toward the communist giants, the USSR and China, with containment directed toward the spread of revolutionary movements, including that of Allende's government in Chile.

The Wars of Watergate

> ### Focus Question
> What political and legal controversies entrapped the Nixon administration, and how did Watergate-related events ultimately force Nixon's resignation?

Nixon's presidency ultimately collapsed as a result of fateful decisions made in the Oval Office. Nixon and his closest aides came to Washington with a view of politics that was as expansive as that espoused by many of the social movements the Nixon White House abhorred. The "new Nixon" endorsed a "new politics"—evidenced in his foreign policy moves toward China and the Soviet Union and in his short-lived enthusiasm for FAP.

At the same time, reminders of the "old Nixon" constantly surfaced. Long known as a political loner, who ruminated about taking revenge against his enemies, Nixon often seemed to be his own greatest foe. Even as his administration publicly built a domestic record that often seemed sympathetic to matters of liberty and equality, it secretly pressed the power of the presidency in constitutionally suspect, and often simply foolish, ways. It ordered the Internal Revenue Service (IRS) to harass prominent Democrats with expensive audits, placed antiwar and Black Power activists under illegal surveillance, and conducted risky covert activities on the domestic front. Some of these activities even rattled the constitutional sensibilities of an old Nixon ally, J. Edgar Hoover, who rarely worried about legal niceties when his own FBI swung into action. The Nixon administration prosecuted leading antiwar activists for allegedly impeding the Selective Service process and on various conspiracy charges. It also encouraged Vice President Spiro Agnew to assail media commentators for daring to criticize White House policies.

Largely isolated from political give-and-take, with a close-knit group of advisers, Nixon eventually created his own secret intelligence unit, which set up shop in the White House. The Nixon administration planned to use this group to undertake secret presidential missions against selected enemies. Its first job, to plug "leaks" of information about Vietnam to the media, soon provided the unit with a name, "the **Plumbers.**"

During the summer of 1971, stories in the *Washington Post* and, later, the *New York Times* enraged the president. These papers had culled their revelations about deceptions and miscalculations by previous presidential administrations from a top-secret history of U.S. involvement in the Vietnam War, popularly known as the *Pentagon Papers*. Daniel

Ellsberg, an antiwar activist who had once worked in the national security bureaucracy, had sent photocopies of this lengthy, classified document, commissioned in 1967 by Robert McNamara, to selected media outlets.

Although the material in the *Pentagon Papers* concerned events that preceded Nixon's presidency, his administration responded angrily. It became determined to make an example of what would happen to anyone else who trafficked in leaked and classified documents. The administration's legal counterattack failed when the Supreme Court rejected, by a 6-3 margin, an attempt to halt through court injunction all media publications based on the *Papers*. More ominously, the White House unleashed its "plumbers." Seeking information that might discredit Ellsberg, this clandestine unit burglarized his psychiatrist's office. Thus began a series of **"dirty tricks"** and outright crimes, sometimes financed by funds solicited for Nixon's 1972 reelection campaign, which would culminate in the constitutional crisis that became known as **"Watergate."**

The Election of 1972

Because Republicans had fared rather poorly in the mid-term elections of 1970, Nixon's political strategists worried that domestic and foreign troubles might deny the president another term. Creating a campaign organization separate from that of the Republican Party, with the ironic acronym of "CREEP" (Committee to Re-elect the President), they secretly raised millions of dollars, much of it from illegal contributions.

As the 1972 presidential campaign took shape, Nixon's chances for reelection dramatically improved. An assassin's bullet crippled George Wallace. Senator Edmund Muskie of Maine, initially Nixon's leading Democratic challenger, made a series of blunders (some of them, perhaps, precipitated by Republican dirty tricksters) that derailed his campaign. Eventually, Senator George McGovern of South Dakota, an outspoken opponent of the Vietnam War but a lackluster campaigner, won the Democratic nomination.

McGovern never seriously challenged Nixon. Early on, opinion pollsters suggested, a majority of voters decided that McGovern

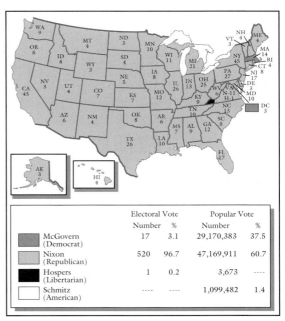

		Electoral Vote		Popular Vote	
		Number	%	Number	%
	McGovern (Democrat)	17	3.1	29,170,383	37.5
	Nixon (Republican)	520	96.7	47,169,911	60.7
	Hospers (Libertarian)	1	0.2	3,673	----
	Schmitz (American)	----	----	1,099,482	1.4

Map 29.3 Presidential Election, 1972 This map shows what is commonly called a landslide election. Less than two years later, however, Nixon would resign from the presidency to avoid facing impeachment charges connected to his role in the Watergate burglary and other "dirty tricks" associated with his presidency.

seemed too closely tied to the antiwar movement, New Left activists, and the Countercul-ture. His key issues—a call for higher taxes on the wealthy, a guaranteed minimum income for all Americans, amnesty for Vietnam War draft resisters, and the decriminalization of marijuana—fell outside of what most potential voters considered the "political main-stream." In foreign policy, McGovern urged deep cuts in defense spending and an immedi-ate peace initiative in Vietnam. Nixon successfully portrayed these proposals as signs of the South Dakota senator's "softness" on communism and "weakness" on foreign policy.

Nixon won an easy victory in November. He received the Electoral College votes of all but one state and the District of Columbia. Although the 26th Amendment, ratified one year before the election, had lowered the voting age to 18, a surprisingly small number of newly enfranchised voters cast ballots. Never seriously interested in helping other GOP candidates, Nixon watched the Democrats retain control of Congress.

Nixon Pursued

In achieving victory, the president's supporters left a trail of crime and corruption. In June 1972, a surveillance team with links to both CREEP and the White House Plumbers had been arrested while fine-tuning eavesdropping equipment in the Democratic Party's head-quarters in Washington's Watergate office complex. Apparently, Nixon and his aides feared that Democratic leaders possessed documents that might hinder the president's reelection drive. In public, Nixon's spokespeople initially dismissed the Watergate break-in as a "third-rate burglary" and, then, as an unseemly incident unconnected to anyone of substance at the White House. Privately, though, the president and his inner circle imme-diately launched a cover-up campaign, which gradually unraveled. They paid hush money to the Watergate burglars and ordered CIA officials to misinform the FBI that any investi-gation by that agency would jeopardize national security operations. The White House succeeded in limiting the political damage until after the 1972 election, but events soon overtook their efforts.

While reporters from the *Washington Post* pursued the taint of scandal around the White House, Democrats in Congress and federal prosecutors sought evidence of illegal activities during the 1972 campaign. In 1973, Judge John Sirica, a Republican appointee presiding over the trial of the Watergate burglars, pushed for additional information, and Senate leaders convened a special, bipartisan Watergate Committee. Headed by North Carolina's conservative Democratic senator Sam Ervin, it enjoyed broad power to investigate election-related issues, including the Watergate break-in. Then, prosecutors uncovered evidence that seemed to link key administration figures, including John Mitchell, Nixon's former attorney general and later the head of CREEP, to illegal activities.

During the spring of 1973, one of the Watergate burglars and other witnesses testified before the Senate's Watergate Committee about various illegal activities committed by CREEP and the White House. Senator Ervin called Nixon's closest aides, though not the president, before the committee, and the televised hearings became a daily political drama that attracted a large and loyal viewer audience. Ultimately, testimony from John Dean, who had been the president's chief legal counsel, linked Nixon to attempts to conceal the Watergate episode and to other seemingly illegal activities. The president steadfastly denied Dean's charges.

Along the way, though, Senate investigators discovered that Nixon had ordered installation of voice-activated taping machines, which had recorded every conversation in his Oval Office. These tapes (now housed at the National Archives) opened the way to determining whether the president or Dean, Nixon's primary accuser, was lying. While maintaining he was not "a crook," Nixon also claimed an "executive privilege" to keep the tapes from being released to either Congress or federal prosecutors, but Judge Sirica, Archibald Cox (a special, independent prosecutor in the Watergate case), and Congress all demanded access to the tapes.

If Nixon's own problems were not enough, his outspoken vice president resigned in October 1973, after pleading no contest to charges of income-tax evasion. Spiro Agnew agreed to a plea-bargain arrangement to avoid prosecution for having accepted illegal kickbacks, which he had not reported as income, while in Maryland politics. Acting under the 25th Amendment (ratified in 1967), Nixon appointed—and both houses of Congress confirmed—Representative **Gerald Ford** of Michigan, a Republican Party stalwart, as the new vice president.

Nixon's Final Days

Nixon's clumsy efforts to protect himself, while retaining his tapes, backfired. During the fall of 1973, Nixon ordered the Justice Department to dismiss Archibald Cox, a move intended to prevent the special prosecutor's office from gaining access to the White House tapes. When Cox's firing only seemed to confirm suspicions of a Nixon cover-up, political pressure forced the president to agree to the appointment of an equally tenacious and independent replacement, Leon Jaworski. Nixon's own release of edited transcripts of some Watergate-related conversations delivered another self-inflicted wound. These flawed documents only helped strengthen the case for independent ears hearing the original recordings. Finally, by proclaiming that he would obey only a "definitive" Supreme Court decision, Nixon all but invited the justices, including ones he had appointed, to deliver a unanimous ruling on the question of the tapes. On July 24, 1974, the Court did just that in the case of *U.S.* v. *Nixon*. A claim of executive privilege could not override the refusal to release evidence required in an ongoing criminal investigation.

Meanwhile, the Democratic-controlled Congress, with support from some Republican members, began steps to impeach Nixon and remove him from office. After televised deliberations, a bipartisan majority of the House Judiciary Committee voted three formal articles of impeachment against the president—for obstruction of justice, violation of constitutional liberties, and refusal to produce evidence. Nixon promised to rebut these accusations before the Senate, the body authorized by the Constitution (Article I, Section 3) to render a verdict of guilty or not guilty after impeachment by the House.

Nixon's aides, however, were already orchestrating his departure. One of his own attorneys had discovered that a tape Nixon had been withholding contained the long-sought "smoking gun," clear evidence of a criminal offense. This recording confirmed, during a 1972 conversation, that Nixon had helped hatch the plan by which the CIA would advance its fraudulent claim of national security in order to stop the FBI from investigating the Watergate break-in. At this point, Nixon's own secretary of defense ordered military commanders to ignore any order from the president, the constitutional commander-in-chief, unless the secretary countersigned it. Now abandoned by almost every prominent Republican, most notably Barry Goldwater, and confronted with enough Senate votes to convict him of the impeachment charges, Nixon capitulated. He went on television on August 8, 1974, to announce his resignation. On August 9, Gerald Ford, who had never even been elected to the vice presidency, became the nation's 38th president.

The events that ended Nixon's presidency have helped to highlight some of the dynamics of historical memory. Shortly after Nixon's departure, most people told pollsters they considered the "Watergate Crisis" to be one of the gravest threats by unchecked power to constitutional liberty in the long history of the republic. As time passed, though, the details of Watergate faded away. Opinion polls conducted on the 20th anniversary of Nixon's resignation suggested that most people already only dimly recalled what had prompted Nixon to leave office.

What specific forces could account for this change? One of these might be that Nixon avoided being prosecuted for his actions. Although nearly a dozen members of his administration—including its chief law enforcement officer, John Mitchell—were convicted or pleaded guilty to having committed criminal offenses, Nixon received an unconditional pardon from his successor. Gerald Ford claimed he wanted to spare the nation another media spectacle: one featuring a former president undergoing a lengthy trial process. Ford's action, however, also prevented any authoritative accounting, in a court of law, of a traumatic political-legal episode.

Another reason for changing memories may be the media's habit of affixing the Watergate label to nearly every political scandal of the post-Nixon era. The suffix-*gate* became attached to apparently grave constitutional episodes and to obviously trivial political events. As the Nixon presidency receded in time, many people came to consider "Watergate" a synonym for "politics as usual." Finally, the specific images of what the historian Stanley Kutler calls the "wars of Watergate" have tended to blend into the broader pictures of the political, social, economic, and cultural turmoil that accompanied U.S. involvement in the nation's longest war.

Conclusion

Attempts to extend the power of the national government marked the years between 1963 and 1974. Lyndon Johnson's Great Society provided a blueprint for waging a War on Poverty, and his administration dramatically escalated the war in Vietnam. This use of governmental power prompted divisive debates that helped polarize the country. During Johnson's presidency, both the war effort and the economy faltered, top leaders became discredited, and Johnson abandoned the office he had so long sought. His Republican successor, Richard Nixon, became implicated in abuses of power that ultimately drove him from the White House. The hopes of the early 1960s—that the U.S. government could aggressively promote liberty and equality both at home and throughout the rest of the world—ended in frustration.

The era of America's longest war was also a time of changing ideas about politics, cultural and racial patterns, and definitions of patriotism. It saw the slow convergence of a wide array of social movements, a veritable movement of movements. As different groups invoked different explanations for the failures of both the Great Society and the war effort, divisions from this era would shape U.S. politics and culture for years to come. Many people became skeptical, some even cynical, about enlarging the power of the federal government in the name of expanding liberty and equality.

SUGGESTED READINGS

On Lyndon Johnson, see **Robert J. Dallek,** *Flawed Giant: Lyndon Johnson and His Times, 1961–1973* (1998), **Irving Bernstein,** *Guns or Butter: The Presidency of Lyndon Johnson* (1996), and **Randall B. Woods,** *LBJ: Architect of American Ambition* (2006).

The many outstanding overviews of U.S. involvement in Vietnam include **George Herring,** *America's Longest War: The United States and Vietnam, 1950–1975* (rev. ed., 2001); **Robert D. Schulzinger,** *A Time for War: The United States and Vietnam, 1941–1975* (1997); **David Kaiser,** *American Tragedy: Kennedy, Johnson, and the Origins of the Vietnam War* (2000); **Frederick Logevall,** *The Origins of the Vietnam War* (2001); **James Mann,** *A Grand Delusion: America's Descent into Vietnam* (2001); and **James H. Willbanks,** *Abandoning Vietnam: How America Left and South Vietnam Lost its War* (2004). *Working-Class War: American Combat Soldiers and Vietnam* (1993) and *Patriots: The Vietnam War Remembered from All Sides* (2003), both by **Christian Appy,** provide a wide range of perspectives. See also, **Odd Arne Wested,** *The Global Cold War* (2005) and **Jussi Hanhimaki,** *The Flawed Architect: Henry Kissinger and American Foreign Policy* (2004). **Jeffrey Kimball,** *The Vietnam War Files: Uncovering the Secret History of Nixon-Era Strategy* (2004) collects and skillfully organizes a revealing set of documents. Finally, **David Maraniss,** *They Marched into Sunlight: War and Peace; Vietnam and America October 1967* (2003) moves back and forth, between Vietnam and the home front, during a single crucial month.

The "movement of movements" during the 1960s can be surveyed, from diverse vantage points, in **David W. Levy,** *The Debate over Vietnam* (rev. ed., 1994); **Lynn Spigel and Michael Curtain,** *The Revolution Wasn't Televised: Sixties Television and Social Conflict* (1997); **Maurice Isserman and Michael Kazin,** *America Divided: The Civil War of the 1960s* (1999); and **Edward K. Spann and David L. Anderson, eds.,** *Democracy's Children: The Young Rebels of the 1960s and the Power of Ideals* (2003).

On the civil-rights movement and its larger context, **Taylor Branch** concludes his multivolume history with *Pillar of Fire: America in the King Years, 1963–1965* (1998), and *At Canaan's Edge: America in the King Years, 1965–1968* (2006). **William L. Van Deburg,** *New Day in Babylon: The Black Power Movement and American Culture, 1965–1975* (1992), along with **Kathleen Cleaver and George Katsiaficas, eds.,** *Liberation, Imagination, and the Black Panther Party: A New Look at the Panthers and their Legacy* (2001) offer useful overviews, while **Robert Self,**

American Babylon: Race and the Struggle for Postwar Oakland (2003) provides a superb local study, as does **Gerald Horne**, *Fire This Time: The Watts Uprising and the 1960s* (1995). See also, **Robin D.G. Kelley**, *Freedom Dreams: The Black Radical Tradition* (2002).

On the late 1960s and early 1970s, begin with the opening portions of **Bruce J. Shuman**, *The Seventies: The Great Shift in American Culture, Society, and Politics* (2001) and **Andreas Hillen**, *1973 Nervous Breakdown: Watergate, Warhol, and the Birth of Post-Sixties America* (2006). The year of 1968 is the subject of numerous volumes, including **Carole Fink, Philipp Gassert, and Detlef Junker, eds**, *1968: The World Transformed* (1998); **Tariq Ali and Susan Watkins**, *1968: Marching in the Streets* (1998); **Mark Kurlansky**, *1968: The Year that Rocked the World* (2003); and the broader account by **Jeremy Suri**, *Power and Protest: Global Revolution and the Rise of Détente* (2003).

On the riddle that was Richard Nixon, see **Richard Reeves**, *President Nixon: Alone in the White House* (2001); **David Greenberg**, *Nixon's Shadow: The History of an Image* (2003); and **Mark Feeney**, *Nixon at the Movies* (2004). **Stanley I. Kutler, ed.**, *Abuse of Power: The New Nixon Tapes* (1997) provides evidence of Nixon's approach to politics and constitutional limits, in his own words, along with commentary that updates Kutler's own *The Wars of Watergate* (1992). **John D. Skrentny**, *The Minority Revolution* (2002) details the bureaucratic activism that expanded rights during the Nixon years, while interpretations of activism on the Supreme Court can be found in **Morton J. Horwitz**, *The Warren Court and the Pursuit of Justice* (1999) and in **Lucas A. Powe, Jr.**, *The Warren Court and American Politics* (2000).

Visit the Liberty Equality Power Companion Web site for resources specific to this textbook: http://www.thomsonedu.com/history/murrin

Also find self-tests and additional resources at ThomsonNOW. ThomsonNOW is an integrated online suite of services and resources with proven ease of use and efficient paths to success, delivering the results you want—NOW!

www.thomsonedu.com/login/

30

Power and Politics, 1974–1992

Following the onset of the Great Depression of the 1930s and the Second World War, the national government continually expanded its power. Most people supported domestic programs intended to cushion against economic downturns and to assist families in distress, and they endorsed national security measures designed to upgrade U.S. military and intelligence capabilities.

Events of the 1960s and early 1970s, particularly the failed intervention in Vietnam and Watergate, shook people's faith in government. Secrecy, corruption, and economic problems bred further disillusionment. During the 1970s and 1980s, people debated questions they did not need to ask a generation earlier: How should the federal government respond to an aging industrial economy, a ballooning federal deficit, and a beleaguered social welfare system? Might conditions improve, as conservatives had long contended, if Washington reduced, rather than continued to enlarge, its role? Emotionally charged issues such as abortion, environmental regulation, and taxation policy also created controversy over the use of governmental power.

Disagreement extended to foreign policy. Should the United States place less emphasis on anticommunism to pursue other goals, as Democratic president Jimmy Carter (1977–1981) initially urged? Or should it wage the Cold War even more vigorously, as his successor, Republican Ronald Reagan (1981–1989), advocated? Had the U.S. extended its power too far or not far enough? After 1989, when the Cold War ended unexpectedly, the United States needed to forge a foreign policy for a post–Cold War world, a task that fell to the post-Reagan generation of national leaders.

Meanwhile, the "movement of movements," a legacy of the 1960s, refused to fade away. Along with a "New Right" movement, activism associated with women's rights, gay pride, and racial and ethnic identities influenced policy discussions and how people defined themselves.

The Caretaker Presidency of Gerald Ford (1974–1977)

Focus Question
How did the legacies of the Vietnam War and Watergate help shape the presidencies of Gerald Ford and Jimmy Carter?

CHRONOLOGY

1968	Indian Bill of Rights enacted by Congress
1969	The Stonewall Inn raid inaugurates a new phase in gay and lesbian activism
1970	Congressional Black Caucus organized
1973	*Roe* v. *Wade* decision upholds women's right to abortion
1974	Nixon resigns and Ford becomes president; Ford soon pardons Nixon
1975	South Vietnam falls to North Vietnam • Ford asserts U.S. power in *Mayaguez* incident • National Conservative Action Political Committee formed
1976	Jimmy Carter elected president • OPEC sharply raises oil prices
1978	Carter helps negotiate Camp David peace accords on Middle East
1979	Soviet Union invades Afghanistan • *Sandinistas* come to power in Nicaragua • U.S. hostages seized in Iran
1980	Reagan elected president • U.S. hostages in Iran released
1981	Reagan tax cut passed
1983	U.S. troops removed from Lebanon • U.S. troops invade Grenada • Reagan announces SDI ("Star Wars") program
1984	Reagan defeats Walter Mondale
1986	Tax Reform Act passed • Reagan administration rocked by revelation of Iran-*contra* affair
1988	George H. W. Bush defeats Michael Dukakis in presidential election • Congress enacts Indian Gaming Regulation Act
1989	Communist regimes in Eastern Europe collapse; Berlin Wall falls • Cold War, in effect, ends
1990	Bush angers conservative Republicans by agreeing to a tax increase
1991	Bush orchestrates Persian Gulf War against Iraq • Clarence Thomas confirmation hearings highlight issue of sexual harassment
1992	Bill Clinton defeats Bush and third-party candidate Ross Perot in presidential race

When Richard Nixon resigned in August 1974, Gerald R. Ford, his vice president, moved from one office to which voters had never elected him to another, the presidency. Emphasizing his long career in the House of Representatives, Ford promised he possessed the experience to "heal the land," but his administration always seemed a stopgap one. This former college football star preferred that the fight song of his alma mater, the University of Michigan, rather than "Hail to the Chief," accompany his public entries. Genial and unpretentious, Ford never attracted the kind of media criticism that enraged Lyndon Johnson and Richard Nixon. Recurrent images of a string of minor presidential mishaps, including tumbles down a ski slope and off an airplane ramp, however, helped reinforce perceptions of Ford as a bumbling, unsteady leader.

Trying to Whip Inflation

Ford's plan to present his administration as an updated version of the moderate Republicanism of the 1950s quickly foundered. His pardoning of former president Nixon, in September 1974, proved widely unpopular, and his appointment of Nelson Rockefeller as vice president infuriated GOP conservatives. Ford's approval rating began skidding downward.

Economic problems dominated the domestic side of the 865-day Ford presidency. Quick-fix policies had helped Nixon win reelection in 1972, but they left his successor with the underlying problems. Ford touted a program called "Whip Inflation Now" (WIN), which included a one-year surcharge on income taxes and cuts in federal spending as his solutions. After both unemployment and prices still crept higher, Ford conceded WIN to be a loser. During 1975, unemployment reached 8.5 percent, and the inflation rate topped 9 percent.

The president continually clashed with the Democratic-controlled Congress. Ford, who vetoed nearly 40 spending bills while in office, finally agreed to a congressional economic package. It included a tax cut, an increase in unemployment benefits, an unbalanced federal budget, and limited controls on oil prices. Democrats charged that Ford could not implement coherent programs of his own, and many Republicans complained that he would not stand up to congressional Democrats.

Foreign Policy

Upon assuming office, Ford pledged a renewal of U.S. military support to the government in South Vietnam, if North Vietnam ever directly threatened its survival. A mood of war weariness in the United States and battlefield conditions that favored North Vietnam, however, made fulfilling this commitment impossible. North Vietnam's armies stormed across the South in March 1975. Congress, relieved that U.S. troops had finally been withdrawn after the 1973 Paris peace accords (see chapter 29), rejected any suggestion of reintroducing them. Conducting their last mission in Vietnam, U.S. helicopters scrambled to airlift U.S. officials and top-ranking South Vietnamese officers off the American embassy's rooftop.

Spring 1975 brought new communist victories in Indochina. In early April, Khmer Rouge forces drove a U.S.-backed government from the Cambodian capital of Phnom Penh, and on April 30, 1975, North Vietnamese troops overran Saigon, renaming the former South Vietnamese capital Ho Chi Minh City. Contention over the history of U.S. policy in Indochina became especially heated in the months that followed.

Operating within this contentious atmosphere, Ford tried to demonstrate U.S. military power. In May 1975, a contingent of Khmer Rouge boarded a U.S. ship, the *Mayaguez*, taking its crew hostage. Henry Kissinger, now Ford's secretary of state, declared that the United States needed to "look ferocious" and convinced the president to order bombing strikes against Cambodia and a rescue operation. This military response, coupled with Chinese pressure on the Khmer Rouge, secured the release of the *Mayaguez* and its crew.

Although the *Mayaguez* rescue cost more lives than it saved, Ford's approval ratings briefly shot up. His other initiatives, which included extending Nixon's policy of détente with the Soviet Union and pursuing peace negotiations in the Middle East, achieved little. Gerald Ford increasingly appeared to be a caretaker president.

The Election of 1976

Ford nearly lost the GOP presidential nomination in 1976. Conservative Republicans rallied behind **Ronald Reagan,** who finally ignited a sputtering campaign by offering himself as a "true conservative" who, unlike Ford, owed nothing to Washington insiders. The president had already won just enough delegates during the early primaries, however, to eke out a narrow first-ballot victory at the Republican Party's national convention. Speaking to this gathering, Reagan accurately predicted, "I shall rise and fight again."

The Democrats, a party in far more disarray than the GOP, did turn to an outsider, **James Earl (Jimmy) Carter.** A retired naval officer, engineer, peanut farmer, and former governor of Georgia, Carter campaigned by stressing personal character. He highlighted his small-town roots and his Southern Baptist faith. To balance the ticket, he picked Senator Walter Mondale of Minnesota as his running mate. In November, Carter won a narrow victory over Ford.

Carter's election rested on a diverse, transitory coalition. Reversing recent Democratic fortunes, this native of the South carried every southern state except Virginia. He ran particularly well among white voters who regularly attended fundamentalist and evangelical churches and among African Americans. Carter also courted former antiwar activists by promising presidential pardons for most Vietnam-era draft resisters. Walter Mondale's appeal to old-line Democratic interests, especially in the labor–union movement, helped Carter narrowly carry New York, Pennsylvania, and Ohio. The final tally remained close, however, and voter turnout sank to its lowest mark, 54 percent of those eligible, since the end of the Second World War.

Jimmy Carter's One-Term Presidency (1977–1981)

Jimmy Carter's lack of a popular mandate and his outsider status proved serious handicaps in Washington. He delighted the inaugural-day crowd and TV viewers by leaving his presidential limousine and walking, hand-in-hand, with his wife Rosalyn down Pennsylvania Avenue. This stroll would remain one of the highpoints of the Carter presidency. After leaving government, Carter reflected on his difficulties: "I had a different way of governing. . . . I was a southerner, a born-again Christian, a Baptist, a newcomer." Moreover, Carter became caught between advisers who claimed that the national government already exercised too much power and those who argued that Washington still did too little to address domestic and foreign problems. The Carter administration, a reflection of a divided Democratic Party in this regard, often seemed unsure of how to view governmental power.

Welfare and Energy Initiatives

Carter puzzled over welfare policy. His own staff differed over whether to increase funding for social-welfare assistance to low-income families or to create several million public service jobs, underwritten by additional federal spending. Ultimately, Carter proposed a compromise that failed to pass Congress, and the impulse to overhaul the nation's social-welfare system continued to flounder.

The president had little choice but to push harder on energy-related issues. The United States obtained 90 percent of its energy from fossil fuels, much of it from imported petroleum. In 1976, as it had in 1973, the Organization of Petroleum Exporting Countries (OPEC), a cartel dominated by oil-rich nations in the Middle East, dramatically raised the price of crude oil and precipitated acute worldwide shortages. As gasoline became expensive and in short supply, drivers in the United States denounced high prices and long lines at the pumps. Carter promised to make the nation less dependent on imported petroleum.

The president charged James Schlesinger, head of a new department of energy, with developing a plan. Schlesinger outlined four ambitious goals to decrease U.S. reliance on foreign sources: (1) use tax incentives and deregulation to increase domestic energy production; (2) raise the federal gasoline tax to discourage consumption; (3) foster conservation; and (4) promote nonpetroleum energy sources, especially coal and nuclear power. Neither Carter nor Schlesinger consulted Congress or even some members of the president's own administration when drawing up these key proposals. Instead, in April 1977, Carter announced that the energy crisis represented "the moral equivalent of war," and he advanced a complicated battle plan, which ultimately included more than 100 interrelated provisions.

Congress quickly rebuffed the president. Gas and oil interests opposed higher taxes. Consumer activists helped block deregulation. Environmentalists charged that greater use of coal would increase air pollution. Carter continued to press for energy conservation, for development of renewable sources, such as solar and wind-generated energy, and for greater use of nuclear power.

The nuclear option generated especially sharp controversy. In theory, nuclear reactors could provide inexpensive, almost limitless amounts of energy. The actual cost of building and maintaining them, however, far exceeded original estimates, and antinuclear activists warned of grave safety risks. In 1979, a serious reactor malfunction at Three Mile Island, Pennsylvania, along with a popular movie about a similar event (*The China Syndrome*), appeared to confirm the worst fears. A nuclear-reactor meltdown at a single facility seemed capable of producing massive environmental damage and substantial casualties. Responding to growing concerns, power companies canceled orders for new reactors, and the nuclear power industry's expansion halted. Meanwhile, OPEC oil prices continued to skyrocket, from $1.80 per barrel in 1971 to nearly $30 a decade later, at the end of Carter's presidency.

A Faltering Economy

Rising oil prices and a lingering case of stagflation, legacies of the Nixon and Ford years, heightened the nation's economic woes. Carter pledged to lower both unemployment and inflation, to rekindle economic growth, and to balance the federal budget (which showed a deficit of about $70 billion in 1976). He ultimately settled on tax cuts and increased public-works spending as the best ways to accomplish these objectives. In addition, the Federal Reserve Board increased the supply of money in circulation and kept the prime interest rate relatively low.

These measures, however, only further aggravated matters. By 1980, government statistics showed virtually no economic growth; unemployment numbers, after temporarily dipping, continued to rise; and the inflation rate topped 13 percent. Stagflation, in turn, brought high interest rates, discouraged investment, and ate away at consumer confidence. Many voters told pollsters that Carter's time in office had coincided with deterioration of their own economic fortunes.

Economic distress spread beyond individuals. New York City, beset by long-term economic problems and short-term fiscal mismanagement, faced bankruptcy. A group of private bankers and public officials managed to secure congressional bailout legislation, which granted special loan guarantees to the nation's largest city. Its troubles were hardly unique. According to one estimate, Chicago lost 200,000 manufacturing jobs during the 1970s. Bricks salvaged from demolished buildings in St. Louis became one of that city's leading products. Soaring unemployment, rising crime rates, deteriorating downtowns, and shrinking tax revenues afflicted most urban areas, even as inflation further reduced the public services that cash-strapped city budgets could afford to finance.

Conservative economists and business interests charged that domestic programs favored by most congressional Democrats contributed to this economic distress. Increasing the minimum wage and vigorously enforcing safety and antipollution regulations, they argued, drove up the cost of doing business and forced companies to raise prices to consumers.

During its last two years in Washington, the Carter administration seemed to agree with some of this analysis. Defying

© Time & Life Pictures/Getty Images

"Is Capitalism Working?"   In 1980, *Time* magazine wondered about the economic future of the United States. Persistent economic problems, especially high rates of inflation and unemployment, dominated the Ford and Carter presidencies.

many Democrats in Congress, the president cut spending for some social programs, sought to reduce capital-gains taxes to encourage investment, and began deregulating various industries, beginning with the financial and transportation sectors.

Negotiating Disputes Overseas

In foreign, as in domestic policy, Carter came to Washington promising new directions. As a symbol of letting go of the Vietnam War issue, he immediately fulfilled his pledge of granting amnesty to most Vietnam-era draft resisters. He soon declared that his presidency would press human-rights issues and would avoid any "inordinate fear of communism."

Pulled in divergent directions, the Carter administration's foreign policy appeared to waffle. Although Carter was a hard worker and a quick study, he possessed little background in foreign-policy issues. Furthermore, his top aides—Cyrus Vance as secretary of state and Zbigniew Brzezinski as national security adviser—advocated (and sometimes tried to pursue) very different agendas. Vance preferred quiet diplomacy and avoidance of confrontations, while Brzezinski favored a hard-line, anti-Soviet policy with an emphasis on military muscle. Carter favored settling disputes through negotiation, rather than military force, and promoting human rights overseas as a major priority.

Carter's faith in negotiations and his personal skills as a facilitator yielded some successes. On the issue of the Panama Canal, the object of diplomatic negotiations for 13 years, Carter secured treaties that granted Panama increasing authority over the waterway and, then, full control in 2000. Carter personally lobbied key members of the U.S. Senate, where he needed a two-thirds majority to ratify any treaty, and finally convinced enough skeptics that ownership of the canal was no longer economically or strategically crucial to the United States.

The "Camp David Peace Talks" of 1978 highlighted Carter's personal diplomatic touch. Relations between Egypt and Israel had been strained since the Yom Kippur War of 1973, when Israel repelled an Egyptian attack and seized the Sinai Peninsula and territory along the "West Bank" (of the Jordan River). Reviving earlier Republican efforts to broker a peace settlement, Carter brought Menachem Begin and Anwar Sadat, leaders of Israel and Egypt, respectively, to the presidential retreat at Camp David. After 13 days of difficult bargaining, the three leaders announced a framework for further negotiations and a peace treaty between Egypt and Israel. Tensions in the Middle East hardly vanished, but these Camp David Accords kept alive high-level discussions, lowered the level of acrimony between Egypt and Israel, and bound both nations to the United States through Carter's promises of economic aid.

In Asia, the Carter administration built on Nixon's initiative, expanding economic and cultural relations with China. The United States finally established formal diplomatic ties with the People's Republic on New Year's Day 1979.

Campaigning for Human Rights Abroad

Carter's foreign policy became best known for its emphasis on human rights. Carter argued that Cold War alliances with unpopular, repressive dictatorships, even in the name of anticommunism, had undermined the international reputation and influence of the United States.

Carter's human-rights policy, however, proved difficult to implement. Judged by its own standards, it appeared that his administration continued to support some dictatorial regimes, such as that of Ferdinand Marcos in the Philippines, when it seemed expedient to do so. Moreover, Carter's critics, especially Republicans, complained that his rhetoric about human rights helped justify uprisings against long-standing pro-American dictators in Nicaragua and Iran. Revolutions in these countries, partially fueled by resentment against the United States, brought anti-American regimes to power and presented Carter with difficult choices.

In Nicaragua, the revolutionary *Sandinista* movement in 1979 toppled the dictatorship of Anastasio Somoza, whom the United States had long supported. The *Sandinistas*, initially a coalition of moderate democrats and leftists, soon veered toward a militant Marxism and began to expropriate private property. Consequently, Carter's opponents at home charged his policies with having given a green light to Marxist-style insurrections throughout Central America, and some pledged to seek the overthrow of the *Sandinistas*.

Confronting Problems in Iran and Afghanistan

If events in Nicaragua marred Carter's foreign-policy reputation, those in Iran and Afghanistan battered it. The United States had steadfastly supported the autocratic Shah Reza Pahlavi, who had reigned in oil-rich Iran since the American-supported coup of 1953. The shah's own ouster in January 1979, by a revolutionary movement dominated by Islamic fundamentalists, signaled a repudiation of the U.S. presence in Iran. When the White House agreed that the deposed shah could enter the United States for medical treatment in November 1979, a militant group of Iranians, acting at the behest of their nation's revolutionary government, seized the U.S. embassy, along with 66 American hostages, in Teheran. They demanded the United States return the shah to Iran in exchange for release of the hostages.

Carter responded with uncharacteristic aggressiveness. He replaced human-rights rhetoric with tougher talk and announced economic sanctions against Iran. Over the objections of Cyrus Vance (who subsequently resigned in protest), Carter also sent a military rescue mission into Iran. When this effort ended in an embarrassing failure, Carter's critics cited the on-going "hostage crisis" as proof of his incompetence. (Diplomatic efforts would finally free the hostages, after Carter's defeat in the 1980 presidential election, but the United States and Iran would remain bitterly at odds.)

Criticism of Carter also focused on the Soviet Union's 1979 invasion of Afghanistan, a move primarily sparked by the Kremlin's fear of the growing influence of Islamic fundamentalists along and within the borders of the USSR. Carter tried to respond in nonmilitary ways. He halted grain exports to the Soviet Union (angering his farm constituency), organized a boycott of the 1980 Summer Olympic Games in Moscow, withdrew a new Strategic Arms Limitation Treaty (SALT) from the U.S. Senate, and revived registration for military service. Still, Republicans (along with some conservative Democrats) charged Carter with allowing U.S. power and prestige to decline.

For a time, after Senator Edward Kennedy of Massachusetts entered the 1980 Democratic presidential primaries, it seemed as if Carter's own party might deny him a second term.

Although Kennedy's campaign challenge eventually fizzled, it popularized anti-Carter themes that Republicans would gleefully embrace. "It's time to say no more hostages, no more high interest rates, no more high inflation, and no more Jimmy Carter," went Kennedy's standard stump speech.

A New Right

By 1976, the idea of preventing another Carter *or* another Kennedy presidency animated a diverse coalition of conservatives: a "New Right." A broadly based movement, this new conservatism succeeded in holding together several different constituencies. The already disparate group that had initially gathered around William F. Buckley's *National Review* during the 1950s provided one of these constituencies. Even as Buckley continued to use his magazine to push conservative ideas, he reached out to new converts through television. His long-running interview show, *Firing Line*, debuted on PBS in 1971 (and ran for another 28 years). The economist Milton Friedman—a frequent Buckley guest, a 1976 Nobel laureate, and creator of a PBS series touting free-market economic principles—provided another important link between the conservatism of the 1950s and that of the 1970s. In addition, many of the then-youthful conservatives who had energized Barry Goldwater's 1964 presidential campaign, such as Patrick Buchanan, came to the New Right after having worked in Richard Nixon's administration.

In contrast, the "neoconservative" (or "neocon") wing of the New Right of the 1970s had generally identified with Democrats, rather than Republicans, during the 1950s and much of the 1960s. Fiercely anticommunist, writers and academics such as Norman Podhoretz, Gertrude Himmelfarb, Jeane Kirkpatrick, and Irving Kristol saw too many Democrats criticizing Lyndon Johnson and, then, rallying behind George McGovern and his theme of "Come Home America." Fearful that the Democratic Party might abandon a strong anticommunist stance, **neoconservatives** also viewed most domestic movements of the 1960s, particularly those displaying countercultural values, as threatening the social stability and intellectual values they admired. This initial generation of neoconservatives, often the offspring of European-Jewish immigrants, also complained that U.S. foreign policy, even under Richard Nixon and Henry Kissinger, failed to support Israel strongly enough. This claim tended to anger some older "paleo-conservatives," those who had never quite shed the anti-Semitism that Buckley's *National Review* had urged all conservatives to abandon.

Conservative business leaders provided another important New Right constituency. Convinced that anticorporate professors and students dominated most colleges and universities, business magnates such as Joseph Coors, of the Colorado brewing family, placed at least some of their fortunes at the service of their convictions. In their view, new regulatory legislation accepted by the Nixon administration, especially measures dealing with workplace safety issues and environmental concerns, threatened "economic freedom" and "entrepreneurial liberty." If colleges and universities could not provide intellectual support for conservative perspectives, then businesses should create counter-institutions in the form of right-leaning think tanks. Conservative business leaders and their philanthropic foundations generously funded research institutions, such as the American Enterprise

Institute (founded in 1943), and created new ones, such as The Heritage Foundation (established in 1973).

Money from New Right businesspeople also financed lobbying efforts, such as those mounted by their own Business Roundtable (created in 1973) and The Committee on the Present Danger (CPD). This bipartisan group, which took its name and much of its leadership from a similarly named group of the 1950s, argued that the foreign-policy establishment of the 1970s, including "realists" such as Henry Kissinger, underestimated the threat that the Soviet Union still posed to the United States. The CPD's successes included persuading Gerald Ford's appointee as CIA director, George H. W. Bush, to order a review of the CIA's assessment of the communist menace by a group of outside analysts. Ultimately known as "Team B" and dominated by people close to the CPD, this panel warned of CIA complacency in the face of Soviet aggressiveness.

Groups such as the CPD also operated effectively outside of the Washington, D.C., beltway. In 1975, activists who had worked for Goldwater's 1964 campaign formed the National Conservative Political Action Committee (NCPAC), the first of many similar movement organizations aimed at mobilizing and organizing at the grassroots. Initiatives such as NCPAC backed conservative political candidates and advocated a wide range of policies. Forging a political strategy aimed at defending "family values," they opposed policies identified with feminist movements, such as legalized abortion, and LGBT (lesbian, gay, bisexual, transgender) lifestyles.

The New Right of the 1970s also attracted grassroots support from Protestants in fundamentalist and evangelical churches. People from these religious groups had generally stayed clear of overtly partisan politics since the 1920s but continued to express concern, exemplified in the work of Billy Graham's organization, about public issues that involved spiritual and social matters. Already angered by Supreme Court decisions that seemed to eliminate sectarian prayers from public schools, many expressed greater outrage over *Roe* v. *Wade* (1973), the landmark abortion ruling. Reaching out to antiabortion Catholics, people whom most members of southern Protestant congregations would have shunned a generation earlier, a "Religious Right" slowly took shape. The Reverend Jerry Falwell of the Thomas Road Baptist Church and *The Old Time Gospel Hour* television ministry declared *Roe* showed the necessity of fighting back on the political front because antireligious elites in Washington "have been imposing morality on us for the last fifty years."

Leaders of the Religious Right insisted that sacred values should actively shape political policy making. The clear separation between church and state, a guiding principle of constitutionalism during the era of Earl Warren's Supreme Court, struck the Religious Right as a violation of a right specifically mentioned in the First Amendment: the "free exercise of religion." Particularly in the South, conservatives embarked on a lengthy legal crusade to prevent the Internal Revenue Service from denying tax-exempt status to the private Christian colleges and academies that opposed racial integration. Challenging older constitutional precedents against state aid to religious institutions, they also urged that government should use tax monies to help fund church-centered education and "faith-based" social programming. Most spokespeople for the Religious Right championed foreign policies that maximized the use of U.S. military power, especially on behalf of Israel. Protestants who embraced "dispensational pre-millennialism," the belief that the Second Coming of Christ would occur in their lifetimes, saw the survival of a Jewish state in the Middle East as crucial to the future they expected to unfold according to Biblical prophesy.

Especially in the South, the process of a political switch to the GOP could almost seem comparable to that of a religious conversion. In 1976 most **evangelicals** and **fundamentalists** from the South, including Jerry Falwell, supported Jimmy Carter. His religious values made him seem less committed to the *Roe* decision than Gerald Ford, whose spouse, Betty Ford, often identified herself with women's issues. Very soon, however, Falwell and others on the Religious Right began realigning their politics with those of the GOP's conservative bloc and embracing a political messiah, Ronald Reagan.

Ronald Reagan (1981–1989)

Focus Question
To what extent did Ronald Reagan's administration represent a victory for the New Right agenda in both domestic and foreign policy?

Ronald Reagan increasingly seemed the best hope of conservative Republicans. Most right-of-center activists had viewed Nixon and Gerald Ford as Eisenhower-style moderates, who only vaguely understood, let alone reliably adopted, conservative perspectives. Their search for a dedicated movement conservative seemed especially urgent after Ford tabbed Nelson Rockefeller, whom many conservative members of the GOP viewed as a crypto-Democrat, as his vice president. "I could hardly have been more upset if Ford had selected Teddy Kennedy," one outraged conservative claimed.

Popular memory now recalls Reagan, particularly after his 2004 death, in glowing terms. Even people who disliked his political ideas and programs often credited him with possessing the presidential aura of FDR, the movie-land charisma of JFK, and the persuasive powers of LBJ. In striking contrast, when Reagan had first run for elective office in 1966, observers from outside the conservative fold tended to dismiss him as a "flake," a washed-up or never-was movie actor, and an intellectual lightweight. Throughout Reagan's entire political career, the tendency to denigrate or, more commonly, underestimate his talents and intellect generally worked to his advantage.

After Reagan had steamrolled a two-term Democratic incumbent to become governor of California in 1966, many political watchers expected he would create havoc once in office. He had campaigned as a political leader who would restore order on university campuses by encouraging police to crack heads—which he *did* do—and as someone who would tear down the state's social-welfare system—which he *did not* do. During his own eight years as California's chief executive, Reagan pursued a moderately conservative path on most issues and generally won praise for a governing style that one historian would later describe as combining "visionary rigidity" with "tactical flexibility."

Still, despite Reagan's promise that the failed 1976 effort to push aside Ford would not mark his last political hurrah, most political observers again discounted his presidential prospects as 1980 approached. Surely, as he neared age 70, Reagan could never redebut in national politics, commentators generally predicted. As Carter's presidency seemed to wander, however, Reagan reemerged as a fresh, new face—an outsider like Carter, but one with better political instincts and a personality that promised to wear well. Using his most obvious asset, the well-practiced ability to communicate across virtually all media, Reagan recorded nearly 1,500 nationally syndicated radio addresses, which he personally drafted in longhand. His domestic priorities well known, Reagan focused many of these speeches on national defense, concentrating on the implications of his major claim: that U.S. leaders had simply stood idly by while the USSR conducted the "biggest military buildup in the history of mankind."

Meanwhile, back in California, angry conservative taxpayers were organizing a grassroots effort to slash the state's property taxes by a ballot initiative labeled Proposition 13. (Ironically, Reagan's agreement to tax hikes during his time as governor had helped fuel the Proposition 13 movement.) This measure, a testament to how effectively conservative activists could mobilize grassroots volunteers and corporate contributors, passed by a large margin in 1978. Always ready to denounce high taxes, Reagan shrewdly elevated the already important tax-cutting issue to a central place in his 1980 presidential campaign.

Still, some on the diverse New Right continued to wonder about Reagan. Where, precisely, did this divorced, one-time Democrat stand on issues such as abortion and school prayer? Pragmatists in the New Right movement, including those with strong ties to the GOP establishment, ultimately viewed Reagan, whether or not he really qualified as a true conservative, as the most conservative presidential hopeful with the best chance of actually winning the White House in 1980.

The Election of 1980

Easily capturing the Republican nomination, and anointing one of his defeated rivals, George H. W. Bush, as a running mate, Ronald Reagan never doubted he could defeat Jimmy Carter. Employing his well-practiced media skills and well-honed message, Reagan sought to transfer his own optimistic vision of a rejuvenated America to the electorate. His standard speech, punctuated with quips inspired by Hollywood movies, stressed opposition to domestic social spending, commitment to significant cuts in federal taxes, and renewed support for the post-Vietnam Pentagon, supposedly short-changed by Democrats and moderate Republicans alike. Speaking before a pro-military audience, Reagan insisted the USSR had surged so far ahead in nuclear capabilities that, during any confrontation with the Soviets, the United States would face a stark choice: "surrender or die." Looking at opinion polls about how people linked their own declining economic circumstances to those of the entire nation during Carter's presidency, Reagan repeatedly asked a simple public policy question: "Are you better off now than you were four years ago?" Quickly offering his own answer, Reagan cited a homemade economic statistic, the "misery index," which added the rate of inflation to that of unemployment.

Reagan also seized issues that the Democratic Party had long regarded as its own—economic growth and increased personal consumption. In 1979, one of Jimmy Carter's advisers had gloomily portrayed the nation's economic problems as so severe that there was "no way we can avoid a decline in our standard of living. All we can do is adapt to it." In contrast, Reagan promised that sharp tax cuts and budget trimming would bring about the return, for the first time since the late 1960s, of robust economic expansion.

The Reagan-Bush team swept to victory. Although it gained only slightly more than 50 percent of the popular vote because John Anderson, a middle-of-the-road Republican, running as an independent, won about 7 percent of the total—the GOP ticket captured the Electoral College tally by a 489 to 49 margin. Carter conceded defeat even before West Coast voting booths had officially closed. Moreover, Republicans took away 12 Democratic Senate seats, including those of George McGovern and Frank Church, widely visible opponents of the foreign-policy vision championed by Reagan. For the first time since 1954, Republicans controlled the U.S. Senate, though not the House of Representatives.

Ronald Wilson Reagan had reinvented himself during the 1960s, supposedly a time dominated by youth. At 70 years of age, he promised to do the same for a nation that seemed to have not yet recovered from the years of polarization.

A "New Morning in America"

Even after his 1980 victory, many political observers continued to underestimate Reagan. Once people experienced President Reagan's actual policies and administrative ineptitude, went a common argument among Democrats, his finely buffed image and well-practiced media skills would count for little. His detractors, with some justification, saw the presidential election representing more of a referendum against Jimmy Carter than a groundswell for Ronald Reagan.

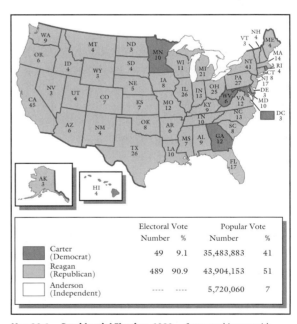

	Electoral Vote		Popular Vote	
	Number	%	Number	%
Carter (Democrat)	49	9.1	35,483,883	41
Reagan (Republican)	489	90.9	43,904,153	51
Anderson (Independent)	----	----	5,720,060	7

Map 30.1 Presidential Election, 1980 Compare this map with the one showing the election of Jimmy Carter four years earlier. What factors might explain such a sudden downturn in Democratic fortunes?

Although conservative think tanks deluged the Reagan administration with policy suggestions, the president and his closest aides focused on three major priorities: (1) cutting federal taxes, (2) reducing the governmental regulatory structure, and (3) boosting national-security capabilities. Implicitly hedging their bets on the depth of their political support and recognizing the desirability of moving quickly, they prepared to take Washington by storm, ironically using FDR's first "100 days" as their model for an anti–New Deal agenda.

Taxes, Supply-Side Economics, and the "Reagan Revolution"

To justify cutting taxes, Reagan continued to endorse a theory widely known as **"supply-side economics."** In this view, the approach that Democrats had favored since the Second World War used ever-increasing tax revenues to finance programs that propped up spending by consumers, thus focusing on the "demand side." Supply-siders leaned in the other direction. Reducing the tax burden on those who paid the most, they argued, would stimulate economic growth by putting more money in the hands of people who supplied the capital needed to stimulate production and increase investment. During the run-up to the 1980 election, a number of top Republican conservatives had pressed this approach, once denounced by Reagan's own Phi Beta Kappa vice president, when he was a rival candidate, as "voodoo economics."

Reagan's administration claimed to support this approach wholeheartedly. The president immediately pressed for a 30 percent reduction in federal taxes, 10 percent in each of the next three years. Dismissing claims that this would produce huge federal deficits, the White House predicted that reductions gained from cutting wasteful programs, and the additional revenues generated by renewed economic growth, would guard against any serious deficit. Lobbying intensely and skillfully with sympathetic Democrats, who had supported limited tax reductions during Carter's presidency, and suspicious old-style Republicans, who were devoted to balanced budgets, Reagan pushed a less ambitious tax-reduction plan through Congress in 1981. He coupled this with a budget bill that aimed at cutting expenditures for social programs.

In the short run, "Reaganomics" appeared to produce a bust rather than a boom. A severe economic downturn in 1981 and 1982, one of the worst since the Great Depression of the 1930s, sent economic indicators and Reagan's approval rating, which reached a low of 35 percent, hurtling downward. Republican losses in the off-year 1982 elections cut into the gains of 1980.

Then, the U.S. economy dramatically rebounded and entered a vibrant period of non-inflationary growth that lasted, without any interruption, until the end of the 1980s. According to one study, the economy added nearly 17 million new jobs; figures on real income, after having declined throughout the 1970s, began to rise; and inflation dropped from double digits to around 2 percent. Although unemployment figures did not fall as sharply, Reagan's supporters would come to talk about a "Reagan Revolution."

This economic resurgence and its precise causes, however, proved controversial. Fiscal conservatives often complained that Reagan failed to match tax cuts to budget reductions, ballooning the U.S. deficit right along with production figures. Reagan constantly inveighed against deficits and "big spenders," but his eight years in Washington, even after he once again displayed his pragmatism by agreeing to a rollback of the initial tax reduction package, saw annual deficits triple to nearly $300 billion. Reagan's own financial guru, David Stockman, later dismissed supply-side economics as more of a rhetorical turn than a prescription for policy. To finance its deficit spending, the United States borrowed abroad and piled up the largest foreign debt in the world. Any Reagan Revolution, critics often charged, brought recovery for the 1980s by courting a long-term budget crisis for the 1990s.

Other economic observers, focusing on the crucial issue of inflation, argued that the policies of the Federal Reserve Board (FRB) under Paul Volcker, a Carter appointee, counted for more than anything done by the White House. By steadfastly keeping interest rates high and the money supply low, from this perspective, Volker's FRB spearheaded the economic boom through its monetary moves.

© Eve Arnold/Magnum Photos, Inc.

Selling off the Farm   Hard economic times during the early 1980s forced the liquidation of many small, family-run farms. Here, neighbors gather at a farm where everything, including a well-used pitchfork, headed to the auction block.

Moreover, a number of critics, especially from Democratic Party ranks, denounced the policies of both the Reagan administration and the FRB as unfair. Partisans of the Reagan Revolution always argued that its effects would ultimately "trickle down" and benefit everyone. In a battle of metaphors, however, its detractors countered that too many people continued to fall through the holes of Reagan's "Swiss-cheese" economy. Reagan's critics noted that farmers in the Midwest, who were holding high-interest loans from the inflation-ridden 1970s, watched falling crop prices hamper their ability to service their debt loads during the early 1980s. A wave of mortgage foreclosures, reminiscent of the 1930s, hit the farm states, and the ripple effect washed over the always vulnerable economies of nearby towns. In urban areas, many of the jobs created during the boom of the 1980s came in the service sector and offered low wages and, at best, meager fringe benefits. The minimum wage, when adjusted for inflation, declined in value throughout the 1980s.

The surge of the Reagan era, then, brought prosperity to many, upward mobility for some, and growing distress for others. If critics desired to emphasize low-wage jobs in the service sector, the so-called McJobs (as at McDonald's and other fast-food outlets), the celebrants of the Reagan Revolution could reply by highlighting the many more well-paid ones for managers and technicians in fields such as electronics and computers. People with solid educational backgrounds and marketable skills generally made significant economic gains during the 1980s.

The number of African American families earning a solid middle-class income, for example, more than doubled between 1970 and 1990. A greater percentage of black women and men completed college than ever before, with black women earning postsecondary degrees at a higher percentage rate than either black men or women of European descent. African American college graduates could expect incomes comparable to those of their white classmates, partly as a result of the Reagan administration's reluctance to overturn affirmative-action hiring plans put in place by the Nixon and Carter administrations. More African American professionals could afford to live in gentrified urban neighborhoods or in suburban areas such as Dekalb County, Georgia. The Reagan administration hailed people, such as Clarence Thomas, who headed the EEOC, as evidence that blacks could not only thrive as Republicans but take pride in being "black conservatives."

The situation looked very different, however, for people who remained persistently un- or underemployed, especially those who lived in declining urban centers or older suburbs. As the construction crews moved in to rehabilitate their urban neighborhood, some financially embattled African American homeowners lost their houses at fire-sale prices. At the end of the 1980s, one-third of all African American families lived in poverty, and the number with an annual income of less than $15,000 per year had doubled since 1970. In inner cities, fewer than half of African American children were completing high school, and more than 60 percent were unemployed. The gap between the very well-off and what one prominent sociologist called the "truly disadvantaged" widened during the 1980s.

Cutting Regulations and Welfare Measures

Meanwhile, Reagan pursued his second major goal: cutting back on the federal regulatory structure. A movement to decrease federal regulations had already taken hold before Reagan ever reached Washington. An early Reagan move, defying the elaborate structure of federal labor law and summarily firing the nation's air traffic controllers, after their union refused to halt a nationwide strike, immediately gladdened conservatives.

Reagan had entered office promising to break OPEC's oil monopoly by eliminating regulations that discouraged development of new sources of supply. Ignoring calls to decrease U.S. dependence on fossil fuels by promotion of renewable sources, the Reagan administration pursued a "cheap oil" policy. The tapping of new oil fields at home and abroad during the 1980s, together with rivalries among OPEC's members, weakened the cartel's hold on the world market and reduced the relative cost of energy.

To encourage conservative interpretations of existing regulatory measures, the Reagan administration worked to place a New Right stamp on the federal legal system. Almost immediately, Reagan nominated a Supreme Court justice, Sandra Day O'Connor (the first woman to sit on the Court), who initially appeared to be a staunch conservative. With the Republican Party controlling the U.S. Senate until 1986, Reagan enjoyed a relatively free hand naming prominent conservative jurists, such as Robert Bork and Antonin Scalia, to lower federal courts. The Senate Judiciary Committee, chaired by Strom Thurmond of South Carolina, gained a reputation for streamlining the confirmation process for White House-favored nominees. An informal network of conservative professors and law students, which had become a feature of every major law school during the 1970s, helped identify right-of-center lawyers for possible appointment to the federal bench. It selected a large number of Catholic jurists, many of whom seemed strong social conservatives. Although the Reagan administration appointed about the same number of women as had that of Jimmy Carter, it found few African American nominees.

This effort at judicial recruitment joined a larger Reagan-era effort to modify, if not overrule, the Warren-era Supreme Court rulings that had consistently supported rights claims. Civil libertarians soon faced the prospect of the federal courts becoming less hospitable to legal arguments made by criminal defendants, labor unions, and political dissenters. By 1990, because of retirements, about half of all federal judges had reached the bench during Ronald Reagan's presidency. His administration also sought out avowedly conservative lawyers for nonjudicial appointments. It staffed the Reagan justice department with young attorneys, such as John Roberts and Samuel Alito, who expressed a desire to assist conservative judges whittle back Warren-era judicial precedents.

On environmental issues, Reagan appointed James Watt, an outspoken critic of governmental regulation, as his first secretary of the interior. Born in Wyoming, Watt supported the so-called sage-brush rebellion, in which entrepreneurs from the Far West demanded fewer governmental restrictions on the use of public lands, especially if they could be used for grazing or tapped for mining and oil-drilling operations. Many people living in the timber-rich states of the Pacific Northwest opposed, with equal vigor, efforts to protect endangered species, such as rare bird populations, if regulations interfered with lumber-related opportunities. Reagan's first two appointees to the Department of Energy actually proposed eliminating the cabinet office they headed—an idea that Congress blocked. Through its appointments to both the interior and energy departments, the

White House achieved some relaxation of the enforcement of safety and environmental regulations.

Overall, however, the Reagan administration pruned rather than clear-cut the regulatory forest. Despite its efforts, most conservatives expressed some disappointment that the Reagan administration had not rolled back even more federal regulations.

Conservatives also pressed the Reagan administration to decrease more drastically its funding for various kinds of public-benefit programs, particularly AFDC. These reductions in food stamps and other programs increased poverty rates and disproportionately affected female-headed households and children. By the end of the 1980s, one of every five children was being raised in a household whose total income fell below the official poverty line.

Reagan, though, steadfastly rejected any suggestion of completely eliminating the basic set of New Deal programs that he called a "social safety net," and he consistently refused to push ideas for revising the popular Social Security program. During the 1970s, Congress had indexed Social Security payments, mandating they would automatically increase along with the rate of inflation. While supporting this practice, the Reagan White House also agreed to congressional legislation raising the payroll taxes for both Social Security and Medicare. Larger Social Security checks, along with continued Medicare benefits, enabled millions of Americans over the age of 65 to do relatively well during the Reagan years. By the end of Reagan's two-term presidency, what the federal government spent on social-welfare programs roughly equaled the amount it had laid out when he entered office.

Despite sometimes sharp debate, especially over the soaring federal deficit and widening income and wealth gaps, Reagan became steadily more popular than he had been in 1980. His genial optimism seemed unshakable. He even appeared to rebound quickly—although close observers noted a perceptible decline in his energies and ability to concentrate—after being shot by a would-be assassin in March 1981. No matter what problems beset other members of his administration, criticism never stuck to Reagan, whom one frustrated Democrat dubbed the "Teflon president."

Routing the Democrats, 1984

Still, many traditional Democrats continued to underestimate Reagan's appeal—a miscalculation that doomed their party's 1984 presidential effort. Walter Mondale, Jimmy Carter's former vice president, ran on a platform that seemed to offer something for nearly everyone. It called for "the eradication of discrimination in all aspects of American life" and for an expansion of national social-welfare programs. Mondale bravely called for higher taxes, while providing few details about from where the revenue might come and to whom it might be channeled. In addition, he chose as his running mate Representative Geraldine Ferraro of New York, the first woman to stand for president or vice president on a major party ticket.

Republican campaign ads—often framed by the slogan "It's Morning Again in America"—portrayed a glowing landscape of bustling small towns and lush farmlands. They attacked Mondale's support from labor unions and civil-rights groups, along with his selection of Ferraro, as a vestige of the "old politics" of "special interests." They labeled his promise to raise taxes as a return to the "wasteful" policies popularly associated with stagflation and the misery index during the 1970s. The 1984 presidential election ended with Mondale carrying only his home state of Minnesota and the District of Columbia.

Reagan's Second Term

Conservatives would eventually almost unanimously hail Ronald Reagan as a giant of their movement, but not during his second term. Then, many activists on the New Right looked balefully at his domestic record, especially on social issues such as abortion and school prayer. His record on judicial politics drew additional criticism. The 1986 resignation of Warren Burger allowed Reagan to elevate William Rehnquist to the position of chief justice and appoint Antonin Scalia, an even more outspoken conservative, to replace Rehnquist as an associate justice. After the 1986 off-year elections gave the Democrats control of the Senate again, however, this body rejected Reagan's 1987 nomination of Robert Bork, a legal and cultural conservative who had become a particular favorite of the New Right, to the High Court.

Bork's lengthy record of legal opinions and scholarly articles, his opponents argued, clearly showed a jurist whose views fell outside the "legal mainstream." To them, Bork not only seemed out of step on current issues such as abortion rights but apparently on settled ones such as the constitutional validity of the 1954 desegregation decision in *Brown*. Some angry conservatives blamed Reagan for not expending his political capital on behalf of his nominee, thereby allowing Democrats and a few apostate Republicans to "Bork" him with a barrage of negative attacks. The battle over the Bork nomination provided a model for the brass-knuckles politics, from both parties, that would become more prevalent during the years that followed.

Meanwhile, many from the Religious Right chafed at what they considered Reagan's halfhearted support of their crusades against abortion and in favor of sectarian prayer in public schools. Many complained that the president and his wife Nancy, who apparently advised on many sociocultural issues, brought some of Tinsel Town's toleration for personal differences, as well as Hollywood-style glamour, with them to Washington. Religious conservatives became increasingly determined to find Republican candidates who would pledge unwavering support for their values.

Although economic growth continued, corruption and mismanagement in the financial industry increasingly loomed as toxic by-products of Reaganomics. The deregulation of financial institutions, supported by Democrats and Republicans alike, had allowed savings and loan (S&L) institutions to assume more risky investments, especially in real estate, using depositors' funds. By 1985, alarmed prognosticators foresaw an impending S&L meltdown, but both the Reagan administration and most members of Congress, hoping to duck the matter until after the 1988 election, ignored obvious warning signs.

Not until 1989 would Congress adopt a bailout plan. It saved some tottering S&Ls and transferred assets from already-failed institutions to still-solvent ones. The arrangement proved astronomically expensive, and taxpayers footed the bill. Meanwhile, the process by

HISTORY THROUGH FILM

THE FIRST MOVIE-STAR PRESIDENT

Ronald Reagan began his presidency in Hollywood. The political career of the "great communicator" built on, rather than broke away from, his days in the entertainment industry. His media advisers could count on directing a seasoned professional. Reagan always knew where to stand, how to deliver lines effectively, how to convey emotions through both body language and dialogue, and when to melt into the background so that other players in the cast of his presidency might carry a crucial scene.

Several of Reagan's actual movies provided rehearsals for roles he would play in the White House. Initially, Reagan's opponents had predicted that his old film parts, particularly in *Bedtime for Bonzo* (1947), in which he co-starred with a chimpanzee, would become political liabilities. Instead of disavowing his days in Hollywood, Reagan accentuated his fluency with film-related imagery. His efforts to cheer on the nation during the 1980s consciously invoked his favorite film role, that of the 1920s Notre Dame football star, George Gipp, whom Reagan played in *Knute Rockne, All American*

(1940). Similarly, when tilting with a Democratic-controlled Congress over tax policy, Reagan invoked Clint Eastwood's famous screen character "Dirty Harry," promising to shoot down any tax increase. "Go ahead, make my day," he taunted. On another occasion, he cited *Rambo* (1982), an action thriller set in post-1975 Vietnam, as a possible blueprint for dealing with countries that had seized U.S. hostages. As he freely drew from Hollywood motion pictures, Reagan occasionally seemed unable to separate "reel" from "real" life. During one session with reporters, he referred to his own dog as "Lassie," the canine performer who had been Reagan's Hollywood contemporary during the 1940s and 1950s.

Life in Hollywood also provided a prologue to President Reagan's conservative policies. Early in his film career, Reagan appeared in four films as the same character, a government agent named "Brass Bancroft." In these B-grade thrillers, Reagan developed an image that he later deployed in politics: an action-oriented character who could quickly distinguish (good) friends from (evil) foes. *Murder in the Air* (1940), one of the Brass Bancroft

which large, well-connected commercial banks purchased the remaining assets of bankrupt S&Ls at bargain-basement prices reeked of corruption and scandal. As a result of the S&L debacle of the 1980s, many people lost at least a portion of their savings, and the banking industry went through a sudden, unplanned consolidation.

Meanwhile, the White House and Congress claimed to have boldly addressed several other domestic issues. First, the Tax Reform Act of 1986 simultaneously lowered the IRS bill of some and raised that of others, with only accountants and tax attorneys being able to determine this complex measure's precise impact on specific individuals and groups. It thus utterly failed to satisfy a major aim of most people: greater simplicity in the tax code. Second, in the 1985 Gramm-Rudman-Hollings Act Congress set a series of targets designed to achieve a balanced federal budget by 1991. (Neither Congress nor the White House, however, seemed to take this goal very seriously, and the government deficit continued to soar.)

Ronald Reagan as the "Gipper" in *Knute Rockne, All American*.

© Bettmann/CORBIS

Second World War, but he served long hours as an Army Air Corps officer, making movies in support of the war effort. He appeared in several films, such as *For God and Country* (1943), and more often provided upbeat voiceovers, once even sharing a soundtrack with President Franklin Roosevelt. He also starred, on loan from the Air Corps, in *This Is the Army* (1943), one of the most successful of wartime Hollywood's military-oriented musicals. After the war, Reagan increasingly directed his energies toward Cold War politics in the film capital. His tenure as the anticommunist president of the Screen Actors Guild—and as a secret FBI informant—likely speeded his conversion from New Deal Democrat to right-leaning Republican. In his final onscreen roles, Reagan usually portrayed the kind of independent, rugged individualist—often in westerns such as *Law and Order* (1953)—whom he would later lionize in his political speeches.

movies, even featured a science-fiction-style "death ray" that resembled SDI (Star Wars) armaments that President Reagan would champion more than 40 years later.

Subsequent film roles refined his Hollywood image. Poor eyesight kept Reagan out of combat during the

Nancy Reagan, who co-starred with her spouse in *Hellcats of the Navy* (1957) and later as the nation's First Lady, offered her close-up view of the relationship between Reagan the actor and Reagan the politician: "There are not two Ronald Reagans." During the 1980s, the cultures of Hollywood and Washington, D.C. became embodied in the same character, Ronald Wilson Reagan.

Finally, Congress passed the Family Support Act of 1988. Largely the work of Daniel Patrick Moynihan (then a Democratic senator from New York), it encouraged states to inaugurate work-training programs and to begin moving people, including mothers receiving AFDC payments, off welfare rolls. Although the measure actually contributed to *raising* federal welfare costs, a pragmatically conservative President Reagan ignored his more ideologically conservative advisers and signed the measure.

Despite complaints from some on the New Right about the White House's often lackadaisical interest in issues such as abortion, the Reagan administration helped change the nation's political vocabulary to the benefit of the larger conservative movement. "Democratic Party programs," to a degree unthinkable in Lyndon Johnson's time, no longer suggested governmental initiatives to stimulate the economy, promote greater equality, and advance liberty for all. Instead, Republicans made "liberal Democrat" a code word for someone devoted to ill-considered social experiments, devised by bureaucrats from a bloated federal government, which gouged hardworking people and squandered their dollars. The term "conservative," as used by New Right Republicans, was coming to stand for economic growth through the curtailment of governmental power; equal treatment for all, rather than "special entitlements" for some; and reverence for traditional sociocultural values. The once-dominant Democratic coalition, forged during the New Deal era, seemed to confront an uncertain future.

Renewing the Cold War

Reagan had campaigned, between 1977 and 1980, on a pledge to reassert U.S. power on the global stage and thus reverse what he characterized as Jimmy Carter's failure to protect national security. Harkening back to the Vietnam War era, Reagan suggested that the U.S. effort had been a "noble cause" and that politicians had refused to allow the Pentagon to win. Renewing the moralistic rhetoric of the early Cold War era and jettisoning the realism of Henry Kissinger, Reagan promised to confront the Soviets with a massively rearmed United States and, soon, denounced the USSR as an "evil empire."

The Defense Buildup

Although tax cuts were reducing federal revenues, the Reagan administration pressed for dramatic increases in military spending. Its initial budget called for increasing military expenditures nearly 30 percent in four years. It allowed the Pentagon to enlarge the Navy and expand strategic nuclear forces, deploying additional missiles throughout Western Europe. At the height of Reagan's military buildup, which contributed significantly to budget deficits, the Pentagon was purchasing about 20 percent of the nation's manufacturing output.

In 1983, Reagan suggested perhaps the most ambitious, and expensive, military system in history. He proposed an elaborate defense shield that would protect the United States against any incoming missiles. Beginning as a vague hope, this **"Strategic Defense Initiative" (SDI),** soon could claim its own Pentagon agency, which initially sought $26 billion, over five years, just in research costs.

Controversy immediately swirled around SDI. Skeptics ridiculed it as something out of the movie *Star Wars*. Budget analysts trained in cost-benefit calculations shuddered at its astronomical costs, especially after most scientists dismissed the plan as impossible to implement effectively. Reagan succeeded in launching, however, a national security initiative that subsequent GOP leaders would loyally follow: faith in the feasibility of constructing, rather than simply imagining "out in the blue," a defensive shield that would eliminate any nuclear threat to the United States. Some in Reagan's administration also suggested that, as the Soviet Union struggled to compete with the United States in the accelerating arms race, the increased burden on the USSR's fragile economy could trigger an economic-political meltdown behind the Iron Curtain. Once proposed, SDI altered strategic debates at home and arms talks with the Soviet Union.

Reagan's foreign-policy agenda also included numerous nonmilitary initiatives. In a new "informational" offensive, the administration funded conservative groups around the world and established Radio Martí, a Florida-based station beamed at Cuba and aimed at discrediting Fidel Castro's communist government. When the Reagan administration and its allies in Congress detected an anti-American tilt in **UNESCO** programs, they simply cut off U.S. contributions that went to fund this UN agency. In addition, the White House championed the benefits of a free and open international marketplace, pressing other nations to minimize tariffs and restrictions on foreign investment. Its "Caribbean Basin Initiative," for example, rewarded with U.S. aid small nations in the Caribbean region that adhered to free-market principles.

The CIA, under the aggressive leadership of Reagan-appointee William Casey, stepped up its covert activities. Some became so obvious they hardly qualified as covert. It seemed no secret, for instance, that the United States was sending aid to anticommunist forces in Afghanistan, many of them radical Islamic fundamentalist groups, and to the opponents of the *Sandinista* government in Nicaragua, the ***contras.***

Deploying Military Power

In renewing the global Cold War, Reagan promised military support to "democratic" revolutions anywhere. This move seemed designed to contain, or even roll back, the Soviet Union's sphere of influence in Third World areas. Reagan's neoconservative ambassador to the UN, Jeane Kirkpatrick, famously wrote that "democratic" forces included almost any movement, no matter how autocratic, committed to opposing communism. The United States thus funded opposition forces in many countries aligned with the Soviet Union. In addition to Afghanistan and Nicaragua, these nations included Ethiopia, Angola, South Yemen, El Salvador, Guatemala, and Grenada. Reagan sometimes called the participants in such anticommunist insurgencies "freedom fighters," although some displayed no visible commitment to such values.

The Reagan administration, on occasion, directly deployed U.S. military power, initially in southern Lebanon in 1982. Here, Israeli troops faced off against Islamic groups supported by Syria and Iran. Alarmed by radical Islamic influence within Lebanon, the Reagan administration convinced Israel to withdraw and sent 1,600 U.S. marines as part of an international "peacekeeping force" to restore stability. Islamic militias, however, turned against the U.S. forces. After a massive truck bomb attack against a military compound killed 241 U.S. troops, mostly marines, in April 1983, a majority in the Reagan administration, overriding dissenting opinions, decided to end this ill-defined undertaking. In February 1984, Reagan ordered the withdrawal of U.S. troops and disengaged from Lebanon.

Meanwhile, another military intervention accomplished its goal. In October 1983, Reagan sent 2,000 U.S. troops to the tiny Caribbean island of Grenada, where a socialist leader appeared to be tilting ever closer to Castro's Cuba. After a brief military operation, which analysts subsequently judged to have been rather ineptly planned and executed, U.S. troops swept aside Grenada's left-leaning government and installed one friendlier to U.S. interests.

Buoyed by events in Grenada, some in the Reagan administration fixed their sights on Nicaragua. Here, the Marxist-leaning *Sandinista* government, seeking to break Nicaragua's historic dependence on the United States, became the target. The Reagan administration marshaled economic pressure, mounted an anti-*Sandinista* informational campaign, and pledged greater military and financial assistance to the *contras*. These early initiatives stirred considerable controversy. Soon, charges by human-rights groups against the *contras*, which highlighted evidence of their corruption and brutal tactics, produced further political discord at home and criticism around the world. Finally, Democrats in Congress successfully pressed to bar additional military aid to the *contras*, a group the president had once compared to America's own "Founding Fathers." Although his administration encouraged wealthy U.S. conservatives and friendly foreign governments to donate money to the *contra* cause, Reagan rebuffed calls to send U.S. troops to Nicaragua.

Violence continued to escalate, meanwhile, throughout the Middle East. As the Israeli-Palestinian conflict remained unresolved and Israel continued its presence in Lebanon, militant Islamic groups increased attacks against Israel and Western powers. Bombings and kidnappings of Westerners became more frequent. Seeing Libya's Muammar al-Qaddafi and Iranian leaders encouraging such activities, the White House attempted, during the spring of 1986, what looked like a long-range assassination attempt against a foreign leader, an action outlawed by Congress. The United States launched an air strike against Qaddafi's personal compound. It killed his young daughter, but Qaddafi and his government survived. Polls suggested broad support at home for using strong measures against nations that sponsored terrorism and those who aided and abetted hostage taking.

The Iran-Contra Controversy

During the 1980 campaign, Reagan had portrayed the hostages held in Iran as tangible symbols of how weak the United States had become under Jimmy Carter's leadership. When Iranian-backed groups continued to kidnap Americans during Reagan's own presidency, members of his administration began seeking clandestine ways to recover hostages. In November 1986, a small Lebanese magazine reported that the Reagan administration was selling arms to Iran in order to secure the release of Americans being held hostage by militants who looked to Iran's Islamic Republic for inspiration and, perhaps, direction. These alleged deals seemingly violated the Reagan administration's own pledges against selling arms to Iran or rewarding hostage-taking by negotiating for the release of captives.

As Congress began to investigate, the story became even more bizarre. The Reagan administration revealed that it had not only sold arms to Iran but had funneled profits from these back-channel deals to the *contra* forces in Nicaragua, thereby circumventing the congressional ban on U.S. military aid for the controversial anti-*Sandinista* forces. Lieutenant Colonel Oliver North, an aide in the office of the national security adviser, directed the effort, working with international arms dealers and private go-betweens. North's covert machinations seemingly violated both the stated policy of the White House and the will of Congress.

Despite its colorful cast of characters, evidence of illegality, and apparent zaniness, the **"Iran-*contra* affair"** played far less visibly in popular political culture than had the earlier Watergate scandal. Oliver North destroyed so many documents and left so many false paper trails that even congressional investigators struggled to compile a simple narrative of his activities. In contrast to Richard Nixon, Ronald Reagan stepped forward and testified, through a deposition, asserting he could not recall any details about either the release of hostages or the funding of the *contras*. His management and oversight skills might deserve criticism, Reagan admitted, but he had never intended to break any laws or presidential promise. Vice President George H. W. Bush, whom a special independent prosecutor personally considered linked to some of North's machinations, also claimed ignorance.

Unable to uncover evidence directly implicating the president or vice president, federal prosecutors pursued others. They secured felony convictions, for offenses that included falsifying documents and lying to Congress, against North and several others in Reagan's administration, but appellate courts later overturned these verdicts on procedural grounds. Finally, in 1992, just a few days before the end of his presidency, George H. W. Bush would pardon six former Reagan-era officials connected to the Iran-*contra* controversy.

The Beginning of the End of the Cold War

After beginning with a renewal of Cold War confrontations, Reagan's presidency ended with a sudden thaw in U.S.–Soviet relations. The economic cost of superpower rivalry was burdening both nations. Moreover, political change swept the Soviet Union and eliminated reasons for continued confrontation.

Mikhail Gorbachev, who became general secretary of the Communist Party in 1985, promised a new style of Soviet leadership. He understood that his isolated country faced economic stagnation and environmental problems brought on by decades of poorly planned industrial development. To redirect his nation's course, he withdrew Soviet troops from Afghanistan, reduced economic commitments to Cuba and Nicaragua, proclaimed a policy of **glasnost** ("openness"), and began to implement **perestroika** ("economic liberalization") at home. Recognizing Gorbachev as a Soviet leader with whom he could deal, Reagan seemed reenergized and worked diligently to forge good relations with the person whom U.S. media often called "Gorby."

Gorbachev's policies gained him acclaim throughout the West. Summit meetings with the United States yielded breakthroughs in arms control. At Reykjavik, Iceland, in October 1986, President Reagan shocked both Gorbachev and his own advisers by proposing a wholesale ban on nuclear weapons. Although negotiations at Reykjavik stumbled over Soviet insistence that the United States abandon SDI, Gorbachev later dropped that condition. Finally, in December 1987, Reagan and Gorbachev signed a major arms treaty that reduced each nation's supply of intermediate-range missiles and allowed for on-site verification, which the Soviets had never before permitted. The next year, Gorbachev scrapped the policy that forbade nations under Soviet influence from renouncing communism. In effect, he declared an end to the Cold War. Within the next few years, the Soviet sphere of influence—and the Soviet Union itself—would cease to exist. Ronald Reagan's final presidential triumph, according to his admirers, was leading the United States to victory in the Cold War.

Reagan's personal imprint on the 1980s, the "Reagan era," has emerged as a mixed one. Even before Reagan sought the presidency and through much of his time in Washington, many people seemed to judge him, apart from his role as "the great communicator," in light of the rather low expectations he had long engendered. Many early accounts of his administration generally adopted an even harsher frame. Most described a remarkably passive, often detached president—the kind of chief executive Reagan admitted to having been while some of his national security advisers were hatching the Iran-*contra* scheme.

After the mid-1990s, as the effects of Alzheimer's kept Reagan out of the public eye, however, other memoirists and biographers offered a more laudatory view. In addition to painting portraits of a public leader who could inspire by personal example, their works expanded on Reagan's own Farewell Address. When leaving office in 1989, Reagan had judged his two greatest accomplishments to have been "economic recovery" and "the recovery of our morale. America is respected again in the world and looked to for leadership."

The First Bush Presidency (1989–1993)

Focus Question
What forces and events contributed to the end of the Cold War? How did the Cold War's end affect U.S. foreign policy?

The Reagan presidency, particularly its initatives in foreign policy, boosted the 1988 presidential prospects of Reagan's heir-apparent, his own vice president, George Herbert Walker Bush. Bush easily secured the Republican nomination.

The Election of 1988

Born into a wealthy Republican family and educated at Yale, Bush had prospered in the Texas oil business, adopted Houston as his home, served in the U.S. House of Representatives, and headed the CIA. To court the New Right, which was decidedly lukewarm to his candidacy, Bush chose Senator J. Danforth (Dan) Quayle, a youthful conservative from Indiana who vaguely resembled the movie star Robert Redford, as a running mate. Quayle, already considered a better golfer than a legislator by most Senate colleagues, quickly acquired a reputation, especially among comedians who specialized in political humor, for off-the-wall comments about issues whose nuances and contexts he apparently failed to grasp.

Governor Michael Dukakis of Massachusetts emerged as the Democratic presidential candidate. After reevaluating Walter Mondale's disastrous effort of 1984 and crediting early polls showing him defeating Bush, Dukakis avoided talk of new domestic programs and higher taxes. Apparently short on larger ideas of any kind, Dukakis engendered little enthusiasm when promising to bring competence and honesty to a White House recently marked by the Iran-*contra* affair. Later, Dukakis seemed genuinely adrift when the GOP launched a series of negative attacks, reminiscent of the infamous LBJ daisy ad of 1964, on his character and gubernatorial record.

Bush emerged the winner, but Democrats retained control of both houses of Congress. Exit polls suggested that neither Bush nor Dukakis thrilled large numbers of potential voters, and the turnout recorded in November seemed to confirm this. It was the lowest, percentage wise, for any national election since 1924.

Once in the White House, Bush began losing crucial support. He angered many New Right Republicans by agreeing to an increase in the minimum wage and by failing to veto a seemingly noncontroversial civil-rights measure, which critics from the New Right charged with establishing "quotas" for the "preferential hiring" of women and people of color. Most importantly, Bush broke a pledge, "no new taxes," on which most conservatives had come to judge his worthiness as Reagan's successor. After the White House and congressional Democrats agreed to an "upward revision" in tax rates, in hopes of dealing with the still-rising federal deficit, activists on the New Right bitterly denounced this accord as one that raised taxes by another name.

Meanwhile, the Democratic-controlled Congress and the Republican-occupied White House deadlocked over how to address several key domestic issues. These included reorganization of the health care and the social-welfare systems. Worse for the president's political future, the economic growth of the Reagan years began to slow, while the budget deficit continued to grow. George H. W. Bush's chances for a second term seemed to depend on his record in foreign, rather than domestic, policy.

The End of the Cold War

During the first Bush presidency, communist states began toppling as if dominoes. In 1989, Poland's anticommunist labor movement, Solidarity, sparked the ouster of the pro-Soviet regime. The pro-Moscow government in East Germany fell in November 1989, and both West and East Germans hacked down the Berlin Wall and, then, began the difficult process of building a reunified Germany. Popular movements similarly forced out communist governments throughout Eastern Europe. Yugoslavia quickly disintegrated, and warfare ensued as rival ethnic groups re-created separate states in Slovenia, Serbia, Bosnia, and Croatia. In the Baltic region, Latvia, Lithuania, and Estonia, all of which had been under Soviet control since the Second World War, declared their independence.

Most dramatically, the major provinces that had anchored the Soviet Union assumed self-government. The president of the new state of Russia, Boris Yeltsin, put down a coup by hard-line communists in August 1991, and he soon solidified his political position. In December 1991, Yeltsin brokered a plan to abolish the Soviet Union and to replace it with 11 separate republics, loosely joined in a commonwealth arrangement. **(See Map 30.2, Collapse of the Soviet Bloc, in the color insert following page 1248.)**

In response, the Bush administration set about redefining U.S. national security in a post–Cold War era. The collapse of the Soviet Union weakened support for the leftist insurgencies in Central America that had so worried many members of the Reagan administration. Nicaraguans voted out the *Sandinistas*, who became just another faction, rather than a revolutionary movement, in a multiparty political system. The Pentagon pondered

Berlin Wall, 1989   Berliners celebrated the end of the Cold War by chiseling away at the Berlin Wall, which the communist East German state had erected in 1962 to prevent the flow of refugees to West Berlin. Pieces of the Berlin Wall became coveted symbols of the fall of communism.

new military missions, imagining rapid, sharply targeted strikes by specially trained forces rather than lengthy, conventional campaigns. The U.S. armed forces might even serve in the "war against drugs," an effort that George H. W. Bush had suggested during his 1988 presidential campaign.

Fighting the drug menace provided a major justification for toppling General Manuel Noriega, the dictatorial president of Panama. Long suspected of being deeply involved in the drug trade, Noriega had continued ruling Panama despite a U.S. indictment against him for international narcotics trafficking, secured earlier by the Reagan administration.

Confronting Noriega posed a potentially embarrassing problem for the Bush administration. The anticommunist general had been recruited as a CIA "asset" during the mid-1970s, when Bush had headed the Agency. Nevertheless, the White House decided the United States needed a friendly, stable, and more competent government in Panama when it completed the transfer of the Panama Canal to Panamanian sovereignty in 2000. Bush decided to topple the mercurial Noriega in "Operation Just Cause." Broadcast live on television, U.S. Marines landed in Panama in December 1989, and they laid siege to the president's headquarters, surrounding it with U.S. troops and round-the-clock ear-splitting rock music. Noriega soon surrendered, faced successful extradition to Florida, and went to prison after a 1992 conviction for trafficking in cocaine.

The Panamanian operation carried major implications. Unilaterally deposing the leader of a foreign government by U.S. military action seemingly raised thorny questions of international law, but this effort, which involved 25,000 U.S. troops and few casualties, provided a new model for post–Cold War strategy. The Pentagon firmed up its plans for creating highly mobile, rapid deployment forces that could undertake similar missions. A partial test of its new strategy came during the Persian Gulf War of 1991.

The Persian Gulf War

On August 2, 1990, Iraq's dictator Saddam Hussein ordered his troops to occupy the neighboring oil-rich emirate of Kuwait. Having been caught off guard about Kuwait, U.S. intelligence analysts now warned that Iraq's next target might be Saudi Arabia, the largest oil exporter in the Middle East and a longtime U.S. ally.

Moving swiftly, President George H. W. Bush orchestrated a multilateral, international response. Four days after Iraq's invasion of Kuwait, he launched "Operation Desert Shield" by sending several hundred thousand U.S. troops to Saudi Arabia. Bush convinced the Saudi government, with which he enjoyed close personal ties, to set aside concerns among some Islamic fundamentalists, including a wealthy businessman named Osama bin Laden, about allowing Western troops on sacred Islamic soil. Saudi Arabia's ruling family finally decided it feared Saddam Hussein more than the Islamic outcry against a U.S. military presence. After consulting with European leaders, Bush approached the UN, which denounced Iraqi aggression, ordered economic sanctions against Iraq, and authorized the United States to lead an international force to Kuwait if Saddam Hussein's troops did not immediately withdraw.

Following the advice of his military strategists, particularly General Colin Powell, Bush then assembled a massive coalition force. Ultimately, it included nearly 500,000 troops from the United States and some 200,000 from other countries. Bush claimed a moral obligation to rescue Kuwait, but his policy makers also spoke frankly about the economic threat that Hussein's aggression posed for the oil-dependent economies of the United States and its allies. These arguments persuaded Congress, after heated debate in the Senate, to approve a resolution backing the use of force.

In mid-January 1991, coalition planes attacked Iraqi targets. After a relatively brief but devastating aerial bombardment, General Norman Schwarzkopf directed a February ground offensive against Iraqi forces. Coalition troops, enjoying air supremacy, decimated Saddam Hussein's armies in a matter of days. U.S. casualties were relatively light (148 deaths in battle). Estimates of Iraqi military casualties, in stark contrast, ranged from 25,000 to 100,000 deaths. Although the entire conflict had lasted scarcely six weeks, it took an enormous toll on highways, bridges, communications, and other infrastructure facilities in both Iraq and Kuwait.

In a decision that aroused dissent from neoconservatives within his own administration, Bush stopped short of ousting Saddam Hussein. The UN had never approved such a step, and U.S. military planners worried about being able to control a post-Saddam Iraq. Instead, the Bush administration, backed by the UN, maintained its economic pressure against Saddam Hussein's regime and ordered the dismantling of its programs for nuclear and biological warfare. In addition, U.S. planes enforced "no-fly" zones over northern and southern Iraq to help protect the Kurds and, less successfully, Shi'a Muslims from continued persecution by Saddam Hussein. The Persian Gulf War temporarily boosted George H. W. Bush's popularity.

Bush's direction of economic foreign policy, although less visible than his leadership during the Iraq war, became of considerable importance. The president pressed, for instance, measures that would assist international economic integration. During the mid-1980s, huge debts owed by Third World nations to U.S. institutions had threatened the international banking system, but most of these obligations had been renegotiated by the early 1990s. Market-based economies, which replaced centrally planned ones, began to emerge in the former communist states; Western Europe moved toward economic integration; and most nations of the Pacific Rim experienced steady economic growth. The president supported (but could not obtain congressional passage of) a North American Free Trade Agreement (NAFTA), which proposed eliminating tariff barriers and joining Canada, the United States, and Mexico together in the largest free-market zone in the world.

When Bush ran for reelection in 1992, however, most potential voters judged even his administration's record on foreign affairs as something of a muddle. The White House had organized an international coalition against Iraq, constructively assisted post–Cold War Russia and Eastern Europe, and embraced global economic integration. On other issues, though, the Bush administration seemed less decisive. The United States remained on the sidelines as full-scale warfare erupted among the states of the former Yugoslavia, with Serbs launching a brutal campaign of territorial aggrandizement and "ethnic cleansing" against Bosnian Muslims. In Africa, after a severe famine wracked Somalia, Bush ordered U.S. troops to secure supply lines for humanitarian aid, but popular opinion in the United States remained wary of this mission in a country without a stable government. After the longtime goal of containing the Soviet Union became irrelevant, George H. W. Bush never succeeded in effectively articulating a new overall vision to guide policy.

The Election of 1992

The inability to portray coherence in either his domestic or foreign policies threatened Bush's reelection. In response, the White House made a series of concessions to the New Right. Vice President Dan Quayle, although clearly a political liability outside of his conservative constituency, returned as Bush's running mate. The president allowed New Right activists, who talked about "a religious war" against Democrats for "the soul of America" and on behalf of "family values," to dominate the 1992 Republican national convention. Conservative Democrats and independents, who had supported Ronald Reagan and Bush in the previous three presidential elections, found the rhetoric of the GOP convention somewhat unsettling.

Bush's Democratic challenger, Governor **William Jefferson ("Bill") Clinton** of Arkansas, stressed economic issues and images of his relative youth. Calling himself a "New Democrat," one who promised fewer governmental programs than had Walter Mondale and who offered more pizzazz than had Michael Dukakis, Bill Clinton promised to create new jobs, reduce the federal deficit, and restructure the nation's health-care system. Sometimes sounding as if he were running as a Republican, Clinton also pledged to shrink the size of government and to "end this [welfare] system as we know it." "People who can work ought to go to work, and no one should be able to stay on welfare forever," he insisted. Rhetoric of this kind frustrated Bush's attempts to label Clinton as a proponent of "big government."

The Democratic focus on the economy also helped deflect attention from sociocultural matters, including rumors of extramarital affairs, on which Clinton seemed vulnerable. As a college student, he had avoided service in Vietnam and, while in England as a Rhodes scholar, had participated in antiwar demonstrations. When Bush, a decorated veteran of the Second World War, challenged the patriotism of his Democratic challenger, Clinton countered by emphasizing, rather than repudiating, his roots in the 1960s. He appeared on MTV, which was promoting a "rock-the-vote" effort aimed at its relatively young audience, and talked about his devotion to (relatively soft) rock music. In addition, he chose Senator Albert Gore of Tennessee, a Vietnam veteran, as his running mate.

The 1992 election brought Clinton a surprisingly easy victory. The self-financed presidential campaign of Ross Perot—a Texas billionaire who spent more than $60 million on a third-party run that emphasized the federal deficit and the necessity for fiscal prudence—probably hurt Bush more than Clinton. With Perot in the race, Clinton garnered only 43 percent of the popular vote but won 370 electoral votes by carrying 32 states and the District of Columbia. Bush gained a majority only among white Protestants in the South. In contrast, Clinton carried the Jewish, African American, and Latino vote by large margins and even gained a plurality among people who had served in the Vietnam War. He also ran well among independents who had supported Reagan and Bush during the 1980s. Perhaps most surprising, about 55 percent of eligible voters went to the polls in 1992, a turnout that reversed 32 years of steady decline in voter participation.

Movement Activism

Focus Question
How did social movements of the post-1960s era affect social life, culture, and the ways people saw their own personal identities during the 1970s and 1980s?

Popular memory often recalls the years between the 1974 resignation of Richard Nixon and the 1992 election of Bill Clinton as ones when social movements of the kind generally associated with the 1960s faded away, sometimes in spasms of self-destructive violence. A few small fringe groups, such as the "Weather Underground" and the "Symbionese Liberation Army" (SLA), did embrace fantasies of revolutionary liberation. The SLA, for instance, briefly made headlines in 1974 by kidnapping Patricia Hearst, the daughter of a wealthy San Francisco newspaper publisher, and committing, sometimes with Hearst's participation, a string of robberies, bombings, and shootings. By the 1980s, the only sociocultural activists still hard at work, from this perspective, toiled for the New Right or for nostalgic and marginal efforts that only vaguely recalled the halcyon days of the 1960s.

Popular pundits constantly looked for symbols of how the 1960s had given way to very different eras, the 1970s and the 1980s. In one popular formulation, the emphasis on social transformation and political empowerment, particularly among people who found well-paying employment, had devolved into a focus on transforming and empowering one's own mind and body. The 1970s, in this view, became the "Me Decade." Extending this story, other observers talked about the "hippies" and "Yippies" of the 1960s morphing, by the mid-1980s, into "Young Upwardly mobile Professionals," or "Yuppies." Self-absorbed, Yuppies supposedly cared little about social values and a great deal about their personal consumption habits.

Recent historical and sociological studies, however, have come to place greater emphasis on the continuation of the kinds of social activism associated with the 1960s. Take, for example, the labor movement. Although contemporary media accounts during the 1970s and early 1980s generally stressed Republican efforts to peel blue-collar workers away from the Democratic Party, the 1960s had spawned a new militancy, particularly among younger workers. As the number of labor strikes reached a postwar high, between 1968 and 1974, dissidents among the rank-and-file also looked askance at their own unions. A number of movements sought to bring the spirit of participatory democracy into union politics.

Grassroots activism would remain a feature of the larger union movement, but the nationwide economic problems of the later 1970s and 1980s eventually acted as a powerful damper on this kind of pressure from below. Ronald Reagan's action against striking air traffic control workers portended aggressive antiunion strategies that both his administration and business interests would pursue during the 1980s. The percentage of unionized workers, by the end of Reagan's presidency, fell to just 16 percent. Seeing the balance of power tilting against them, workers increasingly turned away from strikes as an economic weapon.

Other grassroots movements, however, became more firmly embedded in the daily life of the post-1960s United States. The proliferation of locally based activism, often focused on particular neighborhood-related projects, such as safer streets and cleaner parks, prompted one historian to see a "backyard revolution" taking place during the 1970s and 1980s. Even the U.S. Congress, hardly an institution inclined to fund domestic revolutions, recognized the value of locally based activism and created, in 1978, the National Consumer Cooperative Bank. Legislators charged it with providing loans to support grassroots, cooperative enterprises. Many other public initiatives displayed the influence of activists who represented a constituency or goal that had first become visible during the era of America's longest war, the 1960s.

Mass demonstrations, reminiscent of earlier ones against U.S. policies in Vietnam, remained a feature of the post-1960s movement environment. Both antiabortion and pro-choice forces, for example, regularly demonstrated in Washington, D.C., and in local communities. During the 1980s, the Clamshell Alliance movement conducted a campaign of civil disobedience against a nuclear reactor being built in Seabrook, New Hampshire, and a coalition of West Coast activists waged a lengthy, unsuccessful struggle to close the University of California's Lawrence Livermore National Laboratory, a site for developing nuclear weapons. In nearly every major city and many smaller towns, women's groups staged "Take Back the Night" rallies to call attention to the danger of sexual assaults.

National media, especially network television, however, tended to ignore demonstrations that lacked prominent celebrities or violent conflict. In 1991, for example, 30,000 Korean Americans staged a march for racial peace in Los Angeles. Although it was the largest demonstration ever conducted by any Asian American group, even most local media failed to give it any significant attention. Only C-Span, the niche TV network devoted to public-affairs programming, seemed committed to covering demonstrations intended to dramatize social and political issues.

Women's Issues

In this environment, women's groups adopted a range of methods to rally new supporters and reenergize their core constituencies. Struggles over gender-related issues had emerged within the labor, civil-rights, and antiwar movements of the 1960s. Initially, many of the men involved in these causes complained that issues of gender equality interfered with broader fights to redirect labor, racial, or foreign policies. Women from these movements invariably insisted, though, on calling attention to gender politics, including their own second-class status, in movements that claimed to be egalitarian.

Throughout the 1970s, women continued to promote "consciousness-raising" sessions. These intense personal discussions helped participants consider how *political* empowerment for women often seemed inseparable from *personal* power relationships. The popularity of the birth control pill, for example, allowed greater control over reproductive choices but also complicated the meaning of "sexual freedom." Consciousness-raising also tackled personal-political issues such as sexual preferences, household work routines, child-rearing responsibilities, and economic independence. "The personal is political" became a watchword for many women, especially those who called themselves "feminists."

Although many women kept their distance from overtly feminist organizations, the number of movements addressing issues of concern to women continued to expand during the post-1960s era. The National Organization for Women (NOW), founded in 1966, remained identified with the rights-based agenda of the mainstream of the Democratic Party and the Supreme Court justices who had produced decisions such as *Roe* v. *Wade* of 1973. African American women began forming separate organizations, which emphasized issues of cultural and racial identity. Similarly, Chicana groups coalesced within and alongside most Mexican American organizations. Lesbians also organized their own groups, often allying with an emerging gay rights movement. Organizations in the United States also joined with groups in other nations on behalf of international women's rights.

If particular agendas inevitably varied along lines of race, ethnicity, religion, and economic circumstance, women with differing perspectives also worked together to build new institutions and networks. Their efforts included battered-women's shelters, health and birthing clinics specializing in women's medicine, rape crisis centers, economic development counseling for women-owned businesses, union-organizing efforts led by and directed toward women, organizations of women in specific businesses or professions, women and gender studies programs in colleges and universities, and academic journals and popular magazines devoted to women's issues. Organized pressure for gender equity also affected existing institutions. Country clubs and service organizations began admitting women members. Many Protestant denominations came to accept women into the ministry, and Reform Judaism placed women in its pulpits.

Efforts at empowering women to gain economic self-sufficiency proved an important common concern. By 1990, only about 15 percent of all U.S. households consisted of a fully employed husband and a mother who only worked on tending to home and children. Around twice that percentage consisted of two parents who drew paychecks. Moreover, as the number of single women, including ones heading families, increased, reliance on a male breadwinner, as both ideal and practice, became less viable than ever before. Women wanted—and needed—to find employment that would allow them to support themselves or a family, or to provide additional purchasing power for a multi-income household. The steadily growing number of women entering the paid-labor market helped account for the impressive job-creation statistics of the 1980s.

The labor market these women entered, however, remained laced with inequalities. The average income for women employed full-time continued to lag behind that for men: women earning around 75 cents, in 1990, for every dollar taken home by men. Although this gap largely closed when comparison involved men and women with similar credentials, the overall differential suggested persistent structural inequalities, in educational opportunities and at the entry points to the labor market, that prevented many women from earning a family wage. In addition, professional and business women complained of informal "glass ceilings," gender-based barriers that effectively limited their chances for advancement. And any woman with small children who worked outside her home immediately confronted the two persistent problems of locating and paying for adequate child-care facilities.

The gender gap in pay contributed to another trend—a "feminization of poverty." Homeless shelters, which once catered almost exclusively to single men, began taking in women and children. Women who relied on governmental assistance faced declining prospects. Increases in AFDC payments and expansion of the food stamp program had helped sustain single mothers with children during the 1960s, but economic dislocations of the 1970s and political trends of the 1980s undercut the value, measured in constant dollars, of governmental benefits such as AFDC. Proposals for reshaping the pattern of governmental support through welfare reform, after the failure of Nixon's FAP initiative, generally focused on how to limit direct governmental payment. They also emphasized moving women, even those with young children, into the paid labor force.

Sexual harassment on the job became another highly visible political issue. Most women's groups pressed government and private employers to curtail sexually charged behaviors, which they saw primarily as moves aimed at demeaning women and at further empowering male supervisors and coworkers. The Supreme Court finally ruled in a 1986 decision that sexual harassment constituted a form of discrimination under the Civil Rights Act of 1964.

Several years later, differences over this issue gained national attention when Anita Hill, an African American law professor, testified during 1992 U.S. Senate hearings on the nomination of Clarence Thomas, another African American, to the U.S. Supreme Court. Hill accused Thomas of having sexually harassed her when both had worked in the Reagan administration. Noting how rarely sexual harassment became a public issue, some observers wondered if male senators would have even listened to Hill had Thomas not been otherwise a controversial nominee. Supporters of Thomas, in turn, criticized Hill for being overly sensitive or, perhaps, a "scorned and jealous" woman. In response, feminists denounced the all-male senate judiciary committee for failing even to understand, let alone investigate seriously, the issue of sexual harassment. Although the Senate narrowly approved Thomas for the High Court, political observers credited Hill's testimony with helping women's groups mobilize female voters and with electing four women as U.S. senators in the 1992 elections.

Sexual harassment also became a controversial issue within the U.S. military, which began to recruit women more actively. The service academies accepted female cadets, and women found places within the military hierarchy. Soon, however, revelations about harassment and even sexual assaults against female naval officers by male comrades soon surfaced. Attempts by Navy officials to cover up sexual harassment during the 1991 "Tailhook" convention provoked outrage, and several high-ranking officers were forced to step down.

Sexual Politics

Movements pressing issues involving gays and lesbians also became more public and political as the 1960s turned into the 1970s. In 1969, New York City police raided the Stonewall Inn, an unlicensed bar in Greenwich Village with a largely homosexual clientele. Seeing the liquor license issue as simply a pretext for harassing patrons of the Stonewall, a group of gay and transgendered people in the bar resisted arrest. The resultant confrontation spilled over into the neighborhood and pitted local activists, who viewed themselves as recurring targets for police harassment, against law enforcement officials.

Historians of sexuality have come to criticize what they call "the Stonewall Narrative," a story in which an event at a single Greenwich Village bar ignited what would become known as the Lesbian-Gay-Bisexual-Transgendered (LGBT) movement. Recent studies emphasize that LGBT activism did not suddenly emerge in 1969 but, instead, grew out of earlier movements, such as the Mattachine Society, and cultural communities, including those of the Beats (see chapter 29). Two years before Stonewall, for example, the ACLU reversed its previous stance and declared that legal guarantees of equality prevented authorities from singling out same-sex behaviors as objects for criminal prosecution.

Still, the 1969 events at the Stonewall Inn, because of the prominence they received in mainstream and alternative media, marked an important benchmark in the history of sexual politics. Gay and lesbian activism, though neither nonexistent nor entirely invisible earlier, became an important part of the larger "movement of movements" that continued during the 1970s and 1980s. A number of advocacy and support groups, such as New York City's Gay Activist Alliance (GAA), sprang up. As many individuals "came out of the closet," newspapers, theaters, nightspots, and religious groups proudly identified themselves as activists. LGBT communities emerged, particularly in larger cities, helping to create, and also benefiting from, the general relaxation of legal and cultural controls over the portrayal and the more open practice of a wide range of sexual choices. Activists demanded that law enforcement officials treat attacks against people identifying themselves with an LGBT agenda no less seriously than ones against all other citizens. They also asserted constitutional claims to equal access to housing, jobs, and fringe benefits for partners.

The results of these efforts initially disappointed LGBT activists. In some locales, counter-activism from movements associated with the New Right resulted in battles over the fate of so-called gay rights ordinances. Gradually, during the 1980s, a few states—beginning with Wisconsin and Massachusetts—began enacting statewide antidiscrimination laws. Results at the federal level proved less encouraging to LGBT advocates. Although the EEOC extended the reach of civil-rights laws mandating equality to other "minorities," it refused to do so in response to complaints from LGBT groups. It did not, for example, hold that the refusal to grant spousal benefits between heterosexuals to gays and lesbians violated federal law.

Moreover, in *Bowers* v. *Hardwick* (1986), a divided Supreme Court upheld a Georgia law that made it a crime to engage in sodomy. The majority stressed the lack of any specific mention of sexual liberty in the U.S. Constitution and the long tradition of such measures. LGBT activists took some solace from the recognition that many states had repealed anti-sodomy statutes, that law enforcement officials in other states rarely enforced them, and that opinion polls suggested a majority opposed the sociocultural premises of the *Bowers* decision. (Indeed, in 2003, another divided U.S. Supreme Court would cast aside *Bowers* and declare that state laws criminalizing sodomy violated the Constitution.)

LGBT communities, in contrast, found less comfort when confronting another issue, one with international implications. During the 1970s, public health officials began seeing an apparently new, highly contagious human immunodeficiency virus (HIV). It produced an acquired immunodeficiency syndrome (AIDS), which could become a fatal disease for which medical science offered virtually nothing in the way of cure or treatment. The virus could be transmitted through the careless use of intravenous drugs, tainted blood supplies, and unprotected sexual intercourse. At first, the incidence of **HIV-AIDS** in the United States appeared primarily limited to gay men, and some spokespeople for the New Religious Right viewed HIV-AIDS as a divine judgment against homosexuals. LGBT activists charged

Aids "ACT-UP" Campaign   Health-care issues increasingly galvanized grassroots activists in the late 20th century. In 1989, members of ACT-UP, a group that embraced direct action, protested what they saw as the federal government's inattention to the issue of AIDS during the 1980s.

that the Reagan administration's support from cultural and religious conservatives inclined it to place a low priority on funding efforts to understand the causes of HIV-AIDS, check its spread, or devise viable medical responses.

The AIDS controversy galvanized empowerment efforts among LGBT organizations, such as the "Aids Coalition to Unleash Power" (ACT-UP). Non-LGBT groups joined the effort. Within a relatively short time, new research projects took shape. With the development of prevention programs and drugs that could combat HIV-AIDS, most public figures came to support new efforts both at home and overseas, particularly in Africa, to address HIV-AIDS. Still, it remained a modern scourge that threatened economic advancement and social stability in many parts of the world, but its specific identification with LGBT rights faded.

Race, Ethnicity, and Social Activism

Use of specific group identity as a fulcrum for wider social activism became especially strong within racial and ethnic communities. Building on the model of Black Power activism during the 1960s, groups emphasized pride in their distinctive traditions and insisted cultural differences should be affirmed rather than ignored or merely tolerated. The influx of new immigrants from Third World areas helped focus additional attention on social movements that addressed the question of "multiculturalism."

Activism Among African Americans

African American activists had developed a strong sense of cultural identity during the civil rights and Black Power struggles of the 1960s (see chapters 28 and 29), and activism during the following decades continued to stress pride in African American cultural life. The emphasis on racial pride, for example, showed in Spike Lee's film *Malcolm X* (1991), in rap and hip-hop music, and among educators who advocated an "Afrocentric" curriculum. The Black Entertainment Television network (BET) aimed its programming specifically to African American viewers, attracting a broader audience in the process.

Academics such as Henry Lewis Gates, Jr., who became head of Harvard's Afro-American Studies Department in 1991, sought to integrate study of the black culture into wider frames. In the view championed by Gates and other black scholars, cultural works produced by African Americans should not be seen as "a thing apart, separate from the whole, having no influence on the shape and shaping of American culture." Gates praised African American authors, such as Toni Morrison (who would win the Nobel Prize for Literature in 1993) and Alice Walker, as writers who took "the blackness of the culture for granted" and used this as "a springboard to write about those human emotions that we share with everyone else." The cultural works of African Americans, in short, could simultaneously be seen as unique and different, *and also* be viewed in relationship to broader cultural traditions.

Issues of equal treatment, especially in the legal and criminal justice systems, remained an important part of the agenda for African American activists. Repeated studies suggested, for instance, that police detained African Americans as criminal suspects and stopped black motorists far more often than members of any other ethnic group. Criminologists called this practice **"racial profiling,"** while activists talked about being arrested for a DWB, "driving while black." (In Hispanic communities, DWB came to stand for "driving while brown.") Profiling seemed a reminder, both symbolic and real, of the days of legally sanctioned discrimination and suggested the difficulty of translating formal guarantees of equality into practice.

In addition, differences in the sentencing patterns for convicted felons raised a broader concern. Courts imposed harsher sentences for crimes, for instance, involving crack cocaine, a drug consumed in some African American neighborhoods, than for those involving the more expensive, illegal coca-based products favored by white and suburban drug abusers. Statistical evidence also indicated that African American men in their late twenties were about 10 times more likely than their white counterparts to be imprisoned. Similar statistics showed African Americans who had been convicted of potential capital crimes were far more likely to receive the death penalty than were prison inmates from other ethnic and racial backgrounds.

Other practices viewed as symbolizing the institutionalized racism of the past became the target of activist movements. At the beginning of the 1990s, for instance, the battle flag of the Confederate States of America still flew over public buildings and institutions throughout much of the South. Groups that defended this practice insisted it honored the people who had supported the southern cause during the mid-19th century and said nothing about the system of chattel slavery. Critics, including many African American organizations, wondered how the Confederate cause could ever be separated from the defense of slavery and noted the more recent use of the Confederate flag to symbolize resistance to the civil-rights movement. Was officially displaying the Flag of the Old Confederacy, constitutional lawyers asked, a kind of expression akin to sexual harassment, or was it the sort of symbolic political speech that the First Amendment obviously protected?

African American activists increasingly saw the symbolic politics associated with Confederate flags closely related to efforts at greater empowerment within the country's major political institutions. Symbol and substance, in this view, went together. Beginning about 1970, when less than 1,500 African Americans held elective office in the United States, the number of African Americans in such positions began to increase dramatically. By 1992, there were more than 8,000. In 1970, 13 African American members of Congress established the **"Congressional Black Caucus" (CBC)** as a means of presenting a common front on a wide range of foreign and domestic issues. Picking up the mantle of A. Philip Randolph and Bayard Rustin's "Freedom Budget," the CBC would issue a hypothetical "Alternative Budget," which sought to redirect federal spending toward social initiatives. It also campaigned on behalf of better relations between the United States and African nations.

Activism Among American Indians

American Indians mounted activist movements along two broad fronts. Indians had long-standing identities based on their tribal affiliation, and many issues, particularly those involving land and treaty disputes, turned on specific, tribal-based claims. Other questions, which seemed to require strategies that extended beyond a single tribe or band, became identified as "pan-Indian" in nature.

American Indian activism had burst into the national media, in November 1969, when a group calling itself "Indians of All Tribes" began an extended occupation of the former federal prison on Alcatraz Island in San Francisco harbor. These activists, many of whom had attended colleges in the San Francisco Bay area, hoped to dramatize a history of broken treaty promises. This effort, which lasted for nearly two years, initially attracted extensive media attention.

Expanding on this direct-action tactic, the American Indian Movement (AIM), which had been created in 1968 by young activists from several Northern Plains tribes, adopted even more confrontational approaches. In 1973, they seized control of the small community of Wounded Knee, on South Dakota's Pine Ridge Reservation. This had been the site of a notorious 1890 massacre of Indian people by the U.S. Army, and 83 years later, members of AIM clashed with both federal officials and older American Indian leaders during a military-style standoff that finally ended after several months. In response, federal officials targeted members of AIM with illegal surveillance and a series of controversial criminal prosecutions. The most celebrated trial, which took place in St. Paul, Minnesota, ended after a federal judge dismissed all charges against two AIM members because of improper conduct by governmental officials.

Meanwhile, important social and legal changes had been taking place. A number of tribal Indian organizations, tapping federal funds first made available during the War on Poverty, began a process of empowerment from the grassroots. The U.S. Congress and the White House, pressured by Indian organizations and their supporters, moved to undo the termination and relocation policies of the 1950s. The multipart Civil Rights Act of 1968, for example, contained several sections that became known as the "Indian Bill of Rights." In these, Congress extended most provisions of the constitutional Bill of Rights to American Indians living on reservations, while reconfirming legitimacy of specifically tribal laws and powers.

Federal legislation and several Supreme Court decisions in the 1970s subsequently reinforced the constitutional principle of "tribal self-determination." In 1973, a campaign sparked by supporters of the Menominee tribe, which had been officially disbanded under

© Andre Jenny/The Image Works

Gaming at Potawatomi Casino   During the 1980s, casino style gaming began to emerge as one of the nation's leading entertainment enterprises. Native Americans embraced casinos, such as this one located near Milwaukee, Wisconsin, as important ways to generate jobs and capital on Indian reservations. The Potawatomi complex, which opened in 1991, now juxtaposes traditional style sculptures, an Indian heritage center and gift shop, an imaginatively designed building, more than 1000 slot machines, and a cabaret-style dinner theater patterned after ones in Las Vegas.

the termination policy, succeeded in getting Congress to begin the process of reversing the earlier action. Confirming tribal identification often required extensive legal activity. As litigation proceeded, the federal government came to officially recognize a steadily increasing number of separate tribes and bands.

Tapping the expertise of the Native American Rights Fund (NARF), tribes pressed demands that derived from treaties between tribes and the U.S. government. Some sought recognition of tribal land claims, which could often be traced back to treaty agreements that the U.S. officials had subsequently broken. Others dealt with fishing and agricultural rights. Some of these efforts provoked resistance and resentment among non-Indians, who argued that state and local laws that incidentally affected Indian tribes should not give way to special claims based on federal treaty authority and tribal self-determination. Courts invariably held these state and local laws in conflict with the U.S. Constitution, which established the supremacy of federal treaties. Indians also sued to protect tribal water rights and traditional religious ceremonies, some of which included the ritualistic use of drugs such as peyote. In 1990, responding to pressure from an activist coalition, Congress passed the Native American Graves Protection and Repatriation Act, which required universities and museums to return human remains and sacred objects to tribes who requested them.

Claiming exemption from state gaming laws, many American Indian tribes also began to cash in on self-determination. They opened bingo halls and, then, full-blown, Las Vegas–style gambling casinos. In 1988, the U.S. Supreme Court ruled that states lacked any power to prohibit gambling operations on tribal land, and Congress responded with the Indian Gaming Regulatory Act. As gambling began to emerge as one of the most lucrative sectors of the nation's entertainment business, Indian-owned casinos thrived, generating substantial employment and profit. Ironically, the glitzy, tribal-owned casinos often financed tribal powwows and other efforts to nurture older cultural practices.

To forestall the disappearance of native languages, American Indian movements emphasized the importance of bilingualism and gave renewed attention to tribal rituals. In a related initiative, a 1978 congressional measure provided federal funding for Indian-run educational institutions, which would build job skills and preserve tribal cultures. Indian activists, especially those from AIM, also denounced the use of stereotypical nicknames, such as "Chiefs" and "Redskins," and Indian-related logos in amateur and professional sports.

A steady and substantial increase in the nation's American Indian population provided perhaps the most tangible sign of the renewal of cultural pride: This surging growth rate came not from any increase in birth rates but from a dramatic rise in the number of people of Indian descent who, for the first time in their lives, sought enrollment with a tribe or band and identified themselves as American Indian on the U.S. Census form.

Activism in Spanish-Speaking Communities

Census data showed that the fastest-growing ethnic group in the United States spoke Spanish. Many Spanish-speaking people, especially in the Southwest, came to prefer the umbrella term "Latino," whereas others, particularly in Florida, favored "Hispanic." At the same time, people whom the U.S. Census began (in 1980) labeling "Hispanic" more frequently identified themselves according to the specific Spanish-speaking country or commonwealth from which they or their ancestors had immigrated. People who employed Spanish as their first language, often in the workplace and in their communities as well as at home, thus highlighted the diversity and complexity of identity.

Mexican Americans, members of the oldest and most numerous Spanish-speaking group, could tap a long tradition of political and social activism. The late 1960s saw an emerging spirit of **Chicanismo,** a populist-style pride in a heritage that could be traced back to the ancient civilizations of Middle America. Young activists made "Chicano/a," terms of derision that older Mexican Americans had generally avoided in the past, into symbolic affirmations of their particular heritage. "Crusade for Justice," an organization that first took root in Denver, Colorado, provided a model for other local movements that emphasized getting young people through school and training them for careers in business, education, and social activism. At the same time, many of these groups espoused a view of the past that stressed how, long before the arrival of the Spanish conquistadores and the subsequent incorporation of large parts of an independent Mexico into the United States, the ancestors of *chicanos* and *chicanas* of the 1960s had once controlled vast amounts of land and determined their own destiny. Some even began to talk about regaining control of parts of this territory, which they called *Aztlan.*

Other activists expressed more interest in future politics than old land claims. Beginning in the late 1960s, political and cultural visions of *Chicanismo* gained considerable influence in cities in the Southwest. Members of La Raza Unida, a movement founded in 1967, began to win local elections. At the same time, Mexican American communities experienced a cultural flowering. New Spanish-language newspapers and journals reinforced a growing sense of pride, and many churches sponsored festivals that featured ethnic dancing, mural painting, poetry, and literature. Mexican Americans successfully pushed for programs in Chicano/a Studies at colleges and universities.

The labor organizer Cesar Chavez gained wider media (and, later, historical) attention than any other Mexican American activist, but urban-based movements likely exerted a greater impact on far more people than Chavez's United Farm Workers union (UFW). Developments in San Antonio, Texas, a city with a large Mexican American population, suggested the potential fruits of grassroots political organizing. In the 1970s, Ernesto Cortes, Jr., took the lead in founding Communities Organized for Public Service (COPS), a group that brought the energy and talents of Mexican Americans, particularly women, out of specific neighborhoods and into the city's larger public arena for the first time. Mexican American activists worked with Anglo business leaders and with Democratic politicians such as Henry Cisneros, who became the city's mayor in 1981.

In addition, representatives from the older, political-legal movements, often feeling pressure from younger people who admired the energy of activists such as Cortes and Chavez, embraced new forms of activism. Established organizations such as LULAC, the American GI Forum, and the Mexican American Political Association (MAPA) began demanding that the EEOC take a more proactive approach to job-related issues. In 1967, a multimillion-dollar grant from the Ford Foundation facilitated creation of a Mexican American Legal Defense and Education Fund (MALDEF). This activist legal group gradually abandoned the "other white" due process litigation strategy, used during the 1940s and 1950s (see chapter 27), and began filing lawsuits that charged discrimination against Mexican-descended people, including the kind found in public schools, violated constitutional requirements of equality.

Over time, Mexican American activism became increasingly diverse. After some successes, the UFW confronted greater resistance from growers. It managed to survive, especially as a cultural presence centered on Caesar Chavez and his legacy, but could claim fewer and fewer organizing victories. MALDEF emerged as perhaps the most visible national group, one ready to lobby or litigate. At the local level, organizations formed on the model of COPS, such as United Neighborhood Organization (UNO) in Los Angeles, worked on community and citywide concerns. Mexican Americans, both women and men, often spearheaded urban-based labor-organizing efforts, particularly in the rapidly expanding service sector. Professional women could join organizations such as the National Network of Hispanic Women.

Social activism among Puerto Ricans in the United States emerged more slowly. Many stateside Puerto Ricans focused much of their political energy on the persistent "status"

Mural Art in Chicago   Themes in Mexican history and culture, inspired by the great Mexican muralists, appeared in Mexican American communities throughout the country.

question—that is, whether Puerto Rico should seek independence, strive for statehood, or retain a commonwealth connection to the mainland. New York City's Puerto Rican Day Parade became the city's largest ethnic celebration and an important focus of cultural pride. A 1976 report by the U.S. Commission on Civil Rights, however, concluded that Puerto Ricans remained "the last in line" for government-funded benefits and opportunity programs. In the 1980s, the Puerto Rican Legal Defense and Education Fund and allied groups helped Puerto Ricans surmount obstacles to the ballot box and to political office.

Cuban Americans who had begun arriving in southern Florida during the 1960s, fleeing from Fidel Castro's Cuba, quickly established an important local presence, particularly in Miami. The earliest arrivals generally enjoyed greater access to education and higher incomes than did most Latinos who came later, even from Cuba. This initial wave of Cuban immigrants also tended to be more politically conservative, generally voted Republican, and lobbied for a hard line toward Castro's communist government back in Cuba. This generation created institutions that, taken together, amounted to a government in exile, located in Miami. During the early 1990s, polls consistently revealed that as many as one-fifth of Cubans living in South Florida claimed they would immediately return to Havana once Castro left the scene. Other Cuban Americans, especially the generations born in the United States, became active in Florida politics and civic affairs. Some increasingly questioned their elders' persistent "exile mentality," which took much of its identity and spirit from anti-Castro activities.

Beneath a common Spanish language, then, lay great diversity in terms of economic status, national and cultural identification, political affiliation, and activist goals and organizations. Established communities that identified with Mexico, Puerto Rico, and Cuba developed a wide range of mobilizing and organizing styles.

Activism Among Asian Americans

Americans of Chinese, Japanese, Korean, Filipino, and other backgrounds began to create an Asian American movement. Organizations such as the Asian Pacific Planning Council (APPCON), founded in 1976, lobbied to obtain government funding for projects that benefited Asian American communities. The Asian Law Caucus, founded during the early 1970s by opponents of U.S. intervention in Vietnam, and the Committee against Anti-Asian Violence, created a decade later in response to a wave of racially motivated attacks, mobilized to fight a wide range of legal battles. During the 1970s, Asian American studies programs also took shape at colleges and universities on the West Coast. By the early 1980s, Asian American political activists enjoyed growing influence, especially within the Democratic Party, and began getting elected to public office.

Emphasizing a broad, Asian American identity, however, raised questions of inclusion, exclusion, and rivalry. Filipino American activists, members of the second largest Asian American group in the United States, according to the 1990 Census, often resisted the Asian American label because they believed that Chinese Americans or Japanese Americans dominated groups such as APPCON. Many people of Filipino descent focused on specific goals, particularly an effort to obtain citizenship and veteran's benefits for former soldiers of the Second World War who had fought against Japan in the Philippines. Japanese American groups also lobbied on behalf of specific issues, and in 1988, Congress formally apologized and voted to pay $20,000 in reparations to every living Japanese American who had been confined in internment camps during the Second World War. Similarly, Hmong and Vietnamese groups began pursuing special concerns, many of which stemmed back to the anticommunist ties that had connected the first generation of immigrants to the United States during the Vietnam War era.

Socioeconomic and cultural differences made it impossible to frame a single Asian American agenda. Although many groups showed remarkable upward educational and economic mobility during the late 1980s and early 1990s, for example, others such as Hmong immigrants and Chinese American garment workers struggled to find jobs that paid more than the minimum wage.

The Dilemmas of Antidiscrimination Efforts

How might governmental power best advance the cause of equality? Between the end of the Second World War and about the mid-1960s, antidiscrimination movements and the courts had demanded that the government not categorize individuals according to group identities based on race or ethnicity. On matters such as education, housing, or employment, the law must remain "color-blind" and treat people equally.

Gradually, however, new social-activist agendas envisioned that governmental power should do more than simply eliminate discriminatory barriers to *individual* opportunity. It should take **"affirmative action"** so that *groups* that had historically faced discrimination on the basis of their shared identity could begin to receive an equitable share of the nation's jobs, public spending, and educational programs. Affirmative action, supporters argued, would help compensate for past discrimination and for continued, perhaps hidden, prejudices that laws guaranteeing formal equality failed to reach.

Affirmative action sparked intense controversy. Some beneficiaries of compensatory programs complained that the derogatory label of "affirmative action applicant" tended, inevitably, to throw into question their individual talents and capabilities. More broadly, critics charged that programs to "set aside" jobs or openings in educational institutions for certain racial or ethnic groups smacked of "quotas" and thereby violated the principle of equality. Moreover, was not affirmative action *on behalf of* people in some groups inevitably also "reverse discrimination" *against* those in others? The claim of reverse discrimination became particularly emotional when members of one ethnic group, despite lower scores on aptitude or admissions exams, received preferences for employment or for entry into educational institutions. Supporters of these programs insisted that *any* process of selection would inevitably "affirm" some qualities, such as family or old school lineages, at the expense of others. Efforts at undoing years of discrimination, in this view, required complicated views of what counted as "equality."

The nation's courts struggled to square new affirmative action programs with older antidiscrimination precedents. They tended to strike down as unconstitutional affirmative action plans that contained inflexible quotas and to uphold less rigid ones that made group identity only one of several criteria for making hiring or educational decisions. In the controversial Supreme Court decision of 1978, popularly known as "the *Bakke* case," a majority of the High Court implicitly endorsed the importance of multiculturalism. Affirmative action programs in educational settings could gain constitutional legitimacy because they aimed at redressing past discrimination *and* because they promoted "diversity," a desirable quality that enriched any learning environment. Movements opposed to affirmative action efforts, strongest among people and groups within the broad New Right, redoubled their efforts, in the wake of *Bakke*, to curtail this practice through further litigation and legislative action.

On the local level, the Religious Right mobilized and organized to influence school boards. These activists charged educational bureaucrats from outside their communities with seeking to indoctrinate school children with what they considered anti-Biblical ideas such as feminism, multiculturalism, and evolution. Many rallied behind the ideas of "vouchers" and charter schools, both methods by which financing could be shifted from the public schools and directed toward private educational alternatives. On a wide range of issues, conservative activists wanted tax dollars to directly support the religious and cultural values held by their churches and families.

The New Right also opposed innovations associated with the 1960s in college curricula and in cultural life. It saw colleges contributing to "the closing of the American mind" (the title of a best-selling 1987 book by Allan Bloom) by exposing students only to what was trendy and "politically correct" (PC). Educational conservatives associated with the Reagan administration, most notably William Bennett and Lynn Cheney, warned about what they considered the debasement of intellectual life by trendy and shallow changes masked as innovations. The government-funded National Endowment for the Humanities (NEH) and the National Endowment for the Arts (NEA) came under the New Right's fire when they backed nontraditional projects.

The New Right continued to master the art of publicizing its positions. Well-funded conservative organizations sponsored academic conferences, popular gatherings, and radio and television programs. Pat Robertson, a lawyer turned evangelist, built a multimedia empire, including his popular *700 Club,* a TV program that adeptly merged evangelical religion with New Right politics. Conservative broadcasters such as Rush Limbaugh attracted significant audiences to the talk-radio genre. Not coincidently, Limbaugh's program became national in 1988, the year after the deregulation movement of the 1980s had led to the Federal Communications Commission (FCC) eliminating the "Fairness Doctrine," a rule requiring broadcasters to provide "equal" time for a diversity of viewpoints and opinions.

The New Right, much like other activist groups, hardly moved in lockstep. More traditional members of the New Right coalition, such as the journalist and sometime presidential candidate Patrick Buchanan, decried a new generation of neocons, such as William

Kristol, for hijacking and undermining the conservative movement. Buchanan and his followers denounced the free trade policies and the global military strategy that other conservatives promoted.

While remaining a coalition of disparate parts, the New Right became a powerful force in American life. It successfully challenged the once-dominant political agenda of the Democratic Party, propelled the mainstream of the Republican Party decidedly rightward, established a strong foothold in public-policy and media discussions, and succeeded in re-imagining the nation's cultural and informational landscape.

Conclusion

The "Reagan Revolution" of the 1980s rested on a conservative movement that had been taking shape since the 1950s. New Right Republicans distrusted extending federal government power, advocated sharp tax cuts, and stressed a sociocultural agenda emphasizing traditional values. The dozen years of Republican dominance of the White House, from 1980 to 1992, helped shift the terms of political debate in the United States. In foreign policy, Reagan's military buildup coincided with—and contributed to, according to his admirers—the last years of the Cold War.

Meanwhile, U.S. society seemed to fragment into specialized identifications. Social activism often organized around sexual, ethnic, and racial identities. Celebrants of multiculturalism generally welcomed this fragmentation, while others, especially on the New Right, worried about the nation becoming disunited into warring, even "alien" factions. The New Right's stress on limiting the power of government and promoting conservative social and cultural values increasingly set the terms for public debate, reconfiguring discussions about how government power could best promote liberty and equality.

SUGGESTED READINGS

For differing views of the political trends that came together during the 1980s, see **Garry Wills,** *Reagan's America: Innocents at Home* (rev. ed., 2000); **Burton J. Kaufman,** *The Presidency of James Earl Carter* (1993); **Douglas Brinkley,** *The Unfinished Presidency: Jimmy Carter's Journey to the Nobel Peace Prize* (1998); **John W. Sloan,** *The Reagan Effect: Economics and Presidential Leadership* (1999); **Frances Fitzgerald,** *Way Out There in the Blue: Reagan and Star Wars and the End of the Cold War* (2000); **Lisa McGirr,** *Suburban Warriors: The Origins of the New American Right* (2001); **John Schoenwald,** *A Time for Choosing: The Rise of Modern American Conservatism* (2001); **W. Carl Biven,** *Jimmy Carter's Economy: Policy in an Age of Limits* (2002); **W. Elliott Brownlee and Hugh Davis Graham,** eds., *The Reagan Presidency: Pragmatic Conservatism and Its Legacies* (2003); **Gil Troy,** *Morning in America: How Ronald Reagan Invented the 1980s* (2005); **John Ehrman,** *The Eighties: America in the Age of Reagan* (2005); **Richard Reeves,** *President Reagan: The Triumph of Imagination* (2005); and **Mark Bowden,** *Guests of the Ayatollah, The First Battle in America's War with Militant Islam* (2006). See also, **Bruce J. Schulman,** *The Seventies: The Great Shift in American Culture, Society, and Politics* (2001) and **James T. Patterson,** *Restless Giant: The United States from Watergate to Bush vs. Gore* (2005).

Suggestive studies relevant to themes of social and cultural activism include **Juan P. Garcia,** ed., *Mexican Americans in the 1990s* (1997); **John D'Emilio, William B. Turner, and Urvashi Vaid, eds.,** *Creating Change: Sexuality, Public Policy, and Civil Rights* (2000); **Ellen Messer-Davidow,** *Disciplining Feminism: From Social Action to Academic Discourse* (2002); **Frank Wu,** *Yellow: Race in America Beyond Black and White* (2002); **Larry Nesper,** *The Walleye War: The Struggle for Ojibwe Spearfishing and Treaty Rights* (2002); **Sara Evans,** *Tidal Wave: How Women Changed America at Century's End* (2003); **Van Gosse and Richard Moser, eds.,** *The World the 60s Made: Politics and Culture in Recent America* (2003); **David Carter,** *Stonewall: The Riots that Sparked the Gay Revolution* (2004); **Laura Pulido,** *Black, Brown, Yellow & Left: Radical Activism in Los Angeles* (2006); and **Andreas Hillen,** *1973 Nervous Breakdown: Watergate, Warhol, and the Birth of Post-Sixties America* (2006).

Visit the **Liberty Equality Power** Companion Web site for resources specific to this textbook: http://www.thomsonedu.com/history/murrin

Also find self-tests and additional resources at ThomsonNOW. ThomsonNOW is an integrated online suite of services and resources with proven ease of use and efficient paths to success, delivering the results you want—NOW!

www.thomsonedu.com/login/

Economic, Social, and Cultural Change in the Late 20th Century

The late 20th and the early 21st centuries brought sweeping changes to American life. A dramatic increase in immigration, along with movements of people throughout sprawling metropolitan areas and into states in the West and South, altered U.S. demographic patterns. The continuing transformation away from employment in the manufacturing sector of the economy changed the workplace for many Americans. A digital revolution transfigured systems of information in business and other areas of national life. A vast entertainment-informational complex, with an increasing emphasis on professional sports, also emerged. At the same time, religious life in America became more diverse, more devout, and more intertwined with the nation's politics.

A Changing People

Focus Question
What major demographic trends characterized the post-1970 United States? How did they contribute to changing daily life?

The demographic makeup of the United States changed significantly during the final three decades of the 20th century. The nation's people became older, more metropolitan, and more ethnically and racially diverse. Moreover, important centers of power continued shifting away from the Northeast and toward the South and West.

An Aging, Shifting Population

During the 1950s, the height of the Baby Boom, the population had grown by 1.8 percent per year; after 1970, even with new waves of immigration and longer life expectancies, the growth rate slowed to about 1 percent per year. Younger people generally delayed marriage until well into their 20s, most raised smaller families than had their parents, and more remained unmarried for much of their life. The number of households with at least one child under 18 continually shrank. In 1960, nearly 50 percent fell into this category; by 1999, only about one-third of U.S. households contained even one person under the age of 18. Consequently, by the mid-1980s, people in the 25-to-44 age range constituted a larger slice of the U.S. population than any other category, and the number of those between their teens and early twenties was relatively small.

CHRONOLOGY

1965	Congress passes Immigration Act of 1965
1980	Microsoft licenses its first personal computer software
1981	MTV and CNN debut
1985	Supreme Court rules that home taping of TV programs does not violate copyright law
1986	Immigration Reform and Control Act toughens laws against employing undocumented immigrants
1988	Fox television network debuts
1990	Immigration Act revises conditions for admittance • Census designates "Asian or Pacific Islanders" as single, pan-Asian category
1991	Catch-phrase "surfing the Internet" is coined
1993	Cesar Chavez dies • Number of Internet sites passes the 100,000 mark
1995	Dial-in Internet services begin
1996	Fox News Networks debuts
1997	First Harry Potter book published
1998	E-commerce begins in earnest • German Daimler buys out Chrysler Motors
1999	E-commerce and dot-com stocks surge
2000	Last census of 20th century conducted • Many dot-com enterprises collapse
2001	People classified as "non-Hispanic whites" no longer a majority of California's population • America Online merges with Time-Warner
2005	Final theatrical release in *Star Wars* series

The steady rise of the median age of the population brought public policy, as well as personal, dilemmas. As aging Baby Boomers pondered retirement options, for example, policy makers worried that the projected Social Security and Medicare payouts would bequeath a staggering burden of costs to the smaller post–Baby Boom generations of workers. Trend watchers of the 1960s had talked of a "youth revolt." At the beginning of the 21st century, their counterparts pondered the "graying of America."

Significant change also occurred in the geographic distribution of population, and these transformations helped to shift the regional distribution of political and economic power. After 1970, the vast bulk of the nation's population growth occurred in the South and the West. Nevada, California, Florida, and Arizona became the fastest-growing states, and by 2000, more than one in ten Americans lived in California. Between 1990 and 2001, California gained eight seats in the U.S. House of Representatives, Florida added six, New York lost five, and several other northeastern states lost two or three. Presidential politics increasingly turned on results from Florida, Texas, and California.

Many reasons account for this demographic shift: affordable air-conditioning, the expansion of tourism and new retirement communities in **Sun Belt** areas, businesses attracted by lower labor costs, the absence of strong unions, and the development of high-tech industries connected to military-related spending and the computer revolution. **(See Map 31.1, Population Shifts Toward the Sunbelt, in the color insert following page 1248.)**

The governmentally financed space program, directed by NASA installations in Texas and Florida, symbolized the geographic shift in the research and technology sectors. In 1961, President Kennedy had announced plans for the manned Apollo program, and in July 1969, astronaut Neil Armstrong had stepped from a spacecraft onto the lunar surface. Apollo flights continued until 1972, when NASA began to develop a space station. In the 1980s, NASA started operating **"space shuttles,"** manned craft that served as scientific laboratories in outer space and could be flown back to Earth for reuse. In early 1986, a *Challenger* shuttle craft exploded as it was about to take off, and the program stalled for a few years. Still, the accelerating ripple effect of space and defense spending continued to stimulate technological innovation and population growth in Sunbelt areas.

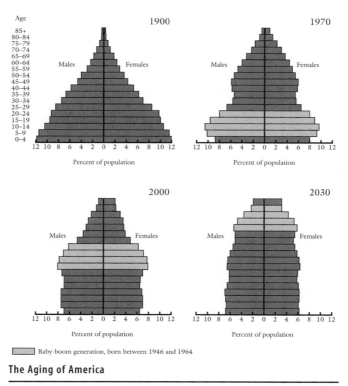

Baby-boom generation, born between 1946 and 1964

The Aging of America

Source: U.S. Census Bureau. Adapted from C. L. Himes, "Elderly Americans," *Population Bulletin 2002*, 56(4): p. 4.

New Immigration

A dramatic increase in immigration from countries mostly to the south and west of the United States accounted for much of the U.S. population growth, particularly in the southern and western parts of the country. The vast bulk of post-1970 immigration came from Asia, Oceania, Latin America, and Africa rather than from Europe, the primary source of immigrants from the 1790s to 1924. In 2000, roughly 12 percent of the U.S. population had been born outside of the United States, compared to the all-time high of 15 percent in 1890.

The largest number of non-European immigrants came from Mexico. Responding to labor shortages in the United States and poor economic prospects at home, both legal and undocumented immigration from Mexico rose substantially during the last 30 years of the 20th century. Many immigrants from Mexico arrived as seasonal agricultural workers or temporary laborers, but most soon formed permanent communities. According to the 2000 census, 90 percent of all Mexican Americans lived in the Southwest, primarily Texas and California.

Most immigrants from Puerto Rico settled around New York City, but sizable Puerto Rican communities developed in Chicago and in cities in New England and Ohio as well. Economic problems on the mainland during the 1970s prompted some to return to the island, but the flow reversed again after about 1980. By 2000, the Puerto Rican population on the U.S. mainland totaled about 3 million, compared to slightly less than 4 million in Puerto Rico.

Cubans had begun immigrating in large numbers in response to Fidel Castro's revolution. After the U.S. Congress, in 1962, designated people fleeing from Castro's Cuba as "refugees" eligible for admittance, more than 800,000 Cubans from every strata of society came to the United States during the next 20 years. They gradually moved northward into many major American cities, but the greatest impact came in south Florida. An agreement with Castro in 1995 brought the first U.S. restrictions on the flow of immigrants from Cuba. In 2000, however, about half of all the people residing in Miami were of Cuban descent.

By the early 21st century, the number of Spanish-speaking people in the United States totaled more than in all but four countries of Latin America. Los Angeles became the second largest "Mexican city" in the world, trailing only Mexico City, and LA's Salvadoran population just about equaled that of San Salvador. More Puerto Ricans lived in New York City than in San Juan, and the Big Apple's Dominican population rivaled that of Santo Domingo.

Changes in immigration patterns began with the landmark **Immigration Act of 1965,** which spurred not only population growth but diversity as well. Since the 1920s, the nature of immigration to the United States had been determined by quotas based on national origins (see chapter 24). The 1965 act abolished these. Instead, it placed a ceiling of 20,000 immigrants for every country, gave preference to those with close family ties in the United States, and accorded priority to people with special skills and those classified as refugees. Although largely unforeseen at the time, this legislation laid the basis not only for a resumption of high-volume immigration but also for a substantial shift in the countries of origin.

International events also affected U.S. immigration policy. In the aftermath of the Vietnam War, for example, U.S. officials facilitated the admittance of many Vietnamese, Cambodians, Laotians, and **Hmong** (an ethnically distinct people who inhabited lands extending across the borders of these three Asian countries). The goal was to resettle people who had allied with the United States during the war and whose families were consequently in peril.

In response to the growing number of people seeking admission to the United States, Congress later passed the **Refugee Act of 1980.** It specified that political refugees, "those fleeing overt persecution," could be admitted more easily but that people seeking simply to improve their economic circumstances could not. In practice, U.S. officials interpreted the terms "political" and "economic" so that they generally admitted people leaving communist regimes but not those fleeing right-wing dictatorships. For example, Cubans and Soviet Jews invariably qualified under the Refugee Act, but Haitians often did not. (The number of undocumented Haitians entering the United States, however, rose rapidly.) Many Guatemalans and Salvadorans, hoping to escape repressive military governments backed by the United States during the 1980s, stood little chance of being admitted as legal immigrants. Thousands of undocumented immigrants from all over Central America, however, entered the United States to look for work.

Chinatown, San Francisco   People navigating many U.S. cities found decoding bilingual signage a useful, if not necessary, skill.

© Richard Cummins/CORBIS

Immigration soon began generating political controversy. As proponents and opponents of restrictions offered conflicting perspectives on how new immigrants, both legal and undocumented, were affecting domestic life, partisan differences emerged. In general, Democrats favored less restrictive policies than their GOP counterparts. Although many congressional Republicans hoped President Ronald Reagan would weigh in on their side, he played a minimal role in the passage of the Immigration Reform and Control Act of 1986. This measure, at first glance, looked fairly restrictive. It granted full residency status to recent immigrants who could prove that they had been living in the United States since 1982, but it included stricter penalties on businesses employing undocumented workers. Lacking effective means of enforcing its penalties on employers, however, the new law did little to halt the flow of immigrants, especially during a time when jobs in the United States remained plentiful.

As a result, the debate over immigration grew more acrimonious and increasingly polarized. Another congressional act, in 1990, raised the number of immigrants who could legally be admitted on the basis of special job skills or the investment capital they could bring to the United States. A 1996 report, by a special congressional Commission on Immigration Reform, called for lowering the total of official immigration slots and for tightening restrictions against undocumented workers, but a wide range of political and social movements opposing such changes blocked such a response by Congress.

Conflicting demands and contradictory claims about the economic impact of immigrant workers helped stalemate further change in policy. Most business interests favored relatively

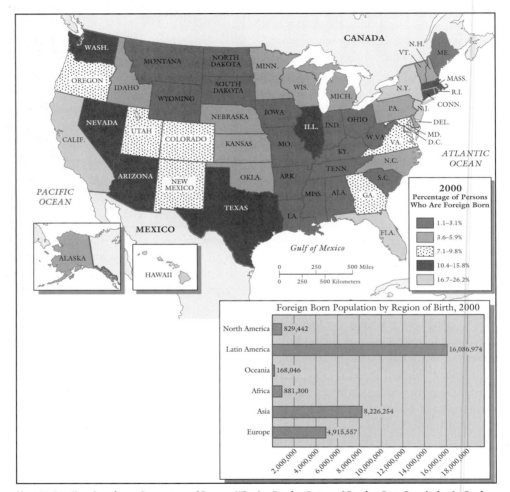

Map 31.2   New Americans: Percentage of Persons Who Are Foreign Born and Foreign-Born Population by Region of Birth, 2000   This map and chart illustrate the wave of new immigration into the United States. Which regions of the world contributed the most immigrants? Which states received the most, and the least, immigration?

Source: U.S. Census Bureau, Census 2000 Summary File 3, Matrix P21; U.S. Census Bureau, Census 2000 American Indian and Alaska Native Summary File, Matrices PCT43, PCT46, and PCT48.

open immigration policies and opposed strict enforcement of rules against hiring undocumented workers. They supported the claim that immigrants, both the highly educated and the skilled, along with those at the entry level, filled job slots that would otherwise remain open. Opponents, on the other hand, cited figures that suggested immigrants were assuming jobs formerly held by U.S. citizens, especially ones with minimal education and job training, and driving down wage rates. Data to sustain any claim about the precise impact of immigration remained thin and highly contested. Moreover, political debate generally turned on reciting emotionally charged, largely anecdotal evidence rather than on closely analyzing available economic numbers.

The new immigration likely changed California more than any other state. (States along the southwestern border of the United States also felt the impact of immigration from Mexico but never experienced the same high level of Asian immigration as did California.) In the Golden Gate State, the counties of Los Angeles and Orange seemed microcosms of world culture. By 2000, fewer than half of schoolchildren in LA could claim proficiency in English, and no single ethnic group comprised a majority of the city's population. As with the earlier surges of immigration, the wave that began during the 1970s produced not only problems and ethnic-based rivalries but also cooperation and hopes for the benefits of multiculturalism.

The Metropolitan Nation

Urban-suburban demographics, too, remained in a state of flux. At the end of the 20th century, more than 80 percent of Americans lived in vast metropolitan areas. With the overall population growing, though more slowly than during the 1950s and 1960s, the relationship between central cities and adjacent suburbs continued to change. Many once-distinct suburban areas melded into **"urban corridors,"** or "metropolitan strips," which ran along freeway links between older cities such as Seattle and Tacoma or Washington and Baltimore. Outlying areas also sprouted "edge cities," shopping and business complexes such as the Tyson's Corner area, just outside of Washington, D.C. Edge cities competed with older urban centers for businesses, jobs, and residents. People living in these new areas, studies showed, rarely found the need to visit the nearby center cities.

Demographic patterns in suburbia also changed. First, greater numbers of people from non-European backgrounds began moving to suburbs, just as more Americans of European descent were relocating in cities. As a result, the percentage of African Americans residing in urban centers steadily declined, and the percentage living in suburbia increased, especially after 1990. With a number of immigrant groups settling outside central cites, some suburbs—even in midsized urban areas such as Minneapolis-St. Paul, Minnesota—came to contain more people identified with non-European ethnic groups than the central cities they surrounded.

Second, many new suburbs sprouted up farther away than ever from either edge or core cities. A frenzy of new construction transformed more and more farmland and small towns into a series of sprawling housing developments, which demographers called "exurbs." Built on relatively inexpensive land, exurbs allowed cost-conscious home buyers, many of them drawn to the tax-cutting policies of the Republican Party, to purchase more space for less money. At the same time, exurban areas of the early 21st century, as had the new suburbs of the mid-20th century, offered families with young children newly built schools and freshly constructed playgrounds. They also, however, allowed anyone commuting to work the opportunity to spend up to several hours every day trapped inside a car, inching in and out of exurban areas.

Meanwhile, the nation's urban cores underwent continual transformation. During the 1970s and much of the 1980s, as manufacturing jobs began leaving urban areas and retail shopping continued to shift to outlying malls, cities focused on becoming financial, administrative, and entertainment centers. Distinct areas in most large cities also faced rising rates of homelessness, crime, and infrastructure deterioration, especially in their sewer and water systems. Big-city mayors complained that the government in Washington did little to address urban problems. Federal funding decreased from $64 per urban resident in 1980 to less than $30 by 1993.

During the late 1980s and 1990s, however, parts of most central cities underwent a stunning revival that reversed the declines of the 1970s. A building boom brought new office towers, residential buildings, and sports and arts complexes to downtowns across the country. Moreover, the population drain away from cities, at least in part, shifted into reverse. People with money to invest in housing and to spend at restaurants and on entertainment began returning to selected areas, which thus became labeled as "gentrified," in most cities.

Many different sources fed the gentrification movement. During the economically troubled 1970s, affluent young people in the rapidly expanding 25-to-44 age category rediscovered cities as interesting, relatively inexpensive places in which to live. Older homes and neighborhoods, which their parents had rejected, suddenly looked potentially "quaint" and "charming," especially when properly renovated. Encouraged by federal laws that provided funds and tax breaks for refurbishing historic buildings, developers and ordinary people looked for workers skilled in dry-walling, tuck-pointing, and kitchen remodeling. During the 1980s and 1990s, the relatively healthy national economy helped the urban revival continue. Innovative urban design schemes skillfully integrated diverse architectural styles with new green spaces and revitalized river- and lakefronts.

At the turn of the 21st century, many U.S. cities seemed to be emerging as exciting, transnational spaces. Community development corporations (CDCs), grassroots efforts indebted to movement cultures of the 1960s and early 1970s, helped finance affordable housing, child-care facilities, and employment opportunities. The Community Reinvestment Act, which obliged banks to invest in low-income areas, stimulated economic activity. Community policing, a trend toward harsher sentencing, and an aging population lowered urban crime rates. Moreover, commuters frustrated by increasingly clogged freeways discovered that they could save both time and money by moving from distant suburbs to revitalizing downtowns. In addition, new immigrants, many bringing marketable skills and significant amounts of capital, also repopulated once-declining neighborhoods, refurbishing property and reviving commercial zones.

Economic Change

Focus Question
What were the most important, post-1970 technological and economic changes?
How did technological change create both new problems and new possibilities?

Most people living in the United States at the turn of the 20th century oriented their lives around technologies that were either unavailable or only in their infancy 30 years earlier. The most technologically sophisticated could awake to some kind of digital device; pop breakfast into a microwave; telecommute to work, at home, on a portable computer; and talk to friends or colleagues over a cell phone. They could interrupt work, or follow it up, by listening to music downloaded from the Internet; watching a movie or television program recorded earlier; and going online to seek information, entertainment, or companionship. The pace of post-1970 technological change, in short, brought astonishing transformations in work routines and the rhythms of daily life.

New Technologies

Some of the most noteworthy technological changes occurred in biotechnology, in high-performance computing machines and software, and in other communications systems.

In one of the most important research projects of the late 20th century, scientists announced in June 2000 that they had successfully mapped the entire human genetic code. This **Human Genome Project** paved the way for new techniques of gene transfer, embryo manipulation, tissue regeneration, and even cloning. Breakthroughs in biotechnology promised new approaches to the treatment of cancer and other diseases. Genetic manipulation in plants seemed able to revolutionize food production, waste conversion, and toxic cleanup. Large food companies heralded the use of genetically modified crops as an extension of the earlier "green revolution," which had boosted agricultural yields.

Serious questions about the role of science in manipulating genetic codes and altering reproductive processes, however, soon arose. Controversy swirled around the impact of genetically modified foods on the planet's biodiversity. Research on fetal stem cells, which could be used to regenerate human tissue, raised a highly politicized religious-ethical debate over the definition of life.

The computer revolution entered a new phase during the 1970s. The introduction of **microchips** boosted the hardware capability and reduced the size and cost of computers. Powerful memory capacities and parallel processors, which allow many operations to run simultaneously, transformed industrial and informational systems, lowering labor costs and making production schedules more flexible. "Artificial intelligence" (AI) capabilities emerged, along with voice interaction between people and machines.

New communications technologies, such as fiber-optic networks and satellite transmission, and the computer revolution also fueled an **"information revolution."**

Libraries replaced card catalogs with computer networks. Voice-mail, fax transmissions, e-mail, and text-messaging came to supplement or simply replace posted mail and conventional telephone conversations. Cellular phone calls became more common than those using land-lines. The speed and accessibility of information thus changed patterns of human interaction. The simple act of "talking to a real person" or to a consumer representative who lived in the same community or even the same country became an increasingly rare occurrence.

Big Business

Other forms of computerized communications helped transform business operations. Although the practice of buying on credit had become increasingly common since the 1920s, vast computer systems greatly assisted the rapid expansion of bank-issued credit cards. Other innovations—automated teller machines (ATMs), automatic depositing, debit cards, and electronic bill payment—moved Americans closer to a cashless economy. Congressional deregulation of financial industries during the 1980s and 1990s, which prompted the Savings & Loan crisis, also permitted banking institutions and brokerage houses to offer similar financial services, accelerating competition among the financial giants that sold stocks, lent money, and offered insurance.

Franchises and chain stores also changed consumption and workplace patterns. McDonald's and Holiday Inn had pioneered nationwide standardization in the fast-food and travel industries during the late 1950s. Other chains soon copied their models. Starbucks elevated a simple beverage into pricey designer commodities. The Arkansas-based Wal-Mart chain became the country's largest private employer. By the early 21st century, one of about every 120 workers and nearly one of every 20 workers in the retail sector received their paycheck from Wal-Mart. Such chains often brought a greater array of merchandise and lower prices, but critics charged them with crushing local, independent retailers in thousands of midsized and small towns.

U.S. chain businesses expanded overseas as well. After the end of the Cold War, McDonald's opened to great fanfare in Moscow and Budapest, while the Hilton chain quickly placed new hotels in Eastern European capitals. Pepsi and Coke carried their "cola wars" into foreign markets. Starbucks created a controversy when it opened a branch in Beijing's imposing Forbidden City.

Amazon.com led another branch of innovation—e-commerce, or the practice of buying and selling products over the Internet. At the end of the 1990s, a wave of new "dot-com" businesses promised to move more and more purchasing to the Internet and set off a short-term bubble in dot-com stocks. During 2000, stock prices for these enterprises collapsed as dramatically as they had risen. Buying and selling on the Web, however, remained an important new feature of consumer culture. Amazon and eBay, the online auction site, became models for doing business in cyberspace.

Production, as well as consumption, turned global. U.S. automakers, for example, increasingly moved their procurement and assembly work offshore, even as foreign car

Lattes in Shanghai   American chain businesses spread throughout the world, part of the controversial process known as globalization.

manufacturers established new assembly plants in the United States. Moreover, the trend toward privatization (the sale of government-owned industries to private business) in many economies worldwide provided U.S. based firms with new opportunities for overseas acquisitions. Conversely, foreign interests purchased many U.S. companies and real estate holdings. In the early 1990s, RCA, Doubleday, Mack Truck, and Goodyear were just some of the traditionally American brands owned by foreign-based corporations. So many industrial giants had become global by the early 21st century that it was difficult to define what constituted a U.S. company or a foreign one.

Postindustrial Restructuring

New technologies and economic globalization helped change the American business structure and the workforce. In the 1970s, citing pressure from international competition and declining profits, many companies began cutting back their workforce and trimming their management staff, moves known as "downsizing." Major steel plants closed, and the auto industry laid off thousands of workers. In the 1980s and 1990s, the steel and auto industries temporarily regained profitability, but other sectors took their turns at downsizing. Business restructuring, together with the government's deregulation of major industries, touched off a merger boom. During the prosperity of the late 1990s, huge mergers, with acquisitions totaling more than $1.6 trillion per year, brought a concentration in corporate power unseen since the 1890s.

Meanwhile, the kinds of jobs held by Americans shifted. As employment in traditional manufacturing and extractive sectors (such as mining) decreased, jobs in the service sector, high-tech fields, and the information and entertainment areas increased. In 1960, the production of goods, as opposed to services, had engaged roughly one-quarter of the U.S. workforce. By the early 21st century, the comparable figure stood at about 15 percent. Moreover, according to one estimate, more than 40 percent of U.S. corporate profits came from the financial services sector, while only about 10 percent came from manufacturing. Financial services, computing, and other high-tech sectors offered relatively high salaries—astronomical ones for top management—but most jobs in the rapidly expanding service sector—such as clerks and cleaners—remained low paying, part-time, and nonunionized.

Many individuals and families maintained their lifestyles by incurring rising levels of personal debt. In addition to discussing the "U.S. deficit," economists began analyzing "the household deficit," the difference between what U.S. households earned and what they actually spent. As late as 1980, the rate of indebtedness for households, though higher than that during the 1950s, still remained lower than it had been during the 1920s. The 1980s, however, inaugurated a trend that would accelerate into the next century: People living in the United States assumed ever-larger financial obligations enabled through various credit arrangements. As more people shouldered greater debt, the number of personal bankruptcies increased. Conversely, opportunities for accumulating one's own rainy day fund declined. The rate of personal savings in the United States fell to the lowest in the industrialized world.

In turn, the nation's business structure came to include a complex set of greatly expanded, often politically influential, financial institutions. (Financial institutions, benficiaries of deregulation, constituted the largest contributors to political parties.) Some pundits called these, taken together, the "Debt and Credit-Industrial Complex" or the "Borrower-Industrial Complex." A wide range of businesses—from international "super banks," such as Citigroup and the Bank of America, to street corner institutions, such as Check 'n' Go and Moneytree, to pawn-shop chains, such as Pawn America, right on down to illegal loan sharking operations—profited from people who never seemed able to balance their personal books. Many neighborhood loan sharks, cynics quipped, operated with only slightly less regulation, while providing more cordial service, than large banking chains. Federal court decisions and regulatory rulings during the 1990s effectively gave credit-card issuers a green light when charging interest rates and imposing other terms. Banks competed for customers from all across the spectrum but placed increasing importance on spreading "plastic" among the college-age population, for whom personal indebtedness was soaring. Observing the growth of a financial sector reined in by fewer and fewer governmental regulations, the head of the U.S. Senate's banking committee rejected any calls for re-regulation. Greater competition among lenders, he claimed, rather than greater oversight by government, provided the best solution to questionable banking practices: We "believe freedom is the answer," he insisted.

As important business sectors, particularly the financial one, flourished, virtually every part of the labor union movement suffered as membership rolls continued to shrink. During the 1950s, more than 30 percent of the U.S. workforce belonged to a union; in the early 1970s, the figure had declined only slightly, to about 29 percent; by 1991, it stood at slightly above 16 percent. By the early 21st century, it slipped further, to around 13 percent. Some unions suffered greater attrition than others. Unions that represented workers in the "needle trades," such as the fabled International Ladies' Garment Workers Union, lost two-thirds of their membership during the last three decades of the 20th century.

Efforts to organize agricultural workers on the West Coast, who were largely of Mexican and Filipino descent, dramatized some of the difficulties of expanding the union movement. **Cesar Chavez,** a charismatic leader who emulated the nonviolent tactics of Martin Luther King, Jr., vaulted the United Farm Workers (UFW) into public attention during the early 1970s. As the union's president and iconic symbol, Chavez undertook personal hunger strikes and instituted well-publicized consumer boycotts of lettuce and grapes to pressure growers to bargain with the UFW. During the later 1970s and the 1980s, however, the UFW steadily lost ground. Strong antiunion stands by growers and the continued influx of new immigrants who were eager for work undercut the UFW's efforts. When Chavez died in April 1993, his union was struggling to recruit new members and to retain those already on its rolls.

The broader union movement faced only slightly less difficulty making inroads into new sectors of the economy. The major growth for organized labor came among government employees and health care workers. Unions launched ambitious organizing drives among clerical, restaurant, and hotel workers, but businesses adamantly fought back. Employers also continued to cut the health and retirement benefits that the leading U.S. firms had once proudly offered.

The system of fringe benefits found in the United States, which many companies had greatly expanded after the Second World War, came under increasing pressure toward the end of the 20th century. An attractive benefit package had once provided an employer, in the relatively competitive job market of the 1940s and 1950s, a way of attracting workers without paying dramatically higher wages and salaries. Moreover, the amount of money a company paid toward its share of a health plan did not count, under federal law, as part of an employee's taxable compensation. Everyone thus stood to gain, it had seemed, from relatively generous benefit programs.

Things had begun to change, however, during the 1960s as U.S. companies faced both increasing foreign competition and rising domestic health care costs. In 1960, only about 5 percent of the entire U.S. GDP went for health care; some 45 years later, the comparable figure reached more than 15 percent, a greater percentage than people paid for food. The annual cost of providing health care for a family, according to most estimates, came to about what a full-time, minimum-wage worker would earn over a year and twice the pay of the average Wal-Mart employee. Any U.S. company facing domestic or foreign competition, such as the large auto manufacturers, found it increasingly difficult to maintain extensive benefit packages that included health care for an aging workforce.

As early as the 1980s, economists warned that the shift to a globalizing "postindustrial" economy was "deskilling" the labor force and eroding living standards in the United States. Critical observers expressed alarm over statistical evidence that so many of the new jobs created in the U.S. economy offered low wages and few benefits. Did the widening gulf between highly paid, highly skilled positions and minimum-wage jobs threaten to undermine the middle-class nature of American society? Wal-Mart, for example, actively resisted the unionization of its enormous workforce, which earned an average of $7 to $8 per hour in 2003 and enjoyed limited or no fringe benefits. Moreover, manufacturers wanting to lower costs to attract the huge Wal-Mart purchasing contracts moved their plants into countries with the least expensive labor costs. This trend further contributed to the disappearance of relatively better-paid manufacturing jobs from the United States.

Other economists painted a different picture. They acknowledged that internationalization and corporate downsizing might temporarily mean lost jobs for some people but insisted that gains in productivity and new jobs generated by innovative industries would eventually translate into lower consumer prices and rising living standards for all. Celebrants of change pointed to many success stories, especially in high-tech industries, where innovation paved a broad avenue of upward economic mobility for those with computer-age skills. Real wages did begin to rise during the 1990s, but this trend would reverse as the economy softened after 2000, and the gap between the highest and lowest income levels continued to grow.

At the beginning of the 20th century, skilled workers had tended to stick to one profession or place of employment throughout their working life. By century's end, even many highly educated professionals likely faced the prospect of switching occupations several times before reaching retirement age. The need for training and retraining programs that served people of all ages, many observers noted, demanded a transformation in the relationship among education, job training, and employment.

The Sports-Entertainment Complex

What might be called a sports-entertainment complex inexorably expanded after 1970. Metropolitan areas competed vigorously to bring a home team to their locale—or retain the ones already located there. Lucrative TV contracts and generous tax write-offs attracted business entrepreneurs, such as George Steinbrenner of the New York Yankees, who decided they might also be interested in running their own sports team. The generation of owners who had relied on revenues from a sports franchise for their primary livelihood, such as the Griffith family in baseball or the Halas family in football, began disappearing. Even professional wrestling, which still bore the imprint of its carnival origins during the 1970s, finally became part of the sports-entertainment complex. During the 1980s, Vince McMahon, Jr., transformed his late father's World Wrestling Federation (later World Wresting Entertainment or WWE) into a multimillion-dollar, worldwide name brand.

Although still unofficially "the national pastime," baseball faced numerous challenges during the post-1970 era. Seeking a better fit with emerging economic, demographic, and social forces, baseball's own leadership tinkered with the structure of their operation. By relocating franchises to burgeoning metropolitan areas, Major League Baseball (MLB) could acquire a fresh supply of fans, advantageous TV deals, and stadiums financed by public money. If moving existing franchises made sense, creating new ones seemed an even shrewder option. In the single decade of the 1970s, for instance, MLB moved teams out of and back into Milwaukee; into, out of, and finally back into Seattle; and out of, back in, and then out again of Washington, D.C.

This kind of franchise reshuffling paled by comparison to that in professional football and basketball, sports that initially claimed greater growth than MLB. The National Football League (NFL) and the National Basketball Association (NBA) had both prospered during the 1960s, in large part because of national television coverage and franchise expansion, especially into the West and South. The NFL's leadership began citing surveys that showed more sports fans narrowly preferred professional football over the slower-moving product of MLB.

Just in time for the 1970 season, the NFL merged with an upstart rival, the American Football League (AFL), with which it had been playing a "Super Bowl" since 1967. Dividing its TV revenues equally, this revamped NFL ensured that a small-market team, such as the Green Bay Packers, enjoyed a secure financial base and the opportunity to compete, over the long run, on a roughly level playing field with larger-market franchises. During the 1970s, ABC began televising an NFL game during prime-time hours, and the instant success of *Monday Night Football* signaled how important sporting events had become to TV and to the nation's popular culture. Noting the obvious, a group of TV entrepreneurs launched, toward the end of the 1970s, ESPN, a new cable network devoted to nothing but sports. In 2006, the flagship *Monday Night Football* offering moved to ESPN.

The NBA rounded out the big three of the sports entertainment business. With its relatively small court making this sport even more TV-friendly than football, professional basketball could expand into new locales and broaden its television coverage. As the NBA's revenues grew, it came to feature high-profile African American stars, such as Julius ("Dr J") Irving, more prominently than either the NFL or MLB. At century's end, the NBA led the sports-entertainment world in promoting African Americans, including its greatest star Michael Jordan, into coaching and management positions.

Promoters aggressively marketed other sports-entertainment operations. These included a greatly expanded National Hockey League (NHL) and revamped tours of the men's Professional Golfing Association (PGA) and a tour for women (LPGA). The nation's love affair with the automobile helped to speed the growth of auto racing. The Indianapolis 500 initially vied with the Super Bowl for recognition as the most spectacular one-day event in sports, but stock-car competition eventually overtook Indy-style racing, expanding from its traditional base in the South. John Kennedy had tried to soft-pedal his fascination with sports, in favor of emphasizing more cerebral pursuits, but later political figures eagerly sought the glamour coming to surround big-time sports. Political candidates rushed to sign up prominent athletes for their campaign squads, and some, including former star quarterback Jack Kemp, successfully made the transition from the sports to the political field. In addition to tapping his family connections, George W. Bush used his part-ownership of the Texas Rangers baseball team as an entrée into electoral politics.

With the business of sports booming, it seemed inevitable that its legal foundations would also begin shifting. Professional players had long complained of receiving a disproportionately small share of profits, but the laws governing sports operations invariably favored owners. A new generation of athletes, armed with union advisers, challenged the old order. In 1970, baseball's owners celebrated when the U.S. Supreme Court narrowly rejected a suit challenging MLB's key contractual arrangement, the reserve clause that bound a player to a team year-after-year, as an unconstitutional form of involuntary servitude. Subsequent rulings, however, created slightly different systems of "free agency" throughout every team-sport enterprise. As a consequence, talented athletes could auction off their services in the marketplace. (The super-talented, such as Bo Jackson, even played off one professional sport against another.) Although some fans grumbled, especially when highly paid players failed to perform up to expectations, owners discovered that steadily rising revenues from TV, tax breaks, and favorable stadium deals could support the new salary structures. Perhaps the most successful examples of unionization in the post-1970 era came in the sports-entertainment field, where labor strikes remained a viable option for unions. Knowledgeable fans found themselves needing to become conversant with labor relations as well as more traditional sports-world matters.

Sports and legal questions also became intertwined with social issues. Feminists condemned big-time sports for promoting sexism—pointing, for example, to the emphasis the NFL placed on female cheerleading squads that resembled Las Vegas chorus lines—and urged inclusion of more opportunities and better financial rewards for women athletes. Colleges and universities, mandated by Title IX of the Educational Amendments of 1972 to achieve equality in sports activities, faced difficult decisions about how to finance and promote women's sports. In women's sports where professionalism prevailed, such as tennis and golf, the trend was unabashedly toward emulating the male model. Prize money, endorsement contracts, and media coverage for women athletes all steadily escalated during the last decades of the 20th century.

As the importance that cultural commentators assigned to Jackie Robinson's struggle to desegregate MLB during the 1940s had underscored, the sports-entertainment complex had long provided a cultural mirror. Sports supposedly reflected and represented larger themes. How much opportunity the sports-entertainment complex really offered to people of non-European descent, a question that had been raised dramatically by a Black Power protest at the 1968 Summer Olympics, remained a persistent issue. By the early 21st century, the number of African Americans playing MLB was declining, while that of Latino ballplayers was soaring. Similarly, as NBA scouts identified talented international players, especially from Eastern Europe, some observers began to fear that the strong African American presence might disappear from professional basketball courts.

As the sports-entertainment complex grew in wealth and visibility, traditionalists inevitably saw signs of decline. Sporting events, such as the Winter and the Summer Olympic Games, no longer amateur competitions in any meaningful sense, seemed awash in commercialism and on-field corruption. Similarly, the surge of interest in MLB at the end of the 20th and the beginning of the next century appeared to owe a great deal to the prodigious feats of homerun hitters, led by Mark McGwire, Sammy Sosa, and

Barry Bonds. It soon became evident, however, that consumption of greater quantities of performance-enhancing drugs was helping players drive balls out of MLB parks. The super-knowledgeable sports fan, it seemed, not only needed a background in legal but now in pharmaceutical matters as well.

Media and Popular Culture

Focus Question
How did new forms of media change the ways in which people received information and entertainment?

A greater range of knowledge could prove handy for fans of all popular culture. New technologies significantly altered how people received and used books, movies, TV, music, and informational resources. By the early 21st century, virtually every home or apartment had at least one television and VCR or DVD player, and about 60 percent had a personal computer. People looked to the Internet for access to newspapers, books, music, and movies. E-mail and text-messaging increasingly became the first choice for contacting friends. The omnipresent video screen, which became ever more portable, seemed the preeminent symbol of American culture.

The Video Revolution

At the beginning of the 1970s, TV broadcasters could still expect a hit program to draw more viewers in a single evening than a hit motion picture attracted over an entire year. The three networks could promise advertisers that a rough cross section of the American public would be in front of their TV sets watching their sales pitches.

During the 1970s, however, the networks found themselves increasingly forced to embrace the strategy called "narrowcasting," fragmenting the viewing audience into carefully targeted segments. CBS replaced several highly watched programs, such as *The Beverly Hillbillies,* with shows aimed toward viewers under the age of 40, those coveted by advertisers because research studies identified them as more likely than older viewers to spend money on products and services. CBS also introduced "edgier" programming. *All in the Family,* a sitcom about a blue-collar family's intergenerational conflicts associated with the 1960s, made its bigoted protagonist, Archie Bunker, a lightning rod for issues involving race and gender. Although *The Mary Tyler Moore Show* rarely took overtly feminist positions, its cleverly constructed storylines and sharp dialogue consistently addressed the personal politics of working women. Other CBS shows, such as the antiwar sitcom *M*A*S*H,* also merged comedy and social commentary.

With CBS leading the way, the entire TV industry prospered during a nearly 10-year period beginning in the mid-1970s. ABC found its niche among high-school and college-age viewers, emphasizing sex-and-action programs (*Charlie's Angels*), mildly risqué sitcoms

(*Three's Company*), and shows about teen life (*Happy Days*). NBC brought the barbed humor of the 1960s Counterculture to network television by nurturing *Saturday Night Live*. At the end of the 1970s, nine of every ten television sets were tuned to a network program during prime-time viewing hours.

A decade later, however, network programmers faced a harsher TV landscape. NBC could claim two now-classic hits, *The Cosby Show* (featuring an affluent African American family) and *Cheers* (set in a Boston tavern where "everybody knows your name"), but its other prime-time programs garnered disappointing ratings. Facing a similar situation, the other two networks joined NBC in slashing budgets and staff, especially in their news-gathering divisions. At the same time, local stations, which formerly limped along without a network affiliation, suddenly thrived. These independents programmed older Hollywood films, sporting events, and reruns of canceled, prime-time shows now being syndicated to individual stations. Several hundred independent television stations debuted during the 1980s.

Capitalizing on the rise of these independents, the Fox television network went on the air in 1988. Using a pattern that was later imitated by other would-be networks, Fox offered a limited schedule to previously nonaffiliated stations. Fox's first big hit, *The Simpsons,* an animated send-up of the standard family sitcom, became a pop cultural phenomenon and mass-marketing bonanza. In 1993, Fox outbid CBS for the rights to carry professional football games. The WB, UPN, and Fox networks featured programs, such as *Buffy the Vampire Slayer, That 70s Show,* and *Malcolm in the Middle,* for audiences that contained more minority, young, and urban viewers than those of the three older networks.

New technologies, which promised viewers greater choice, challenged all of these networks. The remote control, an innovation of the 1960s that finally caught on during the 1980s, created a television aesthetic called "channel surfing," in which viewers flipped rapidly from program to program. Videocassette recorders (VCRs), introduced during the 1980s, became the first of the record-and-view-later technologies allowing viewers even greater control over their television offerings.

The initial challenge to the networks came from cable television (CATV), which was in nearly 75 percent of the nation's homes by 2000. The arrival of CATV accelerated the fragmentation of TV's audience. Atlanta's Ted Turner introduced the Cable News Network (CNN), several movie channels, and an all-cartoon network before his communication empire merged with that of Time-Warner. Companies selling direct satellite transmission challenged both the networks and cable, but the lack of a standard reception format slowed the expansion of this competing medium. By the early 21st century, the percentage of viewers watching prime-time network programs had fallen from 90 percent to under 60 percent. At the 2003 Emmy awards ceremonies, shows initially running on CATV received, for the first time, more awards than those carried on the traditional networks.

The "New Hollywood"

New technologies and changing business practices during the 1970s produced a "New Hollywood." With movie attendance in 1970 about the same as it had been in 1960, Hollywood studios needed to change their mode of operation. They began raising ticket prices, betting

The Family Guy As the once mass U.S. TV audience began to fragment, animated shows increasingly found exceedingly loyal niche markets, especially on cable channels. The FOX network debuted *The Family Guy* in 1999 but canceled the series in 2000 and, again, in 2002. After noting the popularity of *The Family Guy* in re-runs and the strong DVD sales, FOX began producing new episodes for the Cartoon Network. Although the inept anti-hero of the series, "Peter Griffin," recalls "Fred Flintstone" and "Homer Simpson," aficionados of this series prefer to consider his antics and *The Family Guy's* references to popular culture several cuts above those found on *The Flintstones* and *The Simpsons*.

on a few blockbuster films, such as the highly profitable *Star Wars* series (1977–2005), and hoping for a surprise hit, such as *My Big Fat Greek Wedding* (2002). Yet for every blockbuster or unexpected success, there was a super-expensive flop such as *Gigli* (2003).

Volatility in the movie market encouraged most filmmakers to play it safe. Many movie makers recycled titles and special effects that had made money in the past. They transferred popular stories, such as *How the Grinch Stole Christmas* (2000), and TV shows, such as *The Brady Bunch* (1995), to the big screen and produced sequels for any movie, such as *Pirates of the Caribbean* (2003), which even approached blockbuster status. In addition, Hollywood expanded the older practice of targeting younger viewers with movies such as *Ferris Bueller's Day Off* (1986). Meanwhile, celebratory stories that tapped themes in popular history, such as *Braveheart* (1995) and *Titanic* (1997), impressed both ticket buyers and industry insiders.

At the same time, however, relatively small-scale movies also began to flourish. Woody Allen became one of the first U.S. filmmakers to specialize in movies, such as *Crimes and Misdemeanors* (1989) and *Scoop* (2006), which borrowed techniques and themes from European cinema. The actor-director Robert Redford launched the Sundance Film Institute in the hopes of encouraging "offbeat" examples of screenwriting and direction. Held in Park City, Utah, the annual Sundance Festival began attracting Hollywood moguls who sought the next "small" movie, such as *The Blair Witch Project* (1999), which might find a large audience. The CATV lineup soon included several outlets, including the Sundance Channel, for independent films, and the Landmark movie chain featured films that seemed unlikely to play in the multiplex mall theaters. Some major studios even created special divisions, such as Paramount Classics, to specialize in so-called independent films. Moviemakers also experimented with digital technology, and by 2007, digital movies played regularly in commercial theaters, a trend traditionalists condemned for degrading the visual richness of cinematic imagery.

The New Hollywood became increasingly intertwined with the changing television establishment—once its feared rival—and with the emerging VCR, DVD, and iPod industries. Hollywood gained badly needed revenue by licensing its offerings to TV and for VCR and DVD distribution. During the 1980s and early 1990s, before a few chain operations cornered the market, the United States had claimed more video rental outlets than movie theaters. Constantly updated technologies gave viewers improved visual imagery, bonus attractions, such as footage cut from the theatrical release, wide-screen prints, and the kind of expert commentary and analysis hitherto only available at a film school. As Hollywood studios discovered that DVD sales easily matched theatrical receipts, they sought action films with elaborate special effects that promised to sell well on DVD. They also confronted, however, new "pirating" technologies that allowed their movies to appear in illegal, bootlegged editions at virtually the same time they debuted in theaters.

The Changing Media Environment

CATV, VCRs, and digital technology transformed the entire media-entertainment environment, including the pop music industry. The Music Television channel (MTV), initially offering a 24-hour supply of rock videos, debuted in 1981. Critics immediately charged it with portraying women as sex objects and excluding artists of color. Eventually, however, MTV defused complaints, especially after featuring Michael Jackson's 29-minute video based on his hit single "Thriller" (1983). By the early 21st century, MTV and other CATV channels programmed videos that represented the increasingly multiethnic nature of the music industry.

Musical performers of the 1980s, such as Madonna, used MTV to forge a new relationship between music and visual imagery, the "MTV aesthetic." This fast-paced visual style played with traditional ideas about time and space, recycled images from movies and TV programs, and often carried a sharp, satirical edge. The hit series *Miami Vice*, revived as a feature film in 2006, helped introduce the MTV aesthetic to a broader audience. During the 1990s, MTV abandoned its initial all-video format and developed a wide range of youth-oriented programming. Its cult classic, *The Real World,* anticipated the run of "reality" shows that quickly became staples on other CATV channels and on the networks.

Entertainment conglomerates began marketing music in a variety of ever newer formats. The 45-rpm record and the long-play album (LP), associated with the musical revolutions of the 1950s and 1960s, all but disappeared. Digital compact discs (CDs) and iPods changed not only the technology through which pop music was delivered but also the nature of the product and the listening experience. The classic LPs of the late 1960s and early 1970s had featured 10 to 12 songs, split between the two sides and often organized around a core theme. The turn-of-the-21st-century CD player or iPod, by contrast, could hold a hodge-podge of songs, with themes, if any, established by the listener, not the producer.

Taken together, the Internet and digital technology permitted people to obtain, pre-serve, and exchange music in entirely new ways. The commercial music industry and most artists complained about people using the Internet to pirate copyrighted material. After years of legal sparring, while the practice of Internet file swapping soared, the music indus-try tried a carrot-and-stick approach. It began selling songs online and filed an unprece-dented number of lawsuits for copyright infringement against ordinary people who were sharing music files from their personal computers.

The New Mass Culture Debate

New trends in mass commercial culture predictably generated popular controversy. In 1975, the Federal Communications Commission (FCC) ordered the television networks to dedicate the first 60 minutes of prime-time each evening to "family" programming free of violence or "mature" themes. Eventually, federal courts struck down this family-hour requirement as a violation of the First Amendment's guarantee of free expression. Demands that Congress regulate rock lyrics and album covers also ran afoul of complaints that this kind of legislation would be unconstitutional. Eventually, TV programmers, record pro-ducers, and new Internet gaming companies, following the example of the Hollywood film industry, adopted "warning labels" that supposedly informed parents about products with violent and sexually explicit imagery.

Meanwhile, works of commercial culture were attracting serious aesthetic analysis. Unlike the critics of the 1950s, who had dismissed mass culture as trivial and degenerate, analysts who gravitated to the new academic field of Cultural Studies, and its various spin-offs in the journalistic world, often seemed to be unabashed fans of the commercial prod-ucts they studied. Most consequently jettisoned the distinction between lowbrow and highbrow. The music of The Beatles could be studied along with that of Beethoven, and Bob Dylan's lyrics along with poetic classics. The careers of manufactured celebrities such as Britney Spears and Tom Cruise attracted the attention of entertainment journalists and academics. They sought to understand what the popularity of these iconic figures pur-portedly signified about American life. The Cultural Studies approach rejected the elitist-sounding criticism of the 1950s, which had seen consumers as cultural "dupes" who pas-sively soaked up worthless products. Instead, it stressed how people could interact creatively with commercial culture. Scholarly studies of *Star Trek,* for example, examined how, through self-produced magazines (called "fanzines"), conventions, and the Internet, "Trekkies" had created a grassroots subculture that used the TV series of the 1960s and its spin-offs to launch and sustain discussions about social and political issues.

The Cultural Studies approach tended to embrace multiculturalism. It highlighted, and often celebrated, works produced by women, political outsiders, and non-Western writers and artists. It also encouraged students to see traditional texts within their political and historical contexts rather than as timeless works. Traditionalists condemned this "cultural turn" as a legacy of the counterculture of the 1960s and blamed it for eroding settled ideas of artistic quality and value.

Some of the fiercest debates over an alleged decline in the popular arts involved the emergence of an "infotainment" complex, especially on television. An imprecise cultural category, infotainment signaled that the always-delicate balance between informing and merely amusing audiences was now tilting decisively toward the latter side of the equation. TV news operations, for instance, seemed to have headed in this direction with the 1981 retirement of revered CBS newscaster Walter Cronkite, long considered the "most trusted" person in the country. None of Cronkite's successors, including his replacement at CBS, Dan Rather, ever gained his elevated reputation and credibility.

At the same time, the invention and expansion of CATV news brought strains of infotainment to the gathering and dissemination of news about the United States and the world. Images and commentary, to be sure, reached far more households and ran 24/7 on Cable Network News (CNN), which debuted in 1980. None of the anchors or reporters who worked for this path-breaking operation, however, achieved the oracle-like aura that people such as Cronkite had earlier supplied. As initially directed by Ted Turner, the mercurial CATV visionary, CNN sometimes pursued a "hard-news" agenda, from camera crews and correspondents stationed around the globe, but increasingly stressed programs, such as its one-time signature offering *Firing Line,* that relied on the in-studio pyrotechnics of verbally dueling pundits. Its eventual rival, the Fox News Channel (FNS), created in 1996 as a right-leaning alternative to CNN, retrofitted the *Firing Line* approach and used it in much of its programming, which came to feature a recognizable stable of attractive, verbally quick personalities with conservative views.

Moreover, in contrast to the old TV network format, which aimed at a "big-tent" audience, public affairs coverage on CATV adopted an avowedly narrowcasting strategy. With talk- and news-radio, local TV news programs, and most Internet sites offering much the same approach, critics of the new trends stressed how narrowly informed, according to polling data, consumers of the wide array of public affairs programming seemed to be. Infotainment seemed intent on reconfirming the existing perspectives of its core constituencies. In this same vein, public-opinion data suggested that two popular "fake" news programs, *The Daily Show* and *The Colbert Report,* themselves testaments to the Comedy Central network's own limited audience strategy, likely produced—or simply attracted—viewers who were more broadly informed about issues than aficionados of the "real" news programs.

Another "Great Awakening"

The 1960s, according to most cultural historians, ushered in another religious **Great Awakening.** By employing this term, they did not mean that the nation's diverse people suddenly became roused to spiritual enthusiasm. Religiosity had long been a far more powerful component of cultural life in the United States than in European nations. The last decades of the 20th century, however, witnessed the further intensification of always intense religious sentiments. People drawn to the **Religious Right** became particularly vocal about their commitment to seeing the world through religious teachings, but this perspective was hardly limited to political conservatives. Polls taken during the 1990s revealed that more than 75 percent of Americans believed in a divine being who performed miracles on earth.

This latest Great Awakening emerged within a culture of greater religious diversity than the nation had ever witnessed. During the 1950s, for example, Will Herberg could confidently expect his book entitled *Protestant-Catholic-Jew* (1955) to characterize the religious dimensions of the "American Way of Life." A half-century later, however, these three faiths represented only some of the religious dominations in the United States.

The cultural ferment of the 1960s, for example, affected the nation's religious landscape. Popular memory still identifies the 1960s with cultlike movements, such as the "Jesus People," loosely associated with the Counterculture. Embracing a strategy used by earlier groups that aimed at religious purification, some countercultural groups withdrew from secular institutions and sought to create communal retreats organized around religious principles and teachings. Many people drawn to alternative cultures during the 1960s also embraced spiritual and religious impulses outside of the Protestant-Catholic-Jewish triad. Asian-inspired spiritual traditions, such as Transcendental Meditation and Buddhism, also proved appealing. Looking out from his own Harvard University campus into his local community during the mid-1970s, a religion professor claimed to find more than 40 Asian religions being practiced.

More importantly, the Immigration Act of 1965 enabled larger numbers of immigrants from a variety of places—and religious backgrounds—to come to the United States. By the early 1990s, as the array of different faiths continually expanded, the weekly directory of religious services in LA's leading newspaper noted times and places for nearly 600 different denominations.

Immigration swelled the numbers of people in particular religious faiths, especially Islam, which had held only a minimal presence in the United States prior to about 1970. The Black Power impulse had attracted some new converts to the homegrown Nation of Islam during the 1960s, and later immigration from countries with large Islamic populations brought to the United States several million people who practiced more traditional versions of Islam. According to careful estimates—the official U.S. Census does not track religious affiliations—the number of U.S. residents who practiced Islam by the year 2000 surpassed that of Judaism or of individual mainline Protestant denominations such as Presbyterian and Episcopalian.

Gradually adapting to U.S. cultural conditions, mosques began making Sundays, rather than the traditional Friday, the week's major Islamic holy day. In a similar spirit, leading Islamic institutions such as the Islamic Center of Southern California and the Muslim Community Center in Chicago came to offer a variety of religious and nonreligious services for their congregations. They also sought to inform non-Muslims about their faith, which claimed more followers worldwide than any other religion, and to present an organized front against acts of discrimination.

Similar growth spurts came among Protestant evangelicals and Mormons, both of which grew faster than the U.S. population as a whole. Between the 1960s and the 1990s, the Southern Baptist Convention, moving outside of its regional base in the South, added 6 million new members. The Church of Jesus Christ of the Latter Day Saints (the Mormon faith) added more than half that many. In addition to augmenting their membership rolls in the United States, many of these groups greatly expanded their international missionary activities.

Although the fundamentalist and evangelical faiths associated with the Religious Right flourished, religious allegiance varied considerably all across the political spectrum. A number of evangelical groups such as the Sojourners, for example, embraced sociopolitical positions almost diametrically opposed to those espoused by the New Right.

© Rebecca Cook/Reuters/CORBIS

The Islamic Center of America, Dearborn, Michigan Opened in the spring of 2005, this 70,000 square-foot facility dramatized the growing presence of Islam in the United States. It features building materials imported from throughout the world, a gold dome, twin minarets, and a prayer hall that can accommodate a thousand worshippers.

Moreover, many evangelicals began to embrace the cause of environmental stewardship, a policy once associated more with the political left.

Most organized religious groups struggled with questions about the relationship between spiritual faith and the lifestyles celebrated by LGBT movements. Some leaders of the Religious Right, such as Jerry Falwell, mobilized and organized against what they saw as moral decay. In 1979, he and other like-minded fundamentalist ministers formed the Moral Majority, an activist movement devoted to encountering, as Falwell once put it, enemies of Judeo-Christian values "face-to-face and one-on-one" and to bringing "them under submission to the gospel of Christ." Orthodox Judaism, Islam, and Catholicism also considered same-sex relationships as sinful. In stark contrast, a minority of churches, synagogues, and temples—especially in larger cities—reached out to welcome LGBT members. A few accepted gays and lesbians as ministers and rabbis, and recognizable bodies of "gay theology," grounded in reinterpretations of Biblical passages as well as on general principles of religious tolerance, began to emerge.

Religious divisions emerged over foreign policy questions. During America's longest war, devoutly religious people from virtually every denomination spoke out, from seemingly every possible perspective, about the religious implications of U.S. involvement in Vietnam. If many spiritual leaders and lay people, during the post-1960s era, tended to express foreign policy perspectives comparable to the militant anticommunism that dominated the Religious (and the larger New) Right, a somewhat smaller, and equally devout, number of people believed their religious values impelled them to oppose some U.S. initiatives.

The movement to contain the spread of—and, ultimately, to eliminate—nuclear weapons attracted the support of a number of religious groups, including leaders of the U.S. Catholic Church. After prolonged internal debate among differing factions, Catholic bishops in the United States issued a pastoral letter entitled "The Challenge of Peace" (1983). It joined statements

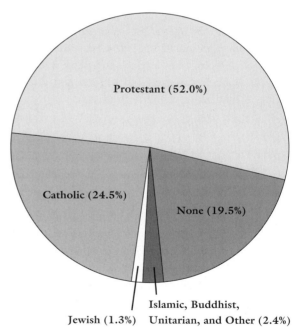

Religion in America, 2001 This chart shows the self-described religious affiliations of the American people compiled through sampling techniques.

Source: Data adapted from *The American Religious Identification Survey,* Graduate Center, City University of New York.

by several Protestant movements and, in effect, declared the nuclear policies of the United States to be in conflict with religious teachings. At about the same time, some Catholic priests joined Protestant congregations in offering sanctuary to undocumented refugees from Latin America, particularly El Salvador and Guatemala, who were fleeing from U.S.-supported military regimes and, once they reached the United States, from immigration authorities.

Three prominent religious figures who entered partisan politics exemplified the diversity of religion's relationship to political action. Father Robert F. Drinan, while a member of the U.S. House of Representatives from 1971 to 1981, generally embraced positions associated with George McGovern's rather than Jimmy Carter's wing of the Democratic Party and, on issues such as abortion, often stood against the pronouncements of his own Roman Catholic Church. Eventually, apparently largely in response to Drinan's political positions, the Church hierarchy ordered that no priest should hold a political office. Espousing political perspectives similar to those of Drinan, the Reverend Jesse Jackson, a Baptist, made two serious bids, in 1984 and in 1988, for the Democratic presidential nomination. He presented himself as part of a "Rainbow Coalition." This movement style of politics looked back, in some ways, to the religious fervor of the civil-rights movement and forward, in other ways, to the secular multiculturalism of post-1960s politics. In contrast, the Protestant evangelist Pat Robertson used his links to the Religious Right to mount an aggressive presidential bid. He hoped to wrest the 1988 GOP presidential nomination away from George H. W. Bush and place it more firmly in the hands of the New Right.

The political campaigns of Jackson and Robertson inevitably revisited charges of corruption that had touched both of their religious movements—and several others as well. The charges against Jackson and Robertson—generally involving sloppy bookkeeping, payrolls heavily staffed with relatives, and ineptly phrased political pronouncements—paled in comparison to the controversies that swamped two other religious movements during the 1980s. Jim and Tammy Faye Bakker of the "Praise the Lord" (PTL) crusade and Jimmy Lee Swaggart, all of whom were prominent celebrities in "the electronic church," saw their multimillion-dollar, multimedia empires collapse when tabloid headlines revealed their well-publicized lapses into the kind of sexual and financial values against which their TV ministries preached. Jim Bakker went to jail, and Swaggart eventually found his TV ministry relegated to public-access CATV channels rather than the top-ranked independent stations on which he once starred.

Far broader and deeper in its appeal than some detractors initially allowed, however, the Religious Right succeeded in establishing itself within the nation's religious-cultural landscape. The crusade led by Billy Graham avoided any hint of financial or moral malfeasance, and Graham remained one of the nation's most admired—and officially nonpartisan—citizens. The Religious Right created cultural-spiritual networks that included publishing enterprises, bookstores, radio and TV outlets, Christian academies and other "charter" schools, an expanded set of religiously affiliated colleges and seminaries, and even schools of law and of public policy.

Emerging early on from this milieu, Hal Lindsey's *The Late, Great Planet Earth* (1970), a best-selling book of the 1970s and 1980s (though not one found on lists compiled by mainstream bookstores and media), prepared the way for other successful apocalyptic novels, particularly the blockbuster *Left Behind* series. Conceived by the Reverend Tim LaHaye, a founder of the Moral Majority, and written by Jerry Jenkins, its 16 entries (1995–2007) featured page-turning tales about Earth's "final days" before the Rapture that would carry true believers to heaven. The actor-director Mel Gibson's *The Passion of the Christ* (2004), a blockbuster movie made outside of the Hollywood studio system, also highlighted the commercial potential of cultural products that tracked the theological-political doctrines of the Religious Right.

This broad movement succeeded in developing a powerful narrative about the history of the United States and of the entire planet, one that could be used to bolster its work on this earth. As articulated by the historian-theologian Francis Schaeffer, a committed evangelical, the people who believed that Christian teachings should shape civil society and the realm of governance had become political outsiders since the Renaissance. In this view of history, the Enlightenment had given birth to **"secular humanism,"** which wrongly separated the secular state from religious values and thus marginalized the true faith. The Religious Right embraced Schaeffer's books, such as *How Should We Then Live* (1976) and *The Christian Manifesto* (1981), as revelatory texts that pointed toward a politics that could reunite the sacred and the secular.

The Republican Party, first in opposition to President Bill Clinton and then in support of George W. Bush, became the primary electoral vehicle of the Religious Right. Religious activists persuaded some state Republican organizations, including that in Texas, to adopt a "Christian" platform that called for curtailing the separation of church and state and radically reorienting the activities of the national government. Also mobilizing and organizing at the local level, the Religious Right created movements that sought to influence the decisions of city and county school boards. From the grassroots to the White House, then, the Religious Right after 1992 played an increasingly important role in an American political culture that revolved around images of hope and fear.

Conclusion

Sweeping changes occurred in demographics, economics, culture, and society during the last quarter of the 20th century. The nation aged, and more of its people gravitated to the Sun Belt. Sprawling urban corridors challenged older central cities as sites for development. Rapid technological change fueled the growth of globalized industries and the restructuring of the labor force to fit a postindustrial economy.

The most prominent development in American popular culture was the proliferation of the video screen. Television, motion pictures, and the Internet increasingly targeted specific audiences, and the fragmented nature of cultural reception was exemplified by the rise of new, particularistic media ventures.

SUGGESTED READINGS

The economic ferment of the late 20th and early 21st centuries may be surveyed, from differing perspectives, in **Daniel Yergin**, *The Commanding Heights: The Battle between Government and the Marketplace That Is Remaking the Modern World* (1998); **Randall E. Stross**, *Eboys: The First Inside Account of Venture Capitalists at Work* (2001); **Kevin Phillips**, *Wealth and Democracy: A Political History of the American Rich* (2003); **Joseph Stiglitz**, *The Roaring Nineties: A New History of the World's Most Prosperous Decade* (2003); and **Paul Krugman**, *The Great Unraveling: Losing Our Way in the New Century* (2003).

An overview of major demographic and social issues can be gleaned, from very different viewpoints, in studies such as **David Hollinger**, *Post-Ethnic America: Beyond Multiculturalism* (1995); **David M. Reimers**, *Unwelcome Strangers: American Identity and the Turn against Immigration* (1998); **Debra L. DeLaet**, *U.S. Immigration Policy in an Age of Rights* (2000); **Joseph Nevins**, *Operation Gate-Keeper: The Rise of the "Illegal Alien" and the Remaking of the U.S.-Mexico Boundary* (2001); **Alice O'Connor**, *Poverty Knowledge: Social Science, Social Policy, and the Poor in Twentieth-Century U.S. History* (2001); and **Hugh Davis Graham**, *Collision Course: The Strange Convergence of Affirmative Action and Immigration Policy in America* (2002).

The much-contested cultural scene comes into view in **Lawrence Grossberg**, *We Gotta Get Out of This Place: Popular Conservatism and Postmodern Culture* (1992); **Fred Goodman**, *Mansion on the Hill: Dylan, Young, Geffen, Springsteen, and the Head-On Collision of Rock and Commerce* (1997); **Robert Kolker**, *Cinema of Loneliness: Penn, Kubrick, Scorsese, Spielberg, Altman* (rev. ed., 2000); **Diana L. Eck**, *A New Religious America* (2003); **Patrick Allitt**, *Religion in America Since 1945: A History* (2003); **Virginia Postel**, *The Substance of Style: How the Rise of Aesthetic Value Is Remaking Commerce, Culture, and Consciousness* (2003); **Sam Roberts**, *Who We Are Now: The Changing Face of America in the Twenty-First Century* (2004); **Reynold Farley and John Haaga**, eds., *The American People: Census 2000* (2005); and **Jon C. Teaford**, *The Metropolitan Revolution: The Rise of Post-Urban America* (2006).

Politics of Hope and Fear, 1993–2007

The 1990s brought an eight-year economic boom, the longest in U.S. history. As the stock market moved steadily, and then swiftly, upward, some economic observers began to talk about a new, depression-proof economy. Others warned, accurately as events turned out, that the good times would eventually end. Still, as the federal deficit began to shrink and, then, to disappear, the administration of Bill Clinton took considerable pride in—and credit for—the unprecedented economic growth.

The first Democratic president in 12 years, Clinton successfully urged his party to limit, rather than expand, social-welfare spending. Meanwhile, however, the conservative wing of the Republican Party regrouped behind an effort to reduce federal programs even more than "New Democrats" such as Clinton desired. Political polarization between the two parties intensified during the 1990s, emblemized by the only impeachment trial of a 20th-century U.S. president and the bitterly disputed 2000 presidential election. Once in office as the nation's 43rd president, George W. Bush pushed the economic and social agenda that the New Right had been advocating, especially on tax cuts.

Both the administrations of Clinton and Bush, following in the wake of Bush's own father, tried to chart foreign policies for a post–Cold War world. Clinton pushed initiatives, sometimes against opposition from within his own Democratic Party, consistent with his view of the inevitability of the "globalization" of economic relationships. Clinton's attempt to address other matters, particularly the use of U.S. military power, produced Republican complaints about the lack of any consistent purpose or clear guideposts in his policy making. Following the attacks of September 11, 2001, the Bush White House found a clear focus for its foreign policy: fighting a "war against terrorism" and attempting to prevail in a war in Iraq.

The Presidency of Bill Clinton (1993–2001)

Focus Question
How did President Bill Clinton seek to reshape the Democratic Party's domestic appeal? How did he try to redesign foreign policy for a post–Cold War world?

William Jefferson Clinton brought images of youth, vitality, and cultural diversity to Washington. The inaugural celebration included different balls, including one broadcast live on MTV, for different musical tastes. Clinton's initial cabinet included three African

CHRONOLOGY

1993	Congress approves North American Free Trade Agreement (NAFTA)
1994	Republicans gain control of both houses of Congress and pledge to enact their Contract with America • Special prosecutor Kenneth Starr takes over the investigation of Whitewater allegations
1995	World Trade Organization (WTO) created
1996	The Personal Responsibility and Work Opportunity Reconciliation Act becomes the first major overhaul of the national welfare system since the 1930s • Clinton defeats Robert Dole in the presidential race
1997	Congress and the White House agree on legislation aimed at reducing taxes and rolling back the federal deficit
1998	Republicans lose House seats in off-year election • Republican-controlled House impeaches Clinton
1999	Senate fails to convict Clinton on impeachment charges • Clinton orders bombing campaign against Serbia
2000	Longest economic expansion in U.S. history continues • George W. Bush defeats Gore in close, hotly disputed election decided by U.S. Supreme Court decision
2001	Large tax cuts passed • al-Qaeda terrorists crash passenger airplanes into World Trade Center and Pentagon on September 11 • USA PATRIOT Act passed • U.S. military campaign ousts Taliban from power in Afghanistan
2002	Midterm elections increase Republican majorities in House and Senate
2003	U.S. invades Iraq and overthrows Saddam Hussein • Huge federal budget deficits return • U.S. Supreme Court overturns *Bowers* v. *Hardwick* • Medicare Drug benefit passes
2004	George W. Bush defeats Democratic nominee John Kerry • Allegations of torture at Abu Ghraib revealed
2005	Price of oil soars • Hurricane devastates U.S. Gulf Coast region, especially New Orleans • Permanent Iraqi Government created
2006	U.S. Supreme Court invalidates Bush administration's trial procedure for Guantanamo detainees

Americans and two Latinos; three cabinet posts went to women. His first nominee to the Supreme Court was Ruth Bader Ginsburg, who subsequently became only the second woman to sit on the High Court. As U.S. representative to the United Nations, Clinton named Madeleine Albright, who would later become the country's first female secretary of state during his second term.

Clinton's First Two Years

Emulating Ronald Reagan, Clinton tried to move quickly on domestic issues. An executive order ended the Reagan era's ban on abortion counseling in federally funded family planning clinics. The White House pushed a family leave plan for working parents through Congress; established "Americorps," a program that allowed students to repay college

loans through community service; and secured passage of the "Brady Bill," which instituted restrictions on handgun purchases. (The U.S. Supreme Court would later rule a part
of this measure exceeded the constitutional authority of Congress.)

Clinton's 1993 deficit-reduction plan also passed, after Vice President **Al Gore** cast a
tie-breaking vote in the Senate. To stimulate economic growth, this measure featured a tax
increase and spending-cut package aimed at reducing the federal deficit and thereby eventually lowering interest rates. It also expanded an existing governmental program, called
the earned tax credit, which assisted low-income workers with children.

In 1994, Congress enacted a Clinton-sponsored anticrime bill that provided federal
funds for placing more police officers on the streets. It also contained money for prison
construction and a controversial "three strikes and you're out" provision, which mandated
a lifetime prison sentence for a third felony conviction.

Clinton's run of domestic successes ended with an ill-fated effort to contain costs and
fill gaps in the nation's health care system. First Lady **Hillary Rodham Clinton** led a task
force that, by trying to incorporate existing institutions into a new structure, produced a
plan so complex that assessments of its potential impact varied widely. The GOP used her
proposal to paint both Clintons as "Big Government Democrats." Talk-radio shows by
New Right personalities such as Rush Limbaugh featured nonstop criticism of Hillary
Clinton and the White House. The Clinton health plan became a hot-button issue on the
increasingly important cable news channels, especially CNN. Conservative pressure
groups and many business associations lobbied heavily against the plan. Sick on arrival,
the proposal died in Congress.

A Republican Congress, a Democratic White House

Congressional Republicans, energized by Representative Newt Gingrich of Georgia and
other southerners, led the GOP to a dramatic, unexpected victory in the 1994 elections.
For the first time in 40 years, the Republicans gained control of both houses of Congress,
ousting 52 Democratic representatives and 10 senators. The GOP also won several new
governorships, gained ground in most state legislatures, and made significant headway in
many city and county elections, particularly across the South. Gingrich claimed a mandate
for the GOP's "Contract with America," an ambitious 10-point program. It aimed at resus-
citating the New Right agenda of the 1980s: drastically rolling back federal spending and
reducing social-welfare programs and governmental regulations.

Congressional Republicans, however, overplayed their hand. Polls suggested that many
people distrusted Gingrich, who became the speaker of the house, more than Clinton.
When conflict between a GOP Congress and a Democratic president over budget issues
forced two brief shutdowns of governmental agencies, most people blamed congressional
Republicans rather than the White House, now advised by Dick Morris, a conservative
who counseled Clinton to stress his independence from both parties.

Most importantly, the revived U.S. economy buoyed Clinton's presidency. Alan
Greenspan, who had succeeded Paul Volker as head of the Federal Reserve Board during

the Reagan administration, gained acclaim as "the Maestro" for helping, through adroit management of the money supply and interest rates, to keep inflation in check. Most economists credited low inflation, declining federal deficits, and increasing productivity with spurring economic growth and creating new jobs. Corporate profits rose, and the U.S. stock markets soared. Some observers talked about a "new economy," one virtually immune to the ups and downs that supposedly always afflicted market-based economies. Most people saw their own economic fortunes improving. Unemployment fell steadily, and statistics on real income began to grow for the first time in nearly 15 years.

The benefits of this Clinton-era expansion, however, seemed almost as inequitably distributed as had been those of the Reagan Boom of the 1980s. The agricultural economy continued to push smaller farmers off the land; the gap between earnings of corporate executives and ordinary workers grew steadily larger; and the wealthiest 10 percent of households owned 90 percent of the nation's stockholdings.

In addition, the corporate scandals of the 1980s mutated into equally virulent ones during what one economist later dubbed the "Roaring Nineties." A Texas-based corporation, Enron, subsequently became the poster firm for this decade's culture of corruption. Before falling into bankruptcy, Enron would manipulate deregulated energy markets, while its top executives skimmed off vast sums from a business with cooked books and inadequately secured pension funds. The role of deregulation in enabling corporate malfeasance and inflated stock values became a matter of heated debate between those who stressed entrepreneurial liberty and those who emphasized governmental power as an essential counterweight to the clout of private corporations.

Meanwhile, Clinton continued to pursue his new Democratic course. He used his 1996 State of the Union address, his last before having to stand for reelection, to declare that "the era of big government is over" and began working with congressional Republicans to fulfill his goal of overhauling the social-welfare system. The **Personal Responsibility and**

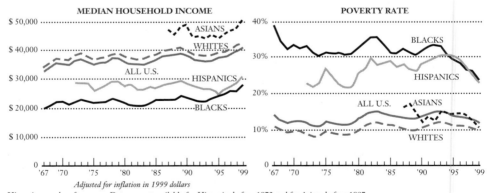

Hispanics may be of any race. Data are not available for Hispanics before 1972 and for Asians before 1987.

Income and Poverty in the Late 20th Century

Two reports by the Census Bureau in 2000 showed the economic expansion of the 1990s reaching all racial and ethnic groups.

Work Opportunity Reconciliation Act of 1996 (PRWORA) represented a series of compromises. Clinton voiced concern over cuts in the food stamp program and in benefits for recent immigrants, but he embraced the law's central feature. It replaced the AFDC program, which had long provided funds and services to poor families headed by single unemployed women, with a flexible system of block grants to individual states. The new program, entitled Temporary Assistance to Needy Families (TANF), allowed the 50 states to design, under general federal guidelines, their own welfare-to-work programs. Senator Daniel Patrick Moynihan, who had been the architect of Richard Nixon's FAP program, called PRWORA "the most brutal act of social policy" since the 19th century.

TANF, which replaced the national welfare system created during the New Deal and the Great Society eras, provoked especially bitter controversy outside Congress. Its proponents claimed that TANF would encourage states to experiment with programs to reduce welfare costs and encourage employment. Critics worried that its limitation of five years of government assistance over a person's lifetime and its authorization that states could suspend benefits if recipients failed to find employment within two years underestimated the difficulty faced by people without job skills. They also feared the impact on children, particularly in states with already minimal child care, nutrition, and medical care programs. By deferring protracted debate over these difficult issues, however, the new law effectively removed the call for welfare overhaul as a campaign issue in 1996, a turn that assisted Bill Clinton's reelection drive.

Victory and Impeachment

In 1996, Clinton and Gore defeated the Republican team of Robert Dole and Jack Kemp by about the same margin they had beaten that of George H. W. Bush and Dan Quayle in 1992. Ross Perot, although running a less aggressive, and less expensive, campaign than he had four years earlier, gained more than 8 percent of the vote, again denying the Democratic ticket a majority of the popular ballots cast. Still, Bill Clinton became the first Democratic president since Franklin Roosevelt to win back-to-back terms. Democrats held a majority of the seats in the 50 state legislatures, but Republicans retained control of Congress and gained several new governorships.

After the election, Clinton and congressional Republicans again cooperated, establishing a timetable for eradicating the federal deficit. The president's 1998 State of the Union address proclaimed that the United States had "a smaller government but a stronger nation," a result he attributed to his administration charting a "third way" between Republicans and most of its fellow Democrats. Clinton also secured a measure extending health care coverage to several million children from low-income families, tried to launch a "national conversation" about racial issues, and proposed programs to improve education. The White House even seemed poised, in early 1998, to work with congressional Republicans on reshaping the Social Security and Medicare programs.

During the rest of Clinton's presidency, however, domestic politics seemed to be geared toward the 2000 election and revolved around the president's personal behavior rather than legislative initiatives. The President and First Lady's joint financial dealings in

Arkansas—particularly those connected to a bankrupt S&L and a failed land development called "Whitewater"—increasingly intrigued critics on the New Right. A special investigation into Whitewater, which Republicans hoped could become this era's Watergate-like scandal, seemed headed nowhere until Kenneth Starr, a conservative Republican jurist, took it over in August 1994, and, then, expanded it to other matters.

Starr's inquiry, which would eventually cost $50 million, finally narrowed to the complex legal implications of a simple question: Had the president been concealing extramartial sexual encounters? Although Clinton unequivocally denied any wrongdoing, Republicans claimed his responses to Starr's inquiry amounted to obstruction of justice. Internet sites and 24/7 cable news channels competed with the print media and talk radio to ferret out the latest tidbits on the Clinton-Starr battle. Meanwhile, with economic statistics continuing to show solid growth, Clinton's approval ratings continued to rise, while Starr's steadily plummeted.

The president's denials crumbled, though, after Starr obtained irrefutable evidence of sexual encounters between Clinton and a young White House intern, Monica Lewinsky. The president, who was already a target for TV's political jokesters and Starr's investigative team, saw his legal problems dramatically escalate. Republicans insisted that Bill Clinton's public actions, particularly a deposition in a private lawsuit for sexual harassment, which a federal judge had already dismissed, justified his ouster. Most Democrats denounced Clinton's personal conduct but insisted that his private failings failed to merit, under constitutional standards, his removal from public office.

Clinton's approval rating, which remained consistently higher than those of his Republican critics, seemingly provided a formidable, nonconstitutional barrier against **impeachment proceedings.** After making Clinton the major issue during the mid-term elections of 1998, in fact, the GOP actually lost five seats in the House of Representatives. Even worse for the New Right, the public revelation of the long-term extramarital affair of Newt Gingrich forced him from office. (Similar problems prompted Gingrich's successor to follow his mentor into retirement.) Even so, the outgoing Republican majority in the House of Representatives sent two articles of impeachment against Clinton, for perjury and obstruction of justice, to the Senate on December 19, 1998. After a dramatic, televised trial, another reminder of Watergate, neither article passed.

With opinion polls suggesting that the constitutional case against Clinton swayed few people not previously inclined to find him guilty, the president's popularity actually grew during and after the impeachment imbroglio. For the first time in more than 30 years, the unemployment rate dipped under 4 percent. The continuing economic expansion, which had begun toward the end of George H. W. Bush's presidency, produced 16 million jobs. Once reviled by Ronald Reagan as the party of the "misery index," the Democrats under Clinton seemed associated with economic growth, full employment, low inflation, and fiscal responsibility. Crime statistics dropped dramatically, and the welfare rolls shrank to one-seventh of their 1994 high, or 2.2 million families. The earned income tax credit provided crucial federal assistance to low-income wage-earners with families.

The Clintons, Bill and Hillary   Stories about personal and temperamental differences have always marked the controversial, interlocking public careers of Bill and Hillary Clinton. Still, the two have remained together, serving as political confidantes and as effective teammates.

On the eve of Clinton's departure from office, nearly 70 percent of poll respondents judged him an effective political leader. Generating bitter enemies, Clinton engendered equally fervent support, particularly among African Americans. Author Toni Morrison joked that Clinton, who had grown up in a multiracial community, might have been the nation's first "black president." The success of the earned income measure also allowed Clinton to retain a strong base among low-income families. Most surprisingly, polls even indicated that people, although disapproving of Clinton's personal behavior, became somewhat less cynical about the national government's performance during his presidency.

Environmental Policy

Clinton's years in office brought an expansion of environmental measures. His administration negotiated plans to manage and protect old-growth forests in the Pacific Northwest, to implement a conservation framework for nine national forests in the Sierra Nevada, and to handle the crowds of tourists in Yosemite National Park. In highly controversial moves, Clinton's secretary of the interior set aside 16 new national monuments and blocked road construction and logging in nearly 60 million acres of wild areas in national forests.

Building on the work of its Republican predecessors, Clinton's administration placed almost 6 million new surface and underwater acres under federal protection. Environmental managers often sought to promote change through incentives rather than penalties. In 1997, for example, the Conservation Reserve Program, a farm subsidy program that had previously paid farmers to remove land from tillage, now extended payment to those who would restore their wetlands, as a means of decreasing polluted runoff into streams and preserving wildlife habitat.

The Clinton administration also highlighted how the U.S. government had often been a flagrant polluter. Throughout the Cold War, governmental nuclear facilities had spewed toxic wastes and inadequately warned workers about the dangers of radiation. In 1993, Clinton's energy secretary released long-secret medical records relating to radiation and promised to inform and compensate victims. The legacy of other military-related pollutants also became evident after Congress ordered, during the 1990s, the shuttering of many of the nation's military installations.

The environmental movement of the 1990s increasingly focused on long-term ecological dangers, which its adherents saw threatening the entire planet. They warned of chlorofluorocarbons (CFCs) causing holes in the ozone layer, climate change associated with deforestation and desertification, pollution of the oceans and seas, the decline of biodiversity in plant and animal species, and, most ominously, "global warming," the gradual increase in temperatures, partly resulting from under-regulated industrial processes. Addressing problems such as these, according to environmentalists, required worldwide cooperation toward "sustainable development."

International meetings on environmental issues became more frequent. World leaders and environmental activists staged a 1992 "Earth Summit" in Brazil, and a convention, held in Japan, in 1997, produced the **"Kyoto Protocol."** This agreement pointed toward establishing international standards on emissions of CFCs and gases that most scientists identified as the primary cause of global warming.

Dissenters within the scientific community, warmly embraced by U.S. conservatives, questioned many of the studies cited by environmentalists. Was there really good scientific evidence *directly* linking environmental changes such as global warming to human causes? Or was a complex set of long-term, cyclical forces, many of them entirely "natural" in origin, producing climatic change? Claiming scientific data to be inconclusive, the New Right became increasingly insistent that environmental regulations limited the economic potential of the United States and disadvantaged the nation with foreign competition. Republicans thus made the Clinton administration's views on international environmental matters another complaint about Democratic foreign policy during the 1990s.

Post–Cold War Foreign Policy

For nearly half a century, anticommunism and rivalry with the Soviet Union had shaped U.S. foreign policy. The Clinton White House tried to articulate a new internationalist vision. It included working on global environmental and health concerns, promoting free-market policies, improving relations with the UN, expanding NATO, advancing human rights and democracy, and reducing nuclear threats.

One of the most perplexing issues facing the United States during the 1990s involved decisions about when, and how, to employ its own military power in localized conflicts. When Clinton took office, U.S. troops, under the umbrella of a UN mission, were already on the ground in Somalia. There, they were attempting to protect humanitarian efforts directed toward providing food and relief supplies in this heavily militarized, deeply divided African nation. After 18 American service personnel died—the result of the entire U.S. force becoming caught in the middle of Somalia's factional warfare— domestic criticism of U.S. involvement, which conservative critics derided as an attempt at "nation building," mounted. Clinton ordered a pullout from Somalia during the spring of 1994, a decision some of his critics would later condemn as an example of "cutting and running."

Somalia provided a backdrop to future U.S. decisions about dispatching military forces. The next year, recalling criticism of the Somalian effort, Clinton refused U.S. support for a UN peacekeeping effort in Rwanda, where 500,000 Tutsis would ultimately die during a genocidal civil war. In Haiti, however, Clinton ordered U.S. troops, in cooperation with the UN, to help reinstall the ousted elected president, Jean-Bertrand Aristide.

The United States, through NATO, also sent troops into the former Yugoslavia to stop Bosnian Serbs from massacring Bosnian Muslims. The U.S. military remained in Bosnia to oversee a cease-fire and peace-building process created in the U.S.-brokered Dayton (Ohio) accords of 1995. Four years later, Clinton supported a NATO bombing campaign to protect Albanian Muslims, nearly 90 percent of the population in the Serbian province of Kosovo, from the "ethnic cleansing" program of Serbia's president, Slobodan Milosevic. In June 1999, after 78 days of bombardment had decimated Serbia's infrastructure, Milosevic withdrew from Kosovo, and Serbs eventually elected a new president, supportive of multiethnic democracy and the West. As in Bosnia, U.S. and other allied troops remained as peacekeepers.

Clinton's actions overseas provoked intense partisan controversy. Republican critics accused the president of lacking clear guidelines for employing U.S. power. Suspicious of cooperating with UN forces, they denounced peacekeeping and nation-building, and demanded that any plan for the overseas deployment of U.S. troops include clear-cut exit strategies. Clinton's defenders, in contrast, continued to view flexibility and cooperation with international initiatives as the strengths, not the weaknesses, of his foreign policy.

Clinton's post–Cold War agenda included several other priorities. The White House successfully encouraged mediation of conflict in Northern Ireland. During the closing hours of his administration, Clinton personally brought Israeli and Palestinian leaders to Camp David but failed to broker a peace agreement. The Clinton administration also supported efforts to stop proliferation of nuclear weapons and ordered the dismantling of some of the U.S. nuclear arsenal. It increased economic aid to Ukraine, then the third greatest nuclear power in the world, in exchange for a pledge that this new nation would disarm the 1,600 Soviet-era warheads it had inherited when the USSR went out of business.

After promises of U.S. help, North Korea also agreed to begin halting its fledgling nuclear weapons program and permitting international inspections—agreements that it later repudiated. The White House successfully pressed for a new Nuclear Nonprolifera- tion Treaty, during the spring of 1995, and three years later neared the brink of war with Iraq to maintain international inspections of **Saddam Hussein's** weapons programs. After enduring punishing air strikes, however, Iraq still expelled the investigators.

A wave of terrorist attacks by Islamic militants emerged as a pressing concern during the 1990s. Terrorists bombed the World Trade Center in New York City in 1993, U.S. embassies in Kenya and Tanzania in 1998, and a U.S. battleship, the *Cole,* docked in Yemen in 2000. These events raised alarm bells throughout the executive branch of government and prompted heightened security efforts, but produced no comprehensive U.S. plan— Clinton's critics would later emphasize—for responding to this new threat.

Globalization

The Clinton administration also pressed for lowering trade barriers and expanding global markets—the economic process called globalization. Implicitly endorsing Reagan-Bush policies, Clinton viewed globalization as boosting prosperity and fostering democracy around the world, to the ultimate benefit of the U.S. economy. A highly visible, emotion- ally impassioned antiglobalization movement, however, took root in most nations during the 1990s.

As part of his globalization emphasis, Clinton enthusiastically promoted the stalled **North American Free Trade Agreement (NAFTA)** among the United States, Canada, and Mexico and pushed it through Congress in late 1993. After a close vote that depended on Republican support, some of the fiercest residual opposition to NAFTA came from within Democratic, especially labor–union ranks. Then, in early 1995, Mexico's severe debt crisis and a drastic devaluation of its currency prompted Clinton to extend a $20 billion loan to Mexico. Unprecedented and controversial, the move stabilized the Mexican economy and, within a few years, had been repaid with $1 billion in interest. When Asian economies began faltering during 1998, Clinton successfully lobbied the International Monetary Fund (IMF) to provide emergency credits to shore up financial systems from Korea to Indonesia.

Clinton's administration, during the eight years it directed U.S. policy, signed more than 300 trade agreements. Promising that expanded trade ties would benefit all nations, trade negotiators completed the so-called Uruguay Round of the General Agreement on Tariffs and Trade (GATT) in late 1993. Then, in February 1994, the United States ended its own 19-year-old trade embargo against Vietnam. Early the following year, a more pow- erful **World Trade Organization (WTO)** replaced GATT. Anxious to move China toward a market economy, Clinton reversed his earlier position and backed China's entry into the WTO, in exchange for its promise to relax its trade policies. Everywhere he went, Clinton extolled the "New Century" in which freer trade would expand prosperity, and "liberty will spread by cell phone and cable modem."

The Presidency of George W. Bush (2001–2007)

Focus Question

How did the presidency of George W. Bush, especially in the wake of the attacks of September 11, 2001, seek to reorient both domestic and foreign-policy priorities?

Opinion polls showed Bill Clinton retaining his popularity as he neared the end of his second term. After one of the closest elections in U.S. history, however, his Republican successor soon began to take the country in different directions. **George W. Bush**, son of the nation's 41st president, seemed determined to move forward the New Right agenda of the 1980s, which the presidencies of his father and of Clinton had interrupted.

The Long Election

A retro aura surrounded the presidential campaign of 2000. Al Gore, Clinton's vice president for eight years, reappeared as the Democratic presidential nominee, and he selected Senator Joseph Lieberman of Connecticut, who practiced Orthodox Judaism, as his running mate. The Republican ballot, for the fifth time in the last six elections, bore the name of Bush. The younger Bush selected **Richard (Dick) Cheney,** a New Right stalwart who had served in his father's administration, as the GOP's vice presidential candidate. The presidential ballot also included a third-party challenger with a familiar name: Ralph Nader, the veteran activist. Running as the Green Party candidate, Nader attracted less than 3 percent of the popular vote, a far less impressive showing than Ross Perot's 1992 campaign or even Perot's less robust effort of 1996.

A listless presidential campaign stirred few passions. Bush claimed his record as the governor of Texas showed he could work with Democrats and might attract a following among African Americans and Hispanics. As president, he promised a "compassionate conservatism." While the Bush camp stayed "on message," Al Gore's disorganized campaign struggled to articulate any coherent theme. By distancing himself from Clinton, the vice president likely squandered two potential assets: Clinton's personal popularity and his record of presiding over eight years of economic prosperity. In contrast, New Right voters who reviled Clinton did turn out—and overwhelmingly favored Bush over Gore.

Barely 50 percent of the eligible voters went to the polls in 2000. Following a pattern evident since the Reagan era, the popular vote displayed discernible gender, racial, and ethnic imbalances. According to exit polls, Bush attracted 54 percent of the votes cast by men but only 43 percent of those from women. He received 38 percent of the votes from Latinos, 37 percent from Asian Americans, and 9 percent from African Americans.

The election of 2000 produced a near dead heat. Republicans narrowly maintained control of the House of Representatives, and the Senate ended up evenly split between the two parties. Gore carried the popular vote, however, by about 500,000 ballots. The only presidential tally that mattered, the one in the Electoral College, remained so close that the

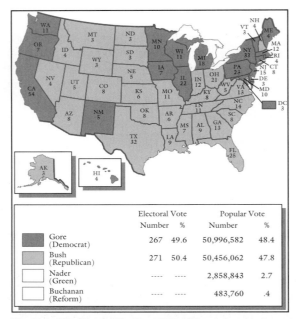

	Electoral Vote		Popular Vote	
	Number	%	Number	%
Gore (Democrat)	267	49.6	50,996,582	48.4
Bush (Republican)	271	50.4	50,456,062	47.8
Nader (Green)	----	----	2,858,843	2.7
Buchanan (Reform)	----	----	483,760	.4

Map 32.1   Presidential Election, 2000   Although Gore won the popular vote, Bush won the electoral vote after a bitter dispute involving ballots in Florida. Note the possible impact of third-party candidates.

identity of the next chief executive turned on the 25 electoral votes from Florida, where Bush's brother Jeb served as governor and Republicans controlled the legislature. The preliminary tally in Florida showed only about 1,000 popular votes separating the two candidates, but Fox Cable News, followed by NBC, soon declared Bush, on the basis of exit polls and samplings, to have been the winner there.

Partisan fervor, largely muted during the campaign, suddenly flared. For a month, no official winner emerged. After counting all absentee ballots, Republican officials in Florida declared, by a margin of 930 votes, that the state had gone for Bush. Democrats complained that many circumstances— including antiquated voting machines, deliberately confusing ballots, and apparent efforts to discourage voting by African Americans—had distorted the tally. They sued to force hand recounts in several counties from which Gore's totals seemed suspiciously low.

More than 50 lawsuits, by Democrats and Republicans alike, quickly dotted court dockets. Both parties, particularly the GOP, flooded Florida with cadres of lawyers and party activists. When the early recounts seemed to be reducing Bush's already slim margin, Republicans charged Democrats with trying to "steal" his "victory." A number of unofficial recounts later suggested Gore, not Bush, had carried Florida, but statisticians also generally advised that no procedure for hand-counting so many disputed ballots, in such a close election, could ever yield a universally agreed-upon result.

In any event, the U.S. Supreme Court, in two 5–4 opinions, chose the new president. The Court's more conservative Republicans (over the dissents of two other Republicans and two Democrats) declared, on December 12, 2000, that conducting recounts only in the contested Florida counties would violate constitutional guarantees of equality. In addition, the same justices insisted that the need of state officials to report to the Electoral College left no time for the alternative solution, a statewide recount. Legally outflanked, Gore conceded political defeat, and George W. Bush became the 43rd president of the United States.

A Conservative Domestic Agenda

As had Bill Clinton, Bush used the Reagan administration's high-octane entry into Washington as a model, one on which he and his advisers hoped to improve. New Right think tanks produced thousands of proposals for policy changes and assembled similar numbers of resumes of reliably conservative appointees. Bush chose a cabinet and White House staff that looked as diverse as Clinton's first one. It included Colin Powell in the key post of secretary of state, three women, two Asian Americans, and even a Democrat (Norman Mineta) who had served in Clinton's administration.

Bush's approach to executive branch operations, however, differed significantly from that of his predecessor. In contrast to Clinton, who reveled in loosely structured intellectual give-and-take, Bush desired brief, highly structured meetings that moved toward clearly delineated decisions. As Bush tacitly admitted and as former members of his administration detailed, this president displayed little interest in exploring, or sometimes even hearing or reading, ideas in conflict with his instincts and hunches. He allowed Vice

The 2000 Presidential Campaign, Phase 2   The inconclusive popular vote in Florida extended the 2000 presidential campaign for an additional month. Partisan activists, especially on the Republican side, became a familiar sight throughout much of Florida and on TV. GOP demonstrators insisted that George W. Bush had carried the Sunshine State and that the Democrats were conspiring to "steal" his victory.

President Dick Cheney and Secretary of Defense Donald Rumsfeld wide latitude to set policy directions. Finally, Bush unabashedly highlighted, especially to people who shared his spiritual views, how his born-again Christianity directly shaped his political outlook. During the 2000 campaign, in a response to a reporter's question about his intellectual roots, he pointedly identified Jesus as the philosopher who had most influenced his intellectual development.

An economic downturn, anticipated by most economists, provided the domestic backdrop to the early days of Bush's administration. Declining economic numbers, accompanied by a plunge in U.S. stock markets, which had been grossly overvalued and riddled with fraud, signaled the end of the 1990s boom. Revenue surpluses, at both the national and state levels, began dwindling and, then, turning into deficits. Consumer confidence slumped as revelations about apparently widespread corporate and accounting dishonesty rocked Wall Street and sent several major companies staggering toward eventual bankruptcy.

Unveiling its own agenda, the Bush administration advanced three controversial proposals, the first two of which the new president had promised while a candidate. First, Bush proposed a tax cut, which Democrats charged favored the wealthiest 1 percent of the population, to provide an economic stimulus. Second, he championed an educational program called "No Child Left Behind." It called for mandatory, nationwide testing of children as a means of determining which schools were teaching effectively. Finally, Vice President Cheney put together an ambitious energy plan, based on easing both restrictions on oil drilling and regulations on pricing. Democrats claimed this proposal, devised behind closed doors, would primarily benefit large oil and gas firms, especially ones headquartered in Texas, and do little to develop alternative sources of energy or encourage conservation.

Bush's initiatives, which seemed bolder than either his campaign rhetoric or his loss of the popular vote might have suggested, confronted a divided Congress and a suspicious public. Congress passed a revised tax plan, which mandated phasing-in substantial cuts gradually, in June 2001. It also enacted, with Democratic support, the No Child Left Behind program. Congressional opponents of the energy bill, however, blocked its passage until 2005. Foreign policy, an area in which Bush conceded his limited background, would soon push most domestic issues to the side.

Foreign Policy Changes Course

Initially, the White House seemed more intent on extracting the United States from existing international initiatives, awaiting ratification by the U.S. Senate, than in offering new proposals of its own. It announced that the United States no longer supported the Kyoto Protocol on global warming and several other international agreements, including a test ban treaty and one establishing an International Criminal Court.

As the White House sorted out its foreign-policy priorities, a small group of Islamic militants provided it with an overriding goal. On **September 11, 2001,** 19 suicide terrorists, divided into separate squads, took over four commercial jetliners, already airborne and loaded with highly flammable jet fuel, for use as high-octane, human-guided missiles. Two planes sliced into the Twin Towers of New York's World Trade Center, toppling them and several adjacent buildings; another ripped into one side of the Pentagon in Washington; and only the courageous actions of passengers on a fourth plane, which crashed in rural Pennsylvania, prevented a second attack in the nation's capital. Nearly five years later, when real-time audio- tapes from September 11 finally surfaced, they suggested disbelief, missed and mixed signals, and chaos among military and civilian officials who seemed mystified by the suicide strategy of the hijackers. The executive branch finally authorized Air Force pilots to shoot down any attacking planes, but its order did not go out until all four hijacked aircraft had hit the ground.

When the confusion ended and the initial shock passed, nearly 3,000 people, including several hundred passengers and an even larger number of police and fire officers in New York City, were dead. Various kinds of toxic materials, as later studies confirmed, covered large parts of lower Manhattan. For several days, activities not related to recovering from the attacks virtually stopped, as people watched wall-to-wall TV coverage.

AP Images/Pablo Martinez Monsivais

George W. Shows Texas Style   George W. Bush emerged victorious despite losing the popular vote to Democrat Al Gore.

Immediately compared to the 1941 Japanese attack on Pearl Harbor, September 11 rallied virtually every U.S. leader and citizen behind the White House. Three days after the attacks, Congress passed a resolution that declared the president, the nation's commander-in-chief, should "use all necessary and appropriate force" to protect the United States from another terrorist assault. In turn, Bush and other members of his administration insisted the nation now faced a very different, "post–September 11 world." Old policies and procedures, including those from the Cold War era and the Clinton years, required drastic revision. No longer facing another superpower, the now-collapsed Soviet Union, the United States could freely deploy its full power, as Clinton had supposedly refused to do—if not restricted by international agreements, other nations, or the UN. Offering himself as the determined leader of an embattled nation, George W. Bush promised to wage an all-out "war against terrorism."

To begin, the United States would retaliate militarily. Knowing the attacks had originated in Afghanistan and with Osama bin Laden, an Islamic fundamentalist from a wealthy Saudi Arabian family who headed a terrorist network called **al-Qaeda,** the Bush administration organized a multinational invasion force. In December 2001, U.S.-led troops toppled the fundamentalist Islamic regime of the Taliban, which had been dominating Afghanistan with bin Laden's help, and installed a pro-U.S. government in Afghanistan's capital city of Kabul. The Afghani effort failed, however, to secure that nation's countryside, which was divided among rival tribal factions, or to capture bin Laden and his top aides.

At the same time, President Bush began detailing other parts of his post–September 11 foreign policy. Denouncing all terrorist networks and any nation sponsoring terrorism or accumulating weapons of mass destruction, he proclaimed a "Bush Doctrine." The United States henceforth claimed the unilateral authority to use its military power for waging preemptive war against any force, including any foreign nation, that endangered its national security. In addition, congressional Democrats joined Republicans in passing legislation popularly known as the **"USA PATRIOT Act"** (Uniting and Strengthening America by Providing Appropriate Tools Required to Intercept and Obstruct Terrorism). This temporary measure gave the executive branch broad latitude to watch over and, then, detain people it considered threats to national security. The president's pre–September 11 approval ratings, which had hovered under 50 percent, soared. The off-year elections of 2002 gave the GOP secure control of the U.S. Senate and an even larger margin than before in the House of Representatives.

Although the White House clearly suggested that fighting a war on terrorism required a reconsideration of the balance between protecting national security and safeguarding civil liberties, it asked for few other sacrifices on the domestic front. Instead, it successfully pressed for adding a complicated—and very costly—prescription drug program, which critics denounced as a disguised subsidy for pharmaceutical companies, to the Medicare and Medicaid programs. The White House also argued for further tax cuts. Downplaying the record federal budget deficit (in part the result of the administration's previous tax reductions) and soaring defense expenditures, supporters of this measure claimed it would guarantee the return of prosperity. Again, Democrats condemned Bush's approach to tax cutting for tilting toward the already wealthy, now in an economy that had recently shed nearly 3 million jobs and in a nation that had seen the gap between rich and poor widen since the end of the 1990s. The partisan pitch of political rhetoric steadily increased, especially in the halls of Congress, on talk-radio, and on the 24/7 news channels.

As Osama bin Laden dropped from sight, the administration invoked the Bush Doctrine against Iraq. Dominated by the regime of Saddam Hussein, the old nemesis of the president's father, Iraq possessed some of the richest oil reserves in the world. It also posed a clear and immediate danger, claimed members of the Bush administration, to the United States. Long before the election of 2000, neo-conservatives who would later join the Bush administration had begun targeting Saddam Hussein. Many from this same group, especially Paul Wolfowitz, an aide to Donald Rumsfeld who had moved between Democratic and Republican administrations and academic life, had repeatedly called throughout the

1990s for "regime change" in Iraq. In this view, Iraq symbolized a broader challenge, one that included other anti-U.S. states such as Iran.

Safeguarding U.S. national security, according to neoconservatives such as Wolfowitz and those working for Vice President Dick Cheney, required the United States to go on the offensive. It could clear away threatening, repressive regimes, beginning with that of Saddam Hussein, and replace them with pro-U.S. democracies. Using its military power to spread liberty around the globe would not only advance U.S. strategic and economic goals but fulfill a moral mission as old as the American republic. Since "the United States is the beacon for freedom in the world," President Bush would later proclaim, it had a "responsibility to promote freedom" in the world that is "as solemn as the responsibility [to protect] the American people, because the two go hand-in-hand."

In addition to strategic-moral arguments, based on Iraq's oil reserves and on a U.S. mission to export democracy, the Bush administration offered two more immediate, pragmatic, and post–September 11 reasons for regime change in Iraq. It highlighted intelligence reports claiming Iraq already possessed, or was actively seeking, **"weapons of mass destruction" (WMDs).** Less strongly, it implied that there had been pre–September 11 ties between Saddam Hussein and al-Qaeda. Citing evidence that became increasingly controversial, the White House asked the UN and other nations to authorize military force for removing the danger Iraq supposedly posed to other nations.

Led by France, Germany, and Russia, most other UN members urged caution. They favored giving weapons inspectors, mandated after the 1991 Gulf War and readmitted into Iraq by Saddam Hussein, additional time to determine what, if any, WMDs Iraq possessed. Avoiding any conclusion to the inspection process and bypassing the UN, the Bush administration assembled, in early 2003, what Secretary of State Powell called a "coalition of the willing." It included small troop contingents from Poland, Italy, Spain, and several other countries, along with a sizeable contribution from Great Britain. Overriding some Pentagon projections, which estimated a need for at least 300,000 U.S. troops, the Secretary of Defense and the White House detailed only a little more than one-third of that total for duty in Iraq.

On March 20, a U.S.-directed air and ground operation, entitled "Iraqi Freedom," targeted Saddam Hussein's government. The White House apparently hoped a massive U.S. bombing campaign, an effort it called "shock and awe," would create physical and psychological confusion, allow British and U.S. troops to secure oil fields and other strategic locations, and permit an Iraqi opposition to organize a new government. Most of the U.S. media, which had rarely doubted the Bush administration's claims about Iraq's arsenal and intentions, enthusiastically covered this military effort, with TV reporters often "embedded" alongside U.S. forces. Far more than Vietnam had ever been, Iraqi Freedom became a "living-room war." After Iraqi troops melted away, to fight another day, Saddam Hussein's regime fell in less than two months.

On May 1, 2003, President Bush proclaimed, from the deck of the aircraft carrier *Abraham Lincoln*, the end of "significant combat" in Iraq. Shortly after this carefully crafted media event, however, it became evident that Iraqi insurgents intended to resist the

American-directed reconstruction, which aimed at creating a pro-U.S. government and an economic order closely tied to U.S. companies. Insurgents also attacked aid workers from the United Nations, the Red Cross, and other international relief agencies. What Americans had viewed as a joint American-Iraqi "liberation" and "reconstruction" effort soon floundered on opposition from Iraqi groups who saw U.S. troops as an unwelcome force of "occupation."

As U.S. officials and cooperating Iraqis worked to create a system of governance, every step in this slowly moving process faced an evolving insurgency that brought rising military and civilian casualties. In part, this carnage stemmed from Saddam Hussein's loyalists who continued to resist. More importantly, ethnic, religious, and regional divisions within Iraq spurred growing conflict. Under Saddam Hussein, Sunni Arabs who primarily lived in areas around Baghdad had dominated political power. The central government had treated Shi'a Arabs, a majority of the nation's population, concentrated in the South, and the northern Kurds, mostly Sunni but non-Arabs, as unwelcome outsiders. Shi'a groups and the Kurds (who had enjoyed de facto independence from Saddam Hussein's regime since the end of the 1991 Gulf War) now wanted a share of governmental power. Divisions also emerged between Iraqis who insisted any new government remain secular (as had been Saddam Hussein's) and those who desired one based on Islamic law. Moreover, Islamic terrorist groups from outside Iraq joined the insurgency to fight against their American enemy.

Struggles between diverse factions and the U.S. occupation often placed American troops, who had little knowledge of Iraq's socioreligious dynamics, in the middle of struggles they hardly understood. U.S. casualties mounted; the pace of military recruitment at home fell off; and the Joint Chiefs of Staff warned of the Iraqi occupation stretching its resources so thin that it might not be able to counter other threats around the globe. Moreover, the paucity of international support for U.S. action meant that, unlike the 1991 Persian Gulf War, U.S. taxpayers directly bore the rising costs of this operation.

Initially, the Bush administration had suggested that Iraqi oil revenues could pay for "liberating" Iraq, but it repeatedly asked Congress for additional billions of dollars to fund ongoing combat and occupation activities in Iraq and in Afghanistan. Iraqi oil revenues remained low; insurgents blew up infrastructure nearly as fast as it could be rebuilt; and unemployment in Iraq soared, further fueling the insurgency. Financial mismanagement, according to later audits, meant that U.S. officials could not account for considerable sums of money, which had been slated for Iraqi redevelopment and channeled to relatively few, politically well-connected U.S. companies.

Meanwhile, the Bush administration's public rationale for invading Iraq and its conduct of the war produced further controversy. Knowledgeable observers found no credible evidence of any significant connection between al-Qaeda and Saddam Hussein. Moreover, an exhaustive and official U.S. government report, issued in April 2005, concluded that Iraq had possessed no biological or nuclear weapons at the time of the U.S.-led invasion. In response to apparent failures in intelligence gathering and assessment, Congress placed existing efforts under a new umbrella agency and created a director of national intelligence as the key coordinating official. Partisans of the Bush administration, however, continued

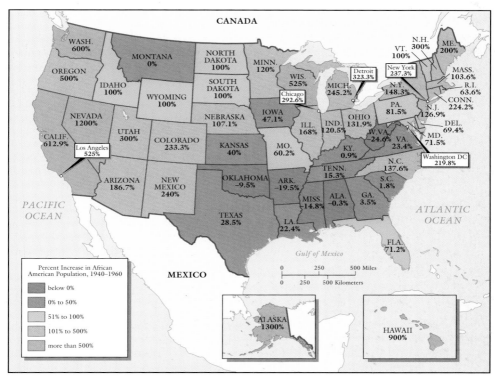

Map 28.1   Shifts in African American Population Patterns, 1940–1960   During and after the Second World War, large numbers of African Americans left the rural South and migrated to new locations. Which states had the largest percentage of outmigration? Which saw the greatest percentage of population increase? How might this migration have affected American life? View an animated version of this map or related maps at http://www.thomsonedu.com/history/murrin.

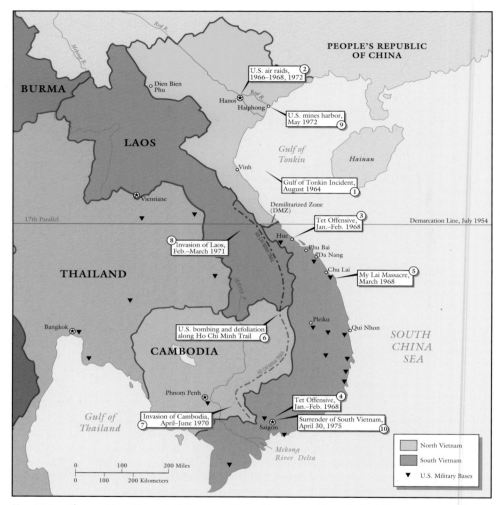

Map 29.1   Vietnam War   The war in Vietnam spread into neighboring countries as the North Vietnamese ran supplies southward along a network called the Ho Chi Minh Trail, and the United States tried to disrupt their efforts. Unlike the Korean War (see map on p. 1023), this guerrilla-style war had few conventional "fronts" of fighting.
View an animated version of this map or related maps at http://www.thomsonedu.com/history/murrin.

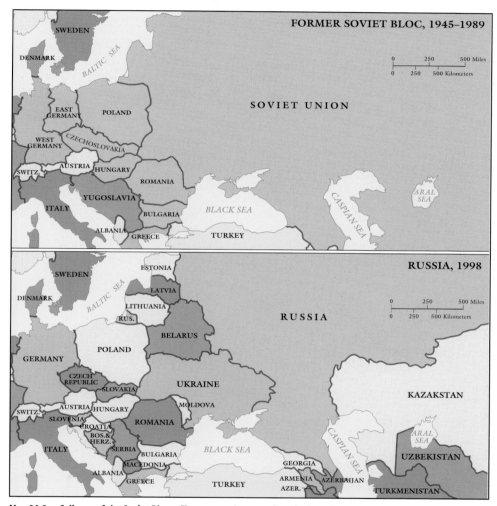

Map 30.2   Collapse of the Soviet Bloc   These contrasting maps show the Soviet Union and the countries it dominated before and after the fall of communist governments. What countries in Eastern Europe escaped Russian control after 1989? What new countries emerged out of the old Soviet Union?

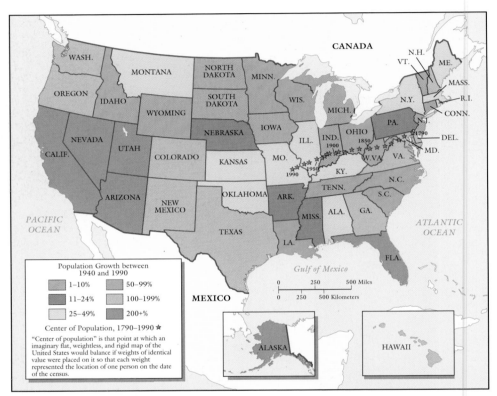

Map 31.1   Population Shifts Toward the Sunbelt   In the era after the Second World War, Americans gravitated toward the South and West. Which states grew the fastest? What might be some of the causes and consequences of such population shifts? View an animated version of this map or related maps at http://www.thomsonedu.com/history/murrin.

AP Images/Khalid Mohammed

Baghdad, Iraq, 2006   Bomb attacks, aimed at both Iraqis and U.S. personnel, followed the fall of Saddam Hussein. In May 2006, a news crew from CBS fell victim to a bomb attack. This incident underscored the danger that journalists confronted whenever they left the relative safety of the U.S.-controlled "Green Zone" in central Baghdad in search of stories about the fate of pacification and reconstruction efforts.

to assert claims about Saddam Hussein's arsenal and his al-Qaeda connections. Opinion polls from 2006 suggested that nearly half of all respondents still erroneously believed that Iraq had been stockpiling WMDs and that a significant number also believed Saddam Hussein had somehow conspired in the September 11 attacks.

As the initial case for war came under fire, so did its conduct. Photographs showing abuse of detained Iraqis, especially at Baghdad's Abu Ghraib prison, and stories of a few U.S. troops deliberately killing civilians fueled domestic debate over the use and definition of "torture" and "war crimes" and over the wisdom of having U.S. forces occupy another country.

Activism at Home during the Second Term

In many ways, the ongoing conflict in Iraq proved a political asset to President Bush during the presidential campaign of 2004. Fine-tuned by consultant Karl Rove, White House political strategy portrayed "staying the course" in Iraq as central to the broader mission to fight terrorism and to spread liberty and democracy. The Democratic nominee, **Senator John Kerry** of Massachusetts, who had served in Vietnam during the 1960s before becoming an antiwar activist, used the Democratic National Convention to highlight his military background. On the campaign trail, Kerry supported the goals of the Iraqi operation but criticized the Bush administration's strategy and tactics. Kerry kept a careful distance from the relatively small antiwar movement.

A fiercely partisan campaign, a contrast to that of 2000, featured intensive use of the Internet and energetic efforts to mobilize key constituencies. The president's supporters attacked Kerry's Vietnam War record and warned that irresponsible dissent could endanger national security. Democrats charged Bush with misleading the country about Iraq, saddling future generations with a horrendous burden of debt, enabling a small percentage of the current generation to enjoy tax cuts, and having failed to show up for military service during the Vietnam years. The election prompted a large turnout and charges of fraud, especially in Ohio.

Bush defeated Kerry and his Democratic running mate, Senator John Edwards of North Carolina, by less than 3 percent of the popular vote and gained only 15 more electoral ballots. As in 2000, Bush did best in suburbia and small towns and among people who attended church regularly. Kerry failed to do as well as had Al Gore in 2000 among white voters, still more than three-quarters of the electorate, or to win enough middle-income people, whom the Democrats had contended were suffering from Bush's economic policies.

The White House immediately claimed a mandate and announced an ambitious second-term agenda. It included a radical overhaul of the Social Security system and a restructuring of the entire tax code. Bush barnstormed the country on behalf of these initiatives, but most people seemed wary. The economy was slowly recovering, but the yawning federal deficit and sharply rising energy prices appeared worrisome signs of greater problems to come. At the same time, a series of scandals also inclined some members of the GOP-controlled Congress to move carefully. Investigations of illegal contributions from lobbyists forced the resignations of several conservative Republican stalwarts, including Tom DeLay, the effective powerbroker in the House of Representatives. The conduct of these members of Congress eroded popular faith in the legislative branch, whose approval ratings fell below that of the Bush White House. Increasingly, activist movements, rather than the White House or the party leadership in

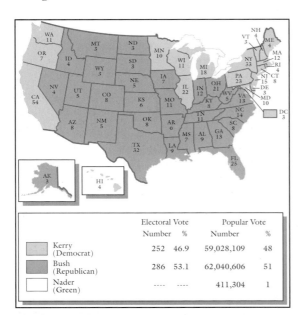

	Electoral Vote		Popular Vote	
	Number	%	Number	%
Kerry (Democrat)	252	46.9	59,028,109	48
Bush (Republican)	286	53.1	62,040,606	51
Nader (Green)	----	----	411,304	1

Map 32.2   Presidential Election, 2004   The 2004 presidential election proved almost as closely contested as that of 2000. Although the Republican ticket carried the popular vote, the Electoral College result turned on the GOP winning a narrow, and controversial, victory in Ohio.

Congress, seemed to be driving domestic politics, especially on several familiar social and cultural issues.

As immigrants had continued to enter the United States in near-record numbers during the 1990s, for example, their settlement patterns had begun to change. Increasing numbers of new arrivals, especially from Mexico, bypassed the western United States in favor of settling in cities and smaller towns elsewhere, particularly in the South. In response, movements that opposed current immigration laws and practices mobilized and organized in most parts of the country. Conservative radio commentators often helped facilitate their efforts. A few people, occasionally with tacit support from local and state officials, took direct action: They formed armed militia-style patrols, fanned out along the southwestern border, and prepared to turn back Mexicans trying to enter the United States. Other organizations mounted intensive lobbying efforts. They demanded new congressional legislation to restrict immigration, tighten border security, and strengthen measures against employing undocumented immigrants. Some also pressed local governments to pass restrictive ordinances.

Pro-immigrant organizations, particularly ones in California and in other states with large Mexican-descended populations, had already become equally active. Tapping the power of Spanish-language radio and TV stations, they staged temporary work stoppages and mounted large demonstrations, pointedly designed to demonstrate the economic importance of immigrant workers and the potential political power of the pro-immigration movement. Citing statistical studies, supporters challenged claims that immigrants "took away" jobs and depressed wage levels.

Political leaders responded cautiously. Republicans in the House, especially those from securely GOP districts, backed legislation favored by anti-immigration activists. Democrats, most of whom opposed these initiatives as too restrictive, gained enough Republican votes in the Senate to block any dramatic legislative response. Confusing matters further, the Bush White House finally promised to send National Guard troops to help secure the U.S.-Mexican border but also angered many congressional Republicans by endorsing some type of "guest worker" arrangement, a course strongly favored by most business organizations. Unable to assess how immigration legislation might affect electoral results in 2006, Republican congressional leaders backed away from taking any significant action.

Meanwhile, other activists pressed other topics. One of the most emotionally charged issues involved "gay marriage." As LGBT communities had gained greater visibility and political clout during the 1990s, some (though not all) activists sought to secure, for both symbolic and very practical reasons, legal recognition of long-term relationships they viewed to be every bit as permanent as heterosexual marriages. When the U.S. Supreme Court, in 2003, overruled its own *Bowers* v. *Hardwick* decision (in *Lawrence* v. *Texas*), its ruling hinted that the same constitutional logic that invalidated anti-sodomy laws might apply to bans against same-sex marriage. Opinion polls suggested sharply divided views about gay marriage but fairly broad support for civil unions or other legal arrangements that would recognize LGBT partnerships. In response to lawsuits supported by civil liberties and LGBT organizations, several courts held that the bedrock principle of legal-constitutional equality guaranteed gays and lesbians a "right to marry."

New Right activists responded vigorously. They tweaked existing marriage statutes and fine-tuned the legal arguments against gay marriage. In response, several judicial tribunals held that carefully drawn laws advanced legitimate public purposes, such as encouraging the best possible child-rearing practices, rather than simply discriminated against same-sex legal relationships. In addition, movements on the New Right sought an amendment to the U.S. Constitution, backed by the Bush White House, which specifically declared marriage as a "union between a man and a woman." During the spring of 2006, Democrats in the U.S. Senate narrowly turned back a GOP-sponsored effort to send such an amendment to the states for ratification.

Clashes between religious beliefs and scientific-medical knowledge also flared. Right-to-Life activists had, since the early 1990s, broadened their agenda beyond opposition to legalized abortion and the *Roe* decision. They condemned all practices that seemed inimical to a "culture of life." These included legislation, court decisions, and administrative rulings appearing to support any "unnatural" means for terminating a person's life, such as "assisted suicide" or removal of feeding tubes; anti-pregnancy drugs, such as "Plan B"; medical research that used stem cells from human embryos; and even regulations that targeted "global warming," considered a "hoax" by some on the New Right.

Differences over these issues encouraged a politics that joined deeply held ethical and spiritual values to media theatrics. In the most spectacular of these, Republicans in Congress and the Bush White House, responding to pressure from the Religious Right, backed an extraordinary 2005 legislative measure. It gave federal courts authority to intervene in a highly publicized Florida case, which involved removal from life-support systems of a young woman who had been in a vegetative state for years. As during the 2000 election controversy, activists from a variety of different movements rushed to the Sunshine State. Eventually, several federal courts refused the invitation to overrule local tribunals. Later, in July 2006, when Congress passed a measure in support of stem cell research, President Bush, standing on "culture-of-life" grounds, responded by issuing, on live television, the first veto of his presidency.

New Right activists and the Bush administration enjoyed perhaps their greatest domestic success in placing judicial nominees on the federal bench. Early in Bill Clinton's presidency, conservatives had begun worrying that an influx of new judges—exemplified by Ruth Bader Ginsburg and Steven Breyer, successfully nominated by Clinton for the U.S. Supreme Court—might cancel out the impact of Reagan-era appointees. Following the GOP surge of 1994, Senate Republicans had managed to block confirmation of a number of judges they considered "liberal activists." When campaigning for the White House in 2000, George W. Bush had declared Antonin Scalia and Clarence Thomas, two of the five Republican justices who would help ensure his presidency in *Bush* v. *Gore,* to be his favorite members of the High Court.

After 2001, the Bush White House and Republican senators seemed, according to their opponents, to want not only conservative judges but a key core of ultra-conservative ones.

Democrats charged several Bush appointees with holding views outside the "legal mainstream" and possessing scant judicial experience. Overriding such complaints, the White House mobilized movements on the New Right and adroitly lobbied wavering GOP and even some Democratic senators. The GOP leadership in the Senate also threatened to change long-standing rules that enabled filibusters, if Democrats continued to block Bush nominees.

These strategies worked. Despite an embarrassing misfire, when a Bush nominee for the Supreme Court, Harriet Miers, met determined opposition not from Democrats but from the New Right, conservative Republicans invariably succeeded in placing their favorites on the lower federal courts. In addition, the White House easily obtained Senate ratifications for two reliably, though reputedly not radically, conservative Supreme Court nominees— John Roberts to replace William Rehnquist as Chief Justice and Samuel Alito to succeed the retiring Sandra Day O'Connor. The Court seemed closer than ever before to having a five-Justice majority for overruling the *Roe* decision.

The Politics of National Security during the Second Term

Meanwhile, continuing its attempt to end the insurgency in Iraq, the Bush administration intensified efforts to create a new Iraqi government. In January 2005, Iraqis elected a 275-member national assembly, charged with establishing a temporary government and drafting a federal constitution. This body, dominated by Shi'a and Kurds, chose an interim prime minister and produced a constitution that, although opposed by many Sunnis, gained popular approval in October 2005. After several false starts and complicated maneuvering among the contending factions, Nouri al-Maliki, a Shi'a, finally emerged as a potentially viable prime minister. Coalition troops continued training Iraqi security forces, but the insurgency seemed to intensify.

Assurances from the Bush administration that U.S. troops would "stand down" whenever Iraq's security forces could "stand up" for Iraqi democracy downplayed obvious difficulties. One problem the White House did emphasize, the strong Iranian presence within Iraq, seemed especially worrisome for those neo-conservatives who had hoped the toppling of Saddam Hussein would increase U.S. power in the Middle East.

In addition, the Iraqi government included factions, such as that led by the fundamentalist Islamic cleric Moqtada al-Sadr, with a thin commitment to Western-style democratic processes and opposed to the American presence in Iraq. Movements such as al-Sadr's participated in electoral politics, held a crucial number of seats in Parliament, and also maintained their own well-armed private militias. This meant that other parliamentary factions could not expect Iraq's struggling central government to enforce policies that religious factions such as al-Sadr's strongly opposed. Contrary to the Bush Doctrine and other neoconservative blueprints, then, it seemed that encouraging democratization in places such as Iraq might not produce stable or pro-American governments, at least not for many years. During 2006, Pentagon officials conceded that Iraq seemed engulfed in what analysts could call a "civil war" and began a thorough review of U.S. tactics.

Elsewhere in the Middle East, the Bush administration confronted the rising power of neighboring Iran, a country whose influence a strong Iraq had once held in check. A new hard-line president, backed by fundamentalist Shi'a clerics, opposed to the United States and seemingly intent on developing nuclear capacities, dominated Iran's political system. Tensions escalated as the United States pressured the UN to adopt stronger measures against Iran. Then, in July 2006, fighting broke out in southern Lebanon between Israel, backed by the United States, and Hezbollah, a fundamentalist Islamic group armed with missiles provided by Iran. A more powerful version of the movement that had likely killed hundreds of the U.S. marines sent to Lebanon by Ronald Reagan in 1982, Hezbollah represented a militant Islamic movement that Lebanon's weak secular government, recently freed from Syrian domination, had lacked the power to control. This short war in Lebanon, ended through UN action, left southern Lebanon devastated and raised tensions throughout the region to new highs.

Previous U.S. administrations, including those as different as Jimmy Carter's and George H. W. Bush's, had seen a pro-Israel stance as consistent with actively facilitating peace arrangements whenever escalating conflict threatened to unhinge Middle Eastern politics. George W. Bush called for a solution that would both recognize Israel's right to exist and also provide for an independent Palestinian state, but, in contrast to his predecessors, he appeared to publicly position the United States as a firm partisan of Israeli policy.

By the end of 2006, meanwhile, military operations in Afghanistan and Iraq had claimed the lives of nearly 3,000 U.S. troops (with more than 15,000 others injured). Some estimates of casualties among Iraqi civilians, statistics that the United States neglected to collect, reached into the hundreds-of-thousands and continued to grow. Independent researchers estimated the monetary cost of the ongoing occupation, to the United States, at $6 billion per month. George W. Bush, who during the 2000 presidential campaign had denounced Democratic attempts at nation building abroad, made Iraq one of the greatest nation-building challenges in U.S. history. With Americans in sharp disagreement over both the justifications and handling of the conflict, popular support for U.S. policy in Iraq and the president's own approval rating dropped below 40 percent.

Hurricane Katrina, slamming into the U.S. Gulf Coast region in late August 2005, had also prompted an intense reevaluation, at least for a time, of nation building and national security on the home front. Local, state, and federal officials from both political parties bumbled through this massive disaster, the first post–September 11 emergency. The Department of Homeland Security, despite its sizable budget and staff, seemed unprepared to assist people in the path of the storm and those who suffered from its aftermath. Although the White House would claim no one had "anticipated the breach of levees" that supposedly protected New Orleans from flood waters, videotapes later showed members of the Bush administration, including the president, receiving precisely such a warning. Katrina exacted an especially heavy toll on the region's truly needy residents, especially those in low-lying—and low-income—neighborhoods of New Orleans. After failing to provide effective

Hurricane Katrina Hits New Orleans, 2005   This photo provides a birds-eye view of post-Katrina New Orleans. Katrina highlighted, at least temporarily, the domestic dimensions of "Homeland Security" and the apparent inadequacy of the social-economic "safety net" that different levels of government supposedly would extend to those in need.

aid to hundreds of thousands of people, authorities could not supply a precise figure, presumably in the several thousands, of those who had lost their lives as a result of Katrina.

Katrina prompted questions that went beyond the inadequacy of preparations for a single hurricane. The "safety net," intended to protect people who were already in distressed circumstances from falling, in this case literally, into desperate circumstances, seemed inadequate or, perhaps, even nonexistent.

More broadly, the Katrina episode raised questions about governmental power. People who expected private insurance companies to help pay for storm damage often discovered that the small print in their policies contained large exemptions. Subsequent studies also raised troubling hints that governmental under-funding for construction and inspection had saddled New Orleans with a badly flawed water-control system. Most controversially, Katrina revived the debate over whether or not global warming might represent the kind of national-security threat that merited, over the long term, a more substantial governmental commitment to remedial measures. Should government action provide appropriate and vital domestic social and public services that private institutions apparently could not provide?

When considering the potential power of the national government, the Bush administration increasingly looked toward expanding the capabilities of the executive branch. It pressed vigorously, and successfully, for a revised version of the "USA PATRIOT Act," which otherwise would have automatically expired in 2006. When a bipartisan coalition blocked the administration's controversial nomination of John Bolton to become ambassador to the UN, Bush placed him in this position through an unprecedented interim appointment, which did not require Senate confirmation. The White House also appointed two new CIA heads, presumably to increase its control over the Agency. On several other key issues, which the White House claimed involved national security and the president's role as commander-in-chief, Bush and his advisers seemed intent on circumventing limitations on the power of the office of the president. Vice President Cheney and Secretary of Defense Rumsfeld, who had served in the executive branch during the immediate post-Watergate era, appeared particularly eager that the Bush administration overcome congressional and judicial restrictions that had initially grown out of Richard Nixon's troubles during the 1970s.

Several constitutional controversies over the scope of presidential power marked Bush's second term. Initially, when dealing with alleged terrorists captured overseas, especially in Afghanistan, the Bush administration chose to operate outside of both domestic and international agreements and to detain hundreds of captives in Cuba, at newly constructed facilities inside the U.S. enclave at Guantanamo Bay. In a related issue, the Bush administration insisted on a loose definition of what constituted "torture" when intelligence operatives questioned people being detained. Later, the administration devised a special legal proceeding for trying detainees being held at "Gitmo," which the U.S. Supreme Court struck down, in a 5-3 decision, during the spring of 2006. In response to the various controversies over detainee treatment and the court's rebuke, the administration successfully pressed Congress in late 2006 to pass the Military Commissions Act of 2006. This act created new procedures for military commissions to try "unlawful enemy combatants" and adopted a controversial view of what constituted "torture."

In another hotly contested move, the Bush administration effectively ignored the Foreign Intelligence Surveillance Act of 1978 (FISA), which mandated special procedures before undertaking domestic wiretaps. The White House insisted the post–September 11 congressional resolution on fighting terrorism and the president's inherent powers as commander-in-chief allowed him to bypass FISA's provisions in order "to save lives."

Finally, and perhaps most strikingly, the White House, very quietly but also very publicly, asserted that all presidents possessed an independent constitutional power to interpret legislation and legal requirements. Invoking a constitutional theory called "the unitary executive," the White House inserted nearly 750 "signing statements" into the *Federal Register* during Bush's first six years in office—after the president had put his name on acts passed by Congress. Although other presidents had issued similar statements, no previous chief executive had done so on such a massive scale or in concert with such a sweeping constitutional vision of presidential authority.

The unitary executive thesis, as formulated by conservative jurists, relied on a section of Article II in the Constitution and the presidential oath of office. Both contain language about "faithfully executing " the duties of the presidency *and* the laws of the United States, magic words that some constitutional theorists read as justifying chief executives to interpret independently and, then, apply unilaterally U.S. laws, even against alternative interpretations by other branches of government. Bush's many signing statements, testaments to an indefatigable White House legal team, included presidential dissents against laws protecting governmental whistleblowers and ones limiting governmental oversight of federally funded research projects.

On the eve of the 2006 mid-term election, the unpopularity of the war in Iraq, the controversies over executive power, several high-profile corruption cases, and schisms within the president's New Right coalition sapped Republican party strength. A re-energized Democratic party capitalized on popular discontent over all of these issues. In the 2006 midterm elections Democrats picked enough senate and house seats to capture control of Congress. Democratic candidates also unseated six Republican governors. In response, the White House announced the resignation of Donald Rumsfeld as secretary of defense.

Conclusion

The end of the 20th century and the beginning of a new one saw the United States seeking to develop domestic policies that could ensure continued economic growth. At the same time, this period witnessed the nation adjusting to the end of a global Cold War and the beginning of an equally broad struggle against terrorism.

Bill Clinton, styling himself a New Democrat, adopted a relatively conservative socioeconomic agenda that included slashing the federal deficit and reshaping the welfare system. During his presidency, Clinton sought to move the Democratic Party away from its big government image. At the same time, however, he supported other issues, such as environmental protection, that were heatedly opposed by many Republicans. Clinton's emphasis on aligning the United States with economic globalization seemed his most forceful attempt to address a post–Cold War world.

The first president to take office—and, then, win a second term—during the 21st century, George W. Bush recalled and promised to re-ignite the conservative surge of the Reagan years. After achieving one of its major domestic goals, tax-cutting, the Bush administration responded to the September 11 attacks with military actions overseas and claims of new executive powers. Its major foreign-policy initiative, a preemptive strike against Saddam Hussein's Iraq, initially prompted widespread support and, later, produced growing controversy.

Clinton and Bush, who used very different images and media skills to become two-term presidents, inspired intense adoration and passionate dislike. Both tried to redraw the political landscape in his own party's favor, yet polling data suggested that the electorate, at the beginning of 2007, remained roughly evenly divided. Against the backdrop of insistent reminders, especially from the Bush White House, that the nation remained under constant threat, an increasingly diverse people continued to negotiate the difficult balances among liberty, equality, and power.

SUGGESTED READINGS

Very different perspectives on the Clinton years appear in **Bob Woodward**, *The Agenda: Inside the Clinton White House* (1994) and *The Choice* (1996); **Theodore Lowi and Benjamin Ginsburg**, *Embattled Democracy: Politics and Policy in the Clinton Era* (1995); **Kenneth Baer**, *Reinventing Democrats: The Politics of Liberalism from Reagan to Clinton* (2000); **Haynes Johnson**, *The Best of Times: America in the Clinton Years* (2001); **David Halberstam**, *War in a Time of Peace* (2001); **Sidney Blumenthal**, *The Clinton Wars* (2003); **John F. Harris**, *The Survivor: Bill Clinton in the White House* (2005); and **Joseph E. Stiglitz**, *The Roaring Nineties* (2003).

The electoral contest that elevated George W. Bush to the presidency is analyzed in **Jack M. Rakove**, ed., *The Unfinished Election of 2000* (2002) and **Jeffrey Toobin**, *Too Close to Call* (2001). For preliminary assessments of how Bush remained in the White House, see **William J. Crotty**, ed., *A Defining Moment: The Presidential Election of 2004* (2005).

The controversy surrounding George W. Bush's presidency, and especially its relationship to the attacks of September 11, is reflected in titles such as **Bob Woodward**, *Bush at War* (3 vols., 2002-6); **Craig Calhoun, Paul Price, and Ashley Timmer**, eds., *Understanding September 11* (2002); **David Frum**, *The Right Man: The Surprise Presidency of George W. Bush* (2003); **Stephen Hess and Marvin Kalb**, eds., *The Media and the War on Terrorism* (2003); **Gerald Posner**, *Why America Slept: The Failure to Prevent 9/11* (2003); **Joanne Meyerowitz**, ed., *History and September 11th* (2003); **Chalmers Johnson**, *The Sorrows of Empire: Militarism, Secrecy, and the End of the Republic* (2004); **Kevin Phillips**, *American Theocracy: The Peril and Politics of Radical Religion, Oil, and Borrowed Money in the 21st Century* (2006); **Michael R. Gordon and General Bernard E. Trainor**, *Cobra II: The Inside Story of the Invasion and Occupation of Iraq* (2006); **Thomas E. Ricks**, *Fiasco: The American Military Adventure in Iraq* (2006); **Ron Suskind**, *The One Percent Doctrine* (2006); and **Vali Nasr**, *The Shia Revival: How Conflicts within Islam Will Shape the Future* (2006).

James T. Patterson, *Restless Giant: The United States from Watergate to Bush v. Gore* (2005) offers an excellent overview of the era from 1974 to 2001. **Godfrey Hodgson**, *More Equal Than Others: America from Nixon to the New Century* (2004) is more impressionistic.

Appendix

The Declaration of Independence

The Unanimous Declaration of the Thirteen United States of America

When in the Course of human events it becomes necessary for one people to dissolve the political bands which have connected them with another, and to assume among the Powers of the earth, the separate and equal station to which the Laws of Nature and of Nature's God entitle them, a decent respect to the opinions of mankind requires that they should declare the causes which impel them to the separation.

We hold these truths to be self-evident, that all men are created equal, that they are endowed by their Creator with certain unalienable Rights, that among these are Life, Liberty and the pursuit of Happiness. That to secure these rights, Governments are instituted among Men, deriving their just Powers from the consent of the governed. That whenever any Form of Government becomes destructive of these ends, it is the Right of the People to alter or to abolish it, and to institute new Government, laying its foundation on such principles and organizing its Powers in such form, as to them shall seem most likely to effect their Safety and Happiness. Prudence, indeed, will dictate that Governments long established should not be changed for light and transient causes; and accordingly all experience hath shewn, that mankind are more disposed to suffer, while evils are sufferable, than to right themselves by abolishing the forms to which they are accustomed. But when a long train of abuses and usurpations, pursuing invariably the same Object evinces a design to reduce them under absolute Despotism, it is their right, it is their duty, to throw off such Government, and to provide new Guards for their future security. Such has been the patient sufferance of these Colonies; and such is now the necessity which constrains them to alter their former Systems of Government. The history of the present King of Great Britain is a history of repeated injuries and usurpations, all having in direct object the establishment of an absolute Tyranny over these States. To prove this, let Facts be submitted to a candid world.

He has refused his Assent to Laws, the most wholesome and necessary for the public good.

He has forbidden his Governors to pass Laws of immediate and pressing importance, unless suspended in their operation till his Assent should be obtained; and when so suspended, he has utterly neglected to attend to them.

Text is reprinted from the facsimile of the engrossed copy in the National Archives. The original spelling, capitalization, and punctuation have been retained. Paragraphing has been added.

He has refused to pass other Laws for the accommodation of large districts of people, unless those people would relinquish the right of Representation in the Legislature, a right inestimable to them and formidable to tyrants only.

He has called together legislative bodies at places unusual, uncomfortable, and distant from the depository of their Public Records, for the sole Purpose of fatiguing them into compliance with his measures.

He has dissolved Representative Houses repeatedly, for opposing with manly firmness his invasions on the rights of the People.

He has refused for a long time, after such dissolutions, to cause others to be elected; whereby the Legislative Powers, incapable of Annihilation, have returned to the People at large for their exercise; the State remaining in the mean time exposed to all the dangers of invasion from without, and convulsions within.

He has endeavoured to prevent the Population of these States; for that purpose obstructing the Laws for Naturalization of Foreigners; refusing to pass others to encourage their migrations hither, and raising the conditions of new Appropriations of Lands.

He has obstructed the Administration of Justice, by refusing his Assent to Laws for establishing Judiciary Powers.

He has made Judges dependent on his Will alone, for the tenure of their offices, and the amount and payment of their salaries.

He has erected a multitude of New Offices, and sent hither swarms of Officers to harass our People, and eat out their substance.

He has kept among us, in times of peace, Standing Armies without the Consent of our legislatures.

He has affected to render the Military independent of and superior to the Civil Power.

He has combined with others to subject us to a jurisdiction foreign to our constitution, and unacknowledged by our laws; giving his Assent to their Acts of pretended Legislation:

For Quartering large bodies of armed troops among us:

For protecting them, by a mock Trial, from Punishment for any Murders which they should commit on the Inhabitants of these States:

For cutting off our Trade with all parts of the world:

For imposing Taxes on us without our Consent:

For depriving us in many cases, of the benefits of Trial by Jury:

For transporting us beyond Seas to be tried for pretended offences:

For abolishing the free System of English Laws in a neighbouring Province, establishing therein an Arbitrary government, and enlarging its Boundaries so as to render it at once an example and fit instrument for introducing the same absolute rule into these Colonies:

For taking away our Charters, abolishing our most valuable Laws, and altering fundamentally the Forms of our Governments:

For suspending our own Legislatures, and declaring themselves invested with Power to legislate for us in all cases whatsoever.

He has abdicated Government here, by declaring us out of his Protection, and waging War against us.

He has plundered our seas, ravaged our Coasts, burnt our towns, and destroyed the lives of our people.

He is at this time transporting large Armies of foreign Mercenaries to compleat the works of death, desolation and tyranny, already begun with circumstances of Cruelty and perfidy scarcely paralleled in the most barbarous ages, and totally unworthy the Head of a civilized nation.

He has constrained our fellow Citizens taken Captive on the high Seas to bear Arms against their Country, to become the executioners of their friends and Brethren, or to fall themselves by their Hands.

He has excited domestic insurrections amongst us, and has endeavoured to bring on the inhabitants of our frontiers, the merciless Indian Savages, whose known rule of warfare, is an undistinguished destruction of all ages, sexes and conditions.

In every stage of these Oppressions We have Petitioned for Redress in the most humble terms: Our repeated Petitions have been answered only by repeated injury. A Prince, whose character is thus marked by every act which may define a Tyrant, is unfit to be the ruler of a free People.

Nor have We been wanting in attentions to our British brethren. We have warned them from time to time of attempts by their legislature to extend an unwarrantable jurisdiction over us. We have reminded them of the circumstances of our emigration and settlement here. We have appealed to their native justice and magnanimity, and we have conjured them by the ties of our common kindred to disavow these usurpations, which, would inevitably interrupt our connections and correspondence. They too have been deaf to the voice of justice and of consanguinity. We must, therefore, acquiesce in the necessity, which denounces our Separation, and hold them, as we hold the rest of mankind, Enemies in War, in Peace Friends.

WE, THEREFORE, the Representatives of the UNITED STATES OF AMERICA, in General Congress, Assembled, appealing to the Supreme Judge of the world for the rectitude of our intentions, do, in the Name, and by Authority of the good People of these Colonies, solemnly publish and declare, That these United Colonies are, and of Right ought to be FREE AND INDEPENDENT STATES; that they are Absolved from all Allegiance to the British Crown, and that all political connection between them and the State of Great Britain, is and ought to be totally dissolved; and that, as Free and Independent States, they have full Power to levy War, conclude Peace, contract Alliances, establish Commerce, and to do all other Acts and Things which Independent States may of right do. And for the support of this Declaration, with a firm reliance on the protection of divine Providence, we mutually pledge to each other our Lives, our Fortunes and our sacred Honor.

The Constitution of the United States of America

We the People of the United States, in Order to form a more perfect Union, establish Justice, insure domestic Tranquility, provide for the common defence, promote the general Welfare, and secure the Blessings of Liberty to ourselves and our Posterity, do ordain and establish this Constitution for the United States of America.

Article I.

Section 1. All legislative Powers herein granted shall be vested in a Congress of the United States, which shall consist of a Senate and House of Representatives.

Section 2 The House of Representatives shall be composed of Members chosen every second Year by the People of the several States, and the Electors in each State shall have the Qualifications requisite for Electors of the most numerous Branch of the State Legislature.

No Person shall be a Representative who shall not have attained to the Age of twenty five Years, and been seven Years a Citizen of the United States, and who shall not, when elected, be an Inhabitant of that State in which he shall be chosen.

Representatives and direct Taxes[1] shall be apportioned among the several States which may be included within this Union, according to their respective Numbers, which shall be determined by adding to the whole Number of free Persons, including those bound to Service for a Term of Years, and excluding Indians not taxed, three fifths of all other Persons.[2] The actual Enumeration shall be made within three Years after the first Meeting of the Congress of the United States, and within every subsequent Term of ten Years, in such Manner as they shall by Law direct. The Number of Representatives shall not exceed one for every thirty Thousand, but each State shall have at Least one Representative; and until such enumeration shall be made, the State of New Hampshire shall be entitled to chuse three; Massachusetts eight; Rhode Island and Providence Plantations one; Connecticut five; New York six; New Jersey four; Pennsylvania eight; Delaware one; Maryland six; Virginia ten; North Carolina five; South Carolina five; and Georgia three.

When vacancies happen in the Representation from any State, the Executive Authority thereof shall issue Writs of Election to fill such Vacancies.

The House of Representatives shall chuse their Speaker and other Officers; and shall have the sole Power of Impeachment.

Section 3. The Senate of the United States shall be composed of two Senators from each State, chosen by the Legislature thereof, for six Years; and each Senator shall have one Vote.[3]

Text is from the engrossed copy in the National Archives. Original spelling, capitalization, and punctuation have been retained.

[1]Modified by the Sixteenth Amendment.
[2]Replaced by the Fourteenth Amendment.
[3]Superseded by the Seventeenth Amendment.

Immediately after they shall be assembled in Consequence of the first Election, they shall be divided as equally as may be into three Classes. The Seats of the Senators of the first Class shall be vacated at the Expiration of the second Year, of the second Class at the Expiration of the fourth Year, and of the third Class at the Expiration of the sixth Year, so that one third may be chosen every second Year; and if Vacancies happen by Resignation, or otherwise, during the Recess of the Legislature of any State, the Executive thereof may make temporary Appointments until the next Meeting of the Legislature, which shall then fill such Vacancies.[4]

No Person shall be a Senator who shall not have attained to the Age of thirty Years, and been nine Years a Citizen of the United States, and who shall not, when elected, be an Inhabitant of that State for which he shall be chosen.

The Vice President of the United States shall be President of the Senate, but shall have no Vote, unless they be equally divided.

The Senate shall chuse their other Officers, and also a President pro tempore, in the Absence of the Vice President, or when he shall exercise the Office of President of the United States.

The Senate shall have the sole Power to try all Impeachments. When sitting for that Purpose, they shall be on Oath or Affirmation. When the President of the United States is tried, the Chief Justice shall preside: And no Person shall be convicted without the Concurrence of two thirds of the Members present.

Judgment in Cases of Impeachment shall not extend further than to removal from Office, and disqualification to hold and enjoy any Office of honor, Trust or Profit under the United States: but the Party convicted shall nevertheless be liable and subject to Indictment, Trial, Judgment and Punishment, according to Law.

Section 4. The Times, Places and Manner of holding Elections for Senators and Representatives, shall be prescribed in each State by the Legislature thereof, but the Congress may at any time by Law make or alter such Regulation, except as to the Places of chusing Senators.

The Congress shall assemble at least once in every Year, and such Meeting shall be on the first Monday in December, unless they shall by Law appoint a different Day.[5]

Section 5. Each House shall be the Judge of the Elections, Returns and Qualifications of its own Members, and a Majority of each shall constitute a Quorum to do Business; but a smaller Number may adjourn from day to day, and may be authorized to compel the Attendance of absent Members, in such Manner, and under such Penalties as each House may provide.

Each House may determine the Rules of its Proceedings, punish its Members for disorderly Behaviour, and, with the Concurrence of two thirds, expel a Member.

---

[4]Modified by the Seventeenth Amendment.
[5]Superseded by the Twentieth Amendment.

Each House shall keep a Journal of its Proceedings, and from time to time publish the same, excepting such Parts as may in their Judgment require Secrecy; and the Yeas and Nays of the Members of either House on any question shall, at the Desire of one fifth of those Present, be entered on the Journal.

Neither House, during the Session of Congress, shall, without the Consent of the other, adjourn for more than three days, nor to any other Place than that in which the two Houses shall be sitting.

Section 6. The Senators and Representatives shall receive a Compensation for their Services, to be ascertained by Law, and paid out of the Treasury of the United States. They shall in all Cases, except Treason, Felony and Breach of the Peace, be privileged from Arrest during their Attendance at the Session of their respective Houses, and in going to and returning from the same; and for any Speech or Debate in either House, they shall not be questioned in any other Place.

No Senator or Representative shall, during the Time for which he was elected, be appointed to any civil Office under the Authority of the United States, which shall have been created, or the Emoluments whereof shall have been encreased during such time; and no Person holding any Office under the United States, shall be a Member of either House during his Continuance in Office.

Section 7. All Bills for raising Revenue shall originate in the House of Representatives; but the Senate may propose or concur with Amendments as on other Bills.

Every Bill which shall have passed the House of Representatives and the Senate shall, before it become a Law, be presented to the President of the United States; If he approve he shall sign it, but if not he shall return it, with his Objections to that House in which it shall have originated, who shall enter the Objections at large on their Journal, and proceed to reconsider it. If after such Reconsideration two thirds of that House shall agree to pass the Bill, it shall be sent, together with the Objections, to the other House, by which it shall likewise be reconsidered, and if approved by two thirds of that House, it shall become a Law. But in all such Cases the Votes of both Houses shall be determined by yeas and Nays, and the Names of the Persons voting for and against the Bill shall be entered on the Journal of each House respectively. If any Bill shall not be returned by the President within ten Days (Sundays excepted) after it shall have been presented to him, the Same shall be a Law, in like Manner as if he had signed it, unless the Congress by their Adjournment prevent its Return, in which Case it shall not be a Law.

Every Order, Resolution, or Vote to which the Concurrence of the Senate and House of Representatives may be necessary (except on a question of Adjournment) shall be presented to the President of the United States; and before the Same shall take Effect, shall be approved by him, or being disapproved by him shall be repassed by two thirds of the Senate and House of Representatives, according to the Rules and Limitations prescribed in the Case of a Bill.

Section 8. The Congress shall have power To lay and collect Taxes, Duties, Imposts and Excises, to pay the Debts and provide for the common Defence and general Welfare of the United States; but all Duties, Imposts and Excises shall be uniform throughout the United States;

To borrow Money on the credit of the United States;

To regulate Commerce with foreign Nations, and among the several States, and with the Indian Tribes;

To establish an uniform Rule of Naturalization, and uniform Laws on the subject of Bankruptcies throughout the United States;

To coin Money, regulate the Value thereof, and of foreign Coin, and fix the Standard of Weights and Measures;

To provide for the Punishment of counterfeiting the Securities and current Coin of the United States;

To establish Post Offices and post Roads;

To promote the Progress of Science and useful Arts, by securing for limited Times to Authors and Inventors the exclusive Right to their respective Writings and Discoveries;

To constitute Tribunals inferior to the supreme Court;

To define and punish Piracies and Felonies committed on the high Seas, and Offences against the Law of Nations;

To declare War, grant Letters of Marque and Reprisal, and make Rules concerning Captures on Land and Water;

To raise and support Armies, but no Appropriation of Money to that Use shall be for a longer Term than two Years;

To provide and maintain a Navy;

To make Rules for the Government and Regulation of the land and naval Forces;

To provide for calling forth the Militia to execute the Laws of the Union, suppress Insurrections and repel Invasions;

To provide for organizing, arming, and disciplining, the Militia, and for governing such Part of them as may be employed in the Service of the United States, reserving to the States respectively, the Appointment of the Officers, and the Authority of training the Militia according to the discipline prescribed by Congress;

To exercise exclusive Legislation in all Cases whatsoever, over such District (not exceeding ten Miles square) as may, by Cession of particular States, and the Acceptance of Congress, become the Seat of the Government of the United States, and to exercise like Authority over all Places purchased by the Consent of the Legislature of the State in which the Same shall be, for the Erection of Forts, Magazines, Arsenals, dock-Yards, and other needful Buildings;—And

To make all Laws which shall be necessary and proper for carrying into Execution the foregoing Powers, and all other Powers vested by this Constitution in the Government of the United States, or in any Department or Officer thereof.

Section 9. The Migration or Importation of such Persons as any of the States now existing shall think proper to admit, shall not be prohibited by the Congress prior to the Year one thousand eight hundred and eight, but a Tax or duty may be imposed on such Importation, not exceeding ten dollars for each Person.

The Privilege of the Writ of Habeas Corpus shall not be suspended, unless when in Cases of Rebellion or Invasion the public Safety may require it.

No Bill of Attainder or ex post facto Law shall be passed.

No Capitation, or other direct, Tax shall be laid, unless in Proportion to the Census or Enumeration herein before directed to be taken.

No Tax or Duty shall be laid on Articles exported from any State.

No Preference shall be given by any Regulation of Commerce or Revenue to the Ports of one State over those of another: nor shall Vessels bound to, or from, one State, be obliged to enter, clear, or pay Duties in another.

No Money shall be drawn from the Treasury, but in Consequence of Appropriations made by Law, and a regular Statement and Account of the Receipts and Expenditures of all public Money shall be published from time to time.

No Title of Nobility shall be granted by the United States: And no Person holding any Office of Profit or Trust under them, shall, without the Consent of the Congress, accept of any present, Emolument, Office, or Title, of any kind whatever, from any King, Prince, or foreign State.

Section 10. No State shall enter into any Treaty, Alliance, or Confederation; grant Letters of Marque and Reprisal; coin Money; emit Bills of Credit; make any Thing but gold and silver Coin a Tender in Payment of Debts; pass any Bill of Attainder, ex post facto Law, or Law impairing the Obligation of Contracts, or grant any Title of Nobility.

No State shall, without the Consent of the Congress, lay any Imposts or Duties on Imports or Exports, except what may be absolutely necessary for executing its inspection Laws: and the net Produce of all Duties and Imposts, laid by any State on Imports or Exports, shall be for the Use of the Treasury of the United States; and all such Laws shall be subject to the Revision and Controul of the Congress.

No State shall, without the Consent of Congress, lay any Duty of Tonnage, keep Troops, or Ships of War in time of Peace, enter into any Agreement or Compact with another State, or with a foreign Power, or engage in War, unless actually invaded, or in such imminent Danger as will not admit of delay.

Article II.

Section 1. The executive Power shall be vested in a President of the United States of America. He shall hold his Office during the Term of four Years, and, together with the Vice President, chosen for the same Term, be elected, as follows:

Each State shall appoint, in such Manner as the Legislature thereof may direct, a Number of Electors, equal to the whole Number of Senators and Representatives to which the State may be entitled in the Congress: but no Senator or Representative, or Person holding an Office of Trust or Profit under the United States, shall be appointed an Elector.

The Electors shall meet in their respective States, and vote by Ballot for two Persons, of whom one at least shall not be an Inhabitant of the same State with themselves. And they shall make a List of all the Persons voted for, and of the Number of Votes for each; which List they shall sign and certify, and transmit sealed to the Seat of the Government of the United States, directed to the President of the Senate. The President of the Senate shall, in the Presence of the Senate and House of Representatives, open all the Certificates, and the Votes shall then be counted. The Person having the greatest Number of Votes shall be the President, if such Number be a Majority of the whole Number of Electors appointed; and if there be more than one who have such Majority, and have an equal Number of Votes, then the House of Representatives shall immediately chuse by Ballot one of them for President; and if no Person have a Majority, then from the five highest on the List the said House shall in like Manner chuse the President. But in chusing the President, the Votes shall be taken by States, the Representation from each State having one Vote; A quorum for this Purpose shall consist of a Member or Members from two thirds of the States, and a Majority of all the States shall be necessary to a Choice. In every Case, after the Choice of the President, the Person having the greatest Number of Votes of the Electors shall be the Vice President. But if there should remain two or more who have equal Votes, the Senate shall chuse from them by Ballot the Vice President.[6]

The Congress may determine the Time of chusing the Electors, and the Day on which they shall give their Votes; which Day shall be the same throughout the United States.

No Person except a natural born Citizen, or a Citizen of the United States, at the time of the Adoption of this Constitution, shall be eligible to the Office of President, neither shall any Person be eligible to that Office who shall not have attained to the Age of thirty five Years, and been fourteen Years a Resident within the United States.

In Case of the Removal of the President from Office, or of his Death, Resignation, or Inability to discharge the Powers and Duties of the said Office, the Same shall devolve on the Vice President, and the Congress may by Law provide for the Case of Removal, Death, Resignation or Inability, both of the President and Vice President, declaring what Officer shall then act as President, and such Officer shall act accordingly, until the Disability be removed, or a President shall be elected.[7]

The President shall, at stated Times, receive for his Services, a Compensation, which shall neither be encreased nor diminished during the Period for which he shall have been elected, and he shall not receive within that Period any other Emolument from the United States, or any of them.

---

[6]Superseded by the Twelfth Amendment.
[7]Modified by the Twenty-fifth Amendment.

Before he enter on the Execution of his Office, he shall take the following Oath or Affirmation:—"I do solemnly swear (or affirm) that I will faithfully execute the Office of President of the United States, and will to the best of my Ability, preserve, protect and defend the Constitution of the United States."

Section 2. The President shall be Commander in Chief of the Army and Navy of the United States, and of the Militia of the several States, when called into the actual Service of the United States; he may require the Opinion, in writing, of the principal Officer in each of the executive Departments, upon any Subject relating to the Duties of their respective Offices, and he shall have Power to grant Reprieves and Pardons for Offences against the United States, except in Cases of Impeachment.

He shall have Power, by and with the Advice and Consent of the Senate, to make Treaties, provided two thirds of the Senators present concur; and he shall nominate, and by and with the Advice and Consent of the Senate, shall appoint Ambassadors, other public Ministers and Consuls, Judges of the supreme Court, and all other Officers of the United States, whose Appointments are not herein otherwise provided for, and which shall be established by Law; but the Congress may by Law vest the Appointment of such inferior Officers, as they think proper, in the President alone, in the Courts of Law, or in the Heads of Departments.

The President shall have Power to fill up all Vacancies that may happen during the Recess of the Senate, by granting Commissions which shall expire at the End of their next Session.

Section 3. He shall from time to time give the Congress Information of the State of the Union, and recommend to their Consideration such Measures as he shall judge necessary and expedient; he may, on extraordinary Occasions, convene both Houses, or either of them, and in Case of Disagreement between them, with Respect to the Time of Adjournment, he may adjourn them to such Time as he shall think proper; he shall receive Ambassadors and other public Ministers; he shall take Care that the Laws be faithfully executed, and shall Commission all the Officers of the United States.

Section 4. The President, Vice President and all civil Officers of the United States, shall be removed from Office on Impeachment for, and Conviction of, Treason, Bribery, or other high Crimes and Misdemeanors.

Article III.

Section 1. The judicial Power of the United States, shall be vested in one supreme Court, and in such inferior Courts as the Congress may from time to time ordain and establish. The Judges, both of the supreme and inferior Courts, shall hold their Offices during good Behaviour, and shall, at stated Times, receive for their Services, a Compensation, which shall not be diminished during their Continuance in Office.

Section 2. The judicial Power shall extend to all Cases, in Law and Equity, arising under this Constitution, the Laws of the United States, and Treaties made, or which shall be made, under their Authority;—to all Cases affecting Ambassadors, other public Ministers and Consuls;—to all Cases of admiralty and maritime Jurisdiction;—to Controversies to which the United States shall be a Party;—to Controversies between two or more States;—between a State and Citizens of another State;[8]—between Citizens of different States,—between Citizens of the same State claiming Lands under Grants of different States, and between a State, or the Citizens thereof, and foreign States, Citizens or Subjects.

In all Cases affecting Ambassadors, other public Ministers and Consuls, and those in which a State shall be Party, the supreme Court shall have original Jurisdiction. In all the other Cases before mentioned, the supreme Court shall have appellate Jurisdiction, both as to Law and Fact, with such Exceptions, and under such Regulations as the Congress shall make.

The Trial of all Crimes, except in Cases of Impeachment, shall be by Jury; and such Trial shall be held in the State where the said Crimes shall have been committed; but when not committed within any State, the Trial shall be at such Place or Places as the Congress may by Law have directed.

Section 3. Treason against the United States, shall consist only in levying War against them, or in adhering to their Enemies, giving them Aid and Comfort. No Person shall be convicted of Treason unless on the Testimony of two Witnesses to the same overt Act, or on Confession in open Court.

The Congress shall have Power to declare the Punishment of Treason, but no Attainder of Treason shall work Corruption of Blood, or Forfeiture except during the Life of the Person attainted.

Article IV.

Section 1. Full Faith and Credit shall be given in each State to the public Acts, Records, and judicial Proceedings of every other State. And the Congress may by general Laws prescribe the Manner in which such Acts, Records and Proceedings shall be proved, and the Effect thereof.

Section 2. The Citizens of each State shall be entitled to all Privileges and Immunities of Citizens in the several States.

A Person charged in any State with Treason, Felony, or other Crime, who shall flee from Justice, and be found in another State, shall on Demand of the executive Authority of the State from which he fled, be delivered up, to be removed to the State having Jurisdiction of the Crime.

---

[8]Modified by the Eleventh Amendment.

No Person held to Service or Labour in one State, under the Laws thereof, escaping into another, shall, in Consequence of any Law or Regulation therein, be discharged from such Service or Labour, but shall be delivered up on Claim of the Party to whom such Service or Labour may be due.

Section 3. New States may be admitted by the Congress into this Union; but no new State shall be formed or erected within the Jurisdiction of any other State, nor any State be formed by the Junction of two or more States, or Parts of States, without the Consent of the Legislatures of the States concerned as well as of the Congress.

The Congress shall have Power to dispose of and make all needful Rules and Regulations respecting the Territory or other Property belonging to the United States; and nothing in this Constitution shall be so construed as to Prejudice any Claims of the United States, or of any particular State.

Section 4. The United States shall guarantee to every State in this Union a Republican Form of Government, and shall protect each of them against Invasion; and on Application of the Legislature, or of the Executive (when the Legislature cannot be convened) against domestic Violence.

Article V.

The Congress, whenever two thirds of both Houses shall deem it necessary, shall propose Amendments to this Constitution, or, on the Application of the Legislatures of two thirds of the several States, shall call a Convention for proposing Amendments, which, in either Case, shall be valid to all Intents and Purposes, as Part of this Constitution, when ratified by the Legislatures of three fourths of the several States, or by Conventions in three fourths thereof, as the one or the other Mode of Ratification may be proposed by the Congress; Provided that no Amendment which may be made prior to the Year One thousand eight hundred and eight shall in any Manner affect the first and fourth Clauses in the Ninth Section of the first Article; and that no State, without its Consent, shall be deprived of its equal Suffrage in the Senate.

Article VI.

All Debts contracted and Engagements entered into, before the Adoption of this Constitution, shall be as valid against the United States under this Constitution, as under the Confederation.

This Constitution, and the Laws of the United States which shall be made in Pursuance thereof; and all Treaties made, or which shall be made, under the Authority of the United States, shall be the supreme Law of the Land; and the Judges in every State shall be bound thereby, any Thing in the Constitution or Laws of any State to the Contrary notwithstanding.

The Senators and Representatives before mentioned, and the Members of the several State Legislatures, and all executive and judicial Officers, both of the United States and of the several States, shall be bound by Oath or Affirmation, to support this Constitution; but no religious Test shall ever be required as a Qualification to any Office or public Trust under the United States.

Article VII.

The Ratification of the Conventions of nine States, shall be sufficient for the Establishment of this Constitution between the States so ratifying the Same.

Done in Convention by the Unanimous Consent of the States present the Seventeenth Day of September in the Year of our Lord one thousand seven hundred and Eighty seven and of the Independence of the United States of America the Twelfth. In witness whereof We have hereunto subscribed our Names,

Articles in Addition to, and Amendment of, the Constitution of the United States of America, Proposed by Congress, and Ratified by the Legislatures of the Several States, Pursuant to the Fifth Article of the Original Constitution.

Amendment I[9]

Congress shall make no law respecting an establishment of religion, or prohibiting the free exercise thereof; or abridging the freedom of speech, or of the press; or the right of the people peaceably to assemble, and to petition the Government for a redress of grievances.

Amendment II

A well regulated Militia, being necessary to the security of a free State, the right of the people to keep and bear Arms shall not be infringed.

Amendment III

No Soldier shall, in time of peace, be quartered in any house, without the consent of the Owner, nor in time of war, but in a manner to be prescribed by law.

Amendment IV

The right of the people to be secure in their persons, houses, papers, and effects, against unreasonable searches and seizures, shall not be violated, and no Warrants shall issue, but upon probable cause, supported by Oath or affirmation, and particularly describing the place to be searched, and the persons or things to be seized.

---

[9]The first ten amendments were passed by Congress September 25, 1789. They were ratified by three-fourths of the states December 15, 1791.

Amendment V

No person shall be held to answer for a capital or otherwise infamous crime, unless on a presentment or indictment of a Grand Jury, except in cases arising in the land or naval forces, or in the Militia, when in actual service in time of War or public danger; nor shall any person be subject for the same offence to be twice put in jeopardy of life or limb; nor shall be compelled in any criminal case to be a witness against himself, nor be deprived of life, liberty, or property, without due process of law; nor shall private property be taken for public use, without just compensation.

Amendment VI

In all criminal prosecutions, the accused shall enjoy the right to a speedy and public trial, by an impartial jury of the State and district wherein the crime shall have been committed, which district shall have been previously ascertained by law, and to be informed of the nature and cause of the accusation; to be confronted with the witnesses against him; to have compulsory process for obtaining witnesses in his favor, and to have the Assistance of Counsel for his defence.

Amendment VII

In suits at common law, where the value in controversy shall exceed twenty dollars, the right of trial by jury shall be preserved, and no fact tried by a jury, shall be otherwise reexamined in any Court of the United States, than according to the rules of the common law.

Amendment VIII

Excessive bail shall not be required, nor excessive fines imposed, nor cruel and unusual punishments inflicted.

Amendment IX

The enumeration in the Constitution, of certain rights, shall not be construed to deny or disparage others retained by the people.

Amendment X

The powers not delegated to the United States by the Constitution; nor prohibited by it to the States, are reserved to the States respectively, or to the people.

Amendment XI[10]

The Judicial power of the United States shall not be construed to extend to any suit in law or equity, commenced or prosecuted against one of the United States by Citizens of another State, or by Citizens or Subjects of any Foreign State.

---

[10]Passed March 4, 1794. Ratified January 23, 1795.

Amendment XII[11]

The Electors shall meet in their respective States and vote by ballot for President and Vice-President, one of whom, at least, shall not be an inhabitant of the same State with themselves; they shall name in their ballots the person voted for as President, and in distinct ballots the person voted for as Vice-President, and they shall make distinct lists of all persons voted for as President, and of all persons voted for as Vice-President, and of the number of votes for each, which lists they shall sign and certify, and transmit sealed to the seat of the government of the United States, directed to the President of the Senate;—The President of the Senate shall, in the presence of the Senate and House of Representatives, open all the certificates and the votes shall then be counted;—The person having the greatest number of votes for President, shall be the President, if such number be a majority of the whole number of Electors appointed; and if no person have such majority, then from the persons having the highest numbers not exceeding three on the list of those voted for as President, the House of Representatives shall choose immediately, by ballot, the President. But in choosing the President, the votes shall be taken by states, the representation from each state having one vote; a quorum for this purpose shall consist of a member or members from two-thirds of the states, and a majority of all the states shall be necessary to a choice. And if the House of Representatives shall not choose a President whenever the right of choice shall devolve upon them, before the fourth day of March next following, then the Vice-President shall act as President, as in the case of the death or other constitutional disability of the President.—The person having the greatest number of votes as Vice-President, shall be the Vice-President, if such number be a majority of the whole number of Electors appointed, and if no person have a majority, then from the two highest numbers on the list, the Senate shall choose the Vice-President; a quorum for the purpose shall consist of two-thirds of the whole number of Senators, and a majority of the whole number shall be necessary to a choice. But no person constitutionally ineligible to the office of President shall be eligible to that of Vice-President of the United States.

Amendment XIII[12]

Section 1. Neither slavery nor involuntary servitude, except as a punishment for crime whereof the party shall have been duly convicted, shall exist within the United States, or any place subject to their jurisdiction.

Section 2. Congress shall have power to enforce this article by appropriate legislation.

Amendment XIV[13]

Section 1. All persons born or naturalized in the United States, and subject to the jurisdiction thereof, are citizens of the United States and of the State wherein they reside. No State shall make or enforce any law which shall abridge the privileges or immunities of citizens of

---

[11]Passed December 9, 1803. Ratified June 15, 1804.
[12]Passed January 31, 1865. Ratified December 6, 1865.
[13]Passed June 13, 1866. Ratified July 9, 1868.

the United States; nor shall any State deprive any person of life, liberty, or property, without due process of law; nor deny to any person within its jurisdiction the equal protection of the laws.

Section 2. Representatives shall be apportioned among the several States according to their respective numbers, counting the whole number of persons in each State, excluding Indians not taxed. But when the right to vote at any election for the choice of electors for President and Vice-President of the United States, Representatives in Congress, the Executive and Judicial officers of a State, or the members of the Legislature thereof, is denied to any of the male inhabitants of such State, being twenty-one years of age, and citizens of the United States, or in any way abridged, except for participation in rebellion, or other crime, the basis of representation therein shall be reduced in the proportion which the number of such male citizens shall bear to the whole number of male citizens twenty-one years of age in such State.

Section 3. No person shall be a Senator or Representative in Congress, or elector of President and Vice-President, or hold any office, civil or military, under the United States, or under any State, who, having previously taken an oath, as a member of Congress, or as an officer of the United States, or as a member of any State legislature, or as an executive or judicial officer of any State, to support the Constitution of the United States, shall have engaged in insurrection or rebellion against the same, or given aid or comfort to the enemies thereof. But Congress may by a vote of two-thirds of each House, remove such disability.

Section 4. The validity of the public debt of the United States, authorized by law, including debts incurred for payment of pensions and bounties for services in suppressing insurrection or rebellion, shall not be questioned. But neither the United States nor any State shall assume or pay any debt or obligation incurred in aid of insurrection or rebellion against the United States, or any claim for the loss or emancipation of any slave; but all such debts, obligations, and claims shall be held illegal and void.

Section 5. The Congress shall have the power to enforce, by appropriate legislation, the provisions of this article.

Amendment XV[14]

Section 1. The right of citizens of the United States to vote shall not be denied or abridged by the United States or by any State on account of race, color, or previous conditions of servitude—

Section 2. The Congress shall have power to enforce this article by appropriate legislation.

Amendment XVI

The Congress shall have power to lay and collect taxes on incomes, from whatever source derived, without apportionment among the several States, and without regard to any census or enumeration.

---

[14]Passed February 26, 1869. Ratified February 2, 1870.

Amendment XVII[15]

The Senate of the United States shall be composed of two Senators from each State, elected by the people thereof, for six years; and each Senator shall have one vote. The electors in each State shall have the qualifications requisite for electors of the most numerous branch of the State legislatures.

When vacancies happen in the representation of any State in the Senate, the executive authority of such State shall issue writs of election to fill such vacancies: *Provided,* That the legislature of any State may empower the executive thereof to make temporary appointments until the people fill the vacancies by election as the legislature may direct.

This amendment shall not be so construed as to affect the election or term of any Senator chosen before it becomes valid as part of the Constitution.

Amendment XVIII[16]

Section 1. After one year from the ratification of this article the manufacture, sale, or transportation of intoxicating liquors within, the importation thereof into, or the exportation thereof from the United States and all territory subject to the jurisdiction thereof for beverage purposes is hereby prohibited.

Section 2. The Congress and the several States shall have concurrent power to enforce this article by appropriate legislation.

Section 3. This article shall be inoperative unless it shall have been ratified as an amendment to the Constitution by the legislatures of the several States, as provided in the Constitution, within seven years from the date of the submission hereof to the States by the Congress.

Amendment XIX[17]

The right of citizens of the United States to vote shall not be denied or abridged by the United States or by any State on account of sex.

Congress shall have power to enforce this article by appropriate legislation.

Amendment XX[18]

Section 1. The terms of the President and Vice-President shall end at noon on the 20th day of January, and the terms of Senators and Representatives at noon on the 3d day of January, of the years in which such terms would have ended if this article had not been ratified; and the terms of their successors shall then begin.

Section 2. The Congress shall assemble at least once in every year, and such meeting shall begin at noon on the 3d day of January, unless they shall by law appoint a different day.

---

[15]Passed May 13, 1912. Ratified April 8, 1913.
[16]Passed December 18, 1917. Ratified January 16, 1919.
[17]Passed June 4, 1919. Ratified August 18, 1920.
[18]Passed March 2, 1932. Ratified January 23, 1933.

Section 3. If, at the time fixed for the beginning of the term of the President, the President elect shall have died, the Vice-President elect shall become President. If a President shall not have been chosen before the time fixed for the beginning of his term, or if the President elect shall have failed to qualify, then the Vice-President elect shall act as President until a President shall have qualified; and the Congress may by law provide for the case wherein neither a President elect nor a Vice-President elect shall have qualified, declaring who shall then act as President, or the manner in which one who is to act shall be selected, and such person shall act accordingly until a President or Vice-President shall have qualified.

Section 4. The Congress may by law provide for the case of the death of any of the persons from whom the House of Representatives may choose a President whenever the right of choice shall have devolved upon them, and for the case of the death of any of the persons from whom the Senate may choose a Vice-President whenever the right of choice shall have devolved upon them.

Section 5. Sections 1 and 2 shall take effect on the 15th day of October following the ratification of this article.

Section 6. This article shall be inoperative unless it shall have been ratified as an amendment to the Constitution by the legislatures of three-fourths of the several States within seven years from the date of its submission.

Amendment XXI[19]

Section 1. The eighteenth article of amendment to the Constitution of the United States is hereby repealed.

Section 2. The transportation or importation into any State, Territory, or possession of the United States for delivery or use therein of intoxicating liquors, in violation of the laws thereof, is hereby prohibited.

Section 3. This article shall be inoperative unless it shall have been ratified as an amendment to the Constitution by conventions in the several States, as provided in the Constitution, within seven years from the date of the submission hereof to the States by the Congress.

Amendment XXII[20]

No person shall be elected to the office of the President more than twice, and no person who has held the office of President, or acted as President, for more than two years of a term to which some other person was elected President shall be elected to the office of the President more than once.

---

[19]Passed February 20, 1933. Ratified December 5, 1933.
[20]Passed March 12, 1947. Ratified March 1, 1951.

But this Article shall not apply to any person holding the office of President when this Article was proposed by the Congress, and shall not prevent any person who may be holding the office of President, or acting as President, during the term within which this Article becomes operative from holding the office of President or acting as President during the remainder of such term.

Amendment XXIII[21]

Section 1. The District constituting the seat of Government of the United States shall appoint in such manner as the Congress may direct:

A number of electors of President and Vice President equal to the whole number of Senators and Representatives in Congress to which the District would be entitled if it were a State, but in no event more than the least populous State; they shall be in addition to those appointed by the States, but they shall be considered, for the purposes of the election of President and Vice President, to be electors appointed by the State; and they shall meet in the District and perform such duties as provided by the twelfth article of amendment.

Section 2. The Congress shall have power to enforce this article by appropriate legislation.

Amendment XXIV[22]

Section 1. The right of citizens of the United States to vote in any primary or other election for President or Vice President, or for Senator or Representative in Congress, shall not be denied or abridged by the United States or any State by reason of failure to pay any poll tax or other tax.

Section 2. The Congress shall have power to enforce this article by appropriate legislation.

Amendment XXV[23]

Section 1. In case of the removal of the President from office or of his death or resignation, the Vice President shall become President.

Section 2. Whenever there is a vacancy in the office of the Vice President, the President shall nominate a Vice President who shall take office upon confirmation by a majority vote of both Houses of Congress.

---

[21]Passed June 16, 1960. Ratified April 3, 1961.
[22]Passed August 27, 1962. Ratified January 23, 1964.
[23]Passed July 6, 1965. Ratified February 11, 1967.

Section 3. Whenever the President transmits to the President pro tempore of the Senate and the Speaker of the House of Representatives his written declaration that he is unable to discharge the powers and duties of his office, and until he transmits them a written declaration to the contrary, such powers and duties shall be discharged by the Vice President as Acting President.

Section 4. Whenever the Vice President and a majority of either the principal officers of the executive department or of such other body as Congress may by law provide, transmit to the President pro tempore of the Senate and the Speaker of the House of Representatives their written declaration that the President is unable to discharge the powers and duties of his office, the Vice President shall immediately assume the powers and duties of the office of Acting President.

Thereafter, when the President transmits to the President pro tempore of the Senate and the Speaker of the House of Representatives his written declaration that no inability exists, he shall resume the powers and duties of his office unless the Vice President and a majority of either the principal officers of the executive department or of such other body as Congress may by law provide, transmit within four days to the President pro tempore of the Senate and the Speaker of the House of Representatives their written declaration that the President is unable to discharge the powers and duties of his office. Thereupon Congress shall decide the issue, assembling within forty-eight hours for that purpose if not in session. If the Congress, within twenty-one days after receipt of the latter written declaration, or, if Congress is not in session, within twenty-one days after Congress is required to assemble, determines by two-thirds vote of both Houses that the President is unable to discharge the powers and duties of his office, the Vice President shall continue to discharge the same as Acting President; otherwise, the President shall resume the powers and duties of his office.

Amendment XXVI[24]

Section 1. The right of citizens of the United States, who are eighteen years of age or older, to vote shall not be denied or abridged by the United States or by any State on account of age.

Section 2. The Congress shall have power to enforce this article by appropriate legislation.

Amendment XXVII[25]

No law, varying the compensation for the service of the Senators and Representatives, shall take effect, until an election of Representatives shall have intervened.

---

[24]Passed March 23, 1971. Ratified July 5, 1971.
[25]Passed September 25, 1789. Ratified May 7, 1992.

Glossary

1919 steel strike Walkout by 300,000 steelworkers in the Midwest demanding union recognition and an eight-hour day. It was defeated by employers and local and state police forces, who sometimes resorted to violence.

40 acres and a mule Largely unfulfilled hope of many former slaves that they would receive free land from the confiscated property of ex-Confederates.

9th and 10th U.S. Cavalry African-American army units that played pivotal roles in the Spanish-American war.

abolitionism Movement begun in the North about 1830 to abolish slavery immediately and without compensation to owners.

abolitionist A person who wanted to abolish slavery.

abrogating a treaty Process of abolishing a treaty so that it is no longer in effect.

affirmative action Program or policy that attempted to compensate for past injustice or discrimination to ensure more employment and educational opportunities.

affluence Abundance of material goods or wealth.

Agricultural Adjustment Administration (AAA) 1933 attempt to promote economic recovery by reducing supply of crops, dairy, and meat produced by American farmers.

Aguinaldo, Emilio Anti-colonial leader who fought for independence of the Philippines first from Spain and then from the United States.

Alamo Battle between Texas revolutionaries and the Mexican army at the San Antonio mission called the *Alamo* on March 6, 1836, in which all 187 Texans were killed.

Albany Congress An inter-colonial congress that met in Albany, New York, in June 1754. The delegates urged the Crown to assume direct control of Indian relations beyond the settled boundaries of the colonies, and they drafted a plan of confederation for the continental colonies. No colony ratified it, nor did the Crown or Parliament accept it.

Algonquians Indian peoples who spoke some dialect of the Algonquian language family.

alien Person from another country who is living in the United States.

American Anti-Slavery Society Organization created by northern abolitionists in 1833 that called for immediate, uncompensated emancipation of the slaves.

American Colonization Society Established by elite gentlemen of the middle and upper-south states in 1816, this organization encouraged voluntary emancipation of slaves, to be followed by their emigration to the West African colony of Liberia.

American System Program proposed by Henry Clay and others to foster national economic growth and interdependence among the geographical sections. It included a protective tariff, a national bank, and internal improvements.

Amerind The forerunner of the vast majority of Indian languages in the Americas.

amnesty General pardon granted to a large group of people.

anarchist Activist who called for the violent destruction of the capitalist system so that a new socialist order could be built.

Anasazi An advanced pre-Columbian cliff-dwelling culture that flourished for two centuries in what are now the states of Arizona, New Mexico, Utah, and Colorado before abandoning these sites in the late 13th century A.D.

Anderson, Marian Black opera singer who broke a color barrier in 1939 when she sang to an interracial audience of 75,000 from the steps of the Lincoln Memorial.

Anglican A member of the legally established Church of England, or that church itself.

Anglos English-speaking people.

anxious bench Bench at or near the front of a religious revival meeting where the most likely converts were seated.

apartheid Legal system practiced in South Africa and based on elaborate rules of racial separation and subordination of blacks.

armistice A temporary stop in fighting. Often in effect before a final peace treaty is signed.

Article X of the Covenant Addendum to the Treaty of Versailles that empowered the League of Nations to undertake military actions against aggressor nations.

artisan A skilled laborer who works with his hands. In early America, artisans often owned their own shops and produced goods either for general sale or for special order.

Association Groups created by the First Continental Congress in local committees to enforce its trade sanctions against Britain. The creation of these groups was an important sign that Congress was beginning to act as a central government.

associationalism Herbert Hoover's approach to managing the economy. Firms and organizations in each economic sector would be asked to cooperate with each other in the pursuit of efficiency, profit, and the public good.

astrolabe A device that permitted accurate calculation of latitude or distances north and south.

Atlantic slave trade A European commerce that led to the enslavement of millions of people who were shipped from their African homelands to European colonies in the Americas.

attrition A type of warfare in which an effort is made to exhaust the manpower, supplies, and morale of the other side.

Auburn system Prison system designed to reform criminals and reduce expenses through the sale of items produced in workshops. Prisoners slept in solitary cells, marched in military formation to meals and workshops, and were forbidden to speak to one another at any time.

Australian ballot (secret ballot) Practice that required citizens to vote in private rather than in public and required the government (rather than political parties) to supervise the voting process.

Aztec The last pre-Columbian high culture in the Valley of Mexico. It was conquered by the Spaniards in 1519–1521.

baby boom Sudden increase in births in the years after World War II.

backcountry Term used in the 18th and early 19th centuries to refer to the western settlements and the supposed misfits who lived in them.

Bacon's Rebellion The most serious challenge to royal authority in the English mainland colonies prior to 1775. It erupted in Virginia in 1676 after the governor and Nathaniel Bacon, the principal rebel, could not agree on how best to wage war against frontier Indians.

balance of trade The relationship between imports and exports. The difference between exports and imports is the balance between the two. A healthy nation should export more than it imports.

This is known as a favorable balance of trade.

bandeirantes Brazilian frontiersmen who traveled deep into South America to enslave Indians. The slaves then were worked to death on the sugar plantations.

banknotes Paper money, issued by banks, that circulated as currency.

barrios Spanish-speaking urban areas, usually separate districts in southwestern towns and cities.

bateau A light, flat-bottomed boat with narrow ends that was used in Canada and the northeastern part of the colonies.

Battle of Lexington The first military engagement of the Revolutionary War. It occurred on April 19, 1775, when British soldiers fired into a much smaller body of minutemen on Lexington green.

Battle of Little Big Horn A battle in eastern Montana Territory on the bluffs above Little Big Horn River on June 25, 1876.

Bay of Pigs Site of an ill-fated 1961 invasion of Cuba by a U.S.-trained force that attempted to overthrow the government of Fidel Castro.

Beatles Preeminent musical group associated with the "British invasion" in the 1960s.

belligerent Country actively engaged in a war.

Beringia A land bridge during the last ice age across the Bering Strait between Siberia and Alaska. It was once an area where plants, animals, and humans could live.

bicameral legislature A legislature with two houses or chambers.

Bill of Rights First ten amendments to the Constitution, which protect the rights of individuals from abuses by the federal government.

Black Codes Laws passed by southern states that restricted the rights and liberties of former slaves.

Black Power Mid-1960s movement that called for modifying integrationist goals in favor of gaining political and economic power for separate black-directed institutions and emphasized pride in African-American heritage.

Black Republicans Label coined by the Democratic Party to attack the Republican Party as believers in racial equality. The Democrats used this fear to convince many whites to remain loyal to them.

blacklist In the postwar years, a list of people who could no longer work in the entertainment industry because of alleged contacts with communists.

blitzkrieg A "lightning war"; a coordinated and massive military strike by German army and air forces.

block grants Part of Nixon's new economic plan in which a percentage of federal tax dollars would be returned to state and local governments to spend as they deemed fit.

blockade runner A ship designed to run through a blockade.

blockade The closing of a country's harbors by enemy ships to prevent trade and commerce, especially to prevent traffic in military supplies.

blockhouse A wooden fort with an overhanging second floor. The white settlers of Kentucky used blockhouses to defend themselves against Indians.

blood sports Sporting activities emphasizing bloodiness that were favored by working-class men of the cities. The most popular in the early 19th century were cockfighting, ratting, dogfights, and various types of violence between animals.

bonanza farms Huge wheat farms financed by eastern capital and cultivated with heavy machinery and hired labor.

Bonus Army Army veterans who marched on Washington, D.C., in 1932 to lobby for economic relief but who were rebuffed by Hoover.

Boone, Daniel A pioneer settler of Kentucky, Boone became the most famous American frontiersman of his generation.

border ruffians Term used to describe proslavery Missourians who streamed into Kansas in 1854, determined to vote as many times as necessary to install a proslavery government there.

Boston Massacre The colonial term for the confrontation between colonial protestors and British soldiers in front of the customs house on March 5, 1770. Five colonists were killed and six wounded.

Boston Tea Party In December 1773, Boston's Sons of Liberty threw 342 chests of East India Company tea into Boston harbor rather than allow them to be landed and pay the hated tea duty.

bounty jumpers Men who enlisted in the Union army to collect the bounties offered by some districts to fill military quotas; these men would enlist and then desert as soon as they got their money.

Boxers Chinese nationalist organization that instigated an uprising in 1900 to rid China of all foreign influence.

braceros Guest workers from Mexico allowed into the United States because of labor shortages from 1942 to 1964.

Brown v. Board of Education 1954 case in which the U.S. Supreme Court unanimously overruled the "separate but equal" doctrine and held that segregation in the public schools violated the principle of equal protection under the law.

"broad" wives Wives of slave men who lived on other plantations and were visited by their husbands during off hours.

Brown, John Prominent abolitionist who fought for the antislavery cause in Kansas (1856) and led a raid to seize the Harpers Ferry arsenal in 1859.

Bryan, William Jennings A two-term Democratic congressman from Nebraska who won the party's presidential nomination in 1896 after electrifying delegates with his "Cross of Gold" speech. Bryan was twice more nominated for president (1900 and 1908); he lost all three times.

Bull Moosers Followers of Theodore Roosevelt in the 1912 election.

bulldozing Using force to keep African Americans from voting.

Burr, Aaron Vice President under Thomas Jefferson who killed Alexander Hamilton in a duel and eventually hatched schemes to detach parts of the west from the United States.

Bush, George H. W. Republican President (1989–1993) who directed an international coalition against Iraq in the Persian Gulf War.

Bush, George W. Republican president (2001–) elected in the highly disputed 2000 contest decided by the Supreme Court.

bushwhackers Confederate guerrilla raiders especially active in Missouri. Jayhawkers were the Union version of the same type of people. Both groups did a tremendous amount of damage with raids, arson, ambush, and murder.

Butternuts Democrats from the southern river-oriented counties of the Northwest region whose name came from the yellow vegetable dye with which they colored their homespun clothing.

Cahokia The largest city created by Mississippian mound builders. Located in Illinois near modern St. Louis, it thrived from A.D. 900 to 1250 and then declined.

californios Spanish-speaking people whose families had resided in California for generations.

camp meeting Outdoor revival often lasting for days; a principal means of spreading evangelical Christianity in the United States.

Capra, Frank Popular 1930s filmmaker who celebrated the decency, honesty, and patriotism of ordinary Americans in such films as *Mr. Deeds Goes to Town* and *Mr. Smith Goes to Washington.*

caravel A new type of oceangoing vessel that could sail

closer to a head wind than any other sailing ship and make speeds of from three to twelve knots per hour.

Carnegie, Andrew A Scottish immigrant who became the most efficient entrepreneur in the U.S. steel industry and earned a great fortune.

carpetbaggers Northerners who settled in the South during Reconstruction.

Carson, Rachel American marine biologist and author best known for *Silent Spring* (1962), a widely read book that questioned the use of chemical pesticides and helped stimulate the modern environmental movement.

Carter, Jimmy Democratic president (1977–1981) whose single term in office was marked by inflation, fuel shortages, and a hostage crisis.

cash and carry U.S. foreign policy prior to American entry into World War II that required belligerents to pay cash and carry products away in their own ships. This arrangement minimized risks to American exports, loans, and shipping.

Cavaliers Supporters of the Stuart family of Charles I during the civil wars.

changing system Elaborate system of neighborhood debts and bartering used primarily in the South and West where little cash money was available.

Chavez, Cesar Political activist, leader of the United Farm Workers of America, and the most influential Mexican American leader during the 1970s.

Cherokee War Between December 1759 and December 1761, the Cherokee

Indians devastated the South Carolina backcountry. The British army intervened and in turn inflicted immense damage on the Cherokee.

Chicanismo Populistic pride in the Mexican American heritage that emerged in the late 1960s. Chicano, once a term of derision, became a rallying cry among activists.

chinampas The highly productive gardens built on Lake Taxcoco by the Aztecs.

CIO The Committee (and then Congress) for Industrial Organization, founded in 1935 to organize the unskilled and semiskilled workers ignored by the AFL. The CIO reinvigorated the labor movement.

circuit court Court that meets at different places within a district.

circuit-riding preachers Methodist ministers who traveled from church to church, usually in rural areas.

Civil Rights Act of 1957 First civil-rights act since Reconstruction, aimed at securing voting rights for African Americans in the South.

Civil Rights Act of 1964 Bipartisan measure that denied federal funding to segregated schools and barred discrimination by race and sex in employment, public accommodations, and labor unions.

Civil Rights Act of 1968 Measure that banned racial discrimination in housing and made interference with a person's civil rights a federal crime. It also stipulated that crossing state lines to incite a riot was a federal crime.

Clay, Henry Speaker of the House, senator from

Kentucky, and National Republican presidential candidate who was the principal spokesman for the American System.

Clinton, Bill Democratic president (1993–2001) whose two-term presidency witnessed rapid economic growth but also a sexual scandal that fueled an impeachment effort, which he survived.

close-order assault Military tactic of attacking with little space between men. In the face of modern weapons used during the Civil War, such fighting produced a high casualty rate.

Clovis tip A superior spear point developed before 9000 B.C. It was in use nearly everywhere in North and South America and produced such an improvement in hunting ability that it contributed to the extinction of most large mammals.

Coercive (Intolerable) Acts Four statutes passed by Parliament in response to the Boston Tea Party, including one that closed the port of Boston until the tea was paid for, and another that overturned the Massachusetts Charter of 1691. The colonists called them the Intolerable Acts and included the Quebec Act under that label.

Cold War The political, military, cultural, and economic rivalry between the United States and the Soviet Union that developed after the Second World War and lasted until the disintegration of the Soviet State after 1989.

collective bargaining Negotiations between representatives of workers and employers on

issues such as wages, hours, and working conditions.

Collier, John Activist head of the Bureau of Indian Affairs who improved U.S. policy toward Native Americans and guided the landmark Indian Reorganization Act through Congress.

colonial economy Economy based on the export of agricultural products and the import of manufactured goods; sometimes used to describe the dependence of the South on the North.

Columbus, Christopher The Genoese mariner who persuaded Queen Isabella of Spain to support his voyage of discovery across the Atlantic in 1492. Until his death in 1506, he believed he had reached East Asia. Instead he had discovered America.

Committee on Public Information U.S. Government agency established in 1917 to arouse support for the war and, later, to generate suspicion of war dissenters.

committees of correspondence Bodies formed on both the local and colonial levels that played an important role in exchanging ideas and information. They spread primarily anti-British material and were an important step in the first tentative unity of people in different colonies.

common law The heart of the English legal system was based on precedents and judicial decisions. Common-law courts offered due process through such devices as trial by jury, which usually consisted of local men.

common schools Tax-supported public schools

built by state and local governments.

Communist Party Radical group that wanted America to follow the Soviet Union's path to socialism. The CP organized some of the country's poorest workers into unions and pushed the New Deal leftward, but was never popular enough to bid for power itself.

commutation fee $300 fee that could be paid by a man drafted into the Union army to exempt him from the current draft call.

compensated emancipation Idea that the federal government would offer compensation or money to states that voluntarily abolished slavery.

competence Understood in the early republic as the ability to live up to neighborhood economic standards while protecting the long-term independence of the household.

Compromise of 1850 Series of laws enacted in 1850 intended to settle all outstanding slavery issues.

Congressional Black Caucus (CBC) Congressional group formed in 1969 that focused on eliminating disparities between African Americans and white Americans.

congressional caucus In the early republic, the group of congressmen who traditionally chose the party's presidential candidates. By the 1820s, the American public distrusted the caucus as undemocratic because only one party contested for power. The caucus was replaced by the national nominating convention.

conquistadores The Spanish word for conquerors.

Conscience Whigs A group of antislavery members of the Whig Party.

Conservation Movement that called for managing the environment to ensure the careful and efficient use of the nation's natural resources.

consumer durable Consumer goods that were meant to last, such as washing machines and radios.

containment Label used to describe the global anticommunist national-security policies adopted by the United States to stop the expansion of communism during the late 1940s.

contraband of war Term used to describe slaves who came within the Union lines.

contras Military force in Nicaragua, trained and financed by the United States, that opposed the Nicaraguan socialist government led by the Sandinista Party.

convention In England, a meeting, usually of the houses of Parliament, to address an emergency, such as the flight of James II to France in 1688. The convention welcomed William and Mary, who then restored the traditional parliamentary system. In the United States by the 1780s, conventions had become the purest expression of the popular will, superior to the legislature, as in the convention that drafted the Massachusetts Constitution of 1780.

cooperatives Marketing groups established by such groups as the Farmers Alliance that eliminated "middlemen" and reduced prices to farmers. The idea also was tried by some labor groups and

included other types of businesses, such as factories.

Copperheads Term used by some Republicans to describe Peace Democrats to imply that they were traitors to the Union.

corrupt bargain Following the election of 1824, Andrew Jackson and his supporters alleged that, in a "corrupt bargain," Henry Clay sold his support during the House vote in the disputed election of 1824 of John Quincy Adams in exchange for appointment as Secretary of State.

Cortés, Hernán The Spanish conquistador who vanquished the Aztecs.

cotton Semitropical plant that produced white, fluffy fibers that could be made into textiles.

Coughlin, Father Charles The "radio priest" from the Midwest who alleged that the New Deal was being run by bankers. His growing anti-Semitism discredited him by 1939.

counterculture Antiestablishment movement that symbolized the youthful social upheaval of the 1960s. Ridiculing traditional attitudes toward such matters as clothing, hair styles, and sexuality, the counterculture urged a more open and less regimented approach to daily life.

coureur de bois A French phrase interpreted as "a roamer of the woods," referring to French colonists who participated in the fur trade with the Indians and lived part of the year with them.

court-packing plan 1937 attempt by Roosevelt to appoint one new Supreme

Court justice for every sitting justice over the age of 70 and who had sat for at least 10 years. Roosevelt's purpose was to prevent conservative justices from dismantling the New Deal, but the plan died in Congress and inflamed opponents of the New Deal.

Covenant Chain of Peace An agreement negotiated by Governor Edmund Andros in 1677 that linked the colony of New York to the Iroquois Five Nations and was later expanded to include other colonies and Indian peoples.

covenant theology The belief that God made two personal covenants with humans: the covenant of works and the covenant of grace.

coverture A common-law doctrine under which the legal personality of the husband covered the wife, and he made all legally binding decisions.

Crazy Horse War chief of the Oglala Lakota (Sioux) Indians, who forged an alliance with Cheyenne chiefs to resist white expansion into the Black Hills in 1874–1875; led the attack on Custer's 7th Cavalry at Little Big Horn.

Credit Mobilier Construction company for the Union Pacific Railroad that gave shares of stock to some congressmen in return for favors.

crisis conversion Understood in evangelical churches as a personal transformation that resulted from directly experiencing the Holy Spirit.

crop lien system System of credit used in the poor rural South, whereby merchants in small country stores provided necessary goods on credit in return for a lien on the crop. As the price of crops fell, small farmers, black and white, drifted deeper into debt.

Cuban Missile Crisis (1962) Serious Cold War confrontation between the United States and the Soviet Union over the installation of Soviet missiles in Cuba.

Custer, George A. Civil War hero and postwar Indian fighter who was killed at Little Big Horn in 1876.

Davis, Jefferson Mississippi planter and prominent leader of the Southern Democrats in the 1850s, who later served as president of the Confederacy.

Dawes Plan 1924 U.S.-backed agreement to reduce German reparation payments by more than half. The plan also called on banks to invest $200 million in the German economy.

Debs, Eugene V. Leader of the Socialist Party who received almost a million votes in the election of 1912.

Declaration of Independence A document drafted primarily by Thomas Jefferson of Virginia; this document justified American independence to the world by affirming "that all men are created equal" and have a natural right to "life, liberty, and the pursuit of happiness." The longest section of the Declaration condemned George III as a tyrant.

deflation Decline in consumer prices or a rise in the purchasing power of money.

Deism Belief that God created the universe but did not intervene in its affairs.

Denmark Vesey Leader of a slave conspiracy in and around Charleston, South Carolina, in 1822.

deskilling Process in which the employment market produces jobs requiring fewer skills (and offering less income) than in the past.

détente An easing of tensions, particularly between the United States and the Soviet Union.

Dewey, John Philosopher who believed that American technological and industrial power could be made to serve the people and democracy.

direct election of senators Constitutional amendment that mandated the election of senators by the people rather than by selection by state legislatures.

dirty tricks Actions designed to destroy the reputation and effectiveness of political opponents of the Nixon administration.

disfranchisement Process of barring groups of adult citizens from voting.

dissenter Person who disagrees openly with the majority opinion.

Dix, Dorothea Boston reformer who traveled throughout the country campaigning for humane, state-supported asylums for the insane.

dollar diplomacy Diplomatic strategy formulated under President Taft that focused on expanding American investments abroad, especially in Latin America and East Asia.

domestic fiction Sentimental literature that centered on household and domestic themes that emphasized the toil and travails of women and children who overcame

adversity through religious faith and strength of character.

Douglas, Stephen A. Senator from Illinois who emerged as a leading Democrat in 1850 and led efforts to enact the Compromise of 1850.

doves Opponents of military action, especially those who wanted to end quickly U.S. involvement in the Vietnam War.

dower rights The right of a widow to a portion of her deceased husband's estate (usually one-third of the value of the estate). It was passed to their children upon her death.

dowry The cash or goods a woman received from her father when she married.

drawbacks Form of rebate offered to special customers by the railroads.

Dred Scott Missouri slave who sued for freedom on grounds of prolonged residence in a free state and free territory; in 1857, the Supreme Court found against his case, declaring the Missouri Compromise unconstitutional.

Du Bois, W. E. B. Leader of the NAACP, the editor of its newspaper, *The Crisis,* and an outspoken critic of Booker T. Washington and his accomodationist approach to race relations.

economy of scale Term used in both industry and agriculture to describe the economic advantages of concentrating capital, units of production, and output.

Eisenhower Doctrine Policy that stated that the United States would use armed force to respond to imminent or actual communist aggression in the Middle East.

Eisenhower, Dwight D. Supreme Commander of the Allied Forces in Europe, orchestrator of the Normandy Invasion, and President of the United States (1953–1961).

elect Those selected by God for salvation.

Electoral College The group that elects the president. Each state receives as many electors as it has congressmen and senators combined and can decide how to choose its electors. Every elector votes for two candidates, one of whom has to be from another state.

emancipation Refers to release from slavery or bondage. Gradual emancipation was introduced in Pennsylvania and provided for the eventual freeing of slaves born after a certain date when they reached age 28.

embargo Government order prohibiting the movement of merchant ships or goods in or out of its ports.

encomienda A system of labor introduced into the Western Hemisphere by the Spanish. It permitted the holder, or *encomendero*, to claim labor from Indians in a district for a stated period of time.

enfranchise To grant the right to vote.

Enlightenment The new learning in science and philosophy that took hold, at least in England, between 1660 and the American Revolution. Nearly all of its spokesmen were religious moderates who were more interested in science than religious doctrine and who favored broad religious toleration.

entail A legal device that required a landowner to keep his estate intact and pass it on to his heir.

enumerated commodities A group of colonial products that had to be shipped from the colony of origin to England or another English colony. The most important commodities were sugar and tobacco.

Environmental Protection Agency (EPA) Organization established in 1970 that brought under a single institutional umbrella the enforcement of laws intended to protect environmental quality.

environmentalism Movement with roots in earlier conservation, preservation, and public health movements that grew in power after 1970, when concern mounted over the disruption of ecological balances and critical habitats.

Equal Rights Amendment (ERA) Proposed amendment to the Constitution providing that equal rights could not be abridged on account of sex. It won congressional approval in 1972 but failed to gain ratification by the states.

Erie Canal Canal linking the Hudson River at Albany with the Great Lakes at Buffalo that helped commercialize the farms of the Great Lakes watershed and channel that commerce into New York City.

Espionage, Sabotage, and Sedition Acts Laws passed in 1917 and 1918 that gave the federal government sweeping powers to silence and even imprison dissenters.

established church The church in a European state or colony that was sustained by the government and supported by public taxes.

evangelical A style of Christian ministry that includes much zeal and enthusiasm. Evangelical ministers emphasized personal conversion and faith rather than religious ritual.

evangelicals Religious groups that generally placed an emphasis on conversion of non-Christians.

excise tax Internal tax on goods or services.

external taxes Taxes based on oceanic trade, such as port duties. Some colonists thought of them more as a means of regulating trade than as taxes for revenue.

factories A term used to describe small posts established for the early slave trade along the coast of Africa or on small offshore islands.

fall line A geographical landmark defined by the first waterfalls encountered when going upriver from the sea. These waterfalls prevented oceangoing ships from sailing further inland and thus made the fall line a significant early barrier. Land between the falls and the ocean was called the tidewater. Land above the falls but below the mountains was called the piedmont.

fascism Type of highly centralized government that used terror and violence to suppress opposition. Its rigid social and economic controls often incorporated strong nationalism and racism. Fascist governments were dominated by strong authority figures or dictators.

favorite son Candidate for president supported by delegates from his home state.

Federal Reserve Act Act that brought private banks and public authority together to regulate and strengthen the nation's financial system.

Federalists Supporters of the Constitution during the ratification process. Anti-Federalists resisted ratification.

feudal revival The reliance on old feudal charters for all of the profits that could be extracted from them. It took hold in several colonies in the mid-18th century and caused serious problems between many landowners and tenants.

fiat money Paper money backed only by the promise of the government to accept it in payment of taxes. It originated in Massachusetts after a military emergency in 1690.

filibuster Congressional delaying tactic involving lengthy speeches that prevent legislation from being enacted.

filibustering A term used to describe several groups that invaded or attempted to invade various Latin American areas to attempt to add them to the slaveholding regions of the United States. The word originated from *filibustero,* meaning a freebooter or pirate.

fire-eaters Southerners who were eager, enthusiastic supporters of southern rights and later of secession.

First Continental Congress This intercolonial body met in Philadelphia in September and October 1774 to organize resistance against the Coercive Acts by defining American rights, petitioning the king, and appealing to the British and American people. It created the Association, local committees in each community to enforce nonimportation.

Five-Power Treaty 1922 treaty in which the United States, Britain, Japan, France, and Italy agreed to scrap more than 2 million tons of their warships.

flappers Rebellious middle-class young women who signaled their desire for independence and equality through style and personality rather than through politics.

flexible response Kennedy's approach to the Cold War that aimed to provide a wide variety of military and non-military methods to confront communist movements.

Ford, Gerald A GOP member of the House of Representatives, Gerald Ford became the first person to be appointed Vice President of the United States. When Richard Nixon resigned in 1974, Ford became President.

Fort Sumter Fort in Charleston's harbor occupied by United States troops after the secession of South Carolina.

Fourteen Points Plan laid out by Woodrow Wilson in January 1918 to give concrete form to his dream of a "peace without victory" and a new world order.

free silver Idea that the government would purchase all silver offered for sale and coin it into silver dollars at the preferred ratio between silver and gold of 16 to 1.

Freedmen's Bureau Federal agency created in 1865 to supervise newly freed people. It oversaw relations between whites and blacks in the South, issued food rations, and supervised labor contracts.

freedom riders Members of interracial groups who traveled the South on buses to test a series of federal court decisions declaring segregation on buses and in waiting rooms to be unconstitutional.

Freedom Summer Summer of 1964 when nearly a thousand white volunteers went to Mississippi to aid in voter registration and other civil-rights projects.

free-labor ideology Belief that all work in a free society is honorable and that manual labor is degraded when it is equated with slavery or bondage.

Free-Soilers A term used to describe people who opposed the expansion of slavery into the territories. It came from the name of a small political party in the election of 1848.

French and Indian War Popular name for the struggle between Britain and France for the control of North America, 1754 to 1763, in which the British conquered New France. It merged into Europe's Seven Years' War (1756–1763) that pitted Britain and Prussia against France, Austria, and Russia.

Friedan, Betty Author of *The Feminine Mystique* (1963) and founder of the National Organization for Women (1966).

frontier An area on the advancing edge of American civilization.

fugitive slaves Runaway slaves who escaped to a free state.

Fulton, Robert Builder of the *Clermont*, the first practical steam-driven boat.

fundamentalists Religious groups that preached the necessity of fidelity to a strict moral code, individual commitment to Christ, and faith in the literal truth of the Bible.

funded national debt The state agreed to pay the interest due to its creditors before all other obligations.

Gabriel's rebellion Carefully planned but unsuccessful rebellion of slaves in Richmond, Virginia, and the surrounding area in 1800.

gang labor A system where planters organized their field slaves into gangs, supervised them closely, and kept them working in the fields all day. This type of labor was used on tobacco plantations.

Garvey, Marcus Jamaican-born black nationalist who attracted millions of African Americans in the early 1920s to a movement calling for black separatism and self-sufficiency.

gas and water socialists Term used to describe evolutionary socialists who focused their reform efforts on regulating municipal utilities in the public interest.

gentleman Term used to describe a person of means who performed no manual labor.

gentlemen's agreement (1907) Agreement by which the Japanese government promised to halt the immigration of its adult male laborers to the United States in return for President Theodore Roosevelt's pledge to end the discriminatory treatment of Japanese immigrant children in California's public schools.

GI Bill Officially called the Serviceman's Readjustment Act of 1944. It provided veterans with college and job-training assistance, preferential treatment in hiring, and subsidized home loans, and was later extended to Korean War veterans in 1952.

girdled trees Trees with a line cut around them so sap would not rise in the spring.

glasnost Russian term describing increased openness in Russian society under Mikhail Gorbachev.

Glorious Revolution The overthrow of King James II by Whigs and Tories, who invited William of Orange to England. William landed in November 1688, the army defected to him, James fled to France, and in early 1689, Parliament offered the throne to William and his wife Mary, a daughter of James. Contemporaries called the event "glorious" because almost no blood was shed in England.

gold bugs "Sound money" advocates who wanted to keep the United States on the international gold standard and believed the expanded coinage of silver was foolhardy.

Gompers, Samuel F. America's most famous trade unionist while serving as president of the AFL (1896–1924). He achieved his greatest success in organizing skilled workers.

Good Neighbor Policy Roosevelt's foreign policy initiative that formally renounced the right of the United States to intervene in Latin American affairs, leading to improved relations between the United States and Latin American countries.

governor-general The French official responsible for military and diplomatic affairs and for appointment of all militia officers in a colony.

graduated income tax Tax based on income with rates that gradually rise as the level of income rises.

Grangers Members of the Patrons of Husbandry (a farmers' organization) and a contemptuous name for farmers used by ranchers in the West.

Grant, Ulysses S. General-in-chief of Union armies who led those armies to victory in the Civil War.

Great American Desert The treeless area in the plains that most Americans considered unsuitable for settlement. It generally was passed over by settlers going to the Pacific Coast areas.

Great Awakening An immense religious revival that swept across the Protestant world in the 1730s and 1740s.

Great Depression Economic downturn triggered by the stock market crash in October 1929 and lasting until 1941.

Great Society Series of domestic initiatives announced in 1964 by President Lyndon Johnson to "end poverty and racial injustice." They included the Voting Rights Act of 1965; the establishment of the Department of Housing and Urban Development, Head Start, and job-training programs; Medicare and Medicaid expansion; and various community action programs.

Great White Fleet Naval ships sent on a 45,000-mile world tour by President Roosevelt (1907–1909) to showcase American military power.

Greeley, Horace Editor of the *New York Tribune*, one of the most influential newspapers in the country.

greenbacks Paper money issued by the federal government during the Civil War to help pay war expenses. They were called greenbacks because of their color.

Greene, Nathanael A general from Rhode Island whose superb strategy of irregular war reclaimed the Lower South for the American cause in 1780–1781.

Greenwich Village Community of radical artists and writers in lower Manhattan that provided a supportive environment for various kinds of radical ideals.

Grenville, George As head of the British government from 1763 to 1765, Grenville passed the Sugar Act, Quartering Act, Currency Act, and the Stamp Act, provoking the imperial crisis of 1765–1766.

Grimke, Sarah Along with her sister Angelina, this elite South Carolina woman moved north and campaigned against slavery and for temperance and women's rights.

gross national product (GNP) Total value of all goods and services produced during a specific period.

Gulf of Tonkin Resolution Measure passed by Congress in August 1964 that provided authorization for an air war against North Vietnam after U.S. destroyers were allegedly attacked by North Vietnamese torpedoes. Johnson invoked it as authority for expanding the Vietnam War.

Gullah A language spoken by newly imported African slaves.

Originally, it was a simple second language for everyone who spoke it, but it gradually evolved into modern black English.

habeas corpus Right of an individual to obtain a legal document as protection against illegal imprisonment.

haciendas Large, landed estates established by the Spanish.

Hale, Sarah Josepha Editor of *Godey's Ladies Book* and an important arbiter of domesticity and taste for middle-class housewives.

Half-Way Covenant The Puritan practice whereby parents who had been baptized but had not yet experienced conversion could bring their children before the church and have them baptized.

Hamilton, Alexander Secretary of the Treasury under Washington who organized the finances of the new government and led the partisan fight against the Democratic Republicans.

Hard Money Democrats Democrats who, in the 1830s and 1840s, wanted to eliminate paper money and regarded banks as centers of trickery and privilege.

Harlem Renaissance 1920s African-American literary and artistic awakening that sought to create works rooted in black culture instead of imitating white styles.

Harpers Ferry Site of John Brown's 1859 raid on a U.S. armory and arsenal for the manufacture and storage of military rifles.

hawks Supporters of intensified military efforts in the Vietnam War.

Haywood, William Labor organizer known as "Big

Bill," who led the radical union Industrial Workers of the World.

headright A colonist received 50 acres of land for every person whose passage to America he financed, including himself. This system was introduced in Virginia.

heathen A term used sometimes by Christians to refer to anyone who was not a Christian or a Jew.

herrenvolk **democracy** Concept that emphasized the equality of all who belonged to the master race—not all mankind.

Hessians A term used by Americans to describe the 17,000 mercenary troops hired by Britain from various German states, especially Hesse.

hidalgos The minor nobility of Spain. Many possessed little wealth and were interested in improving their position through the overseas empire.

High Federalists A term used to describe Alexander Hamilton and some of his less-moderate supporters. They wanted the naval war with France to continue and also wanted to severely limit the rights of an opposition party.

Highway Act of 1956 Act that appropriated $25 billion for the construction of more than 40,000 miles of interstate highways over a 10-year period.

hippies People who identified with the 1960s counterculture. They were often depicted as embracing mind-altering drugs, communal living arrangements, and new forms of music.

Hiroshima Japanese city destroyed by an atomic bomb on August 6, 1945.

Hiss, Alger High-level State Department employee who was accused, in a controversial case, of being a communist and Soviet spy.

Hitler, Adolph German fascist dictator whose aggressive policies touched off the Second World War.

HIV-AIDS Acquired immune deficiency syndrome (AIDS) resulting from infection with the human immunodeficiency virus (HIV). It progressively impedes the body's ability to protect itself from disease.

Hmong Ethnically distinct people who inhabited lands extending across the borders of the Indochinese countries of Vietnam, Cambodia, and Laos.

House of Burgesses The assembly of early Virginia that settlers were allowed to elect. Members met with the governor and his council and enacted local laws. It first met in 1619.

House Un-American Activities Committee (HUAC) Congressional committee (1938–1975) that zealously investigated suspected Nazi and Communist sympathizers.

household industry Work such as converting raw materials into finished products done by women and children to provide additional household income.

Howe, William (General) Howe commanded the British army in North America from 1776 to 1778. He won major victories in New York and northern New Jersey in 1776, but Washington regained control of New Jersey after his Trenton-Princeton campaign. Howe took Philadelphia in

September 1777 but was recalled in disgrace after Britain's northern army surrendered at Saratoga.

Huguenots French Protestants who followed the beliefs of John Calvin.

Hull House First American settlement house established in Chicago in 1889 by Jane Addams and Ellen Gates Starr.

Human Genome Project Program launched in 1985 to map all genetic material in the 24 human chromosomes. It sparked ongoing debate over the potential consequences of genetic research and manipulation.

Hutchinson, Anne A religious radical who attracted a large following in Massachusetts, especially in Boston. She warned that nearly all of the ministers were preaching a covenant of works instead of the covenant of grace. Convicted of the Antinomian heresy after claiming that she received direct messages from God, she and her most loyal followers were banished to Rhode Island in 1638.

hydraulic mining Use of high-pressure streams of water to wash gold or other minerals from soil.

Immigration Act of 1924 (Johnson-Reed Act) Limited immigration to the United States to 165,000 per year, shrank immigration from southern and eastern Europe to insignificance, and banned immigration from East and South Asia.

Immigration Act of 1965 Law eliminating the national-origins quota system for immigration and substituting

preferences for people with certain skills or with relatives in the United States.

Immigration Restriction Act of 1917 Measure that denied any adult immigrant who failed a reading test entry into the United States, and banned immigration from the "Asiatic Barred Zone."

impeach To charge government officeholders with misconduct in office.

impeachment Act of charging a public official with misconduct in office.

imperialists Those who wanted to expand their nation's world power through military prowess, economic strength, and control of foreign territory (often organized into colonies).

impressment Removal of sailors from American ships by British naval officers.

Inca The last and most extensive pre-Columbian empire in the Andes and along the Pacific coast of South America.

indentured servants People who had their passage to America paid by a master or ship captain. They agreed to work for their master for a term of years in exchange for cost of passage, bed and board, and small freedom dues when their terms were up. The number of years served depended on the terms of the contract. Most early settlers in the English colonies outside of New England arrived as indentured servants.

Indian Removal Act (1830) Legislation that offered the native peoples of the lower South the option of removal to federal lands west of the Mississippi. Those who did not take the offer were removed by force in 1838.

indigo A blue dye obtained from plants that was used by the textile industry. The British government subsidized the commercial production of it in South Carolina.

information revolution Acceleration of the speed and availability of information resulting from use of computer and satellite systems.

initiative Reform that gave voters the right to propose and pass a law independently of their state legislature.

Inns of Court England's law schools.

intendant The officer who administered the system of justice in New France.

interchangeable parts Industrial technique using machine tools to cut and shape a large number of similar parts that can be fitted together with other parts to make an entire item such as a gun.

internal improvements 19th-century term for transportation facilities such as roads, canals, and railroads.

internal taxes Taxes that were imposed on land, people, retail items (such as excises), or legal documents and newspapers (such as the Stamp Act). Most colonists thought that only their elective assemblies had the constitutional power to impose internal taxes.

Iran-*contra* affair Reagan administration scandal in which the U.S. secretly sold arms to Iran, a country implicated in holding American hostages, and diverted the money to finance the attempt by the *contras* to overthrow the Sandinista

government of Nicaragua. Both transactions violated acts of Congress, which had prohibited funding the *contras* and selling weapons to Iran.

Iroquois League A confederation of five Indian nations centered around the Mohawk Valley who were very active in the fur trade. They first worked with the Dutch and then the English. They were especially successful in using adoption as a means of remaining strong.

irreconcilables Group of 14 midwestern and western senators who opposed the Treaty of Versailles.

irregular war A type of war using men who were not part of a permanent or professional regular military force. It also can apply to guerilla-type warfare, usually against the civilian population.

itinerant preachers Ministers who lacked their own parishes and who traveled from place to place.

Jackson State (incident) Killing of two students on May 13, 1970, after an escalation in tensions between students at Jackson State University, a historically black institution, and National Guard troops in Mississippi.

Jackson, Andrew President of the United States (1829–1837) who founded the Democratic Party, signed the Indian Removal Act, vetoed the Second Bank, and signed the Force Bill.

Jackson, Thomas J. ("Stonewall") A native of Virginia, he emerged as one of the Confederacy's best generals in 1861–1862.

Jamestown Founded in 1607, Jamestown became England's first permanent settlement in North America. It served as the capital of Virginia for most of the 17th century.

Japanese internment Removal of first- and second-generation Japanese Americans into secured camps, a 1942 action then justified as a security measure but since deemed unjustified by evidence.

Jim Crow laws Laws passed by southern states mandating racial segregation in public facilities of all kinds.

Johnson, Lyndon B. President (1963–1969) who undertook an ambitious Great Society program and a major military effort in Vietnam.

joint resolution An act passed by both houses of Congress with a simple majority rather than the two-thirds majority in the Senate.

joint-stock company A form of business organization that resembled a modern corporation. Individuals invested in the company through the purchase of shares. One major difference between then and today was that each stockholder had one vote regardless of how many shares he owned. The first permanent English colonies in North America were established by joint-stock companies.

journeyman Wage-earning craftsman.

judicial review Supreme Court's power to rule on the constitutionality of congressional acts.

Kansas-Nebraska Act Law enacted in 1854 to organize the new territories of Kansas and Nebraska that effectively repealed the provision of the 1820 Missouri Compromise by leaving the question of slavery to the territories' settlers.

Kennan, George (Mr. X) American diplomat and historian who recommended the policy of containment toward Soviet aggression in a famous article published under the pseudonym "X."

Kennedy, John F. President from 1961 to 1963, noted for his youthful charm and vigor and his "New Frontier" vision for America.

Kent State (incident) Killing of four students on May 4, 1970, by the National Guard at a Kent State University protest against the U.S. incursion into neutral Cambodia.

King George's War Popular term in North America for the third of the four Anglo-French wars before the American Revolution (1744–1748). It is sometimes also applied to the War of Jenkins's Ear between Spain and Britain (1739–1748).

King, Martin Luther, Jr. African American clergyman who advocated nonviolent social change and shaped the civil-rights movement of the 1950s and 1960s.

Know-Nothings Adherents of nativist organizations and of the American party who wanted to restrict the political rights of immigrants.

Korean War Conflict lasting from 1950 to 1953 between communist North Korea, aided by China, and South Korea, aided by United Nations forces consisting primarily of U.S. troops.

Ku Klux Klan White terrorist organization in the South originally founded as a fraternal society in 1866. Reborn in 1915, it achieved popularity in the 1920s through its calls for Anglo-Saxon purity, Protestant supremacy, and the subordination of blacks, Catholics, and Jews.

La Raza Unida Mexican American–based movement that scored some political successes in the Southwest in the late 1960s and early 1970s.

lame-duck administration Period of time between an incumbent party's or office-holder's loss of an election and the succession to office of the winning party or candidate.

League of Women Voters Successor to the National American Woman Suffrage Association, it promoted women's role in politics and dedicated itself to educating voters.

Lee, Robert E. U.S. army officer until his resignation to join the Confederacy as general-in-chief.

legal tender Any type of money that the government requires everyone to accept at face value.

Lend-Lease Act A 1941 act by which the United States "loaned" munitions to the Allies, hoping to avoid war by becoming an "arsenal" for the Allied cause.

levee Earthen dike or mound, usually along the banks of rivers, used to prevent flooding.

Lewis and Clark Explorers commissioned in 1804 by President Jefferson to survey the Louisiana Purchase.

liberal Protestants Those who believed that religion had to be adapted to science and that the Bible was to be mined for its ethical values rather than for its literal meaning.

Liberty bonds Thirty-year government bonds with an annual interest rate of 3.5 percent sold to fund the war effort.

liberty tree A term for the gallows on which enemies of the people deserved to be hanged. The best known was in Boston.

limited liability Liability that protected directors and stockholders of corporations from corporate debts by separating those debts from personal liabilities.

Lincoln, Abraham Illinois Whig who became the Republican Party's first successful presidential candidate in 1860 and who led the Union during the Civil War.

Lincoln-Douglas debates Series of seven debates between Abraham Lincoln and Stephen Douglas in their contest for election to the U.S. Senate in 1858.

Lindbergh, Charles A. First individual to fly solo across the Atlantic (1927) and the greatest celebrity of the 1920s.

lintheads Term used by wealthier whites to describe poor whites who labored in southern cotton mills.

living room war Phrase suggesting that television coverage had brought the Vietnam War into the living rooms of Americans and may have led many to question the war.

lockout Act of closing down a business by the owners during a labor dispute.

Lodge, Henry Cabot Republican Senator from Massachusetts who led the campaign to reject the Treaty of Versailles.

logistics Military activity relating to such things as the transporting, supplying, and quartering of troops and their equipment.

long knives The term Indians used to describe Virginians.

Long, Huey Democratic senator and former governor of Louisiana who used the radio to attack the New Deal as too conservative. FDR regarded him as a major rival.

longhorn Breed of cattle introduced into the Southwest by the Spanish that became the main breed of livestock on the cattle frontier.

Lost Generation Term used by Gertrude Stein to describe U.S. writers and artists who fled to Paris in the 1920s after becoming disillusioned with America.

Louisiana Purchase Land purchased from France in 1803 that doubled the size of the United States.

Lowell, Francis Cabot Wealthy Bostonian who, with the help of the Boston Associates, built and operated integrated textile mills in eastern Massachusetts.

loyalists People in the 13 colonies who remained loyal to Britain during the Revolution.

Ludlow massacre Murder of 66 men, women, and children in April 1914 when company police of the Colorado Fuel and Iron Company fired randomly on striking United Mine Workers.

Luftwaffe German air force.

Lusitania British passenger ship sunk by a German U-boat on May 7, 1915, killing more than 1,000 men, women, and children.

MacArthur, Douglas Supreme commander of Allied forces in the southwest Pacific during the Second World War; leader of the occupation forces in the reconstruction of Japan; and head of United Nations forces during the Korean War.

magistrate An official who enforced the law. In colonial America, this person was usually a justice of the peace or a judge in a higher court.

Mahan, Alfred Thayer Influential imperialist who advocated construction of a large navy as crucial to the successful pursuit of world power.

Malcolm X Charismatic African American leader who criticized integration and urged the creation of separate black economic and cultural institutions. He became a hero to members of the Black Power movement.

mandamus A legal writ ordering a person, usually a public official, to carry out a specific act. In Massachusetts in 1774, the new royal councilors were appointed by a writ of mandamus.

manifest destiny The belief that the United States was destined to grow from the Atlantic to the Pacific and from the Arctic to the tropics. Providence supposedly intended for Americans to have this area for a great experiment in liberty.

manumission of slaves The act of freeing a slave, done at the will of the owner.

Marbury v. Madison 1803 case involving the disputed appointment of a federal justice of the peace in which Chief Justice John Marshall expanded the Supreme Court's authority to review legislation.

maritime Of, or relating to, the sea.

Marshall Plan Plan of U.S. aid to Europe that aimed to contain communism by fostering postwar economic recovery. Proposed by Secretary of State George C. Marshall in 1947, it was known formally as the European Recovery Program.

Marshall, John Chief Justice of the United States Supreme Court from 1801 to 1835. Appointed by Federalist President John Adams, Marshall's decisions tended to favor the federal government over the states and to clear legal blocks to private business.

martial law Government by military force rather than by citizens.

mass production High-speed and high-volume production.

Massachusetts Bay Company A joint-stock company chartered by Charles I in 1629. It was controlled by Non-Separatists, who took the charter with them to New England and, in effect, converted it into a written constitution for the colony.

massive retaliation Assertion by the Eisenhower administration that the threat of U.S. atomic weaponry would hold Communist powers in check.

matrilineal A society that determines inheritance and roles in life based on the female or maternal line.

Maya A literate, highly urbanized Mesoamerican civilization that flourished for more than a thousand years before its sudden collapse in the ninth century A.D.

McCarthyism Public accusations of disloyalty made with little or no regard to actual evidence. Named after Senator Joseph McCarthy, these accusations and the scandal and harm they caused came to symbolize the most virulent form of anticommunism.

McClellan, George B. One of the most promising young officers in the U.S. army, he became the principal commander of Union armies in 1861–1862.

McKinley, William A seven-term Republican congressman from Ohio whose signature issue was the protective tariff. He was the last Civil War veteran to be elected president.

Menéndez, Francisco An escaped South Carolina slave who fought with the Yamasee Indians against the colony, fled to Florida, was reenslaved by the Spanish, became a militia captain, was freed again, and was put in charge of the free-black town of Mose near St. Augustine in the late 1730s, the first community of its kind in what is now the United States.

merger movement Late-19th and early 20th-century effort to integrate different enterprises into single, giant corporations able to eliminate competition, achieve economic order, and boost profits.

Mesoamerica An area embracing Central America and southern and central Mexico.

Metacom's War (King Philip's War) A war that devastated much of southern New England in 1675–1676. It began as a conflict between Metacom's Wampanoags and Plymouth Colony but soon engulfed all of the New England colonies and most of the region's Indian nations.

Mexican repatriation Secretary of Labor William Doak's plan to deport illegal Mexican aliens to Mexico. By 1935, more than 500,000 Mexicans had left the United States.

microchips Technological improvement that boosted the capability and reduced the size and cost of computer hardware.

middle class Social group that developed in the early 19th century comprised of urban and country merchants, master craftsmen who had turned themselves into manufacturers, and market-oriented farmers—small-scale entrepreneurs who rose within market society.

Middle Ground The area of French and Indian cooperation west of Niagara and south of the Great Lakes. No one exercised sovereign power over this area, but the French used Indian rituals to negotiate treaties with their Algonquian trading partners, first against the Iroquois and later against the British.

midnight judges Federal judicial officials appointed under the Judiciary Act of 1801, in the last days of John Adams's presidency.

militia A community's armed force, made up primarily of ordinary male citizens rather than professional soldiers.

Millennium The period at the end of history when Christ is expected to return and rule with his saints for a thousand years.

minstrel show Popular form of theater among working men of the northern cities in which white men in blackface portrayed African Americans in song and dance.

missions Outposts established by the Spanish along the northern frontier to aid in Christianizing the native peoples. They also were used to exploit these peoples' labor.

Missouri Compromise Compromise that maintained sectional balance in Congress by admitting Missouri as a slave state and Maine as a free state and by drawing a line west from the 368 309 parallel separating future slave and free states.

modernists Those who believed in science rather than religion and in moving toward equality for men and women and for whites and nonwhites.

Monroe Doctrine Foreign policy doctrine proposed by Secretary of State John Quincy Adams in 1823 that denied the right of European powers to establish new colonies in the Americas while maintaining the United States' right to annex new territory.

Montgomery bus boycott Political protest campaign mounted in 1955 to oppose the city's policy of racial segregation on its public transit system. The Supreme Court soon declared segregation on public transit unconstitutional.

morale The general feeling of the people toward such events as a war. Good morale greatly enhances an ability to fight or sacrifice for a cause.

Mormons Members of the Church of Jesus Christ of Latter-Day Saints, founded by Joseph Smith in 1830; the *Book of Mormon* is their Bible.

Mourning War An Indian war often initiated by a widow or bereaved relative who insisted that her male relatives provide captives to repair the loss.

muckrakers Investigative journalists who propelled Progressivism by exposing corruption, economic monopolies, and moral decay in American society.

napalm Incendiary and toxic chemical contained in bombs used by the United States in Vietnam.

National American Women Suffrage Association Organization established in 1890 to promote woman suffrage; stressed that women's special virtue made them indispensable to politics.

National Association for the Advancement of Colored People (NAACP) Organization launched in 1910 to fight racial discrimination and prejudice and to promote civil rights for blacks.

National Recovery Administration (NRA) 1933 attempt to promote economic recovery by persuading private groups of industrialists to decrease production, limit hours of work per employee, and standardize minimum wages.

National Security Act (1947) Reorganized the U.S. military forces within a new Department of Defense, and established the National Security Council and the Central Intelligence Agency.

National War Labor Board U.S. government agency that brought together representatives of labor, industry, and the public to resolve labor disputes.

nativism Hostility of native-born Americans toward immigrants.

naturalization Process by which people born in a foreign country are granted full citizenship with all of its rights.

Navajo Signal Corp Navajo Indians who conveyed military intelligence in their native language to preserve its secrecy.

naval stores Items such as pitch, resin, and turpentine that were used to manufacture ships. Most of them were obtained from pine trees.

neoconservatives Group of intellectuals, many of whom had been anticommunist Democrats during the 1950s and 1960s, who came to emphasize hard-line foreign policies and conservative social stances.

neo-Federalists Nationalist Republicans who favored many Federalist economic programs, such as protective tariffs and a national bank.

Neolithic The period known also as the late Stone Age. Agriculture developed, and stone, rather than metal, tools were used.

Neutrality Acts of 1935 and 1936 Legislation that restricted loans, trade, and travel with belligerent nations in an attempt to avoid the entanglements that had brought the United States into the First World War.

neutrality U.S. policy toward World War I from 1914 to 1917 that called for staying out of war but maintaining normal economic relations with both sides.

New Freedom Wilson's reform program of 1912 that called for temporarily concentrating government power so as to dismantle the trusts and return America to 19th-century conditions of competitive capitalism.

New Lights Term used to describe prorevival Congregationalists.

New Nationalism Roosevelt's reform program between 1910 and 1912, which called for establishing a strong federal government to regulate corporations, stabilize the economy, protect the weak, and restore social harmony.

New Sides Term used to describe evangelical Presbyterians.

New York's 369th Regiment Black army unit recruited in Harlem that served under French command and was decorated with the *Croix de Guerre* for its valor.

nickelodeons Converted storefronts in working-class neighborhoods that showed early short silent films usually lasting 15 minutes, requiring little comprehension of English, and costing only a nickel to view.

Nixon, Richard President of the United States (1969–1974) during the final years of the Vietnam War. He resigned the presidency when he faced impeachment for the Watergate scandals.

nonimportation agreements
Agreements not to import goods from Great Britain. They were designed to put pressure on the British economy and force the repeal of unpopular parliamentary acts.

Non-Separatists English Puritans who insisted that they were faithful members of the Church of England while demanding that it purge itself of its surviving Catholic rituals and vestments.

normal schools State colleges established to train teachers.

North American Free Trade Agreement (NAFTA) 1994 agreement that aimed to lower or eliminate barriers restricting the trade of goods and services among the United States, Canada, and Mexico.

North Atlantic Treaty Organization (NATO) Established by treaty in 1949 to provide for the collective defense of noncommunist European and North American nations against possible aggression from the Soviet Union and to encourage political, economic, and social cooperation.

Northwest Ordinance Established the Northwest Territory between the Ohio River and the Great Lakes. Adopted by the Confederation Congress in 1787, it abolished slavery in the territory and provided that it be divided into three to five states that would eventually be admitted to the Union as full equals of the original thirteen.

NSC-68 National Security Council Document number 68 (1950) that provided the rationale and comprehensive strategic vision for U.S. policy during the Cold War.

nullification Beginning in the late 1820s, John C. Calhoun and others argued that the Union was a voluntary compact between sovereign states, that states were the ultimate judges of the constitutionality of federal law, that states could nullify federal laws within their borders, and that they had the right to secede from the Union.

Old Lights Antirevival Congregationalists.

Old Northwest The region west of Pennsylvania, north of the Ohio River, and east of the Mississippi River.

Old Sides Antirevival Presbyterians.

oligarchy A society dominated by a few persons or families.

Olmec The oldest pre-Columbian high culture to appear in what is now Mexico.

Onontio An Algonquian word that means "great mountain" and that was used by Indians of the Middle Ground to designate the governor of New France.

Open Door notes (1899–1900) Foreign policy tactic in which the United States asked European powers to respect China's independence and to open their spheres of influence to merchants from other nations.

Open Skies Eisenhower's proposal that U.S. and Soviet disarmament be verified by reconnaissance flights over each other's territory.

open-field agriculture A medieval system of land distribution used only in the New England colonies. Farmers owned scattered strips of land within a common field, and the town as a whole decided what crops to plant.

pacifist A person opposed to war or violence. The religious group most committed to pacifism is the Quakers.

Panama Canal An engineering marvel completed in 1914 across the new Central American nation of Panama. Connecting the Atlantic and Pacific oceans, it shortened ship travel between New York and San Francisco by 8,000 miles.

parish A term used to describe an area served by one tax-supported church. The term was used primarily in regions settled by members of the Church of England.

Parks, Rosa African American seamstress in Montgomery, Alabama, who, after refusing to give up her bus seat to a white man, was arrested and fined. Her protest sparked a subsequent bus boycott that attracted national sympathy for the civil-rights cause and put Martin Luther King, Jr., in the national spotlight.

parochial schools Schools associated with a church, usually Roman Catholic. The funding of these schools became a major political issue in the 1850s.

passive civil disobedience Nonviolent refusal to obey a law in an attempt to call attention to government policies considered unfair.

patronage The act of appointing people to government jobs or awarding them government contracts, often based on political favoritism rather than on abilities.

patronships Vast estates along the Hudson River that were established by the Dutch.

They had difficulty attracting peasant labor, and most were not successful.

Peace of Paris The 1763 treaty that ended the war between Britain on the one side and France and Spain on the other side. France surrendered New France to Britain. Spain ceded Florida to Britain, and France compensated its ally by ceding all of Louisiana to Spain.

peace without victory Woodrow Wilson's 1917 pledge to work for a peace settlement that did not favor one side over the other but ensured an equality among combatants.

Pearl Harbor Japan's December 7, 1941 attack on a U.S. base in Hawaii that brought the United States into the Second World War.

Penn, William A convert to the Society of Friends in the 1660s, Penn used his friendship with Charles II and James, Duke of York, to acquire a charter for Pennsylvania in 1681, and he then launched a major migration of Friends to the Delaware Valley.

people's capitalism An egalitarian capitalism in which all Americans could participate and enjoy the consumer goods that U.S. industry had made available.

per capita Term used to measure the wealth of a nation by dividing total income by population.

perestroika Russian term describing the economic liberalization that began in the late 1980s.

Perkins, Frances Secretary of Labor under Roosevelt and the first female Cabinet member.

Pershing, John J. Commander of the American Expeditionary Force that began landing in Europe in 1917 and that entered battle in the spring and summer of 1918.

personal liberty laws Laws enacted by nine northern states to prohibit the use of state law facilities such as jails or law officers in the recapture of fugitive slaves.

piedmont A term referring to the land above the fall line but below the Appalachian Mountains.

Pilgrims A pious, sentimental term used by later generations to describe the settlers who sailed on the Mayflower in 1620 and founded Plymouth Colony.

Pitt, William One of the most popular public officials in 18th-century Britain, he was best known as the minister who organized Britain's successful war effort against France in the French and Indian War.

placer mining Mining where minerals, especially gold, were found in glacial or alluvial deposits.

Platt Amendment Clause that the U.S. forced Cuba to insert into its constitution giving the U.S. broad control over Cuba's foreign and domestic policies.

plumbers Nixon's secret intelligence unit designed to stop information leaks to the media.

Plymouth Founded by Separatists in 1620, Plymouth was England's first permanent colony in New England.

political machines Organizations that controlled local political parties and municipal governments through bribery, election fraud, and

support of urban vice while providing some municipal services to the urban poor.

politics of harmony A system in which the governor and the colonial assembly worked together through persuasion rather than through patronage or bullying.

politique A man who believed that the survival of the state took precedence over religious differences.

poll tax A tax based on people or population rather than property. It was usually a fixed amount per adult.

polygamy The act of having more than one wife.

Pontiac An Ottawa chief whose name has been attached to the great Indian uprising against the British in 1763–1764.

pools Technique used by railroads to divide up traffic and fix rates, thereby avoiding ruinous competition.

popular sovereignty The concept that settlers of each territory would decide for themselves whether to allow slavery.

postal campaign Abolitionist tactic to force the nation to confront the slavery question by flooding the mails, both North and South, with anti-slavery literature. Their hope was to raise controversy within an area that was the province of the federal government.

postmillennialism Belief (held mostly by middle-class evangelists) that Christ's Second Coming would occur when missionary conversion of the world brought about a thousand years of social perfection.

powwow Originally, a word used to identify tribal

prophets or medicine men. Later it was used also to describe the ceremonies held by them.

praying Indians The Christian Indians of New England.

predestination A theory that states that God has decreed, even before he created the world, who will be saved and who will be damned.

Presbytery An intermediate level of organization in the Presbyterian church, above individual congregations but below the synod. One of its primary responsibilities was the ordination and placement of ministers.

presidios Military posts constructed by the Spanish to protect the settlers from hostile Indians. They also were used to keep non-Spanish settlers from the area.

Presley, Elvis Known as "the King" of Rock and Roll, he was the biggest pop star of the 1950s.

private fields Farms of up to five acres on which slaves working under the task system were permitted to produce items for their own use and sale in a nearby market.

privateers A privately owned ship that was authorized by a government to attack enemy ships during times of war. The owner of the ship got to claim a portion of whatever was captured. This practice damaged any enemy country that could not dramatically increase naval protection for its merchant ships.

Proclamation of 1763 Issued by the Privy Council, it tried to prevent the colonists from encroaching upon Indian lands by prohibiting settlement west of the Appalachian watershed unless the

government first purchased those lands by treaty.

Progressive Party Political party formed by Theodore Roosevelt in 1912 when the Republicans refused to nominate him for president. The party adopted a sweeping reform program.

Prohibition Constitutional ban on the manufacture and sale of alcohol in the United States (1920–1933).

proprietary colony A colony owned by an individual(s) who had vast discretionary powers over the colony. Maryland was the first proprietary colony, but others were founded later.

protective tariff Tariff that increases the price of imported goods that compete with American products and thus protects American manufacturers from foreign competition.

Protestant Reformation A religious movement begun by Martin Luther in 1517 that led to the repudiation of the Roman Catholic Church in large parts of northern and central Europe.

provincial congress A type of convention elected by the colonists to organize resistance. They tended to be larger than the legal assemblies they displaced, and they played a major role in politicizing the countryside.

public Friends The men and women who spoke most frequently and effectively for the Society of Friends. They were as close as the Quakers came to having a clergy. They occupied special elevated seats in some meetinghouses.

public virtue Meant, to the revolutionary generation,

patriotism and the willingness of a free and independent people to subordinate their interests to the common good and even to die for their country.

Pueblo Revolt In the most successful Indian uprising in American history, the Pueblo people rose against the Spanish in 1680, killed most Spanish missionaries, devastated Spanish buildings, and forced the surviving Spaniards to retreat down the Rio Grande. The Pueblos maintained their autonomy for about a decade, but Spain reasserted control in the early 1690s.

Puritans An English religious group that followed the teachings of John Calvin. They wanted a fuller reformation of the Church of England and hoped to replace The Book of Common Prayer with sermons. They wanted to purify the Church of England of its surviving Catholic eremonies and vestments.

Quakers A term of abuse used by opponents to describe members of the Society of Friends, who believed that God, in the form of the Inner Light, was present in all humans. Friends were pacifists who rejected oaths, sacraments, and all set forms of religious worship.

quasi-slavery Position that resembled slavery, such as that created by the Black Codes.

quitrent A relic of feudalism, a quitrent was a small required annual fee attached to a piece of land. It differed from other rents in that nonpayment did not lead to ejection from the land but to a suit for debt.

R&D Research and development.

racial profiling Law enforcement practice of using racial appearance to screen for potential wrongdoing.

railhead End of a railroad line, or the farthest point on the track.

railroad gauge Distance between the rails on which wheels of railroad cars fit.

"rainfall follows the plow" Erroneous belief that settlement and cultivation somehow changed the weather. It evolved due to heavier-than-normal precipitation during the 1870s and 1880s.

RAND Think tank developed by the U.S. military to conduct scientific research and development.

Reagan, Ronald Republican president (1981–1989) who steered domestic politics in a conservative direction and sponsored a huge military buildup.

real wages Relationship between wages and the consumer price index.

realism Form of thinking, writing, and art that prized detachment, objectivity, and skepticism.

rebates Practice by the railroads of giving certain big businesses reductions in freight rates or refunds.

recall Reform that gave voters the right to remove from office a public servant who had betrayed their trust.

Red Scare Widespread fear in 1919–1920 that radicals had coalesced to establish a communist government on American soil. In response, U.S. government and private

citizens undertook a campaign to identify, silence, and, in some cases, imprison radicals.

redemptioners Servants with an indentured contract that allowed them to find masters after they arrived in the colonies. Many German immigrant families were redemptioners and thus were able to stay together while they served their terms.

redlining Refusal by banks and loan associations to grant loans for home buying and business expansion in neighborhoods that contained aging buildings, dense populations, and growing numbers of nonwhites.

referendum Procedure that allows the electorate to decide an issue through a direct vote.

Refugee Act of 1980 Law allowing refugees fleeing political persecution entry into the United States.

religious bigotry Intolerance based on religious beliefs or practices.

religious right Christians who wedded their religious beliefs to a conservative political agenda and gained growing influence in Republican party politics after the late 1960s.

Republic of Texas Independent nation founded in 1836 when a revolution by residents in the Mexican province of Texas won their independence.

republics Independent Indian villages that were willing to trade with the British and remained outside the French system of Indian alliances.

Restoration era The period that began in 1660 when the Stuart dynasty under

Charles II was restored to the throne of England. It ended with the overthrow of James II in 1688–1689.

restorationism Belief that all theological and institutional changes since the end of biblical times were man-made mistakes and that religious organizations must restore themselves to the purity and simplicity of the apostolic church.

restraint of trade Activity that prevented competition in the marketplace or free trade.

revival A series of emotional religious meetings that led to numerous public conversions.

revolving gun turret A low structure, often round, on a ship that moved horizontally and contained mounted guns.

rifling Process of cutting spiral grooves in a gun's barrel to impart a spin to the bullet. Perfected in the 1850s, it produced greater accuracy and longer range.

Robinson, Jackie African American whose addition to the Brooklyn Dodgers in 1947 began the lengthy process of integrating Major League Baseball.

rock 'n' roll Form of popular music that arose in the 1950s from a variety of musical styles, including rhythm and blues, country, and gospel. Its heavily accented beat attracted a large following among devotees of the emerging youth culture.

Rockefeller, John D. Founder of the Standard Oil Company, whose aggressive practices drove many competitors out of business and made him one of the richest men in America.

Roe v. *Wade* Supreme Court decision in 1973 that ruled

that a blanket prohibition against abortion violated a woman's right to privacy and prompted decades of political controversy.

rolling stock Locomotives, freight cars, and other types of wheeled equipment owned by railroads.

Roosevelt corollary 1904 corollary to the Monroe Doctrine, stating that the United States had the right to intervene in domestic affairs of hemispheric nations to quell disorder and forestall European intervention.

Roosevelt liberalism New reform movement that sought to regulate capitalism but not the morals or behavior of private citizens. This reform liberalism overcame divisions between southern agrarians and northeastern ethnics.

Roosevelt, Eleanor A politically engaged and effective First Lady, and an architect of American liberalism.

Roosevelt, Franklin D. President from 1933 to 1945 and the creator of the New Deal.

Rough Riders Much-decorated volunteer cavalry unit organized by Theodore Roosevelt and Leonard Wood to fight in Cuba in 1898.

royal colony A colony controlled directly by the English monarch. The governor and council were appointed by the Crown.

Russo-Japanese War Territorial conflict between imperial Japan and Russia mediated by Theodore Roosevelt at Portsmouth, New Hampshire. The peace agreement gave Korea and other territories to Japan, ensured Russia's continuing control

over Siberia, and protected China's territorial integrity.

Sacco and Vanzetti Case (1920) Controversial conviction of two Italian-born anarchists accused of armed robbery and murder.

sachem An Algonquian word that means "chief."

Safety-Fund Law New York state law that required banks to pool a fraction of their resources to protect both bankers and small stockholders in case of bank failures.

Salem witch trials About 150 people were accused of witchcraft in Massachusetts between March and September 1692. During the summer trials, 19 people were hanged and one was pressed to death after he refused to stand trial. All of those executed insisted they were innocent. Of the 50 who confessed, none was executed.

Saratoga A major turning point in the Revolutionary War. American forces prevented John Burgoyne's army from reaching Albany, cut off its retreat, and forced it to surrender in October 1777. This victory helped bring France into the war.

saturation bombing Intensive bombing designed to destroy everything in a target area.

scabs Strikebreakers who were willing to act as replacements for striking workers, thus undermining the effect of strikes as leverage against company owners.

scalawags Term used by southern Democrats to describe southern whites who worked with the Republicans.

scientific management Attempt to break down each factory job into its smallest

components to increase efficiency, eliminate waste, and promote worker satisfaction.

secession The act of a state withdrawing from the Union. South Carolina was the first state to attempt to do this in 1860.

Second Continental Congress The intercolonial body that met in Philadelphia in May 1775 a few weeks after the Battles of Lexington and Concord. It organized the Continental Army, appointed George Washington commander-in-chief, and simultaneously pursued policies of military resistance and conciliation. When conciliation failed, it chose independence in July 1776 and in 1777 drafted the Articles of Confederation, which finally went into force in March 1781.

sedentary Societies that are rooted locally or are nonmigratory. Semisedentary societies are migratory for part of the year.

seditious libel The common-law crime of openly criticizing a public official.

seigneurs The landed gentry who claimed most of the land between Quebec and Montreal. They were never as powerful as aristocrats in France.

Seneca Falls Convention (1848) First national convention of women's rights activists.

separation of powers The theory that a free government, especially in a republic, should have three independent branches capable of checking or balancing one another: the executive, the legislative (usually bicameral), and the judicial.

Separatists One of the most extreme English Protestant groups that were followers of John Calvin. They began to separate from the Church of England and form their own congregations.

September 11, 2001 Day on which U.S. airliners, hijacked by Al Qaeda operatives, were crashed into the World Trade Center and the Pentagon, killing around 3,000 people.

serfdom Early medieval Europe's predominant labor system, which tied peasants to their lords and the land. They were not slaves because they could not be sold from the land.

Seward, William H. Secretary of State under Abraham Lincoln and Andrew Jackson. He was best known for his purchase of Alaska from Russia.

share wages Payment of workers' wages with a share of the crop rather than with cash.

sharecropping Working land in return for a share of the crops produced instead of paying cash rent.

Shays's Rebellion An uprising of farmers in western Massachusetts in the winter of 1786–1787. They objected to high taxes and foreclosures for unpaid debts. Militia from eastern Massachusetts suppressed the rebels.

Sheppard-Towner Act Major social welfare program providing federal funds for prenatal and child health care, 1921–1929.

sickle cell A crescent- or sickle-shaped red blood cell sometimes found in African Americans. It helped protect them from malaria but exposed some children to the dangerous and painful condition of sickle cell anemia.

Sir Walter Raleigh An Elizabethan courtier who, in the 1580s, tried but failed to establish an English colony on Roanoke Island in what is now North Carolina.

sit-down strike Labor strike strategy in which workers occupied their factory but refused to do any work until the employer agreed to recognize the workers' union. This strategy succeeded against General Motors in 1937.

sit-in movement Activity that challenged legal segregation by demanding that blacks have the same access to public facilities as whites. These nonviolent demonstrations were staged at restaurants, bus and train stations, and other public places.

Sitting Bull Hunkapapa Lakota (Sioux) chief and holy man who led warriors against the U.S. Army in Montana Territory in 1876, culminating in the Battle of Little Big Horn.

slash and burn A system of agriculture in which trees were cut down, girdled, or in some way destroyed. The underbrush then was burned, and a crop was planted. Men created the farms, and women did the farming. The system eventually depleted the fertility of the soil, and the entire tribe would move to a new area after 10 or 20 years.

Smith, Alfred E. Irish American, Democratic governor of New York who became in 1928 the first Catholic ever nominated for the presidency by a major party.

Smith, John (Captain) A member of the Virginia Council; his strong leadership from 1607 to 1609 probably saved the colony from collapse.

Smith, Joseph Poor New York farm boy whose visions led him to translate the *Book of Mormon* in late 1820s. He became the founder and the prophet of the Church of Jesus Christ of Latter-day Saints (Mormons).

Social Darwinism Set of beliefs explaining human history as an ongoing evolutionary struggle between different groups of people for survival and supremacy that was used to justify inequalities between races, classes, and nations.

Social Security Act Centerpiece of the welfare state (1935) that instituted the first federal pension system and set up funds to take care of groups (such as the disabled and unmarried mothers with children) that were unable to support themselves.

socialism Political movement that called for the transfer of industry from private to public control, and the transfer of political power from elites to the laboring masses.

sodbuster Small farmer in parts of the West who adapted to the treeless plains and prairies, such as the construction of homes out of sod.

southern yeoman Farmer who owned relatively little land and few or no slaves.

sovereign power A term used to describe supreme or final power.

space shuttle Manned rocket that served as a space laboratory and could be flown back to the earth for reuse.

specie Also called "hard money" as against paper money. In colonial times, it usually meant silver, but it could also include gold coins.

spirituals Term later devised to describe the religious songs of slaves.

Spock, Dr. Benjamin Pediatrician who wrote *Baby and Child Care* (1946), the most widely used child-rearing book during the baby-boom generation.

spoils system System by which the victorious political party rewarded its supporters with government jobs.

Sputnik First Soviet satellite sent into orbit around the earth in 1957.

stagflation Condition of simultaneous economic stagnation and price inflation.

Stalin, Joseph Soviet communist dictator who worked with Allied leaders during Second World War.

Stamp Act Passed by the administration of George Grenville in 1765, the Stamp Act imposed duties on most legal documents in the colonies and on newspapers and other publications. Massive colonial resistance to the act created a major imperial crisis.

staple crop A crop grown for commercial sale. It usually was produced in a colonial area and was sold in Europe. The first staple crops were sugar and tobacco.

Starr, Kenneth Republican lawyer appointed as independent counsel to investigate possible wrongdoing by President Clinton.

States General The legislative assembly of the Netherlands.

stay laws A law that delays or postpones something. During the 1780s, many states passed stay laws to delay the due date on debts because of the serious economic problems of the times.

Strategic Defense Initiative (SDI) Popularly termed "Star Wars," a proposal to develop technology for creation of a space-based defensive missile shield around the United States.

Student Nonviolent Coordinating Committee (SNCC) Interracial civil-rights organization formed by young people involved in the sit-in movement that later adopted a direct-action approach to fighting segregation.

subtreasuries Plan to help farmers escape the ruinous interest rates of the crop lien system by storing their crops in federal warehouses until market prices were more favorable. Farmers could draw low-interest loans against the value of these crops.

subversive Systematic, deliberate attempt to overthrow or undermine a government or society by people working secretly within the country.

Sun Belt Southern rim of the United States running from Florida to California.

Sunday schools Schools that first appeared in the 1790s to teach working-class children to read and write but that by the 1820s and 1830s were becoming moral training grounds.

supply-side economics Economic theory that tax reductions targeted toward investors and businesses would stimulate production and eventually create jobs.

sweated Describes a type of worker, mostly women, who worked in her home producing items for subcontractors, usually in the clothing industry.

synod The governing body of the Presbyterian church. A synod was a meeting of Presbyterian ministers and prominent laymen to set policies for the whole church.

table a petition or bill Act of removing a petition or bill from consideration without debate by placing it at the end of the legislative agenda.

Taft, William Howard Roosevelt's successor as president (1909–1913), who tried but failed to mediate between reformers and conservatives in the Republican Party.

tariff A tax on imports.

task system A system of slave labor under which slaves had to complete specific assignments each day. After these assignments were finished, their time was their own. It was used primarily on rice plantations. Slaves often preferred this system over gang labor because it gave them more autonomy and free time.

Teapot Dome scandal Political scandal by which Secretary of Interior Albert Fall allowed oil tycoons access to government oil reserves in exchange for $400,000 in bribes.

Tecumseh Shawnee leader who assumed political and military leadership of the pan-Indian religious movement began by his brother Tenskwatawa.

tejanos Spanish-speaking settlers of Texas. The term comes from the Spanish word *Tejas* for Texas.

temperance Movement that supported abstaining from alcoholic beverages.

tenancy System under which farmers worked land that they did not own.

Tennessee Valley Authority (TVA) Ambitious and successful use of government resources and power to promote economic development throughout the Tennessee Valley.

Tenochtitlán The huge Aztec capital city destroyed by Cortés.

Tenskwatawa Brother of Tecumseh, whose religious vision of 1805 called for the unification of Indians west of the Appalachians and foretold the defeat and disappearance of the whites.

termination and relocation Policies designed to assimilate American Indians by terminating tribal status and relocating individuals off reservations.

Tet offensive Surprise National Liberation Front (NLF) attack during the lunar new year holiday in early 1968 that brought high casualties to the NLF but fueled pessimism about the war's outcome in the United States.

The Man That Nobody Knows Bruce Barton's best-selling, 1925 book depicting Jesus as a business executive.

think tank Group or agency organized to conduct intensive research or engage in problem solving, especially in developing new technology, military strategy, or social planning.

Third Reich New empire that Adolf Hitler promised the German people would bring glory and unity to the nation.

Third World Less economically developed areas of the world, primarily the Middle East, Asia, Latin America, and Africa.

Tierra del Fuego The region at the southern tip of South America.

tithe A portion of one's income that is owed to the church. In most places, it was one-tenth.

toll roads Roads for which travelers were charged a fee for each use.

tories A term for Irish Catholic peasants who murdered Protestant landlords. It was used to describe the followers of Charles II and became one of the names of the two major political parties in England.

total war New kind of war requiring every combatant to devote virtually all his or her economic and political resources to the fight.

totalitarian movement Movement in which the individual is subordinated to the state and all areas of life are subjected to centralized, total control—usually by force.

Townshend Revenue Act Passed by Parliament in 1767, this act imposed import duties on tea, paper, glass, red and white lead, and painter's colors. It provoked the imperial crisis of 1767–1770. In 1770, Parliament repealed all of the duties except the one on tea.

traditionalists Those who believed that God's word transcended science and that

America should continue to be guided by older hierarchies (men over women, whites over nonwhites, native-born over immigrants).

transcontinental railroad Railroad line that connected with other lines to provide continuous rail transportation from coast to coast.

treasury notes Paper money used by the Union to help finance the Civil War. One type of treasury note was known as a greenback because of its color.

Triangle Shirtwaist Company New York City site of a tragic 1911 industrial fire that killed 146 workers who were unable to find their way to safety.

Triple Alliance One set of combatants in World War I, consisting of Germany, Austria-Hungary, and Italy. When Italy left the alliance, this side became known as the Central Powers.

Triple Entente One set of combatants in World War I, consisting of Britain, France, and Russia. As the war went on, this side came to be known as the Allies or Allied Powers.

Truman, Harry S. Franklin Roosevelt's Vice President who became president when Roosevelt died on April 13, 1945.

trust Large corporations that controlled a substantial share of any given market.

Turner, Nat Baptist lay preacher whose religious visions encouraged him to lead a slave revolt in southern Virginia in 1831 in which 55 whites were killed—more than any other American slave revolt.

Turner's frontier thesis Theory developed by historian Frederick Jackson Turner, who argued that the frontier had been central to the shaping of American character and the success of the U.S. economy and democracy.

Twenty Negro Law Confederate conscription law that exempted from the draft one white man on every plantation owning 20 or more slaves. The law's purpose was to exempt overseers or owners who would ensure discipline over the slaves and keep up production but was regarded as discrimination by nonslaveholding families.

U-2 spy plane Aircraft specializing in high-altitude reconnaissance.

Ulster The northern province of Ireland that provided 70 percent of the Irish immigrants in the colonial period. Nearly all of them were Presbyterians whose forebears had moved to Ireland from Scotland in the previous century. They sometimes are called Scots-Irish today.

Uncle Tom's Cabin Published by Harriet Beecher Stowe in 1852, this sentimental novel told the story of the Christian slave Uncle Tom and became a best seller and the most powerful antislavery tract of the antebellum years.

underconsumptionism Theory that underconsumption, or a chronic weakness in consumer demand, had caused the depression. This theory guided the Second New Deal, leading to the passage of laws designed to stimulate consumer demand.

underground railroad A small group who helped slaves escape bondage in the South. It took on legendary status, and its role was much exaggerated.

UNESCO (United Nations Educational, Scientific, and Cultural Organization) UN organization intended to create peace and security through collaboration among member nations.

unicameral legislature A legislature with only one chamber or house.

Union Leagues Organizations that informed African American voters of, and mobilized them to, support the Republican Party.

Unionists Southerners who remained loyal to the Union during the Civil War.

universal male suffrage System that allowed all adult males to vote without regard to property, religious, or race qualifications or limitations.

urban corridors Metropolitan strips of population running between older cities.

vestry A group of prominent men who managed the lay affairs of the local Anglican church, often including the choice of the minister, especially in Virginia.

vice-admiralty courts These royal courts handled the disposition of enemy ships captured in time of war, adjudicated routine maritime disputes between, for example, a ship's crew and its owner, and occasionally tried to decide cases involving parliamentary regulation of colonial commerce. This last category was the most controversial. These courts did not use juries.

Victorianism Moral code of conduct that advocated modesty, sexual restraint, and separate spheres of activity and influence for men and women.

Vietnam War Conflict lasting from 1946 to 1975, with direct U.S. military involvement from 1964 to 1973. Highly controversial, the war devastated the Vietnam countryside, spilled into all of Indochina, and ended in a victory for communist North Vietnam, which then united the country under its rule.

Vietnamization Policy whereby the South Vietnamese were to assume more of the military burdens of the war and allow the United States to withdraw combat troops.

virtual representation The English concept that Members of Parliament represented the entire empire, not just a local constituency and its voters. According to this theory, settlers were represented in Parliament in the same way that nonvoting subjects in Britain were represented. The colonists accepted virtual representation for nonvoting settlers within their colonies but denied that the term could describe their relationship with Parliament.

VJ Day August 15, 1945, day on which the war in the Pacific was won by the Allies.

Voting Rights Act of 1965 Law that provided new federal mechanisms to help guarantee African Americans the right to vote.

Wagner Act (NLRA) Named after its sponsor Senator Robert Wagner (D-NY), this

1935 act gave every worker the right to join a union and compelled employers to bargain with unions in good faith.

Walker, Madame C. J. Black entrepreneur who built a lucrative business from the hair and skin lotions she devised and sold to black customers throughout the country.

War Hawks Members of the 12th Congress, most of them young nationalists from southern and western areas, who promoted war with Britain.

War Industries Board U.S. government agency responsible for mobilizing American industry for war production.

war on terrorism Global effort, adopted after the attacks of September 11, 2001, by the United States and its allies to neutralize international groups deemed "terrorists," primarily radical Islamic groups such as Al Qaeda.

Washington, George A veteran of the French and Indian War, Washington was named commander-in-chief of the Continental Army by the Second Continental Congress in 1775 and won notable victories at Boston, Trenton, Princeton, and Yorktown, where Lord Cornwallis's army surrendered to him in 1781. His fellow delegates chose him to preside over the deliberations of the Philadelphia Convention in 1787, and after the federal Constitution was ratified, he was unanimously chosen the first president of the United States for two terms.

Watergate Business and residential complex in Washington, D.C., that came to stand for the political espionage and cover-ups directed by the Nixon administration. The complicated web of Watergate scandals brought about Nixon's resignation in 1974.

Western development Disproportionate amount of New Deal funds sent to Rocky Mountain and Pacific Coast areas to provide water and electricity for urban and agricultural development.

wheat blast A plant disease that affected wheat and first appeared in New England in the 1660s. There were no known remedies for the disease, and it gradually spread until wheat production in New England nearly ceased.

Wheatley, Phillis Eight-year-old Phillis Wheatley arrived in Boston from Africa in 1761 and was sold as a slave to wealthy John and Susannah Wheatley. Susannah taught her to read and write, and in 1767 she published her first poem in Boston. In 1773, she visited London to celebrate the publication there of a volume of her poetry, an event that made her a transatlantic sensation. On her return to Boston, the Wheatleys emancipated her.

Whigs The name of an obscure sect of Scottish religious extremists who favored the assassination of Charles and James of England. The term was used to denote one of the two leading political parties of late 17th-century England.

Whiskey Rebellion Revolt in Western Pennsylvania against the federal excise tax on whiskey.

whiskey ring Network of distillers and revenue agents that cheated the government out of millions of tax dollars.

Whitney, Eli The Connecticut-born tutor who invented the cotton gin.

wolfpacks German submarine groups that attacked enemy merchant ships or convoys.

Works Progress Administration Federal relief agency established in 1935 that disbursed billions to pay for infrastructural improvements and funded a vast program of public art.

Wounded Knee Site of a shootout between Indians and Army troops at the Pine Ridge Indian reservation in southwestern South Dakota.

XYZ Affair Incident that precipitated an undeclared war with France when three French officials (identified as X, Y, and Z) demanded that American emissaries pay a bribe before negotiating disputes between the two countries.

Yankee A Dutch word for New Englanders that originally meant something like "land pirate."

yankeephobia Popular term describing strong dislike of the United States, whose citizens were referred to as "yankees," in Latin America.

yellow dog contracts Written pledges by employees promising not to join a union while they were employed.

yellow journalism Newspaper stories embellished with sensational or titillating details when the true reports did not seem dramatic enough.

yeoman A farmer who owned his own farm.

"Young America" movement A group of young members of the Democratic Party who were interested in territorial expansion in the 1840s.

Yorktown The last major engagement of the Revolutionary War. Washington's army, two French armies, and a French fleet trapped Lord Cornwallis at Yorktown and forced his army to surrender in October 1781.

Zenger, John Peter Printer of the *New York Weekly Journal* who was acquitted in 1735 by a jury of the crime of seditious libel after his paper sharply criticized Governor William Cosby.

Zimmerman telegram Telegram from Germany's foreign secretary instructing the German minister in Mexico to ask that country's government to attack the United States in return for German assistance in regaining Mexico's "lost provinces" (Texas, New Mexico, and Arizona).

Zion A term used by the Mormons to describe their "promised land" where they could prosper and live without persecution.

Photo Credits

Chapter 1
p. 11: © Mary Evans Picture Library/The Image Works; **p. 18:** Courtesy of the John Carter Brown Library at Brown University; **p. 24:** © Boltin Picture Library/The Bridgeman Art Library; **p. 26:** Theodore de Bry; **p. 33:** Fray Bernardinode Sahagun, General History of the Things of New Spain

Chapter 2
p. 47: Theodore de Bry; **p. 50:** Alliance/Goldwyn/THE KOBAL COLLECTION; **p. 62:** © ARPL/HIP/The Image Works; **p. 67:** The Library Company of Philadelphia; **p. 73** © New York Public Library/Art Resource, NY; **p. 83:** © North Wind Picture Archives; **p. 85:** Library of Congress, Prints and Photographs Division

Chapter 3
p. 103: Courtesy, American Antiquarian Society; **p. 112:** The Connecticut Historical Society, Hartford, CT; **p. 113:** Thomas B. Macaulay, *History of England from the Accession of James II*, ed. by Charles H. Firth (London: Macmillan, 1914); **p. 117:** © Hulton Archive/Getty Images; **p. 119:** The Royal Collection © 2006 Her Majesty Queen Elizabeth II; **p. 123:** Archives Nationales

Chapter 4
p. 138: Chicago Historical Society; **p. 142:** © CORBIS; **p. 146:** Collections of the Newport Historical Society (L93.54) On loan from the MA Charitable Mechanics Ass.; **p. 165:** Collection of the New York Historical Society; **p. 168:** Photo by Archie Carpenter/Courtesy of WQED; **p. 169:** The Historical Society of Pennsylvania

Chapter 5
p. 184: Colonial Williamsburg Foundation.; **p. 189:** The Bostonian Society/Old State House Museum; **p. 198:** Colonial Williamsburg Foundation.; **p. 207:** Courtesy, American Antiquarian Society; **p. 209:** Courtesy of the John Carter Brown Library at Brown University; **p. 211:** Library of Congress, Prints and Photographs Division

Chapter 6
p. 227: Fairfield Historical Society; **p. 236:** Courtesy, American Antiquarian Society; **p. 242:** Colonial Williamsburg, Williamsburg, VA; **p. 249:** Library of Congress, Prints and Photographs Division; **p. 251:** © J. Gilbert Harrington; **p. 259:** © North Wind Picture Archives

Chapter 7

p. 267: © National Portrait Gallery/Smithsonian Institution/Art Resource, NY; **p. 278:** © North Wind Picture Archives; **p. 286:** © The Granger Collection, New York; **p. 290:** *A View of New Orleans Taken from the Plantation of Marigny*, November, 1803 by Boqueto de Woiserie, Chicago Historical Society; **p. 292:** © The Granger Collection, New York; **p. 298:** Collections of Davenport West, Jr.

Chapter 8

p. 310: Lewis Miller (1796-1882). The Historical Society of York County, The York County Heritage Trust, PA.; **p. 314:** The Historical Society of Pennsylvania, *Procession of the Victuallers*, by John Lewis Krimmel (Bc85 K89); **p. 321:** Thomas L. McKenney, *Sketches of a Tour to the Lakes* (1827); **p. 330:** © CORBIS ; **p. 334:** © The New York Public Library/Art Resource, NY; **p. 339:** PBS Video

Chapter 9

p. 343: Collection of the Maryland Historical Society, Baltimore; **p. 349:** Abby Aldrich Rockefeller Folk Art Center, Williamsburg, VA; **p. 356:** The Library of Virginia; **p. 360:** Library of Congress, Prints and Photographs Division; **p. 368:** The Historic New Orleans Collection, Accension #1977.13734311; **p. 369:** © CORBIS SYGMA

Chapter 10

p. 377: © Bettmann/CORBIS; **p. 386:** Courtesy, American Antiquarian Society; **p. 389:** © National Portrait Gallery/Smithsonian Institution/Art Resource, NY; **p. 394:** Courtesy, American Antiquarian Society; **p. 406:** The Library Company of Philadelphia

Chapter 11

p. 423: Library of Congress, Prints and Photographs Division; **p. 431:** Dreamworks LLC/THE KOBAL COLLECTION/Cooper, Andrew; **p. 433:** Woolaroc Museum; **p. 437:** The Historical Society of Pennsylvania; **p. 445:** Collection of the New-York Historical Society; **p. 450:** Library of Congress, Prints and Photographs Division

Chapter 12

p. 466: North Wind Picture Archives; **p. 471:** © American Antiquarian Society, Worcester, Massachusetts, USA/ The Bridgeman Art Library; **p. 476:** Old Sturbridge Village

Chapter 13

p. 491: Courtesy of the Church Archives, The Church of Jesus Christ of Latter-day Saints; **p. 496:** Yale Collection of Western Americana, Beinecke Rare Book and Manuscript Library; **p. 503:** Courtesy of the California History Room, California State Library, Sacramento, California; **p. 508:** Courtesy of The Trustees of Boston Public Library

Chapter 14

p. 525: Library of Congress, Prints and Photographs Division; **p. 527:** Kansas State Historical Society, #FK2.83*15; **p. 529:** © The New York Public Library/Art Resource, NY; **p. 537:** Library of Congress, Prints and Photographs Division; **p. 543:** © CORBIS; **p. 547:** North Wind Picture Archives

Chapter 15

p. 557: Library of Congress, Prints and Photographs Division; **p. 558:** From the Ralph E. Becker Collection of Political Americana, The Smithsonian Institution Neg #49814; **p. 570:** The Everett Collection; **p. 571:** Cook Collection, Valentine Museum, Richmond, Virginia; **p. 579 (top):** Library of Congress, Prints and Photographs Division; **p. 579 (bottom):** © Francis G. Mayer/CORBIS

Chapter 16

p. 592: Library of Congress, Prints and Photographs Division; **p. 601:** Collection of the New-York Historical Society; **p. 610:** Library of Congress, Prints and Photographs Division; **p. 614:** Library of Congress, Prints and Photographs Division; **p. 622:** Library of Congress, Prints and Photographs Division

Chapter 17

p. 629 (left): Library of Congress, Prints and Photographs Division; **p. 629 (right):** Library of Congress, Prints and Photographs Division; **p. 633:** Photographs and Prints Division, Schomburg Center for Research in Black Culture, The New York Public Library, Astor, Lenox and Tilden Foundations.; **p. 637:** Library of Congress, Prints and Photographs Division; **p. 647:** © CORBIS; **p. 649:** © Bettmann/CORBIS; **p. 651:** © Bettmann/CORBIS

Chapter 18

p. 665: © Bettmann/CORBIS; **p. 669:** TM and Copyright © 20th Century Fox Film Corp. All rights reserved. Courtesy: Everett Collection; **p. 674:** Library of Congress, Prints and Photographs Division; **p. 681:** © Bettmann/CORBIS; **p. 687:** © The Granger Collection, New York

Chapter 19

p. 697: Library of Congress, Prints and Photographs Division; **p. 705:** © Bettmann/CORBIS; **p. 712:** Library of Congress, Prints and Photographs Division; **p. 722:** North Wind Picture Archive; **p. 725:** The Kansas State Historical Society Topeka, Kansas

Chapter 20

p. 737: © Lake County Museum/CORBIS; **p. 742:** © Hulton Archive/Getty Images; **p. 751:** © Bettmann/CORBIS; **p. 761:** © Bettmann/CORBIS; **p. 762:** A'Lelia Bundles/Walker Family Collection/www.madamcjwalker.com; **p. 765:** Underwood Photo Archives; **p. 768:** © Bettmann/CORBIS

Chapter 21

p. 774: Culver Pictures; p. 777: Brown Brothers; p. 779: © CORBIS; p. 790: Wisconsin Historical Society; p. 793: © Bettmann/CORBIS; p. 801: Brown Brothers

Chapter 22

p. 815: © The Granger Collection, New York; p. 820 (top): © Bettmann/CORBIS; p. 820 (bottom): © The Granger Collection, New York; p. 825: "*A Philippine Album: American Era Photographs*" by Jonathan Best. (Bookmark, Manila 1998); p. 827: Prints and Photographs Division, Library of Congress; p. 833: North Wind Picture Archive

Chapter 23

p. 846: Wisconsin Historical Society; p. 854: National Archives; p. 855: National Archives; p. 859: Imperial War Museum, London; p. 863: © Bettmann/CORBIS; p. 870: © Paramount Pictures/Courtesy: Everett Collection.; p. 872: Library of Congress, Prints and Photographs Division

Chapter 24

p. 880: © The Granger Collection, New York; p. 886: © Hulton-Deutsch Collection/CORBIS; p. 889: © CORBIS; p. 896: Brown Brothers; p. 903: © John Springer Collection/CORBIS; p. 910: © Bettmann/CORBIS; p. 913: Security Pacific Collection/Los Angeles Public Library

Chapter 25

p. 922: © Bettmann/CORBIS; p. 925: © Bettmann/CORBIS; p. 930: © The Granger Collection, New York; p. 935: FDR Library; p. 936: © Bettmann/CORBIS; p. 939: © Lester Lefkowitz/CORBIS; p. 951: The Michael Barson Collection

Chapter 26

p. 971: © The Granger Collection, New York; p. 981: National Archives #127-N-69559-A; p. 984 (top): © Bettmann/CORBIS; p. 984 (bottom): © Bettmann/CORBIS; p. 987: National Archives; p. 995: Everett Collection; p. 996: © CORBIS; p. 1000: © Universal Pictures/Courtesy: Everett Collection

Chapter 27

p. 1011: © The Granger Collection, New York; p. 1026: © Bettmann/CORBIS; p. 1028: Library of Congress, Prints and Photographs Division; p. 1037: © Margaret Bourke-White/ Time Life Pictures/Getty Images; p. 1041: The Michael Barson Collection

Chapter 28

p. 1062 (top): © Bettmann/CORBIS; p. 1062 (bottom): © Elliott Erwitt/Magnum Photos, Inc.; p. 1068: Library of Congress, Prints and Photographs Division; p. 1077: © Bettmann/ CORBIS; p. 1079: © Don Cravens/Time Life Pictures/Getty Images

Chapter 29

p. 1116: AP Images/Eddie Adams; **p. 1125:** Everett Collection; **p. 1134:** © UPI-Bettmann/CORBIS; **p. 1142:** AP Images; **p. 1145:** © Bettmann/CORBIS

Chapter 30

p. 1160: © Time & Life Pictures/Getty Images; **p. 1169:** © Eve Arnold/Magnum Photos, Inc.; **p. 1175:** © Bettmann/CORBIS; **p. 1182:** © Owen Franken/CORBIS; **p. 1191:** © Reuters/CORBIS; **p. 1194:** © Andre Jenny/The Image Works; **p. 1197:** © Ralf-Finn Hestoft/CORBIS

Chapter 31

p. 1207: © Richard Cummins/CORBIS; **p. 1213:** © Keren Su/CORBIS; **p. 1221:** TM and Copyright © 20th Century Fox Film Corp. All rights reserved./The Everett Collection; **p. 1226:** © Rebecca Cook/Reuters/CORBIS

Chapter 32

p. 1237: AP Images/Dennis Paquin; **p. 1243:** AP Images/Gary I. Rothstein; **p. 1245:** AP Images/Pablo Martinez Monsivais; **p. 1249:** AP Images/Khalid Mohammed; **p. 1255:** © Smiley N. Pool/Dallas Morning News/CORBIS

Index